The —
WESTERN FRONT
COMPANION

Also by Mark Adkin

The Gettysburg Companion

The Trafalgar Companion

The Waterloo Companion

The Sharpe Companion

The Sharpe Companion – His Early Life

The Daily Telegraph Guide to Britain's Military Heritage

The Charge

Urgent Fury

The Last Eleven?

Goose Green

The Bear Trap (with Mohammad Yousaf)

The Quiet Operator (with John Simpson)

Prisoner of the Turnip Heads (with George Wright-Nooth)

THE
WESTERN FRONT
COMPANION

The Complete Guide to How the Armies Fought for Four Devastating Years, 1914–1918

MARK ADKIN

STACKPOLE
BOOKS

To all those who fell and who fought for freedom
in France and Flanders 1914–1918

We Will Remember Them

Copyright © 2013 by Mark Adkin

Published by
STACKPOLE BOOKS
5067 Ritter Road
Mechanicsburg, PA 17055 USA
www.stackpolebooks.com

Produced by
Aurum Press Ltd, 74–77 White Lion Street, London N1 9PF • www.aurumpress.co.uk

Mark Adkin has asserted his right to be identified as the author of this work in accordance with the
Copyright Designs and Patents Act 1988.

ISBN 978-0-8117-1316-0

1 3 5 7 6 4 2
2013 2015 2017 2019 2018 2016 2014

Book design by Robert Updegraff

Printed in China

Colour illustrations of weapons and equipment by Clive Farmer, copyright © 2013 by Clive Farmer
Maps on pages 248, 258, 260, 261, 454 and 499 are reproduced courtesy of the Imperial War Museum, London.
All other maps and diagrams by Robert Updegraff, copyright © 2013 by Aurum Press Ltd
Colour illustrations of aircraft on pages 422–3 reproduced by kind permission of Anova Publishing Ltd.

Picture Acknowledgements
Photographs are reproduced courtesy of the following: pages 300, 361, 516 and 520 (bottom) Alamy; page 295 Alexander Turnbull
Library, Wellington, New Zealand (Royal New Zealand Returned and Services' Association: New Zealand official negatives, World
War I 1914–1918, ref. 1/2-013758-G: permission of the Alexander Turnbull Library, Wellington, New Zealand, must be obtained
before any reuse of this image); page 461 Bridgeman Art Library; pages 16, 19, 28, 36, 92, 122 (bottom), 133, 140 (bottom), 148,
149, 150 (bottom), 155, 190, 296 (bottom), 320, 353, 400 (top), 404, 413 (bottom), 415, 418, 429, 442 and 518 Corbis Images;
pages 25 (top and bottom), 34, 41 (top), 47, 82, 88, 101 (top), 114, 119, 126 (top), 127, 146, 150 (top), 151, 152, 153, 157, 160,
196, 264, 270 (bottom), 377, 400 (bottom), 403, 413 (top), 416, 417 (bottom) and 515 Getty Images; pages 246 and 448
The Heritage of the Great War, www.greatwar.nl/; pages 8, 10, 31, 39, 41 (bottom), 44, 51, 63, 68 (bottom), 70, 80, 98 (top and
bottom), 104 (bottom), 106, 107, 108, 110, 123, 126 (bottom), 140 (top), 147, 156, 159 (top and bottom), 163, 184, 187, 198,
201, 204, 207, 212, 215, 219, 222, 225 (top and bottom), 228, 230, 231 (top and bottom), 232, 235, 241, 250, 261 (top), 262,
265, 270 (top), 280, 285, 314, 315, 318, 322, 323, 330, 332, 333, 334 (top and bottom), 339, 346, 349, 354, 356, 357, 363, 369,
374, 382, 385, 392, 393, 394, 405, 408, 421, 426, 427, 428, 431, 433, 434, 436, 443, 44 (bottom), 446, 451 (top and bottom),
453, 455, 457, 462 (bottom), 464, 467 (top and bottom), 468 (top and bottom), 475 (top and bottom), 476, 477, 480, 483, 486,
491, 492, 498, 500, 502 (bottom), 512, 513 (bottom), 514 and 520 (top) Imperial War Museum, London; pages 2–3 JF Ptak
Science Books; pages 218, 417 (top), 500 (bottom) and 502 (top) Mary Evans Picture Library; pages 1, 462 (top) and 465 National
Archives of The Netherlands; pages 164, 221, 286, 324, 329, 341, 345, 347, 381 and 485 National Library of Scotland; page 170
Press Association Images; 296 (top) The Royal Engineers Museum; page 68 (top) The Royal Hampshire Regiment Trust; pages 367
The Staffordshire Regiment Museum; pages 132, 169, 493 and 519 TopFoto.

Colour photographs (except those on pages 37, 361, 516 and 518)
by Mark Adkin, copyright © 2013 by Mark Adkin

Every effort has been made to trace the copyright holders of material quoted in this book.
If application is made in writing to the publisher, any omissions will be included in future editions.

Contents

Author's Note

The one hundredth anniversary of the start of World War I is fast approaching. For over four years the centenary of battles large and small will be remembered with the publication of books, the production of films and television programmes, and many commemorative military parades and civic events will be held. Thousands will go on pilgrimages to battlefields far and near to pay their respects at memorials and cemeteries to fallen relatives.

With the exception of Russia, by far the greatest number of the fallen of all participating nations fell on the Western Front – that blood-soaked strip of ground, mostly only a few miles wide, that stretched from the mountains and valleys on the Swiss frontier to the flat, flooded fields of Belgium. It was the Western Front that gave such previously unknown names as the Marne, Ypres, the Somme, Verdun, Chemin des Dames, Vimy Ridge, Passchendaele, Arras and Meuse–Argonne a place in the history books of Europe, the Commonwealth and America. On the Western Front the true horror of modern war was exposed to the world for the first time as trenches, barbed wire, massed quick-firing artillery, machine guns, aircraft and tanks combined on the battlefield. The commanders and their armies were ill prepared, and the long process of learning to fight such complex and bloody battles effectively took almost four years.

This book is written as an introduction to the Great War that will, I hope, explain the make-up of the armies and how they fought. It is not a chronological account of events on the Western Front and, like its predecessors the *Waterloo*, *Trafalgar* and *Gettysburg Companions*, does not have to be read from cover to cover. Of course you can do that, but you can equally dip into it section by section, although if you are new to the subject then perhaps the Introduction and Section One: A Western Front Timeline will help in putting the other sections and the battles discussed into context. The theme and construction of the *Companion* is intended to describe and explain how various branches of the armies were commanded, organized and fought, with examples from some of the major battles. The British Army has been used as the primary subject, although efforts have been made to include in the limited space as much as possible of the actions of the armies of Canada, Australia, India, New Zealand, South Africa, the USA, France, Belgium and Germany.

With regard to statistics, especially those relating to casualties, the source relied on most frequently for British losses and other data was *Statistics of the Military Effort of the British Empire during the Great War, 1914–1920*. It was compiled by the War Office and published in 1922 and contains almost 900 pages of statistical information. For other nations considerable effort has been made to secure as accurate figures as possible, but many sources vary or are not readily available, with the result that they must remain realistic estimates. Nations varied in recording losses and did not always distinguish between sick and wounded, or between lightly wounded who returned to duty within a matter of days never having left the front, and those more seriously injured.

No apology is made for the number of maps and diagrams, as this writer is firmly of the opinion that without good maps and diagrams military history books can be both dull and difficult to follow. Relevant photographs add considerably to a reader's interest and understanding, and in this case, in addition to numerous contemporary photographs, a selection of modern, colour photographs of parts of some battlefields is included with explanations of what happened there.

Mark Adkin, March 2013

Acknowledgements

With regard to individuals to whom I owe special thanks, first must come Major J. (Jeff) A. Bennett, a former Royal Artillery officer and member of the Western Front Association, who kindly agreed to check my draft section on the Royal Artillery along with my proposed diagrams. His meticulous response consisted of many pages of detailed comments, explanations and corrections that enabled me better to understand some of the technical points of gunnery at the time and to ensure the section reflects accurately how the Royal Artillery functioned in World War I. Any errors that have crept in despite his help are mine.

Steve Smith, a gold-badged battlefield guide, took me on an extensive tour of the Western Front battlefields in 2009. He was able to take me to all the places I needed to visit along much of the British and French fronts, and to explain in detail what happened at the various sites at which I wished to explore and take photographs. There is little doubt that but for his expert knowledge the *Companion* would not contain the wealth of modern photographs of where events occurred. I much appreciate the efforts he made to make the tour a success.

The third individual was Professor Richard Holmes, a former brigadier, prolific military history author and brilliant lecturer. He most kindly answered all my queries in writing and in full. In particular his lucid explanation of the infantry/artillery tactics of the Western Front was of great benefit, and I am most grateful that he spared some of his time for me. Tragically, Richard Holmes died in 2011.

With regard to organizations that offered considerable support and assistance, I would like to thank the staff at the Records Department of the Imperial War Museum for their excellent service in making available the host of military pamphlets and manuals under the SS Series that I consulted. Without sight of these documents, which were issued during the war and covered so many aspects of the tactics of all arms, it would have been impossible properly to understand and explain how the fighting was conducted and why.

The other main source of information was the Royal United Services Institute library. It was there that I was able to consult so many volumes published just after the war and throughout the 1920s and 1930s that are not readily available elsewhere. The librarian, John Montgomery, who has now retired, was always extremely helpful in finding the information, book or journal that I needed. I owe him my sincere thanks.

Finally I must, yet again, extend my grateful thanks to Robert and Brenda Updegraff, the team that has put this *Companion* together, produced the maps and diagrams so beautifully from my original scrawl, and edited the text so thoroughly and accurately and made so many helpful suggestions of improvement.

Key to Symbols

The symbols shown here are those used most commonly on maps and diagrams throughout the book.
All others have their meaning given in the keys to the individual maps.

National formations, units and positions are shown in the colours used below throughout.

Unit sizes are indicated on top of the unit or sub-unit.

	British and Commonwealth	French	Belgian	American	German
army headquarters					
army	XXXX	XXXX	XXXX	XXXX	XXXX
corps	XXX	XXX	XXX	XXX	XXX
division	XX	XX	XX	XX	XX
brigade	X	X	X	X	X
regiment	││││	││││	││││	││││	││││
battalion	││	││	││	││	││
company	│	│	│	│	│
platoon	•••	•••	•••	•••	•••
section/squadron	•	•	•	•	•
artillery position					

Unit types are all shown in the appropriate national colour – those given here all indicate British units:

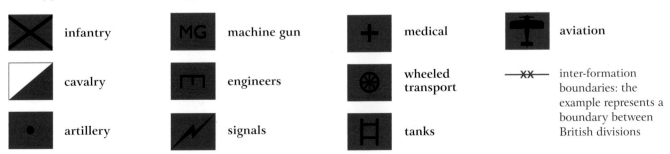

infantry   machine gun (MG)   medical   aviation

cavalry   engineers   wheeled transport   inter-formation boundaries: the example represents a boundary between British divisions

artillery   signals   tanks

I sought them far and found them,
The sure, the straight, the brave,
The hearts I lost my own to,
The souls I could not save.
They braced their belts about them,
They crossed in ships the sea,
They sought and fought six feet of ground
And there they died for me.

A. E. Housman

Archduke Franz Ferdinand and his wife Sophie leaving the town hall in Sarajevo on 28 June 1914.

Introduction

Why the World Went to War

What made World War I so different from every previous conflict was the impact of the Industrial Revolution with its accompanying technical, political, commercial and social changes. This war, known as 'the Great War' until the advent of World War II, was like no other war in history. It rapidly became an all-consuming continental conflict that demonstrated the prodigious strength, resilience and killing power of modern nations. That it developed in this way came as a huge surprise and profound shock to the main participants, with the United Kingdom in particular completely unprepared for a long conflict that was to involve armies numbered in their millions. It would be two years from the outbreak of hostilities in August 1914 before she was able to recruit, expand, train, equip and adequately supply the British Expeditionary Force (BEF) on the unprecedented scale that was required.

By the end of the war over forty countries plus numerous colonies belonging to Belgium, Britain, France, Germany, Italy and Portugal had at some time declared war on behalf of one side or the other (see boxes, pages 29, 39, 51, 58 and 69). However, the principal antagonists at the outset were grouped in two major alliances. The Entente Powers (hereafter called the Allies) consisted of Britain, France and Russia, and the Central Powers of Germany and Austria–Hungary. Forces from the British dominions of Australia, Canada, New Zealand and South Africa, as well as India and small colonial contingents such as the West India Regiment, subsequently contributed to the former. The Allies were also joined by Italy in 1915 and, in the latter part of 1917 and into 1918 were massively reinforced by the United States. The Ottoman Empire (Turkey) joined the Central Powers in 1914, to be followed by Bulgaria in September 1915.

However, this book is directly concerned only with the Western Front, a continuous line of trenches (and later defensive zones) that was, within a matter of months, to wriggle its way from the Swiss frontier to the Belgian coast. This was where the war was eventually won. This was the theatre of operations that would ultimately see 1,554,000 Frenchmen, 1,202,000 British (including dominion and colonial troops), 1,982,000 Americans, 115,000 Belgians and 35,000 Portuguese deployed on the Allied side at the Armistice on 11 November 1918. When Germany finally conceded defeat in Western Europe, she had 2,912,000 of her men in that theatre.

From 2 August 1914, when the Germans marched into Luxembourg, until the end of the war, the fighting on the Western Front never stopped. There were quiet periods and quieter parts of the front, but men were fighting and dying somewhere every hour of

A Family Affair

World War I has sometimes been known, with reason, as 'a family affair' due to the fact that many of the European monarchies – several of which collapsed during the war (for example those of Russia, Germany and Austria–Hungary) – were interrelated.

The British monarch George V's predecessor, Edward VII, was uncle to both the German Kaiser and, via his wife's sister, the Russian Tsar Nicholas II. One of his nieces, Alexandra, was the Tsar's wife. Another, Edna, was queen of Spain, while yet another, Marie, became queen of Romania. Edward's daughter, Maud, meanwhile, was queen of Norway. When King Edward died in 1910, nine kings attended his funeral.

every day of the fifty-two months that the war lasted. From mid-1917, when the French Army was affected by a series of mutinies, the BEF played the central role. By 1916 the armies of Germany, France and the British Empire measured success on the battlefields of France and Flanders in advances of a few thousand, sometimes a few hundred, yards, often gained only after months of virtually continuous fighting. Casualties in such offensives ran into hundreds of thousands for both sides. This was not the kind of war anyone, including the politicians and generals who directed it, had expected or wanted to fight.

Officially, there were ten other theatres of operations apart from the Western Front that in combination swallowed up an even higher number of men. The main ones, with the principal combatants in parenthesis, were: the Eastern Front (Russians against Germans and Austrians); the Balkan Front (British, French, Greeks, Italians and Serbs against Germans and Bulgarians); the Italian Front (Italians against Austrians and Hungarians); the Middle Eastern Front, which included the Dardanelles (Gallipoli), Palestine, Egypt, and Mesopotamia (Iraq) (British against Turks). Useful though these fronts were, particularly the Eastern Front, in dissipating the efforts of the Central Powers, final victory or defeat would occur only in Western Europe, where the Germans soon occupied all but a fraction of Belgium, the whole of Luxembourg and a large slice of France from which they had to be ejected.

To understand why Europe was engulfed in so devastating a conflagration so quickly, the complex tangle of national fears, ambitions and rivalries that had built up in the years prior to war being declared are briefly explained under the headings 'The Fuel', 'The Spark' and 'The Blaze'.

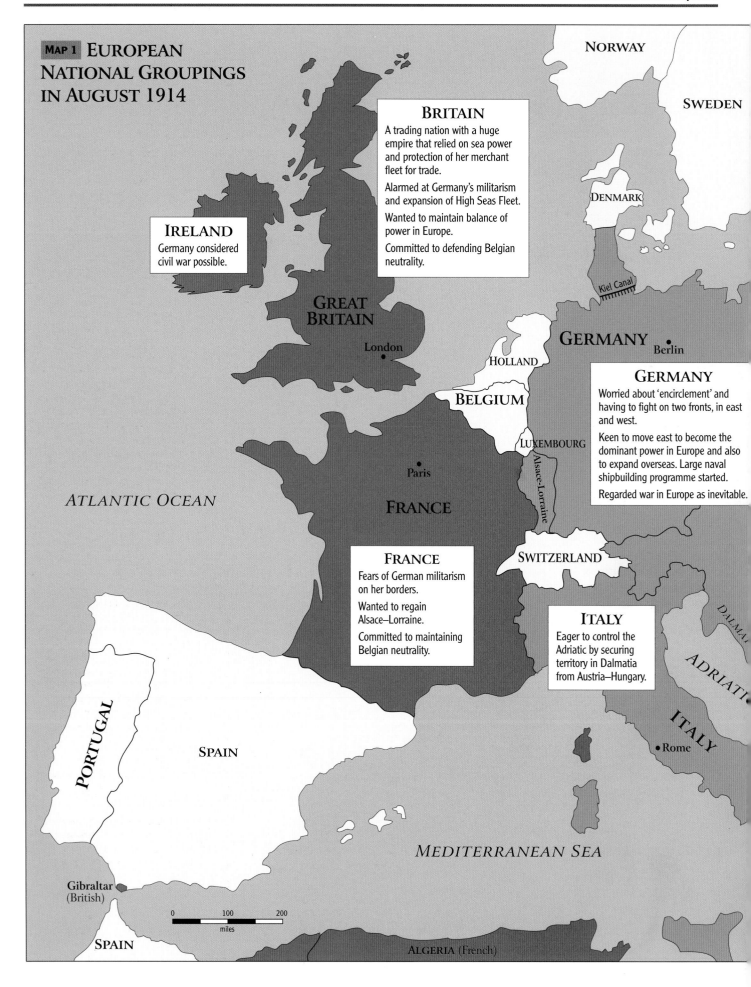

MAP 1 EUROPEAN NATIONAL GROUPINGS IN AUGUST 1914

NORWAY

SWEDEN

DENMARK

Kiel Canal

GERMANY • Berlin

HOLLAND

BELGIUM

LUXEMBOURG

Alsace-Lorraine

BRITAIN

A trading nation with a huge empire that relied on sea power and protection of her merchant fleet for trade.

Alarmed at Germany's militarism and expansion of High Seas Fleet.

Wanted to maintain balance of power in Europe.

Committed to defending Belgian neutrality.

IRELAND

Germany considered civil war possible.

GREAT BRITAIN

London •

GERMANY

Worried about 'encirclement' and having to fight on two fronts, in east and west.

Keen to move east to become the dominant power in Europe and also to expand overseas. Large naval shipbuilding programme started.

Regarded war in Europe as inevitable.

ATLANTIC OCEAN

Paris •

FRANCE

SWITZERLAND

FRANCE

Fears of German militarism on her borders.

Wanted to regain Alsace–Lorraine.

Committed to maintaining Belgian neutrality.

ITALY

Eager to control the Adriatic by securing territory in Dalmatia from Austria–Hungary.

DALMA

ADRIATI

ITALY

• Rome

PORTUGAL

SPAIN

MEDITERRANEAN SEA

Gibraltar (British)

0   100   200
miles

SPAIN

ALGERIA (French)

KEY

THE TRIPLE ENTENTE
(Britain, France and Russia)

THE TRIPLE ALLIANCE
(Germany, Austria–Hungary
and Italy)

NON-ALIGNED COUNTRIES

BALTIC SEA

Petrograd

RUSSIA

Moscow

RUSSIA

Vast country with large
population but lacking in
communications.

Felt isolated from her allies in
the west and concerned about
the internal anti-imperial
revolutionary movement.

Eager to support the Slav
peoples of the Balkans
against Austria–Hungary.

AUSTRIA–HUNGARY

Vienna

AUSTRIA–HUNGARY

Wanted to dominate the Balkans.

Powerful alliance with Germany but
internal difficulties with racial
minorities demanding better
recognition of independence.

ROMANIA

BLACK SEA

BOSNIA
Sarajevo

SERBIA

DALMATIA

MONTE-
NEGRO

BULGARIA

ALBANIA

TURKEY

GREECE

TURKEY

The 'sick man of Europe'
whose Ottoman Empire
was collapsing.

Feared Russia.

Berlin a-Tiptoe for War

W. H. Nevinson was a British
war correspondent for the *Daily
News* in Berlin. He wrote the
following account of his arrest
on 4 August 1914:

> For two days I waited and
> watched. Up and down the
> wide road of 'Unter den
> Linden' crowds paced
> incessantly by day and night
> singing the German war songs
> [such as 'Deutschland,
> Deutschland über Alles'] . . .
> So the interminable crowds
> went past, a-tiptoe for war,
> because they had never
> known it. Sometimes a
> company of infantry,
> sometimes a squadron of
> horse went down the road
> westward, wearing the new
> grey uniforms in place of the
> familiar 'Prussian blue'. They
> passed to probable death
> amid cheering, hand shaking,
> gifts of flowers and of food.
> Sometimes the Kaiser in full
> uniform swept along in his
> fine motor perpetually
> sounding [his horn].
>
> On the morning of the fateful
> 4th, I drove to the Schloss,
> where the Deputies of the
> Reichstag were gathered to
> hear the Kaiser's address.
> Refused permission to enter, I
> waited outside, and gathered
> only rumours of the speech
> that declared the unity of all
> Germany and all German
> parties, in the face of the
> common peril. A few hours
> later, in the Reichstag,
> Bethmann Hollweg announced
> that under the plea of necessity
> the neutrality of Belgium had
> almost certainly been violated.
> Then I knew that the long-
> dreaded moment had come.

In the afternoon Nevinson
heard that war had been
declared and he was turned out
of his hotel as a dangerous
foreigner.

> In front of the hotel entrance
> I could distinguish shouts for
> the English correspondents to
> be brought out . . . Two of the
> armed police seized me at
> once and dragged me out
> holding an enormous revolver
> at each ear. 'If you try to run
> away,' they kept shouting, 'we
> will shoot you like a dog!'

The Fuel

Virulent nationalism; the upsetting of the balance of power in Europe; economic rivalry; the rise of German militarism under Kaiser Wilhelm II (particularly the expansion of the German High Seas Fleet); the instability in the Balkans, where the Turkish Ottoman Empire was dying; and France's desire to regain Alsace and Lorraine, lost to Germany in the Franco-Prussian War of 1870–71 – these were the main ingredients of a highly flammable mix of suspicions and rivalries in Europe during the early years of the twentieth century. By 1914 they had culminated in two supposedly defensive alliances or 'understandings' between the major powers in Europe. These were the Triple Alliance (a formal treaty) between Germany, Austria–Hungary and Italy, and the Triple Entente ('entente' here meaning an understanding rather than a binding agreement) between Britain, France and Russia. Like the North Atlantic Treaty Organization (NATO) of today, they were designed to deter aggression and obliged (or anticipated) mutual assistance if any country in the agreement was attacked. In simplified form, the confused and conflicting aspirations of the main belligerents of the war are summarized below.

The Triple Alliance
Germany

• Under the Kaiser, Germany was determined to remain the dominant power on the European mainland and to 'have a place in the sun', as the chancellor, Prince Bernhard von Bülow, put it. In 1914 her population was 67 million, she was a major industrial country and certainly the most modern military power on the continent. Germany had ambitions to expand her overseas empire for the purposes of trade and securing sources of raw materials. She already had four colonies in Africa (Togo, Cameroon, German Southwest Africa and German East Africa), but in comparison with the worldwide empire of Britain, and to a lesser extent that of France, Germany's handful of overseas possessions was insignificant. She had made her expansionist ambitions plain with her attempts to meddle in French-controlled Morocco in 1905 and again in 1911. During the Second Boer War (1899–1902) she supported the Boer Republics against Britain. But crucial to her expansion was the need to increase her navy – the German High Seas Fleet – into a global striking force that could rival the Royal Navy as the world's leading naval power. This she set out to accomplish by an accelerated shipbuilding programme and the widening of the Kiel Canal so that her new, heavily armoured battleships (the dreadnoughts) could be moved easily from the Baltic to the North Sea. Both activities alarmed Britain and caused her to start an expansionist programme to modernize her own fleet.

• Germany's primary strategic fear was that of 'encirclement'. She was sandwiched between two large and potentially hostile nations – France in the west and Russia in the east. Add to this Britain with her all-powerful navy and huge maritime commercial fleet, and the Kaiser's worries become obvious. It was the realization that if Germany went to war in Europe it was almost certain to involve fighting on two fronts that led to the Schlieffen Plan (see page 19) – a war plan specifically designed to deal with this potentially disastrous situation.

Austria–Hungary

• The Austro-Hungarian Empire was ruled by the same dynasty as the old Holy Roman Empire that it had displaced. In 1914 it was presided over by the eighty-four-year-old Emperor Franz Josef I and embraced a potpourri of ethnic minorities that included Czechs, Dalmatians, Italians, Croats, Bosnians, Germans, Slovaks, Magyars (half the population of Hungary), Romanians and Serbs. Of these it was the Serbs who posed the biggest threat as a landlocked Serbia, independent after 500 years of Turkish rule, strove to expand and seek access to the sea. Austria–Hungary feared unrest among its 23 million subject Slavs if Serbia was permitted to keep developing its power and prestige.

• The objective of the Austro-Hungarian Empire was to dominate the Balkans – surely one of the more unstable regions of the world today as it was then – by crushing the regional pan-Serb movement and, hopefully, Serbia itself, thus securing Austrian control of the route to Salonika (Macedonia) on the Aegean Sea. Its main fear was Russia, to whom the Balkan Slavs looked as their champion and protector. Things have not changed much in this part of the world – Serbia still had Russian backing in the Balkan conflicts of the 1990s. In 1914 Bosnia was ruled by an oppressive Austria–Hungary and looked to Serbia for support. It was in Sarajevo, Bosnia's capital, that the fuse was lit that started the war (see below).

Italy

• Italy had been allied to Germany since 1887 and had ambitions to win territory from Austria, expand to Dalmatia and thus gain control of the Adriatic Sea. However, when war broke out she dithered, and then declared neutrality on the basis that Germany was the aggressor and the Triple Alliance was a defensive treaty. Not until May 1915 did Italy come off the fence and declare war on Austria–Hungary, then three months later on Turkey. But only in August 1916 did she finally decided to complete the process and declare war on Germany, largely on the basis of assurances by the Allies of territorial gains in Austria once the war was won.

Other

Although not signatories of the original Triple Alliance, both Turkey and Bulgaria joined with Germany – the former at the end of October 1914 with the excuse that it was primarily to fight Russia to regain lost Ottoman territory and protect Islam, the latter (Bulgaria was the most powerful of the Balkan states) in September 1915 on the promise of Serbian Macedonia if the alliance was victorious.

The Triple Entente
France

• Although the defeat of France by the Germans in the Franco-Prussian War had occurred over forty years earlier, the loss of the provinces of Alsace and Lorraine and the huge reparations paid to Germany had not been forgotten. France wanted this territory back, and at the same time she became increasingly nervous of Germany's military expansion. This process had accelerated when Kaiser Wilhelm II succeeded to the imperial throne in 1888. A Franco-Russian pact was signed in 1893. However, the delicate balance of power in Europe continued to be threatened by German sabre-rattling, military expansion and interference in French Morocco in 1905 and again six years later.

Britain

• Britain was determined to avoid a continental shift in the balance of power. She was particularly concerned with the shipbuilding programme by the German navy. The result was an agreement with France that Britain's fleet would 'protect' the North Sea and English Channel, thus releasing the French fleet for possible operations in the Mediterranean.

• In 1839 Britain, along with France, Prussia, the Austro-Hungarian Empire and Russia, had signed the Treaty of London, which was designed to guarantee the neutrality of Belgium. Although the Triple Entente was an 'understanding' rather than a formal treaty, Britain was anxious to prevent German control of the Belgian Channel ports close to the English coast. In the event, it was the German invasion of neutral Belgium that decided Britain to declare war and join the French.

MAP 2   THE 'SPARK' – FRANZ FERDINAND IS ASSASSINATED, 28 JUNE 1914

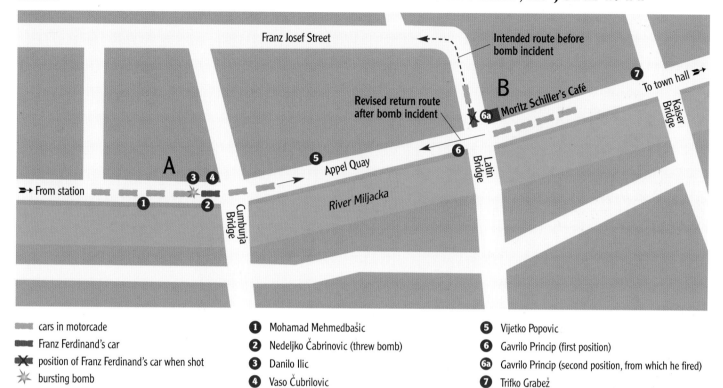

cars in motorcade
Franz Ferdinand's car
position of Franz Ferdinand's car when shot
bursting bomb

1 Mohamad Mehmedbašic
2 Nedeljko Čabrinovic (threw bomb)
3 Danilo Ilic
4 Vaso Čubrilovic

5 Vijetko Popovic
6 Gavrilo Princip (first position)
6a Gavrilo Princip (second position, from which he fired)
7 Trifko Grabež

Notes for Map 2

A The seven-car motorcade with Franz Ferdinand and his wife Sophie in the open third car proceeds along Appel Quay from the station towards the town hall.

At about 10:12 a.m. Nedeljko Čabrinović throws bomb, which bounces off Franz Ferdinand's car and explodes, injuring occupants of fourth car. Franz Ferdinand continues to town hall.

B Franz Ferdinand decides to visit injured officers in hospital after town hall visit. The return route is revised to proceed back down Appel Quay; however, the drivers are not told.

The leading car turns into Franz Josef Street (the intended return route). The drivers are now alerted to the correct route and the archduke's car tries to reverse. Gavrilo Princip steps forward from Schiller's Café and shoots and kills Franz Ferdinand and his wife.

Russia

• Russia entered the war in order to dominate the Balkans and in particular to support Serbia to ensure she was not absorbed by Austria–Hungary.

• The Tsar and the Russian ruling class were fearful of the growing revolutionary movement in Russia and felt a foreign military victory would distract people from internal strife.

The Spark

On 28 June 1914 the spark was struck that lit the fuse that started World War I. That morning the Archduke Franz Ferdinand, heir to the throne of the Austro-Hungarian Empire, accompanied by his morganatic wife, Sophie (see box, page 16), was scheduled to attend a reception in the town hall of the Bosnian capital, Sarajevo, hosted by the mayor. Until 1878 Turkey had governed Bosnia and Herzegovina, but then Austria–Hungary had been given the author-

ity to administer them (by the Treaty of Berlin) after the Turks' disastrous war with Russia. In 1908 Austria–Hungary annexed both provinces. This had aroused the fury of many Bosnian Serbs and the anger of Russia.

On that bright, sunny morning, Franz Ferdinand, who had earlier during the visit completed his inspection of nearby Austrian troop manoeuvres, was dressed in the military finery of a general of hussars, complete with cap crowned with green peacock feathers, blue serge tunic, black trousers, boots and sword. He arrived by train at Sarajevo station, with his wife dressed in white, to be met by the governor, General Oskar Potiorek, and a motorcade of seven cars for the drive to the town hall. The public knew the route they were to take along the Appel Quay beside the river and the curious had come out to watch.

By ten o'clock that morning the Appel Quay was, as it was later called, 'an avenue of assassins'. Spread out in a somewhat haphazard manner, and mingling with the crowds, were seven members of fanatically nationalist Serbian groups, including a secret society called the Black Hand. They were armed with either pistols or hand bombs, or

both, supplied by the Serbian military. Some, more committed and fanatical than others, had cyanide capsules to take after the assassination. The planning, however, seems to have been particularly poor, as none of the plotters appeared to know what the others were doing, where they would be, who was to shoot or throw their bombs or what was to happen if the attack succeeded or if it failed. Individuals appear to have been left to act as just that – individuals.

The archduke was travelling in the third car. He, with his wife on his right, was sitting at the rear of the open vehicle, the hood of which had been pulled down behind them. Opposite and facing Franz Ferdinand was General Potiorek. Beside the driver was Count Franz von Harrach. The target was obvious and exposed, although the use of a bomb was almost certainly going to cause indiscriminate casualties. When the cars approached Mohamad Mehmedbašic (No. 1 on Map 2), at the start of the gauntlet, he had second thoughts and allowed them to pass. As the third car came level with Nedeljko Čabrinović he primed his bomb (a rectangular-shaped flask with a neck) by smashing the top against a lamppost and immediately hurled it at the car. That was his mistake. There would be twelve seconds between striking the primer and the explosion – a long time in those circumstances. In addition, it was not a good throw. The driver accelerated, having seen an object thrown, and the bomb bounced off the hood at the back of the car and rolled into the road. Nedeljko promptly swallowed his poison and jumped down into the shallow waters of the river, where he was soon arrested (and survived – the cyanide proving a far from fatal dose). Meanwhile the bomb exploded in front of the following car, injuring two officers in it and a number of people nearby. The archduke's car kept moving until told to stop. Franz Ferdinand then sent Count Harrach back to check on any injuries. This was a splendid opportunity for one of the other would-be assassins to come forward and make a better attempt, but none did. The injured officers were driven to the hospital while the remaining cars continued to the town hall.

At the reception the mayor began his welcoming speech with the words, 'Your Imperial and Royal Highness, Your Highness. Our hearts are full of happiness on the occasion of your most gracious visit with which your Highnesses have deigned to honour the capital of our land . . .', upon which Franz Ferdinand burst out, 'Herr Bürgermeister, what is the good of your speeches? I come to Sarajevo on a friendly visit and someone throws a bomb at me. This is outrageous.' After some confusion, the archduke calmed down a little and announced, 'Now you can get on with your speech.'

Countess Sophie Chotek – a Morganatic Wife

In 1895 Franz Ferdinand met Countess Sophie Chotek at a ball in Prague and fell in love. To be an eligible marriage partner for a member of the House of Hapsburg, one had to be a member of one of the reigning, or former reigning, dynasties of Europe, which, unfortunately, Sophie was not. However, the relationship flourished secretly for over two years. When it became public knowledge (a photograph of Sophie was discovered in Franz Ferdinand's watch), Sophie was dismissed from her position as a lady-in-waiting. But, deeply in love, Franz Ferdinand refused to consider marrying anyone else.

Finally, in 1899 the Emperor Franz Josef agreed to the marriage provided it would be morganatic – that is, their descendants would not have any rights of succession to the throne. Sophie would not share her husband's rank, title, precedence or privileges. This meant she could not normally appear in public beside him, nor could she sit in the royal box or ride in the royal carriage. Their marriage on 1 July 1900 was a very low-key affair – not even Franz Josef attended. It was nine years before Sophie was 'promoted' in the hierarchy when she was given the title of Duchess of Hohenberg. Nevertheless, at a function attended by royalty she still had to stand far down the line of importance, separated from her husband.

Ironically, when travelling together outside Austria–Hungary Sophie could remain at her husband's side on all occasions. It was this that resulted in her murder in Sarajevo.

After the reception Franz Ferdinand determined on visiting the injured officers in hospital and his wife insisted on accompanying him, despite efforts to persuade her otherwise. In the circumstances it was deemed prudent not to take the narrow streets to the hospital by turning right off the Appel Quay into Franz Josef Street, but to continue on down the much wider Appel Quay. It was then that a disastrous blunder occurred – nobody told the drivers.

In the leading car this time was the mayor, followed by the car containing the archduke, his wife and General Potiorek, with Count Harrach standing on the running board next to Franz Ferdinand. As the motorcade came back down the Appel Quay the mayor's car slowed and turned right into Franz Josef Street and, a few yards behind, the archduke's vehicle followed. Realizing the error, Potiorek shouted for the driver to stop, which he did; he then began to reverse back into the Appel Quay. By pure chance, one of the more determined assassins, Gavrilo Princip, happened to be standing outside Moritz Schiller's café at the road junction. Fate had presented him with a near perfect target. He stepped forward, drew his pistol and fired twice before being seized and set upon by bystanders. What happened is best described in the words of Count Harrach:

> As the car quickly reversed, a thin stream of blood spurted from His Highness's mouth on to my right cheek. As I was pulling out my handkerchief to wipe the blood away from his mouth, the Duchess cried out to him, 'For God's sake! What has happened to you?' At that she slid off the seat and lay on the floor of the car, with her face between his knees. I had no idea that she too was hit and thought she had simply fainted with fright. Then I heard His Imperial Highness say, 'Sophie, Sophie don't die. Stay alive for the children!' At that, I seized the archduke by the collar of his uniform, to stop his head dropping forward and asked him if he was in great pain. He answered me quite distinctly, 'It's nothing!' His face began to twist somewhat but he went on repeating, six or seven times, ever more faintly as he gradually lost consciousness, 'It's nothing!' Then came a brief pause followed by a convulsive rattle in his throat, caused by a loss of blood. This ceased on arrival at the governor's [Potiorek's] residence.

Archduke Franz Ferdinand had been shot through the neck, his wife in the abdomen. Both died within a few minutes of the attack. The spark had been struck, the fuse lit.

Gavrilo Princip is arrested after shooting Franz Ferdinand.

The Blaze

After the bomb and bullets in Sarajevo at the end of June there was no actual clash of arms for over a month. However, by mid-August nation after nation across Europe had declared war in order to fulfil their alliance or entente obligations and the guns were firing for real. They would not fire their last shots for more than four years. The principal events of these calamitous weeks were:

28 June

• Serb fanatics assassinated Archduke Franz Ferdinand, heir to the Austro-Hungarian Empire. Austria–Hungary quickly demanded investigations and punishment of the culprits in deliberately insulting terms that Serbia would, she hoped, reject, giving Austria–Hungary reason to march. The Serbs appealed to the Tsar, who responded that Russia would protect Serbian territory. Austria–Hungary asked for German support.

5 July

• Germany assured Austria–Hungary of 'faithful support' in the event of any Russian aggression.

23 July

• Austria–Hungary demanded that Serbia crack down on dissident Austrian Serbs who were seeking independence and allow Austrian officials into Serbia to take charge of the investigations into the archduke's assassination – hardly onerous demands, to which Serbia's response was placatory. Austria–Hungary, however, was determined to go to war with Serbia and three days later rejected the Serbian reply.

24 July

• Britain urged Germany to mediate with Austria–Hungary.

25 July

• Austria–Hungary mobilized on the Serbian front.

28 July

• Austria–Hungary declared war on Serbia.

• Russia mobilized her forces on her border with the Austro-Hungarian Empire, to the consternation of Germany.

29 July

• Austria–Hungary sent a warship up the Danube to bombard the Serbian capital, Belgrade.

31 July

• Austria–Hungary and Russia ordered full mobilization. The Kaiser sent Russia an ultimatum to demobilize within twelve hours – a demand that was ignored. The Kaiser began to panic, because if Germany declared war on Russia, France would be sure to attack Germany and thus she would be committed to fighting on two fronts simultaneously – something he had always sought to avoid.

1 August

• Germany ordered full mobilization.

• A telegram from the German ambassador in London seemed to indicate that Britain might mediate on the Balkan dispute and thus keep France out of any war. This caused the Kaiser to restrain his chief of the General Staff (de facto commander-in-chief of the German Army) from immediately implementing the German war plans for attacking France (the amended Schlieffen Plan; see page 20) while clarification was sought.

• The clarification arrived at 11:00 p.m. Britain would prevent France going to war if Germany undertook not to go to war with either Russia or France while negotiations took place to solve the Austrian–Serbian dispute. This was unacceptable and Germany declared war on Russia.

• Belgium mobilized.

• France ordered mobilization and the recall of reservists.

• Britain remained uncommitted but sent telegrams to France and Germany asking for assurances that, if hostilities broke out, both countries would respect Belgian neutrality (as we have seen, Britain, France and Germany had all signed the Treaty of London to this effect). France responded positively, but Germany prevaricated and then claimed it was merely 'a scrap of paper'.

2 August

• Germany invaded Luxembourg and demanded free passage for her troops through Belgian territory.

• Britain assured France that her fleet would deny the German fleet access to French ports via the English Channel.

3 August

• Belgium rejected Germany's demands for free passage and King Albert I appealed to King George V for help if Germany invaded. Belgian neutrality was the key factor with Britain. To the mounting alarm of France, Britain appeared to be dithering over technicalities.

• Germany declared war on France.

4 August

• Germany invaded Belgium (although her border had been violated the day before) and Britain ordered mobilization, followed by a declaration of war on Germany late that night.

• Italy declared herself neutral, claiming that her commitment to the Triple Alliance was effective only in a defensive war and that, as Germany was the aggressor, she was not bound to support her.

5 August

• Montenegro declared war on Austria–Hungary.

6 August

• Austria–Hungary declared war on Russia.

7 August

• French troops crossed the frontier and advanced into German Alsace.

• Russian cavalry forces raided into East Prussia.

10 August

• Austria–Hungary invaded Russian Poland (Galicia).

• Leading elements of the BEF left Britain for France.

12 August

• France declared war on Austria–Hungary.

• Britain declared war on Austria–Hungary.

13 August

• Austria–Hungary invaded Serbia.

15 August

• French First and Second Armies attacked into German Lorraine.

16 August

• By this date leading elements of the BEF had arrived in France.

17 August

• Russian forces attacked across the border into East Prussia. Europe was ablaze.

• The bulk of the BEF had arrived in France.

18 August

• Russian forces invaded Galicia in the east.

• America declared herself neutral.

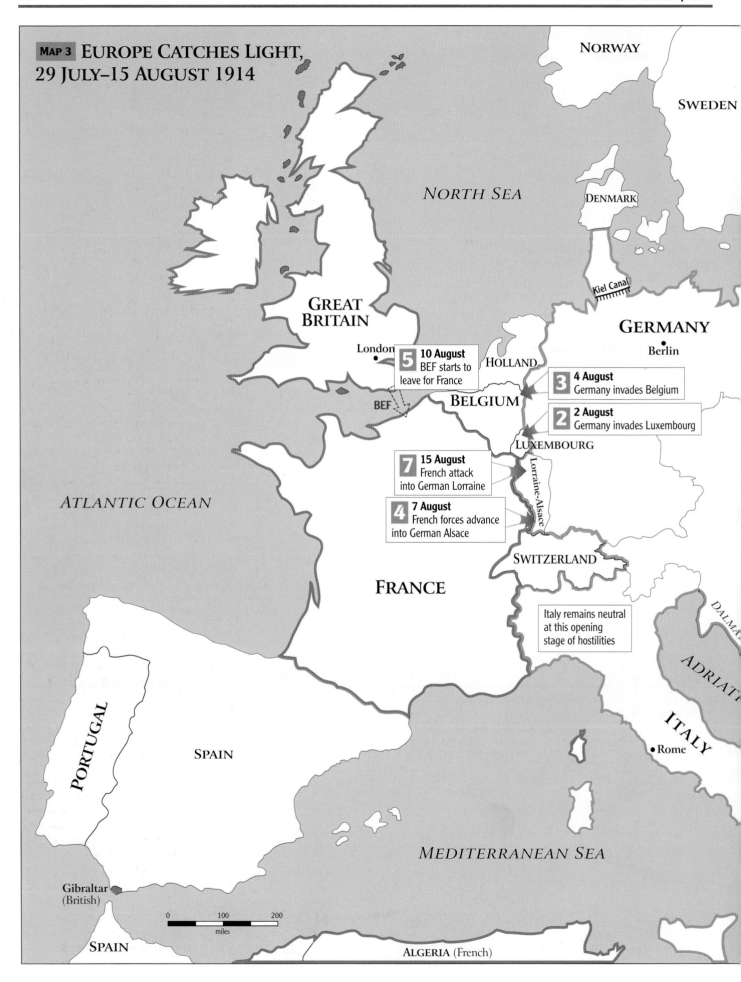

MAP 3 EUROPE CATCHES LIGHT,
29 JULY–15 AUGUST 1914

NORWAY

SWEDEN

NORTH SEA

DENMARK

Kiel Canal

GREAT
BRITAIN

GERMANY

• Berlin

London •

5 **10 August**
BEF starts to
leave for France

HOLLAND

BELGIUM

3 **4 August**
Germany invades Belgium

BEF

2 **2 August**
Germany invades Luxembourg

LUXEMBOURG

7 **15 August**
French attack
into German Lorraine

Lorraine-Alsace

ATLANTIC OCEAN

4 **7 August**
French forces advance
into German Alsace

SWITZERLAND

FRANCE

Italy remains neutral
at this opening
stage of hostilities

DALMA

ADRIATI

PORTUGAL

ITALY

SPAIN

• Rome

Gibraltar
(British)

0   100   200

miles

MEDITERRANEAN SEA

SPAIN

ALGERIA (French)

KEY

⬅ Russian offensive

⬅ German/Austrian offensive

⬅ French offensive

⬅ British movement of forces

1–**9** sequence of events

☐ Triple Entente countries

☐ Triple Alliance countries

8 **17 August**
Russian forces
attack into East Prussia

9 **18 August**
Russian forces
invade Galicia in the east

5 **10 August**
Austria invades
Russian Poland (Galicia)

1 **29 July**
Austria sends
warship up the Danube
to bombard Belgrade

6 **13 August**
Austria–
Hungary invades
Serbia

The German War Plan

In 1891 a fifty-eight-year-old Prussian aristocrat, Count Alfred von Schlieffen, was appointed by the Kaiser as chief of the General Staff of the German Army. He held that position for fifteen years, exercising an extraordinary influence on the development of the German General Staff and Army as a whole. Schlieffen was an experienced soldier, having served in the war of 1866 against Austria–Hungary and in that of 1870–71 against France as a staff officer. During those years as chief of the General Staff (de facto commander of the German Army) he promoted the training of staff officers in the handling of huge armies, urged on technical advances and threw much of his energy into equipping the army with heavy but mobile artillery.

Count Alfred von Schlieffen.

However, Schlieffen is primarily known to history as a war planner. The staff of all armies, including today's, are tasked with producing contingency plans to meet a variety of possible emergencies or operational deployments against potential enemies. Schlieffen's task was to draw up a war plan for Germany to win a full-scale continental war that would almost certainly have to be fought on two fronts simultaneously.

The problem

• The first decision to be made, on the assumption that Germany would be fighting France in the west and Russia in the east, was which to strike first. Germany was in a geographical/strategic 'interior lines' situation – she was located between two enemies, whereas in a war with Germany, France and Russia would be operating on 'exterior lines'. If both attacked simultaneously, the danger for Germany was of being crushed between them. However, as the German railway system was well developed and extensive, she could switch forces quickly from west to east or vice versa. The advantage of interior lines is that, with good communications and good staff work, one opponent can be held at bay with a small force while the main, stronger force concentrates on defeating the other. Having done so, troops can be released to turn on the other enemy.

• When given his instructions by the Kaiser, Schlieffen reversed a previous decision made in 1879 to attack Russia first.

France must now be overrun first in a quick and decisive manner while the Russians were watched and delayed by a comparatively small force deployed in East Prussia. The German war plan was based entirely on this decision. Schlieffen amended and adjusted his plan several times before handing over a final version to his successor, Colonel General Helmuth von Moltke the Younger, in 1906. The thinking was that Russia, weakened and demoralized by her defeat at the hands of the Japanese in 1904–5, would take at least six weeks to mobilize effectively against East Prussia. This timescale of six weeks was precisely the time allowed in the plan for German armies to crush France.

• The next problem was how to defeat France decisively in so short a time. A glance at Map 4 shows the difficulties. In the east the French had protected their border for 200 miles from the Swiss frontier to Verdun with a string of fortifications along the Moselle and Meuse rivers. These fortifications were centred on Belfort, Épinal, Toul and Verdun and were well maintained – from 1877 onwards 160 forts, 250 batteries and a rail network capable of moving fifteen army corps to the German border were built at a cost of around 660 million francs. A small gap was deliberately left between Épinal and Toul to channel an attacker and expose him to attacks into his flanks. France's northern border was neglected, with fortresses such as Maubeuge and Lille poorly maintained, as this frontier was shared with Belgium, which had her own system of fortresses.

• To Schlieffen, an offensive directly across France's eastern frontier could never succeed in six weeks. The defences were too strong and the terrain hugely favoured the defender; in addition, rail communications were insufficient to support a really large offensive. Thus the massing of armies along this frontier followed by deep, decisive thrusts into France were considered impractical and likely to be too costly in men, materials and time. This left the north. An offensive there would need to be a massive wheel into northern France, ignoring Belgian, Dutch and Luxembourg neutrality. Such an attack, with overwhelming strength on the right wing and a static, weaker, defensive left wing, would sweep up the Belgian Army – hopefully before it could retreat into the fortress of Antwerp – as well as any British force that might be rushed across the Channel to assist France. With the use of the extensive Belgian railway network, considerable foraging and much hard marching, such a speedy advance was deemed possible.

The plan

• Schlieffen's plan envisaged a right wing up to seven times the strength of the left wing. It would march south-west through Holland, Belgium and northern France, as Schlieffen explained, 'letting the last grenadier on the right brush the Channel with his sleeve'. The hinge of this vast manoeuvre was the fortress of Metz. It has been likened to the opening of a door that would swing round until it slammed into the wall represented by the French forts on the Franco-German border, with the French armies trapped between. The much weaker left wing would maintain a defensive posture. Alternatively, if a French offensive to recover Alsace and Lorraine were mounted (this was thought highly likely), then it would probably improve the effectiveness of the plan if the German forces opposing the attacks retired gradually.

• Fortresses were to be ignored, bypassed and cut off, to be dealt with by follow-up troops or starved into surrender after the defeat of the enemy field armies. This was also to be the fate of Paris. The objective was to outflank and overwhelm the French armies on their left, with the all-powerful German right wing crossing the Seine below Paris and then wheeling east. Then, in conjunction with the rest of the armies in the wheel, Germany would force a defeat as the French were pushed back against their own line of forts. It was to be all over, bar some mopping up, within six weeks so that large reinforcements could be rushed to the east, where it was anticipated the Russian threat, contained by ten German divisions, would by then be serious.

The plan is modified

• On 1 January 1906 Schlieffen went on to the retired list and was replaced by Helmuth Johannes von Moltke (usually called 'the Younger'), nephew of the famous Count Helmuth Carl von Moltke ('the Elder') who had masterminded the German victory over France in the war of 1870–71. Over the years leading up to 1914 the younger Moltke was instrumental in modifying his predecessor's grand plan – for which many historians have since condemned him. Of the nine new divisions that became available between 1905 and 1914, he allocated eight to the left wing and only one to the right. He also took a more pragmatic look at the problems of implementation and instituted a number of staff studies, particularly on the logistical effort needed to support such a vast undertaking.

• A major change was not to breach the neutrality of Holland. Moltke accepted that Belgium must be invaded, but baulked at having to contend with the Dutch Army as well. Added to the Belgian, French and possibly British forces, the additional fighting could upset the timetable of the 'swinging door'.

• However, this decision brought with it fresh problems. It meant that the right wing of the offensive could not cut through the Maastricht Appendix, that annoying Dutch appendage that hung down from the south of Holland. From the Swiss border in the extreme south, north as far as Verdun, the mountainous terrain, the River Moselle and French fortifications made a swift and successful attack highly unlikely. North of Verdun the River Meuse and Luxembourg blocked the way. Although the neutrality of that insignificant duchy could continue to be ignored, territory to the north consisted of the mountainous Ardennes Forest and then a gap of only some 35 miles before the Dutch frontier was reached. Even this gap was blocked by the Meuse and the fortress of Liège just a few miles inside Belgium.

• Moltke considered that even though the two armies on the far right wing would have to start their advance through this gap, it was practical, with limited roads, for only a single army to assemble opposite the gap. In the event, the German Second Army would assemble at the gap while the First Army would group further north, and both would march through the gap, one behind the other. Liège, the cork in the bottleneck, would possibly be taken by *coup de main* (surprise attack) ahead of the main advance, or would be bypassed.

• The French could be expected to react by attacking in the south with the objective of recapturing Alsace and Lorraine, but, unlike Schlieffen, Moltke was not prepared to give up German territory in that area. For this reason he weakened the right wing in order to bolster the left – indeed a German offensive on the left might create a gigantic pincer movement that would crush the French even more completely.

• Thus the modified plan was devised. In it the right wing was strong, but not as strong as Schlieffen had intended, outnumbering the opposition by three to one instead of seven to one; the wheel of the five most powerful armies was still to hinge on Metz; Dutch territory was not to be entered; and there was no question of German soldiers on the extreme right brushing the Channel with their sleeves. Instead, these right-wing formations would turn south-west at Brussels and swing down over the Seine west of Paris before turning east. Soldiers in these units would have some 600 miles to march – not as far as Schlieffen's plan by at least 100 miles, although still a taxing distance for the men who had to do the marching. The six-week timescale to a French surrender remained. In the event, Moltke also transferred two corps from the west to reinforce the Russian front at the crisis of the August campaign.

• Germany was to commit almost 1.5 million men to the Western Front in 1914, of whom some 580,000 were in the two armies on the right flank. However, as with all military plans, much would depend on what the enemy did, how well they did it, the resistance of the Belgians, the reaction of Britain, the vast German logistical tail functioning smoothly and being able to keep pace with the proposed advance, and also the marching and fighting stamina of the troops.

The French War Plan

Ever since Germany had humiliated France in the Franco-Prussian War the French political and military leadership had been compelled to adapt to a new balance of power in Europe. The emergence of the German Empire on the other side of the Rhine and the loss of Alsace and Lorraine, together with the huge reparations exacted by the victors, had put France at a troubling disadvantage – although the £200 million reparations were paid off ahead of schedule. However, in the event of hostilities breaking out again, France was fairly confident that she could rely on her entente with Russia to ensure that Germany had to face in two different directions – by the 1912 French–Russian Military Protocol, Russia undertook to attack Germany with 750,000 men within fifteen days of mobilization. France also expected Britain immediately to send an expeditionary force to her aid – there had been numerous military 'conversations' as to how this would be done, but no signed political undertaking to cement any arrangements the soldiers made. If anything were to put British troops into France, it would be Germany breaking the Treaty of London and invading Belgium.

In 1898 the French General Staff adopted Plan XIV, as it was known. Taking into account the numerical inferiority of the French Army, this plan envisaged a strategic defensive posture along the Franco-German border making the maximum use of a continuous line of sunken fortifications, rivers and difficult terrain. Besides the increasing disparity in population between France and Germany, there was the problem of reserves. The war of 1870–71 had demonstrated the ability of the Germans to make effective use of their

rail network to deploy armies and mobilize reserves quickly as front-line formations. Plan XIV applied the lessons of railroad use but neglected the use of reservists. In 1903 Plan XIV was superseded by Plan XV, which, while still defensive in character, did include reserves, but only in subordinate roles. Plan XVI replaced this. General Victor Michel, the French commander-in-chief designate, argued that Germany could never achieve a quick victory in Lorraine and through the French chain of modern fortifications, and would therefore attack in strength through Belgium. His answer was to reinforce the French left up to the Channel coast, using reserves, coupled with a pre-emptive move into Belgium up to the River Meuse. Politically, this plan was shouted down as unacceptable. Michel was relieved of his command-designate post and replaced by General Joseph Joffre.

The final plan with which France went to war in 1914 was Plan XVII (see Map 5, page 24), drawn up initially by General Ferdinand Foch and almost wholly offensive. It was adopted and refined by Joffre after he became chief of the General Staff in 1911. It had two fundamental guiding principles: that the only sure way to victory over the Germans was to take the offensive, attacking at both strategic and tactical levels; and that the lost provinces of Alsace and Lorraine should be retaken.

Strangely, the completion of the static defences along the German border saw the birth of an all-pervasive offensive spirit within the French military. It was held that the main reason for the loss of the Franco-Prussian War was lack of this elan, this attacking zeal. Coupled with the national ideal of *la revanche* (revenge) – the desire to erase the shame of defeat – the principle of attacking in virtually all circumstances came to be taught as the only way to victory, while defensive tactics were neglected in military training at all levels. In the critical years before 1914 the gospel of '*l'attaque à outrance*' (attack to excess), promulgated with such enthusiasm by Lieutenant Colonel Loyzeau de Grandmaison, chief of the Operations Branch of the General Staff, took hold throughout the French military, indeed throughout the nation.

Plan XVII

• Despite the two basic principles that ran through French military thinking – take the offensive and recover Alsace and Lorraine – the actual plan with which France went to war in August 1914 was primarily a mobilization one. Joffre wanted to position his armies in the best possible locations so that they could be used for counter-thrusts once the line of the German offensives became

clear. After the war, when Joffre appeared before a parliamentary commission, he went to great lengths to explain the difference between a concentration plan and an operational one. He knew that France's efforts must be inextricably linked to a simultaneous offensive by Russia, but he kept his detailed operational thinking from both his political masters and his military subordinates. He insisted that politicians in particular would 'meddle' – his word – in military matters if they knew the overall plan of operation. An example of this secretiveness was his reluctance to bring even his most senior generals into his operational thinking. It occurred at a meeting of army commanders in early August. When General Yvon Dubail, the First Army commander, asked for more troops to attack into Alsace, Joffre replied, 'That's your plan, not mine.'

• Joffre's mobilization/concentration plan was based on the assumption of the Germans avoiding the fortified line Belfort–Verdun and attacking from the Metz area. He also realized that a German violation of Belgian neutrality in some manner was a virtual certainty – the intelligence indications were clear on this. However, Joffre did not contemplate the sort of wide outflanking sweep by overwhelming numbers that eventually materialized. His belief was that if the Germans marched into Belgium then any advance would be limited to a supporting flank move, probably into eastern Belgium.

• Joffre intended to meet these potential thrusts with a series of strategic offensives. The first would be into German-occupied Alsace and Lorraine by the First and Second Armies, threatening the left flank of an enemy advance. Once this was under way it was intended to launch an equally powerful attack north of Metz. The Fifth Army would attack to the north of that city, while the Third Army would act as a link between these two offensives and undertake the investment (surrounding) of Metz as the advance progressed. The Fourth Army was earmarked as the reserve force to concentrate behind the centre of the line. Its movements depended on how the situation developed and the direction of the main German thrusts. If the Germans moved into Luxembourg and eastern Belgium, then it would support the Fifth Army.

• The essence of the French plan was to take the offensive at the earliest opportunity, relying on the Belgians and, it was hoped, the arrival of the BEF to protect the wide-open left flank of the Fifth Army – there being little apart from some scattered, outdated fortifications and local Territorial troops between it and the sea.

Notes for Map 4

- By 1914 Schlieffen's plan had been somewhat watered down, in that Holland's neutrality was to be maintained. From the all-important right wing Moltke switched troops to the left of the line, an area he considered too weak. Thus, for reasons discussed in the text, Schlieffen's supposed deathbed plea to 'keep the right wing strong' had been modified. Nevertheless, the fundamentals of Schlieffen's plan remained.

- It amounted to a huge, strategic swinging hammer, pivoting at **A**, with the Fifth Army making the shortest inner blow but having to fight around Verdun and across some very difficult terrain that favoured the defence.

- The First and Second Armies provided the hammerhead proper, with some 580,000 men at the end of the hammer. Both armies were to avoid infringing Dutch neutrality and march through the narrow gap between the 'Maastricht Appendix' and the northern edge of the Ardennes Forest, **B**. Because of the restricted space, these two armies were compelled to march one behind the other, with the combined columns stretching back over 100 miles, and had to accept the inevitable delays this caused. The fortress at Liège was to be bypassed and besieged by follow-up troops.

- Soldiers of the First Army on the extreme right were no longer going to 'brush their sleeves on the English Channel' but were to make a tighter wheel, **CCC**, before crossing the Seine well below Paris – a city that was not to be besieged at that stage, if at all.

- The Second, Third, Fourth and Fifth Armies were to cross the River Meuse before beginning to swing south with the object of forcing the French back across the River Marne, **DD**.

- **E** shows the approximate position to be reached by the First Army at the end of six weeks. By then it was anticipated that the French would be crushed, outflanked and forced back against their own fortification along the Moselle. Any small British force that appeared, along with the Belgian Army, was to be knocked back and destroyed by the heavy hammer blows of the right wing.

Technology in World War I

World War I has been characterized as a clash between twentieth-century technology and nineteenth-century tactics and, certainly at the start, that was very true. This situation had disastrous results on the battlefield and was the primary cause of the vast number of casualties on both sides that have become the hallmark of the war. As will become obvious in reading this book, World War I on the Western Front quickly developed into one vast siege operation. In very general terms, the Allies were the besiegers, striving to drive the German besieged from French and Belgian soil.

For much of the war technology favoured the defence. Not until late 1917 and into 1918 did the armies fully succeed in combining the numerous new technologies into effective military tactics capable of breaching the 'wall'. Just how this happened will become clear in the later sections of the book, but a distinction should be made between new technologies and those existing technologies that were improved and better adapted to the awful business of killing. Both these are listed below, together with two non-technical aspects of the war that appeared for the first time.

Existing technologies	New technologies	New non-technical developments
• artillery	• quick-firing artillery of longer range	• millions of men under arms
• machine guns	• aircraft	• the vast scale of the logistical requirements essential to keep these huge armies in the field
• mines	• tanks	
• trenches	• flamethrowers	
• balloons	• gas	
• railways	• rudimentary wireless	
• field telephones		

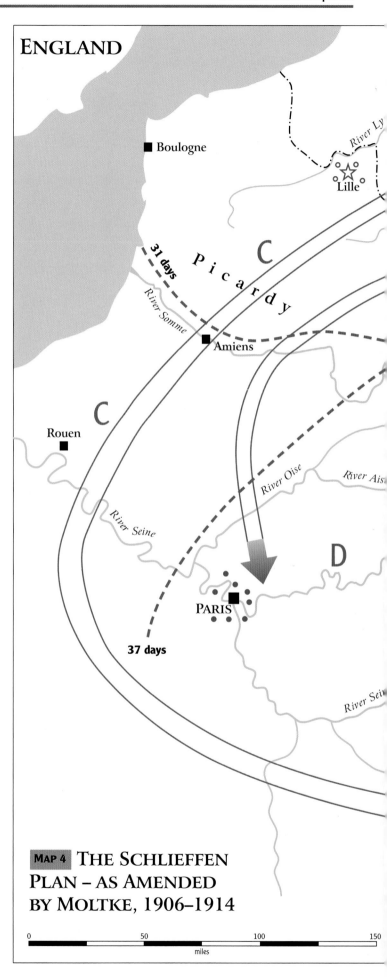

MAP 4 THE SCHLIEFFEN PLAN – AS AMENDED BY MOLTKE, 1906–1914

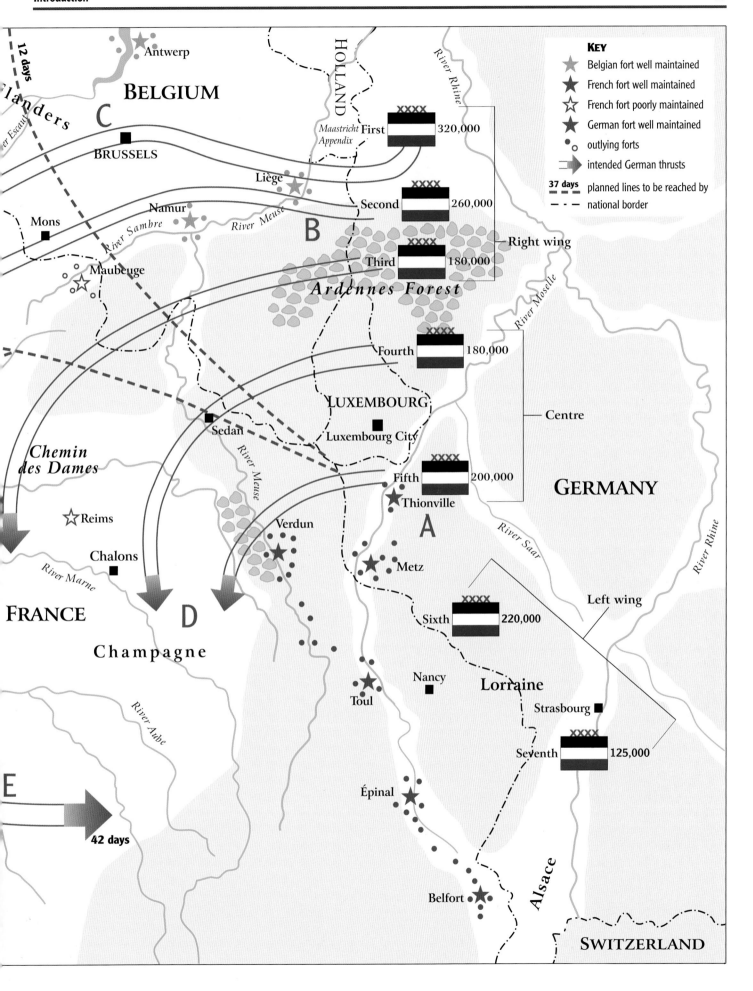

12 days

Flanders

River Escaut

BELGIUM

C

Antwerp

HOLLAND

River Rhine

BRUSSELS

Liège

Namur

River Sambre

River Meuse

Mons

Maubeuge

Maastricht Appendix First 320,000

XXXX

Second 260,000

XXXX

Third 180,000

XXXX

— Right wing

Ardennes Forest

River Moselle

B

Fourth 180,000

XXXX

LUXEMBOURG

Luxembourg City

— Centre

Sedan

Chemin des Dames

River Meuse

Fifth 200,000

XXXX

Thionville

GERMANY

Reims

Verdun

River Saar

Chalons

River Marne

FRANCE

D

Metz

C h a m p a g n e

Sixth 220,000

XXXX

Left wing

Nancy

Lorraine

Toul

Strasbourg

River Aube

Seventh 125,000

XXXX

E

Épinal

42 days

Belfort

Alsace

River Rhine

SWITZERLAND

KEY

☆ Belgian fort well maintained

★ French fort well maintained

☆ French fort poorly maintained

★ German fort well maintained

• ○ outlying forts

➤ intended German thrusts

37 days ----- planned lines to be reached by

—·—·— national border

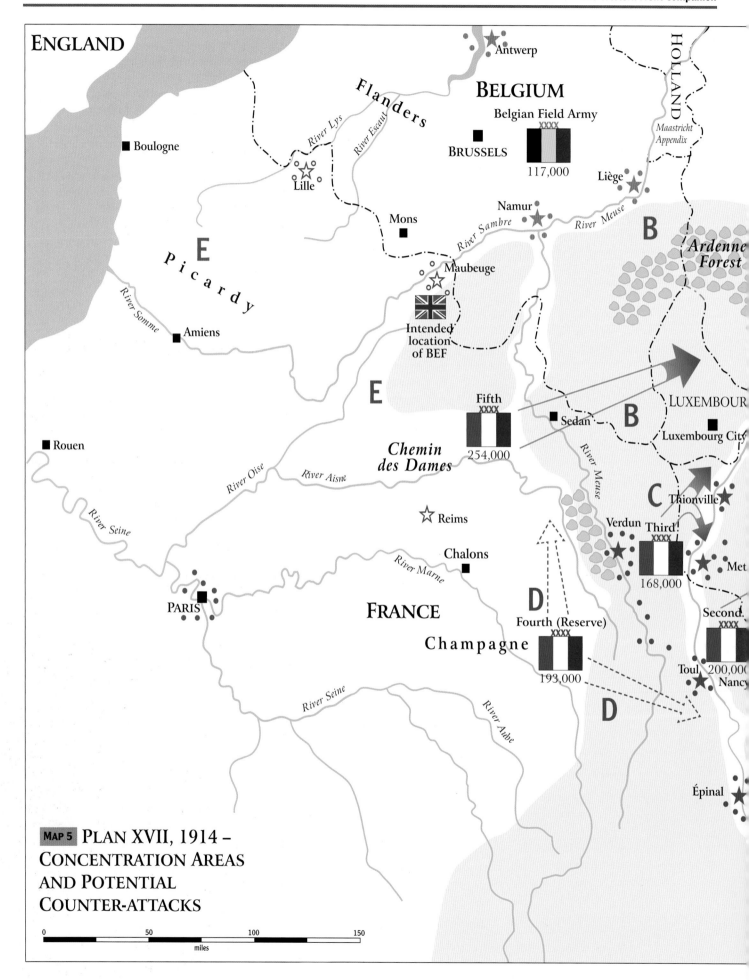

ENGLAND

Flanders

BELGIUM

HOLLAND

Antwerp

Belgian Field Army

Boulogne

BRUSSELS

River Lys

River Escaut

Lille

Mons

River Sambre

Namur

Liège

Maastricht Appendix

117,000

River Meuse

B

Ardenne Forest

E

P i c a r d y

River Somme

Maubeuge

Intended location of BEF

Amiens

E

Fifth

254,000

Sedan

B

LUXEMBOUR

River Meuse

B

Luxembourg City

Rouen

Chemin des Dames

River Oise

River Aisne

C

Thionville

Verdun

Third

River Seine

Reims

Chalons

River Marne

168,000

Met

PARIS

FRANCE

D

Fourth (Reserve)

Champagne

193,000

Second

River Seine

200,00

Toul

Nancy

River Aube

D

Épinal

MAP 5 PLAN XVII, 1914 –
CONCENTRATION AREAS
AND POTENTIAL
COUNTER-ATTACKS

0   50   100   150
miles

Belgian fort well maintained

French fort well maintained

French fort poorly maintained

German fort well maintained

outlying forts

intended French thrusts

national border

River Rhine

River Moselle

GERMANY

River Saar

River Rhine

A

Lorraine

First
XXXX

56,000

Strasbourg ■

Belfort

Alsace

SWITZERLAND

Notes for Map 5

• The French war plan was primarily a mobilization and concentration one. Once hostilities began and the Germans' intentions became known for certain, the French (under Joffre) intended first to strike to the south of Metz into Alsace and Lorraine with the First and Second Armies, **A**. The Fifth Army would attack to the north of Metz and south of the Ardennes Forest, **BB**, to counter the German advance that was expected through Luxembourg and eastern Belgium. Linking these two offensives would be an advance by the Third Army, **C**, which would also have the task of investing Metz. Joffre intended to keep the Fourth Army in reserve behind the centre, able to move either north or south as circumstances required, **DD**.

• The large gap that stretched to the sea on the left of the Fifth Army, **EE**, was an obvious potential weakness. However, Joffre did not believe that if Belgian neutrality was breached it would involve a wide sweep by the Germans through the north of that country. In consequence, the defences in this area were thin. Reliance was placed on a number of outdated and neglected fortifications, such as those at Maubeuge and Lille, and on some poor-quality Territorial formations. Apart from the small Belgian Army, there was also the expectation that the BEF would arrive in time to concentrate on the French left.

• A glance at Map 4 reveals how the German offensive, after crashing through Belgium, was planned to hit the most exposed and vulnerable part of the French line.

Belgian troops prepare for the defence of Antwerp in trenches near the city, 1914.

The British War Plan

As noted above, the UK, unlike Russia, which was committed by a separate treaty – was not obliged to go to war if France was attacked by Germany. Nevertheless, certainly within the military leadership on both sides of the Channel, there was an understanding that Britain would send troops to support France. A series of regular military planning meetings had been held and an understanding of the likely British role and area of deployment had been agreed.

Britain, unlike the continental powers, did not have universal military service. Thus mobilization was limited to the regulars, fleshed out with a small number of immediately available reserves. It was intended that this force would consist of two army corps of three divisions each, a cavalry division and supporting artillery and services. It would become the British Expeditionary Force and would be shipped to France to form on the left flank of the French line near Maubeuge. It was intended that this BEF would be deployed in France twenty-one days after mobilization. That was the British war plan.

The Belgian War Plan

The commander-in-chief of the Belgian Armed Forces was King Albert I. In 1914 Belgium's field army consisted of 117,000 men organized into six infantry divisions and one cavalry division. It was supported by around 65,000 garrison troops in Antwerp, Namur and Liège. The plan was for these field divisions to concentrate west of the Meuse and be available to delay any advance, but to avoid battle against superior forces. Antwerp was to be defended at all costs and the field army was intended to keep in touch with the city.

General Sir John French and his secretary Major Watt leaving the War Office after a crisis Cabinet meeting in the period before the outbreak of war.

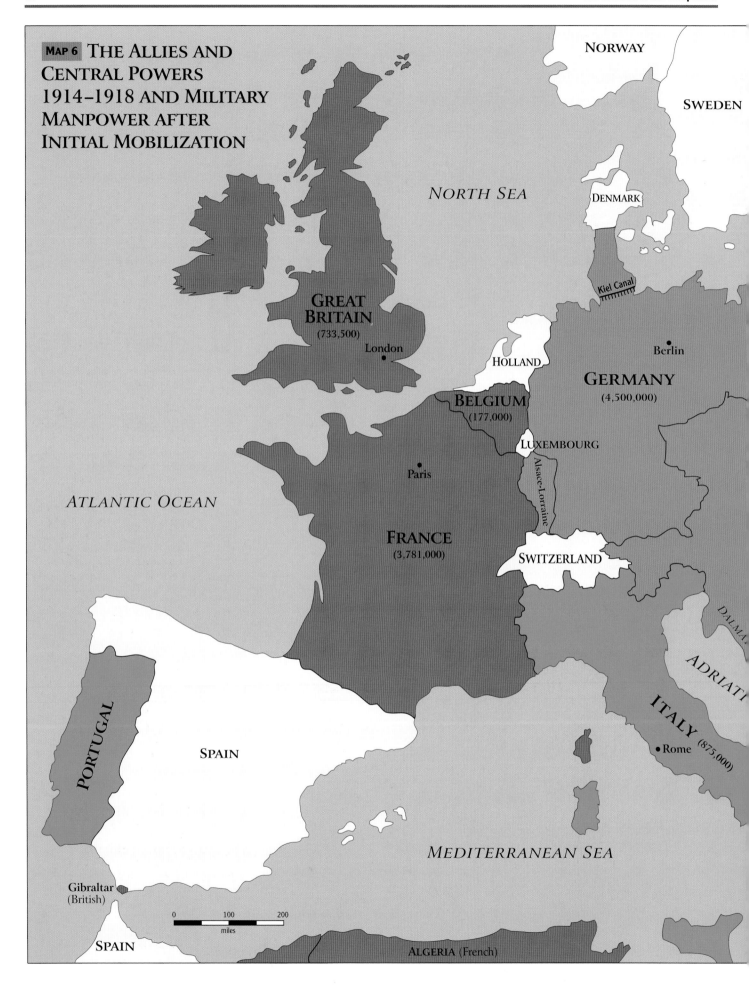

MAP 6 THE ALLIES AND
CENTRAL POWERS
1914–1918 AND MILITARY
MANPOWER AFTER
INITIAL MOBILIZATION

NORWAY

SWEDEN

NORTH SEA

DENMARK

Kiel Canal

GREAT
BRITAIN
(733,500)

London

HOLLAND

Berlin

GERMANY
(4,500,000)

BELGIUM
(177,000)

LUXEMBOURG

Alsace-Lorraine

Paris

ATLANTIC OCEAN

FRANCE
(3,781,000)

SWITZERLAND

DALMA

ADRIATI

PORTUGAL

SPAIN

ITALY (875,000)

Rome

MEDITERRANEAN SEA

Gibraltar
(British)

0   100   200
miles

SPAIN

ALGERIA (French)

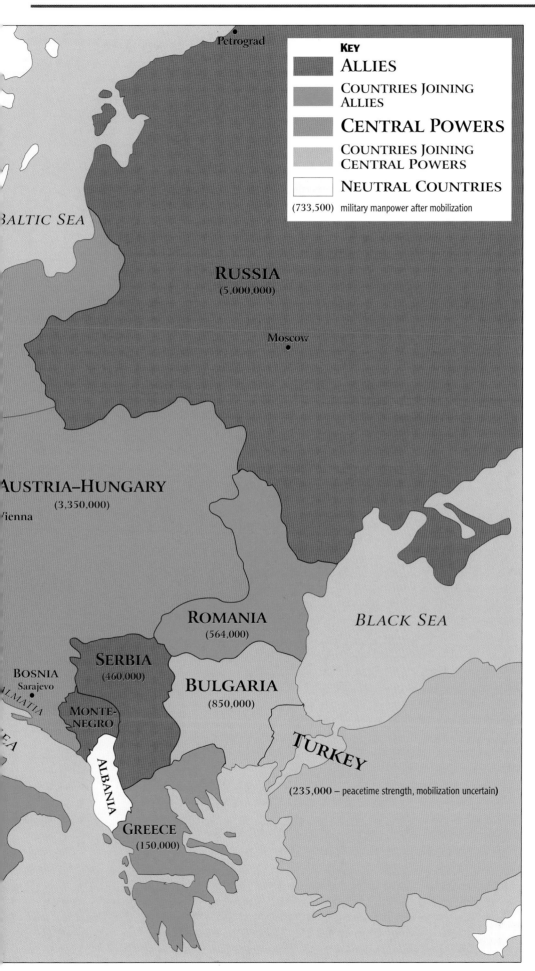

Paris in Shock

Philip Gibbs, the *Daily Chronicle* correspondent in Paris in early August 1914, described the atmosphere when war become inevitable – a great contrast to the scenes in London and Berlin at the same time (see boxes, pages 13 and 96).

There was no wild outbreak of Jingo fever, no demonstration of bloodlust against Germany in Paris or any town in France [as] the people waited for the fateful decision . . .

On August 1 there was a run on one of the banks. I passed its doors and saw them besieged by thousands . . . in a long queue waiting with a strange quietude . . . to withdraw the savings of a lifetime . . . There were similar crowds outside other banks, and on the faces of these people was a look of brooding fear, as though all they had fought and struggled for . . . might suddenly be snatched from them. The cashiers had been withdrawn from their desks and cheques could not be paid.

'We are ruined already,' said a woman. 'This war will take all our money. Oh my God!' She made her way through the crowd with a fixed white face.

The call to arms came without any clamour of bugles or orations. Unlike the scenes in the early days of 1870 [when Germany last invaded France], there were no street processions of civil enthusiasts. No painted beauty of the stage waved the tricolour to the shout of '*À Berlin!*' No mob orators jumped on café tables to wave their arms in defiance of the foe.

The quietness of Paris was astounding, and the first mobilization orders were issued with no more publicity than attends the delivery of a trade circular through the halfpenny post. Yet in hundreds of thousands of houses through France . . . there was a drama of tragic quietude when the [mobilization] cards were delivered to young men in civilian clothes.

A company of Canadian soldiers going 'over the top' from a World War I trench. Note the shell bursts overhead.

A Western Front Timeline

Battles, even in these ages, are transacted by mechanisms;
men now even die, and kill one another, in an artificial manner.

Thomas Carlyle, *The French Revolution*, 1837

In May 1921 the Battles Nomenclature Committee published its report, and although this *Companion* has not specifically followed the phases of the war set out by the committee, it may be useful to enumerate their conclusions in order to help the reader understand the sequence (or phasing) of major events that occurred during the four years of continuous fighting on the Western Front.

Phase 1 The German invasion in 1914.

Phase 2 Trench warfare, 1914–1916.

Phase 3 The Allied offensive in 1916 (the Battles of the Somme and the French defence of Verdun).

Phase 4 The German retreat and the Allied advance to the Hindenburg Line.

Phase 5 The Allied offensives of 1917 (Arras, Vimy, Chemin des Dames, Third Ypres (Passchendaele), Cambrai.

Phase 6 The German offensive, spring 1918.

Phase 7 The Allied advance to victory, August–November 1918.

Before describing in detail how the war on the Western Front was fought, a look in outline at the critical events and battles that took place year by year will help in putting the later, more detailed, accounts of smaller-scale actions into context. The timeline is in the form of a year-by-year diary of events, illustrated by maps showing the battles fought and the line of the Western Front at the end of each year. More detailed maps with accompanying notes explain two or three of the more important battles fought during each year.

1914

Never in the history of warfare had so large a concentration of military forces assembled in Europe. In round numbers, the Germans initially deployed 1.5 million; the French had over 1 million, with 3 million reservists on call; the Austrians and Russians each had 1.25 million on their frontiers; and by the end of the year 1 million volunteers in the UK had come forward to serve. By Christmas, as an unofficial truce was celebrated on parts of the Western Front, the expectation of a short, sharp war of manoeuvre had evaporated. The Kaiser had told departing troops, 'You will be home before the leaves have fallen from the trees.' In Britain the urgency of the patriotic rush to volunteer was due to the prevailing view that the great adventure would 'be all over by Christmas'.

Only Lord Kitchener, the British war minister, warned the Cabinet that the war would not be short – he anticipated it would last three years. The first weeks of fighting in the west were clashes of encounter and movement (the Battles of the Frontiers), which saw the Allies forced to retreat in the face of a massive German onslaught. This opening phase of the war was what both sides had planned for – a type of war their commanders understood and for which their armies were trained. However, Moltke's variation of the Schlieffen Plan had, by the end of 1914, failed to provide the decisive, overwhelming and speedy victory envisaged by the Germans. Worried by reports of Russian advances into East Prussia, Moltke had weakened the all-powerful right wing by detaching troops to the Eastern Front and had failed to appreciate how the blazing heat of summer, continuous forced marching over extensive distances, combat and heavy losses, coupled with immense logistical problems, would exhaust his armies before any decisive victory could be achieved.

When General Alexander von Kluck, commanding the German First Army on the extreme right wing, had been forced to turn his tired troops south-east and march north of Paris instead of swinging south of it, he

Declarations of War 1914

Every year from 1914 to 1918 at least five declarations of war were made, many by tiny countries like Haiti and Honduras, both of which declared only a few months before the Armistice. In 1914 they were:

28 July	Austria on Serbia
1 August	Germany on Russia
3 August	Germany on France
4 August	Germany on Belgium
	UK on Germany
5 August	Montenegro on Austria–Hungary
6 August	Austria–Hungary on Russia
	Serbia on Germany
8 August	Montenegro on Germany
12 August	France on Austria–Hungary
	UK on Austria–Hungary
23 August	Japan on Germany
25 August	Japan on Austria–Hungary
28 August	Austria–Hungary on Belgium
2 November	Russia on Turkey
	Serbia on Turkey
5 November	UK on Turkey
	France on Turkey

The First British Rifle Shot of the War

On 22 August 1914 C Squadron of the 4th Dragoon Guards were part of the cavalry screen advancing ahead of the BEF and about to take part in the first action by British soldiers on the continent of Europe since Waterloo ninety-nine years earlier. Suddenly, over the crest of a hill, a body of lance-carrying German Uhlan cavalry appeared.

The squadron commander, Major Tom Bridges, gave permission for Captain Hornby with the 1st Troop to make a mounted charge. In the resulting melee, the British swords proved far more effective than the Germans' unwieldy lances. The Germans scattered and the 1st Troop, supported by the 4th, careered off in pursuit for about a mile before the Germans rallied and turned to open fire. Trooper (Drummer) Edward Thomas left an account of how he fired the first British rifle shot of World War I:

Captain Hornby gave the order, '4th Troop, dismounted action!' We found cover behind a chateau wall and, possibly because I was rather noted for my quick movements and athletic ability, I was first in action. I could see a German cavalry officer some four hundred yards away, gesticulating to the left and to the right as he disposed of his dismounted men and ordered them to take up their firing positions to engage us. Immediately I saw him I took aim, pulled the trigger and automatically, almost instantaneously, he fell to the ground.

Thomas was later promoted Sergeant and awarded the Military Medal.

The 'Old Contemptibles'

This was a title proudly adopted by the soldiers of the original BEF, who saw service in France and Flanders from Mons to the First Battle of Ypres. It is said to have originated from a translation from the Kaiser's Order of the Day of 19 August to the German First Army commander, Alexander von Kluck, at the outset of hostilities. He wrote:

It is my Royal and Imperial command that you concentrate your energies for the immediate present upon one single purpose, and that is that you address your skill and all the valour of my soldiers to exterminate first the treacherous English; walk over French's contemptibly small army . . .

It was used by post-war veterans' associations as a highly suitable title.

Timeline 1914

Date	General	Western Front
28 June	Franz Ferdinand assassinated	
2–4 Aug.	Declarations of war	
4 Aug.	Germany invades Belgium	
7–10 Aug.		Battle of Mulhouse (opening French attack of the war) – French defeat
14–25 Aug.		First Battle of Lorraine (Battles of Morhange and Sarrebourg) – French defeat
15 Aug.	Russia invades East Prussia	
17 Aug.		Liège surrenders to Germans
18 Aug.	America declares neutrality	
19–20 Aug.	Battle of Gumbinnen – Russians force German retreat	
20 Aug.		Germans occupy Brussels
21–23 Aug.		Battle of the Ardennes – French retreat
21–23 Aug.		Battle of Charleroi – French defeat
23–24 Aug.		Battle of Mons – BEF retreat
23 Aug.–5 Sept.		BEF retreat from Mons
25 Aug.		Namur surrenders to Germans
		French garrison abandons Lille
26 Aug.		Battle of Le Cateau – BEF retreat
26–30 Aug.	Battle of Tannenburg – Russians decisively defeated by Germans	
29–30 Aug.		Battle of St-Quentin (or Guise) – French withdrawal
4–12 Sept.		Second Battle of Lorraine (Grand Couronne, Nancy) – French repulse German assaults
7–14 Sept.	Battle of Masurian Lakes – Russians driven from East Prussia	
7–10 Sept.		First Battle of the Marne – Allies defeat Germans
8 Sept.		Maubeuge surrenders to Germans
12 Sept.		Germans take Lille
12–21 Sept.		First Battle of the Aisne – stalemate
22–26 Sept.		Battle of Picardy (Noyon, Péronne and Bapaume) – indecisive
25–29 Sept.		Battle of Albert (part of the end of the Battle of Picardy) – indecisive
27 Sept.–10 Oct.		First Battle of Artois –indecisive
10 Oct.		Antwerp surrenders
10 Oct.–2 Nov.		Battle of La Bassée – indecisive, BEF hold the line
12 Oct.–2 Nov.		Battle of Messines – indecisive
13 Oct.–2 Nov		Battle of Armentières – BEF hold the line
16–31 Oct.		Battle of the Yser – French and Belgian forces secure Belgian coastline
17 Oct.	First contingent of Australian Imperial Force (AIF) embarks for France	
19 Oct.–22 Nov.		First Battle of Ypres ends Race to the Sea. BEF halts German attacks at Langemarck (21–24 Oct.), Gheluvelt (29–31 Oct.) and Nonne Bosschen (11 Nov.)
31 Oct.	Turkey joins Central Powers	
20 Dec.		First Battle of Champagne begins

German infantry advancing in 1914 – making an excellent target for rifle or machine-gun fire, or for artillery firing shrapnel.

exposed his own right to a flank attack from Paris by the French governor, General Joseph-Simon Gallieni. General Joffre, the French commander-in-chief, ordered the French Sixth, Fifth and Ninth Armies (under Generals Michel-Joseph Maunoury, Louis Franchet d'Espèrey and Foch), together with the BEF (Field Marshal Sir John French), to counter-attack across the River Marne. This resulted in the so-called 'Miracle of the Marne', which saw the entire German advance halted and pushed back as far as the River Aisne. Here the Germans stabilized the line and both sides started to dig. At this stage Lieutenant General Erich von Falkenhayn replaced a demoralized Moltke as chief of the German General Staff.

In Belgium the German victory had been swift and decisive, with the Belgian field army compelled to fall back on the vital port of Antwerp. The critical importance of Antwerp was appreciated by Britain, and after a visit by Winston Churchill, the First Sea Lord, the hastily assembled and poorly trained Royal Naval Division reinforced it. Antwerp held out only until 9 October, although the bulk of the Belgian field army was able to withdraw by way of Ghent and Bruges to the canalized line of the River Yser. The Belgians eventually opened the sluice gates at Nieuport and brought in the North Sea to help check the Germans.

While Antwerp was under siege, the Allies and the Germans became involved in a complex series of movements aimed at outflanking their adversary. For the Allies, there was the added need to cover the Channel ports – their critical link with their home base. This was the 'Race to the Sea'. The BEF was marched north from the Aisne to Flanders, where by mid-October they had taken up a salient position around Ypres, Armentières and Neuve Chapelle. There they defeated the Germans' final attempts to break through and capture Calais and Boulogne at the First Battle of Ypres (19 October–22 November).

By the winter of 1914 the war on the Western Front had stabilized with a continuous 460-mile ribbon of makeshift opposing trenches wriggling all the way from the North Sea to Switzerland. Until 1918 the fighting on this front became one gigantic, neverending siege operation. The task of the Allies was primarily that of the besieger trying to force a breach in the ever-thickening walls. This offensive role (in a war with developing technology favouring defensive operations) was forced on them, as the Germans occupied a tenth of metropolitan France, including the main French coalfields, all but a small fraction of Belgium and the whole of Luxembourg – only an offensive could drive them out or force a capitulation.

The five months of fighting in 1914 exhausted both the Allies and the Germans. For Britain it was the loss of so much of its pre-war Regular Army (some 86,000 since August) that would prove so damaging. In particular, the loss of so many regimental officers and senior NCOs was to be a huge hindrance in the months and years to come.

A British View of the Retreat from Mons

The exhaustion experienced by all ranks during the retreat in late August was described by Second Lieutenant C. F. Hodgson, Royal Field Artillery:

We were moving in feet. There was no proper movement. You moved a few yards and halted. Another few yards, halted. My big trouble was that I was so exhausted that I couldn't keep on my horse; I kept going to sleep so then I tied the stirrups under my horse's tummy and, of course, as I fell forward my feet didn't spread out so I kept on the saddle and this went on all night. It was lack of food that concerned me more than the fear of the Germans harassing us. The Army Service Corps people had dumped piles of biscuits and bully beef but we hadn't got the time to open the boxes.

Notes for Map 7

- **The Battles of the Frontiers** represented a collision between the German Schlieffen/Moltke and French XVII plans. There were six main clashes:

Battle of Mulhouse 7–10 August. The first French attack of the war in Alsace. The French under Gen. Bonneau took Mulhouse but were soon driven out by Gen. Josias von Heeringen's Seventh Army. Gen. Paul Pau replaced Bonneau.

First Battle of Lorraine (Battles of Morhange and Saarbourg) 14–25 August. Part of the main French offensive in the west. The French First Army under Gen. Auguste Dubail was to advance on Saarbourg while the Second Army under Gen. Noel Édouard Castelnau headed for Morhange. Opposing them were the German Sixth and Seventh Armies under Crown Prince Rupprecht of Bavaria and Gen. Heeringen respectively. The French attacks were driven back by strong German counter-attacks authorized by Moltke. The French were forced to withdraw to the line Belfort–Épinal–Toul.

Battle of the Ardennes 21–23 August. Joffre ordered an attack through the Ardennes Forest to support the French advance into Lorraine. Two sets of armies joined in battle. The French Third Army under Gen. Pierre Ruffey and the French Fifth Army commanded by Gen. Charles Lanrezac advanced against the German Fourth and Fifth Armies, the former under Gen. Archduke Albrecht von Württemberg and the latter under Maj. Gen. Crown Prince Wilhelm of Prussia. The French aim was to strike the German advance in the flank as it passed through the forest. There were heavy losses on both sides, but the French were soon forced into a disorderly retreat.

Battle of Charleroi 21–23 August. The French Fifth Army under Lanrezac was ordered to attack across the River Sambre, but before he could do so the German Second Army under Bülow attacked first and established two bridgeheads. After offering a strong resistance, Lanrezac, fearing being cut off, ordered a withdrawal.

Battle of Mons 23–24 August. The first major action of the BEF, under Field Marshal Sir John French, deployed on the left of the French Fifth Army. When the Fifth Army withdrew from Charleroi, French agreed to hold the line of the Mons–Condé Canal for 24 hours. The BEF faced the advance of Kluck – the extreme right wing of the entire German offensive. After halting the enemy advance and inflicting heavy losses on the leading units, the BEF was compelled to retreat (the start of the exhausting, and later famous, British retreat from Mons) to conform to the French withdrawal on its right. (See also Map 8.)

Second Battle of Lorraine (Grand Couronne or Nancy) 4–12 September. The German Sixth Army's objective here was to break through the gap in the French fortified line south of Toul. Its way was barred by the ridge of the Grand Couronne east and north-east of Nancy, defended by Castelnau's Second Army. The Germans launched repeated attacks but, despite their being reinforced, the French were able to drive them off.

- **Battles during the Allied retreat to the Marne and advance to the Aisne:**

The Battle of Le Cateau 26 August. A rearguard action fought by the BEF's II Corps under Gen. Sir Horace Smith-Dorrien against the advance of Kluck's First Army. The British rifle and artillery fire punished the Germans severely and the II Corps was able to check the enemy advance and then withdraw in generally good order, although 38 British guns were taken from batteries that had sacrificed themselves to cover the retreat.

Battle of St-Quentin (or Guise) 29–30 August. The battle was launched by Lanrezac's Fifth Army to delay Bülow's advance and give sufficient time for Joffre to deploy the newly formed French Sixth Army on the northern extremity of the Western Front. Unfortunately, the French plans fell into enemy hands and Bülow was waiting to strike. However, despite the German counter-attack

Continued on page 34

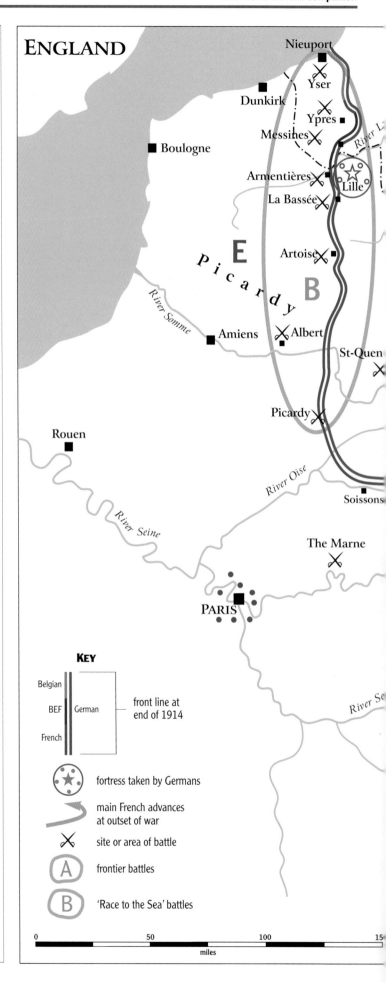

ENGLAND

Nieuport
Yser
Dunkirk
Ypres
Messines
Boulogne
Armentières
Lille
La Bassée
Artois
Picardy
E
B
Amiens
Albert
St-Quen
Rouen
Picardy
River Somme
River Oise
Soissons
River Seine
The Marne
PARIS
River Se

KEY

Belgian
BEF / German
French
front line at end of 1914

★ fortress taken by Germans

main French advances at outset of war

✕ site or area of battle

Ⓐ frontier battles

Ⓑ 'Race to the Sea' battles

0   50   100   15
miles

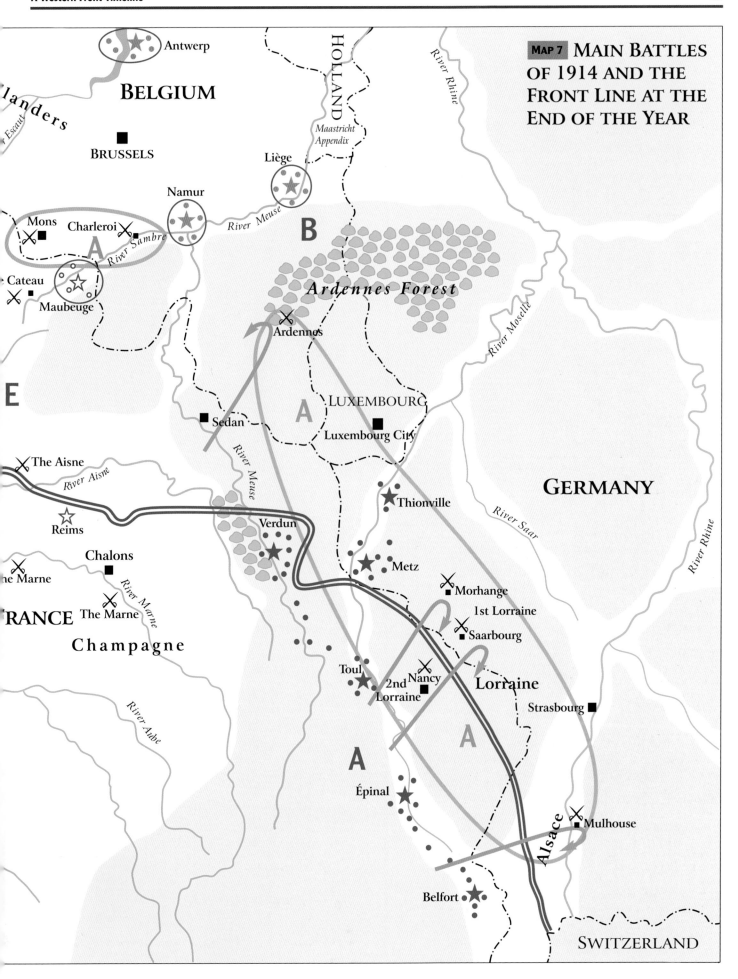

Antwerp

BELGIUM

HOLLAND

*Maastricht
Appendix*

BRUSSELS

Liège

Namur

River Rhine

l)anders

River Escaut

Mons   Charleroi

A

River Sambre

Cateau

Maubeuge

E

Sedan

River Meuse

B

Ardennes Forest

A

LUXEMBOURG

Luxembourg City

River Moselle

GERMANY

The Aisne

River Aisne

Reims

River Meuse

Verdun

Thionville

Metz

River Saar

Chalons

River Marne

he Marne

The Marne

RANCE

Champagne

Morhange

1st Lorraine

Saarbourg

Toul

2nd
Lorraine

Nancy

Lorraine

Strasbourg

River Aube

A

A

Épinal

Alsace

Mulhouse

Belfort

River Rhine

SWITZERLAND

Continued from page 32

pushing back his left, Lanrezac made good progress, but Joffre was forced to authorize a withdrawal due to the increasing weight of the German assaults. Nevertheless, the delay had allowed him time to patch up the French line.

First Battle of the Marne 7–10 September. The first full-scale battle of the war that saw the French and BEF halt and drive back the German armies of Kluck and Bülow. It finally broke the Schlieffen/Moltke plan. (See also Maps 9 and 9a.)

First Battle of the Aisne 12–21 September. The Allied follow-up offensive against the German right wing after victory on the Marne. The Germans began to dig in on the north bank of the river, basing their defences on the Chemin des Dames ridge. The Allies were unable to attack these positions successfully. Both sides dug in and the outflanking Race to the Sea began.

• **Battles during the Race to the Sea**, which saw the Germans and Allies leapfrogging each other northwards. The main battles in these unsuccessful outflanking attempts were as follows, although in several cases they merged into each other and took place simultaneously:

Battle of Picardy 22–26 September. The Germans attacked Castelnau's right flank at Roye while his army was advancing across the Somme. The French advance was checked.

First Battle of Albert 25–29 September. The end part of the wider Battle of Picardy, where the French Second Army (Castelnau) clashed with the German Sixth Army (Prince Rupprecht). The Germans made limited progress, but their attempt to take Albert failed. Both sides moved north to continue their search for an open flank.

Battle of Artois 27 September–10 October. Prince Rupprecht was ordered to attack at Arras and succeeded in causing a crisis in the Allied position. Joffre was compelled to reorganize the northern armies and form the new French Tenth Army. His energy reinvigorated the Allied defence line around Arras; the line held and the fighting moved north into Flanders.

Battle of La Bassée 12 October–2 November. This involved both the French and BEF holding the line of the La Bassée Canal.

Battle of Messines 12 October–2 November. The battle began with the British Cavalry Corps advancing, then developed into the defence of the Messines Ridge. However, this action merged into the Battle of Armentières to the south.

Battle of Armentières 13 October–2 November. Officially this battle was fought by III Corps of the BEF between the River Douve and a line between Estaires and Foumers, but in reality it was part of the ongoing fighting at Messines and La Bassée. III Corps advanced for six days against the German Sixth Army before action merged into the First Battle of Ypres.

Battle of the Yser 16–31 October. This was the northernmost battle of the Race to the Sea. The River Yser runs between high banks into the sea near Nieuport, the port that was the key to the defence line as opening the sluice gates would flood the surrounding area. The line was defended by the Belgian Army, supported by some French units and a Royal Navy squadron. The Belgians felt compelled to open the gates (see box, page 126) but, although the German attacks drove the Belgians west of the Yser, the line was stabilized and remained so for the rest of the war.

First Battle of Ypres 19 October–22 November. This was the last major battle of 1914, and along with the Battle of the Yser marked the end of the Race to the Sea, which had no winner. First Ypres was actually a series of battles that included those of Langemarck (21–24 October), Gheluvelt (29–31 October) and Nonne Bosschen (11 November), all of which were primarily heavy German attacks and several British counter-attacks. By mid-November the German assaults had been held and Ypres was to remain in British hands for the next four years, although two more battles were to bear its name. (See also Map 10.)

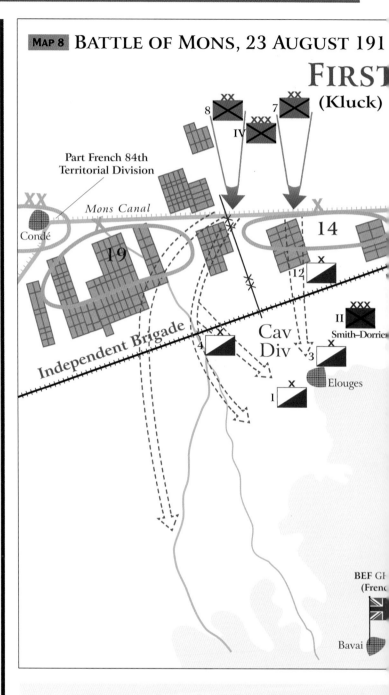

MAP 8 BATTLE OF MONS, 23 AUGUST 191

FIRST
(Kluck)

Part French 84th
Territorial Division

Mons Canal

Condé

19

14

12

II
Smith–Dorrie

Cav
Div

Independent Brigade

4

3

Elouges

1

BEF GI
(Frenc

Bavai

A German View of the Pursuit from Mons

Captain Walter Bloem in the German 12th Grenadier Regiment was pleased to be alive after the fight at Mons:

We were all tired to death, and the column just trailed along anyhow. I sat on my war-horse like a bundle of wet washing; no clear thought penetrated my addled brain, only memories of the past two appalling days . . . a sad melancholy for all the dead friends seemed to pervade us all, strangely mixed with a hazy feeling of pleasure still to be in the land of the living oneself . . . still to be the master of one's weary limbs, still to feel a horse's back between one's legs.

German troops in the Grand Place, Mons, 28 August 1914.

GERMAN ASSAULTS AND REARGUARD ACTION AT ELOUGES, 24 AUGUST

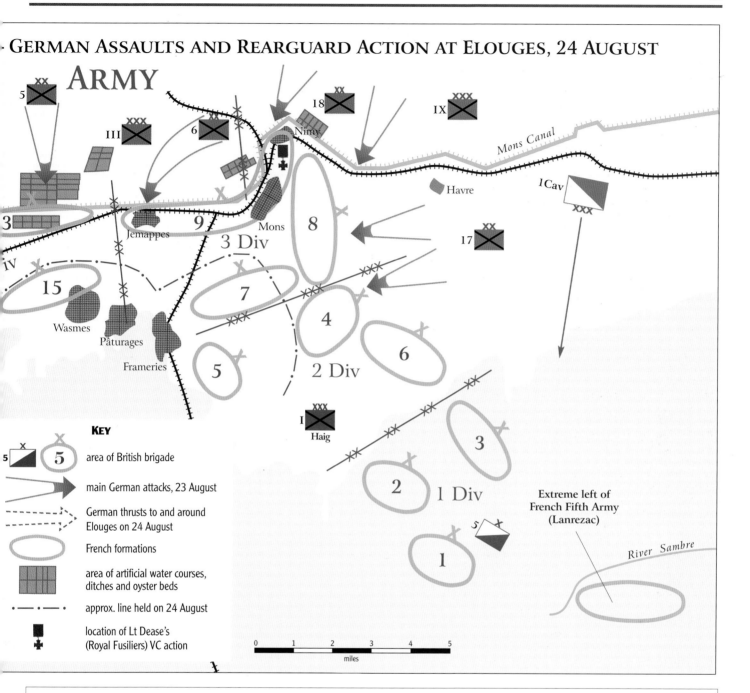

ARMY

Mons Canal

5

III

6

18

Nimy

IX

1 Cav

Havre

3

Jemappes

9

Mons

3 Div

8

17

IV

15

7

4

Wasmes

Pâturages

5

6

Frameries

2 Div

I

Haig

3

2

1 Div

Extreme left of
French Fifth Army
(Lanrezac)

River Sambre

1

5

KEY

5	area of British brigade
→	main German attacks, 23 August
- - - →	German thrusts to and around Elouges on 24 August
◯	French formations
▦	area of artificial water courses, ditches and oyster beds
– · – ·	approx. line held on 24 August
■ ✠	location of Lt Dease's (Royal Fusiliers) VC action

0   1   2   3   4   5
miles

Notes for Map 8

	British	German
Belligerents:	BEF	First Army
	4 infantry divisions	8 infantry divisions
	1 cavalry division	3 cavalry divisions
	70,000 men	160,000 men
	300 guns	600 guns
Commanders:	Field Marshal Sir John French	General Alexander von Kluck
Casualties:	1,600	5,000 (estimate)

Result: German advance checked for a day, but then the BEF forced to retreat to conform with the withdrawal of the French Fifth Army (Lanrezac) on its right (east).

Summary: On 22 August the BEF began its advance into the line of battle on the left of the French Fifth Army and thence into its first battle of the war. When deployed in its position along the Mons–Condé Canal south-east of Mons, it was spread thinly over nearly 30 miles. The German attacks were heavy and repeated, despite huge losses – largely due to their use of massed formations and the exceptionally high rate of rifle fire from the British regulars and artillery, often firing over open sights. The British in the Nimy salient were particularly hard pressed, and this position became untenable once the German 17th Division had crossed the river further east at Havre and attacked westwards. A general withdrawal of the BEF became necessary to avoid being isolated, as the French Fifth Army was at this time withdrawing from the line of the River Sambre. On 24 August a successful rearguard action was fought around Elouges and the BEF and French Armies began the retreat that was to end on the River Marne.

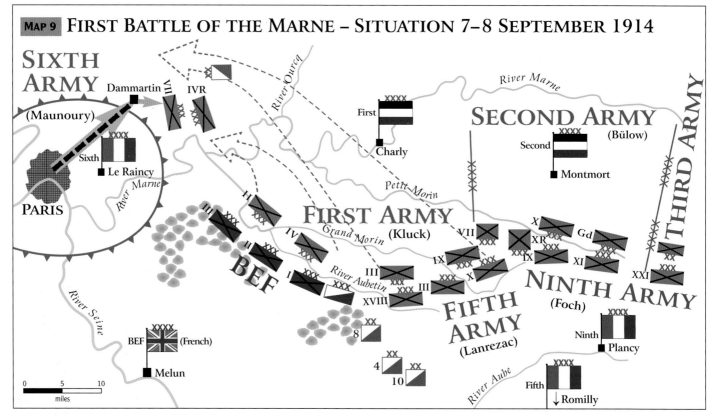

MAP 9 FIRST BATTLE OF THE MARNE – SITUATION 7–8 SEPTEMBER 1914

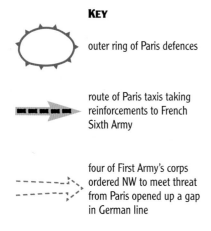

KEY

⬭ outer ring of Paris defences

▰▰➤ route of Paris taxis taking reinforcements to French Sixth Army

- - -➤ four of First Army's corps ordered NW to meet threat from Paris opened up a gap in German line

Notes for Map 9

Belligerents	Allies (1,071,000 men)	German (1,485,000 men)
	French Fifth, Sixth and Ninth Armies	First, Second and Third Armies
	BEF	
Commanders	French: Marshal Joffre	Gen. Helmuth von Moltke
	BEF: Field Marshal Sir John French	
Casualties	French: approx. 250,000 (80,000 dead)	approx. 250,000
	BEF: approx. 13,000 (1,700 dead)	

Result Allied victory with Germans driven back behind the Aisne.

Summary The first Battle of the Marne saw the whole of the Germans' advancing right wing and centre halted and then forced to withdraw to a defensive line behind the River Aisne.

• Instead of driving south and round to the west of Paris as intended, Kluck's First Army had swung south-east before passing Paris. This had exposed his right flank to attack from the French Sixth Army, reinforced by troops rushed from Paris in taxis (see box below).

• To counter this threat, on the 7th Kluck turned his four southern corps north-west. This opened up a 25-mile gap in the German line, guarded only by a thin screen and cavalry patrols. Kluck's hope was to outflank and crush the French Sixth Army before the Allies discovered and exploited the gap.

The Marne Taxis

On 6 September 1914, with the rail system overloaded, the military governor of Paris, General Joseph-Simon Gallieni, sought alternative means of transporting the French 7th Division from the frontier to join the Sixth Army defending the city. An acute shortage of military vehicles and drivers caused him to suggest the use of taxis, so all Parisian taxis were assembled at the Esplanade des Invalides. On being told their task, one driver is alleged to have shouted out, 'What about the fare?' Nothing was forthcoming at the time, although eventually compensation was paid at a rate of 27 per cent of the meter reading.

About 150 empty taxis left Paris that night under the charge of a Lieutenant Lefas. Progress was slow, breakdowns occurred, but by the early hours of 7 September the column had swollen to 400 vehicles and the harassed Lefas was

Marne taxis outside the École Militaire in Paris.

having problems rationing his tired and disgruntled drivers – he was shocked to discover that some twenty of them did not drink wine, especially as there was no water available. The convoy was directed to Dammartin-en-Goële while more taxis arrived from Paris. From Dammartin the convoy, which by then contained assorted trucks, limousines and racing cars, drove to a railway siding to load up with arriving troops of the 103rd and 104th Infantry Regiments. Each cab took five soldiers and departure for the front began at dusk, making the night drive without headlights an extremely stressful journey. Within two days Gallieni's taxis transported about 4,000 urgently needed reinforcements to a critical point of the battle near Nanteuil. A typical Marne taxi is on display at the Invalides Museum in Paris.

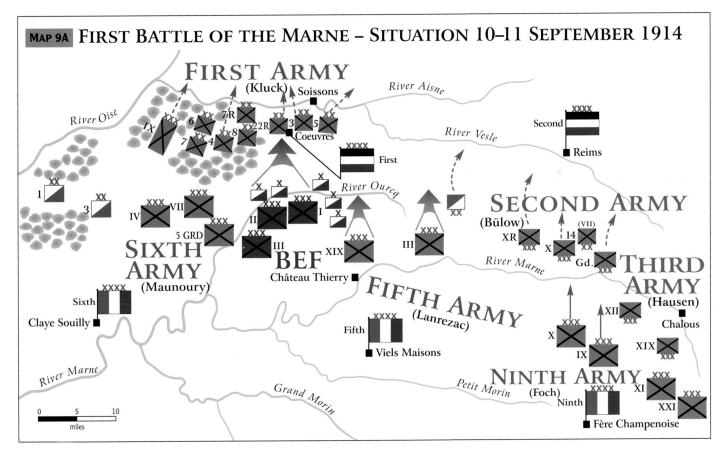

MAP 9A FIRST BATTLE OF THE MARNE – SITUATION 10–11 SEPTEMBER 1914

KEY

- - - → Germans in retreat to the Aisne

⟩⟩→ BEF and French Fifth Army exploit the gap and advance somewhat slowly northwards

Notes for Map 9A

Summary Allied aircraft spotted the gap and Joffre ordered its exploitation by the French Fifth Army and the BEF. However, the French Sixth Army was in danger of being overwhelmed, despite the reinforcements rushed from Paris, and for a time the battle was touch and go.

• The French Fifth Army and BEF drove into the gap and on 9 September Moltke had a nervous breakdown, panicked and ordered the German Second Army to withdraw. This exposed the First Army to being cut off and thus Kluck was forced to retreat as well. On the 10th the German Third and Fourth Armies were ordered to pull back, to be followed on the 13th by the Fifth as well (the Fourth and Fifth Armies are off the map to the east and south-east).

• The Allied pursuit lacked vigour and the Germans were allowed to fall back behind the Aisne. By this time both armies were utterly exhausted and had suffered very heavy losses.

• The Moltke-modified Schlieffen Plan was in ruins. What the British were to call the 'Miracle of the Marne' had happened. Moltke was dismissed and replaced by Falkenhayn on 14 September.

The Victoria Cross in 1914

Forty-three Victoria Crosses were won in 1914. Of these, five were won on 23 August during the Battle of Mons, the first going to Lieutenant Maurice James Dease of the 4th Royal Fusiliers.

B and C Companies of the battalion were responsible for defending the road and rail bridges over the Mons–Condé Canal. C Company set up a section of two machine guns under the command of Lieutenant Dease. One was knocked out by intense German fire, which inflicted heavy losses. Dease took over firing the remaining gun and continued to operate it, despite being wounded several times. The fifth wound was mortal; Dease died shortly after being carried to safety.

Lieutenant K. Tower, Royal Fusiliers, watched Dease in action and later recorded:

> The enemy started to advance in mass down the railway cutting, about 800 yards off, and Maurice Dease fired his two machine guns into them and absolutely mowed them down. I should judge without exaggeration that he killed at least 500 in two minutes. The whole cutting was full of bodies and this cheered us all up.

The machine gun was then manned by Private Sidney Godley, who, although wounded, continued to fire until he ran out of ammunition. He dismantled his gun and threw the pieces into the canal before being captured. He was awarded the second Victoria Cross (and the first to a private soldier) of the war. He survived, and in 1938 was presented with a special gold medal by the citizens of Mons. He died in 1957, aged sixty-eight.

The third was Corporal Charles Garforth, 15th Hussars, who, when his troop was immobilized by wire, volunteered to cut it, allowing his troop to escape while he came under heavy fire. He survived the war, dying in 1973, aged eighty-one.

The others were Captain Theodore Wright and Lance Corporal Charles Jarvis, both Royal Engineers, who won their VCs for their combined efforts under heavy fire while laying and firing charges that destroyed the bridge at Jemappes, near Mons (see page 287). Wright was mortally wounded the following month while assisting a wounded man. Jarvis died in 1948, aged sixty-seven.

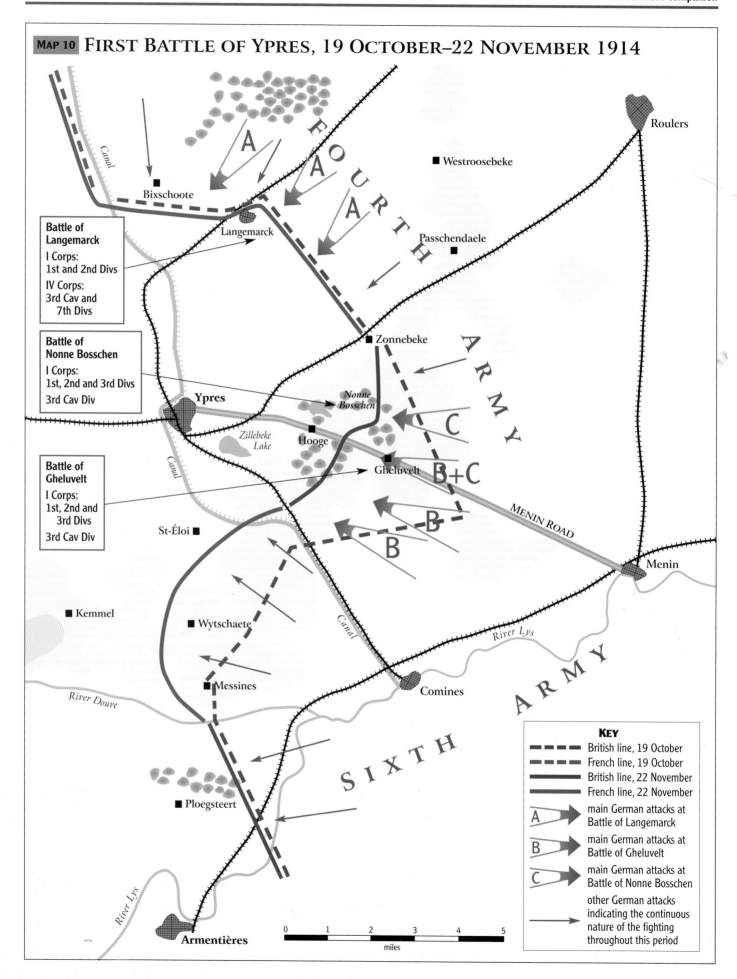

MAP 10 FIRST BATTLE OF YPRES, 19 OCTOBER–22 NOVEMBER 1914

FOURTH ARMY

Roulers

■ Westroosebeke

Bixschoote

Canal

A

A

A

Langemarck

Passchendaele

Battle of Langemarck

I Corps:
1st and 2nd Divs

IV Corps:
3rd Cav and
7th Divs

Zonnebeke

ARMY

Battle of Nonne Bosschen

I Corps:
1st, 2nd and 3rd Divs

3rd Cav Div

Nonne Bosschen

Ypres

C

Zillebeke Lake

Hooge

Gheluvelt

B+C

Battle of Gheluvelt

I Corps:
1st, 2nd and 3rd Divs

3rd Cav Div

Canal

St-Éloi ■

B

B

MENIN ROAD

Menin

■ Kemmel

■ Wytschaete

River Lys

Canal

ARMY

■ Messines

SIXTH

Comines

River Douve

■ Ploegsteert

River Lys

KEY

British line, 19 October

French line, 19 October

British line, 22 November

French line, 22 November

A	main German attacks at Battle of Langemarck
B	main German attacks at Battle of Gheluvelt
C	main German attacks at Battle of Nonne Bosschen
	other German attacks indicating the continuous nature of the fighting throughout this period

Armentières

0   1   2   3   4   5
miles

Notes for Map 10

• First Ypres was the last major conflict of the first year of the war and consisted of a series of battles starting on 19 October and ending (according to the British) on 22 November. This battle and the Battle of the Yser marked the end of the Race to the Sea. The Germans called it the 'Massacre of the Innocents', as eight German units, composed mainly of university student volunteers exempt from the draft, were killed (according to some sources as many as 25,000 young men). In 1917 the British instituted the Mons Star medal for those surviving troops who had served in France or Belgium prior to the end of the battle – the last surviving holder of this medal, Alfred Anderson, died in November 2005.

• The belligerents were the BEF under Field Marshal French, the French IX Corps (Second Army) with the II Corps and Gen. Mitry's Cavalry Corps, and the 87th and 89th Territorial Divisions, all under Foch. The Germans deployed their Fourth and Sixth Armies under Falkenhayn.

• The fighting raged over a 25-mile front for more than a month, with the Allies, seriously outnumbered, particularly in heavy artillery, seeking to hold the high ground east of Ypres. The British Battlefields Nomenclature Committee highlights three battles within the period:

Battle of Langemarck 21–24 October. The German Fourth Army launched a series of assaults either side of Langemarck. It was here that the massed ranks of the German students were mown down, many now resting in the German Langemarck War Cemetery. The major German attack on 22 October was held with difficulty and the help of a French counter-attack.

Battle of Gheluvelt 29–31 October. A German assault by six divisions came the closest to breaking the British line around Ypres until 1918. On 31 October the Germans broke through the British lines south of Gheluvelt and the situation was restored only by a magnificent bayonet charge by the 2nd Worcestershires against 1,200 Germans around Gheluvelt Château – the Worcestershires thereafter celebrated Gheluvelt Day annually on 31 October. This attack, combined with another by the 7th Division, plugged the gap in the British line.

Battle of Nonne Bosschen 11 November. The main threat came from an attack by some 10,000 Germans of the Guards and 4th Divisions that penetrated as far as the Nonne Bosschen woods. They were finally driven back by well-directed artillery fire and a counter-attack by the 2nd Oxfordshire Light Infantry.

Casualties The British suffered just over 58,000, of whom almost 8,000 were killed. It is sometimes said the pre-war professional army died at First Ypres. The French lost around 50,000 and the Germans an estimated 134,000 (including what the Germans called the Battle of the Yser, which covered the fighting from Gheluvelt to the sea).

1915

This year saw Germany change her grand strategy for the war. Ever mindful of the potential problems of fighting on two fronts, and with the west solidified, she decided, with the exception of Ypres in April, to remain on the defensive in the west and attack the Russians in the east, moving troops accordingly. The Allies on the other hand, again with the exception of Ypres, sought a breakthrough in the west and the year saw a succession of unsuccessful attempts to achieve this objective. It was also the year in which Britain opened another front, against Turkey in Gallipoli.

With the realization that the war would be prolonged, thus demanding huge additional resources of both manpower and materials, 1915 was a year of expansion for all the nations engaged on the Western Front. This was particularly so for the British. But despite the increase in the size of the BEF from 10 divisions to 37 (including two Canadian), the main weight of the war in the west would still be borne by the French Army. Its strength in France rose to 107 divisions and the German Army's to 94 out of a total of 159 on all fronts. With the virtual destruction of her Regular Army in the first five months of the war, the UK had now to rely first on Territorial and then on New Army (Kitchener) formations hastily raised and mostly inadequately equipped and trained.

It was also a year when the realities of fighting positional trench warfare over such vast distances and involving so many men were fully appreciated by political and military leaders. The problems of scale came as a shock to the military system not only in terms of manpower but with regard to casualties, medical requirements, supply, training, lack of experienced officers (both commanders and staff) and senior NCOs at all levels, and desperate shortages of arms, ammunition, equipment and guns (particularly artillery high-explosive shells). Details of these deficiencies and the means adopted to remedy them will be explained in the appropriate sections.

On the battlefields it was a year of experimentation, of learning, of trying to grasp the realities of how to break into, fight through, and then break out to exploit the resultant gap in the enemy's multiple defen-

Declarations of War 1915

23 May	Italy on Austria
3 June	San Marino on Austria
21 August	Italy on Turkey
14 October	Bulgaria on Serbia
15 October	Britain on Bulgaria
	Montenegro on Bulgaria
16 October	France on Bulgaria
19 October	Russia on Bulgaria
	Italy on Bulgaria

sive lines. This became the all-encompassing objective that frustrated generals on both sides until 1918. The fighting in 1915 saw the first use on a large scale by the Germans of poison gas, at the Second Battle of Ypres in April. The BEF followed

Winter in the trenches – the 2nd Royal Scots at La Boutillerie, 1915.

An Indian Soldier's Experience at Neuve Chapelle

Rifleman Amar Singh Rawat, Garhwal Rifles, wrote to a friend some two weeks after the Battle of Neuve Chapelle while recovering in Kitchener's Indian Hospital, Brighton:

I have been wounded in the head but hope to get better soon. My fate is now very lucky [in] that I am alive while all my brethren have been killed . . . Up to now the war has been as follows – the Germans kept firing from their trenches and we from ours. But on the 9th and 10th of March we attacked the Germans . . . When we reached their trenches we used the bayonet and the kukri, and blood was shed so freely we could not recognize each other's faces . . . The scene was indescribable. If I survive I will tell you all. But if I get killed it does not matter, when so many of my brethren have been slain it would not matter about me, but my great scene has been enacted . . .

The Germans Attack at Loos

Second Lieutenant John Easton, 12th Royal Fusiliers, using the pseudonym Broadchalk, described the heroic death of Major Parsons, the officer commanding C Company during a German counter-attack:

The next hour was a nightmare of muddle and confusion. Parsons had lost his company, and had taken up his position on the parapet as the only field officer known to be alive in the area.

He was a big man, nearly stone deaf, and the enemy was barely two hundred yards away – to get orders was no mean feat; Broadchalk stood on his toes and shouted in his ear, and the snipers' bullets whizzed past his head continuously.

The organisation of the line and the check of any suspicion of a rout was largely due to Parsons: he stood on the top of the trenches with his arms folded, a great monument of a man, collecting the men as they were driven in and guiding them to this or that trench. A faint smile played over his lips and hinted at the deaf man's oblivion to the rattle and noise, or the infection of shaken nerves.

Broadchalk told him about the field message. 'You had better prospect for a gap, and if you find it stay there. You can't do anything here, we're jammed solid as it is. If you find my company let me know!' Ten minutes later he fell, shot through the head.

Timeline 1915

Date	General	Western Front
4 Feb.	Germany begins submarine warfare on merchant shipping	
7–22 Feb.	Russia defeated at Second Battle of Masurian Lakes	
16 Feb.–18 March		First Battle of Champagne continues
19 Feb.	British and French naval attack on the Dardanelles – Gallipoli campaign begins	
10–13 March		BEF launches Battle of Neuve Chapelle
22 April–25 May		Second Battle of Ypres – German attacks (battles) at Gravenstafel Ridge, St-Julien, Frezenberg Ridge and Bellewaarde Ridge
25 April	Allied forces land in Gallipoli	
1–3 May	Germans defeat Russians at Battle of Gorlice-Tarnów	
7 May	British liner *Lusitania* sunk by German U-boat.	
9 May		British attack at Battle of Aubers Ridge
9 May–18 June		French begin Second Battle of Artois
15–25 May		British attack at Battle of Festubert
1 Sept.	Germany suspends unrestricted submarine warfare (to keep US out of war)	
15 Sept.–4 Nov.		French launch Third Battle of Artois (Loos/Artois offensive)
25–28 Sept.		British attack at Battle of Loos
25 Sept.–6 Nov.		French attack at Second Battle of Champagne
27 Oct.	French Army lands at Salonika and, with help of British and Italian troops, sets up a Balkan Front	
10 Dec.	Allies begin withdrawal from Gallipoli (complete by 9 Jan. 1916).	
18 Dec.		Haig replaces French as British commander-in-chief on Western Front
20 Dec.		Falkenhayn (German chief of General Staff) issues memorandum for operations for 1916 containing the phrase 'the forces of France will bleed to death' – referring to Verdun

The Victoria Cross in 1915

Sixty-seven Victoria Crosses were awarded during the year. An outstanding award went to Piper Daniel Laidlaw of the 7th King's Own Scottish Borderers (KOSBs) for his gallantry on 25 September at the Battle of Loos. The battalion was waiting to go 'over the top' but could not to do so until after the release of the gas and smoke that was to precede the attack. Unfortunately, the wind began to blow the gas into the British positions. Despite this, the order was given to advance, but there was some reluctance to move and considerable hesitation among the men. Laidlaw's company officer, Second Lieutenant Martin Young, turned to him and shouted, 'For God's sake, Laidlaw, pipe 'em together.' Laidlaw clambered up on to the parapet and, disregarding both the gas and the shelling, marched up and down playing 'Blue Bonnets over the Border'. This inspiring action launched the assault by the entire battalion, which, led by the skirl of Laidlaw's pipes, advanced on the enemy. When close to the German trenches he was hit by shrapnel in the left leg and ankle. Undeterred, he continued to hobble painfully forward with the sound of his pipes still audible amongst the din of battle. He was then hit again in the same leg but continued to play until he saw his comrades secure their objective, whereupon he dragged himself back to his own lines.

His inspiring gallantry won him the VC and the French *Croix de Guerre* with Palms. He died in 1950 and is buried in St Cuthbert's churchyard, Norham, Northumberland.

Wounded French troops at a farm in Champagne after the Battle of Loos, 1915.

suit and used gas for the first time in combination with large smokescreens at Loos in September. All belligerents began to appreciate the crucial role of artillery in every operation. Commanders came to realize that without massive artillery support neither the attacker nor the defender could achieve much. It quickly became a question not just of massing the guns but of how they should best be used tactically, while at the same time ensuring enough ammunition was available. The use by both sides of increasing numbers of aircraft for bombing, artillery-spotting and aerial photography, as well as aerial combat, became one of the most obvious developments of warfare on the front during the year. These technologies and the tactics involved, together with the problems associated with them, are highlighted below in the sections dealing with the various Arms and Services.

Most of the 1915 operations were in some way related to Joffre's grand plan for the elimination of the so-called Noyon salient (see Map 11, page 42), the apex of which thrust threateningly to within 75 miles of Paris. He proposed a huge strategic pincer movement to remove this salient by launching large-scale offensive thrusts from Artois to the north and Champagne to the south. Similarly, the Germans sought to crush the much smaller British salient around Ypres and, they hoped, secure the Channel ports of Le Havre, Rouen and Boulogne upon which the BEF depended. All the battles associated with these operations involved the problem noted above – that of punching a hole in the enemy front and then

rushing troops (primarily cavalry) through it. Apart from Ypres, where the BEF (with French support) was fighting a defensive action, the other battles involving British divisions were offensive operations designed to support the main French strategic plan.

This was a bad year for the British in terms of losses. Although not nearly as bloody as the following three years, it came as a sobering shock that over 267,000 men had been listed as casualties on the Western Front during these twelve months. The Germans suffered over 110,000, the inequality highlighting the fact that, from early in

the war, an attacker was more likely to be hit than a defender. The Germans had held the Allies in check in the west and appeared to have succeeded in the east, with the Russians pushed back into Belorussia. Meanwhile, by the end of the year the British expedition to Gallipoli had proved a disaster. In general terms, 1915 belonged to the Germans.

In December General Sir Douglas Haig, commander of the British First Army, replaced Field Marshal Sir John French as commander-in-chief of the BEF. He was to remain in that position until the end of the war.

Four Years in a Frenchwoman's Cupboard

This is the astounding story of how an extraordinarily brave and resourceful Frenchwoman, Madame Marie Belmont-Gobert, sheltered Trooper Patrick Fowler of the 11th Hussars in her house and cupboard from January 1915 to November 1918. Fowler spent many hours cramped up in the cupboard with German troops sometimes sitting in the same room.

Fowler had been cut off from his regiment after the Battle of Le Cateau in 1914 and had spent four months wandering behind German lines before being given indefinite shelter. He later gave a detailed account of his unique experiences, of which this is an example:

A week later they [the Germans] came – eight of them. They occupied the upper part of the house, but spent much of their time drinking coffee and gossiping

in the room where I was hidden . . . One night I must have moved slightly for the woodwork creaked. To me it sounded like the crack of a pistol; certainly it was enough to make madame spring up from her chair by the fireside and, with great presence of mind, exclaim to the soldiers sitting round and playing cards, 'Ah, ces bêtes souris' [Oh, those wretched mice!]. And with quick resourcefulness, I heard her advance and flick around the outside of the wardrobe in mock pursuit of a phantom mouse.

Madame Belmont-Gobert later received a grant from the British government and the Order of the British Empire (OBE). Her famous cupboard is an exhibit in the museum of the King's Royal Hussars (a successor regiment of the 11th Hussars) in Winchester.

Notes for Map 11

The first five months of the war had seen continuous fighting, at the end of which it solidified, starting the seemingly endless and bloody siege that was to be the fate of the Western Front until 1918. However, the French commander-in-chief, Joffre, had visions of achieving a major breakthrough during the year with offensives from Artois in the north and from Champagne in the south, **AA**, to pinch out the huge German bulge in the line that threatened Paris and to sever vital German rail communications. He anticipated support from the BEF in these offensives. In the event, this grandiose scheme came to nought as both the Allies and the Germans found themselves enmeshed in battles of attrition, paying a staggering cost in casualties for a few thousand yards of ground gained. By December any changes to the front line in 1915 were noticeable only on large-scale maps.

The important offensives/battles fought during 1915 were:
- **First Battle of Champagne** 16 February–18 March. Gen. Fernand Langle de Cary's French Fourth Army attacked over the Champagne hills in the area of Perthes-lès-Hurlus. These assaults continued for a month against well-defended German strongpoints but gained a mere 3,000 yards at a cost of some 40,000 casualties before shuddering to a halt.
- **Battle of Neuve Chapelle** 10–13 March. A British attack in the Artois region of France, with the aim of breaching the German lines at the village of Neuve Chapelle, then seizing the La Bassée–Aubers Ridge, followed, optimistically, by an advance to Lille – a key German communications centre. The IV Corps and Indian Corps of the British Second Army under Smith-Dorrien made the assault against the German VII Corps and part of the XIX Corps, both belonging to Prince Rupprecht's Sixth Army. It was the first time aerial photography was used extensively, and the initial attack secured Neuve Chapelle. Primitive communications hindered progress and on 12 March the Germans launched a heavy and partially successful counter-attack. Both sides claimed a victory, with the British managing to hang on to the village. (See also Map 12.)
- **Second Battle of Ypres** 22 April–25 May. The German forces involved were the XV, XXII Reserve, XXVI Reserve and XXVII Reserve Corps. The fighting started with an attack – using gas on a large scale for the first time – by the German XXII Reserve and XXVI Reserve Corps on the northern French-held sector of the Ypres salient. The French 45th Algerian Division and some Territorial units were panicked by the gas and fled. The attack was eventually checked by a counter-attack by battalions of the 2nd and 3rd Brigades of the Canadian 1st Division. This action developed into the Battle of Gravenstafel Ridge, 22–23 April, to be followed by the Battle of St-Julien, 24 April–4 May; the Battle of Frezenberg Ridge, 8–13 May; and the Battle of Bellewaarde Ridge, 24–25 May – each of these actions forming a part of Second Ypres. The result of the German assaults was a shrinking of the Ypres salient held by the BEF and the French, to such an extent that the front line was, in places, within 2 miles of the town. Smith-Dorrien was sacked as Second Army commander on 6 May, replaced by Gen. Sir Herbert Plumer. (See also Map 13.)
- **Second Battle of Artois** 9 May–18 June. Joffre had planned this offensive to start in March, supported by a BEF attack on La Bassée. Instead, the British attacked at Neuve Chapelle, forcing Joffre to postpone his Artois offensive against the German Sixth Army (Rupprecht), supported by their Second Army in the south, until May. The primary objective of the French, after a six-day preparatory bombardment, was the dominating Vimy Ridge. The BEF's Fourth Army, attacking at Festubert (see page 44), supported this operation, as did Castelnau's French Second Army in the south. Vimy Ridge was taken by the French 77th and Moroccan Divisions, but held only briefly. Some six weeks later this tortuous advance ground to a halt, having gained a mere 4,000 yards of territory at the appalling cost of 300,000 casualties, a third of whom were dead. The vital, dominating Vimy Ridge was still in German hands.

Continued on page 44

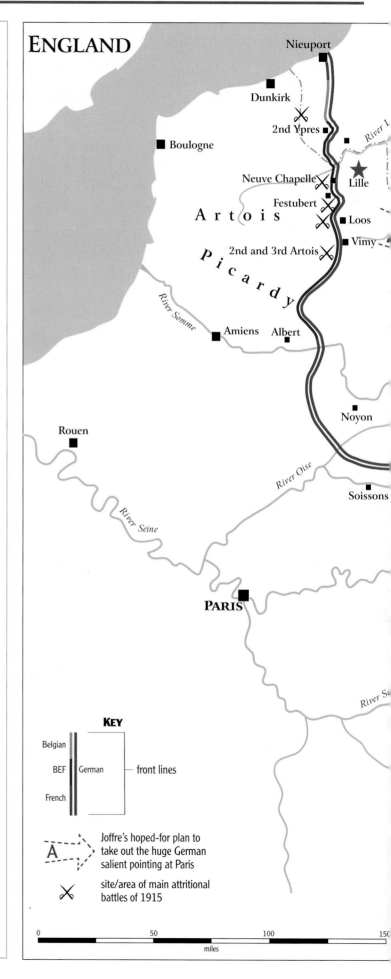

ENGLAND

Nieuport

Dunkirk

2nd Ypres

Boulogne

River L

Neuve Chapelle

Lille

Festubert

Artois

Loos

Vimy

2nd and 3rd Artois

Picardy

River Somme

Amiens   Albert

Noyon

Rouen

River Oise

Soissons

River Seine

PARIS

River S

KEY

Belgian

BEF | German

French

— front lines

A — Joffre's hoped-for plan to take out the huge German salient pointing at Paris

✕ site/area of main attritional battles of 1915

0   50   100   150

miles

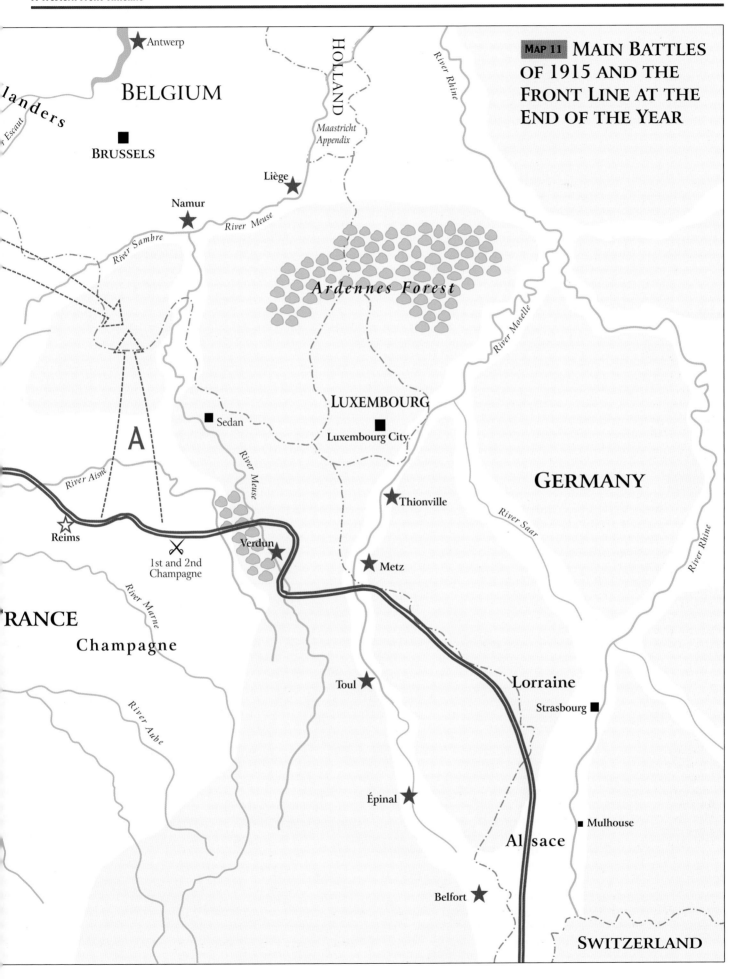

Antwerp

BELGIUM

landers

River Escaut

BRUSSELS

HOLLAND

Maastricht Appendix

River Rhine

Liège

Namur

River Meuse

River Sambre

Ardennes Forest

River Moselle

A

Sedan

LUXEMBOURG

Luxembourg City

River Meuse

River Aisne

GERMANY

Reims

1st and 2nd Champagne

Verdun

Thionville

River Saar

Metz

FRANCE

Champagne

River Marne

Toul

Lorraine

River Aube

Strasbourg

Épinal

Mulhouse

Alsace

Belfort

River Rhine

SWITZERLAND

Continued from page 42

- **Battle of Aubers Ridge** 9 May. This was part of the overall Allied offensive strategy for 1915 and thus part of the BEF's contribution to the French Artois attacks. It achieved nothing and was beaten back with the loss of around 10,000 men.
- **Battle of Festubert** 15–25 May. Under pressure from the French, this was really a renewal of the Aubers Ridge offensive. The assault included the first British night attack (by the 2nd Division) and was partially successful. However, the subsequent British and 1st Canadian Division attacks achieved little. After attacking for five days the Canadians had advanced 600 yards on a one-mile front, losing 2,500 men in the process, mainly due to superior German artillery fire. The battle ended inconclusively, although the Germans lost the village of Festubert.
- **Third Battle of Artois (Loos/Artois offensive)** 15 September–4 November. In September Joffre launched two more simultaneous offensives in Artois and Champagne. The British, after some argument, agreed to participate by attacking at Loos. The French attack once again had Vimy Ridge as a principal objective, but after very determined German resistance and having suffered disproportionate losses, Joffre called off the French Tenth Army's offensive.

- **Battle of Loos** 25–28 September. The British component of the Allied Loos/Artois offensive. The battle was conducted by Gen. Sir Douglas Haig, commander of the British First Army, and marked the first occasion the British used (ineffectively) poison (chlorine) gas during the war. The British assault on the first day succeeded in capturing the town of Loos and reaching as far as Hill 70, a mile east of the town. However, the positioning of the British reserves too far back, resupply and communication difficulties, plus the failure of British artillery fire to cut much of the German wire, inhibited further progress against sustained enemy machine-gun and artillery fire. Renewed attacks the next day were soon halted and the British were forced to retreat to their starting positions. (See also Map 14.)
- **Second Battle of Champagne** 25 September–6 November. Joffre regarded this offensive as the most promising and accordingly gave priority in men and guns to Castelnau's Centre Group of Armies (Second and Fourth), which together mustered 27 divisions, 1,300 field and 650 medium or heavy guns. The German first line was taken, but fresh reserves were unable to secure the second. A halt was called by Joffre, which the Germans used to bring up reinforcements. The renewed attack against a defensive system some 3 miles deep with numerous concrete pillboxes was easily frustrated, with murderous losses for the French, whose 75mm guns began to run out of ammunition at the critical stage.

Notes for Map 12

Belligerents	British	German
	First Army	Sixth Army
	IV and Indian Corps	VII and part XIX Corps
	40,000 men	25,000 eventually (estimate)
Commanders	Field Marshal	Crown Prince Rupprecht
	Sir John French	of Bavaria
Casualties	11,650	12,000 (estimate)

Result Stalemate, although both sides claimed victory.

Summary The first British offensive against the German trench system. Phase 1 was to take Neuve Chapelle and the Smith-Dorrien Trench, phase 2 to exploit the gap and capture the La Bassée–Aubers Ridge.

- Careful planning and a short but intense artillery barrage on targets previously spotted by aircraft surprised the enemy and both village and trench were taken. Success was fairly easy, although the 2nd Middlesex were held up by machine guns south of the Moated Grange.
- Communication failures and hesitation by corps commanders on the 11th allowed German reserves to be rushed forward. At dawn on 12 March they counter-attacked all along the line. The British held on with difficulty, a serious problem being shortage of artillery ammunition.
- Other problems were vulnerable communications, difficulty in bringing forward reserves quickly and insufficient artillery observation posts (OPs). The critical tactical importance of achieving surprise with artillery preparation was not fully appreciated until later in the war.

The village of Neuve Chapelle after the battle, 1915.

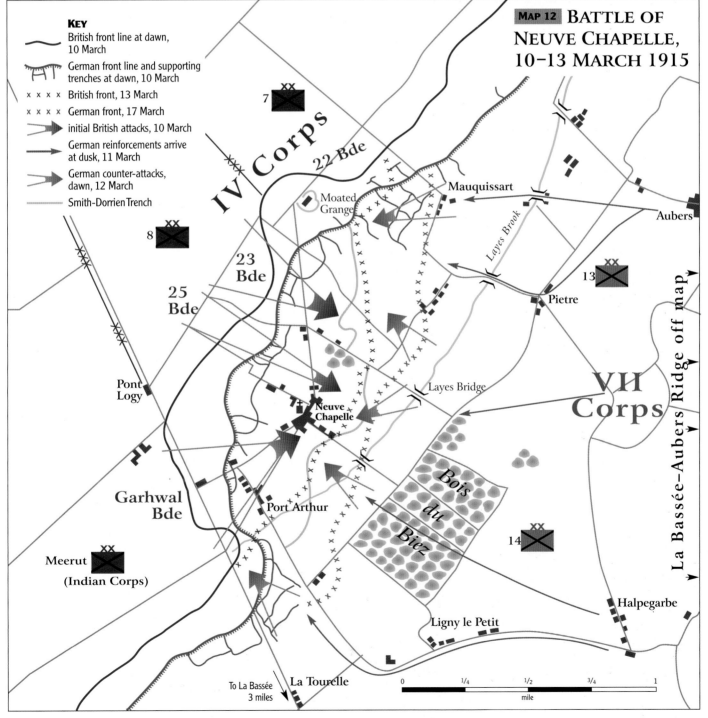

Neuve Chapelle, looking from the south-west towards where the German strongpoint 'Port Arthur' was located. This was assaulted by the right-hand battalion of the Garhwal Brigade, 1/39th Garhwalis, and was captured with difficulty due to the attackers' mistaking the direction of the assault.

Port Arthur' area

Bois de Biez

MAP 12 BATTLE OF NEUVE CHAPELLE, 10–13 MARCH 1915

KEY

British front line at dawn, 10 March

German front line and supporting trenches at dawn, 10 March

x x x x British front, 13 March

x x x x German front, 17 March

initial British attacks, 10 March

German reinforcements arrive at dusk, 11 March

German counter-attacks, dawn, 12 March

Smith-Dorrien Trench

IV Corps

7

8

22 Bde

23 Bde

25 Bde

Moated Grange

Mauquissart

Aubers

Layes Brook

13

Pietre

Pont Logy

Layes Bridge

VII Corps

Neuve Chapelle

Bois du Biez

Garhwal Bde

Port Arthur

14

Meerut (Indian Corps)

Halpegarbe

La Bassée–Aubers Ridge off map

Ligny le Petit

To La Bassée 3 miles

La Tourelle

0   1/4   1/2   3/4   1
mile

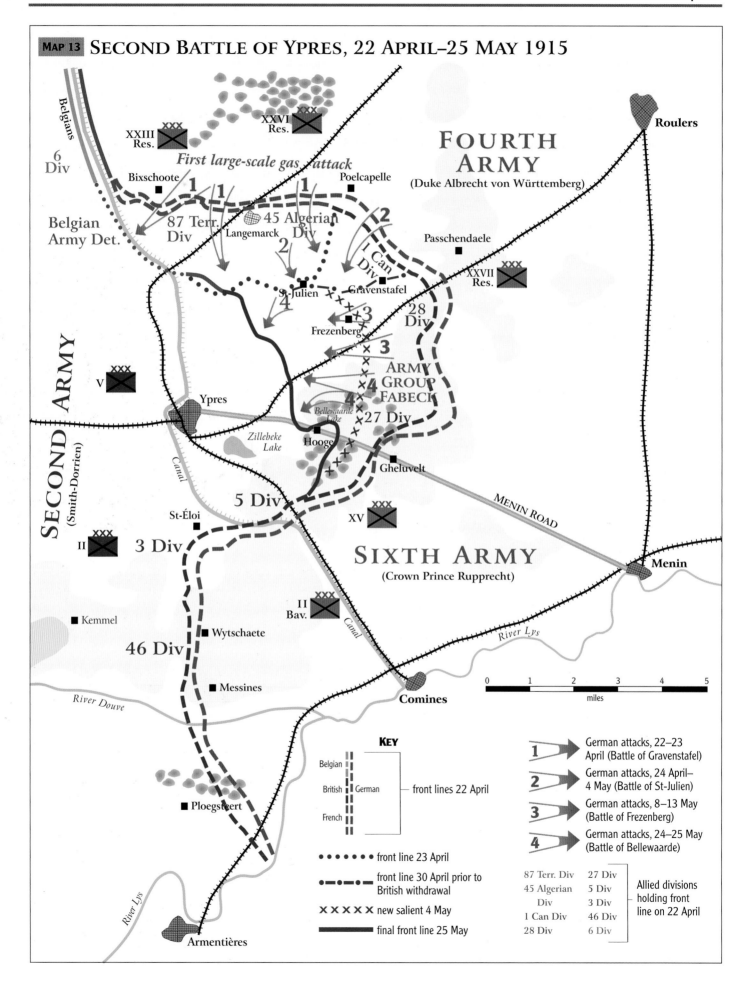

MAP 13 SECOND BATTLE OF YPRES, 22 APRIL–25 MAY 1915

Belgians

6 Div

XXIII Res.

XXVI Res.

First large-scale gas attack

Bixschoote

Belgian Army Det.

87 Terr. Div

45 Algerian Div

Langemarck

Poelcapelle

FOURTH ARMY
(Duke Albrecht von Württemberg)

Passchendaele

1 Can Div

St-Julien

Gravenstafel

XXVII Res.

28 Div

Frezenberg

ARMY GROUP FABECK

Bellewaarde Lake

27 Div

Ypres

Zillebeke Lake

Hooge

Canal

SECOND ARMY
(Smith-Dorrien)

V

Gheluvelt

MENIN ROAD

5 Div

St-Éloi

XV

3 Div

II

SIXTH ARMY
(Crown Prince Rupprecht)

Menin

Kemmel

Wytschaete

II Bav.

46 Div

Messines

Canal

River Lys

Comines

0   1   2   3   4   5
miles

River Douve

Ploegsteert

River Lys

Armentières

Roulers

KEY

Belgian

British ┃ German

French

front lines 22 April

••••••••• front line 23 April

—•—•—•— front line 30 April prior to British withdrawal

××××× new salient 4 May

——— final front line 25 May

1 German attacks, 22–23 April (Battle of Gravenstafel)

2 German attacks, 24 April– 4 May (Battle of St-Julien)

3 German attacks, 8–13 May (Battle of Frezenberg)

4 German attacks, 24–25 May (Battle of Bellewaarde)

87 Terr. Div	27 Div	
45 Algerian Div	5 Div	Allied divisions holding front line on 22 April
1 Can Div	3 Div	
28 Div	46 Div	
	6 Div	

The Germans' Use of Gas

When Lord Kitchener first heard of the Germans using gas he telegrammed Sir John French expressing the view that 'the use of asphyxiating gasses is, as you are aware, contrary to the rules and usages of war'. The secretary of state for foreign affairs, Viscount Grey, had written that the use of poison gas by the Germans was 'an offence not only against the rules of war, but against all humane considerations'. There was some argument whether the Hague Convention of 1907 forbade the use of asphyxiating as distinct from poisonous gas, although most considered it was inferred if not specifically barred.

The German government certainly felt the need to conceal its use from its people and the world by omitting all reference to it in its communiqués. In 1917 the German War Ministry and High Command issued an official apologia, claiming that before the war the French Army possessed and had used a rifle grenade filled with bromic acid and a hand grenade filled with a lachrymatory liquid called ethyl bromo-acetate. Their justification at the time, when it was common knowledge that they had used gas, was that they had merely got in a first strike in anticipation of the Allies using it.

French troops wearing an early form of gas mask in the trenches during the Second Battle of Ypres. Note the excessive length of the French cruciform cross-section bayonets – impossible to use effectively in a trench.

Notes for Map 13

Belligerents	Allies	German
	BEF: II, V, and Cav. Corps (part of Fourth Army)	XXIIIR, XXVIR, XXVIIR, XV and II Bav Corps
	French: Belgian Det. (87 Terr. and 45A Divs)	
	Belgian: 6 Div	
Commanders	British: Gen. Horace Smith-Dorrien; from 7 May Lt Gen. Sir Herbert Plumer	Gen. Archduke Albrecht von Württemberg
	French: Gen. Gabriel Putz	
	Belgian: Gen. A. L. T. de Ceuninck	
Casualties	British: 59,275	34,933
	French: 10,000 (estimate)	
	Belgian: 1,530	

Result Allies forced to reduce salient frontage from 16 to 10 miles.

Summary The five weeks' fighting began with a large-scale gas attack by the Germans in the north of the salient. It was a complete surprise and sent the 45th Algerian and some of the 87th Territorial Division fleeing in panic. Only a gallant Canadian counter-attack stopped a possible breakthrough. The Germans pressed their attacks from the north and east, causing the British to withdraw to a shorter line on 4 May. This was also pushed back so that the final perimeter was only 2 miles east of Ypres down the Menin Road. There were four distinct German assaults during the battle:

Battle of Gravenstafel 22–23 April. At around 5.00 pm on 22 April the Germans released 168 tons of chlorine gas on the line held by the French. Many were killed or blinded while the rest fled en masse, leaving a 4-mile gap in the Allied line. A hasty defence and a brilliant counter-attack by the Canadians, coupled with the inability of the Germans to follow up their advantage, prevented disaster (see also page 311).

Battle of St-Julien 24 April–4 May. On 24 April the Germans attacked the village of St-Julien behind another cloud of gas. The Canadian defenders were told to urinate on their handkerchiefs and place them over their noses. This was ineffective and the Canadians were driven from the village. Counter-attacks by the 50th (Northumberland) Division failed to retake it. Further British attacks, including two by the Indian Lahore Division, stabilized the line.

Battle of Frezenberg 8–13 May. The German successes in the north had made the salient narrower and very extended and thus vulnerable on both flanks. After some argument between Foch and French it was accepted that a withdrawal and contraction of the front must take place. The new line was established by 4 May. The Battle of Frezenberg began with attacks on the 27th and 28th Divisions, followed by another gas attack on 10 May. After six days' fighting the Germans had gained about 1,000 yards.

Battle of Bellewaarde 24–25 May. The German assault began by launching yet another gas cloud on a front of some 4 miles. The British held the line initially but were then pushed back another 1,000 yards to the north of Bellewaarde Lake.

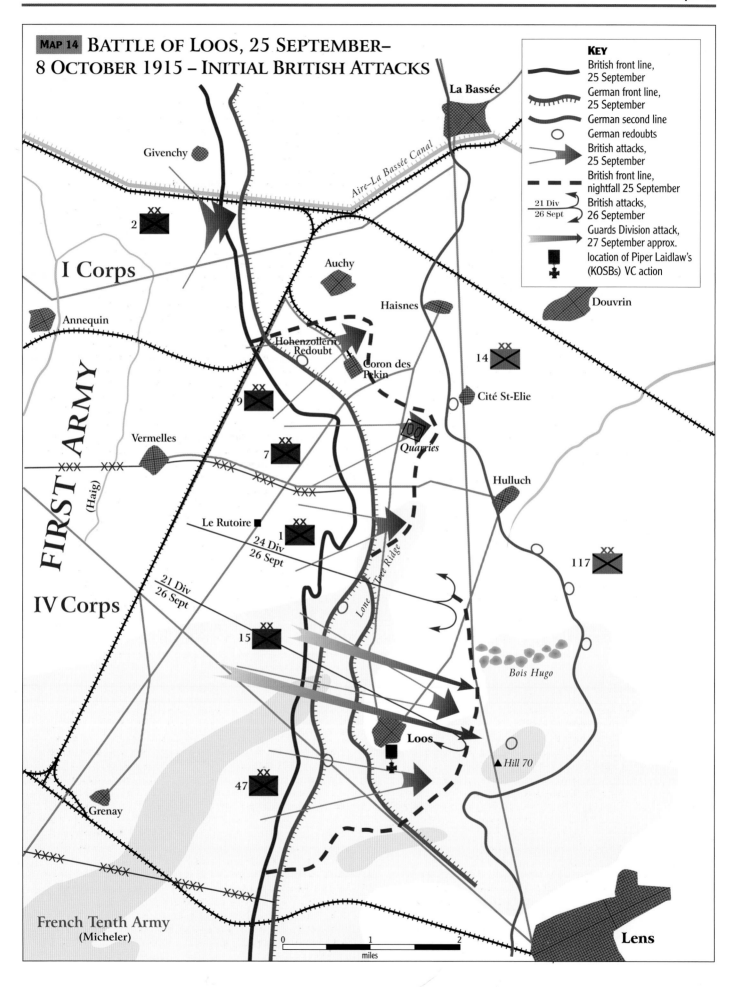

MAP 14 BATTLE OF LOOS, 25 SEPTEMBER–
8 OCTOBER 1915 – INITIAL BRITISH ATTACKS

KEY

British front line,
25 September

German front line,
25 September

German second line

German redoubts

British attacks,
25 September

British front line,
nightfall 25 September

21 Div / 26 Sept British attacks,
26 September

Guards Division attack,
27 September approx.

location of Piper Laidlaw's
(KOSBs) VC action

La Bassée

Givenchy

I Corps

Auchy

Haisnes

Douvrin

Annequin

Hohenzollern
Redoubt

Coron des
Pekin

14

Cité St-Elie

9

Quarries

Vermelles

7

Hulluch

FIRST ARMY

(Haig)

Le Rutoire

1

24 Div
26 Sept

117

21 Div
26 Sept

IV Corps

Lone Tree Ridge

15

Bois Hugo

47

Loos

Hill 70

Grenay

French Tenth Army
(Micheler)

0　　　1　　　2
miles

Lens

Notes for Map 14

Belligerents	British	German
	First Army	Sixth Army
	I, IV, Indian and Cav. Corps	In forward defences four regiments of the 14th and 117th Divisions plus a Jäger battalion. In reserve the Guards Reserve and 8th Divisions
	75,000 men	11,000 initially
Commanders	Gen. Sir Douglas Haig	Crown Prince Rupprecht of Bavaria
Casualties	almost 45,000 (inc. three maj. gens: Capper, Thesiger and Wing)	20,000 (estimate)
Result	A major British offensive halted.	

Summary Loos was part of the long-delayed simultaneous Allied offensives in Artois and Champagne. Because of acute shortages of British artillery and munitions, and the dangers of a narrow frontal attack exposing vulnerable flanks, Haig had devised two plans to achieve what was hoped would be a significant breakthrough. The first would be a wide frontal attack, with all six divisions advancing in line, with gas and smoke used to cover areas that could not be covered adequately by artillery – this would be the first use by the British of gas (chlorine) in the war. If the wind was unfavourable for gas and smoke, a narrow attack with the maximum artillery support would be carried out by the 9th (Scottish) Division (I Corps) against the Hohenzollern Redoubt, while the 15th (Scottish) Division attacked the enemy strongpoints on Lone Tree Ridge. The GHQ reserve (Guards, 21st and 24th Divisions) plus the Cavalry and Indian Corps were held back to be used only on the authority of the British commander-in-chief (French).

• On 25 September, despite doubts about the wind, Haig ordered gas from 5,000 cylinders and smoke from 7,870 smoke candles to be released along the 8-mile front. Thus a wide attack was launched following a four-day artillery bombardment that had consumed 250,000 shells, as well as extensive use of the Royal Flying Corps (RFC) on bombing and observation flights behind enemy lines. Although the attackers outnumbered the German defenders, the latter held the dominating ground and had built a strong second line, in places up to 4,000 yards behind the first. Additionally, they had constructed numerous redoubts and machine-gun posts in the small villages, miners' cottages and quarries that were prominent features of this coal-mining area.

• In IV Corps' area the gas released at 5:00 a.m. was largely effective and, combined with a smokescreen from Stokes mortars, allowed the 47th (London) Division, a Territorial formation, to make good progress south of Loos (the Irish Rifles went over the top kicking a rugby football ahead of them). The 15th (Scottish) Division was even more successful and had entered Loos by 8:00 a.m., and later in the day pushed on to reach Hill 70. The 7th King's Own Scottish Borderers (KOSBs) had been encouraged from their trenches that morning by the sight and sound of Piper Daniel Laidlaw calmly walking up and down the parapet playing 'Blue Bonnets Over the Border', for which gallantry he received the Victoria Cross (see box, page 40). The 1st Division had mixed fortunes attacking Lone Tree Ridge. A few small units reached Hulluch village before being driven out, but the bulk of the attackers were held up by uncut German wire.

• On the northern flank of I Corps' area the wind was definitely unfavourable for gas and the officer responsible on the 2nd Division's front declined to release it until given a direct order from the corps commander. The result was that much of it blew back on to the men, causing numerous casualties and confusion. The attack was halted. However, the 7th and 9th Divisions made satisfactory progress, with the enemy front-line trenches being taken. The former division advanced to the La Bassée–Loos road and secured the area of the quarries. The latter took the Hohenzollern Redoubt and fought its way east into the mining area and slag heaps around Caron des Pekin.

• By the end of the day a substantial hole had been punched in the German first line around Loos, but heavy losses, particularly among officers and NCOs, and local enemy counter-attacks, uncut wire and dwindling artillery support had forced the assaulting divisions to halt in front of the enemy's second line. It was time for the army reserve divisions to move through and open a breach in the second line. Unfortunately, they had been held back some distance behind the British front and required the authority of Field Marshal French before these three divisions could be placed under Haig's command. This was given at around 11:00 a.m. on 25 September, but the 21st and 24th were already tired from long marches on 24 September and were subjected to much delay during their approach march. It was not until the afternoon of the second day that they attacked between Loos and the Vermelles–Hulluch road. They were both untried New Army (Kitchener) divisions and moved forward in extended lines as if on some gigantic parade, to be cut down in their hundreds by a German second line that had been heavily reinforced during the lull. A German regimental history stated: 'Never had machine guns such straightforward work to do, nor done it so effectively. With barrels burning hot and swimming in oil, they traversed to and fro along the enemy's ranks unceasingly; one machine gun fired 12,500 rounds that afternoon.' These two divisions lost over 8,000 men. It was only the arrival and subsequent attack by the Guards Division towards Hill 70 on 27 September, during which 2nd Lt John Kipling, son of the poet, serving with the Irish Guards, was killed (see box below). The fighting dragged on into October, ending on the 8th when a German counter-attack along most of the front was beaten off.

The Mystery of Second Lieutenant John Kipling

John Kipling, the eighteen-year-old son of the author and poet Rudyard Kipling, was reported missing on 27 September at the Battle of Loos while serving with the 2nd Irish Guards. He was later presumed killed in the Guards' attack towards Bois Hugo (see Map 14). His distraught father never recovered from his death (Rudyard Kipling had used his influence to get his son accepted into the army after he was originally rejected due to poor eyesight) and spent years scouring the battlefield searching for his son's body or grave. By the time of his death in 1936 he had not succeeded.

In June 1992 the Commonwealth War Graves Commission (CWGC) announced that it had succeeded beyond reasonable doubt in establishing that John Kipling is buried in St Mary's Field Hospital Cemetery at Loos, in a grave commemorating an unknown 'Lieutenant of the Great War, Irish Guards'. This body was recorded as being found about 6,000 yards (a considerable distance) from where he was actually fighting. The Commission claimed that no other Irish Guards lieutenant was killed on that spot that day, therefore the body must be that of John Kipling.

In 1992 a book written by Tonie and Valmai Holt, the founders of Holts Battlefield Tours, dismissed the Commission's findings, largely on the basis that John was still a second lieutenant when he died and the body found had a lieutenant's rank badge on it. Only eight days before he was killed John had written to his father giving his rank as second lieutenant and, although his promotion had been officially decided three months earlier, it was not published in the *London Gazette* until two months after he went missing. The Holts also state that a study of the field hospital's burial returns shows that its team searched the area where John was fighting and found nothing before searching the area where the unknown lieutenant was found. The Holts say that the Commission's claim that the hospital's team confused the two areas 'stretches the imagination'. The Guards Museum curator supported the Holts' views, as did an experienced magistrate who said the Commission's proof failed to meet the standards of a criminal or civil court.

As a final twist, in June 2002 the Ministry of Defence (MOD), after a ten-month inquiry, stated that it was satisfied that the Commission had properly identified Lieutenant John Kipling's grave. The mystery remains.

1916

By December 1915 the Allied situation on all fronts was disturbing. The year had seen two major offensives on the Western Front (Artois and Champagne) fail with a shockingly high butcher's bill and no real impression made on the German front lines. All belligerent nations now had to call on their total manpower resources to conduct the war. Thus, in January 1916 the UK passed the first of the Military Service Acts, introducing conscription for the first time in her history.

On the Eastern Front the Germans had driven the Russians back and now occupied a huge tract of her territory. Italy, fighting with the Allies, had made no appreciable headway against Austria–Hungary – Italy had yet to declare war on Germany. Bulgaria,

The Road (*La Voie Sacrée*)

This supply route to Verdun was not named *La Voie Sacrée* until after the war; in 1916 military personnel commonly called it *La Route* (the Road). It was 38 miles long, running from Bar le Duc to Verdun, and from what was a narrow, two-lane, local road surfaced with crushed stone there is now a Route Nationale maintained by the French government as a military monument.

Some 8,800 military labourers were employed throwing 700,000 tons of crushed stone on the surface during the ten-month battle. The freight system consisted of 3,900 vehicles, including about 3,000 trucks with solid tyres carrying around 50,000 tons a week. Heavy freight consisted mostly of artillery ammunition with separate trucks for the powder charges for the large-calibre projectiles. The traffic crawled along at about 15 miles per hour, day and night, with an average of one vehicle passing a given point every fourteen seconds. Broken trucks were pushed off the road to be recovered by repair vehicles posted at intervals along the route.

Some 90,000 troops were also transported in and out of Verdun every week, often under air attack. To deter enemy aircraft, machine-gun posts were set up alongside the road and several airfields were located nearby, with seven fighter squadrons, including the famous *Escadrille Americaine*, tasked with route protection.

However, it is a myth that this road alone supplied the Verdun salient during 1916, as a metric-gauge railway running parallel to the road carried some 22 per cent. By July a newly built standard-gauge track had been constructed, relegating the road to lighter vehicles. Between the road and railway it was possible to rotate 221 French infantry divisions (some 2 million men) in and out of Verdun during that year.

Timeline 1916

Date	General	Western Front
9 Jan.	Gallipoli evacuation completed	
27 Jan.	UK introduces conscription	
21 Feb.–15 Dec.		Battle of Verdun
23 April	Easter Rising by Irish rebels against UK	
31 May–1 June	Battle of Jutland, the only major naval battle of the war – inconclusive	
2–13 June		Battle of Mount Sorrel
5 June	Lord Kitchener, British minister for war, drowns when HMS *Hampshire* sinks off the Orkneys	
1 July–18 Nov.		Battle of the Somme
1–13 July		Battle of Albert (opening phase of the Somme)
14–17 July		Battle of Bazentin Ridge (start of second phase of the Somme)
15 July–3 Sept.		Battle of Delville Wood (intermediate phase of the Somme)
23 July–3 Sept.		Battle of Pozières Ridge (intermediate phase of the Somme)
27 Aug.	Italy declares war on Germany Romania declares war on Austria–Hungary	
29 Aug.		Paul von Hindenburg replaces Falkenhayn as chief of German General Staff
3–6 Sept.		Battle of Guillemont (intermediate phase of the Somme)
9 Sept.		Battle of Ginchy (intermediate phase of the Somme)
15–22 Sept.		Battle of Flers-Courcelette (start of final phase of the Somme) – tanks used for first time in war by British
23 Sept.		Germans begin construction of the Hindenburg Line
25–28 Sept.		Battle of Morval (part of final phase of the Somme)
26–28 Sept.		Battle of Thiepval Ridge (part of final phase of the Somme)
1–18 Oct.		Battle of the Transloy Ridges (part of final phase of the Somme)
1 Oct.–11 Nov.		Battle of the Ancre Heights (part of the final phase of the Somme)
13–18 Nov.		Battle of the Ancre (final phase of the Somme)
5–7 Dec.	Prime Minister Henry Asquith resigns and is replaced by David Lloyd George	
13 Dec.		General Robert Nivelle replaces General (promoted Marshal 26 Dec.) Joseph Joffre as French commander-in-chief

Declarations of War 1916

9 March	Germany on Portugal
15 March	Austria–Hungary on Portugal
27 August	Romania on Austria–Hungary
28 August	Italy on Germany
30 August	Turkey on Romania
1 September	Bulgaria on Romania
14 September	Germany on Romania

fighting with the Central Powers, had overrun Serbia and Montenegro, while in Mesopotamia British forces were bottled up under siege in Kut. And the much-vaunted Gallipoli expedition against Turkey had ended in total failure. It was in these depressing circumstances that the Allied commanders-in-chief met at Chantilly between 6 and 8 December 1915 to decide plans for the following year.

The overall strategic decision was that the Allies should launch simultaneous offensives on all the main fronts (Western, Eastern and Italian), thereby crushing the Central Powers from all sides and hopefully negating their geographical advantage of interior lines. In January 1916 General Joffre, now commander of all French armies, agreed to the BEF making its main attack in Flanders, which is what Haig wanted as it would be close to the British supply routes through the Channel ports. However, after further discussions this was changed to the Allies mounting a major joint offensive astride the Somme in the summer, with the British (and one French corps) to the north and the French to the south of the river. It was to be a massive effort with no fewer than twenty-five British and forty French divisions earmarked for the initial assault.

However, as these plans were being put in hand, the Germans launched a large-scale attack on Verdun in the south-east, where the French defences had been seriously weakened to replace shortages of

A German soldier takes cover beside the body of a dead Frenchman, 1916.

manpower and guns in her more active armies. In Germany, General Falkenhayn had returned from his triumphs in the east with a determination to 'bleed white' the perceived weakened French by attacking a place that, for reasons of national prestige, France would defend to the end – the fortress of Verdun.

As the French became sucked ever more deeply into the defence of Verdun, so their capacity to fight alongside the British on the Somme diminished rapidly – as time progressed one of the objects of the BEF's efforts in maintaining the offensive on that river was to relieve the pressure on the French at Verdun who were hard pressed to hold their own. In the event, the war on the Western Front in 1916 consisted of these two major offensives – the Germans at Verdun, a struggle that was to become the longest battle of the war; and the British (with some French support) attacking on the Somme, which became the most costly battle of the war.

The fighting around Verdun lasted ten months, at the end of which the French had clung on to the town and had pushed the Germans back from some, but not all, of their initial gains. Both sides were utterly worn out and to an extent demoralized by crippling losses, highlighting the sheer horror of the destruction of men and material by modern war. The battle had ended in stalemate. On the Somme the fighting began on 1 July and ended in mid-

November with the British and French having advanced a maximum of 7 miles, and with even greater losses than either side sustained at Verdun. There had been no Allied breakthrough.

By the end of 1916 the Western Front had cost the BEF 600,617 casualties – well over twice the number for the previous year. For the Germans the year's loss had been 297,351 – 2.7 times that of 1915. These horrific figures would be eclipsed by those of 1917, with 1918, the year the war ended, seeing the worst losses of all.

A German View of Verdun

A German officer at Verdun, Lieutenant Ernst Jünger, later described the devastation wrought by artillery fire:

> The sunken road now appeared as nothing but a series of enormous shell-holes filled with pieces of uniform, weapons and dead bodies. The ground all round, as far as the eye could see, was ploughed by shells . . . Among the living lay the dead. As we dug ourselves in we found them in layers stacked one on top of the other. One company after another had been shoved into the drum-fire and steadily annihilated.

A French View of Verdun

A French officer at Verdun, Major Roman, wrote of the appalling scene at the entrance to his bunker:

> On my arrival, the corpse of an infantryman in a blue cap partially emerges from this compound of earth, stones, and unidentifiable debris. But a few hours later, it is no longer the same; he has disappeared and has been replaced by a *Tirailleur* [light infantryman] in khaki. And successively there appear other corpses in other uniforms. The shell that buries one disinters another. One gets acclimatized, however, to this spectacle; one can bear the horrible odour of this charnelhouse in which one lives, but one's *joie de vivre*, after the war, will be eternally poisoned by it.

Some Verdun Statistics

Verdun was defended by nineteen main forts and forty redoubts, but many were poorly equipped with guns.

The Germans deployed some 1,400 heavy, medium and field guns in their assault. These included thirteen 'Big Bertha' 420mm mortars. They employed about 1,300 trains to stockpile 2.75 million rounds of gun and howitzer ammunition for the initial attack. In the three months from 21 March to 20 June almost 17 million rounds of all types were fired and by the end of the battle this number had risen to an estimated 32 million.

The Germans assembled 150 aircraft, four airships and several artillery observation balloons for the assault.

Nine villages were obliterated and whole swathes of woods and ground so pulverized and contaminated with the detritus of war – human and material – that the land was declared irrecoverable.

Casualties in the ten months of fighting were for the Germans 330,000, of whom 143,000 were dead. The French suffered 351,000 total losses, composed of 56,000 dead, 100,000 missing (mostly killed) or prisoners and 195,000 wounded.

The bones of about 130,000 of the unknown dead of both sides are gathered in a specially built ossuary on Douaumont Ridge, the site of Fort Douaumont.

Some Somme Statistics

The average casualties per division (each approximately 10,000 strong) for the four and a half months' fighting were: British and dominion troops combined 8,026; the three Australian divisions 8,960; the forty-three British divisions 8,133; the four Canadian divisions 6,324; and the New Zealand division 8,133.

The Allied average daily loss during the 142-day battle was 4,366, with the British losing 2,976 and the French 1,390 per day. The German daily loss averaged 3,099.

The British used the creeping barrage (page 254) for the first time.

Preparations for the offensive saw the use of seven trains a day to bring up artillery ammunition.

For the preparatory bombardment 1,537 guns and howitzers were available – that translated into one field gun for every 20 yards of front and one heavy piece for every 58 yards.

The Royal Flying Corps lost 782 aircraft and 526 aircrew.

The British losses of 57,470 on 1 July consisted of: officers – 993 killed, 1,337 wounded, 96 missing, 12 prisoners – total 2,438; other ranks – 18,247 killed, 34,156 wounded, 2,056 missing, 573 prisoners – total 55,032.

The Victoria Cross in 1916

Sixty-four Victoria Crosses were awarded during the year, nine for acts of gallantry on 1 July. Of those, that of twenty-one-year-old Private William McFadzean, 14th Royal Irish Rifles, is particularly remarkable. McFadzean was in a crowded trench near Thiepval Wood when a box of bombs (grenades) fell down, spilling its contents on the floor. He saw that the pins of two of them had come loose, meaning there was about five seconds before they exploded and killed or wounded a large number of his comrades. In a supreme act of self-sacrifice, McFadzean threw himself on the two bombs, covering them with his body. He was blown to pieces, but only one of the other soldiers in the trench was wounded, in the leg. It is said that as his remains were carried away his comrades saluted and several wept. McFadzean is commemorated on the Thiepval Memorial and at Newtonbreda Presbyterian Church, Belfast.

As recently as 2008 a Royal Marine did the same in Afghanistan, but because he turned on his back and the blast was absorbed by his pack and body armour he survived with minor injuries. He was awarded the George Cross, second only to the VC for gallantry.

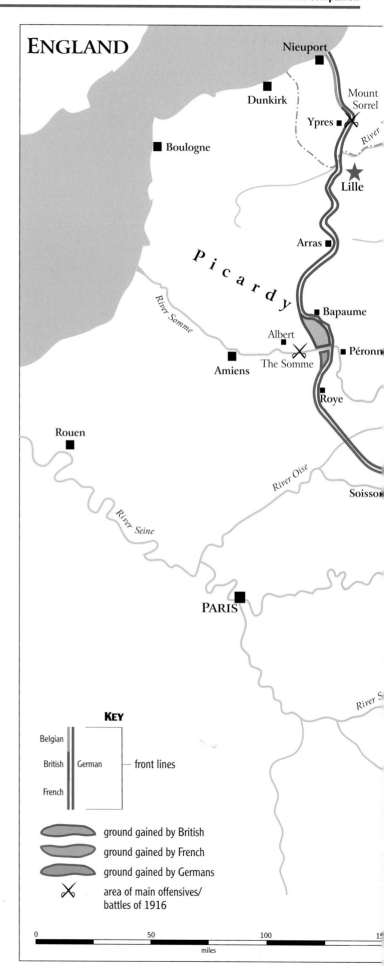

ENGLAND

Nieuport

Dunkirk

Mount Sorrel

Ypres

Boulogne

Lille

Arras

P i c a r d y

River Somme

Bapaume

Albert

The Somme

Péronne

Amiens

Roye

Rouen

River Oise

Soissons

River Seine

PARIS

River S

KEY

Belgian

British | German — front lines

French

ground gained by British

ground gained by French

ground gained by Germans

area of main offensives/ battles of 1916

0   50   100   15

miles

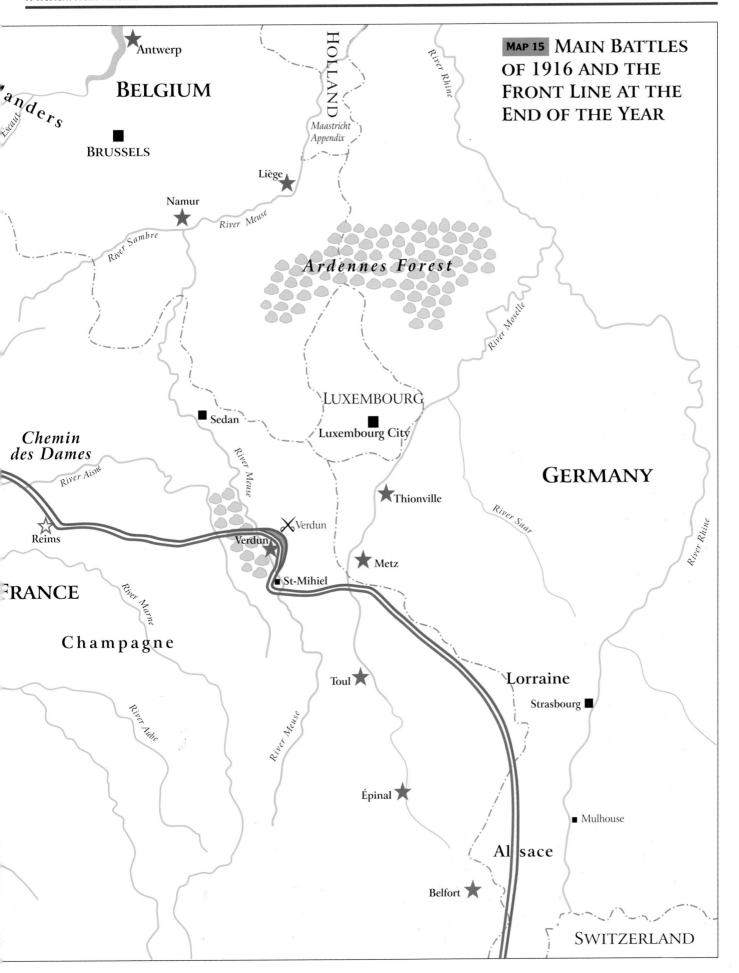

MAP 15 MAIN BATTLES OF 1916 AND THE FRONT LINE AT THE END OF THE YEAR

Antwerp

BELGIUM

HOLLAND

River Rhine

Flanders

Escaut

BRUSSELS

Maastricht Appendix

Liège

Namur

River Meuse

River Sambre

Ardennes Forest

River Moselle

LUXEMBOURG

Sedan

Luxembourg City

Chemin des Dames

River Aisne

GERMANY

River Meuse

Thionville

River Saar

Reims

Verdun

Verdun

Metz

River Rhine

FRANCE

St-Mihiel

River Marne

Champagne

Toul

Lorraine

River Aube

Strasbourg

River Meuse

Épinal

Mulhouse

Alsace

Belfort

SWITZERLAND

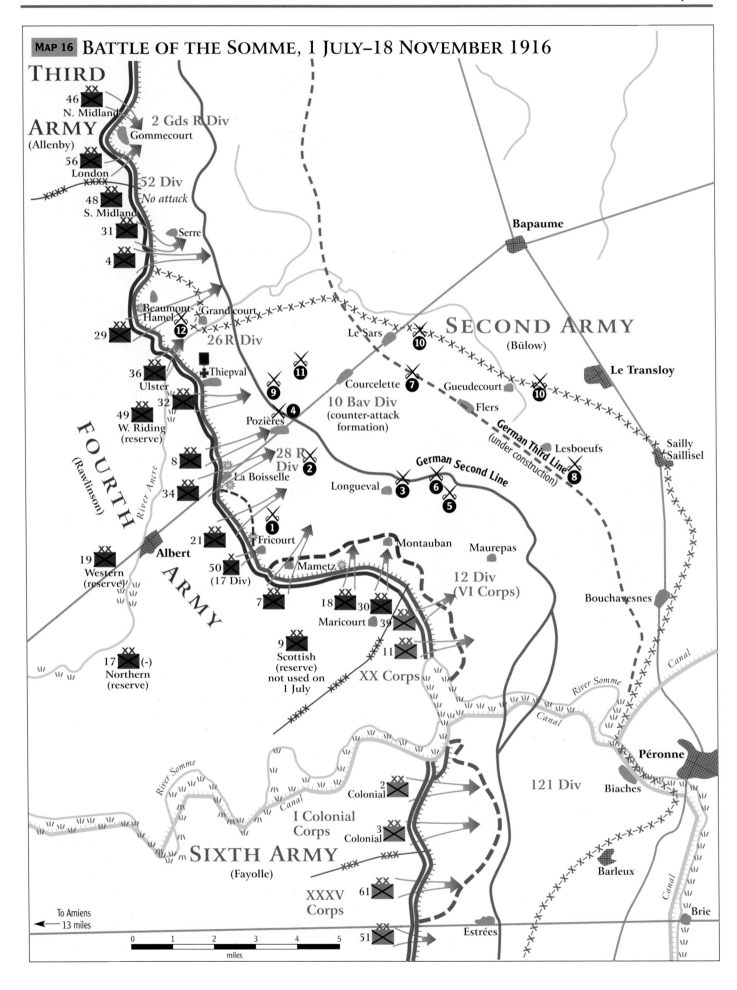

MAP 16 **BATTLE OF THE SOMME, 1 JULY–18 NOVEMBER 1916**

THIRD
ARMY
(Allenby)

46 N. Midland

2 Gds R Div
Gommecourt

56 London

52 Div
No attack

48 S. Midland

31

4

Serre

Beaumont-
Hamel

Grand court

26 R Div

Le Sars

SECOND ARMY
(Bülow)

Bapaume

Le Transloy

29

36 Ulster

Thiepval

10 Courcelette

Gueudecourt

11

9

Pozières

4

10 Bav Div
(counter-attack
formation)

7

Flers

10

German Third Line
(under construction)

49 W. Riding
(reserve)

32

FOURTH
(Rawlinson)

River Ancre

8

34

28 R
Div

2

La Boiselle

Longueval

3

German Second Line

6

5

Lesboeufs

8

Sailly
Saillisel

21

1

Fricourt

Albert

19 Western
(reserve)

50
(17 Div)

ARMY

7

Mametz

18

30

Maricourt

39

Montauban

Maurepas

12 Div
(VI Corps)

Bouchavesnes

11

17 (-)
Northern
(reserve)

9 Scottish
(reserve)
not used on
1 July

XX Corps

River Somme

Canal

Péronne

River Somme

Canal

121 Div

Biaches

2 Colonial

I Colonial
Corps

Colonial

SIXTH ARMY
(Fayolle)

3 Colonial

Barleux

XXXV
Corps

61

Brie

To Amiens
← 13 miles

Estrées

0   1   2   3   4   5
miles

Notes for Map 16

Belligerents	British	French	German
Armies	initially Fourth, with some Third Army support in the north	Sixth Army	Second Army
Divisions engaged 1 July	17	6	6 + 3 reserve
Guns	2,800	1,200	uncertain
Commanders	Gen. Sir Douglas Haig (BEF) Gen. Sir Henry Rawlinson (Fourth Army)	Gen. Ferdinand Foch (Army Group North) Gen. Marie Fayolle (Sixth Army)	Gen. Max von Gallwitz (Army Group Gallwitz) Gen. Fritz von Bülow (Second Army)
Casualties 1 July	57,470 (19,240 killed)	uncertain	uncertain
by 18 November	430,000	196,000	660,000 (estimate)

Result Allies fail to achieve breakthrough. Massive losses on both sides and armies exhausted.

Summary

Although the French played an important role in the Somme offensive, it was the British and dominion troops who provided the main effort. It was a massive battle of grinding attrition lasting four and a half months, at the end of which the Allies had advanced a maximum of 7 miles but failed to achieve a breakthrough. The Germans had occupied the area since 1914 and had constructed a deep defensive position of three lines, mostly on the high ground facing the British. Villages were fortified and redoubts built, all surrounded by wide belts of wire. Despite firing about 1.7 million shells in the seven-day preparatory bombardment, the British assault on 1 July by 17 divisions achieved little. The staggering losses by the British on the first day were never to be equalled on one day until the fall of Singapore in World War II when over 80,000 were captured. To say that both sides were exhausted by November is a huge understatement. Of the German Army, which saw 95 divisions pass through the horrors of the Somme, some of them twice or even three times, Ludendorff said, 'The army had been fought to a standstill and was utterly worn out.'

Twelve actions were officially classified by the British as battles:

Battle of Albert 1–13 July. The opening phase of the Somme offensive by both British and French Armies, and primarily the attacks on the German front line on 1 July, for which the British had virtually nothing to show except the appalling casualty lists. However, the French south of the Somme achieved a more substantial advance at far less cost. The remaining days were spent in small-scale attacks of little significance.

Battle of Bazentin Ridge 14–17 July. The start of the next phase of the offensive involving the Fourth and Reserve Armies, which saw the capture of Longueval, Trones Wood and Ovillers, and attacks at Fromelles and High Wood.

Battle of Delville Wood 15 July–3 September. This bitter and intense struggle for the splintered stumps and tangled wire of 'Devil's Wood', where four VCs were won, lasted over six weeks. It is particularly associated with the attacks by the South African Brigade (see page 115). The wood was finally captured on 15 September on the first day of the Flers-Courcelette battle.

Battle of Pozières Ridge 23 July–3 September. A long struggle for the ridge on which the village stands, remembered mainly as an Australian battle. Australia's official historian, Charles Bean, recorded that this ridge was 'more densely sown with Australian sacrifice than any other place on earth.' Pozières was captured but the British advance did not exceed a mile.

Battle of Guillemont 3–6 September. A combined British (Fourth Army) and French attack, with the British advancing on Guillemont and the French on Maurepas. It resulted in some limited British success.

Battle of Ginchy 9 September. Another Fourth Army attack, which saw the 16th (Irish) Division capture the village, thus depriving the Germans of several observation posts that had overlooked the entire battlefield.

Battle of Flers-Courcelette 15–22 September. The Fourth and Reserve Armies attacked in the last large-scale battle of the Somme offensive. It saw the first use of tanks in the war by the British (see page 388), but their performance was patchy. Although gains were made by British, Canadian and New Zealand formations, there was still no breakthrough.

Battle of Morval 25–28 September. In part a continuation of the Flers-Courcelette battle, this attack on the villages of Morval, Combles, Lesboeufs and Gueudecourt saw the capture of the last three by the Fourth Army.

Battle of Thiepval Ridge 26–28 September. An attack by the Reserve Army designed to coincide with the Battle of Morval. It saw the fall of the German Thiepval fortress, which had held out since 1 July.

Battle of the Transloy Ridges 1–18 October. This battle involved formations from both Fourth and Reserve Armies. The attacks were hampered by the arrival of wet autumn weather and minimal progress was made, although the villages of Eaucourt l'Abbaye and Le Sars were taken.

Battle of the Ancre Heights 1 October–11 November. This was a long battle of attrition conducted by the Reserve Army, resulting in gains of about 1,000 yards. However, it saw the capture of the Schwaben and Stuff Redoubts by the British, while the Regina Trench finally fell to the Canadian Corps after four bloody attempts on 11 November.

Battle of the Ancre 13–18 November. The final battle of the Somme offensive, in which the main attacking force was the Fifth Army (formerly the Reserve Army), which advanced north and south of the Ancre. The 31st Division failed in its attack over the same ground it had advanced over on 1 July, although at last Beaumont-Hamel was secured by the 51st (Highland) Division. This was sufficient for Haig to proclaim a success when attending the commanders-in-chief conference at Chantilly on 17 November to plan operations for 1917. The Battle of the Somme was over.

KEY

┅┅┅┅ front lines, 1 July	
━━━━ front line, 2 July	
X–X–X–X–X– front line, 15 December	
⊠→ planned British divisional attacks, 1 July	
⊠→ French divisional attacks, 1 July	
26 R Div front-line German division, 1 July	

☀ main British mines out of 17 planted

■ approx. location of Pte McFadzean's VC action

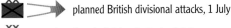

❶ Battle of Albert, 1–13 July

❷ Battle of Bazentin Ridge, 14–17 July

❸ Battle of Delville Wood, 15 July–3 September

❹ Battle of Pozières Ridge, 23 July–3 September

❺ Battle of Guillemont, 3–6 September

❻ Battle of Ginchy, 9 September

❼ Battle of Flers-Courcelette, 15–22 September

❽ Battle of Morval, 25–28 September

❾ Battle of Thiepval Ridge, 26–28 September

❿ Battle of Transloy Ridges, 1–18 October

⓫ Battle of the Ancre Heights, 1 October–11 November

⓬ Battle of the Ancre, 13–18 November

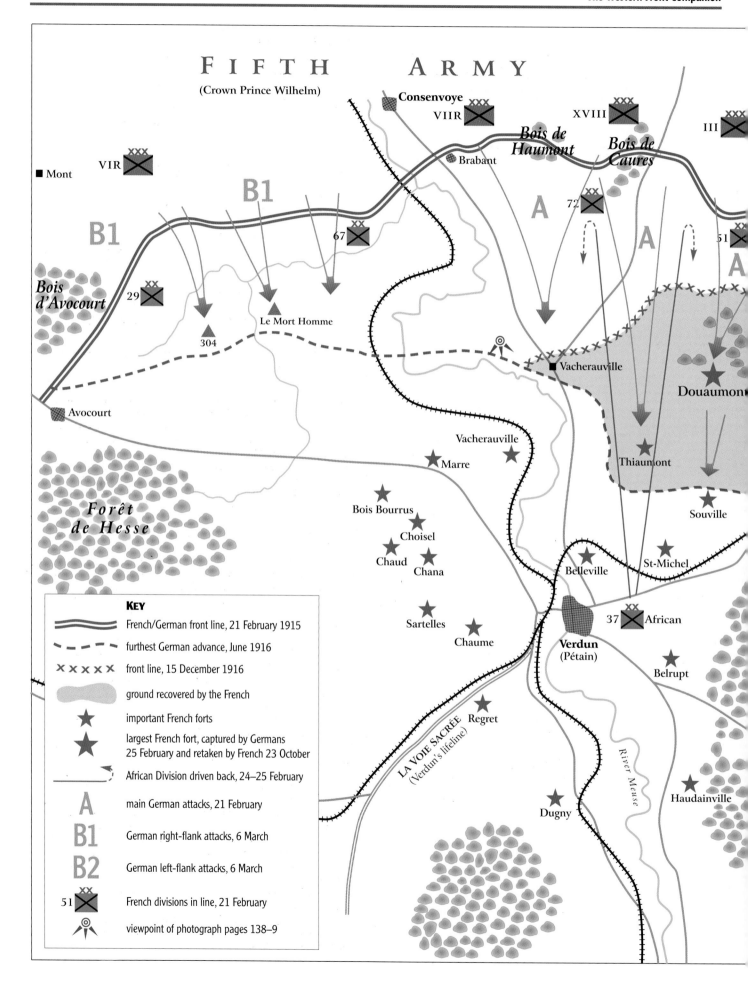

F I F T H A R M Y
(Crown Prince Wilhelm)

■ Mont

VIR

Bois
d'Avocourt

29

B1

B1

B1

304

Le Mort Homme

Avocourt

Forêt
de Hesse

Consenvoye

VIIR

Brabant

*Bois de
Haumont*

*Bois de
Caures*

XVIII

III

A

72

A

51

A

67

A

Vacherauville

■ Vacherauville

Douaumont

Thiaumont

Souville

Marre

Bois Bourrus

Choisel

Chaud

Chana

St-Michel

Belleville

37 African

Sartelles

Chaume

Verdun
(Pétain)

Belrupt

LA VOIE SACRÉE
(Verdun's lifeline)

Regret

River Meuse

Dugny

Haudainville

KEY

French/German front line, 21 February 1915

furthest German advance, June 1916

× × × × front line, 15 December 1916

ground recovered by the French

★ important French forts

★ largest French fort, captured by Germans
25 February and retaken by French 23 October

African Division driven back, 24–25 February

A main German attacks, 21 February

B1 German right-flank attacks, 6 March

B2 German left-flank attacks, 6 March

51 French divisions in line, 21 February

viewpoint of photograph pages 138–9

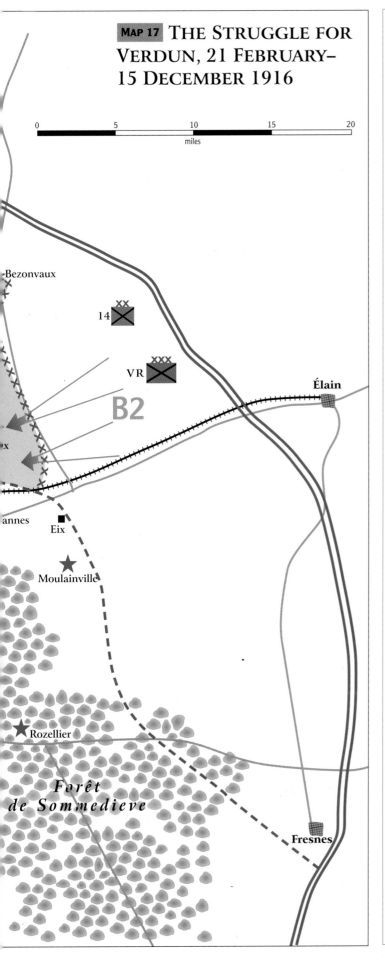

MAP 17 THE STRUGGLE FOR VERDUN, 21 FEBRUARY–15 DECEMBER 1916

Notes for Map 17

Belligerents	French	German
	Second Army	Fifth Army
	XXX and VI Corps	III, VIIR and XVIII Corps

Divisions 21 Feb. for initial German assault

	French	German
	2 divisions in line	6 divisions
	1 reserve	
	34 battalions	72 battalions

Guns	fewer than 300	1,300, inc. many heavy guns and mortars

Commanders

on 21 Feb:	Gen. Frédéric-Georges Herr;	Maj. Gen. Crown Prince Wilhelm of Prussia
from 25 Feb:	Gen. Philippe Pétain	Lt Gen. Konstantin von Knobelsdorf (chief of staff, de facto commander)
from 1 May:	Gen. Robert Nivelle	

Casualties (during 10 months):

	351,000	330,000
	(156,000 dead/ missing/prisoners)	(143,000 dead)

Result The French retained Verdun but both armies were crippled and utterly exhausted.

Summary

• According to the post-war memoirs of the German chief of staff Erich von Falkenhayn, the objective for the year was to attack the French at a place from which they could not retreat for reasons of national pride. His stated aim was not so much to achieve a breakthrough but to bleed the French Army white by relentless attrition. The place chosen was Verdun, which in February 1916 was weakly defended by second-rate troops and had been denuded of some 50 gun batteries. The entire Verdun salient was exposed to artillery fire from three sides.

• The battle started on 21 February with a nine-hour artillery bombardment of over 1 million shells (including gas) and flamethrowers. By 22 February the massive German infantry assault, with the troops storming forward with rifles slung and grenades in hand, had advanced 3 miles. The French XXX Corps was only just saved from disaster by the arrival of XX Corps. The next day Pétain, commander of the French Second Army, was put in command at Verdun and the defenders lost their most important fort, Douaumont, to a bold German *coup de main* (see page 136). The 33rd Regiment – in which Captain Charles de Gaulle, the Free French leader in World War II and later French president, was a company commander – defended the village of Douaumont. The arrival of the Second Army halted the German advance in the centre, so they turned to attack the flanks. Launched on 6 March, the right assault focused on Avocourt and the Mort Homme/Point 304 features, while on the left the attack was towards Fort Vaux. Again the fighting was exceptionally fierce and bloody; the Mort Homme did not fall until the end of May, and Fort Vaux not until 7 June. By this time both sides were exhausted and had suffered staggering losses in what became known as the 'hell of Verdun'.

• It was during this phase (on 1 May) that Pétain was promoted to command the Central Group of Armies and his place was taken at Verdun by Nivelle – an extreme exponent of all-out offensive warfare. On 7 June Fort Vaux fell after a magnificent defence by the garrison under a Maj. Sylvain-Eugène Raynal, during which his men's thirst had compelled them to lick moisture from the walls and drink their own urine. Nivelle then turned to the offensive and, after more prolonged and bitter fighting, with the ground now just a lunar landscape of overlapping shell holes and craters, retook Fort Douaumont on 23 October and Fort Vaux on 3 November. The Germans had been driven back some 5 miles north of Douaumont and the fighting finally ceased by mid-December. Verdun had been saved; Nivelle was the hero.

1917

Declarations of War 1917

6 April	US on Germany
7 April	Panama on Germany
	Cuba on Germany
13 April	Bolivia severed relations with the US
23 April	Turkey severed relations with the US
27 June	Greece on Austria–Hungary, Bulgaria, Germany and Turkey
22 July	Siam (Thailand) on Germany and Austria–Hungary
4 August	Liberia on Germany
14 August	China on Germany and Austria–Hungary
6 October	Peru severed relations with Germany
7 October	Uruguay severed relations with Germany
26 October	Brazil on Germany
7 December	US on Austria–Hungary
8 December	Ecuador severed relations with Germany
10 December	Panama on Austria–Hungary
16 December	Cuba on Austria–Hungary

The year 1917 was marked by two prodigious events that had huge consequences for both the Germans and the Allies. The first was the fall of the Tsarist autocracy in Russia and then, in November, the Bolshevik seizure of power in Petrograd, causing Russia's virtual withdrawal from the war and the opening of peace negotiations that would lead to the signing of the Treaty of Brest-Litovsk in March 1918. This event had potentially enormous implications for the Western Front in terms of the Germans being able to bring large numbers of troops and guns westwards.

The second occurrence was the entry of America into the war on the Allied side, the formal declaration being made in April. Her massive manpower and industrial potential would more than compensate for the Russian exit from hostilities provided she could deploy her army to France quickly enough. This became the problem, as the American Regular Army was tiny and the need to expand tenfold and more would take many months.

The year anticipated an increase in British manpower, with up to sixty-five divisions (including two Portuguese) expected on the Western Front by the end of March; however, this total was not achieved and at the end of the year the number of divisions had reached only sixty. This very considerable force of five armies was complemented by a vast administrative and supply network that delivered (among countless other items) arms, ammunition, stores, food and equipment, fodder for almost 450,000 horses and mules, and 6 million gallons of petrol every month.

There was also a marked improvement in tactics (particularly in infantry/artillery/tank/aircraft cooperation), both offensive and defensive, with meticulous planning, training and the realization of the importance of the achievement of surprise by the attacker. For the defending Germans the emphasis was on a flexible defence in great depth, with a network of machine-gun emplacements, concrete bunkers and the coordinated use of artillery and counter-attacks (see relevant sections below).

Since 1916 the Germans had been constructing new defensive lines, or rather defensive zones, behind their front line south-east of Arras. The Germans called this the *Siegfriedstellung*, although the British came to call it the Hindenburg Line after General Paul von Hindenburg who, with General Erich Ludendorff, conceived the idea (see opposite). The Allied plan at the start of the year was French. General Robert Nivelle, the new French commander-in-chief (appointed largely due to his success in recapturing Fort Douaumont at Verdun), persuaded his government and the British (with difficulty, as several senior political and military leaders were sceptical) that with surprise and properly coordinated

Timeline 1917

Date	General	Western Front
16 Jan.	Germans send telegram to Mexico proposing an alliance with Germany against the USA – this becomes the primary reason for America joining Allies	
1 Feb.	Germany resumes unrestricted submarine warfare	
3 Feb.	US severs diplomatic ties with Germany	
23 Feb.–5 April		Germans withdraw to Hindenburg Line
8–11 March	British capture Baghdad	
12 March	Russian Revolution begins	
15 March	Tsar Nicholas II of Russia abdicates	
6 April	US declares war on Germany	
9 April–17 May		Battles of Arras
16 April–20 May		French (Nivelle) offensive on the Aisne and in Champagne
29 April–10 June	Series of mutinies in French Army	
10 May	Gen. John Pershing appointed commander of American Expeditionary Force (AEF)	
15 May		Nivelle replaced by Pétain as French commander-in-chief
7–14 June		Battle of Messines
25 June.		First American troops land in France
31 July–10 Nov.		Battles of Third Ypres
15–25 Aug.		Battle of Hill 70
23 Oct.–1 Nov.		Battle of Malmaison
5 Nov.	Allies agree to establish a Supreme War Council	
7 Nov.	October Revolution in Russia – Bolsheviks seize power	
20 Nov.–7 Dec.		Battle of Cambrai
7 Dec.	US declares war on Austria–Hungary	
23 Dec.	Russia signs armistice with Germany	

creeping barrages he could punch a hole in the German defences on the Chemin des Dames ridge within hours rather than days. The British would support this effort with an attack east from Arras. The withdrawal of the Germans in late February and March to their newly fortified Hindenburg Line complicated Nivelle's plans, but postponed rather than prevented them. The attacks in April/May, however, failed with unacceptable losses and were the immediate cause of Nivelle's dismissal and a series of mutinies in the French Army (see box, page 128).

The British Arras offensive gained about 5 miles but achieved no breakthrough. However, it did have two striking, if comparatively minor, successes. The first was the capture of Vimy Ridge by the Canadians in April (see Section Two, page 102), followed by the British Second Army (including Australians and New Zealanders) taking Messines Ridge in June (see Section Seven, pages 307–10). The latter attack preceded Haig's offensive from the Ypres salient, which has become commonly known as the Battle of Passchendaele – although officially called the Third Battle of Ypres. It was intended to take the ridge of that name and then strike deep behind the German lines with the ultimate (highly optimistic) objective of destroying the German U-boat bases on the Belgian coast – Germany had resumed unrestricted submarine war.

The year ended in November with an initially highly successful attack by the Third Army at Cambrai (see Section Thirteen), using new offensive tactics and employing several hundred tanks. Unfortunately, the British were unable to exploit this success.

Total losses on the Western Front for the year were almost 760,000 British and just under 450,000 German.

The Hindenburg Line

Although General Nivelle's offensives on the Aisne and in Champagne were postponed due to the German withdrawal to the Hindenburg Line from February to March 1917, this was not because the new defensive system was unknown to the Allies. The Germans had started construction as early as September the previous year and the new works taking shape were spotted by Royal Flying Corps (RFC) reconnaissance flights in October 1916. German prisoners also supplied information on its development. The surprise was the timing of the withdrawal.

The German High Command decided that after their huge losses on the Somme there was a need for a strong fall-back defensive position behind that front. Of equal importance was the desire to shorten the front generally, thus freeing up troops to constitute a larger reserve force. As a glance at Map 18 shows, there were two salients in the German line. One in the north extended almost 10 miles west of Bapaume, while the second much larger one to the south extended west of Roye. In the event, the withdrawal shortened the line by some 25 miles and involved the front line of April being from 10 to almost 30 miles behind that of February 1917. The saving in troops holding the line was fourteen divisions.

The Germans called the new line the *Siegfriedstellung*, a *Stellung* being a fortified position or area. It was much more a defensive zone than a line, running for 100 miles between Lens and Reims. There was a second defensive zone about 1½ miles behind the first and it too consisted of fire and support trenches some 200 yards apart. As far as possible it was sited on reverse slopes, with artillery observation posts at least 500 yards behind the front trenches and overlooking them.

The whole system was divided into a 'battle' zone and a 'rear' zone, and as labour became available yet another system was constructed to complete the rear zone. In front of the battle zone was an outpost zone about 600 yards deep to deny the attacker observation over it. This consisted mostly of small groups of men armed with light machine guns. In the battle zone there was a chequered arrangement of fortified posts containing concrete machine-gun emplacements.

A sustained industrial effort had been made in the construction of these works. For example, sawmills had produced thousands of identical dugout doors, while other factories produced ferro-concrete shelters of the same pattern.

Fronting these positions was a forest of barbed wire fixed to iron corkscrew pickets. The wire was usually sited in three belts, each 10–15 yards in depth and 5 yards or more apart, with the belts laid out in a zigzag pattern and flanking machine guns tasked to fire along the wire. Observation posts were similarly protected and were linked by buried cable to the guns or headquarters; and a network of light railway track was built to service the new zones. This huge defensive zone was divided into five sectors or operational areas from north to south.

Continued on page 68

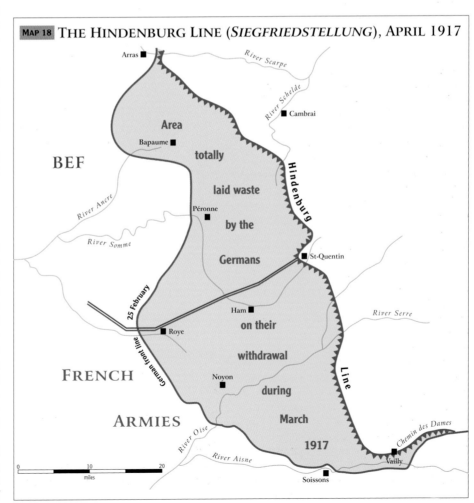

MAP 18 THE HINDENBURG LINE (*SIEGFRIEDSTELLUNG*), APRIL 1917

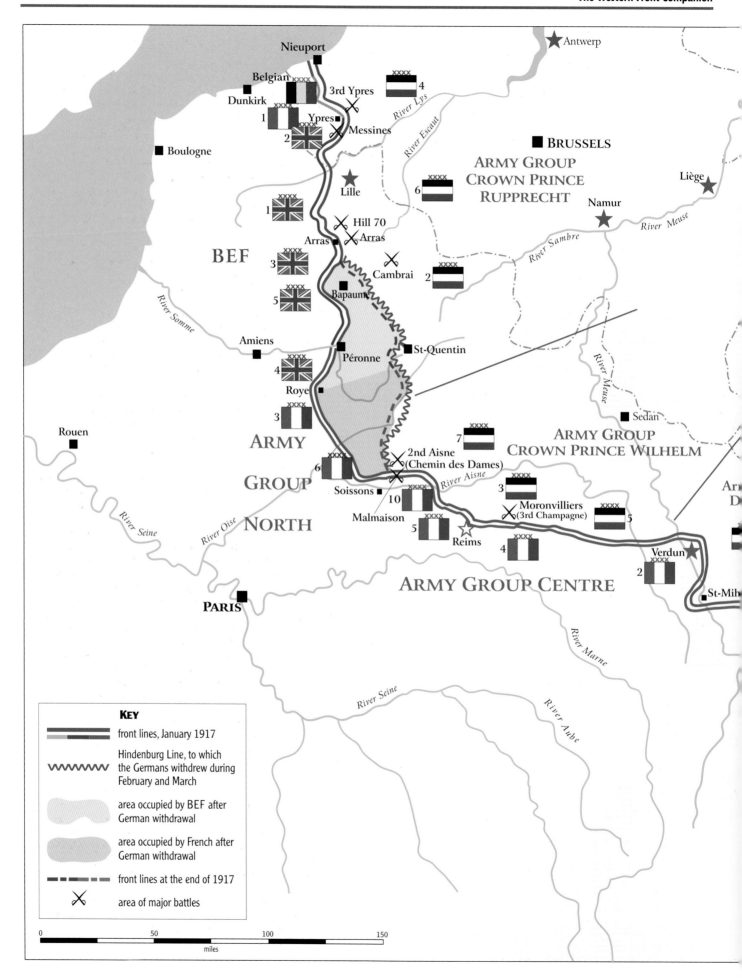

Antwerp

Belgian

Dunkirk

3rd Ypres

4

1

Ypres

River Lys

2

Messines

Boulogne

BRUSSELS

ARMY GROUP
CROWN PRINCE
RUPPRECHT

Liège

Lille

6

Namur

1

Hill 70

River Meuse

Arras

Arras

BEF

3

Cambrai

River Sambre

5

2

Bapaume

River Somme

Amiens

St-Quentin

4

Péronne

Roye

3

Sedan

ARMY

ARMY GROUP
CROWN PRINCE WILHELM

Rouen

7

2nd Aisne
(Chemin des Dames)

GROUP

6

Soissons

River Aisne

3

River Seine

River Oise

NORTH

10

Moronvilliers
(3rd Champagne)

5

Malmaison

Verdun

5

4

St-Mih

River Seine

Reims

2

PARIS

ARMY GROUP CENTRE

River Marne

River Aube

KEY

front lines, January 1917

Hindenburg Line, to which
the Germans withdrew during
February and March

area occupied by BEF after
German withdrawal

area occupied by French after
German withdrawal

front lines at the end of 1917

area of major battles

0   50   100   150

miles

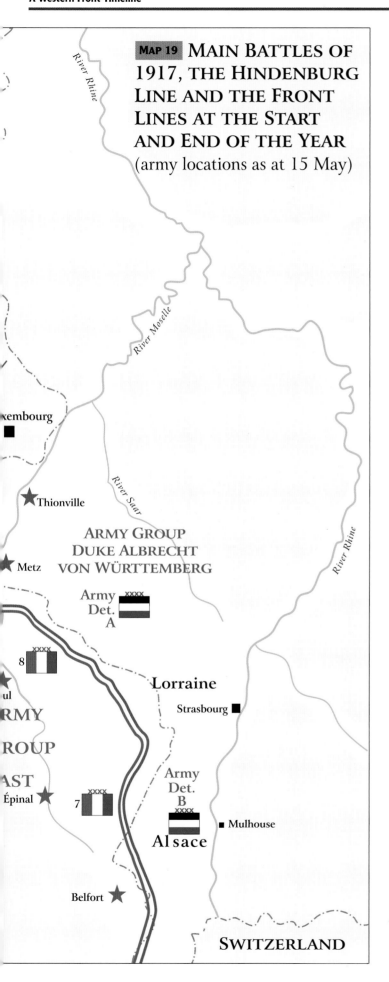

MAP 19 MAIN BATTLES OF 1917, THE HINDENBURG LINE AND THE FRONT LINES AT THE START AND END OF THE YEAR (army locations as at 15 May)

River Rhine

River Moselle

River Saar

River Rhine

xembourg

Thionville

ARMY GROUP DUKE ALBRECHT VON WÜRTTEMBERG

Metz

Army Det. A

8

ul

RMY

ROUP

AST

Épinal

7

Lorraine

Strasbourg

Army Det. B

Mulhouse

Alsace

Belfort

SWITZERLAND

Going Over the Top at Third Ypres

Captain J. F. Lucy had served as a corporal and sergeant in the Royal Irish Fusiliers before being commissioned into the same regiment. Arriving back as an officer, Lucy describes a typical series of events as seen by a platoon commander as he prepared to lead his platoon, in this case one he had never met, over the top. The objective was a fortified heap of rubble in the Ypres salient, formerly the village of Westhoek.

Another half-mile of mud brought me to a small trench in which two officers were seated – the OC 'B' Company, Captain Collins, and a Lieutenant Malone, both Wexford men. Collins was very cheerful. He warned me not to knock over the little wall of mud along the parados which was keeping out the surface water.

'Come in,' he then said, 'and have something to eat.' An orderly appeared with cold bully beef stew, potatoes, a bottle of sauce and some earthy bread and promised a cup of tea to follow. I had to fish for saliva before I ate. Rain began to fall steadily . . .

The Germans knew we were going to attack them. Night came and with it definite orders for the advance in the morning, and I moved out to a nearby trench to find my platoon and make myself known to them. I collected the sergeant and section commanders and explained the plan of attack, which was very simple.

The battalion would go forward in an hour or so and take over a section of trenches from the English holding the front line. At the first streak of dawn a British creeping barrage would come down on our front and we would go forward at once and follow the barrage, and occupy the German first line . . .

Extra shovels were issued and strapped to the backs of selected men. Empty sandbags were dished out, extra grenades and bandoliers of ammunition, and water bottles were filled from petrol tins. Greatcoats were rolled and dumped at company headquarters trench.

We arrived thirty strong in the front line, and the English went out, back to support. Rations, tobacco and rum came up and were distributed, and a double tot of rum was saved up to be taken by each man just before zero hour. I was glad to see my sergeant cheerful and carrying himself well. One of the corporals also attracted me. He made a bet he would reach the second German line before me. I took him on . . .

Hardly anyone slept that night. There was too much coming and going. Runners, stretcher-bearers, gunner officers, signallers, Stoke mortar teams and others made perpetual traffic during the darkness. I sat up and wrote a last letter home by a shaded torchlight . . . The sergeant roused everyone an hour before zero and repeated orders. Rum was issued. I went along to inspect the men. Bayonets were fixed, cartridge clips and grenade pins loosened. Some men had collected boxes, others had dug holes in the trench side, or placed small ladders to help them clamber out. They stood facing the parapet, jaw muscles rigid, bayonet-points under cover – waiting.

At two minutes to zero I took a good swig of whisky, saw the nearest men all tensed and ready to climb out, and I put my whistle to my lips. My heart thumped heavily. Exactly to the second pandemonium broke loose. I blew my whistle and was up and over, looking back to see my trench emptying rapidly. Only two men were still struggling to get out – slipped off boxes or something. Good enough for me. I broke forward into a trot, gripped my whistle between my teeth, pulled a bomb from my haversack and threw away the pin. With my ready bomb in my right hand and my revolver in my left I speeded up. Concussions jostled me in my stride. The German counter-barrage was down.

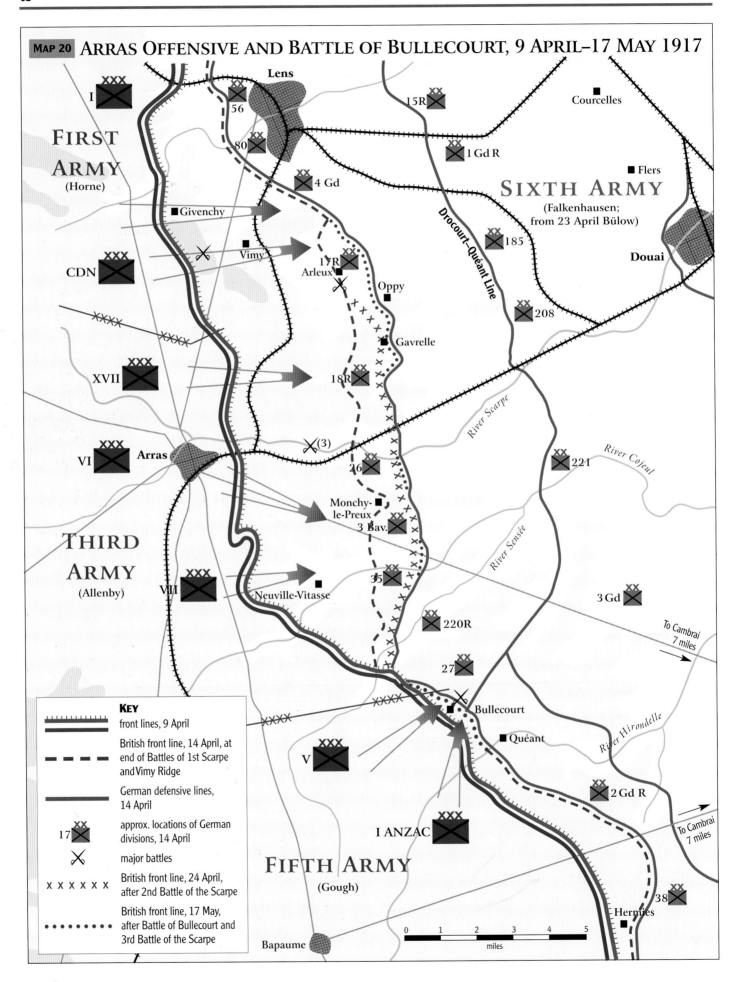

MAP 20 ARRAS OFFENSIVE AND BATTLE OF BULLECOURT, 9 APRIL–17 MAY 1917

I

FIRST
ARMY
(Horne)

Lens

56

80

4 Gd

■ Givenchy

CDN

✕

Vimy

17R
Arleux

18R

XVII

VI Arras

15R

1 Gd R

SIXTH ARMY
(Falkenhausen;
from 23 April Bülow)

185

Oppy

Gavrelle

River Scarpe

26

Monchy-
le-Preux

3 Bav.

THIRD
ARMY
(Allenby)

VII

35

Neuville-Vitasse

220R

27

Bullecourt

V

Quéant

I ANZAC

FIFTH ARMY
(Gough)

Bapaume

■ Courcelles

■ Flers

Douai

208

221

River Cojeul

3 Gd

To Cambrai
7 miles

River Sensée

River Hirondelle

2 Gd R

To Cambrai
7 miles

38

Hermies

KEY

front lines, 9 April

British front line, 14 April, at
end of Battles of 1st Scarpe
and Vimy Ridge

German defensive lines,
14 April

17 approx. locations of German
divisions, 14 April

✕ major battles

✕ ✕ ✕ ✕ ✕ British front line, 24 April,
after 2nd Battle of the Scarpe

British front line, 17 May,
after Battle of Bullecourt and
3rd Battle of the Scarpe

Drocourt-Quéant Line

0   1   2   3   4   5
miles

British infantry climb out of the trench to advance during the Battle of Arras.

'His nerves were in rags'

Philip Gibbs (later knighted) was one of the official British reporters during the war. Below is his description of meeting a young artillery officer he had known before the war as a journalist in Fleet Street. The meeting occurred early in the Arras offensive.

even Divisional Generals were embittered by these needless losses [a costly brigade attack near Neuville-Vitasse].

Their language was mild compared with that of some of our young officers. I remember one I met near Henin. He was one of a group of three, all gunner officers, who were looking about for better gun positions not so clearly visible to the enemy . . . Some of their guns had been destroyed; many of their horses killed; some of their men. A few minutes before our meeting a shell had crashed into a bath close to their hut where men were washing themselves. The explosion filled the bath with blood and bits of flesh.

The younger officer stared at me under the tilt forward of his steel helmet and said: 'Hello Gibbs.' I had played chess with him at Groom's Café in Fleet Street before the war. I went back to his hut and had tea with him . . . I had heard some hard words before about our generalship and Staff work, but never anything so passionate, so violent, as from that gunner officer . . . He raged against the impossible orders sent down from Headquarters, against the brutality with which men were left in the line week after week [this was rare – see page 458], and against the monstrous, abominable futility of all our so-called strategy.

His nerves were in rags, as I could see by the way in which his hand shook when he lighted one cigarette after another. His spirit was in a flame of revolt against the misery of his sleeplessness, filth, and imminent peril of death. Every shell that burst near Henin sent a shudder through him. I stayed an hour with him in his hut . . .

Notes for Map 20

Belligerents	British	German
	First Army: I, XIII and Canadian Corps	Sixth Army I Bavarian Reserve Corps
	Third Army: Cavalry, VI, VII and XVII Corps	IX Reserve Corps
	Fifth Army (Bullecourt area): I ANZAC, IV and V Corps	
Guns	2,817 artillery pieces	1,014 artillery pieces
Commanders	First Army: Lt Gen. Sir Henry Horne	Gen. Ludwig Freiherr von Falkenhausen; from 23 April Gen. Otto von Bülow
	Third Army: Gen. Sir Edmund Allenby	
	Fifth Army: Gen. Sir Hubert Gough	
Casualties	just under 150,000	130,000 (estimate)

Result A British advance of up to 5 miles had been made in places but no breakthrough achieved.

Summary

The British offensive at Arras was conceived in conjunction with the French High Command, which was simultaneously embarking on a similar massive attack in the south against the Chemin des Dames and to a lesser extent in Champagne. These offensives formed the new French commander-in-chief Nivelle's grand strategic plan for the year, aimed at a decisive breakthrough of the Hindenburg Line to which the Germans had retreated during February and March. The BEF's Arras offensive is officially divided into six major battles:

Battle of Vimy Ridge 9–12 April. The Canadian Corps launched a carefully planned assault on the key feature of Vimy Ridge (see Section Two, pages 102–4). Moving behind a creeping barrage, the Canadians succeeded in advancing some 4,000 yards and securing the crest of the ridge within a few hours. It was a brilliant triumph.

First Battle of the Scarpe 9–14 April. The major British attack of the first day of the offensive east of Arras. When the assault went in it was snowing heavily and the wind blew the sleet into the faces of the Germans in the first line, who were largely overwhelmed. By the 14th the attackers had advanced about 3 miles on a 15-mile front.

Second Battle of the Scarpe 23–24 April. Another attempt by the British to advance eastwards astride the River Scarpe. Stiff German resistance meant the attack was called off on the 24th.

Battle of Arleux 28–29 April. A British and Canadian attack on the enemy positions between Arleux and Oppy to secure the Canadian position on Vimy Ridge. The Canadians captured the village of Arleux and, with British assistance, held it against German counter-attacks. A resumption of the offensive the next day failed to achieve any further gains, and with mounting losses the attack was halted.

Third Battle of the Scarpe 3–4 May. Yet another British advance east along the river to try to break through the *Wotanstelllung*, a major defensive part of the Hindenburg Line. The attack was to coincide with a second assault at Bullecourt. However, heavy losses forced the operation to be abandoned on the second day.

Battles of Bullecourt 10–11 April and 3–17 May. The first battle involved an assault by the 4th Australian (see Section Two, pages 110–12) and 62nd (West Riding) Divisions on either side of the village of Bullecourt. The participating tanks were delayed by bad weather and on the 11th many broke down, leaving only a few to take part. The Germans had been alerted to the impending attack and the slight gains made at the start had to be given up. The Australians suffered severely. The second battle again involved the Australians and British in a bloody struggle for the village that lasted for two weeks, but little progress was made apart from the capture of the ruins of Bullecourt. These two battles cost the British over 14,000 casualties, more than half in 1 ANZAC Corps.

Notes for Map 21

Belligerents	French	German
	Reserve Army Group: Fifth Sixth and Tenth Armies	Seventh Army
Divisions	47 (7 cavalry)	26
Guns	over 5,000	1,000 (estimate)
Tanks	128 tanks	

Commanders

Overall: Gen. Robert Nivelle   Gen. Max von Boehn
Fifth Army: Gen. François Mazel
Sixth Army: Gen. Charles Mangin
Tenth Army: Gen. Denis Duchêne

Casualties (inc. Third Battle of Champagne – Moronvilliers)
183,000   163,000

Result A French gain of a maximum of 3 miles that included the Chemin des Dames itself. No breakthrough was achieved and the appalling losses for so little led to the sacking of Nivelle and the collapse of French morale, which manifested itself in the army mutinies in May and June (see Section Two, page 128).

Summary

• Nivelle's grand plan for early 1917 envisaged a massive French attack on the Aisne (Chemin des Dames); another, smaller, to the east of Reims in Champagne; and a British offensive to tie down German divisions and free up French formations for his main effort. Haig was not enthusiastic, preferring the British assault to be in Flanders, close to his vital supply routes to the coast. The British eventually, and reluctantly, accepted attacking in their southern sector at Arras.

• On the Aisne, Nivelle believed a combination of overwhelming artillery bombardments supporting carefully planned infantry assaults would carry the day, as it had at the recapture of Fort Douaumont at Verdun. As this map shows, the French had a formidable task attacking uphill to take the Chemin des Dames plateau. The attack was launched on a 30-mile front a week after the BEF began their Arras offensive. The Germans were well prepared – the attack was no surprise, as a copy of the French plan giving details of objectives and timings had been captured; and the weather was foul – the assault began in driving sleet and rain. German guns and scores of machine guns wreaked havoc among the gallant attackers. The French bombardment did comparatively little damage to the deep bunkers and caverns in which the Germans sheltered. The French loss of around 40,000 on the first day was only slightly less of a bloodbath than that suffered by the British on the Somme on 1 July the previous year. Nivelle refused to accept failure and the attacks continued until the third week of May with depressingly similar results.

• The futility of the attacks for minimal gain and no promised breakthrough led, at the end of April and later in May and June, to the French Army mutinies and the dismissal of Nivelle.

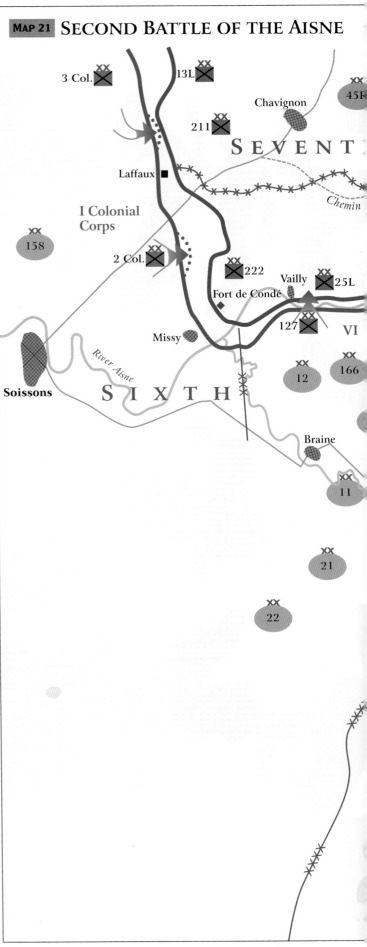

MAP 21 SECOND BATTLE OF THE AISNE

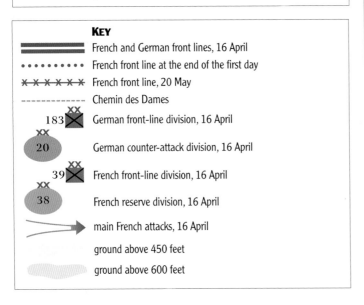

KEY

▬▬▬	French and German front lines, 16 April
••••••••	French front line at the end of the first day
✕✕✕✕✕	French front line, 20 May
------------	Chemin des Dames
183 ✕	German front-line division, 16 April
20	German counter-attack division, 16 April
39 ✕	French front-line division, 16 April
38	French reserve division, 16 April
→	main French attacks, 16 April
	ground above 450 feet
	ground above 600 feet

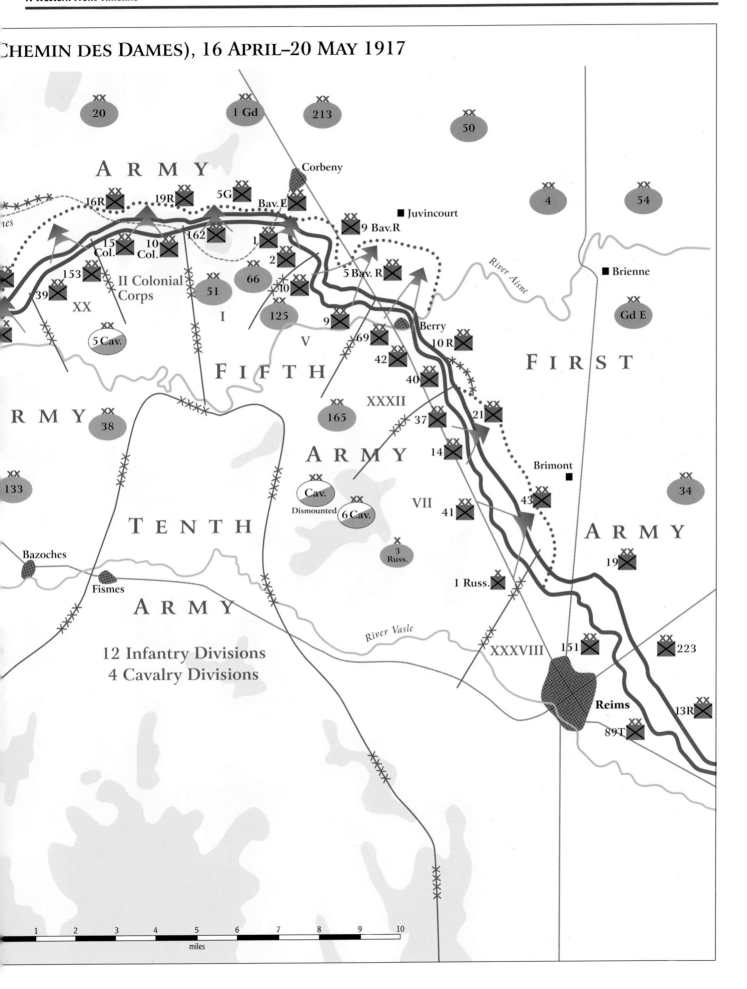

(CHEMIN DES DAMES), 16 APRIL–20 MAY 1917

20

1 Gd

213

50

A R M Y

Corbeny

16R 19R 5G

Bav. E

■ Juvincourt

9 Bav. R

4

54

15
Col.

10
Col.

162

1

2

5 Bav. R

River Aisne

■ Brienne

153

II Colonial
Corps

51

66

10

125

39

XX

I

9

V

69

Berry

10 R

Gd E

5 Cav.

42

40

FIFTH

F I R S T

A R M Y

38

165

XXXII

37

21

14

Brimont ■

34

133

Cav.

Dismounted

6 Cav.

A R M Y

VII

41

43

T E N T H

3
Russ.

19

Bazoches

Fismes

A R M Y

1 Russ.

River Vasle

12 Infantry Divisions
4 Cavalry Divisions

XXXVIII

151

223

Reims

13R

89T

miles

1 2 3 4 5 6 7 8 9 10

MAP 22 THIRD BATTLE OF YPRES (PASSCHENDAELE), 31 JULY–10 NOV. 1917

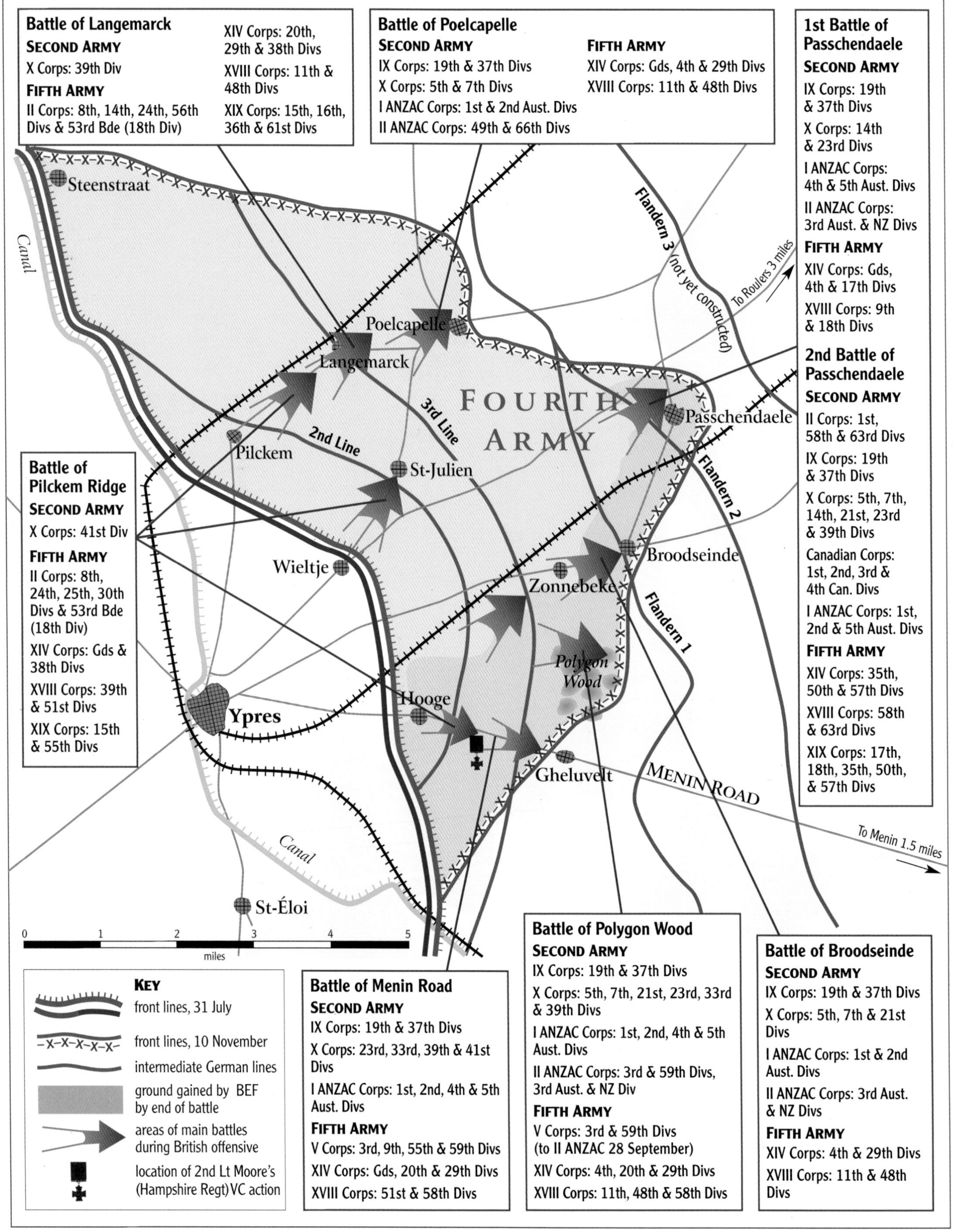

Battle of Langemarck

SECOND ARMY

X Corps: 39th Div

FIFTH ARMY

II Corps: 8th, 14th, 24th, 56th Divs & 53rd Bde (18th Div)

XIV Corps: 20th, 29th & 38th Divs

XVIII Corps: 11th & 48th Divs

XIX Corps: 15th, 16th, 36th & 61st Divs

Battle of Poelcapelle

SECOND ARMY

IX Corps: 19th & 37th Divs

X Corps: 5th & 7th Divs

I ANZAC Corps: 1st & 2nd Aust. Divs

II ANZAC Corps: 49th & 66th Divs

FIFTH ARMY

XIV Corps: Gds, 4th & 29th Divs

XVIII Corps: 11th & 48th Divs

1st Battle of Passchendaele

SECOND ARMY

IX Corps: 19th & 37th Divs

X Corps: 14th & 23rd Divs

I ANZAC Corps: 4th & 5th Aust. Divs

II ANZAC Corps: 3rd Aust. & NZ Divs

FIFTH ARMY

XIV Corps: Gds, 4th & 17th Divs

XVIII Corps: 9th & 18th Divs

2nd Battle of Passchendaele

SECOND ARMY

II Corps: 1st, 58th & 63rd Divs

IX Corps: 19th & 37th Divs

X Corps: 5th, 7th, 14th, 21st, 23rd & 39th Divs

Canadian Corps: 1st, 2nd, 3rd & 4th Can. Divs

I ANZAC Corps: 1st, 2nd & 5th Aust. Divs

FIFTH ARMY

XIV Corps: 35th, 50th & 57th Divs

XVIII Corps: 58th & 63rd Divs

XIX Corps: 17th, 18th, 35th, 50th, & 57th Divs

Battle of Pilckem Ridge

SECOND ARMY

X Corps: 41st Div

FIFTH ARMY

II Corps: 8th, 24th, 25th, 30th Divs & 53rd Bde (18th Div)

XIV Corps: Gds & 38th Divs

XVIII Corps: 39th & 51st Divs

XIX Corps: 15th & 55th Divs

Battle of Menin Road

SECOND ARMY

IX Corps: 19th & 37th Divs

X Corps: 23rd, 33rd, 39th & 41st Divs

I ANZAC Corps: 1st, 2nd, 4th & 5th Aust. Divs

FIFTH ARMY

V Corps: 3rd, 9th, 55th & 59th Divs

XIV Corps: Gds, 20th & 29th Divs

XVIII Corps: 51st & 58th Divs

Battle of Polygon Wood

SECOND ARMY

IX Corps: 19th & 37th Divs

X Corps: 5th, 7th, 21st, 23rd, 33rd & 39th Divs

I ANZAC Corps: 1st, 2nd, 4th & 5th Aust. Divs

II ANZAC Corps: 3rd & 59th Divs, 3rd Aust. & NZ Div

FIFTH ARMY

V Corps: 3rd & 59th Divs (to II ANZAC 28 September)

XIV Corps: 4th, 20th & 29th Divs

XVIII Corps: 11th, 48th & 58th Divs

Battle of Broodseinde

SECOND ARMY

IX Corps: 19th & 37th Divs

X Corps: 5th, 7th & 21st Divs

I ANZAC Corps: 1st & 2nd Aust. Divs

II ANZAC Corps: 3rd Aust. & NZ Divs

FIFTH ARMY

XIV Corps: 4th & 29th Divs

XVIII Corps: 11th & 48th Divs

KEY

front lines, 31 July

-x-x-x-x- front lines, 10 November

intermediate German lines

ground gained by BEF by end of battle

areas of main battles during British offensive

location of 2nd Lt Moore's (Hampshire Regt) VC action

Map labels

Steenstraat

Canal

Poelcapelle

Langemarck

Pilckem

2nd Line

3rd Line

St-Julien

FOURTH ARMY

Passchendaele

Flandern 3 (not yet constructed)

To Roulers 3 miles

Broodseinde

Zonnebeke

Flandern 2

Wieltje

Polygon Wood

Flandern 1

Hooge

Ypres

Gheluvelt

MENIN ROAD

To Menin 1.5 miles

Canal

St-Éloi

0   1   2   3   4   5
miles

Notes for Map 22

Belligerents	British		German

Belligerents

British
Second and Fifth Armies:
II, V, IX, X, XIV, XVIII, XIX,
Canadian, I and II Anzac Corps

German
Fourth Army:
initially III Bavarian and IX Reserve Corps, but another
73 divisions deployed by end of the battle in November

Divisions

51 British, 6 French
2,868 guns

88
1,556 guns

Commanders

Second Army: Gen. Sir Herbert Plumer
Fifth Army: Gen. Sir Hubert Gough

Gen. Sixt von Armin

Casualties

BEF: 260,000 (estimate)
French (attacking on British left): 112,000 (estimate)

260,000–300,000 (estimate)

Result The Ypres salient was extended by a maximum of 5 miles and the rubble that was once Passchendaele secured, but all at huge cost. The Germans had suffered almost as much but prevented a British break-out.

Summary

Haig's plan was to advance from Ypres, first to secure the Passchendaele Ridge and then to push through to Roulers and beyond. A preliminary operation was the taking of Messines Ridge (see Section Seven, pages 307–10) south of Ypres. The main initial assault would be by the Fifth Army east of Ypres, with flanking operations on the right by the Second Army and on the left by the French First Army. The preliminary bombardment started on 16 July, with the guns firing 4.5 million rounds by the time the leading troops advanced.

• The Germans had constructed deep defences – as the map shows, in places six lines deep (although the Flandern 3 line was not yet constructed). Their tactics had changed from 1916 and they employed an elastic defence with a chequerboard system of machine-gun emplacements backed up by plentiful guns and units trained in, and designated as, counter-attack roles. In addition, they used mustard gas for the first time.

• The British attack started on 31 July on an 8-mile front, but gains were small and the French were halted in the north. Successive attempts to renew the offensive over the following weeks were severely hampered by the worst rains for 30 years, which, combined with the massive shelling by both sides, destroyed drainage ditches and churned the ground into a vast quagmire of mud and ponds, making movement by tanks, guns and infantry a Herculean task.

Eight main official battles made up Third Ypres:

Battle of Pilckem Ridge 31 July–2 August. This was the start of the battle of Third Ypres and included attacks towards Pilckem, St-Julien, Zonnebeke and up on to the Gheluvelt plateau. About 2,000 yards were gained, but at a cost of over 30,000 casualties.

Battle of Langemarck 16–18 August. An attack involving XIV and XVIII Corps, well supported by artillery, with observers directing fire from Pilckem Ridge that succeeded in taking Langemarck.

Battle of the Menin Road Ridge 20–25 September. Plumer (Second Army) was directed to take the Gheluvelt plateau with support from the Fifth Army on his left. The preliminary and creeping barrage that supported this attack was provided by 1,295 guns – one to every 5 yards of frontage. This was a well-planned assault in depth that succeeded in advancing about a mile and defeating the inevitable German counter-attacks with protective artillery barrages.

Battle of Polygon Wood 26 September–3 October. This action saw Plumer's Australians take Polygon Wood and Gough's Fifth Army the village of Zonnebeke.

Battle of Broodseinde 4 October. A successful, though costly (8,000 casualties), attack by I and II ANZAC Corps with British support that took the village of Broodseinde, thus bringing the Second Army within striking distance of Passchendaele itself.

Battle of Poelcapelle 9 October. An advance at Poelcapelle ended in dismal failure, with poor staff work, poor infantry–artillery coordination, mud and enemy counter-attacks. The result was another 9,000 casualties and little ground gained.

First Battle of Passchendaele 12 October. An attack by the II ANZAC Corps developed into a shambles, much of the chaos due to the horrendously muddy condition of the ground and the consequent near impossibility of bringing forward either the supporting guns or ammunition, leaving the infantry to struggle forward without proper support. The losses were appalling, with the 3rd Australian Division suffering almost 3,000 casualties in just a few hours.

Second Battle of Passchendaele 26 October–10 November. This attack saw the Canadian Corps, considered something of an elite force after its success at Vimy Ridge, tasked with finally taking Passchendaele. The corps commander, Gen. Arthur Currie, expressed strong misgivings but was persuaded to comply. By 10 November, with British assistance, the grinding slog to take the village was over and several heavy counter-attacks repelled. It was a Canadian success that had cost them dear – 12,403 killed, wounded and missing. The Third Battle of Ypres was over at last.

On the Receiving End of the British Preparatory Barrage at Third Ypres

Georg Bucher, a German infantry officer, described some of the unspeakable horrors that shelling could inflict while he crouched in a dugout on 31 July under an endless bombardment of HE shells.

'Georg!'

I jumped up at Gaaten's resounding cry. He rushed down into the dugout, blood streaming from his mouth.

'You're hit!' I cried hoarsely.

He burst into wild laughter, spitting blood and fragments of tooth.

'Nothing – a tiny splinter! But outside . . .' He hesitated, and then broke into horrible curses. The signs were so unmistakable that Riedel quickly grasped his arm and held it like a vice. Gaaten broke free from him with a wild cry. 'Keep your hands off me!' he shouted fiercely and gripped his trench dagger. 'Sonderbeck is finished,' he added in a choking voice. 'Left leg off nearly to the stomach – he's asking for you' . . . Gaaten's voice sank to murmured curses. We rushed after him out of the dugout. For us at the moment drum-fire didn't exist.

We found Sonderbeck to the right of the huge crater. Blood was streaming from him. He did not shriek – but his hands were clutching a ghastly fragment of himself, his severed leg which still wore a wide-shafted talisman boot. It lay across him – he held it to him as a mother might hold her child.

A shell landed close by and covered us with dirt, but I scarcely noticed it as I knelt by Sonderbeck. He recognized me in spite of his agony.

'My leg, Georg, my leg, my leg!'

Riedel knelt down beside me. 'Kurt . . . mate,' he said hoarsely. Sonderbeck turned to him his deathly pale distorted face: 'My leg, Riedel . . . O God!'

I couldn't bear to look at the dead limb in his arms – I tried to take it away from him but he held on to it so fiercely and moaned so imploringly that Riedel pulled me away. 'Leave him alone, God damn you!' he shouted.

The Victoria Cross in 1917

There were 141 Victoria Crosses awarded in 1917. Second Lieutenant Montague Shadworth Seymour Moore was a twenty-one-year-old officer in the 15th Hampshires when, on 20 August, he volunteered to lead some seventy men in an attack on a collection of bunkers, dugouts and pillboxes on a small spur near Tower Hamlets. This enemy location, south of the Menin Road and about three quarters of a mile west of Gheluvelt, had already repulsed a previous attack by the Hampshires.

By the time Moore neared the objective only a sergeant and four men remained with him. He rushed forward to the nearest bunker under intense fire and lobbed a bomb inside, capturing twenty-eight prisoners, a machine gun and a field gun. Eventually several officers and about sixty men joined him, enabling Moore to organize the defence of the position for thirty-six hours, during which several German counter-attacks were beaten off. Finally, when down to about ten men, Moore was compelled to withdraw. His actions were an outstanding example of personal courage and leadership by a very junior and inexperienced officer.

Moore survived the war and was discharged with the rank of major. Later he became a game ranger and warden in East Africa (Tanganyika) from 1926 to 1951. When he died in 1966, aged seventy, his ashes were scattered in a game park.

Moore was educated at Bedford School – as was the present writer.

Continued from page 59

The demands made by the construction on labour and materials were immense. About 65,000 men were employed daily – Russian prisoners, Belgian civilians and German reserve troops – but the German firms that made the concrete emplacements and dugouts usually sent out their own skilled workmen to install them. Materials were brought forward by barge and train (some 1,250 trainloads of engineer stores were needed).

The code name for the withdrawal was Operation Alberich; it began in late February and continued until the beginning of April. During this time there was the systematic creation of a desert over the ground the Germans abandoned. This laying waste is best described by the *History of the Great War Based on Official Documents* (known as the *British Official History* of the war) – *Military Operations: France and Belgium 1917*, Vol. I:

Not only were all military buildings to be dismantled and depots to be withdrawn, but railways to be torn up, craters to be blown in the roads; but, so far as possible, every town and village, every building in them, was to be destroyed by fire or explosive; every tree, even the fruit trees, were to be cut down, or 'ringed' to ensure it died; civilians were to be removed; and the wells were to be filled up or polluted, but not poisoned . . . On the British Fourth Army front instructions were captured [that instructed] the 6th Cuirassier regiment . . . [to] ensure that plenty of horse-dung should be left near the wells – in order, of course, that pollution might be carried out at the last possible moment.

Crown Prince Rupprecht [of Bavaria] objected strongly to the methods and extent of this devastation. Not only was it utterly repellent to his nature . . . It would, he thought, give Germany a bad name throughout the world . . . He feared the effect upon the discipline of the troops, and not without cause; for childish barbarities, such as the breakage of crockery and mirrors and the searing with hot irons of upholstered chairs, in houses not destroyed, and the wholesale looting in the few towns left intact, were almost certainly the results of indiscipline and not of orders. So deep was his repugnance that he was anxious to resign his command and was only prevented from doing so by the representation that this would appear to the world to mark a breach between Bavaria and the *Reich*.

Eventually it was decided to refrain from destroying the houses of Nestle, Ham, Noyon and one or two smaller places, and to collect in them a number of civilians, who would be allowed to await the advance of the allies . . . The ten to fifteen thousand persons left behind were almost all children, their mothers and the aged. Ten times as many were moved back behind the Hindenburg Line . . . these included practically all who were capable of work in field or factory.

A stretch of the Hindenburg Line defences.

1918

Declarations of War 1918

23 April   Guatemala on Germany
23 May   Costa Rica on Germany
12 July   Haiti on Germany
19 July   Honduras on Germany

This was the year the war finally ended. Armistice Day – eleven o'clock on 11 November 1918 – the eleventh hour of the eleventh day of the eleventh month. At the start of the year there were few politicians or soldiers on either side prepared to make a prophecy of the outcome. The year was to be one of high drama, with first the Germans coming within a whisker of victory, followed by an unstoppable Allied offensive that ended the war – an offensive that saw the greatest succession of victories by the British Army in her history.

For Germany the situation during the early months of the year was promising in only one major respect – the Russians stopped fighting. The Bolsheviks seized power in Moscow in November 1917 and their leaders (Lenin, Trotsky and Stalin) wanted time to cement Communist control over 180 million Russians. They therefore sued for peace and an armistice was agreed on 16 December 1917, although the final peace treaty at Brest-Litovsk was not signed until 3 March 1918. The cessation of fighting in the east transformed the strategic balance of the war, as it gave Germany the opportunity to switch many divisions and thousands of guns and munitions to the west. This transfer took place during the two and a half months between the armistice and the treaty. However, the heavily reinforced German armies on the Western Front had to be used quickly before the arrival of American formations swung the numerical advantage irreversibly in the Allies' favour (the Americans had around 300,000 troops in France by March 1918 and 1.25 million by August). Germany needed a decisive victory in the west, and needed it fast – hence the massive offensive, the *Kaiserschlacht* (the Kaiser's Battle), that began on 21 March.

There were other events that made the Germans' March offensive something of an all-or-nothing throw of the dice. By 1918 there was an all-pervasive war-weariness at home, much of it caused by the crippling effect of the British naval blockade, now in its fourth year. Hunger was an ever-present enemy of the German civil population – as early as 1916 there had been food riots in thirty-one cities and towns, including Berlin. It is estimated that over 760,000 deaths in

Germany can be attributed to the naval blockade of her ports. Add to this acute food shortage the bitter winter weather, the Spanish flu then sweeping Europe and the fearful losses on all fighting fronts, and the dire situation at home is clear. The general atmosphere of gloom and doom had sapped civilian morale to the extent that leaflets were distributed in Berlin saying, 'Down with the Kaiser and the government'.

There was also disaffection in Austria–Hungary, with constant clashes between the different nationalities of that empire. Turkish troops were deserting in droves in Palestine and a peace movement was spreading in Bulgaria. All political, economic and military factors underlined the urgency of a major, decisive, offensive victory on the battlefields in the west – nothing less could save Germany from eventual defeat.

For the UK and France, 1918 started with the grim realization, certainly by the British, that they must hang on until sufficient Americans arrived to warrant further major offensives. Haig, knowing a German offensive was inevitable, planned to adopt the German defence-in-depth system that had been his undoing at Passchendaele, using forward, battle and rear zones. The problem was that, while his enemy was receiving a continuous stream of reinforcements during the winter 1917/18, quite the reverse was happening with the BEF. By January 1918 well over 600,000 troops were waiting in England for a role, prevented from crossing the Channel by the prime minister, David Lloyd George. He was appalled by the seemingly pointless and horrific casualties (some 760,000) during 1917 and was at loggerheads with Haig – he wanted to replace Haig, but was unable to do so as there was no suitable successor. As far as the prime minister was concerned, Haig had sufficient troops to hold the line

Timeline 1918

Date	General	Western Front
3 March	Peace treaty between Germany and Russia signed at Brest-Litovsk	
21 March–5 April		German *Kaiserschlacht* or Operation Michael offensive begins
26 March		Marshal Foch appointed Supreme Allied Commander
9–29 April		Germans launch Operation Georgette in Flanders
27 May–6 June		Germans launch Operation Blücher-Yorck (Third Battle of the Aisne)
9–19 June		Germans begin final phase of spring offensive – Operation Gneisenau
15–17 July		Operation Marne–Reims ends German offensives on the Western Front
20 July–2 Aug.		French counter-attack in Champagne (Second Battle of the Marne)
8–11 Aug.		Battle of Amiens starts the Allies' Hundred Day offensive that will end the war
12 Sept.–12 Oct.		Allies break through Hindenburg Line
26 Sept.–11 Nov.		US Meuse–Argonne offensive
3 Oct.	British enter Damascus	
20 Oct.	Germany suspends submarine warfare	
29 Oct.	German High Seas Fleet mutinies	
30 Oct.	Turkey signs Armistice of Mudros	
4 Nov.	Austria–Hungary signs armistice with Italy	
9 Nov.	Kaiser Wilhelm II abdicates	
11 Nov.	Between 5:12 and 5:20 a.m. the Armistice is signed, hostilities to cease at 11:00 a.m.	

German infantry attacking in the spring offensive, 1918.

eventual American successes in their Meuse–Argonne offensive to the south.

For Germany there was bad news from every direction. Bulgaria capitulated after the French broke through on the Salonika front; General Sir Edmund Allenby entered Damascus on 3 October and the Turks began to sue for peace; Austria–Hungary was induced to seek terms after the Italians, with British and French support, launched an offensive on the River Piave in late October. Meanwhile, the Allied advance, although slowed by exhaustion, had continued to push the Germans back all along the Western Front. By November bread riots, revolution and a mutiny in the German High Seas Fleet convinced the German High Command that the war must be ended – and on 11 November the German delegation signed the Armistice.

Despite the Allies' war-winning successes, 1918 saw the BEF suffer 805,844 casualties – the heaviest loss for any year of the conflict. The Germans lost only marginally more – 825,130.

A British Nurse's Experiences

Nurse Catherine Black, MVO, MBE, RRC, was on duty during the retreat to Amiens and later told of her experiences during that time:

> General Gough's Fifth Army was unable in the face of overwhelming odds to hold the line any longer, was falling back fighting inch by inch of the ground.
>
> And hard on the heels of its disciplined orderly retreat straggled a medley of panic-stricken villagers, ambulances, carts and lorries of every description . . .
>
> At Villers Bretonneux we passed whole battalions who had come straight out of the trenches, slouching along almost asleep on their feet, but still cheery, whistling and smoking.
>
> Many of them were good-naturedly helping the fleeing villagers, pushing prams for harassed mothers, loading bundles of homely household possessions, pots and pans and tables on to handcarts.
>
> Two stalwart artillerymen were carrying between them a crippled woman who looked half-dead with fright, but was still keeping a firm grip on the rope attached to a cow that ambled after them.

Sister Black became well known after the war for her devoted nursing of King George V from the time of his illness in 1928 until his death in 1936.

until the Americans flooded in – only enough men (about 100,000) were earmarked for France to replace the normal wastage of sickness and casualties.

Nevertheless, Britain was experiencing something of a new industrial revolution – mass production, with 200 factories producing munitions, explosives, aero-engines and aircraft among a host of other vital war supplies. A million women were playing a key role in the war effort. The Allies had virtually total control of the air, with over 22,000 aircraft available. By early 1918 the British Army was the best equipped on the Western Front.

Operation *Kaiserschlacht* began on 21 March and lasted until 17 July (see Map 24). The opening bombardment from 6,500 guns, howitzers and mortars delivered 1.2 million shells in five hours. The main thrusts were on the Somme and were codenamed Michael I, II and III. They hit the ill-prepared British Fifth Army, employing flexible stormtrooper tactics (see Section Twelve, pages 482–5) and outnumbering the British by three to one. By 4 April Albert had been taken and the Germans were on the River Avre, having smashed through the British line and advanced some 35 miles. Only then did they run out of momentum and the British and French finally held their attackers. Major General Erich Ludendorff switched his effort northwards to Flanders with Operation Georgette, aimed at breaking the line with the usual objective of taking the Channel ports. This time the German advance was limited to a maximum of 12 miles, but no fewer than seven battles were fought before the line was again stabilized.

Once more the Germans transferred their offensive to a new area. This time it was against the French, codenamed Blücher-Yorck and launched on 27 May; it was followed by

the Marne– Reims attacks in mid-June. By July the Germans were once more on the Marne and within 45 miles of Paris – although their furthest actual penetration of the Allied front was near Montdidier. However, by this time the American presence had made itself felt with two divisional attacks at Cantigny on 28 May and Belleau Wood on 2 June. The German offensive was a great tactical success but it failed to achieve any strategic aims, outran its logistical support and cost a staggering 690,000 casualties.

From August to November it was the Allies' turn. The Germans, exhausted, disappointed at failing to achieve a decisive victory and with morale sinking in many units, faced a massive Allied onslaught – which included the American Expeditionary Force (AEF) – along the entire front, with offensives launched from St-Mihiel southeast of Verdun to the Channel coast.

On 20 July the French counter-attacked on the Marne; on 8 August the British, supported by the French to their south, launched the Battle of Amiens – a date that was to go down as the 'Black Day of the German Army'; on 21 August the British attacked north of Arras on the River Scarpe; and finally in mid-September the Americans attacked at St-Mihiel. The Allies were now employing coordinated, all-arms tactics with infantry, artillery, tanks, cavalry and aircraft cooperating in every offensive. There was a vastly improved system of training, meticulous planning, improved weapons, overhead machine-gun barrages, with artillery firing off the map and aircraft spotting for the guns from overhead (see Sections Twelve and Thirteen). Despite these immense improvements, there followed stiff battles with heavy losses to break into and through the Hindenburg Line, but by the end of September this was achieved, along with

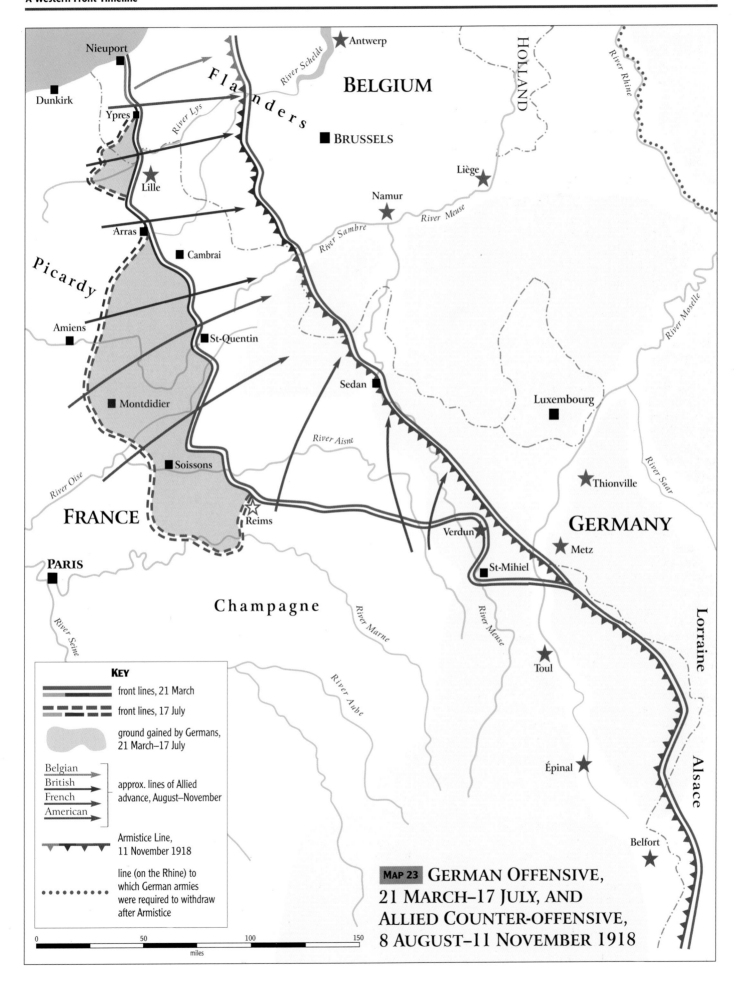

KEY

front lines, 21 March

front lines, 17 July

ground gained by Germans, 21 March–17 July

Belgian
British
French
American

approx. lines of Allied advance, August–November

Armistice Line, 11 November 1918

line (on the Rhine) to which German armies were required to withdraw after Armistice

0   50   100   150
miles

MAP 23 GERMAN OFFENSIVE, 21 MARCH–17 JULY, AND ALLIED COUNTER-OFFENSIVE, 8 AUGUST–11 NOVEMBER 1918

MAP 24 *KAISERSCHLACHT* OFFENSIVE, 21 MARCH–17 JULY 1918

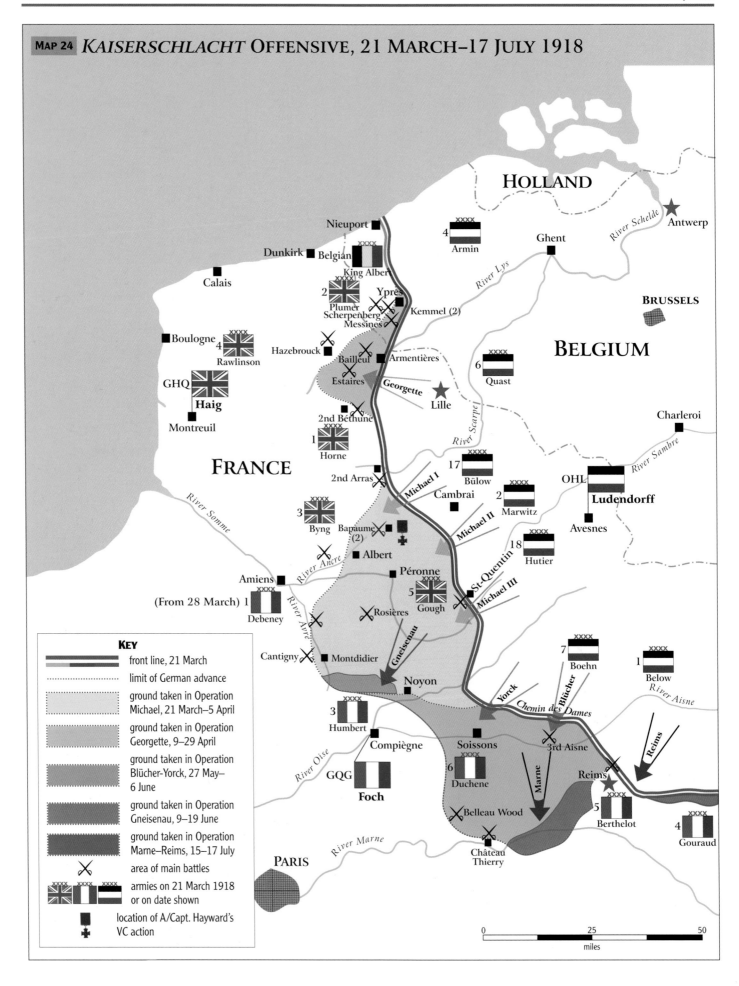

KEY

— front line, 21 March

⋯⋯ limit of German advance

ground taken in Operation Michael, 21 March–5 April

ground taken in Operation Georgette, 9–29 April

ground taken in Operation Blücher-Yorck, 27 May–6 June

ground taken in Operation Gneisenau, 9–19 June

ground taken in Operation Marne–Reims, 15–17 July

✗ area of main battles

armies on 21 March 1918 or on date shown

location of A/Capt. Hayward's VC action

Notes for Map 24

The German spring offensive of 1918, named the *Kaiserschlacht* (Kaiser's Battle), was a series of heavy attacks which marked the deepest advances of either side since 1914. There were four major German attacks codenamed Michael (I, II and III), Georgette, Gneisenau and Blücher-Yorck. By this time each side had refined both offensive and defensive tactics (see Section Twelve), with the German attackers using stormtrooper units to bypass strongpoints and infiltrate through the enemy lines to attack headquarters, artillery units and supply depots, with points of strong resistance being taken by follow-up troops. Defensive positions were no longer simple trench lines but elaborate defensive zones.

Michael I (Seventeenth Army), Michael II (Second Army), Michael III (Eighteenth Army)

BATTLES OF THE SOMME 21 March–5 April:

Battle of St-Quentin 21–23 March. A colossal German onslaught, helped by an early-morning fog, against the ill-prepared British Fifth Army under Gough. The Germans broke through at several points and after two days the British were in full retreat.

First Battle of Bapaume 24–25 March. Ludendorff was convinced he had dealt a mortal blow, so modified his plans and sought to separate the British and French Armies with his subsequent attacks. The British were forced further back and Bapaume was evacuated.

Battle of Rosières 26–27 March. The Germans exploited a large, 9-mile gap that straddled the Somme and a series of confused, vicious actions involving six British divisions being attacked in front flank and rear by eleven German divisions. The Rosières–Bray line was held temporarily as British units continued to retire. Gough was dismissed and replaced by Rawlinson.

Second Battle of Arras 28 March. In the days following 21 March, considerable numbers of German heavy-gun batteries were moved north to the Arras front to blast through the British Third Army defences astride the Scarpe. However, the defenders were generally well prepared and expecting attack. Huge numbers of Germans were cut down by artillery and machine-gun fire and, despite being forced back some distance, the line was held.

Battle of the Avre 4 April. The Germans switched their main effort back south, with Amiens as their objective. Their Second Army was shifted south and some 17 divisions on a 15-mile front south of the Somme threatened units of the French First Army and British formations covering Amiens. Three German assaults were held, but a fourth pressed the British 18th Division back, a breakthrough being prevented by a determined counter-attack by the 36th Australian Battalion. The line was held.

Battle of the Ancre 5 April. The German attacks had become more spasmodic and less determined as losses mounted. This battle was a final attempt by them to reach Amiens, this time from the north-east. The main assault fell on the 4th Australian Division. There was bitter fighting as the Germans initially forced a breakthrough, which was checked only by a dramatic Australian counter-attack. The Germans had made small gains but sustained huge losses. Ludendorff ordered a halt to further attacks – his Michael offensive was over.

Georgette (Sixth Army)

BATTLE OF THE LYS 9–29 April:

Battle of Estaires 9–11 April. The German attack by the Sixth Army sought to take advantage of the fact that both Allied Armies had sent divisions south to support the Third and Fifth Armies. The assault by nine divisions, with five in reserve, fell on the First Army, with only four divisions in line and two in reserve. The recently arrived Portuguese Division collapsed and by nightfall the British had been forced back 3 miles to the River Lys.

Battle of Messines 10–11 April. The German offensive was widened and involved a powerful attack on Plumer's Second Army with the aim of taking the Messines–Wyschaete Ridge captured by the Second Army the previous year. After a fierce defence the attackers were driven back. On the 11th, Haig issued his famous order of the day: 'With our backs to the wall and believing in the justice of our cause, each one of us must fight on to the end.'

Battle of Hazebrouck 12–15 April. A German attack towards the critical logistics centre of Hazebrouck, which if lost would have opened the way to the Channel ports. This attack was slowed by determined British resistance and finally stopped by the 1st Australian Division only 5 miles from the town.

Battle of Bailleul 13–15 April. The Germans took the town of Bailleul after a stiff fight and Plumer was given the authority to withdraw another 3 miles. There was a determined defensive action at Neuve Église, but Bailleul was not retaken until 30 August.

Battles of Kemmel Ridge 17–19 April and 25–26 April. French units reinforced the British defenders and were positioned to defend the key position of Kemmel Ridge. While holding off the initial German attacks, the French were compelled to surrender the ridge on 25 April after an attack preceded by a very heavy gas bombardment for which the French were ill-prepared. A British counter-attack by the 25th Division the next day reached Kemmel village, but it was forced to withdraw when French support failed to materialize.

Second Battle of Béthune 18 April. This engagement involved four divisions from I Corps and one from XI Corps, as well as the 1st Division's defence of Givenchy. The German heavy attacks at Givenchy made slight progress but those south of Kemmel were repulsed.

Battle of the Scherpenberg 29 April. Violent German attacks halted. This repulse by the French brought an end to the Battle of the Lys. On 29 April the Georgette offensive ground to a halt

Blücher-Yorck and Gneisenau

With the offensives on the Somme and the Lys halted, the Germans turned their attention to another river, the Aisne, where their opponents would primarily be the French. With the Gneisenau operation Ludendorff sought to extend the offensive westwards.

Third Battle of the Aisne 27 May–6 June. The German First and Seventh Armies attacked the French Sixth, which had British (four divisions of IX Corps) and Americans under command. Success on the Aisne would put the Germans within striking distance of Paris. Following a 4,000-gun bombardment, 17 German divisions attacked. IX Corps was routed and the Germans reached the river in six hours on a line between Reims and Soissons, pushing the Allies back to the River Vesle with the loss of the Chemin des Dames ridge. The heavy Allied losses were mostly attributable to the French Gen. Duchene insisting on massing most of his troops in the front trenches – a decision that cost him his job. By 30 May the Germans had taken 50,000 prisoners and 800 guns and were within 35 miles of Paris.

Battle of Cantigny 28 May. This was a minor action, but significant in that it saw the first sustained American offensive of the war. Their 1st Division, with French air, artillery and tank support, captured the village and held it against repeated counter-attacks.

Battle of Château-Thierry 3–4 June. A successful defensive battle fought by a French colonial division, assisted by the 7th American Machine Gun Battalion (48 guns). They beat off several German attempts to cross to the south bank of the Marne.

Battle of Belleau Wood 1–19 June. This battle was fought by the 2nd and 3rd American Divisions (the former containing the 4th US Marine Brigade) against an advance by elements of five German divisions. A bitter and costly struggle developed for Belleau Wood. The Marines attacked into the wood six times, resorting to hand-to-hand combat before the Germans finally withdrew. Two famous remarks originated at this battle. Captain Lloyd Williams, 2/5 Marines, when advised to retreat by the French, retorted, 'Retreat? Hell, we only just got here!' The second was by Gunnery Sergeant Dan Daly, who got his men on their feet to start an attack by shouting, 'Come on, you sons of bitches, do you want to live for ever?' Many lived only a matter of hours, as this action cost the Marines over 9,000 casualties, making it one of the bloodiest and most ferocious battles the Americans would fight in the war.

The Second Battle of the Marne started on 17 July with attacks east and west of Reims (the last German offensive of the war). Some small territorial gains were made, but they precipitated strong and successful counter-attacks on the 20th which are shown on Map 25.

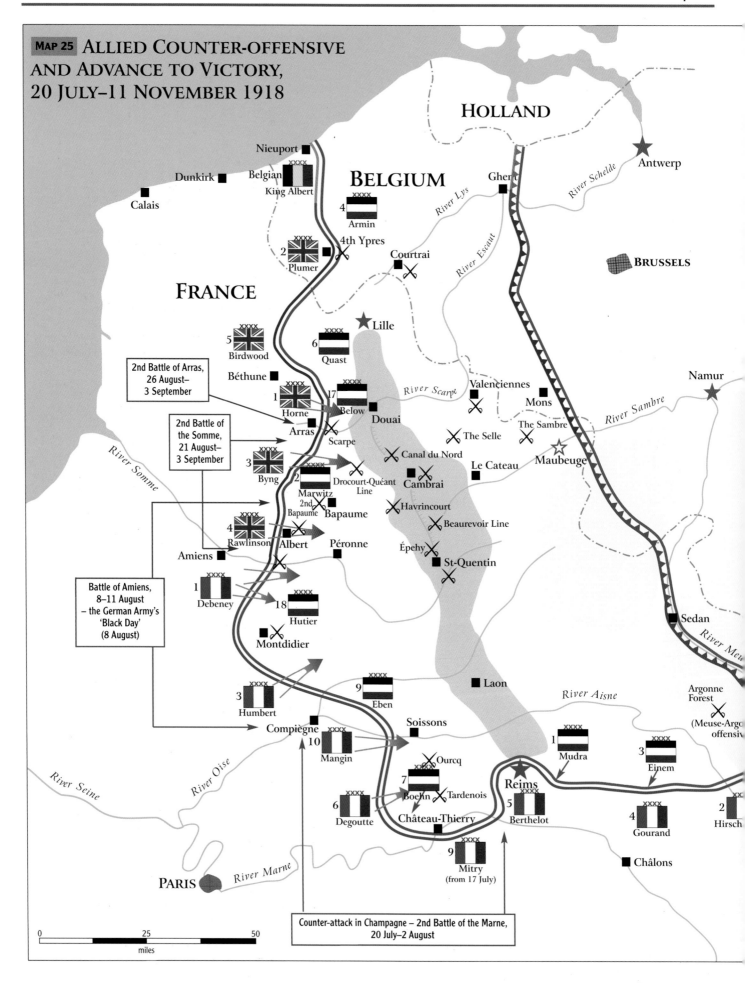

MAP 25 ALLIED COUNTER-OFFENSIVE
AND ADVANCE TO VICTORY,
20 JULY–11 NOVEMBER 1918

HOLLAND

Antwerp

Nieuport

Dunkirk

Belgian
King Albert

BELGIUM

Ghent

River Schelde

Calais

4
Armin

BRUSSELS

River Lys

4th Ypres

River Escaut

FRANCE

2
Plumer

Courtrai

Lille

5
Birdwood

6
Quast

River Scarpe

Valenciennes

Namur

Béthune

River Sambre

2nd Battle of Arras,
26 August–
3 September

1
Horne

17
Below

Mons

Douai

The Sambre

Arras

The Selle

Maubeuge

2nd Battle of
the Somme,
21 August–
3 September

Scarpe

Canal du Nord

3
Byng

Le Cateau

River Somme

2
Marwitz

Drocourt-Quéant
Line

Cambri

Havrincourt

2nd
Bapaume

Beaurevoir Line

4
Rawlinson

Bapaume

Amiens

Albert

Péronne

Épehy

St-Quentin

Sedan

Battle of Amiens,
8–11 August
– the German Army's
'Black Day'
(8 August)

1
Debeney

18
Hutier

River Meu

Montdidier

Laon

River Aisne

Argonne
Forest

3
Humbert

9
Eben

(Meuse-Argo
offensiv

Compiègne

Soissons

1
Mudra

3
Einem

River Oise

10
Mangin

Ourcq

Reims

River Seine

7
Boehn

Tardenois

5
Berthelot

2
Hirsch

6
Degoutte

Château-Thierry

4
Gourand

9
Mitry
(from 17 July)

Châlons

PARIS

River Marne

Counter-attack in Champagne – 2nd Battle of the Marne,
20 July–2 August

0   25   50
miles

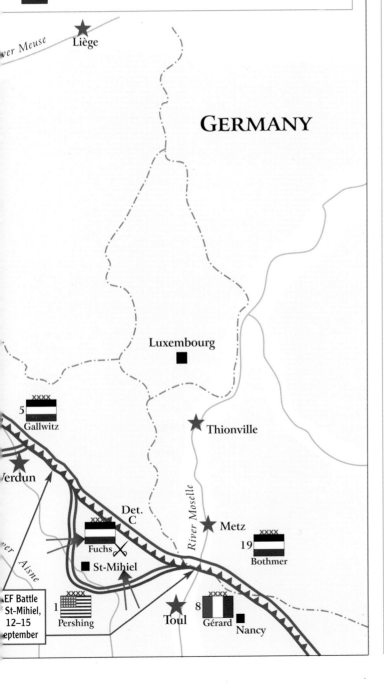

KEY

front lines, 17 July 1918

front lines, 11 November 1918

main German defensive zone, including the Hindenburg Line

approx. location of main battles

main Allied attacks at the start of their advance to victory, 20 July–3 September, including American offensive at St-Mihiel

German attacks at start of 2nd Battle of the Marne

area of armies at end of July and early August with commanders at that time

GERMANY

Liège

river Meuse

Luxembourg

5 Gallwitz

Thionville

Verdun

Det. C

Fuchs

River Moselle

Metz

19 Bothmer

St-Mihiel

Aisne

EF Battle St-Mihiel, 12–15 eptember

1 Pershing

Toul

8 Gérard

Nancy

Notes for Map 25

This map covers the period from the first French counter-attacks in July in Champagne through to the end of the war on 11 November. The Allies' Hundred Day advance to victory included the Second Battle of the Marne; the Battle of Amiens – the 'Black Day of the German Army' (8 August); the assault and breaching of the Hindenburg Line; and the final advance to the Armistice Line. Significant offensives/battles included:

Second Battle of the Marne 20 July–2 August. The German failure to break through east and west of Reims prompted Foch, then the Allied Supreme Commander, to authorize a major counter-offensive on 18 July. The French Tenth Army under Mangin led the attack, with 18 divisions (including two American and two British), 345 light tanks, 2,000 guns and 500 aircraft; leading the advance were units of the French Foreign Legion. Degoutte's Sixth Army with nine divisions, 145 tanks, 1,000 guns and 350 aircraft attacked to the south of Mangin. The weight of the attack forced the Germans to retire slowly, inflicting devastating losses on the French with battles at Tardenois (20–31 August) and Soissonnais and the Ourcq (23 July–2 August) being particularly fierce. Lack of support from the French Ninth and Fifth Armies east of the salient enabled the exhausted German Seventh Army to retreat in an orderly manner to a line between the Vesle and the Aisne. For his victory on the Marne, Foch was promoted marshal.

Battle of Amiens 8–11 August. See Map 26 and accompanying notes.

Battle of Montdidier 8–11 August. The summer offensive of 1918 was an Allied affair and this battle saw the start of the advance of the French First and Third Armies against the German Eighteenth Army. Montdidier was found deserted and destroyed, but the advance was delayed east of the town by stiffening resistance. By the end of the fourth day the First Army had pushed the Germans back some 8 miles along an 18-mile front, with the Third averaging 4 miles on a 15-mile front.

Second Battle of the Somme 21 August–3 September. This was the main British counter-offensive by the Third and Fourth Armies in response to the four-month German onslaught of the spring, and formed the central part of the Allies' advance to the Armistice Line of November 1918. It involved a major offensive against the German Second Army and opened with the Battle of Albert (21–23 August). This was followed by the Second Battle of Bapaume (31 August–3 September), with the town falling on 29 August.

Second Battle of Arras 26 August–3 September. This offensive by the British First and Third Armies started when the First Army struck on a 6-mile front east of Arras, resulting in the Battle of the Scarpe, 1918 (26 August–30 August), which achieved a 4-mile advance. By 3 September the First Army was closing up to the Hindenburg Line when the Canadian Corps penetrated and took control of the Drocourt–Quéant Switch Line north of Bullecourt (3 September).

Battles of the Hindenburg Line 12 September–12 October. These were a succession of battles that had to be fought to breach the centre of the Hindenburg Line – mainly by the British First, Third and Fourth Armies. Six engagements classified as battles were involved in breaking through this line, or rather zone, of formidable defences. They were as follows, with national formations other than British that played a prominent part in parenthesis:

Battle of Havrincourt 12 September

Battle of Épehy 18 September

Battle of the Canal du Nord 27 September–1 October (Canadians)

Battle of the St-Quentin Canal 29 September–2 October (Australians and Americans)

Battle of the Beaurevoir Line 3–5 October

Battle of Cambrai, 1918, 8–9 October (Canadians).

Battle of St-Mihiel 12–15 September. This battle was part of the series of offensives by the Allies on the Western Front that drove the Germans back to the final Armistice Line. It involved the AEF and

Continued on page 76

Continued from page 75

some 48,000 French troops, all under the command of the American Gen. John J. Pershing. The objective was to pinch out the St-Mihiel salient and drive for Metz. It delivered a strong blow, but the attack faltered after the advance outdistanced food and artillery supplies. The attack on Metz was impossible as the Germans refortified their line, and the American efforts were switched to the Meuse–Argonne offensive. (See also Section Two, page 120.)

Meuse–Argonne Offensive (Battle of the Argonne Forest)
26 September–11 November. Here the primary role was given to the American First Army, supported by the French Fourth Army. The first phase, which lasted until 3 October, saw some progress made, but German reinforcements resulting in several strong counter-attacks halted progress, forcing the Americans into making frontal attacks on formidable defensive positions. Phase 2 saw fresh American divisions finally break through the defences and by 28 October they had advanced 10 miles, breaking out of the Argonne Forest. The final phase saw the American forces reorganized into two armies, the First led by Gen. Hunter Liggett and the Second by Lt Gen. Robert Bullard. The former advanced on Sedan and the latter on Metz. (See also Map 32.)

Battles of the Final Advance 28 September–11 November. The last six weeks of the war saw the Allies drive the demoralized Germans back along the entire Western Front from St-Mihiel to the Channel coast (see also Map 25), with continuous operations by all armies and the fighting mostly in open country. In Flanders the two battles primarily involved the British Second Army, although the Belgians were also attacking and liberating the Belgian coast. These battles were the Fourth Battle of Ypres (28 September–2 October) and the Battle of Courtrai (14–19 October). Between 2 October and 11 November the British First and Fifth Armies advanced from Artois, while the advance from Picardy saw the First, Third and Fourth Armies engaged at the Battle of the Selle (17–25 October), the First Army at the Battle of Valenciennes, and the First, Third and Fourth again at the last battle of the war, the Battle of the Sambre (4 November).

Ludendorff Assesses the Situation after 8 August 1918

Major General Erich Ludendorff considered the Allied success at Amiens on 8 August the turning point – the point at which he knew Germany would be defeated. He later wrote:

> Six or seven divisions, which could certainly be described as battle-worthy, had been completely broken . . . The losses of the 2nd Army had been very heavy . . . The infantry of some divisions had had to go straight off the lorries, whilst their artillery had been sent to some other part of the line . . . The report of the Staff officer I had sent to the battlefield as to the condition of those divisions that had met the first shock of the attack on the 8th perturbed me deeply. I summoned divisional commanders and officers from the line to Avesnes [his headquarters] to discuss events . . .
>
> I was told of deeds of glorious valour, but of behaviour which I should not have thought possible in the German Army; whole bodies of our men had surrendered to single troopers or isolated squadrons. Retiring troops, meeting a fresh division going bravely into action, had shouted out things like 'blackleg', and 'You're prolonging the war', expressions that were to be heard again later. The officers in many places had lost their influence and allowed themselves to be swept along with the rest.
>
> The 8th of August put the decline of the fighting power beyond all doubt, and in such a situation as regards reserves I had no hope of finding a strategic expedient whereby to turn the situation to our advantage. The fate of the German people was for me too high a stake. The war must be ended.

Notes for Map 26

Belligerents

Allies	German
British: Fourth Army	Second Army
French: First Army	Eighteenth Army

Divisions

British: 12 (inc. 5 Australian, 4 Canadian); 8 in initial attack	25 (10 in front line)
French: 12; 7 in initial attack	

Tanks   600

Guns 2,000 (all types)	1,000 (estimate)
Aircraft 1,900	365

Commanders

Fourth Army:	Second Army:
Gen. Sir Henry Rawlinson	Gen. of Cav. Georg von
III Corps: Lt Gen.	der Marwitz
Sir Richard Butler	Eighteenth Army:
Australian Corps:	Gen. Oskar von Hutier
Lt Gen. Sir John Monash	
Canadian Corps: Lt Gen.	
Sir Arthur Currie	
French First Army:	
Gen. Marie-Eugène Debeney	

Casualties 8–11 August

British: 22,200	74,000 (47,000 prisoners),
French: uncertain	600–700 guns

Result

A decisive Allied victory at the start of what become known as the Hundred Days campaign to Armistice Day on 11 November.

Summary

• This map shows the first day of the Battle of Amiens, which was part of the 1918 Allied counter-offensive along the Western Front (see also Map 25). By 10 August the British Fourth Army had over 441,000 men and almost 100,000 animals in the field. A key factor in the planning was secrecy, with the assaulting battalions not told the plan until three days beforehand. Artillery-reinforcing batteries deployed at night, registered targets off the map and dispensed with preliminary bombardments. The guns would open fire at zero hour with the assaulting troops advancing behind a creeping barrage fired by a third of the artillery batteries, with the bulk of the remainder committed to counter-battery fire. The attack would include exceptionally large numbers of tanks – some 360 Mk V and MkV*, 184 supply tanks and 96 Whippets (light tanks) with the cavalry. The attackers would have virtually total control of the air over the battlefield, with the Allies' planes far outnumbering those of the Germans. The French First Army in the south would start its advance 45 minutes later than the British, supported by 72 Whippet tanks and numerous aircraft.

• The attack started at 4:20 a.m. on 8 August, with the main effort made by the Australian and Canadian Corps in the centre. By about 7:30 a.m. the first German positions were taken and supporting divisions were passed through to continue the attack. Cavalry and light tanks pushed forward and by 11:00 a.m. the leading units were 3 miles from their start line. There was less success north of the Somme, where the terrain was difficult and tank support minimal. III Corps was held up by the steep wooded ridge of Chipilly spur, which was taken on 10 August with the assistance of several units from the American 33rd Division (the corps reserve). To the south, the French main effort was by XXXI Corps. By the end of the first day a gap of over 12 miles, up to 8 miles deep, had been punched through the enemy defences, with the British taking 13,000 prisoners and the French another 3,000. It was indeed a 'black day' for the German Army and marked the beginning of the end of the war.

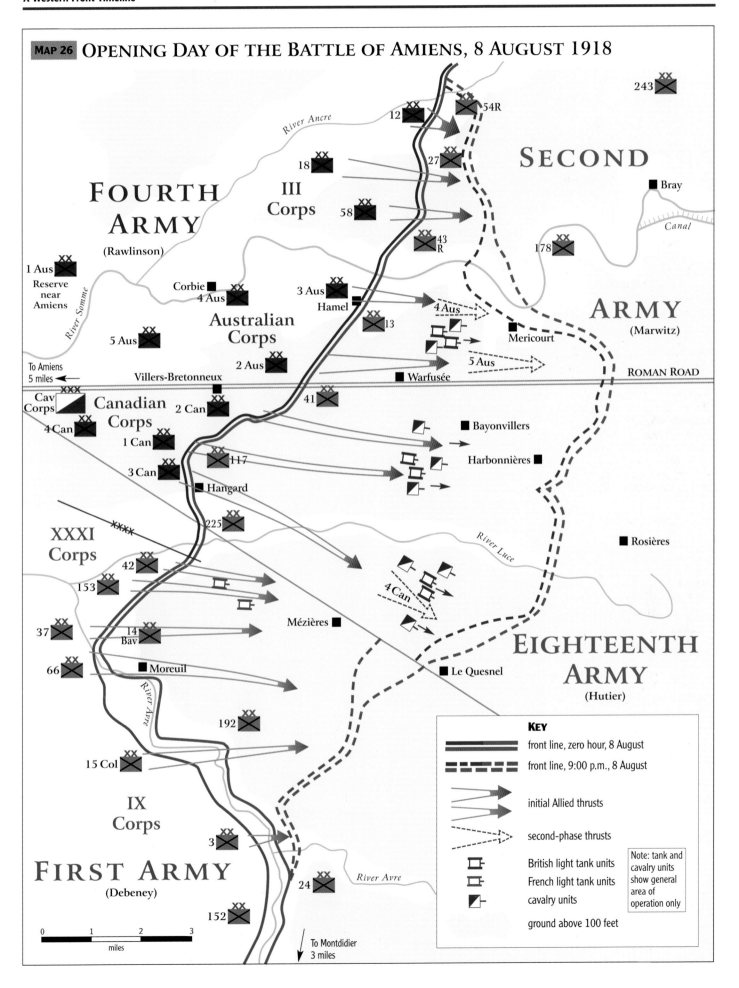

MAP 26 OPENING DAY OF THE BATTLE OF AMIENS, 8 AUGUST 1918

243

River Ancre

12

54R

SECOND

18

27

Bray

III
Corps

58

Canal

43
R

178

FOURTH
ARMY

(Rawlinson)

1 Aus
Reserve
near
Amiens

Corbie

4 Aus

3 Aus

ARMY

Hamel

4 Aus

(Marwitz)

Australian
Corps

13

5 Aus

5 Aus

Mericourt

To Amiens
5 miles

Villers-Bretonneux

2 Aus

Warfusée

ROMAN ROAD

Cav
Corps

Canadian
Corps

2 Can

41

Bayonvillers

4 Can

1 Can

Harbonnières

3 Can

117

Hangard

225

River Luce

Rosières

XXXI
Corps

42

153

4 Can

37

14
Bav

Mézières

66

Moreuil

Le Quesnel

EIGHTEENTH
ARMY

192

(Hutier)

15 Col

KEY

front line, zero hour, 8 August

front line, 9:00 p.m., 8 August

IX
Corps

initial Allied thrusts

3

second-phase thrusts

FIRST ARMY

British light tank units

(Debeney)

French light tank units

24

River Avre

cavalry units

Note: tank and
cavalry units
show general
area of
operation only

152

ground above 100 feet

0   1   2   3
miles

To Montdidier
3 miles

River Somme

River Avre

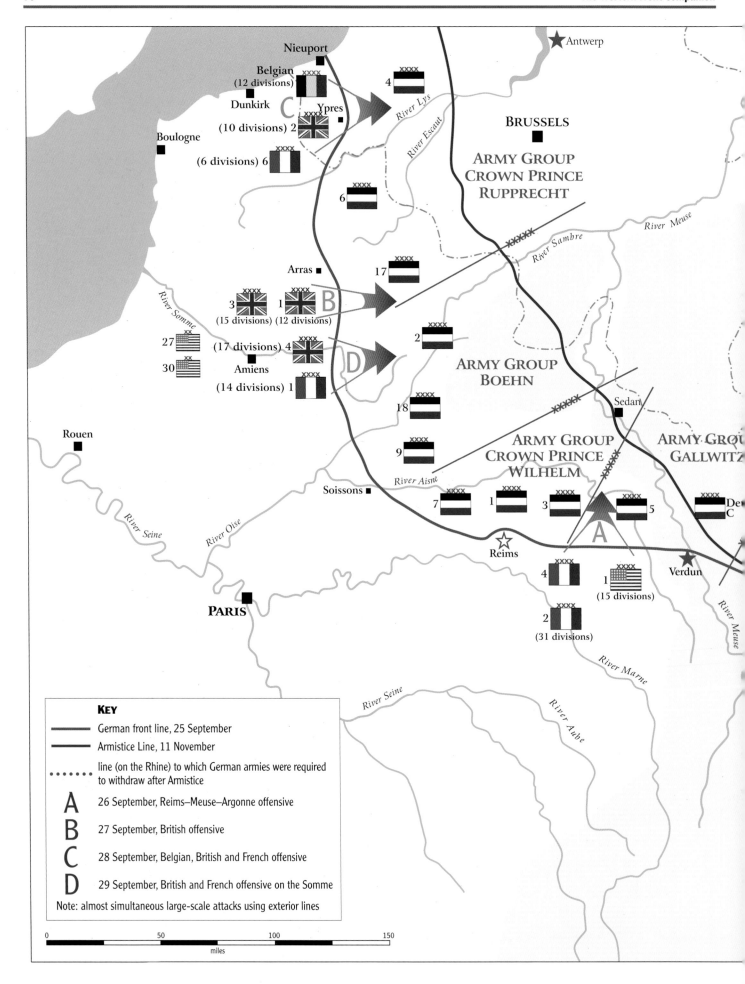

Nieuport

Belgian
(12 divisions)

Antwerp

Dunkirk C

Ypres

4

Boulogne

(10 divisions) 2

BRUSSELS

River Lys

River Escaut

ARMY GROUP
CROWN PRINCE
RUPPRECHT

(6 divisions) 6

6

River Meuse

River Sambre

Arras

17

River Somme

3

1 B

(15 divisions) (12 divisions)

2

27

(17 divisions) 4

30

Amiens

(14 divisions) 1

D

ARMY GROUP
BOEHN

18

Sedan

9

Rouen

ARMY GROUP
CROWN PRINCE
WILHELM

ARMY GROUP
GALLWITZ

River Aisne

Soissons

7

1

3

5

De
C

River Seine

River Oise

Reims

A

4

1

Verdun

(15 divisions)

PARIS

2

River Meuse

(31 divisions)

River Marne

River Seine

River Aube

KEY

German front line, 25 September

Armistice Line, 11 November

line (on the Rhine) to which German armies were required
to withdraw after Armistice

A 26 September, Reims–Meuse–Argonne offensive

B 27 September, British offensive

C 28 September, Belgian, British and French offensive

D 29 September, British and French offensive on the Somme

Note: almost simultaneous large-scale attacks using exterior lines

0   50   100   150

miles

MAP 27 WESTERN FRONT, 25 SEPTEMBER 1918: THE FINAL FOUR ALLIED OFFENSIVES

River Rhine

River Moselle

embourg

River Saar

★Thionville

Lorraine

ARMY GROUP
DUKE ALBRECHT
VON WÜRTTEMBERG

Metz 19

River Rhine

Det. A

Nancy

Strasbourg

Det. B

pinal ★

Mulhouse

Alsace

Belfort ★

SWITZERLAND

The 'Aussies' Attack Péronne and Mont St-Quentin

Lieutenant H. R. Williams described some of his experiences in the bitter fighting to break into the Hindenburg Line on 1 September 1918:

I got out of the trench, and before I was into my stride, the machine-gun bullets went 'zip-zip' around me. Half-way across I turned to see that my team were following. Suddenly I was bowled over as if a sledge-hammer had struck me. My tunic was on fire, and the fumes of cordite made me cough and splutter. Some machine-gun bullets had struck the pannier that was over my left breast. The metal of the pannier had turned the bullets, which cut through perhaps eight or ten cartridges that were in the pannier and set fire to them. I beat out the fire by banging the panniers on the ground and crushed the burning tunic in my hand. To my surprise I was not wounded. A few more yards and instinct caused me to adopt the prone position; a shell landed so close that its explosion covered my face with earth, and knocked my steel helmet off. Again unscathed, I arose and continued on my way . . .

Passing along the sunken road were stretcher parties carrying the badly wounded . . . They were all in a pitiful condition, drenched with rain, shivering and with faces pale from loss of blood. But when spoken to each man would summon a wan smile and never a word of complaint was heard from them.

There were some ghastly wounds among them. Shells had smashed bones and cut flesh in a manner sickening to behold. One chap had stopped a burst of fire from a machine-gun, which had torn part of his stomach away. How he lived long enough to be carried back to the sunken road was little short of miraculous; still, he lay among us for some time and smoked cigarettes unceasingly, these being fed to him by our fellows.

The Victoria Cross in 1918

There were 177 Victoria Crosses awarded during the year, making a total of 492 for operations on the Western Front in the war. On the second day of the German spring offensive, Acting Captain (later Lieutenant Colonel) Reginald Frederick Johnson Hayward was commanding a company of the 1st Battalion, the Wiltshire Regiment, near Frémicourt, just east of Bapaume on the Cambrai road, working on improving the defensive positions. The German barrage pounded Hayward's company, burying Hayward under earth and debris, wounding him in the head and rendering him deaf. He nevertheless insisted on staying to lead his company in the ferocious defensive battle that saw the Wiltshires defeat three enemy assaults. The next day his right arm was shattered and he received a second head wound. Despite this, Hayward still continued to encourage his men and supervise the defence of the company position, moving from trench to trench until he collapsed from loss of blood and exhaustion. He was evacuated on the night of the 25th. (See Map 24.)

Hayward survived the war and in addition to the VC received the Military Cross (MC) twice and later the Territorial Efficiency Decoration (ED). He served in World War II in the Anti-Aircraft (AA) Command and as commandant, prisoner of war camps. He died in January 1970, aged seventy-eight, and was cremated at Putney Vale, London. He is commemorated on the Arras Memorial.

Brigadier John Campbell, VC, stands on a damaged bridge over the St-Quentin Canal at Riqueval to address the 37th Staffordshire Brigade, 46th (North Midland) Division, at the place where it crossed the canal on 29 September 1918 during the battle to breach the Hindenburg Line in this area.

Section Two

The Western Front Armies

Send for the boys of the Old Brigade,
To keep Old England free.
Send for me father and me mother and me brother,
But for Gawd's sake don't send me!

Anon., 'Song of World War One'

Manpower Deployed on the Western Front

Although this book is concerned with the Western Front, it is useful to look at the overall manpower available in terms of total populations at the start of the war, how many were initially mobilized, as well as the total called up during the war. With the hostilities lasting over four years and with unexpectedly heavy losses on all sides, the belligerent nations were forced to expand their forces to unprecedented levels. Not only was the war long but it rapidly became a world war, involving all of continental Europe, including Russia, as well as the British dominions and, finally, the United States of America. Although the Western Front was where the war was eventually won, huge armies were engaged in prolonged and bitter fighting on the Eastern Front, the Italian Front, in the Balkans and in Mesopotamia.

Most historians accept that it will never be possible to collate absolutely accurate figures for the number of men mobilized, the number who fought on a particular front or the casualties suffered. This is due, apart from the length of the war, to the wide variance between the belligerents in the accuracy of their statistics, and the fact that some included all casualties while others did not – Germany, for example, did not count minor wounded who received treatment at the front and quickly returned to their units, whereas the British did. This being so, the statistics below and throughout this book are the best efforts of the present writer to source as reliable figures as possible.

The table below lists the nations whose troops fought on the Western Front, showing the population and initial mobilization during August 1914 (where applicable); the total mobilized during the war; and a comparison of the combatant troops available in August 1914 with those deployed in the field in November 1918.

Military Manpower in August 1914 and November 1918

Country	Population	Initial Mobilization 1914	Total Mobilized 1914–18	Strength 1918	WF Combatants August 1914	WF Combatants November 1918
Australia	4,872,000	65,000	416,800 (8.5)	298,000	–	94,000
Belgium	7,517,000	177,000 (30% in fortresses)	267,000 (3.5)	145,000	177,000	115,000
Canada	7,400,000	32,000	620,000 (8.4)	364,000	–	154,000
France	39,600,000	3,781,000	8,660,000 (22)	2,794,000	1,071,000	1,554,000
India	316,000,000	223,700 (75,000 British)	1,680,000 (0.53)	654,000	–	16,000
New Zealand	1,050,000	8,430	128,500 (12.2)	30,000	–	25,000
Portugal	6,000,000	150,000	200,000 (3.3)	35,000	–	35,000
South Africa	6,000,000	50,000	231,000 (3.8) (85,000 Africans)	9,000	–	3,000
UK	46,400,000	733,500	5,704,000 (12.2)	3,196,000	117,000 (BEF)	1,202,000
USA	92,000,000	208,000	4,355,000 (4.7)	1,982,000	–	1,982,000
Germany	67,000,000	4,500,000	13,400,000 (20)	4,200,000	1,485,000	2,912,000

* Unless otherwise explained, figures in brackets denote percentage of population.

Note Not all these troops fought on the Western Front, though the majority did. The table illustrates clearly the enormous strain placed on the populations of France, the United Kingdom and Germany, countries that bore the brunt of the slaughter in that theatre for well over four years.

Discounting the Americans for the moment, although their intervention in large numbers on the battlefields in 1918 was crucial to the Allies' victory, it is interesting to note the total number of troops mobilized as a percentage of the total populations of the main Western Front belligerents. As shown in the table, France mobilized the highest, then Germany, followed by the United Kingdom (not counting dominion troops). Among the dominion countries, New Zealand, with a tiny population of just over one million, managed to mobilize as great a percentage of her population as the United Kingdom.

During the first clashes in August 1914, the number of Allied troops almost equalled the German invaders (1,365,000 to 1,485,000). At the Armistice Germany still had nearly 3 million men on the Western Front, but with the arrival of the Americans the Allies had well over 5 million.

Numbers, however, tell only part of the story. Napoleon claimed that God was on the side of the big battalions, which is true only if all else is equal – which it seldom is. Generalship, middle-level and junior leadership, training, morale, equipment, weapons and tactics are all part of the mix that brings success or failure on the battlefield.

The principal Allied army commanders in 1918. From left to right: Marshal Pétain, Field Marshal Haig, Marshal Foch and General Pershing.

Comparative British, French and German Ranks

The table below shows the main infantry ranks for the various levels of command during the war. The Germany Army rank structure was extremely complex, with differing rank titles for various arms and military administrators – for example, the equivalent of an infantry captain, *Hauptmann*, in the cavalry was a *Rittmeister*.

Command	British	French	German
Army Group	Field Marshal	*Maréchal*	*Generalfeldmarschall*
Army	General	*Général*	*Generaloberst*
Corps	Lieutenant General	*Général de Corps*	*General der Infanterie/Kavallerie*
Division	Major General*	*Général de Division*	*Generalleutnant*
Brigade	Brigadier General	*Général de Brigade*	*Generalmajor*
Regiment	–	*Colonel*	*Oberst*
		Lieutenant Colonel	*Oberstleutnant*
Battalion	Lieutenant Colonel	*Commandant*	*Major*
Company	Major/Captain	*Capitaine*	*Hauptmann*
Platoon	Lieutenant/	*Lieutenant/*	*Oberleutnant*
	2nd Lieutenant	*Sous Lieutenant*	*Leutnant*
Non-commissioned ranks			
Platoon	–	–	*Feldwebelleutnant* **
Platoon	–	–	*Offizierstellvertreter* **
–	Regimental Sergeant Major	*Adjutant Chef*	*Etatmässige Feldwebel*
–	Company Sergeant Major	*Adjutant*	*Feldwebel*
–	Staff Sergeant	–	*Vizefeldwebel*
–	Sergeant	*Sergent*	*Sergent*
Section/squad	Corporal	*Caporal*	*Unteroffizier/Kaporal*
–	Lance Corporal	*Soldat Première Classe*	*Gefreiter* (commanded a *Gruppe*)

*Originally called sergeant-major general.

** Due to heavy officer casualties, the *Feldwebelleutnant* (sergeant-major lieutenant) and *Offizierstellvertreter* (acting officer) were used by the Germans as platoon and sometimes company commanders.

Army Structure

For a full understanding of the remaining sections of this book, it is worth having some knowledge of the structure of the armies on the Western Front – the various formations and units of which they were composed, their approximate strength and the rank of the person who normally commanded them. A comparison of the ranks and command of the British, French and German armies is given in the box above. An explanation of army structure is fairly straightforward as all the belligerents used the same basic organizations of roughly the same size and commanded by officers of similar if not identical ranks; variations are explained in the paragraphs describing the national armies below. The armies that marched to war in August 1914 were very different to those in the field in November 1918 in terms of numbers. They were, in several cases, smaller than in 1917 (although their structure had not changed dramatically), but they were equipped, armed and supplied on a scale not dreamed of four years earlier.

The following brief notes on army structure are based primarily on the British Army at the time.

General Headquarters

GHQ was the location of the commander-in-chief along with his large operational and administrative staff – more details are given in Section Three. During a major battle the commander-in-chief often had a forward headquarters separate from his main one. All belligerents had an equivalent.

Army Groups

As the title implies, this was the grouping together of several armies under one overall commander. The British did not have the need for this, but both the French and Germans had army groups on the Western Front as the numbers of men under arms expanded to millions. In 1915 the French had Army Group North, Army Group Centre and Army Group East, of which Army Group Centre was the largest with four armies under command. By the spring of 1917 they had added a Reserve Army to the other three. In the same year the Germans had deployed three army groups named after their commanders – Army Group Crown Prince Rupprecht, Army Group Crown Prince Wilhelm of Prussia and Army Group Archduke Albrecht of Württemberg. By 1918 the Germans had twelve army groups, their deployment divided between all fronts. It was rare for an army group to be moved from its area of operational responsibility. It was sometimes reinforced by armies being added to it or reduced by the transfer of an army to a more critical part of the front.

Armies

An army consisted of several corps – the British (BEF) increased from two in August 1914 to five in 1918. During the Allied offensive of August 1918 Haig had command of five armies (in all but name a large army group), all of which had four corps, apart from the Fifth Army, which had two. Other nations had virtually identical organization of armies, although the Germans adopted a somewhat confusing system of creating 'army detachments' – an example being in 1917 when Army Group Albrecht consisted of Army Detachments A, B and C, each of which was also known by its commander's name. The Allies fielded seventeen armies along the Western Front by mid-1918. When their final offensive began in August, ten German armies and three army detachments opposed them. All armies were capable of sustained independent action in that they had their own supporting Arms (artillery, aircraft and engineers) and Services (transport, supply, medical, veterinary and ordnance) under direct command, as well as infantry and cavalry formations. By 1917–18 both the British and French armies had large numbers of tanks. Depending on the number of corps, an army would vary in strength from around 100,000–300,000 men and would be commanded by a full general or equivalent.

Corps

Prior to mobilization, the British Army had no corps in its structure but rather fielded large divisions to conform to the Indian Army organization. However, when the BEF took the field, corps were adopted in order to conform to its far more powerful French ally. Under a lieutenant general, a corps would average about 40,000 men when at full strength, while the number of corps making up an army, as noted above, would vary from two to four. Corps, like armies, were a mixture of all Arms and Services, and like them had a strong back-up in supporting arms, such as heavy artillery, directly under corps headquarters rather than as an integral part of the divisions within the corps.

As the size of armies expanded, so the composition of corps changed. Within the British Army a corps commander initially commanded two divisions but later often had up to four. Whereas corps headquarters usually remained fixed, its divisions were frequently switched to other areas, other corps. As the war progressed, corps were given control over more supply arrangements and over specialist units such as heavy artillery (from early 1916 onwards). British infantry corps were numbered I–XXIV, to which were added the Indian Corps (on the Western Front until the end of 1915), the Australia and New Zealand Army Corps (ANZAC), the Canadian Corps and the Cavalry Corps. All fought in France at some stage except for the XII and XVI (Salonika), XX and XXI (Palestine), and XXIII and XXIV (formed in England in 1918).

Divisions

Just over a hundred years earlier, during Napoleonic times, the strength of an army had normally been assessed by counting the number of regiments or battalions of infantry and cavalry. However, on the Western Front and elsewhere the number of divisions was used to gauge an army's strength. How many divisions do we have? How many does the enemy have on our front? How do we defend so wide a frontage with so few divisions? How do we allocate our divisions to the front line or to reserve or counter-attack roles? All these were common questions for commanders at GHQ, army or corps headquarters. Each belligerent nation used the division as the building block of its armies.

Divisions were split into infantry and cavalry (by World War II the latter had become armoured divisions), with the overwhelming majority being the former. The type of troops that initially predominated in their composition further categorized them. Within the British Army they were the following active field, as distinct from Home Service, divisions, with the number formed shown in brackets: Guards (1), Regular Army (11), First Line Territorial (16), New Army (Kitchener) (30), Second Line Territorial (8) and Royal Naval Division (1). Other divisions were known by the country that supplied them for the Western Front: Australia (5), Canada (4), New Zealand (1) and India (1). All except eight British divisions served at least some time on the Western Front. Over a period of several years, individual divisions gained unofficial ratings as to competence and reliability, and, although opinions were subjective, by the end of the war there was only one regular division, the Guards Division, in the top ten.

Commanded by a major general, a British or Belgian division usually had three brigades (there were exceptions, such as the British Cavalry Division, which went to war in 1914 with four), while French, American and German divisions had two. All had supporting Arms and Services under direct command, making divisions capable of operating independently for limited periods. At full strength they contained around 18,000 men, but as the war progressed, and after a major offensive resulting in very severe losses, the average fell to much nearer 10,000–12,000 until they were reinforced.

Both Belgium and America fielded much larger divisions than either their allies or Germany (see below). Similarly, from May 1917 to February 1918 the New Zealand Division had sixteen battalions in four brigades rather than the usual twelve in three brigades, making this one of the largest on the Western Front. However, during 1918 battle losses and sickness had reduced the average size of divisions to: American 25,500, British 11,800, French 11,400 and German 12,300.

British Armies on the Western Front

First Army Formed in France on 26 December 1914, initially under the command of Sir Douglas Haig. It remained on the Western Front, coming under the command of Sir Henry Horne when Haig was promoted to commander-in-chief in December 1915.

Second Army Formed in France on 26 December 1914 under the command of Sir Horace Smith-Dorrien. Later commanded by Sir Herbert Plumer. Apart from four months (November 1917–March 1918) in Italy, it was always associated with the Ypres salient.

Third Army Formed in France on 13 July 1915, initially commanded by Sir Edmund Allenby but later taken over by Sir Julian Byng when Allenby was sent to command in Palestine.

Fourth Army Formed in France on 5 February 1916 under the command of Sir Henry Rawlinson. Renamed Second Army when Plumer moved to Italy, but reverted to Fourth Army on his return.

Fifth Army On 22 May 1916 the Reserve Corps under General Sir Hubert Gough became the Reserve Army, which was then renamed the Fifth Army. Destroyed by the great German offensive in March 1918, it was renamed Fourth Army on 2 April 1918 and its HQ became HQ Reserve Army again. It was restored as Fifth Army on 23 May 1918 under command of General Sir William Birdwood.

Unlike higher formations, divisions were transferred around from corps to corps and army to army as certain parts of the front needed reinforcing or to meet other operational imperatives. In lengthy offensives such as that on the Somme in 1916, which lasted four and a half months, fifty-four British divisions were involved in twelve individual battles. During this period, as in other offensives, divisions were rotated in and out of the fighting, with a number being engaged several times – for example the 18th (Eastern) Division six times and the 56th (London) Division five.

Certainly within the British Army, as the division was the formation that the High Command moved around, it became the largest formation to which the soldiers retained any sort of corporate identity or loyalty. Although a soldier's primary loyalty was always to his own battalion (regiment), his second was to his division, as the units within it by and large remained constant.

Because of their importance in the structure of forces on the Western Front, details of the organization of divisions and a brief comparison between nationalities is given in diagrammatic form (pages 85–95), showing them as they were when they went to war in 1914 – the exception being the Americans, whose troops did not start arriving in France until late 1917. There is also a note on the main changes that had occurred by 1918.

Brigades

A brigadier general commanded an infantry or cavalry brigade. With the infantry it usually consisted of four battalions (the French had three) of infantry and three regiments of cavalry (the French two) in a mounted brigade. If up to establishment (maximum permitted strength), an infantry brigade would have around 4,500 men, a cavalry brigade considerably fewer. The manpower crisis of 1917 forced a reduction to three battalions in the infantry brigades of the British and German Armies. The brigade – or in some instances a regiment (see below) – was the smallest formation in all the armies; all subordinate or smaller forces were termed units or sub-units. Unlike a division, a brigade had no supporting Arms or Services under command and could therefore not operate independently as a fighting formation.

The British used the term 'brigade' to describe both artillery and later tank units in a somewhat complex system that will be described in the relevant sections.

Regiments

French Army regiments were the equivalent of brigades. A French infantry regiment had three infantry battalions under command. In the British Army things were more confusing. A British infantry regiment was not a tactical unit deployed on the battlefield but an administrative and recruiting organization that produced infantry battalions for operations. However, in the cavalry a regiment was the tactical equivalent of a battalion. Thus in the French Army a regiment would be commanded by the equivalent of a brigadier general or a full colonel and would be of a similar strength to a British brigade. The German system was different again, as shown in the diagram on pages 94–5.

Battalions

At full strength a battalion consisted of about 1,000 men commanded by a lieutenant colonel (in the German Army a major). The detailed organization is discussed in Section Four; here it is sufficient to note that its basic structure was four infantry companies. Initially French and German battalions were the same, but in 1916 the French reduced to three companies. It was the infantry battalions of all armies that bore the brunt of the fighting and the casualties of the war. The battalion was normally classified as a unit.

Companies

The infantry company (the cavalry equivalent was a squadron, the artillery a battery) was commanded by a major – or more likely, as losses mounted, a captain (in the French and German Armies always a captain). With four platoons in the company it could be up to 250 men strong at full strength – a rare circumstance when sick, wounded and detached personnel are taken into account. A company was a sub-unit.

Platoons

Four platoons under a second lieutenant or lieutenant (subalterns in the British Army) made up an infantry company. Each was up to fifty strong initially and was the smallest sub-unit normally commanded by a commissioned officer.

Sections

In the British Army four sections of twelve men each under a corporal were the smallest sub-units in the infantry.

As an example of how an army was structured, the diagram opposite shows the BEF (infantry and cavalry only) in August 1914.

The Divisional System

The table below compares the number of combat divisions in the different armies on the Western Front on 15 September 1914 (after the Battle of the Marne) and on Armistice Day, 11 November 1918, including all combat divisions and their equivalent in independent brigades:

Number of Combat Divisions

	1914			1918		
	Infantry	**Cavalry**	**Total**	**Infantry**	**Cavalry**	**Total**
France	78	11	89	110	–	110
Belgium	6	1	7	12	–	12
Australia	–	–	–	5	–	5
Canada	–	–	–	4	–	4
New Zealand	–	–	–	1	–	1
South Africa	–	–	–	1 bde	–	1 bde
Portugal	–	–	–	2	–	2
UK	6	1	7	42	3	45
USA	–	–	–	23	–	23
Total Allies	**90**	**13**	**103**	**199+1 bde**	**3**	**202+1 bde**
Germany	**86**	**9**	**95**	**192**	**1**	**193**

The diagrams on pages 85–95 show how an infantry division was structured in the armies of the belligerents on the Western Front early in 1914. An actual example of a British division is shown, including the names of the senior commanders and the designations of the various units within it. So much detail is not provided for Belgian, French, German or American divisions.

UK

The 1st Division (pages 86–7) went to war as one of the two divisions of I Corps under Lieutenant General Sir Douglas Haig.

The divisions that fought at Mons were very different from those that broke through the Hindenburg Line in 1918 and brought the war to an end. The initial flood of volunteers, followed by conscription in 1916, ensured that the strength of British divisions peaked in September 1916 – when at full establishment the 1st Division had 19,372 all ranks. However, the critical manpower shortages in 1917 caused by the horrendous losses due to sickness and casualties led to the reduction of brigade establishment from four to three battalions – nine instead of twelve in a division, plus a tenth designated as the pioneer battalion. This meant the theoretical establishment of a slimmed-

Outline Structure of the BEF in France, August 1914

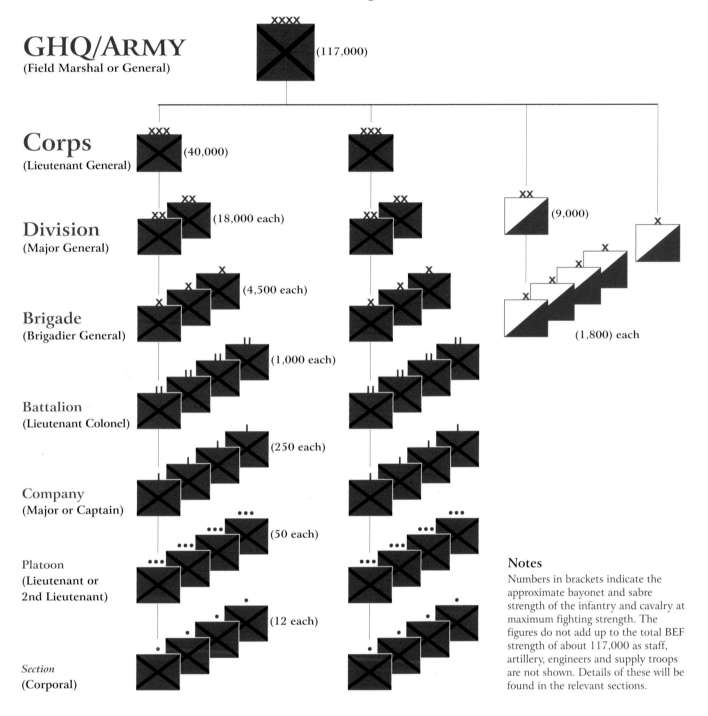

GHQ/ARMY
(Field Marshal or General)

(117,000)

Corps
(Lieutenant General)

(40,000)

Division
(Major General)

(18,000 each)

(9,000)

Brigade
(Brigadier General)

(4,500 each)

(1,800) each

Battalion
(Lieutenant Colonel)

(1,000 each)

Company
(Major or Captain)

(250 each)

Platoon
(Lieutenant or
2nd Lieutenant)

(50 each)

Section
(Corporal)

(12 each)

Notes
Numbers in brackets indicate the approximate bayonet and sabre strength of the infantry and cavalry at maximum fighting strength. The figures do not add up to the total BEF strength of about 117,000 as staff, artillery, engineers and supply troops are not shown. Details of these will be found in the relevant sections.

down division of April 1918 barely reached 16,000, although the average actual strength was around 4,000 fewer (see page 86). However, the Australian divisions retained twelve battalions and by the end of the war both Australian and Canadian divisions were larger than their British counterparts.

But it was in weaponry that the differences were most striking. By 1918 the division no longer had direct command over as many guns as four years earlier (it had dropped from fifty-four 18-pounders to thirty-six, and from eighteen 4.5-inch howitzers to twelve; and the 60-pounder howitzer battery had been transferred to the heavy artillery) as the emphasis was now on heavy artillery regiments, which were controlled from corps or army headquarters. However, within the division there were thirty-six heavy mortars where there had been none, and a machine-gun battalion of the Machine Gun Corps with sixty-four Vickers heavy machine guns had been brought in from April 1917. Giving another

major boost to firepower had been the introduction of the light machine gun (the Lewis gun) to the infantry at platoon level – by 1918 there were 336 in a division.

The cavalry squadron and cyclist company had been withdrawn, the number of horses required had shrunk from over 5,000 to just under 4,000 and there were twenty-one motor ambulances within the division.

The table overleaf shows how the full establishment of a British infantry division changed during the war.

The 1st Division of the BEF, August 1914

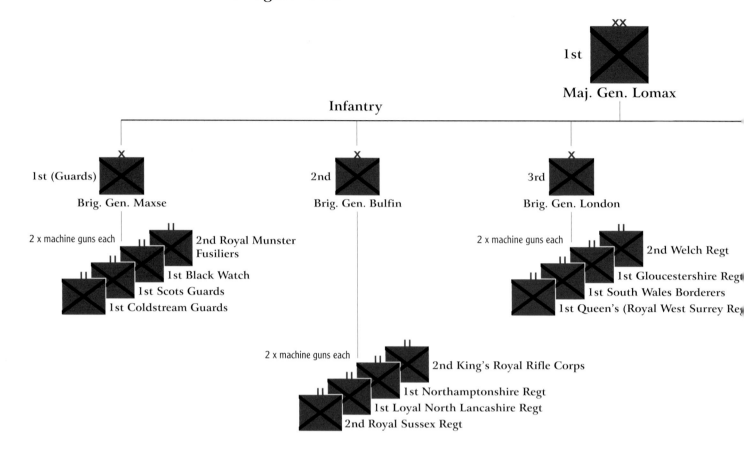

1st — **Maj. Gen. Lomax**

Infantry

1st (Guards) — **Brig. Gen. Maxse**

2 x machine guns each

2nd Royal Munster Fusiliers
1st Black Watch
1st Scots Guards
1st Coldstream Guards

2nd — **Brig. Gen. Bulfin**

2 x machine guns each

2nd King's Royal Rifle Corps
1st Northamptonshire Regt
1st Loyal North Lancashire Regt
2nd Royal Sussex Regt

3rd — **Brig. Gen. London**

2 x machine guns each

2nd Welch Regt
1st Gloucestershire Regt
1st South Wales Borderers
1st Queen's (Royal West Surrey Reg

The Thiepval memorial arch on the Somme.

The beautifully peaceful setting of the British cemetery in Ploegsteert Wood, Belgium.

British Infantry Division Establishment

	1914	1915	1916	1917	1918
All ranks	18,179	18,122	19,372	18,825	16,035
Horses	5,594	5,174	5,145	4,342	3,838
Guns	76	56	64	48	48
18-pdrs	54	48	48	36	36
4.5-in how.	18	8	16	12	12
60-pdrs	4	–	–	–	–
Trench mortars	–	–	40	40	36
Stokes	–	–	24	24	24
Medium (2-in)	–	–	12	12	12
Heavy (9.45-in)	–	–	4	4	–
Machine guns	24	48	200	264	400
Vickers	24	48	48	64	64
Lewis Guns	–	–	152	200	336
Carts and vehicles	877	834	878	845	822
Cycles	382	521	372	388	341
Motorcycles	9	17	24	22	44
Motor cars	9	11	13	11	11
Motor lorries	–	5	3	3	3
Motor ambulances	–	21	21	21	21

Notes

- **Division HQ**   Commander: major general; senior staff officer: colonel; Commander Royal Artillery (CRA): lieutenant colonel; Commander Royal Engineers (CRE): lieutenant colonel
- **Infantry**   3 brigades of 4 battalions (12,000 all ranks)
- **Artillery**   3 field artillery brigades each under a lieutenant colonel and each with a brigade ammunition column (BAC); 54 x 18-pdr field guns (9 batteries of 6 guns); 1 field artillery howitzer brigade of 18 x 4.5-inch howitzers under a lieutenant colonel with a howitzer BAC (3 batteries of howitzers); heavy battery, Royal Garrison Artillery (RGA), 4 x 60-pdrs; 1 divisional ammunition column (DAC)
- **Mounted Troops**   1 divisional cavalry squadron and 1 cyclist company

Totals   3,750 all ranks, 76 guns and about 5,600 horses

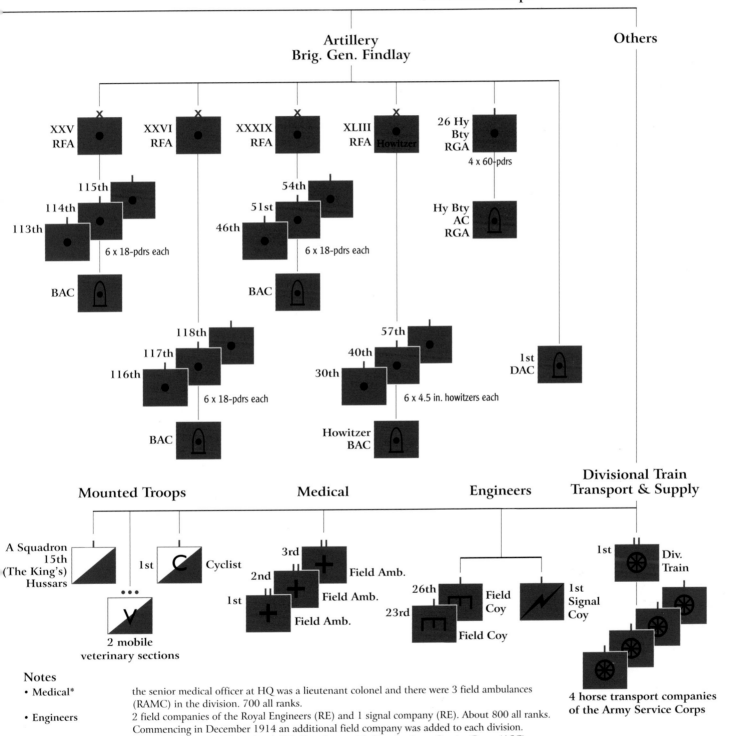

Notes

- **Medical***   the senior medical officer at HQ was a lieutenant colonel and there were 3 field ambulances (RAMC) in the division. 700 all ranks.
- **Engineers**   2 field companies of the Royal Engineers (RE) and 1 signal company (RE). About 800 all ranks. Commencing in December 1914 an additional field company was added to each division.
- **Transport & Supply**   1 divisional train totalling about 430 all ranks provided by the Army Service Corps (ASC).

Divisional Totals   18,000 all ranks with 76 guns and almost 5,600 horses

* A small Army Veterinary Corps (AVC) mobile section was added to a division by the end of 1914.

Belgium

The major change within the Belgian Army was that in January 1918 all the six infantry divisions were divided in two to create twelve much smaller formations.

Outline Organization of a Belgian Infantry Division in the Field Army, August 1914

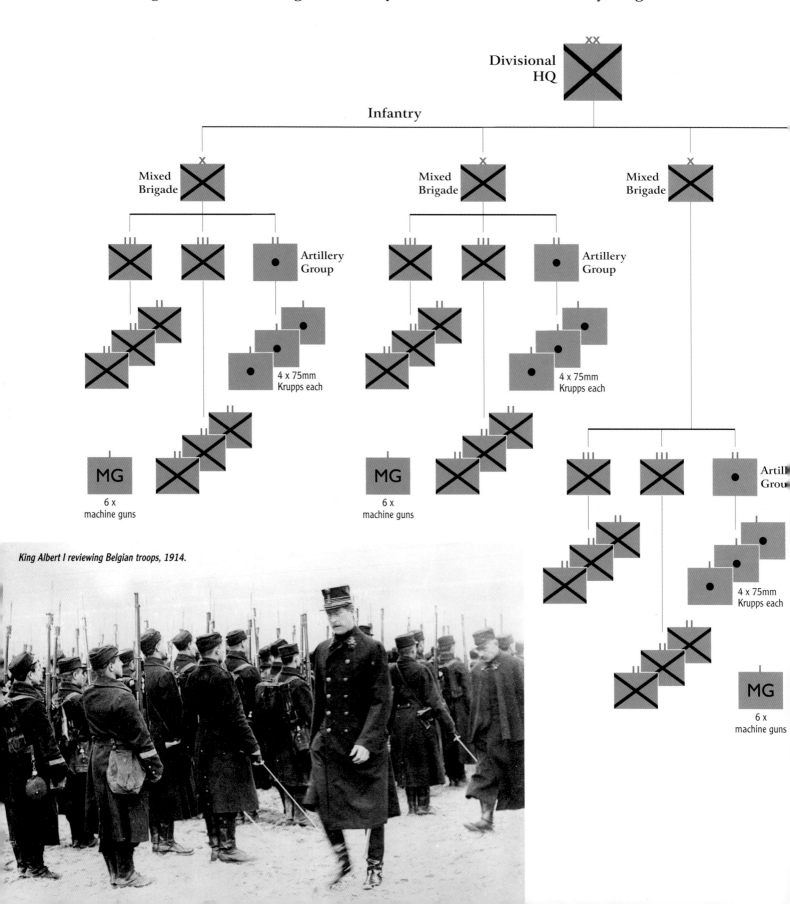

King Albert I reviewing Belgian troops, 1914.

Notes

• This division is a three-brigade division as were four of the six Belgian infantry divisions at the outbreak of the war. The two larger divisions had four brigades.

• The division was particularly weak in machine guns, having only one machine-gun company of six guns in each brigade.

• The total strength at full establishment was 25,500, with the four brigade divisions having an all-ranks strength of 32,000, with 5,200 horses, making it the equivalent of a corps in other armies.

• Although the artillery had the excellent 75mm field gun, it was numerically weak for its overall size, having only 48 guns (or 60 in the larger divisions).

• It was also weak in communications, with only one section of telegraphists.

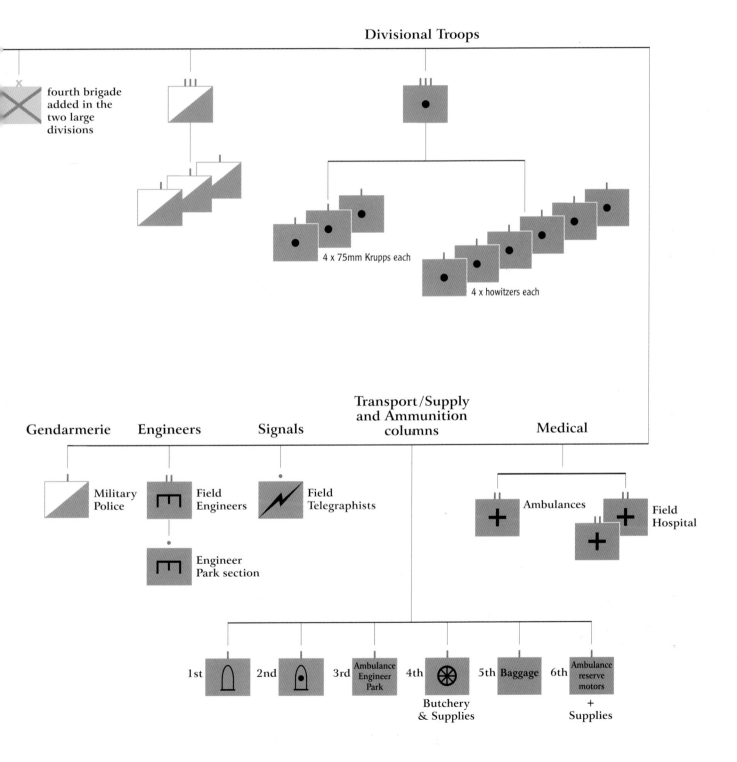

Divisional Troops

fourth brigade added in the two large divisions

4 x 75mm Krupps each

4 x howitzers each

Gendarmerie   Engineers   Signals   Transport/Supply and Ammunition columns   Medical

Military Police

Field Engineers

Engineer Park section

Field Telegraphists

Ambulances

Field Hospital

1st   2nd   3rd Ambulance Engineer Park   4th   5th Baggage   6th Ambulance reserve motors

Butchery & Supplies

+ Supplies

France

The main structural change within the division was the reduction from four regiments to three, although this was still not complete by the end of 1917. The artillery was reorganized, with a regiment now having three field batteries of four 75mm guns, a trench artillery battery, a field howitzer battery and a mortar company. Each infantry battalion had a machine-gun company and each company a machine-gun section. The divisional engineers were increased with the addition of two mining

Outline Organization of a French Regular Infantry Division, August 1914

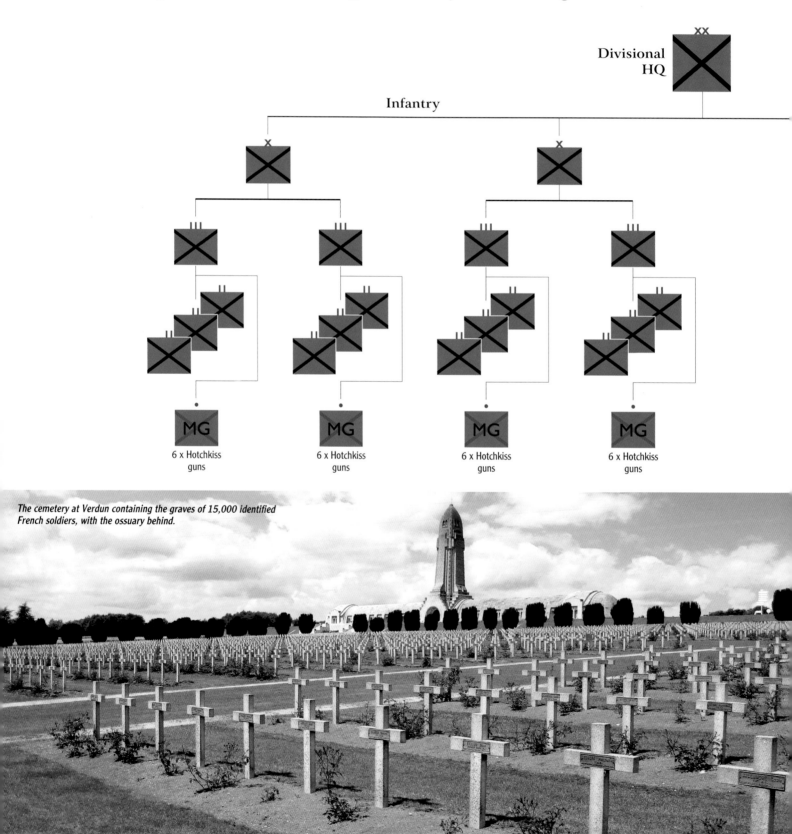

The cemetery at Verdun containing the graves of 15,000 identified French soldiers, with the ossuary behind.

companies, a field park company and a signals section.

As with other armies, the French infantry division relied on horsepower to move heavy equipment, guns, ammunition and most of the seriously wounded. As noted in Section Six, the French for the most part neglected horse management. Subsequent heavy losses from enemy action, sickness, fatigue and neglect caused considerable problems, many of which might have been avoided. There is no indication of any veterinary sub-unit in this divisional organization, and the present writer has been unable to discover whether any existed during the early part of the war.

Notes

• The usual organization of a regular French infantry division with only two brigades (12 battalions), as compared to the Belgian division with 18 battalions.
• The French division was, like all Allied divisions in August 1914, poorly equipped with machine guns.

• The average strength was around 15,900 all ranks, making it the smallest division establishment of the Allies at the start of the war.
• Its artillery groups were equipped with 36 of the quick-firing 75mm field guns.
• Telephone, telegraph and field park and bridging units were attached at corps level.

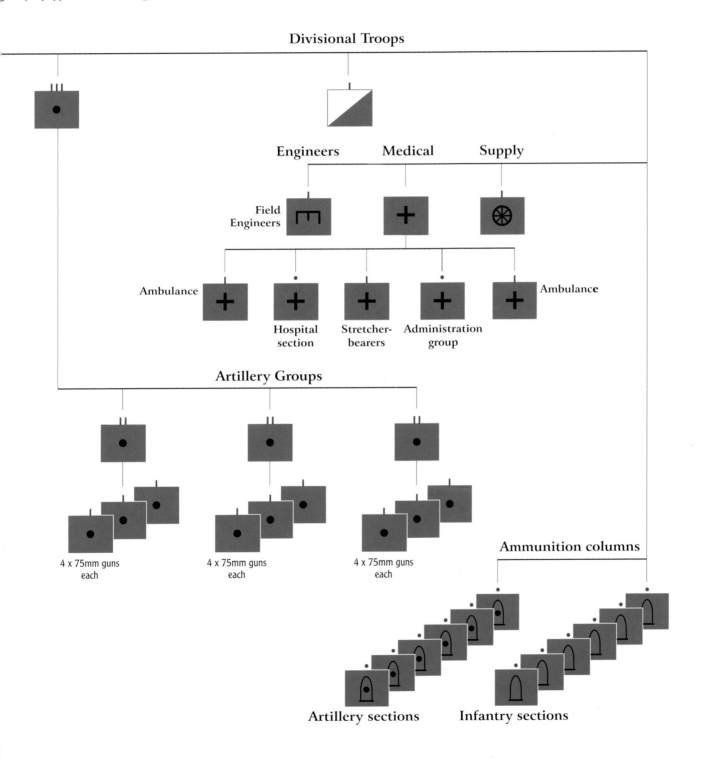

Divisional Troops

Engineers   Medical   Supply

Field Engineers

Ambulance   Hospital section   Stretcher-bearers   Administration group   Ambulance

Artillery Groups

4 x 75mm guns each   4 x 75mm guns each   4 x 75mm guns each

Ammunition columns

Artillery sections   Infantry sections

America

The AEF did not play any major part in the fighting before 1918, but by the end of the war it had twenty-three combat divisions in the field, forming two armies. As noted in the diagram, all their divisions were, with 28,000 all ranks, about twice the size of most of the by this time shrunken Allied formations.

Outline Organization of an American Infantry Division, November 1917

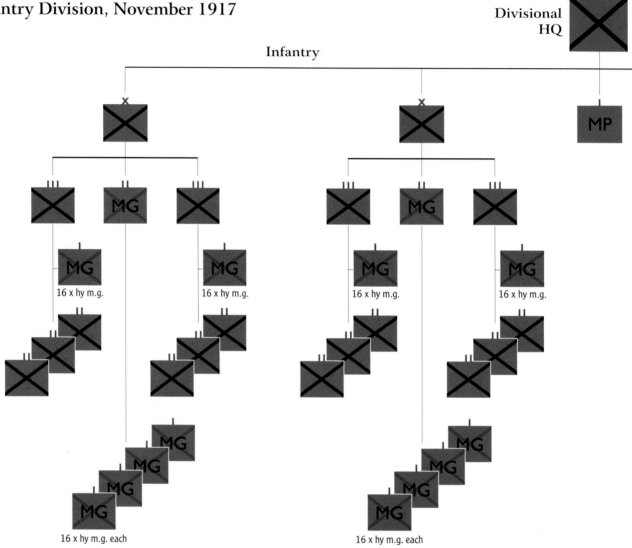

US recruits undertake bayonet training at Fort Worth, 1918.

Divisional Troops

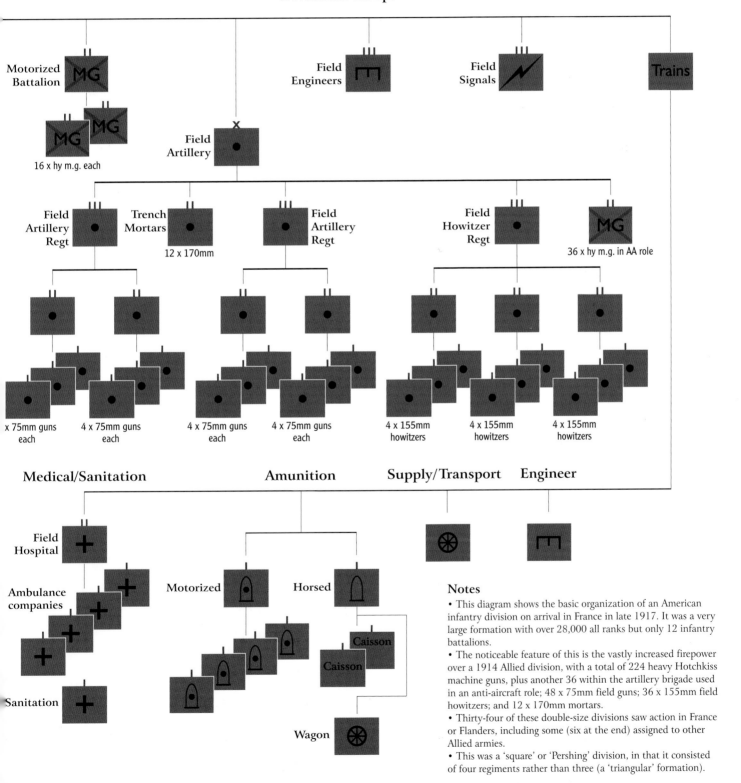

Motorized Battalion MG

MG MG

16 x hy m.g. each

Field Engineers

Field Signals

Trains

Field Artillery

Field Artillery Regt

Trench Mortars
12 x 170mm

Field Artillery Regt

Field Howitzer Regt

MG
36 x hy m.g. in AA role

x 75mm guns each

4 x 75mm guns each

4 x 75mm guns each

4 x 75mm guns each

4 x 155mm howitzers

4 x 155mm howitzers

4 x 155mm howitzers

Medical/Sanitation   **Amunition**   **Supply/Transport**   **Engineer**

Field Hospital

Ambulance companies

Sanitation

Motorized

Horsed

Caisson

Caisson

Wagon

Notes

• This diagram shows the basic organization of an American infantry division on arrival in France in late 1917. It was a very large formation with over 28,000 all ranks but only 12 infantry battalions.

• The noticeable feature of this is the vastly increased firepower over a 1914 Allied division, with a total of 224 heavy Hotchkiss machine guns, plus another 36 within the artillery brigade used in an anti-aircraft role; 48 x 75mm field guns; 36 x 155mm field howitzers; and 12 x 170mm mortars.

• Thirty-four of these double-size divisions saw action in France or Flanders, including some (six at the end) assigned to other Allied armies.

• This was a 'square' or 'Pershing' division, in that it consisted of four regiments rather than three (a 'triangular' formation).

Germany

By 1917 basic changes had been made with the reduction from two brigades to one, but with regiments within each brigade increased from two to three. This reduction in the over-all number of infantry regiments was necessary due to the very severe losses sustained during the previous two years and it enabled the creation of additional, if smaller, divisions – the strength of an average German division in 1918 was about 12,300 all ranks.

As with other nations, the critical importance of machine guns was reflected in the 1918 division having 130 heavy and 216 light machine guns. These included those of the specialist marksman machine-gun detachment that most divisions had

Outline Organization of a German Regular Infantry Division, August 1914

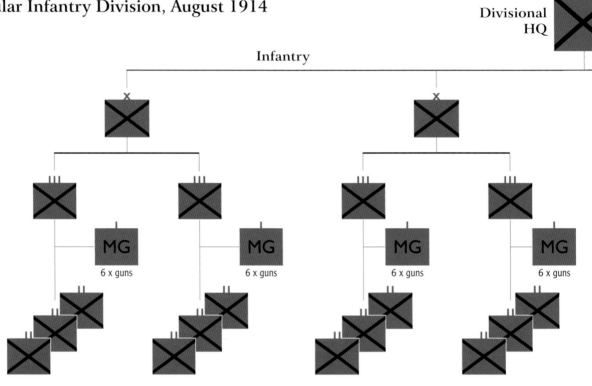

Divisional HQ

Infantry

MG — 6 x guns
MG — 6 x guns
MG — 6 x guns
MG — 6 x guns

German burial site inside Fort Douaumont – 679 Germans are buried behind the cross.

acquired by the end of the war. The divisional artillery command controlled a field-gun regiment of two battalions (*Abteilungen*) each of three batteries and a field howitzer battalion. In addition, the division had seventy-six trench mortars and a company of medium mortars, the latter being grouped with the new (from 1917) divisional pioneer battalion, which also included a searchlight detachment.

Grouped with the divisional troops were a field hospital, veterinary hospital, motor transport column and a telephone detachment. A major change was the removal of the ammunition columns from divisional to sector control by 1917 and also the reduction of the cavalry from a regiment to a squadron.

Notes

• On mobilization the German regular infantry divison was a powerful force, with about 17,500 all ranks, the infantry element numbering some 12,000. There were over 4,000 horses within the division.

• The artillery was divided into two regiments, each with two *Abteilungen* or groups which were the approximate equivalent of a battalion or regiment in the British Army. The total number of guns was 72 (54 field guns and 18 light field howitzers).

Divisional Troops

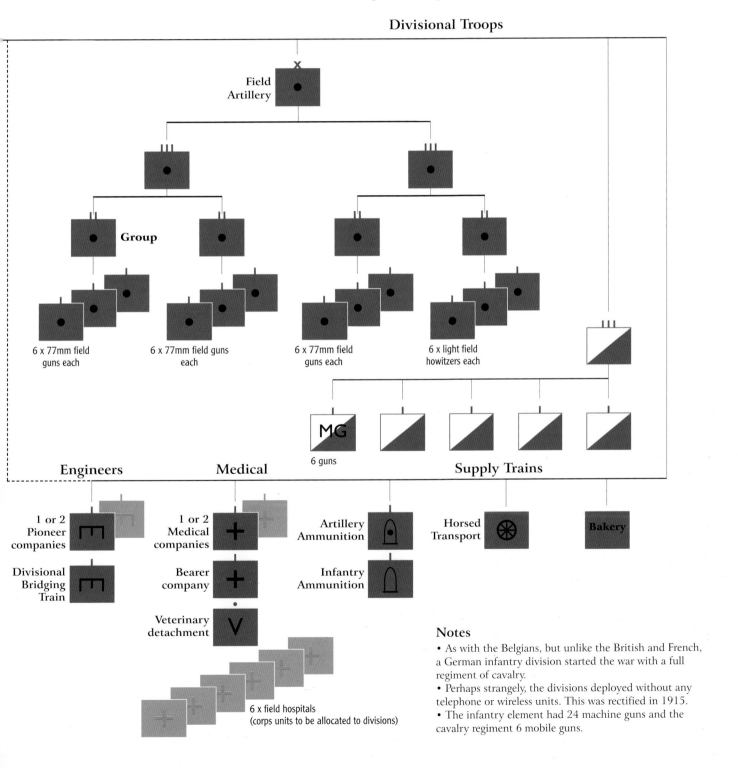

Field Artillery

Group

6 x 77mm field guns each

6 x 77mm field guns each

6 x 77mm field guns each

6 x light field howitzers each

MG — 6 guns

Engineers

1 or 2 Pioneer companies

Divisional Bridging Train

Medical

1 or 2 Medical companies

Bearer company

Veterinary detachment

6 x field hospitals (corps units to be allocated to divisions)

Artillery Ammunition

Infantry Ammunition

Supply Trains

Horsed Transport

Bakery

Notes

• As with the Belgians, but unlike the British and French, a German infantry division started the war with a full regiment of cavalry.

• Perhaps strangely, the divisions deployed without any telephone or wireless units. This was rectified in 1915.

• The infantry element had 24 machine guns and the cavalry regiment 6 mobile guns.

The Armies

The pages that follow give a brief picture of each of the armies that fought on the Western Front, as well as the contributions of Australia, Canada, India, New Zealand and South Africa – although none of these fielded an army. Each account includes a look at mobilization, recruitment and associated problems, along with some comment on how the different forces expanded and developed during the course of the fighting. This is followed by a brief description of a battle (along with a map) in which the force in question played a prominent part – the exception being the British Army, as Section Thirteen will examine the attack of the British 29th Division at the Battle of Cambrai in 1917 in considerable detail. For British, dominion and Indian forces, the numbers quoted are taken from *Statistics of the Military Effort of the British Empire during the Great War, 1914–1920*, published in 1922.

The British Army

The UK declared war on Germany at 11:00 p.m. on 4 August 1914, committed to sending an expeditionary force to France. In theory she had an army of 247,432 men of all ranks, almost half of whom were serving overseas, mostly in the crown jewel of the British Empire – India. The cutting edge of the army was the infantry, organized into 157 battalions – 9 battalions of Foot Guards and 148 battalions of regular infantry of the line – of which 81 battalions were at home and 76 abroad (51 in India). Additionally, Britain had 31 cavalry regiments (9 in India) as well

as supporting Arms and Services (artillery, engineers, medical, supply, etc.). The other professional army, at least available to take on duties on the subcontinent and thus freeing some British units for France or elsewhere, was the 150,000 strong Indian Army (quite separate from British units stationed in that country), a fifth of which was cavalry.

Britain was primarily a naval power. It was the Royal Navy that controlled the oceans and ensured security of the shipping lanes of empire, while much of the nation's small army was scattered around the world on policing and garrison duties. With the exception of the Second Boer War (South African War) of 1899–1902, the army's primary role had been the protection and control of overseas dependencies. In addition to those in India, 41,545 men were sprinkled in penny packets in Aden, South and West Africa, Bermuda, Ceylon, China, Cyprus, Egypt, Gibraltar, Hong Kong, Jamaica, Malta, Mauritius, the Straits Settlements (Singapore) and Sudan. Although it was small in size, the British Army's leaders had enjoyed a varied and practical application of soldiering in the handling of small columns in colonial expeditions – those on the northwest frontier of India (now Pakistan) being particularly frequent. Such experience was not available to continental armies on anything like the same scale. However, valuable as this type of soldiering was to all ranks, it in no way prepared the British Army, or any army, for the horrendous experience of modern war, the scale and complexity of which was unknown to history.

The immediate concern was that most units were up to 60 per cent under war establishment, a situation that demanded the immediate recall of tens of thousands of reservists to the colours and the withdrawal of regular units from overseas (where their strength had been at least partially maintained by drafts from home) and, if possible, their replacement with some category of reservists. In August 1914 the various categories of reservists and the Territorial Force could, theoretically, provide 479,000 men of all ranks, thus making a possible total available military manpower of just over 726,000. Reservists came from the following organizations:

The Army Reserve

This consisted of former regular soldiers who, when they originally signed on for seven or nine years with the colours (full-time service), had also committed themselves to serve on the Reserve for five years. There were three categories of army reservists, with those in the top category liable to be recalled first and those in the others to be recalled only after all those in the category above them had rejoined. In 1914 there were just over 145,000 such reservists. These men were destined to reinforce existing regular units directly.

The Special Reserve

The Regular Army could also call on the Special Reserve. It was formed out of the

The British Ultimatum to Germany Expires

Michael MacDonagh was the parliamentary correspondent of *The Times* in 1914 and recorded his experience in London on 4 August when at 11:00 p.m. the United Kingdom went to war with Germany.

It was in the streets, on August 4, 1914, after the House of Commons had adjourned, that I found myself in an atmosphere of real passion. Parliament Street and Whitehall were thronged with people highly excited and rather boisterous . . . All were already touched with war fever. They regarded their country as a crusader – redressing all wrongs and bringing freedom to oppressed nations. Cries of 'Down with Germany' were raised . . . The singing of patriotic songs, such as 'Rule Britannia', 'The Red White and Blue', and also 'The

Marseillaise', brought the crowds still closer together . . .

Suddenly, amidst the cheering and booing [against a small number of anti-war protestors], a cry was raised, 'The King! On to Buckingham Palace!' And at once we streamed out of Trafalgar Square into the Mall and out of Whitehall into Birdcage Walk . . . At Buckingham Palace the crowd sang 'God Save the King' with tremendous fervour. His majesty came out onto the balcony overlooking the forecourt, wearing the uniform of an Admiral of the Fleet. He was joined by the Queen, the Prince of Wales and Princess Mary. The crowd greeted the king by singing, that homely British song 'For He's a Jolly Good Fellow' . . .

At the approach of the decisive hour of eleven (midnight German time) when the ultimatum to Germany was to expire, we returned in our thousands to Whitehall . . . From the Clock Tower of the Houses of Parliament came the light and gladsome chimes of the four quarters . . . Then came the slow and measured strokes of Big Ben proclaiming to London that it was eleven o'clock. We listened in silence. Perhaps it was but a reaction to the mood we were in, but I thought Big Ben was tolling the hour with an even more solemn note, for the pause between each stroke and its reverberation seemed unusually prolonged . . . At the eleventh stroke of the clock, the crowd, swarming in Downing Street, Parliament Street and Parliament Square, burst with one accord into 'God Save the King'.

Reservists Cause Problems for the Regulars

Lyn Macdonald in her book *1914* quotes the comments of Bandsman H. V. Shawyer, a regular soldier in the 1st Battalion, The Rifle Brigade, on discovering his barrack room had been taken over by reservists during his absence:

We found the barracks full of Reservists – many still in civilian dress – and more flocking in by almost every train. Fitting them out with uniform, boots and equipment was proceeding rapidly, but in some cases it was no easy job. Quite a few men had lost the soldierly figure they had taken with them into civil life. I remember one man in particular who must have weighed all of eighteen stone.

In fact the Quartermaster's staff couldn't fit him out, and he had to stay behind in England for several weeks until the training and the exercise – not to mention less sumptuous feeding! – tore about four stone off him.

It was hard on the Reservists, leaving good jobs and comfortable homes to come back to coarse uniforms and heavy boots. Even so, I found it hard to forgive them. Our Band Rooms were the showpiece of the Battalion, but after *they* took them over they looked like an old clothes shop down Petticoat Lane. All our review order tunics had been tossed into heaps in corners and our carefully creased black trousers were just lying around wholesale.

All our spare kit, our grey shirts and our socks and pants, had been pinched – we'd left in such a hurry there was no time to put things away securely.

Even so, we'd left our barrack rooms spick and span – hand-scrubbed floors, kit precisely folded and everything neat and tidy. I could hardly believe it was less than a week ago. I just stood inside the door with all my full kit still on and stared at it. I don't know what expression was on my face – disgust I suppose! – but one man who was stretched out smoking on *my* bed-cot had the cheek to say to me 'Never mind, kid. The war won't last long enough for you to get hurt. You're too young to worry.'

---

old militia and during recent reforms had been organized into formed units. Thus a third battalion of a two-battalion regular regiment became the reserve battalion. There were also several categories of these reservists, details of which are not necessary here; suffice it to say that these men were expected to have completed six months' recruit training and a month's annual camp, during which time they received the same pay as their regular comrades and a small bounty. They were subject to immediate recall to the colours, but only the top category was liable for overseas service. At the time of mobilization, the strength of the Special Reserve was almost 64,000 all ranks.

The Territorial Force (TF)

This organization was formed in early 1908 and was a key part of the army reforms instituted by the then secretary of state, the energetic Richard Haldane. This force replaced the old Volunteers raised in Napoleonic times to defend the country from invasion by the French. Originally intended to be used to reinforce regular units after six months' training, by 1914 the emphasis by the government had swung towards using it for home defence.

Territorial Force volunteers were expected to sign up for four years, complete a fixed number of drills (training days) and attend an annual two-week camp. Like army reservists, they were paid while in uniform and received an annual bounty. The force numbered just over 270,000 men and was organized in fourteen infantry divisions, including supporting Arms and Services, and fourteen cavalry brigades made up of yeomanry units. The TF also had several cyclist battalions which were employed patrolling the coast.

The New Armies

It was quickly recognized by the British government that, even with the call-up of the various categories of reservists, only a comparatively small expeditionary force could be sent to France in August 1914. There was a need to tap an entirely new source of voluntary manpower and thereby create a 'New Army' on a scale never before seen in Britain. This new force would be raised under the direction of the new secretary of state for war, Field Marshal Earl Kitchener (appointed on 6 August), a popular figure for his previous victories in Egypt and the Sudan.

The famous poster of Lord Kitchener's stern, moustachioed military face and pointing finger with the statement 'Your Country Needs You' was soon to be seen in towns and railway stations all over the country. It became (and probably still is) the most successful army recruiting poster ever printed. Kitchener got government agreement to raise 500,000 men in phases, the first 100,000 being known as the Kitchener 1, or, more commonly, the K1 group (K2–K6 would follow eventually). The plan was to form six divisions out of each group of 100,000 and every regular battalion was instructed to send a captain, two subalterns, two sergeants and thirteen reservist NCOs to regimental depots to organize and train the volunteers. These men were enlisted for three years or the duration of the war, and to distinguish them from regular, reserve or Territorial Force battalions they were termed Service Battalions.

There was no shortage of volunteers, with hundreds of somewhat elderly, unfit former officers and senior NCOs among them. Thousands rushed to join, spurred on by a wave of patriotic enthusiasm and spirit of

A TF Battalion Suffers Loss on British Soil

The 1/7th Battalion of the Royal Scots was the victim of the worst rail disaster ever to have occurred in Britain. The tragedy happened on 22 May 1915 near a small farmstead called Quintinshill, close to Gretna Green. A distracted signalman forgot about a stationary local train he had shunted on to the opposite line (the up line) to let through an express train on the down line, as both of the passing loops were already occupied. This led to a collision between a special troop train on the up line and the local train. Immediately afterwards, just as shocked and injured soldiers were leaving their train, the express train ploughed into the wreckage. In total 226 people died and 246 were injured. Of the two companies of the 1/7th, only sixty answered the roll

call next day. The exact number of soldier deaths is not known, as the roll of the regiment was destroyed in the fire. The conflagration was made worse as the troop train carriages were built with wooden bodies and frames and were gaslit. The fire burned for two days.

At the trial the jury reached its verdict in just eight minutes and the two signalmen, James Tinsley and George Meakin, were sentenced to three years' and eighteen months' imprisonment respectively for culpable homicide due to gross neglect of duties. The Board of Trade inquiry reported that if the signalmen had followed basic operating rules the accident would not have happened. Both men were released after a year but neither was called up to join the army.

British recruits taking the Oath of Allegiance.

adventure, and fuelled by the belief that the war would be short – probably over by Christmas. Then came news of the BEF having to retreat from Mons, information that caused the rush of volunteers to become a flood. By the end of December Kitchener's men numbered just over 800,000. By mid-1916 thirty New Army divisions had been raised, numbered from 9 to 26 and from 30 to 41. All but two of these, the 10th (Irish) and 13th (Western) Divisions, would see service on the Western Front at some stage during the war.

Locally raised (Pals) battalions

These also formed part of Kitchener's New Armies, but instead of being raised by the War Office (the predecessor of our Ministry of Defence) they were raised by wealthy and influential individuals or municipalities who undertook to clothe, billet and feed the recruits. The aim was to have units comprising friends, men with a common background or similar employment – often all three – hence the name Pals Battalions. They would enlist together, train together, fight together and countless thousands would die together at a devastating cost to particular industries, professions, businesses, towns, streets and even sports. For example, Leyton Orient Football Club were the first footballers to answer the call and enlisted in what became the 17th Battalion, the Middlesex

Regiment, which became known as 'The Footballers Battalion'.

Two examples illustrate how popular these Pals units were. The mining community of Barnsley produced several. Roni Wilkinson, in his book *PALS on the Somme 1916*, describes the raising of one such battalion:

> In Little Houghton, another pit village in the Barnsley coalfield, men completing the day shift flocked to the recreation ground to hear their local branch representative of the Yorkshire Miner's Association address them:

> *I put my weight behind Lord Kitchener's recruiting drive and I hope that miners will respond to the call. Colonel Hewitt has just told me that if at Houghton we get a company's strength, or two companies, that our men will be kept together. He assures me that just as you have worked together in the pit, you will be able to work together as soldiers.*

> After singing the National Anthem the men surged to the colliery offices and upwards of 200 handed in their names. The following morning they were taken by motor coaches to the outskirts of Barnsley. There they were formed up into four ranks and marched, as best they could, to the Public Hall to join other volunteers already gathered there. Along the way they sang with great gusto 'It's a Long Way to Tipperary'.

The second example occurred in the City of London. Here a reserve officer, Major the Hon. Robert White, a veteran of the Sudan Campaign of 1884–5 and the Second Boer War, volunteered to raise a battalion of a thousand men from City workers employed in the various financial houses. His recruiting office in Throgmorton Street was swamped with recruits and within a week some 1,600 had attested to become the 10th (Stockbrokers') Battalion of the Royal Fusiliers.

In all, 144 Pals or City battalions raised by local authorities or private organizations fought during the war. Of these, ninety-six were Pals/City units, such as the 1st or 2nd Liverpool, Barnsley or Bradford Pals; there were four Manchester Pals battalions. The Ulster Volunteer Force provided thirteen battalions (see box, page 214), the Tyneside Scottish and Irish eight, Public Schools and Sportsmen five each, and there was even one Church Lads' Brigade. As the huge losses mounted and the demand for replacements became ever more urgent, the height requirement for recruits was reduced several times so that eventually men under 5 feet could enlist in Bantam Battalions, which were grouped in the 35th (Bantam) Division.

The grimmest single day for Pals was suffered by the 34th Division on the opening day of the Somme. All twelve battalions that attacked that morning were Pals. Of the three brigades, the four battalions of the 102nd were Tyneside Scottish battalions of the Northumberland Fusiliers, while the four in the 103rd were Tyneside Irish bat-

Kitchener's famous recruiting poster.

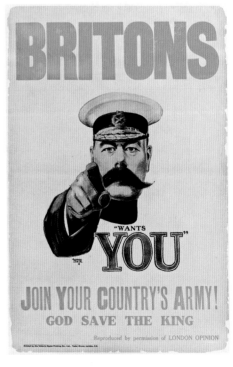

Old and New Divisions on the Somme, July 1916

As John Keegan points out in his book *The Face of Battle*, the seventeen divisions that attacked on 1 July 1916 illustrated the extent to which the British Army was a mixture of the old and new. Four of the divisions were regular. In the 4th Division five of its twelve fighting infantry battalions were Midland or North Country, two were Irish, two West Country, one Scottish, one East Anglian and one London. In the 7th and 8th Divisions one of the three brigades contained Kitchener New Army battalions, while the 29th Division contained the Newfoundland Regiment and the so-called Public Schools Battalion, but was otherwise regular. Three of the New Army divisions, the 21st, 30th and 32nd, had a regular battalion in each brigade. In the 18th, 31st, 34th and 36th New Army Divisions every battalion was a Kitchener battalion. And every man going forward into the hell that was the first day on the Somme, whether regular or New Army, was a volunteer.

talions of the same regiment. The brigades assaulted Sausage Valley and La Boiselle in column of battalions rather than extended line. The British preparatory barrage failed to cut the enemy's wire or destroy his positions, so the Pals were met with a storm of artillery and machine-gun fire that cut them down in their hundreds. It is said they lost 80 per cent of their number in just ten minutes. Certainly this division had the highest casualty count for 1 July – 6,380 killed, wounded and missing – of any attacking division. There was barely a street on Tyneside that was not in mourning as a result of this disaster.

Conscription

The ever-lengthening casualty lists caused acute manpower problems for all armies, not just the British, but only the British had relied solely on volunteers from the start. By the end of 1914 about 1.2 million men had enlisted and throughout the early months of the following year 100,000 a month had joined. However, it fast became apparent that this rate of recruitment could not be sustained by purely voluntary means, particularly with Kitchener stating that he needed 35,000 men a week as replacements. Lord Derby, under-secretary of state for war, drew up a scheme to register voluntarily every male aged between eighteen and forty. They would be grouped according to age, marital status and type of

employment, and would be called up in batches – the younger single men first. The results were poor, with many of those registered not appearing. A series of Military Service Acts was therefore passed which gradually imposed conscription, the first coming into force on 27 January 1916. By the end of the war, of the 5.7 million men who had worn uniform, just over half were conscripts.

The huge numbers of men enlisting during the first two years of the war had knock-on effects in every other area of the military machine. The country was not geared up industrially for war. Endless problems over accommodation, lack of uniforms and weapons, outdated weapons, insufficient ammunition and munitions for the artillery, a dearth of heavy artillery and inadequate medical facilities are just a few of the material difficulties that could not be overcome quickly. The personnel problems revolved around insufficient time for proper training, a lack of officers and senior NCOs for command, staff and training roles – a situation that the appalling casualty lists aggravated tenfold. On the Western Front, British officer deaths (including dominion and Indian) from all causes had risen to 36,722 by November 1918. Most of these difficulties are discussed further in the relevant sections of this book.

The BEF in August 1914 and 1918

The British Regular Army that took the field in France in August 1914 did so speedily after a largely seamless, well-planned and well-executed mobilization. It was superbly trained, with high morale, but it was incredibly small compared with the armies that France and Germany had already deployed. By the end of August it had six infantry and one cavalry division across the Channel and was fighting hard on the left of the French, to whom it was much the junior partner. The many months and battles that followed saw not only huge increases in manpower, heavy artillery and machine guns, but also commanders faced with the massive tactical problems associated with trench, or rather siege, warfare on a scale never dreamed of. These difficulties were largely brought about by the introduction of modern technology to warfare, of new weapons such as quick-firing artillery, gas, tanks and aircraft. All armies had to learn the new ways of war on the battlefield, and it was a hugely costly process; but by 1918 both Allies and Germans fought very different battles from the experimental slogging matches of 1915, 1916 and some of 1917. The table on the right shows statisti-

cally just how the British Army (excluding colonial forces) expanded, developed and changed during those four years.

The most striking thing shown by the table is the huge increase in percentage terms of the 'tail' (excluding the Labour Corps) compared to the 'dog'. While the infantry and artillery saw massive growth in overall numbers, in percentage terms the rise was a comparatively modest one. Note the cavalry's small increase as their role on the battlefield became so limited. By 1918 there were almost 3.5 million men under arms, so the demand for logistical support was monumentally increased. The extent to which technology and mechanization had begun to dominate the battlefield with new weapons of war is clear from the figures for the Royal Flying Corps, with a staggering personnel increase of almost 12,000 per cent, the Machine Gun Corps (infantry) jumping almost 3,300 per cent and the Tank Corps about 2,250. Apart from the Royal Flying Corps, the Veterinary Corps had the most spectacular percentage rise. This reflects the often forgotten fact that without horses and mules no army of that period could move or fight, and that animals were just as, if not more, vulnerable to sickness and wounds as any soldier. Finding remounts and their fodder became an all-consuming task for the remount and supply services. In August 1914 the army had 25,000 animals (horses and mules), four years later 735,409. By this date there were also 56,287 camels, bullocks and donkeys in the various theatres of war.

British Army Expansion 1914–1918

(figures are for all ranks, all theatres)

Branch of the Army	August 1914	August 1918	% increase
Cavalry	46,496	75,342	62
Infantry	306,654	1,684,039	449
Artillery (all branches)	86,041	529,068	515
Royal Engineers	24,035	357,389	1,387
Army Service Corps	14,491	326,388	2,152
Royal Army Medical Corps	17,840	138,017	673
Royal Army Veterinary Corps	508	27,471	5,307
Royal Army Pay Corps	578	14,549	2,417
Royal Army Ordnance Corps	2,505	30,446	1,115
Army Cyclist Corps	4,280 (Sept. 1914)	15,094	252
Machine Gun Corps			
Motorized	496 (Jan. 1915)	2,396	383
Infantry	3,536 (Feb. 1916)	119,986	3,293
Cavalry	676 (June 1916)	7,883	1,066
Tank Corps	1,202 (May 1916)	28,299	2,254
Royal Flying Corps (RAF from March)	1,200	144,078	11,906
Totals	**510,538**	**3,500,445**	**585**

The Canadian Army

In early 1914 Canada, with a population of fewer than 8 million, had no Regular Army, only a cadre of just over 3,000 professional soldiers whose primary duty was to garrison several coastal fortresses and train the militia. Within this Permanent Force, as it was called, was just one infantry battalion (the Royal Canadian Regiment); two cavalry regiments of two squadrons each (the Royal Canadian Dragoons and Lord Strathcona's Horse); two batteries of the Royal Canadian Horse Artillery; and five companies of the Royal Canadian Garrison Artillery. Various small administrative units supported this force. At best this represented one very weak brigade. By the end of the war this tiny force had expanded into the Canadian Expeditionary Force (CEF), consisting of four strong divisions of the Canadian Corps with supporting Arms and Services. Canadians had fought in every major battle on the Western Front, suffered some 232,000 casualties and were awarded sixty-nine Victoria Crosses. Along with the Australians, Canadian soldiers had gained a reputation as second to none in terms of fighting ability.

During the decade before the war, strenuous efforts had been made to expand and improve the training and organization of the Non-Permanent Active Militia. Canada had provided 8,000 men from various militia units to fight in the Second Boer War, during which four Canadians won the Victoria Cross. This success was the catalyst for a steady improvement in the effectiveness of the militia. By mid-1914 the establishment was just over 77,000 all ranks, with 17,410 horses. However, no force can fight without sufficient arms and equipment, and it was here that the Canadians, like all other nations, were confronted with serious difficulties. There were shortages of guns (only 200 modern pieces were available), British .303 Lee-Enfield rifles, horse-drawn and motor transport, uniforms and a host of other items.

With the outbreak of war the Canadian government telegraphed London to offer Canadian troops and set about raising an expeditionary force and solving the associated problems. The initial objective was to raise an infantry division of around 20,000 men, and on 6 August the minister of militia informed all militia commanding officers that the CEF would be mobilized and that their quota of volunteers should assemble at Camp Valcartier, then being constructed by engineers, for training. This camp was a marvel of what could be achieved in three weeks. A mile of rifle ranges, a telephone system, waterworks, electric lighting, stores, offices and even a cinema had sprung up. By the end of August over 30,000 volunteers had arrived

– far more than expected or asked for, and almost every unit was over strength. Many individuals had jumped on the troop trains without authority and came on their own responsibility. Several regiments, such as the Queen's Own of Toronto and the Royal Highlanders of Montreal, sent an entire battalion, while the Fort Garry Horse of Winnipeg arrived unexpectedly on two privately chartered troop trains. However, Canada's English- and French-speaking populations were divided, with enthusiasm to fight stronger in the former than the latter. Of the first contingent of volunteers assembled for

The Ross Rifle

This was the weapon with which the Canadian infantryman went to war in 1914 and used until the British Lee-Enfield finally replaced it in late 1916. Arguments as to the merits and demerits of these two rifles were protracted, with the subject repeatedly discussed in the press and Canadian parliament. The final verdict of the infantryman was that the British weapon was far more reliable for everyday use in the trenches, but that for long-range sniping the Ross was better because of its greater accuracy and superior sights – although the rounds had to be spotlessly clean or the weapon would jam.

By 1914 numerous defects found in the first versions of the Ross had supposedly been eliminated. However, problems soon surfaced. The 30½-inch barrel was cumbersome and difficult to use in a narrow trench, particularly with a bayonet fixed. When fired with a fixed bayonet it was not uncommon for the bayonet to fall off. But its worst defect was its tendency to jam when used in the dirty, muddy conditions of the trenches. The bolt could be disassembled for cleaning and inadvertently reassembled in such a way that the bolt would fail to lock but would still allow a round to be fired, causing the bolt to fly back and injure the firer – although this was a rare occurrence. Many Canadians in the 1st Division who held the line against the German gas attack at Ypres in 1915 retrieved Lee-Enfields from British casualties to replace their Ross rifles.

The famous Canadian sniper Captain Herbert W. McBride, who served in the 21st Battalion of the CEF, considered several of the problems more related to the poor quality of much of the ammunition supplied for the rifle. He claimed that 'some brands would not work at all and many others were woefully deficient, causing many stoppages and breakages, often at extremely critical times.'

Only when the Canadian minister of militia and defence, Colonel Sam Hughes, an inflexible advocate for the Ross, was forced to resign in November 1916 did the Canadians all finally replace their Ross rifles with British Lee-Enfields.

training at Valcartier, at least two thirds were British-born. Recruiting was always more difficult among the French-Canadian population, although one regiment, the 22nd (the Van Doos), was French-speaking.

Unsurprisingly, the first few weeks in camp were chaotic. All was confusion as the military authorities sought to place the thousands of men into units, and to accommodate, feed, equip and provide uniforms for the ever-growing numbers. However, by mid-September a proper training programme had begun, with the emphasis on weapon training. Although the initial intention was to send just one division, it was decided that all 83,000 men under training would go to England.

By the third week in September a flotilla of thirty-one transport ships had been assembled at Quebec to take the first contingent. The loading, which began on 27 September, was something of a disaster due to a total lack of planning and communications. Units were embarked on to one ship but their equipment went to another, guns were loaded with their wheels on and so took up too much room; stores that would be needed first on arrival were put on first and ended up buried under less urgent items. In the end much equipment was left behind. On 3 October, escorted by British warships, the convoy sailed in three parallel lines to be joined out at sea by a ship that carried the Newfoundland Regiment (see box opposite). After a two-week voyage, fortunately undisturbed by German submarines, the transports arrived at Plymouth.

Further training was to be carried out on Salisbury Plain in southern England (still the main training area for the British Army in that part of the country). It was to be a miserable experience, due entirely to appalling weather. Within days of arrival the clouds opened and for day after day the rain poured down, converting the ground into a morass and drenching tents, uniforms and men. Everything was soaked and impossible to dry. Life became a wretched existence, training was impossible and sickness mounted until the local hospitals were overflowing – in many ways it foreshadowed conditions most of the men would soon experience in France. The rain, mud and boredom took their toll on discipline. Hundreds went absent without leave, some to the hotels and fleshpots of London, returning when their money ran out to face their punishment, others not returning until after their unit had left for France.

Apart from a hospital unit, the first troops to go to France were the Princess Patricia's Canadian Light Infantry (PPCLI), usually known as 'Princess Pats'. It was named after the daughter of the Canadian governor general, the Duke of Connaught, and it was she who had personally embroidered the regiment's colours. This regiment had been raised separately from the main Canadian contingent due to the generosity of one of its officers, the Montreal millionaire Captain Andrew Hamilton Gault. It was mainly composed of British reservists and veterans, some of whom had seen service in the Second Boer War. It was regarded as an elite unit and was sent to France in December 1914 to join the British 27th Division. It would not rejoin its compatriots for a year.

The 1st Canadian Division did not arrive in France until early February 1915. A Canadian Corps of two divisions was formed there later that year, and in 1916 it reached its full strength of four divisions. On 9 June 1917 the Canadian Corps got its first Canadian commander, Lieutenant General Sir Arthur Currie, former commander of the 1st Division. A fifth division was also formed in England, but only its divisional artillery and certain specialist units were sent to the front. The CEF eventually numbered 262 infantry battalions, thirteen mounted rifle regiments, thirteen railway troop battalions, five pioneer battalions, plus field and heavy artillery batteries, ambulance, medical, dental, forestry, labour, tunnelling, cyclist and various supply and line of communication units. A special unit within the CEF was the Canadian Machine Gun Corps, consisting of

Newly arrived Canadian troops on their way to Plymouth station, 1914.

The Royal Newfoundland Regiment

Newfoundland became a self-governing dominion of the British Empire on 26 September 1907 so, like other parts of the empire, was bound by British foreign policy and entered the war on 4 August 1914. From a tiny population, the 1st Newfoundland Regiment of one battalion was raised to fight alongside the British Army. It initially acquired the nickname the 'Blue Puttees' as a shortage of material prevented the soldiers wearing the standard olive drab ones. A total of 6,241 Newfoundlanders served with the regiment during the war and another 5,747 served in other units.

The regiment was initially sent to Gallipoli, landing at Suvla Bay in September 1915. In three months there the regiment lost forty men killed or died of disease, while at least 150 were treated for frostbite and exposure. It was among the last to withdraw from Gallipoli in early January 1916 en route to the Western Front.

On the opening day of the Battle of the Somme some 800 Newfoundland soldiers went over the top at Beaumont-Hamel just north of Albert. The regiment was scheduled to attack as part of the follow-up wave to reinforce the hoped-for success of those who had gone before. It did not happen like that. The Newfoundlanders discovered the forward trenches from which they were to start

jammed with dead and dying men from the first waves, so they were forced to jump off from secondary trenches, which meant their exposed advance would be over a greater distance than planned. The advance was a disaster. Despite incredible courage, devastating machine-gun and artillery fire cut them down in swathes. The Newfoundland Regiment never made it past its own barbed wire. That day the regiment lost 255 dead, 386 wounded and 91 missing. Every officer who tried to advance that day was either killed or wounded, and the following day only sixty-nine men answered the roll call. The regiment had been all but wiped out. Newfoundlanders (now Canadians) commemorate 1 July not just as Canada Day but also as Memorial Day.

The regiment was brought back up to strength within six weeks. It fought in Flanders and again on the Somme in October 1916. But it was at Monchy-le-Preux during the Battle of Arras in late April 1917 that Newfoundlanders were once more crippled by heavy losses. Here they lost 485 men in one day while holding off a massive German assault. Then at the Battle of Cambrai in November 1917 they stood their ground although outflanked, an achievement that won them the honour of being called the 'Royal' Newfoundland Regiment – the only regiment of the British Empire to be granted that honour during the actual war.

On 14 October 1918 seventeen-year-old Private Thomas Ricketts of the regiment became the youngest soldier to win the Victoria Cross during the war when he exposed himself to heavy machine-gun fire while doubling back to find more ammunition for a Lewis gun during an attack on an enemy gun battery. This selfless action was instrumental in the capture of four field guns, four machine guns and eight prisoners. Ricketts was also in receipt of the Distinguished Conduct Medal and the French *Croix de Guerre* with Golden Star. He died in St John's, Newfoundland, on 10 February 1967.

four three-company battalions, bringing the divisional complement of heavy Vickers machine guns to ninety-six. One battalion was attached to each division in the corps.

The Canadian Corps fought with great distinction on the Western Front and became recognized as one of the elite formations within the Allied armies. The major battles in which it was heavily engaged included:

1915 Battles of Ypres (including Gravenstafel Ridge, St-Julien, Frezenberg Ridge and Bellewaarde Ridge), Festubert and Loos.

1916 Battles of Mount Sorrel and the Somme (Bazentin Ridge, Pozières Ridge, Flers-Courcelette, Thiepval Ridge, Le Transloy Ridges, Ancre Heights and the Ancre).

1917 Battles of Arras (Vimy Ridge, Arleux and Third Scarpe), Hill 70, Ypres (Second Passchendaele) and Cambrai.

1918 First Battles of the Somme (St-Quentin), Battles of the Lys, Second Somme, Second Arras (the Scarpe and Drocourt–Quéant Canal), Battles of the Hindenburg Line (Canal du Nord, St-Quentin Canal, Beaurevoir Line and Cambrai), Valenciennes and the Sambre.

According to Colonel G. W. L. Nicholson's *Canadian Expeditionary Force 1914–1918*, the official history of the Canadian Army in the First World War, 619,636 Canadian men and women served in Canada's army during the war. Losses included 51,748 soldiers or nursing sisters who were killed in action or died of wounds, as well as 7,796 who died of other causes such as sickness or accidental injuries. Army fatalities totalled 59,544 – almost 10 per cent of those who served – while total casualties of all types amounted to 232,494.

Inside the Grange Tunnel at Vimy Ridge. This tunnel was 800 yards long with side bays for headquarters, signal centres and water-storage points, and with standing room for waiting soldiers. It was part of the 6 miles of tunnels dug before the battle. The Canadian attack here was made by the 7th Brigade of the 3rd Division.

The Canadians take Vimy Ridge

The Canadian attack on Vimy Ridge was part of the opening phase of the larger Battle of Arras, which was in turn a diversionary attack for the French offensive on Chemin des Dames. The Canadian objective was to capture the German-held high ground (Vimy Ridge) that dominated the Plains of Douai, allowing the southern flank of the Arras offensive to advance without being fired on from the flank. The Germans had held this ridge since October 1914 and its 4-mile length was honeycombed with tunnels, concrete bunkers and machine-gun nests, with the front line consisting of three trench lines behind heavy belts of barbed wire. The three German divisions in the line were part of the Sixth Army and were determined not to relinquish control over this magnificent observation platform, which also sheltered the Lens coalfields, essential for their war effort. This was the first time the four Canadian divisions had attacked as a corps and its success became a national symbol of sacrifice and triumph.

Undoubtedly one of the primary reasons for this success was the meticulous planning and preparation carried out beforehand:

• **Artillery** After seeking advice from the French on their experiences at Verdun (their recapture of Fort Douaumont in particular), the Canadian plan envisaged an advance on to four coloured linear objectives (consecutively Black, Red, Blue and Brown), the infantry proceeding close behind a creeping barrage fired by light field guns on a tightly timed schedule of 100-yard increments. The heavier howitzers would fire standing barrages further ahead of the infantry against known strongpoints and enemy gun batteries. The infantry battalions would leapfrog through each other from one objective to the next and reserves would be pushed through, after a pause on the Red Line, to maintain the momentum. The artillery force delivering this fire plan was formidable: twenty-four brigade artillery groups consisting of 480 18-pounders, twenty-four 9.45-inch mortars, ninety-six 2-inch trench mortars and 245 siege guns and heavy mortars. The artillery plan included a two-week preliminary bombardment of German strongpoints, batteries and trenches staring on 20 March. The second phase began on 2 April with every single gun or mortar available to the corps.

• **Training** In February 1917 the neglected tactical doctrine of fire and movement was officially proclaimed as the tactics for infantry in a new training pamphlet. The Canadians adopted it and trained in its use enthusiastically and repeatedly prior to the assault. All battalions practised walking in

blob formation (small dispersed groups) behind a simulated creeping barrage over and over again until most of the troops were thoroughly fed up with it – but the procedure became second nature.

• **Trench raids** The Canadians carried out fifty-five trench raids, the largest involving a full brigade, in the four months before the attack. In this way they dominated the enemy and secured valuable information from prisoners and observation of the enemy's defences.

• **Tunnelling/mining operations** In the soft, porous but stable chalk of the area around Vimy mining and tunnelling warfare had been a prominent feature of the fighting since 1915. This had resulted in nineteen mine craters along the Canadian front before the coming battle. British tunnelling companies, with Canadian assistance, had placed thirteen mines under German forward positions, although only three were detonated in support of the assault. An extensive underground system of twelve subways – the longest (The Grange) was almost three quarters of a mile long and 30 feet deep – was built to connect the reserve lines to the front lines. These allowed attacking troops to move to the front unharmed and unseen.

Notes for Map 28

Belligerents

British	German
First Army	Sixth Army
Canadian Corps	I Bavarian Reserve Corps

Divisions

5 (inc. British 5th Division)	3

Commanders

Lt Gen. Sir Julian Byng	Gen. Ludwig, Freiherr von Falkenhausen

Casualties

10,600 (3,600 killed, 7,000 wounded)	uncertain (4,000 prisoners)

Result

The Canadians took control of Vimy Ridge. This was the first time in her history that Canada had fielded a corps-sized formation.

Summary

Under cover of a carefully planned barrage of over 1,100 cannon of all types, almost 100,000 men were involved in taking this vital, dominating ridge which the Germans had held for so long. All four Canadian divisions attacked, with the British 5th Division in support. In less than two hours three of the four Canadian divisions had taken their objectives; the 4th Division was held up by machine-gun nests on Point 145. However, the 85th Nova Scotia Highlanders took Point 145 later on 9 April. By the end of the day on the 12th the ridge belonged to the Canadians – a triumph that involved the 10th Canadian Brigade attacking the Pimple in a snowstorm.

MAP 28 THE CANADIANS CAPTURE VIMY RIDGE, 9–12 APRIL 1917

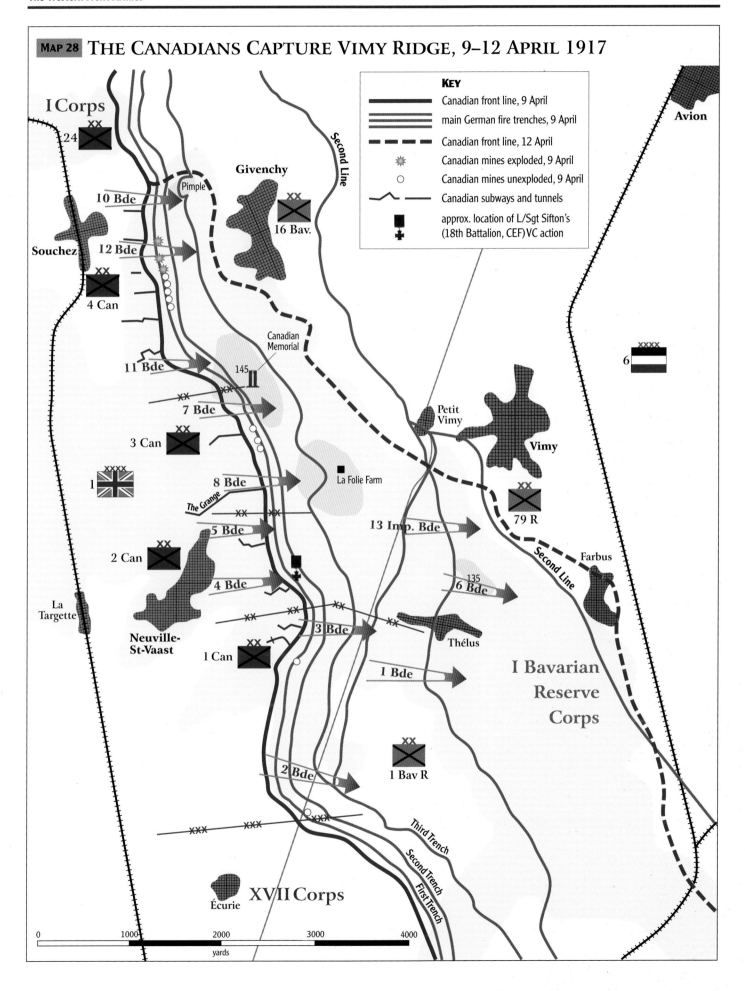

KEY

- ——— Canadian front line, 9 April
- ===== main German fire trenches, 9 April
- - - - - Canadian front line, 12 April
- ✳ Canadian mines exploded, 9 April
- ○ Canadian mines unexploded, 9 April
- ∿∿— Canadian subways and tunnels
- ■✠ approx. location of L/Sgt Sifton's (18th Battalion, CEF) VC action

I Corps

124

Souchez

4 Can

10 Bde

12 Bde

Pimple

Givenchy

16 Bav.

Second Line

11 Bde

145

Canadian Memorial

7 Bde

3 Can

1

8 Bde

La Folie Farm

Petit Vimy

Vimy

79 R

The Grange

5 Bde

2 Can

4 Bde

13 Imp. Bde

Farbus

Second Line

La Targette

Neuville-St-Vaast

1 Can

3 Bde

135

6 Bde

Thélus

1 Bde

I Bavarian Reserve Corps

2 Bde

1 Bav R

Third Trench

Second Trench

First Trench

Écurie

XVII Corps

6

Avion

0   1000   2000   3000   4000

yards

Canadian Victoria Crosses

Sixty-nine members of the Canadian Expeditionary Force were awarded the Victoria Cross on the Western Front, four of them for actions at Vimy Ridge.

Lance Sergeant Ellis Wellwood Sifton was in C Company, the 18th Battalion (West Ontario Regiment) on the morning of 9 April 1917. During the attack his company was held up by withering enemy machine-gun fire inflicting heavy losses. The citation for Sifton's VC reads:

. . . having located the gun he charged it single handed, killing all the crew. A small enemy party advanced down the trench, but he succeeded in keeping these off until our men had gained the position. In carrying out this gallant act he was killed, but his conspicuous valour undoubtedly saved many lives and contributed largely to the success of the operation.

What the official wording omits was that Sergeant Sifton killed the German crew in close hand-to-hand combat with his clubbed rifle and bayonet, and that shortly after, as he was supervising the surrender of more enemy, one of the wounded Germans reached for his rifle and shot Sifton at point-blank range, killing him instantly.

• **Air support** The Royal Flying Corps deployed twenty-five squadrons with 365 aircraft to gain control of the air for artillery-spotting, observation and photography behind enemy lines. The enemy was outnumbered two to one in the air and although the RFC lost 131 aircraft it did not prevent it achieving its objectives in the weeks prior to the offensive.

The Canadian Corps was commanded by the British Lieutenant General Sir Julian Byng. His four divisions and one reserve were supported in the north by the British 24th Division and to the south by XVII Corps. His plan was for the 4th Canadian Division in the north to take Point 145 and later the heavily defended knoll known as the Pimple. The 3rd Canadian Division was responsible for the narrow central section of the ridge,

Part of Vimy Ridge from the German rear area, taken from the D51 road midway between Vimy and Givenchy. It shows how important to both sides it was to hold such a prominent feature for observation.

including La Folie Farm, while the 2nd Canadian Division, later supported by the British 13th Brigade from the 5th British Division, was tasked to capture the small town of Thélus. The veteran 1st Canadian Division, under Major General Arthur Currie (as he then was), was ordered to take the southern section of the ridge – a task that involved the longest advance of all.

Under cover of the fire of over 1,100 guns of all calibres, including several enormous rail-mounted naval guns, the leading waves of some 15,000 infantry advanced in the frosty dawn of 9 April, Easter Monday. The troops kept close to the creeping barrage (known as the 'Vimy Glide') and, with machine-gun barrages arching overhead, made good progress in all areas except the north. Within less than two hours, and after some bitter and bloody fighting, all divisions except the 4th had taken their objectives. Although in many cases the German trenches had been obliterated, the 4th Division had been held up by the machine-gun nests on the highest point of the ridge around Point 145. Here the 87th Battalion suffered 50 per cent casualties and it was not until the 85th Nova Scotia Highlanders were sent in that the hill was finally taken by the end of the day.

On 12 April, in darkness and a raging snowstorm, the 10th Canadian Brigade attacked the Pimple, by then defended by Prussian guardsmen rushed forward as reinforcements. Within two hours the strongpoint was taken and many prisoners captured.

By 12 April the Canadians had control of the ridge at a cost of 3,598 killed and 7,002 wounded. The number of German casualties is uncertain, except that over 4,000 prisoners were taken along with 54 artillery pieces, 124 machine guns and 104 trench mortars. King George V signalled that 'Canada will be proud that the taking of the coveted Vimy Ridge has fallen to the lot of her troops.'

Vimy Commemoration

The Vimy Memorial, Canada's largest war monument, commemorates the 11,285 missing dead from Canada who fell in France; those missing in Flanders (7,024) have their names inscribed on the walls of the Menin Gate at Ypres. The memorial stands on what was Hill 145, the highest point on the ridge and the strongest point of the German defences. In 1922 the land for the battlefield park was granted in perpetuity by the French nation to the people of Canada in recognition of Canada's contribution to the war. The memorial took eleven years to build and cost $1.5 million; it was unveiled by King Edward VIII on 26 July 1936, shortly before his abdication, in the presence of President Albert Lebrun of France and over 50,000 Canadian and French veterans and their families.

The ninetieth anniversary of the battle for Vimy Ridge was commemorated on 9 April 2007 (Easter Monday) in towns and cities across Canada and at the recently restored memorial itself. Some 25,000 people, mostly Canadians (including over 5,000 students), attended a rededication ceremony at the memorial. Queen Elizabeth II performed the rededication, as Queen of Canada, and speeches were given by the prime ministers of Canada and France.

German troops surrender to the advancing Canadians on Vimy Ridge, April 1917.

The Armies of Australia and New Zealand

To British 'Tommies' Australian soldiers were known as 'Diggers' (former goldminers), while New Zealanders were called 'Kiwis' after their national bird. The Australians and New Zealanders called each other 'Digger'. Both Australia and New Zealand made a massive contribution to the Allied war effort when the size of their populations at the time is considered. The Australians, with fewer than 5 million people, sent 14 per cent of her male population to fight overseas, of whom some 203,100 became casualties (54,600 killed and 148,500 wounded) on the Western Front. An even greater percentage sacrifice was made by New Zealand. From a population of just over a million, 128,500 enlisted (including 2,688 Maoris and 346 Pacific Islanders), of whom 103,000 served overseas, about 20 per cent of the male population. Of these 16,710 were killed or reported missing and 41,820 were wounded or taken prisoner, with the Western Front accounting for 12,500 of the killed. In addition, nearly 3,400 served in the Australian or Imperial forces.

Recruitment began on 10 August 1914 after the Australian government undertook to put the 20,000 men in its Regular Army and 45,000 part-time militia at the disposal of the British government. A volunteer force called the Australian Imperial Force (AIF) was created for service overseas. At the same time in New Zealand the government used its 600 regular soldiers and 25,000 Territorials as the basis for forming the New Zealand Expeditionary Force (NZEF). The first contingents from both countries left for Europe on board troopships in early November 1914, with the second convoy sailing at the end of the year. Initially destined for the Western Front, they were diverted to Egypt for training as there was an acute shortage of accommodation in England (swamped with New Army volunteers). While they were in Egypt further reinforcements arrived and it was decided that the Australian and New Zealand forces should be combined into what was to be known as the Australia and New Zealand Army Corps (ANZAC). From Egypt the ANZAC was sent not to Europe but to take part in the disastrous Gallipoli campaign, which cost it around 30,000 casualties, including 10,000 dead. It was withdrawn back to Egypt in December 1915 for further training, rest and expansion.

As a result of being substantially reinforced in Egypt, the combined Australian and New Zealand forces were divided into two army corps: I ANZAC, consisting of the 1st and 2nd Australian Divisions – a formation that sailed for France in February 1916; and II ANZAC, consisting of the 4th and 5th Australian and New Zealand Divisions, which left Egypt the following May. The 3rd Australian Division, which was forming in Australia, joined II ANZAC after training in England in late December 1916. An ANZAC mounted division containing the New Zealand Mounted Brigade and an Australian mounted division (the latter formed in early 1917) were deployed to participate in the ultimately successful campaign against the Turks in the Sinai Peninsula and Palestine.

Once in France, the ANZAC was under the command of General Sir William 'Birdy' Birdwood, an Indian Army cavalry officer, until 30 May 1918 when Lieutenant General John Monash became the first Australian to command it. On arrival on the Western Front it became part of the BEF and was sent to a quiet part of the line near Armentières nicknamed the 'Nursery' to conduct raids and learn the new ways of war in the trenches. A brief look at ANZAC divisional records on the Western Front is given below. The casualty figures are best estimates.

The New Zealand Memorial at Broodseinde, showing part of the area over which the New Zealand Divisions attacked on 4 October 1917 – it was the first bound in what became known as the Third Battle of Ypres (Passchendaele). Overall the battle was a great success, with 5,000 prisoners taken (the New Zealanders 1,150) and recovered the southern end of the Passchendaele Ridge.

New Zealand Memorial

part of New Zealanders' attack

I ANZAC

- **1st Division AIF** First saw serious action in 1916 on the Somme when it was sent to reinforce the front near Albert and was thrown in on 23 July to take the ruined but fortified village of Pozières on the Thiepval–Pozières Ridge. It was a bloody introduction. The Australians took most of their objective but at a high price – in four days they lost 5,285 all ranks. The division was again in action on the Somme at Flers-Courcelette in October 1916.

It was moved to the Ypres sector and given time for recovery and reinforcement before becoming part of the general advance to follow up the German withdrawal behind the Hindenburg Line in the spring of 1917. In May of that year it fought in the Second Battle of Bullecourt, followed by the Third Battle of Ypres (Menin Road) in September and Broodseinde in October.

April 1918 saw the division defending the line at Hazebrouck during the German offensive of 21 March. It then rejoined I ANZAC for the British counter-offensive at Amiens in August and took part in the fighting that broke through the Hindenburg Line and ended the war.

The 1st Division suffered about 51,000 casualties (15,000 killed and 36,000 wounded) during the war. Its divisional memorial is at Pozières.

- **2nd Division AIF** First went into battle to relieve the 1st Division in late July 1916 on the Somme and succeeded in taking Pozières Ridge at a heavy cost. It continued to be involved in intense fighting on the Somme in August and November. In 1917 it was involved in the pursuit of the Germans when they withdrew to the Hindenburg Line.

This culminated in its participation in the Second Battle of Bullecourt. Like the 1st Division, it fought at Menin Road in September and Broodseinde in November.

1918 saw the division participating in the halting of the German spring offensive and the subsequent Allied advance from Amiens in August. However, its most remarkable success was the capture in August of the strongly fortified Mont St-Quentin feature – an action that has been described by some as 'the finest single feat of the war'. In an extremely skilfully planned and conducted assault, the division took its objective at a cost of 3,200 casualties while inflicting some 15,000 on the enemy. It then saw action in the breaking through of the Hindenburg Line and the final advance beyond. It was the last ANZAC formation to be withdrawn from the fighting on the Western Front.

Estimated total losses for the war amounted to 50,500 all ranks (12,600 killed and 37,900 wounded). The divisional memorial is at Mont St-Quentin.

II ANZAC

- **3rd Division AIF** Arrived in France at the end of December 1916 and, like its compatriot formations, spent some months in the 'Nursery'. It saw action at Messines in July 1917 and with the 1st and 2nd Divisions at Broodseinde in October, but at Passchendaele later in the same month its attack was repulsed with severe losses.

The next year it fought to halt the German advance in late March, then took part in the successful driving of the Germans back to and beyond the Hindenburg Line, playing a prominent part in the Battles of Amiens, Hamel, the breaking of the

Hindenburg Line and Mont St-Quentin. Of particular note were the skilful tactics employed by the division in the attacks around Sailly-le-Sec near the River Somme.

Losses on the Western Front (the division did not participate in the Gallipoli campaign) amounted to 31,000 (6,800 killed and 24,200 wounded). Its memorial is at Sailly-le-Sec.

- **4th Division AIF** In August 1916 this division moved from the Armentières area to the Somme with the 1st and 2nd Divisions and later relieved the 2nd Division on the Pozières Ridge. On 6 August it entered the battle to hold the ground that its fellow Australians had gained against enemy counter-attacks. It also attacked Mouquet Farm (known invariably as 'Mucky' Farm) a mile north-west of Pozières and became involved in bitter and extremely costly fighting in the area for another month without making further progress. The *Australian Official History* of the war states that 'The Pozières windmill site is more densely sown with Australian sacrifice than any other place on earth.' There is now a memorial on the site of that windmill. This division took part in the Battle of Flers-Courcelette in October 1916.

It played a major role in the First Battle of Bullecourt in April 1917 (see page 110). The division was then moved to Flanders, where it was involved in the successful action at Messines in June and in September at Polygon Wood in the Passchendaele offensive.

1918 saw it on the Somme helping to stem the German offensive at Hebuterne and Dernancourt in March, followed by a successful counter-attack at Villers-Bretonneux in April. The division fought at Hamel, Amiens and the breaching of the Hindenburg Line, with its final action of the war taking place at Bellenglise, part of the German defences behind the St-Quentin Canal.

Western Front casualties (the division did not fight in the Gallipoli campaign) were 38,900 (11,800 killed and 27,100 wounded). Its memorial is at Bellenglise.

- **5th Division AIF** In July 1916, after only a few days in the 'Nursery', the division was ordered to attack the high ground held by the Germans at Fromelles. Attacking on a narrow front in daylight under extremely heavy machine-gun and artillery fire, the Australians broke into part of the enemy defences and held on against several counter-attacks coming in from the flanks. A withdrawal became inevitable and the cost incurred in twenty-four hours of incessant and bloody fighting was a quarter of the division's strength – over 5,500 killed, wounded and missing. In October the division fought at Flers-Courcelette on the Somme.

The 45th Australian Battalion attacking the Hindenburg Line, 18 September 1918.

Left: *The first use of tanks, 15 September 1916. There were four tanks under 2nd Lieutenant H. G. F. Brown supporting the 2nd New Zealand Brigade (2nd Auckland and 2nd Otago) in the attack west of Flers on 15 September 1916. Brown's tank, D8, was to advance along the extreme left flank of the divisional sector to the Flers–l'Abbaye road, known as Abbey Road, north-west of Flers village. This was a distance of around 2 miles and involved crossing three separate German trench lines.*

During the advance D8 operated on its own, as the other three tanks became embroiled in the fighting through the enemy positions south-west of Flers.

Right: *D8 continues its fighting advance, swinging left (west) of Flers towards Abbey Road. As shown on Map 28, this tank advanced some distance beyond its objective before turning back.*

Captain Jacka, VC, MC and Bar, 14th Battalion, AIF

Captain Albert 'Bert' Jacka won his Victoria Cross as a lance corporal in Gallipoli and his two MCs as an officer in France. A native of Victoria, Jacka came from a humble background with only a basic elementary schooling. He had worked as a labourer before enlisting as a private in the 14th Battalion in September 1914. His exploits and VC quickly made him famous in Australia. His likeness was used on recruiting posters and his deeds featured in numerous newspapers. The acts that gained him his two Military Crosses illustrate vividly his exceptional courage, even more perhaps than the action that won him the VC.

In early August 1916 the 1st Australian Brigade had captured part of the Pozières Ridge near a ruined windmill. This had caused a salient that the Germans were determined to retake. On the night of 14 August the salient in which Second Lieutenant Jacka's battalion was defending was subjected to a hurricane of shellfire from three sides. Australia's official historian, C. E. W. Bean (who was present), described it as 'the crowning bombardment of the whole series'. Jacka's platoon had spent the night sheltering in an old German dugout and the thunder and crash of the German barrage had kept them below ground as the first wave of enemy rolled over their position. The first Jacka knew of the Germans' arrival was a bomb lobbed down the steps of the dugout. The shock of the concussion was tremendous. A dazed Jacka stumbled up the steps armed with a revolver to be confronted by the second wave of German attackers milling about, with a group of them escorting some forty Australian prisoners to the rear.

With only seven surviving members of his platoon, Jacka determined to fight his way out by attacking the sixty or more Germans nearby. Jacka and his men charged the enemy; two of his group immediately fell dead and the others were wounded, Jacka himself seven times. Each time he fell he miraculously picked himself up and charged on with his men, emptying his revolver in all directions before picking up a rifle and bayonet and personally accounting for as many as twelve Germans. The Australian prisoners turned on their captors, and men from nearby platoons joined in, with the result that some fifty enemy were turned from captors to captured. As the casualties were brought in Sergeant (later Captain) E. J. Rule asked a stretcher-bearer, 'Who've you got there?' The soldier replied, 'I don't know who I've got, but the bravest man in the Aussie Army is on that stretcher just ahead. It's Bert Jacka, and I wouldn't give a Gyppo [Egyptian] piastre for him: he's knocked about dreadfully.' Most witnesses considered Jacka should have got a second Victoria Cross rather than a Military Cross for this exploit. Bean was later to describe Jacka's action at Pozières as 'the most dramatic and effective act of individual audacity in the history of the AIF.'

After recovering in England Jacka refused an offer to return to Australia and instead rejoined his battalion in December 1916. He was promoted captain and became the battalion intelligence officer. He won his second MC during the Battle of Arras and in particular the first Battle of Bullecourt in early April 1917 (see Map 30). Two hours before his battalion was due to advance, Jacka was crawling around in no-man's-land trying to check on the German wire while his men lay in the snow (it was dreadfully unseasonable weather) when he spotted a German officer and soldier who could clearly see the waiting troops. Jacka leapt up, raised his revolver and pulled the trigger, but the weapon misfired. Undaunted, Jacka captured the two and brought them back to Australian lines.

The previous night on another patrol Jacka had found the German wire uncut by the artillery bombardment and had reported to the brigade commander that it was 'pure murder to attempt the operation'. Like his previous disputes with senior officers, such comments did not endear him to higher command. Nor did his critical after-battle report on the use of tanks – a report which, it was later accepted, highlighted valuable tactical lessons.

In May 1918, near Villers-Bretonneux, Jacka received the wound that ended his combat career. On his return to Australia in September 1919 he was greeted by a large welcoming crowd and described in one newspaper as 'the symbol of the spirit of the ANZACs'. His civilian career included running an electrical goods business and being elected mayor of St Kilda (a suburb of Melbourne) in 1929. However, after his business failed in 1930 his health deteriorated and he died of kidney disease in 1931, aged thirty-nine. He was buried with full military honours in St Kilda cemetery. Over 6,000 people filed past his coffin as it lay in state. It was borne to its final resting place by eight Victoria Cross holders at the head of a procession of over a thousand former soldiers and watched by thousands of silent onlookers.

New Zealanders in a communication trench at Flers, September 1916.

The New Zealand Division at Flers

The Battle of Flers-Courcelette was the third phase of the Battle of the Somme. It is best known as the first time in history that tanks appeared on a battlefield. It was to involve the British Fourth Army and part of the Reserve Army (later the Fifth Army). The plan was for XV Corps to break through the German lines north-east of Flers, allowing the cavalry to get into the enemy rear. The New Zealand Division, deployed on a narrow front, was to force a break in the German line held by the 4th Bavarian Division immediately west of Flers. The opening attack was scheduled for 15 September. The advance was preceded by a prodigious artillery bombardment – one field gun to every 10 yards of front and one heavy gun to every 29 yards. The New Zealand Division was one of twelve divisions attacking that day, but only thirty-two of the forty-nine tanks available to support the infantry in fighting through the German trench lines made it to the start line. The tanks were spread out in penny packets across the whole front being attacked. Four of them attacked with the Kiwis and did valuable work in fighting through the Brown Line and north-west of Flers. Tank D8 penetrated as far as Grove Alley and survived the day; D10 and D12 were knocked out earlier in the day and D11 on 16 September.

In March 1917 it took part in the follow-up of the Germans as they retreated behind their new defences on the Hindenburg Line and captured the town of Bapaume. In May it relieved the 1st Australian Division and fought in the First Battle of Bullecourt, an action that included repulsing several enemy counter-attacks. The highlight of its success that year took place in September when its action was crucial in the Allied success in capturing Polygon Wood.

In 1918, like the other Australian divisions, the 5th took part in checking the German spring offensive and fought well, defending several Somme bridges. In April it launched a counter-attack that secured Villers-Bretonneux. In July it was involved in the fight for Hamel and the next month at Amiens at the start of the great British counter-offensive. It forced a crossing of the Somme in September and took part in the breaking of the Hindenburg Line.

Recent research has indicated that it was a rifle or machine gun from the 5th Australian Division that shot down the famous German fight ace Captain Baron Manfred von Richthofen – the Red Baron (see page 444).

The division's Western Front losses were 48,500 (8,300 killed and 23,300 wounded). The divisional memorial is in Polygon Wood.

C The 2nd and 3rd Rifle Battalions advance to take the third objective – the Blue Line (Flers Support Trench and north-west corner of Flers).

D The 1st Battalion was tasked with taking the final objective, the Red Line (Grove Alley), and protecting the exposed left flank. Although a number of this battalion took parts of Grove Alley and were reinforced, they eventually had to withdraw in the face of heavy German counter-attacks.

Although the four tanks were late arriving, and overall throughout the larger battle their performance was disappointing, they effectively supported the Canadians, particularly during the fighting through the Brown Line and north of Flers.

Notes for Map 29
Belligerents

British	German
Fourth Army	First Army
XV Corps	II Bavarian Reserve Corps
New Zealand Division	4 Bavarian Division
(about 16,000)	(about 12,000)

Commanders
Maj. Gen. Sir Andrew Hamilton Russell — Gen. Fritz von Below

Casualties
24,000 during the Somme, of which about 7,230 sustained at Flers-Courcelette — uncertain

Result The New Zealanders took all their objectives on 15 September but were forced to withdraw from the final Red Line objective north-west of Flers at the end of the day.
Summary This battle saw the first use of tanks on the battlefield, four of them allocated to the New Zealand Division's front. It was a carefully planned operation, with the infantry leapfrogging forwards under cover of precisely timed creeping artillery barrages (see page 254) and supported by tanks moving just ahead of the infantry. The attack was divided into four phases:

A The 2nd NZ Brigade (2nd Otago and 2nd Auckland Battalions leading) take the Green Line (Switch Trench).

B The NZ Rifle Brigade passes through the 2nd Brigade and the 4th Rifle Battalion assaults the Brown Line (Flag Lane–Fat Trench).

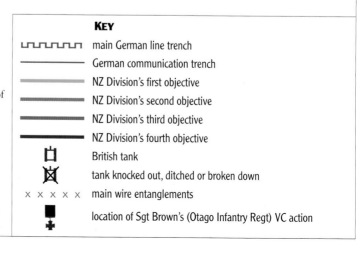

KEY
- main German line trench
- German communication trench
- NZ Division's first objective
- NZ Division's second objective
- NZ Division's third objective
- NZ Division's fourth objective
- British tank
- tank knocked out, ditched or broken down
- × × × × × main wire entanglements
- location of Sgt Brown's (Otago Infantry Regt) VC action

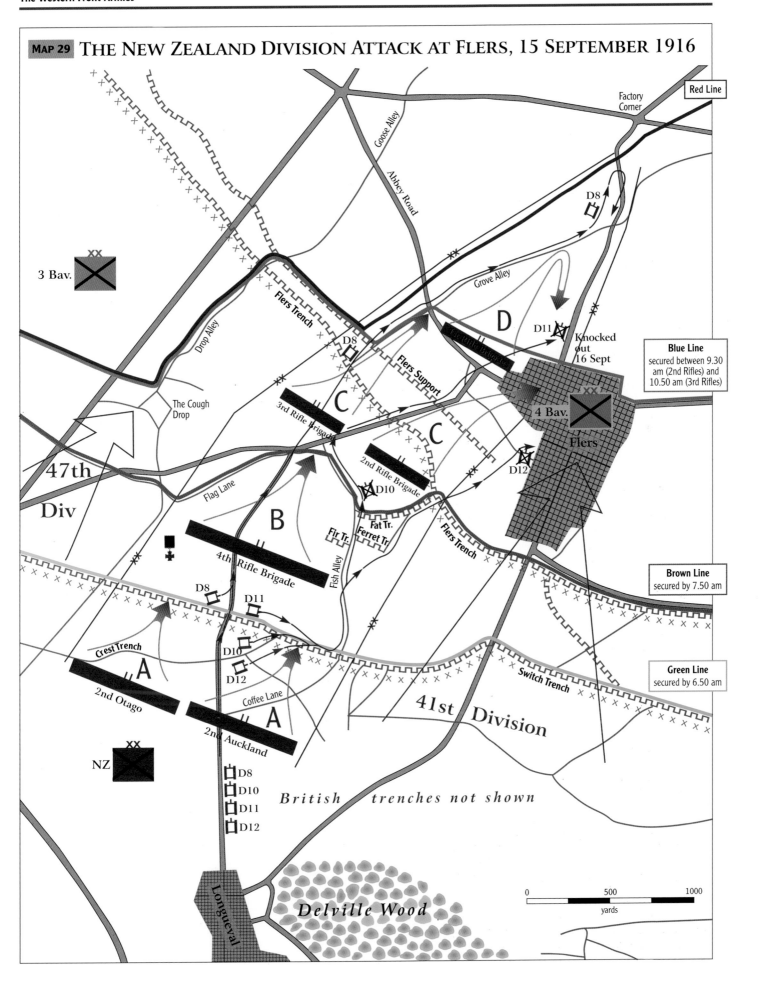

MAP 29 THE NEW ZEALAND DIVISION ATTACK AT FLERS, 15 SEPTEMBER 1916

Red Line

Factory Corner

3 Bav.

Goose Alley

Abbey Road

D8

Grove Alley

Flers Trench

Drop Alley

D8

Flers Support

D

D11

Knocked out 16 Sept

1st Rifle Brigade

Blue Line
secured between 9.30 am (2nd Rifles) and 10.50 am (3rd Rifles)

The Cough Drop

3rd Rifle Brigade

C

C

4 Bav.

Flers

2nd Rifle Brigade

D12

47th

Div

Flag Lane

B

D10

Fat Tr.

Fir Tr. Ferret Tr.

Flers Trench

4th Rifle Brigade

Fish Alley

D8

D11

Brown Line
secured by 7.50 am

Crest Trench

D10

D12

Coffee Lane

A

Switch Trench

Green Line
secured by 6.50 am

2nd Otago

41st Division

A

2nd Auckland

NZ

D8

D10

D11

D12

British   trenches   not   shown

Longueval

Delville Wood

0   500   1000

yards

The 4th Australian Division at the First Battle of Bullecourt

Sir Douglas Haig's plan for attacking the Bapaume salient in the spring of 1917 collapsed with the German withdrawal to the Hindenburg Line. The British followed up and General Gough's Fifth Army was instructed to attack the elaborate German defences between Bullecourt and Quéant in conjunction with an offensive by the Third Army to the north (the Battle of Arras). The final plan for the 4th Division's attack on 10 April envisaged considerable reliance being placed on surprise and the effectiveness of twelve tanks (one never made it) that were to lead the infantry. The artillery would not open fire until the tanks had breached the heavy wire entanglements in front of the German line. However, Bullecourt itself would be bombarded and subjected to a heavy gas attack. The tanks would line up in front of the infantry and penetrate the wire ahead of them. Once the Hindenburg Line had been taken, four tanks would swing westwards into Bullecourt, followed by an Australian battalion (the 48th), and another four tanks with the Australians on the right would advance on Riencourt.

However, due to patrol reports that in many areas the German wire was not sufficiently cut and that an attack without planned artillery support was too risky, the attack was first postponed from 9 to 10 April. By 1:00 a.m. on the 10th the Australian infantry were lying out in the open only 700 yards from the enemy wire, shivering and soaked under a blinding snowstorm waiting for the tanks. The appalling and unseasonable weather had seriously delayed the tanks; there was no prospect of their reaching the infantry in time for the 4:30 a.m. jump-off. Yet again, at the last moment, the attack was postponed for another twenty-four hours.

At 4:30 a.m. on 11 April the tanks leading the 4th Brigade arrived on time and the infantry advanced. However, the tanks with the 12th Brigade were late and, due to a misunderstanding, the commanding officer of the 46th Battalion thought he was to advance fifteen minutes after the tanks had passed. The resultant confusion meant that it was not until 5:15 a.m. that the 46th Battalion advanced, just as it was getting light and the artillery barrage on Bullecourt was lifted. The tanks proved ineffective, as most were disabled one way or another early on without breaking through the enemy wire, so although the infantry advanced and, fighting under great difficulties, captured the first- and second-line trenches, it was only after very considerable losses. Urgent requests for supporting artillery fire beyond the German line to block off enemy reinforcements were refused, as artillery commanders at the rear thought the tanks were through and would be hit by 'friendly fire'. There was a heated telephone exchange between Brigadier Charles Briand, commanding the 4th Brigade, and the gunner

Notes for Map 30

Belligerents

Australian	German
British Fifth Army	
I ANZAC Corps	XIV Reserve Corps
4th Australian Division	27th Division

Commanders

| Maj. Gen. William Holmes | Lt Gen. Otto von Moser |

Casualties

| 3,289 out of 5,000 engaged (66%) | 749 |

Result Initial, but costly, Australian success in taking the first line of their Hindenburg Line objectives, but they were unable to make further progress. They were driven back later in the day by fierce German counter-attacks.

Summary The plan envisaged the 4th and 12th Australian Brigades, supported by 11 (originally 12) tanks, attacking the Hindenburg Line defences between Riencourt and Bullecourt with the 4th Brigade on the right of the Central Road, the 12th to the left. The leading battalions would take the first two lines of trenches (**A A A**) and the following three would pass through the leading battalions – those on the right to take Riencourt and the 48th on the left to attack into Bullecourt (**A1 A1 A1**). Due to the late arrival of some tanks and the very heavy German fire, the attackers succeeded only in taking the trenches shown on the map. Very heavy counter-attacks from different directions (**B B B B**) against the weakened defenders, some of whom were running out of ammunition, forced a withdrawal of the survivors. The tanks proved largely ineffective and all eleven were at one stage or another disabled. The approximate final location of each tank is shown on the map.

Australian artillery observers watch the barrage as the Australians attack at Bullecourt, April 1917.

commander, with the argument going back as far as the corps commander (Birdwood). The request was refused.

The Australians were embedded in the Hindenburg Line and their flanks exposed to heavy fire from both Riencourt and Bullecourt. Then came numerous German counter-attacks from different directions, including from the uncaptured trenches on either flank and down Ostrich Avenue and Emu Alley. Now running short of ammunition and losing heavily, the order was given for an Australian withdrawal. Shortly after midday they walked out the way they had come, carrying their wounded.

First Bullecourt was something of a shambles. Staff failures, communication failures, delays, commanders refusing to accept what front-line officers told them, ineffective tanks and lack of proper artillery support when needed all led to the Australians losing 66 per cent of the 5,000 men engaged and achieving nothing.

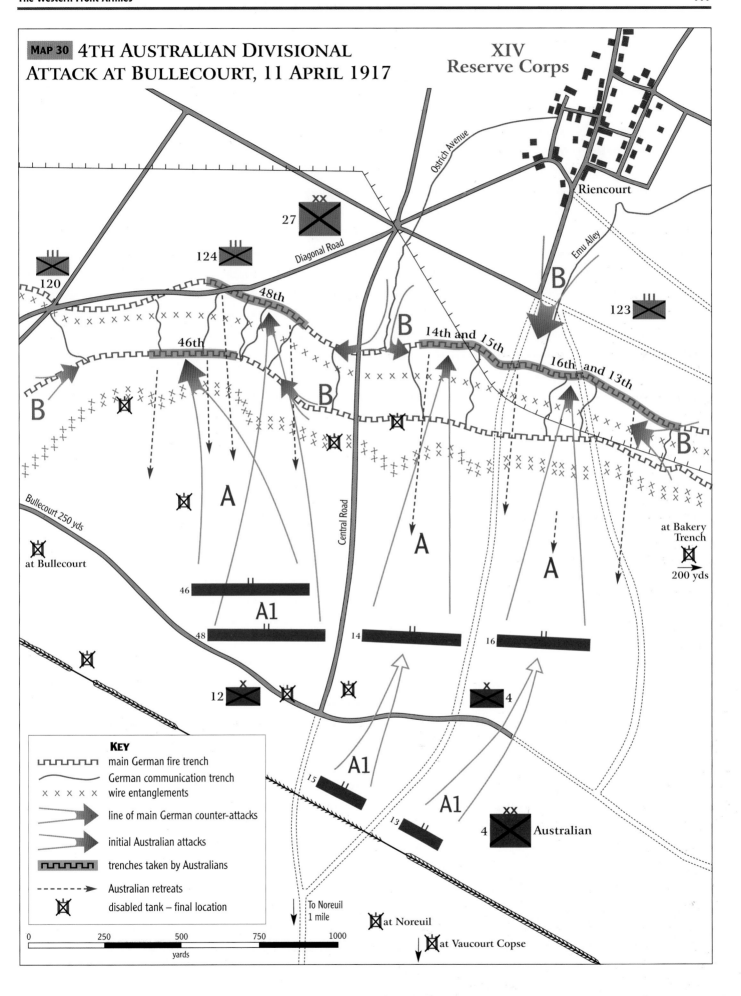

MAP 30 **4TH AUSTRALIAN DIVISIONAL ATTACK AT BULLECOURT, 11 APRIL 1917**

XIV
Reserve Corps

Ostrich Avenue

Riencourt

27

124

Diagonal Road

Emu Alley

120

B

48th

123

46th

14th and 15th

B

B

16th and 13th

B

B

B

Bullecourt 250 yds

at Bullecourt

at Bakery
Trench

200 yds

A

A

A

46

A1

48

14

16

Central Road

12

4

A1

A1

15

A1

13

4 Australian

KEY

⊔⊔⊔⊔⊔ main German fire trench

〰〰 German communication trench

× × × × × wire entanglements

line of main German counter-attacks

initial Australian attacks

trenches taken by Australians

- - - → Australian retreats

disabled tank – final location

To Noreuil
1 mile

at Noreuil

at Vaucourt Copse

0   250   500   750   1000

yards

Bullecourt

Riencourt

The Australian 4th Division attack at Bullecourt, 11 April 1917. This panorama shows the leading elements from their start line, with the German front-line trenches on the rising ground about halfway to the village of Riencourt. This attack was something of a disaster, through no fault of the Australians, who showed great courage and determination before a shortage of ammunition and heavy counter-attacks forced the withdrawal of the survivors. Australian losses included about 3,300 battle casualties and 1,170 prisoners.

ANZAC Victoria Crosses

Seventy-seven recipients of the Victoria Cross served with the AIF on the Western Front and another nine received it for their gallantry in Gallipoli; these included the posthumous VC to Captain Alfred John Shout, MC, a New Zealander and Boer War veteran serving with the 1st Battalion (NSW) AIF. Excluding Shout, eighteen New Zealanders were awarded the VC during the war, fifteen of them for their actions on the Western Front. Of the other three, two were awarded for bravery in Gallipoli and one at sea.

Sergeant Donald Forrester Brown, VC, 2nd Otago Regiment NZEF
During the New Zealand Division's attack through the German trench system east of Flers on 15 September 1917, Sergeant Brown was involved in his battalion's attack on Coffee Trench. After this had been secured, the advance on Crest Trench was checked by heavy German machine-gun fire. Sergeant Brown and a comrade crawled to within 30 yards of the gun and then rushed forward to kill the four crew and capture the gun. The attack continued on the next objective, Switch Trench, where Brown led another charge on another machine gun, again destroying it with bombs and the bayonet. On 1 October the 2nd Otago were ordered to attack another strongly defended trench system east of the small village of Eaucourt l'Abbaye called Circus Trench. Yet again Brown rushed a machine-gun nest and captured it, this time almost single-handedly, before being shot dead on the parapet of a trench. According to a comrade writing to Brown's father:

[Brown] shot the lot with one of their own pistols, which he was carrying and still remained unhurt when the rest of the men

caught up on him. To reach their objective they had to go further and that is where one of the best men I ever saw met his death – he was the first to get on the parapet and got sniped. The mate I got the account from saw him fall but he [Brown] told them that morning that he would not come back.

Sergeant Brown was buried on the battlefield but later exhumed and lies in the Warlencourt British cemetery. His parents later received a posthumous VC on behalf of their son.

Sergeant John Woods Whittle, VC, DCM, 12th Battalion AIF
In early April 1917 the 3rd Australian Brigade, 1st Division, was involved in the attacks on the Hindenburg Line. On 9 April the 12th Battalion, in which Sergeant Whittle was a platoon commander, was tasked with attacking the village of Boursies on the Bapaume–Cambrai road. Whittle's platoon had just captured an enemy trench near a ruined windmill north of the road when it was attacked by a strong German force determined to retake the mill. The Germans succeeded in taking some of the position, but when they reached Whittle's trench he organized a spirited defence that drove the enemy back. Six days later, when the Germans had broken through the New Zealand line, they brought up a machine gun to enfilade the defenders' position. Whittle immediately charged across open fire-swept ground and attacked the enemy with bombs, killing all of them and capturing the gun.

Whittle, who was from Tasmania, survived the war and died in Sydney in 1946, aged sixty-two. He is buried in Rookwood Cemetery, Sydney.

16th Battalion

14th Battalion

The Indian Army

This man in his own country prayed
we know not to what Powers.
We pray Them to reward him for
his bravery in ours.

Rudyard Kipling, 'Hindu Sepoy in France',
from *Epitaphs of the War*, 1919

By November 1918 the Indian Army had made a major contribution to the defeat of the Central Powers. By that date Indian troops had fought in France and Belgium; in Gallipoli, Salonika and Palestine; in Egypt and the Sudan; in Mesopotamia and Aden; in Somaliland, Cameroon and East Africa; in north-west Persia and Kurdistan, the Persian Gulf and North China. However, the three main theatres of operations for the Indian Army were, in order of numbers of troops involved, Mesopotamia (675,000), Egypt (144,000) and the Western Front (138,000).

In 1914 India's Regular Army was a colonial force of around 150,000 all ranks, but added to the country's military capability were the private armies of the Indian princes and the Imperial Service (British) troops stationed in India – in total a formidable force of trained soldiers, all volunteers, known collectively as the 'Army in India'. In peacetime the ranks were mostly filled with illiterate peasants from the rural areas in the north and north-west of the subcontinent – the provinces of Punjab,

Uttar Pradesh, the North-West Frontier and Nepal – as these were thought to provide hardier and more warlike recruits than the urban areas and the 'softer' south. Some 15–20,000 recruits were taken in every year and paid 11 rupees a month. The Indian Army had three main functions – defence of the North-West Frontier (at the time of writing, mostly Taliban territory), the maintenance of internal security throughout the country and the provision of a field force against possible Russian or Afghan incursions. The field force normally consisted of two infantry divisions and a cavalry brigade with attached British units.

An Indian regiment/battalion was either a 'class' or 'class-company' type, with the men of class regiments being all of one caste or religion, such as the 47th Sikhs. In a class-company regiment men of several different religions were recruited, but each company contained men of the same religion – an example being the 57th Wilde's Rifles (Frontier Force) with companies of Sikhs, Dogras, Punjabi Muslims and Pathans. Each battalion usually had twelve British officers (holding the King's Commission): the commanding officer, a major (second in command), adjutant, quartermaster and four captains commanding the companies, each perhaps assisted by a lieutenant. Indian officers (holding the Viceroy's Commission) commanded the platoons (*jemadars*, equating to a subaltern), with *subedars* (captains) and a *subedar-major* – the senior Indian officer in an infantry battalion and adviser to the commanding officer on all matters relating to the customs and religion of the men.

The 1st and 2nd Garhwalis Reach the Western Front

On 13 October 1914 these battalions landed at Marseilles and in just over two weeks were in the front-line trenches near Neuve Chapelle. Philip Mason describes their situation:

The trenches were very shallow, hardly deep enough to cover a man kneeling; they started digging at once and, having no sandbags, used timber from ruined houses in the village behind them to improve the trenches . . . They had a long spell, twenty days without relief; they worked at night, often bare-legged in icy water, to clear ditches and get the water away. Twenty

years later, at home in Garhwal, men showed me feet without toes [caused by trench foot]. The men were 'marvellously steady under shellfire'. They were terribly short of everything; they had at first no bombs [grenades] and the supporting battery was limited to eighteen shells a day. The 2nd Battalion had 1,100 yards of trench to hold with 600 men; the German front line was only 50 yards away.

The Garhwalis were relieved on 18 November but found themselves back in the line near Festubert five days later.

The army was organized on British lines, with four battalions to a brigade, three brigades to a division, plus all the supporting arms. However, there was an important difference within the infantry brigades, as at least one battalion was always British. This was an outdated hangover of lack of trust from the time of the Indian Mutiny in 1857. As an example, the Jullundur Brigade (Lahore Division) contained the 1st Manchester Regiment, 15th Ludiana Sikhs, 47th Sikhs and 59th Scinde Rifles (Frontier Force).

In 1914 the Indian Army initially sent the Lahore and Meerut Infantry Divisions and the Secunderabad Cavalry Brigade to France. They formed the Indian Corps, under Lieutenant General Sir James Willcocks, with the Ferozepore, Jullundur and Sirhind (joined December 1914) Brigades forming the Lahore Division and the Dehra Dun, Garhwal and Bareilly Brigades forming the Meerut Division. Each division had a cavalry regiment, three field artillery brigades (regiments), a heavy battery and its accompanying ammunition columns, engineers (two companies of the Indian Sappers and Miners, one of the rare units primarily recruited in the south), signals, medical, pioneers, and supply and transport units.

The Indian Corps arrived in France dressed, trained and equipped for colonial campaigns. The supporting artillery was British and there was no mechanical transport. There were also acute shortages of medical supplies, signals equipment and for some months suitable winter uniforms (some were still in light khaki drill by Christmas 1914). Before being sent into the line, the *sepoys* (private soldiers) had to

Indian Victoria Crosses

In the year that the Indian Corps was on the Western Front five Victoria Crosses were awarded to its Indian members. The first was to Sepoy Khudadad Khan, 129th Duke of Connaught's Own Baluchis, whose battalion was in the line near Ypres on 31 October 1914. On that day the Baluchis were engaged in some desperate and confused fighting as they tried to halt heavy and frequent German attacks. Khudadad Khan was a member of the crew of one of the two machine guns in the battalion that drew a particularly heavy enemy fire. In the course of the battle both machine guns were cut off. The British officer in command of the section was wounded and the other gun was put out of action by a shell. Khudadad Khan, although wounded himself, continued to work the remaining gun after all the other five men of his detachment had been killed. He was left for dead by the enemy but later recovered sufficiently to crawl back to his unit.

Khudadad Khan was from what is now the Pakistani half of the Punjab. He survived the war and became a very distinguished soldier, rising to the rank of subadar. He died in Rykhan village, Pakistan, in March 1971, aged eighty-three, and is buried in the village cemetery.

exchange their rifles for the unfamiliar pattern of Lee-Enfields used by the British Army. Although tough physically and used to biting cold, intense heat and long marches, week after week of the wet cold of a European winter had a debilitating effect on many. The Indian contingents arrived in Marseilles in September 1914 and were fed piecemeal into the line as quickly as possible thereafter. The losses they suffered were severe, sometimes with whole companies being wiped out and battalions coming out of the line at less than half their original strength. Sickness claimed as many victims as bullets and shells. The 47th Sikhs, an average-strength Indian battalion, arrived in France with 764 all ranks, but by the end of November had only 385 fit for duty. Problems arose with replacements. Reinforcements arriving from India were often older and less fit, while drafts from other regiments might not speak the same language or eat the same food. But it was the loss of so many of their British officers that was particularly keenly felt, as they knew their men, knew their customs, spoke their language and above all were trusted by their soldiers. Their replacements had not grown up and trained with their soldiers and had to earn their trust by learning their customs and language while fighting in the trenches.

Despite these disadvantages, the Indians fought superbly. Philip Mason, in his book on the Indian Army, *A Matter of Honour*, quotes a German soldier as writing:

Today for the first time we had to fight against the Indians and the devil knows those brown rascals are not to be underrated. We at first spoke with contempt of the Indians. Today we learned to look on them in a different light – the devil knows what the English put into those fellows . . . With a fearful shouting thousands of those brown forms rushed on us . . . At a hundred metres we opened a destructive fire which mowed down hundreds but in spite of that the others advanced . . . in no time they were in our trenches and truly those brown enemies were not to be despised. With butt ends, bayonets, swords and daggers we fought each other and we had bitter hard work.

The Indian Corps fought on the Western Front until the end of 1915, when it was transferred to the Middle East (except for the 2nd Indian Cavalry Division, which remained), a more suitable theatre of war for Indian troops whose morale was fragile and whom it was thought unwise to expose to another winter in France. However, they had fought exceptionally well and continuously during that year, being heavily involved at corps or divisional level in 1914 in the Battles of La Bassée and Messines and the defence of Festubert and Givenchy. In 1915 they fought at Neuve Chapelle (see Map 12), Ypres, Aubers Ridge, Festubert and Loos. During their time on the Western Front the Indians suffered over 21,400 casualties.

An Indian soldier fires a machine gun in an anti-aircraft role, 1915.

The South African Army

The principal component of South Africa's contribution to the war on the Western Front was the 1st South African Infantry Brigade. However, there were also South African units integrated into the British Imperial Armies and divisions in the field. These included the Cape Corps (infantry and a labour battalion), mounted and dismounted rifles, heavy and field artillery, engineer, signals, supply, medical, veterinary and native labour contingents. All ranks were volunteers and were part of the South African Overseas Expeditionary Force (SAOEF), which fought in four campaigns.

Before moving to the Western Front the 1st SA Infantry Brigade fought in Egypt against the Sennusi in the Battles of Halazin and Agagiya during the first three months of 1916. A large South African contingent of divisional strength, sometimes more, of infantry, mounted brigades and field artillery under South African generals (Lieutenant Generals Jan Smuts and Sir Jacob van Deventer) fought in the German East African Campaign from 1916–18. From 1917–18 the Cape Corps and South African field artillery participated in the Palestine Campaign alongside British forces against the Turks. During the war South Africa mobilized 231,000 men (213,000 served overseas), of whom 85,000 were black Africans, from a population of around 6 million. Of these, just over 19,000 white soldiers became casualties (7,120 killed) and at least 38,700 Africans died in East Africa while serving as labourers and porters.

On the Western Front the South African contribution to trench warfare was primarily heavy artillery and the 1st SA Infantry Brigade. They fought on the battlefields of the Somme in 1916; Arras, Ypres, Menin, Passchendaele and Cambrai in 1917; and at the Hindenburg Line, Messines, Mount Kemmel and the Selle in 1918. The infantry brigade consisted of the 1st (Cape of Good Hope) Regiment, 2nd (Natal and Orange Free State) Regiment, 3rd (Transvaal and Rhodesia) Regiment and the 4th (South African Scottish) Regiment, the latter representing the strong Scottish military tradition in the country. The brigade commander, Brigadier General H. T. (Tim) Lukin, was a veteran who had seen service in most of the South African campaigns during the past thirty-five years. When the brigade embarked from Cape Town it numbered 160 officers and 5,648 other ranks. After a period of training in England, they were sent to fight in Egypt (see above) before transferring to France, where they arrived in the Somme area in early June 1916 as part of the 9th (Scottish) Division. This was a reserve division during the infamous 1 July attack, so the South Africans were not committed to battle until two weeks later.

The struggle for Delville Wood

The attack on Longueval and Delville Wood was part of the next phase of the British Somme offensive, when XIII Corps was given the task of taking the village and establishing a strong defensive flank around it. The assault on Longueval was allotted to the 9th (Scottish) Division and was scheduled for dawn on 14 July following a night approach march. The actual assaulting formations would be the 26th and 27th Brigades, with the 1st SA Brigade in reserve. However, by around 8:00 a.m. the fighting was so intense that the 1st SA Regiment, under Lieutenant Colonel F. S. Dawson, was sent into the village as reinforcements. A *South African Military History Journal* article by I. S. Uys, from which the quotations in these paragraphs are taken, quotes Private Martin Carey of D Company in that regiment:

> Then I began to see things were getting bad. Then another [bullet] went over. Then another. Then I thought, 'It's my turn next.' There were machine gun posts at the flour mill at Longueval and we got it very heavy from there. I got hit at the beginning of the wood. The lower part of my jaw was shot away, they reckon by a ricochet. It felt like a mule kick.

The next day, the 15th, the remaining three battalions received the following order: 'you will capture and consolidate the outer edge of the whole of Delville Wood'. The operation was under the command of Lieutenant Colonel William Tanner (2nd SA Regiment), about whom a soldier would say, 'We'd have followed him through any fire anywhere . . . He was a trim, wiry man, and a great smiler: I never think of him but I think of his smile.' His plan was to attack with the 2nd and 3rd Regiments, the latter commanded by Lieutenant Colonel E. F. Thackeray, leading, and the 4th Regiment, under Lieutenant Colonel F. A. Jones, in support. The advance through the wood was accomplished comparatively easily and the troops set to digging in along the perimeter to face the inevitable German bombardment and counter-attacks. The South Africans were now in a salient that, as one observer commented, was shaped rather like a dog's head (see Map 31) and thus terribly vulnerable to enemy fire and attack from three sides.

Former Enemies' Last Stand in Delville Wood

Privates Lawson and Breytenbach were two old soldiers serving in D Company, 3rd Battalion, the former a veteran of the First Boer War, the latter also a veteran of the same war but fighting on the opposite side. Now they were friends, fighting on the same side in Delville Wood. Lawson recounted the events of his last day in the wood:

> The enemy launched an attack in overwhelming numbers . . . As the Germans came on they were mown down; every shot must have told. Our rifles smoked and became unbearably hot . . . when the enemy broke they were reinforced and came on again. We again prevailed and drove them back. Only one German crossed our trench, to fall shot in the heart a few yards behind it . . .
>
> Exhaustion now did what shell fire and counter-attacks had failed to do, and we collapsed in our trench, spent in body and at last worn out in spirit . . . What happened during the next two hours or so I do not know. Numbed in all my senses I gazed vacantly into space. From this state of coma I was rudely awakened by a shell which exploded just over me, and instantaneously I passed into unconsciousness. When I regained consciousness a few minutes after, my first sensation was that of being thoroughly refreshed by sleep. But on moving I found that the fight for me was over.
>
> I tried to rouse my friend, who had fallen face downwards beside me. Getting no response I lifted his head, calling upon him by name, but I could not arouse him. I then commenced with pain and difficulty to walk down the line. I found the last two hours of shelling had done its work – only six remained alive in the trench. I aroused some of the young, brave worn-out sleepers and told one of them I had been badly hit and was going to try to walk out. He faced me for a second and asked me what he was to do. I said there was nothing to do but carry on . . . His brave last 'Right-o!' were the last words I heard there.
>
> I returned to Breytenbach and shook him gently and again raised his head. Then I realised that the shell which had put me out of the fight had put him to rest.
>
> With a last look at my friend I turned to face that painful walk out of the stricken wood . . .

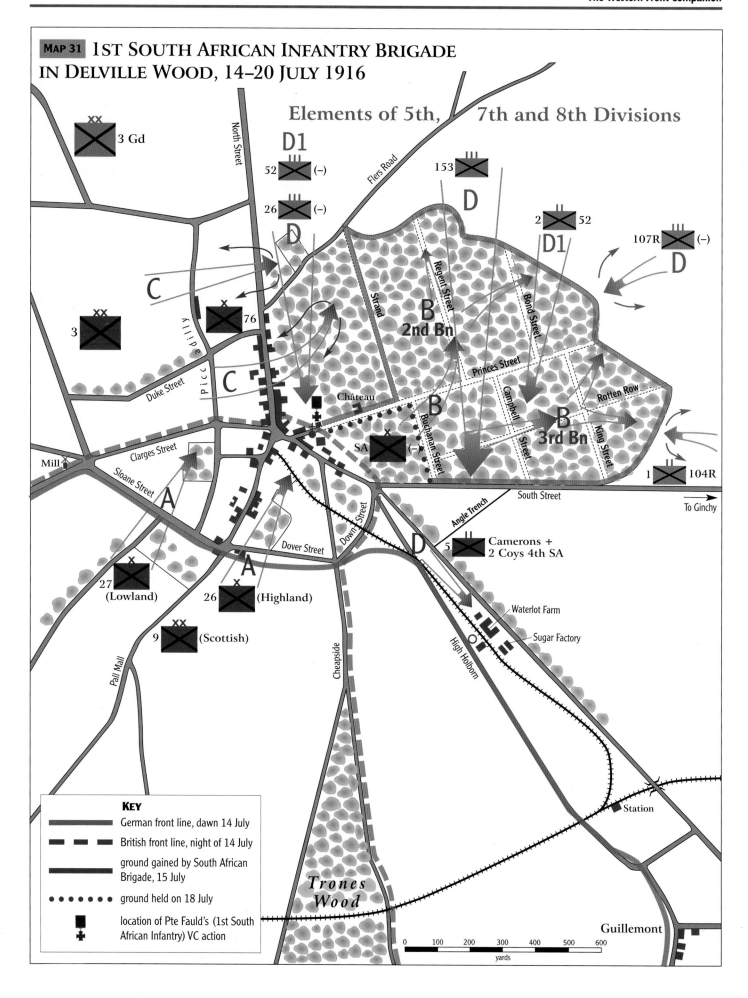

MAP 31 1ST SOUTH AFRICAN INFANTRY BRIGADE
IN DELVILLE WOOD, 14–20 JULY 1916

Elements of 5th, 7th and 8th Divisions

3 Gd

North Street

D1

52 (–)

Flers Road

153

D

26 (–)

D

2 52

D1

107R (–)

C

D

3

76

Regent Street

Strand

Bond Street

C

B
2nd Bn

Piccadilly

Duke Street

Princes Street

Campbell Street

Rotten Row

Château

B

King Street

Mill

Clarges Street

SA (–)

B
3rd Bn

1 104R

Sloane Street

South Street

To Ginchy

A

Buchanan Street

Angle Trench

Dover Street

Down Street

D

5 Camerons +
2 Coys 4th SA

A

27
(Lowland)

26 (Highland)

Waterlot Farm

Sugar Factory

9 (Scottish)

Pall Mall

Cheapside

High Holborn

Station

KEY

German front line, dawn 14 July

British front line, night of 14 July

ground gained by South African
Brigade, 15 July

•••••• ground held on 18 July

■ location of Pte Fauld's (1st South
✠ African Infantry) VC action

*Trones
Wood*

Guillemont

0 100 200 300 400 500 600

yards

Princes Street in Delville Wood. This photograph is taken looking east along the main ride (much wider than during the battle) of the wood, which saw much of the bitter fighting. First the South Africans (2nd Battalion) attacked across it from right to left and later the Germans counter-attacked from left to right.

Shortly after noon Lieutenant Elliot (2nd SA Regiment) sent a somewhat overly polite message to his commanding officer: 'Enemy shelling wood heavily and their rifle fire getting very brisk. Reinforcements are being supplied to them. Please send some more ammunition and if you can get artillery on the enemy trenches it would be a great help to us.'

The 16th and 17th were largely days of trying to consolidate positions and endure the dreadful pounding of the wood by artillery, which was not only reducing the trees to an almost impenetrable tangle of matchwood but was also tearing the brigade to shreds. But it was on the 18th that the Germans, heavily reinforced, made their main effort to retake the wood. The attacks were preceded by a concentration of fire on to the one square mile of wood that was unlike anything witnessed before. At least 20,000 shells fell on the South Africans in the space of seven hours – an average of forty-eight arriving every minute. At times there were seven explosions every second. At 2:50 p.m., after the wounding of Colonel Tanner, Colonel Thackeray was placed in command and endeavoured to control the chaos from his headquarters dugout near the junction of Buchanan and Princes Streets. The frantic desperation of the defenders is clear from the message sent by Lieutenant Thomas at 5:30 p.m.:

One Lewis gun crew has been blown up. Can you send another crew? I have wounded men lying all along my front & have no stretchers left, and they are dying for want of treatment, my field dressings being all used up. Can you obtain stretcher bearers? Urgent. I consider my position is now untenable, and have had my breastworks all blown in [tree roots prevented deep trenches and the soil had to be used for flimsy breastworks]. It is impossible to spare men to take wounded away, and my front is now very lightly held with many gaps . . . Most of the men are suffering from shell shock and I do not consider we are fit to hold the position in the event of an enemy attack.

Notes for Map 31

Belligerents

British	German
Fourth Army	Second Army
XIII Corps	IV Corps
9th (Scottish) Division	elements of 5th, 7th
1st South African Infantry Brigade	and 8th Divisions
3,153 all ranks initially	number uncertain

Commanders

Gen. Sir Henry Rawlinson (Fourth Army)	
Lt Gen. Sir William Congreve (XIII Corps)	Gen. Fritz von Below
Maj. Gen. W. T. Furse	(Second Army)
(9th (Scottish) Division)	Lt Gen. Sixt von Armin
Maj. Gen. Sir H. T. Lukin	(IV Corps)
(1st South African Infantry Brigade)	

Casualties

2,536 (1st SA Brigade), or 80%.	uncertain, but the 26th Regiment mustered only 160 out of 5,800 on 20 July – loss of 97%

Result The South Africans took the wood on 15 July and hung on until relieved on 20 July, when the southern half was recaptured.

Summary The 1st South African Infantry Brigade was part of the 9th (Scottish) Division, committed to the British attack on the Longueval–Delville Wood sector of the German line during the Somme offensive. The brigade consisted of the 1st (Lt Col F. S. Dawson), 2nd (Lt Col Willliam Tanner), 3rd (Lt Col E. F. Thackeray) and 4th (Lt Col F. A. Jones) SA Regiments (battalions). Their defensive action constitutes one of the finest examples of endurance and raw courage of the war.

14 July. The 9th Division attacked Longueval at dawn with the 26th and 27th Brigade and the 1st SA Brigade in reserve **A**. Heavy resistance and the problems of street fighting led to the 1st SA Regiment being committed. The southern part of the village was secured.

15 July. The remainder of the SA Brigade, less the 1st SA Regiment, was ordered to take Delville Wood. Lt Col Tanner, who deployed the 2nd and 3rd Regiments in the assault with the 4th in reserve, commanded the operation **B**. They entered the wood from the south-west corner and by the end of the day had reached the perimeter and secured the wood except for the north-west corner.

16–17 July. Consolidation days during which the wood was subjected to continuous heavy shelling, causing mounting losses and reducing the wood to a chaotic mass of twisted branches and splintered stumps. Several enemy counter-attacks were beaten off. On 17 July Tanner was wounded and Thackeray assumed command in the wood, with his headquarters in a dugout at the junction of Buchanan and Princes Streets.

Night of 16/17 July. The north-west corner of the wood was unsuccessfully attacked by the 27th Brigade and the 1st SA Regiment **C**. At 8:00 a.m. on the 17th the 5th Cameroon Highlanders, with two companies of the 4th SA Regiment, captured Waterlot Farm **D**.

18 July. Delville Wood was subjected to a horrendous artillery barrage, lasting about seven hours. Some 20,000 shells fell in an area of under a square mile. The Germans, having created a hellish inferno inside the wood, launched a series of heavy massed attacks. Those from the east were driven off; that from the north forced the surviving South Africans back **D**. Bitter hand-to-hand fighting with the 4th SA Regiment bolstered the defence. The German attacks were reinforced by the battalions of the 52nd Regiment **D1**.

19 July. Renewed German assaults on the remnants of the 3rd SA Regiment on the eastern edge of the wood were taken in the rear by elements of the enemy's 52nd and 153rd Regiments and overrun. Thackeray desperately appealed for relief, with the survivors clinging on to the Buchanan Street trench against ever-increasing pressure.

20 July. After a failed attempt in the early morning, the SA Brigade was finally relieved by the 76th Brigade (3rd Division) in the evening.

Old trenches in Delville Wood.

South African Victoria Crosses

Two Victoria Crosses were awarded to South Africans on the Western Front. The first went to Private (later Captain) William Frederick Faulds, 1st SA Regiment, for great gallantry on two occasions. On 18 July a bombing party under Lieutenant Craig attempted to rush over 40 yards of ground between the opposing trenches in Longueval. Under heavy rifle and machine-gun fire, most of the party were killed or wounded. Unable to move, Craig lay on open ground midway between the trenches. Faulds and two other men ran out and carried him back, one man being badly wounded. Two days later Faulds again went out to bring in a wounded comrade and carried him half a mile to the dressing station.

After commissioning in May 1917 he was awarded the Military Cross for further bravery, but was wounded and captured during the German offensive of March 1918. However, he survived the war and moved to Salisbury in Rhodesia, but served again in East Africa during World War II. He died in August 1950, aged fifty-five, and is buried in Salisbury Pioneer Cemetery.

The Delville Wood Memorial

The Delville Wood Cemetery lies immediately south of the Longueval–Ginchy road but contains the graves of only 113 identified South Africans who died fighting in the village or wood. The central avenue of the cemetery is continued across the road by a wide grass clearing or avenue that runs north through the wood to the memorial situated in the centre of the wood, which was replanted after the war. The wood itself is also a burial ground for those 538 soldiers who died there but were never found. The original memorial was unveiled in October 1926 by the widow of General Louis Botha and consisted of a screen (wall), two shelters on each side and a central arch surmounted by a horse, with a figure on either side representing the two races of the South African Union. After World War II the Stone of Sacrifice was added, and in 1986 a museum was constructed in the rear of the memorial following the story of the South Africans from World War I to Korea.

By the end of the day the Germans had succeeded to retaking the wood, except for the south-west corner and a small strip along the perimeter in the east.

By the end of 19 July the Germans had overrun the wood except for Buchanan Street, where a last-ditch stand was being made by survivors who had retreated from the perimeter defences. Many South Africans had been captured as Private Victor Wepener, B Company, 3rd Battalion, later described:

> We were shelled from all sides. At times men were killed next to me while I was talking to them. Though I always had ammunition, the rain and mud got into our rifle bolts and caused them to jam . . . When the Germans overran us, I was impressed by a very aristocratic officer who wore a hat instead of a steel helmet. He kept his hand over his pistol holster whilst us 'remnants' were being collected in an open glade . . . We were then marched through their lines and we saw many Germans lying there waiting to attack. A

couple of our chaps carried a German with a stomach wound on a groundsheet. Our artillery opened up and we were amused to see our guards ducking away and running for cover. After all we had been through we didn't worry about shellbursts any more.

Not until the following day were the survivors of the brigade finally relieved by a counter-attack that regained the southern half of the wood. The official historian of the 9th (Scottish) Division wrote that 'the defence of Delville Wood by Lieutenant Colonel Thackeray's small band rightly takes its place as one of the classic feats of the war.'

The Portuguese Army

In February 1916, following a British request, Portugal interned German ships anchored in her ports. This resulted in Germany declaring war on Portugal on 9 March. In mid-July the British government formally invited Portugal to take an active part in the military actions of the Allies and the CEP (*Corpo Expedicionario Portugues* or Portuguese Expeditionary Corps) of 30,000 men under General Norton de Matos was formed. During August 1916 a force of some 55,000, plus 1,000 artillerymen, was raised to be sent to France. This amounted to three infantry divisions earmarked to man some 10 miles of front. In the event only two divisions were landed in France, as the

need to transport American troops had dramatically reduced the Allies' shipping capacity. However, Portugal fielded troops in her African colonies – Mozambique and Angola – against German colonial forces in the former and German-inspired unrest in the latter.

In January 1917 it was agreed that the CEP would be integrated with the BEF and that, at the request of France, a Portuguese Independent Artillery Corps be formed to man twenty-five heavy artillery batteries. It was not until 30 May that a Portuguese brigade occupied a sector of the battle front, coming under attack a few days later. On 10 July the CEP 1st Division assumed responsibility for a sector of the front under XI Corps, British First Army. With the arrival of the 2nd Division in the autumn, Portuguese command assumed responsibility for its sector in early November.

As the third division was never sent to France, the Portuguese did not receive reinforcements and consequently their troops had to serve long periods at the battle front with little rest. The German offensive in March 1918 aggravated this situation and by April it was recognized that the exhausted units must be withdrawn from front-line duty to reorganize and recover. However, further German attacks prevented this and the Portuguese were forced to fight on.

In this battle on 9 April (the Battle of Estaires to the British, Operation Georgette to the Portuguese), the attack by eight German divisions, supported by intensive artillery fire, hit some 20,000 Portuguese, supported by eighty-eight guns, virtually annihilating the 2nd Division. The CEP lost 327 officers and 7,098 men, or 35 per cent of its strength. It was the last Portuguese action of the war.

The American Army

When America entered the war in April 1917 she was faced with the monumental task of forming an army numbering millions and shipping it overseas. At that time her Regular Army was less than 135,000 strong, scattered in small detachments all over the country. There was not a single division that could be put in the field. Ten months later she had only one division in the line in France. Not until 10 August 1918 was the American Expeditionary Force (AEF) able to deploy an American Army – the First – for the Meuse–Argonne offensive. Eventually three armies were formed, although the third was used for occupation service only. In addition to the Regular Army, which had been fortified by Federal National Guardsmen called up for the Mexican War in 1916, there were around 100,000 National Guards in state service. To raise a force of 2 or 3 million a selective form of conscription had to be introduced – the draft. To recruit, equip, arm, organize and train such a force from such small beginnings was a Herculean task. Inevitably it required many months, at a time on the Western Front when reinforcements were becoming critical to bolster the exhausted Allies in holding the line as German troops poured west from the Eastern Front.

Solving a chronic lack of equipment was, as with other Allied armies at the outset, an ever-increasing headache. In terms of artillery, tanks and aircraft, the problem could not be solved before the war ended. The Americans possessed only 600 outdated 3-inch guns and, despite unprecedented production efforts, it was with the excellent French 75mm gun, of which France supplied over 3,800 (and some 10 million rounds of ammunition), that the AEF joined the war. In the first large-scale battle in which American troops played the leading role, at St-Mihiel on 12–13 September 1918, not a single gun was of American manufacture. It was the same with tanks and aircraft. The first American-built tank, a two-man 2½-tonner, arrived in France in October 1918 – only fifteen were ever built. Again the French met the deficiency, supplying their Renault light tank. In August 1918, 144 of these arrived to add to the twenty-five already received. They were organized into two light tank battalions under Colonel George S. Patton – destined to become one the most forceful and successful tank commanders of World War II. Similarly, the American Air Force was fully effective only during the last weeks of the war, and in order to be so acquired almost 2,700 aircraft from the French.

The commander of the AEF, General John J. Pershing, arrived in France with a small staff in June 1917 determined to build up an independent American Army under American command as soon as practical. This could not happen until all units had first been trained by Allied instructors and given front-line experience under Allied commanders in quiet sectors. Not until more than four months after Pershing's arrival did the honour of firing the first American artillery round go to Battery C, 6th Field Artillery Battalion, on 23 October 1917.

The build-up of divisions in France was a seemingly interminable process, not helped by the fact that America lacked sufficient transport shipping and had, somewhat belatedly, to call on Britain's merchant fleet for help. Pershing had insisted on the reorganization of his divisions into formations at least twice the size of the other belligerents. American divisions eventually went to war with an establishment of over 28,000 all ranks (see diagram, pages 92–3).

One of the immediate decisions to be taken was what part of the front would become the AEF's responsibility. With the British covering the Channel ports and the French covering Paris, the communications systems in these areas were already heavily overburdened. The answer was for the Americans to deploy in Lorraine, for which they could have priority use of the ports south of Le Havre and where the existing road and rail links were less busy.

Before an American army in France could take its place as a fighting force, it had to sort out a bewildering number of administrative and logistical problems. Staffs had to be assembled and trained; docks, railways, roads, depots, hospitals and signal networks had to be constructed; and at the same time huge dumps of supplies and ammunition had to be established. Without this enormous tail the dog would be unable to bite. Not until 12 September 1918 was the American Army ready for its first large-scale attack as an independent

Little-known American Statistics

- 2,057,675 military personnel had served in France by the Armistice, of whom about half were combat troops.
- Around half of the expected AEF had not left America by the end of the war.
- Some 180,000 members of the AEF in France were black Americans.
- At the Armistice the US Air Service was operating in forty-five squadrons with 740 aircraft (mostly purchased from the French).
- 42,644 civilian employees and volunteers supported the AEF overseas.
- Of the 4.7 million Americans mobilized during the war, the majority – about 4 million – served in the army (including the Air Service), 600,000 in the navy and 79,000 in the marines.

army. Below is a summary of the American combat operations of 1918:

6 April Over 2,000 troops join the British in the defence of Amiens.
9–29 April 500 troops involved with the British at Kemmel.
27 May–5 June American troops help the French halt German attacks at Château-Thierry.
9–15 June Over 27,000 troops involved in driving back the German advance and retaking Belleau Wood.
18 July–6 August 270,000 troops play a prominent part in the first Allied advance of the year north of the River Marne.
8 August 54,000 troops take part in the British offensive on the Somme.
19 August 108,000 troops join the Allied advance in the Ypres sector.
12–16 September 550,000 troops form the first independent American command in the attack on the St-Mihiel salient.
26 September–11 November 1.2 million troops forming the First and Second American Armies conduct the costly but successful Meuse–Argonne offensive.

US troops in action in the Meuse–Argonne offensive, 1918.

The Meuse–Argonne Offensive

The American First Army's attack was on a 20-mile front between the Meuse on the right and the Aisne of the left, with French troops on either flank. The objective was Sedan, 35 miles distant and the strategic hub of lateral German rail communications. The German Fifth Army provided most of the defenders at the start. Although only five weak divisions opposed the Americans on 26 September, they had the advantage of a 10-mile deep, entrenched sector of the Hindenburg Line that passed through ideal defensive terrain. This was especially so on their right, where the steep gullies and valleys, densely wooded, of the Argonne Forest posed a daunting obstacle to any attacker. In the centre was the towering, 500-foot high Monfaucon bastion, dominating the ground for miles around.

After a prolonged bombardment, the initial assault on 26 September by nine American divisions initially made good progress, and

Colonel Patton was able to watch his tanks drive forward from the summit of Vauquois Hill. However, the attackers were unable to take the Monfaucon Heights until the second day, while the exhausting terrain and poor visibility in the Argonne Forest slowed progress considerably for the 28th and 77th Divisions. Seeing a crisis developing on his Fifth Army's front, the German Army Group commander, General Max von Gallwitz, deployed six reserve divisions to shore up the line. Their arrival ended all hopes of a quick American victory in the Argonne.

By 1 October the attackers were forced to halt and regroup. Pershing replaced several of his green divisions with more experienced troops – a necessary decision, but one that aggravated the chaotic logistical problems. On 4 October the American assault was resumed, but against a ferocious defence made little progress. It was during this phase that the 77th Division's famous 'Lost Battalion' made its stand, and Corporal Alvin York won the Medal of Honor (see box, page 122).

On 10 October Pershing gave command of the First Army to Major General Hunter Liggett with orders to push on while he formed the Second Army under Major General Robert L. Bullard to attack east of the Meuse. From 13–16 October the Americans made further progress and, at considerable cost, finally breached the Kriemhild Line – a first-day objective. During a halt to regroup, an attack by the 78th Division took the town of Grandpré.

On 1 November, following a massive bombardment, the First Army attacked again all along the line, making large gains – 5 miles by V Corps in the centre – forcing the Germans into headlong retreat. On 5 November the 5th Division crossed the Meuse, frustrating the enemy's intention of making it a new defensive line. Three days later the Germans contacted the Allied commander-in-chief, Foch, about an armistice, but the Americans continued to drive the enemy before them. On 11 November the war ended.

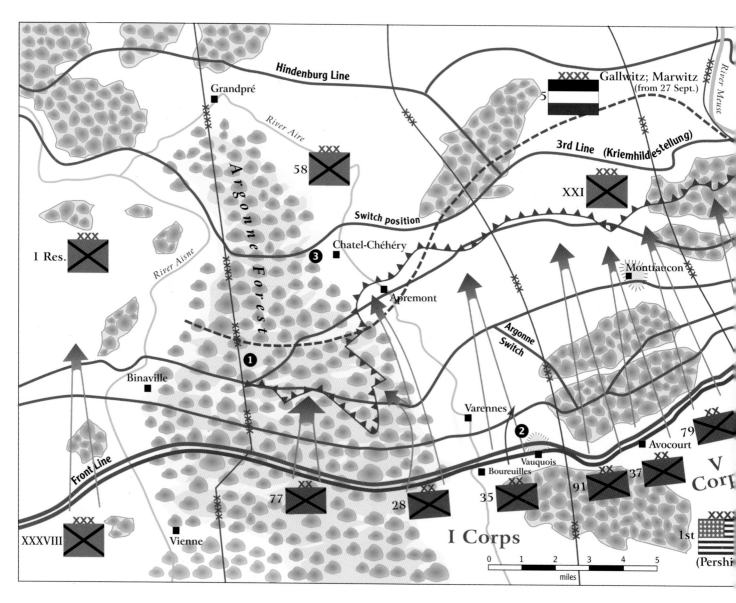

The Lost Battalion was actually an ad hoc group of six under-strength companies (A, B, C, E, G and H) of the 308th Infantry Regiment, Company K from the 307th Infantry and Companies C and D from the 306th Machine Gun Battalion – in total, some 700 men.

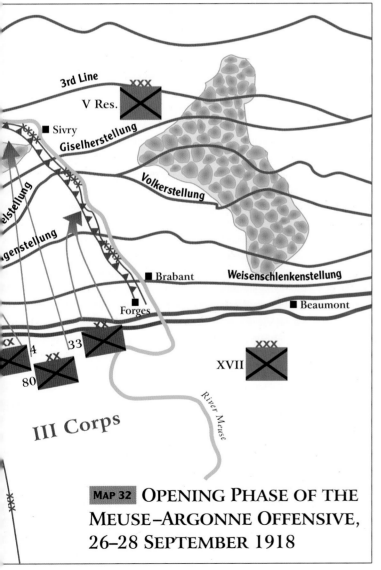

MAP 32 **OPENING PHASE OF THE MEUSE–ARGONNE OFFENSIVE, 26–28 SEPTEMBER 1918**

Notes for Map 32

Belligerents

American	German
First Army	Fifth Army

Divisions

9 initially; by 11 Nov. 24 infantry divisions had been committed	5 initially, but eventually approx. 450,000 men

Commanders

Gen. John J. Pershing, then Maj. Gen. Hunter Liggett*	Gen. Georg von der Marwitz

Casualties

122,000 all ranks (26,300 killed)	120,000 (28,000 killed)

Result As part of the final Allied offensive of the war, the American forces drove the Germans back to the line of the Meuse from Verdun to Sedan. On this line the war ended.

Summary The Meuse–Argonne offensive was the southern part of the great Allied offensive that finally broke the German lines on the Western Front and ended the war. This map shows only the start of the opening phase of the American participation that developed into the biggest AEF battle of the war, sucking in 1.2 million American soldiers, and leaving 26,277 dead and 95,786 wounded.

Phase 1 26 September–3 October. Supported by almost 4,000 guns (which fired over 4 million shells during the seven-week battle), 324 tanks (both guns and tanks supplied by the French) and 840 aircraft, the Americans jumped off at 5:30 a.m. on 26 September with the objective of penetrating the German defensive lines to a depth of up to 10 miles. Extremely difficult terrain on the left (the Argonne Forest), and well-prepared defences manned by a determined enemy, meant that progress was erratic and slow, particularly on the left. On 29 September the Germans deployed six new divisions and counter-attacked – initially successfully. By the end of the month the offensive halted to replace the 35th, 37th, 79th and 80th Divisions. It was during this phase that elements of the 77th Division attacking north in the Argonne Forest became cut off on 2 October and held out against all the odds for five days, for ever after being known as the 'Lost Battalion'.

Phase 2 4–28 October. A series of costly frontal assaults finally broke through the third defensive line (*Kriemhildestellung*) between 14 and 17 October. By the end of October the Americans had advanced 10 miles and had finally cleared the Argonne Forest. It was during this phase that Corporal York made his famous capture of 132 prisoners (see box, page 122).

Phase 3 26 October–11 November. This saw the final push by the American forces, now reorganized into two armies (the second led by Maj. Gen. Robert L. Bullard*) close up to the River Meuse. On 6 November the key German communications link – the Sedan–Metz railway line – came under artillery fire. The American 1st Division's final advance on Sedan was halted to allow the French to take the city, which had been in German hands since the French defeat in the Franco-Prussian War. The Armistice on 11 November halted all fighting.

* Promoted lt gen. on 1 November 1918.

KEY

▬▬▬▬▬	German front line
〰〰〰	main German defensive lines
▬▬▬▬▬	French–American front line
– – – – –	American objective, 26 September
▲▲▲▲▲	American front line, 28 September
28 ⊠	American divisions in initial attacks
➊	the 'Lost Battalion'
➋	Patton's tank attack
➌	Sergeant York's exploits

Cheppy village

direction of
tank advance

Montfaucon Wood

This panorama shows a portion of the ground over which Lieutenant Colonel George Patton led forward his French tanks (crewed by Americans) in their drive for Cheppy on 26 September 1918. Patton led his tanks forward on foot, waving a stick and yelling encouragement until he was wounded in the leg.

The Medal of Honor

The Medal of Honor is the highest award that the American government can give for great gallantry in battle and is the equivalent of the British Victoria Cross. During the war 124 were awarded; ninety-six to the army, twenty-one to the navy and seven to the marines. During the Meuse–Argonne battles there were fifty-three recipients, eight in the 'Lost Battalion', although certainly the most famous was Corporal Alvin Cullom York.

York was born into an impoverished Tennessee family on 13 December 1887, the third of eleven children. He grew up, with little education, into something of a hard-drinking saloon brawler, despite the fact that his mother was a devout member of the Church of Christ in Christian Union. Not until shortly before the war, when he saw a friend killed in a drunken fight, did York heed his mother's pleas and quit drinking, becoming a practising Christian. However, this reformation did not diminish his skill at shooting with both rifle and pistol, mostly for the family pot but also at local shooting matches.

On 5 June 1917, at the age of twenty-nine, York received notice to register for the draft as America had joined the war two months earlier. His application to seek conscientious-objector status was refused and York was ordered to attend basic military training at Camp Gordon in Georgia, although he was still hoping to be excused fighting. He was posted to Company G, 2nd Battalion, 328th Infantry, a part of the 82nd Division. During training he soon became noticed for his skill with weapons and as a marksman of outstanding ability. It was during this time that he was able to reconcile his Christian reluctance to fight with his patriotic duty as a soldier by the counselling of both his battalion and company commanders.

York first saw action in the first completely American operation of the war in the St-Mihiel battle on 12 September. He proved himself a good soldier, was promoted corporal and became a squad leader. On 8 October 1918 York's regiment was heavily involved in fighting near Hill 223, close to the village of Chatel-Chéhéry in the Meuse–Argonne battle. The 328th Regiment's mission was to sever the narrow-gauge railway supplying the Germans surrounding the 'Lost Battalion' (see Map 32). The battalion's advance was soon held up by heavy enemy machine-gun fire from three sides and the attack stalled. A Sergeant Bernard Early was detailed to take sixteen men, including Corporal York's squad, to outflank and eliminate the machine guns. This patrol moved forward through dense forest and, whether by accident or design, got behind the German positions, surprising and capturing a number of Germans in a clearing well behind their lines. However, while contending with the prisoners the patrol came under heavy machine-gun fire which killed Corporal Savage and five others, as well as wounding three more, including Sergeant Early and the other squad leader, Corporal Cutting. This put Corporal York in command of the remaining seven. The time had come for him to make use of his marksmanship skill. In his own words:

Sergeant Alvin York

> Those machine guns were spitting fire and cutting down the undergrowth all around me something awful. And the Germans were yelling orders. You never heard such a racket in all your life. I didn't have time to dodge behind a tree or dive into the bush . . . As soo as the machine guns opened fire on me I bega to exchange shots with them. There were over thirty of them [it's uncertain if he meant thirt machine guns or thirty Germans – the latter i more likely] in continuous action, and all I could do was touch off [shoot] the Germans just as fast as I could. I was sharp shooting . . All the time I kept yelling at them to come down. I didn't want to kill any more than I had to. But it was they or I.

York's brief account does not do hi justice. He was so close to the enem that they had to expose their head to fire at him and his men, at the same time avoiding hitting their comrades. Every time a Germar head appeared, York shot at it. settle the matter, an exasperate German lieutenant led a charge on York's position. For York thi was life or death, snap-shooting moving targets, albeit at very clo range. Coolly he downed the soldiers from the rear first so that those at the front would not realize what was happening. York's rifle magaz took only five rounds, but having shot f of the enemy he pulled out his pistol, killed the remaining attackers and wounded the lieutenant in the stomach. At this point the Germans surrendered. During the march out wi the prisoners they encountered more enemy wh joined the increasingly large band of captives. T total count of prisoners York and his men broug out was 132.

York was promoted sergeant and received th Medal of Honor. He was also awarded the Fren *Croix de Guerre* and *Légion d'honneur*, while Ital and Montenegro awarded him the *Croce di*

Butte de Vauquois

uerra and War Medal respectively. On his return
the United States in April 1919 he was greeted
a national hero.

After the war he founded the Alvin C. York
gricultural Institute in Jamestown, Tennessee,
d opened a Bible School with the proceeds of the
m made about his exploits. During World War II
served on the Tennessee Draft Board and
came a colonel in the Tennessee State Guard.
rk died at the veterans' hospital in Nashville,
nnessee, on 2 September 1964, aged seventy-six.
s name is commemorated as follows:

The Alvin C. York Veterans' Hospital in
urfreesboro, Tennessee.

His original York Institute continues as
mestown's High School.

Sergeant York, a 1941 film starring Gary Cooper.

York Avenue in the Upper East Side of
anhattan.

In 1983 the Sergeant York M 247 Divisional Air
efense Gun was delivered for service. It had twin
mm anti-aircraft guns mounted on a tank chassis
th tracking and surveillance radar. However, the
ogramme was terminated after it was discovered
at the radar could not distinguish between a
mp of trees and a low-flying helicopter.

On 5 May 2000 the US Postal Service issued a
ries of 'Distinguished Soldiers' stamps in which
rk was honoured.

The riderless horse in former President
eagan's funeral procession in 2004 was named
rgeant York.

A Sergeant York Historic Trail in the Argonne
lows visitors to explore the site of his exploits.

A Tennessee football trophy is named after him.

The 229th Military Intelligence Battalion, A
mpany, Monterey, California, dedicated their
ldiers' hall in honour of Sergeant York.

In 1968 a bronze statue of York was placed in
e grounds of the Tennessee State Capitol.

The Belgian Army

As explained in the Introduction, the
German plan to destroy the French field
armies involved breaching Belgian neutrality
(the primary reason for the UK entering the
war). On 2 August 1914 Germany issued her
ultimatum demanding access through Belgian
territory and the use of the fortresses of Liège
and Namur. Belgium's refusal led to immediate invasion, which found the Belgian Army
completely unready for a major war and in
the midst of a drastic reorganization. Her
government had previously agreed that the
country needed an army of 350,000 men,
composed of a 150,000 field army, 130,000
fortress garrisons and 70,000 reserves and
auxiliary troops. The problem was that these
figures would not be achieved until 1925.

Prior to 1913, recruitment was partly by
voluntary service and partly by limited conscription. In that year the principle of compulsory military service was accepted, requiring one man from each household to serve
fifteen months with the colours for infantry,
twenty-one months for field artillery and
twenty-four for horse artillery – although
married men with families served only four
months. The consequent expansion, the
reform of training, and the upgrading of
arms and equipment was to be well under
way by 1918, which meant that by August
1914 little had been done and few, if any,
improvements made.

The Belgian Army comprised the Regular
Army, Gendarmerie and Garde Civique. The
Gendarmerie was recruited from selected personnel and formed an elite cavalry formation,
whereas the Garde Civique was not part of
the military but was administered by the
Home Department rather than the War
Department and included all able-bodied
men between the ages of twenty and thirty-
two not in the army or reserve. They were
primarily to be used to deal with civil disturbances and around 35,000–40,000 were
available for service in 1914. The Germans
did not regard them as military personnel –
something that prompted the local gardes to
pile their arms in town halls to prevent the
occupying Germans treating them as soldiers
rather than police, albeit paramilitary ones.

Like her allies, the Belgian Army went to
war with serious deficiencies. Most units
were not up to strength, particularly with
regard to officers – some companies went
into battle commanded by senior NCOs –
and the average age for the soldiers was, initially, about thirty. Training was often poor
and lack of physical fitness a problem, with a
10-mile march producing far too many stragglers. Some basic equipment, such as field
kitchens, was unavailable. Despite this, army
morale was high, with a fervent desire to
confront the Germans in defence of the
country. However, there were other problems of a material nature. The most serious
included the army possessing only 324
obsolete Krupp field guns and no heavy
guns at all. For infantry weapons only some
93,000 rifles and 105 machine guns were
immediately available.

On the outbreak of war Belgium's available military manpower and resources were
split between the field army and the garrisons of fortresses, the important ones
being Antwerp, Liège and Namur. The field
army was able to put around 117,000 men

Belgian carabiniers, with their traditional Tyrolean hats and with dogs pulling machine guns on carts, moving towards the front in August 1914.

into action in August 1914, made up of six large infantry divisions and one small cavalry division of about 6,000 men – in reality a brigade. The fortresses had second- or third-rate troops as defenders, numbering some 85,000 all ranks – 56,000 in Antwerp, 15,500 in Liège and 13,500 in Namur. These fortresses were lacking in modern, long-range heavy guns, whereas the Germans were able to bring up siege guns firing concrete-busting projectiles. These huge pieces stood well back from their target, immune to enemy counter-battery fire, and pounded the defences to pieces. Liège was the first to fall, on 17 August; Namur followed on 25 August, but Antwerp was not forced to surrender until 9 October.

Antwerp was a special case. It was an entrenched national refuge into which retreated the field army as it was forced to withdraw, along with thousands of civilian refugees. Its ring of outer forts and defences were more extensive than the other fortresses, and its garrison was also boosted not only by the Belgian field army but also by a British naval brigade of 6,000 men (at the insistence of Winston Churchill as first lord of the admiralty). During the siege the Belgian Army mounted two major sorties designed to divert German forces from their advance into France. These occurred from 25 to 26 August and 9 to 13 September, the latter costing almost 8,000 casualties. From 28 September to 9 October, beginning with the outer ring of forts, the Germans bombarded the defenders into submission. The city of Antwerp itself was shelled continuously for thirty-six hours from midnight on 7 October and the military governor finally surrendered at 3:00 p.m. on 10 October, by which time the field army had withdrawn south to maintain the fight and was to meet the enemy onslaught again on the River Yser.

The Belgian Army, despite its serious deficiencies and facing a more numerous and far better armed, trained and equipped enemy, was able to check, to slow the massive German advance for a few days. This was enough to throw the German war plan behind schedule. Under their commander-in-chief, King Albert I, the Belgians held the line along the Yser sector of the Western Front for the remainder of the war, defending the small area of Belgium that remained free from German occupation. By conscripting from the area still held, the Belgians were able to maintain their army at around 170,000 and by November 1918 had mobilized 267,000 men, of whom they lost 38,000 dead, 44,700 wounded and 10,200 prisoners.

The Battle of the Yser

Following the siege of Antwerp, the Belgian Army was forced into the far south-western corner of the country, where it made a stand along the 20-mile Yser river/canal as the Germans tried to reach the French Channel ports of Calais and Dunkirk. Just to the south, the First Battle of Ypres took place at the same time as the Battle of the Yser, both battles concluding the series of outflanking manoeuvres by the belligerents known as the Race to the Sea, and led to the establishment of the trench lines that characterized the Western Front until almost the end of the war.

Notes for Map 33

Belligerents

Belgian/French	German
Belgian Army	Fourth Army
I French Division	III, XXII and XXIII
and Marine Brigade	Reserve Corps

Divisions 7 infantry   initially 12

Commanders

King Albert I	Archduke Albrecht
of Belgium	von Württemberg

Casualties

Belgian: 15,000	uncertain
French: 8,000	

Result The German advance was held on the line of the Yser.

Summary On 18–19 October the German offensive by the Fourth Army drove back Allied outposts **A**. On 20 October heavy German assaults between Nieuport and the coast almost broke through but were repulsed with the help of a British naval bombardment **B** and a further German attack near Dixmude was repulsed **B1**. During the night of 20/21 October the Germans were able to secure a small bridgehead over the Yser at Tervaate **C** which could not be destroyed by counter-attacks, even with the arrival of reinforcements from the French 42nd Division on 23 October which allowed local counter-attacks to be made **D**. This was the day on which the last bridge over the Yser was blown. The town of Dixmude was subjected to particularly severe bombardments and some 15 separate attacks, which were driven off on the 24th **E**. On 26 October the continuous enemy assaults forced the Belgians to withdraw behind the Nieuport–Dixmude railway embankment. During periods of high tide between 28 and 30 October the sluice gates at Nieuport were opened and the low ground between the Yser and the railway embankment was slowly flooded, making large-scale military operations impractical. On 29 October Dixmude finally fell to the Germans, but their decisive attack planned for 30 October was called off and the front stabilized, with the German High Command abandoning attempts to crush the Belgians and transferring its efforts to the south. The Belgians maintained this front until 1918, when they retook their country during the Allies' final advance to victory.

Belgian Refugees Flee Antwerp

J. M. N Jeffries was correspondent for the *Daily Mail* in Antwerp during the siege of the city and witnessed the final despairing trek to refuge of the civilians as they fled south from the city:

We quitted Antwerp between ten and eleven . . . away before us a stream of fugitives stretched to the village of Eeckeren, three miles beyond. To the right over more bare country, flowed another great stream of mankind. Seen from afar this was so sombre and moved so little that it had the likeness of something cut deep in the soil, of some vast drain.

The number of those departing was so great that I gave no thought to estimating it. If huge crowds had left the city I might have tried to reckon how many they were. But what I perceived now was not a mere escape or withdrawal of huge crowds. Departure was universal. Antwerp was like a box which had been opened and its population had fallen out of it . . .

All the time the afflictions of the route encompassed me . . . Enormous wagons occupied half the road bearing twenty, twenty-five, thirty persons pent in a heap, girls huddled listlessly together upon heaps of bedding, aged brown women like shrunken walnuts buried in shawls, children fitfully asleep and querulous, and babies crying interminably . . . Perambulators, too, were filled with children on whom clothes and linen had been piled . . . Sons wheeled old fathers along in wheelbarrows, and strong men were carrying (for how long?) chairs slung from their shoulders in which daughters or wives, ill or with child, sat gripping the arms of the chair rigidly . . . mixed with [these] was a surf, an undersurf of domestic beasts, clogging every pore of progress; bevies of wretched hoof-weary ba-aing sheep; dogs barking distractedly; bellowing cattle in droves . . . Some of the legions of dogs dragged little carts . . . numbers of women cradled cats in their arms.

The awful slowness of movement wore out the soul. Hundreds upon hundreds gave up, flung themselves down by the roadside or formed camps by the trees by the border . . . An extraordinary sight stays in my mind still, seen when I had struggled forward to learn the cause of a long delay in the ranks. In mid-roadway was a group of women, all clothed in black, leaning humped together, as the old masters draw women at the foot of the Cross, and moaning in unison like Jews under the walls of Jerusalem, crying: '*Donnez-nous à boire! Sainte Vierge, donnez-nous à boire!*' ['Give us something to drink! Holy Virgin, give us something to drink!']

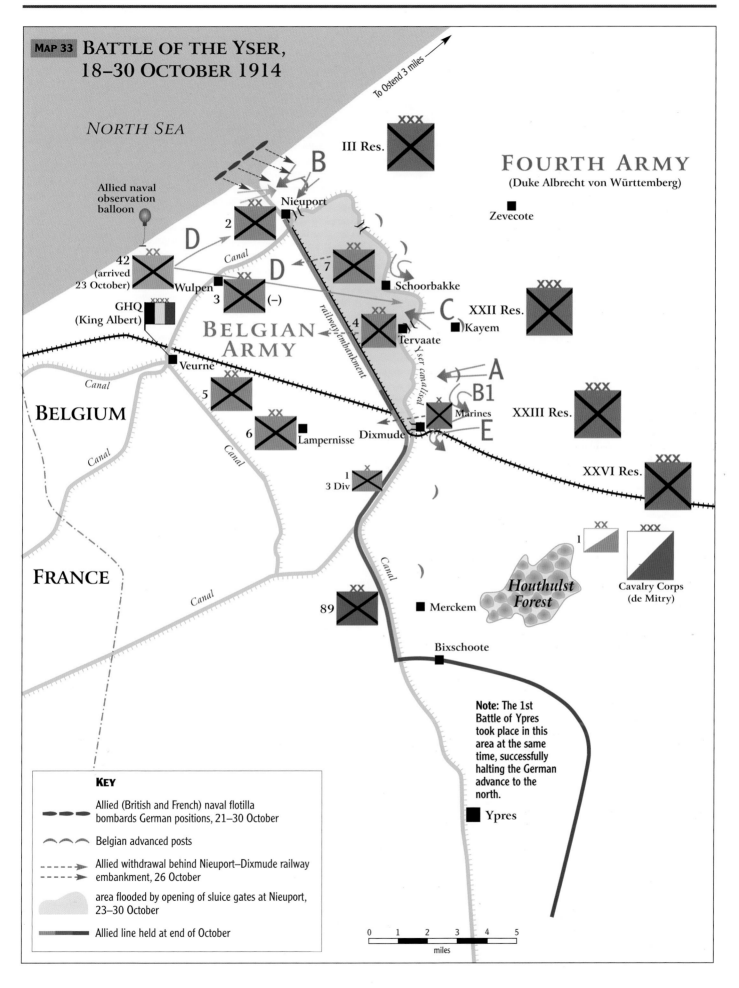

MAP 33 BATTLE OF THE YSER,
18–30 OCTOBER 1914

To Ostend 3 miles

NORTH SEA

III Res.

FOURTH ARMY
(Duke Albrecht von Württemberg)

B

Allied naval
observation
balloon

Nieuport

Zevecote

2

D

Canal

D

42
(arrived
23 October)

Wulpen

7

Schoorbakke

C XXII Res.

3   (–)

Kayem

BELGIAN
ARMY

4

GHQ
(King Albert)

Tervaate

Veurne

Canal

railway embankment

Yser canalized

5

A

Canal

B1

BELGIUM

6

Lampernisse

Dixmude

Marines

XXIII Res.

Canal

E

Canal

1
3 Div

XXVI Res.

FRANCE

Canal

Canal

1

Cavalry Corps
(de Mitry)

89

Merckem

Houthulst
Forest

Bixschoote

Note: The 1st
Battle of Ypres
took place in this
area at the same
time, successfully
halting the German
advance to the
north.

Ypres

KEY

Allied (British and French) naval flotilla
bombards German positions, 21–30 October

Belgian advanced posts

Allied withdrawal behind Nieuport–Dixmude railway
embankment, 26 October

area flooded by opening of sluice gates at Nieuport,
23–30 October

Allied line held at end of October

0 1 2 3 4 5
miles

Belgian infantry advancing over open ground.

The entire Belgian Army was deployed to defend the front, with three infantry divisions forward and three in reserve. The troops were exhausted and low on ammunition after two months of fighting and retreating. France reinforced the Belgians with an infantry division (the 42nd) and a marine brigade, while the British Royal Navy provided a flotilla of warships and three armoured, shallow-draught monitors, each carrying two 6-inch guns and two 4.7-inch howitzers. This flotilla (reinforced by two French warships) kept the coastal strip under constant bombardment, seriously disrupting German operations and causing many casualties.

The outline and sequence of the battle are shown on Map 33. Some of the most protracted and bitter fighting, at times hand to hand, took place in and around Dixmude. The defenders fought with exceptional gallantry and determination, on 24 October repelling fifteen separate German assaults.

However, on the night of the 21/22 October the Germans gained a bridgehead by simply walking across an unguarded footbridge at Tervaate – not a shot had been fired at them. This bridgehead could not be destroyed and on 26 October the Belgians pulled back behind the Nieuport–Dixmude railway embankment and opened the sluice gates. The consequent flooding persuaded the Germans to close down offensive operations and turn their attentions to Ypres.

The Flooding of the Polders

The north-western coastal area of Belgium was flat, reclaimed land known as 'polders'. Intersected with canals and ditches, it could be flooded by opening a series of sluice gates at the canal complex at Nieuport and the Belgians had planned to use this if need be as a defence against a German advance. A major engineering task had been the damming of the twenty-two culverts that ran below the Nieuport–Dixmude railway embankment. This done, the plan depended on the right high tides, the force and direction of the wind and the feasibility of opening the old sluice of Veurne, which consisted of two gates that needed to be held open constantly, with one set of ebb-tide doors free to move with the rise and fall of the water. At the other sluices the doors and gates had to be operated manually. Careful planning was needed to avoid flooding the area while it was still occupied by the 2nd Division. On 26 October 1914 attempts to open the Veurne sluice failed, but two days later the second try succeeded and slowly the waters began

to rise and flooding spread. More sluices were opened on the 29th and 30th to take advantage of high tides.

While these aquatic operations were in hand, bitter fighting continued as the Germans maintained the pressure, but as the flood rose so the troops found themselves moving through water inches deep over the whole region between the Yser and the railway embankment. Eventually the flooding covered an area some 8 miles long and nearly 3 miles wide.

As the water gradually spread, the Belgians began to run out of ammunition, with field guns down to their last 100 rounds. The French commander, Foch, advised King Albert to withdraw behind the Veurne–Ypres Canal (see Map 33) – but he refused, as it would have meant giving up virtually the entire country. It was the correct decision, as by 31 October the rising waters and strong resistance drove the Germans to switch their efforts southwards.

JAN		1
		2
FEB		③
		4
		5
MAR		6
		7
		8
APR		9
		10
		11
MAY		12
		13
JUNE		14
		15
		16
JULY		17
		18
AUG		19
		20
		21
SEPT		22
		23
		24
OCT		25
		26
		27
NOV		28
		29
DEC		30
		31

DATE DUE

To help keep track of your borrowed items, please use the reverse of this slip to record titles.

A hole has been punched next to the month and day your books are due. You are responsible for returning them on time.

Stolen or lost card? Contact your branch or call 403-260-2608 (24 hrs.)

Calgary Public Library

The French Army

The French Army was the cornerstone of the Allies' effort on the Western Front from August 1914 at least until mid-1917. By the end of the war French fatalities were almost half a million more than those of Britain and her empire, and wounded more than twice as numerous. Since her disastrous defeat in the Franco-Prussian War the French had introduced the concept of universal military conscription. Under the 'Three Years Law' of 1913, the original period of active service was increased from two to three years.

There were four categories of service. First was in the active army, where all fit nineteen-year-old Frenchmen were liable for three years' duty. After this a man would spend another eleven in the Active Reserve. Then came a period of seven years in the Territorial Army and finally another seven in the Territorial Reserve. Thus a man would be about forty-eight before he could no longer be called to don a uniform. The Territorial formations were intended as garrison troops and were required to put in forty days' training each year, but once in the Territorial Reserve this dropped to a paltry single day – an amount that was of no military value. Call-up was on a regional basis under the control of the general commanding the eighteen joint military regions and corps headquarters of Metropolitan France and the nineteenth in Algeria. For the 173 active-line infantry regiments there was an equal number of affiliated reserve regiments, numbered by adding 200 to the number of their parent regiment. There were also thirty-one light infantry (*chasseurs à pied*) battalions, each with a linked reserve battalion. The Territorial Army could raise 145 infantry regiments of three or more battalions.

In a similar way to Britain, Metropolitan France was able to call on the services of her overseas possessions for duty on the Western Front. This second army was an extraordinary and colourful mix of colonial troops, of whom the great majority was based in North Africa (Morocco, Algeria and Tunis). The French Metropolitan and North African Armies of 1914 were composed of the regiments shown in the table above.

In addition, France had sixteen colonial regiments raised from French citizens in France or the colonies to garrison the latter (including China, West Africa and Indochina). A further nineteen regiments were reservists or recruited from scratch from a mixture of Europeans and Senegalese – the best known being the highly decorated *Régiment d'Infanterie Coloniale du Maroc* (Moroccan Colonial Infantry), originally recruited from personnel stationed in Morocco in 1914. Added to these were the regiments raised from the indigenous people of Africa and Indochina. At the start of the war there were twenty-one battalions of Senegalese, ten of Malagasies and one of Somalis, plus two Congolese and five Indochinese regiments – all in all a varied and colourful mixture. Also, organized on military lines were the Gendarmerie (a national police force), the Republican Guard (a semi-military police force to maintain public order in Paris), the *Chasseurs Forestiers* (gamekeepers, rangers and bailiffs used in wartime as guides and intelligence agents) and the Customs Corps (on mobilization helped garrison fortresses and defended ports).

Metropolitan and Colonial Troops, 1914

Cavalry	Infantry	Artillery
12 *cuirassiers*	173 line regts	62 regts field artillery
32 dragoons	31 batts *chasseurs à pied*	10 groups horse artillery
21 *chasseur à cheval*	4 regts Zouaves	2 regts mountain artillery
14 hussars	9 regts *tirailleurs Algériens*	11 regts foot artillery
6 *chasseurs d'Afrique*	2 regts *Étrangers* (Foreign Legion)	5 regts heavy field artillery
4 *spahis* (light cavalry)	5 batts *Légère d'Afrique*	10 groups *artillerie d'Afrique*
	12 regts *colonial*	3 regts *artillerie coloniale*
	7 batts *de marche coloniale*	
	5 batts *Auxiliaires Marocaines*	

The peacetime strength of the French Army was 817,000 French and around 67,000 North African troops – in all 884,000 men – and these numbers were increased on mobilization to 3,683,000, the great majority being conscript peasants from the countryside. Of these some 2,670,000 were available for service in the field or in the fortified areas along the eastern and northern frontiers. The French field armies that counter-attacked the Germans in August 1914 numbered well over a million men. They were divided into five armies with a total of 62½ infantry and ten cavalry divisions (see Map 5, pages 24–5, for the strength of each). They went to war full of patriotism, elan and a determination to avenge their defeat of forty-three years earlier, a significant element of which was the reclaiming of the lost provinces of Alsace and Lorraine. However, apart from being outnumbered by a more powerful force of seven armies, they went into battle with four distinct disadvantages:

• **Uniforms** When French soldiers went into action in 1914 they provided conspicuous targets for their enemy. Neither infantry nor cavalry would have looked out of place on a Napoleonic battlefield of a hundred years earlier. The metropolitan infantryman wore a dark blue jacket with polished buttons, red trousers and red kepi. On the outbreak of war a less conspicuous

French troops at a listening post in advance of the front line, winter 1917. Note the excessive and awkward length of the Lebel rifle when the bayonet was fixed.

uniform had been suggested by, among others, General Gallieni, the military governor of Paris, but had been rejected mostly on the extraordinary claim by Eugène Étienne, minister of war in 1913, that 'Red trousers are France.' A cavalry regiment on the march to battle made an even more spectacular sight, the cuirassiers taking the prize with their gleaming breastplates and burnished, plume-topped helmets. Within a matter of weeks it was realized that some form of camouflage uniform was vital and the 'horizon blue' – a light blue-grey colour – was agreed. Kepis and puttees were the first to be made of this material, but in April 1915 it was ordered that all troops at the front should wear a complete uniform of this colour, which, when dirtied by the chalky mud of Champagne and Artois, produced a reasonable camouflage. However, it was not until November 1915 that all soldiers wore the complete new uniform.

• **Small arms** The principal rifle was the 8mm Lebel, originally adopted in 1886 and modified in 1893 (it was still in use in some units at the end of World War II). It was much too long for trench fighting and was made virtually useless in such circumstances when the long spike bayonet, which broke easily, was attached. Perhaps worse was that initially, although it could hold eight 8mm rounds and a ninth in the breach, the magazine was a long tube under the barrel into which each round had to be loaded separately. It was replaced in 1916 by the Berthier (a development of the cavalry carbine), which when modified could be loaded from five-round clips. The 1914 machine gun was the Hotchkiss, which was fed by long, straight clips of thirty rounds rather than by belts. Its weight, with tripod, was over 53 lb (24kg), making it unpopular with those who had to carry it and the ammunition over long distances – the concession given to machine-gun teams was that they were armed with a pistol instead of a rifle.

• **Artillery** Here the French started the war with probably the best field gun of any army – the quick-firing (up to twenty rounds a minute in an emergency) 75mm, designed in the 1880s. The problem was the neglect of heavier guns and mortars that were seen initially as primarily armament for fortresses. In 1914 France had 616 field

The French Army Mutinies, April–June 1917

Early summer 1917 saw what any military commander dreads – mutiny. Sixty-eight divisions of the French Army were ultimately affected, although not all to the same extent – a figure representing over half the army. The great majority of the outbreaks occurred in the infantry, with only seven artillery and no cavalry regiments involved, reflecting the fact that it was the infantry that bore the bulk of the horrors of war.

The causes were the sum of several factors. First and foremost was the perceived futility of the slaughter of the previous twelve months in terms of bringing the war to an end. To the hundreds of thousands of casualties of Verdun and the Somme were added those of General Nivelle's disastrous offensive on the Chemin des Dames in April 1917. French soldiers were bitterly disillusioned and had come to view any offensive as a useless waste of life – some regiments had advanced into battle bleating like a herd of sheep. On top of this was the French Army's neglect of the soldiers' personal welfare and morale. Genuine grievances over poor food, lack of proper rest periods, primitive conditions out of the line and above all lack of home leave – something that Nivelle had curtailed even further.

The first signs of trouble came in June 1916, when the average monthly desertion rate rose to 1,620, up from 620 in April. Although the mutinies began in mid-April 1917 and peaked in early June, they rumbled on, with minor instances occurring until January 1918. The first major outbreak was in the 21st Division on 3 May, while the futile Nivelle offensive was still going on. These troops refused to attack. The ringleaders were identified and summarily shot or sent to a living death on Devil's Island off the coast of French Guiana. Next, two other regiments (the 120th and 128th) disobeyed orders to move into the line and the mutiny quickly spread to units throughout the army, with around 20,000 men deserting during its course. Men with exemplary battlefield records were not immune, although it was rare for NCOs to join in actively. In most units the disturbances were more like those in an angry and militant trade union than armed soldiers turning on their officers (although some were roughly handled). Usually it was resting regiments that would mount angry demonstrations, demand redress of grievances, wave red flags of

A French soldier is executed near Verdun for desertion during the mutinies of 1917.

revolution, sing the 'Internationale' and elect 'councils' to make decisions and represent them to the authorities. There were ominous similarities to the revolution taking place in Russia that particularly frightened the French government and High Command. Threats were made to march on Paris, but the only case of violence to a senior officer was when the 23rd and 133rd Regiments roughed up General Bulot, ripped off his rank badges and threw stones at him. He was widely regarded by his troops as a callous butcher of men.

Amazingly, the news of the mutinies did not apparently reach the Germans, perhaps partially due to the fact that, apart from a few exceptions, units in the line remained steady – they would not attack, but they did not abandon their positions and were prepared to resist any enemy attack. Nevertheless, for several weeks the situation was potentially disastrous. The government turned to Marshal Philippe Pétain to restore order. This he did with a firm but fair combination of toughness and moderation. Courts martial dealt with arrested mutineers, of whom 499 were sentenced to death, although only about fifty-five such sentences were carried out; most of the others received prison sentences varying from three years to life. Alongside these heavy punishments on individuals, some regiments were disbanded and others were stripped of their colours. Two generals and nine lieutenant colonels were sacked. However, Pétain fully understood that many of the soldiers' grievances contained much truth and he immediately put in hand reforms to improve food standards, refurbish barracks, and ensure that rest periods and leave were fairly and properly organized, including facilities for travelling home and an entitlement of seven to ten days for every four months at the front. Pétain visited dozens of units to see that the reforms were taking place, to speak to the soldiers, distribute tobacco and award medals – particularly the newly instituted *Croix de Guerre*.

Pétain had surely saved the day, but the French Army was no longer able to mount the large-scale offensives of the earlier years, and the primary burden of fighting on the Western Front passed to the British while both countries anxiously awaited the arrival of the Americans.

Driant's command post in the Bois des Caures.

artillery and thirty horse artillery batteries, compared with fifty-eight of heavier guns (all of four guns).

• **The gospel of *l'attaque à outrance***
Literally translated, this means 'attack to excess'. At both the strategic, operational and tactical levels it was ingrained in all commands from general to corporal that an attack in virtually all circumstances would ensure success. Throughout the military, this cult of the offensive carried with it a corresponding neglect of the defensive. A Lieutenant Colonel Loyzeau de Grandmaison first expounded this doctrine in 1906. He was head of the General Staff's 3rd Bureau, Operations and Training, responsible, among other things, for tactical theory. The violent assault conducted by soldiers imbued with *élan* (dash) and *cran* (guts) could, he believed, overcome any enemy, regardless of the firepower of modern weapons. It was all about the will to win, with rigidly disciplined regiments advancing behind officers waving swords and shouting, '*En avant à la baïonette*' ('Forward with the bayonet'). This theory was adopted by the army in the years prior to the war and was incorporated in the tactical and infantry training manuals. Field artillery would advance with the infantry to support the attack rather than bombard the enemy in preparation for it. Cavalry would fight mounted and charge home at the first opportunity. Officers and NCOs were not required to think further than the assault: if in doubt, attack or counter-attack – it was simple.

At the start of the war a combination of these four factors – conspicuous uniforms, second-rate rifles, lack of heavy and medium guns and a tactical theory that invited disaster – was to cost France a million casualties (300,000 dead) in five months – a staggering loss for a nation of 39.6 million.

Like the other belligerents, France was forced to adapt to trench (siege) warfare and to new technologies on the battlefield, and to evolve better tactics at least to lessen the horrendous losses. These last are discussed in the relevant sections below. It is sufficient here just to outline the manpower difficulties that France had to overcome during the course of the war. They were no different from those of the other participants, but will serve as an example of the tremendous burden those nations had to endure in human terms.

As noted above, the French Army suffered an extremely costly shock during the early months of the war. Nevertheless, despite these losses, 1915 saw the number of divisions rise to ninety-two, with 2.6 million men under arms. However, that year saw casualties averaging over 130,000 a month up to June, with those of the autumn Champagne offensive reaching 180,000. In addition, the vastly increased demand for supplies and munitions necessitated the withdrawal of large numbers (339,000 by the end of the year) of combatants for industrial work. Add in another 100,000 sent to Salonika and it is extraordinary that the army managed to increase in size so that at the start of 1916 it had some 2.86 million men. However, as for other nations, 1916 was another dreadful year for losses, with Verdun and the Somme between them inflicting over 600,000. But yet again the French Army at the front had marginally more men at the end of the year than at the beginning.

The tipping point was reached in 1917 with the failure of the Nivelle offensive and the withdrawal of more men for industry and agriculture, which resulted in the overall size of the army shrinking for the first time. Coupled with poor morale and the mutinies of that year (see box opposite), 1917 was a grim year for the French. The next year saw France once again bringing her army up to 102 divisions, although they now consisted of three regiments of nine battalions instead of the previous twelve. However, the German spring offensive and the Allied summer advance saw close to another million losses. Nevertheless, by the end of the war France still had 2.6 million men in the field – about the same number as in early 1915 – a remarkable, if crippling, achievement.

For the French Army, Verdun became the furnace in which almost every division on the Western Front was burned at some time during 1916. It was the longest and most costly battle of the war, lasting from 21 February to 18 December. The primary objective of the German Operation Gericht (Scaffold) was to bleed the French Army to death – not necessarily to take Verdun itself (although the German commanders involved thought it was), but to suck in tens of thousands of French troops and pulverize them. It was to be the ultimate battle of attrition. The German chief of staff, General Erich von Falkenhayn, assembled over 1,200 guns, howitzers and mortars (with a stock of 2.5 million shells), seven army corps and large numbers of aircraft for the offensive.

Inside Driant's command post.

The French defence of the Bois des Caures (Verdun)

The Bois des Caures was a key position in the defences of Verdun, located just over 20 miles north of the city and on the east, or right, bank of the River Meuse. Its defence was entrusted to the 56th and 59th Battalions of chasseurs à pied commanded by Lieutenant Colonel Émile Driant. The troops had been deployed in these woods following the Battle of the Marne in 1914, and Driant had tried to prepare his defences as well as his limited manpower and resources (particularly barbed wire) would allow. There was considerable depth to the position, with the defenders located in a series of bunkers and strong-points linked by communication trenches, mostly on high ground and in thick woods. The outer line of bunkers was supported by a second line about 200 yards to the rear (numbered S1–9 on Map 34). About 1,000 yards further back was the more extended third, or reserve, line with concrete bunkers numbered R1–5. Three companies manned the forward area. From the left, 7 Company under Captain Sequin; in the centre 9 Company under Lieutenant Robin; and on the right 10 Company commanded by Captain Vigneron. In each of these company localities (two in 7 Company) there was a well-developed strongpoint called a *Grande Garde*, labelled **GG 1–4** on the map. The reserve, 8 Company under Lieutenant Simon, was positioned around Driant's command post near the Flabas– Ville–Verdun road junction. With only around 1,200 men and a position 2,000 yards wide and 1,500 yards deep, Driant had to spread his men very thinly.

During 1915 the Verdun defences had been stripped of manpower, guns, ammunition and supplies, which were switched to other fronts as the French High Command did not consider Verdun would face a major,

sustained assault. Major General Herr, the military governor of Verdun, had repeatedly but in vain called for reinforcements to implement the works needed to repair the neglected defences. Driant himself had written to a friend, Paul Deschanel, president of the Chamber of Deputies, asking him to intervene directly with the minister of defence to secure more men and resources. Driant's letter caused outrage. It reached Marshal Joffre, who responded, 'I cannot be a party to soldiers under my command bringing before the Government, by channels other than the hierarchic channels, complaints or protests concerning the execution of my orders.' Had Driant survived he might well have been court-martialled for his temerity.

The German build-up before Verdun for the aptly codenamed Operation Gericht had been carefully and largely successfully concealed from the French. However, despite the shortcomings of French intelligence, as the start date approached rumours were spreading, fed by an increasing number of German deserters (mostly Alsatians), who spoke of increased offensive preparations. The Germans were amassing a huge force of men and guns. Opposed to the Verdun defences, manned by XXX Corps supported by some 270 artillery pieces, were the German VII Reserve, XVIII and III Corps, with the V Reserve and XV Corps in reserve supported by over 1,200 guns, many of them heavy, some super-heavy. The general attack on Verdun was due to start on 12 February, but a blinding blizzard reduced visibility to a few yards and the attack was postponed. The appalling weather continued for day after day as the troops on both sides froze in their bunkers and trenches.

Not until the 21st was there a let-up in the snow and freezing rain that had lashed the woods and all who huddled and shivered in them. On that morning the German barrage opened and shells lashed down on the Bois des Caures, smashing dugouts, burying,

MAP 34

MAP 34 LIEUTENANT COLONEL ÉMILE DRIANT'S DEFENCE OF THE BOIS DES CAURES, 21–22 FEBRUARY 1916

Bois
Sau

Bois
d'Haumont

R5

R4

Sergeant Léger's bunker on the western edge of the Bois des Caures.

Notes for Map 34

Belligerents

French	German
XXX Corps	XVIII and III Corps
72nd and 51st Divisions	21st and 25th Divisions
56th and 59th Battalions Chasseurs à Pied	81st, 87th, 115th and 117th Infantry Regiments
1,200 all ranks	4,000+ (estimate)

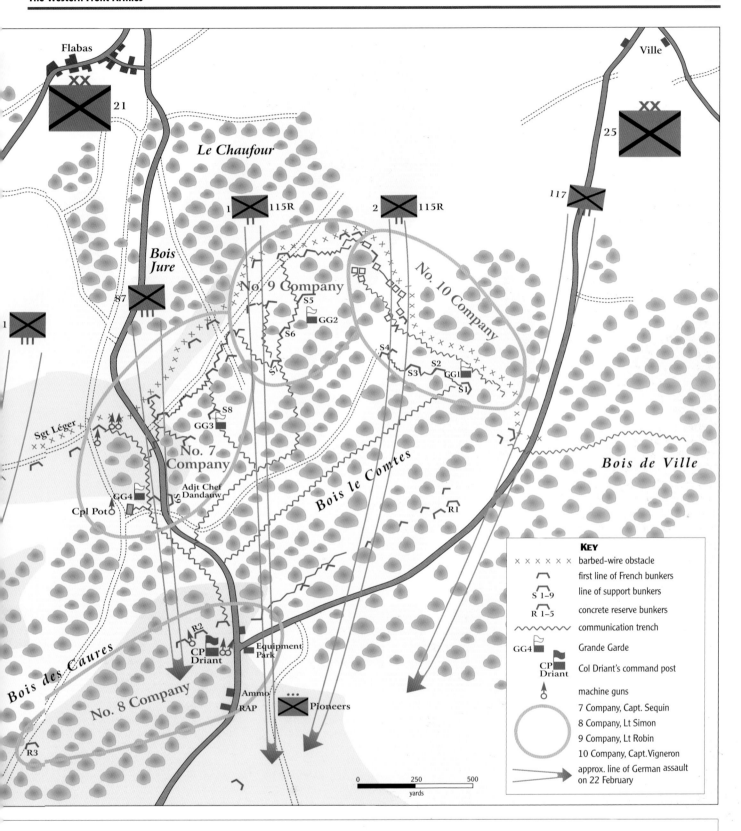

Flabas

XX
21

Ville

XX
25

117

Le Chaufour

1 ✕ 115R

2 ✕ 115R

Bois
Jure

87

No. 9 Company

S5

GG2

S6

No. 10 Company

S1

S4

S2

S3

GG1

S1

Sgt Léger

S8

GG3

No. 7
Company

Bois le Comtes

Bois de Ville

Adjt Chef
Dandauw

R1

GG4

Cpl Pot

Bois des Caures

R2

CP
Driant

Equipment
Park

No. 8 Company

Ammo

RAP

Pioneers

R3

KEY

✕ ✕ ✕ ✕ ✕ ✕ barbed-wire obstacle

⌐ first line of French bunkers

S 1–9 line of support bunkers

R 1–5 concrete reserve bunkers

〜〜〜 communication trench

GG4 Grande Garde

CP
Driant Col Driant's command post

machine guns

7 Company, Capt. Sequin

8 Company, Lt Simon

9 Company, Lt Robin

10 Company, Capt. Vigneron

approx. line of German assault
on 22 February

0   250   500
yards

Commanders

Lt Col Émile Driant
(Fifth Army)

Maj. Gen. Crown Prince
Wilhelm of Prussia

Casualties

700+

uncertain

Result After a magnificent defence the
Germans overran the French position and
Col Driant was killed.

Summary After the German assault on Verdun
was first delayed by appalling weather, the Bois des
Caures defenders were subjected to a whirlwind
bombardment, estimated at 80,000 shells, which
destroyed many bunkers and turned the wood into
matchwood. The initial German attack on
21 February was mostly of a probing nature to
locate weak points. The main assault on the next
day was also preceded by an intense barrage, with
a box barrage sealing off the defended area from
reinforcements. The German attackers, supported
by several flamethrower detachments, soon
penetrated gaps on the left and right of the
position and, although their units in the centre
became confused and intermixed in the wood, the
gravely depleted French defenders were eventually
forced back, overwhelmed or taken prisoner.
Col Driant died defending his command post.

Lieutenant Colonel Émile Driant, 1855–1916

Émile Driant was born in the Champagne region of France. His father was a lawyer, but Émile chose a military career, entering the French military academy of St-Cyr in 1875. Two years later he was commissioned into the 54th Infantry Regiment, serving with it until 1883 when he was transferred to the 4th Regiment of Zouaves in Tunis. There he was appointed to the staff of the controversial soldier-cum-politician Major General Marcelle Boulanger, who was commanding the occupation division. Driant later accompanied Boulanger to Paris when the general became minister of war, and in 1888 married his daughter. (Boulanger was later charged with treason but fled to England, eventually shooting himself on the grave of his mistress in Brussels in 1891.)

Driant was promoted captain in 1892 and was well known on account of his marriage, his position on his father-in-law's staff and his authorship of a stream of well-received patriotic military novels under the pseudonym 'Capitaine Danrit'. His first book was *La Guerre de Demain* (*The War of Tomorrow*) and his subsequent literary output included *La Guerre en Ballon* (*Balloon Warfare*) and *Guerre Fatale: France–Angleterre* (*The Fatal War: France–England*). The theme of devotion to duty, love of France and military honour predominated in all his works – which was precisely what readers of that time wanted.

For six years, 1899–1905, Driant commanded the 1st Battalion of chasseurs, becoming much respected for his leadership and concern for his men, of whom he was immensely proud. However, due to his close connection with the Boulanger family, he was passed over for promotion in five consecutive years. Seeing no future in the army, he resigned and devoted his energies to writing and calling on the government to remedy the deficiencies of the army. In 1910 Driant was elected to the Chamber of Deputies for Nancy and increased his calls to strengthen national defence. He espoused powerful nationalism, Catholic values and a fervent wish to see France regain the lost provinces of Alsace and Lorraine.

Driant was recalled to the army in 1914, aged fifty-eight, in the rank of captain, but was soon promoted to lieutenant colonel and given command of the 56th and 59th Battalions of chasseurs à pied. He also remained a deputy and was involved in drafting the legislation that instituted the *Croix de Guerre*. His letter to the minister of war complaining about the state of the Verdun defences and the lack of men and materials, together with his key role in the defence of the Bois des Caures and his death in that battle are detailed in this section.

The gallant defence of Bois des Caures by Driant and his chasseurs is commemorated every year on 21 February in la Place du Colonel Driant in Nancy with a parade and a gathering of military and civil dignitaries in front of a memorial plaque to the Heroes of the Great War. There is a rue du Colonel Driant in Paris and an avenue named after him in Valencia. In 1956 France issued a postage stamp bearing his portrait.

He was initially buried by the Germans, and a German baroness, whose husband had found Driant's body, sent his personal belongings back to his widow via Switzerland. He was reburied by the French at the place in the wood where he fell, where a memorial to him and his chasseurs now stands.

killing and wounding scores of chasseurs, at the same time uprooting trees and reducing the woods to a dense tangle of branches and splintered matchwood stumps. There was a short pause around midday, followed by a heavy mortar bombardment while the guns lifted to more distant targets and to seal off the area with box barrages – a surprisingly short preparatory barrage by World War I standards. Nevertheless, under this concentrated hailstorm (10,000 shells are thought to have fallen on Driant's positions during the two days), Driant's defenders suffered severely. Among the many smashed defences were shelters **R4** and **R5**, which received direct hits that killed all the occupants, while **R2** was partially damaged. Some sources consider up to half of the defenders were killed or wounded by this opening barrage. At 4:00 p.m. numerous small groups of German stormtroopers in field grey, the spikes removed from their helmets, surged forward tasked with finding the weak spots in the defences.

Within minutes Lieutenant Robin had his forward positions overrun. He informed Driant by runner and desperately called for artillery support – it was not forthcoming, as so many French battery positions had already been neutralized. With enemy infiltrating behind his bunker, Robin, after some vicious hand-to-hand encounters, pulled back to **S6**. Nightfall saw him, now wounded, withdrawing again with the rem-

nants of his company. On Captain Sequin's 7 Company's left flank two key machine guns were posted under Sergeant Léger and Corporal Pot. The latter had withdrawn unnecessarily to Adjutant Chef Dandauw's blockhouse (**S9**). With Germans closing in, Dandauw panicked and retreated down the communication trench to near Driant's command post; he was stopped and ordered to retake his position next morning. It was only the gallantry of Léger and his detachment holding out that prevented a complete collapse of 7 Company's left flank. Darkness brought the fighting to an end, but signalled the renewal of the dreaded artillery barrage. Despite this and his own wound, Robin led a bayonet charge that recaptured two of his support positions and a section of front-line trench, taking several prisoners.

At 7:00 a.m. the German pounding of the splintered wood and remaining French positions began again. At midday the infantry assault resumed, this time in overwhelming numbers. On the right of the position masses of Germans belonging to the 117th Infantry Regiment swept forward, using the road from Ville as their axis, and broke through, uncovering the whole of the right and centre of the French position. Frantic firing of flares for artillery support was again unavailing; complete disaster was forestalled only by the courageous and skilful work of several chasseur machine-gun positions. A similar situation developed on

the left where the German 81st Infantry Regiment was able to penetrate the gap between 7 Company and the French in Bois d'Haumont. Captain Sequin had his arm blown off and moments later his position was overrun. Meanwhile Robin too had been forced to surrender, unable to offer further resistance with a handful of men.

Those chasseurs who were able had now converged on Driant's command-post area for a final stand along the reserve line of redoubts. Germans attacking from the rear took **R1**, and at around 1:00 p.m. tried to rush **R2** but were driven off by Driant firing his rifle and encouraging those around him to do likewise. The Germans infiltrated between **R2** and **R3**, and the officer commanding the latter was forced to abandon it, leaving just Driant and **R2** still resisting. With the arrival of a German 77mm gun able to fire directly into the **R3** defences, the command post was no longer tenable. Driant ordered a final withdrawal, in the process of which the pioneer sergeant saw him suddenly throw up his arms and collapse, killed outright by a shot through his head.

Of some 1,200 men in the two chasseur battalions, about 500 managed to struggle further back to French lines, including many wounded. Their stand had checked the German advance, inflicting heavy and unexpectedly high losses. His inspiring leadership and courage made Colonel Driant one of France's most famous heroes of the war.

The German Army

The German Empire was a confederation of twenty-six states that included duchies, principalities, free cities and the kingdoms of Prussia, Bavaria, Saxony and Württemberg. Of these, Prussia was the most important, with 40 million people out of Germany's total of 67 million. Prussia's Hohenzollern king was the Kaiser, or Emperor, under whose aegis the empire had been formed. In 1914 Kaiser Wilhelm II, known as 'Kaiser Bill' to the British, had been on the imperial throne for twenty-six years. In peacetime the armies of the four kingdoms remained relatively distinct, as each was controlled by its own war ministry. However, in war there was a unified command under the Kaiser as commander-in-chief, with only Bavaria maintaining a separate establishment, although its staff coordinated planning with the Prussian General Staff. The proportion of army contingents to be provided by the four kingdoms was fixed by law in accordance with relative populations: Prussia and the smaller states 78 per cent; Bavaria 11 per cent; Saxony 7 per cent; and Württemberg 4 per cent (percentages approximately maintained during the war).

Germany, with the exception of Bavaria, was divided into eight army inspectorates.

Each was considered an army command and controlled a number of corps (two or more divisions with support troops). The corps covered a specific geographical area and were responsible for maintaining reserve forces within their area. By 1914 there were twenty-one corps areas under Prussian jurisdiction, plus three Bavarian army corps, as well as the Guard Corps, which controlled the elite Guard formations. Some corps areas also contained fortress troops and aviation battalions.

Like the other European countries, except the UK, Germany required its able-bodied men to undergo compulsory military service. It was an extremely comprehensive, if not complex, system. At the outbreak of war there were five classifications of military service: Regular (Active), Reserve, *Landwehr*, *Landsturm* and the *Ersatz* (Supplementary) Reserve, with the first being the Regular Army personnel. From the age of seventeen to twenty, men were liable to serve in the Landsturm (a Home Guard-type force); from twenty they served for two years in the regular infantry or active army, followed by five in the Reserve (three and four years respectively for the cavalry and horse artillery). From the age of twenty-seven the man was transferred to the Landwehr (1st Class) and at thirty-two to the Landwehr

Ernst Jünger Goes to War

Ernst Jünger, who died in 1998 at almost 103 years old, was a prolific writer who served throughout World War I and most of World War II. In his book *Storm of Steel* he described how many young German men felt as they marched to war in August 1914 – feelings not dissimilar to those of his enemies in those heady days before the grim reality of modern war was revealed.

We had come from lecture halls, school desks and factory workbenches, and over the brief weeks of training, we had bonded together into one large and enthusiastic group. Grown up in an age of security, we shared a yearning for danger, for the experience of the extraordinary. We were enraptured by war. We had set out in a rain of flowers, in a drunken atmosphere of blood and roses. Surely the war had to supply us with what we wanted; the great, the overwhelming, the hallowed experience. We thought of it as manly, as action, a merry duelling party on flowered, blood-bedewed meadows. 'No finer death in all the world than . . .' Anything to participate, not to have stayed at home!

Jünger was later commissioned and successfully led an infantry company with great gallantry on the Western Front. His company's attack on 21 March 1918 is described in brilliant detail in *Storm of Steel*.

German recruits on parade during training.

German Stormtrooper Battalions

The most famous of the stormtrooper units, named after its commander, was *Sturmbataillon Nr 5 (Rohr)* – Stormtrooper Battalion No. 5. It was formed in March 1915 at the training ground near Cologne with men from a pioneer battalion. In September Captain Willi Rohr took command of the unit and reorganized it. When completed, the unit consisted of two pioneer companies (assault companies), a 37mm gun section, a machine-gun platoon with six guns, a *Minenwerfer* (mortar) section with four light trench mortars and a *Flammenwerfer* (flamethrower) detachment. Many more stormtrooper units were formed later, primarily from pioneer or *Jäger* (light infantry) units. They were expanded in size and by the end of 1916 each army had its attached storm battalion (eighteen in all), which was in practice a mixed battalion battle group comprising up to five assault companies, one or two machine-gun companies, a mortar company, a howitzer battery, a flamethrower platoon and a horse transport column. Stormtrooper units spearheaded attacks at Verdun, counter-attacking at Cambrai, Riga (in Russia), in the Twelfth Battle of Isonzo (Italy) and in the German offensive of March 1918.

Sturmbataillon Nr 5 (Rohr) and Jäger-Sturmbataillon Nr 3, two of the original units, were later split into companies or platoons to be attached to various units for specific missions. According to Bob Lembke, whose father fought in the large *Garde-Reserve-Pionier-Regiment (Flammenwerfer)* – Guards Reserve Pioneer Regiment (Flamethrowers) – this unit was detached as sub-units in this way. In preparation for Operation Michael in March 1918, he explains that each company of this regiment had a special platoon for loan to the eighteen established storm battalions and that the platoon's machine guns were replaced with more flamethrowers. Lembke states that his father fought on several occasions with Rohr's battalion.

Lembke also added an interesting aside which shows how unpopular or corrupt senior ranks were sometimes dealt with in his unit:

My father, who was at war with a corrupt company command structure as well as the French, used a semi-live firing exercise as an opportunity to shoot a sergeant in the butt with a wooden blank, which he had modified. In another live-fire exercise, he and others shot a drunken, corrupt, and cowardly company commander to death on a manoeuvre ground.

The modern expression for this type of behaviour is 'fragging' – a practice elevated to a fine art by the Americans in Vietnam.

(2nd Class) for another seven years. From the age of thirty-nine to forty-five he was required to return to the Landsturm. The Ersatz Reserve consisted of men fit for active service but excused on grounds of minor physical defects, family or financial reasons – these reservists had to complete periods of annual training for twelve years before passing to the Landsturm. Men who were medically downgraded for active service did not escape altogether – they were liable for service in the Landsturm for three training periods annually from the age of seventeen to forty-five.

There was an annual intake of recruits based on year of birth; thus men born in 1894 would be called up as the class of 1914 on reaching the age of twenty. In time of war things changed, in that all classes could be called up and sent to the front before reaching the age of twenty; all transfers (except for men incapacitated by wounds or sickness) from one category to another were suspended; there was no release from service at the age of forty-five and all men previously graded medically unfit were re-examined. Recruits were classified as fit for active service, fit for garrison duties, fit for labour employment or permanently unfit. In 1914 these methods produced fifty-one regular (active) divisions at established strength and thirty-two reserve divisions. However, these were just the small beginnings of what would be required. The huge numbers needed on mobilization, and subsequently to feed the fighting on three fronts, meant that recruiting had to be dramatically increased and accelerated. As with

other belligerent nations, it became a never-ending and increasingly insoluble problem, certainly as far as quality was concerned.

The initial expansion in 1914 absorbed most of the Reserve and Landwehr and by September large numbers of Ersatz Reserve men were arriving at the training depots. Although the 1914 class of recruits was called up towards the end of September (the usual time), from then on the annual intake of young men was made progressively earlier. The 1915 class joined in April, May and June of that year, and the 1916 class from August to November. In the same year heavy losses forced a drastic combing out of previously exempt men among agricultural labourers, followed by industrial workers. The 1917 class was called up in early 1916, eighteen months early; some of them were rushed to the front after only three months' training. The 1918 class was summoned to the depots two years early and the 1919 class in mid-1917, two and a half years early. The composition of new divisions formed during 1917 was about 50 per cent class of 1918 recruits and 25 per cent each of trained soldiers withdrawn from the front and recovered wounded from the depots. Finally, the 1920 class was mustered in the spring of 1918.

The German Army had a peacetime strength of 880,000, which, after full mobilization, expanded to 4.5 million. By the end of the war it still had 4.2 million under arms (2,912,000 were on the Western Front). During the war years some 13.4 million men had served – more than any other belligerent nation, including Russia. The

table below shows the categories and numbers of the 236 infantry divisions of the German Army raised during the war.

The German Army in 1914 had a justifiably strong reputation for rigid discipline, administrative competence and a highly trained, thoroughly professional General Staff and officer corps (see Section Three). Like other nations, its soldiers went to war singing enthusiastically on a wave of patriotism, convinced that God was on their side and would ensure a quick victory. But also like other belligerents, German basic infantry tactics were outdated and clumsy,

Wartime Infantry Divisions

Division	Total formed	Served on WF*
Guards	5	5
Guards *Ersatz*	1	1
Regular	121	111
Reserve	44	43
Landwehr	32	20
Ersatz	5	5
Bavarian Regular	10	10
Bavarian Reserve	7	7
Bavarian *Landwehr*	3	2
Bavarian *Ersatz*	1	1
Marine	3	3
Alpine	1	1
Baltic	1	1
Jäger	1	1
Franke	1	1

* Denotes divisions that fought for at least part of the war on the Western Front. Many switched between fronts, an example being the 26th Division, which fought on the Western Front, then in Russia, Serbia and Italy. The table shows 212 divisions which spent some time in the west. There were also eleven cavalry divisions, including one Guards and one Bavarian, all except one of which served on the Western Front.

resembling those of the Franco-Prussian War more than forty years earlier. Despite the fact that the army was far better financed, armed and equipped with more machine guns and particularly medium and heavy artillery than its opponents, German field artillery, though plentiful, was inferior to the British 18-pounder or the French 75mm. However, trench warfare was as big a shock to the German soldier as it was to the French *poilu* or British 'Tommy'. Before the war, the German Army's annual manoeuvres were visually impressive affairs in which tens of thousands of troops participated in mock battles, often with the Kaiser commanding one side – the results being distorted by the fact that he was never allowed to lose. Although improvements had been made by 1914, the comments of the military correspondent of *The Times* after watching these war games in 1911 are revealing, and go some way to discounting the widely held belief that the German Army was, as one author has described it, 'the most powerful, well-trained and well-equipped [army] the world had ever seen':

> The Infantry lack dash, display no knowledge of the ground, are extremely slow in their movements, offer vulnerable targets at medium ranges, ignore the service of security, perform the approach marches in old-time manner, are not trained to understand the connection between fire and movement and seem totally unaware of the effect of modern fire. The Cavalry drill well and show some beautifully trained horses, while the Cavalry of the Guard is well handled. But the Army was in many ways exceedingly old-fashioned, the scouting is bad and mistakes are made of which our Yeomanry [Territorial cavalry units] would be ashamed.

That there was a degree of truth in this opinion is borne out by Corporal William Holbrook of the 4th Royal Fusiliers who, after he and his comrades opened rifle fire on massed waves of attacking German infantry at Mons in August 1914, later commented:

> Bloody Hell! You couldn't see the earth for them there were that many. Time after time they [his own officers] gave the order 'Rapid Fire'. Well, you didn't wait for the order really! You'd see a lot of them coming in mass on the other side of the canal and you just let them have it. Of course, we were losing men and a lot of the officers, especially when the Germans started this shrapnel shelling and, of course they had machine guns –

masses of them! But we kept flinging them back. You don't have time to think much. You don't even feel nervous – you've got other fellows with you, you see. I don't know how many times we saw them off. They didn't get anywhere near us with this rapid fire.

As with other armies, the Germans slowly adapted their formation and unit organizations and tactics through experience – largely a costly process of trial and error in countless battles and lesser engagements. For example, the number of machine guns had doubled by 1916; in 1914 there were 72 guns or howitzers in a division, by 1918 there were 358; within four years the number of infantry battalions had risen from 670 to 2,300 and artillery batteries (field and heavy) had jumped from 1,040 to 5,150. In 1915 heavy casualties and the dominance of artillery caused the reduction of the infantry component of divisions from four to three regiments. Similarly, in 1917 the number of men in a rifle platoon was cut. But one of the major changes at unit level (also adopted by other armies) was the development of special detachments of 'storm troops' and infiltration tactics (see box opposite).

By 1918 German Army morale had deteriorated considerably through a combination of the failure of their March offensive and the subsequent summer victories of their enemy, staggering losses (at least 6.4 million,

including over 2 million dead in all theatres) and depressing news from home of families going hungry and a naval mutiny. Despite this, the army was shocked and embittered by the sudden capitulation of the High Command – something that the soldiers, for many years to come, would consider a stab in the back forced on the generals by politicians. In fact it was something of a myth that the army had not been beaten on the battlefield, but it was used by Hitler in later years to bolster his bid for power backed by army support. In reality the German field army had been beaten. As Wilhelm Deist in his book *The Military Collapse of the German Empire* points out, 'the military instrument for the conduct of the war, the army, was in the process of disintegration'. At the end of October 1918 Ludendorff's replacement as first quartermaster, Lieutenant General Wilhelm Groener, noted that 'the formations at the base were corrupted through and through, and even the Army in the field showed signs of disintegration. Corps in a state of dissolution, and hordes of deserters, to the number of many thousands, were storming the railways at Liège and Namur.'

Unlike the Allied national armies, the German Army fought in every battle on the Western Front, large and small. The small but brilliantly successful attack on Fort Douaumont, part of their meat-grinder assault on Verdun, illustrates it in action.

German trench and wire on the summit of the Butte de Vauquois.

The summit of Fort Douaumont.

75mm turret   observation turret   ventilation shaft   machine gun turret

properly convey the tangle of woods, ravines, hills and gullies that covered the ground to within 500 yards of the fort. Supported by another thunderous bombardment, the German assault troops advanced to find most of the opposition melting away before them and they were able to push on beyond their original more modest objectives to within striking distance of the fort. Apart from the crews manning the 75mm and 155mm, which fired at nothing in particular, the garrison was sheltering well below ground from the ear-shattering, mind-numbing noise of the hundreds of explosions landing on the fort.

The attacking companies got inextricably mixed up as they struggled through the woods and along the ravines. As they closed on the fort they came under fire from a machine gun in Douaumont village church, but the main danger was from their own

Fort Douaumont falls to the Germans

From the German viewpoint, Fort Douaumont looked a frighteningly difficult nut to crack. Its low, menacing shape sat atop the highest hill in the area and seemed to dominate every approach. They might have been reassured somewhat had they known the situation inside.

Physically, Douaumont was indeed a tough nut that even the German heavy artillery (and later the French) failed to break. It has been estimated that during the course of the Verdun battle (February–December 1916) the fort was hit by at least 120,000 shells, of which some 2,000 were heavy or the super-heavy 420mm mortar projectiles. None penetrated a roof that was constructed of a sandwich of reinforced concrete with a 4-foot thick filling of sand, all topped by 8 feet of earth. Polygon-shaped and over 400 yards across, the fort was protected by two belts of barbed wire 30 yards deep. Behind that were spiked railings 8 feet high and below them was a 24-foot-wide dry moat.

Enfilading the moat from the corners of the wall were concrete galleries built to house light cannon, searchlights and machine guns designed to illuminate and slaughter any enemy that got into the moat. Inside were two-storeyed barrack accommodation for 500 men and a labyrinth of deep passages and tunnels connecting the gun positions, ammunition bunkers, stores, offices and barracks. The centrepiece was the artillery guns mounted in retracting turrets that were moved up and down to fire by huge counterweights. These consisted of twin 75mm pieces mounted in the escarpment in the north and the heavy, short-barrelled 155mm

facing east. There were also three machine-gun turrets and four steel observation domes.

However, by February 1916 the fort had been stripped of both its impressive armaments and almost the entire garrison, leaving it virtually undefended. As early as 1914 the process of cannibalization began with the removal of some ammunition stocks for other parts of the front. This process continued during 1915, involving not just Douaumont but all the other forts that ringed Verdun. It is estimated that by October 1915 fifty-four gun batteries had been removed from the Verdun forts and other defensive outposts, along with ammunition and supplies. Douaumont lost all its guns except the 75mm and 155mm. By February 1916 the garrison was less than sixty reservist gunners commanded by a sixty-year-old *gardien de batterie* (a sergeant major) named Chenot.

The German assault on the defences of Verdun began on 21 February under cover of the fire of some 1,200 artillery pieces, ranging in size from 420mm mortars to 77mm field guns. They were also operating under the first air umbrella in aviation history, which consisted of 168 aircraft, fourteen balloons and four zeppelins. Ten miles north of Douaumont the attackers overwhelmed Lieutenant Colonel Driant and his chasseurs after an heroic defence in the Bois des Caures (see page 130), causing huge losses and forcing them back in disorder.

Four days later the attack by the 2nd and 3rd Battalions of the 24th Infantry Regiment (the Brandenburgers) on Fort Douaumont was opposed by critically weakened, and for the most part exhausted and demoralized, French units defending Hills 378 and 347 and Hassoule Wood about a mile to the north. Map 35 shows their approximate positions but cannot

Notes for Map 35

Belligerents

French	German
XXX Corps, XX Corps	III Corps
2nd and 3rd Battalions Zouaves (–)	8th *Liebgrenadiers*
95th Infantry Regiment (–)	12th Grenadiers
2nd and 4th Battalions Chasseurs (–)	2nd and 3rd Battalions, 24th Infantry Regiment
1st Battalion, 208th Infantry Regiment (–)	1st and 3rd Battalions, 20th Infantry Regiment

Commanders

Gen. Andrien Chrétien (XXX Corps) relieved on night 23/24 Feb.; Gen. Maurice Balfourier (XX Corps)	Lt Gen. Edwald von Lochow

Casualties

uncertain	uncertain

Result French driven back in confusion and Fort Douaumont fell to the Germans.

Summary By 24 February the French had already lost very heavily from the German attacks that started on the 21st. They had been driven back and morale was generally poor. French commanders had run out of reserves. The German assault behind a massive bombardment on the 25th met little resistance and the 24th Brandenburg Infantry Regiment pushed forward through Hassoule Wood and the ravines with companies becoming mixed. Fort Douaumont had been stripped of most of its guns and garrison. Only a 155mm and a 75mm gun remained with a tiny garrison of 56 Territorial gunners under Warrant Officer Chenot. Small parties of Germans were able to enter the fort unopposed. The first group, led by Lt Eugen Radtke (6 Company 2/24th), the second by Capt. Hans Haupt ((7 Company 2/24th), secured the fort and once inside took the garrison prisoner without further loss.

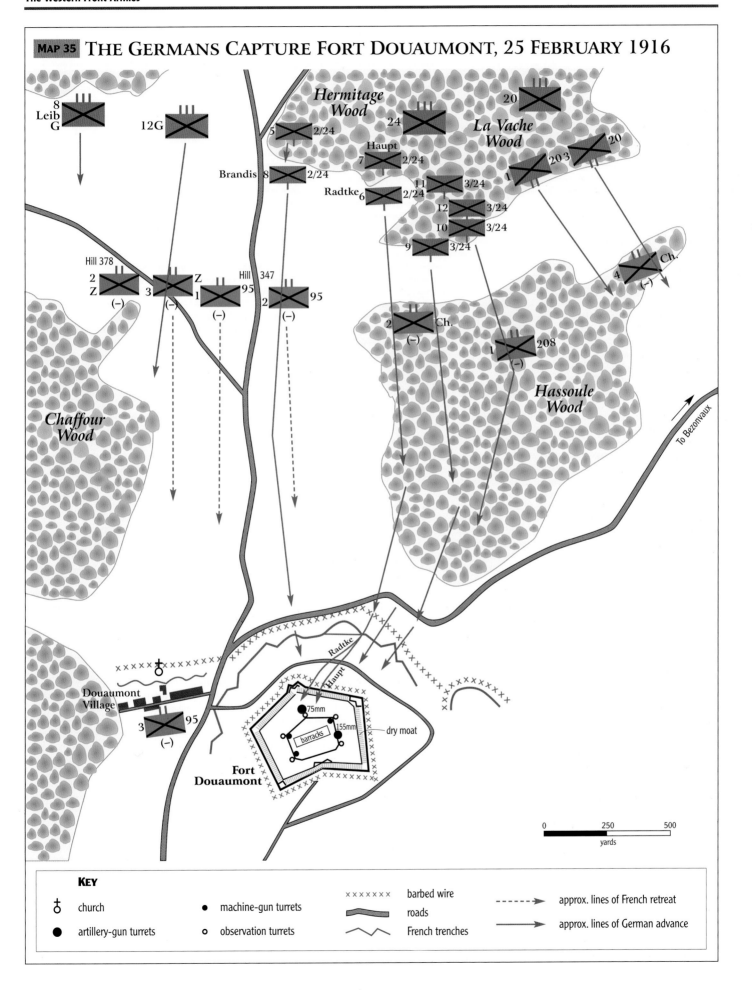

MAP 35 THE GERMANS CAPTURE FORT DOUAUMONT, 25 FEBRUARY 1916

Hermitage Wood

La Vache Wood

8 Leib G

12G

5   2/24

24

20

Haupt 7   2/24

20 3   20

Brandis 8   2/24

Radtke 6   2/24

11   3/24

1   20

12   3/24

10   3/24

9   3/24

4   Ch. (−)

Hill 378
2 Z   3   Z
2   Z   (−)   1

Hill 347
95
(−)

95
2   95
(−)

Chaffour Wood

2   Ch. (−)

1   208 (−)

Hassoule Wood

To Bezonvaux

Radtke

Haupt

Douaumont Village

3   95 (−)

75mm

155mm

barracks

dry moat

Fort Douaumont

0   250   500
yards

KEY

✝ church

● artillery-gun turrets

● machine-gun turrets

○ observation turrets

××××××× barbed wire

〰〰 roads

⌃⌄⌃⌄ French trenches

- - - → approx. lines of French retreat

——→ approx. lines of German advance

The German Douaumont Controversy

For many years afterwards controversies dogged the story of the capture of Fort Douaumont. They revolved around the gallantry awards given to the officers and troops, and the question of which individuals should be given the main credit for the capture. Within weeks of the triumph a large number of Iron Crosses was sent forward for distribution, mostly to soldiers of 7 and 8 Companies, including, according to at least one writer, the cobblers, clerks and bakers. This grossly unfair distribution caused heated protests and some fighting among the men who had been involved.

Lieutenant Cordt von Brandis, commander of 8 Company, had arrived at the fort after its fall, but it was he who had been sent back by Captain Hans Haupt, commander of 7 Company, to battalion headquarters to convey the news that the fort was in German hands. Major von Klufer, commander of the 2nd Battalion, sent Brandis back to regimental headquarters to report the success personally – a mission that was to give the German authorities a wholly distorted understanding of the role Brandis had played. The divisional war diary stated that 7 and 8 Companies, led by Haupt and Brandis, had stormed the fort, with the two officers fighting their way into it at different places, and that they were equally deserving of distinction. Both were decorated with Germany's highest award for gallantry, the *Pour le Mérite*. Lieutenant Eugen Radtke was not mentioned. Although later he received the Iron Cross 1st Class, it did not reflect that his initiative and gallantry had been primarily responsible for the fort's capture as the first person to enter under heavy German artillery fire.

The 155mm gun turret on Fort Douaumont.

For protesting that this was unjust, Major von Klufer was first ignored and then removed from command and posted to remote garrison duties at Neuruppin. Brandis became a public hero, wrote a book about the storming of the fort and became a favourite of the Crown Prince – all of which caused much bitterness for years after the war. Not until 1925, when war diaries revealed that the leaders of the attack were Radtke and Haupt (the latter had faded into obscurity), was Brandis's account called into question. In 1934 Radtke wrote his own version of the action, the publication of which brought him a signed self-portrait of the Kaiser – and promotion.

The next stage of the controversy was the reappearance of Major von Klufer. He wrote another version of the Douaumont affair in which an entirely new character was given the honour of almost single-handedly capturing the fort. Klufer seemingly accepted the version of a Sergeant Kunze, who had commanded a section of pioneers in the assault. Kunze told of finding a breach in the eastern side of the fort through which he and two comrades succeeded in entering via a tunnel that led to the 155mm gun, the crew of which he captured. He then got lost in the passageways but took more prisoners, whom he locked in a room before finding a tempting array of food and stopping to eat. The obvious question is why did it take so many years for this version of events to emerge? Klufer highlighted it in his book and a number of modern accounts claim that Sergeant Kunze was first into the fort and responsible for its capture. Nobody will know for sure who was right, but to the present writer Kunze's account is unconvincing.

Poste de
Belle Épine   Fort de Marre   Fort de Bois Bourris

auville

A view of the French defences from north of Verdun. This panorama was taken from the high ridge north-west of the village of Vacherauville, north of the Meuse, looking out to Verdun and the French forts defending the city from the north-west. This location was the furthest reached by the Germans during 1916 in this part of the battlefield – none of the French forts shown were taken by the Germans, although the ridge provided them with excellent observation and gun positions.

guns, the crews of which were unaware of how far they had advanced. Despite the frantic firing of flares and waving of a flag, the thunderstorm of shells persisted. First into the fort was a small group led by Lieutenant Eugen Radtke, commanding 6 Company 2/24th, closely followed by Captain Hans Haupt, commanding 7 Company of the same regiment. Others quickly followed from various companies, amazed at the lack of resistance, and then at the smallness of the garrison and how easy it was to affect their surrender. The most important fort in the Verdun defences had fallen without a fight.

Fortunately for the French, the German attack halted to allow reorganization and for the supporting artillery to be moved forward. This delay was sufficient for the French to reinforce and stabilize the line. The recapture of Fort Douaumont, however, took another eight months of horrendous bloodshed.

The German cemetery at Langemarck. Under each stone between two and eight named soldiers are buried.

Field Marshal Hindenburg, Kaiser Wilhelm II and General Ludendorff confer.

A meeting of French and British leaders: (left to right) Marshal Joffre,
President Poincaré, King George V, Marshal Foch and Field Marshal Haig.

Section Three

Commanders and Staff

I have always believed that a motto for generals must be
'No regrets', no crying over spilt milk.

Field Marshal Viscount Slim, *Defeat Into Victory*, 1956

This section is divided into two parts – Commanders and Staff – and deals mainly with the British system of both, with some comparison where necessary with the French and Germans. A commander can be of any rank, from a field marshal commanding a group of armies with over a million men to a lance corporal in charge of a listening post with three. The commander receives instructions from his superior, makes his plan, gives his orders and is responsible for the success or failure of his mission. Two levels of command will be discussed – generals commanding formations (from brigade upwards), and regimental officers and non-commissioned officers (NCOs) commanding anything from a battalion to a section of infantry or the equivalent in other Arms and Services. However,

no commander can function without being able to disseminate orders, to facilitate and coordinate the movement of his troops, and to ensure that they have the right equipment, arms, ammunition, food, medical services and a host of other administrative needs. All this requires an efficient communication, control and supply system that is the responsibility of the various headquarters' staff to implement and oversee.

While brief comments will be made on some individual commanders, both senior and junior, only those who served as commanders-in-chief have biographical notes included as boxes.

Government Structure

Before discussing the commanders, it is useful to look at the overall direction of the war effort under which the commanders-in-chief on the Western Front operated.

Britain

In London

The King   King George V took a very active interest in the progress of the war, maintained a close personal contact with all branches of the fighting Services and frequently visited the Western Front – on one occasion while in France he was injured when he fell from his horse and it rolled on him. He and Queen Mary took considerable interest in the welfare of the troops and, from the early days of the war, even opened up Buckingham Palace for tea parties for hundreds of wounded soldiers from hospitals in and around London. Wearing their hospital blue, the men were brought by cars and motorbuses to the palace. Every detail of these parties was carefully thought out and many willing helpers, including members of the Royal

Family (on at least one occasion Sub-Lieutenant Prince Albert, the future King George VI), served tea and food.

Prime Ministers   Herbert Asquith until December 1916, then David Lloyd George.

War Cabinet   This was responsible to the Cabinet and eventually to parliament and was charged with directing the war effort of the British Empire in all theatres. This entailed consulting with allies and relying heavily on military advice, all of which led to its issuing somewhat vague guidelines rather than firm directions.

War Office   The Army Council at the War Office consisted of:

Secretary of State for War: Kitchener/Lloyd
  George/Derby/Alfred Milner
Chief of the Imperial General Staff (Dec 1915–
  Feb. 1918): Sir William Robertson*
Adjutant General: Henry Sclater/Nevil
  Macready/George Macdonogh
Quartermaster General: John Cowans
Master General of the Ordnance: Stanley von
  Donop/William Furse
Parliamentary Under-secretary of State for War:
  Harold Tennant/Derby/Ian Macpherson
Finance Member: H. T. Baker/Henry Forster
Director General of Military Aeronautics (from
  February 1916): David Henderson/John
  Salmond
Director General of Movements and Railways
  (from February 1917): Guy Granet/Sam Fay
Surveyor General of Supply (from May 1917):
  Andrew Weir
Deputy Chief of the General Staff (from
  December 1915): Robert Whigham/Charles
  Harington

In France

Commander-in-chief: French until December 1915, then Haig

---

* General Sir William 'Wully' R. Robertson was the only man in the British Army to rise through the ranks from trooper (private) to field marshal.

War Office Staff

In practice there were two major divisions within the British staff corps, the first deployed in France and other theatres and the other at the War Office in London. The latter was a mixture of military and civilian personnel and, like every headquarters, grew from comparatively modest beginnings to an enormous organization employing almost 22,000 people. They consisted of the following:

In August 1914	In November 1918
187 military officers	1,352 military officers
28 retired officers as senior clerks	1,673 warrant officers, NCOs and men
255 former soldiers as junior clerks	5,664 male civilian staff
635 civilian staff	13,090 female civilian staff
55 female typists	**Total 21,779**
50 messengers	
Total 1,210	

Note The above does not include 1,500 transferred to the Ministry of Pensions, 450 to the Ministry of National Service and 1,100 to the Air Ministry during 1917 and 1918.

The Allied headquarters at Souilly.

France

President Raymond Poincaré
Premier René Viviani/Aristide Briand/
Alexandre Ribot/Paul Painlevé/
Georges Clemenceau
Council of Ministers
GQG (*Grand Quartier Général* – General
Headquarters). This was the headquarters
of the French commanders-in-chief –
Joffre/Nivelle/Pétain.

USA

In the USA

President Overall commander-in-chief –
Woodrow Wilson
**Secretaries of State for State, Treasury,
Navy, War and Army**

In France

AEF commander Pershing

Germany

On the Western Front

The Kaiser Overall commander-in-chief
– Wilhelm II
Great General Staff Inner ring of staff
officers working directly with the
Kaiser and chief of the General Staff
in the field.
General Headquarters This was the
headquarters of the chief of the
General Staff, the principal military
adviser to the Kaiser and in practice
the field army commander on the
Western Front – Moltke/Falkenhayn/
Hindenburg.
First Quartermaster General This
position was created in August 1916
and was effectively deputy chief of the
General Staff – Ludendorff.

In Berlin

Military Cabinet Appointments,
promotions, honours and awards.
Ministry of War Military administration
and finance. The minister had no
military command over troops except for
the Home Army.
War Bureau Created in October 1916
when the Ministry of War and General
Staff were reorganized, and charged with
utilizing the full resources of the nation
for war.

Note There was an overlapping and blurring of the
functions between the *Oberste Heeresleitung* (OHL) – the
Supreme Command of the field army – and GHQ.

Field Commanders

General Officers

These were senior officers ranking from a
brigadier general commanding a brigade of
around 3,000 men to a field marshal (the
French equivalent being a marshal) as commander-in-chief of several armies or groups
of armies. The Centre for War Studies at
Birmingham University has calculated
(more may be revealed with further
research) that 1,257 British generals served
in the BEF during the war, including not
just field commanders but senior artillery,
engineer, medical, supply, administrative
and staff officers. The French and German
Armies had many more, and by adding the
Belgians and Americans it is likely that
between 5,000 and 6,000 general officers of
all nationalities served at some time on the
Western Front in a variety of capacities.

On 8 August 1918, at the start of the
great Allied offensive, British (and dominion) generals were commanding, staffing
and administering 69 divisions (59 British,
5 Australian, 4 Canadian and one New
Zealand), with approaching 2 million men
in nineteen corps deployed in five armies.
This immense force had become the most
efficient and highly trained in Europe. In
the so-called Hundred Days campaign following this date, it secured a stunning series
of victories that included the Battles of
Amiens, Albert, the Scarpe, Havrincourt,
Hindenburg Line, the Selle and the Sambre
Crossing. During these battles the BEF took

almost 190,000 prisoners and 2,840 guns –
considerably more than any other Allied
army. It was this Allied advance, involving
not only the BEF but also French, American
and Belgian armies, that brought about the
final collapse of the Germans.

French generals came from far more contrasting social backgrounds than their
British counterparts, who invariably were
from upper- or upper-middle-class families.
France produced generals from rural peasant backgrounds, such as General, later
Marshal, Pétain, and from aristocratic families, such as General Charles Lanrezac. The
one thing most of them had in common in
1914 was that they were elderly men in
their sixties. Anthony Clayton, in his book
on the French Army in World War I, *Paths
of Glory*, puts the number of French generals
on all fronts in 1916 at 502 of divisional
commander rank, of whom thirty-eight
were commanding a group of armies or an
army, ninety-five were commanding an
army corps or equivalent, and forty were
serving on the staff. The French rank structure at this level was confusing, as there was
no rank between major general and marshal
(a hangover from Napoleonic days). Thus a
major general could command a division, a
corps, an army or even a group of armies –
it was the appointment, not the rank, that
gave him his authority – with the rare elevation to marshal being reserved for overall
commanders-in-chief such as Joffre, Pétain
and Foch.

The German rank structure for their generals was more straightforward, rising consecutively from a major general commanding a brigade, a lieutenant general a division, a general of infantry (or cavalry or
artillery) a corps, a colonel general an army,
and a field marshal a group of armies, with
the Kaiser as overall commander-in-chief.

The table below compares the number of
combat formations from army group to divisional level on the Western Front in
November 1918, including cavalry but
excluding depot, training or arriving divisions.

Formations at Armistice

	Army Group	Army	Corps	Division	Total
British*	–	5	19	66	90
French	3	7	29	108	147
American	–	2	9	31	42
Belgian	–	1	–	12	13
Portuguese**	–	–	1	2	3
German	4	11	48	193	256

* Includes Australian, Canadian and New Zealand formations.
** Under British Fifth Army.

These figures mean that there were 558
generals commanding combat formations of
divisional size or larger at the end of the
war. Adding generals of major general rank
and higher in the artillery, engineers, ordnance, supply, medical and the staff would
at least double this number.

The generals, particularly brigade and divisional commanders, suffered not inconsiderable losses in killed and wounded, it being something of a myth that they (the more junior ones at any rate) seldom visited the front line; this casts doubt on the veracity of the opening lines the old marching song of the trenches sung to the tune of 'Onward Christian Soldiers':

Forward Joe Soap's army, marching without fear,
With our old commander, safely in the rear.

According to Davies and Maddocks in *Bloody Red Tabs*, some 232 generals became casualties during the war, seventy-eight of whom were killed (sixty-two on the Western Front), mostly by small-arms fire, with eight generals being wounded twice. At the Battle of Loos in 1915 four British generals were killed, two wounded and one captured. However, a far more common cause of their removal from command was being 'degummed' or 'Stellenbosched' (Stellenbosch was the site of a base camp in the Second Boer War to which incompetent officers were sent) – that is, being dismissed for perceived failure. The French equivalent was to be sent to Limoges. By the time of the First Battle of the Marne, Joffre had already sacked two out of five army commanders, ten out of twenty corps commanders and forty-two out of seventy-four divisional commanders.

Within the BEF this 'incompetence' not infrequently meant failing to achieve the impossible on the battlefield, or being regarded as 'sticky' – reluctant to drive their troops forward regardless of losses – as opposed to a 'thruster'. An example of a so-called 'sticky' general was Brigadier General H. J. Evans, commanding the 115th Brigade, which was ordered to attack Mametz Wood in July 1916. After suffering heavily, the brigade was ordered to renew the assault over open ground in broad daylight. Although there was a preliminary bombardment, the anticipated smokescreen never materialized and the guns failed to mask the enemy machine guns firing from the flanks. Lieutenant Wyn Griffith, attached to brigade headquarters, later wrote:

> The time was drawing near for the renewal of the attack, for another useless slaughter. Casualties in officers had been extremely heavy, and the battalions [the two attacking units] were somewhat disorganized. 'This is sheer lunacy,' said the General. 'I've tried all day to stop it. We could creep up to the edge of the wood by night and rush it in the morning, but they won't listen to me . . . it breaks my heart to see all this.'

Eventually, with communications cut, Evans managed to get through again on an artillery telephone and described the folly of repeating the attack; after some acrimonious exchanges he succeeded in getting authority to pull back. Evans then told Griffith: 'You mark my words, they'll send me home for this; they want butchers not brigadiers. They'll remember now that I told them, before we began, that the attack could not succeed unless the machine guns were masked. I shall be in England in a month.' Six weeks later Evans went home.

Another example from the Somme battle was Brigadier General Thomas Jackson (he was still only a substantive major), who commanded the 55th Brigade in the 18th (Eastern) Division on the Somme. At the end of September 1916 his brigade was ordered to take over the front opposite the Schwaben Redoubt, still partially held by the Germans. At this juncture Jackson began to disagree directly with his divisional commander, Major General Ivor Maxse. Private Robert Cude, the battalion runner of the 7th Buffs (East Kent), recorded in his diary:

> Just now an interesting situation arises, for Gen Maxse, Officer Commanding 18th Div. gives orders that the Buffs are to make a frontal attack on the system of trenches held by Jerry. This order our Brig Gen Jackson refuses to carry out under the plea that he had insufficient troops at his disposal and that it was impractical.

There was further disagreement between the brigade and divisional commanders, although Jackson did reluctantly order a bombing raid that resulted in a number of casualties. Maxse then ordered him to 'Capture the remains of the Schwaben Redoubt, and occupy the high ground to the north of it.' In this action the 55th Brigade lost heavily and little ground was gained. Jackson was sacked. In Maxse's words, 'the 55th Brigade was not handled with firmness, and the attacks were too partial. The situation should have been grasped more firmly by the brigade commander concerned, and he was so informed.' Maxse regarded Brigadier Jackson's actions as 'sticky'. Private Cude was outraged at this dismissal and wrote:

> Brig Gen Jackson is relieved of his command and returns to England [he later returned to the front to command a battalion of the Manchester Regiment]. For what – being a human man. He will carry with him the well wishes of the whole Bde and we can never forget the man who would wreck his career rather than be a party – however unwillingly to the annihilation of troops under his command . . .

Lieutenant Colonel John F. Elkington

On 25 August 1914 Lieutenant Colonel Elkington, commanding officer of the 1st Royal Warwicks, found himself in charge of the remnants of his 10th Infantry Brigade as, after four days of no sleep or food, they stumbled and straggled back from Mons. Among the men in his battalion were a junior officer called Bernard Law Montgomery, the future Field Marshal Montgomery of Alamein, and the well-known cartoonist Bruce Bairnsfather. When Elkington, now joined by Lieutenant Colonel A. E. Mainwaring commanding the 2nd Royal Dublin Fusiliers, and their men arrived at the village of St-Quentin they hoped to obtain food and supplies. However, in order to prevent the destruction of the village and many casualties amongst the women and children, the mayor pleaded with both colonels not to fight against the rapidly approaching Germans. Elkington and Mainwaring were persuaded to sign a surrender letter, which they handed to the mayor. Shortly afterwards the British rearguard of two squadrons of the 4th Dragoon Guards under a Major Bridges arrived. Without speaking to the colonels, and with the help of a subaltern of the 4th Hussars, Bridges rallied the stragglers, retrieved the surrender letter from the mayor and organized the retreat of the column.

Elkington and Mainwaring were tried by a General Court Martial for 'behaving in a scandalous manner unbecoming the character of an officer and gentleman'. The president of the court was the then Brigadier General 'Hunter-Bunter' Hunter-Weston. Both officers were found guilty and sentenced to be cashiered (dismissed from the army in disgrace, losing their rank and pension rights). Mainwaring disappeared into obscurity, but within a short time Elkington enlisted as a private in the French Foreign Legion. He fought with great gallantry (he was awarded the *Médaille Militaire* and *Croix de Guerre*) during the spring and summer of 1915 before being badly wounded in the leg by machine-gun fire. He spent the next ten months in hospital at Grenoble before being invalided home to England.

In 1916, at the instigation of the now corps commander Hunter-Weston, who had heard of his exploits with the French, a pardon and restoration of rank were successfully negotiated for both Elkington and Mainwaring. On 30 October 1916 Elkington attended a private investiture at Buckingham Palace were the King presented him with the DSO.

Cude was hopelessly, and unjustifiably, prejudiced against Jackson's successor, but in November 1917 he got a brigade commander who was very much the warrior, and of whom he thoroughly approved. This was Brigadier General Edward A. Wood, a man who had served as a private in the 17th Lancers and the 2nd Dragoon Guards before becoming an officer in the Bechuanaland Border Police, the Matabeleland Mounted Police and the British South African Police. In 1914 he was short, fat, a boozer and forty-nine years old, but after stating his age as forty-two he was given a temporary commission as a captain in the 6th King's Shropshire Light Infantry. His war record was outstanding. He won four DSOs, was mentioned in despatches seven times, wounded five times, gassed twice and buried once, while in September 1918, unarmed and alone, he captured some twenty Germans by throwing rocks and old boots at them. Little wonder Cude would write that he would 'serve in hell, so long as General Wood was in command of the Brigade'. Wood was a 'thruster' of the 'follow me' type. Unfortunately, for too many true warriors after any war civilian life proves difficult and disappointing, and so it was with Wood – his later life disintegrated. He failed to repay loans, went bankrupt twice, all largely due to drink, and died on 20 May 1930 from cirrhosis of the liver, aged sixty-five.

Haig once stated that he had dismissed over a hundred brigadier generals during the war, many in 1916. Their replacements were usually headhunted from the best regular commanding officers – only eleven Territorial officers became brigade commanders.

If the prime minister, Lloyd George, had had his way, Haig himself would have been sacked after Passchendaele (Third Ypres) in late 1917. After the butcher's bill for that battle the British GHQ was purged of senior officers – the chief of staff, Lieutenant General Launcelot Kiggell, and the head of intelligence, Brigadier John Charteris, along with the quartermaster general, chief engineer and director general of medical services, were all sent home. In early 1918 Lloyd George sent a member of the War Cabinet (General Jan Smuts) and its secretary (Colonel Maurice Hankey) to France to find a suitable replacement for Haig. They failed to do so.

It was at brigade level that the influence of a general was usually felt most by the troops. Brigade headquarters were close behind the lines, so it was the brigade commander who was most frequently seen visiting battalions in the forward trenches, supervising, inspecting or fussing over petty details. However, as the war progressed, these were mostly men with many months of practical experience of trench warfare. The insatiable demand for officers to command units and formations of the New Army meant that senior commanders tried to cherry-pick the best regimental officers for promotion from the ranks of battalion and company commanders.

A typical thruster, who quickly rid his brigade of officers he judged to be sticky, was Brigadier General Frank Crozier, who aptly entitled his book *A Brass Hat in No Man's Land*, reflecting his frequent personal excursions beyond the wire and his continual demand for aggressive patrolling and raids. One of his junior officers regarded him as a 'callous and overbearing martinet'. He had been promoted from commanding a somewhat unruly battalion (the 9th Royal Irish Fusiliers, known as the Shankill Road Boys), where he got results by leading attacks from the front – as he did on the first day of the Somme, despite specific orders to remain at the rear.

An outstanding example of a regular officer who reached brigade command was Brigadier General Frederick Lumsden, the most decorated officer of the war, who commanded the 14th Infantry Brigade in 1918. Formerly a Royal Marine artillery officer, he was awarded the Victoria Cross in April 1917 while a major, but was shot and killed near Arras in June the following year. At the time of his death, in addition to his VC, he was a Commander of the Order of the Bath (CB), had four DSOs, four mentions in despatches (MIDs) and had been awarded the Belgian *Croix de Guerre*.

The major generals commanding divisions were, in most cases, the most senior commanders known by at least a fair proportion of their men. A division that might have contained 18,000 men in 1914 probably had only 12,000 or fewer by the end of the war, but it was still the main building block of all armies. While a British divisional commander (and corps and army commanders) was invariably a regular, this was not true of dominion formations, whose pre-war armies had been so small that the promotion to high rank of able Australian, Canadian and New Zealand citizen-soldiers was commonplace – and produced some of the best commanders on the Western Front. As with generals of all grades there was, certainly during the middle part of the war, a mix of good, mediocre and poor divisional commanders, these last often elderly 'dugouts' who were unable to adapt to the new ways of war or were physically unable to withstand the pressure.

The Death of Brigadier General F. A. Maxwell, VC, CSI,* DSO and Bar

Francis Aylmer Maxwell was one of many brigade commanders on the Western Front who were frequently seen in the front-line trenches. He had been awarded the Victoria Cross in the Second Boer War when, as a young lieutenant, he went out five times under heavy fire to help bring in two guns and limbers that had been left exposed and were in danger of being captured. On 21 September 1917 Maxwell was commanding the 27th Brigade during the Passchendaele offensive and was shot by a sniper while inspecting an outpost in no-man's-land. One of the men with him at the time was his orderly, Lance Corporal A. Laird, who wrote a letter to Maxwell's widow describing what happened. That letter, given below, is taken from Philip Warner's book *Passchendaele*.

27 Brigade,
5 October, 1917

Dear Madam,
I was very glad to hear from you. I will try and tell you about the fateful 21st, when I lost my beloved General. There was Major Ross and myself along with him. We went up to the front line to see if everything was alright and carried on down the line of our brigade front. We went out into 'no man's land', as the General wanted to have a good look round. We were from 80 to 100 yards in front of our front line. A captain of the Scottish Rifles came along with us to his 'out-post'. The General was showing him the land. I think the General wanted to have a machine-gun posted at this particular part. I was about five yards in front watching for any movement in the shell-holes. I was lying flat with my rifle ready to shoot. The first bullet that was fired by the Huns went right into the ground below my left elbow. I shouted to the General to get down, as he was standing at the time, and he did so. He sat for about two minutes, then he got up again to show what he was saying to this Captain, and he was just opening his mouth to speak when he got shot. I caught him as he was falling, and jumped into a shell-hole with him. I held his head against my breast till all was over. Madam, I cried till my heart was like to burst. If I could only see you I could tell you something about the General. He was a King among men and loved by everyone; in fact, Madam, next to yourself, I miss him more than anyone, for I would have done anything for him.

Perhaps I can speak better than anyone of his personal bravery, for I was his personal orderly in all the fighting the brigade did.

I can say no more just now, but if God spares me, I will come and see you some day.
I am,
Your faithful servant,
(signed) A. LAIRD
L/Corporal

* Commander of the Star of India

Sentry Duty at GHQ

When Haig succeeded French as commander-in-chief, he moved his headquarters from St-Omer to Montreuil, where for a time the guard duties were undertaken by a battalion of the Artists' Rifles – while also sending a flow of young officers to the front. One such person was Captain Allbeury, MC, who before commissioning was a private doing guard duties at GHQ. Here he recounts an amusing incident while he was manning the gate barrier.

A large car suddenly approached. My barrier was fast down, and I advanced secure in my own righteousness to examine the pass. Judge my surprise when the window was let down with a bang and a large crimson face surmounted by a wealth of scarlet and oak leaves appeared at the aperture.

'And what the devil do you want?' said the face.

'Your pass, sir.'

'Pass? What pass?'

'This is G.H.Q., sir,' I said politely. 'A pass is required before you can enter the town.'

'Oh, is it?' came the answer, working up into a fury. 'Do you know who I am? . . . Do you know who I am?'

'No sir.'

This was undoubtedly the wrong answer. My *vis-à-vis* had intended to overawe a mere sentry by indicating his badges as a major-general, not to enquire if I was acquainted with his august name. I remained unimpressed as major-generals at Montreuil were as thick as roses in

June, and I was quite used to them by this time. I stood respectfully silent.

'I am a general!'

'Yes, sir. Your pass please, sir.'

'Dammit, man!' he yelled. 'I tell you I am a general. And how the devil do you think I am going to keep my appointment with the Director of What-not, if some silly fool of a sentry keeps me hanging about? Drive on chauffeur!!' he shouted at the imperturbable figure at the wheel.

'Don't move, driver!' I called, bringing my rifle down to the load and slipping a cartridge into the chamber. 'If you move an inch I will blow your tyres off!'

My opponent fell back upon his seat with a strangled sound, a deep purple, his eyes rolling fearfully. Fortunately he was beyond speech, otherwise I should have been shrivelled to a cinder as I stood. Fearing to look at him farther, my eyes shifted to his companion in the opposite corner.

What I saw was hard to credit. My first impression was a colossal wink. My second, carefully hidden from my outraged victim, containing the desired pass . . . I stepped back smartly, raised my barrier, and performed the world's finest 'present arms'.

'Bloody fool!' The remark floated out of the window as the car gathered speed . . . I would have liked to have met that ADC again. After all, the whole performance had been conducted entirely for his enjoyment.

An example of a successful commander at this level was Major General Sir Hugh Tudor, who had fought as an artillery officer in the Second Boer War. He served on the Western Front throughout the war, during which time he rose from captain to temporary major general commanding the 9th (Scottish) Division. He was an innovative general. As a brigade commander he was the first to make use of smokescreens; was one of the first advocates of predicted artillery fire; and the famous creeping barrage first used on 14 July 1916 at Longueval was his brainchild while acting as Commander Royal Artillery (CRA) at 9th Division headquarters. He was also a man of considerable courage. While at the front during the Third Battle of Ypres in October 1917 he was hit on his helmet by a shell fragment, and was then almost captured during the German spring offensive the following year.

Of less obvious ability was Major General George Gorringe, whose claim to fame was being the only British major general at the Armistice (commanding the 47th

Division) who had been in the same rank at the outbreak of war. He was an arrogant, ruthless thruster (nicknamed 'Blood Orange'), calm in a crisis but detested and feared by most of the officers and men under him. However, the future Field Marshal Montgomery of World War II served under Gorringe as a staff officer and spoke well of him.

By 1917 in the German Army a divisional commander took command of all troops within his sector. As the German training manual makes clear, 'regardless of seniority, both the front-line division and the counter-attack division will be under the undivided command of the front divisional commander'.

The next level up was that of corps commander (there was no such formation in the peacetime British Army) – a lieutenant general. At this level the personal influence of the general usually ended. It was seldom (there were notable exceptions) that a corps commander was seen further forward than divisional or perhaps brigade headquarters.

As a result of both this and the frequent movement of divisions from one corps or army to another, very few soldiers even knew the name of their corps commander (one exception being Lieutenant General the Earl of Cavan, commanding XIV Corps) – not that most were particularly interested anyway. At this level the generals and their staff were primarily occupied with planning and coordinating in accordance with instructions from their army commander. In the German Army their manual stressed that army and corps commanders' main tasks were to 'Secure favourable conditions for their troops before the battle, to ensure cooperation, to bring up reserves in men and material, to arrange reliefs and to undertake immediate further preparations in accordance with the course of the battle.'

A number of British corps commanders stood out as well above average. Prominent among them was a pre-war civil engineer, the Australian Lieutenant General Sir John Monash (ANZAC Corps commander in 1918), and the Canadian former insurance broker, estate agent and militia officer Lieutenant General Sir Arthur Currie. King George V knighted Monash in the field within four days of his corps' successes at the start of the Battle of Amiens in 1918. Monash later wrote of the achievements of his command:

During the advance, from 8th August to 5th October, the Australian Corps recaptured and released no less than 116 towns and villages. Every one of these was defended more or less stoutly . . . The total number of enemy divisions engaged was 39. Of these, 20 were engaged once only, 12 were engaged twice, 6 three times and 1 four times . . .

All this was accomplished for the loss of 5,000 dead – a remarkably low figure for the Western Front.

After the war it was alleged that both Monash and Currie had been considered as possible replacements for Haig as commander-in-chief – this speculation owed its origin to the memoirs of David Lloyd George. Neither of these generals was tested at army command but at commanding a corps they proved highly capable and earned genuine respect and loyalty from their men. Both were fortunate to command troops with an excellent fighting reputation and Currie's Canadians were always kept up to strength, making them probably the most powerful Allied corps in 1918. The two corps attacked side by side, spearheading the BEF's offensive south of the Somme on 8 August 1918 – the German Army's 'Black Day'. They were chosen for this key role due to the quality of both commanders and troops.

However, some corps commanders found it hard to keep up with the way changes in tactics had been brought about as new technologies were introduced on to the battlefield. Such an individual was Lieutenant General Sir George Harper, commanding IV Corps (appointed 11 March 1918). On one occasion Brigadier General John Hardress Lloyd, commander of the 3rd Tank Brigade, tried to explain to him the importance of infantry advancing in 'worm' or single-file formation behind tanks instead of in waves. The incident quoted below is from Tim Travers' book *How the War Was Won*:

> 'Now', exclaimed the old ass [Harper] 'if you were walking down the road with a girl how would you go?' 'Arm in arm', answered H.L. [Hardress-Lloyd]. 'There you are', exclaimed old Harper . . . 'Well general', replied H.L., 'if you and the late Oscar Wilde were walking down a street together where do you think he would go?'

Harper was very nearly taken out of the room in an ambulance.

A corps commander who managed to keep his rank and position despite his record of failures was Lieutenant General Sir Aylmer Hunter-Weston, commander of VIII Corps. He was universally known as 'Hunter-Bunter' but was also referred to as 'the Butcher of Helles' for his seeming total disregard for the welfare of his troops and incompetent battle plans during the Gallipoli Campaign. Hunter-Weston advocated broad frontal attacks in daylight. When they failed, as in the Second Battle of Krithia (6–8 May 1915), he merely repeated the failed attack on the second and third days – a classic example of reinforcing failure. When he launched the inexperienced 156th Brigade (52nd Lowland Division) into an attack during the Battle of Gully Ravine (28 June 1915) without artillery support and half the

brigade became casualties, he claimed he was 'blooding the pups'. Sent home sick from Gallipoli, he got himself elected an MP before being recalled to the Western Front in time for his divisions to suffer the worst losses and fail to capture any of their objectives on the opening day of the Battle of the Somme. A splendid anecdote about this pompous and incompetent general, who retained his appointment almost certainly due to his longstanding friendship with Haig, is told by Richard Holmes in *Tommy*. During the bitter winter of 1917–18 'Hunter-Bunter' decided to wish troops departing on leave trains a happy Christmas:

> An aide de camp would open the carriage door and the general would intone: I am Lieutenant General Sir Aylmer Hunter-Weston MP, your Corps Commander, and I wish you a happy Christmas.' From the smoky fug of one of the carriages a disembodied voice declared: 'And I'm the Prince of Wales, and wish you'd shut the bloody door.'

The five British army commanders at the time of the August offensive of 1918 had all proved themselves at least competent at lower levels of command. At army level their responsibility was to implement the directives of the commander-in-chief, a function that involved coordinating and overseeing the planning of the corps under their command (of the five armies, only the Fifth had two rather than four).

The First Army was initially commanded by Haig, who handed it over to General Sir Charles Monro at the end of 1915, who passed it to General Sir Henry Horne in September 1916. Horne, who kept command until the end of the war, was formerly an artillery officer and the only gunner to command an army – something he did without attracting undue criticism or praise;

indeed his name appears very infrequently in books on the war.

General Sir Horace 'S.D.' Smith-Dorrien commanded the Second Army for only four months before being dismissed by French, who had a longstanding antipathy to Smith-Dorrien that came to a head during the Second Battle of Ypres for supposedly failing to get a proper 'grasp' of the situation; he was sent to command in East Africa. General Sir Herbert Plumer then assumed command for the remainder of the war. Plumer looked a typical caricature of a World War I 'Colonel Blimp' – short, red-faced, with a large fluffy white moustache hiding his mouth. However, appearance can be deceptive, as many consider Plumer the best of the army commanders. He was a meticulous planner and organizer, his main success being at Messines Ridge in June 1917, where careful planning and the exploding of nineteen mines under the German lines at the start of the battle resulted in a victory at a fraction of the usual cost in lives. The day before the attack Plumer remarked to his staff, 'Gentlemen, we may not make history tomorrow, but we shall certainly change the geography.' Plumer was well known by all ranks and affectionately nicknamed 'Daddy' by his soldiers, who valued the way he looked after them. Colonel W. N. Nicholson records an illustration of this in his book *Behind the Lines*:

> There was an officer in my regiment who was transferred to General Plumer's staff; and they gave him a batman from his last formation, an old soldier who had done his share of trench duty. 'General Plumer, Sir; he'll know me,' said the man. And he did. Picked him out on a parade and spoke to him as he passed down the ranks. Moreover whenever he saw him in the streets, crowded with soldiers, he stopped and addressed him by name.

Plumer was made a field marshal after the war, Governor of Malta, president of the MCC and he unveiled the new Menin Gate at Ypres in 1927. He died in 1932 and is buried in Westminster Abbey.

The Third Army was not formed until July 1915 and its first commander was General Sir Charles Monro, but only until October, when General Sir Edmund Allenby took over. Allenby was something of a fierce martinet, nicknamed the 'Bull'; as Richard Holmes relates, when Allenby left his headquarters on a visit, his staff used to warn subordinates by the Morse letters BBL for 'Bloody Bull Loose'. Allenby's performance on the Western Front was mediocre and it was not until he was moved to command in Palestine in the spring of 1917, where more

The King and his generals in 1918: (left to right) Birdwood (Fifth Army), Rawlinson (Fourth Army), Plumer (Second Army), King George V, Field Marshal Haig, Horne (First Army) and Byng (Third Army).

Field Marshal Sir John Denton Pinkstone French, 1852–1925

French was the son of a Royal Naval officer who died when he was only two and shortly afterwards his mother was confined to a mental home. French joined the Royal Navy in 1866 as a young cadet at the Eastman's Naval Academy, Portsmouth, but transferred to the army as a lieutenant in the 8th (King's Royal Irish) Hussars in 1874, leaving that regiment soon afterwards for the 19th Hussars. Coming from a family of modest means, French found it expensive to maintain the lavish cavalry lifestyle he enjoyed and eventually got into serious debt, avoiding resignation only by accepting a loan of £2,000 from a brother officer, Douglas Haig. He was a keen polo player and, although married twice, was something of a serial womanizer.

French took part in the Sudan expedition of 1884–85, seeing action at the Battle of Abu Klea, where his dismounted regiment formed part of the British square that, after some desperate hand-to-hand fighting, beat off massed charges by the dervishes. He then received quick promotion and commanded the 19th Hussars between 1889 and 1893, before becoming assistant adjutant general, during which time he was promoted to colonel and then brigadier general. In 1897 he received command of the 2nd Cavalry Brigade, which he exchanged for the 1st Cavalry Brigade two years later. He commanded this brigade in the Second Boer War, notably commanding the troops that relieved the Siege of Kimberley. He also played a significant role in the defeat of the Boers at the Battle of Paardeberg. As a lieutenant general he was commander-in-chief Aldershot after the war until 1907, when he was promoted full general and became inspector general of the army (1907–12).

From March 1912 to April 1914 French served as chief of the Imperial General Staff (being promoted field marshal in 1913), but resigned after the Curragh Mutiny in Ireland. The problem was that the British government's Home Rule Bill, intended to give the whole of Ireland independence, was violently resisted by the Protestant north, to the extent that the 3rd Cavalry Brigade in Dublin under Brigadier General John Gough, VC, was ordered to prepare to march on Belfast and quell any rebellion by force. Many officers resigned in protest, including French and the then secretary of state for war (Colonel Jack Seely), although most officers withdrew when not compelled to enforce home rule.

The outbreak of war saw French appointed commander-in-chief of the BEF. As a die-hard cavalryman of the old school who still believed in the use of the *arme blanche* (sword-armed cavalry), he found it hard, like many of his contemporaries in 1914, to adapt to the new ways and technologies of warfare. He was not helped by his fiery temper and having to cooperate with the French. Together these combined to make the task beyond him and he resigned in December 1915 after the costly Battle of Loos (and Haig's backstage scheming) to become commander-in-chief of Home Forces. Douglas Haig replaced him.

In 1916 French oversaw the suppression of the Irish Uprising and in May 1918 was appointed Lord Lieutenant and commander of the British Army in Ireland. In 1919 a band of the Irish Republican Army (IRA) ambushed his three-car motorcade. Believing French was in the second car, the IRA forced it off the road, but in fact he was in the leading vehicle, which managed to drive through the ambush. A gun battle developed as the third car arrived and joined in firing rifles and a machine gun at the ambushers, killing one and wounding another. The British convoy continued with several wounded (French was unscathed) and as reinforcements approached the IRA withdrew.

French kept his post in Ireland until his retirement in 1921. He died, aged seventy-two, the following year.

---

open warfare suited his cavalry background, that he became successful, achieving a decisive victory over the Turks, which culminated in a triumphal entry into first Jerusalem and then Damascus. His successor in the Third Army was General the Hon. Sir Julian Byng, Bt, who led it to the Armistice. Previously Byng had successfully overseen the Allied forces' withdrawal from Suvla Bay, Gallipoli. He proved another competent planner, insisting on scrupulous organization, thorough training, rehearsals and briefing of all ranks, the best example being his meticulous supervision of the preparations before the successful Canadian attack on Vimy Ridge on Easter Monday 1917. The other notable success of the Third Army under Byng was during the second phase of the Battle of Amiens in August 1918 when it advanced 60 miles in eighty days, breaking through the Hindenburg Line in the process and capturing 67,000 Germans by 11 November 1918. After the war, he became successively Viscount Byng of Vimy, Governor General of Canada, Commissioner of the Metropolitan Police and a field marshal in 1932. He died two years later.

The Fourth Army was commanded by General Sir Henry 'Rawly' Rawlinson for most of its existence, after his short spell in Gallipoli. Recalled to the Western Front in 1916, he played a leading role in the British Somme offensive, where his arguments for a limited offensive (bite-and-hold tactics) contrasted sharply with Haig's breakthrough aims. Rawlinson served in every rank from major general to army commander during the war. As this was despite the fact that Field Marshal French had disliked him and Haig distrusted him, he must surely be regarded as at least a competent general. After the war he briefly commanded the Murmansk Expedition sent to assist the White Russians in their civil war against the Reds (Bolsheviks). He was later made Commander-in-Chief India and died in post in 1925.

The reconstituted Fifth Army took part in the Somme offensive of 1916 under General Sir Hubert 'Goughie' Gough. In 1917 he was for some time in charge of the Ypres offensive, where his conduct of operations received considerable criticism. The brunt of the great German offensive in March 1918 fell on his troops, who were unable to withstand the pressure and fell back with heavy loss in men and material. Gough's dispositions over a wide front under virtually impossible circumstances were arguably appropriate, but he was relieved of his command. Lloyd George denied his demands for an inquiry on what Gough claimed was an unjustifiable sacking. He left the army in 1922 to go into farming and business, and was a pall-bearer at Haig's funeral in 1928. He commanded a Home Guard unit during World War II and in later years wrote his memoirs, in which, with considerable justification, he defended his conduct in command on the Western Front. He died in 1963, aged ninety-three – outliving his contemporary generals by many years. For the remaining months of the war the Fifth Army was commanded by General Sir William Birdwood. Previously he had spent much of his time commanding the Australians at Gallipoli, on the Somme and at Bullecourt. During this period a strong mutual understanding and respect developed between the archetypical British Indian Army general and his militarily unconventional 'Diggers', who usually referred to him as 'Birdy'. He was an efficient commander whose genial and somewhat indulgent style of leadership was perhaps more effective with Australians than it would have been with British troops – although he came under a temporary cloud

Field Marshal Sir Douglas Haig, 1861–1928

Haig was born in Edinburgh, the son of John Haig, head of the family's Haig & Haig whisky distillery. He studied at Brasenose College, Oxford, but left without graduating due to sickness and the need to enter the Royal Military College at Sandhurst before being barred by age. He was commissioned into the 7th (Queen's Own) Hussars in 1884. He saw overseas service in India as adjutant of his regiment from 1887 to 1888. He took part in Kitchener's Omdurman campaign in 1898 as a captain, attached to the cavalry of the Egyptian Army as a staff officer. He had several administrative posts with the cavalry during the Second Boer War and was mentioned in despatches four times, his performance being noted by both Kitchener and French. He was promoted major in 1899 and lieutenant colonel in 1901, when he became the commanding officer of the 17th Lancers for two years. This was followed by the prestigious appointment as ADC to King Edward VII with the rank of colonel. Then followed another period in India, where he became the youngest major general in the British Army (he was forty-five), having risen from captain in five years. During this time he was inspector of cavalry while Kitchener was commander-in-chief, India.

In July 1905 Haig married the Hon. Dorothy Vivian, a lady-in-waiting at King Edward VII's court, and the following year took up his duties in the War Office as director of military training. During this time Haig assisted the secretary of state for war, Richard Haldane, in his reforms of the British Army. After a short period as director of staff duties he returned once more to India in 1909, this time as a lieutenant general and chief of the Indian General Staff. He was appointed General Officer Commanding (GOC) Aldershot from 1912 to 1914 and ASC to King George V in the same year. His close royal connections undoubtedly helped with promotion, and later to deflect Lloyd George's efforts to sack him.

Haig was commander of the BEF from December 1915 and thus oversaw the massive and ineffective offensives on the Somme in 1916 and at Third Ypres in 1917, but also the great advance to victory in 1918. There is no room in this book to discuss the pros and cons of his generalship (others have done this at considerable length), apart from repeating that he won, and that no general of any nation avoided horrendous losses, especially when attacking as the Allies were compelled to do most of the time. Haig, like his

contemporaries, was a product of British Empire colonial warfare, and of the pre-war upper-class-dominated officer corps. Although often inarticulate – in 1912, when presenting prizes at Aldershot garrison, he said, 'I congratulate you on your running. You have run well. I hope you will run as well in the presence of the enemy' – he was nevertheless intelligent and showed a keen interest in the newly developing technologies. It says much for his conduct of the war and the monumental responsibilities he bore that Lloyd George had to admit that he could not find a better candidate to replace Haig in 1917–18, despite his determined efforts to do so.

After the war Haig was created 1st Earl Haig and was voted the thanks of both Houses of Parliament. Following a period as commander-in-chief of the Home Forces, he devoted his remaining years to the welfare of ex-servicemen, travelling throughout the British Empire to promote their interests. He established the Earl Haig Fund for the financial assistance of former servicemen, and the Haig Homes charity to provide proper housing for them. He was also involved in the creation of the Royal British Legion, of which he was president until his death on 29 January 1928, aged sixty-six.

Haig was given a state funeral. Huge crowds lined the streets on a cold February day. His coffin was carried on the gun carriage that had borne the Unknown Warrior (see Epilogue, page 518) to his grave and had fired the first British shot of the war. As the cortège moved slowly from St Columba's Church, Pont Street, where he had lain in state, to Westminster Abbey, the gun carriage was followed by three royal princes, and the pall-bearers included two marshals of France – Foch and Pétain. The cortège was accompanied by five guards-of-honour marching in slow time with muffled drums and arms reversed; two officers and fifty other ranks from each of the three services; fifty men from the French Army I Corps; and sixteen men of the Belgian Regiment of Grenadiers. After the funeral service the procession re-formed to escort the field marshal to Waterloo Station for the rail journey to Edinburgh, where he lay in state for three days at St Giles Cathedral. Haig was buried at Dryburgh Abbey in the Scottish Borders, his grave marked by a simple white Commonwealth War Graves headstone. His memorial is an equestrian statue in the centre of Whitehall; due to controversy, it was not unveiled until just before Armistice Day 1937.

---

after the Australian losses at Bullecourt. The Australians gave him a rousing welcome when he toured their country in 1920. Promoted field marshal in 1925, he spent the last five years of his service as commander-in-chief of the Army in India. He died in 1951 at Hampton Court Palace and is buried in Twickenham Cemetery. His field marshal's baton is on display in the Australian War Memorial, Canberra.

The BEF on the Western Front was not subdivided into army groups, as were the French and Germans, as the number of armies did not justify it. Thus the pinnacle of military command was that of commander-in-chief, held by Field Marshal Sir John French until December 1915, and from then on by Field Marshal Sir Douglas Haig. French was sacked as a result of a failure in the handling of the reserves at the costly (for

that time) Battle of Loos in September 1915 – it was seen as a disappointing culmination of his mediocre performance thus far. There was a bitter post-mortem over who was to blame for the Loos failure, with Haig telling King George V when he visited France in October that 'the C-in-C was a source of great weakness to the army'.

Numerous books and articles have been written for and against the contention that responsibility for the seemingly senseless slaughter of the British in the attrition battles on the Western Front, particularly the Somme in 1916 and Passchendaele in 1917, lay primarily with one man – Field Marshal Haig. It is not the intention of this book to explore these arguments in detail but merely to record that the public perception of Haig as the head 'donkey' of the Western Front seems now to have been dispelled as some-

thing of a myth. In support of this more modern, informed view are the quotes below.

Charles Carrington, who enlisted at the age of seventeen in 1914 and was commissioned into the 1/5th Territorial Army battalion of the Royal Warwickshire Regiment a year later, wrote in his book *Soldier from the Wars Returning*:

> I wish to place on record that never once during the war did I hear such criticisms of Sir Douglas Haig as are now current when his name is mentioned [1960s] . . . He was trusted, and that put an end to discussion.

James Jack rose from captain to brigadier general during the war and later published *General Jack's Diary 1914–1918*. His diary entry for 16 December 1918 describes Haig's farewell to senior officers:

Before departing Sir Douglas said: 'Thank you, gentlemen.' Then passed from us a redoubtable, well-liked Chief, who for nearly four years had calmly borne a crushing load of responsibility.

It should be added that this huge responsibility was made doubly difficult by the persistent criticisms and behind-the-scenes intrigues to replace him by the prime minister, Lloyd George.

John Baynes, in *Morale: A Study of Men and Courage*, wrote:

Throughout all my investigations, and all my reading about the War, I have been struck by the fact that criticism by fighting soldiers of every other senior General can be found somewhere, but never of Haig.

And finally Marshal Foch, the Allied Generalissimo in 1918, was to write of Haig's victories that year:

Never at any time in history has the British Army achieved greater results in attack than this unbroken offensive . . . The victory was indeed complete, thanks to the Commanders of the Armies, Corps and Divisions and above all to the unselfish, to the wise, loyal and energetic policy of their Commander-in-Chief, who made easy a great combination and sanctioned a prolonged gigantic effort.

It seems Haig passed the ultimate test of any general in war – he won.

Before one judges the generals on either side, it is imperative to look at the circumstances on the Western Front during those four and a half years, and not to condemn them solely because of the horrendous losses all armies suffered. Every commander, high and low, had to learn how to fight successfully on a battlefield beyond any previous experience – this applied equally to professional and citizen soldiers. Obviously blunders occurred – a military maxim that has stood the test of time is that it is usually the side that makes the fewest mistakes that wins, and that side invariably has more instances of good luck thrown in as well. The generals commanding in 1917–18 had mostly learned from their own experience and that of others how to fight battles on the Western Front.

With millions of men under arms, the senior commanders and their staffs faced immense, previously undreamt-of problems of scale. For example, almost 170.4 million rounds of artillery ammunition were fired by the BEF alone during the war, and almost 25.5 million tons of stores (including ammunition) were shipped to France to keep it fighting. The horrors and brutality of the war, the responsibility for the seemingly endless death and maiming of so many millions for so little territorial gain have, at least in the general public's perception, most often been laid at the door of the generals – the 'donkeys leading the lions'. This view is encapsulated in General Sir

John Hackett's book *The Profession of Arms* when he describes the British attack at the Battle of Loos in 1915 – the one that cost Field Marshal French his job:

Then twelve battalions, 10,000 men, on a clear morning, in columns, advanced up a gentle slope towards the enemy's trenches. The wire behind which these lay was still unbroken. The British advance met with a storm of machine gun fire. Incredulous . . . the Germans mowed the attackers down, until, three and a half hours later, the remnants staggered away . . . having lost 385 officers and 7,681 men. The Germans as they watched the survivors leave, stopped firing in compassion. Their casualties at the same time had been nil.

The opposite view is that, by and large (there were exceptions), the generals did their best in coping with circumstances totally outside their experience, and that all commanders in all armies at every level had to undergo a hugely costly learning curve. This view has now gained considerable support among modern military historians. The British Army on the Western Front that surged forward in a series of successive victories in August 1918 was a very different army, not just in size but also in training, tactics and equipment, from the one that General Hackett described at Loos three years earlier.

Maréchal Joseph Jacques Césaire Joffre, 1852–1931

Joffre, the son of a cooper, was born in Rivesaltes in the Eastern Pyrenees and entered the army in 1870, aged eighteen. While still a cadet he took charge of an artillery battery during the Siege of Paris in the Franco-Prussian War. He saw much service in the French colonies of Indo-China, West Africa and Madagascar. As a lieutenant colonel he won distinction in 1894 by leading a column across the desert from West Africa to capture Timbuktu. Joffre made his name as a competent engineer and organizer, and rose rapidly in rank after the turn of the century. After a period as director of engineers in the War Ministry in 1907, he commanded an infantry division and the following year became a corps commander. In 1911 he was appointed chief of the General Staff (a position that would in effect be commander-in-chief in war) and was responsible for the flawed French Plan XVII.

By 1914 Joffre had gained a reputation as a devotee of the offensive and had weeded out senior officers who were less than enthusiastic about this doctrine. He gained the credit, despite the failure of Plan XVII, for regrouping the French Armies and for halting the German advance on the Marne and then pushing it back. His calmness, imperturbability in a crisis and refusal to admit defeat were qualities that gave him his credibility. These characteristics, along with his appearance and popularity with his troops, gave him his nickname

of 'Papa Joffre'. At this point it is impossible to resist including a brief quotation on Joffre from Alistair Horne's book *The Price of Glory*:

But the really outstanding (in more than one sense) physical feature of Joffre was his belly. His appetite was legendary; staff officers often observing him consume a whole chicken at a sitting, and one, explaining his taciturnity at table, remarked that he never left himself time to speak, even had he wanted to. Joffre maintained his appetite to his death bed; in the final coma, when a hospital orderly tried to insert a few drops of milk between his lips, he opened his eyes abruptly, seized the glass and drained it, then went back to sleep. Once when criticizing a general he remarked, tapping his own, that the man had 'no stomach'.

After the Somme Joffre was replaced by General Nivelle, promoted Marshal of France and brought back to Paris in an advisory/diplomatic role. In 1917 he headed a military mission to the United States. Between 1918 and 1930 he held a number of posts at the Ministry of War. He died in 1931, aged seventy-nine. His main memorial is an equestrian statue in Place Joffre in Paris. There is also a Mount Joffre in British Columbia, a Rue Joffre in Quebec, a Joffre Avenue in Milltown, New Jersey, and a Joffre Street in Pascoe Vale, Victoria, Australia.

Général Robert Georges Nivelle, 1856–1924

Nivelle was born in the French provincial town of Tulle to a French father and an English mother. He graduated from the *École Polytechnique* as an artillery officer in 1878. Despite serving with distinction in the Boxer Rebellion in China, in Algeria and Tunisia, it was thirty-five years before he was promoted colonel.

He fought with great gallantry at the First Battle of the Marne, when his artillery regiment fired at point-blank range over open sights to halt an attack about to overwhelm an infantry unit. Thereafter promotion was rapid – brigade command in October 1914, a division in early 1915 and a corps by the end of the year. In 1916 he took command of one of the French armies at Verdun and gained great credit for recapturing Fort Douaumont and planning and executing a series of counter-attacks. His success at Verdun was the main reason he replaced Joffre as commander-in-chief in December 1916. His boastful powers of persuasion secured support for what was to become the infamous Nivelle offensive at Chemin des Dames. This costly failure ensured his replacement by General Pétain in May 1917 and he was shunted off to the African war in December of that year. He retired in 1921 and died three years later, aged sixty-eight.

Charles Carrington again:

On the whole, as I have grown older, I find myself willing to accept the general incompetence of human beings, and I no longer expect a superman to emerge with a solution for every unforeseen problem. I am inclined to think that the First War [Carrington was a lieutenant colonel in World War II] commanders did pretty well, according to their lights, and the tendency to blame them for the crimes and follies of a whole generation now seems to be disingenuous.

So what were those unforeseen problems that have so often been forgotten by those who condemn the Western Front generals – who must include French, American, Russian and German as well as British, as all their armies suffered on much the same scale – as callous butchers of their men?

• The first factor, already mentioned, was the one of scale. The battle lines from late 1914 onwards extended for 460 miles; to man and supply such a front was inconceivable to the generation of generals commanding on the Western Front. Many of them had to be plucked from retirement to take the field in 1915 to cope with the unforeseen and dramatic expansion of the army. It was way beyond their experience in previous colonial wars and in the Second Boer War, although those professional soldiers who had studied the Russo-Japanese War of 1904–05 might have seen what was coming.

Such a man was Major General James Montagu Stuart-Wortley, who commanded the 46th Division on the opening day of the Battle of the Somme. Educated at Eton and commissioned into the King's Royal Rifle Corps in 1877, his medal ribbons illustrated active service in the Afghan War (1878–79); First Boer War (1881); Egypt and the Nile Expedition (1882–85), taking part in the Battles of Tel-el-Kebir, Abu Klea and Gubat; with the Sudan Frontier Force at the action at Giniss (1886); in the Nile Expedition (1897–98), where he won a DSO commanding a gunboat flotilla; commanding Egyptian troops at the capture of Omdurman (1898); and finally commanding the 2nd Battalion the King's Royal Rifle Corps in the Second Boer War (1900–01). All this did not, could not, adequately prepare Stuart-Wortley or any of his peers for the battles they faced on the Western Front. The 46th Division's diversionary assault on the German salient at Gommecourt on 1 July 1916 was repulsed with heavy losses, with nothing achieved, largely due to lack of surprise and enemy flanking fire. Stuart-Wortley, who was suffering from sciatica, was sacked. His corps commander reported that he was 'not of an age,

Maréchal Henri Philippe Pétain, 1856–1951

Pétain was born in Cauchy-à-la-Tour in the Pas-de-Calais and entered St-Cyr Military Academy in 1876. He became a captain, but unlike many of his contemporaries did not serve in the colonies. Instead he had six years on the staff of the military governor of Paris (1893–99). He was promoted major in 1900 and in the following years became known for his unfashionable criticism of the offensive doctrine, recognizing its dangers in the face of modern weapons. In 1911 he was a colonel commanding an infantry regiment in which a Lieutenant Charles de Gaulle (future general and French president) was serving.

On the outbreak of war Pétain commanded a brigade creditably during the retreat to the Marne, where he was given a division. By October 1914 he had been elevated to corps command and in July 1915 he was made an army commander (Second Army). He was given command of Army Group Centre during his defence of Verdun. His success in halting the German assaults by July 1916 transformed him into a national hero. It was Pétain's firm but fair handling of the French mutinies in 1917 that saved the situation from spiralling out of control. He became commander-in-chief, replacing Nivelle, in May 1917. However, the German offensive in March 1918 saw the Allies wavering and Pétain was put under the orders of the new Allied overall commander and coordinator, General Foch. This did not prevent Pétain's promotion to Marshal of France nor his riding through Paris on a white horse during the 1919 victory parade while being cheered to the echo.

In 1920 Pétain, who had always been an ardent womanizer, finally, at sixty-four, married an ex-lover, Madame Eugénie Hardon. During the inter-war years the aged Pétain was instrumental in shaping French military policy based on the superiority of the defence in the form of the Maginot Line fortifications.

When the Germans attacked France in 1940 (bypassing the Maginot Line) he was recalled from Spain to become the French premier and, as his first act, made peace with Germany. The seat of government was moved from Paris to Vichy and thereafter Pétain headed a totalitarian French government cooperating fully with the German authorities – something that included sending thousands of Jews to death camps in the east.

On 15 August 1945 Pétain, the hero of World War I, was tried for treason in World War II. He was convicted and sentenced to death by firing squad. His former subaltern of many years before, and now president of the Provisional Republic, Charles de Gaulle, commuted the sentence to life imprisonment. Pétain soon became senile and was in need of constant care until he died in prison on 23 July 1951, aged ninety-five. He was buried at a cemetery nearby. Calls are sometimes made for him to be reburied at Verdun.

neither had he the constitution, to allow him to be as much among his men in the front lines as is necessary to imbue all ranks with confidence and spirit . . .'

• Britain, with her tiny Regular Army scattered around the world and her historical and economic emphasis on naval power, was in no way prepared or geared up industrially to meet the demands of mass production, mass logistics and the mass of administrative tasks required to keep the ever-expanding armies in the field. For example, the acute shortage of munitions in 1915 (see also Section Five) that cost many lives was in no way the fault of the generals, but instead typical of political parsimony in times of peace. Of equal, if not greater, consequence at the outset was that for over two years Britain was the junior partner to the French. At the end of 1914 the BEF was responsible for a mere 24 out of the 460 miles of front. This imbalance placed considerable constraints on first French and then Haig as British commanders-in-chief whose hands were often tied by the need for a coalition war. An example was the continuance of the costly offensive on the Somme, on ground not of Haig's choosing, in order to draw German reserves from their attacks on the French at Verdun, which might otherwise have fallen.

• Senior and junior commanders had been trained for, and expected to fight, a mobile war that would be over comparatively quickly – the Germans were banking on it, so that they could turn their attention eastwards to the Russian Front. This did not happen. Within five months commanders faced what rapidly developed into a gigantic siege operation with the protagonists either defending the walls (trenches) or trying to make a breach in them. For the remainder of the war generals on both sides were forced to try to find a solution largely by trial and error. This was admitted by Brigadier General Sir James Edmunds, compiler of the *British Official History of the War*, in a private letter to the Australian historian Charles Bean quoted in Denis Winter's book *Haig's Command*: 'In viewing 1914–1916 you must remember that from the highest to the lowest, we were all amateurs. Generals and staffs of the regular army, though professionals in name, had never been trained to fight continental armies or deal with such masses of troops.'

• A number of war-fighting technologies were deployed for the first time during the war and commanders needed time to train their troops and to adopt appropriate tactics for their use. These included aircraft, poison gas, flamethrowers, tanks, quick-firing artillery, massed use of machine guns, motorized transport and rudimentary wireless telegraphy. The employment of each one of these had huge consequences for both the attacker and the defender of the 'siege' lines. Again, commanders had to learn on the job how to handle all these innovations, and how to combine their use effectively to achieve or prevent a break-through (the evolution of tactics is discussed in the relevant sections).

• These new technologies, certainly during 1915 and through to late 1917, tended to favour the defender. Once the front solidified, the Germans occupied all of Luxembourg, most of Belgium and a large portion of France. The Allies had to drive them out. To do so meant taking the offensive and striving to breach the ever-deepening trench systems and defensive zones such as the Hindenburg Line. The attackers faced dense wire obstacles, concrete dugouts, machine-gun posts and massive defensive fire from enemy guns. In the end the Allied generals succeeded in developing all-arms tactics that breached the walls – but inevitably it took a long time for tactics to catch up with technology. Until it did, as the French General Charles Mangin bluntly put it, 'Whatever you do, you lose a lot of men'.

• Probably the most acute battlefield problem for commanders, particularly for the generals, was the frequent impossibility of communicating quickly with their units actually engaged with the enemy. John Terraine, in his book *The Smoke and the Fire*, quotes from a Lieutenant Colonel C. F. Jerram (Royal Marine Light Infantry), who was the senior staff officer at the headquarters of 46th Division:

> [Some writer] ignores or simply hasn't noticed the *only* thing that matters and without which you cannot begin to

Maréchal Ferdinand Foch, 1851–1929

Foch was born at Tarbes in the Pyrenees into a devout Catholic family. He enlisted in the infantry in 1870 during the Franco-Prussian War and in 1871 entered the *École Polytechnique*. He was commissioned into the artillery in 1873. After reaching captain he entered the *École de Guerre* (Staff College) in 1885. In 1890 he was selected to join the elite Third Bureau (Operations) of the General Staff, where he obtained a professorship of military history. He was very much a military thinker and was author of several works on the conduct of war. It was to his regret that the cult of the offensive came to dominate French military thought. By 1898 he had risen only to lieutenant colonel, but thereafter his career accelerated. He was a colonel commanding a regiment in 1903, then a brigadier general in 1907 when appointed commandant of the *École de Guerre*. In 1911 he was commanding a division and two years later the XX Corps at Nancy.

Given command of the newly formed Ninth Army, he handled it skilfully during the First Battle of the Marne and prevented a breakthrough with a well-organized counter-attack that liberated Châlons – he was given a rapturous welcome and formally received by the bishop. By 1915 he was commanding the Northern Army Group and conducted the Artois offensive, then in 1916 the French part of the Battle of the Somme. His tactics and the heavy losses were strongly condemned, resulting in his being removed from command by Joffre and sent to Italy. However, when Pétain was appointed commander-in-chief Foch was recalled and promoted chief of the General Staff. In March 1918, at the Allies' Doullens Conference, Foch was appointed Supreme Allied Commander. Under his guidance the Allies halted the German March offensive and, along with Haig, Foch planned the great combined Allied advance that was to win the war. In August 1918 Foch was made a Marshal of France.

At the cessation of hostilities in November Foch refused to shake hands with the Germans. At the Paris Peace Conference in January 1919 he recommended that Germany's western frontier should be the Rhine. Although the conditions imposed on Germany were severe, Foch's proposal was not accepted, leading him to regard the Treaty of Versailles as a 'capitulation' and a 'treason'. As the treaty was signed he declared (with remarkable precision), 'This is not peace. It is an armistice for twenty years.'

Foch was made a British field marshal in 1919 and a marshal of Poland in 1920. He died, aged seventy-eight, in 1929 and was buried in Les Invalides next to Napoleon and other famous French soldiers. His statue was erected at the Compiègne Armistice site (it was the only feature remaining after the German destruction of the area in 1940) and there is another near Victoria Station in London. Several streets bear his name, including Avenue Foch in Paris and places in Poland, Ecuador, Lebanon, the USA and South Africa.

criticize, i.e., the fact that it was the *only* war ever to be fought without voice control; which came back in World War II with Walkie-Talkie and without which the modern soldier is as completely lost as we were. Nobody recognizes that once troops are committed to the attack, *all* control was over. Why didn't you and I and our generals go up and take charge? – See for ourselves and give the necessary orders? – What the hell use would we have been? The ONLY place where it was possible to know what was going on was at the end of a wire, with its antennae to Brigades and Artillery.

One of the oft-repeated jibes at the generals was that they lived safely in luxury in magnificent chateaux, dined well with fine wine while their soldiers led a troglodyte existence in flooded trenches or bunkers, freezing cold in winter and forever caked in mud (see Map 36 for locations of General Headquarters). What is forgotten is that an army headquarters with several hundred staff and junior ranks required extensive accommodation in order to function and, like all headquarters, expanded rapidly along with the increasing size of the armies. In 1914 the official estab-

Advanced GHQ

Considerable misunderstanding has arisen regarding Haig, as commander-in-chief of the BEF, being more or less permanently ensconced at GHQ at Montreuil, miles behind the front. This is incorrect. Haig frequently operated from an advanced headquarters, which was a much smaller affair than main GHQ (some 300 staff officers worked at GHQ, with another 240 in outlying directorates). With Haig at advanced GHQ would be his chief of staff, heads of the operations and intelligence branches, and such other senior staff officers he might need to consult, along with the necessary supporting liaison officers, clerks and orderlies. The movements of this headquarters in 1917 and 1918 are revealing. During the Battle of Arras, advanced GHQ moved from Beauquesne to Bavincourt, then in June it resided in a train that stood in a siding at Godewaersvelde for the Third Battle of Ypres. In October Haig moved into a house in Cassel alongside General Plumer's army headquarters. For Cambrai he returned to Bavincourt. In March 1918 he was centred at Dury in the Somme area, and for the final offensive he toured the front in his train. All this mobility prompted a staff officer at main GHQ to say, 'when Haig did appear at Montreuil all felt they had the right to go to the window to catch a glimpse of him.'

King Albert I of the Belgians, 1875–1934

Born in Brussels, Albert was fourth in line of succession to the Belgian throne. However, the early deaths of his uncle King Leopold II's only legitimate son and of Albert's older brother made sixteen-year-old Albert unexpectedly heir-presumptive (after his father, Prince Philippe, Count of Flanders, who died in 1905). He was a studious boy and set about preparing himself for kingship. This included travelling around the poor districts incognito to see for himself the conditions of the working classes. He was a devout Catholic and keen sportsman who became a skilled mountaineer with an interest in engineering and mechanics. He attended the Belgian *École Militaire* and spent some time as an officer in the Grenadier Regiment. He was married in Munich to Duchess Elisabeth Gabrielle Valérie Marie, second daughter of the Duke of Bavaria, and they had two sons and a daughter – in 1915 their eldest son, Leopold, then only fourteen, was allowed to enlist in the Belgian Army as a private and fight in the ranks.

Albert succeeded to the throne on the death of Leopold II in December 1909. He travelled widely, took considerable interest in improving the lot of the poor and in laying out plans for the reorganization of the army – intended to produce an effective force of 350,000 men. During a reception while on a visit to Germany in 1913 (he was honorary colonel of the Hanover Dragoons), the Kaiser and Moltke told him that war with France was imminent – a message he immediately passed to the French ambassador. In August 1914 he famously replied to the German ultimatum to be allowed to march through his country with the words 'I rule a nation, not a road!'

The outbreak of war saw him assume his constitutional role of commander-in-chief of the Belgian Army in the field. King Albert led his army in delaying the right wing of the German advance, through the Siege of Antwerp and at the Battle of the Yser when the Germans were finally halted with just a thin strip of Belgian soil unoccupied and the front solidified. Although his children had been sent to England, King Albert remained with his troops and shared their dangers, while Queen Elisabeth worked for the welfare of the soldiers as a nurse and in organizing canteens for their benefit. After almost four years behind the Yser canal, King Albert was given command of Army Group Flanders, consisting of Belgian, French and British divisions, for the final offensive of the war that liberated occupied Belgium. The King, Queen Elisabeth and their children re-entered Brussels to a hero's welcome.

King Albert attended the Paris Peace Conference, where he insisted on war reparations to enable Belgium to recover economically but opposed excessive humiliation of defeated Germany. He spent much of the remainder of his reign assisting in the post-war reconstruction of his country. On 17 February 1934 he was killed in an accident while climbing alone on the Roche du Vieux Bon Dieu near Namur; he was fifty-nine.

In 2009, celebrating 175 years of Belgian dynasty and the 100th anniversary of his coronation, Albert I was selected as the main motif of a high-value collector's coin, the Belgian 12.5 euro, the obverse of which has his portrait.

lishment of GHQ was 31 officers and 106 ORs (other ranks), but by 1918 it had swollen to 83 officers and 250 ORs. Thus to put a divisional, corps or army commander in a forward bunker would render him unable to fulfill his responsibilities as a general – he would in effect become a superfluous battalion commander quite unable to exert any authority over the larger battlefield, or indeed to have the remotest knowledge of what was happening outside his immediate area. A general needed secure, sheltered accommodation for himself and his staff to plan and work, and he needed to be at the end of the then rudimentary and cumbersome wireless communication system. Aside from this, it is also often forgotten that even front-line bunkers could be made deep and relatively comfort-

able – the Germans were particularly adept at this: see Section Twelve – although the food remained grim. During a major battle Haig and all army commanders would operate from an advanced headquarters (Haig often used a train) closer to the front.

Regimental Officers and NCOs

A military truism that applies to armies of all nationalities and to all wars down the ages is that there are no bad soldiers but only bad officers. This broad generalization applies especially to regimental officers from lieutenant colonel to second lieutenant – the men who are responsible for training, administering, supervising and leading men on the battlefield. Of these, a key personality is the commanding officer. At unit (regiment or battalion) level, the commanding officer's personality and efficiency are decisive in creating high morale, trust and regimental spirit. His decisions directly affect every man in his command, and from him subordinate officers and NCOs take their lead. In *My War Memoirs 1914–1918*, the German General Ludendorff had this to say of regimental commanders:

> The duties of regimental commanders were varied and exceptionally arduous. They were everywhere responsible for their troops, and had to answer to their superiors for the appearance and MORAL[E], the success or failure, the

weal or woe, of every single man under their command . . . He had to inspire his officers and men with his own spirit; he was their example and their stay, their counsellor and friend in periods of inactivity as in battle.

By 1918 the foremost German battalion commander (*Kampftruppenkommandeur* – KTK) within a regiment, when in defence, was the key man irrespective of rank (sometimes he was only a captain). He had total powers of command within his area and could summon troops from the supporting unit in his rear as he saw fit. Once they were in his area they were under his command, even if their commander outranked him. The KTK directed artillery-fire support and was responsible for the supply and casualty evacuation of all

troops then under command. This method of command often gave huge responsibility to comparatively junior officers.

Throughout the fighting on the Western Front an infantry battalion's effectiveness and morale was usually a reflection on the leadership ability and character of its commanding officer. This point is well made by Colonel W. N. Nicholson in his book *Behind the Lines*:

> A Lancashire battalion for example had many ups and downs. After the Somme where in the first attack the battalion lost 16 officers and 600 men they were badly in need of a commanding officer, when Magnay, a young captain of the Royal Fusiliers, was posted to the command. At Arras the battalion (thanks to him) did wonderfully; but a

General John Joseph Pershing, 1860–1948

Pershing was born near Laclede, Missouri, one of nine children of a railway foreman. He graduated from West Point into the 6th Cavalry in 1886 and was sent to the frontier, where he saw service in the final campaign against Geronimo's Apaches in Arizona. In 1893 he attended the University of Nebraska as a military instructor and to study law. Two years later came, after nine years, promotion to first lieutenant and a posting as a troop leader in the 10th Cavalry, a unit of black 'buffalo soldiers' in Montana. In 1897 he was back at West Point as a tactics instructor where he gained the nickname 'Nigger Jack' on account of his service with the 10th Cavalry. This derogatory name was converted into 'Black Jack', a nickname that would remain with him throughout his career. When the Spanish-American War began in 1898, Captain Pershing rejoined the 10th Cavalry and fought at San Juan Hill in Cuba alongside the future president Theodore Roosevelt. A posting to the Philippines followed in 1903 in which he made a name for himself in helping to put down an insurrection by fanatical Moro tribesmen and, it was alleged, fathering several children with Philippino women.

In January 1905 Pershing married Helen, daughter of Civil War veteran and Medal of Honor recipient Senator Francis E. Warren; President Roosevelt was the premier guest. He was then posted as military attaché in the US Embassy in Tokyo, during which time he was able to observe operations in Manchuria in the Russo-Japanese War. Captain Pershing had built up a reputation as a competent junior commander and staff officer. September 1906 saw the birth of his daughter in Tokyo and in the same month news that Roosevelt, using his presidential prerogative, had promoted him from captain to brigadier general. This elevation, jumping three ranks over the heads of 862 officers, was unprecedented since the Civil War and caused something of an outcry over what was seen by many as flagrant political promotion.

In early 1914 Pershing took command of the 8th Infantry Brigade, responsible for security on the US–Mexican border. From there he led the unsuccessful hunt for the Mexican revolutionary Pancho Villa. Shortly after this came the catastrophic news that a fire at his home in San Francisco had killed his wife and three daughters; only his six-year-old son, Warren, survived. Pershing never really recovered from this huge personal disaster.

He was promoted major general in May 1916 and chose to command the AEF on the country's entry into the war. He arrived in France in June 1917 with a small headquarters staff to organize the build-up of

the US forces over the coming months. From the start he insisted that the integrity of the US Army be preserved and that ultimately it would fight in cooperation with, but independent of, other nations.

Although while the build-up was taking place American formations were deployed under other Allies' command in order to experience trench warfare and learn the tactics, Pershing was rightly determined to resist any attempt to scatter his divisions around the front. His policy was not fully consummated until the US First Army fought its first entirely independent and successful operation in September 1918 at St-Mihiel.

Pershing has been heavily criticized for his lack of personal magnetism and the gulf between him and his soldiers, many of whom detested him for his aloofness and authoritarian methods. One 'Doughboy' (the word equates to British 'Tommy') described how 'That sonofabitch roared past our column in his big staff car, spattering every one of us with mud and water from head to foot.' Pershing insisted on training that emphasized the rifle and bayonet rather than the bomb and machine gun. There is little doubt that the average Doughboy initially went into the fight inadequately trained, with little knowledge of tactics or the need for all-arms cooperation that the British and French had developed by 1918. Pershing, who was promoted full general in October 1917, launched his final offensive with two armies in the Meuse–Argonne area in the final weeks of the war. It was a major victory for American arms, with all objectives reached – but at an unnecessarily high cost of 120,000 casualties in six weeks. Pershing controversially ordered his troops to continue fighting after the Armistice had been signed. This resulted in some 3,500 US casualties on the last day of the war, an act that was likened to murder by several officers under his command.

In September 1919, in recognition of his achievements, which included creating, almost from nothing, the vast structure of a national army of some 3 million men, Congress approved the re-creation of the rank of General of the Armies for Pershing – a rank that had previously been held only by George Washington. There was no prescribed insignia, so Pershing chose the four stars of a full general, but in gold rather than silver. In 1921 he was appointed chief of staff, and during his tenure designed a new framework for the US Army. After 1941 he lived in retirement in quarters built for him at the Walter Read Hospital in Washington DC, where he died on 17 July 1948, aged eighty-eight. He was buried in the Arlington National Cemetery.

Lieutenant Colonel Henry William Murray, VC, CMG, DSO and Bar, DCM, 5 MIDs, *Croix de Guerre*

Henry Murray, the most decorated Australian soldier of World War I, won his Victoria Cross as a captain commanding a company of the 13th Battalion of the AIF on 4/5 February 1917. He was a superlative example of a soldier from humble background commissioned from the ranks (he was promoted from lance corporal to sergeant to second lieutenant on one day while serving in Gallipoli) who at every level displayed magnificent leadership and courage. Quoted below is his commanding officer's recommendation for the VC:

Capt Murray commanded the Right flank Coy in the attack by the 13th Battn on Stormy Trench, N.E. of Guedecourt on night of 4-5/2/17. I placed him on the Right flank because it was the most dangerous and critical. He led his Coy to the assault with great skill and courage and the position was quickly captured. Then followed the severest fighting in the history of the 13th Battn and I am sure that the position could not have been held and our efforts crowned by victory but for the wonderful work of this officer. His Coy beat off one counter-attack after another, three big attacks in all, although one of these consisted of no less than five separate bombing attacks. All through the night the enemy concentrated the fire of many 4.2s and 5.9s on the sector of trench held by this Coy, and in 24 hours the fighting strength dwindled steadily from 140 to 48, 92 casualties including 1 Officer killed and 2 Officers wounded. On one occasion the men gave ground for 20 yards but Capt Murray rushed to the front and rallied them by sheer valour, with his revolver in one hand and a bomb in the other he was ubiquitous, cheering his men, heading bombing parties, leading bayonet charges or carrying wounded from the dangerously shelled areas, with unequalled bravery. So great was his power of inspiration, so great was his example that not a single man in his Coy reported himself shell shocked although the shelling was frightful and the trench at times was a shambles that beggars discription [*sic*]. His Coy would follow him anywhere and die for him to a man. He won the D.C.M. at Anzac and the D.S.O. at Mouquet Farm in France. I most strongly recommend Capt Murray for the Victoria Cross.

Murray was wounded twice in Gallipoli and twice more at Mouquet Farm. He was promoted to major and then to lieutenant colonel in March 1918 to command the 4th Machine Gun Battalion. In April he won his second DSO at Bullecourt, in October 1918 was awarded the French *Croix de Guerre* and the following May he was promoted to Commander of St Michael and St George (CMG). In World War II he commanded the 26th Battalion – part of the force defending north Queensland from possible invasion. He died of a heart attack following a car accident in January 1966, aged eighty-six.

and twenty-one wounded). These included six acting commanding officers (five majors and a captain). These figures give a clear illustration of the scale of replacement problems that produced an almost daily crisis throughout the war for all belligerents, and at every level.

A battalion normally consisted of four companies of 100–200 men, each commanded in the British Army by a major but in others by a captain. Its equivalent in the cavalry was a squadron and in the artillery a battery. A company/squadron/battery sergeant major assisted the company commander, in the same way as the battalion commander relied on the regimental sergeant major as a vital link with his soldiers on matters of morale, discipline and welfare. Company commanders led from the front and, like their platoon commanders, suffered disproportionately for doing so. This was particularly true during the first year or so of the war, when officers went into action conspicuously wearing shiny boots, Sam Browne belts and waving revolvers or canes; many French officers were similarly dressed even down to the wearing of white gloves. On 10 March 1915 at the Battle of Neuve Chapelle, at least one company commander of the 2nd Scottish Rifles (Cameronians), Captain E. B. Ferrers commanding B Company, led his men forward with drawn sword. He was badly wounded at the first German trench but propped himself up against the parapet, lit a cigar and continued to urge his company on – he survived the war and commanded the 1st Cameronians in the 1920s. He was the only company commander to survive that assault at Neuve Chapelle; the other three, all majors, died. By 12 March every other officer of the 2nd Scottish Rifles had been killed or wounded except for a Second Lieutenant W. F. Somervail, and the horribly depleted companies were commanded by sergeants. As infantry officer losses mounted they were ordered to dress more like their men, with puttees round their legs, and to carry rifles, although this instruction was far from universally followed.

The commanders of the leading companies going over the top at 7:30 a.m. on the Somme were invariably first up the trench ladders. One even climbed out early, as Private Robert Cude described in his diary:

Punctual to time 7:28 a.m. two minutes before the line advanced Captain [Billy] Neville [a former professional footballer], 8th E. Surreys, kicks off the football that is to take the boys across to Jerry. He is killed as his leg is uplifted after kicking the ball. E. Surreys and Queens go over singing and shouting and the ball is punted from one to another . . .

heavy howitzer shell made a direct hit on his battalion headquarters, killing Magnay and his adjutant. Then came bad times again; till eventually a New Army officer was posted to the command. Once again the battalion became as good as any in the division. The stuff was there all the time; but the right leader was essential. It had to be the right man, for every battalion varied somewhat in its requirements.

The type of successful battlefield leader for both officers and NCOs has usually been the 'come on' rather than the 'go on' leader. After World War II General George Patton, the commanding officer who led his tanks into the attack in September 1918 on foot and waving a stick (see caption, page 122), succinctly described leadership thus: 'If you want your men to fight to the death then lead them. Troops are like spaghetti; you can't push them around you have to pull them.'

In the Allied armies of 1914 a battalion was normally commanded by a lieutenant colonel (in the German Army a major). It was the official policy that when a battalion was attacking, going over the top, the commanding officer should not lead but remain at his headquarters, perhaps in the support line, until the objective had been secured. Although this might be sensible to facilitate control of events, it was frequently ignored, with battalion commanders deliberately putting themselves in the attacking waves. On 1 July 1916, on the opening day of the Somme, some 202 British battalions were earmarked as attacking units; at the end of the day, fifty-one battalion commanders had fallen (thirty killed or died of wounds

Within a company of infantry there were usually four platoons (German *Zug*) under a junior officer, although as the war dragged on the Germans commonly used an acting officer or senior NCO (see page 197). Each platoon (the word derives from the French word *peloton*, meaning group) had three or four sections/squads under a junior NCO. It is argued by some that, once battle was joined, success depended more on the leadership of the platoons than on anything else – if they failed, no amount of skilful generalship would bring victory. As Colonel Nicholson wrote, 'The thirty men whom he leads take their inspiration from him; they will be lions or lizards in harmony with the tune he pipes.' Fifty years after the Somme, S. A. Boyd, a former lance corporal in the 10th Royal Fusiliers, recalled, 'My lasting impression of the Somme battle is the fine young officers who led us so well. They were extremely brave but so young, many under the age of twenty.' Private George Morgan, 1st Bradford Pals, had this to say of the same battle:

There was no lingering about when zero hour came [on 1 July]. Our platoon officer blew his whistle and he was the first up the scaling ladder, with his revolver in one hand and a cigarette in the other. 'Come on boys,' he said, and up he went. We went up after him one at a time. I never saw the officer again . . . He was only young but he was a very brave man.

The average life of an infantry subaltern in the trenches in 1916 was reckoned to be two weeks.

Among the senior NCOs the determined leadership of so many of the infantry sergeant majors and platoon sergeants merits a special mention. Normally the second in command of a platoon, the sergeants (and sergeant majors) were men of considerable front-line experience and as such were relied upon for advice and guidance by countless young, newly joined second lieutenants given a platoon for the first time – the same is true today. The present writer's son, arriving to take command of a troop of three 'Warrior' armoured vehicles during frequent fierce clashes in Iraq in 2007, often sought guidance from his more experienced troop sergeant and corporal. As noted above, so many of these subalterns did not last long, thus necessitating the sergeant taking command, if only for short periods. In the great majority of cases they performed admirably, winning countless decorations for gallantry.

An example of sergeants undertaking most of the key leadership positions within a company was C Company (nicknamed the 'Half-moon Company'), 1/5th Sherwood Foresters, in September 1918 for its attack on the Hindenburg Line. In this case there were just two officers in the company, with all four platoon commanders sergeants. Of these, three were to die on 24 September. Sergeant R. H. Ford, DCM, MM, was riddled with bullets as he attempted to find a gap in the enemy wire; Sergeant C. Loomes, DCM, was badly wounded early in the attack and died later that day; and Sergeant G. H. Holmes, MM, was killed instantly with a bullet through his head as he led his men in a charge on a German post. Such men were hard to replace.

The general situation and problems associated with regimental/battalion leadership as the war on the Western Front expanded are outlined below. The situation for the British Army is examined in some detail, but the problems were virtually identical for both France and Germany – the main protagonists on the Western Front until mid-1918. Put simply, the requirement was to find a continuous flow of battalion, company and platoon leaders to cope with the ever-increasing size of the armies and the ever-lengthening casualty lists – by 1917 the British required about 10,000 officers a year. The figures used to illustrate the difficulties are from *The Statistics of the Military Effort of the British Empire during the Great War, 1914–1920*, published by the War Office in 1922.

The approximate number of British officers (excluding the Indian Army and dominion contingents) available at the outbreak and end of the war was as follows:

Generaloberst Helmuth Johann Ludwig von Moltke, 1848–1916

Moltke was born in Gersdorf, Mecklenburg, and named after his uncle, Helmuth Karl Bernhard von Moltke, future field marshal and architect of the victories over the Austrians in 1866 and the French in 1870. In order to distinguish between the two, they are often referred to as Moltke the Elder and Moltke the Younger. The latter was commissioned in 1870 and, while serving in the 7th Grenadier Regiment in the Franco-Prussian War, was cited for bravery. He attended the War Academy from 1875 to 1878 and joined the General Staff in 1880. Two years later he became personal adjutant to his uncle, then chief of the General Staff. In 1891, on the death of his uncle, Moltke became ADC to Kaiser Wilhelm II, thus becoming part of the Kaiser's inner circle. In the late 1890s he commanded a brigade and then the 1st Division of the Guards Corps before finally being promoted lieutenant general in 1902. In 1904 Moltke was made quartermaster general – in effect, deputy chief of the General Staff. In 1906, on Schlieffen's retirement, he became chief – an appointment not without its critics, who felt it was due to the strength of his name and friendship with the Kaiser.

Moltke inherited Schlieffen's grand plan for the massive invasion of France through Belgium while keeping the Russians in check in the east with far smaller forces. As explained on pages 19–23, he tinkered with this plan and in the event strengthened the left wing of the advancing armies at the expense of the right; he also withdrew six divisions earmarked for the west and sent them to the east. In 1914 Moltke was sixty-six and in generally poor health (from 1911 he had suffered from heart trouble and shortness of breath), made worse by a clash with the Kaiser just before the outbreak of war. He quickly lost control of events in August 1914 and the culminating German defeat on the Marne was the final straw that broke him. On 8 September, in his daily letter to his wife he wrote: 'I cannot find words to describe the crushing burden of responsibility [that] weighs upon me today. The appalling difficulties of our present situation hang before me like a dark curtain through which I can see nothing. The whole world is in league against us . . .' At the end of the Marne campaign, his report to the Kaiser contained the phrase 'Majesty, we lost the war.'

With his health seriously undermined and no longer able to cope mentally, Moltke was replaced on 14 September 1914 by the War Minister, Lieutenant General von Falkenhayn, although for political reasons until 3 November Falkenhayn acted only as deputy. Moltke's health continued to deteriorate and he died in Berlin on 18 June 1916, aged sixty-eight.

British Officer Numbers

4 August 1914		11 November 1918	
Regular	12,738	Regular and New Army	74,200
Special Reserve	2,557	Special Reserve	28,000
Territorial	9,563	Territorial	60,055
Reserve of officers	3,202	Reserve of officers	2,000
Total	**28,060**	**Total**	**164,255**

During the war the approximate number of British combatant commissions granted for all theatres was 229,316. In addition, 17,745 non-combatant officers were commissioned (Royal Army Medical Corps 12,692 and chaplains 5,053), making a total

General von der Infanterie Erich von Falkenhayn, 1861–1922

Falkenhayn was born in Burg Belchau, West Prussia, into an aristocratic if somewhat impoverished family with a strong military tradition. He entered the army at nineteen and spent some ten years at the Berlin War Academy. He served as a military instructor to the Chinese Army and took part in the march to relieve Peking during the Boxer Rebellion in 1900. His reports from China were well received by the Kaiser and when he returned to Germany in 1903 he was appointed to the General Staff. Thanks to the Kaiser's patronage Falkenhayn rose rapidly in rank and authority. In 1913 he became the Prussian war minister – at fifty-two an unheard-of event – and in September 1914 succeeded the mentally crushed Moltke as chief of staff.

It was under Falkenhayn, who controlled the German efforts to outflank the Allies in the Race to the Sea (see pages 31 and 34), that the Western Front saw the start of the stagnation into siege warfare. In the east he had succeeded in alienating General von Ludendorff by halting a promising German offensive just as a decisive victory seemed within reach. However, it was an event initiated by him on the Western Front that brought about his downfall. He proposed to defeat the French by a meat-grinder offensive to 'bleed the French white' at Verdun – the

aim being to compel the French to keep committing an endless stream of reserves into the defence of Verdun and then to destroy them in a massive battle of attrition. The slaughter at Verdun lasted for most of 1916 and cost the Germans over 250,000 dead without destroying (although it was dreadfully mauled) the French Army. The German failures of 1916, along with the hostility towards Falkenhayn of Hindenburg and Ludendorff, brought about his removal and replacement by Hindenburg in September of that year.

Falkenhayn was sent to command the Ninth Army to confront the Romanians, who had just entered the war on the Allies' side. Within four months his troops had taken the capital, Bucharest, in a skilfully conducted offensive. Following this success, he was sent to help the Turks recapture Mesopotamia. When this proved impossible, he was sent to Palestine, but eventually failed to prevent General Allenby's advance and triumphal entry into Jerusalem in December 1917 – an event that sealed his replacement by General Otto Liman von Sanders in February 1918. His final, one might almost say punishment, posting was to see out the remainder of the war in obscurity as commander of the Tenth Army in Lithuania. He died near Potsdam on 8 April 1922, aged sixty-one.

of those posted as missing were eventually recorded as dead, but some were prisoners released after the war. However, both wounded and missing were casualties that required replacement at the time. The figures below show the approximate casualties in all categories for the BEF, including the Royal Naval Division, dominion and colonial formations, on the Western Front from August 1914 to November 1918:

Deaths (all causes)

Officers	ORs
36,722	611,654

Wounded

Officers	ORs
83,580	1,755,435

Missing and prisoners

Officers	ORs
10,816	313,432

Total

Officers	ORs
131,118	2,680,521

These figures show that the overall casualty ratio of officers to other ranks was 1:20.

The figures for officer losses by November 1918 reveal the daunting magnitude of maintaining a constant flow of regimental-level officers for all branches of the army, particularly the infantry, who suffered over 84 per cent of all casualties. Just to replace deaths required an average of 580 officers a month for the British Army alone. If other casualties are included on the assumption that they all needed replacing, then the monthly average would be 2,521. Major offensives or battles caused officer (and soldier) deaths to spike dramatically, leading to days, if not weeks, when units were desperately short of middle and junior leaders. Listed below are some of these battles, showing the officer casualties and the average daily rate of losses:

of 247,061. Thus eight times the August 1914 total of combatant officers' commissions were granted during the following fifty-two months at an average of some 4,400 a month. The ratio of officers to other ranks at the start of the war was around 1:24 and this was more or less maintained on average throughout.

As far as the Western Front was concerned, the approximate figures of deaths on the battlefield and due to sickness are compared below for the BEF officers and other ranks (excluding those missing) as reported for the period 4 August 1914 to the end of November 1918.

Many officers and soldiers died long after the war from war-related wounds, but the numbers are almost impossible to obtain. From the table below, the overall ratio of officer to other rank battlefield deaths was 1:16.6 – a significantly high ratio. For every officer who died from sickness, over sixteen died on the battlefields of the Western Front. Due to weather and climate, almost as many Indian soldiers died of sickness as in battle.

With the wounded it is not possible to know how many eventually returned to duty, but British casualty returns did not include officers or men who were lightly wounded and did not leave their units. Similarly, most

Causes of Death

	Killed/died of wounds		Sickness/other causes		Total deaths	
	Officers	ORs	Officers	ORs	Officers	ORs
Regular/Territorial/New Army	28,467	438,554	1,682	43,861	30,149	482,415
Dominion/colonial	5,572	107,203	516	9,945	6,088	117,148
Royal Naval Division	314	5,264	12	315	326	5,579
Indians	146	3,446	13	3,066	159	6,512
Total	**34,499**	**554,467**	**2,223**	**57,187**	**36,722**	**611,654**

Offensive/battle	Dates	Officer casualties	Average daily rate
1914			
First Ypres	19 Oct.– 21 Nov.	2,057	60
1915			
Second Ypres	22 April–24 May	3,213	97
Loos	25 Sept. –15 Oct.	3,082	147
1916			
Somme	1 July–17 Nov.	22,042	157
1917			
Arras	9 April–16 May	7,776	205
Messines	7–14 June	1,902	238
Cambrai	20 Nov.–7 Dec.	3,226	179
Third Ypres (Passchendaele)	31 July–6 Nov.	14,514	147
1918			
German offensive	21 Mar.–5 April	9,829	614
Third Aisne	27 May–2 June	2,318	331
Allied Hundred Days offensive	8 Aug.–11 Nov.	19,341	201

• The most intense period of losses was during the sixteen days of the German offensive, mostly against the British Fifth Army, in March 1918. Over 9,800 officers fell (many captured) at a crippling daily rate of 614 – the highest such rate on the Western Front during the war.

• The two most notorious battles of the Western Front were the Somme and Third Ypres (Passchendaele). The former lasted for 142 days, during which over 22,000 officers became casualties at an average daily rate of 157. However, it was the opening day of the British offensive that is remembered for the most appalling losses on one day. On 1 July 1916, of the 57,420 casualties 2,456 were officers. Nine Victoria Crosses were won (six by officers or NCOs) – a total of fifty-one were awarded during this offensive, of which thirty-two went to officers or NCOs. By the end of the first day, thirty-two of the attacking infantry battalions had lost over 500 men – an unprecedented experience for the British Army – and all four commanding officers of the 103rd Brigade (Tyneside Irish) had been killed. In the New Zealand Division, the 1st Otago Regiment suffered thirty officer and 207 NCO casualties – losses that compelled

the divisional commander, Major General Russell, to tour his division interviewing men for commissions.

• Third Ypres, lasting ninety-nine days with an average daily officer loss of 147, was in a slightly different league from the Somme, mainly in terms of duration. Nevertheless, the intensity of the fighting in some of the most dreadful conditions encountered during the war resulted in the award of sixty-one VCs, eighteen to officers and thirty to NCOs (many for taking over leadership roles after officers fell). Fourteen of these were won for actions on 31 July, the first day, including Captain Noel Chavasse, who posthumously gained a bar to his Victoria Cross (see box, page 361).

The Statistics of the Military Effort of the British Empire during the Great War, 1914–1920 contains a comparative table of British and German officer casualties for the period February 1915–October 1918, but without figures for 'died of wounds' or 'died of disease', as the German records for these casualties were unavailable. These casualties occurred where the two armies were engaged on the Western Front. Extracts for officer casualties are given at the foot of the table.

1915 (exc. January)	**British**	**German**
Killed	2,854	592
Wounded	7,780	1,465
Missing/prisoners	757	198
Total casualties	**11,391**	**2,255**
1916		
Killed	6,506	1,396
Wounded	19,452	3,889
Missing/prisoners	1,524	867
Total casualties	**27,482**	**6,152**
1917		
Killed	9,187	2,482
Wounded	25,948	6,493
Missing/prisoners	2,379	1,891
Total casualties	**37,514**	**10,866**
1918		
Killed	7,558	5,522
Wounded	26,159	16,739
Missing/prisoners	5,637	5,684
Total casualties	**39,354**	**27,945**

Total officer casualties during this period:

115,741   47,218

or approx. British to German 5:2

Generalfeldmarschall Paul Ludwig Hans Anton von Beneckendorff und von Hindenburg, 1847–1934

Hindenburg was born in Posen, Prussia (modern Poland), the son of a Prussian aristocrat. After attending the Berlin cadet schools he was commissioned at eighteen into the Prussian Foot Guards. He fought in the Austro-Prussian and Franco-Prussian Wars and was decorated for bravery in 1870, three years later securing a place at the *Kriegsakademie* (War Academy). Over the next thirty years he rose steadily, reaching general of infantry rank in 1903 after long periods on the staff interposed by shorter periods commanding troops. However, his prospects of further promotion were somewhat blighted by his defeating the Kaiser at the 1904 annual military manoeuvres – seen as exceptionally bad form. He received no more promotion and retired, aged sixty-four, in 1911.

By the third week of August 1914, with events in the east against Russia deteriorating, Hindenburg was recalled from retirement and given command of the German Eighth Army in East Prussia, with General Ludendorff as his chief of staff. The Russian advance was massively defeated at the Battles of Tannenberg and the Masurian Lakes in August, although much of the credit for this triumph was due to the brilliant planning of a staff officer called Colonel Max Hoffman. Hoffman's opinion of his commander was not high. After the war, when escorting cadets round the Tannenberg battlefield, he is alleged to have said, 'See – this is where Hindenburg slept after the battle, and this is where Hindenburg slept before the battle, and this is where Hindenburg slept during the battle.' However, Hindenburg became a national hero and was promoted field marshal. Thus the Hindenburg–Ludendorff partnership that was to oversee the German efforts for the final two years on the Western Front was formed. This partnership continued to bring success in the east during 1915 and 1916, although Hindenburg was in reality no more than a mediocre

general who was fortunate to have a team of talented staff and able subordinates, including Ludendorff. Nevertheless, it was these successes that transformed Hindenburg into Germany's most popular general, regarded as the embodiment of German honour, decency and strength. He was used as a rallying symbol to boost flagging German morale. Wooden statues of him were erected all over Germany to which people nailed money or cheques for war bonds, and the government programme of all-out industrialization was called the Hindenburg Programme.

In September 1916, when Falkenhayn was deposed, Hindenburg was made chief of the General Staff with Ludendorff as his first quartermaster general (deputy). From this point onwards, the focus of power slipped from the government into the hands of the army, with Ludendorff the *éminence grise* exercising the real power behind the hugely popular Hindenburg – Germany was being run by a military dictatorship. This situation continued until shortly before the Armistice when Ludendorff resigned, followed on 9 November by the Kaiser's abdication and flight to Holland, which had remained neutral throughout the war. Hindenburg, however, remained as head of the army until 1919.

In the years following the war, Hindenburg's credibility remained high among the ordinary German people and he was elected president of the German Weimar Republic in 1925 at the age of seventy-eight. He later attempted to limit the power of Hitler, whom he despised intensely, but in January 1933 he was compelled to appoint Hitler as chancellor. Hindenburg died in August 1934, aged eighty-seven, before the catastrophe of the Hitler regime became apparent. He was given a full state funeral and was buried near Tannenberg, scene of his greatest military triumph.

The British suffered many more officer losses than their enemy – about 116,000 to roughly 47,000. For every five British officers only about two Germans fell – a very considerable, potentially crippling, statistic. In 1915 the disparity was at its worst, with over five British officers being lost for every German, but with matters evening up considerably by 1918 with a ratio of 1:1.4. There were several reasons for this:

• The British Army commissioned, albeit with temporary wartime commissions, many more regimental officers than the Germans. A New Army British battalion going into action for the first time on the Somme would expect to have twenty-five combatant officers, whereas a German equivalent would have nine or ten. German platoons at this stage were normally commanded by acting officers, sergeant-major lieutenants, sergeant majors, or staff sergeants, none of whom ranked as a commissioned officer. Casualties among these men were therefore not deemed officer losses.

• With more officers as targets, inevitably many more would get hit than among the German officers, where it was common for only the company commander to be a commissioned officer in the rank of captain or lieutenant. Thus a British subaltern was expected to perform many duties that would be the responsibility of an NCO in the German Army. A simple example was the raid carried out by the 1/4th East Yorkshires on the night of 26–27 June 1916. Two subaltern officers were sent out to cut the German wire where the attackers hoped to enter the enemy position. This was done successfully but put the lives of two officers at considerable risk; this sort of task would have been unthinkable for a German officer. Although British NCOs took over when their officer became a casualty, a commissioned officer replacement was invariably sought immediately and the NCO seldom remained in command for long. The comments of the *British Official History of the War* on the Battle of Arras in 1917, during which an average of 205 British officers fell every day for thirty-eight days, are relevant:

> When British troops lost their officers they were . . . apt to fall back, not because they were beaten but because they did not know what to do and expected to receive fresh orders. Perhaps the large number of officers commissioned and the fact that a sergeant rarely held command of a platoon for more than a few days lessened the prestige of the non-commissioned officer . . .

• Another factor was the need for the British units to take the offensive for much of the war, and before assault tactics on successive trench lines and bunkers had been developed to include the proper combination of infantry, artillery, aircraft and (later) tanks. With the attacker compelled to attack frontally, the machine gun, the quick-firing field artillery piece, barbed wire and deep bunkers all favoured the defender – a combination that invariably led to a much higher proportion of attacker losses of all ranks.

Before looking at methods of obtaining the officers needed, it is worth recapping the statistics. The British Army started the war with just over 28,000 officers, over half of whom belonged to the Special Reserve, Territorial Force or Reserve. Some 229,000 new combatant officers had been commissioned by the war's end (the great majority for the New Armies) – that is, an average of 4,400 every month: an incredible achievement. Expansion and then replacement problems grew together and exacerbated each other from August 1914 onwards. The call to raise the New (Kitchener) Armies went out that month. The first 100,000 volunteers were called K1; in September K2 followed; K3 and K4 came later, with conscription necessary in 1916. As early as the end of September 1914 Sir John French, commanding the BEF, wrote to Kitchener, 'The proportion of reliable leaders to the men they have to direct and lead is becoming most serious throughout the Whole Force'. One divisional commander was more specific, writing that the four battalions in one of his brigades had only four, six, seven and nine company officers (there should have been at least twenty in each) and that, 'The great pressing need is for officers. Without them the reinforcements are practically wasted.'

This was the winter of 1914/15, about which the *British Official History* commented:

> Such was the emergency in France in the winter of 1914–1915 that instead of being used as training cadres, a framework on which to build new battalions and batteries, the last of the Regular soldiers from overseas stations were formed into the 27th, 28th and 29th Divisions. The first two of them were sent to Flanders as soon as possible . . . Thus there was only a very small leaven of trained officers and non-commissioned officers for the New Armies, and these when from foreign stations or the Reserve not always up to date. Battalions were built up on a nucleus of two or three officers and a dozen NCOs or less [for battalions of 1,000 untrained civilian volunteers].

So how was this neverending crisis solved?

Permanent regular officers

Prior to the outbreak of war, Regular Army officers were commissioned from the Royal Military College (RMC), Sandhurst, and the Royal Military Academy (RMA), Woolwich. The RMC provided some two-thirds of newly commissioned regular officers for the Infantry, Cavalry and Army Service Corps, while the RMA did the same for 99 per cent of the technical arms – the Artillery and Engineers. The course at the former was eighteen months and at the latter two years. On the outbreak of war these were cut to three and six months respectively. However, war necessitated the granting of the great majority of regular commissions as second lieutenants from the sources listed below, with the figures in brackets showing the intake in 1913:

RMC	5,013	(343)
RMA	1,928	(112)
RMC (Canada)	172	(6)
Special Reserve	1,008	(67)
Territorial Force	335	(9)
Temporary commissions	1,109	(nil)
Universities	246	(78)
Colonial	20	(3)
From the ranks	6,713	(7)
Total	16,544	(625)

Special Reserve

The number of commissions granted in the Special Reserve between August 1914 and 1 December 1918 was 30,376, compared with 81 in 1913.

Territorial Force

In August 1914 the number of officers holding commissions in this force was 9,563. The number of commissions granted from that date to 1 December 1918 was 60,044.

Officer Cadet Battalions (OCBs)

From February 1916 the issue of direct commissions to the Special Reserve and Territorial Force had practically ceased. Commissions after this were granted only to cadets who passed the four-and-a-half-month course at OCBs (although some battlefield commissions were still granted). By the Armistice there were thirty-eight such units in which almost 108,000 cadets had been trained, the great bulk (69,000) being commissioned into the infantry or artillery (19,000). A Lieutenant A. P. White wrote of one:

> The . . . school is a fairly new institution. The fellow who is running it describes it as 'a sort of working holiday.' You spend nearly a month . . . hearing lectures, working out field schemes, etc., then you

The Sinking of HMS *Hampshire*

HMS *Hampshire* was an armoured cruiser detailed by the Admiralty to take Lord Kitchener, the secretary of state for war, to Russia to confer with the Tsar. On 5 June 1916, in a raging storm off the Orkneys, *Hampshire* struck a mine and sank in less than fifteen minutes. Eight hundred officers and men, including Kitchener and his staff, were drowned. There were only twelve survivors, one of whom was Walter Farnden, a stoker. He later described the final moments of the ship as she began to sink.

Orders 'Abandon ship' were given, and as the hatches were opened men poured up from below on to the deck and took up their positions at the boat stations. I was among them.

There was no panic, but a great deal of confusion; shouted orders were lost in the howling wind and booming seas. It was found impossible to launch the boats; the derricks were electrically controlled and the current had failed.

One boat which was got away by cutting its lashings was immediately caught by a tremendous wave and dashed to pieces against the *Hampshire*'s side. Between fifty and sixty men were flung into the water.

Men now began jumping overboard from the quarterdeck in their lifebelts and life-saving waistcoats. All around the fast-sinking vessel men could be seen clutching pieces of wreckage in frantic efforts to save themselves. Some were badly injured or scalded for a boiler had been burst by the force of the explosion.

Farnden got away by clinging to one of the Carley floats (large, cork-filled, oval lifebelts with rope handles round the edges). He watched the final plunge of his ship:

Many of the crew, when it had been found impossible to lower the boats, had remained in them as they hung from their davits, thinking that as the ship went down under them the boats would float. Instead, when the *Hampshire* gave a final plunge and, turning a somersault forwards, disappeared, she carried down with her all the boats and those in them . . . There were between thirty and forty men on the circular raft when the ship went down, but one by one they disappeared . . . An hour passed, two hours, and nearer and nearer to land the storm hurled us. Men were still dying in the agony of it all until there were but four of us left alive.

Presently our raft was flung against the shore, and smashed, leaving us clinging to the rocks. Between me and the shore was a strip of calmer water, perhaps twelve feet wide, perhaps more. And I could not swim. But I somehow managed to get across it. I was saved.

Field Marshal Earl Horatio Herbert Kitchener, 1850–1916

Kitchener was educated in Switzerland and at the Royal Military Academy, Woolwich. His family lived in France and in 1870 Kitchener briefly joined a French field ambulance in the Franco-Prussian War. However, he caught pneumonia after ascending in a balloon to watch the French Army in action and returned to England, where he was commissioned into the Royal Engineers in January 1871. He served in Palestine, Egypt and Cyprus as a surveyor, learned Arabic and prepared topographical maps of the areas.

As a captain in 1883 he was attached to the Egyptian Army and took part in the Nile Expedition that unsuccessfully attempted to save General Gordon surrounded at Khartoum – he was promoted brevet major and lieutenant colonel for his services. At this time his fiancée died of typhoid in Cairo; Kitchener subsequently never married. In the late 1880s he was a colonel and Governor of the Red Sea Territories (Suakin). In 1890 he led the cavalry in action against the dervishes at Gamaizieh and Toski. In 1892 he become the *sirdar* (commander) of the Egyptian Army, and in 1896, as a British major general, he led another expedition up the Nile. He ultimately defeated the Sudanese at the Battle of Omdurman (in which a young subaltern called Winston Churchill took part in a victorious cavalry charge). For this triumph he was created Baron Kitchener of Khartoum (he later acquired the nickname 'KK'), received the thanks of Parliament and was awarded £30,000.

As a lieutenant general he was initially chief of staff to Lord Roberts in the Second Boer War and in late 1900 succeeded him as commander-in-chief. He was responsible for conducting the guerilla war against the Boers that saw thousands confined in grim conditions in what were the first concentration camps – for which many condemned him. Nevertheless, with the Boers capitulating, Kitchener was made a viscount and received another £50,000. After a spell as commander-in-chief in India, during which he established the Indian Staff College at Quetta, he became consul general in Egypt, where he put in place numerous beneficial reforms in agriculture, the cotton markets, sanitation and education.

At the outbreak of hostilities in August 1914, Kitchener, now a field marshal, was appointed secretary of state for war and became the man of the hour, his reputation and iron will enabling the government to meet its obligations to the Allies in Europe. He set in train the mobilization and expansion of a British Army (Kitchener's New Army of volunteers – see page 97) that eventually defeated all its enemies – his 'Your King and Country Need You' poster remains well known and is occasionally adapted for use today. Unfortunately, Kitchener drowned when HMS *Hampshire*, on which he was travelling to Russia, sank off the Orkneys after hitting a mine on 5 June 1916 (see box above).

Several memorials to Kitchener were established after the war, including the renaming of a town in Ontario, and the naming of Mount Kitchener in the Canadian Rockies. In addition, the Lord Kitchener Elementary School was founded near Vancouver; it continued to function up to 2007. The Kitchener Memorial Hospital was named in his honour in Geelong, Victoria, Australia. In England the Kitchener National Memorial Fund was set up by the Lord Mayor of London to assist casualties of the war, and the Kitchener Memorial Homes in Chatham were built from public subscriptions for ex-servicemen and women who had seen active service. On the rugged Marwick Head, Orkney, a 48-foot tower was built in his memory, overlooking the Brough of Birsay where *Hampshire* sank. The plaque on the tower was unveiled on 2 July 1926 as the battleship *Royal Sovereign* steamed over the exact spot where *Hampshire* lies and fired a salute from its massive guns.

Generalleutnant Erich Friedrich Whilhelm Ludendorff, 1865–1937

Ludendorff was born in Kruszewnia near Posen (now Poland) into a merchant family that had no pretensions of Prussian military aristocracy. His acceptance into the Cadet School at Plon was largely due to his flair for mathematics and his enthusiastic work ethic – the latter being a lifelong characteristic. In 1885 he was commissioned into the 57th Infantry Regiment. During the next eight years he served with the 2nd Marine Battalion at Kiel and the 8th Grenadier Guards at Frankfurt, obtaining high praise in all his reports. After doing well at the War Academy, Ludendorff was appointed to the General Staff in 1894. In 1905 he joined the Second Section of the Great General Staff in Berlin, working under Schlieffen on the mobilization aspects of his invasion plan. By 1911 he was a colonel and agitating vociferously and persistently for an increase in army manpower and funding. By early 1913 his agitations had become politically too embarrassing; he was removed and sent to command the 39th Fusiliers at Düsseldorf, where he became a well-respected commander, popular with the younger officers – this despite his reputation as a dour, unapproachable and friendless staff officer.

On the outbreak of war Ludendorff, then a brigade commander, was transferred as deputy chief of staff to the German Second Army. The first setback to the German attack through Belgium came at the fortress of Liège, where artillery and machine-gun fire had decimated the frontal attacks of the German infantry. Ludendorff, who had made a detailed study of the defences while on Schlieffen's staff, was given command of the 14th Brigade, cut off Liège and, with skilful use of siege artillery, demolished all the surrounding forts, thus allowing the First Army to advance. This action earned him Prussia's highest military decoration, the *Pour le Mérite*.

Ludendorff was appointed Hindenburg's chief of staff in August 1914 and both were despatched to the Eastern Front to take command of the faltering German forces opposing the Russians. Thus began the association that was to form probably the most important command partnership of the war. Ludendorff assumed the title of first quartermaster general in August 1916 and became the de facto controller of the war, although Hindenburg was certainly more than just a popular figurehead. These two took the Germans through the remainder of the war, including launching the massive attack on the Western Front on 21 March 1918 that so nearly succeeded in breaking the Allied front. However, its failure, and the subsequent Allied counter-attack on 8 August 1918 that produced what Ludendorff called the 'Black Day of the German Army', broke his will to the extent that he considered Germany's only option was to sue for peace while the German forces stood on the defensive. The continued Allied advances crushed him, bringing on a near mental breakdown. Despite this, he changed his mind when he disapproved of the terms of the peace being discussed, forcefully advocating that negotiations cease and the army hold out until the winter when defence would be easier. When the government continued to negotiate, Ludendorff resigned. Shortly after the Armistice he fled to Sweden in disguise.

Ludendorff wrote several books and articles about Germany's conduct of the war in which he established the myth that the German Army had been stabbed in the back by the government, as well as undermined by civilian strikes and the general home-front collapse. He saw the conditions of the Treaty of Versailles as an unacceptable humiliation of Germany. He returned to Germany in 1920 and his ultra-nationalistic views soon involved him in right-wing politics and approval of the rising Nazi Party and its leader Hitler. Ludendorff was persuaded to participate in Hitler's infamous Beer Hall Putsch in 1923. The plot failed and Ludendorff was among those arrested, although acquitted by the trial that followed. In 1924 he was elected to the Reichstag (German parliament) and in the following year ran (very unsuccessfully) in the presidential election against Hindenburg. After 1928 he retired and went into seclusion, having fallen out with the Nazi Party and Hitler, whom he now regarded as just another manipulative politician.

In 1935 Hitler paid Ludendorff an unexpected visit and offered to make him a field marshal – an offer that he furiously rejected. He died in 1937, aged seventy-two, and, against his wishes, was given a state funeral attended by Hitler.

---

go on a tour which includes Divisional headquarters, brigade headquarters, a battery of artillery, an aerodrome, etc. The object is to give the infantry an idea of how other branches of the army work . . . We have lectures from various Johnnies who show us 'how the wheels go round' in the Supplies Department, Medical Services, etc., etc.

In addition, sixteen cadet battalions were established for training Royal Flying Corps (RFC) officers and they granted commissions to some 37,700 cadets. Overall, these OCBs provided almost half the combatant commissions (including RFC) granted during the war. Corporal Ernest Parker, Durham Light Infantry, who served from 1914 through Loos, Ypres and the Somme before being sent to an OCB, later wrote favourably of his experience there in early 1917 and of the quality of most of the men commissioned:

At the Officer Cadet Battalion at Kimmel Park, near Rhyl, some hundreds of NCOs from the Expeditionary Force were assembling. They were men who had voluntarily joined Kitchener's Army, and now, after many battles in which they had won their stripes, they had been selected by their commanding officers to undergo four months' training before being commissioned in the New Armies.

They were keen serious students of the art of war and first-rate instructors, some of whom had already won coveted decorations, including at least one VC, trained them. When they finally returned to the battlefronts they brought an entirely new spirit into the ranks of the junior officers.

Parker was commissioned, won an MC, survived the war, was discharged in 1919 aged twenty-two and served in World War II.

Initially the problem was the acute shortage of officers for the K1 and K2 armies forming in August and September 1914, compounded by the heavy losses incurred by the BEF at Mons, Le Cateau and the retreat to the Marne. Small cadres of regular, Territorial Forces and reserve officers and NCOs were taken from their units to fill the basic command and training posts for the thousands of volunteers responding to 'Your King and Country Need You' posters. In September Kitchener appealed in the press for 2,000 men of good education and former cadets who had attended a university OTC to come forward. Retired, somewhat elderly, officers and NCOs were recalled for duty – the 'dugouts' from the Second Boer War or earlier among them. Officers on leave from units stationed overseas, mostly in India, were prevented from returning and posted to new units. Sandhurst and Woolwich commissioned cadets who were in their final term immediately, shortening their courses. University OTCs and the Inns of Court OTC provided a significant number. However, the majority of junior officers were commissioned directly, having merely to attend a selection board where university or public school OTC experience was usually regarded as sufficient qualification to be recommended to the War Office for a commission – those with technical qualifications or degrees going mostly to the engineers and to a lesser extent the artillery.

The problem was exacerbated by forming, and sending across the Channel, New Army battalions such as those from public schools, the Honourable Artillery, the Artists' Rifles, the London Scottish and the London Rifle Brigade, composed almost entirely of upper- and middle-class young volunteers. This was quickly seen as a dreadful waste of potential officers and these units soon began to be milked of men for commissioning; one Public Schools' Battalion alone had had 350 men taken for this purpose by the end of 1914. This was not popular with commanding officers, one of whom claimed that 95 per cent of his battalion was suitable to be officers so he might as well convert his unit into an OTC. There was also a fairly widespread commissioning of senior warrant officers. Charles Messenger, in his book *Call-to-Arms*, cites the 2nd Royal Welsh Fusiliers commissioning the regimental sergeant major (RSM), the regimental quartermaster sergeant (RQMS) and a company sergeant major (CSM) at the end of October 1914. Second Lieutenant Murphy, previously the RSM, was unhappy: 'There was I, a thousand men at my control, the Commanding Officer was my personal friend, the Adjutant consulted me, the Subalterns feared me, and now I am only a bum-wart and have to hold my tongue in the Mess.'

Despite Murphy's grumbling, many of these former warrant officers did extremely well, rising in rank and being decorated for gallantry. An example was a pre-war soldier, Warrant Officer J. F. Plunkett of the Royal Irish Rifles, who was recommended for the Victoria Cross in 1914, was commissioned and rose to be a lieutenant colonel commanding a battalion by early 1917, and was recommended yet again for a VC at Cambrai. By November 1918 he was one of the most decorated officers in the army: three DSOs, an MC, a DCM and the French *Croix de Guerre*.

The solution in most Pals battalions was to select those with managerial experience as officers, and former supervisors or foremen as NCOs. Colonel Nicholson explained the situation as he saw it as a senior staff officer – his view appears slightly at odds with that of Captain (formerly Corporal) Parker above.

As the war progressed the shortage [of junior officers] became more and more acute, the quality worsened . . . in January 1917 we were ordered to find fifty candidates a month from the 17th Division. To obtain these we depended on the recommendations of the unit commanders. But only the best unit commanders were prepared to lose their best NCOs, for they did not necessarily come back to them as officers. Moreover many of these NCOs declined to leave the home they knew; so that our fifty candidates did not necessarily represent the pick of the bunch. It is open to question whether an improvement in the NCO status [like the German system] would not have met this shortage more satisfactorily.

One commanding officer forwarded the names of two sanitary orderlies who had fought in the Second Boer War and the brigade commander eventually, under protest, had to accept them. Nevertheless it should be recorded that over fifty officers commissioned after the start of the war rose to the rank of lieutenant colonel, most of them to command infantry battalions, while at least four became brigadier generals.

Certainly the British system meant that the old pre-war class distinctions within the officer corps all but disappeared in most units. A War Office survey of some 144,000 officer demobilizations categorized by civil occupations showed that while 60 per cent were middle class, such as teachers, students, clerical or from commerce, a significant number of the remainder had been in working-class jobs, such as seamen, fishermen, warehousemen, porters, coalminers and carters. At the end of the war, in the 33rd Machine Gun Battalion the company commanders were a medical student (DSO and MC), a wool salesman (MC and Bar), a Scots Guard sergeant (MC and DCM) and the son of a miner (MC and Bar, and DCM), and the adjutant was the son of a land agent (MC and Bar). However, this situation did not survive the war and the British Regular Army reverted to commissioning mostly men of upper-middle or upper class – a system which was again found totally inadequate in World War II and which has no substance in today's army.

To summarize the common experience of an infantry battalion with regard to the standard of experience and training of its officers, the performance of the 1st South Staffordshire Regiment on the Western Front from 1914–18 is briefly described below. Its source is the article by Chris Baker in the April/May 2009 issue of *Stand To!*, the journal of the Western Front Association.

1914 The 1st South Staffords was a regular battalion, part of the 7th Division. When it landed at Zeebrugge, the commanding officer was Lieutenant Colonel Robert Ovens, described as a 'short, fiery, red-headed northern Irishman' with twenty-five years' commissioned service that included the Second Boer War. Two of the company commanders were also veterans of the same war, while the other two had some thirteen years' service each. Among the subalterns, all regulars, about a quarter were inexperienced and with less than four years in the army. One had been commissioned only on 26 August and had received practically no training prior to the war. There was a similar situation with the warrant officers and NCOs. The battalion was to be comparatively fortunate with the continuity of its commanding officers and RSMs during the next four years, in that, apart from a short period in 1915, it had only three commanding officers, assisted by five RSMs, of whom two were commissioned. New officers joining the battalion undoubtedly benefited from the quality of the leadership and high standards maintained by the regulars.

The battalion was all but destroyed at First Ypres, including Lieutenant Colonel Ovens wounded, when the reality of trench warfare and the devastating effect of massed artillery fire, which nobody had anticipated or trained for, exacted its unforgiving toll on all ranks.

1915 By the end of 1914 the battalion no longer had a leavening of pre-war junior officers. Most of the replacements had been directly commissioned as wartime volunteers with little, if any, military experience apart from school or university OTCs. Along with these novices came a few elderly regulars, 'dugouts' from the Special Reserve, Indian Army or from forgotten corners of the empire. It was fortunate that in this period of early 1915 the battalion was not committed to any major action, and spent the weeks digging and dodging the sniper's bullet and the occasional salvo of shells.

Not until May, when the battalion was involved in the Festubert battle, was its leadership severely tested again. By this time a substantial number of the Ypres replacements had gone – sick or removed for various reasons. A number of the gaps thus created in the chain of command were filled by returned officers and NCOs wounded at Ypres and by several men commissioned from the ranks, including a former RSM and tin-plate worker with eighteen years' service, William Cooper. For the attack at Festubert a captain, four subalterns and 131 men were left out of battle as a nucleus on which to re-form if losses were heavy. This practice soon became the standard procedure throughout the BEF. The Staffords' attack was launched behind a hurricane barrage instead of the previous long preparatory one that warned the Germans what to expect. It was a success. The battalion took the enemy trenches, secured their position and beat off several counter-attacks during the next three days. Its success came primarily from achieving surprise and the determined leadership within the battalion.

Four months of front-line experience followed before the Loos attack started in late September. By then more Ypres wounded had returned, including Lieutenant Colonel Ovens. In addition to the commanding officer, every company commander, the adjutant and machine-gun officer were Ypres veterans. Nevertheless, over half the subalterns were as untrained and inexperienced as their counterparts of early in the year. As Chris Baker described it in his article, Loos was a bitter experience:

> The battalion officers had little chance to innovate or show their character at Loos. Divisional and Brigade orders were much more detailed, prescriptive and rigid than hitherto. In the case of the Staffords they required a frontal assault against a strongpoint – the Pope's Nose – that in the event was barely touched by the preliminary bombardment and invisible through the gas cloud.

The battalion war diary described the attack:

> the gallant 1st South Staffords rose to their feet at 0628, advanced in extended order – about 3 paces interval between each man – and moved steadily forward against this almost impregnable position. They stormed it, and took the second or support line. And what remained of this magnificent old regiment moved on, and with other units mixed up with them, captured the Quarries. Some of them, with their CO, went on, up to about 50 yards from the German position in Cite St. Elie [see Map 14, pages 48–9].

Losses were horrendous. Some 400 men became casualties, including eighteen of the twenty-one officers, necessitating a complete rebuilding of the battalion. However, replacement officers were no longer completely green in the ways of war. In late 1915 the 7th Division set up a training school for officers to learn the rudiments of leadership and tactics. These schools soon became the norm and together with the commissioning of three NCOs, the Staffords' Loos replacements were much better equipped to lead their men than those arriving nine months earlier.

1916 From early in the year it was common for officers and NCOs to be away from the battalion attending courses or specialist schools. By the time the Staffords attacked

Mametz on 1 July, practically all the officers had at least experienced a setpiece trench raid and a number were returned wounded. Chris Baker again:

> It was a wilier battalion that faced Mametz. But it was also a more empowered battalion, for its officers and those at the higher levels of command in 7th Division were learning their trade and being given increased freedom of action. Whilst Fourth Army might feel the need to issue prescriptive, restricting orders to formations of the New Armies under its command, XV Corps and 7th Division were experienced enough to adapt its orders to their own needs . . . in consequence the battalion's successful attack consisted of a short rush from a position taken up deep into no man's land whilst the bombardment continued . . .

1917–18 The 1st South Staffords continued to have many hard fights and lose many officers for the remainder of the war, with the average age of officer replacements being twenty-three – well above that of the young boys straight from school or university who had volunteered in late 1914 or through much of 1915. Now these new subalterns were the product of the much improved training at the OCBs, or else they were experienced NCOs given battlefield commissions.

The Staff

Britain

The staff are the channels through which a senior commander ensures that his orders, both operational and administrative, are issued, delivered and understood. Without this oil the military machine cannot function. Of equal importance is that the staff exists for the welfare of the troops. Without good staff work the soldiers go short of ammunition, food, water, clothing, equipment, transport, mail, adequate rest or leave periods, decent billets, baths and many other needs. Staff officers worked at the headquarters of all formations from brigade, division, corps and army, and at GHQ as well. They were also to be found at the headquarters of commands and districts at home, at bases or administrative areas on the lines of communication, as well as at the War Office. They were responsible for assisting the commander in making operational or logistical plans for all the units in the formation and disseminating the appropriate orders, both operational and administrative.

Like many British generals of World War I, the staff have come in for considerable, often unfounded, criticism from writers with the benefit of hindsight and lacking relevant military experience. If staff work on the Western Front had been consistently poor, the overall morale of the fighting soldier could not have been maintained and ultimately victory would have been impossible, as the troops would have given up. Bad staff work would have meant lack of food, lack of ammunition, poor arrangements for casualty evacuation and treatment, shortages of equipment, bad deliveries of mail from home, being sent to the wrong places, no facilities for rest, clean clothes or baths, and inadequate opportunities for leave. Certainly some of these things happened in some formations sometimes, but they were neither general nor continuous. Staff officers had to learn to handle administrative situations of a scale and complexity undreamt of in the pre-1914 army. Most had to learn on the job, from their own experience and that of others. That they did so and that the

nearly 2 million men of the BEF in 1918 were able to undertake a full-scale advance to victory reflects as creditably on the staff as on the commanders and troops. However, in fairness it must be said that this Allied advance could have continued but was ultimately halted for logistical reasons, certainly for the French, as the administrative tail needed to catch up with the dog.

Charles Carrington had this to say of BEF staff work:

> The build-up for a battle required such masses of supplies and munitions, such elaboration of movements by road and rail, that it could not be concealed and, once set on foot, could change direction only at the cost of chaos. As a feat of organization the staff work of the BEF was supremely efficient, far more so than in the armies of any of our allies.

Despite the overall efficiency of the staff, there was a general feeling of animosity between them and the regimental officer. This had its roots in the old Regular Army, when to attend Staff College (at Camberley) was often regarded as disloyalty to the regiment and indicated a self-seeking individual. There was an anti-staff attitude in many regimental officers' messes fostered by crusty old captains and majors who were probably too lazy and mentally incapable of coping with complex staff problems. Siegfried Sassoon put his feelings thus in his poem 'Base Details':

> *If I were fierce, and bald, and short of breath,*
> *I'd live with scarlet majors at the Base,*
> *And speed glum heroes up the line to death.*
> *You'd see me with my puffy petulant face,*
> *Guzzling and gulping in the best hotel,*
> *Reading the Roll of Honour. 'Poor young chap,'*
> *I'd say – 'I used to know his father well;*
> *Yes, we've lost heavily in this last scrap.'*
> *And when the war is done and youth stone dead,*
> *I'd toddle safely home and die – in bed.*

The wearing by staff officers of red tabs on their collars, red bands round their hats and special armbands – so that they could be easily recognized when bringing forward orders – caused considerable resentment as it gave the impression that the wearer was a superior being and emphasized that he lived in a different, invariably much safer, more comfortable world than the regimental officer. These uniform embellishments were normally worn only by colonels and above and after the war, when their negative effect was recognized, they were abolished for all more junior officers.

The duties of staff officers were broadly divided into three main categories:

General Staff (GS) Not created in Britain until 1904. Responsible for all matters of operations, training, intelligence and the overall coordination of all staff work within the headquarters. Referred to as 'G' Staff.

Adjutant General's (AG) Department Responsible for questions of manpower, recruiting, pay, discipline, medical services and chaplains. Referred to as 'A' staff.

Quartermaster General's (QMG) Department Responsible for the supply of food, equipment, animals, transport, barracks and billets. Referred to as 'Q' staff.

In addition, the term 'staff officers', although not strictly correct, is generally applied to all officers at a headquarters. These would include those holding personal appointments such as aides-de-camp (ADCs), officers holding special appointments such as camp commandants, and provost marshals, as well as those heading the administrative services and departments – medical, pay, supplies, transport, ordnance services, works, etc. – each of whom would have deputies and assistants. The system of grading staff officers was, and still is, complex and that for the Western Front is described briefly below:

Headquarters of the 21st Infantry Brigade during the Battle of Neuve Chapelle, March 1915.

• Those holding the most senior staff appointments as heads of their branches at GHQ were all lieutenant generals. They were the Chief of the General Staff (CGS), Adjutant General (AG) and Quartermaster General (QMG).

• The deputy heads of branches at GHQ and heads of branches at army headquarters were normally major generals. These included a Major General General Staff (MGGS), Deputy Adjutant General (DAG) and Deputy Quartermaster General (DQMG). However at army headquarters there was a Deputy Assistant Adjutant and Quartermaster General (DAA&QMG) to coordinate the work of both branches.

• There was a Brigadier General General Staff (BGGS) who was deputy to the MGGS at GHQ or to the senior General Staff officer at corps headquarters. The senior A&Q staff officer at corps was a DAA&QMG, also a brigadier general.

• The heads of administrative services were directors (D Supplies, D Transport, etc.). At GHQ they were normally major generals (e.g. Director of Veterinary Services) or more often brigadier generals (e.g. Director of Railways). Elsewhere they would be either brigadier generals or colonels.

• A deputy director would be one rank lower than director. If the director was at GHQ the deputy director would be at a base on the line of communication or vice versa. Many administrative services had a deputy director at army headquarters.

• The lower grades of staff officers (lieutenant colonels, majors and captains) were found at all headquarters and bases from division to army – a brigade headquarters did not merit a lieutenant colonel. Lieutenant colonels were either General Staff Officers Grade 1 (GSO1) or assistants such as Assistant Adjutant General (AAG) or Assistant Quartermaster General (AQMG). Majors were General Staff Officers Grade 2 (GSO2) or deputy assistants such as Deputy Assistant Adjutant General (DAAG) or Deputy Assistant Quartermaster General (DAQMG). Captains were either General Staff Officers Grade 3 (GSO3) or working in an administrative role as a staff captain. At brigade headquarters the senior General Staff Officer was called a brigade major, although on the Western Front most were captains.

The larger the headquarters, the more staff were required – by 1918 GHQ consisted of 1,169 officers and 6,076 ORs. A formation headquarters would also contain the commanders of the supporting arms, such as the artillery, engineers, signals and tanks, each with their own staff. At the other end of the scale was an infantry brigade headquarters with a brigade major (BM), usually a captain, responsible for 'G' matters and a staff captain responsible for both 'A' and 'Q' matters. At battalion level no staff officer was attached to the headquarters, although the adjutant was effectively the commanding officer's 'G' and 'A' staff officer, with the quartermaster responsible for 'Q' affairs. Also at battalion headquarters were the medical officer, machine-gun officer, signalling officer and transport officer with the duty of coordinating the activities of their respective 'supporting arms' or 'services'. See diagram, page 166.

The Staff at Work

It was usually the contention by regimental officers and soldiers that the staff had an idle, safe and comfortable time. As noted above, they needed a degree of the latter two in order to function, but as regards their workload, this contention is way off the mark. A staff officer at GHQ working in the 'Q' branch had this to say of a critical juncture of the war:

> During the worst of the German offensive in the Spring of 1918 Staff officers toiled from 8.30 am to midnight, with half-hour intervals for meals. I have seen a Staff officer faint at table from sheer pressure of work, and dozens of men, come fresh from regimental work, wilt away under the fierce pressure of work at G.H.Q.

Colonel Walter Nicholson was DAA and QMG of XIII Corps in 1918, responsible for planning and coordinating the supply for four divisions and corps troops during the British advance to victory. He later wrote:

> I sat at a table with a map in front of me. The map gradually became more and more attenuated as we advanced; for our railheads remained fixed, while our front reached further and further away from them. All my interest was centred on the long thin line which joined my railheads with the front, and hardly any of my interest concerned actual fighting. I spent many hours calculating the number of lorries I could raise, working out the amount of ammunition that could be carried forward, planning roads and traffic circuits, watching the light railway gradually move forward and the repairs to the broad gauge. All my attention turned on the ammunition supply, the food supply and roads – and all my time was completely occupied. The number of complications in such a problem is inconceivable. A time mine on the railway, the wrong side of Epehy, which delayed an ammunition train some twenty hours, lost me one hundred and fifty lorries and robbed me of an ammunition reserve just before a battle. The craters that the Germans had blown in all the main roads affected my transport calculations.

Field Marshal Haig leaves his headquarters train.

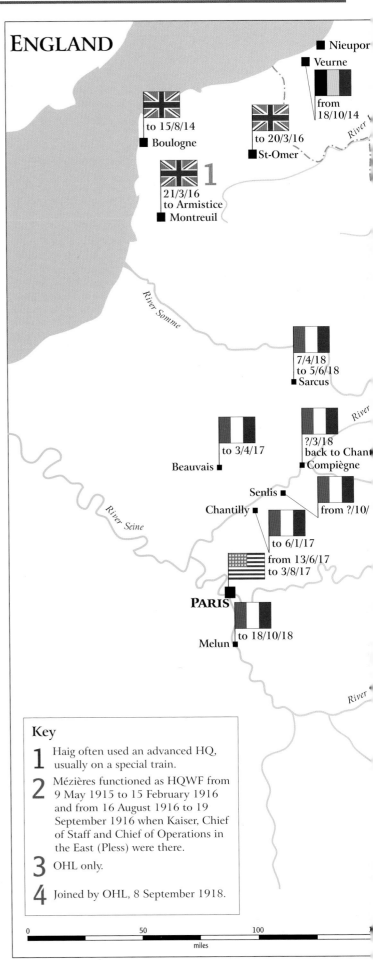

ENGLAND

to 15/8/14
Boulogne

to 20/3/16
St-Omer

Nieupor
Veurne
from 18/10/14

21/3/16
to Armistice
Montreuil

River Somme

7/4/18
to 5/6/18
Sarcus

to 3/4/17
Beauvais

?/3/18
back to Chan
Compiègne

Senlis
Chantilly

from ?/10/

to 6/1/17

from 13/6/17
to 3/8/17

PARIS

Melun

to 18/10/18

River Seine

Key

1 Haig often used an advanced HQ, usually on a special train.

2 Mézières functioned as HQWF from 9 May 1915 to 15 February 1916 and from 16 August 1916 to 19 September 1916 when Kaiser, Chief of Staff and Chief of Operations in the East (Pless) were there.

3 OHL only.

4 Joined by OHL, 8 September 1918.

0   50   100

miles

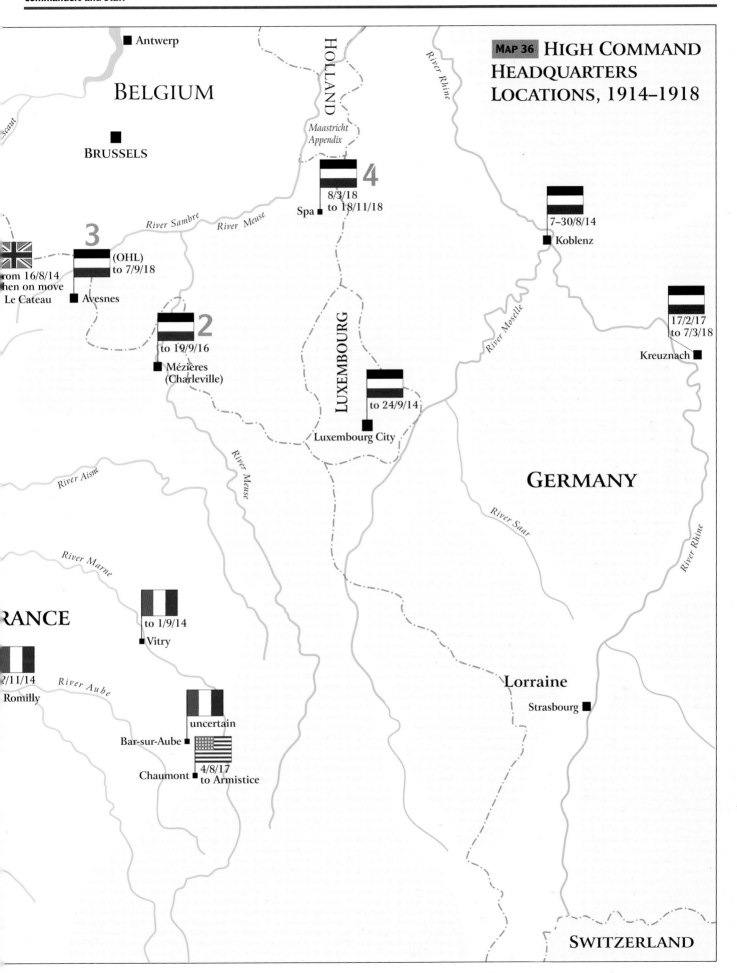

■ Antwerp

BELGIUM

HOLLAND

River Rhine

MAP 36 HIGH COMMAND
HEADQUARTERS
LOCATIONS, 1914–1918

■

BRUSSELS

*Maastricht
Appendix*

4

8/3/18
to 18/11/18

Spa ■

7–30/8/14

■ Koblenz

3

River Sambre   *River Meuse*

(OHL)
to 7/9/18

from 16/8/14
then on move
Le Cateau
■ Avesnes

River Moselle

17/2/17
to 7/3/18

Kreuznach ■

2

to 19/9/16

■ Mézières
(Charleville)

LUXEMBOURG

to 24/9/14

River Aisne

River Meuse

Luxembourg City ■

GERMANY

River Saar

River Rhine

River Marne

RANCE

to 1/9/14
■ Vitry

/11/14

Lorraine

Romilly

River Aube

Strasbourg ■

uncertain

Bar-sur-Aube ■

4/8/17

Chaumont ■ to Armistice

SWITZERLAND

BEF General Headquarters – France, 1914–1918

Commander-in-Chief
(Field Marshal)

'MS'

Military Secretary
(Maj. Gen.)

Honours

Awards

Appointments
(colonels+)

Appointments
(officers to staff)

Brevets

General Courts Martial

'G'

Chief of General Staff
(Lt Gen.)

Deputy Chief of General Staff
(Maj. Gen.)

Operations
(Maj. Gen.)

Policy

Plans

Liaison

Despatches

Movement control

Maps/topography

Situation reports

Personnel

Intelligence/information on:
- enemy artillery
- enemy plans
- enemy communications
- enemy defences
- enemy orbat
- enemy tactics
- enemy armaments

Secret Service

Agents' reports

Counter-espionage

Control of civilians

Staff Duties
(Maj. Gen.)

Personnel

Establishments

New units

Supply policy

Anti-aircraft

Searchlights

Training and tactics

Educational training

Censorship

Publicity

Press

Line of Communication Area

Inspector General of Communications
(replaced by Director General
Transportation late 1916)
(Lt Gen.)

Main British bases:
- **Boulogne** (Brig. Gen.)
- **Calais** (Brig. Gen. from April 1915)
- **Le Havre** (Brig. Gen.)
- **Rouen** (Brig. Gen.)
- **Marseilles** (Brig. Gen.)
- **Advanced base** (Col)

There were also bases at:
- **Amiens**
- **Brest**
- **Cherbourg**
- **Dieppe**
- **Dunkirk**

Infantry Divisional Headquarters Staff, 1918

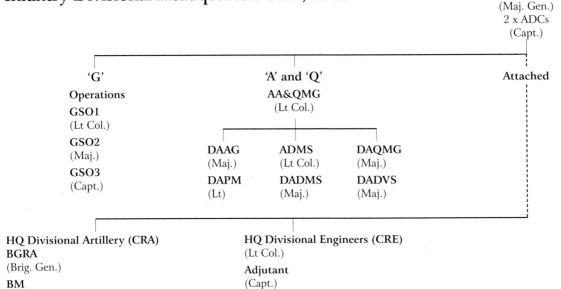

General Officer Commanding (GOC)
(Maj. Gen.)
2 x ADCs
(Capt.)

'G'

Operations

GSO1
(Lt Col.)

GSO2
(Maj.)

GSO3
(Capt.)

'A' and 'Q'

AA&QMG
(Lt Col.)

DAAG	ADMS	DAQMG
(Maj.)	(Lt Col.)	(Maj.)
DAPM	**DADMS**	**DADVS**
(Lt)	(Maj.)	(Maj.)

Attached

HQ Divisional Artillery (CRA)

BGRA
(Brig. Gen.)

BM
(Maj.)

AS03 (Artillery Staff Officer) – Intelligence
(Capt.)

Staff Lieutenant – Reconnaissance

HQ Divisional Engineers (CRE)
(Lt Col.)

Adjutant
(Capt.)

Notes
- In comparison to General HQ, an infantry division's staff had increased from four to 15 (not counting the artillery and engineer commanders) officers by the end of the war and by then had around 80 ORs, including clerks, batmen, drivers, military police, cooks and postal workers.
- The CRA, a brigadier general, was the commander of the artillery units within the division. Similarly, the CRE was the commander of the engineer units.

'A'

Adjutant General
(Lt Gen.)

Personal services (from Sept. 1917)
(Brig. Gen.)

Paymaster-in-Chief
(Brig. Gen.)

Demobilization (from Oct. 1918)
(Brig. Gen.)

Provost Marshal
(Brig. Gen.)

Director General Medical Services
(Lt Gen.)

Notes

• This shows the division of GHQ into the four main branches 'MS', 'G', 'A' and 'Q' and the attached supporting arm staff in outline, as well as the main British bases. The ranks shown are those held by the officer in charge in 1918.

• It shows five lieutenant generals, 10 major generals and 26 brigadier generals. There were many more junior staff officers of all grades in virtually all branches or directorates. In total GHQ in 1918 had almost 1,200 officers and over 6,000 other ranks.

• The QMG branch was by far the largest, with two director generals (Transportation and Medical), 15 directors and two controllers. The clear division between the General Staff dealing with operational matters and the Administrative Staff is obvious – at least 70% of GHQ personnel were employed in the latter role.

• In October 1916 transportation matters were taken from the QMG and given to a separate department under Sir Eric Geddes, a railway expert, as Director General of Transportation. In June 1918 these matters were transferred back to the QMG.

• The diagram does not attempt to show the host of more junior staff officers or ADCs.

'Q'

Quartermaster General
(Lt Gen.)

Director General Transportation
(under QMG from June 1918)
(Maj. Gen.)

Director of Transport
(Brig. Gen.)

Director of Roads (from Oct. 1916)
(Brig. Gen.)

Director of Inland Water Transport
(Brig. Gen.)

*Director of Railways
(Brig. Gen.)

Director of Railway Traffic (from March 1918)
(Brig. Gen.)

Director of Docks
(Brig. Gen.)

*Director of Works
(Maj. Gen.)

Director of Supplies
(Brig. Gen.)

*Director of Ordnance Services
(Brig. Gen.)

Controller of Labour (from Dec. 1916)
(Col)

Controller of Salvage (from Dec. 1916)
(Brig. Gen.)

*Director of Army Postal Service
(Brig. Gen.)

Director of Hirings and Requisitions (from Jan. 1915)
(Maj. Gen.)

Director of Engineering Stores (from June 1918)
(Brig. Gen.)

*Director of Veterinary Services
(Maj. Gen.)

*Director of Remounts
(Brig. Gen.)

Director of Forestry (from May 1916)
(Brig. Gen.)

* These directorates generally received instructions from the IGC and had their offices at his HQ, although directly under the command of the QMG and GHQ.

Attached

Artillery

Major General Royal Artillery
(MGRA)

Brigadier General Royal Artillery
(BGRA)

Engineer-in-Chief
(Maj. Gen.)

Director of Gas Services
(from March 1916)
(Brig. Gen.)

Director of Army Signals
(Maj. Gen.)

Inspector of Mines
(from Jan. 1916)
(Brig. Gen.)

Inspector General of Training
(from July 1918)
(Lt Gen.)

Inspector Machine Gun Corps
(from March 1918)
(Brig. Gen.)

Outline Organization of French Army Staff, 1918

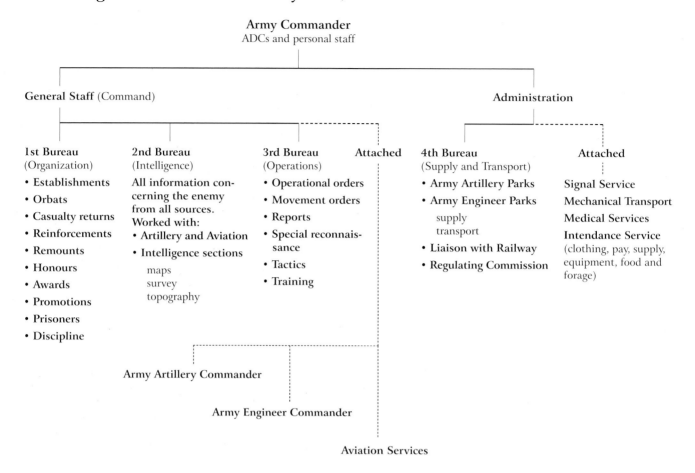

Army Commander
ADCs and personal staff

General Staff (Command)

Administration

1st Bureau
(Organization)
• Establishments
• Orbats
• Casualty returns
• Reinforcements
• Remounts
• Honours
• Awards
• Promotions
• Prisoners
• Discipline

2nd Bureau
(Intelligence)
All information concerning the enemy from all sources.
Worked with:
• Artillery and Aviation
• Intelligence sections
  maps
  survey
  topography

3rd Bureau   Attached
(Operations)
• Operational orders
• Movement orders
• Reports
• Special reconnaissance
• Tactics
• Training

4th Bureau
(Supply and Transport)
• Army Artillery Parks
• Army Engineer Parks
  supply
  transport
• Liaison with Railway
• Regulating Commission

Attached

Signal Service
Mechanical Transport
Medical Services
Intendance Service
(clothing, pay, supply, equipment, food and forage)

Army Artillery Commander

Army Engineer Commander

Aviation Services

France

About half the potential officers destined for the French infantry, cavalry or colonial regiments were trained for two years at the *École Spéciale Militaire* at St-Cyr. The others were mostly commissioned senior NCOs, together with some young men from the larger prestigious technical colleges or from reserve subalterns. Like the UK, France sent her potential artillery and engineer officers to a different school. They attended the Paris *École Polytechnique* along with future state civil servants and naval officers. Staff training was carried out at the *École Supérieure de Guerre* at the *École Militaire* building in Paris. There were two courses. The first, for captains and subalterns under the age of thirty-five, lasted two years and was a strictly staff training course. The second, for more senior officers (majors and lieutenant colonels), was for ten months' training in command of higher formations up to army or even army group level.

Control of the French army groups rested with the commander-in-chief operating from the *Grand Quartier Général* (GQG) or General Headquarters, assisted by a chief of staff. The branches of the General Staff within GQG were divided initially into three bureaux, each headed by a general, with another general as Director of Staff Duties coordinating the running of the headquarters. The 1st Bureau was responsible for organization, establishments, supply, munitions, orders of battle, honours, promotions and discipline, and corresponded roughly with the British adjutant general's branch. The 2nd Bureau was responsible for all intelligence matters and the 3rd Bureau for operations. Later in the war a 4th Bureau was found necessary to take over responsibility for supply and transport from the 1st Bureau, becoming the equivalent of the British quartermaster general's branch. The lines of communication and system of supply in the rear of field armies were the responsibility of a *Directeur de l'Arrière* (Director of the Rear Area). His superior at GQG was the Director of the Rear Zone.

An example of a French Army headquarters staff in 1918 is shown in the diagram above. The staff was divided between the General Staff, which had approximately the same duties as the British, and the Administrative Staff. Heads of supporting Arms and Services with their staff were attached to the headquarters.

Germany

With the Kaiser as overall commander-in-chief, the German military system fell broadly into three divisions or branches, all with large and complex staffing systems.

Military Cabinet Responsible for appointments, promotions, transfers, retirements, honours and awards, corresponding closely with the British Military Secretary's branch of the staff. The Chief of the Military Cabinet was the senior personal aide to the Kaiser.

War Ministry Each of the four sovereign states (Prussia, Bavaria, Saxony and Württemberg) had its own war ministry, but in war it was the Prussian War Ministry that had overall authority. The minister of war was appointed by the Kaiser and was the highest administrative authority in the German Army, but had no command authority over troops in the field (although he did control the Home Army). During the war there were eight departments – Central, General War, Army Administration, Quartering, Pensions and Law, Remount Inspection, Medical and War Bureau (recruiting, labour, munitions, raw materials, exports, imports and food supply).

General Staff Under the chief of the General Staff of the field army, who was the principal adviser to the Kaiser on all military operations. Early in 1915 General Helmuth von Moltke handed over this key position to Lieutenant General Erich von Falkenhayn. He was succeeded in August 1916 by Field Marshal Paul von Hindenburg. General Erich Ludendorff was offered the post of second chief of the General Staff, which he refused as he considered himself second to none, and instead assumed the title of first quartermaster general. It was these two that controlled the German war effort on the Western Front from August 1916 onwards, with Ludendorff very much in the driving seat.

The General Staff (*Generalstab*) provided staff officers for the whole army. With few exceptions every staff officer had undergone three years' staff training at the *Kriegsakademie* (War College). This training was exhaustive and rigorously structured, not only to weed out the less able but also to produce a body of professional military experts with common methods and outlook and dedication to their profession. Although their careers included periodic duty with troops, as staff officers they represented an elite corps within the army, distinguished by wide, double carmine trouser stripes. In 1914 the General Staffs of the German Armies totalled 625 officers, of whom only 239 were available for service at

the headquarters of field formations. Such officers were called *Truppengeneralstab* (General Staff with troops) and were perforce spread very thinly indeed. The chief of the General Staff of the field army issued operational orders on behalf of the Kaiser.

Senior General Staff officers held key positions at all formation headquarters in the field. They had the right to disagree, in writing, with the plans or orders of the commander and to appeal to the commander of the next higher formation – which could ultimately be the Kaiser – who would be guided by the head of the Great General Staff (see below). This served as a check on incompetence and allowed the dissenting officer to disassociate himself from a flawed plan. Even at a higher formation headquarters it was possible for a comparatively junior officer to hold the position chief of the General Staff. An example was the Supreme Command East (Russian Front) – initially held by Field Marshal Hindenburg and then Field Marshal Prince Leopold of Bavaria – which had a colonel (Max Hoffmann) as chief of the General Staff for over a year before he was promoted. The Second Army on the Western Front, commanded by a colonel general, had a major as chief of staff for several months in 1917.

There was also a select inner ring of staff officers called the Great General Staff

Adolf Hitler (right) as a regimental messenger. His dog, Fuchsl, originally belonged to the British, but Hitler caught him when he jumped into a German trench while chasing rats in no-man's-land.

(*Grosser Generalstab*), working directly under the chief of the General Staff at General Headquarters (*Grosses Hauptquartier* or GHQ). All orders for the field army were issued from GHQ except those of an administrative or technical nature that emanated from the Ministry of War in Berlin.

The staff at an army headquarters is shown in outline in the diagram below.

Outline Organization of Staff at German Army Headquarters, 1918

Army Commander

Chief of the General Staff (CGS)

General Staff (directly under CGS) — **Administrative Staff** (under Quartermaster General) — **Attached**

I(a)
- Operations
- Orders
- Orbats
- Tactics
- Training

I(c)
- Intelligence
- Signals
- Air Service

I(d)
- Ammunition (Infantry and Artillery)

II(b)
- Establishments
- Strengths
- Returns

III
- Military Law
- Provost Marshal
- Discipline
- Courts Martial

IV(b)
- Medical
- Anti-gas Measures

I(b)
- Movements
- Billeting
- Salvage

II(a)
- Personnel
- Promotions
- Honours
- Supply
- Transport

II(c)
- Interior Economy
- Routine Orders
- Returns

IV(a)
- Intendance
- Rations
- Clothing
- Pay
- Requisitions
- Civilians

IV(c)
- Veterinary

Artillery Commander

Pioneer Commander

Engineer Commander

Signals Commander

Mechanical Transport Commander

AA Commander

Ammunition Train Commander

Staff Officer for machine-gun troops

Camp Commandant

British troops advancing at the Battle of the Somme, 1 July 1916.

Section Four

Infantry and Their Weapons

*Look into an infantryman's eyes
and you can tell how much war he has seen.*

William H. Maudlin, *Up Front* (1944)

Three days before he bled to death on 16 October 1915 a German soldier, Alfred E. Vaeth, a former philosophy student at Heidelberg University, sent a letter home in which he wrote:

> The attack was terribly beautiful. The most beautiful and at the same time most terrible thing I have ever experienced. Our artillery shot magnificently and after two hours the position was sufficiently prepared for the German infantry. The storm came, as only German infantry can storm! It was magnificent the way our men, especially the youngest, advanced! Magnificent! Officers belonging to other regiments, who were looking on, have since admitted that they had never seen anything like it! In the face of appalling machine-gun fire they went on with a confidence which nobody could ever attempt to equal . . . The attack was glorious!

On 1 July 1916 Private Roy Bealing, MM, 6th Wiltshires, went over the top (the slang for which was 'hop the bags') on the most disastrous day of the war for British infantry:

> Captain Reid came along the top of the trench – right out in the open! . . . he must have had a couple of machine gun bullets through his water bottle because the water was spouting out of it. He yelled down. 'Fix your bayonets and get ready to go over when you hear the whistle.'
>
> I was beside a young chap called Lucas and he was a bundle of nerves. He was simply shivering and shaking like a leaf. He could hardly hold his rifle, never mind fix his bayonet. So I fixed mine and then I said, 'Here you are, Lucas,' and I fixed his for him . . .

The worst of waiting in the trench was that the Germans had a machine-gun trained on it going backwards and forwards . . . coming round every couple of minutes, and the bullets were cutting the sandbags on the parapet just as if they were cutting them with a knife. And if the bullet didn't get you, this shower of sand and dirt was going straight into your eyes . . .

When the whistle went, I threw my rifle on top of the trench and clambered out of it, grabbed the rifle and started going forward. There were shell-holes everywhere. I hadn't gone far when I fell in one. There were so many shell-holes you couldn't get round them. But you had to go on so, every time I stumbled and fell in a shell-hole, I just waited a quarter of a minute, had another breath, then out of it and on again. I must have fallen half a dozen times before I got to the first [German] line, and there were lads falling all over the place. You didn't know whether they were just tripping up, like me, or whether they were going down with bullets in them, because it wasn't just the shells exploding round about, it was the machine guns hammering out like hell from the third German line because it was on slightly higher ground. Lucas went down.

Lieutenant D. W. J. Cuddeford, commanding a company of the 12th Highland Light Infantry on 9 April 1917, described two dying infantrymen, one British, one German.

The British:
Among the victims that fell to the German riflemen just then was a young lad in McLean's platoon . . . He was only a boy, obviously not more than about seventeen years of age, but he had always refused to be sent back to the Base Depot along with the other 'under ages.' The bullet struck him in the belly, and as is usual with

abdominal wounds he rolled about clawing the ground, screaming and making a terrible fuss. Certainly, to have one's guts stirred up by a red-hot bullet must be a dreadful thing . . . they got the boy back to the trench, opened his clothes and put a bandage around his middle over the wound, but of course we could see from the first it was hopeless . . . as I passed he half opened his eyes and said something to me. I had to stoop down to catch what he said; it was 'Good luck to you, sir!'

The German:
He was a long, lanky fair-haired fellow, and he had been struck by a bullet just under the nose. As he sat propped up against the side of the trench, with his eyes closed and his funny little round German forage cap perched on the extreme crown of his head, his old-

The Dead on the Battlefield

Most of the dead left on the battlefields of the Western Front were infantry. In *A Natural History of the Dead*, Ernest Hemingway wrote:

> Until the dead are buried they change somewhat in appearance each day. The colour change in Caucasian races is from white to yellow, to yellow-green, to black. If left long enough in the heat the flesh comes to resemble coal-tar, especially where it has been broken or torn, and it has quite a visible tar-like iridescence. The dead grow larger each day until sometimes they become quite too big for their uniforms, filling these until they seem blown tight enough to burst. The individual members may increase in girth to an unbelievable extent and faces fill as taut and globular as balloons.

fashioned 'lug-hook' spectacles had toppled down to the tip of his nose, and in struggling to breathe through the great gash in his nose and palate the poor devil was making a loud snoring noise. Not a very comical sight perhaps . . . but our men at the time seemed to think it was.

Unsurprisingly, it was the Western Front that generated the title 'PBI' (Poor Bloody Infantry) for the foot soldier of all nations of all wars – including today's. In August 1914 the British infantry (regular and Territorial Force) was 306,654 strong; by November 1918 it had almost 1,684,039, an expansion of five and a half times, and it represented 45 per cent of the entire army. The BEF went to war with 72 infantry battalions and ended it with over 700, although they were substantially smaller units than their predecessors. With by far the largest numbers doing by far the most fighting, inevitably the infantry suffered in proportion. This was not unique to the Western Front, World War I or indeed to any war fought throughout history. The infantry always bears the brunt and always suffers the worst. In all theatres, British infantry casualties (killed, died of wounds, wounded, missing/prisoners) reported up to March 1920 totalled 1,372,117. In France, British infantry losses constituted 84.39 per cent of all the BEF's battle casualties. The Australian infantry in France fared even worse, with 87.8 per cent of battle casualties. Figures for Belgian, French, American and German infantry losses on the Western Front were not available to the present writer, but were undoubtedly in the order of 80–85 per cent.

Infantry Weapons

The notes below cover rifles and bayonets, bombs/grenades, revolvers/pistols, machine guns (heavy and light), flamethrowers and other makeshift weapons. Trench mortars will be discussed in Section Five: Artillery, and gas in Section Seven: Engineers. As the size of all armies increased so rapidly, the BEF, and to a similar extent the armies of the other belligerent nations (although Germany was better prepared), suffered acute shortages of the latest rifles, grenades and machine guns as their manufacture took months, if not years, to catch up with demand.

Rifles and Bayonets

From the day of the musket up to the modern infantryman in Afghanistan, the rifle and bayonet have been the foot soldier's basic personal weapons. In 1914 the standard-issue British rifle was the bolt action .303 Short Magazine Lee-Enfield (SMLE) with an extreme range out to 2,000 yards – roughly the standard maximum range of the rifles of all nations. Battlefield use, however, was almost invariably at far shorter ranges, often at distances of 5–10 yards, although hits at 1,000 yards were possible. The magazine took ten rounds, which could be loaded quickly with two five-round chargers by placing them in the breach and thumbing them down. Rounds could also be loaded singly, so a fully loaded weapon could have eleven. The regular British infantryman prided himself on his marksmanship – the better he was, the more he was paid – and on his ability to fire up to fifteen rounds a minute, a rate that was mistaken for machine-gun fire at Mons.

Like all weapons, the rifle did not like the mud and the breach was often covered with a cloth when not likely to be needed quickly. However, it was a robust and reliable weapon that was preferred by the Canadians to their Ross rifle and was issued to other dominion troops as supplies became available. Nevertheless, as the British Official History states, 'the lack of them [SMLE rifles] was a main factor in limiting the number of men put into the fighting line in 1915.' In 1914, 1,381,000 were ordered, including 200,000 from America, with another 1.5 million, also from America, in April 1915. But the effect of these arrangements was not felt for many months, although by the end of 1918 the daily production rate was up to 10,000.

When America entered the war in 1917 she was desperately short of all military equipment and weapons. Her first troops to arrive in France had the 1903 Springfield rifle, while factories were mass-producing the American Enfield .300-calibre weapon – in other respects virtually a replica of the British SMLE. By the end of the war America had produced some 2.5 million rifles, of which only 313,000 were Springfields. However, the US 93rd Division, which operated under French command, was armed with the French rifle and wore the French helmet.

The French initially opted for the Lebel Model 1886 (modified in 1896), firing an 8mm bullet. Its serious disadvantage was the slow reloading process, as the eight rounds had to be fed one at a time into a tubular magazine under the barrel. This was made even slower by the need to be wary of hitting the primer in the base of the round in front too hard, thereby causing an unwelcome explosion. As rounds were fired, the centre of balance changed, making a careful aim adjustment necessary after each shot. Two years into the war the French produced an improvement – the Berthier Model 1907 – although the magazine of the initial issue held only three rounds and it was not until 1916 that the modified Berthier could be loaded by a clip or charger which held six rounds.

The Belgians relied on the Mauser Model 89 rifle, the distinguishing feature of which was the five-round, single-column box magazine projecting beneath the wrist stock. It was loaded either singly or with a clip. The Germans seized large quantities in 1914 (a number being adapted to fire from their own version of the Mauser), and for the remainder of the war the Belgian Army relied on their rifles being manufactured in the USA and England.

The German soldier had the .323-calibre Mauser Gewehr 98. It was a reliable weapon, noted for its accuracy but suffering from the disadvantages of the magazine holding only five rounds and the bolt arrangement being unsuited to rapid fire, in that the long bolt pull meant that the rife had to be clear of the face when reloading, thus disturbing the firer's aim. It was also 4 feet long, making it very unwieldy in the confines of a trench, especially with a bayonet fixed.

This quotation is from the German novel *All Quiet on the Western Front* by the veteran Erich Maria Remarque, and was published in English in 1929. The original sold some 2.5 million copies in the first three months after publication, and was later burned and banned by the Nazi regime.

> In any case, the bayonet isn't as important as it used to be. It's more usual now to go into the attack with hand-grenades and your entrenching tool. The sharpened spade is a lighter and more versatile weapon – not only can you get a man under the chin, but more to the point, you can strike a blow with a lot more force behind it. That's especially true if you can bring it down diagonally between the neck and the shoulder, because then you can split down as far as the chest. When you put a bayonet in, it can stick, and you have to give the other man a hefty kick in the guts to get it out.

Lee-Enfield Mark III (British)

Springfield M1903 (US)

Ross Mark III (Canadian)

Lebel M1886 (French)

Mauser M1889 (Belgian)

Mauser M1898 (German)

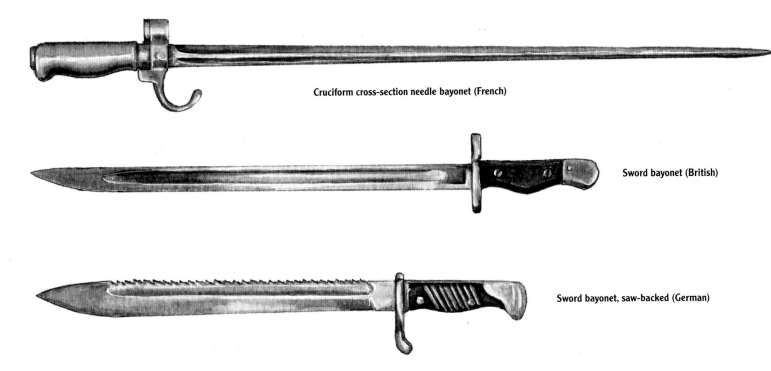

Cruciform cross-section needle bayonet (French)

Sword bayonet (British)

Sword bayonet, saw-backed (German)

All rifles had a clip-on bayonet, varying in length up to the British 21-inch sword bayonet. The French favoured the excessively long cruciform cross-section type, while the Germans devised a number of different patterns, including a fearsome saw-backed blade. All armies encouraged the use of the bayonet as an offensive close-quarter weapon, fostering the aggressive spirit. The World War II field marshal Bernard Montgomery wrote in his memoirs:

> In my training as a young officer I had received much instruction in how to kill my enemy with a bayonet fixed to a rifle. I knew all about the various movements – right parry, left parry, forward lunge. I had been taught how to put the left foot on a corpse and extract the bayonet, giving at the same time a loud grunt.

However, it is estimated that a bayonet was responsible for only 0.3 per cent of British casualties, as on the end of a rifle in the confines of a trench or bunker it was an almost impossibly awkward weapon to wield. It was nevertheless used in close combat in trenches. The Canadian Captain Herbert McBride, who was a firearms expert (see also page 468), considered that the slim French needle bayonets, when hand-held, were 'terribly effective weapons [and] perfectly adapted to this stealthy night work [trench raids].' After the war a trench at Verdun that had been filled in by a bombardment was discovered with bayonets protruding at regular intervals – beneath each rifle was a corpse. The French named it *la Tranchée des Baionnettes*.

Battery Sergeant Major Douglas Pegler, Royal Field Artillery (RFA), has described the result of a bayonet fight to the death on the Somme:

> What ghastly sights there are to be seen here! Two men, a Prussian and a Coldstreamer, each transfixed with the other's bayonet remaining standing, each dead body supporting the other. On each dead face can be seen the grin of triumph which he could not suppress when he saw his opening and took it, leaving himself open, killing and killed.

Bombs/Grenades

Alfred O. Pollard of the 1st Battalion, The Honourable Artillery Company, who was to become a captain with a VC, MC and Bar, and DCM, described a bombing fight in Sanctuary Wood, near Hooge, Ypres, in 1915:

> Tall trees were all about us, their green foliage making a strange setting for our savage sport. The bombs burst with a curious hollow sound, the explosion deadened by the tree trunks.
>
> Bang! Bang! Bang! Zunk! Zunk! Zunk! The bombers were getting down to it with a will. The worthy Royal Scots were joining in as fast as they could pick up their bombs and pull the safety pins.
>
> For three minutes or so we had it all our own way. Then a shout from one of the men warned me that retaliation had commenced. A thing like a jam tin on the end of a stick came hurtling through the air; landed on our parapet; a moment whilst it lay hissing – crack! Instantly it

was followed by another. Then another and another. Fritz could give as good as he received.

> This was all very well, but as long as we were confronted by that barricade progress was impossible. The affair was degenerating into a sort of snowball match except the snowballs were deadly missiles.

Being able to lob a bomb (grenade) into an enemy trench or over a traverse (a buttress built to prevent enfilade fire along the length of a trench), barricade or into a bunker was, and still is, an effective way of dealing with an enemy you cannot see. Bombing became an essential part of the tactics of clearing enemy trenches, dugouts and machine-gun posts at close range.

In early 1915 each infantry brigade formed a bombing company of thirty selected men from each of the four battalions. They were trained initially by the Royal Engineers, although High Command schools were soon established and instruction manuals issued. In an attack, twenty bombers from the brigade company usually accompanied each battalion, with the remainder held in brigade reserve.

In 1915 Private (later Captain) Ernest Parker of the 10th Durham Light Infantry joined the battalion bomb squad. He later wrote:

> I became a member of the toughest crowd in the Battalion. As a bomber life became one long escape from fatigues and rifle drill. While rifles were sloped, presented, ordered, ported, canted, trailed and bayoneted we stole off to fill jam tins with mud in order to shy them

at a target. Now and then fresh recruits were returned to duty when it was found that bad nerves made them fumble with lighted bombs. We got rid of them with relief, for they were unpleasant neighbours to have around.

Captain Pollard, as a potential bombing officer, was sent on a two-week course at Second Army Grenade School – a course that he later considered had surely saved his life:

I acquired a complete knowledge of every bomb and grenade in use by either ourselves or the Hun at that time. They also taught me a method of trench clearing for a bombing party . . . It consisted of eight men. Two ordinary riflemen with fixed bayonets led the way. Their job was to protect the bomb-throwers from surprise and tackle any of the enemy they came across. Behind them came the first bomb-thrower followed by a man carrying a supply of bombs for him to throw. Then came another bomb-thrower and another carrier. Then the leader of the party and lastly a spare man who acted as an extra carrier or could be used to replace casualties according to circumstances.

The greatest grenade battle of the war took place between the Australians, with British support, and the Germans on Pozières Heights on 26–27 July 1916, when both sides hurled grenades of every conceivable type at each other for twelve and a half hours. By the end of the night the Australians and British had thrown some 15,000 bombs and many men had collapsed with exhaustion.

British bombs

As the value of grenades in the fighting on the Western Front became apparent, the UK was caught unprepared and, until 1916, British bombs were very much a hotchpotch of makeshift devices, several of which were highly unsafe and caused worrying numbers of casualties among the users. By the end of 1914 the demand for bombs by the BEF had reached 10,000 a week and improvisation became the order of the day, with Royal Engineer workshops and individual units producing some fifteen different types based on designs by Colonel Louis Jackson, the assistant director of fortifications and works.

All bombs were either percussion (exploded on hitting the ground or other solid obstacle); ignition (lit by a friction lighter); or mechanical (a spring-loaded mechanism inside the bomb was released by the removal of a pin that struck and ignited a detonator) – it was this type that ultimately proved the most effective.

Among the early grenades was the percussion Mark I, with a brass body containing the explosive attached to a 16-inch cane handle; its detonator was secured by a removable safety pin. It was fitted with cloth streamers intended to ensure that the bomb fell on its nose. Instructions for use emphasized the need to throw it well up into the air. The danger with these percussion bombs was that, in throwing back his arm, the user could hit the rear of the trench, with disastrous consequences to himself and nearby comrades. Ernest Parker described a serious accident with the so-called Newton Pippin grenades, which he said had to be struck on the end of the handle of an entrenching tool to light the fuze (military spelling).

We had good cause to remember these primitive weapons, for once, when the whole Battalion was halted in column of route in the narrow streets of Poperinghe, one of our comrades, Private Hoare, dropped all his Newton Pippins on the cobbled roadway while stooping down to tighten his puttees. The consequent explosions just ahead of A Company caused forty or fifty casualties in the crowed ranks.

The most well-known friction version was the 'jam-tin bomb'. A ration 1-lb jam tin was stuffed with an explosive, such as guncotton or ammonal (more powerful), around which was packed nails, metal scrap

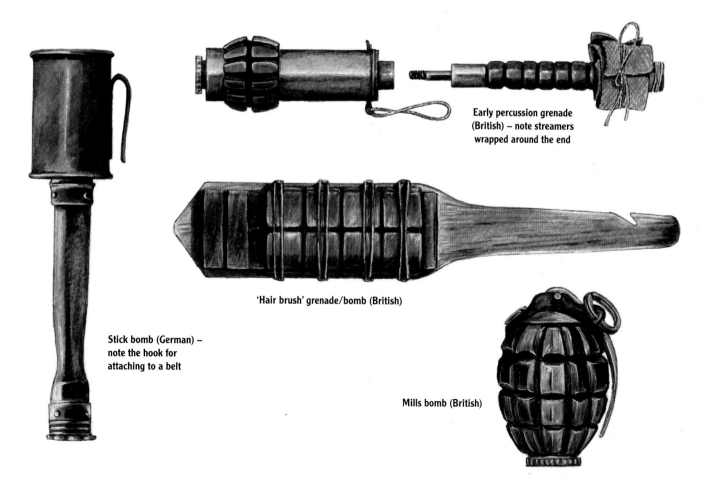

Early percussion grenade (British) – note streamers wrapped around the end

'Hair brush' grenade/bomb (British)

Stick bomb (German) – note the hook for attaching to a belt

Mills bomb (British)

or stones. A length of Bickford's fuze was attached, leading to an internal No. 8 detonator. The fuze was to be lit with a 'match, pipe, cigar or cigarette'. The trick was to cut the fuze to the appropriate length – too long and it might be thrown back, or its intended victims would have time to retire; too short and the thrower was the loser.

A 'hairbrush' bomb was also introduced. A slab of gun-cotton was fixed by wire to a flat piece of wood shaped like a hairbrush, thus providing a handle for throwing. It was ignited in the same way as the jam-tin version. At a demonstration before a gathering of generals and their staff, when the officer in charge threw his bomb only the handle went forward and the charge dropped to the ground. Some spectators fled, while others crouched down. There was no explosion.

Like the jam-tin type, the 'cricket ball' bomb required the fuze to be lit by the thrower. Private Harold Dolden of the London Scottish did not think much of them:

we were issued with eight cricket ball bombs which were carried in pockets in an apron strapped round our kilt. The bombs had a detonator jutting out of the top covered with a piece of sticking plaster. On our wrist a band was worn, to which was attached the striking part of a box of matches [it was a larger

Nicknames of Servicemen

The following nicknames were used by British soldiers for the servicemen of other nations:

Australians and New Zealanders from the Australian and New Zealand Army Corps: ANZACs.

Americans: Yanks. (US soldiers called themselves Doughboys.)

Australians: Aussies, Diggers.

British: Tommies (also used by the Germans), Fred Karno's Army, Old Contemptibles (for the original BEF – see box, page 30).

Canadians: Canucks.

French: Frenchies, Frogs. (French soldiers called themselves *Poilus* – bearded ones.)

Germans: Alleyman, Boche, Huns, Jerries, Fritz, Krauts (from *Sauerkraut*).

Italians: Ities, Macaronis.

Indians from North-West Frontier Province (now Pakistan): Pathans, Forty Thieves.

New Zealanders: Diggers, Kiwis, Fernleafs (from NZ cap badge).

Portuguese: Antonios, Geese, Pork and Cheese.

South Africans: Africaaners, Boers.

version], and we were also supplied with matches. The procedure was as follows – to take the bomb from the pocket of the kilt apron, tear off the sticking plaster on the detonator, strike a match on the wristband and light the charge, hold the bomb for three or four seconds, then throw as far as possible. I do not know what genius devised this bomb with its farcical method of ignition, but I'm very doubtful whether he ever spent a night in the pouring rain and tried to strike a match on his wristband . . .

The most effective bomb was the No. 5 Mills bomb (devised by the Scottish inventor William Mills), which was of the spring-mechanism type (modern grenades still use this method). It weighed about 1.5 lb and had a segmented iron case. Apart from the bursting charge, the case contained a spring-operated striker and a fixed detonator. The top of the striker protruded and was held in place by a lever that lay flat against the body of the grenade. This lever was in turn held in place by a retaining pin. When the pin was pulled, the lever was kept down by the thrower's hand. Only when thrown did the lever fly off, releasing the spring to bring down the striker on the detonating cap. Some fuzes burned for four seconds, others for seven. The bombs were carried in special bombers' waistcoats, pouches or canvas buckets. Mills bombs came in boxes of twelve, but were coated in protective grease that had to be cleaned off before use. They started to be issued by mid-1915 and soon made all other types redundant. Production by July 1916 was 800,000 a week and during the war exceeded 50 million. An updated version, the 36 Grenade, was still in use in the British Army well after World War II.

Like the British, the French experimented with several bombs during the first two years of the war; not until 1916 did they produce a satisfactory grenade. It was lemon-shaped and operated on the same mechanical system of spring, striker, lever and safety pin as the Mills. The only drawback was the French habit of carrying grenades loose in a haversack, where the pins and levers tended to become entangled – with unpleasant consequences.

American grenades were largely copies of British or French models.

The most common German bomb was the 'stick grenade', a cylinder filled with explosive and with a hollow wooden handle attached that increased the range it could be thrown. It contained its own friction lighter and had a burning fuze of either three or seven seconds – the time was

stamped on the handle. By 1917 the Germans were also issued with the 'egg grenade', a small, egg-shaped 11 oz bomb that could be thrown up to 50 yards, fitted with five- or eight-second fuzes. Being so small, the explosive effect was limited. Both these grenades relied primarily on blast rather than fragmentation and so were more effective in confined spaces.

Incendiary bombs were also produced, notably the 'P' for phosphorus or the 'Fumite' for smoke. They were both effective in setting alight woodwork in bunkers and the clothing or flesh of soldiers inside. The official pamphlet SS 119, entitled *Preliminary Notes on the Tactical Lessons of Recent Operations (July 1916)*, stated, 'The most effective weapon for clearing dug-outs is the "P" grenade, which drives out or suffocates the occupants . . .' The modern phosphorus grenade makes an effective smokescreen but is officially banned as an anti-personnel weapon, as burning phosphorus on flesh is almost impossible to put out, making it a particularly terrifying weapon. In battle the ban is sometimes ignored by hard-pressed infantry, as it is such an effective grenade in a confined space – as was discovered on the Somme.

Bomb-throwers and rifle grenades

The desirability of being able to launch a bomb further than the 30 yards that can be achieved by a man quickly became obvious to the British and a variety of improvised 'bomb-throwers' were devised. Several types of trench catapults were constructed on the lines of the schoolboy 'Y' catapult. A 6-foot-high version was developed and supplied to the BEF by the sports department of Gamages, the London store. It was supplied at the rate of twenty per division and was able to hurl a grenade up to 160 yards. Because the elasticity of the twelve bands of twisted rubber tended to deteriorate quickly, its use was usually confined to major operations. The British also produced the longer-range West Spring Gun, which was basically a modern version of the Roman ballista or medieval trebuchet with a long throwing arm held back under great tension by banks of steel springs. It could hurl a grenade about 250 yards. Both these throwers were discontinued in 1916.

More reliable were rifle grenades – although they were not always accurate as they were fired with the rifle at an angle and the butt on the ground, because in the shoulder the huge kick would have broken bones. The principle was to attach a grenade to a rod that was inserted in the barrel of a rifle and fired using a blank cartridge. The most common British version was called the Hales grenade and had a range of over 200 yards. Another problem was that continual use damaged the rifle barrel. By the end of 1914 the BEF was receiving about 630 rifle grenades weekly.

The other version, which preserved the barrel, was a Mills bomb fired from a cup discharger fixed to the muzzle of the rifle. By early 1918 every platoon was expected to have a section of rifle grenadiers as well as one of hand-grenadiers (bombers) – thus around half the infantry were designated as bombers. The Germans ceased using rifle grenades in 1916 (they restarted in 1918), but the British and French persisted with cup grenades, even increasing their range to 400 yards by using fin grenades.

The French rifle grenade (also used by the Americans) was the Viven-Bessières, which differed from most other such grenades in that the fuze ignition was caused by a live bullet fired through a tube that passed through the centre of the grenade, using the gas that propelled the bullet to drive the grenade forward.

Rifle grenades could be very effective if used in batteries, as Captain Pollard (now a battalion bombing officer) explained:

> I found some rifle racks that took six rifles each. By tying all the triggers together with string, I succeeded in firing them all at once . . . I provided each of the three Companies with a similar machine and gave orders that the bombers were to fire not less than two hundred rifle grenades per day per company. After a few tries we got the range . . .
>
> Six hundred rifle grenades per day! My requisitions to the Brigade bombing officer were terrific. After a few days he asked me to ease up. His supply was unequal to my demand.

Pistols and Revolvers

A fervent advocate of the automatic pistol as a weapon of choice for trench fighting was the Canadian Captain Herbert McBride. He firmly believed every soldier not armed with a rifle should carry a pistol. Below are four short quotes from his book *A Rifleman Went to War.*

> I unhesitatingly choose the automatic for actual use in war . . . the great advantage of the automatic lies in the ease and rapidity with which it can be reloaded – especially in the dark . . . there is really no comparison between slipping a fresh magazine into the butt of the pistol, and fumbling with six small cartridges in trying to get them into six *different* revolver chambers.

> Those of us in the Machine Gun Section who were fortunate enough to have pistols thoroughly appreciated the advantage of such weapons and were much envied by the others who were not so armed. No pistol was ever permitted to be taken to the rear on a dead or wounded man; someone always grabbed for it as soon as the owner was picked up.

> I had the prisoner climbing out, and we all picked up our loads and started on when that Heinie [slang for German] slid back into the trench and reached for those grenades. Very fortunately, the last man in our party carried a pistol – he dropped his load, made one of the quickest draws I have ever seen, fired twice, and shot that smart Dutchman through the knee joint, almost smashing his leg apart.

> During my war experience, which extended from September 1915 to February 1917 and included innumerable little 'contacts' with the enemy and several major battles, I fired exactly seven shots at an enemy with my pistol. *Seven* – count 'em. I used up quite a lot of ammunition, shooting at rats, rabbits and tin cans but as to shooting Germans, well, I've told you seven was all and the longest range at which I fired at these individuals was never more than ten feet.

In the BEF pistols were officially the officers' weapons, but were later issued to machine-gunners, tank crews, despatch riders and Royal Engineers. Nevertheless, they were often acquired by infantrymen for close combat. The most common were the .45 Webley, Colt, and Smith & Wesson. The Webley Mark IV was popular, packed an enormous punch, was easy to clean and reliable – over 300,000 were issued during the war. However, a much-prized piece of loot was the German Luger (see below). French officers and adjutants carried either the regulation 1892 revolver or privately purchased pistols. American officers and senior NCOs carried .45-calibre handguns, the most well known being the single-action, semi-automatic Colt M1911, which held seven rounds in a detachable box magazine, and the Smith & Wesson M1917 six-shot revolver.

The Germans replaced their 1883 model revolver with the 1908 Luger pistol, which took eight .354 rounds. It was renowned for its reliability and became the world's most used pistol – about 1.5 million were produced during World War I and it was also used extensively during the early part of World War II. A removable stock was developed to enable it to be fired from the shoulder, thus increasing its accuracy.

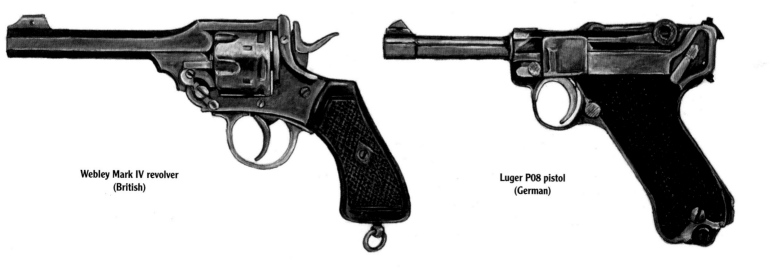

Webley Mark IV revolver
(British)

Luger P08 pistol
(German)

Machine Guns

Underneath the inscription to the fallen on the Machine Gun Corps Memorial in Hyde Park are the words:

> Saul hath slain his thousands
> But David his tens of thousands

On 1 July 1916, Private W. J. Senescall, 11th Battalion the Suffolk (Cambridgeshire) Regiment, while waiting to advance watched as the leading waves of the 10th Lincolns walked forward into German machine-gun fire on the opening day of the Somme offensive:

> The long line of men came forward, rifles at the port [carried diagonally across the chest] as ordered. Now Gerry started. His machine guns let fly. Down they all went. I could see them dropping one after another as the gun swept along them. The officer went down at exactly the same time as the man behind him. Another minute or so and another wave came forward. Gerry was ready this time and this lot did not get so far as the others.

Lieutenant Geoffrey H. Malins was an official cameraman attached to the 29th Division on that day. He later described filming infantry of the Lancashire Fusiliers going over the top towards Beaumont-Hamel into a hurricane of machine-gun fire:

> Then the signal rang out, and from the trenches immediately in front of me our wonderful troops went over the top. What a picture it was! I could see while I was exposing that numbers were shot down before they reached the top of the parapet; others just the other side. They went across the ground in swarms, and, marvel upon marvel, still smoking cigarettes. One man actually stopped in the middle of No Man's Land to light up again.

It is quotes such as these that have given rise to the myth that the machine gun was the dominant killer on the Western Front. Appalling losses were inflicted on all armies by machine guns, heavy and light, by countless millions of bullets spewed out by tens of thousands of machine guns during the four-year struggle. The *British Official History 1916*, Volume I, states British casualties caused by machine guns and rifles as 39 per cent and by artillery and mortars as 51.5 per cent – leaving the king of the battlefield in terms of destruction and death the artillery/mortar combination.

The primary reason for these figures was that machine guns required an exposed body as a target, which meant troops out in the open for some reason, mostly attacking or making daylight raids. Even among Allied units, who were obliged to take the offensive

Relief in the Line, March 1915

In March 1915 Lieutenant Colonel E. P. Cawston was the battalion machine gun officer (MGO) of the Queen Victoria Rifles (9th London Regiment, QVR), a Territorial Force unit. Many years later he wrote about how he got the job, describing an amusing incident that occurred shortly after they had taken over the trenches from the 2nd King's Own Scottish Borderers:

> QVR-HQ was on the South side of the main street [of Neuve Eglise] and it was there that our near perfect Adjutant Culme-Seymour, KRR [King's Royal Rifles] informed OC 11 Platoon [Cawston] that he would take over MG Section in place of that very efficient and smart MGO Fargus, who had been shot through the head while on reconnaissance in Douve Valley. The Platoon Commander said that he had no knowledge whatsoever of machine-gun

mechanism but was assured that that was not material, as the two Sergeants Macmorran knew all there was to know about M-G.

> Not long afterwards the QVR took over the part of the line occupied by KOSB.

> Talking of reliefs, I recall when our M-G Section relieved KOSBIES in Trenches 1, 2 and 3. I told the [Brigade] MGO what a darned good lot the KOSBIE MG Section were; that they stayed in the trenches for quite a time after we arrived; insisting on placing our squirts [guns] and ammo in the right places and telling us all about the position. 'They would do that,' he said. But on his visiting us later that morning I had to tone down my appreciation, for, after they had gone, we found they had gone off with the whole of our rum issue.

to win the war, individual infantrymen spent only a small fraction of their time attacking or out in the open exposed to small-arms fire. With artillery (and mortars), however, high-explosive shells or bombs were a constant source of death or wounding in varying degrees of intensity for twenty-four hours of every day in the whole frontal zone. Troops were vulnerable in their billets, bunkers, buildings or trenches, as well as on working parties or when attacking.

Private Senescall and Lieutenant Malins were, of course, watching the start of the Battle of the Somme, when it was indeed the enemy machine guns that wrought unrivalled havoc among the advancing infantry – estimated at some 90 per cent of almost 60,000 British casualties that day. A German machine gunner wrote:

> We were amazed to see them walking, we had never seen that before . . . The officers were at the front. I noticed one of them was strolling along carrying a walking stick. When we started firing we just had to load and reload. We didn't have to aim, we just fired into them.

The machine gun was a fearsome weapon, and in certain circumstances the dominant and most dangerous one, but it never caused as much terror or as much horrendous damage to human flesh and bone by jagged lumps of red-hot metal as was delivered by the artillery.

On the Western Front machine guns were usually categorized as either heavy or light, although the Vickers machine gun discussed below, which was in service with the British Army until 1968, was later regarded as a medium machine gun.

Heavy machine guns

The British Vickers machine gun was based on the successful Maxim gun of the late nineteenth century. After purchasing the Maxim Company in 1896, Vickers improved the design of the gun that was formally adopted for the British Army in November 1912 for use alongside their Maxims. However, the BEF went to war in 1914 with Maxims, which were replaced by Vickers as and when sufficient numbers were manufactured. This took some time, as at the outbreak of war only 1,963 machine guns were in service (only 105 of them Vickers). Orders were placed in November 1914 for 200 guns a week to be delivered by July 1915. This could not be achieved, as the manufacturing capacity did not exist, so America was contracted to produce 2,000. Initially, Vickers was threatened with prosecution for war profiteering because of the exorbitant price charged for each gun. The price was then slashed, and by 1918 a gun was being manufactured for just under £67 – a very reasonable price for a weapon with over 130 parts, each of which was machined from high-grade steel. The Ministry of Munitions, under Lloyd George, was established in May 1915 and when Sir Eric Geddes was put in charge of machine-gun and rifle production, output rose from 266 in 1914 to 2,405 in 1915; 7,429 in 1916; 21,782 in 1917; and 21,782 in 1918. By November 1918 Vickers' total output for the war was 71,355 guns (machine guns and rifles).

The Vickers was a water-cooled, belt-fed machine gun with a maximum range of 3,500 yards (extended to 4,500 in 1916 with the introduction of streamlined ammunition)

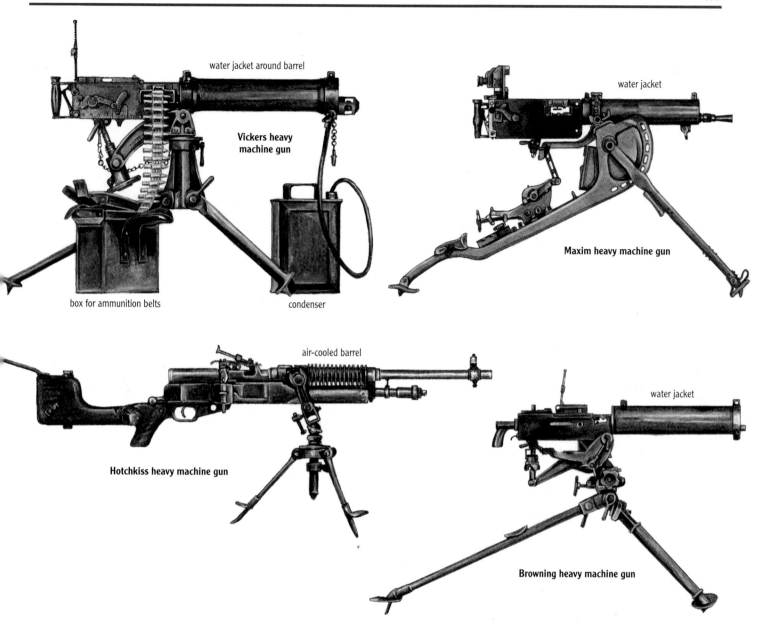

water jacket around barrel

Vickers heavy machine gun

box for ammunition belts

condenser

water jacket

Maxim heavy machine gun

air-cooled barrel

Hotchkiss heavy machine gun

water jacket

Browning heavy machine gun

and a theoretical rate of fire of 450–550 rounds per minute (rpm). The normal firing rate was 125 rpm, fired in bursts of 5–6 that could be maintained for about half an hour. Rapid fire was 250–300 rpm, which could not be maintained for long periods, and the slow rate for barrage fire about 60–75 rpm. Harassing fire targets usually received 1,000 rounds an hour – 17 rpm. The webbing ammunition belt held 250 rounds of .303 ammunition. The barrel was enclosed in a jacket containing 7.5 pints of water for cooling purposes. Firing at the rate of about 200 rpm caused the water to boil after about 600 rounds. This boiling water set up convection currents that created an efficient transfer of heat. It also caused evaporation at the rate of 1½ pints per 500 rounds – two belts of ammunition. The steam was passed from the jacket via a rubber tube into a condenser can, enabling

the re-use of water and avoiding the steam giving away the gun's position. In circumstances of heavy firing for prolonged periods, this produced insufficient water and stories of men risking their lives to get more, and even urinating into the can, abound. Captain McBride's comments on this difficulty are revealing:

And how that water does boil away! In spite of the most careful use of the condenser, it evaporates at a rapid rate and then the problem is how to replenish it. Even though the action may be literally on the bank of a river it may be impossible to go the few feet and back . . . more than a few times the members of the gun crew have been called up to 'make water', and there is a sort of grim humor in the fact that on such occasions few, if any, could produce the goods: no, not a drop.

The barrel was supposed to be changed after firing 10,000 rounds – in theory one hour of continuous firing.

The weight of the gun varied according to the gear attached, but was generally about 42 lb (including the water in the jacket), with a 48-lb tripod. The boxes for the 250-round belts of ammunition weighed 22 lb each. In 1916 GHQ directed that there should be eight belts of ammunition with each gun, a belt-filling machine and 4,000 rounds per gun in unopened boxes held centrally (usually at or near battalion headquarters). With the addition of spare barrel, other spares, reserve ammunition belts and tools, the total weight was considerable and the gun required a crew of six men and a limbered wagon drawn by two draught horses or pack animals – the Belgians used a pair of large dogs to pull their Maxims (see page 123). The crew could carry the gun for limited periods, with the

No. 1, the firer, carrying the tripod, the No. 2 the gun and the others the ammunition, spares and other kit.

The Vickers, despite some drawbacks, was an extremely reliable and effective machine gun that could be used to fire indirectly at targets with plunging fire (see page 182). Its most incredible test of reliability came on 24 August 1916 at High Wood, when ten guns fired continuously for twelve hours (see box below). On many a battlefield since, the familiar tac-tac-tac-tac-tac-tac-tac of long bursts from a Vickers has reassured hard-pressed British infantry. It was widely sold commercially and saw service with many nations after alteration for their own ammunition. It also served as a base for many other weapons – for example, Italian, German, Dutch, Swiss, French, American and Russian guns. There is a splendid story that, when the gun was declared obsolete in 1968, a farewell ceremony was held at the Small Arms School, Hythe. While a gun was fired down the range, a band played the hymn 'O God, our help in ages past' in tribute to a remarkable weapon.

The French heavy machine gun was the 1914-pattern Hotchkiss, which was fed by strips of thirty rounds and mounted on a tripod for firing. Gun and tripod together weighed about 110 lb and, because of the weight, the three-man crew were individually armed with pistols. The gun ejected the strip as soon as it was empty, leaving the bolt open for a new one to be inserted; this triggered the release of the bolt forward and firing resumed. However, the clip system was found to be impractical for a single gunner firing in a tank, aircraft or from a confined space, so a 250-round articulated metal belt was adopted in 1917. It was a gas-operated, air-cooled weapon with a maximum range of 4,150 yards and a theoretical rate of fire of 450 rpm. With continuous firing, the barrel could attain a temperature of 400°C and glowed dark red. The Hotchkiss Company delivered around 47,000 1914 model guns to the French Army during the war.

The Belgians and Americans (they purchased 7,000) also used the Hotchkiss. The Americans also used some Vickers (made by Colt in the USA) and, in the last months of the war, the water-cooled US-manufactured M1917 Browning. The Hotchkiss was last used in Algeria and Indochina in the 1950s.

Another air-cooled gun was the American-made Colt machine gun, initially used by the CEF. This .300-calibre gas-operated gun had the arm that operated the action under the barrel, which, if used close to the ground, made contact with it, leading to its being nicknamed the 'Potato Digger'. However, mounted on a tripod it gave satisfactory service, despite not much liking British ammunition. Captain McBride thought well of it, stating that it was 'the best and safest ever invented for firing, at low elevation, over the heads of your own troops'. It was phased out during 1917–18.

The Germans were armed with the 1908-pattern water-cooled Maxim machine gun, which had the same calibre as their rifles and was mounted on a sledge with four legs – the height of the gun in action could be altered by adjusting the spread of the legs. It had an extreme range of 4,400 yards, fired at a theoretical rate of 500 rpm from 250-round belts of ammunition. The gun weighed 55 lb, the sledge 75 lb and a belt of ammunition 16 lb, making the gun and its sledge-mounting some 40 lb heavier than the British Vickers and its tripod. Its transport was a two-horse gun carriage and limber, or a handcart drawn by two men.

The British Machine Gun Corps (MGC)

In 1914 all infantry battalions contained a machine-gun section of two guns (Maxims). It quickly became obvious during the First Battle of Ypres that more machine guns were needed and that they required special tactics and organization. This led to the BEF establishing a Machine Gun School at Wisques in France and a training centre at Grantham in England. In October 1915 the Machine Gun Corps was created by withdrawing guns and teams from battalions and forming them into three specialist machine-gun companies (one to each brigade). The soldiers in the new corps were specialists, wearing the new cap badge of crossed Vickers guns. In the infantry battalions the Vickers was replaced by the light Lewis gun (see page 187). The changeover was gradual, as it depended on the availability of Lewis guns, but was complete by the start of the Battle of the Somme.

In 1917 a fourth, reserve, company was added to each division and early the following year these four divisional companies were formed into machine-gun battalions. The MGC would eventually consist of infantry machine-gun companies, cavalry machine-gun squadrons and motor machine-gun batteries. The Motor Branch formed motorcycle and light armoured-car batteries (for use with the cavalry to exploit hoped-for breakthroughs), and the first tanks into action at Flers in September 1916 were crewed by members of the Heavy Branch of the MGC. In July 1917 the Heavy Branch became the Tank Corps – now the Royal Tank Regiment.

MGC soldiers won seven Victoria Crosses (six on the Western Front). A total of 170,500 officers and men served in the corps, of whom 62,049 were killed, wounded or missing.

High Wood and the 100th Machine Gun Company

High Wood featured prominently in the British Somme battle from July to September 1916. It was heavily and stoutly defended by the Germans during this period – no fewer than seven major assaults where halted before the wood was finally cleared on 15 September by the 47th (2nd London) Division, at a cost in casualties (between 10 and 22 September) of 4,554 all ranks. Sergeant Bill Hay, 1/9th Royal Scots, later described the unsuccessful night attack on 22/23 July:

This was a stupid action, because we had to make a frontal attack on bristling German guns and there was no shelter at all . . . There were dead bodies all over the place where previous battalions and regiments had taken part in previous attacks. What a bashing we got. There were heaps of men everywhere – not one or two men, but heaps of men, all dead. Even before we went over, we knew this was death. We just couldn't take High Wood against machine-guns. It was ridiculous. There was no need for it. It was just absolute slaughter.

For the attempt on 24 August the 100th Machine Gun Company fired perhaps the most incredible machine-gun barrage on the Western Front. The ten guns had the task of firing indirectly on to a selected area about 2,000 yards behind the crest on which High Wood stood to check an anticipated German counter-attack from across this ground. It was an extraordinarily ambitious task that would test the staying power of both the guns and their teams – two companies of infantry were drafted in just to ferry ammunition, rations and water. The intention (which was achieved) was to maintain continuous firing for twelve hours with two men on each gun keeping up a supply of ammunition from another two working a belt-filling machine. In those twelve hours just short of a million rounds were fired – something that required the use of a hundred new barrels and every drop of water in the neighbourhood, including from the men's water bottles and even latrine buckets – and not one gun failed. The German verdict on this barrage was 'annihilating'. The maximum fired by one gun was 120,000 rounds, a record that earned its crew a reward of 5 francs! As noted above, the wood was not finally secured until 15 September. Although exceptional, this barrage proved what could be achieved with Vickers guns by the summer of 1916.

An Infantry Battalion Vickers Machine Gun Section, 1915

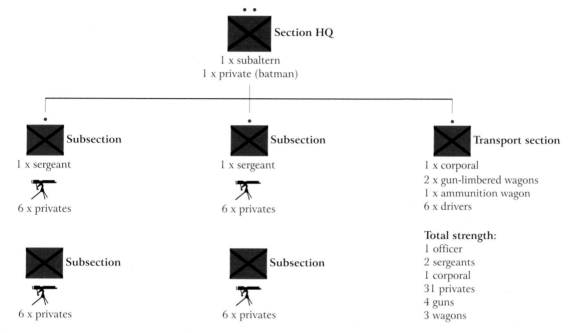

Section HQ

1 x subaltern
1 x private (batman)

Subsection

1 x sergeant

6 x privates

Subsection

1 x sergeant

6 x privates

Transport section

1 x corporal
2 x gun-limbered wagons
1 x ammunition wagon
6 x drivers

Subsection

6 x privates

Subsection

6 x privates

Total strength:
1 officer
2 sergeants
1 corporal
31 privates
4 guns
3 wagons

Notes

Duties:
• Officer to command in accordance with his orders; select gun positions, observe, control fire and regulate ammunition supply.
• Sergeants to supervise guns coming into action.
• Corporal responsible for packing and contents of wagons, supervising ammunition supply and filling of belts and sandbags as required.

• Privates with the guns:
No. 1 The firer. On going into action carried the tripod, positioned it and assisted No. 2 in mounting the gun. Repeated all orders received, observed his fire and made alterations of elevation or direction as needed.
No. 2 Carried the gun into action. While firing he attended the feeding of the ammunition, watched for signals from the section commander and assisted the No. 1.
Nos. 3 & 4 No. 3 took the first supply of ammunition to the gun, assisted by No. 4, and ensured the spare-parts wallet was brought to the gun position. No. 4 brought extra ammunition from the limber to No. 3 when necessary. No. 3 was responsible for the condenser, ensuring it was fitted to the gun before the water boiled. No. 4 placed the rifles of Nos. 1, 2, 3 and his own on the limber.
No. 5 Acted as scout as directed by the section commander (he retained his rifle while the gun was in action).
No. 6 The range-taker. Prepared the range cards and was the spare man to assist as required.

A Machine Gun Corps Battalion, 1918

Notes

By 1918 a MGC battalion had 64 guns in four companies, with one attached to each brigade and the fourth as a divisional reserve. There was a maching-gun officer at brigade and divisional HQ.

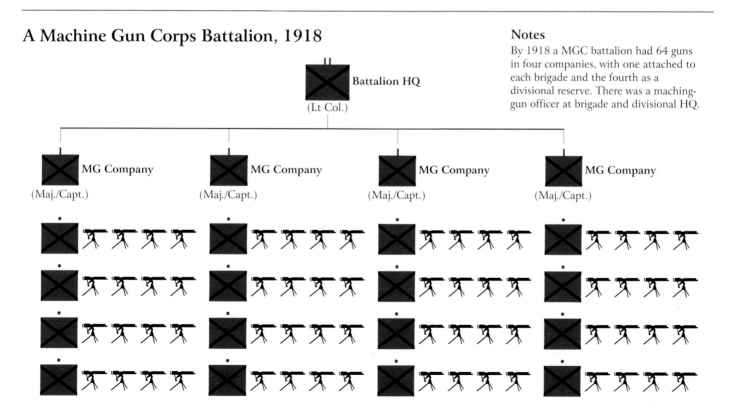

Battalion HQ

(Lt Col.)

MG Company
(Maj./Capt.)

MG Company
(Maj./Capt.)

MG Company
(Maj./Capt.)

MG Company
(Maj./Capt.)

Types of fire and tactics

The notes and diagrams below concern the principles for the use of heavy machine guns on the Western Front by all belligerents, using the British Vickers gun as an example.

Like all tactics, those of the machine gun evolved and improved considerably during the war. By mid-1917 the Allies' use of barrage fire had improved to a marked degree in both direct and indirect fire situations; this was true in attack and also in defence. The Germans, however, never made the same use of barrages as the British, and in fact never used them at all until late 1917.

Differing roles were ascribed for the attack and defence. In the attack, machine guns were divided into two classes. Forward guns were allotted to infantry brigades to move forward to support the attacking battalions under command of the brigade commander; rear guns would supply barrage and other forms of covering fire.

Definitions and Types of Fire

Trajectory The curved path a bullet takes in flight.

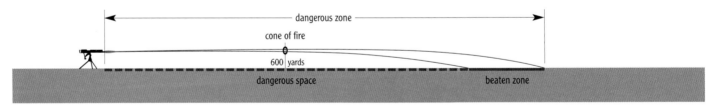

Cone of fire When the group of trajectories from a burst of fire hits a vertical target the rounds form a pattern, oval in shape, with the density of shots decreasing towards the edges.
Beaten zone The pattern formed when a burst of fire strikes the ground in a cigar shape, with the density decreasing towards the edges.

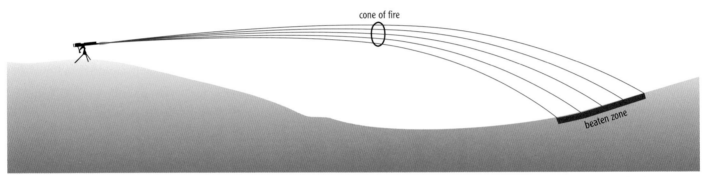

Dangerous zone From the muzzle to where the last round hits the ground.
Dangerous space From the muzzle to the point where the lowest round hits the ground.
Grazing fire On level ground where the centre of the cone does not rise above a metre – this occurs at 600 yards' range.

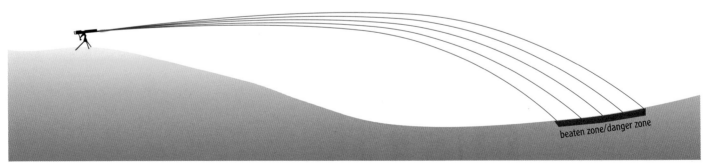

Plunging fire Where the danger zone is confined to the beaten zone.

Different types of fire included:

• **Standing barrage** Could be placed on or beyond various objectives and remain there until the infantry advance rendered it necessary for it to move forward. There could be frontal or flanking barrages, depending on the tactical situation, but in most large-scale attacks only frontal ones were practical. Likely target areas included enemy lines of communication, likely routes of enemy counter-attacks, or open ground over which the enemy must retire or bring up reinforcements.

• **Creeping barrage** Designed to move in front of the artillery barrage, lifting on a timed basis.

• **Neutralizing fire** Placed on ground from which enemy observers could direct fire on to the attackers or on positions which, not being directly attacked, were holding up the attack.

• **SOS barrage** Arranged to provide a complete belt of fire along the whole front of the operation as soon as the attackers reached their final objective.

• **Harassing fire** Usually fired at night to prevent movement and dislocate enemy supply of the front line.

Direct fire At fixed-point target.

Searching fire Range slightly increased to 'search' a fixed linear linear target of some depth.

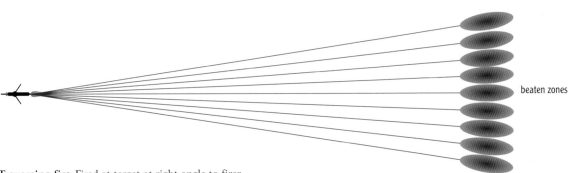

Traversing fire Fired at target at right angle to firer.

Firer starts by firing a burst at either left or right of target, then by tapping the breech with either left or right hand moves the line of sight by 2 inches for each tap – often more efficient if tapping is irregular.

Traversing and searching fire Used to hit oblique targets. Combines tapping (traversing) with relaying the gun after each tap and then firing another burst.

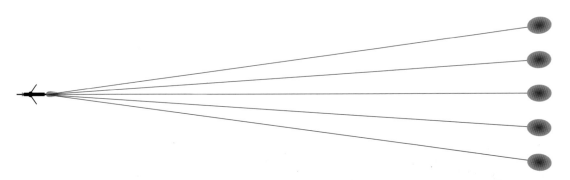

Swinging traverse The gun is traversed from left to right and back, firing continuously. Only used in emergencies when the enemy is close and in large numbers (not normally above 300 yards).

Frontal, Flanking and Enfilade Fire – the Theory

Notes

This diagram shows a platoon of 35 men in extended line at 5-yard intervals advancing on the machine gun at **A**.

The gun is 1,000 yards away. At this distance the beaten zone is 160 yards long and 10 yards wide at its widest point.

All three guns are the same distance from the target and the beaten zones are drawn to scale, with each gun firing one burst of 6–8 rounds.

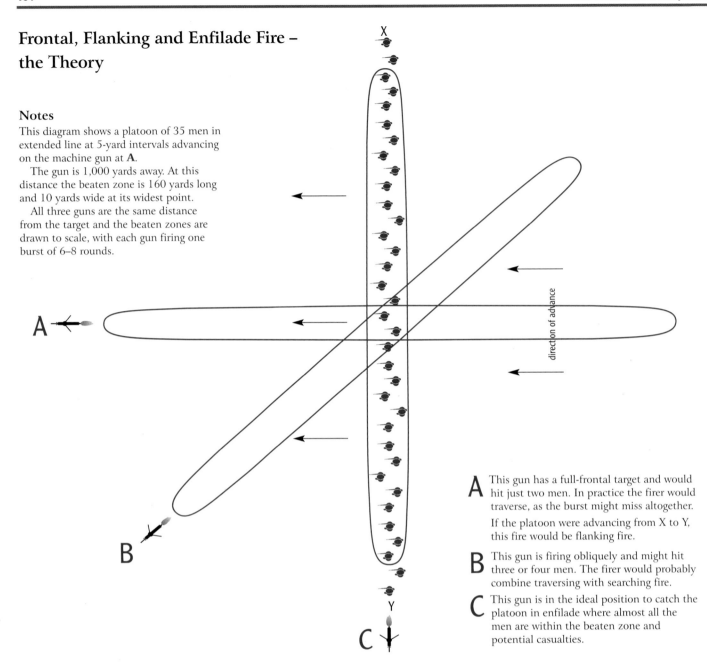

X

direction of advance

A

B

Y

C

A This gun has a full-frontal target and would hit just two men. In practice the firer would traverse, as the burst might miss altogether.

If the platoon were advancing from X to Y, this fire would be flanking fire.

B This gun is firing obliquely and might hit three or four men. The firer would probably combine traversing with searching fire.

C This gun is in the ideal position to catch the platoon in enfilade where almost all the men are within the beaten zone and potential casualties.

British soldiers of the Machine Gun Corps firing a Vickers gun, Arras, 1917. This appears to be a gun set up or about to fire in an anti-aircraft role – note the crew are looking up into the sky. The Vickers was fairly effective in this role against low-flying aircraft.

An old British machine-gun bunker in Ploegsteert Wood.

By 1917 a British defensive zone normally consisted of an outpost zone (forward line), a support line (second line) and a main line of resistance or reserve line. Behind these were other positions, such as strongpoints, woods or villages prepared for defence (see also Section Twelve). An example of how machine guns were decisive in halting a massive German attack occurred in the sector defended by the 56th (1st London) Division (part of the British First Army) on 28 March 1918 when it was hit by five German divisions. The 193rd Machine Gun Battalion, MGC was part of the divisional defences between the villages of Gavrelle and Oppy, where its guns played a crucial role in decimating the attacking infantry and checking the German attack in that sector in what was otherwise a successful offensive.

Unfortunately for the British First and Fifth Armies during late March 1918, the 193rd Battalion's success was the exception rather than the rule, as the commanding officer of the 9th Battalion, MGC reported:

It had long been known that a German attack was impending, and it came in no sense as a surprise. The S.O.S. barrage had been carefully coordinated with the artillery – it was not too ambitious and was undoubtedly of adequate density. It was placed where the 18-pdr. barrage was thin or non-existent, covering the valley between Gonnelieu and Villers-Guislain. At neither of these places did the enemy succeed in penetrating our line until after our troops [infantry] had been withdrawn. The guns of the Battalion were distributed in depth . . . Although all positions had been selected primarily for direct fire over the sights up to 1,000 yards and over, each gun had been, where possible given an indirect S.O.S. line on the ground in front of our front line. The fields of fire were in all cases good – in many excellent – and the protection for gun teams fair . . . It is a matter for regret that no opportunity was afforded for testing these defences, which would I think have provided the enemy with a difficult nut to crack.

From the example of the 193rd Battalion, he was probably right.

The general deployment/tactical principles on which they operated were (see also diagram left):

• If possible, the forward guns were arranged in pairs, rather than in batteries of four or more as when supporting an attack, and deployed between the front and support lines. The aim was to direct belts of flanking or oblique fire in front of posts in the outpost zone (first line).

• Rear guns, sometimes in groups of four, were usually positioned behind the main line of resistance (reserve line). Primary tasks were to provide a complete SOS barrage line along the whole front (or at least on selected parts), using overhead fire and normally beyond the range of the artillery barrage line. As with all guns, they were used to fire indirectly at night at crossroads, communication trenches and road junctions – any target that might disrupt or cause casualties to the enemy, as darkness was used to carry out resupply and repair work to trenches.

• SOS barrages were particularly important and planned in conjunction with the artillery and trench-mortar units. They were called for by the firing of a predetermined Very light (flare) signal, usually by the infantry being threatened. Response had to be immediate (if possible before the Very lights had burned out and before the enemy had reached the defensive wire obstacles).

• If possible, guns were always sited so that their arcs of fire interlocked with other guns on their flank (see Map 39), the object being to criss-cross the fire over no-man's-land, thus catching attackers obliquely or in enfilade. All major fire plans (defensive or offensive) were drawn up in conjunction with the supporting artillery and trench-mortar batteries.

• Emplacements. Machine-gun emplacements varied in the detail of design, materials used and degree of sophistication, but were basically either covered or open emplacements – this applied to all belligerents. The role of the gun, the lie of the ground, the labour available, the type of soil and the proximity of the enemy governed the type constructed. All had some form of shelter or dugout nearby – with overhead protection and a covered approach from there to the gun emplacement – which had room for two gunners and recesses for the storage of ammunition. The notes below refer to British emplacements and are based on War Office pamphlet SS 192, *The Employment of Machine Guns*, January 1918:

Covered loophole emplacements By 1918, when built into a clearly defined trench system, this type was regarded as less suitable, as even using concrete it no longer withstood a heavy bombardment. Also, the loophole face got knocked about or blocked or masked by bombardment debris. In the confined space, cordite fumes often forced the crew to fire wearing respirators. Despite these problems, firing under cover reduced minor injuries and gave added confidence to the crew. These emplacements were still suitable in places such as woods, buildings or on reverse slopes where construction was not visible to the enemy.

Open emplacements These were connected by a covered or open trench with neighbouring emplacements and a central dugout (it had to be fairly close to the emplacements) to shelter crew members resting or during a bombardment. Their advantage was ease and speed of construction, which enabled several alternative positions to be prepared in advance. They were particularly suited to battery positions, as they facilitated fire control.

German emplacements As the Germans were mostly on the defensive, their defensive works, including machine-gun posts, became deeper, more elaborate and better protected, with considerable use made of concrete in their construction. This was particularly true of the Hindenburg Line defensive zone. Each stretch of the line had an outpost zone about 600 yards deep in which were built numerous concrete machine-gun posts and dugouts. Behind this was the 2,500-yard-deep main battle zone, which included the first and second trench/strongpoint lines with a network of more concrete machine-gun emplacements to provide interlocking belts of fire across no-man's-land, many firing down the line of massive belts of protective barbed wire, often 100 yards thick.

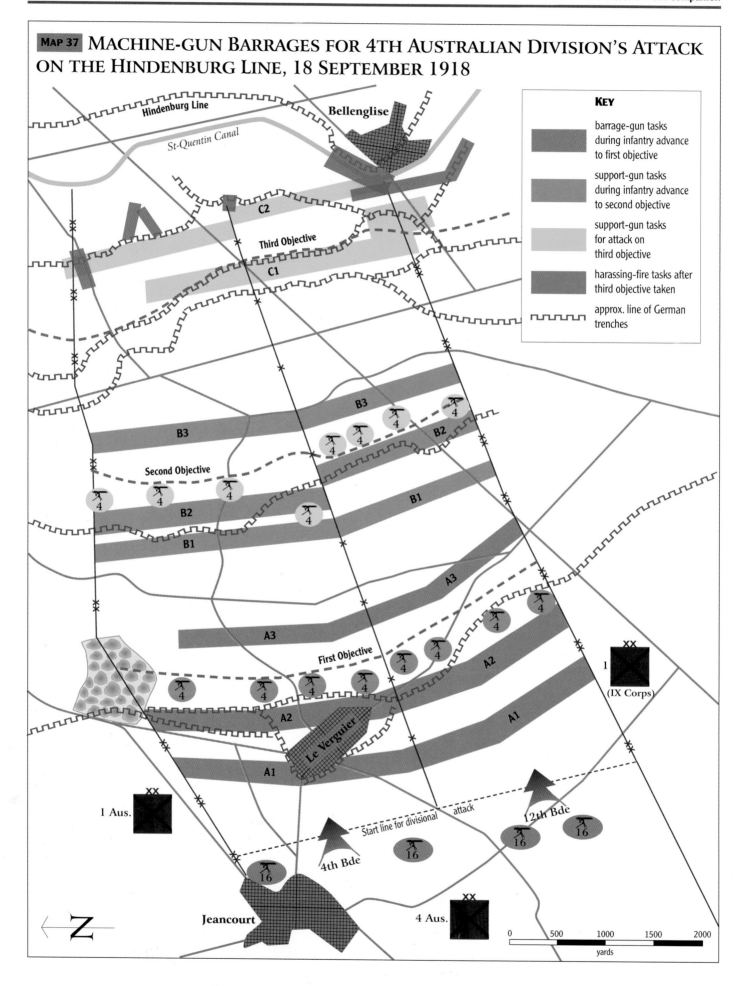

MAP 37 MACHINE-GUN BARRAGES FOR 4TH AUSTRALIAN DIVISION'S ATTACK ON THE HINDENBURG LINE, 18 SEPTEMBER 1918

German machine-gun organization

Pre-1914, every German infantry regiment (equivalent to a British brigade) had a machine-gun company of six guns. The war brought about expansion and new companies were formed, consisting of an officer and up to forty men with three or four machine guns, wagons and draught horses for the guns, ammunition, supplies (food and forage) and a field kitchen. These companies were absorbed into the regiments of the expanding army, although by the end of 1915 some regiments had acquired two companies. During the winter of 1915–16, specialist marksmen machine-gun companies were formed from selected machine-gunners who trained at machine-gun training centres.

Notes for Map 37

A machine-gun battalion of 64 Vickers guns was deployed to support the attack of the 4th Australian Division on the forward defences of the Hindenburg Line. Its timed barrages were to precede and complement those of the artillery. There were three main belts of fire, one for each of the infantry objectives, each divided into three or two (third objective) narrow belts.

First objective All 64 guns were involved as barrage guns and were deployed over some 3,000 yards of frontage, giving about 50 yards per gun firing at a range of 1,000 yards at targets in belt **A1** on the map. The guns would probably be traversing. At a specific time the firing would lift to belt **A2** and, as the infantry approached the first objective, the guns would fire on belt **A3** to block any German attempt to reinforce their position.

Second objective Two companies (32 guns) moved up to provide support for the infantry advance on the second objective. Again, guns would fire in advance of the artillery and the two belts **B1** and **B2** were laid on the main German trench lines, the range this time being about 1,500 yards. The belt **B3** was designed to help isolate the objective.

Third objective Here the infantry objective was limited to the first two German trench lines – the division was not required to attack the main Hindenburg defences behind the St-Quentin Canal. Another two companies of guns were to advance to support the attack on this objective and were to fire the belts **C1** and **C2** at ranges from 2,000 to 2,500 yards. After this objective had been secured, harassing fire tasks were planned, as shown on the map, to hit known or likely enemy strongpoints, outposts or routes forward west of the canal.

This was a highly successful attack, with the machine-gun barrage being described by German prisoners as 'frightful'. By midnight the whole of the third objective was in Australian hands and they now overlooked the canal.

By the start of 1916 there were over 8,000 (rising to 11,000 by July) German machine guns on the Western Front, but without any properly coordinated organization. This reorganization began in August 1916, when companies were standardized with six guns and every infantry regiment had three (one per battalion). The special marksmen companies were grouped into marksmen detachments of three companies and kept as a GHQ reserve – one was usually allocated to any division actively engaged. In 1917 the number of machine guns increased, and although the number of companies in a division did not, each company saw the number of its guns raised from six to eight, then to ten and finally to twelve.

Light machine guns

Private A. D. Haslam was a member of a Lewis-gun team that faced the German onslaught of March 1918. He left an account of an episode in early April.

I was awakened by the voice of Raikes [Lance Corporal Raikes was the No. 1 on the gun], as he called into the dug-out, 'Frank, Frank.' I scrambled out. 'Come on,' he said, 'we're for the advanced post again. Where's Joe Miller?' 'Just up there,' I answered. 'I'll tell him. We'll be with you in a minute. You go on.'

I roused Joe, the victim of a sentry's bomb. He slept heavily, and kept answering, 'Yes, coming,' and dropping off to sleep again, until I leaned into his shelter and shook him. We doubled to our shell-hole [often used as an advanced post in front of the line], and found Raikes firing. Looking out I saw the enemy advancing. 'Column of lumps,' Raikes had said during the night, and now it was column of lumps again, ragged masses of grey-clad, helmeted riflemen, in no definite order, though they seemed to keep to their sections

[the Germans were using stormtrooper tactics – see Section Twelve].

We kept the gun firing merrily. No fancy work was needed. Raikes was gazing down the sights and traversing. I was watching the effect of the fire for a while, then asked him for the distance and put up the backsight of my rifle. After firing a few shots, the thought stole into my head that this was a very queer battle . . . We were firing three-quarters right, at two hundred and fifty. 'Why the deuce,' I thought, 'haven't we got a target in front?' . . .

I heard another Lewis gun tapping away on our left. That was encouraging, but I had expected more. I was not sure of our company's armament, but it was stuck in my head that we had four Lewis guns, and rifles by the dozen. Yet I heard no rifle fire.

Meanwhile our ammunition was disappearing . . .

Out of ammunition and unable to get more, Haslam and his team were later captured.

The Lewis gun was the first practical light machine gun to be produced. Its distribution within the British Army started with two guns per company in early 1916 (four for all front-line battalions at the start of the Somme battle) and expanded by 1918 to eight. It was the gradual issue of Lewis guns that enabled the heavy Vickers to be progressively withdrawn from infantry battalions and brigaded into specialist machine-gun battalions and the formation of the MGC. In March 1916, at one of Haig's Army Commanders' Conferences, it was recorded:

we discussed the use of Lewis guns in an advance. A few of these guns can develop as great a volume of fire as a considerable number of infantry. They are far less vulnerable and can find cover more easily. I emphasised the necessity

A German machine-gun crew in action with an MG08, 1918.

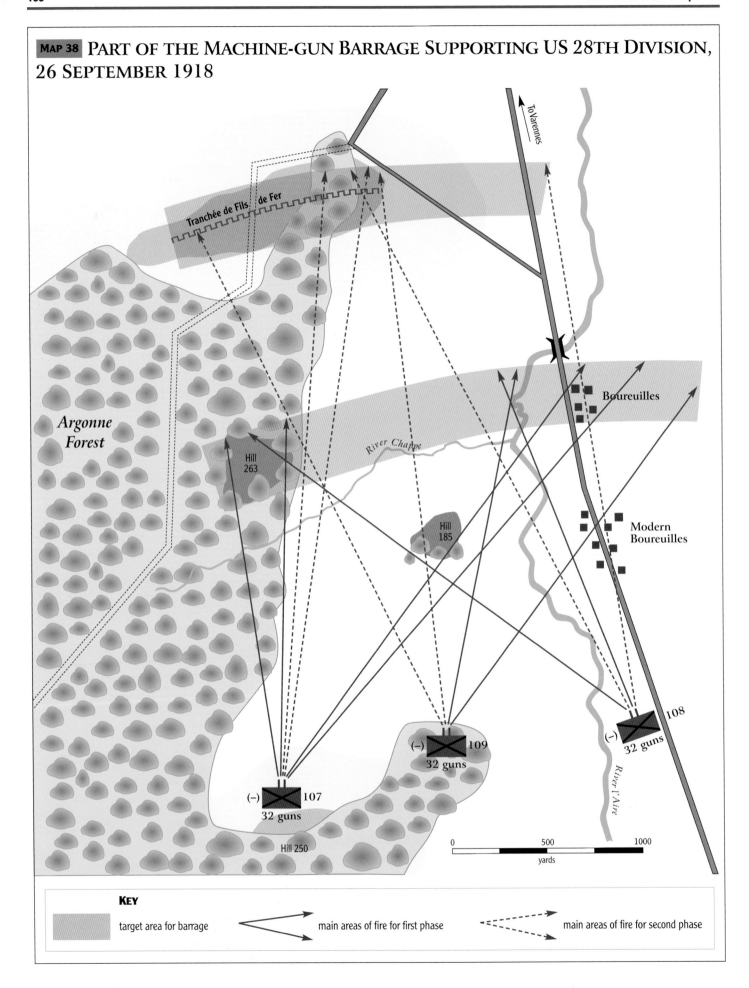

MAP 38 PART OF THE MACHINE-GUN BARRAGE SUPPORTING US 28TH DIVISION, 26 SEPTEMBER 1918

To Varennes

Tranchée de Fils de Fer

Argonne
Forest

Boureuilles

River Chappe

Hill
263

Hill
185

Modern
Boureuilles

108

(−)
32 guns

River l'Aire

(−) 109
32 guns

(−) 107
32 guns

Hill 250

0   500   1000

yards

KEY

target area for barrage   main areas of fire for first phase   main areas of fire for second phase

2 companies 107th MG Bn.

Mont de Villiers

Argonne Forest

Phase 1 targets

Phase 2 targets

Boureuilles village

2 companies 109th MG Bn.

2 companies 108th MG Bn.

D946 road from Neuvilly-en-Argonne

The site of the US 28th Division machine-gun barrage, 26 September 1918. The photograph was taken from the position of the two companies of the 108th Machine Gun Battalion alongside the road south of Boureuilles. Each of the six companies shown had an establishment of sixteen heavy machine guns and a supply of an extra 60,000 rounds of ammunition per company – almost a million rounds. Their target was the German line from Boureuilles west to Hill 263 (see Map 38). The barrage would then lift in Phase 2 to targets in rear.

for company and platoon commanders being trained in the use of these guns in tactical situations. At present only a comparatively few officers of infantry realise the great addition of fire-power which has been given them by the formation of machine-gun companies and Lewis gun detachments.

Britain had not been geared up for mass production and by mid-July 1915 only 621 Lewis guns had been delivered from an order of 1,500. Nevertheless, over the following months it gradually changed the way the British fought the war on the Western Front

Notes for Map 38

This machine-gun barrage was fired on the first day of the American Meuse–Argonne offensive. It was in support of the US 28th Division attack immediately east of the Argonne Forest and involved two companies each from the 107th, 108th and 109th Machine Gun Battalions – a total of 96 guns. The barrages involved overhead fire, were at long range (up to 3,000 yards) and involved considerable indirect laying for much of the target area. Some 360,000 rounds of extra ammunition were made available to the guns (60,000 per company). During the first phase of the attack the four companies of the 108th and 109th fired at the enemy line between Hill 263 and Boureuilles village and then lifted to the second *fils de fer* position. One company of the 107th was directed to fire initially on Boureuilles and the other on Hill 263, after which both were to fire in enfilade along the eastern edge of the forest.

At 2:30 a.m. the artillery barrage began and shortly before 5:30 a.m. all 96 machine guns opened up with a continuous roar, pouring tens of thousands of bullets into the German positions. After strong resistance, the Americans had successfully penetrated the enemy positions by the end of the day.

(particularly in providing support in the leading waves of an attack), although initially many infantrymen were disturbed to see the Vickers removed from their control. Once distributed in larger numbers, however, the Lewis gun proved its worth, and by the war's end 133,104 had been made.

The Lewis became the most sought-after light machine gun of the time, to the extent that Russia purchased 10,000 in 1917, and its effectiveness on the battlefield was a serious concern to the Germans (they called it the 'Belgian Rattlesnake', as they had first encountered it in that country), who quickly converted any captured weapons for their own use. Not only was it used extensively on the ground by the army, but it had also been chosen and ordered by the Royal Flying Corps in 1913 for use in the air (see Section Eleven). Although not without its faults – heavy magazines that were awkward to load, difficult to keep clean in the mud and required a wheeled carriage 'resembling a coffin' to move it around – its general success prompted the Australian General Monash to remark in 1918, 'so long as they have 30 Lewis guns per battalion it doesn't much matter what else they have'.

The basic elements of the Lewis gun were first invented in 1910 by an American, Samuel Maclean, who sold the patents to the American Automatic Arms Company. It was found impractical to produce, so the company asked a serving American officer, Colonel Isaac Newton Lewis, to re-engineer it. Colonel Lewis demonstrated his reworked gun (including firing from an aircraft) to a gathering of high-ranking American generals – who rejected it. Lewis resigned and took his new gun to Belgium in 1913 to demonstrate it to Belgian generals – who accepted it. A new company, the *Armes Automatiques Lewis*, was formed in Liège and began to manufacture the guns, choosing .303 as the calibre, the same as the British rifle ammunition. Needing a light machine gun, the British

secured a licence and production started at the Birmingham Small Arms Company.

The Lewis gun was an air-cooled, gas-operated, .303-calibre, fully automatic weapon that weighed 28 lb and could be carried and fired by one man if necessary. Originally the guns were to be transported on a wheeled trolley drawn by a mule, but men on foot frequently caught this duty. By 1918 SS 197, *The Tactical Employment of Lewis Guns*, specified a horse-drawn company wagon carrying four guns, 176 filled magazines, 9,000 loose rounds and various spare parts.

Lewis guns were mounted on a bipod for normal firing in the prone position or standing in a trench, but could be fired from the shoulder (as an automatic rifle) or from the hip on the move with the aid of a sling. The barrel was enclosed in a cooling system comprising an aluminium, finned, tubular sleeve, giving the gun its unusual appearance. Its rate of fire was 500–600 rpm and the gun took a circular, pan-shaped magazine holding forty-seven rounds (ninety-seven when used in an aircraft). Its effective range was up to 600 yards and it was best fired in short, aimed bursts rather than continuously, which would empty a magazine in five seconds. High rates of fire required at least a two-man gun team, although five was initially the recommended number – the No. 1 firing the gun, the No. 2 changing magazines and Nos. 3, 4 and 5 carrying the spare magazines in special, circular canvas bags each containing two. However, this team composition was soon increased. The training manual SS 143 dated February 1917 specified one gun per platoon operated by a section of nine men carrying thirty magazines of ammunition containing 1,410 rounds. The No. 1 was armed with a revolver while his comrades carried their rifles and grenades to protect the firers. Eventually, such was the importance of the gun that most infantrymen were trained in its use.

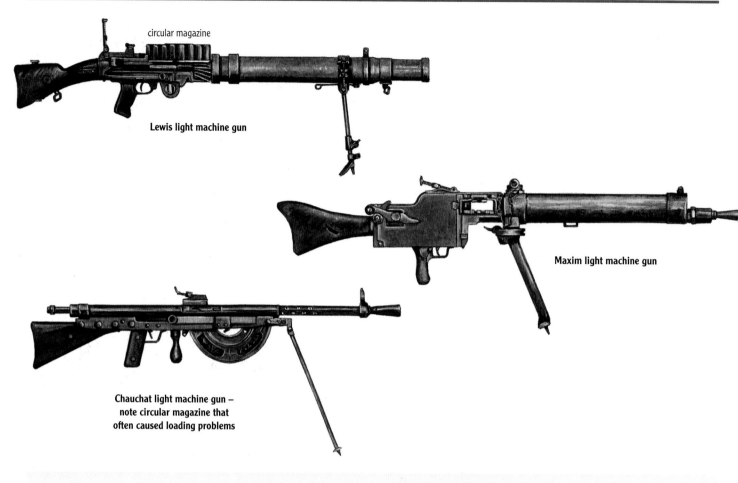

circular magazine

Lewis light machine gun

Maxim light machine gun

**Chauchat light machine gun –
note circular magazine that
often caused loading problems**

Private Harry Patch, *Légion d'honneur*

On Saturday, 25 July 2009 the former Private Harry Patch died, aged 111, the last surviving British soldier who fought in the trenches of World War I. After being conscripted at eighteen and completing basic training, Patch landed in France in June 1917 to become a Lewis-gunner in C Company, the 7th Duke of Cornwall's Light Infantry. He was to spend four months in the trenches at Ypres. He vividly recalled the fear and bewilderment of going over the top, of crawling forward because to stand up meant the certainty of being cut down by enemy machine-gun fire. As his battalion advanced from Pilckem Ridge that summer he remembered the wounded crying out for help – 'But we weren't like the Good Samaritan. We were the robbers who passed them by and left.'

At Passchendaele his platoon came across a member of the battalion lying in a pool of blood, ripped open from shoulder to waist. The man was pleading to be shot. But before anybody could do so he died with the word 'Mother' on his lips. Patch recalled, 'It was a cry of surprise and I'll always remember that death is not the end.' When they reached the German second line, four Germans stood up and one ran forward pointing his bayonet at Patch, who had only three rounds left in his revolver (as No. 1 on the gun he had a revolver rather than a rifle). He fired twice at the man's leg, knocking him down – he always refused to kill deliberately if humanly possible.

On 22 September 1917 Patch's five-man Lewis-gun team was moving back over open ground to the battalion's support line when a shell exploded beside them, blowing the three ammunition carriers to pieces; a red hot piece of shrapnel wounded Patch in the groin. The wound was painful but not serious and it was not until the following evening that the medical officer in the dressing station told

Patch that he could remove the 2-inch piece of metal but that there was no anaesthetic available. After some hesitation, Patch agreed and was held down by four men as the shrapnel was removed with tweezers. It took about two minutes, and he remembered that during that time he could have happily killed the doctor.

By the time he had fully recovered, the war had ended and Patch eventually qualified as a sanitary engineer. During World War II he joined the Auxiliary Fire Service and spent his time fighting fires in Bath, Bristol and Weston-super-Mare, on occasion having to dive under his engine to escape the bullets of a strafing enemy aircraft. He also became a machine-gunner again; and if the Germans had invaded Patch would this time have been manning a Vickers rather than a Lewis gun.

Patch was married twice but both his wives predeceased him, as did two sons from his first marriage. He went into an old peoples' home aged 100 and soon became a reluctant television celebrity, persuaded after all those years to speak of his Western Front experiences, about which he had remained silent for so long. He had a cider, Patch's Pride, named after him and he was awarded an honorary degree by Bristol University, where he had worked on the Wills memorial tower over eighty years earlier. He also received the *Légion d'honneur* from the French government. To the end, it was the loss of his three friends on 22 September 1917 that haunted him most. 'Those chaps are always with me. I can see that damned explosion now,' he would say.

Asked about a state funeral as the last surviving 'Tommy', Harry Patch insisted, 'It's not for me.' His wish was to be buried alongside his family in the village churchyard at Monkton Combe. 'Why,' he asked, 'would I want to be anywhere else?'

MAP 39 LEWIS-GUN ZONES OF BATTALION IN RESERVE TO BRIGADE IN THE LINE, 20 JULY 1918

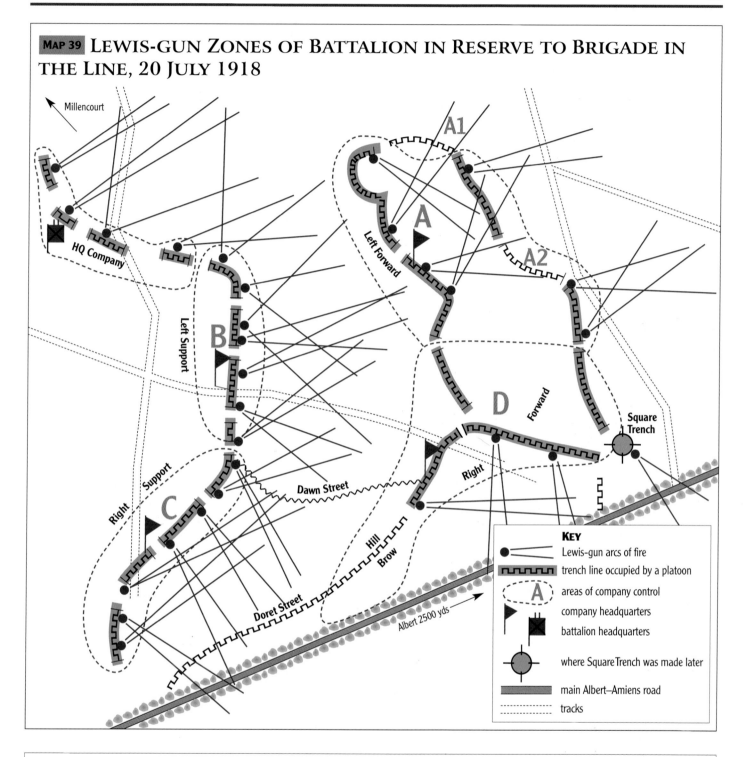

Notes for Map 39

This map has been copied, with certain modifications to improve its clarity, from a sketch map drawn by Lt Col E. P. Cawston in his *Personal Reminiscences of Incidents in the Kaiser War 1914–1918*. Col Cawston was then commanding the 2/10th Londons, deployed in a defensive position just under 2 miles south-west of Albert, immediately north of the Albert–Amiens road. The map was part of the handing-over notes Cawston gave to the relieving battalion on 20 July 1918, showing the arcs of fire of 29 Lewis guns. It gives a clear picture of how these guns could be sited to produce a complex criss-crossing of arcs of fire within a battalion defensive position. Particular points to note are:

• The typical battalion layout, with two companies forward and two in support but holding three trench lines, the support (or third) line being the most strongly held and having the great majority of the Lewis guns – 18 out of 29 if Headquarter Company guns are included.

• There are only three guns (one in A Company and two in D Company) firing directly to the battalion front. Of the four guns in A Company's second trench line, one is directed at the gap in the occupied trench at **A1**, and another through the gap at **A2**. All D Company's four guns are with the two platoons guarding the battalion's right flank and directing their fire across or obliquely along the Amiens–Albert road.

• B and C Companies have seven guns each and have the capacity to produce a massive weight of interlocking arcs of fire across the ground in front of B Company, and from C Company's trenches over the main road and across the company front.

• The four guns with Headquarter Company are positioned mainly to cover A Company's left flank and to the north-east.

Other nations' light machine guns were:

• France The Chauchat-Sutter-Ribeyrolles-Gladiator, or Chauchat for short, was the French attempt to produce what they considered an automatic rifle that would give a good volume of fire in an easily portable form. Like all light machine guns, it was air-cooled and gas-operated. It weighed 20 lb (its lightness being its main advantage), fired the same ammunition as the Lebel rifle at a maximum rate of 250 rpm with a light (2 lb) magazine containing twenty rounds. It was distributed in the field in 1915 and found to be a disappointment. It was very prone to stoppages, partly because the magazine, semicircular in shape and attached under the gun, prevented a smooth feed. The magazine was flimsy and easily damaged, and the bipod weak. When firing prone, the soldier had to be careful to avoid being hit in the face by the long recoil action. Despite these problems, the gun could, and did, work well on some notable occasions, although overall it cannot be rated more than very mediocre. Teams of two, who had also to carry all their personal equipment, initially operated the Chauchat; however, by early 1918 two additional men were added, mainly to carry ammunition. Despite its drawbacks, some 225,000 were produced between 1914 and 1918.

• Belgium The first country to use the Lewis gun.

• America The AEF was issued with the Chauchat, chambered to accept the US .300 round, despite the availability of better weapons, particularly the Lewis gun. The Chauchat's problems, noted above, made it unpopular and it was not unknown for it to be discarded in favour of a rifle. Only in the final weeks of the war did some US troops get issued with the Browning Automatic Rifle (BAR) M1918, weighing just under 20 lb and with a rate of fire of 500 rpm.

• Germany In 1915 the Germans began work on their MG08 heavy machine gun to produce a lighter version. In the meantime they created several *Musketen-Bataillone* – automatic rifle battalions – armed with the Danish-manufactured Madsen, an air-cooled, twenty-round, curved-magazine, bipod-mounted, 20-lb weapon that had been captured from the Russians in large numbers. These battalions consisted of three companies, each with thirty of these light machine guns, each operated by a four-man team. It was an inferior gun to the Lewis, and by the end of the British Somme offensive enough Lewis guns had been captured to re-equip these battalions with converted British weapons.

By the end of 1916 the Germans had introduced their own so-called light (its weight of 43 lb being its main drawback) machine gun, although some units retained the modified Lewis gun until the end of the war. The new weapon was the water-cooled (it needed 5 pints) Maxim 08/15, which was not much different to the heavier MG08, except that it was bipod-mounted with a wooden butt and pistol grip. It was fed by belts of 100 or 250 rounds and could therefore produce a far heavier weight of fire than either the Lewis or Chauchat guns – it was really a medium machine gun that could, at a pinch, be operated by one man. It was first encountered on the Western Front in March 1917 when it was issued on a scale of three to a company – later raised to six, giving two to every platoon, each with an eight-man section under an NCO. Battalions were provided with a wagon to transport these guns.

In the final few months of the war, the Germans issued their stormtrooper battalions with what was effectively the world's first sub-machine gun – the MP18. It was developed by Hugo Schmeisser at the factory of Theodor Bergmann and by the

Armistice some 30,000 had been produced. The small drum magazine held thirty-two 9mm parabellum rounds and the weapon was fired from the open bolt – pulling the trigger sent the bolt forward, a system that led to occasional accidental firing. It weighed 11 lb when loaded, and fired effectively at ranges up to 150 yards at a maximum rate of 450 rpm. It was a popular weapon and the forerunner of the German sub-machine guns of World War II.

Flamethrowers

Although the Germans had used flamethrowers against the French at Malancourt, near Verdun, on 26 February 1915 – not particularly successfully – it was not until their attack at Hooge (Second Ypres) on 29–30 July that year that these weapons were first used against the British. This occurred in their assault on the 8th Rifle Brigade defending the Hooge crater area immediately north of the Menin Road. Although this was a more spectacular, surprise action, the number of burn casualties was comparatively small, as appears to be borne out by the following two accounts. Lieutenant G. V. Carey's platoon was holding a position near the edge of the crater:

> There was a sudden hissing sound, and a bright crimson glare over the crater turned the whole scene red. As I looked I saw three or four distinct sheets of flame – like a line of powerful fire-hoses spraying fire instead of water – shoot across my fire trench. How long this lasted is impossible to say – probably not more than a minute; but the effect was so stupefying that, for my part, I was utterly unable for some moments to think collectedly.

Private A. P. Hattan also witnessed this attack:

> We first heard sounds as of a splashing to our front, then there was a peculiar smoky smell just like coal-tar; next a corporal of C Company cried out that he had been hit by a shell; yet when we went to look at him we found that a huge blister as from a burn was on his forehead, while the back of his cap was smouldering.
>
> We had no time to notice anything else, for after that preliminary trial the Boches loosed their liquid fire upon us with a vengeance. It came in streams all over the earthworks, while shells containing star lights ignited the black fluid. Sandbags, blankets, top-coats, and anything of that sort that was handy smouldered and then flared. We were choked by the smoke and half scorched by the heat.

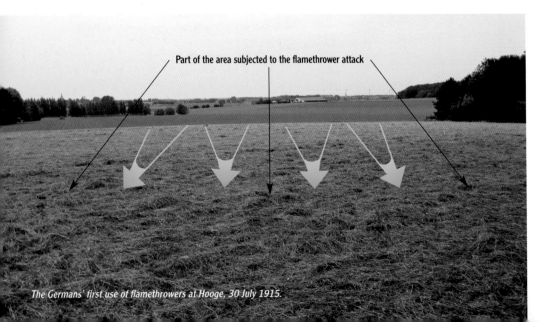

Part of the area subjected to the flamethrower attack

The Germans' first use of flamethrowers at Hooge, 30 July 1915.

Not until late 1914 did the Germans produce a flamethrower for use in the field. Major Bernhard Reddemann, an engineer commanding a Landwehr Engineer Company, designed them with fellow engineer Richard Fiedler. They developed a portable model, which belched forth a stream of a burning mixture of petrol and oil up to about 20 yards for under two minutes. It was intended to be carried by one man with another operating the nozzle and control valve. The second model was much larger and designed to operate from a stationary position, what it lacked in mobility being made up by its increased range and longer burning time.

The perceived success at Hooge prompted the High Command to develop the arm further and men (mostly firemen) were recruited into the 3rd Guard Engineer Battalion, which had between nine and twelve companies equipped with flamethrowers. By April 1916 a Reserve Guard Engineer Regiment under Reddemann's command was established. This was a substantial unit with three battalions, each with four companies, as well as a training company and experimental company. With each company having thirty–forty portable flamethrowers, up to 480 weapons were available. Fuel and replacement flamethrowers were carried in a transport unit attached to each company, which also had twelve–fifteen heavy flamethrowers. This regiment was usually stationed near GHQ, with units or subunits attached to armies for particular operations. A lightweight one-man model called the Wex came into service in 1917.

The flamethrower is potentially a potent weapon, especially for its effect on morale, in that it can inflict the most dreadful injuries or a horrific death. It did, however, have several serious drawbacks. The first was its weight – around 80 lb or more – which limited mobility, and its recognizable bulky shape, which made the carrier an obvious target. Coupled with the shortness of range, which meant the operator had to be close to the enemy position before he could open fire, these problems ensured his vulnerability. Because of the fearsome nature of the weapon, it was seldom that men caught carrying flamethrowers were taken prisoner – most could expect summary execution. The best attacking tactic was to combine them with machine-gunners and grenadiers. If they reached a trench line, dugout, bunker or building, their use could be decisive. Specific flamethrower attacks during the war are estimated to have risen from 32 in 1915 to almost 300 by 1918. They became far more effective when mounted in armoured vehicles or tanks.

After the Hooge incident, the British and French began a flamethrower development programme. The former initially produced a knapsack type for one man, with a range of some 30 yards, which was little used. A further development, by Captain Livens of the Royal Engineers, was the two-man model, with a range of 50 yards and a twenty-second burst. However, this was heavy (220 lb) and could only be termed semi-portable. In readiness for the Somme, four large models,

weighing 2 tons each and with a range of 90 yards, were constructed piece by piece into a forward trench only 60 yards from the German lines. Two were destroyed by enemy shelling while the others operated successfully on 1 July, albeit only in their local area. The British did not use them in action again after 1916.

The French had a portable model, called the Schilt, with a maximum range of just over 100 yards for one long burst. It was used effectively against pillboxes in attacks during 1917–18.

Other Weapons

Soldiers of all nations resorted to makeshift weapons for close-quarter combat in trenches and bunkers where the rifle and bayonet were found to be unwieldy – such weapons were often taken by night-raiding parties. Many favoured short-handled spades or entrenching tools with sharpened blades. Daggers, knives, knuckledusters, wooden clubs with nails embedded in the head or metal maces were also common. Some Americans used the pump-action shotgun, as it was such a formidable weapon at close range. The Germans lodged a formal complaint concerning its use two months before the end of the war, stating, 'every prisoner found to have in his possession such guns or ammunition belonging thereto forfeits his life.' Some ANZAC and British troops carried sawn-off shotguns, although they were sporting models and not officially issued.

Infantrymen

Infantry Battalions and Platoons

The battalion was the infantryman's home on the Western Front. It was initially around 1,000+ strong in all armies and was the unit upon which the higher command primarily depended to achieve its aim in either defence or attack. In 1914 it was basically a rifle- and bayonet-armed unit with little in the way of integral heavier or specialist weapons. By 1918 it had developed into a very different unit, not so much in terms of manpower, which had generally decreased substantially due to losses, but in having greatly enhanced firepower with numerous light machine guns (one Lewis-gun team could produce the equivalent fire of fifteen–twenty riflemen) and rifles adapted for throwing grenades. The diagrams on pages 194–7 show the basic organization of national infantry battalions in 1914.

If the battalion was his home, then the platoon was the infantryman's family. It was with these close comrades that he ate, slept, worked, fought and in so many cases died. These men shared the most horrific experiences and developed a bond that, if they survived, could never be broken. In many instances they came to know each other better than their parents ever would. Little has changed with most infantry soldiers on operations today. The men in a platoon in Iraq or Afghanistan fought first and foremost for their mates. They trusted each other, they depended on each other, and so often they endangered, or sometimes sacrificed, themselves for their comrades. It has always been that the soldiers of an infantry platoon do the actual fighting, if necessary hand to hand. For many infantry officers who rise much higher in rank, commanding a platoon was the best and most enjoyable command in their military career. The good officer has

always developed a special bond of loyalty and respect – and in many cases devotion – between himself and the men of his platoon. On the Western Front, as in today's conflicts, this mutual respect was established by the platoon commander setting the example, putting the welfare of his soldiers before his own and leading from the front.

However, it was the platoon, as a small sub-unit, that could be destroyed in a few minutes by machine guns and shellfire. It was the platoon that fought with rifle butt, bomb and bayonet for a bunker or a few yards of trench. It was the platoon that crouched shaking and terrified under the indescribable horror of neverending artillery bombardment. And it was the platoon that saw the most obvious changes in tactics and weaponry during more than four long years of fighting.

Platoon organization towards the end of the war was as shown in the diagrams on pages 194–7.

A British Infantry Battalion, 1914

(1,007) Lieutenant Colonel

A B (227) C D MG (18)
Major Subaltern

1 2 3 (37) 4
Subaltern

2 x Maxim/Vickers machine guns

1 2 (12) 3 4
Corporal

Total at full establishment:
1,007 all ranks
(30 officers and 977 ORs)

Notes

• This shows a battalion at full strength, including a rear party that would remain at its depot when the battalion went to war.
• Battalion HQ contained the commanding officer (lieutenant colonel), second-in-command (major), adjutant (captain), quartermaster (captain or lieutenant) and medical officer (captain) attached from the Royal Army Medical Corps (RAMC). It also included the regimental sergeant major (RSM) and several sergeants with specialist roles (provost, quartermaster, drummer, cook, pioneer, transport, signals, armourer and orderly-room clerk).
• Also in the battalion HQ were:
  • a corporal and four soldiers attached from RAMC

• a corporal and 15 privates as signallers
• 10 privates employed as pioneers
• 11 privates used as drivers for horse transport
• 16 bandsmen acting as stretcher-bearers in the field
• 6 privates serving as batmen (servants) for officers
• 2 privates acting as medical orderlies.
• Companies were lettered A–D, each with a major commanding; a captain as second-in-command; a company sergeant major (CSM); a company quartermaster sergeant (CQMS); and several privates as batmen, drivers or storemen.
• The machine-gun section was commanded by a subaltern and had a sergeant, corporal, two drivers, a batman and 12 privates divided into two 6-man gun teams.

• Each platoon in each company was numbered 1–4 (as were the sections) and was composed of 1 officer, 1 sergeant, 1 batman/runner and four sections each of 12 men under an NCO – usually a corporal.
• **Transport** This consisted of 13 riding (for certain officers) and 43 draught and pack horses – they provided the pulling power for 6 ammunition carts, 2 water carts, 3 general service wagons (for tools and machine guns) and the medical officer's Maltese cart. The signallers had 9 bicycles.
• **Ammunition** Battalion transport carried 32 boxes of 1,000 rounds and each soldier carried 120 rounds. The machine guns were each supplied with 41,500 rounds, of which 3,500 were with the gun and 8,000 in the battalion reserve, the great bulk being carried in brigade or divisional transport.

A British Infantry Platoon, 1917–18

(41) Subaltern

(9) (9) MG (9) (9)

Bomber section
1 x Corporal
8 x ORs (inc. 2 throwers and 2 bayonet men)

Rifle section
1 x Corporal
8 x ORs (best shots, scouts, bayonet fighters)

Lewis-gun section
1 x Corporal
8 x ORs (inc. Nos. 1 and 2 on gun)

Rifle-grenade section
1 x Corporal
8 x ORs (inc. 4 grenade firers)

Notes

• This strength and organization appeared in GHQ OB/1919, dated 7 February 1917 and set out the recommended platoon organization for the latter part of the war. It includes specialist sections where tactical roles had been developed to incorporate the changed tactics of that time (see Section Twelve). The numbers shown indicate an almost full establishment platoon but this organization could be used with platoons down to 28 ORs (exclusive of platoon headquarters).
• In an attack the following ammunition was to be carried as a minimum:
  • bombers, runners, scouts, Lewis-gunners: 50 rounds each; remainder 120
  • Lewis-gun section (6 men): 30 drums (5 drums each)

  • bombing section: each thrower 5 bombs; remainder 10 each
  • rifle grenade (bomb) section: 6 or more rifle grenades/bombs
  • flares distributed throughout the sections
• This gives an approximate holding of ammunition within a platoon advancing to attack and for the immediate consolidation on, and defence of, the objective:
  • rifle ammunition: 3,300+
  • Lewis-gun ammunition: 860+
  • grenades/bombs in section: 70+; at least the same number carried by individuals in the remainder of the platoon
  • rifle grenades/bombs: 48+

A French Infantry Battalion, 1914

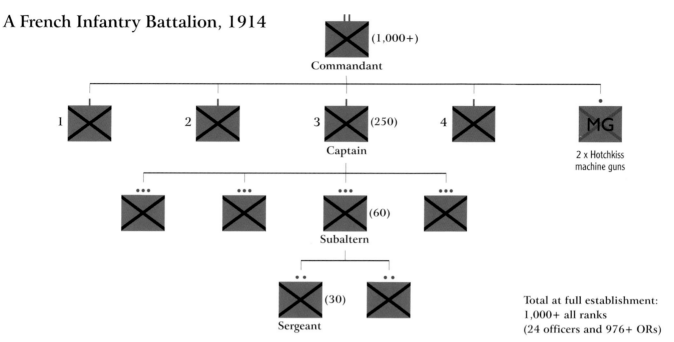

Total at full establishment:
1,000+ all ranks
(24 officers and 976+ ORs)

Notes

• Each company had a headquarters with a captain commanding and an adjutant (company sergeant major), a quartermaster sergeant and a corporal, plus 15 soldiers.
• The four platoons (the French called them sections) were each commanded by a subaltern officer with a platoon sergeant as second in command. The platoon had two half-sections of about 30 men, each under a sergeant; these were again divided into two squads (equivalent to a British section) composed of one corporal and 14 privates.

• The machine-gun section changed little from 1915–18. During that period it consisted of one officer and 29 men if at full strength. It was divided into three sections:
  • firing section consisting of the lieutenant, a senior NCO, two corporal gun commanders and eight men (two firers, two loaders, two ammunition carriers, one range-finder and one gunsmith
  • combat train with a corporal, two conductors (drivers) and four horses pulling a caisson of some 22,000 rounds
  • echelon (supply section) composed of a corporal, four suppliers and nine conductors, with two gun mules, six munition mules carrying six crates each, plus one spare mule
• The total ammunition with the section amounted to about 30,000+ rounds.

A French Infantry Platoon, October 1917–October 1918

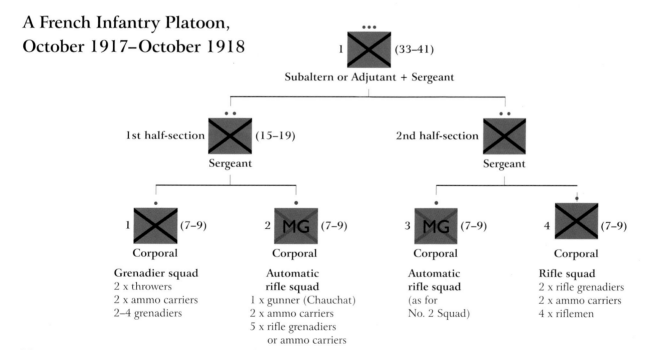

Notes

• By this stage officer losses meant the platoon (French section) could be commanded by either a junior officer or an adjutant (sergeant major).
• At this stage of the war, as in other armies, the infantry platoon contained specialist sections. Automatic-rifle squads had the Chauchat light machine gun.

• For the last two months of the war platoon organization was again altered. The squad was abolished and instead a section (platoon) was composed of three combat groups.

US Infantry Battalion, November 1917

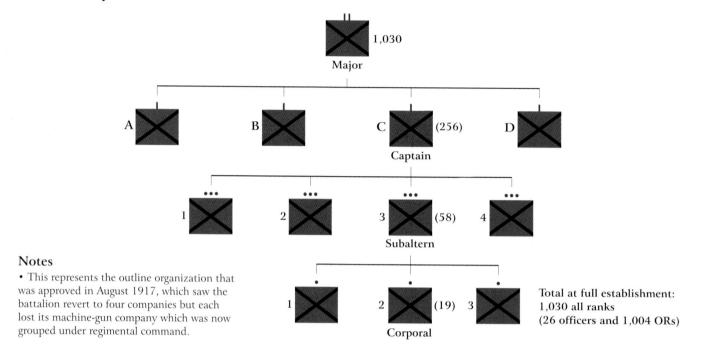

Notes

• This represents the outline organization that was approved in August 1917, which saw the battalion revert to four companies but each lost its machine-gun company which was now grouped under regimental command.

Total at full establishment:
1,030 all ranks
(26 officers and 1,004 ORs)

US Infantry Platoon, November 1917

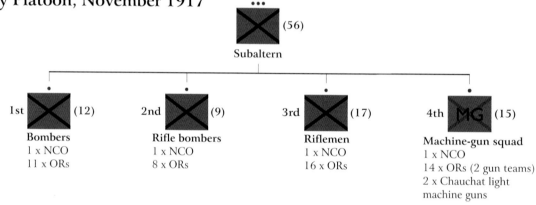

1st (12)
Bombers
1 x NCO
11 x ORs

2nd (9)
Rifle bombers
1 x NCO
8 x ORs

3rd (17)
Riflemen
1 x NCO
16 x ORs

4th MG (15)
Machine-gun squad
1 x NCO
14 x ORs (2 gun teams)
2 x Chauchat light
machine guns

Notes

• At full strength this was a large platoon with considerable firepower.
• Unusually, the four squads/sections varied in numbers.

An American machine-gun platoon creeping along a small road near the front line, 1917.

A German Infantry Battalion, 1914

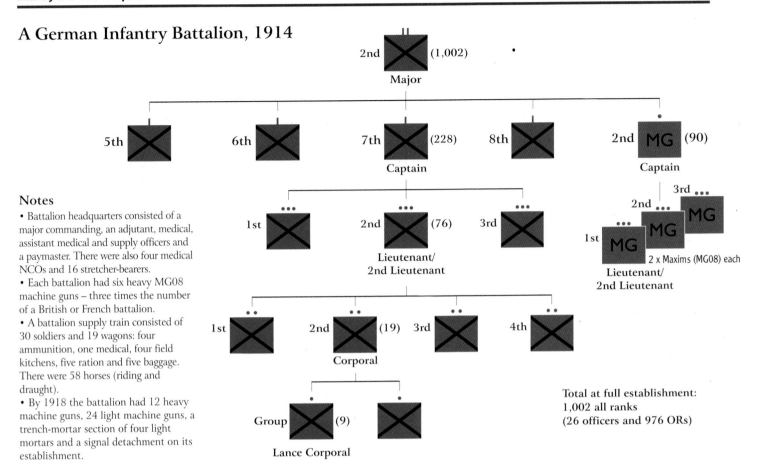

Notes

• Battalion headquarters consisted of a major commanding, an adjutant, medical, assistant medical and supply officers and a paymaster. There were also four medical NCOs and 16 stretcher-bearers.

• Each battalion had six heavy MG08 machine guns – three times the number of a British or French battalion.

• A battalion supply train consisted of 30 soldiers and 19 wagons: four ammunition, one medical, four field kitchens, five ration and five baggage. There were 58 horses (riding and draught).

• By 1918 the battalion had 12 heavy machine guns, 24 light machine guns, a trench-mortar section of four light mortars and a signal detachment on its establishment.

Total at full establishment:
1,002 all ranks
(26 officers and 976 ORs)

A German Infantry Platoon, 1918

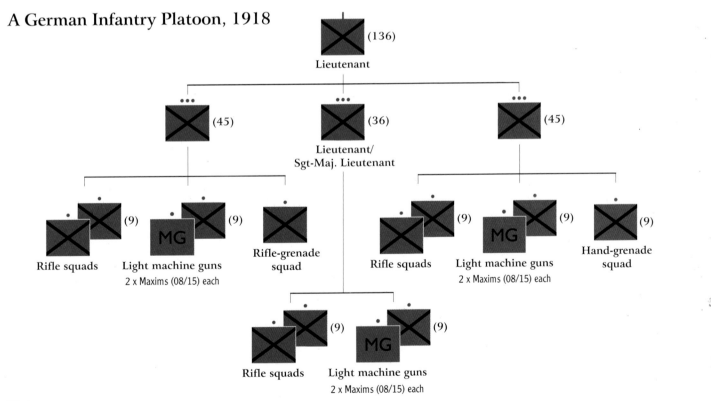

Notes

• The high casualty rate amongst officers meant that a company was lucky to have a lieutenant in command, with perhaps all platoons commanded by sergeant-major lieutenants or acting officers. The corporals still commanded the sections and the lance corporals the groups or squads of eight men.

• As with other nations, the German platoon by this late stage of the war was a mixture of riflemen, rifle-grenade throwers, grenadiers (bombers) and light machine guns, although the platoons in a company did not have an identical composition.

Uniforms and Equipment

In all armies the infantry soldier's equipment was designed to do the same – facilitate the carrying of ammunition, water, food and various personal items. This required either a leather or a webbing belt, together with pouches, pack, haversack, steel helmet and gas helmet, as well as greatcoat, groundsheet, weapon and entrenching tool. When all these were worn, the soldier was in full marching order, carrying some 65–70 lb. However, this complete load was not worn in a defensive position, nor in a raid (raiders took the bare minimum), nor in an attack, when the greatcoat and large pack were left behind in what was termed 'fighting order'. Nevertheless, this reduction in weight was often more than made up for by the need, particularly by supporting waves, to carry additional ammunition of all types, heavier weapons, wire-cutters, flares, barbed-wire coils and sandbags for immediate use in defending and consolidating enemy positions taken.

The *British Official History of the War 1916*, Volume I, with reference to the failures of 1 July on the Somme, has this to say on the subject of the weight of equipment carried:

> The total weight carried per man was about 66 lbs., which made it difficult to get out of a trench, impossible to move much quicker than a slow walk, or rise and lie down quickly . . . This overloading of the men is by many infantry officers regarded as one of the principal reasons of the heavy losses and failure of their battalions; for their men could not get through the machine gun zone with sufficient speed.

Saying that carrying 66 lb prevented movement at 'much quicker than a slow walk' is a questionable excuse for failure. That weight is by no means crippling for a reasonably fit soldier, especially when he had to advance only 500 yards, and in some cases considerably less, and considering that no-man's-land was fairly firm and, on 1 July 1916, was not yet a mangled mass of countless thousands of shell holes. The present writer, and the soldiers of his platoon, carried at least 60 lb for hour after hour, day after day, up and down the steep, jungle-clad hills of Malaya – utterly exhausting. A 500-yard walk at even a fast pace with 66 lb (although many of the follow-up troops on the Western Front carried considerably more in the way of wire, trench stores and ammunition) would have been regarded as something of a 'doddle'. There was much more to the losses on 1 July than carrying too much weight.

An item of equipment of which each of the three major antagonists had a noticeably different type was the helmet. During the first year of the war soldiers of all nations went into battle in a variety of soft caps or, in the case of the Germans, the traditional spiked leather *Pickelhaube*, none of which offered any protection against head wounds. The French were the first to react to the need for a helmet and in 1915 initially distributed some 700,000 steel skullcaps to be worn under their distinctive kepi. The problem with the skullcaps was primarily one of weight, and by the summer of that year the French had started to issue the steel Adrian helmet (designed by General Louis Auguste Adrian), which was later adopted by the Belgian, Italian and other armies. It was a four-piece construction (initially painted sky blue and later khaki), on the front of which was a sheet-metal badge – a flaming grenade for infantry, a horn for light infantry, crossed cannon for artillery and a miniature breastplate for the engineers. Each badge incorporated the letters 'RF' for *République Française*. Winston Churchill favoured this helmet and there is a well-known photograph of him wearing one when he was serving at the front.

Meanwhile, Britain had also seen the need for a helmet and requested samples of the French type for trials. Almost 500 were received, but it was considered insufficiently strong and too complex to mass-produce quickly. This led to the adoption of the Brodie helmet (designed by John L. Brodie). After a change from the original mild steel to a harder steel with a 12 per cent manganese mix, the Type B Brodie helmet, weighing 2 lb, began to be issued – 140,000 were received in France by March 1916 for front-line troops. This helmet was of a 'soup-bowl' shape with a fairly shallow crown, a chin-strap, liner and wide brim – a helmet designed to protect the head from shrapnel fragments falling from above (the British authorities claimed it would stop shrapnel travelling at 750 feet per second), but it offered minimal protection to the lower part of the head or neck. It was painted matt khaki and finished off with sand or sawdust to prevent it shining. It was a success, in that the number of head wounds dropped to a quarter of the previous level, and an accelerated supply was demanded by GHQ. About a million had been received by the first week of July 1916 and by the end of the war some 7.75 million were produced, of which 1.5 million were supplied to the Americans.

The German infantry went to war wearing the *Pickelhaube* (1895 model), black in colour, with a massive gilded helmet plate in front. By 1915 the spike was made detachable, as in the trenches the spiked helmet made a splendid aiming mark for snipers and it also snagged branches when moving through woods. Other materials such as Vulkan Fibre (vulcanized fibre), cloth-covered cork and even papier mâché were tried, none of which afforded any protection. Demands by the Medical Department for a helmet that reduced head wounds eventually resulted in the production of the *Stahlhelm* (steel helmet), with its coalscuttle appearance, which gave greater protection to the neck than other types. It had been tested on an artillery range and found to be resistant to shell splinters and shrapnel, so went into immediate production, with some 30,000 being issued to front-line troops at Verdun in February 1916. When it was also found to be successful on the battlefield, the subsequent general issue saw the *Pickelhaube* replaced on the Western Front within a matter of months.

As noted above, the Americans opted for the British Brodie helmet and all dominion troops were also issued with it.

Roll call of the 2nd Battalion, the Seaforth Highlanders, on the afternoon of the first day of the Battle of the Somme near Beaumont-Hamel. They are equipped with haversack, rolled groundsheet and mess tin instead of the large pack. The insignia on their sleeves indicates that they were part of the attacking force.

A British infantryman *c.*1916

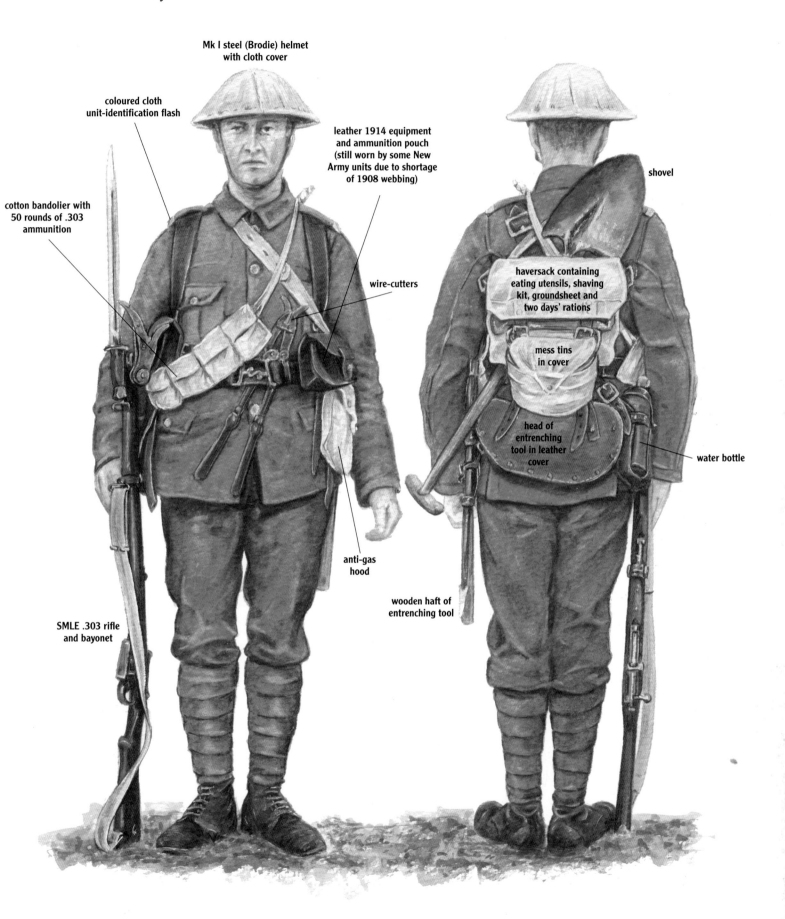

Mk I steel (Brodie) helmet with cloth cover

coloured cloth unit-identification flash

leather 1914 equipment and ammunition pouch (still worn by some New Army units due to shortage of 1908 webbing)

cotton bandolier with 50 rounds of .303 ammunition

wire-cutters

SMLE .303 rifle and bayonet

anti-gas hood

shovel

haversack containing eating utensils, shaving kit, groundsheet and two days' rations

mess tins in cover

head of entrenching tool in leather cover

water bottle

wooden haft of entrenching tool

A German infantryman *c.*1916

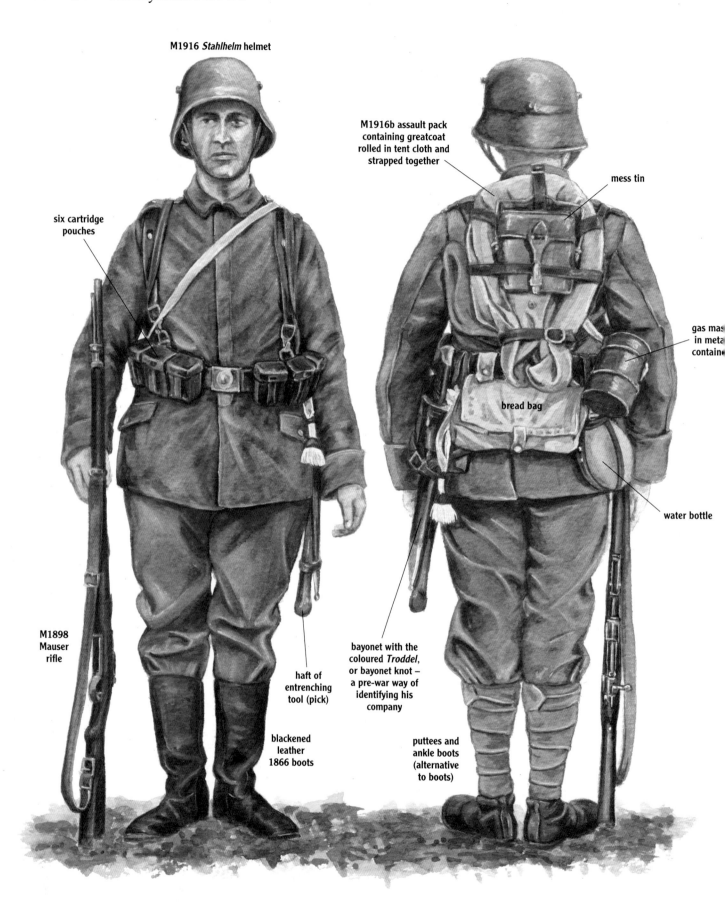

M1916 *Stahlhelm* helmet

M1916b assault pack
containing greatcoat
rolled in tent cloth and
strapped together

mess tin

six cartridge
pouches

gas mask
in metal
container

bread bag

M1898
Mauser
rifle

water bottle

haft of
entrenching
tool (pick)

bayonet with the
coloured *Troddel*,
or bayonet knot –
a pre-war way of
identifying his
company

blackened
leather
1866 boots

puttees and
ankle boots
(alternative
to boots)

1 July 1916 – the Worst Day for British Infantry

Dutch Courage

The fear men felt when waiting to go over the top, the dreadful realization that they faced imminent agonizing mutilation or had only minutes to live, was usually worse than when physically advancing with their comrades. Martin Middlebrook in *The First Day on the Somme* quotes such a situation confronting Private G. Brownbridge, 13th Northumberland Fusiliers:

I found that I wasn't alone, as a second-lieutenant was standing beside me, shaking like a jelly, which nearly made me jittery myself. He was just a youngster, about my own age, and had just joined the battalion a few days before. I shouted at him to get over the top but he just looked at me forlornly and couldn't seem able to speak. I whipped out my bottle of rum, I had been saving it for several days, and offered it to him but he must have been a teetotaller as he only took a sip. I told him to take a good drink, which he did. You never saw a man find his courage so quickly. He pulled out his revolver, climbed the ladder and went charging after the men like a hare. If we hadn't had our rum we would have lost the war.

The British Fourth Army under General Sir Henry Rawlinson was a New Army formation, far from fully trained, packed with Kitchener's volunteers, with only four of its sixteen divisions being regular – the 4th, 7th, 8th and 29th. Rawlinson was to commit fifteen of these divisions (the 9th Scottish remained in reserve), supported by two divisions from the Third Army in the north, into an attack along a front of 16 miles from just north of the River Somme (see Map 16), against strong German defences manned by six divisions of the German Second Army under General Fritz von Below (12th, 52nd, 10th Bavarian, 2nd Guards Reserve, 26th Reserve and 28th Reserve Divisions). On the right, immediately north of the river, two French divisions would also attack, as would another six divisions of General Marie Émile Fayolle's French Sixth Army south of the Somme. Held in reserve to exploit any gap was the Reserve Army, consisting mostly of cavalry. Each attacking British division had twelve battalions (one of which was a pioneer battalion). This meant that the Fourth Army's attack involved 204 battalions either in the first waves or in support. With

battalions averaging about 750–800 men (10 per cent were always deliberately left out of battle to form a nucleus around which a new unit could be built if losses were severe), some 153,000–163,200 British infantrymen advanced at 7:30 that morning or were involved later in the day.

1 July 1916 would become the bloodiest single day of the war for the British Army. Total losses were 57,470 (all but 685 were infantrymen), of which 19,240 were dead and 2,152 missing. Unusually, it was enemy machine guns that caused some 60 per cent of these casualties rather than artillery fire – the biggest killer of the war. Thirty-two battalions lost over 500 all ranks, with the 10th West Yorkshires (17th Division) being virtually wiped out when it lost 710 – only one officer, Lieutenant Philip Howe, and twenty men remained unscathed. Commanding officers, who were supposed to remain to the rear until an objective was secured, largely ignored this instruction and went forward with their men. They paid the same price, with fifty-one of them becoming casualties (thirty killed or died of wounds and twenty-one wounded). Brigadier General C. B. Prowse, commanding 11th Brigade, 4th Division, was killed and Brigadier General N. J. G. Cameron, commander of 103rd Brigade, 34th Division, was wounded. Nine men were awarded the Victoria Cross.

The strategic thinking that resulted in the attack on the Somme had been agreed in December the previous year when the Allies determined on major offensives on the Western, Eastern and Italian fronts aimed at crushing Germany from three directions. The

British and French contribution to this, agreed at Chantilly on 14 February 1916, involved a massive joint attack, side by side along the Somme. A week after this conference the Germans began their assault on Verdun with the objective of bleeding the French Army to death, and by May it had begun to look as though they might succeed. On the 26th of that month Joffre told Haig, who wanted to launch the Somme attack in August, that by then there might be no French Army left. The result was that the British attacked earlier than intended and the anticipated French support south of the river was weakened by the needs of Verdun.

The area selected for the attack had been relatively quiet thus far in the war and the Germans, although not strong in numbers due to their commitment at Verdun, had had plenty of time to construct formidable defences in the chalk uplands of the Pozières Ridge. Rawlinson faced two completed defensive lines, with a third under construction. Villages like Gommecourt, Serre, Beaumont-Hamel, Thiepval, Pozières and Fricourt were virtual fortresses; dugouts and bunkers, some 30 feet deep (virtually impervious to anything but a direct hit by a heavy shell), had been constructed and every trench line was fronted with dense belts of barbed wire covered by interlocking machine-gun arcs.

The Fourth Army plan envisaged the methodical destruction of German strong-points, wire and trenches through a five-day (extended to seven when bad weather led to a postponement from 29 June) continuous bombardment by a huge concentration of guns and mortars – over 460 of them heavy –

Men of the Royal Warwickshire Regiment, their rifles stacked nearby, lying exhausted in the grass in a rear area on the Somme.

throwing 1.7 million shells. After the explosion of five massive mines (Hawthorn Ridge, Y Sap, Lochnagar, Triple Tambour and Kasino Point) under enemy strongpoints in the front line, the infantry were to advance in successive waves. They would walk forward under cover of a series of artillery barrages falling in a timed programme on successive predetermined targets in a methodical 'bite-and-hold' operation. This was the first large-scale attempt to use a creeping barrage – first tried (successfully) at Loos but then neglected. There were practical problems, and its implementation was patchy on 1 July, but by the end of the battle in November the BEF had developed the creeping barrage to a high degree (see page 254). The overall objective was to secure the German second line from the north at Serre south to Pozières, and then a line from that village to Montauban in the south-east, on day one. Haig hoped there would be a breakthrough, a gap, through which he could launch his cavalry.

In the event, it was generally a disastrous day for the British. Only in the extreme south, next to the French, did two divisions succeed in taking all their objectives. For the rest it was mostly failure as infantrymen were cut down or blown up in their thousands. The guns had failed to crush all the bunkers or cut enough gaps in the enemy wire, and the German machine-gunners won the 'race for the parapet' to fire at targets it was impossible to miss. In contrast, the French both north and south of the Somme were far more successful, partly due to their concentrating many more guns on half the frontage and because their infantry advanced more quickly in looser formations rather than in semi-parade-ground lines. In the words of Captain Edward Spears, a liaison officer with the French who watched the attack, 'The French had already adopted the self-contained platoon as a unit. Tiny groups, taking advantage of cover, swarmed forward . . .'

Highlights of this day of infamy for most, but not all, British infantry are summarized below.

XIII Corps

Both the attacking divisions achieved remarkable success in comparison with most others, in that they were the only divisions to take all their objectives and they did so with the fewest casualties.

30th Division

Major H. F. Bidder, commanding the divisional machine-gun company, later described the start of the advance:

> There was a wonderful air of cheery expectancy over our troops. They were in the highest spirits, and full of confidence. I have never known quite the same universal feeling of cheerful eagerness.

French Successes on 1 July

The French Sixth Army (General Fayolle), astride the Somme on the British right, secured all its objectives on 1 July, and in some instances had gone beyond them and engaged the Germans' second position. This was in part due to the French advancing at 9:30 a.m., two hours after the British, and thus surprising the Germans, who thought no French attack was imminent; and in part because they attacked in more mobile groups rather than steadily advancing in waves in long lines. However, the most important factor in their success was their more effective artillery preparation. They deployed a huge preponderance of heavy guns (eighty-five batteries south of the Somme) on a far smaller frontage, which ensured more direct hits on bunkers and dugouts than the British achieved. Progress beyond the first day's objectives was limited by the fear of exposing the flanks to counter-attack and enfilade fire. Nevertheless, the French captured over 4,000 prisoners – half taken by the Colonial Corps – on the first day.

The moment came, and they were all walking over the top, as steadily as on parade, the tin discs on their backs (to show the guns where they were) glittering in the sun . . . Very soon

---

Notes for Map 40
British Order of Battle (infantry)
XIII Corps
(Lt Gen. W. N. Congreve, VC)

18th (Eastern) Division	**55th Brigade**	**30th Division**	**90th Brigade**
(Maj. Gen. F. I. Maxse)	7th Queen's	(Maj. Gen. J. S. M. Shea)	2nd Royal Scots Fusiliers
53rd Brigade	7th Buffs	**21st Brigade**	16th Manchester (P)
8th Norfolk	8th East Surrey	18th King's (P)	17th Manchester (P)
8th Suffolk	7th Royal West Kent	2nd Green Howards	18th Manchester (P)
10th Essex	**Pioneers**	2nd Wiltshire	**Pioneers**
6th Royal Berkshire	8th Royal Sussex	19th Manchester (P)	11th South Lancashire
54th Brigade		**89th Brigade**	
10th Royal Warwickshire		17th King's (P)	(P) indicates a Pals battalion. The British 18th Division was made up entirely of English county regiments from the eastern half of the country, while in the 30th Division 8 of the 12 attacking battalions were Pals battalions.
7th Bedfordshire		19th King's (P)	
6th Northamptonshire	9th (Scottish) Division in reserve (off map) – did not attack on 1 July.	20th King's (P)	
12th Middlesex		2nd Bedfordshire	

The German defences had considerable depth, with their second line being some 2,000 yards in rear of their first. The village of Montauban was heavily fortified and in the front line the enemy had constructed three redoubts (Pommiers, The Castle and Glatz); however, the attackers heavily outnumbered the defending German infantry.

This attack by XIII Corps on the extreme right of the Fourth Army's offensive was the only real success on 1 July. The attack would be made 'in successive waves or lines, each line adding fresh impetus to the preceding one when this is checked and carrying the whole forward to the objective' (GHQ memorandum on divisional offensive action, dated 8 May 1916). The corps objective was to secure the German first line, including Montauban, and this had been achieved by around midday all along the line. On the right, 30th Division attacking with the French advanced with two brigades (21st and 89th) to take its first-phase objective of the Dublin Trench – D Company, 20th King's, even pushing north beyond the objective to secure the brickworks. This was followed by the 90th Brigade advancing to take Montauban. The 18th Division had about 2,000 yards to go to its objective of Montauban Alley, about twice the distance of its sister division. Also, because of the width of its sector (2,000 yards), this division advanced with all its three brigades in line. The first phase of its attack was to take the line of the Pommiers Trench–Train Alley, before moving on Montauban Alley to the north.

The French on the right also achieved complete success.

Casualties in the 18th Division amounted to 3,115 (killed 912) and in the 30th Division to 3,011 (killed 828). Apart from the 46th (North Midland) Division in the Third Army at the northern extremity of the line, these were the lowest losses of any attacking division that day.

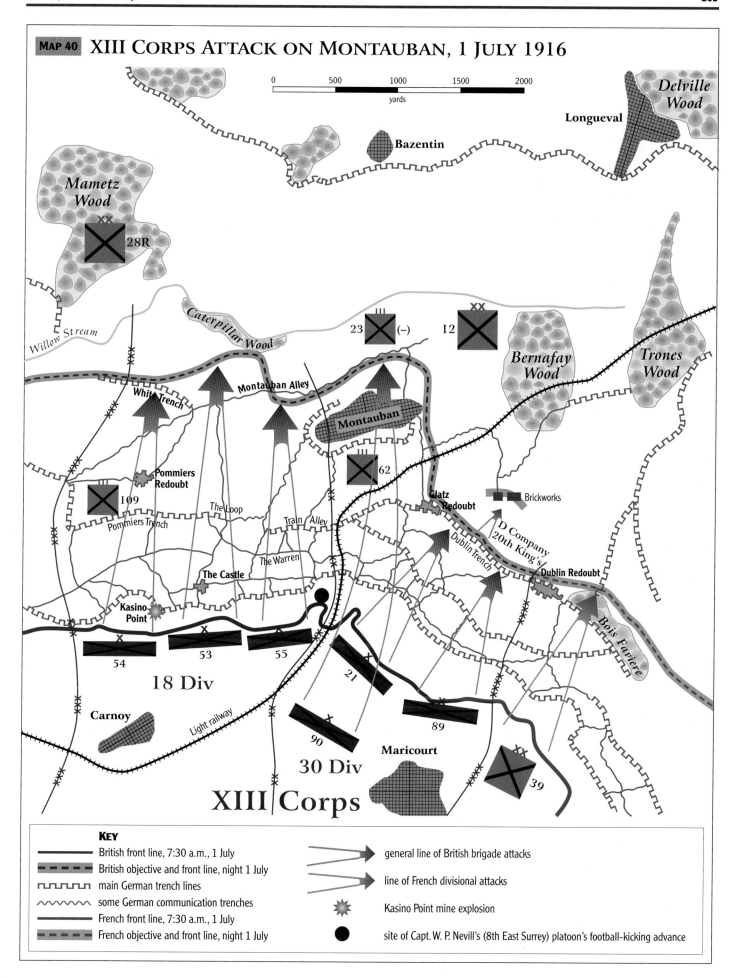

MAP 40 XIII CORPS ATTACK ON MONTAUBAN, 1 JULY 1916

Delville Wood

Longueval

Bazentin

Mametz Wood

XX
28R

Caterpillar Wood

Willow Stream

White Trench

Montauban Alley

23 ‖ (–)   12 XX

Bernafay Wood

Trones Wood

Montauban

Pommiers Redoubt

62 ‖

109 ‖

The Loop

Pommiers Trench

Train Alley

Glatz Redoubt   Brickworks

D Company 20th King's

The Warren

Dublin Trench

The Castle

Dublin Redoubt

Kasino Point

Bois Faviere

54   53   55

21

18 Div

Carnoy

Light railway

89

90

Maricourt

30 Div

39 XX

XIII Corps

KEY

——— British front line, 7:30 a.m., 1 July	general line of British brigade attacks
▦▦▦ British objective and front line, night 1 July	line of French divisional attacks
⊓⊔⊓⊔ main German trench lines	
⋀⋀⋀ some German communication trenches	Kasino Point mine explosion
——— French front line, 7:30 a.m., 1 July	
▦▦▦ French objective and front line, night 1 July	● site of Capt. W. P. Nevill's (8th East Surrey) platoon's football-kicking advance

Montauban village in ruins after the attack on the opening day of the Battle of the Somme.

German prisoners began to come back, and we could see our leading lines topping the German support lines.

At 7:22 a.m. there was a hurricane bombardment by six Stokes mortar batteries positioned along the front on the right of this division. These mortars were located close to the enemy trench line at the end of Russian saps (shallow tunnels projecting forward from the British front-line trenches), the ends of which had been broken open during the night. The infantry's task had also been greatly facilitated by the support of large numbers of French heavy artillery pieces. The extreme right-hand leading battalion was the 17th King's, whose commanding officer, Lieutenant Colonel B. C. Fairfax, stepped over the parapet together with his French opposite number on the right, Commandant Le Petit, commanding the 3rd Battalion, 153rd Regiment. They were in the second wave and eventually led the advance arm in arm.

As the leading waves advanced across the 500 yards to the enemy line they were relieved to see that the medium mortars had done a good job of cutting the German wire. The defenders were not out of their bunkers and dugouts in time to man their positions before the British infantry arrived and so offered a mostly feeble resistance. Some 300 prisoners and four machine guns were captured by the following 'mopping-up' parties of the 2nd Bedfordshires. A successful tactic used by some more merciful bombers for a dugout whose occupants failed to surrender was to throw a large rock in one entrance and catch them as they rushed out at the other. The 89th Brigade reached its first objective, Dublin Trench, within an hour to find it crushed and unoc-cupied. Simultaneously, the French took Dublin Redoubt, where Lieutenant Colonel Fairfax and Commandant Le Petit embraced. On the left of the division the 21st Brigade had taken Glatz Redoubt, where a heavy shell had penetrated and destroyed a regimental headquarters.

The second phase of the attack involved the 90th Brigade advancing through the leading brigades and attacking Montauban. This started shortly after 8:30 a.m., with the 16th and 17th Manchesters in the lead. Both these battalions suffered heavily through a machine gun catching them in enfilade from a position in The Warren on their left flank. It was eventually silenced by a Lewis-gun crew from the 16th Manchesters. The attack on Montauban was screened by a heavy smokescreen – a German diary entry described visibility as only 2–3 yards in Montauban. The village was a total ruin, having received the attention of a French 240mm mortar battery for seven days during which a deep artillery headquarters dugout had been destroyed.

The cost: 3,011 casualties (828 killed).

18th Division

Precisely at 7:30 a.m. Captain W. P. Nevill of the 8th East Surreys in the 54th Brigade blew his whistle to start his inter-platoon football-kicking competition. He had given a football to each of his four platoons and offered a prize to the first one to kick its ball into a German trench.

About 1,400 yards to the left of Nevill's company, the firing of the Kasino Point mine was the scene of some drama, as the tunnelling officer's and the infantry commander's watches were seemingly not synchronized. The engineer officer was horri-fied to see the infantry clambering from their trenches at a time he considered too early, with the mine unexploded. With the leading attackers only about 200 yards from the mine, the officer had seconds to make a critical decision. He pressed the plunger. The huge explosion impressed Lance Corporal E. J. Fisher of the 10th Essex:

> I looked left to see if my men were keeping a straight line. I saw a sight I shall never forget. A giant fountain, rising from our line of men, about 100 yards from me. Still on the move I stared at this, not realizing what it was. It rose, a great column nearly as high as Nelson's Column, then slowly toppled over. Before I could think, I saw huge slabs of earth and chalk thudding down, some with flames attached, onto the troops as they advanced [they caused some casualties].

The enemy machine-gun post at Kasino Point was obliterated and the attacking waves moved steadily forward over the German front-line trench; however, the following waves were now caught in a defensive artillery barrage falling on the ground between the opposing lines. Despite considerable loss, the attack pressed on and entered The Warren and then Train Alley. Here the 7th Queen's captured ninety Germans from the 62nd and 109th Regiments. It was in these actions that the determination of the German machine-gunners was demonstrated. One was a grey-haired, elderly man found dead with a pile of empty cases as high as the gun beside him; another, a wounded Bavarian, had chained himself, or been chained to, his gun and was found by the 6th Royal Berkshires when they finally took The Loop, capturing sixty prisoners. During this action one of the battalion's company sergeant majors shot and killed a German sniper who had caused several casualties to the attackers. Pommiers Redoubt fell and bombers from the 10th Essex fought their way down the communication trench leading to the division's second objective – White Trench, which was reached by 3:30 p.m. Two hours later the division had consolidated along the line of White Trench and Montauban Alley. The 8th Norfolks and 6th Royal Berkshires established positions just north of these trenches on the ridge overlooking Caterpillar Wood.

A Captain A. E. Percival, commanding a company of the 7th Bedfords, was awarded the Military Cross for his actions that afternoon. Twenty-six years later, Lieutenant General Arthur Percival surrendered Singapore to the Japanese – the 18th Division was among the 80,000 troops taken into captivity.

The cost: 3,115 casualties (912 killed).

XV Corps

This Corps' forward trench line bent round the exceptionally strong German defences of the Fricourt salient with opposing trenches only 100 yards apart in places. It was commanded by a particularly hard-driving 'thruster' in the form of Lieutenant General Sir Henry Horne, who was to sack the commander of 17th Division (Major General Thomas Pilcher) on 11 July (only its 50th Brigade was involved on 1 July) for failing to be sufficiently ruthless in committing his battalions regardless of losses. Horne was promoted to command the First Army in October. The initial attacks were to be on either side of Fricourt, with the 7th Division on the right and the 21st on the left. Fricourt was to be attacked later by the 50th Brigade from the 17th Division attached to the 21st. Final objectives included the Quadrangle and White Trenches, between 2,000 and 3,000 yards from the start line. As with other divisions, the troops were ordered to walk steadily forward to occupy shattered and supposedly empty trenches.

The corps artillery orders included reference to a creeping barrage for the attack. On 14 June they stated, 'When lifting, 18-pds. should search back [away from the advancing infantry] by increasing their range, but howitzers and heavy guns must lift directly on to the next objective.'

7th Division

On the right the 91st Brigade came under heavy enfilade machine-gun and rifle fire from Mametz village ruins and Danzig Alley. Despite this, by 8:00 a.m. the 1st South Staffords were in Cemetery Trench, with a few individuals in the outskirts of the ruins of Mametz, and the 22nd Manchesters were nearing Danzig Alley. German resistance thus far had been patchy, with some machine-gun posts holding out tenaciously and inflicting heavy losses (one in Mametz was later found to be concealed in a house, constructed of concrete and with 4-inch-thick steel loopholes), but with many infantrymen surrendering as the advance progressed. Nevertheless, Mametz itself proved a tough nut to crack. Three attacks were needed, with considerable hand-to-hand fighting, before it was finally cleared. Each attack was preceded by an artillery bombardment that pounded and churned over the heaps of bricks and stone that was all that remained of the village. Private J. Kirkman of the 20th Manchesters later graphically described his experience in this fighting:

I went over the top at 2.30 p.m. in the second wave with our bombers. Just as I

was about to jump into the German trench, a Jerry made a lunge at me with his bayonet, but I stepped back a little and he just took a small piece out of my thigh. Instead of a rifle I had a knobkerrie, which the bombers used for trench fighting. I hit out at him and sank it deep into his forehead [it was probably studded with nails]. In the scuffle his helmet came off and I saw that he was a bald-headed old man. I have never forgotten that bald head and I don't suppose I ever will. Poor old devil!

With the fall of Pommiers Redoubt to the 18th Division of XIII Corps on the right, Horne ordered a greater effort to secure Danzig Alley and Fritz Trench. After another artillery bombardment, the attack made progress, at one stage killing the crew of a German field gun battery who had remained in position firing over open sight.

The 20th Brigade was intended to advance to form a defensive flank on the left, while the right-hand battalion, the 2nd Gordon Highlanders, was to secure the western half of Mametz – the ultimate aim being for the attacking battalions to link up along Orchard and Bunny Alleys. In the centre, the 9th Devons were instantly hit by a hail of machine-gun fire from several different locations. They were caught by long-range fire from Fricourt Wood, at short range from the enemy support trench and in enfilade by guns in the trenches south of Mametz. Despite losing all their officers, the Devons pressed grimly on and secured the enemy front trench.

At 3:00 p.m. the 7th Division made its final major effort of the day after yet another artillery bombardment. More bitter fighting saw Mametz secured and the division was able to reach the line of Orchard Alley–Bunny Alley–Fritz Trench by around 5:00 p.m. Though still a little short of their intended objective, the important stronghold of Mametz had been taken and, with the success of the XIII Corps, the British first-day objectives along a 3-mile front had been secured, including the villages of Montauban and Mametz.

The cost: 3,380 casualties (1,032 killed).

21st Division

This division had four brigades, including the 50th Brigade attached from the 17th Division. The plan was for the initial assault to be made by the 63rd and 64th Brigades, with the 62nd in reserve. The 50th was to remain in its trenches initially and to attack Fricourt later when progress had been made on the flanks of the village. However, one battalion of this brigade, the 10th West Yorkshire, was to attack in the

first phase to secure a defensive flank on the right of the 63rd Brigade towards Fricourt. This assault proved a disaster. The leading two companies took the German front trench with little loss and pressed on towards the northern end of Fricourt. However, the following two companies and battalion headquarters were caught in a storm of machine-gun fire from Fricourt and the area of the Tambour crater by gunners who had survived the bombardment in deep dugouts. As the British barrage had moved on, they were able to destroy the follow-up companies in their entirety, as well as the battalion's commanding officer, Lieutenant Colonel A. Dickson, its second-in-command, its adjutant and all its headquarters staff. The leading companies were then isolated in the northern outskirts of Fricourt and were overcome later in the morning – only Lieutenant Philip Howe and twenty men made their way back to British lines.

The 63rd and 64th Brigades had as their first objective Crucifix Trench, but on leaving their trenches the 63rd Brigade was hit immediately by six machine guns untouched by the bombardment. All the officers of the leading companies went down and only about forty men reached Lonely Trench (a sunken road). Behind them, the supporting companies and the 8th Somerset Light Infantry on the left managed only to reach the Germans' front-line trench. Despite further reinforcements from following battalions, machine-gun fire from Fricourt stalled the 63rd Brigade's attack at Lonely Trench. On the left, the 64th Brigade was caught in heavy machine-gun fire from the front and in enfilade from the higher ground south of La Boiselle. Nevertheless, the three battalions of Yorkshiremen and the one from Durham secured Lonely Trench and then sent parties forward to occupy part of Crucifix Trench.

In the afternoon little further progress could be made, and at 4:33 p.m. the divisional commander ordered both brigades to consolidate and hold the positions gained.

The cost: 4,256 casualties (1,182 killed).

50th Brigade

The intention of 'squeezing' out Fricourt village in the morning by advancing on its flanks had failed and it had been machine guns in the ruins that had inflicted horrific losses by firing in enfilade into the attacking battalions to the north and east. It had become the unenviable task of the 50th Brigade to take this troublesome village in the afternoon. There was nothing much left of the 10th West Yorkshires, so the task fell to the 7th East Yorkshires, 7th Green Howards (only three companies strong, as

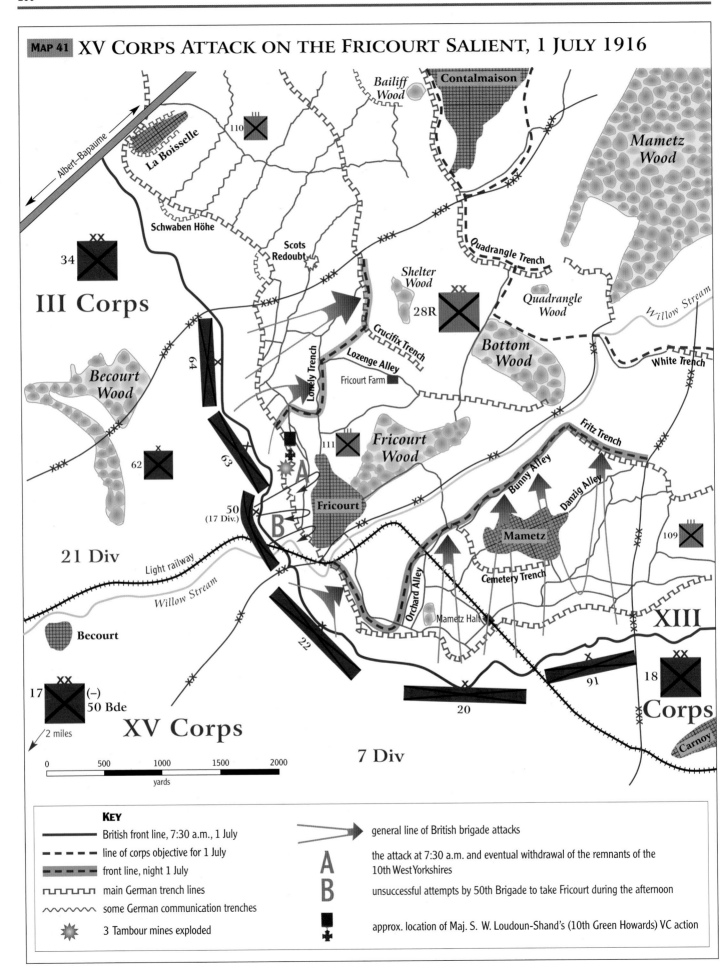

MAP 41 XV CORPS ATTACK ON THE FRICOURT SALIENT, 1 JULY 1916

KEY

— British front line, 7:30 a.m., 1 July

- - - line of corps objective for 1 July

front line, night 1 July

main German trench lines

some German communication trenches

3 Tambour mines exploded

general line of British brigade attacks

A the attack at 7:30 a.m. and eventual withdrawal of the remnants of the 10th West Yorkshires

B unsuccessful attempts by 50th Brigade to take Fricourt during the afternoon

approx. location of Maj. S. W. Loudoun-Shand's (10th Green Howards) VC action

an earlier mistake had sent the fourth company into an attack in which it had been almost destroyed) and 6th Dorsetshires, with the former two battalions in the lead. The whistles blew at 2:33 p.m. after an inadequate artillery bombardment. In the 7th Green Howards the rum ration had not been issued in the rush to get ready at short notice, prompting one soldier to complain, 'What about the rum issue, sir?' To which his officer replied that he was taking the jar with him to celebrate in the enemy position, although the odds on being able to do so were not high. As the East Yorkshires scrambled out of their trench, they were caught by the inevitable machine gun traversing along the parapet at close range. Men collapsed on the parapet, some tumbled back into the trench and none got further than 20 yards towards the enemy. Within two or three minutes over 120 were hit, and the survivors were ordered back into their trench – the attack had never got

British troops in the entrance to a German dugout in the Danzig Alley trench at Fricourt.

started. At the end of the day Fricourt remained at the tip of a much narrower German salient and the gallant and tenacious defenders were vulnerable to converging fire from three directions. Such vulnerability made their situation untenable and they withdrew the next night.

The cost: 1,155 (killed 557).

Notes for Map 41
British Order of Battle (infantry)
XV Corps
(Lt Gen. H. S. Horne)

7th Division
(Maj. Gen. H. E. Watts)
20th Brigade
  8th Devonshire
  9th Devonshire
  2nd Border
  2nd Gordons
22nd Brigade
  2nd Royal Warwickshire
  2nd Royal Irish
  1st Royal Welch Fusiliers
  20th Manchester (P)

91st Brigade
  2nd Queen's
  1st South
    Staffordshire
  21st Manchester (P)
  22nd Manchester (P)
Pioneers
  24th Manchester (P)

21st Division
(Maj. Gen. D. G. M. Campbell)
62nd Brigade
  12th Northumberland
    Fusiliers
  13th Northumberland
    Fusiliers
  1st Lincolnshire
  10th Green Howards
63rd Brigade
  8th Lincolnshire
  8th Somerset Light Infantry
  4th Middlesex
  10th York & Lancaster

64th Brigade
  1st East Yorkshire
  9th King's Own
    Yorkshire Light
    Infantry
  10th King's Own
    Yorkshire Light
    Infantry
  15th Durham Light
    Infantry
Pioneers
  14th Northumberland
    Fusiliers

17th (Northern) Division
(Maj. Gen T. D. Pilcher) –
Corps reserve
50th Brigade (attached to
  21st Division)
  10th West Yorkshire
  7th East Yorkshire
  7th Green Howards
  6th Dorsetshire

(P) indicates a Pals battalion.

XV Corps was deployed on a frontage of 5,000 yards facing the German Fricourt salient. Their defences of both Fricourt and Mametz were exceptionally strong, with these villages well fortified. The Germans had deployed six battalions of their 28th Reserve Division in the trenches and there were numerous machine-gun emplacements throughout the area. Some bunkers were two storeys deep and supplied with electric light.

XV Corps had the 7th Division on the right and the 21st Division on the left, divided by the Willow Stream. The 17th Division was in reserve but its 50th Brigade had been attached to the 21st Division for the attack. The plan envisaged a three-phase attack, in the first phase of which the 7th and 21st Divisions would clear the high ground on either side of the Willow Stream, including the village of Mametz. It was hoped that, with the 7th Division attacking on the right of Fricourt and the 21st on the left, the Germans in the village would be cut off, making the second phase, the taking of Fricourt by the 50th Brigade (17th Division), easier. The final phase was to secure the line Quadrangle Trench–Bottom Wood–White Trench by the end of the day and thus link up with III Corps on the left and XIII Corps on the right. The assault was to be preceded by an intense bombardment starting at 6:25 a.m. from some 200 field guns and howitzers and 86 heavy pieces, the latter including some French guns. Gas was to be

released in the centre of the corps front where there would be no initial assault. At 7:22 a.m. Stokes mortars would join the bombardment and at 7:27 a.m. a smokescreen would be released to protect the inner flanks of the two attacking divisions. At 7:28 a.m. the three mines (49,000 lb of explosive) under the Tambour salient would be fired. At 7:30 a.m. the infantry would go over the top.

On the right the 7th Division had to make three attacks on Mametz before it was secured, but it was not until around 7:00 p.m. that the line Bunny Alley–Fritz Trench had been taken – the division was still 750 yards short of its objective. On the left the 21st Division used the 10th West Yorkshires from the 50th Brigade to attack on the right of the 63rd Brigade to secure its flank from enfilade fire from Fricourt. Despite elements reaching the northern outskirts of Fricourt, the battalion was virtually wiped out. The other two brigades (63rd and 64th), after suffering very severely, managed to advance only to the line of Crucifix and Lonely Trenches by night – between 1,000 and 2,000 yards from their final objective. All attempts to take Fricourt by the 50th Brigade during the afternoon failed with heavy losses.

Casualties in the 7th Division amounted to 3,380 (1,032 killed), in the 21st Division to 4,256 (1,182 killed) and in the 50th Brigade to 1,155 (557 killed). The 10th West Yorkshires had the highest battalion casualty rate for 1 July – 710.

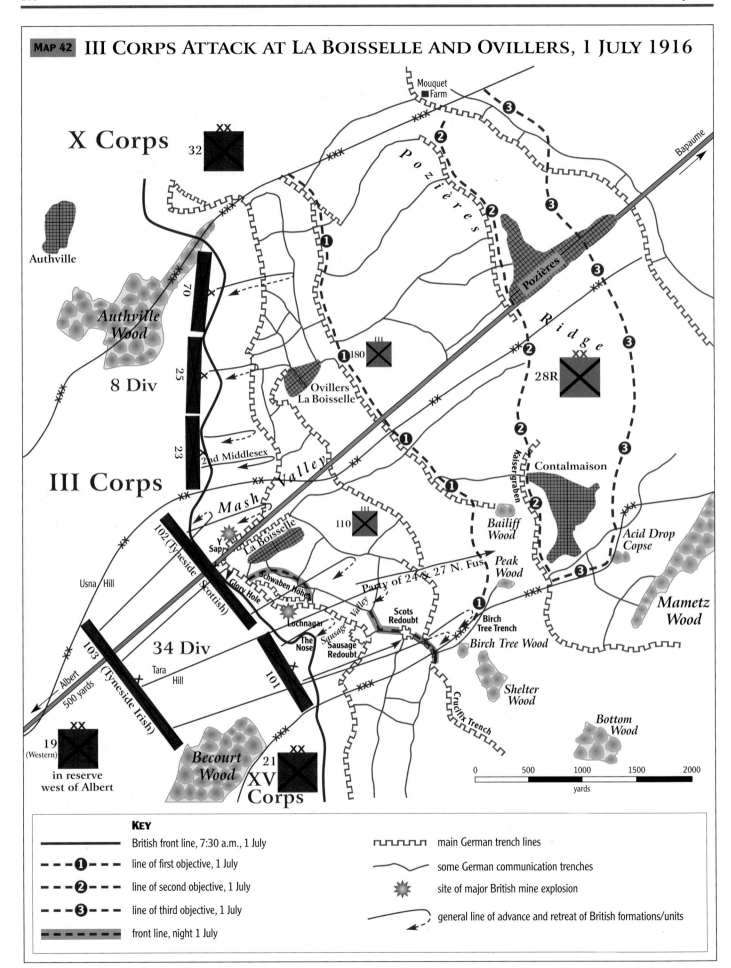

MAP 42 III CORPS ATTACK AT LA BOISSELLE AND OVILLERS, 1 JULY 1916

X Corps

32

Mouquet
Farm

Bapaume

P
o
z
i
è
r
e
s

Poziéres

R
i
d
g
e

Authville

Authville
Wood

8 Div

70

25

23

III Corps

2nd Middlesex

180

Ovillers
La Boisselle

28R

Kaisergraben

Contalmaison

Mash Valley

Bailiff
Wood

Acid Drop
Copse

110

Party of 24 & 27 N. Fus

Peak
Wood

Mametz
Wood

102 (Tyneside Scottish)

Usna Hill

Y
Sap
La Boisselle

Schwaben Höhe

Glory Hole

Lochnagar

The
Nose

Sausage Valley

Sausage
Redoubt

Scots
Redoubt

Birch
Tree Trench

Birch Tree Wood

Shelter
Wood

Bottom
Wood

103 (Tyneside Irish)

Albert
500 yards

34 Div

Tara
Hill

101

Crucifix Trench

0   500   1000   1500   2000

yards

19
(Western)

in reserve
west of Albert

Becourt
Wood

21

XV
Corps

KEY

———————— British front line, 7:30 a.m., 1 July	⌐⌐⌐⌐⌐ main German trench lines
– – –**❶**– – – line of first objective, 1 July	——— some German communication trenches
– – –**❷**– – – line of second objective, 1 July	✸ site of major British mine explosion
– – –**❸**– – – line of third objective, 1 July	general line of advance and retreat of British formations/units
front line, night 1 July	

III Corps

The battalions in the leading waves of this corps' attack had some 4,000 yards to their final objective, the key Pozières Ridge that dominated the British front lines. An objective that it was planned to take in one day was not captured until after a bloody and prolonged struggle lasting from 23 July until 3 September. Those units in the 103rd Brigade had 6,000 yards to advance, all in view of the enemy. The whole attack got off to a poor start due to the artillery barrage which, having crushed many enemy trenches and turned the villages into unrecognizable heaps of debris, had however failed to destroy the deep dugouts in which many Germans sheltered. A German in the 180th Reserve Regiment, in the Ovillers sector facing the 8th Division, best described the situation as wave after wave of British infantry advanced in broad daylight. His account of what happened that morning could fit virtually the entire corps front – indeed most of the front of the Fourth Army – and is quoted in the *British Official History of the War 1916*, Volume I:

The intense bombardment was realized by all to be the prelude to an infantry assault sooner or later. The men in the dug-outs therefore waited ready, belts full of hand grenades around them, gripping their rifles and listening for the bombardment to lift from the front defence zone onto the rear defences . . . Looking towards the British trenches through the long trench periscopes held up out of the dug-out entrances there could be seen a mass of steel helmets above the parapet, showing that the storm-troops were ready for the assault. At 7.30 a.m. the hurricane of shells ceased as suddenly as it had begun. Our men at once clambered up the steep shafts leading from the dug-outs to daylight and ran singly or in groups to the nearest shell craters. The machine guns were pulled out of the dug-outs and hurriedly placed in position, their crews dragging the heavy ammunition boxes up the steps and out to the guns. A rough firing line was thus rapidly established. As soon as the men were in position, a series of extended lines of infantry were seen moving forward from the British trenches. The first line appeared to continue without end to right and left. It was quickly followed by a second line, then a third and fourth. They came on at a steady easy pace as if expecting to find nothing alive in our front trenches . . . The front line, preceded by a thin line of skirmishers and bombers, was now half way across No Man's Land. 'Get ready!' was passed along our front from crater to crater, and heads appeared over the crater edge as final positions were taken up for the best view, and machine guns mounted firmly in place. A few moments later . . . the rattle of machine-gun and rifle fire broke out along the whole line of shell holes. Some fired kneeling so as to get a

---

Notes for Map 42
British Order of Battle (infantry)
III Corps
(Lt Gen. Sir W. P. Pulteney)

8th Division		**34th Division**	
(Maj. Gen. H. Hudson)		(Maj. Gen. E. C. Ingouville-Williams)	
23rd Brigade	**70th Brigade**	**101st Brigade**	**103rd Brigade (Tyneside Irish)**
2nd Devonshire	11th Sherwood Foresters	15th Royal Scots	24th Northumberland Fusiliers
2nd West Yorkshire	8th King's Own Yorkshire Light Infantry	16th Royal Scots	25th Northumberland Fusiliers
2nd Scottish Rifles	8th York & Lancaster	10th Lincolnshire	26th Northumberland Fusiliers
2nd Middlesex	9th York & Lancaster	11th Suffolk (Cambridgeshire)	27th Northumberland Fusiliers
25th Brigade	Pioneers	**102nd Brigade (Tyneside Scottish)**	Pioneers
2nd Lincolnshire	22nd Durham Light Infantry	20th Northumberland Fusiliers	18th Northumberland Fusiliers
2nd Royal Berkshire		21st Northumberland Fusiliers	
1st Royal Irish Rifles		22nd Northumberland Fusiliers	
2nd Rifle Brigade		23rd Northumberland Fusiliers	

This corps had responsibility for attacking along a 5,000-yard frontage and was deployed on the forward slope of a low ridge, of which Tara and Usna Hills formed part, providing the gunner observers with an excellent view over the German lines, which were easily identified by the grey chalk parapets. The distance between opposing lines varied between 50 and 800 yards. The divisional artillery was dug in en masse in the open fields on either side of the Amiens road just west of Albert and behind the British ridge. The 34th Division on the right faced the fortified village of La Boisselle and the strongpoints of the Schwaben Höhe, as well as the Sausage (or Heligoland) and Scots Redoubts. On the left the 8th Division faced the equally well-fortified village of Ovillers. The 19th (Western) Division was held back west of Albert in reserve, although their guns participated in the preparatory bombardment. Two minutes prior to zero hour, two mines were exploded under German defences at Lochnagar (60,000 lb) and Y Sap (40,000 lb). The German defenders belonged to the 28th Reserve Division.

The corps plan was ambitious and envisaged a total advance of some 4,000 yards from the British front line to the Pozières Ridge. The three phases to achieve this objective, which included the taking of most of Pozières, are shown on the map as objectives 1, 2 and 3.

At 7:30 a.m. the advance began along the entire corps front, except at the Glory Hole, as it was intended to attack either side of La Boisselle initially. On the right, all three brigades of the 34th Division attacked or, with the 103rd Brigade on the Tara and Usna Hills, began their advance.

Once again it was primarily enemy machine guns that were the problem, particularly those firing from the rubble of La Boisselle and the strongpoints or redoubts. On the right, the 101st Brigade eventually consolidated their hold on the Scots Redoubt, while the 102nd took the Schwaben Höhe. However, although small mixed parties from various battalions penetrated deeper (one was last seen disappearing towards Contalmaison), little progress was made towards even the first objective line and Sausage Redoubt remained in enemy hands. The advance of the 103rd Brigade down the open forward slope of the ridge resulted in crippling losses, as the waves of Tyneside Irish made near perfect targets for machine-gun fire and the survivors of these battalions were unable to advance beyond the leading brigades (see page 476).

On the left, the 23rd Brigade of the 8th Division was caught between heavy machine-gun fire from both La Boisselle and Ovillers and managed to hold only some 300 yards of the German front-line trench for two hours before being driven out by counter-attacks. The 25th Brigade was hit by the same machine guns as the 23rd and, although they secured a hold in the enemy trench line and attempted to advance further, they were ultimately driven back to their own line. The 70th Brigade got as far as the second German trench, but heavy losses and lack of support forced them to withdraw. The entire division ended the day in its own front line.

Casualties in the 34th Division amounted to 6,380 (2,480 killed) and in the 8th Division to 5,121 (1,927 killed).

Schwaben Höhe (redoubt)

Bloater Trench

Bloater Trench

10 Lincolns

Bloater Trench

11 Suffolks

Sausage

'Sausage Valley' – the scene of the 11th Suffolks' attack on 1 July 1916. The panorama is taken from the eastern edge of the Lochnagar Crater, looking across Sausage Valley from north-east to south-east. It shows the approximate line of Bloater Trench and Sausage Redoubt (Heligoland), which was a formidable strongpoint that resisted all attempts to take it on 1 July. The 34th Division attack on the right was undertaken by the 101st Brigade with the 10th Lincolns (Grimsby Chums) and the 15th Royal Scots leading, supported by the 11th Suffolks (Cambridge) and 16th Royal Scots respectively. The attack failed, with all battalions suffering huge losses, particularly from flanking fire from the Schwaben Höhe on the left and Sausage Redoubt on the right. Fifteen officers and 512 men of the 11th Suffolks fell that day.

better target over the broken ground, whilst others, in the excitement of the moment, stood up regardless of their own safety, to fire into the crowd of men in front of them. Red rockets were sped up into the blue sky as a signal to the artillery, and immediately afterwards a mass of shell from the German batteries in the rear tore through the air and burst among the advancing lines. The advance rapidly crumpled under this hail of shells and bullets. All along the line men could be seen throwing up their arms and collapsing . . . The extended lines, though badly shaken and with many gaps, now came on all the faster. Instead of a leisurely walk they covered the ground in short rushes at the double. Within a few minutes the leading troops had advanced to within a stone's throw of our front trench, and whilst some of us continued to fire at point-blank range, others threw hand-grenades among them. The British bombers answered back, whilst the infantry rushed forward with fixed bayonets . . . The shouting of orders and the shrill cheers as the British charged forward could be heard above the violent and intense fusillade of machine guns and rifles and the bursting of bombs and above the deep thunderings of the artillery and shell explosions. With all this were mingled the moans and groans of the wounded, the cries for help and the last screams of death.

Despite the utmost gallantry, the 8th Division was beaten back in the manner described, having gained nothing but huge losses by the end of the day. The fate of the 2nd Middlesex was typical of the battalions leading this attack. It was formed up on the extreme right of the division and had some 750 yards to advance up Mash Valley to the first German trench (manned by the 180th

British troops try to snatch some sleep in a trench at Ovillers on the Somme. One man, the sentry, is kneeling on the firestep, while several others are trying to get some rest at the bottom of the trench.

Sausage Redoubt (Heligoland)

10 Lincolns

15 Royal Scots

16 Royal Scots

11 Suffolks

Valley

KEY

intended advance

actual advance

Regiment) – the longest approach of any battalion that morning. The well-respected commanding officer, Lieutenant Colonel E. T. F. Sandys, had become extremely agitated and worried that his battalion would be attacking against uncut wire and enemy posts that would survive the bombardment. He had spent hours gazing at the enemy lines through field glasses and, unable to sleep, had wandered aimlessly around his assembly area prior to moving forward to the front trenches. His pessimism was not shared by most, who considered few, if any, Germans would live through the bombardment; all ranks had been briefed to expect the attack to be a walkover. Unfortunately, as described above, Sandys was proved correct and his battalion was cut to pieces, losing 540 all ranks in the attempt to reach and briefly secure a part of the enemy front trench. Sandys followed his men up Mash Valley and became one of the wounded evacuated to the rear and later to England to recover. Although he recovered physically, mentally he had been destroyed by seeing his beloved battalion decimated, for which he blamed himself. He wished he had been killed with his men. In a letter to a fellow officer he wrote, 'I have come to London to take my life. I have never had a moment's peace since July 1st.' In the Cavendish Hotel on 6 September 1916 he shot himself through the head with his revolver, dying in hospital a week later.

On the right, the 34th Division had more to show at the end of the day than their comrades to the north. However, the capture of Schwaben Höhe and the Scots Redoubt cost the division the highest casualty list of any attacking division on 1 July in either the Fourth or Third Armies – 6,380 all ranks, 628 more than the next highest division, the 4th. III Corps had lost 11,501 men, virtually the equivalent of an entire division.

X Corps

Six members of the corps winning the Victoria Cross on this day, four in the 36th (Ulster) Division, underlines the intensity of the fighting on this front. The two leading divisions suffered over 9,000 casualties. And, although by nightfall the attackers had managed only two small toeholds in the German line, some Ulstermen had advanced over a mile from their own lines during the morning, taking the Schwaben Redoubt in the process.

The corps plan was ambitious and envisaged the capture of the German second position, the Mouquet Farm–Grandcourt line, on the first day – an advance of 2,500 yards through four German defence lines and the taking of six redoubts and Thiepval village, all by 10:10 a.m. When these objectives had been secured, the 49th (West Riding) Division was to form part of the 'army of pursuit' and push through the hoped-for gap. One heavy gun for every 57 yards of frontage

and one field gun for every 28 yards had been amassed for the preliminary bombardment and covering barrages, along with a 9-inch heavy mortar lent by the French. The support would take the form of six timed lifts for the heavy guns and ten for the 18-pounders searching from trench to trench, with the 4.5-inch howitzers concentrating on specific strongpoints. The weakness proved to be the lack of flexibility in this elaborate programme – it could not be changed quickly to meet unforeseen delays to the infantry's progress, nor switched to troublesome pockets of resistance that were holding up an attack. The artillery support moved forward faster than the infantry could keep up and, although it was eventually brought back, this was a lengthy process involving communication up the chain of command.

The 36th (Ulster) Division was composed entirely of Protestant Ulstermen, mostly members of the Ulster Volunteer Force (UVF) – a number of men wearing the orange ribbon of the Orange Order and encouraged by the fact that 1 July was the anniversary of the Battle of the Boyne. The 109th Brigade tactic of leaving their trenches fifteen minutes before the bombardment ended and creeping forward to within 100 yards of the first German trench paid huge dividends, as when the guns lifted the infantry were able to rush the trench through well-cut wire before many of the enemy had time to leave their bunkers

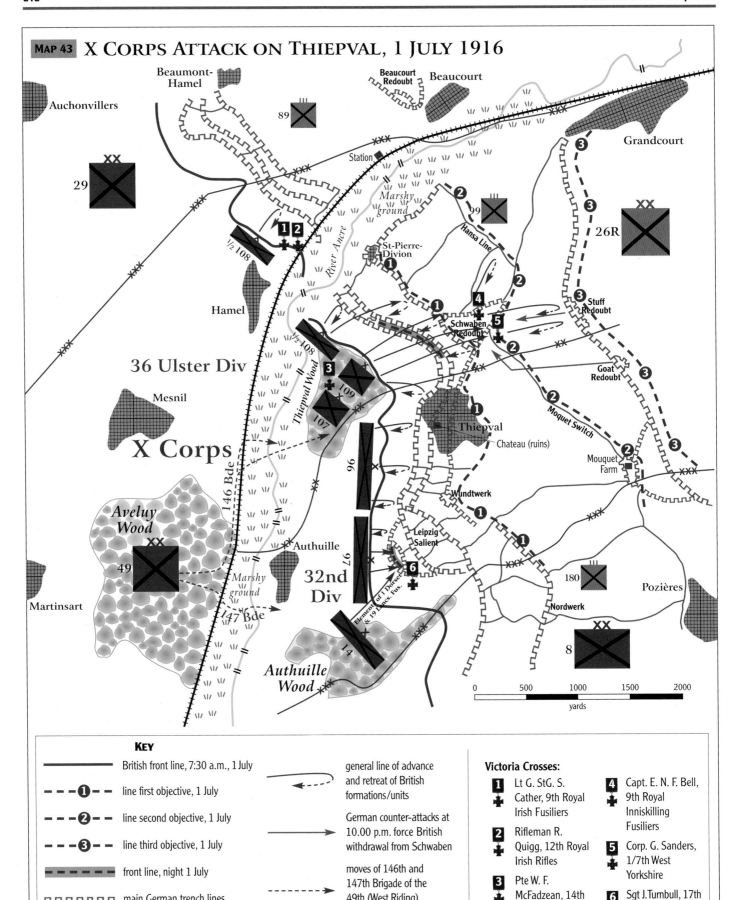

MAP 43 X CORPS ATTACK ON THIEPVAL, 1 JULY 1916

Auchonvillers

Beaumont-Hamel

Beaucourt Redoubt   Beaucourt

89

Grandcourt

Station

29

Marshy ground

99

26R

½ 108

St-Pierre-Divion

Hansa Line

Stuff Redoubt

½ 108

36 Ulster Div

Schwaben Redoubt

Goat Redoubt

Hamel

River Ancre

Mesnil

109

107

Thiepval

Chateau (ruins)

Moquet Switch

X Corps

96

Mouquet Farm

146 Bde

Aveluy Wood

Authuille

Wundtwerk

Marshy ground

Leipzig Salient

180

Pozières

49

32nd Div

97

Martinsart

147 Bde

Element of 1 Dorset & 19 Lncs. Fus.

Nordwerk

14

8

Authuille Wood

0   500   1000   1500   2000
yards

KEY

———— British front line, 7:30 a.m., 1 July

— ❶ — line first objective, 1 July

— ❷ — line second objective, 1 July

— ❸ — line third objective, 1 July

▬▬▬ front line, night 1 July

⊓⊔⊓⊔ main German trench lines

〜〜 some German communication trenches

general line of advance and retreat of British formations/units

German counter-attacks at 10.00 p.m. force British withdrawal from Schwaben

moves of 146th and 147th Brigade of the 49th (West Riding) Division preparatory to supporting 32nd Division

Victoria Crosses:

❶ Lt G. StG. S. Cather, 9th Royal Irish Fusiliers

❷ Rifleman R. Quigg, 12th Royal Irish Rifles

❸ Pte W. F. McFadzean, 14th Royal Irish Rifles

❹ Capt. E. N. F. Bell, 9th Royal Inniskilling Fusiliers

❺ Corp. G. Sanders, 1/7th West Yorkshire

❻ Sgt J. Turnbull, 17th Highland Light Infantry

Notes for Map 43
British Order of Battle (infantry)
X Corps (Lt Gen. Sir T. L. N. Morland)

32nd Division
(Maj. Gen. W. H. Rycroft)
14th Brigade
  19th Lancashire Fusiliers
  1st Dorestshire
  2nd Manchester
  15th Highland Light Infantry
96th Brigade
  16th Northumberland Fusiliers
  2nd Royal Inniskilling Fusiliers
  15th Lancashire Fusiliers
  16th Lancashire Fusiliers
97th Brigade
  11th Border
  2nd King's Own Yorkshire Light Infantry
  16th Highland Light Infantry
  17th Highland Light Infantry
Pioneers
  17th Northumberland Fusiliers

36th (Ulster) Division
(Maj. Gen. O. S. W. Nugent)
107th Brigade
  8th Royal Irish Rifles
  9th Royal Irish Rifles
  10th Royal Irish Rifles
  15th Royal Irish Rifles
108th Brigade
  11th Royal Irish Rifles
  12th Royal Irish Rifles
  13th Royal Irish Rifles
  9th Royal Irish Fusiliers
109th Brigade
  9th Royal Inniskilling Fusiliers
  10th Royal Inniskilling Fusiliers
  11th Royal Inniskilling Fusiliers
  14th Royal Irish Rifles
Pioneers
  16th Royal Irish Rifles

49th (West Riding) Division
(Maj. Gen. E. M. Perceval)
146th Brigade
  1/5th West Yorkshire
  1/6th West Yorkshire
  1/7th West Yorkshire
  1/8th West Yorkshire
147th Brigade
  1/4th Duke of Wellington's
  1/5th Duke of Wellington's
  1/6th Duke of Wellington's
  1/7th Duke of Wellington's
148th Brigade
  1/4th King's Own Yorkshire
Light Infantry
  1/5th King's Own Yorkshire
Light Infantry
  1/4th York & Lancaster
  1/5th York & Lancaster
Pioneers
  1/3rd Monmouthshire

X Corps front was some 4,500 yards long, with the northernmost part cut off from the southern section by the River Ancre and the marshy ground on either side. The corps had two divisions up front, the 32nd on the right and the 36th (Ulster) on the left, with the 49th (West Riding) in reserve. A number of bridges, some makeshift, over the river were in place and in assembling for the attack the Ulstermen were able to obtain some concealment in Thiepval Wood and the 14th Brigade of the 32nd Division in Authuille Wood, while the 49th assembled west of the river in Aveluy Wood.

The German position was one of considerable strength, manned by eight battalions of the 26th Reserve Division. Their front line consisted of three trench lines in which were positioned several strongpoints, in addition to the pile of rubble on a spur that was once the village of Thiepval. Many houses had cellars that could withstand everything except a direct hit from a heavy shell; these converted easily into bunkers in which machine-gun crews and riflemen could shelter. From the south, the first redoubt was the Nordwerk, outside the corps area but able to bring fire to bear on an attack on the Leipzig salient. This salient was a large and imposing defensive work with the forward trenches only 200 yards from the British front line. Next in the north was the Wundtwerk Redoubt, just south of Thiepval in the German third trench line. Immediately north of the village was the Schwaben Redoubt, a huge triangular strongpoint on a forward slope. Finally, the tiny hamlet of St-Pierre-Divion on the right of the German line had been converted into a strongpoint able to fire on targets north and south of the river. Behind these forward defences was the German second line, running north from Mouquet ('Mucky') Farm (a redoubt) to the Ancre, with Goat and Stuff Redoubts in the centre.

The corps plan envisaged three objective lines as shown on the map, the third being the enemy's second line. All attacks had to be frontal and they were supported by the usual, pre-planned timed artillery lifts, which were difficult or impossible to change once the battle was under way.

32nd Division
At 7:23 a.m. the 17th Highland Light Infantry (HLI) of 97th Brigade crept forward to within 40 yards of the enemy trenches and, when the barrage lifted at 7:30 a.m., they rushed the Leipzig Redoubt and, with the Germans slow to leave their

bunkers, the redoubt was taken. Supports following an hour later were caught in heavy machine-gun fire from Nordwerk and only a few got to the redoubt, the rest having to crawl back to their own lines. The 96th Brigade assault on Thiepval began with a football booted ahead of the leading wave, but suffered severely as it attempted to cross no-man's-land. Further attempts, with support from 14th Brigade, failed to make progress and at the end of the day the pile of ruins that had been Thiepval remained in German hands and only a toehold in the Leipzig Redoubt remained in the division's possession.

36th (Ulster) Division
This division began the day with remarkable success. The 109th Brigade advanced to the sound of bugles across the 500 yards of no-man's-land and, finding the German wire well cut, pushed through to take the front and support trenches with few losses. The attack was continued and, despite being hit by accurate machine-gun fire from Thiepval, by 8:30 a.m. the Schwaben Redoubt had been secured and the Mouquet Switch reached. The right-hand battalion of 108th Brigade (11th Royal Irish Rifles), under cover of a smokescreen, had reached part of the Hansa Line, but the remainder of the brigade on either side of the river failed to make progress after being hit by intense machine-gun fire from St-Pierre-Divion. The 107th Brigade followed through in support and, although suffering heavily, got within 100 yards of Stuff Redoubt when they were caught in their own barrage as well as machine-gun fire from Grandcourt that halted progress. The division held out for the rest of the day, but by night, running short of ammunition and bombs, and faced with a series of strong enemy counter-attacks, they were forced to fall back. By 10:30 p.m. only about 750 yards of the German front trench line was still occupied by the division.

Efforts were made to bring the 49th Division across the river and the 146th Brigade moved into Thiepval Wood and 147th Brigade to south of Authuille. However, only two companies of the 1/7th West Yorkshires were committed late in the evening near the Schwaben Redoubt and, despite a party of 30 under Corporal Sanders putting up a desperate defence, nothing was achieved and they were forced to withdraw.

Casualties in the 32nd Division amounted to 3,949 (1,283 killed), in the 36th Division to 5,104 (1,856 killed) and in the 49th Division to 590 (131 killed).

and man their weapons. The result was that the front and support trenches were taken with few losses. More men pushed forward and the successful struggle for the Schwaben Redoubt began. However, in the 108th Brigade on the extreme left only the right-hand battalion (11th Royal Irish Rifles) was equally successful; the other leading battalions on either side of the river made little progress against the machine guns in St-Pierre-Divion. When the 107th's four West Belfast battalions moved forward to support the leading brigades and attack the German second line at around 9:00 a.m., they were caught in a welter of machine-gun fire from Thiepval, as well as in the German defensive artillery barrage. Nevertheless, with encouragement from Major George Gaffikin, a company commander, who waved aloft his orange sash and yelled the Boyne battlecry of 'Come on boys! No surrender!', the battalions pushed on and by around 10:00 a.m. came within 100 yards of the Grandcourt line and Stuff Redoubt. Here they became victims of their own artillery barrage, which began firing on that German line, and of machine guns in Grandcourt, and they were also confronted by much uncut wire. A German in Stuff Redoubt recalled:

I was down in a dug-out in the *Feste Staffen* when someone shouted down to me in an amazed voice 'The Tommies are here.' I rushed up and there, just outside the barbed wire, were ten or twenty English soldiers with flat steel helmets. We had no rifle, no revolver, no grenades, no ammunition, nothing at all; we were purely artillery observers. We would have had to surrender but, then, the English artillery began to fire at our trench; but a great deal of the shells were too short and hit the English infantrymen and they began to fall back. If the English could have got through, they would only have met clerks, cooks, orderlies and such like. For a distance of several hundred metres to right

and left from us there were no German soldiers. It was a decisive moment.

A few of the 107th Brigade did manage to get into the Grandcourt trench line, but most were caught exposed in no-man's-land under intense fire. These men were forced to pull back as best they could to the Schwaben Redoubt, by then in Irish hands. German counter-attacks began in the afternoon and, although initially repulsed, the defenders of the redoubt were running out of bombs and ammunition, were severely depleted in numbers and under fire from three directions – frontally and from Thiepval and Beaucourt and St-Pierre-Divion, as there had been no progress on either of their flanks. By 10:00 p.m., with further heavier counter-attacks from several directions, the reluctant survivors were compelled to pull back and relinquish almost all the ground gained at such a high price.

Meanwhile, the 32nd Division on the right had attacked the Thiepval spur and the Leipzig Salient. The leading battalion of the 97th Brigade opposite the Leipzig Salient (17th Highland Light Infantry) had crept forward to within 30 yards of the enemy position while the guns were still firing on it, and at 7:30 a.m. rushed forward to overrun the first trench almost without loss. However, in attempting to advance further into the salient they were caught by flanking fire from the redoubt known as the *Wundtwerk* (Wonder Work) and halted. At 8:30 a.m. the reserve battalion (11th Border), moving forward in support, was also caught in this fire and those unhurt joined those already in the forward tip of the salient (called the Leipzig Redoubt). On the left, the 96th Brigade met with disaster early on. The two leading battalions were exposed to a hail of machine-gun fire from the ruins of Thiepval and the chateau, and were pinned down in no-man's-land, losing men every minute. The British barrage had moved on and some German defenders were

An Officer's Ultimate Sanction

Lieutenant Colonel (later Brigadier General) F. P. Crozier, a battalion commander of the 9th Royal Irish Rifles (107th Brigade) on 1 July 1916, described attempts to halt the unauthorized retreat of several groups of demoralized and exhausted soldiers:

At that moment a strong rabble of tired, hungry and thirsty stragglers approach me from the east. I go out to meet them. 'Where are you going?' I ask. One says one thing, one another. They are marched to a water reserve, given a drink and hunted back to the fight. Another more formidable party cuts across to the south. They mean business. They are damned if they are going to stay, it's all up. A young sprinting subaltern heads them off. They push by him. He draws his revolver and threatens them. They take no notice. He fires. Down drops a British soldier at his feet. The effect is instantaneous. They turn back to the assistance of their comrades in distress.

seen to be so bold as to stand up or kneel to get a better view of their targets.

At 8:45 a.m. the 14th Brigade, with orders to take the Mouquet Farm objective, began its advance in the belief that all was going to plan. Once again, the leading battalion (1st Dorsetshire) was exposed to the hurricane of machine-gun fire from the Wundtwerk and only about sixty survivors of the leading two companies were able to reach the Leipzig Redoubt. A similar fate awaited the 19th Lancashire Fusiliers when they tried to come up in support. The British in the Leipzig Salient were unable to make further progress during the afternoon. By nightfall, the ground remaining in British hands had shrunk to the two small areas shown on Map 43.

The 36th (Ulster) Division

In September 1914 the Ulster Division was formed from the Ulster Volunteer Force (UVF) which raised thirteen battalions for the three Irish regiments based in Ulster – the Royal Irish Rifles, Royal Inniskilling Fusiliers and Royal Irish Fusiliers. The UVF was a Protestant organization with over 80,000 members, formed by Sir Edward Carson to oppose the passing of the Home Rule Bill and because of this there was some delay in the British government granting authority to form an Ulster Division.

The UVF was already a semi-military, armed organization and in August 1914 was in a high state of readiness due to the home rule debate earlier in the year. It was thus able to convert quickly into infantry battalions in an army division. However, it was not until early October 1915 that the division moved to France, where it spent the winter 1915/16 in training before taking over a section of

the front in February. Its first battle was on 1 July 1916 and involved the storming and capture of the Schwaben Redoubt, although failure of attacking units on either flank forced a retreat later in the day. A Captain W. Spender, a staff officer at Divisional Headquarters, watched the attack and was quoted as saying, 'I am not an Ulsterman but yesterday, the 1st July, as I followed their amazing attack, I felt that I would rather be an Ulsterman than anything else in the world.'

In November 1921 the Ulster Memorial Tower was unveiled on the site of the Schwaben Redoubt. It is a replica of Helen's Tower at Clandeboye, County Down, where the men of the newly formed division drilled and trained at the beginning of the war. World War I cost the 36th (Ulster) Division 32,186 killed, wounded or missing. Nine members of the division were awarded the Victoria Cross.

VIII Corps

This corps suffered almost 14,600 casualties and one brigade (the 92nd, 31st Division) was not even involved in the attack, while the Germans give their casualty figure as just over 1,200 in the three regiments defending this sector. This means that the Germans inflicted twelve casualties for every one they received. For this terrible price the British infantry had secured a tiny part of the Quadrilateral, which they were compelled to vacate the next day. The troops that held out so tenaciously in this area were almost entirely a mixed bag of Lancashire and Irish Fusiliers and Seaforth Highlanders under Lieutenant Colonel J. O. Hopkinson of the Seaforths. These men fought to retain their position all afternoon but were slowly pushed back, and by the small hours of 2 July only a company of the 1st Royal Irish Fusiliers remained in the German front line. They withdrew at 11:30 a.m. next day, bringing all their wounded and three prisoners with them.

At 7:20 a.m. the 40,000 lb of ammonal in the Hawthorn mine had gone up. The German 119th Regiment account described it:

During the intense bombardment there was a terrific explosion which for the moment completely drowned the thunder of the artillery. A great cloud of smoke rose up from the trenches of No. 9 Company, followed by a tremendous shower of stones, which seemed to fall from the sky all over our position. More than three sections of No. 10 Company were blown into the air, and the neighbouring dug-outs were broken in and blocked [in some cases Germans entombed inside were rescued after the British attack was defeated]. The ground all round was white with the debris of chalk as if it had been snowing, and a gigantic crater, over fifty yards in diameter and some sixty feet deep [actually 130 feet in diameter and 58 feet deep] gaped like an open wound in the side of the hill. This explosion was a signal for the infantry attack, and everyone got ready and stood on the lower steps of the dug-outs, rifles in hand, waiting for the bombardment to lift. In a few minutes the shelling ceased, and we rushed up the steps and out into the crater positions. Ahead of us wave after wave of British troops were crawling out of their trenches, and coming forward towards us at a walk, their bayonets glistening in the sun.

These Germans had taken advantage of what appeared to be a serious error in the timing of the British supporting heavy artillery fire – it lifted from the German front-line trenches at 7:20 a.m. (the same time as the Hawthorn mine was blown), but the main infantry advance did not begin for another ten min-utes. This gave the Germans sheltering in their dugouts ample, indeed far too much, time to scramble out to set up their machine guns and man the shell holes. This problem was compounded by the field artillery (18-pounders) lifting at zero hour as well. The mine exploding ten minutes before the infantry advance also warned the Germans that an attack was about to be launched and prompted a flurry of signal flares that brought down the defensive artillery barrages – some hitting British front, support and reserve trenches as the attackers began to advance. It was largely these errors, plus the fact that they advanced in broad daylight, that accounted for thousands of British lives as they attempted to cross no-man's-land all along the corps sector in the face of a storm of steel. This fire also caught the supporting battalions, such as the 1st KOSB and 1st Border Regiment, as they came up to the front trench and crossed the duckboard bridges over it – there was no escape for the leading waves or for those following in support.

As noted above, the only temporary success was the taking of the Quadrilateral in which the German engineers had mistakenly blown themselves up with their own mine. Sergeant A. H. Cook, 1st Somerset Light Infantry, found himself a platoon commander five minutes after starting the advance. He had this to say of his experiences that day at the Quadrilateral:

[The Quadrilateral was] about the size of Piccadilly Circus. Communication trenches were everywhere, and just in front was a communication trench up which some British troops were moving . . . I noticed some Germans with fixed bayonets, and then realised that our fellows were prisoners, so I started picking off the escorts; this was very successful and quite good fun . . . our men could have escaped, but I suppose they were fed up with it all, and only too glad to be out of the fighting

. . . Colonel Hopkins[on] of the Seaforths was doing excellent work, he seemed to be the only officer here, and was seen walking around the Quadrilateral [encouraging] all. He saved a dangerous situation; someone gave the order to retire, there was an immediate panic, and some four or five hundred retired, in spite of great efforts to stem the rush by the colonel and us sergeants. The colonel then ordered a bugler [Drummer Ritchie, VC] to sound the 'charge' this had the immediate effect and saved the situation . . .

There were many casualties amongst those that retired . . . In places where enfilade fire caught them they were three or four deep . . . it is extraordinary how some men die. I slipped into a shell hole and on getting out saw a man sitting up apparently doing his puttee up. I entered into conversation and was getting annoyed at no reply; he was dead.

Sergeant Cook was among a small group that hung on to part of the Quadrilateral until late at night. Part of the fight involved a deadly bombing encounter:

now commenced another grenade contest, and the only bombs we had were the German stick bombs. We could see each other as the bombs were thrown, and we were actually throwing back what they threw before they burst. The time fuse seemed much longer than our Mills bomb of four seconds . . . we were relieved about 11 p.m. and ordered back. We needed no second telling . . . How I escaped I do not know. I tripped over dead bodies, fell head-long into shell holes full of dead, my clothes were torn to ribbons by barbed wire. I lost all sense of direction and eventually fell sprawling, dead beat to the world.

Thus ended 1 July for a survivor. Hunter-Weston's VIII Corps had been devastated.

The Hawthorn Redoubt mine explodes under the German strongpoint, 1 July 1916.

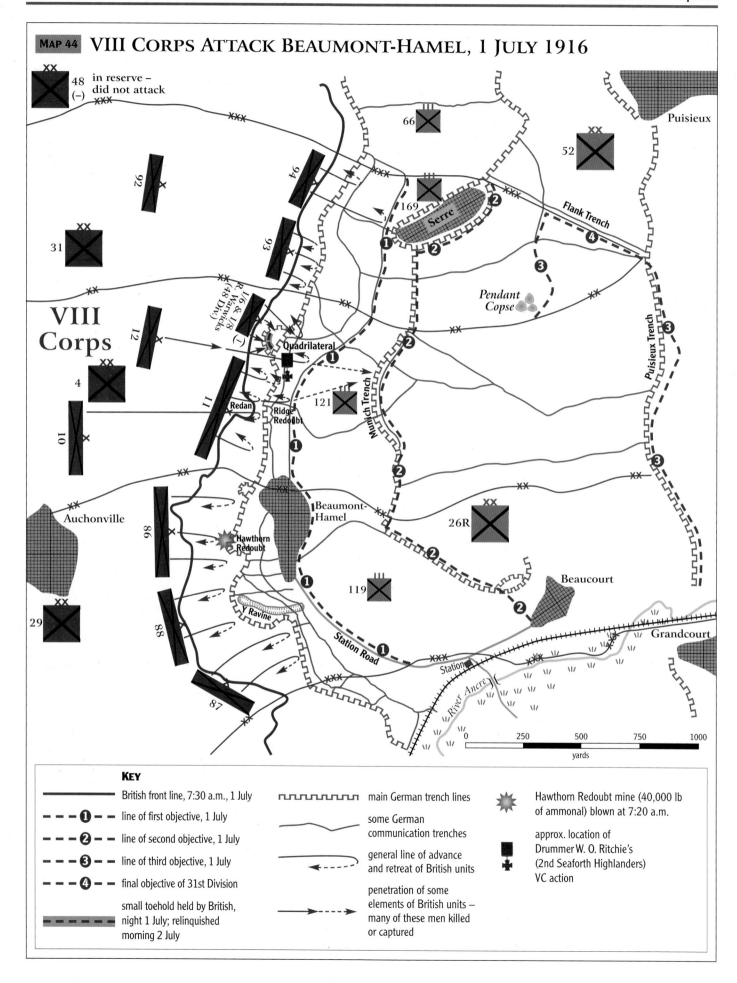

MAP 44 VIII CORPS ATTACK BEAUMONT-HAMEL, 1 JULY 1916

48 (–) in reserve – did not attack

66

52

Puisieux

92

94

169

Serre

Flank Trench

31

93

VIII Corps

R.1/6 & 1/8 Warwicks (48 Div.)

Pendant Copse

Puisieux Trench

12

Quadrilateral

4

121

Munich Trench

Redan

Ridge Redoubt

11

10

Auchonville

86

Hawthorn Redoubt

Beaumont-Hamel

26R

Beaucourt

119

29

88

Y Ravine

Station Road

Grandcourt

87

Station

River Ancre

0   250   500   750   1000

yards

KEY

——— British front line, 7:30 a.m., 1 July

– – –**①**– – – line of first objective, 1 July

– – –**②**– – – line of second objective, 1 July

– – –**③**– – – line of third objective, 1 July

– – –**④**– – – final objective of 31st Division

▬▬▬ small toehold held by British, night 1 July; relinquished morning 2 July

⊓⊔⊓⊔⊓⊔ main German trench lines

∿ some German communication trenches

general line of advance and retreat of British units

penetration of some elements of British units – many of these men killed or captured

Hawthorn Redoubt mine (40,000 lb of ammonal) blown at 7:20 a.m.

approx. location of Drummer W. O. Ritchie's (2nd Seaforth Highlanders) VC action

German positions and Y Ravine   'Lone' or 'Danger' tree

The Newfoundland Regiment at Beaumont-Hamel. Taken from the Caribou Memorial in the Newfoundland Memorial Park, this photograph shows the British front-line trenches over which the Newfoundlanders attacked on 1 July 1916. Their objective was the German line and part of Y Ravine some 300 yards down the slope. Due to the 1st Essex, the other assaulting battalion, being delayed, the Newfoundlanders advanced in isolation. No sooner had they left cover than their ranks were swept by fire from machine guns, rifles and artillery. The majority of men were hit before getting much beyond the British wire, although a few reached the German trenches before being killed or captured. The 'Lone' or 'Danger' Tree shown indicates the maximum distance most of the attackers reached before being hit. This battalion suffered the second highest casualty rate of any on 1 July.

Notes for Map 44

British Order of Battle (infantry)

VIII Corps (Lt Gen. Sir A. G. Hunter-Weston)

4th Division
(Maj. Gen. W. Lambton)
10th Brigade
 1st Royal Warwickshire
 2nd. Seaforth Highlanders
 1st Royal Irish Fusiliers
 2nd Royal Dublin Fusiliers
11th Brigade
 1st Somerset Light Infantry
 1st East Lancashire
 1st Hampshire
 1st Rifle Brigade
12th Brigade
 1st King's Own
 2nd Lancashire Fusiliers
 2nd Duke of Wellington's
 2nd Essex
Pioneers
 21st West Yorkshire

29th Division
(Maj. Gen. H. de B. de Lisle)
86th Brigade
 2nd Royal Fusiliers
 1st Lancashire Fusiliers
 16th Middlesex
 1st Royal Dublin Fusiliers
87th Brigade
 2nd South Wales Borderers
 1st King's Own Scottish Borderers
 1st Royal Inniskilling Fusiliers
 1st Border
88th Brigade
 4th Worcestershire
 2nd Hampshire
 1st Essex
 Newfoundland Regiment
Pioneers
 1/2nd Monmouthshire

31st Division
(Maj. Gen. R. Wanless O'Gowan)
92nd Brigade
 10th East Yorkshire
 11th East Yorkshire
 12th East Yorkshire
 13th East Yorkshire
93rd Brigade
 15th West Yorkshire
 16th West Yorkshire
 18th West Yorkshire
 18th Durham Light Infantry
94th Brigade
 11th East Lancashire
 12th York & Lancaster
 13th York & Lancaster
 14th York & Lancaster
Pioneers
 12th King's Own Yorkshire Light Infantry

48th (South Midland) Division
(Maj. Gen. R. Fanshawe)
Only the 1/6th and 1/8th Royal Warwickshire attached to the 4th Division took part in the day's operations.

VIII Corps front was extended over some 2,750 yards, with the distance between opposing lines varying from 350 yards in the south to 100 in the extreme north. No-man's-land was open with little cover, while beyond the German wire was a formidable enemy position with three main trench systems, the second (Munich Trench) being around 500 yards behind the first, with the third (Puisieux Trench) another 1,000 yards further to the rear. It was this Puisieux Trench that formed the final corps objective for the day. As with other parts of the Somme front on 1 July, the Germans had constructed several strongpoints, the most prominent being, from the south, Y Ravine, Hawthorn and Ridge Redoubts and the Quadrilateral. However, the strongest were the exceptionally well-fortified villages (ruins) of Serre and Beaumont-Hamel. The fortress of Beaumont-Hamel dominated the valley parallel to the front that the corps must cross in order to advance. This village was to defy all attempts to take it, not just on 1 July, but for over four months afterwards, and then it fell only when the attackers employed tanks and gas.

The corps had three divisions earmarked for the attack, with two additional battalions from the 48th Division, which was held in reserve, attached to the 4th Division. On the right the 29th Division faced Y Ravine, Hawthorn Redoubt and Beaumont-Hamel; in the centre the 4th initially attacked the Ridge Redoubt and the Quadrilateral; on the left the 31st had to take Serre and then swing left to take Flank Trench to secure the corps' left flank, as there was to be no advance by the 48th Division. The 4th and 29th Divisions were to advance the 2,000 yards to their final objectives in three and a half hours. The corps had the support of one heavy gun for every 44 yards of front, and one field gun per 20 yards, firing to a timed programme that consisted of five lifts – the last one being off the final objective three and a half hours after zero hour. At 7:20 a.m. the

Hawthorn Redoubt mine was exploded and two platoons with machine guns and Stokes mortars occupied the crater.

The 29th Division faced considerable uncut enemy wire and furious machine-gun fire, particularly from Y Ravine and Beaumont-Hamel. All three brigades were halted after losing hundreds of men – the Newfoundland Regiment suffered 710 casualties. By 9:30 a.m. the divisional attack had failed.

The 4th Division also sustained disastrous losses, as, although the wire was well cut and the front trenches smashed, the Germans in the deep bunkers were untouched and quickly manned their machine guns. They brought a storm of enfilade fire on the advancing infantry from the Ridge Redoubt and long-range overhead fire from the Beaucourt spur. At the same time, German defensive artillery fire was brought down first on no-man's-land and then on the British front-line trenches. Some attackers managed to enter the Quadrilateral (the Germans called it *Heidenkopf* after a local commander), as the occupants had mistakenly blown themselves up by prematurely exploding a mine. At 9:30 a.m. the 10th Brigade was supposed to advance through the leading battalions, but due to the crippling losses sustained by the forward units the order was given to halt its advance. This did not reach the leading battalions and their attack went ahead – some even reaching Munich Trench.

The 31st Division advanced at 7:30 a.m. into a hurricane of artillery and machine-gun fire from a seemingly undamaged enemy. Progress was minimal, although a few men were reported to have disappeared into Serre. The attack had failed and the 92nd Brigade was not sent to reinforce failure. By night the corps had nothing to show for its gallantry but horrendous losses.

Casualties in the 29th Division amounted to 5,240 (1,642 killed), in the 4th Division to 5,752 (1,883 killed) and in the 31st Division to 3,600 (1,349 killed).

VII Corps (Third Army)

This was another corps that, by the end of the day, had lost what small territory it had taken at a dreadful price. In the 46th Division the 1/7th Sherwood Foresters lost 73 per cent, while in the 56th the London Scottish lost 71 per cent. Some 6,769 men had fallen in an attack that was merely a diversion. The evidence that this attack had any significant effect on the overall result of the Fourth Army's offensive is negligible. The attack on either side of Gommecourt was defeated by the same combination of frontal attacks in bright sunlight against strong positions where deep dugouts protected enemy machine-gun crews and allowed many of them to surface before the attackers reached them. Where the British succeeded despite the dugouts remaining untouched was when the preparatory bombardment blocked the entrances and either delayed or prevented a quick exit by the occupants. It was all about the race for the parapet – whoever won that race invariably won the ensuing encounter.

Part of the report of the German 170th Regiment reads:

> The general effect of the British bombardment was good, so that the front trenches were levelled and the wire shot away, but the losses of men, in consequence of there being plenty of deep dug-outs, were small. The sector opposite the 56th Division was held by the 170th Regiment, with four companies and the left company of the 55th Reserve Regiment in the front line. Here the smoke completely hid the start of the attack, and, owing to the damage done to the entrances of the dug-outs, the men could not get out quickly enough, and were overrun by the Londoners.

Gommecourt chateau in ruins. It was briefly held by the 56th London Division on 1 July.

On the 46th Division's front, the 1/5th battalion of the Sherwood Foresters was attacking between Little Z and Gommecourt Wood. The following extracts from *The War History of the Fifth Battalion Sherwood Foresters Notts & Derby Regiment* by Captain L. W. de Grave illustrate the experiences of many infantrymen that day:

> Companies were organized in four waves, each of two platoons, with two platoons in immediate support. D Company, Major Naylor, was on the right; A Company, Captain H. Claye, in the centre; C Company, Major Wragg, on the left; and B Company, Captain Kerr, as a carrying party . . .
>
> Companies moved up to the front about midnight, disposing themselves in Retrench [a waiting trench]. Shortly afterwards Col. Wilson, with headquarters, including police, runners, pioneers and scouts, moved over the open to Battle Hd. Qrs. The trenches were impassable – mud, water and traffic [1 July was bright but the previous week had seen torrential rain]. The party was continually tripping over wire and dropping on machine guns and trench mortar positions, moving in single file, and not making much more than half-a-mile an hour. This head-quarter party was fully loaded with consolidating gear, latrine pails, notice boards, direction arrows, charcoal, picks and shovels . . . Mention must also be made of a basket of pigeons, which in the end did serve a useful purpose, but not their legitimate one . . .
>
> At 3.30 a.m. it was found that all the Companies were in position. Hot coffee, with a tot of rum added, was brought up at 4.45 in petrol tins, eight per company, and was very acceptable, everyone without exception being wet through and perished with cold . . .
>
> Our barrage commenced at 6.25 . . . Enemy machineguns were clipping the top of the parapet, or rather where it had been an hour previously . . .
>
> The smoke screen was very dense and seemed to cling to the earth and our sodden clothing. No sooner was the parapet crossed than everyone was lost to view, and it was only by bumping into anyone that companionship was recognized.
>
> The enemy set up a triple barrage of artillery, trench mortars and machine guns as soon as our attack was launched. The first three waves attacked with great dash, but casualties during the advance were very heavy . . .
>
> The fourth wave was delayed by their heavy loads and the muddy state of the

A British View of the Somme

The quotation below is from *The Battle of the Somme* by the writer and poet John Masefield, published in 1919. Masefield, who was born in 1878 and was thus exempt by age from military service, none the less volunteered for the Western Front as a medical orderly.

> The field of Gommecourt is heaped with the bodies of Londoners; the London Scottish lie at the Sixteen Poplars; the Yorkshires are outside Serre; the Warwickshires lie in Serre itself; all the great hill of the Hawthorne Ridge is littered with Middlesex; the Irish are at Hamel, the Kents on the Schwaben, and the Wilts and Dorsets on the Leipzig. Men of all the towns and counties of England, Wales and Scotland lie scattered among the slopes from Ovillers to Maricourt. English dead pave the road to La Boisselle, the Welsh and Scotch are in Mametz. In gullies and sheltered places, where wounded could be brought during the fighting, there are little towns of dead in all these places: 'Jolly young Fusiliers, too good to die.'

Masefield survived the war to become Poet Laureate from 1930 until his death, aged ninety-two, in 1967. His ashes were placed in Poets' Corner in Westminster Abbey.

trenches, which caused them to be 15 minutes late in moving over the top. The carrying company was still more delayed, but made a splendid effort to get through although carrying loads almost too much to attempt on a good track, they advanced at 8.10 a.m., when the smoke screen had to a great extent dissolved. They were met consequently with a withering machine gun fire from several directions. This completely checked any advance, with the result that the 6th and 7th Battalions were unable to move . . .

Sergt. Bowler, Bombing Sergt., was one of many killed immediately before advancing from the jump off trench, and if it were possible to ascertain the casualties before the advance, it would probably be found that companies were reduced to practically platoon strength before they started . . .

The attack by the 137th Brigade was held up and a retirement made [followed by the remainder of the assaulting units] . . .

Thus ended a disastrous day . . . Our strength in the morning had been 28 officers and 706 others. On the roll being called at the end of the engagement we were three officers and 237 others.

British wounded at an advanced dressing station behind the Somme front.

The Reckoning

Of the fifteen British infantry divisions that attacked at 7:30 on the morning of 1 July, only two still held their day's objectives by midnight. These were the two on the southern (right) flank – the18th (Eastern) and 30th Divisions. Of the remainder, several had had partial initial success but could not hold their gains. This was the bloodiest day of the war for the British infantry, the great majority of whom were Territorial and New Army (Kitchener's volunteers). Many people think of the Battle of the Somme as just this dreadful day, whereas the struggle continued until mid-November. It quickly developed into a slogging match of attrition, with General Rawlinson's 'bite-and-hold' tactics gradually forcing back the Germans, who had been ordered to hold their ground and immediately to recover losses with counter-attacks. The overall casualties for nearly five months' fighting are seemingly impossible to calculate with real certainty. However, the *British Official History*, published in 1938, used German sources to estimate their losses as about 660,000, with the Anglo-French total being somewhat less than 630,000. As the French have been estimated to have suffered some 200,000 losses on the Somme, this gives British casualties of about 430,000.

Two points require emphasis. First, that overall the German losses grew rapidly after the first day, until by November they had suffered more than the Allies. Second, that the offensive lasted for another 141 days after 1 July, giving the average British daily loss of (in round numbers) 2,650 compared with nearly 60,000 on the first day – figures that explain why this day will always be remembered as such a catastrophe for the British infantry.

Why were losses so high? A combination of factors, some avoidable, some not, was responsible:

• There was no surprise – the Germans knew the attack was coming.

• The attack was frontal in broad daylight and the smokescreen was not fully effective.

• The preparatory bombardment failed to destroy most of the deep, well-constructed enemy bunkers and dugouts.

• The artillery support was inflexible, tied to a fixed, timed programme that took far too long to change. This led to the supporting gunfire moving on too quickly and leaving the infantry behind. The creeping barrage had yet to be properly refined with the rate of progress of the infantry.

• The British tactic of advancing elements of the attacking units forward into no-man's-land to get as close as possible to the barrage before zero hour and before it lifted was proved effective. Where it was used, these attackers usually won the race for the parapet. However, these troops were few and the supporting units were caught in a hurricane of defensive machine-gun and artillery fire – much of the latter from the flanks.

• German positions were strong and deep, coupled with some very determined defenders who invariably counter-attacked vigorously.

• There was a general (there were exceptions) British sense beforehand that it was going to be 'a walk in the park', that nothing much would survive the preparatory pounding.

There is no doubt that the Somme taught the British in particular many lessons. The coming months and years saw a steady improvement in tactics and inter-arm co-operation that ultimately produced the series of victories in 1918 that concluded the war.

An Infantryman's Ordeal

The survival for fourteen days by a seriously wounded soldier in no-man's-land was surely unique. This was the experience of Private A. Matthews of the 1/4th City of London Regiment in July 1916. He later described what happened when, on 1 July, after reaching the second German trench, he and another soldier were detailed to escort some German prisoners to the rear:

We had hardly got 50 yards away when I was hit in the thigh by a bullet and collapsed in a heap. It was obviously impossible for my comrade to have seen what had occurred; therefore he went on and I was left to my fate. Near by was an officer with a few men in an old disused trench, and I shouted to him and he immediately came and dragged me into this trench, bound up my wound to the best of his ability, and gave me a drink of water as my own water-bottle had emptied owing to a bullet passing through it . . . I was left alone. I found it utterly impossible to move, even a few inches as my wound was very serious, being a compound fracture of the thigh.

A company runner was the next man I saw, later in the day, and he very generously left me his water-bottle . . . Shells were bursting all round me, and it was only the shelter of the trench I was lying in which saved me from being blown to atoms, but it had the disadvantage of hiding me from anybody passing by . . . I tried once to crawl, but it was futile, I might as well have been chained to the ground for all the movement I could make . . . Night came on . . . I shouted at intervals, but all to no purpose . . . in my

haversack was my iron ration, consisting of five hard biscuits and a tin of bully beef . . . I ate and drank sparingly . . . Still I shouted at intervals, but the third day passed and nobody came . . . and I had come to the end of my food . . . it was on the fourth night that I fancied I could hear footsteps, so I shouted again and was rewarded by seeing the forms of men coming towards me . . . they could not help as they were wounded . . . They had been feeding on the iron rations they found on the dead men lying about, and they got me a stock before leaving . . .

The following morning I woke to find that a shell had burst above me, blown in a part of the trench, and partly buried me. I managed to clear the worst of the earth away, but found to my dismay that the biscuits were buried and a piece of the shell had penetrated my water-can . . . For two days I was without any means of sustenance, then it rained heavily and I caught some of it in my steel helmet, and when that had gone I drank from the filthy pools of water I was able to reach in the trench . . . The time dragged on . . . occasionally I would shout . . . I was becoming by this time very weak, and this went on for about ten days . . .

I began to feel I was dying . . . I had lost all count of time, when in the darkness I was awakened by the shuffle of feet, and I managed to call out . . . it proved to be an officer . . . with a party of NCOs of the London Scottish . . . I was nearly delirious with joy at having been rescued . . . For two weeks I remained in hospital in France and my wound took exactly twelve months to heal.

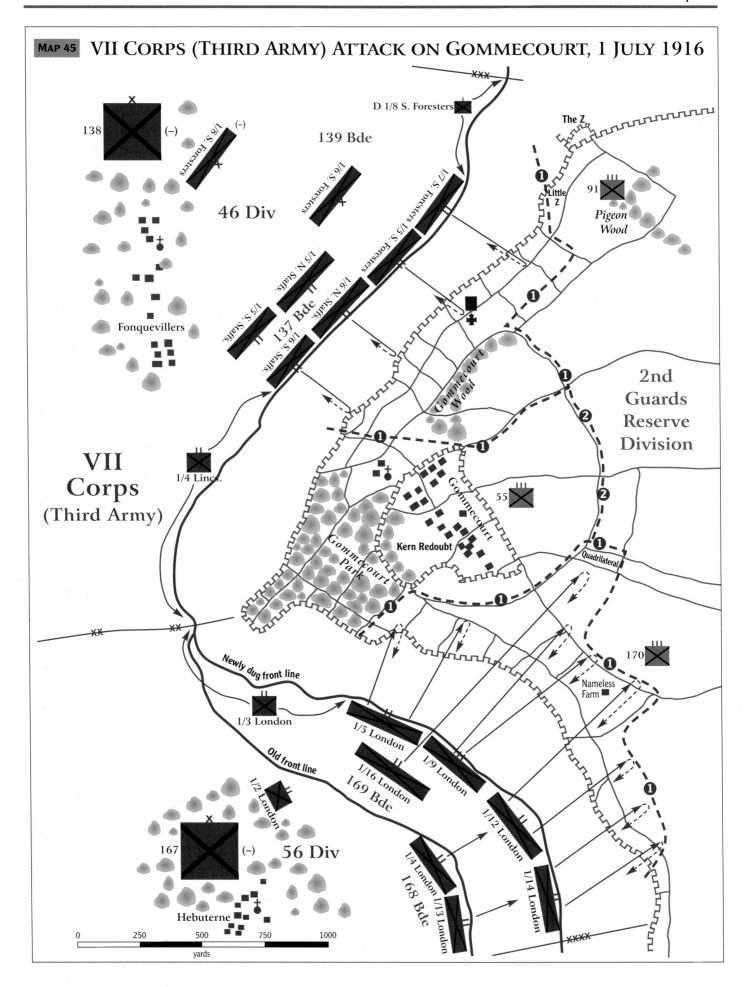

MAP 45 **VII CORPS (THIRD ARMY) ATTACK ON GOMMECOURT, 1 JULY 1916**

138 (−)

D 1/8 S. Foresters

139 Bde

1/8 S. Foresters

The Z

91

Pigeon Wood

Little Z

46 Div

1/5 S. Foresters

1/7 S. Foresters 1/5 S. Foresters

1/5 N. Staffs.

1/6 N. Staffs.

137 Bde

1/5 S. Staffs.

Fonquevillers

1/6 S. Staffs.

2nd
Guards
Reserve
Division

VII
Corps
(Third Army)

1/4 Lincs.

Gommecourt Wood

Gommecourt

55

Gommecourt
Park

Kern Redoubt

Quadrilateral

Newly dug front line

1/3 London

170

Nameless
Farm

Old front line

1/5 London

1/9 London

1/16 London

169 Bde

1/12 London

1/2 London

167 (−)

56 Div

1/4 London 1/13 London

1/14 London

168 Bde

Hebuterne

0   250   500   750   1000

yards

Notes for Map 45
British Order of Battle (infantry)
VII Corps (Third Army)
(Lt Gen. Sir T. d'O. Snow)

46th (North Midland) Division
(Maj. Gen. Hon. E. J. Montagu-Stuart-Wortley)

137th Brigade	**139th Brigade**
1/5th South Staffordshire	1/5th Sherwood Foresters
1/6th South Staffordshire	1/6th Sherwood Foresters
1/5th North Staffordshire	1/7th Sherwood Foresters
1/6th North Staffordshire	1/8th Sherwood Foresters

138th Brigade	**Pioneers**
1/4th Lincolnshire	1/1st Monmouthshire
1/5th Lincolnshire	
1/4th Leicestershire	
1/5th Leicestershire	

56th (London) Division
(Maj. Gen. C. P. A. Hull

167th Brigade	**169th Brigade**
1/1st London	1/2nd London
1/3rd London	1/5th London (London Rifle Brigade)
1/7th Middlesex	1/9th London (Queen Victoria's Rifles)
1/8th Middlesex	1/16th London (Queen's Westminster
	Rifles)

168th Brigade	**Pioneers**
1/4th London	1/5th Cheshire
1/12th London (Rangers)	
1/13th London (Kensington)	
1/14th London (London Scottish)	

The British plan was that an attack either side of Gommecourt would 'assist in the operations of the Fourth Army by diverting against itself the fire of artillery and infantry which might otherwise be directed against the left flank of the main attack near Serre.' It was to be an isolated affair, as the gap between VII Corps and VIII Corps on the right was some 2 miles. The German defences in the Gommecourt salient were immensely strong and the village itself resembled a fortress. The corps plan involved a two-prong assault on either side of the village in the first phase, and a link-up behind it in the second. Both divisions were Territorials; on the right was the 56th (London) Division attacking with two brigades and on the left the 46th (North Midland) Division also attacking with two brigades forward. The gap between, directly opposite Gommecourt, was occupied by the 1/4th Lincolns from the reserve brigade (138th Brigade) and the 1/3rd London from the 167th Brigade. The 37th Division formed the corps reserve.

The Londoners had the benefit of a smokescreen laid down at 7:20 a.m. This enabled the leading companies to start their 400–500-yard advance by moving out five minutes before the supporting barrage lifted and forming up on the white tape well out into no-man's-land. The full advance started at 7:30 a.m. and, despite heavy defensive artillery fire, the first two German trenches were overrun with comparatively small loss, as the enemy wire was mostly well cut. The third trench line proved a tougher proposition, as the defenders manned several machine guns and there were large numbers of enemy riflemen manning the parapets. Nevertheless, by bombing their way up communication trenches, the third line was eventually taken, although Nameless Farm was never captured. The failure of the 46th Division to make any headway meant that by the afternoon the Germans were able to concentrate on driving back the Londoners. Due to the intense enemy barrage and machine-gun fire from the Park, the leading battalions were cut off from reinforcements and a resupply of bombs and ammunition. Desperate signals were made for bombs, but all attempts to support the troops in the third German line failed, with heavy loss. By 4:00 p.m. the number of wounded coming back had reached some-

thing of a flood, and by nightfall the first and second lines had been vacated and the remnants of the division were back where they started.

The 46th Division's attack was a disaster. Many men in the 137th Brigade became disorientated in the dense smokescreen, so the advance was not uniform and the Germans were able to man their positions when the attackers were only halfway across no-man's-land. An intense artillery barrage and enfilade machine-gun fire from The Z caught the follow-up waves, causing heavy casualties, confusion and loss of control. Without the support of the follow-up troops, the leading elements were soon forced back. The brigade attack had failed. The 139th Brigade did somewhat better. The first three waves reached the German front trench, although at considerable cost, and some even managed to reach the second line. In the afternoon various plans were made to renew the attack, but the start was postponed several times due to lack of smoke bombs. Only a few were eventually forthcoming, but by this time confusion and indecision were rife so no coordinated attack was mounted and survivors of the leading assault battalions (1/5th and 1/7th Sherwood Foresters) withdrew during darkness.

Casualties in the 46th Division amounted to 2,455 (853 killed) and in the 56th Division to 4,314 (1,353 killed). German losses are given as 1,241 – a ratio of 1:5.4 defenders to attackers.

Entrances to two German dugouts in their support line at Gommecourt. Note they are on either side of a traverse with timber supports to the entrances. The trench sides have been revetted with brushwood and the roofs of the dugout covered with a substantial thickness of earth.

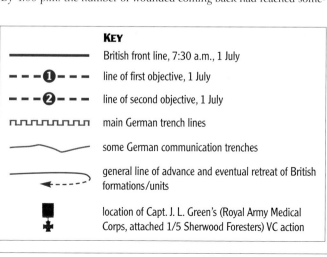

KEY

—————— British front line, 7:30 a.m., 1 July

– – –❶– – – line of first objective, 1 July

– – –❷– – – line of second objective, 1 July

⊓⊔⊓⊔⊓⊔⊓⊔ main German trench lines

∿ some German communication trenches

←- - - - general line of advance and eventual retreat of British formations/units

▮✠ location of Capt. J. L. Green's (Royal Army Medical Corps, attached 1/5 Sherwood Foresters) VC action

The desolation of the guns: Chateau Wood, Ypres, October 1917.
A duckboard track leads across the mud and the water-filled shell holes.

Section Five

Artillery

Then shook the hills with thunder riven,
Then rushed the steed to battle driven,
And louder than the bolts of Heaven
Far flash'd the red artillery.

Thomas Campbell, 'Hohenlinden', *Poems*, 1903

At 3:45 a.m. the great bombardment commenced in full power along the whole front from Warneton to Bixschoote. I went out at 3:55 a.m. to watch it from the hill near here and human eyes never saw a more terrible yet grand sight. The guns were flashing in thousands and one could see the big bursts of shrapnel. Flashes of every kind of explosion were seen and were of different colours. High in the air I could see the Germans' frantic signals – for artillery assistance – clusters of red rockets. They were going up in an absolute frantic manner one after another. The noise was frightful. My word – what a bombardment! It was the very greatest massed artillery shoot of this war.

This was how Sapper David Low described the British opening bombardment on the first day of the Third Battle of Ypres, 31 July 1917. Now a German view:

There was an absolute downpour of earth and shell splinters . . . Three men were plastered on the walls of the trench or lying in fragments on the ground . . . There was a terrific explosion and a hissing column of flame and earth rose from the trench . . . a dug-out and four men in it had ceased to exist . . .

By the evening the parapets had disappeared . . . Forty-one dead, all blown to shreds. All through the night the soil of Flanders was lacerated by most furious shellfire. In the morning we reported fifty-nine dead, all unrecognizable . . .

About midday the ground heaved and rocked. I staggered out of my shelter and worked my way along the ruins of the trench while shell splinters hummed around me. Where the company

commander's dug-out had been twelve steps deep and reinforced with baulks of timber was now a huge smoking crater. There was nothing to be seen in it but wreckage and a little blood-soaked earth. . . . We laid the remains of our eighty-four dead in the huge crater but not for a moment did the shells leave them alone.

Sapper Low called this bombardment the 'greatest massed artillery shoot of this war' and few Germans at the receiving end would have disagreed. Lieutenant Georg Blücher, an infantry officer, is quoted above describing what happened to even a deep bunker when suffering a direct hit from a heavy artillery shell in that bombardment. And in case the reader has the impression that artillery detachments had a relatively easy and safe existence compared to the infantry, the following description is taken from the history of the 8th Division (*The Eighth Division 1914–1918*), and concerns the 5th Battery, XLV Artillery Brigade (18-pounders), during the Battle of the Aisne in May 1918. The battery had to remain in action continuously while under heavy German counter-battery fire and the detachments eventually resorted to being infantrymen before being virtually wiped out when the German assault closed in.

The battery was carrying out its counter-preparation work when the deluge from the enemy's guns broke over it. Gas masks were instantly adjusted [invariably gas shells were mixed with high explosive (HE)] and about ten minutes later the rocket sentry reported S.O.S. rockets on the front [the infantry were signalling for supporting fire]. The call was immediately responded to by our gunners, Capt. J. H. Massey

controlling the fire of the battery, while Lieut. C. E. Large and 2nd Lieut. C. A. Button commanded their sections. To continue to serve the guns indefinitely during such a terrific bombardment was a physical impossibility for any one man, and Capt. Massey, realizing this, organized a system of reliefs, two gunners and one NCO manning each gun. The remainder of the personnel took cover until their turns came round to take their places at the guns.

After the customary period of fire on the S.O.S. lines, guns were once more laid on 'counter-preparation' lines and a steady rate of fire was continued during what seemed an interminable night . . .

The Guns Salute the New Year, 1916

Philip Gibbs, in his book *From Bapaume to Passchendaele, 1917*, describes how a British gun battery welcomed in the New Year of 1916:

An artillery officer up in the Ypres salient waited for the tick of midnight by his wrist-watch . . . and then shouted the word 'Fire!' . . . One gun spoke, and then for a few seconds there was silence. Over in the German line the flares went up and down, and it was very quiet in the enemy trenches, where, perhaps, the sentries wondered at that solitary gun. Then the artillery officer gave the word of command again. This time the battery fired nine rounds. There was silence again, followed by another solitary shot, and then by six rounds. So did the artillery in the Ypres salient salute the birth of the New Year . . .

By about 5 a.m. No. 4 gun had been put out of action . . .

The strain on all concerned was terrific, but at last at about 6.45 a.m. the enemy's barrage lifted clear of the position. Instead, however, of the expected respite, large numbers of German infantry and gunners came into view less than 200 yards from the battery position. A few rounds were fired at point-blank range, but it was then reported that Germans were coming up in rear. There was nothing left but to resort to rifles and the Lewis guns. Capt. Massey, realizing the situation a little earlier, had called for volunteers and pushed off with 4 gunners and a Lewis gun to a small eminence to the eastward in an endeavour to protect the flank . . . Lieut. Large, although wounded in the foot, took the other Lewis gun, 2nd Lieut. Button, after having destroyed all maps, papers and records, was last seen moving off with a rifle to assist Capt. Massey. The remainder of the battery fought to the last with their rifles till overwhelmed by sheer weight of numbers.

Only three unarmed gunners, and one with a rifle, survived and this account was compiled from their statements. All three battery officers were reported killed in action along with the two forward observation officers (Second Lieutenant C. Counsell and Second Lieutenant H. Reakes) and their telephonists. This battery, along with the 2nd Devonshires, shared the honour of being cited in the French Fifth Army orders and awarded the *Croix de Guerre*.

Gunner Gilbert Frankau encapsulated the impersonal horror of the artillery in his poem 'The Voice of the Guns':

> We are the guns, and your masters!
>   Saw ye our flashes?
> Heard ye the scream of our shells in the
>   night, and the shuddering crashes?
> Saw ye our work by the roadside,
>   the shrouded things lying,
> Moaning to God that He made them –
>   the maimed and the dying?
> Husbands or sons,
> Fathers or lovers, we break them.
>   We are the guns!

There is much truth in the belief that the struggle on the Western Front was 'an artillery war'. Attack plans revolved around the availability of guns, mortars and ammunition stocks. Guns invariably decided the issue as so little could be achieved without them. Soldiers were crushed, terrified and shell-shocked by the blind violence of the artillery (including mortars). They killed and maimed far more men than any other weapon, indeed all other weapons combined, with some 67 per cent of casualties attributed to them. The low-velocity jagged lumps of shell casings tore tissue far more than bullets, producing horrendous wounds that invariably went septic due to the dirt taken into the body, with the result that a survivor was vulnerable to gangrene. Even a near miss could be fatal, as the blast could cause death by concussion, with kidneys and spleen being ruptured without leaving any outward marks on the body.

From the first Battle of the Marne in 1914, where the French 75mm field gun played a crucial role in the Allied victory, to the Germans' long-range pieces that bombarded Paris in 1918, the gun was the military machine par excellence, blind and tireless, surrounded by its detachment and ammunition caissons. It was around it that battlefield tactics revolved until the massed use of the tank removed some, but by no means all, of its tasks in 1917.

To keep the guns firing required the urgent expansion of foundries and factories in Britain and other belligerent countries, as well as the capacity of the supply chains to deliver the guns and shells to the front. The growth in both manpower and guns within

At the Receiving End of a German Bombardment

Private Cecil Thomas vividly described his experience of being under continuous bombardment on Vimy Ridge on 21 May 1916:

We crowd into the dug-out, Lew and I now being half-way down the entrance passage, squatting on one of the steps . . . with a crash and a roar the previous shelling, heavy as it was, is more than doubled . . . Although nearly midday, the brilliant sunshine is turned to semi-darkness by the dust, the smoke, and the gas, the whole earth shakes and trembles, clods and stones fly through the air, and those at the entrance to the dug-out push their way inwards away from the inferno.

Surely it can never last at this rate! But it does. On and on it goes, without pause between the bursts – just one long roar and upheaval . . . Lord how we pray for ourselves . . . now we are really praying for the first time, in the full realization of our own microscopic smallness and the impossibility of all protection save from above.

What senseless fool, what short-sighted imbecile planned these dug-outs and trenches? Four dug-outs, dug-outs for men, officers and stores, all placed together at the junction of the communication trench with the support trench, like desirable suburban villas round a railway station . . .

Crash! Darkness is upon us; the whole passage and dug-out sway from side to side like a ship on a rough sea; the four sides seem to contract, the timbers bellying inwards as if in an endeavour to crush us. Clouds of dust pour downwards from the entrance, and upwards from the dugout itself, coming into the latter from the hole in the roof . . .

Sometime later the men in the dugout were ordered out to man the trench.

I take my end place and look for the rifle, but it has been blown up and only a broken portion is sticking out of the ground. Another is passed along and, leaning it against the parapet, I follow the example of all the rest, save the lookout at the periscope, and lie flat on the fire-step squeezing myself as tightly as possible against the protecting sand-bags of the trench side . . .

How the earth shakes! Pressing against the parapet, I can feel it move from side to side, away from me and again into me as it reels in its torture this way and that under the sometimes simultaneous explosions . . .

After again withdrawing into a dugout, Thomas continued:

On and on goes the shelling . . . Again the earth is suddenly darkened. That was a big one and near. A sound of awful screams and of fierce scuffling outside follows. A man comes tearing past me down into the deepest depths of the dug-out, moaning piteously, holding both his hands over a face which is featureless under a swelter of blood. Blindly he knocks his head against the cross-beams of the roof as he stumbles past . . .

Horrified we draw aside as another, even worse follows him, like a madman flying from a pursuing demon. A third and fourth force their way past us and we hear them yelling, screaming and stamping as they rush madly backwards and forwards at the bottom of the dug-out, while to their clamour is added the noise of those, some of them wounded, who were lying down there and who are now being trampled upon in the darkness.

The result of this horrendous yet common experience for men of both sides was that the trench was captured and Thomas and his surviving comrades taken prisoner. He remained in captivity for the rest of the war.

the British Royal Artillery will serve as an example of the rapid growth of this arm – something that happened in all armies (the French expanded from 420,000 artillerymen in 1914 to over a million four years later; the Germans from 642 field batteries to nearly 3,000). There were some 93,000 all ranks (4,000 officers) in the Royal Artillery in August 1914, but by November 1918 the numbers had rocketed six times to almost 549,000, of whom 30,000 were officers. From 486 British guns and mortars in France in 1914 there were 6,437 (excluding anti-aircraft artillery) by the end of the war; of these, over 2,200 were heavy. For the Somme battle the British assembled 1,537 guns and howitzers, and in the preliminary seven-day bombardment hurled some 1,733,000 shells of all calibres at the German defences. As noted previously, this did not ensure success on 1 July, and the number of guns and ammunition used was dwarfed by the battles of a year or so later. During August 1916 at Verdun, over a period of three days French artillery fired 3 million rounds. On 26 September 1918, in order to break through the German defences in Champagne, they fired 1,375,000 75mm shells. The massive eleven-day preparatory bombardment for the British assault on Messines Ridge in

At least one heavy shell has made a direct hit on this German trench. The effects have been devastating, with the occupants blown to pieces and the trench itself smashed.

June 1917 required 2,200 guns and howitzers firing 3.5 million shells, including 120,000 gas and 60,000 smoke shells. During these prolonged battles the gun batteries were manned continuously for twenty-four hours a day, with relays of detachments staggering with exhaustion, deafened by the din and often under enemy shelling – few gunners on the Western Front had an easy life.

The Royal Regiment of Artillery, 1914–1918

'The Gunners', or Royal Regiment of Artillery, is one of the oldest regiments in the British Army, having been formed in 1716 when the artillery companies were first established in the army on a permanent basis. Six years later they adopted their official title and in 1756, reflecting the importance of guns on the battlefield, the Gunners were given precedence (seniority) over all infantry regiments, including the Foot Guards. The Royal Artillery, unlike infantry and cavalry regiments, carry no colours or guidons, but give their guns the same status as colours. The Gunners' motto, borne on their badges, is '*Ubique quo fas et Gloria ducunt*' ('Everywhere that Right and Glory lead'), which appropriately encapsulates the fact that guns have been present on all major (and most minor) battlefields from the first use of gunpowder to the present day.

The Royal Artillery (including dominion artillery) that fought on the Western Front was divided into three branches.

Men of the Royal Garrison Artillery roll a 15-in howitzer shell along rails, Engelbelmer Wood, west of Thiepval, 1916.

• **Royal Horse Artillery (RHA)** This branch came officially into being in 1793 to provide artillery support to the cavalry. When parading with guns, it formed on the right of the line, taking precedence over all other regiments or corps in the army; this privilege remains today. In 1914 the appropriate level of support to a cavalry brigade was a battery of six 13-pounder guns with all battery personnel mounted. In September 1914, L Battery RHA gained three Victoria Crosses for its action at the small village of Néry (see box, page 244). With the role of cavalry in trench warfare being limited, the expansion

of the RHA during the war was minimal and by the Armistice it had only six and a third batteries (fifty-six 13-pounders) in France.

The King's Troop of the RHA, which today performs ceremonial duties, was originally called the Riding Troop, but King George VI, on a visit to the unit in 1947, signed the visitors' book and crossed out the word 'Riding', substituting 'King's'. When Queen Elizabeth came to the throne she ruled that the troop retain the title 'King's' as a tribute to her father. Today the guns drawn by the King's Troop on ceremonial occasions are some of the original 13-pounders from World War I.

• **Royal Field Artillery (RFA)** This branch was the most numerous within the artillery and provided the 18-pounder gun and 4.5-inch howitzer batteries supporting the infantry divisions, and from November 1916 the army field artillery (AFA) brigades withdrawn from divisional control. By the end of hostilities the RFA in France fielded 527 batteries of 18-pounders (3,162 guns) and 162 howitzer batteries (972 howitzers).

• **Royal Garrison Artillery (RGA)** This branch provided coastal defence, mountain, siege and heavy batteries, as well as some anti-aircraft (AA) batteries. On the Western Front these included 60-pounder, 6-inch, 9.2-inch, 12-inch and 14-inch guns and 6-inch, 8-inch, 9.2-inch, 12-inch and 15-inch howitzers. By the end of the war heavy artillery in France totalled some 633 guns and 1,578 howitzers.

Artillery Weapons

Types of Gun

Artillery pieces were all breech-loaded and divided into two categories. This was broadly the same for all nations, although the gun types and their characteristics, such as range, varied slightly from army to army. The basic division was between guns and howitzers – both could be light or heavy. The former fired projectiles at a high velocity with a flat trajectory (the 18-pounder could fire only up to 16 degrees above the horizontal), while the howitzers fired at a much higher angle and were thus used against targets hidden behind obstacles such as low hills or ridges. Mortars (discussed below, page 240) fired at even steeper angles, which considerably reduced their range but enabled them to hit targets behind high obstacles. It was often possible to watch the flight of a mortar bomb and even dodge it at the last moment. The diagram below illustrates the different trajectories.

These two categories were further subdivided into three types (ignoring further subgrouping into medium or super-heavy pieces): field (mostly light) artillery, including howitzers; heavy guns and heavy howitzers. They were classified according to either the diameter of the bore (measured in inches by the British and centimetres or millimetres by the French and Germans) or the weight of

the projectile. The British light field artillery consisted of the 13-pounder, 15-pounder and 18-pounder guns and 4.5-inch howitzers. By 1916 heavy guns included the 4.7-inch, 60-pounder, 6-inch, 9.2-inch and 12-inch pieces. By the end of the war there were no fewer than twenty-three different types of guns, howitzers and mortars with the British in France, totalling over 10,000 pieces. Heavy howitzers included 6-inch, 8-inch, 9.2-inch, 12-inch and 15-inch weapons. The problem with the first three was that their shells had an aiming error of at least 25 yards and insufficient explosive power to collapse really deep bunkers – some German bunkers were 30 feet deep.

All these heavy pieces had to be movable and were therefore mounted on carriages to facilitate transportation. The lighter-wheeled pieces were horse-drawn – later in the war some were pulled by motor tractors. Super-heavy pieces were moved on railway trucks, most requiring specially laid tracks. A British example was the 14-inch naval gun, which fired a shell weighing 1,586 lb, and the French 37mm mortar, which weighed 30 tonnes and threw a projectile weighing 1,300 lb. Towards the end of the war the Germans deployed their three so-called 'Paris guns' (*Kaiser Wilhelmgeschütz* – Emperor William's gun) – not to be con-

fused with the 'Big Bertha' 75-tonne howitzers that pounded the Belgian forts at Liège and Antwerp and required a detachment of around 280 – manufactured by Krupp and designed to shell the French capital. The Paris guns were manufactured by inserting 21cm liners in 35cm naval gun barrels. As these barrels wore out they were re-bored, at first to 22.4cm and then to 23.2cm. They were able to fire 280-lb shells at ranges up to 80 miles, although accuracy at that distance was poor. However, according to General Michel it was the 280mm howitzers that were the most effective in smashing defences. He has described their effect on Fort Suarlée, one of the ring of forts protecting Namur:

> The bombardment of Fort Suarlée commenced on Sunday morning, August 23, and it fell on the 25th at five in the afternoon. Three German batteries armed with the 28cm howitzer fired 600 shells each weighing 750 lb on the 23rd; 1,300 on the 24th, and 1,400 on the 25th against it. These destroyed the whole of the massive structure of concrete and wrecked all the turrets, and further resistance was impossible . . . The German fire literally swept off the face of the earth forts and improvised defences, troops and guns.

Trajectories of Different Artillery Pieces

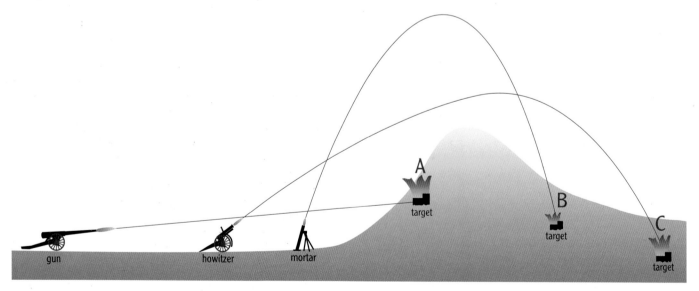

Notes

• The gun, with a high muzzle velocity, produces a flat trajectory and has a long range compared to the other pieces. However, it can hit target **A** only.

• The howitzer, with a lower muzzle velocity, fires at a higher angle than the gun to clear the hill and hit target **C**. Targets **A** and **B** are less suitable.

• The mortar, with an even lower muzzle velocity, fires at a very steep angle, but with a limited range, in order to clear the hill and hit target B, hidden on the steep reverse slope.

The Application of Artillery Fire

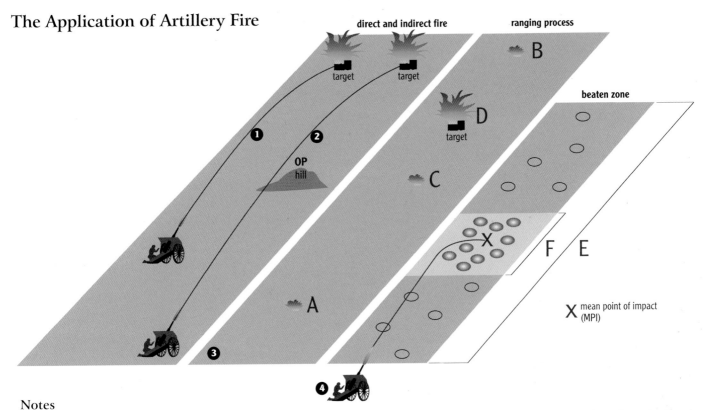

direct and indirect fire

target target

① **②**

OP hill

③

④

ranging process

B

D
target

C

A

beaten zone

X

F E

X mean point of impact (MPI)

Notes

1 Direct fire is aiming and firing over 'open sights', where a target is visible to the detachment. It was used primarily in the early weeks of the war, such as at the Battle of Le Cateau and the action at Néry.

2 Indirect fire had to be used when an obstruction such as a hill prevented the gunners seeing the target. In this case an observer (OP) on the hill with communications (mostly telephone) to the guns was able to direct the fire on to the target.

3 'Ranging' was the firing of single shots, the observer adjusting them laterally and in range on to the target. Lateral adjustments were easy. Range adjustments were called 'bracketing'. In this case shot **A** is 'short'. The observer needs to see a shot 'over' the target to establish a bracket. He orders 'Add 400' (meaning 400 yards) and shot **B** lands 'over' the target. He then splits the bracket by ordering 'Drop 200.' Shot **C** is 'short'. The bracket is split again – 'Add 100.' Shot **D** hits the target. (If **D** had been 'short' or 'over', the bracket would be split again). The whole battery now fires using the same range and bearing and hits the target.

4 When a gun fires, there are round-to-round variations. If it fires 100 shots at the same spot, the shots will be dispersed around that spot. The mean point of impact (MPI) of the shots is in the imagined rectangle **E**. **E** is much longer than it is wide. The spread of the hits within **E** is called the 'zone' or '100% zone' of the gun. Most hits are near the centre, their density decreasing towards the edges. About 50% of all hits fall within the central area **F**, which is called the '50% zone'. **F** is a quarter of the area **E**. The length of the '100% zone' varied with the type of gun and range. An 18-pdr at 3,000 yards had a '100% zone' of 140 yards; for a 6-inch howitzer at 5,000 yards, it was 200 yards. Every shot was affected by zone. In barrage planning it was a vital consideration – batteries fired in terms of football pitches!

To the above types must be added guns modified for an anti-aircraft role – examples being the British 13-pounder and 3-inch, the French 75mm and the German 8.8cm – the gun that was to cause such grief to Allied armour in World War II.

Before looking at a number of types of gun or howitzer used on the Western Front, three important aspects of the application of artillery fire to a target are explained in the diagram above.

The differing models of guns and howitzers deployed on the Western Front were extensive, as virtually all those in the field in 1914 were modified and improved during the war – for example, the British 18-pounder field guns with the BEF in August 1914 were the Mark I and II versions, but by 1918 the Mark IV was being developed. Space prevents all types being discussed in this book so, with the emphasis on the

British, four guns and three howitzers (four British, one French and two German) are described below – all were common field artillery pieces in use in France and Flanders.

The smallest and commonest tactical grouping of these guns was called a battery (six or four pieces) and this was common to the artillery of all armies. There were several changes in the number of guns or howitzers in British field batteries during the war. The regular divisions had six guns/howitzers in 1914, and continued with six in a battery for the rest of the war. Territorial units (initially equipped with obsolete 15-pounder guns) and some New Army field batteries had four guns until the start of 1917.

At the end of 1916 and into 1917 the field artillery of the BEF underwent its final reorganization. Batteries were restored to a six-gun or six-howitzer establishment, usually by breaking up one of the artillery brigades

in each division and using it to bring the others up to the new strength. Thus a division's artillery consisted of two brigades, each of three batteries of six 18-pounders (thirty-six guns) and one battery of 4.5-inch howitzers (twelve howitzers). Experience on the battlefield had shown a critical need for army commanders to have a reserve of field artillery in order to rest divisional artillery personnel, who up until then had been unable to be properly rested out of the line as infantry battalions were. This reserve was created from the reduction in numbers of divisional artillery brigades and an extra thirty-four batteries of 18-pounders that were formed in England (most initially with only four guns) and sent to France by mid-1917.

At much the same time, the heavy artillery under corps or army control was regrouped. The previous system of artillery 'groups' had meant batteries could be moved around individually, with consequent loss of identity with a parent unit and a lowering of soldiers' morale. This, coupled with an inadequate command structure allied to administrative shortcomings, dictated change. The changes made in 1917 led to the creation of heavy artillery brigades (HABs) at army and corps level.

Corps

Mobile brigades – two 60-pounder batteries, each of six guns, and two 6-inch howitzer batteries of six guns each.
Howitzer brigades – 8-inch howitzer brigades of three batteries of six guns each and one of 8-inch howitzers; 9.2-inch howitzer brigades of three batteries of 6-inch and one of 9.2-inch howitzers.
Mixed brigades – two 60-pounder, two 6-inch howitzer, one 8-inch howitzer and one 9.2-inch howitzer batteries.

Army

Army brigades responsible administratively for the 6-inch, 12-inch and 14-inch guns and 9.2-inch, 12-inch and 15-inch howitzers.

All except the 6-inch guns and some 12-inch howitzers were on railway mountings. Apart from the 6-inch batteries with four guns each, all army batteries were formed of two pieces, except that a battery of 15-inch howitzers had only one piece. The 8-inch and 9.2-inch howitzers and 6-inch guns were moved by caterpillar tractors driven by Army Service Corps personnel.

These changes meant that an army headquarters had overall control of all heavy batteries and several reserve brigades of field artillery. These were mostly allocated to corps commanders when preparing for a major offensive. For example, for the attack at Cambrai in November 1917 the Third Army allotted III Corps some forty batteries of heavy guns and howitzers as well as four reserve field artillery brigades – almost 260 pieces in addition to the eight field artillery brigades in its four divisions.

The detailed organization of a British field artillery battery and its method of operating are described in the 18-pounder paragraphs as representative of the general principles of the way any battery functioned – differences being mostly in crew numbers and more advanced technology.

British 18-pounder QF (quick-firing) field gun

This was the standard British field gun of the war, which, with modifications, saw service with British forces until 1942. It was classified as a 'quick-firing' gun, meaning the propellant was in a cartridge fixed to the shell, and it had a rapid-action breech and a highly effective recoil system. These guns had a barrel that recoiled within a jacket, slowed by a hydraulic buffer and then returned to the firing position by powerful springs – it was these factors that hugely speeded up loading. Guns of this type were classified as QF. However, having the projectile and propellant together in one casing was not possible with very heavy shells. With these it was necessary first to load the shell into the breech, then the propellant, in a combustible bag, was placed behind it. This type of artillery was known as a BL or breech-loading piece.

The gun, hooked up to its two-wheeled ammunition limber (cart), was drawn by a team of three pairs of light draught horses, with a driver riding the left-hand horse of each pair. It was serviced by a gun detachment of six men who actually operated it in action, while four others were responsible for ammunition supply; all rode either on their own horse or on the limber or ammunition wagon. Initially, while operations were still fairly fluid, the ammunition limber was positioned immediately to the left of the gun in action, but once static trench warfare became established more ammunition was needed close to hand, so it was usually dumped in specially prepared locations by the gun pits (dug-in positions). Once guns were deployed, all teams, limbers, wagons and battery transport were found at the wagon line.

A battery at full establishment of six guns under a major had a captain as second-in-command and three subaltern officers, each commanding a section of two guns. A sergeant commanded each gun and its detachment with a corporal, as 'coverer', who was second-in-command and in charge of the teams and wagons. A simplified organization of an 18-pounder battery deployed for action is shown in the diagram opposite – it does not show all personnel, and depicts one ammunition wagon and limber remaining with each gun but the teams withdrawn.

The 18-pounder had been in service since 1905 and initially was supplied only with shrapnel ammunition; it was not until late 1914 that some high-explosive (HE) shells began to be issued as well. The 1914 *Field Service Pocket Book* states that a battery of six guns should have 1,056 rounds immediately available, made up of 144 in the gun limbers and 912 in the twelve ammunition wagons and limbers.

The 18-pounder range of only some 6,500 yards at the start of the war was eventually increased to 9,000 yards. The problem with this initial comparatively short range was partially overcome by digging in the single pole trail so that it did not obstruct the recoil of the breech when firing and thus allowed an increase in elevation and range. The rate of fire is shown as 4 rpm in the table on page 233, but it was capable of firing much faster (up to 20 rpm) than this if necessary for short periods. The problem, common to all guns, was that rapid or prolonged firing wore out the barrel, which had then to be replaced – a long process. Following the experience of the Battle of the Somme, from January 1917 the 18-pounder was normally restricted to 4 rpm.

This gun, firing shrapnel or HE, was particularly suited to certain tasks or targets. They are best illustrated by quoting an

18-pounder field guns of the 24th Battery, Australian Field Artillery, in action near Ypres, September 1917. Note how the shells are stacked in the gun pit.

18-pounder Field Battery in Action, *c.*1914

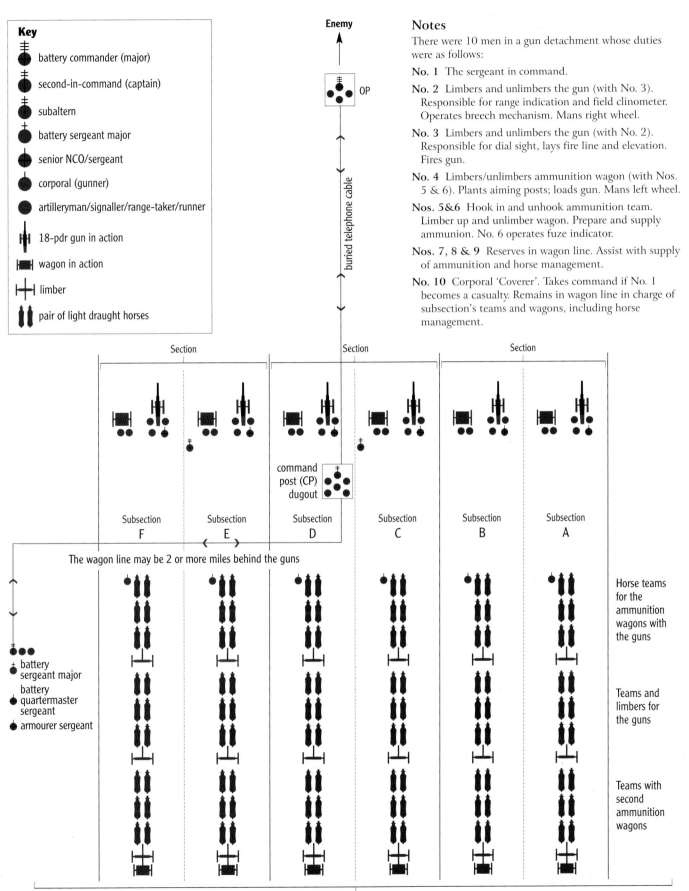

Key

- ‡ battery commander (major)
- ‡ second-in-command (captain)
- ‡ subaltern
- † battery sergeant major
- senior NCO/sergeant
- corporal (gunner)
- artilleryman/signaller/range-taker/runner
- 18-pdr gun in action
- wagon in action
- limber
- pair of light draught horses

Enemy

OP

buried telephone cable

Section   **Section**   **Section**

command post (CP) dugout

Subsection F   Subsection E   Subsection D   Subsection C   Subsection B   Subsection A

The wagon line may be 2 or more miles behind the guns

- ‡ battery sergeant major
- battery quartermaster sergeant
- armourer sergeant

Horse teams for the ammunition wagons with the guns

Teams and limbers for the guns

Teams with second ammunition wagons

wagon lines

Notes

There were 10 men in a gun detachment whose duties were as follows:

No. 1 The sergeant in command.

No. 2 Limbers and unlimbers the gun (with No. 3). Responsible for range indication and field clinometer. Operates breech mechanism. Mans right wheel.

No. 3 Limbers and unlimbers the gun (with No. 2). Responsible for dial sight, lays fire line and elevation. Fires gun.

No. 4 Limbers/unlimbers ammunition wagon (with Nos. 5 & 6). Plants aiming posts; loads gun. Mans left wheel.

Nos. 5&6 Hook in and unhook ammunition team. Limber up and unlimber wagon. Prepare and supply ammunion. No. 6 operates fuze indicator.

Nos. 7, 8 & 9 Reserves in wagon line. Assist with supply of ammunition and horse management.

No. 10 Corporal 'Coverer'. Takes command if No. 1 becomes a casualty. Remains in wagon line in charge of subsection's teams and wagons, including horse management.

extract from the XV Corps instructions for a preliminary bombardment on 1 July 1916:

B. Divisional Artilleries.

(i) 18 pr. Batteries:-

1. Wire-cutting
2. Searching trenches, villages, woods, OPs [observation posts] and hollows by day and night.
3. Destruction of machine gun emplacements, OPs and dug-outs within the power of the gun [see below under ammunition, page 234].
4. Interruption of communications especially by night.
5. Preventing enemy repairing damage.

Fire-planning will be discussed below (page 247), but a small extract from a divisional artillery timetable for the same day shows how 108 18-pounders were used to bombard their targets for sixty-five minutes prior to the infantry going over the top (0 indicates zero hour, with other figures indicating minutes):

9 wire-cutting 18-pr. batteries [54 guns]	0 minus 65–0	Front line trenches.
5 forward (9th Div.) 18-pr. batteries [30 guns]	ditto	Support line trenches.
4 other 18-pr. batteries [24 guns]	ditto	Selected communication trenches.

A perilous perch for an artillery observation post, on top of the wall of a ruined farm at Havrincourt, taken by the 62nd (West Riding) Division on 20 November 1917.

In 1914 a major commanded a British field battery at full establishment of around 200 men. At battles such as Le Cateau or the action at Néry, when his guns came into action in the open using direct fire and had to be able to change position rapidly, the major was normally located in the gun line, with the limbers and teams close behind. Trench warfare changed all that: the battery commander then went forward with several signallers and runners to establish an observation post (OP) from which he could see the target and observe and adjust the fall of shot. From there he controlled the indirect fire of his battery. This was best done by field telephone, the cable of which was normally buried in a narrow trench sometimes up to 6 feet deep. Alternative methods included flags, lights or runners. This system was the theory. In practice, with losses and perhaps with no suitable OP site other than the foremost infantry trench, duties changed, with the battery commander located in the infantry battalion command post (CP) bunker and a subaltern or captain observing as best they could alongside the infantry in the trenches, and with some gun detachments commanded by junior NCOs.

Assuming a full complement of officers, the second-in-command, a captain known as the 'battery captain', was in command of the wagon line. There were found the teams for the ammunition wagons with the guns, the teams and limbers for the guns themselves, and the teams and second wagons for each gun. Again, the favoured means of communication with the guns was by telephone or, if that failed, a mounted orderly. The wagon line would also have the remaining gun detachment personnel: the battery sergeant-major, battery quartermaster sergeant, armourer staff sergeant, fitters, farriers, shoesmiths, wheelers, cooks, drivers and other administrative personnel. In addition to the official vehicles, every battery acquired a variety of extra wagons and carts to carry the little luxuries, such as tables, chairs, beds, cooking stoves, etc. The wagon line could be several miles in the rear of the guns, which meant a lengthy and difficult journey, usually over appalling roads or tracks, for ammunition re-supply or to move the guns, so it was common for a forward wagon line of limbers and teams to be established.

In action, the gun line was commanded by the senior of the three subalterns, known as the 'battery leader', who set up a CP in a dugout close to the guns. In the CP would be linesmen/signallers manning the telephone links to the OP and wagon line,

A Forward Observation Officer (FOO) at Loos

Major C. J. C. Street, RFA, described the activities in a forward artillery observation post as he registered his battery on different targets:

Up in the observation post things are very different. There the observing officer sits, watching the black and yellow smoke clouds of the bursting high explosive, or the cotton-wool-like puffs of the shrapnel. 'No. 1 fired, sir!' The words of the telephonist seem to come from another world. Here she comes, far away behind, the whistle of the shell shrieking louder as she passes right overhead – splendid! In the very trench itself; see the black smoke spread out and rise slowly from a long section of trench, while the green vegetation grows white with the falling chalk. No correction can be made to that, 'No. 1, repeat!' 'No. 2 fired, sir!' Here she comes, ah, a little to the right – 'No. 2, ten minutes more left, fire!'

So it goes on, until this particular section of trench has practically disappeared, leaving only a white scar. Then a change of target and a repetition of the destruction. A fascinating business this on so fine an autumn day . . . The only thing in the world is the measured fall of the shell and the swift framing of the consequent order, the only pleasure the deep satisfaction of a well placed round . . .

range-takers and runners. When not firing, the gun's detachment personnel would shelter or rest in nearby bunkers.

The gun battery in 1914 had several specific methods of fire, namely:

• **Battery fire** The guns were fired in succession from the right at five-second intervals, unless a different interval was ordered.

• **Section fire** The guns of each section were fired at an interval ordered by the battery commander.

• **Gunfire** Each gun was fired independently, usually for a specific number of rounds, either at an interval ordered by the battery commander or as rapidly as possible (gunfire was not used in heavy batteries). If no interval was ordered, the gun fired when ready.

The 18-pounder was by far the most numerous British gun, with some 3,162 in use in France alone by the end of the war.

British 60-pounder gun BL Mark I

This was the main British heavy gun (it weighed 4.5 tons) on the Western Front, firing a powerful 60-lb shrapnel or HE shell and designed to be pulled by a team of eight Shire carthorses or a tractor. It had a quick-firing recoil, in that the carriage did not move when the gun was fired, but it fired separated rounds (the shell and bagged cartridge were loaded separately). These guns were withdrawn from divisional command in February 1915 and thereafter were normally allocated and tasked by senior artillery commanders at corps and army level.

With its greater range and hitting power, this gun was invariably tasked with targets deeper into enemy defences. This is illustrated by the XV Corps' targeting instructions for the preliminary bombardment on 1 July on the Somme. The list includes:

- destruction of trenches and strongpoints further back
- distant wire-cutting
- bombardment of villages, woods, railways and stations
- counter-battery work
- interrupting communications
- bombarding distant billets by day and night
- preventing enemy repairing damage

By the Armistice 456 60-pounders were in use in batteries in France.

British 4.5-inch QF field howitzer

This field howitzer served the British Army from 1909 to 1942 and was the standard light howitzer for all British Empire formations throughout the war. It had a sliding breechblock, a box trail and variable recoil to allow operation with the barrel elevated to 45 degrees; with the barrel horizontal the recoil was some 40 inches, but at high elevation only 20 inches, thus preventing the breechblock hitting the ground. Its role in early 1917 was described as neutralizing guns with gas shells, enfilading communication trenches, bombarding weaker defences, barrage work (especially at night) and wire-cutting in places field guns could not reach.

A notable action fought with just two howitzers under the command of twenty-four-year-old Sergeant Cyril Edward Gourley of D/276 Battery, Royal Field Artillery, was fought close to Little Priel Farm east of Épehy on 30 November 1917 during the Battle of Cambrai. The citation for Gourley's incredible Victoria Cross reads:

A British 60-pounder Mark II in action in the open, shelling the advancing Germans during their March 1918 offensive.

For most conspicuous bravery when in command of a section of howitzers. Though the enemy advanced in force getting within 400 yards in front, between 300 and 400 yards on one flank and with snipers in the rear, Sergeant Gourley managed to keep one gun in action practically throughout the day. Though frequently driven off always returned, carrying ammunition, laying and firing the gun himself, taking first one and then another of the detachment to assist him. When the enemy advanced he pulled his gun out of the pit, and engaged a machine gun at 500 yards, knocking it out with a direct hit. All day he held the enemy in check, firing with open sights at enemy parties in full view at 300 and 800 yards, and thereby saved his guns, which were withdrawn at nightfall.

Gourley was also awarded the Military Medal and survived the war. He died in 1982 and a lane leading from his old school, Caldy Grange Grammar School, Wirral, has been named Gourley's Lane.

There were 984 4.5-inch howitzers in service on the Western Front at the Armistice.

British BL 6-inch 26-cwt howitzer

The 6-inch 26-cwt (weight of barrel and breech together) howitzer, a siege gun of the Royal Garrison Artillery (see page 225), replaced the BL 6-inch 30-cwt howitzer and became the most numerous and lightest of the heavy howitzers used by the BEF. It was in service from late 1915 to the end of World War II. It was able to fire a 100-lb shell at a steep angle and thus bring a devastating

A British 4.5-inch howitzer stuck in a shell-hole gun position.

plunging fire on its targets out to a distance of 10,000 yards. It was particularly effective against enemy artillery in a counter-battery role or firing against strongpoints, bunkers, supply dumps, roads or railways behind enemy lines.

It had a detachment of ten and was initially drawn by horses, but from 1916 was commonly towed behind a four-wheel-drive 3-ton lorry. It was sufficiently mobile to serve alongside the 60-pounder field gun.

At the end of the war 1,042 were in service in France.

French 75mm field gun

The French 75mm gun, the famous *soixante-quinze*, was the first genuine quick-firing gun in history, having been adopted by the French Army in 1898 after five years of secret trials. It was first seen in public during the Bastille Day parade on 14 July 1899, although none of the people watching knew what a revolutionary weapon it was. It was the first gun to have the smooth-operating sliding breech and recoil system that returned the barrel forward to its original position after each shot. Previously, with the old artillery guns, the recoil made the gun jump backwards after firing and so this weapon had to be resighted in order to stay on target. The French 75 easily delivered 15 aimed rounds a minute and could fire much faster for limited periods (although the normal rate was 6 rpm). This, together with the use of fixed ammunition, mobility, accuracy and a maximum range (with buried trail) of up to 9,000 yards, made it superior to any other field gun in the first years of the twentieth century. By 1914, apart from its rapid-

ity of fire, it was matched by its contemporaries. However, at maximum range the strike of HE shells could not be seen, so was largely ineffective and risked damaging the recoil system. The maximum effective range for shrapnel was 4,500 yards, the limiting factors being the difficulty in observing the fall of shot and the maximum fuze (military spelling) setting. French artillery doctrine was based on firing shrapnel out to 3,500 yards; beyond that, HE became increasingly necessary. Like most guns, the 75 was improved during its service, with final variants after World War I ranged to 12,000 yards.

Although unable to elevate the barrel above 18 degrees unless the trail was dug deeply into the ground, it was able to traverse laterally 3 degrees to right or left. This, along with slight adjustments in elevation while firing, enabled a four-gun battery firing shrapnel (each shell contained 290 lead balls) to deliver some 17,000 projectiles over an area 400 yards long and 100 yards wide in one minute. Although other nations caught up with the technology, and indeed surpassed the 75 in terms of weight of shell, in sheer numbers it dominated the battlefields (over 21,000 were produced during the war) and was largely responsible for halting the Germans on the Marne in 1914. It was at this battle that the Germans gave the French 75mm gunners the nickname 'Black Butchers' for the way they decimated attacking German infantry. Despite this the gun was primarily designed for mobile warfare and advancing to support infantry in the attack, and was thus fully in accordance with the French tactical doctrine of the supremacy of the offensive. Its flat trajectory, the light-

ness of the gun and its shells were therefore less effective once fighting bogged down into a vast siege operation where heavier guns, howitzers and mortars came into their own – weapons of which the French had woefully insufficient numbers until 1916. Part of the reason for the failure of Nivelle's offensive at Chemin des Dames in 1917 was that the high ridge was a series of slopes, with the resultant dead ground that the 75s could not reach. Another problem with the 75 was that there was considerable wastage due to wear on the bore with excessive firing over long periods, the wear being much increased when heavier charges were fuzed to get longer range. An equally serious problem was the frequency of shell bursts in the bore, again due to the use of heavier charges. The French Army's *Artillery Journal* for January–February 1924 records that between 1 July and 24 October 1916, 746 guns in their Sixth Army were burst or worn out – 4.5 a day. In just over a year, from September 1917 to October 1918, 926 75s were destroyed by bursts in the bore, 853 were swelled, 511 were destroyed by enemy fire and 3,758 were worn out – revealing statistics

Nevertheless, with America so short of modern weaponry, this was the field gun supplied to the American National Guard formations as they arrived in France from 1917 onwards. Captain Harry S. Truman, the future president of the United States, commanded Battery D of the 129th Field Artillery Regiment, which was equipped with 75s. On 26 September 1918 his battery participated in the opening barrage of the Meuse–Argonne offensive and, as he stood beside his guns, Captain Truman remarked, 'I

A German 77mm gun firing, probably on a practice range.

Comparison of Gun Characteristics

| | British | | | | French | German | |
	18-pdr gun (Mk II)	60-pdr gun	4.5-in howitzer	6-in howitzer	75mm gun	77mm gun (1896 M)	10.5cm howitzer
Maximum range (yards)	6,525	12,300	7,300	11,400	8,400	6,500	9,000+
Shell weight (lb)	18	60	35	100	16	15	34.5
Rate of fire (normal per min.)	4	2	4	26 (15+)	4	4	
Crew	6	10	6	10	6	5	6
Number made	10,500+	1,756 (Mk I)	3,359	3,633	21,000+	5,000+	5,000+
Elevation (degrees)	−5 to +16	−5 to +21	−5 to +45	0 to +45	−11 to +18	−12 to +16	−13 to +40
Used by	Britain and Dominions				France, Belgium, USA	Germany and Empire	

would rather be here than be President of the United States'. His guns fired so rapidly that wet blankets had to be wrapped around the barrels for ten minutes every hour to cool them down. That day, French and American 75s fired 1,375,000 rounds. Overall, the French supplied the Americans with more than 3,800 field pieces and 10 million rounds of ammunition.

German 77mm field gun 1896

This gun, designed and built by the firm of Krupp and Erhardt, was the workhorse of the German field artillery for the first half of the war, after which the improved 1916 model superseded it. It was a quick-firing gun using fixed ammunition and, as such, the equivalent of the French 75mm and the British 18-pounder, although it was never the equal of the French gun in rapidity of fire or accuracy, nor the equal of either in weight of shell. However, it was lighter than the Allies' guns, as in 1914 the Germans placed considerable emphasis on tactical mobility. It was the gun that originated the name of 'whiz-bang' among the British, as the first they knew of it was the shell arriving unannounced by the sound of the report at the gun. Although originally intended to have six guns in a battery, the need for rapid expansion in 1914 led to batteries being steadily reduced to four. In December 1914 there were some 600 six-gun batteries so by reducing them to four another 300 batteries were created.

By 1916 the Germans were producing an improved 77mm, one that would be used by the stormtroopers in their counter-attack at Cambrai, employing infiltration tactics and accompanied by 77mm batteries to provide close support. This new model used a smaller shell (13.4 lb) and an increased powder charge, which in combination improved the maximum range to over 11,000 yards. Although the weight of the gun in action was also increased, it was able to elevate the barrel up to 40 degrees instead of only 16 degrees in the 1896 model. In order to give it a lower silhouette, stormtrooper units often put smaller wheels on the carriage despite it making the gun more difficult to move across broken ground. This later model was to prove effective as an anti-tank gun in 1917, when guns were manhandled out of their gun pits and successfully took on British tanks over open sights, something repeated in 1918.

To overcome the difficulty of moving the 77mm over rough, shell-pitted ground, Krupp produced the light 37mm *Sturmkanone*, which supposedly could be manhandled more easily. These were infantry guns intended to provide close support, mainly in an anti-tank role. However, they proved cumbersome and vulnerable – the first unit to use them had 30 per cent losses in a series of minor attacks. They were mostly replaced by cut-down captured Russian field guns with an effective range of 1,200 yards but which could be manhandled more easily, rather than dragged behind vulnerable horses.

German 10.5cm howitzer 1916

This was another Krupp artillery piece that became the standard German field howitzer from 1916 onwards, seeing service, with modifications, up to 1945. It replaced the 10.5cm light field howitzer 98/09 but fired the same ammunition and was a longer piece, using a heavier charge and thus having a considerably increased range.

The basic characteristics of the above guns/howitzers are summarized and compared above.

Anti-aircraft Defence and Guns

World War I saw the advent of air warfare on an ever-increasing scale (see Section Eleven) and with it came the need for ground defence, if not to destroy enemy aircraft, at least to frighten them away from their targets or from their reconnaissance or photographic missions. This proved to be more difficult than expected. It was not so much that artillery guns could not, in time, be modified for the role of this high-angle firing, but the problem of aiming and deflection firing to hit a target that operated in three dimensions and was able to move at speed and manoeuvre. Much of this revolved around the difficulty of accurately judging the height (range) and making the necessary adjustments to cater for rapid changes of altitude by the pilot. This was particularly difficult with high-flying aircraft. Aiming at low-flying targets was easier; they were frequently shot at by riflemen and machine guns used in an anti-aircraft role. It has been established beyond much doubt that the famous German air ace Manfred von Richthofen (the Red Baron) was finally brought down by a combination of machine-gun and rifle fire while flying very low (see pages 444–5).

With aircraft flying low in the vicinity of balloons where the length of their cable was known, it was easier to assess heights. Allied to judging the height of the target was the need to have ammunition that was effective, not just through direct hits but also through damaging the aircraft with near misses. There was much debate over what projectile to use. Shrapnel was commonly selected but was not found entirely satisfactory, partly due to the difficulty of setting the timing fuze.

Britain had no anti-aircraft (AA) organization within the army in 1914. However, it soon became apparent that the defence of London and other key facilities required protection from Zeppelin bombing raids. It was the Admiralty that led the way in the development of what became the 3-inch, high-angle (it could be elevated to 90 degrees), quick-firing gun for the Royal Navy, and it assumed responsibility for the AA defence of London, setting up thirty guns and twelve searchlights on the roofs of buildings in central London, Woolwich Arsenal, Waltham ordnance factory and on the Medway. Guns of various types and ages were also co-opted for the defence of naval establishments, such as at Dover, Harwich and on the Tyne and Humber.

The War Office became responsible for the defence of other key facilities, including munitions factories, and in 1914 AA sections were formed with the intention of providing one for each division in France – something not achieved until 1916. The first section arrived in France in September 1914, equipped with one (supposedly two) 1-pounder Vickers pom-pom gun. On 23 September No. 2 AA Section, commanded by Lieutenant O. Hogg, managed to shoot down the first enemy aircraft after firing seventy-five shots at it – the pom-pom was never going to be up to the task. During 1915 experiments were carried out to find a better gun. These resulted in the adoption of the Mark III QF 13-pounder mounted on a lorry chassis. Another version was the 18-pounder with the barrel modified to accept 13-pounder shells. These became the standard British AA guns (13-pounder, 9 cwt) on the Western Front. They fired shrapnel shells with time fuzes at a rate of 18 rpm up to a height of 19,000 feet, with a maximum elevation of 90 degrees and traverse of 360.

By July 1916, 113 AA guns were in service in France, grouped into four-gun batteries, along with two searchlight sections operated by the Royal Engineers (RE). In addition to protecting the forward area, batteries were deployed to guard the lines of communication. Each army had its AA group HQ staff and the front was divided into areas, each having an AA defence commander responsible for coordinating all AA defences (called an AA group) within his area. By the end of 1916 there were seventy-four AA Sections, Royal Garrison Artillery, and twenty-two searchlight sections in France. For the Battle of Cambrai (see Section Thirteen) AA guns formed an integral part of the battle plan, with seven AA batteries giving covering fire that swept up to 3,500 yards ahead of the attacking infantry. By November 1918 the BEF had 234 13-pounder, 10 12-pounder and 103 3-inch AA guns in France.

The French were able to adapt their 75mm gun, mount it on a vehicle and produce a reasonably satisfactory AA gun, with a vertical range of 16,500 feet and a maximum elevation of 70 degrees. The Germans developed an extensive AA organization, based mainly on the 88mm and 77mm guns, the former having a rate of fire of 10 rpm, a vertical range of 12,500 feet and 70-degree elevation, and the latter 8 rpm, 14,000 feet vertical range and the same elevation. They were called anti-aircraft defence guns – *Fliegerabwehrkanone*, or *Flak* – a name that became all too familiar to Allied airmen in World War II. German batteries usually had two guns. By the end of the war they had amassed an impressive number of flak batteries. Hermann Cron, in his *Imperial German Army 1914–18*, lists them as 116 heavy motorized batteries, 168 horse-drawn batteries, 166 fixed batteries, 3 railway batteries, 183 machine flak detachments, 49 horse-drawn flak detachments, 173 fixed flak detachments and 80 individual motorized vehicle flak. These were supplemented by numerous anti-aircraft machine-gun detachments.

Overall, anti-aircraft defence proved to be more of a deterrence than an effective way of destroying aircraft due to the complexities of securing a hit and sketchy training in what was very much an experimental form of gunnery. As an example of the difficulties, in the week ending 27 April 1918 British AA guns engaged 2,039 enemy aircraft but managed to shoot down only ten and damage five.

Artillery Ammunition
Ammunition and fuzes – types and tasks

All armies fired variants of the same basic types of shell, but with differing weights according to the size of the gun, and their fuzes were all designed with the same function: to explode the shell at the required moment. As mentioned above, a shell could be 'fixed' – that is, the projectile and explosive charge that propelled it were within the same casing, like a rifle bullet – or 'separate', with the projectile loaded first, followed by the bagged charge. The fuze's task was to explode the shell at the right moment over (timed), on impact (percussion), or when it had penetrated the target or ground (delayed).

The two most common shells were shrapnel and HE, with others including smoke, incendiary, gas, illuminating and coloured flares/star shells. Until the introduction of proximity fuzes after World War I, the airburst timed fuze was mostly used in what are technically termed 'cargo munitions' such as shrapnel, smoke, gas and illuminating shells. These airbursts had the fuze length (running

time) set on them. This was done just before firing. HE rounds requiring a burst 20–30 feet above ground also needed a timed fuze, and if the setting was just slightly wrong the rounds would hit the ground or burst too high.

From the above, the crucial importance of using the right type of gun or howitzer, firing the correct type of shell with the right fuze for particular targets becomes obvious – there was plenty of room for error.

Shrapnel shells

By far the most common type of shell held by the field batteries of the BEF in 1914 was the shrapnel shell. It was a munition that threw several hundred lead balls at its target, normally troops in the open, when the bursting charge exploded – the timing of which, as noted above, depended on that set on the fuze. The lethality of the balls depended almost entirely on the height of burst of the shell. It was found to be ineffective against even light to moderate protection such as sandbags or compacted earth, so it could not destroy defensive positions. It could, however, be used against a trench parapet, not to destroy it but to ensure it was not manned by enemy troops. It was used by field artillery in barrages (see page 250) and was found to be less hazardous to attacking British infantry than HE when supporting an advance – as long as the shells burst ahead of them. It was also useful against enemy counter-attacks, working parties or other exposed troops. Multiple bursts produced a smokescreen that helped to conceal attackers while forcing defenders to stay under cover, and at the same time they did not crater the ground – something that would hugely hinder subsequent forward movement by artillery and infantry, especially when combined with muddy soil.

Another problem of shrapnel ammunition, apart from its poor penetration, was that it was also frequently unsatisfactory in wire-cutting. Barbed wire, usually in extensive and thick belts, defended every fighting (as opposed to communication) trench, and field artillery lacked the range to tackle the deep wire defences, often thousands of yards behind the enemy front line. Extensive wire-cutting required many guns and a prolonged bombardment – the original Somme bombardment plan included five days for wire-cutting. Things improved with the introduction of the 106 percussion fuze in 1917, its first serious use being during the Battle of Arras in April. It had a sensitive 'graze' action – the slightest contact would trigger the detonation. This allowed it to cut wire entanglements far more effectively. The shell burst the instant the ground was touched and its force was expended horizontally and upwards, rather than being partially buried in the ground.

High-explosive (HE) shells

As the war progressed, HE ammunition began to replace shrapnel. Not only could it be used to smash defences, but it also had an anti-personnel capability – although it was arguably not as effective a killer of troops in the open. HE shells could be fitted with airburst fuzes, as it was found that the bursting explosion (using the right explosive) fragmented the shell casing effectively – for example, a 10.5cm shell produced hundreds of high-velocity small fragments that were lethal at close range. However, using airburst fuzes meant that the shells could not be fired as close to attacking troops as shrapnel, because the fragments were scattered in all directions, not just forwards. Nevertheless, they were simpler to make and, with percussion or delay fuzes, could destroy defences as well as kill the occupants. A drawback was that with soft ground shells tended to bury themselves before exploding, something that dramatically reduced their lethality. Here again, the use of the 106 fuze resulted in increased effectiveness, in that an HE barrage did not crater the ground.

Smoke and light

Smoke shells and the screens they produced soon became a feature on most Western Front battlefields, the white cloud obscuring any object or person behind or within it. Being dependent on a favourable wind was often a decisive limitation on their use, and they required a continuous 'topping up', particularly if the breeze was fresh or blowing in an awkward direction. They were used to screen assaulting troops, to block enemy observation or to deceive them about where an attack might to launched. Frequently smoke shells were mixed with gas to cause even greater confusion and discomfort.

Light, or illuminating, shells were introduced to complement or supersede the soldier's hand-held Very pistol, which fired a coloured flare or light to a height of about 1,000 feet (*in extremis*, these pistols were deadly anti-personnel weapons). The more sophisticated illuminating shells could be made to explode at a predetermined height and then float slowly down on a parachute, brightly lighting up the battlefield. Any movement was quickly spotted and the training for a soldier caught in the open – it is the same today – was immediately to remain perfectly still until the light went out. Coloured flares were used for signalling, and various simple signals were incorporated into operation orders. On any night at the front, illuminating flares went up from both sides at frequent intervals. Often another shell was fired to explode just before the first died, thus giving prolonged light during which nervous sentries strained their eyes for movement. Any sign of serious enemy activity caused a frantic flurry of signal flares calling for defensive fire tasks from machine guns, mortars or artillery.

Shells, probably HE, bursting over an enemy position.

Gas

Another wind-dependent weapon. Early British gas shells were called T-shells and contained tear gas, followed by K-shells containing diphosgene and later 'cocktail shells', which had a mixture. In July 1917 the Germans introduced liquefied mustard-gas shells. More details of the types, usage and effects are given in Section Seven, as in the British Army it was the Royal Engineers who were initially responsible for delivering gas from cylinders.

Some of the effects of firing shrapnel and HE shells with varying fuzes are illustrated in the diagrams overleaf.

Wire-cutting

Creating and maintaining sufficient gaps in enemy wire obstacles before an infantry assault was one of the never-ending problems facing the artillery on the Western Front. The number of miles of wire laid must have run into millions during the four years of fighting, as it quickly became one of, if not *the*, most important feature of any defensive position. Its destruction by artillery fire was always problematic, largely due to the guns or howitzers not having suitable ammunition until the widespread use of the British 106 percussion fuze in 1917, along with the increased use of mortars for this purpose. Before any attack, much of the field artillery's task was wire-cutting; as we have seen, the planners of the Somme offensive allocated five days for the task. Destruction required accurate information on its location and on the length and depth of the belts – normally the task of infantry patrols for the foremost enemy defences, and of observers in balloons or aerial photography for the wire protecting deeper positions. Just to bombard the wire for days on end and hope that gaps would be created was seldom enough. It was essential that patrols and observers checked the results of the shelling and, where wire was destroyed, arrangements must be made to fire harassing tasks at night to deter repair.

General Staff Notes for June 1916 has this to say about the problem:

It is now generally agreed that 18-pounder shrapnel is the most effective projectile, burst as close to the wire and as low down as possible. Experiments with H.E., whether burst on graze or with No.100 delay action fuze, have given practically no effect against wire, but about 10 or 15 per cent H.E. mixed with shrapnel is sometimes useful for dispersing the posts and the wire when cut. On hard ground percussion shrapnel is very effective.

The best ranges have been found to be from 1800 yards to 2400 yards, and five or six rounds per yard are then required for an entanglement ten yards deep [many were considerably deeper]. Wire can be cut up to about 3200 yards with a much larger expenditure of ammunition, but at longer ranges the 18-pounder gives little, if any, effect. In all cases close observation is essential . . .

The 6-inch howitzer has been effectively employed against wire between 3000 and 5000 yards, and distant wire has been cut by 60-pounders firing H.E. with aerial observation. Trench mortars should also take part in wire-cutting; the 2-inch is particularly useful.

The notes went on to describe some of the problems in destroying wire. These included:

• Heavy coils of wire on iron posts or on broken ground are particularly difficult to destroy.
• The effect [of gunfire] on trestle wire is easier to observe than on staked wire.
• Wire among bushes is hard to see, and it is difficult to tell if it is cut or not.

By late 1917 this task had become easier, as not only were the new fuzes now in plentiful supply, but tanks had appeared, able to crush or drag away wire entanglements (see Section Ten).

Factors Affecting the Firing of Shrapnel Shells

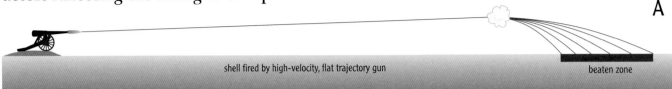

A

shell fired by high-velocity, flat trajectory gun

beaten zone

Notes
- Shrapnel, mostly an anti-personnel shell using a timed fuze.
- In this case the airburst throws the shrapnel balls forward due to the flat trajectory of the gun, resulting in the comparatively long beaten zone.

- Note all bursts produced a puff of smoke that, with multiple bursts, produced a smokescreen, which in many cases at least partially concealed attacking troops.

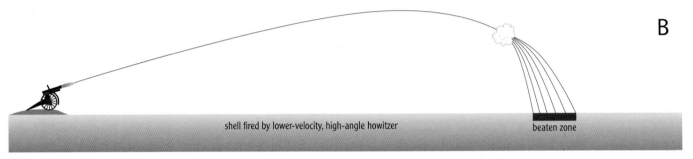

B

shell fired by lower-velocity, high-angle howitzer

beaten zone

Notes
- Here the shell is descending steeply when it bursts. The shrapnel balls are still thrown forward, but they are directed towards the ground and the beaten zone is much smaller than in diagram **A**.

- Against troops in the open, the flat trajectory is the more effective, but the howitzer shell can seek out targets behind obstacles.

C

the shell burst has little effect

Notes
- Here the firer has set the correct range, but the fuze setting is too 'long'. The shell detonates on the ground with little effect.

- All British fuzes included a percussion element.

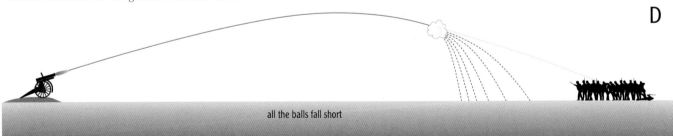

D

all the balls fall short

Notes
- If the range is set correctly but the fuze setting is too 'short', the shell bursts too early. Its effect is wasted.

- The cone of shrapnel from a burst follows the line of the trajectory. The cone widens rapidly, but as the force of the burster charge dissipates, the balls lose momentum and effectiveness.

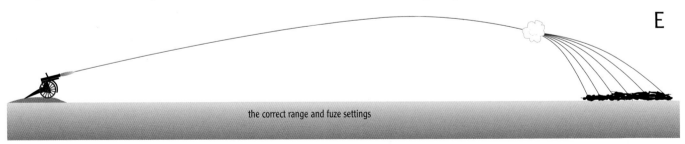

E

the correct range and fuze settings

Notes
- In this example of the importance of setting the range and fuze, both have been done correctly.

- The burst is just in front of, and above, the advancing troops, ensuring all are in the beaten zone.

The Effect of High-explosive Shells with Varying Fuzes on Different Targets

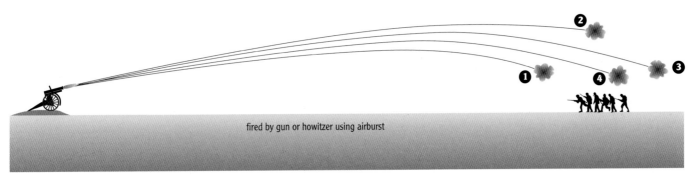

fired by gun or howitzer using airburst

Notes
• Used in an anti-personnel role, the high-explosive (HE) shell was often less effective than shrapnel, as the fragments were scattered in all directions rather than being thrown forward.

• Here the only burst likely to be effective is no. **4**, but even then many fragments are wasted. Nos. **1** and **3** have burst too far ahead or behind the target, and no. 2 is too high.
• Using the correct time fuze and assessing the range accurately are critical.

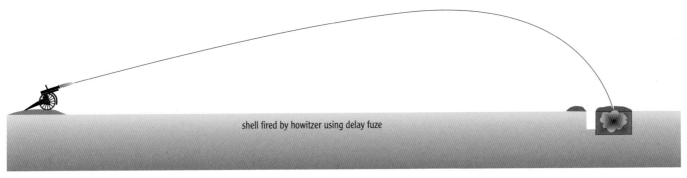

shell fired by howitzer using delay fuze

Notes
• This shows high-angle plunging fire by a howitzer, using a delay fuze that allows the shell to penetrate the roof of the bunker/dugout before exploding.

• Even heavy shells failed to penetrate many of the very deep and reinforced shelters used by the Germans.

Notes
• Bursts nos. **1** and **2** have used the older percussion/impact fuze, which has allowed the shell to penetrate the ground before detonating. The effect on the wire is minimal.
• Shell no. **3** has used an airburst fuze and the effect is virtually nil.
• Shells nos. **4** and **5** have used the 106E percussion fuze and just touching the wire is enough to cause detonation. The explosions in the midst of the wire before hitting the ground blow apart the wire effectively.

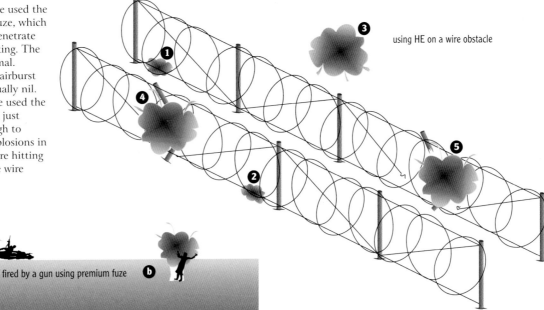

using HE on a wire obstacle

fired by a gun using premium fuze

Notes
• As the war progressed, HE became the accepted ammunition for most targets using percussion fuzes.
• The HE shell had the advantage of a blast effect, as well as producing splinters that caused casualties, disorientation and shell shock.
• In this case, the HE shell with a percussion fuze has hit men in the open **a** and struck the trench at **b**. In both cases, casualties would have been caused.

Artillery Ammunition Supply for a Division, 1914–1916

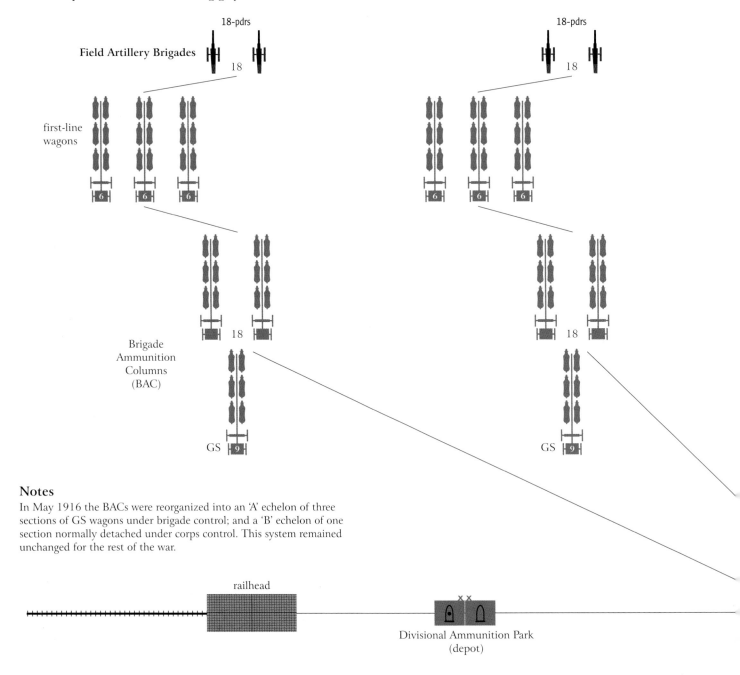

Notes

In May 1916 the BACs were reorganized into an 'A' echelon of three sections of GS wagons under brigade control; and a 'B' echelon of one section normally detached under corps control. This system remained unchanged for the rest of the war.

Ammunition supply

Field Marshal Haig, in his final despatch of 21 March 1919, summing up the critical features of the war, had this to say about artillery ammunition:

> It was not until mid-summer 1916 that the artillery situation became even approximately adequate to the conduct of major operations. Throughout the Somme battle the expenditure of artillery ammunition had to be watched with the greatest care ... Only in 1918 was it possible to conduct artillery operations independently of any limiting consideration other than that of transport.

Haig was referring to the fact that the success or otherwise of all major operations depended on having enough guns and ammunition available, as it was around these assets that all planning revolved. For the first two years on the Western Front, artillery ammunition stocks in France suffered from two major defects: a woefully inadequate supply and too many defective fuzes. On more than one occasion in 1915 (at the Battles of Aubers and Festubert), the Chief of the General Staff reported 'the battle must now cease' for lack of ammunition. This was the year of the 'Munitions Crisis' that brought about the fall of the British Liberal government when it became public

that ammunition supply (of all categories, not just artillery shells) was totally inadequate for sustained operations. The basic problem, like most problems on the Western Front in the early years, was due to the ever-expanding scale of demand for everything, from men to all weapons, items of military equipment, uniforms, stores or ammunition. In 1915 a new front was opened up in the Dardanelles, which hugely increased pressure on an already overburdened manufacturing base. Munitions factories were too few, experience in the manufacture of ammunition was limited and workers were still sticking to union rules. In 1915 there were 707 trade disputes in the United Kingdom, resulting in

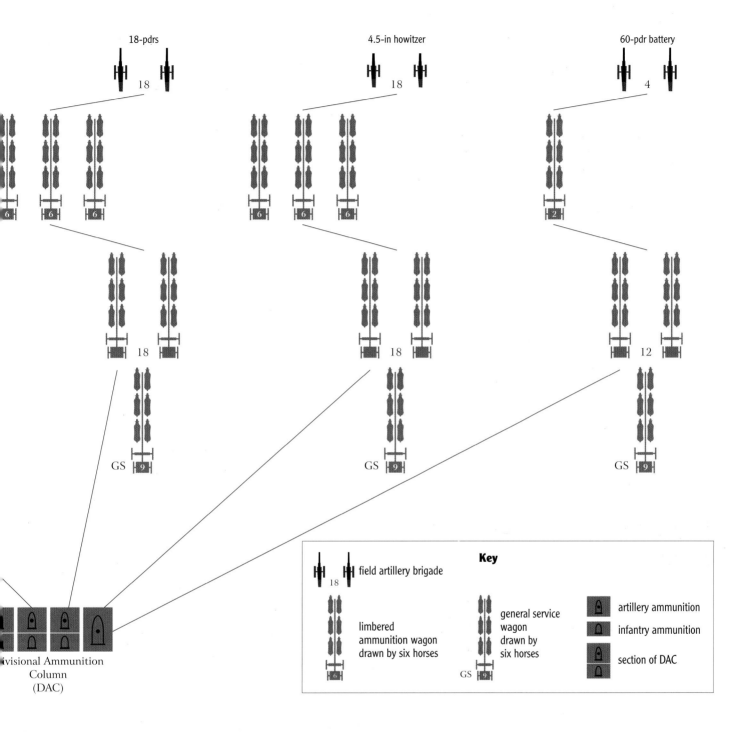

the loss of over 3 million working days, and in 1916, as thousands died on the Somme, another 2.6 million were lost. An extreme example occurred in a munitions factory in 1916 when there was a refusal to work with two female overseers who would not join a boycott of the canteen. More labour troubles came in 1917. Strikes of shipyard workers also affected delivery of supplies, including ammunition, to France. As Kipling put it in his poem 'Batteries Out of Ammunition':

If any mourn us in the workshop, say
We died because the shift kept holiday.

The crisis led to the formation of the Ministry of Munitions, under Lloyd George, on 1 July 1915 to oversee a steady expansion of munitions manufacture, including new factories and the use of every other possible institution, even school workshops (see box, page 240), to meet demand. Many months were to elapse before production began to catch up, as demand was rising spectacularly. For example, in July 1915 the weekly minimum requirements for 18-pounder ammunition (shrapnel and HE) was 340,000 rounds; in September 767,000; in October 1917 1,400,000; and by that

time the requirement for 6-inch howitzer ammunition had risen from 50,000 to 330,000 a month. As well as insufficient shells, there was a worse shortfall of fuzes. By the end of May 1915, 870,000 of the No. 80 fuze for the 8-inch howitzer had been delivered instead of the contracted 1,770,000. By August 1916 there were, according to the *British Official History of the War 1915*, Volume I, 25 million 18-pounder shells in stock awaiting fuzes. Even when fuzes were available, too high a proportion malfunctioned. This problem was just as acute with the heavy guns. Major Franklin

Lushington, RGA, described the situation in 1915:

> for some months after Festubert all siege batteries were reduced to a maximum of twelve rounds a day. At that time the only ammunition supplied to these batteries was some 6-inch gun shell from Gibraltar, which had been condemned as unserviceable . . . To ensure safety these were fired by means of a specially long lanyard, all the gun crew being ordered out of the gun-pit except the hero who pulled the string. A premature detonation occurred in a neighbouring battery, which blew the whole of the front of the barrel off. But owing to the care that was taken when firing these condemned shells, no casualties occurred.

Throughout the following year there was a growing increase in the number of premature explosions in proportion to the number of rounds fired. Not only were there too many bursts in the gun, but also too many rounds that failed to explode on arrival at the target – what the military term 'blinds'. The fuze on the 8-inch howitzer failed so often to ignite the bursting charge that parts of the Somme battlefield were reported to be littered with blinds – or 'duds' as the soldiers called them. German shells had the same problem. Lieutenant-Colonel Neil Fraser-Tytler, a gunner officer, has described one incident:

> Our dugouts were merely little scratchings in a bank under a hedge, and on this afternoon I heard a dud land in the bank. On investigation I found it had gone through ten feet of earth (in the bank) into a dugout where three men were lying; it passed over one man, slightly bruising his ribs, and came to rest with the fuse touching the clay of the far wall. Three scared men crawled out of their hole very speedily, and I looked and saw lying there a silvery 5.9-inch shell, polished by its passage through the earth.

The British preparatory bombardment for the Somme offensive consumed over 1.7 million shells of all types – of these it is estimated that an incredible 30 per cent were duds.

Britain was not alone with supply difficulties, as the French and Germans experienced serious shortages of artillery ammunition after the Battle of the Marne due to the number of engagements and the rapidity of fire. The French had a greater initial supply than the Germans. They started with 1,300 rounds per gun on hand for their 75s, and even after the Marne 500 remained, the average expenditure being 800. Nevertheless, this was still inadequate and by the end of September 1914 General

Foch, commanding the new Ninth Army, sent a staff officer to his commander-in-chief, Joffre, to plead for more ammunition. On hearing the plea, Joffre responded:

> 'What has come over you all, to keep asking me for ammunition I don't have? At the end of October, we shall be producing five thousand shells a day. Today is only the 27th of September. For a month therefore, we'll have to do some faking. Three shells per gun! Tell Foch to stop bothering me.'

The Germans had made the initial error of supplying the QF field guns with less ammunition than the heavy, slower-firing, field howitzers. According to the German artillery paper *Artilleristische Monatshefte* in early 1914, their original supply was 987 per field gun, 973 per light field howitzer, but 4,000 per heavy field howitzer.

Production and delivery invariably lagged behind requirements on the battlefield. Many weeks of stockpiling were needed by all belligerents before any major offensive. Two examples illustrate the problem. First, on 1 July 1916 on the Somme the French fired 270,000 rounds of 75mm ammunition, including 80,000 rounds from heavy pieces and 30,000 from trench mortars. To transport this to the front required twenty-seven trains of thirty cars every day. Second, during the period 21 March to 20 June 1916 at Verdun, the Germans fired almost 17 million rounds of all types of artillery and mortar ammunition – an average of 190,00 rounds a day. There have been claims that German development of artillery was faster than that of the Allies, but the evidence of this is hard to find. All artillery developed along similar lines in differing circumstances. They all benefited from the innovations of friend and foe. German artillery ascendancy in the first half of 1918 was lost to the Allies from July of that year onwards.

Trench Mortars

Mortars are discussed separately from guns and howitzers to avoid confusion, as although they started out as infantry weapons, the British later gave heavier versions to the Royal Artillery while the lighter ones continued to be crewed by infantrymen, but were separated from battalion command and allocated to brigades.

The average infantryman in a front-line trench loathed mortars – German or Allied. The former were *Minenwerfer* (literally, mine-throwers) of varying sizes that threw large black bombs called 'minnies', which shattered trenches and men with seeming impunity. These German projectiles were

the size of a 2-gallon oildrum filled with a wet yellow paste that smelled of marzipan and burst with a massively destructive force. Their range was over 1,000 yards and the canister would make a 'woof, woof' noise as it turned over and over in the air. A typical shoot would put a bomb on every 10 yards of the designated trench line every three minutes. Richard Holmes, quoting from Robert Graves, succinctly illustrates the British hatred of this weapon:

> Opposite Fricourt on the Somme, 2/Royal Welch Fusiliers were repeatedly shelled by a mortar firing a two-gallon drum of explosive . . . When they took the village they found a wooden cannon buried in the earth and discharged with a time-fuse. 'The crew offered to surrender,' wrote Robert Graves, 'but our men had sworn for months to get them.' Nearby a German frantically sought to have his surrender accepted by shrieking '*Minenwerfer* man, *Minenwerfer* man' in the hope that this might make him seem less hostile, but his opponent quietly remarked: 'Then you're just the man I've been looking for,' and ran him through with his bayonet.

The general dislike of Allied mortars was because, when positioned close to forward positions, as they had to be due to range limitations, their firing invariably brought down a deluge of retaliatory fire on the infantry – usually after the mortar detachment had

A store of British 'toffee apple' mortar bombs in an old German trench at Gommecourt, March 1917.

departed. The divisional historian of the British 33rd Infantry Division (G. S. Hutchison) puts this sentiment vividly:

> We feel sure that if Sir William Stokes, when he so patriotically offered his wonderful drainpipe [the Stokes mortar, see below] to the British Government, had he known what a volcano of unpopularity and lava flow of oaths he would call down, not only upon his own head, but upon the heads of those unfortunates who were called upon to manipulate his weapon, he would have confined his inventive genius to something which irritated the Hun less.

Despite the above, experienced soldiers could, if lucky, contrive to avoid an incoming mortar bomb provided they spotted it in flight. Soldiers learned to listen for the distinctive 'cough' of firing and immediately scan the sky, as due to the low velocity and very high angle it was often possible to watch the bomb approaching, rather like a cricketer on the boundary watching the descent of a high catch. Once seen, there was time to rush down the trench away from the likely impact area, or to dive into a nearby dugout. This method also worked at night, as a trail of sparks marked the path of its flight. Shrewd mortar men fired at dusk when it was too light to see the burning fuze but dark enough to make the bomb invisible.

A mortar was basically a smooth-bore steel tube on a base plate supported at a high angle by a bipod. The bomb/shell was dropped down the barrel from the muzzle end, which then hit a striker in the base plate that fired the charge to propel the bomb in its steep climb, but over a comparatively short range. Because of the steep descent of the bomb, the mortar was able to hit targets that were more difficult for other artillery, such as infantry sheltering down behind the parapet of a trench. The lighter versions were easily portable and could be set up concealed in, and fired from, trenches. As front-line trenches were seldom more than 800 yards apart, mortars were a deadly and effective addition to trench warfare – hence their name. As well as a maximum range, mortars also had minimum safe ranges for friendly troops – fired vertically, the bomb would theoretically fall on the firer – that varied from 150–200 yards.

In 1914, after observing their effectiveness in the Russo-Japanese War of 1904–1905, the Germans had some 150 mortars available to their field army compared to the Allies' nil and their introduction of the *Minenwerfer* at Ypres in October 1914 came as an unpleasant shock. The French had to scramble around to assemble an ancient collection of more or less useless Napoleonic mortars, while the British had largely to resort to various ingenious contraptions to throw bombs put together hastily in engineer and ordnance workshops in France. These included giant catapults and crossbows, the design of which owed much to the Roman legions. The first British mortars were crude improvisations known as 'drainpipes', the crew of which took cover while the firer, also under cover, pulled a long lanyard. However, with the personal intervention of Lloyd George, the production of effective mortars progressed and the British ended up with a 2-inch spigot mortar, which had a large bomb on the end of a shaft that was inserted into the barrel for firing (known as the 'toffee apple'). This was eventually classified as a medium mortar, along with the 3.7-inch (an unsatisfactory weapon) and 4-inch and 6-inch Newton mortar (introduced to replace the 2-inch in 1917). The 9.45-inch was classified as a heavy mortar, firing bombs known as 'flying pigs' that weighed 150 lb. However, it was the light 3-inch Stokes mortar (there was also a 4-inch Stokes, primarily used for firing gas) that became the most common British mortar, used extensively by dominion, American and French units. The 3-inch mortar of World War II and the 81mm mortar of modern times are both basically Stokes mortars with increased range and other added refinements.

By 1 July 1916 mortars were being used on a variety of tasks. The preliminary bombardment instruction for XV Corps for that date gives them as follows (light mortars would have been tasked at divisional and brigade level):

C. Trench Mortars

(i) Heavy and Medium:-
    1. Destruction of enemy defences and bombardment of villages within range.

(ii) Medium:-
    1. Wire-cutting [at which they were usually effective].
    2. Preventing enemy repairing work at night.
    3. Night firing on front system.

The Stokes mortar, introduced in 1915, took the name of its inventor, Frederick Wilfred Scott Stokes (later knighted), who, despite initial rejections, persevered and designed a simple and effective weapon that became the British infantryman's mortar for several decades. It consisted of a smooth-bore metal tube fixed to a base plate to absorb recoil, with a lightweight bipod mount. When the bomb was dropped into the barrel an impact-sensitive primer in the base of the bomb hit the firing pin at the bottom of the barrel and detonated the propellant charge.

The range was determined by the angle of the barrel and the amount of propellant charge used. The basic charge was used with all firings and covered short ranges. Up to four additional propellant 'rings' were supplied with the cartridge, to be used for incremental range increases. The firer discarded the rings that were not needed.

Overleaf are three extracts from a Stokes mortar range table that illustrate this; the figures for range are given in yards, the time in seconds.

Stokes Mortar Ranges

Cartridge only			1 Ring		2 Rings		3 Rings		4 Rings	
Degs	Range	Flight time	Range	Flight time	Range	Flight time	Range	Flight time	Range	Flight time
45	240	7.1	420	9.6	550	11.6	660	13.2	800	15.0
65	170	8.9	313	12.2	409	14.8	499	16.9	586	19.0
75	102	9.4	197	13.0	259	15.7	320	18.0	364	20.1

The table shows that to get maximum range the mortar had to be fired with the barrel at 45 degrees with the cartridge and all four rings of propellant. For very close targets, the opposite was the case, with a 75-degree angle and a cartridge dropping the bomb only about 100 yards in front of the firer – any steeper angle was decidedly risky. This mortar could fire as many as twenty-five bombs a minute, with a skilled firer able to get seven or eight bombs in flight simultaneously.

Production, particularly of ammunition, took some time to catch up with demand. The output of trench mortars in 1915 was 945, of which 524 were produced in the last quarter. With ammunition, the total for that year was 411,234, of which 182,880 were in the last quarter. This means only 435 bombs per mortar – an amount that could disappear in a few hours' firing. However, there was a huge improvement during winter 1915/16, and in the first quarter of 1916 over a million were produced, a number doubled the following quarter in time for the start of the Somme offensive. By the Armistice there were nearly 1,700 Stokes mortars in service on the Western Front with British and dominion troops.

Within the BEF there was considerable confusion during the first two years of the war over whether mortars should be operated by infantrymen or gunners. Not until December 1915 was it finally agreed to classify batteries (of four mortars each) as light, medium and heavy, with the infantry manning the light and medium and the artillery the heavy. Then in June 1916 the artillery took over medium, leaving the Stokes as the light infantry mortar. None the less, although they were manned by infantrymen, the Stokes were removed from infantry battalion control and organized as one trench-mortar company of two four-mortar sections under a captain in each brigade. According to Lord Moran, a battalion medical officer during the war, 'when a battalion was ordered to send men to a trench mortar company . . . it often seized the chance to get rid of its rubbish'. This may not have been universal, but there was always a temptation to get rid of troublesome or incompetent individuals to postings from which they were unlikely to return. Also in June 1916, the Royal Artillery established the post of divisional trench mortar officer (DTMO) at divisional headquarters to coordinate the activities of the three medium mortar batteries allotted

to each division, along with a battery of four heavy mortars firing 'flying pigs'.

As with the Allies, the Germans divided their *Minenwerfer* into light, medium and heavy, with the 1916-pattern light firing out to a maximum range of 1,400 yards and minimum of 175 yards. The heavy 25cm *Minenwerfer* could manage 930 yards maximum down to 260 yards minimum. The British called the 150mm German mortar the 'Jack Johnson', because when the shell exploded a dense cloud of black smoke was produced and Jack Johnson was the world heavyweight champion boxer at the time.

The Germans were the only belligerents who went to war in 1914 with mortars. They were theoretically manned by pioneers rather than infantry (although in practice many were drawn from the infantry) or artillery, and organized in sections of two (heavy) or six (medium or light) *Minenwerfer*, formed into companies and battalions. Each division had a *Minenwerfer* company attached, consisting of one heavy section of four mortars and two medium sections each comprising eight *Minenwerfer* – a total of twenty mortars and about 250 all ranks. Light mortars were issued to infantry battalions. In addition, some thirteen *Minenwerfer* battalions of four companies formed a reserve at the disposal of General Headquarters. Further reorganization took place after Hindenburg became supreme commander in late 1916. All light mortars passed from pioneer to infantry control, and divisional companies had an establishment of four heavy and eight medium *Minenwerfer*. There was a *Minenwerfer* officer attached to every regiment and special training schools set up behind the front. By the end of the war, the Germans had deployed some 708 *Minenwerfer* companies.

Artillery Development 1914–1918

This section aims to give a general overview of artillery on the Western Front and in doing so to paint a broad picture of how the use of this crucial arm developed.

The artillery of the main belligerents was organized as follows:

• **BEF** At the Battle of Mons the artillery support for each of the four infantry divisions comprised fifty-four 18-pounder guns in three brigades, each of three six-gun batteries; eighteen 4.5-inch guns in three batteries of six guns; and a battery of four 60-pounder guns. The Cavalry Division had five batteries of six 13-pounder guns. Two batteries were in each of the Royal Horse Artillery (RHA) brigades – the fifth battery supported the 5th Independent Cavalry Brigade.

• **French** Each first-line division had thirty-six 75mm guns in three *groupes* of three batteries of four guns. There were also twenty regiments of corps' artillery, each of four *groupes* of three batteries and five regiments of heavy artillery.

• **Germans** Their artillery was divided into field artillery (including horse and foot artillery), which consisted of all medium and heavy batteries of guns and howitzers. Each first-line division's artillery was normally (there were variations) made up of two regiments. One regiment comprised two battalions, each of three batteries of six 77mm guns (36 total). The second regiment manned three batteries, each of six 10.5cm howitzers (18 total). In addition, there was

in each corps a battalion of 12.15cm howitzers and in each army a number of 21cm heavy howitzers.

The types of equipment in use by the three powers did not vary much. All proved deficient in range, the British artillery being initially at the greatest disadvantage in this respect. The French lack of a field howitzer was due to the failure of the government to provide the funds – it was partially compensated for by the excellence of their field gun, the *soixante-quinze*. The Germans had a marked advantage in having large numbers of howitzers capable of assisting in both field and siege operations. All three nations had divisional artillery commanders, but at this stage only France had one at corps level.

Viewed with hindsight, it appears the British and French tactical doctrine unduly emphasized mobility at the expense of firepower, with the Germans slightly better balanced in this respect. All belligerents grossly underestimated the quantity of ammunition that would be required. Britain had estimated a likely expenditure of seven rounds a day per 18-pounder, a figure that in practice often rose to over 500 a day. No country had fully appreciated the effect on artillery of the development of railways, motor traction, aircraft, telephones, wireless and survey.

Evolution of Equipment

The artillery of all nations developed from an arm trained to dash about the battlefield, firing mostly over open sights at a target the gunners could see, to one that could fire thousands of tons of ammunition in barrages lasting days, with guns capable of firing accurately from a map – predicted fire. By 1917 this ability to employ predicted fire restored a degree of surprise to attacks, which, together with infantry, tanks and aircraft, saw the beginning of modern battle-group warfare. The main command and technical developments that brought about the very considerable advances in gunnery, particularly counter-battery work, are given below. They do not include the technical advances made to the actual guns.

• **Command and Control** In 1914 the senior artillery officer at a corps headquarters was called the Brigadier General Royal Artillery (BGRA), but he was an adviser to the corps commander, not a commander of the heavy artillery supporting his corps, which was commanded by higher headquarters. During 1915 some corps started to give command responsibilities to their BGRAs. This arrangement was officially recognized at the end of the Somme battle in late 1916, and enabled much improved coordination of the heavy artillery tasking for the crucial 'deep battle' and counter-battery fire, as opposed to the battle at the front line, largely fought by field artillery and mortars.

• **Ranging/registration** The firing of ranging shots to register the target for a battery was time consuming and warned the enemy of what was coming. Two methods were developed to overcome this problem:

Sound-ranging. This was designed to locate enemy guns by setting up listening stations with six 'Tucker' microphones, named after a corporal in the Royal Engineers, distributed across a wide area and introduced in 1916.

It was possible, using the time taken for each microphone to register the sound of each gun firing, to calculate how far away the gun was and the bearing to it. Corporal Tucker had found a way of eliminating the sonic boom of the shell in the recording, thus ensuring the microphones were listening only to the report at the gun. C and H Sound-ranging Sections RE would eventually be involved in locating up to 90 per cent of the Germans' batteries without the need of a single ranging shot.

Flash-spotting. With this method of locating enemy guns, an observer watched the muzzle flash and then timed how long it took to hear the report at the gun. By using a bearing on the guns and the fact that light and sound travel at different speeds, it was possible to calculate the range. However, when the Germans introduced flashless powder for their propellants in 1917 this method was thwarted and reliance was placed on sound-ranging and aerial photography.

• **Battery boards** Another response to the need for indirect fire was a board mounted on a tripod and covered with gridded paper at a scale corresponding to the maps in use, supported by telephone or wireless reports from ground or airborne observers. The board was a graphical device to convert the target location and observer's information, expressed as grid references, into ranges in yards and bearings in degrees that could be passed to the guns. The positions of the guns and observer were marked on the paper. Pinned to the board over the guns was a pivot carrying a steel range-arm marked in yards. The far end of this ran along a steel arc marked in degrees and minutes, also pinned to the board. When a target grid reference was received it was pencilled in on the board and the range arm swung over the spot, enabling the range and bearing to be read off. The line from the observer to the target was also pencilled in so that the observer's corrections, expressed in yards left or right or add or drop, could be incorporated after the fall of shot had been observed.

• **Aerial observation** The use of aircraft as spotters hugely increased the ability of the artillery to locate German batteries and strongpoints. In particular, aerial photographs provided artillery and other planners with accurate, up-to-date information that would otherwise be virtually impossible to obtain. Not only were enemy positions more easily pinpointed, but aerial photography also became vital for accurate, up-to-date map-making. A considerable number of observation balloons were used for this purpose, as well as aircraft.

• **Surveying** The whole success of the counter-battery and long-range artillery effort depended heavily on good mapping of the front. From small beginnings in late 1914, a topographical section was eventually established at every corps headquarters. By using aerial photographs, it was possible during the latter part of 1915 to produce a comprehensive series of 1:10,000 maps, to keep updating them, and to print off detailed barrage and target maps for specific operations (see pages 248–9 and 258–61 for examples). This facilitated predicted firing entirely off a map, which enabled a fire plan to be implemented when required without the ranging or registration that so often gave away intentions – surprise became possible.

• **Meteorological data** Considerable understanding was gained of how the variables of temperature, humidity, wind, elevation of the target in relation to the gun and wear on the barrel affected accuracy. Tables were supplied to battery officers enabling alterations incorporating these factors to be made.

Evolution of Tactics

The evolution of artillery organization and equipment and the evolution of tactics were interdependent. During the first clashes on the Western Front in 1914 it quickly became evident that the power of small-arms fire in defence meant that attacks must be well prepared by artillery. Tactical mobility had become dependent on firepower, but initially neither side had the artillery or ammunition to provide that power in adequate measure. At Le Cateau, the British learned the dire consequences of deploying their batteries in the open in close support of the foremost infantry. The urgent need for more medium and heavy artillery soon became apparent.

With the advent of trench warfare during the winter of 1914/15, new developments, including the large-scale introduction of barbed-wire entanglements, night firing by artillery, the use of defensive bombardments, the need to distribute guns in depth and the value of using aircraft for observation began to develop. The increasing accuracy and range of the artillery meant there was a need to camouflage gun positions and to protect them and their gunners either with concrete or with 12–15 feet of solid earth. To these must be added the growing requirement for HE ammunition to supplement, and in many cases replace, shrapnel as the more effective shell against a variety of targets, particularly when used by heavier guns or howitzers.

The Battle of Neuve Chapelle (see Map 12, page 45) on 10 March 1915 formed

Three Victoria Crosses in One Morning at Néry

On the evening of 31 August 1914 the British Brigadier General C. J. Briggs, commanding the 1st Cavalry Brigade consisting of the 2nd and 5th Dragoon Guards and the 11th Hussars, supported by L Battery RHA commanded by Major W. D. Sclater-Booth, was ordered to billet for the night in the small village of Néry. They were expected to continue the general retreat from Mons at 4:30 the next morning. During the night, and unbeknown to the British, the German 4th Cavalry Division, under Major General von Garnier, had crossed the River Automne at Béthisy-St-Martin and moved up the hill to Le Plessis Châtelain, arriving in the early morning while it was still dark and with a thick mist developing. A patrol of the 17th Dragoons reported the village of Néry occupied by the British, but apparently not prepared for defence. Garnier resolved to attack.

L Battery RHA was bivouacked in a hayfield immediately south of the village. The mist had meant a delayed start for the brigade, and a number of the battery's horse teams had been sent to water at the sugar factory where the battery headquarters was billeted. Shortly after 5:00 a.m. a hurricane of machine-gun, rifle and artillery fire hit the village and L Battery from the heights some 800 yards to the east. The scene in L Battery's field quickly became one of devastation as a hail of shrapnel and bullets hit men and horses. Sergeant D. Nelson, the No. 1 of F gun, later wrote:

> During the awful carnage of dying men and horses was audible amidst the terrific thundering of the cannon . . . One man in full view of me had his head cut clean off his body, another was literally blown to pieces, another was practically severed at the breast, loins, knees and ankles. One horse had its head and neck completely severed from its shoulders. So terrific was the hail of shrapnel that I was bespattered with blood from men and horses.

Captain E. K. Bradbury had led the rush to man the guns, but only four (B, C, D and F) could be brought into action with the officers serving as crew members. Nelson's account continues:

L Battery, Royal Horse Artillery, at Néry. In this field the battery's six 13-pdr guns, limbers and some 200 horses bivouacked on the night of 31 August/1 September 1914. Here the battery fought its epic duel with the enemy over open sights, with the German guns overlooking this exposed field from the ridge (mostly obscured behind trees). Three VCs were won.

> I took cover by the wagons, momentarily dumbfounded, and awaiting orders, but after a second volley of shrapnel, seeing no officers near, I called Gunner Darbyshire and with his assistance unlimbered my gun and directed it on the enemy's guns and opened fire.
>
> Just then Captain Bradbury, Lieut Mundy, Corpl Payne and Driver Osborne arrived and we kept up a destructive fire for some time. Gnr Darbyshire and Dvr Osborne heroically carrying ammunition from other wagons to augment the supply already in the gun limber.

At that stage F gun detachment consisted of Lieutenant Mundy acting as observer, Captain Bradbury laying, Sergeant Nelson setting the range, Darbyshire in the firer's seat and Osborne fetching ammunition from the wagons some 20 yards away across ground swept by fire. Corporal Payne's duties are unclear, but he was eventually reported killed bringing ammunition to the gun. When C gun was knocked out, Lieutenant J. D. Campbell, although wounded, dashed over to help with F gun, the only one still in action, and assisted Osborne with fetching ammunition. Darbyshire had this to say of his time as firer:

> As soon as we got No. 6 Gun (F gun) into action I jumped into the seat and began firing, but so awful was the concussion of our own explosions and the bursting German shells that I could not bear it for long. I kept it up for about twenty minutes, then my nose and

ears were bleeding because of the concussion, and I could not fire any more, so I left the seat and got a change fetching ammunition.

> Immediately I left the seat, Lieutenant Campbell, who had been helping with the ammunition, took it . . . but he had not fired more than a couple of rounds when a shell burst under the shield. The explosion was awful, and the brave young officer was hurled about six yards from the very seat in which I had been sitting a few seconds earlier. He lived for only a few minutes.

This same shell also fatally wounded Lieutenant Mundy and Corporal Payne. Seeing the situation, Battery Sergeant-Major G. T. Dorrell, who had been firing his rifle at the enemy, ran across to join the remaining F gun team. At this stage the three men serving the gun were Captain Bradbury, Sergeant Major Dorrell and Sergeant Nelson, who had already been wounded twice but refused to leave the gun. Despite the efforts of Darbyshire and Osborne, ammunition had become critical and Captain Bradbury went to fetch more. Gunner Darbyshire's account describes what happened:

> When I felt a little better I began to help Driver Osborne to fetch ammunition from the wagons. I had just managed to get back to the gun, with an armful of ammunition, when a lyddite shell exploded behind me, threw me to the ground and partially stunned me.
>
> When I came round I got up and found that I was uninjured. On looking round, however, I saw that Captain Bradbury . . . had been knocked down by the same shell that floored me, and was mortally wounded [he had both legs blown off at the knees]. Though the Captain knew that death was near, he thought of his men to the last, and begged to be carried away, so that they should not be upset by seeing him, or hearing the cries which he could not restrain.

However, Captain Bradbury did not die immediately. Sometime after the action ended, Colour Sergeant E. M. Lyons of the Warwickshire Regiment, who was searching for wounded, found Bradbury. 'There was one we couldn't put in the ambulance he was so badly wounded so we borrowed a farm cart and packed it with straw. It was the battery commander Capt. Bradbury, who I'm sorry to say died soon'.

F gun remained in action until after 7:00 a.m., but the Germans did not finally withdraw until they had come under attack from the Dragoon Guards, 11th Hussars, Queen's Bays, I Battery RHA and the arriving infantry of the 1st Middlesex.

L Battery's casualties amounted to eight officers and forty-seven men killed, with undoubtedly a number of men suffering from deafness and bleeding from the nose and ears (both common problems on a gun line). Captain Bradbury, Battery Sergeant Major Dorrell and Sergeant Nelson each received the Victoria Cross. Dorrell, who had enlisted as a boy of fifteen to fight in the Second Boer War, rose to the rank of brevet lieutenant colonel and commanded a Home Guard detachment in World War II. He died aged ninety-one in 1971. Nelson was also commissioned and was killed as an acting major in 1918. Gunner Darbyshire and Driver Osborne were awarded the French *Médaille militaire*. One of the 13-pounders from L Battery, along with the three Victoria Crosses, is on display at the Imperial War Museum, London. L Battery was given the honour title of 'Néry' and served in North Africa and Italy during World War II. At the time of writing (January 2010) it is part of 1RHA, based at Tidworth in Wiltshire.

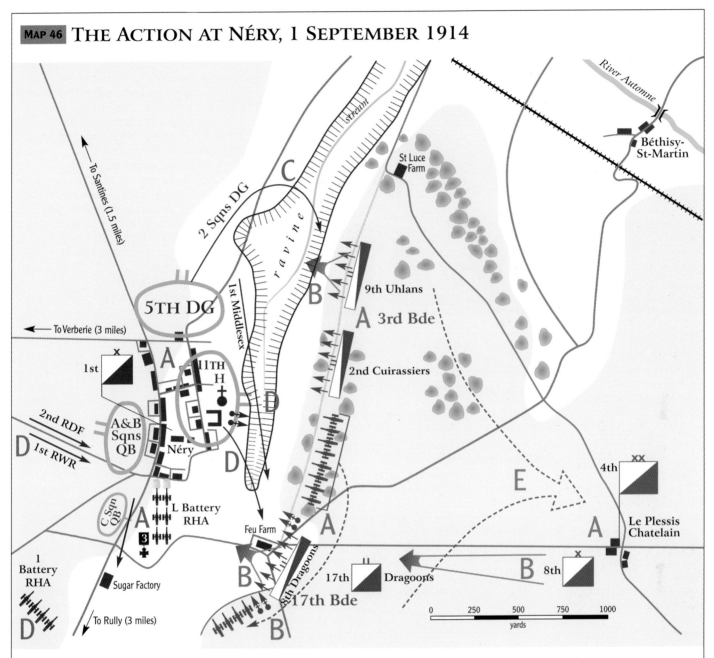

MAP 46 THE ACTION AT NÉRY, 1 SEPTEMBER 1914

River Automne

Béthisy-St-Martin

To Santines (1.5 miles)

stream

St Luce Farm

2 Sqns DG

C

ravine

5TH DG

9th Uhlans

1st Middlesex

B

A   3rd Bde

To Verberie (3 miles)

1st   X

A

11TH H

2nd Cuirassiers

2nd RDF

A&B Sqns QB

D   Néry

D

1st RWR

C Sqn QB

A

4th   XX

L Battery RHA

3

Feu Farm

A

E

A   Le Plessis Chatelain

1 Battery RHA

Sugar Factory

B

8th Dragoons

17th   Dragoons

B   8th   X

D

To Rully (3 miles)

17th Bde

B

0   250   500   750   1000

yards

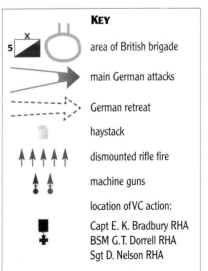

Notes for Map 46
• The 1st British Cavalry Brigade was billeted in and around Néry on the night of 31 August 1914, as shown by **AA** on the map. L Battery RHA was bivouacked in a field to the south. The German 4th Cavalry Division arrived during the early morning darkness and mist of 1 September, took up the positions on the high ground shown by **AAA** and prepared to attack.
• The German artillery, machine-gun and rifle fire caught the brigade completely by surprise: the exposed and unprepared L Battery was quickly reduced to a shambles of dead and wounded men and horses. Initially four guns were able to come into action but they were soon reduced to just F gun, which kept firing despite the crew being reduced to three (Capt. Bradbury, BSM Dorrell and Sgt Nelson).
• The German attempts to attack on both flanks were half-hearted, despite reinforcements and shifting the guns north of Feu Farm to join the battery in the south – see **BBBB**.
• Two squadrons of the Dragoon Guards were launched to counter-attack in the north and checked the German Uhlans' advance – indicated by **C**.
• British reinforcements arrived at 8:00 a.m. and I Battery RHA opened fire with great effect on the German guns. The 11th Hussars charged towards the Germans around Feu Farm and the Queen's Bays attacked the Germans, who had reached the sugar factory, while at much the same time the 1st Middlesex, arriving from the north, attacked southwards – **DDDD**.
• The Germans, who had suffered severely, retreated hastily, leaving behind their guns – **E**.

KEY

5   X   area of British brigade

main German attacks

German retreat

haystack

dismounted rifle fire

machine guns

location of VC action:

Capt E. K. Bradbury RHA

BSM G.T. Dorrell RHA

Sgt D. Nelson RHA

A German gun has been knocked out, with two of its crew killed. A third gunner falls as another shell hits the position.

something of a landmark in artillery tactical evolution, although the lessons of the initial success were not universally followed up. In this British penetration attack some 340 guns and howitzers were to concentrate their fire along a narrow 2,000-yard front, the narrowness being due to the limited amount of ammunition and the realization that what was available must be concentrated and targeted. Aircraft were used for observation and the guns were in position by 5 March, with registration completed. The 240 13- and 18-pounders were tasked with destroying the German wire and trenches on the flanks of the attack, as part of an intense thirty-five-minute bombardment before the infantry assault. The sixty 4.5-inch and 6-inch howitzers were to attack the trenches and selected targets, while the 4.7-inch and 6-inch guns had a counter-battery role. The village of Neuve Chapelle was to be hit by three heavy 9.2-inch howitzers (see photograph, page 44). The first and second phases of the attack were, except on the extreme left, remarkably successful; the third phase failed due to a delay in bringing up infantry reserves caused by communication failures. Careful planning and target allocation, and above all surprise – achieved by registering the guns several days before the assault and by the preparatory bombardment lasting only 35 minutes – were the key factors in the initial success.

Some six months later at Loos, the lessons of surprise and concentration of fire at Neuve Chapelle were seemingly forgotten as the British plan envisaged an attack on a front some five times longer but with a similar number of guns/howitzers. Consequently, a lengthy preparatory bombardment of four days was employed, with the obvious loss of surprise. Another factor in the lack of success

was the failure of the wind to cooperate with the first British use of gas discharged from cylinders. As with the attacks at Festubert and Givenchy earlier that year, the objective of the artillery was to destroy and kill rather than merely to neutralize or paralyse – that is, to prevent enemy activity interfering with the attackers' progress until they had arrived close to or on their objective. The French fell into the same error of neglecting surprise in Champagne and Artois.

The prolonged battles on the Somme and at Verdun in 1916, with their massive preparatory barrages lasting days rather than hours or minutes and ending with an intense hurricane of fire immediately prior to the infantry advance meant there could be no attempt at surprise; the former warned of a major offensive in that area, and the latter signalled the precise time of the actual attack. New experiments with differing barrages were incorporated into the Somme battles, the details and effectiveness of which are discussed below (page 250). During this year it became clear that a well-planned and well-supported attack could be fairly certain of taking enemy positions to a depth of 1,000–2,000 yards, but that progress much beyond this was seldom achievable. This type of offensive became known as the 'bite-and-hold' attack. Limited objectives were all that could be expected, as a clean breakthrough of the deep defensive lines or zones was just not practical. More and more heavy artillery was needed and the crucial importance of effective counter-battery fire to protect the advancing infantry from defensive artillery fire became ever more apparent. These were still the tactics of destruction on a massive scale, requiring huge tonnages of ammunition – the amount available was the determining

factor in the size, and certainly the frontage, of an operation. All this gunfire churned up the ground and created the moonscapes of millions of shell craters, splintered tree trunks that had once been woods, and piles of rubble that were once villages such as those seen in the photographs on pages 44 and 204. Such cratering and destruction, especially when coupled with unseasonable torrential rain and deep mud, rendered impossible the speedy forward movement of artillery to support anything but a very limited advance.

Some examples of the increasing numbers of guns, and the proportion of heavy to medium pieces, illustrate the dominance of heavier artillery in the middle and later part of the war. At the Somme on 1 July 1916 there was approximately one gun or howitzer to every 20 yards of front attacked, with the proportion of heavy to medium pieces being one in every three. At the Battle of the Scarpe on 4 April 1917 there was a gun or howitzer to every 10 yards of front, with the proportion of heavy to medium slightly more than one in three. In the British attack at Amiens on 8 August 1918 there was again one gun or howitzer every 10 yards, but the proportion of heavy to medium had risen to seven to twelve. On the parts of the front the Germans considered decisive for their offensive in April 1918, they deployed an artillery piece for every 5 yards of front.

The first half of 1917 saw a continued reliance on destruction and limited objectives. The successful setpiece assault by the Canadians on Vimy Ridge in April is a good example of how, despite appalling weather, the attackers could take a limited objective. General Currie's division captured the entire forward defence system of three trenches within half an hour – the German trenches had been obliterated by the gunfire of the standing barrage, reducing them to what has been described as a 'muddy pudding'. However, this resounding victory could not be followed up, as the supporting artillery could not fire further into the enemy defences without moving forward to new positions. Pierre Berton graphically describes the insurmountable artillery difficulties in his book *Vimy*:

> The irony was that the very arm of the service that had made the capture of Vimy Ridge possible – the artillery – had rendered itself impotent. The guns had given the battlefield such a harrowing that they could not be hauled forward to hammer the fleeing enemy. The melting snow completed the work of the barrage. The heavier guns were bogged down. It took as many as a hundred horses and

eight men to haul a single 60-pounder a quarter of a mile, and the horses were dying under the strain. It was almost as difficult to move the lighter field guns . . . Most guns had to be withdrawn until new roads were built, old craters, trenches, and shell holes filled with rubble, piles of cut brush laid under the new thoroughfares, and a narrow-gauge rail line extended to the ridge top. Five thousand men were set to work to repair the famous plank road; it was so slippery that no gun could negotiate it. The only hope the artillery had of keeping the pressure on the fleeing Germans was to use their own captured guns. By then, the enemy was consolidating near Lens and any hope of a breakthrough was lost.

The same massive destructive barrages were employed at the Third Battle of Ypres in July 1917, as they alone held out any hope of destroying the dense belts of wire fronting the German defences. Again the area was saturated with shells, but what little progress the infantry subsequently made was checked by enemy counter-attacks. And again it was established that the tactics of destruction were not the way of achieving that longed-for breakthrough.

The major change in tactics occurred at Cambrai in November 1917 (see Section Thirteen). Here the technical advances noted above were combined to produce accurate predicted fire from maps, indirect fire was routine, while gas and smoke shells could be combined effectively to neutralize and screen rather than just using HE to smash enemy positions. The accuracy and range of guns had been considerably improved and artillery commanders and staffs were now experienced planners. In combination with the extensive use of aircraft for spotting and bombing, the employment of several hundred tanks and the planners' rigid insistence on concealment of all preparations, this produced the key to most successes – surprise.

The German successes on the Western Front in 1918 were in a large part due to the skilful artillery tactics, for the development of which Lieutenant Colonel Georg Bruchmüller, Ludendorff's artillery adviser, was chiefly responsible. He ran a sort of mobile gunnery team that travelled up and down the Western Front advising and co-ordinating the new tactics.

Georg Bruchmüller had retired from the army in 1913 after a riding accident, but was recalled at the end of 1914 to become the artillery commander of the 86th Infantry Division on the Eastern Front. There he developed the new technique for artillery support of infantry attacks, which involved the centralized direction of fire from Army High Command. Until then, direction of fire had been delegated to divisions. Bruchmüller's employment of massed concentrations of fire, controlled at a higher level, brought impressive results. The British and French were also evolving towards a similar philosophy. Bruchmüller's primary objective was surprise. Secondly, he neutralized the enemy. He targeted head-quarters, command posts, batteries and infantry positions to paralyse the enemy's resistance, not necessarily destroy it. Gas shells, part of the neutralization, constituted a large proportion of the ammunition expended. Gas compensated for lack of accuracy in hitting targets with HE or shrapnel. Barrages were of short duration, many shifting backwards and forwards, surprising the enemy when they returned to, or emerged from, their positions.

His methods were brilliantly demonstrated in March 1916 at the Battle of Lake Naroch, where the German Army destroyed Russian General Alexei Evert's force, and then again at Riga in September 1917 when Bruchmüller was artillery adviser to the commander of the German Eighth Army (in all but name, commander of the artillery), using 27 per cent gas shells in his bombardments. By this time he had acquired the nickname *Durchbruchmüller* (Breakthrough Müller). For his part in these victories he was awarded the prestigious *Pour le Mérite*, with the Kaiser visiting the front in March 1918 to decorate Bruchmüller personally. He was one of only four senior artillery officers to receive it. His methods were so successful that in 1918 the Supreme Army Command assigned him as artillery adviser to Army High Command for the offensive in the West. By now a colonel, he oversaw the successful use of German artillery during their spring offensive that year. He retired again in 1919, subsequently writing several books on his artillery techniques. He died in 1948, aged eighty-five.

Artillery Fire-planning and Barrages

Planning

From 1916 through to the Armistice the advancing technology of artillery and the need for precise coordination with other arms made artillery fire-planning the most complex part of an offensive, ultimately involving hundreds of staff officers at all headquarters from army to brigade, in addition to the exacting workload of the officers and men in the batteries. To this must be added hundreds more planners and thousands of soldiers and labourers on the lines of communication, moving guns and enormous tonnages of ammunition forward from railheads to stockpile at dozens of dumps. The story of all artillery-offensive planning revolved around the number of guns, having enough ammunition and a very extensive programme of target acquisition.

Apart from ground observers, aircraft of the Royal Flying Corps played a crucial role in the acquisition of intelligence on enemy positions. For artillery planning for the Somme battle, each corps had two aircraft tasked with locating enemy batteries, while one was earmarked to observe the accuracy and effectiveness of the fire of the heavy howitzers on intermediate lines and the second enemy position. Corps also had a kite balloon available. This acquisition was followed by a painstaking intelligence analysis and assessment of targets – what guns were best used to destroy or neutralize them. This led to target allocation and tasking down to individual batteries and the preparation of minute-by-minute timetables for the actual firing. Map 47 (overleaf) shows the probable locations of German artillery positions, headquarters and defensive fire tasks on the Hindenburg Line – the information it contains was gathered from captured German maps dated 10 February 1917.

These hugely complex bombardment plans frequently covered several days, during which the artillery would be in action virtually continuously. Bombardments were usually the preliminary preparation for a major battle and were planned at army and corps level. Barrages, however, were more concerned with the actual battle in progress, particularly the opening stages, and were normally planned at divisional or lower level. Planning involved conferences at higher headquarters before operation orders were prepared, along with target and barrage maps that were copied and distributed to all infantry and artillery units involved.

Not until 1918, after years of trial and error, had the respective responsibilities for

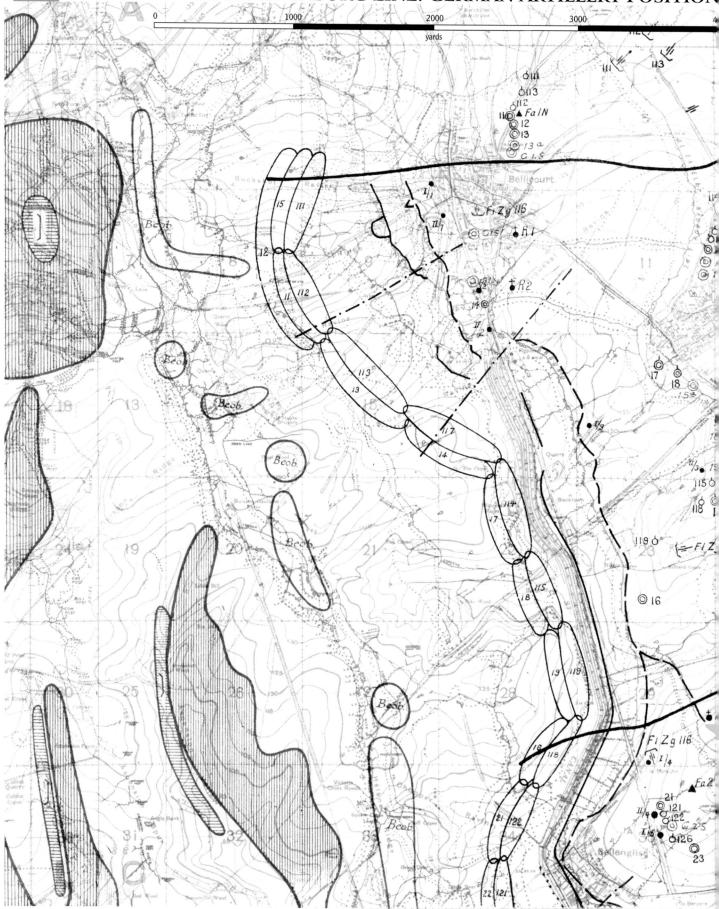

MAP 47　DEFENCE OF THE HINDENBURG LINE: GERMAN ARTILLERY POSITION

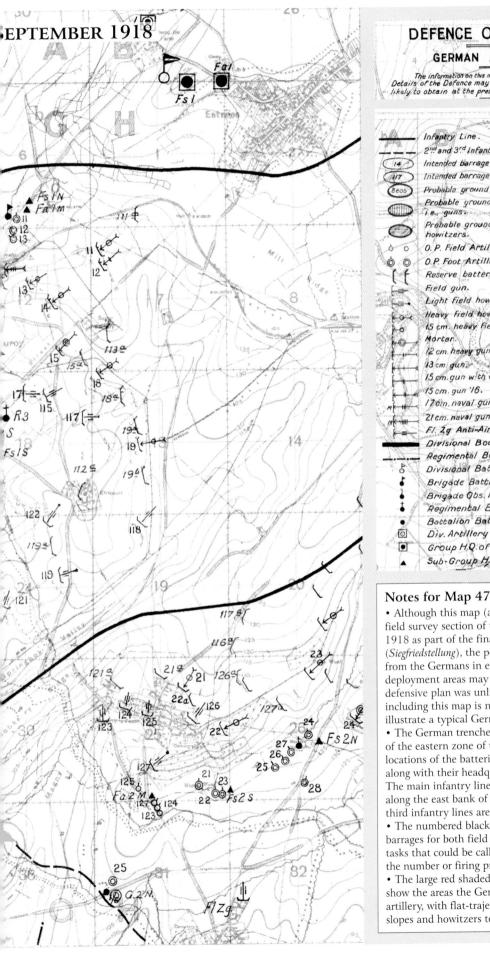

DEFENCE OF HINDENBURG LINE
GERMAN ARTILLERY POSITIONS

The information on this map is taken from captured German maps dated 10·2·17
Details of the Defence may have been modified since that date, but the General Plan is
likely to obtain at the present day

REFERENCE

	Infantry Line.
	2nd and 3rd Infantry Lines.
14	Intended barrage area of a heavy battery (figures under 100).
117	Intended barrage area of a field battery (figures over 100).
Beob	Probable ground for enemy O.Ps.
	Probable ground for enemy flat-trajectory artillery (Field Art.) i.e., guns.
	Probable ground for enemy high-trajectory artillery, i.e., howitzers.
	O.P. Field Artillery.
	O.P. Foot Artillery.
	Reserve batteries and reserve battery positions.
	Field gun.
	Light field howitzer.
	Heavy field howitzer.
	15 cm. heavy field howitzer.
	Mortar.
	12 cm. heavy gun.
	13 cm. gun.
	15 cm. gun with chase rings.
	15 cm. gun '16.
	17 cm. naval gun on platform mounting.
	21 cm. naval gun.
	Fl. Zg Anti-Aircraft gun.
	Divisional Boundary.
	Regimental Boundary.
	Divisional Battle H.Q.
	Brigade Battle H.Q.
	Brigade Obs. H.Q of 7th Infantry Division.
	Regimental Battle H.Q.
	Battalion Battle H.Q.
	Div. Artillery H.Q.
	Group H.Q. of Foot and Field Artillery.
	Sub-Group H.Q. of Foot and Field Artillery.

Notes for Map 47

• Although this map (a section of a larger one) was prepared by a field survey section of the British Royal Engineers in September 1918 as part of the final assault on the Hindenburg Line (*Siegfriedstellung*), the positions shown are from maps captured from the Germans in early 1917. As stated on the map, the deployment areas may have been modified but the overall defensive plan was unlikely to be very different. The purpose of including this map is not to show the British attack but to illustrate a typical German defensive artillery plan.

• The German trenches are in blue and show the detailed defence of the eastern zone of the Hindenburg Line. Note the pinpoint locations of the batteries of field, foot (heavy) and mortar artillery along with their headquarters from divisional to battalion level. The main infantry line is shown by black lines; much of it runs along the east bank of the St-Quentin Canal. The second and third infantry lines are indicated by black dashes.

• The numbered black lozenges indicate a series of standing barrages for both field and heavy pieces. These are numbered SOS tasks that could be called for by the infantry merely by quoting the number or firing predetermined light signals.

• The large red shaded sections on the western half of the map show the areas the Germans considered likely locations for enemy artillery, with flat-trajectory field guns largely on the forward slopes and howitzers to the rear (west) on reverse slopes.

A 9.2-in howitzer in action in the ruins of Tilloy-lès-Mofflaines, east of Arras, April 1917. The layer (third from left) is adjusting the sights while the gunners on the right are setting fuzes.

decisions and planning between the infantry and artillery commanders and staff been satisfactorily agreed and all the necessary personnel put in place. As noted above, in 1914 the senior artillery officer at a formation headquarters was an adviser who had no responsibility for implementing the operational plan. As the war progressed, this system was exposed as woefully inadequate. The growing problems of scale (particularly of heavy artillery), the advent of static trench warfare, the logistics, the need for close liaison between infantry, artillery and the RFC, and the overriding requirement for cooperation and coordination were slowly recognized and resolved. By the end of 1916, GHQ had a MGRA and army and corps headquarters had General Officers Commanding Royal Artillery (GOCRA) with staff.

For the Somme offensive, planning began at the Fourth Army Headquarters in February (for a June attack) under the MGRA, Major General J. F. N. Birch, and for the first time operation orders dealing solely with artillery matters were issued. According to artillery instructions at the time, the objectives of a preliminary bombardment and subsequent support were to prepare the way for the infantry and to support and protect the infantry throughout its progress. The preliminary bombardment was specifically tasked with:

• overpowering the hostile artillery

• the physical and moral reduction of the enemy's infantry

• the destruction of material obstacles to the infantry's advance and other defences

With the British Somme offensive, the preliminary bombardment was planned to last for six days, and its complexity is readily appreciated when the general instruction for the overall programme – shown on pages 252–3 – is examined. 'Z' Day (or Z-day) is the day the infantry assault began.

From this general day-to-day army instruction, the GOCRA at corps headquarters was responsible, in accordance with the corps commander's plan and in consultation with the divisional commanders, for allocating artillery resources (guns, howitzers and mortars) and deciding detailed targets and timings for all heavy artillery batteries. Throughout the assault, the overall artillery fire plan remained in the hands of the corps commander, although divisional commanders were normally given a call on some field batteries to meet unforeseen problems arising on their front; they could also delegate some of this authority to brigade commanders. With planning at divisional level, artillery commanders and staffs had to coordinate the field artillery assets into the daily bombardment plan.

From the field artillery barrage maps, each battery could draw up its own barrage tables (something that could take up to five hours for a complex barrage) of ranges, angles of elevation, type of ammunition, number of rounds to be fired at every lift or stage of the barrage. These had to be calculated for every gun in the battery and the section commanders and Nos. 1 given a copy. Some registration by the guns was usually necessary and invariably rehearsals were carried out without ammunition so that every gun detachment and all battery officers were familiar with the timings and procedures.

The Fourth Army programme demonstrates the thoroughness of such a lengthy preliminary bombardment. All artillery resources, including infantry trench mortars, divisional units and heavy guns and howitzers from corps and army units, were involved – a complete orchestra of guns combining to play a highly complex piece of music. The targets ranged from trenches, strongpoints, machine-gun posts, villages and communications to longer-range tasks such as railways, food and water distribution points, billets and counter-battery work. Note the importance given to wire-cutting – an all-day task every day up to and including the day before Z-day. However, the only task classed as 'very active' was counter-battery work, it being crucial to destroy or neutralize enemy guns capable of hitting the infantry assaults. The remaining targets were to be engaged as normal, with no giveaway increase of intensity. The shelling of targets to disrupt communications, working parties and resupply efforts was largely a night task, as it was during darkness that many of these activities had to take place. The shells hitting these targets came in concentrations rather than barrages, with the divisional field artillery taking on the closer ones and the heavy guns and howitzers firing at enemy batteries and deeper targets, often using gas shells after they became widely available from 1917.

Throughout this period intensive efforts were made to check the effectiveness of the bombardment. Forward observers from infantry and artillery, aircraft, observation balloons and infantry patrols all reported on the shelling and on any new targets; the infantry patrols particularly sought information on the effectiveness of the wire-cutting and damage to forward trenches.

Barrages

The word 'barrage' comes from the French for barrier and meant a curtain of continuously bursting shells, always linear but of any length. Barrages were mostly associated with the artillery, although in the latter part of the war machine-gun barrages were often fired to supplement the artillery. They supported the infantry in their advance and in the fight through to their objectives – their purpose being to destroy, neutralize, screen, harass and protect the infantry from hostile fire of all types while, and after, they secured these objectives. The overall plan invariably included concentrations of fire in combination with a variety of precisely timed barrages fired at, during and after the different phases of the attack. Selection of the most effective type of artillery for particular targets was a key element of planning concentrations or barrages. There was always some overlapping of tasks, as most guns, howitzers or mortars could take on several types of target provided they were within range. However, in general terms, the most common allocation of targets is given below, bearing in mind that, in the latter part of the war, most could fire smoke or gas shells if required as part of a bombardment or barrage.

• **Field guns** Primarily employed in barrage fire in close support of the infantry, repelling attacks in the open, raking communication trenches, wire-cutting. Also for neutralizing fire against enemy batteries within range and to assist in the destruction of weak enemy defences that were vulnerable to the HE shells of a field gun, such as breastworks or barriers. They were often employed to prevent the enemy working parties repairing damage to trenches or gaps in wire obstacles.

• **Field howitzers** Employed for the bombardment of weaker defences, against troops poorly entrenched and for enfilading communication trenches. They were effective against ill-protected batteries in range, neutralizing targets with gas and for wire-cutting, using the 106 fuze from 1917 onwards.

• **Medium/heavy guns** Used for counter-battery work, raking communication trenches and forming protective barrages (see page 254) beyond the range of field guns. The 6-inch, 9.2-inch and 12-inch guns were particularly effective for use against villages, camps, supply dumps, railway stations and for long-range counter-battery tasks.

• **Medium/heavy howitzers** Used for the destruction of defences, strongpoints and entrenched troops, and for neutralizing fire against hostile batteries. The 6-inch howitzer with the 106 fuze could be used effectively for wire-cutting. The 8-inch and 9.2-inch were used against enemy batteries that were well protected and for the destruction of strong defences. Super-heavy howitzers (12-inch and 15-inch) could be used effectively in counter-battery tasks and against especially strong and deep defensive structures and bridges.

• **Mortars** Light mortars such as the Stokes were often used to harass the enemy in the final stages of a bombardment against trenches and machine-gun posts – the Fourth Army programme overleaf shows them employed in a 'hurricane' bombardment of the enemy front line on Z-day, with the 4-inch providing smokescreens on the flanks of the attack. Heavier varieties could take on more distant targets, such as wire-cutting, with the 240mm mortar firing on villages, deep dugouts and strongpoints.

Before looking at the different types of barrage and how they were used, several points need clarification:

• There was a huge difference between the mobile use of guns, firing over open sights, in 1914 and the massive barrages involving thousands of guns in 1916, 1917 and early 1918. However, for the final months of the war, once the Hindenburg Line was breached and the more fluid operations of the British Hundred Day offensive were under way, artillery tactics had almost come full circle. Batteries were once again on the move and often well forward, supporting the infantry with direct fire, lifting barrages and concentrations on specific targets that were holding up the advance.

• The enormous ammunition requirement for bombardments and barrages was of particular concern in 1915 during the shell shortage and always dictated a bombardment's length or intensity. For the opening of the Somme battle the stocks had been built up by 20 June and rounds per 18-pounder gun amounted to just over 1,800: some 350 at the guns, 1,000 dumped nearby and the remainder at divisional and corps dumps. As a general guide to the number of guns for field artillery barrages, official sources stated in autumn 1916 that one 18-pounder for every 25 yards of front was needed to produce an effective barrage. However, the amount of ammunition in relation to specific tasks is even more indicative of the vast number of shells fired, bearing in mind that only a small proportion would be direct hits and neutralization was often as effective as destruction. Examples of planning figures were:

• To destroy selected points in a trench about 30 yards apart required 100 rounds per point from a 2-inch mortar or 80 rounds from 6-inch or 8-inch howitzers.

• A machine-gun emplacement with a roof of three rows of pit props covered with not more than 3 feet of earth needed 80 rounds from a 2-inch mortar or 65 from a 6-inch or 8-inch howitzer.

• Strongpoints with concrete roofs or deep dugouts required heavy howitzers – 130 rounds from an 8-inch, 100 from a 9.2-inch and 75 from a 12-inch.

• To prevent repair of damaged defences, an 18-pounder would need 250 rounds every twelve hours for every 300-yard length of the target.

• For night firing on communications, the 18-pounder required 50 rounds per target per hour.

• Smoke barrages fired by 18-pounders needed 2 rounds for every 10 yards per minute.

The scale of ammunition expenditure is illustrated by the huge figures for the BEF between 8 August and 6 September 1918 – the opening phase of the Hundred Days offensive:

13-pounders	225,100
3-inch 20 cwt	5,400
18-pounders	5,372,000
4.5-inch howitzers	1,443,400
60-pounders	750,400
6-inch howitzers	1,566,800
6-inch guns	108,200
8-inch howitzers	170,500
9.2-inch howitzers	145,700
0.2-inch guns	5,300
12-inch howitzers	11,700
12-inch guns	1,100
14-inch guns	175
15-inch howitzer	1,225
Total	**9,807,000**
	with a total weight
	of 242,350 tons

Out of a total expenditure of just over 9.8 million rounds, averaging almost 327,000 a day, just over 28 per cent were fired by the heavy artillery.

• The type and mix of ammunition for barrages became more complex from 1917 onwards and more use was made of the 106 fuze for HE shells (which were effective wire-cutters and did not crater the ground), smoke and gas. Prior to the Somme, 18-pounder barrages were usually entirely shrapnel, but by April 1917 at Arras the creeping barrage was fifty–fifty shrapnel and HE, while the 9th Division fired the first mixed creeping barrage with 75 per cent HE and 25 per cent smoke. From Cambrai in November 1917 to the Armistice it became common to have varying percentages of shrapnel, HE and smoke in creeping barrages.

• It was invariably a lengthy, difficult and extremely frustrating undertaking to try to alter a timed barrage programme once it had started. If an attacking unit was held up and the barrage moved on in accordance with the timetable, then those infantry had 'lost the barrage' and suffered the consequences. Units on either flank that continued to advance soon created salients and the flanks of the troops in them became vulnerable to enfilade or flanking fire. The invariably poor communications and the need to get higher authority to agree a change in the programme, plus the time taken to make the change if accepted, meant that the progress of the advance was often patchy. In the latter part of the war this difficulty was largely overcome by earmarking reserve batteries to deal with unexpected resistance from specific strongpoints.

The Somme Fourth Army Artillery Program

Tasks	'U' Day	'V' Day	'W' Day
Wire-cutting	**All day**	**All day**	**All day**
Bombardment: Trench system, fortified localities and strongpoints, OPs and machine-gun emplacements, water supply, etc.	No increase beyond the normal except for registration.	All day and at intervals during the night by all natures of howitzers. Concentrated bombardment for 1 hour 20 minutes from 3 p.m. to 4.20 p.m.	All day by all natur howitzers. Concent bombardment for 1 20 minutes from 8 to 9.20 a.m.
Bombardment: billets	No increase beyond the normal except for registration.	Concentrations of fire and intermittent fire.	As for 'V' Day
Shelling of: Communications, approaches, railways, working parties, etc., with the object of preventing replenishment of ammunition, food and water.	All night	All night. By day as required.	As for 'V' Day
Counter-battery work	Very active	Very active	Very active
Villages, strongpoints, etc., by 240mm mortars.	No increase beyond the normal.	As required	As required
Wire-cutting and bombardment of front-line trenches by 2-in medium mortars.	As required for wire-cutting.	As for 'U' Day	As for 'U' Day
Front-line trenches and machine-gun emplacements by 3-in Stokes mortars.	No increase beyond the normal.	As required	As required
The establishment of smoke barrages by 4-in Stokes mortars (smoke).	No increase beyond the normal.	As required	As required
To lead enemy to believe that an assault is about to be made and induce him to man his front trenches. 'P' bombs and candles.	No increase beyond the normal.	As required with the gas discharge if it takes place on this night.	As required with the discharge if it takes on this night.
Flammenwerfer to burn out hostile trenches when within range.	No increase beyond the normal.	As required with the gas discharge if it takes place on this night.	As required with the discharge if it takes on this night.
Gas: To inflict loss on enemy by taking him by surprise at night.	No increase beyond the normal.	On night 'V'/'W' if wind is favourable, i.e. W or SW as per programme. Hour to be notified by AHQ to corps by 5 p.m.	If wind is favourable discharge was not p ble on night 'V'/ Hour to be notifiec 5 p.m.

Note 1: At Zero on 'Z' day the Artillery will lift off the front trenches and the Infantry will deliver the assault. The hour of Zero will be notified to Corps on 'W' or 'X' day.

2: Our trenches during 'U'–'Y' days to be kept as empty as possible especially during the discharge of gas and smoke.

3: Villages in which our troops are usually billeted should be kept as empty as possible and troops bivouacked in the open if weather is suitable.

Preliminary Bombardment, 5 June 1916

'X' Day	'Y' Day	'Z' Day	General Instructions
All day	All day		
...ay by all natures of ...zers. Concentrated ...ardment for 1 hour ...nutes from 3.30 a.m. ...50 a.m., and again ...5.30 p.m. to 6.50 p.m.	All day by all natures of howitzers. Concentrated bombardment for 1 hour 20 minutes from 5 a.m. to 6.20 a.m., and again from 3 p.m. to 4.20 p.m.	Concentrated bombardment −65 to Zero. Subsequently as per corps artillery programme.	Arrangements should be made for heavy howitzers to cease firing during a certain period every day in order to permit of photography, verification of fire and examination of equipment. The pause for photography should not be previous to the concentrated bombardment. The enemy system of water mains should be destroyed as soon as possible.
...r 'V' Day	As for 'V' Day	From −65 under constant fire.	By day and night: (a) Sudden concentrations of fire, e.g. for a few minutes, 10 to 15 minutes subsequent to discharge of gas. (b) Intermittent bursts of fire on billets and approaches, especially at night.
...r 'V' Day	As for 'V' Day	From −65 under constant fire.	Demands co-operation of field artillery, machine guns and rifles on an inner zone and that of heavy artillery and long-range guns on an outer zone.
...active	Very active	Concentration of gas shells on hostile gun positions before the assault. Very active	Special batteries detailed for the destruction of hostile artillery personnel and material and the neutralization of fire in conjunction with aircraft.
...quired	As required	Concentrated bombardment −65 to Zero. Subsequently as per corps artillery programme.	Special batteries detailed for the destruction of hostile artillery personnel and material and the neutralization of fire in conjunction with aircraft.
...r 'U' Day	As for 'U' Day	As per corps artillery programme.	Special batteries detailed for the destruction of hostile artillery personnel and material and the neutralization of fire in conjunction with aircraft.
...quired	As required	Hurricane bombardment of front-line system from −8 including ranging rounds.	Care must be taken that detachments are kept fresh for 'Z' Day, and that guns and personnel are not knocked out by too free a use of these mortars on previous days.
...quired	As required	As required for flank barrage.	Care must be taken that detachments are kept fresh for 'Z' Day, and that guns and personnel are not knocked out by too free a use of these mortars on previous days.
...quired with the gas ...arge if it takes place ...is night.	½ hour smoke commencing at 6.20 a.m. all along the line if direction of wind permits.	As required for flank barrage.	To be accompanied by heavy shrapnel barrage on front-line trenches, searching of communication trenches and heavy bombardment of reserve billets and communications.
...quired with the gas ...arge if it takes place ...is night.	½ hour smoke commencing at 6.20 a.m. all along the line if direction of wind permits.	As required commencing at −10.	To be accompanied by heavy shrapnel barrage on front-line trenches, searching of communication trenches and heavy bombardment of reserve billets and communications.
...r 'W' Day	As per 'W' Day	As required commencing at −10.	Programme: 4 cylinders White Star simultaneously per bay – 0 to 4 1 cylinder Red Star per bay every 10 minutes – 4 to 1.56 4 cylinders White Star per bay – 1.56 to 2.0 To be accompanied by heavy shrapnel barrage on front-line trenches, searching of communication trenches and heavy bombardment of reserve billets and communications. The noise of the initial discharge to be covered by rapid fire of rifles and machine guns all along the line.

Standing barrages

A standing barrage was static, and in this respect was a linear concentration. It was usually employed to hit each infantry objective as it was to be assaulted; on the Western Front these were invariably irregular linear features such as trench lines or wire obstacles. This barrage could lift, usually at a predetermined time, from one objective to the next and thus became a 'lifting barrage'. When a standing barrage was used to prevent, or target, possible enemy counter-attacks against an objective that had been secured by hitting a line or ground beyond the objective, it was called a 'protective barrage'. These could be made to conform with tactical or terrain features and were thus not always in straight lines. If deployed to a flank they were sometimes useful for bringing down enfilade fire along the axis of zig-zag communication trenches. A form of protective barrage was the 'box barrage', which normally involved three standing barrages fired along the three sides of an open 'box', inside which the infantry were operating. Their objective was to prevent enemy reinforcing a position to be attacked, or to screen the flanks while the assault was in progress. From 1917 it was common to include considerable quantities of smoke shells in box and protective barrages to screen the attackers from effective fire and observation.

A standing barrage could be converted into a 'back barrage'. In this instance the barrage might have lifted from the first to the second objective and 'stood' on it for some time before lifting back to comb, or sweep, the ground between the two objectives for a certain period, then moving back to stand again on the second objective. This type was intended to confuse enemy who had thought the barrage had moved on, and catch them exposed.

In defence, the defenders would arrange for predetermined and registered SOS targets. These were artillery (and machine-gun) targets on which batteries were laid when not on other tasks. These emergency-fire tasks could be called for immediately, usually by the infantry firing coloured flare signals, in the event of a sudden enemy threat.

Creeping barrages

There is some controversy over when the first true creeping (sometimes called a 'walking' or 'rolling') barrage was employed, although Loos in 1915 is usually credited as the first battle to see a form of creeping or lifting barrage on the Western Front. However, it was on the Somme in July 1916 that it came into use on a much wider scale, although with different divisions employing local variants. By that September it had become the most common form of barrage and had been adopted

Advancing Behind a Creeping Barrage

Second Lieutenant D. W. J. Cuddeford, 12th Highland Light Infantry, advanced behind a creeping barrage on 15 September 1916 at the Battle of Flers-Courcelette. In the early 1930s he wrote of the experience in his book *And All For What?*

> The line [zone] of bursting shells jumped forward at the rate of fifty yards a minute, and we, being the first wave of the attack, had to regulate our pace so as to keep just fifty yards behind this barrage . . .
>
> I wonder how many people at home, who in 1916 read in their newspapers all about creeping barrages, realize exactly what advancing under a creeping barrage meant to the leading waves of infantry. Fifty yards is a very short distance to be from a line of bursting shells, whether German or British. If the line of shellfire could possibly have been kept absolutely exact . . . there would still be plenty of splinters coming back, but even supposing the artillerymen to be infallible in the gun-laying (which they were not) many guns were worn and inaccurate, and the shells fell short.
>
> I don't think I'm exaggerating in saying, at least, as far as our own brigade was concerned, that in the early part of the attack quite a third of the very heavy casualties we suffered were caused by our artillery fire. However, the fault did not lie entirely with the artillerymen; many of our men would insist on pressing on too fast . . .
>
> Fifty yards a minute was our rate of advance, a mere snail's crawl [the ground was firm], and as we went on, the men of the first line of the attack threw forward smoke-producing bombs ('pea-bombs') to create a mask of smoke screening the advance. The effect was most weird. A haze of smoke hung over the whole scene; here and there added to by the black greasy smoke from the heavy howitzer shells which the Germans soon started putting over.

See the 'beaten zone' in the diagram on page 236 for an illustration of the dangers.

by the French. A creeping barrage became a highly sophisticated fire plan, the aim of which was to get the advancing infantry to within 40–50 yards of the enemy position before it lifted off the objective. It was hoped that the attackers could then rush the position, before the defenders realized that shellfire had ceased hitting their trenches and began manning their parapets and machine-gun posts. The 'wall' of shell bursts (shrapnel or HE, or a mixture of both) would move forward in short bounds on a rigid timetable, with the infantry closed up to within 40 yards of the shells and accepting the loss of a few men to 'friendly fire' as a price well worth paying if they could thereby win the 'race to the parapet'; although if the infantry caught up the barrage, they would usually kneel down to wait for it to move on. The word 'wall' is in quotes because, although commonly used to describe the bursting shells, in fact they formed a carpet or zone of fire, often hundreds of yards deep, in front of the attackers. By the Battle of Arras in 1917, the creeping barrage could have five or six lines of fire covering a depth of 1,000 yards ahead of the infantry – a truly enormous carpet of bursting shells. Each of these lines could be moved independently back and forth so the enemy infantry would never know when it was safe to come up from their shelters to man their positions.

Creeping barrages on to the first infantry objective were usually fired by the shorter-range field guns and howitzers, with more distant objectives and enemy guns being targeted by medium or heavy batteries. When the opposing trench lines were very close

and the enemy had no advanced posts, it was not uncommon for the guns just to fire a standing barrage on the German front line while the infantry advanced to within 40–50 yards of the shells; the barrage then lifted to allow the assault to rush in.

The speed at which the barrage advanced was always a matter of considerable importance to the artillery planners and the infantry. Much depended on the state of the ground, particularly obstacles that the infantry had to negotiate – a mass of shell craters or waterlogged ground with deep mud such as at Passchendaele. If the ground was firm, then 100 yards in two minutes was possible; however, if it was extremely broken and muddy, then the infantry would struggle to make 100 yards in ten minutes. Assuming reasonable ground, 100 yards in four minutes was a rate that was commonly used when preparing timetables. Even then the advance to second or deeper objectives invariably moved at a slower rate to take account of casualties, delays and the inevitable confusion of all attacks, and above all the need for the field batteries to move forward.

When Second Lieutenant Alexander Aitken, a New Zealander in the 1st Otago, was informed of the barrage timings for the attack on 27 September 1916 near Flers, he was not happy:

> The timetable . . . was even more discouraging. The careful arrangements of the 25th had allowed twenty-three minutes for the crossing of 700 yards [30 yards a minute]; these of the 27th allowed a bare eight minutes for the

MAP 48 BARRAGE MAP, *c*.1917

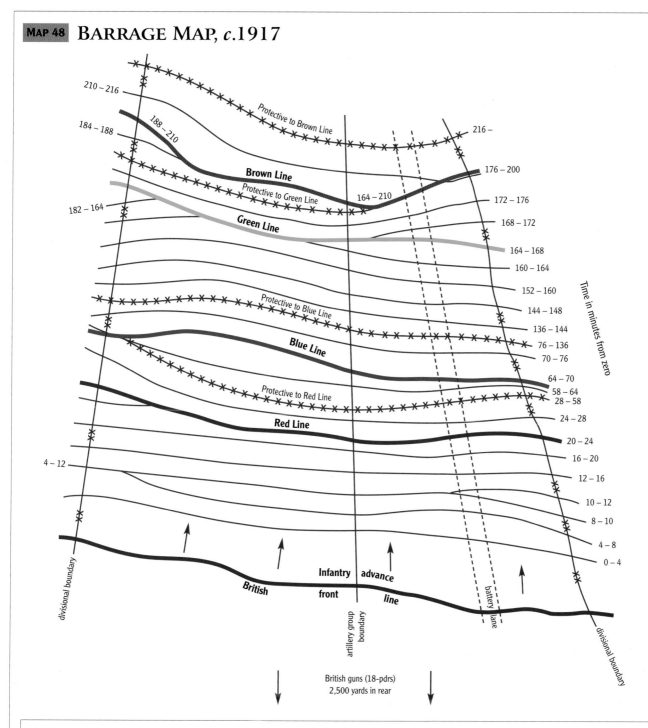

210 – 216
184 – 188
188 – 210
Protective to Brown Line
216 –
Brown Line
176 – 200
Protective to Green Line
164 – 210
172 – 176
Green Line
168 – 172
182 – 164
164 – 168
160 – 164
152 – 160
Protective to Blue Line
144 – 148
136 – 144
Blue Line
76 – 136
70 – 76
64 – 70
Protective to Red Line
58 – 64
28 – 58
Red Line
24 – 28
20 – 24
16 – 20
4 – 12
12 – 16
10 – 12
8 – 10
4 – 8
0 – 4

Time in minutes from zero

divisional boundary

Infantry advance line
British front line
artillery group boundary
battery lane
divisional boundary

British guns (18-pdrs)
2,500 yards in rear

Notes for Map 48

• This shows a simplified possible barrage map plan for a creeping barrage for the divisional field artillery supporting a British divisional attack typical of *c*.1917. The infantry have four objectives, marked Red, Blue, Green and Brown Lines, with the Brown being the final one, over 2,000 yards into the enemy defensive zone. Two artillery groups are firing and the map will have been divided into battery lanes (only one is shown).

• The guns, probably firing mostly shrapnel but with a small percentage of HE and possibly some smoke, are shown firing with the lifts every four minutes, allowing the infantry that amount of time to advance about 100 yards – they would hope to be closed up to within 40 yards of the falling shells and prepared to rush the German positions of the first objective and subsequent objectives as the guns lifted beyond them.

• About 200 yards beyond each objective a protective barrage (standing barrage) is fired while the infantry consolidate and reorganize for their continued advance. The protective barrage, which might contain more smoke, is fired for much longer periods than the creeping lifts – for Red it is 30 minutes, for Blue 60 minutes and for Green 24 minutes, illustrating that these barrages do not always lift at regular intervals. Their purpose is to disrupt counter-attacks and screen the infantry while re-forming. The intermediate lift between the objective and the protective barrage is to hit any enemy positions between the two lines.

• The protective barrage beyond the Brown Line has no finishing time: there are no further lifts as the infantry have secured their final objective, and the time the artillery support is to finish is not yet known.

crossing of 1,000 yards far more exposed to fire of all kinds. We should have to move at 150 paces a minute. As for barrages, there was nothing remotely resembling the elaborate creeping and stationary barrages of the Monday; little more than the bare statement that the barrage would lift and go forward at zero time, when we should make our dash.

An example of the differing timings of the advance for a successful three-phase attack is afforded by the 9th Division at Frezenburg on 20 September 1917. The speed in Phase 1 was 100 yards in four minutes, Phase 2 in six minutes and Phase 3 in eight minutes.

The ultimate disaster for the infantry was to 'lose the barrage' – to see it moving further and further ahead of them, allowing the Germans to man their positions unhindered. Sometimes, however, if the infantry advanced too fast for the timetable, they had to wait for the barrage to move on. This was much less of a problem than losing the barrage, but could be dangerous and confusing

if successive waves of attackers (usually with different tasks from the leading one) caught up with it. With the wide frontages of attack, and with enemy trenches not being in regular straight lines, it was common that some units would reach their objective before those on their flanks. This difficulty was dealt with in one of three ways, or in a combination of some or all of them:

• **Straight barrage** (see diagram below). The lines of fire are parallel and the infantry axis of advance is parallel to the

Straight, Piled-up and Standing or Protective Barrages

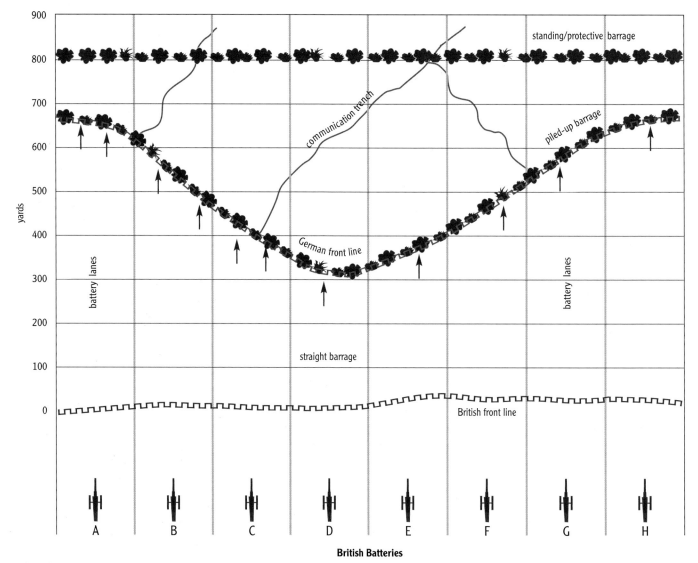

Notes

• This illustrates 'straight', 'piled-up' and 'standing'/'protective' barrages. Eight batteries fire, each with its own 'lane' or sector of the barrage for which it is responsible. The lifts are 100 yards every four minutes. The infantry objective is the German front-line trench.
• All batteries start with straight, parallel barrages at 100 yards and lift progressively every four minutes. At the third lift, at 300 yards, Battery D's shells hit the enemy trench and remain firing on this section of trench when the remaining batteries lift their fire. When this happens, the fire of Batteries C and E hits their section of trench

before the 400-yard line is reached. These two batteries now continue to fire on the trench and do not move on after four minutes. Meanwhile the 'piled-up' barrage has started as Battery D is continuing to fire on the trench. This process is repeated as fire from the batteries hits the trench (as shown by the red arrows).
• When all the batteries are firing in the trench, then, according to a timed programme, they all lift their fire to 700 and then 800 yards, with the final lift providing a standing or protective barrage against counter-attacks.

The Criss-cross Barrage Supporting 2nd Middlesex at Biache-St-Vaast, 7 October 1918

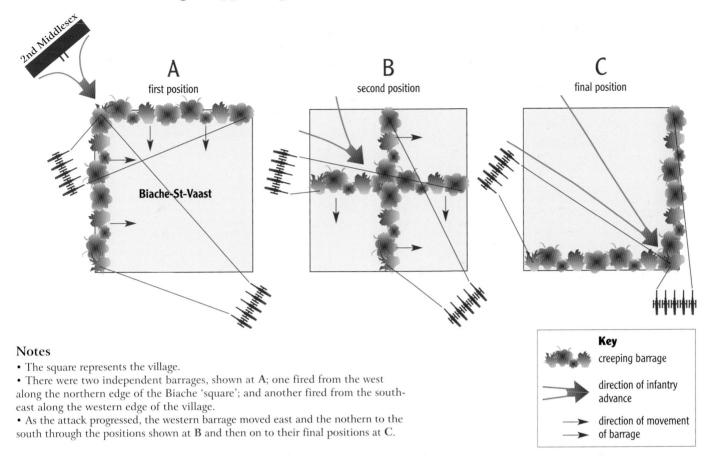

A first position

B second position

C final position

Biache-St-Vaast

Key

creeping barrage

direction of infantry advance

direction of movement of barrage

Notes

• The square represents the village.
• There were two independent barrages, shown at **A**; one fired from the west along the northern edge of the Biache 'square'; and another fired from the south-east along the western edge of the village.
• As the attack progressed, the western barrage moved east and the nothern to the south through the positions shown at **B** and then on to their final positions at **C**.

---

line of fire. The problems are that the whole enemy line is not engaged simultaneously and sectors of the attack are exposed to hostile fire. This barrage is best employed against more or less straight sections of enemy trenches.

• **Piled-up barrage** (see diagram left). The lines of fire are parallel, but fire piles up when it reaches the enemy position. The difficulty for the infantry is that they cannot assault until the whole position is engaged. Infantry with the furthest to go must then advance first so that the enemy is assaulted simultaneously. A difficult barrage to coordinate with the infantry, who are liable to suffer heavily from unknown positions.

• **Creeping barrage paralleling enemy trenches** (see Map 49 overleaf). Here the lines of fire are parallel but matching the shape of the enemy defensive line. An effective variation, but the infantry may have to advance at different times to close up behind the barrage together.

The planning of a creeping barrage was never simple, requiring extensive coordination, meticulous calculation of timings, a complete understanding by both infantry and gunners at all levels and huge amounts of ammunition. To achieve all this, bar-

rages were planned at corps level and could take between eighteen and twenty-four hours to organize.

An indication of how sophisticated barrages had become by late 1918 was the 'criss-cross' barrage employed by the 8th Divisional Artillery under Brigadier General J. W. F. Lamont for the attack by 2nd Middlesex on Biache-St-Vaast village in October (see diagram above). In addition to the guns, three batteries of eight machine guns were grouped under the control of a single officer (a Second Lieutenant Aspinall) to support the attack. The advance started at 5:00 a.m. and within three hours the Middlesex had taken the village: 'A magnificent artillery barrage was put down and all objectives were quickly reached with but little opposition and with very few casualties . . .'

Chinese barrages

These were artillery barrages fired to deceive or confuse the Germans about the true time or location of an attack. They were a common feature of planning by 1916 and included false starts of the creeping barrage, the bombardment of parts of the line that were not to be attacked and the use of smoke mixed with gas, sometimes on a flank.

Wytschaete barrage maps

The British Second Army captured the vital Wytschaete–Messines Ridge in a two-phase attack in early June 1917, its success being to a large extent due to the massive, well-planned preliminary artillery bombardment and barrages on Z-day. The artillery made available for the attack numbered 2,266 guns and howitzers, of which 756 were heavies and mediums. The latter were divided into forty groups with between eighteen and twenty pieces in each. The field artillery comprised sixty-four field artillery brigades, of which thirty-three were army field artillery brigades controlled by Army Headquarters. As with the heavies, these guns and howitzers were split into artillery groups and sub-groups with, in the 19th Division, for example, each infantry brigade having the support of two sub-groups (twelve 18-pounder or 4.5-inch howitzer batteries, seventy-two guns/howitzers). Some 144,000 tons of artillery ammunition was brought forward by rail to dumps behind the front. In addition, 120,000 gas and 60,000 smoke shells were made available.

Planning and control was at the highest level. The Major General Royal Artillery (MGRA), Major General George McKenzie

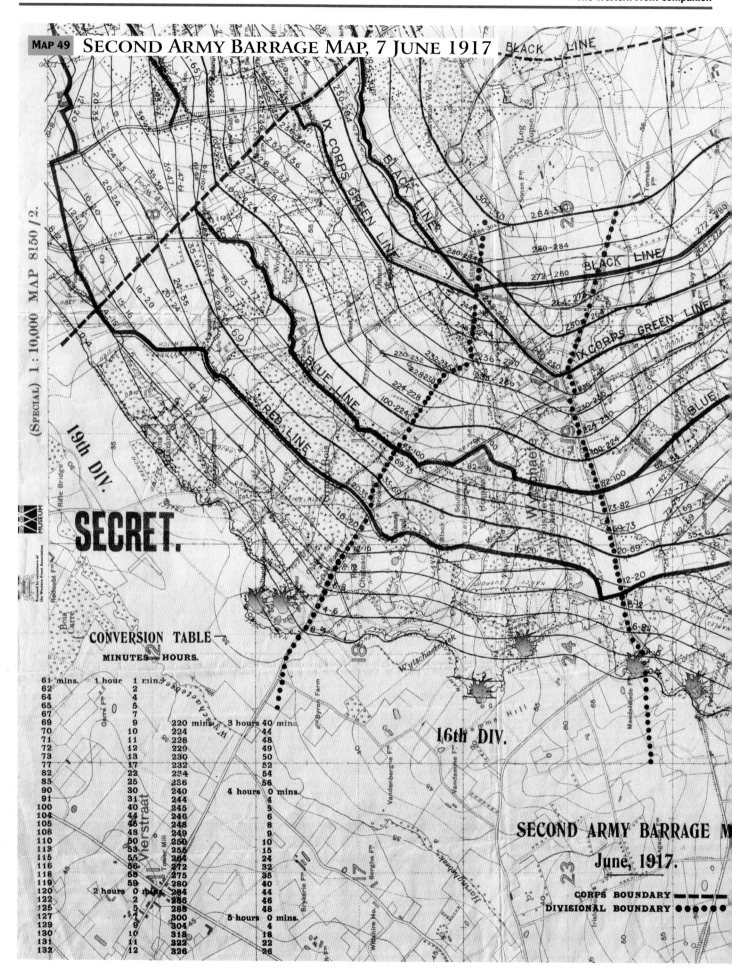

MAP 49 SECOND ARMY BARRAGE MAP, 7 JUNE 1917

SECRET.

CONVERSION TABLE

MINUTES — HOURS.

61 mins.	1 hour	1 min.			
62		2			
64		4			
65		5			
67		7			
69		9	220 mins.	3 hours 40 mins.	
70		10	224		44
71		11	228		48
72		12	229		49
73		13	230		50
77		17	232		52
82		22	234		54
85		25	236		56
90		30	240	4 hours 0 mins.	
91		31	244		4
100		40	245		5
104		44	246		6
105		45	248		8
108		48	249		9
110		50	250		10
113		53	255		15
115		55	264		24
116		56	272		32
118		58	275		35
119		59	280		40
120	2 hours 0 mins.		284		44
122		2	286		46
125		5	288		48
127		7	300	5 hours 0 mins.	
129		9	304		4
130		10	318		18
131		11	322		22
132		12	326		26

SECOND ARMY BARRAGE M

June, 1917.

CORPS BOUNDARY ▬ ▬ ▬

DIVISIONAL BOUNDARY ● ● ● ● ●

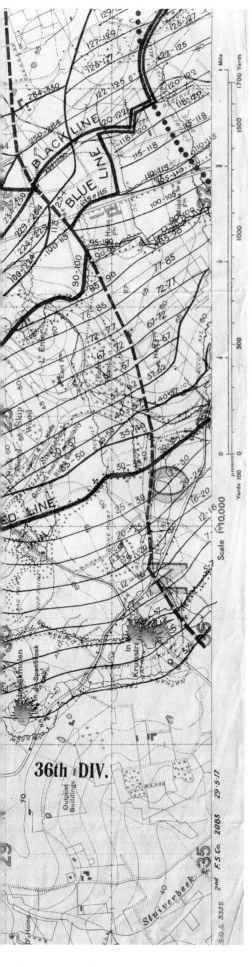

Franks at Second Army Headquarters, coordinated the corps plans, with corps counter-battery areas divided into zones and allotted to heavy-artillery groups. These zones were subdivided into map squares and allocated to batteries. Eight kite balloons and around 300 aircraft would provide observation of target location and effectiveness of firing. The plan envisaged a preliminary bombardment lasting ten days, from 28 May to 6 June – in the event, this bombardment consumed over 3.5 million rounds. On Z-day, 7 June, pre-planned barrages and concentrations by the heavy artillery would hit enemy batteries and deep targets while the field artillery brigades concentrated on providing creeping and standing/protective barrages to get the infantry on to their objectives.

IX Corps had the task of taking the Wytschaete sector of the ridge and planned to attack with three divisions abreast – the 19th Division on the left, the 16th in the centre and the 36th on the right, with the 11th in reserve. In addition to the divisional artillery brigades, the corps had the support of ten army field artillery brigades. The heavy support for IX Corps was organized into five bombardment groups and four counter-battery groups under the control of a lieutenant colonel at corps headquarters.

Maps 49–52 are four of the barrage maps for this attack. The map notes provide a detailed explanation of how this vital ridge, which dominated the German-occupied ground to the east, was taken by the end of the day.

Notes for Map 49

• This comprehensive parallel barrage map shows the creeping and standing barrages for Phase 1 for all three assaulting divisions of IX Corps from zero hour through to the infantry consolidation on the Black Line just east of Wytschaete. The 16th Division in the centre was tasked with taking Wytschaete itself, considered to be a particularly difficult operation, so its attack was on a much narrower frontage than those of the divisions on either side. Ten mines were set to be detonated just prior to the infantry advance and their locations have been superimposed on the map for completeness (see Section Seven for mining at Messines).

• The successive infantry objectives for this first phase are shown by the four lines Red–Blue–Green–Black. The parallel lines, or rather zones, of fire of the creeping barrage advanced in a series of four-minute lifts (there were local minor variations of this) of 100 yards. The barrage 'stood' on each of the objective lines, sometimes for considerably more than four minutes – e.g. in the 19th Division's sector it was to stand for 15 minutes on the Red Line, and in the 16th Division on the Blue Line for 27 minutes on the left but only for nine in the centre. These variations were for local tactical reasons to allow the infantry time to complete their advance.

• As each objective line was taken, the barrage advanced beyond to a distance of 100–200 yards and became a standing/protective barrage while the infantry consolidated and reorganized for the next advance. The standing barrage beyond the Red Line varied from 34 minutes in front of the 16th and 19th Divisions to 49 minutes on the left of the 36th Division. The final protective barrage line beyond the Black Line stood for 46 minutes along part of the 16th Division's front. At this stage its purpose was primarily to deter or halt German counter-attacks and allow sufficient time for the units undertaking Phase 2 to move up.

• Note the narrowness of the front anticipated for the 16th Division when fighting through Wytschaete and therefore how intensely concentrated the barrage would be at that stage.

The beautiful Pool of Peace in the Spanbroekmolen mine crater, created on 7 June 1917. The location is marked by the fourth flare symbol from the right on the map.

MAP 50 **HEAVY ARTILLERY ATTACK ON WYTSCHAETE, 7 JUNE 1917**

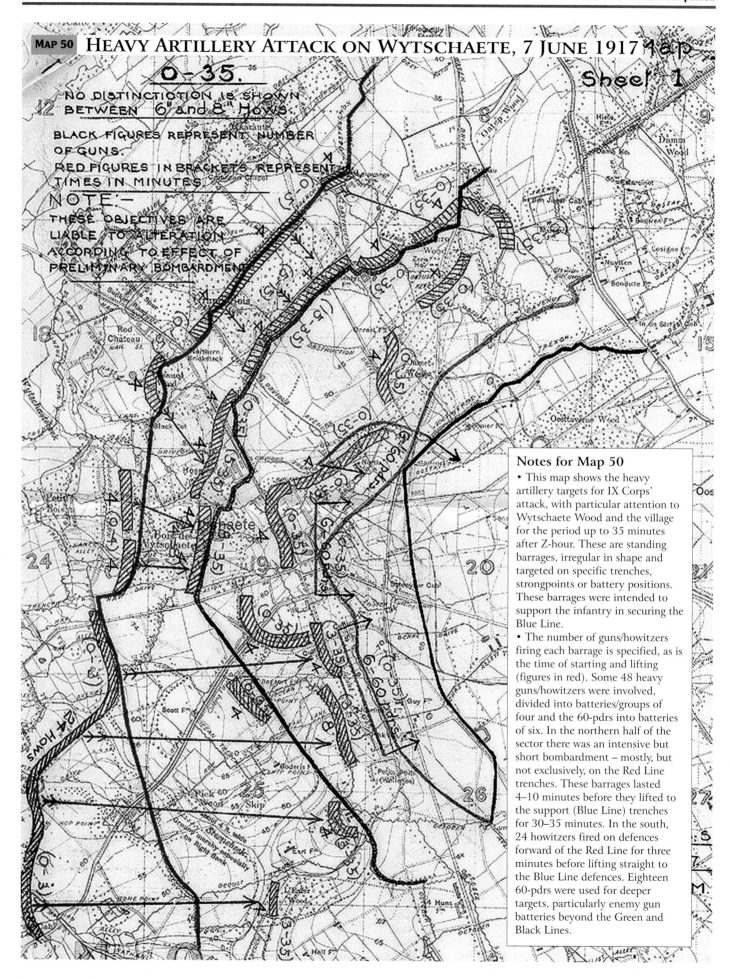

Sheet 1

O-35.

NO DISTINCTIOTION IS SHOWN
BETWEEN 6" and 8" HOWS.

BLACK FIGURES REPRESENT NUMBER
OF GUNS.

RED FIGURES IN BRACKETS REPRESENT
TIMES IN MINUTES.

NOTE:-
THESE OBJECTIVES ARE
LIABLE TO ALTERATION
ACCORDING TO EFFECT OF
PRELIMINARY BOMBARDMENT.

Notes for Map 50

• This map shows the heavy artillery targets for IX Corps' attack, with particular attention to Wytschaete Wood and the village for the period up to 35 minutes after Z-hour. These are standing barrages, irregular in shape and targeted on specific trenches, strongpoints or battery positions. These barrages were intended to support the infantry in securing the Blue Line.

• The number of guns/howitzers firing each barrage is specified, as is the time of starting and lifting (figures in red). Some 48 heavy guns/howitzers were involved, divided into batteries/groups of four and the 60-pdrs into batteries of six. In the northern half of the sector there was an intensive but short bombardment – mostly, but not exclusively, on the Red Line trenches. These barrages lasted 4–10 minutes before they lifted to the support (Blue Line) trenches for 30–35 minutes. In the south, 24 howitzers fired on defences forward of the Red Line for three minutes before lifting straight to the Blue Line defences. Eighteen 60-pdrs were used for deeper targets, particularly enemy gun batteries beyond the Green and Black Lines.

MAP 51 HOWITZER BOMBARDMENT, WYTSCHAETE

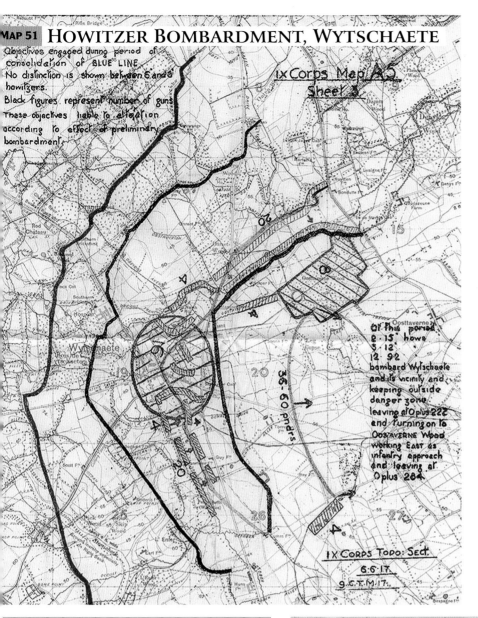

Objectives engaged during period of
consolidation of BLUE LINE.
No distinction is shown between 6 and 8
howitzers.
Black figures represent number of guns
These objectives liable to alteration
according to effect of preliminary
bombardment.

IX Corps Map A5
Sheet 3

Of this period
2 · 15" hows
5 · 12"
12 · 9·2"
bombard Wytschaete
and its vicinity and
keeping outside
danger zone
leaving at O plus 222
and turning on to
Oostaverne Wood
working East as
infantry approach
and leaving at
O plus 284

IX Corps Topo: Sect.
6·6·17.
9.C.T.M.17.

A howitzer on the Western Front.

Notes for Map 52

• This is a divisional field artillery straight creeping barrage map for the second phase of the Wytschaete attack by IX Corps. The artillery of all three divisions is involved and the attack is on a far narrower front than the initial one (Map 49). The black line just east of the village corresponds to the Black Line, or final objective of Phase 1 on Map 49. The Blue Line shown here is the same as the final protective/standing barrage on Map 49. The Purple Line here corresponds to the dotted black line on Map 49.

• The infantry objective was the Oostaverne Line, shown as the Green Line here, just beyond the Odonto Trench (the actual objective to be secured), which was protected by a double belt of thick wire. The barrage was in straight lines, lifting by 100 yards every 3 minutes until it reached the Odonto Trench when it was to pile up, starting on the northern part of the trench. When the infantry assaulted the position, the barrage would lift and pile up again on the Green Line (Oosttaverne Line) for 15 minutes before advancing two more lifts and forming a standing/protective barrage against enemy counter-attacks for 47 minutes.

Notes for Map 51

This shows the use of the heavy batteries of howitzers, under Second Army control, to be employed during the infantry consolidation of the Blue Line. Note that although there is a heavy concentration on Wytschaete, specific trench lines in the village are targeted as well. These barrages on the village are timed to lift 222 minutes after Z-hour – that is, two minutes before the field artillery standing/protective barrage lifts at 224 minutes and becomes again the creeping barrage for the advance on the Green Line. The reason for the early lift was the much longer zone and splinter distances of the heavies.

These heavy batteries lift on to Oosttaverne Wood, the Black Line, and move slowly east as the infantry approach. Thirty-six 60-pdrs are superimposed on deeper targets, primarily enemy gun batteries and strongpoints.

The village of Wytschaete today, seen from the position of the British troops on 7 June 1917.

MAP 52 CREEPING BARRAGE, WYTSCHAETE

The 11th Hussars on the march from the Aisne to Flanders, October 1914.

Section Six

Cavalry

There seems to be nothing to look forward to – only trenches. Nothing one has learnt seems to be of any use to one. We can only exercise the horses in half sections along a road, as the men are away digging. Nobody knows how to use us or where. Indeed cavalry in this sort of war seems to be an anachronism.

An officer of the 18th Lancers, July 1915

The first clash between troops of the BEF and the advancing Germans occurred between opposing cavalry units on 22 August 1914, in the little Belgian village of Casteau just 5 miles north-east of Mons on the Brussels road. The first German to be injured at the hand of a British soldier was wounded by a cavalry officer's sword cut, and the first to die by a bullet was shot by a cavalry corporal.

The 4th (Royal Irish) Dragoon Guards (2nd Cavalry Brigade) was part of the cavalry screen covering the advance of the BEF through Belgium. It was about to meet some of the leading elements of the German First Army, the extreme right wing of the German sweep through that country. Major Tom Bridges, commanding C Squadron, had bivouacked the previous night on either side of the road near Casteau, his task being to gain information on enemy movements and report back – a traditional cavalry role, and something that for best results meant capturing a prisoner. The account of what happened that morning is described by two participants.

The first was Trooper Benjamin Clouting, a sixteen-year-old lad who had been a stable boy before enlisting.

At about 6.30 a.m., we arrived at a farm on the corner of a staggered crossroads and began watering our horses in a trough. There were already a few people about and as we waited, a farm worker came in saying he'd seen four German cavalrymen coming down the road.

There was a flurry of activity, and a plan was hatched to capture the patrol as it passed. Four men from 4th Troop were dismounted and ordered to fire a volley of shots into the patrol at close quarters. This would be followed by 2nd Troop charging forward and bagging the remainder. I, along with the rest of 4th

Troop, was placed out of sight, mounted, waiting with drawn sword. I believe a man was sent out behind a hedge to signal when the Germans were about to arrive, but in his excitement he ran to grab his horse and gave the position away. The Germans probably observed the horse for they were seen to stop for a moment, then pull their horses round and return the way they had come. There was consternation among the Dragoons, until Captain [Charles] Hornby made an appeal to his squadron leader, Major Tom Bridges, to give chase. A brief nod, and assent was given.

The 1st Troop with Captain Hornby at their head went after them, and the rest of the squadron followed on in support with drawn swords. Our troop officer, Lieutenant Pigeon, led the troop at a fast canter, and everyone was highly excited. As the Germans retired into the village they met up with a larger group of cavalrymen, and, owing to the congestion, were soon caught by the 1st Troop. A fight immediately broke out, swords clashing with lances [it was a Uhlan unit]. The German lances proved too unwieldy at close quarters and several of the enemy were downed. However, we arrived just after the Germans had scattered, with the main body splitting off and carrying on up the main road . . . We continued to give chase, our horses slipping all over the place as we clattered along the road's square-set stones.

Our chase continued for perhaps a mile or more, until we found ourselves flying up a wide rising road, tree-lined on both sides. The Germans, reaching the road's crest turned, and, although they were still mounted, began firing back down the hill. 'Action front, dismount,' rapped Captain Hornby. 'Get the horses under cover!' In

one movement the troop returned their swords, reached for their rifles and dismounted, dashing for cover, lying flat on their stomachs behind the trees.

It was during this first close-quarter mounted clash that Captain Hornby slashed a German across the body with his sword – an action in which he subsequently took considerable pride. Corporal Edward Thomas fired the first BEF shot that brought down a German after the squadron had dismounted – see box, page 30.

A plaque commemorating this first encounter by the BEF was unveiled in the village in August 1939 just a month before the outbreak of World War II. Present on that occasion were both Major (Captain) Hornby and Benjamin Clouting, who, although he survived the war, had been wounded twice. The sword that did the damage is now held in the Regimental Museum of the Royal Dragoon Guards in York. By an extraordinary coincidence, some 50 yards away is another plaque commemorating the last shot of the war on the Western Front, fired by the 116th Canadian Infantry Regiment.

A Surprise Attack

During the retreat from Mons a number of minor cavalry skirmishes occurred. On 28 August Captain J. K. Gatacre, advancing over a crest with a troop of the 4th Hussars, caught some German cavalry by surprise 200 yards away down the slope. Gatacre's troop drew swords and advanced at a canter. The surprised Germans retreated, but when about 80 yards from them the Hussars gave a wild yell and charged downhill. The Germans started to flee but, being mounted on faster horses, Gatacre's men were soon among them, using the points of their swords to skewer eight or nine enemy, Gatacre himself accounting for two or three.

The Value of Cavalry on the Western Front

The minor clash of C Squadron, 4th Royal Dragoons, was typical of the sort of brief mounted encounters experienced by cavalry of all nations fighting on the Western Front. Indeed, there were to be no large-scale cavalry battles from the winter of 1914 through to August 1918. Cavalry were mostly used as infantry or on labouring duties while waiting for infantry and artillery to make a gap in the enemy defensive zones that cavalry could then exploit. As will be seen below, sometimes the glimmer of a gap appeared, but for various reasons a breakthrough – through which large bodies of mounted troops could dash to cause havoc in the enemy's rear and possibly bring about a general collapse of the front – never occurred. The reasons for this revolved around the difficulty of identifying the gap in the confusion of battle, and also the great depth of the German defences, especially in the latter part of the war. These difficulties were compounded by the invariable failure or slowness of communications and the need to have cavalry formations grouped close behind the front at the right place ready to exploit at the right moment.

It is no great exaggeration, however, to say that throughout the war on the Western Front the High Command of the Allies, and to a much lesser extent that of the Germans, was fixated on creating such a breakthrough – it was certainly the ultimate objective of Haig in all major British offensives. The fighting, as emphasized before, was a gigantic siege operation and the only arm with

Interpreters and Paul Maze

French interpreters were attached to British units on arrival in France. They were mostly reservists from a variety of regiments and appeared in French uniforms, though these were soon changed for British khaki. One of those attached to the 7th Dragoon Guards was a retired French brigadier, who remained with the regiment throughout the war. Their value varied from being a nuisance to being held in high regard. They were particularly useful in making billeting arrangements in the towns and villages behind the lines and sometimes being sent on foraging missions – the 18th Hussars had one that invariably came back with fresh meat, bread and vegetables. Some were not so useful, and one with the 15th Hussars was suspected of cowardice. During the retreat from Mons in September 1914 Sergeant Hanna of that regiment wrote in his diary, 'Jew French interpreter has his sixth horse shot under him. I think he shoots them himself – he doesn't like them.'

Perhaps the best-known interpreter was the artist Paul Lucien Maze, DCM, MM and *Croix de Guerre*, who wrote of his experiences during the war in *A Frenchman in Khaki*. He was born in 1887 in Le Havre of Anglo-French parentage and at twelve was sent to England to finish his education. He later worked for his father until deciding to devote himself to art, then he served in the French Army before working with the British. Initially he attached himself to the Royal Scots Greys, acting as an informal interpreter and liaison officer – although he was never actually commissioned. During the retreat from Mons he became separated from the Greys and was arrested as a possible spy after approaching Major General Charles

Monro and asking the whereabouts of the regiment. He was searched, handcuffed and marched off with German prisoners in fear of being shot. The next day he was saved by the timely arrival through the village of a squadron of the Scots Greys, whose commander recognized him and persuaded the provost marshal to release him.

Later in the war Maze was serving with the 17th Lancers – of Charge of the Light Brigade fame – where he was much respected, dining with the officers and keeping them entertained with his fund of amusing stories. On one occasion when the 17th came under shellfire Maze happened to be riding with the colonel. He described his reaction as follows:

I saw some shells burst near one of our squadrons . . . then more . . . Horses and men were going up in the air, I closed my eyes . . . I said to the Colonel, 'But it is folly to remain where we are; let's go.' But these British are funny – he didn't answer. I said; 'If you wish to get killed, I don't,' so I turned my fat pony and galloped away . . . A General was coming up on his horse. 'Don't go there,' I said, you'll get killed.' Well, what do you think? That funny man spurred his horse to where I told him not to go.

Maze, however, was a courageous man, as proved by his decorations. It was while he was with the Scots Greys that he met Winston Churchill. They became lifelong friends and Maze encouraged him to paint. In 1939, when Maze had become a well-established artist, it was Churchill who wrote the foreword to the catalogue of his first New York exhibition. He served again in the British Army during World War II and died in 1979, aged ninety-two.

Cavalrymen of the York Hussars rest their horses, 1915.

the mobility to exploit a breach was the mounted arm. Even by November 1917 when tanks were deployed in large numbers, only cavalry had the necessary speed. Tanks crawled along at around 4 miles an hour at best, and at the Battle of Amiens in 1918 British heavy tanks had to be led on to the battlefield by mounted officers. It was for this reason that Haig resolved to keep a cavalry corps in being, despite many attempts by politicians (Lloyd George and Churchill) to pressurize him into abandoning it. The Battle of Cambrai in late 1917 was the nearest cavalry came to exploiting an opening gap, but timidity by the High Command and poor communications saw the opportunity evaporate (see Section Thirteen).

If cavalry needed open warfare to fulfil its potential, there were four short periods in which it might conceivably have done so. These were the retreat from Mons in 1914;

the advance to the Hindenburg Line in March 1917; the spring retreat from the German offensive a year later; and the general Allied advance of the Hundred Days offensive that ended the war. For reasons that will be explained below, on none of these occasions were anything other than comparatively small-scale cavalry operations mounted. At the start of the war the French cavalry in particular – who, with their splendid uniforms and gleaming cuirasses, were men steeped in the exploits of Napoleon's dashing cavalry leaders, such as Murat, Kellerman and Lasalle – found their inability to emulate their forebears deeply disappointing. The lancer officer quoted at the start of this section neatly sums up the frustration of the cavalry for much of the war.

This lack of opportunity or ability to fulfil the traditional cavalry roles of reconnaissance, screening, patrolling, exploitation, pursuit and – a cavalryman's dream – executing a full-blooded charge, not only frustrated the mounted men but caused many infantry units to complain bitterly that the cavalry were failing to pull their weight. The problem was that a horseman was exceptionally vulnerable to rifle, machine-gun and artillery fire. He made a large target and if his horse was hit the rider became immobilized; even if he dismounted to fight, at least one man in four had to remain out of the action as a horse-holder. Exacerbating these vulnerabilities was barbed wire. Horses have difficulty seeing strands of wire strung between pickets and, approaching at speed, will avoid the pickets and either run into the wire or see it at the last moment and try to leap over it, fail, and land on it. Deep belts of wire were an even more impenetrable barrier to cavalry than to infantry. The suffering of horses – not just those of the cavalry, which in fact had a minority of the animals on the Western Front – will be discussed in greater depth in Section Nine, but a description by Lieutenant Colonel A. Beaman, 4th Queen's Own Hussars, of horses' vulnerability under artillery fire in 1918 illustrates their often pitiable circumstances:

Things were not pleasant with the squadron. It was strung out and closely hugging the low bank . . . waiting for our new attack to begin. In addition to the fragments of crumps from the shells that fell so fast in the valley, we were now and then directly saluted by salvos of whiz-bangs. Few men were hit by these as they lay close against the bank holding their reins; but soon were busy with their revolvers putting mutilated horses out of their agony. My own poor mare had both her forelegs shot away above the knees, and lay screaming like a child until Dano gave her the coup de grace.

The horrendous losses among the infantry in all armies soon necessitated not only the drastic reduction of recruiting into cavalry units but also the use of dismounted cavalry as infantry or as labourers working on the construction and repair of roads and tracks behind the lines. The problems for cavalry acting as infantry were several, but primarily their lack of manpower, as even at

Lieutenant General Sir Adrian Carton de Wiart, VC, KBE, CB, CMG, DSO, *Croix de Guerre* (Belgium), *Croix de Guerre and Légion d'honneur* (France), 1880–1963

De Wiart was a truly exceptional and courageous cavalryman. During the course of the war he was wounded eight times, won the Victoria Cross, lost the sight of an eye and his left hand, but continued to serve, going on to reach the age of eighty-three having led an almost unbelievably adventurous life.

He was born in Brussels, the son of a Belgian barrister, and spent much of his early childhood in Cairo. After attending the Oratory School, Edgbaston, and spending an unsuccessful period at Balliol College, Oxford, he ran off and joined a yeomanry regiment as a trooper. While serving with this regiment during the Second Boer War he was badly wounded, invalided out and returned to Balliol for a second, equally unsuccessful, period. De Wiart then returned to South Africa, again enlisting as a trooper. However, he was later commissioned into the 4th Dragoon Guards without ever having to attend Sandhurst. A period spent in India and South Africa allowed him to indulge to the full his tastes for cavalry sports and hunting.

In July 1914 de Wiart volunteered for service in Somaliland, where he joined the Camel Corps and saw action in the fighting against rebels led by the 'Mad Mullah'. It was in a cavalry charge during this time that he was badly wounded in his left eye, which later had to be removed at the World War I emergency hospital at 17 Park Lane, London. From then on he wore a black patch. On recovery, now a major, he rejoined the 4th Dragoon Guards in Belgium and during the Second Battle of Ypres received the first of his Western Front wounds – this one necessitating the amputation of his left hand. When he was once more fit, and after some hard words with medical boards, he returned to the front as second-in-command of a Lancashire infantry battalion before being promoted to command a battalion of the Gloucesters. On 2–3 July 1916 Lieutenant Colonel de Wiart, then commanding the 8th Gloucesters, took command of the 57th Brigade, 19th Division, at La Boiselle after the other commanding officers became casualties. For 'organizing the positions to be held, he exposed himself fearlessly to enemy fire', receiving a slight wound to his ear and later the Victoria Cross. In 1917, by then a brigadier general, another wound brought him back to 17 Park Lane and three months' recuperation. The following year he arrived back in France just in time for the Germans' March offensive, during the course of which de Wiart was severely wounded in the leg, necessitating yet another stay at 17 Park Lane, which was now said to keep a bed permanently reserved for him.

From 1918 to 1924 he commanded the British Military Mission in Poland and after leaving the army he spent much of his time living there. Shortly before the Germans invaded Poland in 1939 he had been reappointed head of the Military Mission there; however, there was little to do, so he was recalled to Britain and given command of a Territorial division and in April 1940 found himself conducting a skilful withdrawal of British troops from Norway. After this he was appointed by Churchill to head the Military Mission in Yugoslavia. However, his aircraft was shot down into the sea and de Wiart was captured. He and General Richard O'Connor managed to escape disguised as peasants (O'Connor spoke Italian), but were recaptured after eight days, only to be released and sent to Lisbon to assist negotiate the Italian surrender in August 1943. Churchill then despatched de Wiart to China as his personal representative to General Chiang Kai-shek, where he remained until the Japanese capitulation – on his way home he managed to break his back!

De Wiart was a true battlefield leader. As Dr Anthony Clayton, a former senior lecturer at Sandhurst, has said, 'de Wiart . . . commanded a personal respect among the men he led in battle, soldiers could see that he was a man who had been to where he was asking them to go.'

full establishment a cavalry regiment had little over half that of a full-strength infantry battalion. Nevertheless, as infantry they gave a good account of themselves and generally accepted fighting on foot, digging trenches and constructing tracks as unavoidable and necessary evils for much of their time on the Western Front. Cavalrymen were not infrequently exposed to the horrors of trench warfare, conditions which were described by Lieutenant Colonel Beaman during the winter of 1917/18:

> When Purple [a Captain F. A. Sykes] had been going round the positions previous to our taking over, the officer who guided him had protested that it was impossible to walk down Spade Trench. Purple, however, feeling that he ought to see for himself, had insisted on trying. After a few steps his guide had sunk up to the waist in clinging mud from which the united efforts of Purple and himself had been powerless to extricate him. Fortunately, the unhappy officer was wearing thigh gum boots, and, having undone the attachments to his braces buttons, he was eventually, after nearly an hour's strenuous labour, pulled out of them by five stalwart men, leaving the boots behind him . . .

On another occasion Beaman went out at night to check on the progress of a wiring party in no-man's-land:

> At this moment a man who was softly tapping in a picket made a bad shot in the dark and hit the fingers of the man holding it for him. The injured man let out a roar of pain and a volley of blasphemy loud enough to awaken the dead. Instantly a machine gun opposite opened fire.
>
> I sprang into a large mine crater a yard or two away. My right arm sunk up to the shoulder and half my shoulder into a soft woozy substance like a soufflé. Hastily drawing it out, I began to slide down the side of the crater and clutched wildly in the dark. My hand again slipped along some inches of slime, then, sinking through it, closed on something hard and stick like. Grasping this firmly, I checked my descent for a moment, and then my support gave way, and I rolled to the bottom of the crater with the lower part of a human leg in my hand.

Cavalry Organization

On the Western Front the British (including some dominion forces), the French, the Belgians and the Germans deployed cavalry as a separate arm supported by horse artillery. The Portuguese, when they entered the conflict in 1917, provided only infantry and artillery. Likewise the Americans, although commanded by a former cavalryman (General Pershing) who advocated their inclusion in the expeditionary force, had to give far higher priority to the enormous task of assembling, training and shipping the other essential arms and services to France – cavalry was way down the list.

Cavalry regiments in all armies were deployed in two groups or categories, each with its own distinctive role. The first was the cavalry division or cavalry corps with its horse artillery and administrative units in support providing a strategic mobile reserve – the hoped-for deep-exploitation formation. The BEF initially fielded one division of four brigades and a fifth independent brigade (see diagram, pages 268–9); this was later expanded into a strategic force, the Cavalry Corps, its deployment kept very much under Haig's personal authority. The French started with ten cavalry divisions and the Belgians with one. The Germans launched their massive wheel into Western Europe with ten cavalry divisions, including one Bavarian, all of which were used to head the advance of their invading armies. From the right wing of the wheel, riding ahead of the German First and Second Armies, were the 2nd, 4th and 9th Cavalry Divisions; leading the Third Army were the Guards and 5th Cavalry Divisions; preceding the Fourth and Fifth Armies rode the 3rd and 6th Cavalry Divisions; while the 7th, 8th and Bavarian Cavalry Divisions headed the Sixth Army. Only the Seventh Army was not allocated a separate cavalry division.

The second cavalry grouping was termed 'divisional' cavalry. These were regiments attached to infantry divisions as their own reconnaissance force, used for patrolling, escorting, checking roads and supply routes, providing details to the provost marshal for traffic control, escorting prisoners and supplying mounted orderlies for divisional and brigade headquarters. British cavalry regiments doing these duties within the BEF in the autumn of 1914 were A and C Squadrons of the North Irish Horse and B Squadron of the South Irish Horse (Special Reserve regiments), all of which were under army headquarters control. Marching with the infantry divisions were two regiments, divided as follows:

1st Division	A Squadron, 15th (King's) Hussars
2nd Division	B Squadron, 15th (King's) Hussars
3rd Division	C Squadron, 15th (King's) Hussars
4th Division	B Squadron, 19th (Queen Alexandra's Own Royal) Hussars
5th Division	A Squadron, 19th (Queen Alexandra's Own Royal) Hussars
6th Division	C Squadron, 19th (Queen Alexandra's Own Royal) Hussars

Within a short time these squadrons were found insufficient for the multitude of duties, so cyclist companies, with personnel from infantry units, were attached to each squadron of divisional cavalry. With the arrival of the Kitchener infantry divisions in France, the attached divisional cavalry units were provided by yeomanry (Territorial Force) regiments.

Britain

In 1914 the British Army had 31 regular cavalry regiments and another 55 yeomanry regiments. Regular regiments consisted of 2 household cavalry, 11 dragoons (including 7 dragoon guards), 12 hussars and 6 lancers. In August 1914 the BEF's Cavalry Division and independent Cavalry Brigade were composed of regular regiments totalling 9,000 men and 9,800 horses – on the line of march on a single road such a cavalry division would extend about 11½ miles.

On 13 September the 2nd Cavalry Division was formed in France from the independent 5th Brigade and the 3rd withdrawn from the original Cavalry Division, now named the 1st Cavalry Division. At the same time, the 3rd Cavalry Division was forming in England from regiments still remaining there and from others returning from overseas. Initially this division, like the 2nd, had only two brigades. It was sent to France in October 1914 and the divisions were brought up to three brigades as yeomanry regiments arrived on the Western Front. On 9 October the 1st and 2nd Cavalry Divisions formed the Cavalry Corps under Allenby. When the 3rd joined from IV Corps later in the month, it made the Cavalry Corps the largest British cavalry force ever assembled under one commander. Late in 1914 two Indian cavalry divisions arrived at the front as part of the Indian Corps and when the corps left the Western Front in early 1916 its cavalry divisions remained and were renumbered the 5th and 6th Cavalry Divisions. From July that year Lieutenant General Charles Kavanagh commanded the Cavalry Corps. In early 1918 the two Indian divisions left for Palestine, bringing the British cavalry force down again to three divisions. See diagram, pages 268–9.

In August 1914 the cavalry strength represented almost 8 per cent of the BEF. With the development of static trench warfare and the huge expansion of the force on the Western Front, cavalry numbers increased: in 1916 there were five divisions (including the two Indian), but their proportion to the rest of the army was shrinking dramatically so that by September that year it was only 2.5 per cent. By the Armistice in November 1918, with the two Indian divisions in Palestine, the Cavalry Corps represented only just over one per cent of the British

Army on the Western Front – in terms of numbers this was around 27,400 out of over 1.9 million men. British cavalry casualties in France totalled just over 19,000, of which some 4,420 were killed. As a percentage of the total BEF casualties of 2.1 million, 19,000 is just 0.9 per cent, reflecting the comparatively small numbers of cavalry and their relatively short exposure in front-line trenches or operations.

A British regular cavalry regiment in 1914 consisted of a headquarters, three squadrons (called 'sabre squadrons' – an unofficial title that still exists today for tank squadrons in cavalry regiments) of four troops, each of two sections (see diagram below).

The second-largest cavalry contingent on the Western Front, one that remained until early 1918, were the two Indian divisions that formed the Indian Cavalry Corps, commanded from 18 December 1914 by Lieutenant General Michael Rimington. The Marquess of Anglesey in his definitive *A History of the British Cavalry*, Volume 8, quotes a lieutenant of the 18th Lancers having this to say on Rimington in 1916:

He may have been excellent in command of a squadron – but absolute murder having him in command of a corps – a gallant officer but useless GOC [General Officer Commanding] and universally disliked by the Indian portion of his command – not unnatural as on one occasion he was known to have remarked 'they were only fit to feed pigs and so forth' – a nice thing to say about two thirds of his command.

The 1st Indian Cavalry Division comprised the Sialkot, Ambala and Lucknow Cavalry Brigades (named after the locations in India at which they were based in peacetime). The 2nd Indian Cavalry Brigade contained the Mhow, Meerut and Secunderabad Cavalry Brigades. Each division had three batteries of horse artillery, a brigade ammunition column (BAC) and engineer, signals, supply and medical units under command. In each brigade of three regiments one regiment was British – for example, the Lucknow Brigade had the British 1st (King's) Dragoon Guards serving alongside the Indian 29th Lancers (Deccan Horse) and 36th Jacob's Horse. This system,

British Cavalry Regiment at Full Strength, August 1914

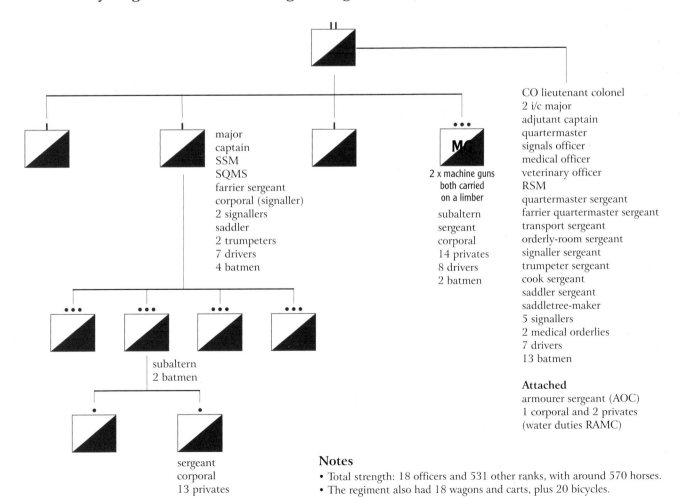

major
captain
SSM
SQMS
farrier sergeant
corporal (signaller)
2 signallers
saddler
2 trumpeters
7 drivers
4 batmen

2 x machine guns
both carried
on a limber

subaltern
sergeant
corporal
14 privates
8 drivers
2 batmen

CO lieutenant colonel
2 i/c major
adjutant captain
quartermaster
signals officer
medical officer
veterinary officer
RSM
quartermaster sergeant
farrier quartermaster sergeant
transport sergeant
orderly-room sergeant
signaller sergeant
trumpeter sergeant
cook sergeant
saddler sergeant
saddletree-maker
5 signallers
2 medical orderlies
7 drivers
13 batmen

Attached
armourer sergeant (AOC)
1 corporal and 2 privates
(water duties RAMC)

subaltern
2 batmen

sergeant
corporal
13 privates

Notes
• Total strength: 18 officers and 531 other ranks, with around 570 horses.
• The regiment also had 18 wagons and carts, plus 20 bicycles.

British Expeditionary Force Cavalry, August 1914

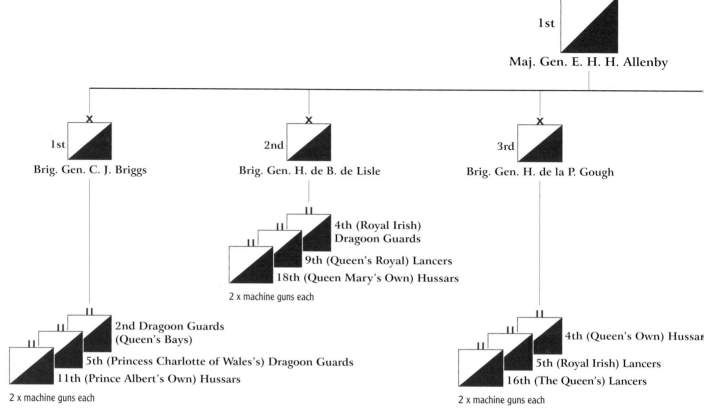

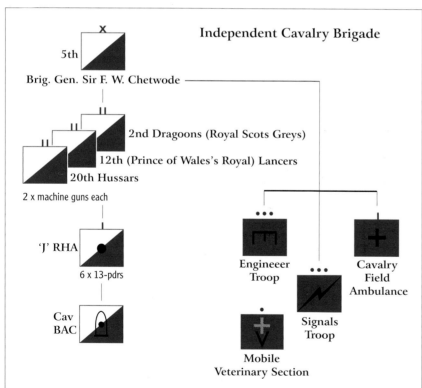

Notes

• The cavalry element of the BEF in August 1914 comprised the 1st Cavalry Division of four brigades and a fifth independent brigade. This represented some 9,000 men and 9,800 horses, which on the line of march would have occupied almost 12 miles of road.

• Each brigade had an attached battery of the RHA, with six 13-pdr guns, a troop of engineers and signals, plus a field ambulance and veterinary sections.

• This force had 15 regiments of cavalry, 30 x 13-pdr guns and 30 machine guns.

which applied equally within Indian infantry formations, was a hangover from the 1857 Indian Mutiny after which it was deemed prudent to have a British unit within Indian formations for security reasons. During oper- ations on the Western Front it was unusual to have an Indian officer above platoon/troop commander level in an Indian unit. An Indian cavalry division had over 5,000 all ranks, a similar number of horses and several hundred mules used as pack animals. The Jodhpur Lancers acted as corps troops and the 15th Lancers (Cureton's Multanis) and the 4th Cavalry acted as divisional cavalry to the Lahore and Meerut Divisions respectively.

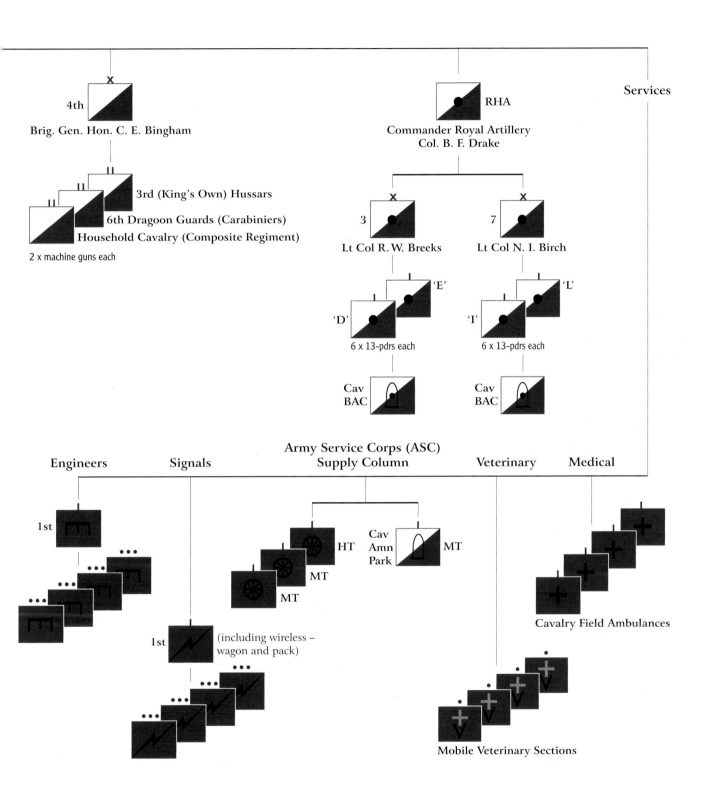

4th
Brig. Gen. Hon. C. E. Bingham

3rd (King's Own) Hussars
6th Dragoon Guards (Carabiniers)
Household Cavalry (Composite Regiment)
2 x machine guns each

RHA
Commander Royal Artillery
Col. B. F. Drake

Services

3
Lt Col R. W. Breeks

7
Lt Col N. I. Birch

'D' 'E'
6 x 13-pdrs each

'I' 'L'
6 x 13-pdrs each

Cav
BAC

Cav
BAC

Engineers Signals
Army Service Corps (ASC)
Supply Column
Veterinary Medical

1st

HT
MT
MT

Cav
Amn
Park
MT

Cavalry Field Ambulances

1st
(including wireless –
wagon and pack)

Mobile Veterinary Sections

The present author has been unable to trace the native Indian cavalry losses in France, but overall there were 20,854 (all ranks) native Indian casualties on the Western Front, of which 3,869 were killed, 15,321 wounded and 1,664 missing or taken prisoner.

Another cavalry formation serving with the BEF was the Canadian Cavalry Brigade. Formed in February 1915, it consisted of the Royal Canadian Dragoons, Lord Strathcona's Horse and the 2nd King Edward's Horse (a unit of the British Special Reserve) – replaced by the Fort Garry Horse in 1916 – and, except for two months in mid-1917, was

An Indian troop commander consults his map near Vraignes, 1917, while his troop sergeant looks on anxiously.

Front) with sword-armed opponents, as the lance was easily parried and was then virtually useless against a sword cut or thrust. It was also a real hindrance when moving through woods.

France

Like the Germans, the French started the war on the Western Front with ten cavalry divisions, divided initially as follows:

First Army	6th and 8th Cavalry Divisions
Second Army	2nd and 10th Cavalry Divisions
Third Army	7th Cavalry Division
Fourth Army	9th Cavalry Division
Fifth Army	4th Cavalry Division
GHQ Reserve	Cavalry Corps (under General J. F. A. Sordet): 1st, 3rd and 5th Cavalry Divisions (Generals Buisson, de Lastour and Bridoux)

A second Cavalry Corps under General Conneau was formed in September.

A French cavalry division consisted of three brigades of two regiments of four squadrons, a regiment having 35 officers and 734 other ranks, making it substantially larger than its British counterpart (see diagram opposite). From November 1914 these divisions contained a 'light group' mounted on bicycles, formed of men detached from the squadrons; it was normally used in a light infantry role.

In total there were 89 active French cavalry regiments – which included 13 cuirassier, 14 hussars, 21 chasseurs à cheval, 31 dragoons, 6 chasseurs d'Afrique and 4 spahis – dressed for the most part in Napoleonic-style uniforms, which made a splendid sight on the line of march but were positively disastrous on Western Front battlefields. There was plenty of patrolling work for these regiments in the last three months of 1914 and innumerable minor, and some not so minor, clashes occurred in Belgium and across France as French and German cavalry screened their advancing armies. However, as with other nations, France soon found that the traditional roles of cavalry were mostly obsolete, and with the huge overall losses many cavalry units had to convert to being infantrymen. In 1916 six cuirassier regiments were converted to infantry but called themselves cuirassiers à pied, and by 1918 the number of cavalry divisions had been reduced to six.

An ongoing problem with the French cavalry was poor horse management. Unlike the British, the French cavalryman seldom walked his horse even when the animal was exhausted, while at night girths

commanded by Brigadier General Jack Seely. Like other cavalry brigades, it had a machine-gun section and was supported by a horse-artillery battery, a field ambulance, engineer, signals, veterinary and supply sub-units. For provost duties, a squadron of the Royal Canadian Mounted Police formed part of brigade headquarters.

Australia raised fifteen regiments of light horse organized into five brigades. Each regiment was composed of around 600 men divided into three squadrons with two machine guns (Vickers) and the usual supporting sub-units. All except the 13th Light Horse and one squadron of the 4th and 14th Light Horse served in Gallipoli, Libya, the Sinai and Palestine, mostly as mounted infantry. The 13th Light Horse and the two squadrons of the 4th and 14th served on the Western Front, first as the divisional squadrons for the 2nd, 4th and 5th Australian Divisions, and then as the 1st ANZAC Corps

Mounted Regiment. A squadron of the 4th provided the divisional cavalry for the 1st Division and the one from the 14th Light Horse for the 3rd Division. In combination with some New Zealand mounted troops the squadron of the 4th became part of the II ANZAC Corps Mounted Regiment. After the formation of the Australian Corps in November 1917, the I ANZAC Corps Mounted Regiment once again became known as the 13th Light Horse Regiment.

British cavalry, when deployed at the front as distinct from waiting in reserve to exploit the hoped-for breakthrough, mostly did so as mounted infantry – that is, they used their horses for movement and dismounted to fight. Equally, cavalry regiments were put in the trenches and fought as normal infantry, handing in their horses for the duration of their stay in the line and receiving bayonets and digging tools – initially there were not enough of the latter to go round and locally requisitioned tools, bayonets, mess tins and broken plates were used to scratch rudimentary trenches. All cavalrymen were issued with the same .303 rifles as the infantry. In the mounted role they were also armed with the 1908 cavalry-pattern sword until it was withdrawn in 1915 (Indian cavalry kept their swords, except for sergeants and above, who received revolvers instead). In 1915 all British cavalry regiments, not just light ones, were issued with the lance. This was a splendid weapon for use in a charge – provided the rider had mastered the knack of thrusting and not being dragged from his horse by the weight of a transfixed enemy, and for skewering a man in pursuit. However, it was far from ideal in a close-quarter melee (a rare but not unknown occurrence on the Western

A German lancer, 1917, with lance and gas mask – old and new forms of war together.

French Cavalry Division, August 1914

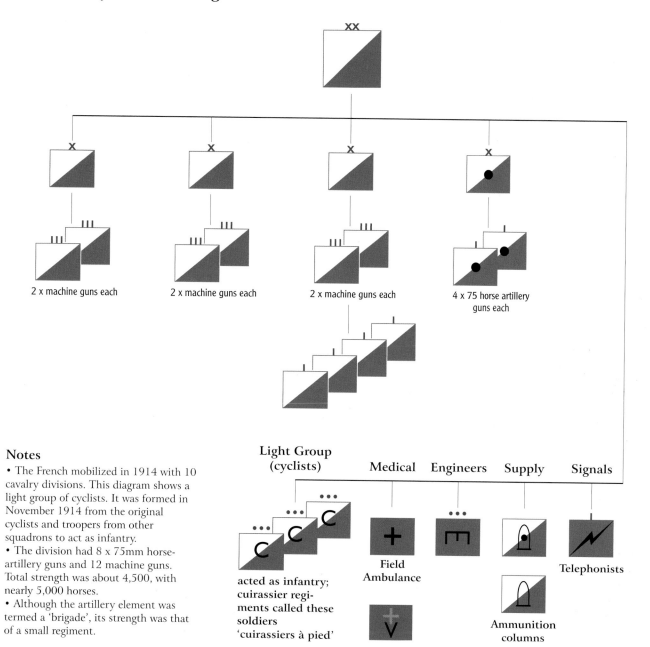

2 x machine guns each

2 x machine guns each

2 x machine guns each

4 x 75 horse artillery
guns each

Light Group
(cyclists)

Medical   Engineers   Supply   Signals

Field
Ambulance

Telephonists

Ammunition
columns

acted as infantry;
cuirassier regi-
ments called these
soldiers
'cuirassiers à pied'

Notes
• The French mobilized in 1914 with 10 cavalry divisions. This diagram shows a light group of cyclists. It was formed in November 1914 from the original cyclists and troopers from other squadrons to act as infantry.
• The division had 8 x 75mm horse-artillery guns and 12 machine guns. Total strength was about 4,500, with nearly 5,000 horses.
• Although the artillery element was termed a 'brigade', its strength was that of a small regiment.

often remained unloosened. To see a French cavalryman dismounted even during a comparatively long halt was a rarity. The result was a large number of sick and worn-out animals, many with large, foul-smelling sores on their backs. The Marquis of Anglesey quotes an officer who witnessed a body of French cavalry resting:

an hour in the saddle at the halt, with corn stooks twenty yards away from them, without a thought of dismounting or giving their horses a mouthful of food . . . One morning I saw a wounded horse lying on a heap of burning litter. He was groaning and struggling to get up but fell back each time on the burning stuff. The

yard was full of French troops, but not one took the slightest notice of the horse which was slowly roasting to death in front of their eyes. I put him out of his misery with a bullet from my pistol.

The main weapons were the sword and the 1890-model 8mm cavalry carbine, known as a *mousqueton* – a decidedly inferior weapon to the British rifle and German carbine due to its short range. Dragoon regiments also had lances, as did a number of chasseurs à cheval regiments. These were originally made of ash or bamboo, but in 1914 were replaced by tubular steel. In all cavalry regiments, officers, senior NCOs, trumpeters and machine-gunners were armed with sword and revolver.

Germany
The Germans mobilized eleven cavalry divisions on the outbreak of war, ten of which spearheaded their invasion of Belgium and France (see pages 22–3). These ten were grouped into four cavalry corps as follows:

I Corps Guards and 5th Cavalry Divisions (General von Richthofen)

II Corps 2nd, 4th and 9th Cavalry Divisions (General von der Marwitz)

III Corps 7th, 8th and Bavarian Cavalry Divisions (General von Frommel)

IV Corps 3rd and 6th Cavalry Divisions (General von Hollen)

German Cavalry Division, August 1914

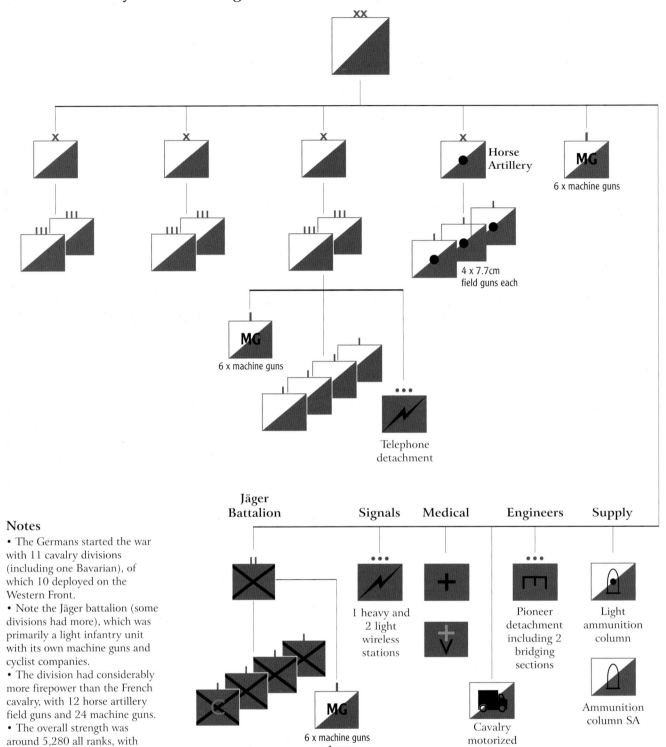

Horse Artillery

6 x machine guns

4 x 7.7cm field guns each

6 x machine guns

Telephone detachment

Jäger Battalion

Signals

Medical

Engineers

Supply

1 heavy and 2 light wireless stations

Pioneer detachment including 2 bridging sections

Light ammunition column

6 x machine guns + 1 spare

Cavalry motorized vehicle column

Ammunition column SA

Notes
• The Germans started the war with 11 cavalry divisions (including one Bavarian), of which 10 deployed on the Western Front.
• Note the Jäger battalion (some divisions had more), which was primarily a light infantry unit with its own machine guns and cyclist companies.
• The division had considerably more firepower than the French cavalry, with 12 horse artillery field guns and 24 machine guns.
• The overall strength was around 5,280 all ranks, with some 5,590 horses and 216 wagons/vehicles.

In peacetime the cavalry was not organized into divisions but, except for the guard cavalry, consisted of two or three cavalry brigades in each of the Army Corps Districts into which the country was divided. From these brigades the eleven cavalry divisions were formed, with surplus regiments earmarked as divisional cavalry for the infantry. These cavalry divisions represented a powerful force of nearly 60,000 men and around 65,000 horses (riding and draught). The cavalry division was a well-balanced formation with three brigades each of two regiments of five squadrons (on mobilization one squadron remained behind to act as a depot squadron). It had the support of twelve horse-artillery field guns, twenty-four machine guns and at least one Jäger (light infantry) battalion mounted on bicycles, making it into something resembling, in modern terms, a cavalry battle group (see diagram above).

The divisional cavalry attached to the infantry originally comprised two or three squadrons, but as the demand for manpower in other arms grew it was reduced to one squadron. These men frequently took turns in the trenches and when not so employed undertook patrols, pickets, provost, escorts, or orderly or manned observation duties.

On mobilization, 110 active, 33 reserve, 2 Landwehr and 1 Ersatz cavalry regiments were allotted to the field army, as well as 38 Landwehr and 19 Ersatz squadrons. As the war developed, 39 reserve cavalry regiments were formed along with numerous Landwehr and Ersatz units and sub-units for duty as divisional cavalry. The 110 active regiments comprised 10 cuirassier, 28 dragoon, 21 hussar, 24 Uhlan, 13 *Jäger zu Pferde* (mounted rifles), 2 Saxon (guard and carabineer) and 12 Bavarian (2 Uhlan,

2 heavy cavalry and 8 light horse) regiments. A regiment forming part of a cavalry division in the field consisted of four squadrons and a machine-gun squadron with six guns. Each squadron had 4 officers, 163 other ranks, 178 horses and 3 wagons. A regiment had a war establishment of 36 officers, 688 other ranks, 709 riding horses, 60 draught horses, 2 bridge wagons, 1 telephone wagon, 1 medical wagon and 5 each of baggage, supply and fodder wagons – a total of 19 wagons.

As with other armies, the Germans quickly found that cavalry was unsuited to trench warfare and those units not required behind the lines began to be converted to infantry. The huge demand for horses for other arms and services, particularly draught horses for the artillery, accelerated

this process. From 1917 these dismounted cavalry regiments used as infantry began to be called cavalry *Schützen* regiments, and although expected to fight as infantry were considerably below the strength of an ordinary infantry unit. By the spring of 1918, fifty-one such regiments formed the three cavalry *Schützen* divisions on the Western Front.

In 1914 the armament was the same for all mounted regiments. Officers and senior NCOs were armed with sword and revolver; corporals with lance, sword and revolver; and privates with lance, sword and carbine. The lance was 10 feet 6 inches long and made of tubular steel; the revolver was gradually replaced by the 9mm automatic pistol; the carbine was the 9mm 98 pattern model, similar in design to the rifle.

Cavalry Actions on the Western Front, 1914–1918

The following paragraphs give a summary of a few of the cavalry actions on the Western Front by year, remembering that most cavalry units spent the great majority of their time fighting dismounted as infantry or, particularly with the British, waiting in reserve to exploit any breakthrough in the trench systems. The actions below were all comparatively small scale, when the cavalry of at least one side fought mounted.

1914

In the late summer and autumn there were countless minor clashes between cavalry units of all three belligerent nations over the 450-mile arc from the Belgian coast in the north to Alsace in the south. Ahead of the marching infantry columns, cavalry squadrons screened their advance, probed for information, endeavoured to drive in opposing cavalry patrols and capture prisoners. All this was true cavalry work, and tens of thousands of horsemen were thus employed during those weeks in August and September 1914.

On 11 August a French reconnaissance in force pushed the Germans out of the frontier village of Lagarde in Lorraine. In the action that followed the Bavarians won their first battle honour of the war. A Uhlan brigade from the Bavarian Cavalry Division charged the enemy positions, which included artillery batteries, and drove the French back, capturing 1,467 prisoners, six machine guns, two batteries of artillery and the French operation order, which was found on the body of the French commanding general. This remarkable success came at a price. The Uhlans lost fourteen officers (including the brigade commander, General

von Redwitz, and his brigade major), 250 men and 319 horses.

On the same day some 2,000 German cavalry engaged and defeated a regiment of Belgian lancers. However, at Aineffe a regiment of German dragoons charged a Belgian infantry position and were driven off after several hours of fighting that cost the Germans 250 casualties and left the Belgians in control of the village. The following day saw a more dramatic and bloody battle between German and Belgian horsemen, which also involved considerable use of artillery and machine guns, at Haelen, a small market town lying on the axis of advance of von der Marwitz, which would provide a convenient crossing place for the Germans over the River Gete. To block the German advance, the Belgians sent their single cavalry division under Lieutenant General Leon de Witte to secure the bridge over the river. Witte decided to fight dismounted. Through communication intercepts the Belgians learned that the Germans were heading for Haelen and sent their 4th Infantry Brigade to reinforce the cavalry in the early hours of 12 August.

Fighting started about 8:00 a.m. when the German vanguard of the 4th Cavalry Division, with the aid of artillery, drove about 200 Belgian troopers from their position in the old brewery at Haelen. Although the bridge had been blown, it only partially collapsed and allowed the Germans to send about 1,000 cavalry into the town. Emboldened by this success, the Germans then began a series of cavalry charges with lance and sabre, involving cuirassiers, Uhlans and dragoons, against de Witte's dismounted troopers whose main position was

just to the west of the town. Belgian rifle, machine-gun and artillery fire decimated the attackers, whose assaults continued with great gallantry but little success until early evening. The Germans eventually withdrew, having lost some 150 dead, 600 wounded and 200–300 prisoners – the Belgians later called this victory the 'Battle of the Silver Helmets' due to the large number of cavalry helmets scattered around the battlefield. Although celebrated as a brilliant achievement by the Belgians, Haelen had no real effect on the Germans' overall advance. The clash was an early indication of the futility of horsemen charging dismounted cavalry (infantry) in prepared positions.

The first, very minor, British cavalry action on 22 August has been described at the start of this section. On 24 August the British 2nd Cavalry Brigade was in position to assist in covering the retreat of the 5th Infantry Division from its positions along the south bank of the Mons–Condé Canal (see Map 8). When the Germans successfully attacked across the canal, the Cavalry Division was ordered to support the 5th Division's left flank to allow it to retire. As part of this, the 9th Lancers, supported by the 4th Dragoon Guards (both 2nd Cavalry Brigade), were ordered to halt the enemy's advance from the village of Quievrain (see Map 53). The brigade commander, Brigadier General Beauvoir de Lisle, ordered Lieutenant Colonel D. G. M. Campbell of the 9th Lancers to check the enemy at all costs, adding, 'It may be necessary for you to charge.' He also told Lieutenant Colonel R. L. Mullens of the 4th Dragoon Guards to support the 9th. L Battery RHA, firing over

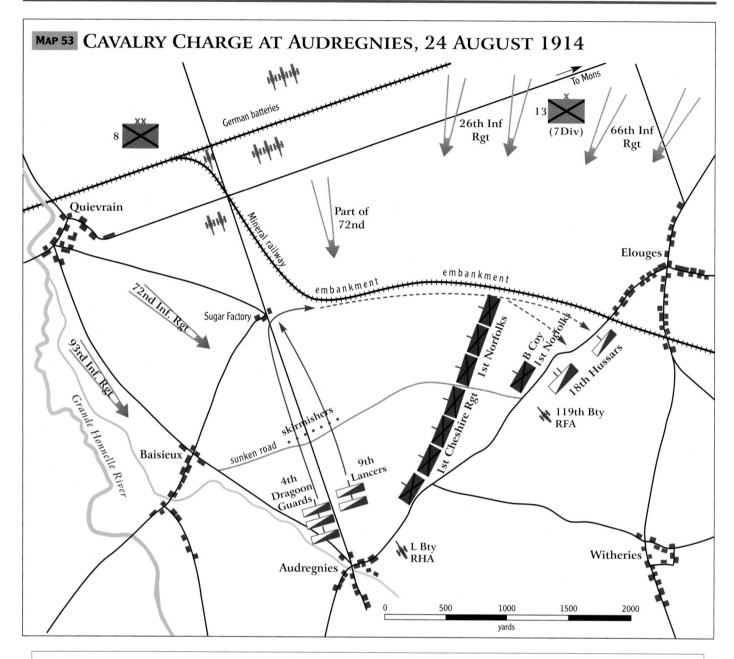

MAP 53 CAVALRY CHARGE AT AUDREGNIES, 24 AUGUST 1914

Notes for Map 53

• This map shows the situation about 1:00 p.m. on 24 August, with an attack developing by two German divisions against the left flank of the British, who were in the process of withdrawing. There was a danger of the Cheshires and Norfolks being outflanked and overrun, so the 9th Lancers and 4th Dragoon Guards were ordered to charge to check the enemy advance. They were supported by L Battery RHA.

• The charge overran some German skirmishers in the sunken road but was subjected to heavy rifle fire and shelling from up to nine enemy batteries, causing considerable loss. On reaching the area of

the sugar factory, wire fences and a steep railway embankment brought both regiments to a confused halt. Some riders dismounted and returned fire from the sugar factory, but the majority, now inextricably mixed, were forced to swing right and gallop along the line of the railway, still under heavy fire, with the survivors eventually rallying in the 18th Hussars' position just south of Elouges.

• The charge achieved little and cost the cavalry 169 men and over 300 horses. It was a classic example of how, no matter how gallant the cavalry, they charged infantry and artillery at their peril.

---

the cavalry's heads, was to support their advance, although the Germans had nine batteries in action opposite them east of Quievrain. The actual attack was made by two squadrons of the 9th Lancers with three of the 4th Dragoon Guards echeloned to their left, with the riders knee to knee in column of squadrons.

Corporal Harry Easton of the 9th Lancers thought the squadrons in 'a very disordered mess – horses anyhow' as they began their advance. Shortly after moving forward Colonel Campbell give the signal to canter. Second Lieutenant R. Chance, a troop commander in the 4th Dragoon Guards, remembered being unable to hear a shouted order

from those to his front because 'all I can hear is the whistlecrack of bullets and the "whee-ump" of shells. All I can do is follow my [squadron] leader, who forms troop into squadron columns and we are off at the gallop, swords pointed.' The charge had about 1,200 yards to go over ground that sloped gently down towards the enemy, with the fields of corn cut and stooked, but with some hedges and wire fences to cause problems. The horsemen were charging into a storm of rifle fire and the shells of nine enemy batteries straight ahead. As the 9th Lancers scrambled across the sunken road between Baisieux and Elouges, several German skirmishers were ridden down and speared. Chance continued:

> A cloud of dust erupts ahead, pierced by the flash of shell bursts. If there is a hail of bullets I am not aware of it as, with the men thundering behind, I endeavour one-handed to control my almost runaway steed . . . Sergeant Talbot has gone down, dead or alive, in a crashing somersault, and no sooner is he lost to us than I am among those who, halted by wire, veer in disorder, like a flock of sheep.

It was not a barbed-wire defensive obstacle but rather farmer's fencing and a steep railway embankment that caused the charge to be halted in a chaotic tangle of mixed-up riders from both regiments. On the left was a sugar factory at which a number of horsemen dismounted, took shelter and returned fire, while the majority of fragmented survivors who still had horses swung right and retired along the line of the mineral railway line towards Elouges, where they sought to rally among the 18th Hussars. The cavalry had attempted to charge an unknown number of infantry supported by nine batteries of guns over ground that was criss-crossed with obstacles. As a French general who had witnessed the charge of the Light Brigade against Russian guns in the Crimea sixty years earlier remarked, 'It was magnificent, but it was not war.' The losses of the two regiments were 169 men killed, wounded and missing, as well as over 300 horses.

French cavalry were frequently engaged in minor skirmishes with the Germans along the River Lys and around Lille on the French–Belgian border. At Lassigny in mid-October French chasseurs à cheval charged German infantry and gun positions successfully, and on 5 October French cuirassiers crossed the River Lys and fought with German cavalry hand to hand in a series of clashes along the bank. On 14 October the British 1st Life Guards (Household Cavalry) clashed (mostly dismounted) with a number of German Uhlans in the village of Gheluwe about 10 miles south-east of Ypres, just north of the Lys. In his autobiography, *Troop, Horse & Trench*, Trooper R. A. Lloyd describes two incidents from that fight:

> Soon the party of Uhlans was wiped out, all except two. One of these managed to reach his horse, sprang into the saddle and galloped away. He went tearing along a straight road at full speed and

was gradually becoming a mere speck in the distance when Sergeant Johnny Arthurs of the Skins [Inniskillings] took his rifle, sighted it at twelve hundred yards, and shot the Uhlan dead.

> [Another] one took to running across country and was pursued by Hon. Gerald Ernest Francis Ward [a lieutenant] and a couple of mounted men. Soon he stopped, raised his carbine and aimed straight at the officer. As the latter rode directly at him, he changed his mind, threw the gun down and put up his hands. A wild fellow, named Bellingham, galloped at him and ran him through the body with his sword. He then calmly wiped his sword on his horse's mane and remarked: 'That's the way to serve them bastards.'

On 11 October, south of the Somme near Noyon, the 6th Pomeranian Infantry, thinking the French were retreating, rushed forward to pursue, only to be charged by French dragoons with lances lowered. The Germans, in the open, were given the time-honoured order from Napoleonic battlefields for infantry to receive cavalry: 'Form square.' Despite this, the disorganized Germans were overrun, scattered and their regimental colour captured.

During the series of battles that was First Ypres (October–November 1914) the British cavalry got their first real taste of fighting as mobile infantry on the flanks of what became known as the Ypres salient. The two cavalry divisions under Allenby were able to put only around 6,000 men in the line as riflemen and machine-gunners against a far superior enemy. However, this thin line, by a combination of bluff and superb shooting, held its own.

The extent of the numerical weakness of the cavalry is explained by the Marquess of Anglesey in Volume 7 of his *A History of the British Cavalry*:

> the numbers of men available in a regiment for action in the trenches was greatly limited. Most of the regiments were below strength due to mounting casualties. Several could hardly muster half-strength at about 180 men. After subtracting one man as horse-holder for four animals, the farriers and the essential non-commissioned officers, a brigade of three regiments could rarely produce more than 600 men to man the trenches. Nevertheless more often than not a cavalry brigade was expected to hold the same length of line as an infantry brigade . . . When the 6th Cavalry Brigade took over the 3rd Infantry Brigade's trenches on 5 November it numbered 1,200 rifles and

five machine guns. This entailed leaving one man to look after fifteen to twenty horses. All this took place in atrociously vile weather, the beginning of one of the worst winters ever known in Flanders.

One of the highlights of the cavalry's dismounted defensive battles that year was the successful defence of Messines town on 31 October by the 1st Cavalry Division. Twelve squadrons faced a determined assault by twelve battalions of enemy infantry supported by sustained artillery fire. Some of the action involved house-to-house fighting in the streets of the town. Afterwards Major General de Lisle issued the following order:

> The G.O.C. 1st Cavalry Division has been highly complimented both by the Commander of the Corps and by the Field-Marshal, Commander–in-Chief, [French], on the gallant manner in which the 1st Cavalry Division defended Ypres [Messines] today. The G.O.C. wishes this conveyed to troops tonight if possible. 7.40. 31st.

1915

Throughout the year the British cavalry, apart from some patrolling, was not involved in any mounted action. Rather it was a year devoted to life in billets behind the lines, interspersed with periods as infantry in the trenches or working as pioneers – the latter being something the cavalry loathed. During the offensive battles at Neuve Chapelle, Festubert and Loos, cavalry formations waited behind the front for the anticipated breakthrough that never came. However, during the Second Battle of Ypres that spring cavalry units were constantly rushed from place to place in the line as a convenient 'fire brigade' with which senior commanders plugged gaps. In the five and a half weeks between 22 April and 31 May the 1st, 2nd and 3rd Cavalry Divisions' casualties amounted to over 3,000 all ranks. Captain L. R. Lumley's *The Eleventh Hussars (Prince Albert's Own) 1908–1934* recounts some of the bitter trench fighting that involved that regiment and others in the German attack on Hooge on 24 May, during which the British defences were subjected to a heavy gas attack.

> The first intimation that the Germans were bombing down the trench towards A Squadron was the arrival of wounded men of the Durham Light Infantry and of the 9th Lancers. In the words of an eyewitness: 'wounded came streaming down the trench, shouting for a doctor, one poor devil badly wounded in the throat, quite conscious and aware that he had to die; one could do little or nothing for him, and he was a long time a-dying'...

MAP 54 2ND INDIAN CAVALRY DIVISION AND THE 'GAP', 14 JULY 1916

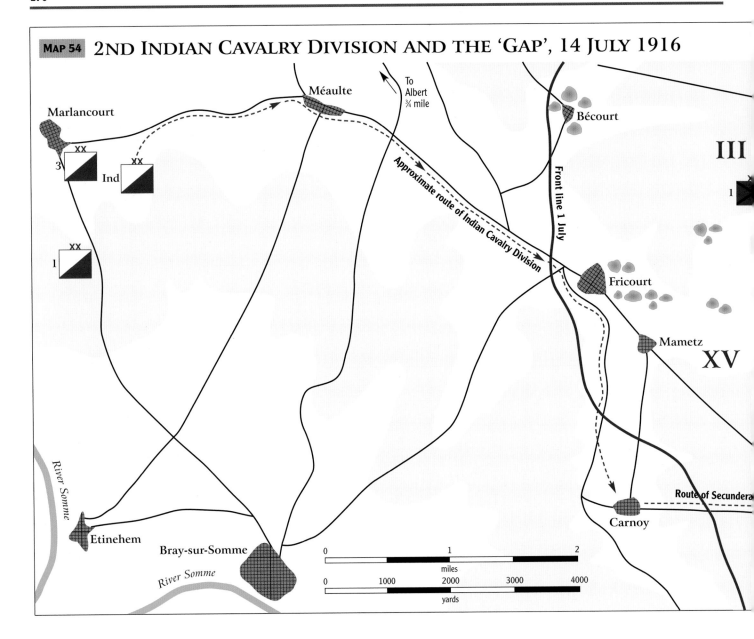

The Germans had captured a portion of
trench from the 9th Lancers . . . They now
rushed a machine gun into this trench and
started firing into the back of the trench
held by A Squadron. Then desperate
messages come down from the 9th
Lancers for more bombs and ammunition
. . . It was not long before the Germans
reached the beginning of A Squadron's
trench. The Durham Light Infantry and
the 9th Lancers were driven back and all
their wounded came crowding in to the
squadron, causing some confusion . . . The
Germans continued to bomb their way
down the trench. At every traverse a
barricade was hastily made and defended,
but with the aid of their plentiful supply
of bombs, each one was blown up by the
Germans in time. At length the last
traverse before the stream was reached,
and here the squadron held the enemy

with a most gallant defence, led by the
squadron leader. Captain Lawson himself
took a hand in throwing bombs . . . among
others who distinguished themselves were
Lance-Corporal H. J. Skipper, who
displayed magnificent courage; besides
defending the traverse with his rifle, he
and Captain Lawson several times caught
German bombs in the air and hurled
them back before they burst. Lance-
Corporal J. P. Howells also displayed great
gallantry; a German bomb fell in the mud
amongst a group of men; he rushed to
pick it up and it burst just as he reached
it, but fortunately it only stunned him.
Thanks to the bravery of men such as
these, the German advance down the
trench was held up.

In comparison life behind the lines, with
access to occasional hot baths, being bil-

leted in villages, farms and barns and even,
for some, getting home leave to England,
was a very comfortable and safe existence –
there was even a branch of the exclusive
London store Fortnum & Mason selling
expensive food in Ypres for the earlier part
of the year; it was well frequented by cavalry officers. Popular activities included
games for the soldiers, with football competitions being the most popular. For officers,
there was some polo, partridge-shooting and
hunting hares with beagles brought back
from England by officers returning from
leave. The 17th Lancers persuaded a French
farmer with a kennels nearby to loan them
some Artois hounds, which, mixed with
English hounds, made for a pack of about
sixty couple. The regiments tried to keep
fox-hunting hidden from the High
Command, but after three brigadiers were
out of action injured at the same time it

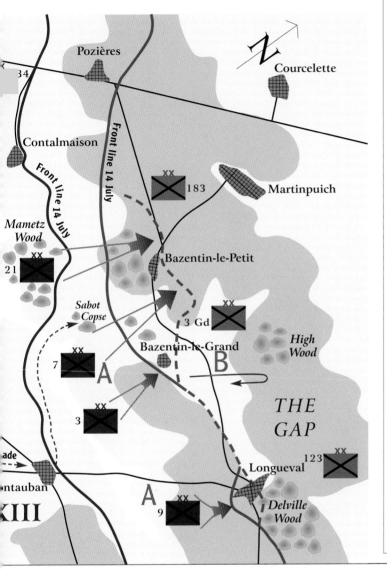

Pozières
Courcelette
Contalmaison
Front line 14 July
XX 183
Martinpuich
Mametz Wood
XX 21
Bazentin-le-Petit
Sabot Copse
3 Gd XX
Bazentin-le-Grand
B
High Wood
XX 7 A
XX 3
THE GAP
ntauban
Longueval
123 XX
XIII
XX 9 A
Delville Wood

Notes for Map 54

- The infantry assault (**AA**) began at 3:25 a.m. with the ultimate objective of securing the dominating ridge running south-east from Pozières. The three cavalry divisions waited near Marlancourt for an order to move forward. By 6:00 a.m. Bazentin-le-Petit had been entered, but half an hour later misleading messages were received that Longueval had been cleared. Elsewhere the attackers had been largely successful, particularly on the 7th Division's front.
- At 7:40 a.m. XIII Corps ordered the Indian Cavalry Division forward. They moved off at 8:20 a.m. with the Secunderabad Cavalry Brigade leading; the divisional objective was High Wood. The ground over which the cavalry advanced, particularly between the front line of 1 July and 14 July, was badly cratered and criss-crossed with a network of smashed trenches and rusting wire obstacles that made progress painfully slow.
- At around 10:00 a.m. several senior officers were able to walk forward as far as High Wood without seeing signs of the enemy or being shot at (**B**). It seemed a gap had opened from High Wood to Delville Wood. The commander of the 7th Division requested authority to commit his reserve brigade (the 91st) to exploit the situation – the 3rd Divisional commander supported the request. It was refused, as corps wanted to await the cavalry.
- By noon the cavalry had not appeared, so the 7th Division was authorized to attack. This was, however, stopped when it was realized that Longueval had not yet been taken. Sometime after midday the Indian Cavalry Division arrived in the Carnoy area and, apart from sending forward patrols beyond Montauban, which reported enemy still in Longueval, the division waited in this area for well over four hours.
- At 3:10 p.m. another erroneous message was received at corps that Longueval was clear and again the attack on High Wood was put in motion. The 7th Division would attack with the Secunderabad Cavalry Brigade protecting its right flank. However, the advance, initially scheduled for 5:15 p.m., was postponed, first to 6:15 and then 7:00 p.m., to give the infantry time to get organized. By about 5:40 p.m. the Secunderabad Cavalry Brigade had moved forward to the Montauban area, where the two armoured cars in the brigade got bogged down. There, a little later, the brigade commander was ordered to send two regiments forward to Sabot Copse from where they would support the infantry's assault. He sent the 7th Dragoon Guards and the Deccan Horse.

was officially forbidden – not that this by any means stopped the sport. In true cavalry fashion, horse shows were arranged. One in particular was described as a 'unique occasion' with cavalry regiments from all over the Empire participating (26 British, 5 Yeomanry, 3 Canadian and 11 Indian).

The above relaxing activities represented only a small proportion of the cavalry's time out of the line. The majority was spent in infantry training, exercising and looking after their horses, and constructing defensive works in the rear of the combat zone, burying dead or building 'cavalry tracks' – tracks that the cavalry would use to move forward to the front line and intended primarily for their own use. Sometimes volunteers would help French farmers with harvesting, ploughing and sowing crops such as wheat and oats – something of a busman's holiday for many cavalry troopers.

1916

During May and June the New Army divisions saw their divisional cavalry squadrons withdrawn and formed into corps cavalry regiments, and during the winter 1916/1917 cavalry recruiting was curtailed and many men diverted to the infantry.

However, this was the year of Verdun and the Somme, offensives that have gone down in history as the most prolonged and horrendous series of battles of the war. Both developed into slogging matches between massed artillery supporting endless infantry assaults, with the French at Verdun desperately trying to hang on to their positions and then counter-attacking to regain lost ground. For the British offensive (with some French assistance) on the Somme there was always the hoped-for breakthrough, but primarily the struggle continued in order (successfully) to

take some of the pressure off Verdun, where at one stage the French looked near to defeat. In all these engagements there was virtually no scope for cavalry in any role, except as infantry or providing endless working parties. However, for the British there was a rare and fleeting exception on 14 July in the High Wood–Delville Wood area, just two weeks into the Somme battles (see Map 54). There was no exploitation, but the action illustrates the host of difficulties in getting the cavalry forward to the right place at the right time. Problems included poor communications, false messages concerning enemy positions, the slowness of movement over difficult ground, the time taken to organize a fresh infantry attack and the urgent need for speed in decision-taking – if necessary, forward at divisional level.

The Fourth Army's XIII and XV Corps were to attack the Germans' second-line defences between Bazentin-le-Petit in the west and Delville Wood (Longueval) in the east and secure the Bazentin Ridge. This was a front of some 5,000 yards, with the four divisions in the initial assault sending about 22,000 men over the top at dawn. The three cavalry divisions were to be ready to move forward at 4:00 a.m., with their objectives being: 2nd Indian Cavalry Division, High Wood; 1st Cavalry Division, Leuze Wood; 3rd Cavalry Division, Martinpuich – this last being 1½ miles behind the front line (in the event, the Indian Cavalry Division was the only one ordered forward). General Rawlinson, the army commander, attached considerable importance to the capture of High Wood, which occupied a dominating position on the crest of the Bazentin Ridge. He had issued specific instructions regarding the decision to use the cavalry: 'the final decision as to whether the suitable time has come for launching them will rest in his [own] hands.' However, with the 2nd Indian Cavalry Division's task of taking High Wood, 'the Army Commander feels that he must leave this to the G.O.C. XIII Corps to decide'.

In the event, the infantry attacks all along the front were mostly a success, due primarily to the use of an accurate five-minute hurricane bombardment followed by the new creeping barrage taking the infantry forward. By 9:00 a.m. the Bazentin villages were in British hands, although on the right the struggle for Longueval continued unabated. By 10:00 a.m. reports arriving at army and corps headquarters indicated that the enemy had melted away. Several senior officers (including the 9th Brigade commander, Brigadier General H. C. Potter) actually walked up the slope towards and into the southern edge of High Wood without being shot at and saw no Germans. The much sought-after 'gap' seemed as though it had finally opened up in the enemy lines. It was time for the cavalry to exploit, in partic-

ular the 2nd Indian Cavalry Division, whose objective was High Wood. However, the nearest available troops were infantry – the reserve brigades of the 7th Division (91st Brigade) and the 3rd Division (73rd Brigade). Both divisional commanders requested authority to use their respective brigades to advance – it was refused, to the former because it was felt necessary to await the cavalry, to the latter in order to keep his brigade in hand for possible enemy counter-attacks.

The 2nd Indian Cavalry Division had been held in readiness but it had encamped at Morlancourt, 4 miles south of Albert, and would have to negotiate the churned-up battlefield over which the British had advanced during the past two weeks. The division started at 8:20 a.m., but it proved an exceedingly slow process. By noon the cavalry had not arrived, so at 12:15 p.m. the Fourth Army sanctioned the advance of the 7th Division. The actual move was postponed by corps headquarters, as Longueval had still not been cleared, so German guns would be able to enfilade the approach to High Wood across the valley. Meanwhile the Indian cavalry, led by the Secunderabad Cavalry Brigade (7th Dragoon Guards, Deccan Horse, Poona Horse, a squadron of Fort Garry Horse with trench bridges, a field troop of Royal Engineers, N Battery RHA and two armoured cars from the 9th Light Armoured Car Battery) arrived in the vicinity of Carnoy. There they waited for several hours. At 3:10 p.m. an erroneous report reached XV Corps that Longueval was now clear of Germans and at 3:30 p.m. the commander of XV Corps informed XIII Corps that the 7th Division would advance on High Wood at 5:15 p.m. The cavalry was to cooperate by covering the right flank, and at 5:40 p.m., with the 7th Dragoon Guards leading the Deccan Horse, both regiments moved forward to the Montauban area. Brigadier General C. L. Gregory, commanding the Secunderabad Cavalry Brigade, was

then told that the infantry would not advance until 6:15 p.m. Some time afterwards he received orders to send two regiments (7th Dragoon Guards and Deccan Horse) forward to Sabot Copse (the Poona Horse remained in reserve). Not until 7:00 p.m. did the attack start, as a further delay was necessary – the previous timing being unrealistic for the infantry.

Thus a potential gap had been discovered at 10:00 a.m. and the infantry commanders on the spot had urged action, but not until nine hours later were troops ready to exploit it. Unfortunately, the opportunity for a possible easy breakthrough at High Wood had gone. The Germans had regrouped and, supported by artillery, filtered back into the wood and the standing cornfields between it and Delville Wood.

The overall plan was for the 7th Division to advance on High Wood with the Secunderabad Cavalry Brigade protecting its right flank, while a simultaneous infantry attack by the 9th Division took place to clear Delville Wood. Within the cavalry the 7th Dragoon Guards would be on the left, aiming for the south-western edge of High Wood, while the Deccan Horse on the right made for the open ground between the woods before wheeling right (east) to threaten Delville Wood from the rear. In both regiments their lancer squadrons were in the lead.

The cavalry moved forward via Sabot Copse to make their attack (Map 55). B and C Squadrons of the 7th Dragoon Guards advanced into the Longueval valley south of High Wood and then charged at the gallop north over the open ground towards the wood. A watching officer of the Royal Artillery described it as 'an incredible sight, an unbelievable sight. They galloped up with their lances and pennants flying, up the slope to High Wood.' After jumping a bank they ran down and speared some fifteen enemy machine-gunners and riflemen, capturing over thirty prisoners before being forced to retire and dismount behind the

The scene of the charge of the Deccan Horse, 14 July 1916, during the Battle of the Somme. The regiment had orders to advance to a position north and north-west of Delville Wood, and from that higher ground to attack the wood and thus facilitate the 9th Division's efforts to capture it. The photograph shows the direction of their charge, through standing corn in which numerous Germans were encountered. Despite heavy flanking fire from the wood, they secured the position, but due to their isolation they were compelled to withdraw after dark.

Delville Wood

High Wood

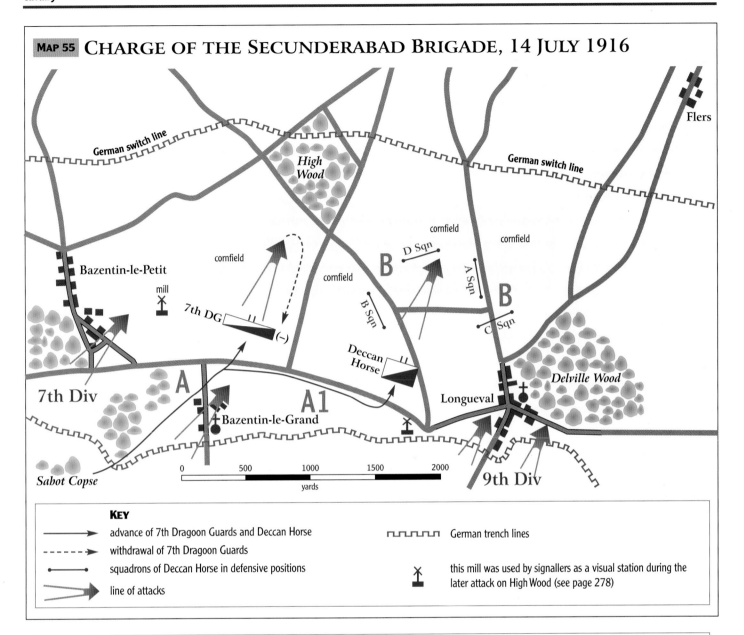

MAP 55 CHARGE OF THE SECUNDERABAD BRIGADE, 14 JULY 1916

KEY

→ advance of 7th Dragoon Guards and Deccan Horse

- - -► withdrawal of 7th Dragoon Guards

•— squadrons of Deccan Horse in defensive positions

➤ line of attacks

ᒥᒥᒥᒥ German trench lines

☓ this mill was used by signallers as a visual station during the later attack on High Wood (see page 278)

Notes for Map 55

• From their assembly area at Sabot Copse, the two regiments moved forward past Bazentin-le-Grand, with the 7th Dragoon Guards leading the Deccan Horse (**A**); the Poona Horse remained at Sabot Copse in reserve. Having cleared the village, the Deccan Horse swung right and proceeded towards Longueval (**A1**).

• At around 7:00 p.m., as the 7th Dragoon Guards crossed the German trench line they were greeted with cheers by infantry and gunners – cavalry moving forward to attack was a sight not seen since the start of trench warfare. After crossing a track they were confronted by cornfields stretching up to High Wood about 1,000 yards away. B and C Squadrons advanced at a gallop and after 200 yards jumped a low bank, then, wheeling slightly right, charged some enemy machine-gunners and riflemen in the corn. According to Capt. F. J. Scott, commanding C Squadron, some 15 Germans were ridden down by the lancers and 32 surrendered. All this time the horsemen had been under heavy rifle and machine-gun fire from High Wood and the German switch line trench, as well as continuous shelling from enemy guns. With the intensity of the firing and with High Wood occupied, the 7th were forced to retire to the bank and dismount. During this period Lt H. W. Pope, a B Squadron troop leader, won the Military Cross for personally going back to bring in two wounded men.

• The Deccan Horse, like the 7th Dragoon Guards, were led by their lancer squadron (A Squadron), commanded by Capt. F. Jarvis. The advance was initially along a narrow track that caused some delay, but as the squadrons cleared this obstacle they formed line and charged up the slope through the corn and into the supposed 'Gap' between High and Delville Woods (see photograph opposite). As the horsemen crashed through the corn, a number of Germans popped up and tried to surrender – unsuccessfully in most cases. During the attack, heavy machine-gun fire from Delville Wood had caused losses and as the squadrons reached their objective on the crest of the slope the Germans in the switch line opened fire. At this moment enemy shells began arriving as well. The plan had envisaged the Deccan Horse advancing on the north-western edge of Delville Wood, but this was now impossible, so Lt Col E. Tennant, the commanding officer, organized his squadrons in a position of all-round defence (**BB**). The regiment was now isolated and out of contact with the 9th Division on the right and the 7th Dragoon Guards to the left and was unable to contact brigade headquarters. With the arrival of darkness, and with C Squadron still under heavy machine-gun fire from Delville Wood, Tennant decided to withdraw. They pulled out just in time to avoid a heavy concentration of shellfire and took up a position in the first German trench line.

Members of the Deccan Horse in Carnoy, just prior to their attempt to make a breakthrough between High Wood and Delville Wood on 14 July 1916.

bank in the face of sustained machine-gun and rifle fire. To their right the Deccan Horse advanced, with A Squadron (lancers) leading into the standing cornfields between the woods. The other squadrons followed in line, all moving at a gallop. A number of Germans popped out of the corn to surrender, some embracing the horses' necks while begging the rider for mercy. The Deccan Horse took its objective, but was unable to swing right to attack Delville Wood due to flanking machine-gun fire from the trees and artillery fire that opened on them as they regrouped. Instead, all four squadrons took up a defensive position between the woods. After dark the regiment withdrew into the valley, narrowly escaping a heavy artillery bombardment that fell on their previous position.

Losses among the 7th Dragoon Guards were light, with three killed and twenty-four wounded. The Deccan Horse suffered more, with nine killed and forty-one wounded.

The last battle of the year of the Somme offensive in which it was hoped cavalry would have a key role to play was that of Flers-Courcelette on 15 September. Tanks were to be used for the first time and it was the intention that they would help create a gap through which at least two of the five cavalry divisions would pour to attack the German railway communications in their rear. Things, as usual, did not go according to plan, as of the forty-nine tanks seventeen ditched on the way to the front and of the remainder only thirteen played any real part in the fighting. The five cavalry divisions that had moved forward in anticipation of the gap materializing received no orders until 18 September, when the three British divisions were sent back, leaving only the Indian divisions forward. On

25 September there was a brief moment in the Battle of Morval when it appeared that the very effective use of the creeping barrage and tanks had created an opportunity for the cavalry near the village of Gueudecourt. A squadron of the 19th Lancers and South Irish Horse rode forward to take the village, but could only hold it with difficulty.

1917

Haig was strongly opposed to the diversion of cavalry recruits to the infantry that was in full swing during the winter of 1916/1917. He wanted to maintain a powerful, well-trained cavalry corps as the only force capable of the speed required to exploit the elusive breakthrough. The result of this diminution of the mounted arm was that his force in the field was shrinking, as replacements were insufficient to counteract the daily wastage of men and horses.

This was the year of the German retreat to the Hindenburg Line in March, the failed Nivelle offensive in April and the subsequent large-scale offensives of Arras, Third Ypres (Passchendaele) and Cambrai. The German withdrawal to the Hindenburg Line supposedly opened up the prospect of cavalry performing its more normal role in a pursuit. However, as noted above, the ground over which they retired was subjected to massive destruction by the Germans, who conducted their retirement behind a network of strongpoints and machine-gun posts. These rearguards were supplemented by German divisional cavalry units and three cavalry brigades brought down from Belgium. The state of the ground, sub-zero temperatures, blizzards and non-existent or disintegrating tracks caused prolonged delays in bringing forward supplies (including fodder for the horses), with the overall result that the British and French follow-up was slow, with no real chance of exploiting the situation.

For the British 1917 offensive, Haig planned to attack with General Horne's First Army in the north, General Allenby's Third Army in the centre and General Gough's Fifth Army in the south. The 350,000 men in Allenby's Third Army were to thrust eastwards from Arras (just north of the northern end of the Hindenburg Line) on 9 April. This would be called the First Battle of the Scarpe (9–14 April). The weather was still appalling, the winter having been the worst and longest in living memory. The horses suffered even more then the men, as Trooper Sam Bailey, 1st Life Guards (5th Cavalry Brigade) described after spending the night of 9/10 April on the Arras racecourse:

> [Awoke] to a pitiful sight. The horses had pulled up their heel pegs and were huddled together. Some were dead

through exposure; others had chewed their saddle blankets to pieces. It was impossible to release the head chains as they were completely frozen, and so were our fingers . . . After a while came the order to saddle up and mount. What with the freezing night which had weakened the horses and our combined weight, many of them just collapsed and died.

VI Corps (3rd, 12th, 15th, 17th, 29th and 37th Divisions), immediately east of Arras, was to take three German defensive lines (codenamed Black, Blue and Brown), the last one being the Monchuriège Trench between Wancourt and Feuchy, some 3,500–4,000 yards from the British line – an ambitious undertaking. The three assault divisions were the 15th on the left, 12th in the centre (both north of the Arras–Cambrai road), and the 3rd on the right to the south of it (see Map 56). Six brigades would form the initial assault along a 3,000-yard front. The attacks AAA on the map were largely successful; however, it was north of the Scarpe on 9 April where the infantry of XVII Corps had made the best progress, and it was felt that an opportunity had opened up for the cavalry on the front of the 34th Division. Unfortunately, the overall plan had envisaged the cavalry being used south of the river, and although the 1st Cavalry Division was warned to be prepared to send a brigade north of the Scarpe, no order was given that day for the move. The 2nd and 3rd Cavalry Divisions were south of Arras and in no position to exploit a fleeting opening in the north.

Further advances by VI Corps infantry took place on 10 April. By nightfall the infantry had reached well beyond the Brown Line, taking Orange Hill, and VI Corps was on the line BB on Map 56, facing the village of Monchy sitting atop some dominating high ground. The final effort to achieve a breakthrough came on 11 April, with the objective of reaching the Green Line (east of Monchy) and beyond. General Allenby telegraphed corps commanders:

> The A.C. [Army Commander] wishes all troops to understand that Third Army is now pursuing a defeated enemy and that risks must be freely taken. Isolated enemy detachments in farms and villages must not be allowed to delay the general progress. Such points must be masked and passed by.

It was on the 11th, as part of this final push, that units from the 6th and 8th Cavalry Brigades (3rd Cavalry Division) carried out a cavalry charge in an attack on Monchy. It took place in a snowstorm, with most of the horses already seriously weakened by exposure and lack of food. Early that morning the infantry was reported to have reached the

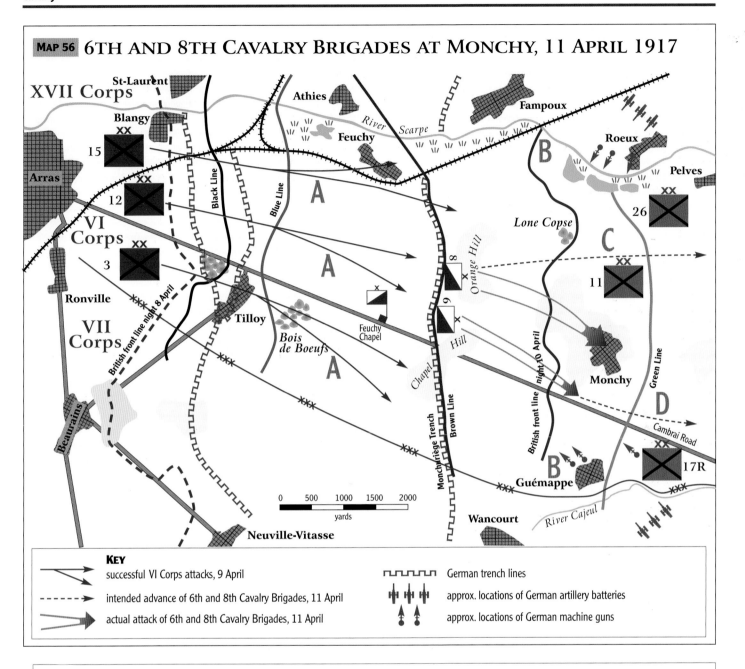

MAP 56 6TH AND 8TH CAVALRY BRIGADES AT MONCHY, 11 APRIL 1917

KEY

successful VI Corps attacks, 9 April

intended advance of 6th and 8th Cavalry Brigades, 11 April

actual attack of 6th and 8th Cavalry Brigades, 11 April

German trench lines

approx. locations of German artillery batteries

approx. locations of German machine guns

Notes for Map 56

• On 9 April 1917, as part of the Arras offensive, the British VI Corps' three forward divisions attacked (**AAA**), aiming to secure the Brown Line or the Monchuriège Trench. This was mostly successful and deep penetrations were made. However, the cavalry was earmarked for possible exploitation north of the Scarpe so was not ready to react quickly to the opportunity south of the river.

• On 10 April the infantry made further progress and by nightfall had secured the Brown Line and reached the line **BB**. There was some confusion over whether infantry had managed to secure Monchy, but cavalry patrols from the 8th Cavalry Brigade confirmed the enemy still held the village in some strength. In early evening, the 3rd and 6th Cavalry Brigades moved forward through Tilloy and spent another miserable, freezing night in the open, west of Orange Hill, with brigade headquarters in Feuchy Chapel.

• At 5:00 a.m. on 11 April the infantry attacked again and two hours later the 3rd Dragoon Guards (6th Brigade) reported Monchy secured – in fact the infantry had gained only a toehold on the western edge. The chance for the cavalry had seemingly arrived and the 6th and 8th Brigades were ordered forward: the 8th to advance north of Monchy and exploit up to and beyond the Green Line; the 6th to do the same to the south of the village (**C** and **D**).

• As the 8th Brigade came over the crest of Orange Hill, a brief clearing of the snow flurries revealed to the watching infantry the splendid sight of the Essex Yeomanry and 10th Hussars cantering forward. However, they also came into the sights of German machine-gunners and artillery north of the Scarpe in the Roeux area and suffered accordingly. As they charged forward they swung half right, making for and entering the village. Attempts to get beyond it were frustrated by heavy enemy fire and, joined by the rest of the brigade, the regiments set about defending Monchy from threatened enemy counter-attacks. The village was then subjected to a hurricane of artillery and machine-gun fire that caused large numbers of casualties, particularly to the horses. Among those killed was the brigade commander, C. B. Bulkeley-Johnson, hit in the face by a bullet. Meanwhile the 6th Brigade, headed first by the 3rd Dragoon Guards, had been forced by fire from Guémappe to dismount and join with infantry units when they reached the Cambrai Road south of Monchy.

• Cavalry foot patrols established the Germans digging in just 300 yards east of the village. By midnight the infantry had taken over the defence of Monchy and a much depleted and exhausted cavalry withdrew to Arras.

western edge of Monchy but had yet to secure the eastern side. Awaiting its opportunity was the 3rd Cavalry Division, with the leading brigades, the 6th (Brigadier General A. E. W. Harman) and the 8th (Brigadier General C. B. Bulkeley-Johnson) formed up just east of the Wancourt–Feuchy line north of the Cambrai road. The cavalry's moment had seemingly arrived. The 8th Brigade, with the Essex Yeomanry leading the 10th Hussars, would make the attack north of the village (C on map). The Royal Horse Guards were in reserve. Bulkeley-Johnson ordered his brigade to exploit as far as a line from Pelves village to Bois de Sart, with the Essex Yeomanry on the right and the 10th Hussars on the left. However, he added the proviso that, should they come under heavy fire from the north-east across the Scarpe, they should make straight for Monchy. The 3rd Dragoon Guards would lead the 6th Brigade's attack south of the village (D on map). An officer in the Highland Light Infantry later described the cavalry's advance:

> During a lull in the snowstorm an excited shout was raised that our cavalry were coming up! Sure enough, away behind us, moving quickly in extended order down the slope of Orange Hill was line upon line of mounted men as far as we could see. It was a thrilling moment for us infantrymen, who had never dreamt that we should live to see a real cavalry charge, which was evidently what was intended.

As the 8th Brigade topped Orange Hill they came under an ever-increasing rain of shells and machine-gun fire from the area of Roeux as they surged forward, first at the canter and then the gallop. A number of the nearby Northamptonshire Yeomanry (the VI Corps' cavalry regiment) joined the attack. Among them was Trooper Bertie Taylor, who years later recalled:

> The snow was laying [sic] thick and I remember at this point some of our horses collapsed, buckling the swords of their riders. We extended into one long line [others thought it a loose open formation], a bugle sounded and we charged! Over open ground, jumping trenches, men swearing, horses squealing – a proper old commotion! The bugle sounded three times – and we had come under quite heavy shell fire and some of the saddles had been emptied . . . Mine, poor devil, had been wounded badly in the coronet so I pulled up and dismounted and had a look at him . . . Another one came flying past me with half his guts hanging out, I'd never seen anything like that. Well, my horse perked up, so off we galloped after the

rest. The riderless horses were still leading the charge. Eventually I caught up with our officer, Mr. Humphriss, who was riding a few yards ahead when a shell exploded just beneath his horse and split him like a side of beef hanging up in the butcher's shop.

The Essex Yeomanry, followed by the 10th Hussars, had been forced by the fire from north of the Scarpe to veer to the right, enter Monchy and dismount; any attempts to push beyond the village were met with fierce enemy fire and could make no progress. The remainder of both regiments arrived in Monchy along with the machine guns and a few infantrymen and endeavoured to consolidate their hold on the village, which had become the target for a deluge of artillery fire that appeared to herald a German counter-attack. Casualties mounted, particularly among the horses, and several mounted messengers were sent back for reinforcements. A squadron of the Royal Horse Guards with more machine guns was sent forward, but was driven back by the intensity of the shelling with heavy loss. Most of the defences in the village were taken over by infantry during the night and, leaving two squadrons behind with the machine guns, the remnants of the 8th Brigade withdrew. An infantry officer later described the scene in Monchy:

> Heaped on top of one another and blocking up the roadway for as far as one could see, lay the mutilated bodies of our men and horses. These bodies, torn and gaping, had stiffened into fantastic attitudes. All the hollows of the road were filled with blood. This was the cavalry. I walked up the hill, picking my way as best I could and often slipping in the pools of blood, so that my boots and the lower parts of my puttees were dripping with blood by the time I reached the top. Nor, I discovered on my way up, were all the men and animals quite dead. Now and then a groan would strike the air – the groan of a man who was praying for release . . . A small party of stretcher-bearers was, obviously unequal to their task, doing what they could to relieve the suffering.

To the south of Monchy the 3rd Dragoon Guards had led the attack of the 6th Brigade and, although suffering from shellfire, had reached the Cambrai road south of the village by shortly after 9:00 a.m. The leading squadron dismounted and was joined by the North Somerset Yeomanry and a machine-gun section. By midnight infantry had relived them and all the regiments withdrew to the Arras racecourse.

The cavalry had earned the admiration of all, including that of the commander-in-

chief, for their occupation and defence of Monchy. Haig's message of congratulations read, 'the action of the cavalry probably saved the many thousands of lives it would have cost to retake Monchy had the Boche got back in there.' The casualties in the two brigades are estimated at over 600 all ranks, the Essex Yeomanry and 10th Hussars taking the heaviest losses. Losses among the horses cannot have been much less than 900.

The Third Battle of Ypres (Passchendaele), which started in July, was a horrific infantry affair lasting several months in which the cavalry had no role other than providing endless working parties to repair road and rail links or manning trenches as infantry.

The late-November Battle of Cambrai, in which the mounted arm had a role to play, is described in Section Thirteen as part of what was very much an all-arms battle.

1918

The final year of the war saw three major events on the Western Front. The first was the German offensive starting on 21 March that almost broke through General Gough's Fifth Army – a near disaster that saw Gough removed from command. Next came the big British victory at Amiens on 8 August (the Germans' 'Black Day') and the breaching of the Hindenburg Line, and finally, at long last, the open warfare that marked the Hundred Days campaign as the Allies drove the Germans back, bringing about their final defeat on 11 November.

Potentially there was scope for the cavalry of both sides in the British retreat in March and April. However, Lloyd George and his government had had enough of the butchers' bills of Passchendaele and the like and set about restricting the flow of reinforcements to France. The prime minister coupled this with demands that cavalry recruits should now be sent to the Royal Flying Corps (RFC) and armoured car units, as there was no purpose in the mounted arm. Haig appeared before the War Cabinet on 7 January 1918 and argued forcefully for the retention of the Cavalry Corps on the basis of their mobility, and because once disbanded it would take too long to build and train them again. A compromise was reached. The two Indian Cavalry Divisions would be sent to Palestine, leaving Haig with three in France.

Due to the fragile state of the French Army after the mutinies (see page 128), the BEF was required to take over another 28 miles of the line from the French, further stretching Haig's manpower resources. Of the cavalry remaining with Haig, only about a third were still mounted, the others forming weak dismounted divisions ill-equipped for the infantry role, or for converting to

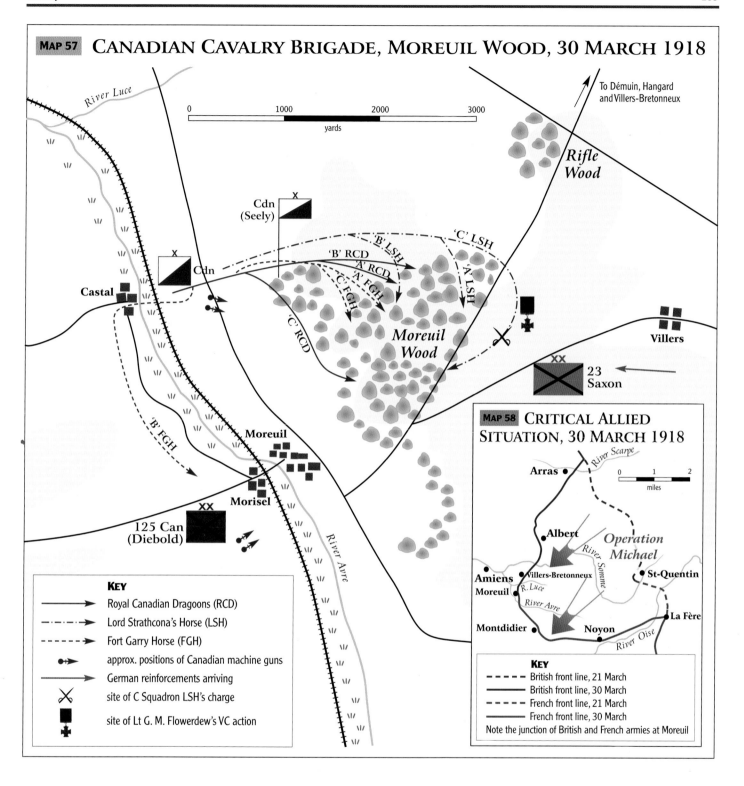

MAP 57 CANADIAN CAVALRY BRIGADE, MOREUIL WOOD, 30 MARCH 1918

To Démuin, Hangard and Villers-Bretonneux

Rifle Wood

Cdn (Seely)

Cdn

Castal

'C' LSH

'B' LSH

'A' LSH

'B' RCD

'A' RCD

'A' FGH

'C' FGH

'C' RCD

Moreuil Wood

Villers

23 Saxon

'B' FGH

Moreuil

Morisel

125 Can (Diebold)

KEY

→ Royal Canadian Dragoons (RCD)

---→ Lord Strathcona's Horse (LSH)

- - -→ Fort Garry Horse (FGH)

•→ approx. positions of Canadian machine guns

→ German reinforcements arriving

✕ site of C Squadron LSH's charge

▆✝ site of Lt G. M. Flowerdew's VC action

MAP 58 CRITICAL ALLIED SITUATION, 30 MARCH 1918

Arras

River Scarpe

Albert

Amiens

Moreuil

Villers-Bretonneux

R. Luce

River Avre

Operation Michael

River Somme

St-Quentin

La Fère

Montdidier

Noyon

River Oise

KEY

- - - British front line, 21 March

——— British front line, 30 March

- - - French front line, 21 March

——— French front line, 30 March

Note the junction of British and French armies at Moreuil

machine-gun units or for use as a labour force. Thus when the Germans struck in March there was a desperate scramble to remount cavalry regiments and re-form the 2nd and 3rd Cavalry Divisions. Before that could be completed, a number of ad hoc mounted detachments were thrown together from a mixture of units, taking their name from their commanding officer – examples being the Harman's, Brooke's or Cooke's Detachments. This last comprised six squadrons from several brigades under the commanding officer of the 20th Hussars. These detachments were rushed around as mounted infantry to plug holes in the crumbling front, or to act as rearguards to cover the British retreat. However, between 25 and 27 March the 2nd and 3rd Cavalry Divisions were remounted. Meanwhile, on the 24th, about 150 men (a troop each from the 3rd Dragoon Guards, 10th Hussars and the Royals, part of the 6th Cavalry Brigade) took part in a highly successful charge at the village of Collezy, where, with very little loss, up to a hundred of the enemy were ridden down and put to the sword while another hundred were captured.

A much more important cavalry action took place on 30 March some 10 miles south-east of Amiens, just south of the main Amiens–Roye road (Maps 57 and 58).

Map 58 (inset above) shows the seriousness of the Allied situation in the face of the German Michael offensive, which was threatening Amiens via the junction of the British and French front lines. At that junction was the village of Moreuil on the River Avre, over-looked by the Moreuil Ridge and the wood of the same name on it (Map 57). The French 125th Division under General Diebold held the line at this point, but there were few British units until Villers-Bretonneux 10 miles to the north. By 30 March the Germans had taken Moreuil Ridge, occupied Moreuil Wood and appeared poised to thrust through the gap. If they succeeded, Amiens would probably fall and the Allied front be split apart. This grave situation was saved by the delay forced on the Germans by the Canadian Cavalry Brigade under Brigadier General J. E. B. 'Galloper Jack' Seely in what was arguably the most important cavalry action on the Western Front.

The Canadian Cavalry Brigade consisted of the Royal Canadian Dragoons (RCD), Lord Strathcona's Horse (LSH) and the Fort Garry Horse (FGH), in all some 850 all ranks. The brigade was part of the British 2nd Cavalry Division under Major General T. T. Pitman. At 8:30 a.m. on 30 March, Pitman visited the Canadians bivouacked in woods 10 miles west of Moreuil and gave Seely his instructions. 'The Germans,' said Pitman, 'have captured Mezieres and are rapidly advancing on Amiens. I want you to cross the Avre as quickly as possible and delay the enemy . . . Go to the support of the infantry just beyond Castel. Don't get too heavily involved – you will be needed later.'

Having ordered his brigade forward, Seely rode ahead with his brigade major and his ADC, Captain Prince Antoine of Orléans, an officer of royal blood whom French law prohibited from serving in the French Army. At Castel they fortuitously met General Diebold, commanding the 125th Division responsible for that part of the line. After a hurried consultation, the Frenchman, who had been about to order a withdrawal of his men from Moreuil, agreed to command them to hold on at all costs while the Canadians

attacked Moreuil Wood and attempted to secure the ridge – although he thought the chances of Seely succeeding remote.

When the leading regiment, the Royal Canadian Dragoons (Lieutenant Colonel C. T. van Straubenzie), arrived at Seely's head-quarters, which he had established at the edge of a small, unoccupied wood adjoining the north-west corner of Moreuil Wood, its task was to send A and B Squadrons to the left round the northern face of the wood to try to take the north-eastern corner and then encircle it. C Squadron was sent to the right, round the western face, to endeavour to link up with A and B Squadrons and to make contact with the French in Moreuil. In the event, both these squadrons (A and B) were forced by accurate rifle and machine-gun fire to enter the wood's northern side and become embroiled in a close-combat struggle through the trees and undergrowth. C Squadron was also forced into the wood's western edge by fire from enemy near Moreuil.

The next regiment to come up was Lord Strathcona's Horse (Lieutenant Colonel D. J. MacDonald). Supported by the fire of four machine guns, it was told to send A and B Squadrons into the wood to support the Royal Canadian Dragoons, while C Squadron, under Lieutenant G. M. Flowerdew, was ordered to circle round the wood to the north at a gallop and cut off the Germans. When Seely emphasized the importance of the task, the young lieutenant replied, 'I know, sir, I know, it is a splendid moment. I will try not to fail you.' The third regiment, the Fort Garry Horse (Lieutenant Colonel R. W. Paterson), was initially held in reserve. Thus the plan was to encircle the wood and at the same time drive out the enemy with a dismounted attack through the trees from the west. In practice, six squadrons became embroiled in fighting inside the wood against a fiercely resisting enemy who was rushing reinforcements in from the east.

Flowerdew led his four troops thundering round the wood, but as they came to the eastern face he was confronted with a steep bank held by Germans, who had been forced out of the wood by the Canadians inside. Behind the bank was another unit of the enemy, marching to join the fight. Flowerdew later described the situation as 'two lines of enemy, each about sixty strong, with machine guns in the centre and flanks; one line being about two hundred yards behind the other.' He immediately wheeled three troops into line and charged both lines, turning and charging again, scattering the enemy and inflicting around seventy casualties. However, his squadron had suffered grievously and only a handful survived unscathed to join the fourth troop in the wood. Flowerdew had been shot through both thighs and in the chest but continued to encourage his men until he collapsed, dying of his wounds on 2 April. He was awarded a posthumous Victoria Cross.

At this stage Seely committed the Fort Garry Horse. A and C Squadrons were sent into the wood to reinforce the other two regiments, which were in danger of being pushed back, while B Squadron with a section of machine guns retraced its steps through Castel and rode south to establish a position on the higher ground near Moreuil from which to fire on the Germans in the southern part of the wood.

Throughout the morning aircraft of the RFC had been circling overhead attacking the enemy with bombs and machine guns. By 11:00 a.m. the centre and southern parts of the wood were still in enemy hands and the Canadians were having considerable difficulty making further progress, despite being reinforced by the arrival of the 3rd Cavalry Brigade, which had crossed the Avre behind the Canadians. As night fell the German artillery increased their pounding of the wood with both gas and high-explosive shells. Not until the early hours of 31 March was the cavalry relieved by the arrival of infantry. Later that day the Germans secured the wood, but the Canadians had delayed the enemy's advance long enough for French and Australian reinforcements to check the threat to Amiens.

The cost to the Canadian cavalry at Moreuil Wood and in a later dismounted attack to retake Rifle Wood on 1 April was extremely high, amounting to 488 casualties – almost 50 per cent of the brigade.

One of the reasons for the failure of the Germans' massive offensive in the spring of 1918 was their lack of a credible cavalry force. Their mounted arm had been emasculated by conversion to infantry, leaving only the squadrons with infantry divisions – in no way a viable independent force. Had they possessed two or three cavalry divisions able

Brigadier General Jack Seely with his famous horse Warrior.

British cavalry pass the ruined basilica of Notre-Dame de Brebières, Albert, 8 September 1918, during the Allies' Hundred Days offensive.

to exploit the gap opening at the junction of the Allied line at Moreuil, the result of the battle might well have been very different.

Ludendorff's 'Black Day' for the Germans was 8 August 1918, when the Allies launched their counter-offensive east of Amiens – an offensive that turned out to be the start of the advance to the Rhine. The British plan envisaged a surprise attack on a 7-mile front by Rawlinson's Fourth Army, with the Canadian Corps on the right and the Australian Corps on the left. There would be no preliminary bombardment. At zero hour (4:20 a.m.) the barrage, the tanks and the infantry would start together, the final objective for the infantry being the old Amiens defensive line some 6 to 8 miles beyond the British front. The three cavalry divisions would follow close behind the infantry to the second intermediate objective and then pass through to take the final one and hold it until the infantry caught up.

Space prevents recounting the details of the battle, but the 1st Cavalry Division worked with the Australians and the 3rd with the Canadians, both with a battalion of whippet light tanks in support. The 2nd Cavalry Division was held in reserve. By early afternoon the 3rd Cavalry Division had advanced almost 8 miles and reached the final objective. Lieutenant-Colonel Paterson of the Fort Garry Horse later wrote, 'Once our men were on top of the enemy they put up no fight and appeared completely demoralized.' A surrendering German officer exclaimed, 'Look, look! Wherever you look you see British cavalry.'

It was a similar situation with the advance of the 1st Cavalry Division together with the Australians. By 12:30 p.m. the opportunity

was open for the cavalry to push ahead beyond the infantry's final objective and make for the Roye–Chaulnes railway line 5 miles further east, as specified in their original orders. Indeed, at this time Rawlinson ordered the Cavalry Corps commander, Kavanagh, to push on. However, whether due to misunderstandings coupled with poor communications, it did not happen. Nevertheless, the cavalry had advanced at a remarkably rapid rate, taking at least 3,000 prisoners, and they had proved their value against a shaken enemy over open ground that had not been pitted beyond recognition with shell holes. At times the whippet–cavalry cooperation had proved difficult, as they had not trained together; and when not under fire the cavalry moved too fast for the tanks, whereas under heavy machine-gun fire the cavalry could not follow the tanks. Much of the problem stemmed from the whippets being held back initially and put under the

command of the cavalry; had they been acting independently they might have been better able to exploit and advance earlier. However, one whippet, called the 'Musical Box', did penetrate far behind the German lines, causing considerable chaos and alarm – its adventures are described in Section Ten.

The cost to the cavalry for the three days 8, 9 and 10 August was over 1,000, of whom 117 were killed. Losses among the horses had been exceptionally severe, to the extent that by mid-August the corps was 1,100 short.

The period from August to the Armistice in November saw the breaching of the Hindenburg Line and the Hundred Days offensive, but with the cavalry too weak to play an effective role as the pursuer of a beaten enemy. However, the British, who began their war on the Western Front with a cavalry charge, managed to end it in the same way at a bridge over the river at the village of Lessines (see box below).

The 7th Dragoon Guards at Lessines, 10:50 a.m., 11 November 1918

Early on the morning of 11 November 1918 the following message was sent to all British armies on the Western Front:

Hostilities will cease at 11 hours today, November 11th. Troops will stand fast on the line reached at that hour, which will be reported by wire to Advanced GHQ. Defensive precautions will be maintained. There will be no intercourse of any description with the enemy until receipt of instructions from GHQ.

The much-reduced cavalry had a brigade attached to each of the First, Second, Third and Fourth British Armies. Due to the narrowing of the front from about 100 miles in August to 65 miles in November, the armies were deployed in some depth, and congestion on the roads forward was considerable. This meant that most cavalry units were up to 8 miles behind the leading infantry, making it extremely difficult to get forward quickly.

At around 9:30 a.m. the 7th Dragoon Guards (7th Cavalry Brigade) was ordered by the commander of the 88th Infantry Brigade, Brigadier General B. C. Freyburg, VC, to get forward at once and capture the bridge over the River Dendre at Lessines, 18 miles north of Mons in Belgium, in order to prevent its demolition and to seize the river crossing before the Armistice came into effect.

The dragoons had about 10 miles to cover and 90 minutes in which to complete their task. The cavalry commanding officer detailed a squadron as the advance party and, led by Freyburg and his groom, they spurred away. It was a wild ride, with the horsemen galloping at every opportunity. Shortly before 11:00 a.m., as they approached the bridge, the leading troop came under fire from machine-gunners and riflemen and several horses were hit. As they thundered down the main street of Lessines, shots were fired from windows and a bullet struck Freyburg's saddle. However, Belgian civilians took the opportunity to rise up and attack the Germans in the houses, forcing them into the streets. There was no stopping the cavalry, who charged for the steel-girder bridge and clattered across before it could be demolished just a few minutes before 11:00 a.m.

Three German officers, along with 103 soldiers, were captured. Several of the officers cried foul, claiming they had been taken after 11:00 a.m. While this argument was going on a German fired from a house, killing a horse – it was quickly commandeered by villagers, who immediately began to skin and cook it.

By an extraordinary coincidence, the BEF had both started and finished the war on the Western Front with a cavalry charge, and both had taken place in Belgium within 15 miles of each other.

Engineers and men rebuilding a destroyed bridge in the Somme area of the Western Front, c.1918.

Section Seven

Engineers

No Corps was more constantly in demand,
so much master of so many tasks.

General Sir David Fraser

Only a few minutes to go. 3.5 a.m. At the firing posts stand officers; their pale faces show unmistakable signs of the strain of suspense. 3.6 a.m. Innumerable watches are consulted. 3.7 a.m. A hasty wipe of clammy hands. 3.8 a.m. Watches are held to the ear. 3.9 a.m. Hands tremble slightly as fingers close around switch and exploder handle; complete silence broken only by laboured breathing. Eyes staring at synchronized watches. Three hours . . . nine minutes . . . 59 seconds ... ZERO!

The supreme moment at last! With almost the same grim feeling as a soldier plunges his bayonet into the belly of his enemy, the Tunnellers banged in switches and slammed home plungers. Instantaneously the leads carry the message of destruction to the charged mines, hundreds of yards away. The long hibernation was ended.

The above, taken from *Tunnellers* by Captain W. G. Grieve, Royal Engineers, and B. Newman, vividly describes the acute tension experienced by demolition officers in the moments before blowing the mines under the German positions at Messines in June 1917. However, as emphasized in General Fraser's quotation, tunnelling and detonating mines was just one – if perhaps the most spectacular – of the dozens of different tasks undertaken by engineers on all sides on the Western Front, some of which are described in this section. While most examples of the duties use the activities of the British Royal Engineers (RE), French, German and later American engineers or pioneers had identical or very similar responsibilities.

Royal Engineers – whose lowest rank was a 'sapper', as he was originally a soldier tasked with digging 'saps', or tunnels towards enemy fortifications – fulfilled roles ranging from fighting as infantry to

that of specialist artisan. As with other arms and services, the scale of expansion necessary to provide engineer support to the fighting front was totally unexpected, and the Royal Engineers of 1918 bore little resemblance to the corps of four years earlier either in its size or in its roles. At the end of August 1914 the RE had some 7,500 all ranks in France and were organized as in the diagram on pages 288–9. There were twelve field companies and one field squadron with the cavalry, and two fortress companies (whose title indicates their origin) for work on the lines of communication with the BEF, but the fortress companies were gradually increased and re-named 'army troops' companies. In early 1916 one of these companies per division was authorized to be available for work in army and corps areas. By the end of the year there were fifty-one army troops companies on the Western Front.

Including all theatres, the four years from 1914 saw the Royal Engineers expand from 25,000 to just over 314,000, of whom around 15,000 were officers. Some 50,000 all ranks had become casualties (killed, wounded and missing) in France by the end of the war. At the Armistice 1,189 RE units of sixty-eight different types (including transportation units) were deployed on the Western Front. The largest number (163) was that of the field companies (see diagram, pages 288–9), which were distributed throughout the army with, for most of the war, three attached to every infantry division. Similarly, the Royal Engineers provided all signal units (the Royal Corps of Signals was not formed until 1920), of which, by November 1918, seventy-seven different types were deployed with the BEF.

Engineers were responsible for the design and construction of fortifications and field defences, frequently supervising labour provided by other units. Engineer units con-

structed and maintained hundreds of miles of road and railway tracks (including the light railway system used immediately behind the front line) and operated canal barges – all tasks critical for the forward movement of many thousands of tons of supplies every month. They were tasked with repairing or building bridges (often pontoon), repairing road and rail tunnels and, particularly during the retreat from Mons in 1914, the demolition of the same. During this period two engineers (Captain T.

Pioneer Battalion Duties

These infantry battalions had an establishment of twenty-four officers and 859 other ranks, and performed a host of vital duties in their divisional areas, as the following list illustrates: digging and draining trenches; shovelling mud from tracks; constructing dugouts and machine-gun posts; revetting trenches; making trench boards for flooring; building or repairing roads, mule tracks and light railways; erecting wire obstacles; digging communication trenches and saps; laying and burying telephone cable; tunnelling and mining duties; building camp huts; repairing bridges; burying corpses; neutralizing booby traps; clearing captured bunkers; and on occasion providing stretcher-bearers. Although work was done at night if possible, casualties from shelling were not uncommon and in emergencies pioneer battalions could revert to infantry fighting. An example was the 1/7th Durham Light Infantry (Pioneers), who covered the withdrawal of the 149th Brigade on 26 March 1918 and during a counter-attack the next day lost heavily. Again, on 10 April the battalion was called on to make another counter-attack, followed by several days of digging and wiring under fire, during which three company commanders were killed.

The Royal Engineer Component of the BEF, August 1914

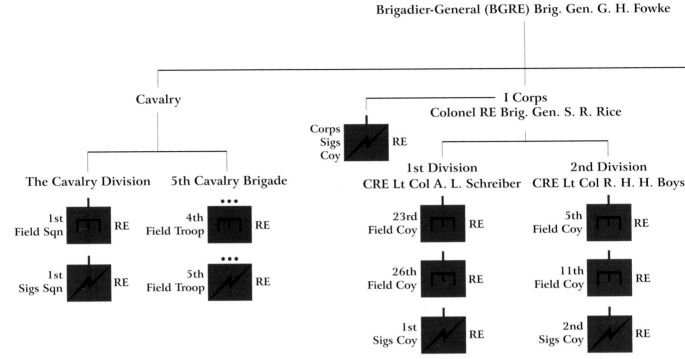

GHQ ————
Brigadier-General (BGRE) Brig. Gen. G. H. Fowke

Cavalry

I Corps
Colonel RE Brig. Gen. S. R. Rice

Corps Sigs Coy — RE

The Cavalry Division   5th Cavalry Brigade

1st Division
CRE Lt Col A. L. Schreiber

2nd Division
CRE Lt Col R. H. H. Boys

1st Field Sqn — RE

4th Field Troop — RE

23rd Field Coy — RE

5th Field Coy — RE

1st Sigs Sqn — RE

5th Field Troop — RE

26th Field Coy — RE

11th Field Coy — RE

1st Sigs Coy — RE

2nd Sigs Coy — RE

Notes

• RE and RE Signal Service sub-units serving with the cavalry are termed 'squadrons', whereas the same sub-units with the infantry are 'companies'.
• The senior RE officer at GHQ is a brigadier-general, but the commanding RE (CRE) at division was a lieutenant-colonel.
• Air-line sections were responsible for telegraph overhead communications and cable sections for telephone communications.

• The total RE strength with the BEF by the end of August 1914 was over 7,500 all ranks, or about 6.4% of the BEF.
• A third field squadron RE was allocated to each infantry division in 1915 so that there was one for each brigade.

A Royal Engineer Field Company

Field HQ

Company HQ vehicles
1 water cart
1 cook's wagon
2 pontoon wagons
1 trestle wagon
4 general service (GS) wagons
1 bicycle

1 major	1 shoeing smith
1 captain	1 trumpeter
1 CSM	1 bugler
1 CQMS	21 drivers
1 farrier sergeant	4 batmen
2 sergeants	2 sappers
1 corporal	2 RAMC
1 2nd corporal	41 in total

Section vehicles (each)
2 tool carts
1 forage cart
1 pack horse
8 bicycles

Field Sections

1 subaltern
1 sergeant
1 corporal
2 2nd corporals
1 batman
4 drivers
34 sappers
44 in total

Notes

• Full strength: 6 officers, 211 other ranks.
• The 2nd corporal rank was peculiar to the RE and AOC (Army Ordnance Corps).
• Note the predominance of carpenters, bricklayers, masons and blacksmiths.
• The GS wagons carried stores and baggage.
• There were 76 horses (17 riding, 55 draught and 4 pack).

Tradesmen	Coy HQ	1 Sect.	2 Sect.	3 Sect.	4 Sect.
blacksmiths	1	4	3	4	3
bricklayers		5	5	5	5
carpenters		10	10	10	10
clerks	1	1	1	1	1
coopers	1		1		
draughtsmen			1		1
electricians		1			1
engine drivers		1	1	1	1
fitters & turners		2	2	2	2
labourers	1	1	2	1	2
masons		3	3	3	3
painters		2	1	2	1
plasterers		1		1	
plumbers & gasfitters		2	2	2	2
saddlers & harness-makers	1		1		1
slaters			1		1
shoemakers	1				
surveyors		1		1	
tailors		1	1	1	1
wheelwrights	1	1	1	1	1

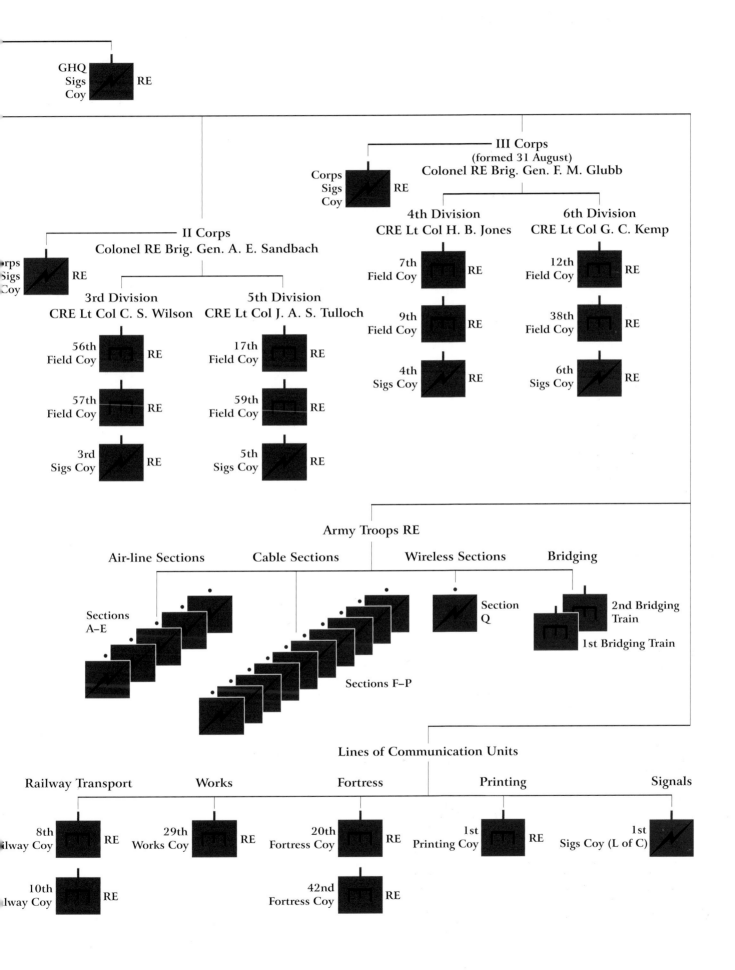

GHQ Sigs Coy RE

III Corps
(formed 31 August)
Colonel RE Brig. Gen. F. M. Glubb

Corps Sigs Coy RE

4th Division
CRE Lt Col H. B. Jones

6th Division
CRE Lt Col G. C. Kemp

7th Field Coy RE

12th Field Coy RE

9th Field Coy RE

38th Field Coy RE

4th Sigs Coy RE

6th Sigs Coy RE

II Corps
Colonel RE Brig. Gen. A. E. Sandbach

Corps Sigs Coy RE

3rd Division
CRE Lt Col C. S. Wilson

5th Division
CRE Lt Col J. A. S. Tulloch

56th Field Coy RE

17th Field Coy RE

57th Field Coy RE

59th Field Coy RE

3rd Sigs Coy RE

5th Sigs Coy RE

Army Troops RE

Air-line Sections

Cable Sections

Wireless Sections

Bridging

Sections A–E

Sections F–P

Section Q

2nd Bridging Train

1st Bridging Train

Lines of Communication Units

Railway Transport

Works

Fortress

Printing

Signals

8th Railway Coy RE

29th Works Coy RE

20th Fortress Coy RE

1st Printing Coy RE

1st Sigs Coy (L of C)

10th Railway Coy RE

42nd Fortress Coy RE

Wright and Lance Corporal C. A. Jarvis) won the Victoria Cross for their gallant attempts to blow bridges (see pages 291–2 for an account of Wright's award). Among the tasks that were soon to fall on the Royal Engineers were maintaining stores depots, workshops, operating water supply and its sterilization, manning searchlights, surveying land and making maps, printing, and running training schools, one of which taught camouflage techniques. They built hutted camps and established quarrying and forestry companies for the production of the vast tonnages of stone and timber required for construction and repair. Of particular importance to the troops in the trenches were the RE specialist companies devoted to tunnelling, mining and the use of, and protection against, poison gas (see page 295).

Like the British, both the French and German armies started the war with modest engineer establishments. In 1914 the French had 71 field engineer companies split between infantry and cavalry divisions, along with 15 fortress, 16 railway, 12 telegraph, 21 searchlight and 2 wireless companies. As the war progressed they undertook extensive tunnelling and mining, and in 1915 a team of designers, sculptors and painters were coopted into the 1st Engineer Regiment to oversee camouflage work.

The Germans had a slightly different way of organizing their engineer support to the field armies. The duties corresponding to those of the Royal Engineers were performed by the Corps of Engineers (*Ingenieur-Korps*), fortress construction officers (*Festungsbau Offiziere*) and the Corps of Pioneers (*Pionier-Korps*). The first two consisted of officers only and were engaged solely with design, planning, overseeing construction, maintenance and the organization of fortresses. However, they and Pioneer Corps officers received the same training and were largely interchangeable. All three operated under a general of the Engineers and Pioneer Corps at the Great Headquarters who was adviser to the Kaiser, and generals of pioneers at each army headquarters. The Signal Service was separate; by 1917 it had embraced all means of communication, including telegraph, telephone, wireless, visual and sound signalling and carrier pigeons.

The principal units within the German Pioneer Corps were connected with field engineering tasks and comprised field companies, mining companies, bridging trains, searchlight sections and park (engineer equipment) companies. The Pioneer Corps also provided personnel for trench-mortar units (except for an infantry unit's light *Minenwerfer*), gas projectors and flamethrowers. Details of the structure and personnel of a pioneer field battalion 1914–16 and company and divisional pioneer battalions in 1917 are shown in the diagrams below.

German Pioneer Battalion, 1914–1916

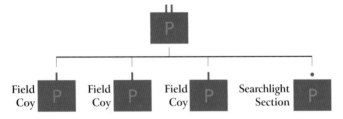

Notes
• Pioneer battalions were allocated to corps at the outbreak of war.
• Strength: 8 officers and just over 300 other ranks.
• The number of pioneer companies was increased considerably as the war progressed by the addition of Ersatz, Landwehr and Landsturm units.
• By the end of 1914 there were almost 600 pioneer field companies with the field army and a year later nearly 700.
• They were mostly used on field works.

German Divisional Pioneer Battalion, 1917

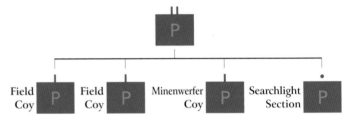

Notes
• In 1917 the pioneer units were regrouped and reorganized in a divisional pioneer battalion. The main change was the reduction of one field company and the addition of a Minenwerfer company, the weapons (heavier) being operated by pioneers. In 1916 there were 217 of these companies.
• Light Minenwerfers were operated by infantry in 1916.

German Pioneer Field Company, 1917

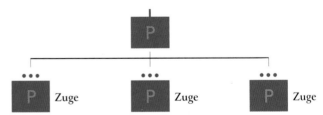

Notes
• Full establishment: 4 officers plus a medical officer and paymaster, 262 other ranks, 20 horses and 7 vehicles.
• Vehicles: 1 pioneer stores wagon (4-horsed)

3 pioneer stores wagons
1 baggage wagon
1 mobile kitchen   } 2-horsed
1 supply wagon
1 pack horse

• By 1917 the number of field companies in a division was fixed at two, with the remainder allocated to army and army groups for construction of rear defensive zones.

An observation tower built by German engineers from the ruins of the village church at Montfaucon.

The huge diversity of British Royal Engineer responsibilities is clear from the diagram on pages 288–9, which sets out the structure of GHQ by the end of the war. Not only was there an engineer-in-chief – a major general, with the directors of army signals and gas services and an inspector of mines reporting to him – but a number of directors working (from June 1918) to the quartermaster general. These officers were engineer brigadier generals responsible for overseeing the work of constructing, expanding and developing roads, railways, inland waterways, docks, engineer work-shops and stores, forestry, quarrying, works and postal services.

All these tasks required Royal Engineer advice, planning and supervision, but with the bulk of the tens of thousands of manual workers provided by infantry or cavalry units when out of the line 'resting', or by the infantry pioneer battalion in each division (from 1915), or by specific labour units (military and civil) that are discussed in detail below (page 321). Space prevents examining every different type of engineer unit, but they can be very broadly divided, with some overlap, into the divisional field engineer and signal companies that worked in the forward area, and the remainder – the corps, army and line of communication units that were controlled and tasked by higher command (the army troops companies), with base areas coming under the works directorate. For ease of understanding the remainder of this section will explain the Royal Engineers' roles under the headings Field Companies, Specialist RE Units (Tunnelling and Gas), Signalling, and Construction and Labour. Examples from specific battles will illustrate the scale and type of the work done.

RE Field Companies

From 1915 there were normally three field companies – in round figures, just over 600 men – allocated to every infantry division; it was common practice for one company to be attached to each brigade. Engineering policy normally rested with the divisional commander, and the commanding royal engineer (CRE), a lieutenant colonel, drew up the programme of work. From early 1915 infantry divisions also had their own pioneer battalion, which provided much, but by no means all, of the muscle for fetching, carrying and digging that engineering work entailed – although they were still infantrymen who on occasion had to fight as such. Cavalry field engineer squadrons attached to the cavalry divisions were seldom economical units, as they could produce only about seventy-five dismounted men. They did, however, carry out numerous bridge demolitions during the BEF's retreat from Mons. Once trench warfare set in, they usually accompanied cavalry working parties in a supervisory role, installed water points for the horses and undertook in a more limited way the tasks of their infantry field company comrades.

Many field company tasks were common to all operations at and behind the front, but the more usual ones are described below.

Defence and withdrawal

In defence or during quiet periods at the front, divisional field engineer units were normally based close behind the support line of trenches, spending much of their time constructing defences. Dugouts, machine-gun posts, observation posts, wire entanglements, headquarters bunkers, dressing stations, water supply points, light bridges, roads, duckboard tracks, trenches, expanding billets and establishing supply dumps all required continuous work, as well as the provision of engineer stores, timber, wiring pickets and a host of smaller items and tools. Much of the time the front was under sporadic and sometimes intense bombardment that caused not only casualties to engineers and working parties (the infantry called them 'fatigue parties' – because they invariably involved yet more work for already tired men – until a High Command order prohibited it and insisted on 'working parties'), but also considerable damage to defences, trenches, roads and other structures that necessitated continuous repair, much of which had to be done at night to avoid providing an easy artillery target. In addition, engineers were kept busy experimenting with and producing makeshift bombs, grenades, trench stores, periscopes and mortars, for which the demand was acute once trench warfare became established.

Over the winter of 1914/15 constant shelling and heavy traffic caused so much damage to the roads behind the front that they became virtually impassable. Divisional engineering field units were given the task of solving the problem. They devised a wooden 2-foot-gauge tramway to carry stores and ammunition forward from refilling points to the front line. The rails were made from 3-inch x 2-inch planks and the sleepers from 1-inch planking. By May 1915 the tramways were also being used to evacuate wounded stretcher cases as well as to remove the spoil from tunnels.

Demolition has always been a traditional military engineer's task, and so it was on the Western Front, particularly when a withdrawal was necessary, as in late August 1914. However, field companies had gone to war with only basic demolition kits containing gun-cotton and gunpowder, no instantaneous exploder fuze and only one exploder per section, so reliance was placed on electrical firing equipment and limited amounts of safety fuse. With the BEF's defensive line along the Mons Canal under intense pressure from the Germans to the north, and with the French pulling back on the right, it became obvious that a general withdrawal was imminent. In the early hours of 23 August, II Corps gave orders for the numerous bridges over the canal to be prepared for demolition, while at the same time a second defensive line was being selected and reconnoitred to the rear. Often this instruction arrived too late and the Germans succeeded in taking a number of bridges intact. When 56 Field Company arrived at the canal that morning, its first bridge was already under sniper fire and the section sent on to the bridge to lay the charges was rushed by the enemy and captured, and their officer killed.

The 57 Field Company had eight bridges to prepare, but despite gallant attempts under fire only one bridge could be destroyed, although the actions of Captain T. Wright and Lance Corporal C. A. Jarvis won them both the Victoria Cross. The bridges from Jemappes railway station to Mariette were allotted to Lieutenant P. K. Boulnois (57 Company), who took with him four NCOs and four sappers on bicycles, with his forage cart loaded with explosives and a drum of cable. He divided up his small party and stores, and arranged to return with the exploder and blow up each bridge in turn. The bridge at Mariette was prepared by Sergeant Smith and Sapper Dabell. About 2 p.m. Lieutenant Boulnois, accompanied by Sergeant Smith, went off on their bicycles to visit the other bridges.

The *Royal Engineer Journal* of March 1932 gives a fascinating account of what happened.

> [On their way] they met Captain Wright (Adjutant, 3rd Divisional RE) coming back from Loch 2 where he had been wounded in the head by shrapnel . . . No orders had yet been received for the destruction of the bridges, but they stopped a despatch-rider (searching for the Scots Fusiliers) and learned that he was carrying orders for a general

retirement. They at once realized that they were faced with the problem of instantly blowing up five bridges on a front of 3 miles with one exploder.

Wright started off in a car to order the destruction of Day's bridges [Lieutenant A. F. Day had been tasked with blowing the road and rail bridge over the canal north-west of Mons], and told Boulnois to get on with his as best he could. Boulnois bicycled with Sergeant Smith to his furthest bridge, close to Jemappes station, and successfully destroyed it at around 3 p.m. He then decided that as there was no time to lose he would omit the bridges at Loch 2 and the two next to it (Lance-Corporal Halewood's), and make for the Mariette bridge which carried a main road. On their way they again met Wright and, after a short consultation, it was decided that he should take the exploder and drum in his car and, accompanied by Sergeant Smith, go to Mariette while Boulnois went to Corporal Halewood's bridges. Here he succeeded in joining up his leads with the local electric supply in an adjoining house, hoping that the current that was still running the lights would set off the detonator if he switched it on suddenly. By this time, however, the village had been deserted, and at this very moment the current failed.

Captain Wright and Sergeant Smith on reaching Mariette made most gallant attempts to get at the free ends of the leads, which only just reached the towpath. B Company of the 1st Northumberland Fusiliers was still holding out at the barricade on the south side of the canal, but the towpath was separated from the barricade by the subsidiary canal, here spanned by a girder bridge fifteen to twenty feet wide. Captain Wright bridge-laddered under this subsidiary canal bridge with extra leads tied on to him, and time and again tried to get at the ends of the leads on the towpath. Each time his hands or head appeared above the level of the towpath he was fired at from about thirty yards off, so eventually he gave up the attempt. In swinging himself back under the girder across the subsidiary canal, he lost his grip owing to exhaustion, and was pulled out of the water by Sergeant Smith.

The result was that of the eight bridges allotted to the 57th Company only the one close to Jemappes station was blown up.

Wright was awarded the Victoria Cross posthumously, as he was mortally wounded

just three weeks later at Vailly (where he is buried in the British Military Cemetery) when assisting the passage of the 5th Cavalry Brigade over a pontoon bridge and helping a wounded man into shelter.

As the Germans withdrew to the Hindenburg Line in the spring of 1917, laying waste the ground as they went, the field squadrons were heavily involved, particularly with road and bridge repairs and construction. With the major German offensive a year later, it was back to demolitions as the enemy advance forced the BEF back. Much use was made of the mobility of the field squadrons with the Cavalry Corps. As an example, 2 Squadron prepared sixteen demolitions on 22 and 24 April and blew them all successfully on the 25th. On 22 March Second Lieutenant C. L. Knox of 150 Field Company was entrusted with the demolition of twelve bridges. He successfully carried out his task, but with one steel-girder bridge the time fuze failed, so Knox ran out on to the bridge under fire and with the Germans actually on it. He reached the charge, tore out the time fuze and lit the instantaneous fuze, to do which he had to get under the bridge. His gallantry earned him the Victoria Cross. Knox survived the war, spent several of the inter-war years as a flight lieutenant in the Royal Auxiliary Air Force and died in 1943.

Finally, field companies were sometimes required to fight in both defensive and offensive roles. During the bitter battles at Ypres in late 1914, 5 Field Company, under Major A. H. Tyler, was involved every night in working on the defences of Polygon Wood, when on 11 November Tyler was told the Germans had broken through the 1st Black Watch and 2nd Connaught Rangers and that he should take his men to plug the gap. The company deployed partially in the wood and partially in a disused trench in the open. Heavy fighting against a Prussian Guard attack took place, in which Major Tyler and two subalterns were killed. Eventually the German attack was driven back and the overall position restored by a counter-attack by the 2nd Oxford Light Infantry. Even the engineers' company cooks became embroiled in the fight. They had been left behind near a French gun battery that came under rifle fire from a nearby house. Sapper Vye led his five cooks forward in skirmishing order to drive five Germans from the house, capturing two. No. 5 Field Company gained seven DCMs for its exploits that day – a record for so small a unit.

At the Battle of Loos in September 1915, 73 Field Company was involved in the attack on Hill 70 in support of the 10th Gordon Highlanders. Two sections under

Captain E. D. Carden advanced behind the infantry and on reaching the crest of the hill saw the strongpoint known as the Keep about to fall to the enemy. They rushed forward and tried to enter it, but heavy machine-gun fire drove them back. Carden and Second Lieutenant F. H. Johnson gathered together a machine gun and ten sappers, then advanced on the Keep again. This time they retook it, but were soon driven out, Captain Carden being badly wounded and Johnson hit in the leg. Despite his wound, Johnson took command, rallied his men and throughout the day led several charges to try to retake the Keep, although it remained in German possession. For his actions Johnson was awarded the Victoria Cross. He died of wounds as a major at Ypres on 26 November 1917.

Preparations for attack

The complexity and scale of the work of field companies in preparing for a major offensive is amply demonstrated in the preparations for the attack on the Somme in 1916. Overall 320 field companies (some 60,000 men) and eighteen infantry pioneer battalions (over 10,000 men) were available to support the British offensive of eighteen divisions and associated artillery brigades assembled for 1 July.

In early April the 31st Division opposite Serre received instructions to prepare for an attack at the end of the month, which was subsequently postponed several times until 1 July. The RE and the pioneer battalion (12th King's Own Yorkshire Light Infantry) worked under the CRE. Two RE field companies each had one company of the pioneer battalion at its disposal and worked in the forward area. The third field company had two sections working in the forward area, while another two sections were involved with back-area tasks. Of the remaining two pioneer companies, one assisted the artillery in constructing gun emplacements and dugouts and cutting timber for them. The other had an assortment of tasks, such as repairing roads, sinking wells, constructing medium-mortar emplacements and army and corps signal dugouts.

Two cross-country roads were marked out from Colincamps to the front trenches for the use of forward and return traffic. Trenches on the route were bridged to take motor ambulances, while a large number of stores and tools, such as wire-cutters, hedging gloves, trench bridges and ladders and sandbags, were issued to units. Each brigade had access to four small RE stores dumps and four infantry ones for food, water and small-arms ammunition, as shown in the diagram opposite.

RE Field Companies and Pioneer Units, 31st Division, Prior to Attack, 1 July 1916
(not to scale)

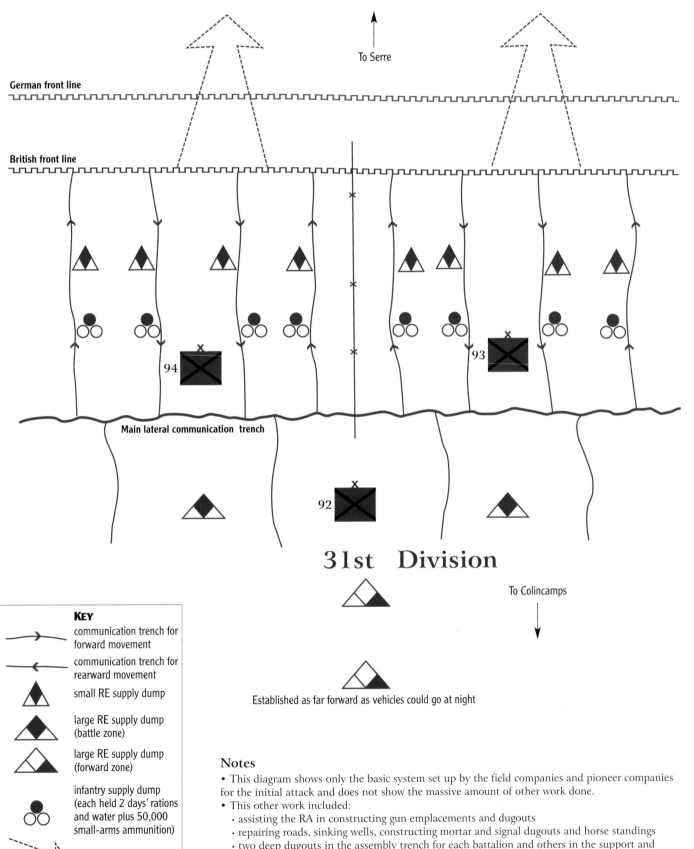

Notes
- This diagram shows only the basic system set up by the field companies and pioneer companies for the initial attack and does not show the massive amount of other work done.
- This other work included:
  - assisting the RA in constructing gun emplacements and dugouts
  - repairing roads, sinking wells, constructing mortar and signal dugouts and horse standings
  - two deep dugouts in the assembly trench for each battalion and others in the support and reserve trenches
  - constructing two deep dugouts with adjoining OP for each brigade battle HQ
  - five large dugouts each for wounded and the Advanced Dressing Station at Colincamps

Major works completed by the RE companies, assisted by the pioneers and others, in the forward area of just one division during the three months' preparation included:

- 8 miles of new trenches
- 30 miles of other trenches cleared, deepened, improved and restored
- 86 dugouts constructed, plus 16 for RFA batteries and 21 for medium trench mortars near the front line
- 34 observation posts
- 36 emplacements for 360 gas cylinders made in the front line
- 22 tramway trenches
- 6 sets of water tanks placed in trenches and connected to water pipes
- 5 deep-mined approaches totalling 2,500 feet run to within 30 yards of the German line and 20 Stokes mortar emplacements constructed off them
- name- and noticeboards made and erected in all trenches, particularly at junctions and along cross-country road routes

Work in the back area included:

- 100 wooden huts to accommodate four battalions along with 2 wells for water
- 2 deep, 130-foot, wells sunk with motor pump, tanks and standpipes to fill water carts
- 2 reservoirs holding 21,000 gallons, along with over 3 miles of piping to form a water point with troughs for horses
- 2 RA ammunition dumps and one grenade and mortar dump constructed
- 2,600 trees felled for timber; branches used to make revetment posts and fascines
- 2,500 yards of flint quarried for road repair

During and after an attack

Again, the start of the Somme offensive provides a good example. The key principle was to get engineers on to captured enemy positions immediately after they had been secured, as it was wasteful of specialist personnel to be caught up in the fighting for the objective. Thus the orders for 1 July stated that no portion of the divisional field companies was to take part in the assault. One section could be placed at the disposal of the commander of each assaulting brigade, but it was not to be ordered forward until the objective had been gained. The remainder was to be held back for work on, and improvement of, forward roads and water supply, as well as for consolidation of strongpoints at night. This instruction was not always complied with on 1 July, nor on the 23rd when the 48th Division attacked up Mash Valley, as it seems some engineers were involved – or were so close behind as to

make no difference – in the infantry assault. Sapper E. E. Comer later recorded:

My lot went up with the troops and we had to go over with rifles. Our own bombardment was terrific. This place, Pozières, was up on top of the ridge and in front of us there was nothing but one sheet of explosives. We went straight up. You grip your rifle and you say, 'Come on, you silly fool, you've got to go.' But all you could do was drop down as the shells came around, then up again and on, and down again. The only thing you thought of was getting out of it. We engineers had to be there, because the idea was that as soon as we captured a trench we would consolidate it, reverse the parapet so that we'd be able to fire at the Germans from that side. What was even worse than going forward, was trying to keep on working. You drove yourself to it. You made yourself go on but they were firing at you all the time.

I admit that I was windy. I remember being in a shell hole and I was clawing at the ground to get my head into it. That's all I was interested in, to get my head right down in the ground. We captured one trench, and then a bit of another. But we didn't get much further.

The orders given on 21 June by Major General J. S. M. Shea for 30th Division's assault show clearly what was expected of the engineers. The division was to take Dublin Trench, Glatz Redoubt, and if possible exploit these to take the *briqueteries* (brickworks) in the first phase, with the leading brigades of the 89th on the right and the 21st on the left. The second phase was the capture of Montauban by the 90th Brigade (see Map 40). Paragraph 9 of the divisional order reads:

The C.R.E. will tell off 1 section Fd. Coy. R.E. and 1 platoon of Pioneers, which with 2 platoons to be detailed by 89th Bde will make the 'Strong point party' to follow the 89th Bde. He will also tell off another section Field Coy. R.E. to assist in the Briqueterie operation.

He will tell off another section Fd. Coy R.E. and 1 platoon of Pioneers which, with 1 platoon to be detailed by 21st Bde, will make the 'Strong point party' to follow the 21st Bde.

These 'Strong Point Parties' will be under the command of the Brigadiers whose brigades they are to follow. Their first duty is to construct Nos. 1 and 2 Strong Points 89th Bde. Area, and No. 1 Strong point in 21st Bde. Area . . . after which they will be available to assist in the completion of the other 'Strong Points' as ordered [there were more required, but those specified above had priority] . . .

The C.R.E. will arrange for the maintenance of communication trenches within our own lines, the digging of new ones where necessary, and the repair for use as communication trenches certain German trenches . . . He is also responsible for (i) preparation for the use of the Maricourt-Montauban road (ii) formation of R.E. dumps other than the forward dumps that are under the Brigadiers (iii) issue of R.E. stores as necessary to the Bdes.

The emphasis is clearly to get specifically detailed parties of engineers, pioneers and infantry forward quickly to construct several strongpoints in the captured enemy trench system in preparation for resisting the anticipated counter-attacks that were an automatic feature of German tactics if a position was lost. The second priority was the maintenance of communication by using British and German trenches for the forward movement under cover of reinforcements and supplies.

Appendix C of these orders allocates subunits to tasks and spells out who is to do what and where. For example, in the 89th Brigade the Strong Point Party would consist of 1 Section, 200 Field Company, one platoon of pioneers and two platoons of infantry, and was to build the strongpoints at specific map references. Communication, road and trench maintenance parties and divisional engineer reserves were detailed. In this appendix the commander of the 11th South Lancashire (divisional pioneer battalion) received instructions for supplying the communication maintenance parties. The platoon responsible for the maintenance of the Support and West Avenue Trenches had 1,000 sandbags, ten rolls of wire netting, fifty sheets of expanded metal, fifty 7-foot pickets, 100 long-angle iron posts and two rolls of plain wire at its disposal.

With an objective secure, there was still much work for engineers and pioneers. A training manual of January 1918 makes clear that an engineer officer should be attached to brigade headquarters during and after an attack to advise the brigadier on the work and stores necessary. Some of the tasks were:

- supervision of strongpoint construction
- construction of boarded tracks
- arrangements for bridging trenches, filling shell holes to allow artillery to get forward
- finding and opening sources of water supply
- providing and fixing signboards and direction lamps for use at night
- forming dumps of engineer stores near the objective
- checking captured enemy dugouts for mines, then repairing and improving them for use as headquarters or regimental aid posts

Specialist RE Units

Tunnelling Companies

For the purpose of clarification, 'tunnelling' is taken to mean boring shafts and digging tunnels (usually referred to as galleries) more or less horizontally, while 'mining' is the placing and firing of explosives.

> Sap-heads had been dug out from our line to within three metres of the enemy position . . . From the ten sap-heads in the zone of the attack, mines were laid under the enemy's trenches, each charged with 50 kilogrammes of explosive.
>
> To ensure the ignition of the mines, the attack was arranged for 9.0 a.m. so that the leads could be tested by the company commander and his second-in-command, and that any improvement which appeared necessary could be made in daylight. A mine was also laid under a house, held by the enemy on the right of the front of attack (Quinque Rue), and was charged with 300 kilogrammes (66 lbs) of explosive. All telephone communications were manned to ensure the neighbouring units commencing the attack simultaneously in the event of there being any delay in the explosion. Actually the explosion did not take place till 10.25 in the morning owing to special difficulties in connection with one of the leads. When it was reported to the senior pioneer officer on the front of the attack that all the mines were ready, he had three flare signals fired simultaneously. This signal was only meant for pioneers, who then fired all the mines.

This extract is from the report of the German VII Corps on the success of its attack on 20 December 1914 on the Indian Corps holding the Givenchy–Festubert front. The detonation of the ten small mines (except Quinque Rue) caught the Sirhind Brigade by surprise and the following infantry assault drove it back 500 yards to the reserve line. The first honours in mine warfare had gone to the Germans, although on a minute scale compared with what was to come.

Alarm bells sounded in the British GHQ and armies were ordered to switch from what had been tentative defensive tunnelling to detect enemy activity to offensive mining. However, RE field companies were already overburdened and initially the best that could be achieved was to scour units at the front for men with mining experience and group them into brigade mining sections of one officer and around fifty men. However,

their efforts were unable to compete with the better-equipped, more experienced and more numerous enemy pioneers. Demands from armies along the British front for miners to protect their sectors, especially at Givenchy and in the vicinity of Ypres, became urgent. On 19 February 1915 a previous suggestion by a Major J. Norton Griffiths, an engineer in the 2nd King Edward's Horse who had approached Lord Kitchener directly, that coal miners and other underground workers should be specially enlisted was accepted, and eight companies of tunnellers or 'moles' were authorized. Griffiths, acting as liaison officer to the army engineer-in-chief, Brigadier General George Fowke, began the job of recruiting former miners and excavators into specialist tunnelling companies. Many, but not all, of these men were experienced 'clay-kickers' (see page 297), previously employed digging the tunnels for the London Underground or for sewers in the larger cities. On 21 February the first party of tunnellers, who five days before had been in the sewers below Manchester, were burrowing into the clay at Givenchy. Their conversion from civilians to very sloppy 'soldiers' with no military training had been exceptionally swift and traumatic. In five days they had been given rifles but no training, ill-fitting uniforms and thigh-length gumboots, and had been horribly seasick crossing the Channel, followed by an equally appalling rail journey in cattle trucks. Then

within hours of arrival at the front they were once again underground. With these men and other ex-miners from several infantry battalions, the nucleus of 170 (Tunnelling) Company, RE, was complete.

From then until the end of June 1916 expansion continued apace, helped by the fact that there was a vast pool of around a million coal miners in Britain. Specialist volunteers were encouraged by the idea of receiving 6 shillings (30p) a day compared with the ordinary sapper's 2/6d (12½p) and the infantry private's just 1 shilling (5p). By the start of the Somme offensive twenty-five British tunnelling companies with a lower establishment of nineteen officers (including a medical officer) and 325 other ranks, together with three Canadian, three Australian and one New Zealand company were deployed in France; by the war's end 1,516 'moles' had lost their lives. The mining effort for the Somme offensive started many months before July 1916 and included reluctant infantrymen drafted for non-specialist duties such as concealing spoil or manning windlasses and air pumps. By June 1916 over 20,000 men were employed on underground work. The command set-up comprised an inspector of mines (brigadier general) at GHQ and a controller of mines (lieutenant colonel) at each army HQ; the latter was the principal executive officer for mining operations in an army area. Additionally, an army mine school was established under a captain.

Christchurch Tunnel, dug by the New Zealand Tunnelling Company, was one of a series of tunnels and caverns beneath Arras named after towns and cities in their homeland.

Sapper William Hackett, VC

Known as the 'Tunnellers' VC', William Hackett was the only tunneller to be awarded this distinction for an outstanding example of self-sacrifice. He enlisted in the Royal Engineers tunnelling companies in October 1915 aged forty-two; he had previously been rejected three times by the York and Lancaster Regiment because of his age. However, the fact that he had worked as a miner for twenty-three years in the Nottingham and Yorkshire coalfields made him very acceptable as a tunneller.

On the morning of 22 June 1916, Hackett was one of five miners from 254 Tunnelling Company driving an attacking tunnel towards the German line near Givenchy. The tunnel was about 35 feet below the surface and connected to a single shaft known as the Shaftesbury Shaft. Work had progressed about a third of the way to its objective when, at 2:50 a.m., the Germans blew a mine that collapsed the roof of nearly 30 feet of tunnel behind Hackett and his comrades, entrapping them. The crater thus formed became known as the Red Dragon Crater.

Digging desperately for some twenty hours, the rescue party made an escape hole through the earth and fallen timbers and contact was made with the five men. Hackett helped three men to crawl to safety but, although unhurt, he refused to leave until the last, seriously injured man – Thomas Collins, 14th Battalion, the Welch Regiment (Swansea Pals) – was rescued. When urged to leave, Hackett replied, 'I am a tunneller, I must look after the others first.' The rescue party worked on despite many interruptions by enemy shells falling around the shaft head, and still Hackett refused to leave his comrade. Finally the gallery collapsed again and, although the rescuers worked frantically for four days, they failed to reach the two men. Both men still lie together, but, strangely, are remembered apart, with Hackett's name on the Ploegsteert Memorial and Collins's on the Thiepval Memorial.

King George V presented Hackett's Victoria Cross to his widow at Buckingham Palace on 29 November 1916 and it is now in the Royal Engineers' Museum, Gillingham, Kent.

Digging the tunnels

The first information needed concerned the geology of the ground through which the tunnel would be dug. This was obtained by sinking boreholes with the object of determining the type and thickness of the strata and thus the depth at which tunnelling was possible – sandy, wet soil making such work virtually impossible. The British sector of the Western Front could be roughly divided into two geological areas.

First, to the north of the Vimy Ridge lies the heavy blue-clay stratum of Flanders, at varying depths but up to 400 feet thick. The advantage of tunnelling through the clay was that it was comparatively easy to dig, which led to good progress and also meant that the digging was almost noiseless. However, galleries had to be supported by timber to prevent collapse and, as clay readily absorbs moisture, intense pressure was put on these timber supports.

The second area extended south-west of Vimy, past Arras to the River Somme, and was primarily white chalk; some men who worked at a chalk tunnel face for long periods developed snow blindness. Chalk was comparatively hard, so tunnels were often self-supporting with timber needed only for roof support. The problem was that digging could not be done by the clay-kicker method but required the use of specially adapted hand tools – so silence was obtained with difficulty and progress was slow. One solution was to sink the shaft deep and drive forward the tunnel at a depth where it was hoped no German listening post could hear any noise. As the war progressed so shafts tended to get deeper, with a depth of over 100 feet being common.

The shaft

This was the entrance to the tunnel system and had to be selected with care. It was important to conceal the shaft house, either by camouflage, use of existing buildings or preferably within a concealed dugout. Shaft heads were tempting targets for shelling or for destruction in raids if near the front line, so their location had to be hidden from the air. Other factors affecting siting were the distance from the enemy target if the tunnel was one in which mines were to be laid – the further back the shaft, the easier it was to conceal but the longer the tunnel would take to dig.

The first construction was the shaft house, in which were located the windlass for hauling up the sacks of spoil, air pump, other equipment and the personnel to work at the shaft head. Occasionally the entrance shaft would be driven almost horizontally into a hillside, but more often it would slope down at an angle (this more often in chalk strata). The usual (it could vary) six-hour shift consisted of an NCO and twelve men, of whom often only the NCO and three or four men working at the gallery face would be Royal Engineers. The remainder would be infantrymen drafted in to provide the muscle for what was mostly labour-intensive work. On occasion up to 300 infantrymen would be attached to a tunnelling company. Within a shift up to four men might be employed at the face, kicking, erecting timber supports and bagging spoil, four hauling spoil back on the rubber-wheeled trolley, two hoisting the bags up the shaft and two manning the pumps. Further labour was needed to dispose of the spoil. In good, dry soil wooden shafts were used, but if the ground was soft or wet

A British chalk tunneller working at the face.

then sectional steel cylinders were required (in a process known as tubbing) to seal the shaft until a harder strata or clay was reached – the Germans often used concrete for this purpose. A ladder was fixed to the side of a vertical shaft for access and the windlass, pulley and rope were normally used to haul up the sacks of spoil. Of critical importance was the air pump, often operated by a man using a blacksmith's bellows, which was found effective and could be operated quietly. Fresh air was blown through a 6–9-inch diameter tin piping with canvas joints, often fixed to the roof of a tunnel. An officer directly supervised the air pump, as any failure to get oxygen to the face caused severe headaches, light-headedness and loss of energy leading to unconsciousness. If candles went out it was a sign that oxygen levels were dangerously low.

The removal of spoil was an important task for those working above ground, especially when digging through chalk, as loose spoil thrown around or piled up was an instant giveaway. It was arduous work and was usually done by infantry, whose term for the Royal Engineers was the 'press gang'. With aerial reconnaissance the problem became acute and disposal had to be pre-planned. It was dumped to the rear in old shell holes, disused trenches, inside ruined buildings or in natural hollows and then covered in loose soil or camouflaged with a large cloth suspended on poles. Handling spoil bags was a filthy, backbreaking task loathed by all involved.

Several feet above the bottom of the shaft was a chamber and entrance to the main tunnel or gallery. This provided space for two men to offload bags from the trolley and hitch them to the rope to be taken to the surface. A poor alternative to the trolley was to drag the bags along the floor of the tunnel. The bottom of the shaft served as a covered sump from which water could be pumped to the surface, sometimes by a pump fixed on a platform halfway down the shaft. Electric pumps installed by the end of 1916 could keep a mine system clear of water with an hour or two's pumping a day.

Galleries

Galleries were driven forward in clay by a procedure known as 'clay-kicking', as the actions of the man at the face resembled kicks. It was a method of driving a tunnel that was usually so small that the miner had no room to do more than crouch. Use of the legs on a special type of spade with a curved blade and sharp cutting edge provided the energy. Some inches above the shoulders of the blade, on either side of the handle, were projections that received the force of the thrust by the 'kicker'. To obtain the necessary leverage the kicker had to have support for his back. This came in the form of a strong wooden cross set up in the tunnel at an angle of 45 degrees. The kicker sat on an improvised seat, leaned his shoulders against the arms of the cross and drove his spade home into the clay with his legs. The lumps of clay were loaded into sacks by a 'bagger' lying beside him and were then placed on a trolley with rubber-tyred wheels by the 'trammer'; the trolley was pulled by

British Tunnel System – Basic Plan (not to scale)

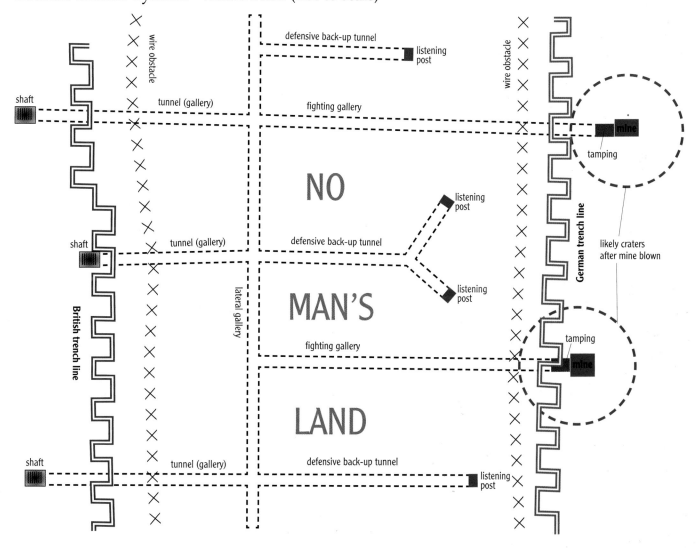

Simplified Cross-section of Shaft and Fighting Gallery Workings (not to scale)

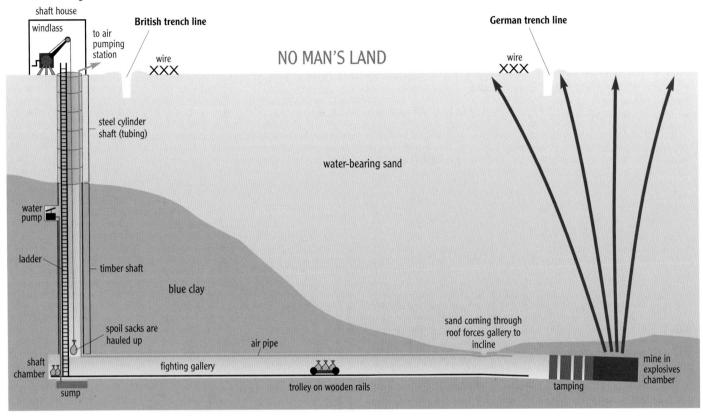

cover for windlass and
personnel camouflaged or
in concealed dugout

shaft house

windlass

to air
pumping
station

British trench line

wire
XXX

NO MAN'S LAND

German trench line

wire
XXX

steel cylinder
shaft (tubing)

water-bearing sand

water
pump

ladder

timber shaft

blue clay

spoil sacks are
hauled up

air pipe

sand coming through
roof forces gallery to
incline

shaft
chamber

fighting gallery

trolley on wooden rails

mine in
explosives
chamber

tamping

sump

Notes

• The shaft through wet sand is constructed of steel cylinders. Timber is used through the clay layer below.
• A six-hour shift usually comprised:
  • at the shaft house – NCO + 7 (4 hauling sacks and removing spoil, 2 on the windlass and 1 on the air pump)
  • at the shaft bottom – 2 men offloading trolleys, hitching sacks of spoil to the rope and hauling trolleys
  • at the tunnel face – 3 men (1 clay-kicker, 1 filling sacks, and 1 loading and pulling trolley
• Note the spaces between the sandbag tamping which will force the explosion upwards.

A tunneller descending a shaft wearing Proto breathing apparatus.

rope along wooden tramlines to the shaft chamber – a process called 'tramming'. After cutting a few feet, the kicker paused to erect four pieces of thick, broad timber already sawn to the right length to form a box to protect him against collapse, in which he worked until the proper timber supports could be erected. Lighting was by candles or torches, and in some cases electric light cable was installed. In good conditions, working in clay without interruptions, British 'moles' could excavate over 25–30 feet in a day.

In contrast, working at a face of hard chalk, progress of 2 or 3 feet a day was considered satisfactory. Cutting through chalk silently was almost impossible once the enemy lines were approached or where counter-mining was suspected. In the La Boiselle area this tunnelling was carried out with bayonets fitted with a special spliced handle; the men were barefoot and the floor of the gallery was carpeted with sandbags (alternatively, the tunnellers' boots were wrapped in sacking). The man at the face inserted the point of the bayonet in a crack in the chalk or alongside a flint, gave it a twist and dislodged a lump of chalk, which he caught in his other hand and laid on the floor; if he had to use both hands on the bayonet, his companion caught the chalk as it fell. All this had to be done in a tunnel about 4½ feet high and 2½ feet wide. Here the sacks of spoil were sometimes lined against the wall to be used later to 'tamp' the explosive charge in the mine chamber, although trolley removal was also used. In some tunnels spraying it with vinegar softened the surface of the chalk.

The mine chamber

Once the gallery was under the enemy position, the mine chamber was dug out and packed tight with explosive. Initially gunpowder was used, but it was soon found that ammonal, blastine and gun-cotton were more than three times as powerful.

The memorial to the 1st Australian Tunnelling Company. Between 9 November 1916 and 7 June 1917 approximately thirty men of the company lost their lives on Hill 60. The worst loss occurred on 25 April 1917, when a detonator exploded and brought down the underground headquarters, killing three men and suffocating seven others.

A Pioneer Battalion at Work

Ernest Parker joined up at the age of seventeen in 1914, was wounded twice and ended the war as a captain with the Military Cross. When serving with the pioneer battalion of the Durham Light Infantry near Arras, he worked under the orders of the New Zealand tunnellers. In his book *Into Battle, 1914–1918* he describes a typical experience of men being involved in the vital chore of hiding spoil:

Towards evening we daily journeyed to the front line and there, in shifts of eight hours, worked under the orders of a company of New Zealand sappers who were tunnelling under the German trenches. At the top of the sap we hauled a continuous stream of chalk-filled sandbags, carrying them outside and unloading the chalk some distance from the sap head. By special favour I was sometimes allowed to crawl down the deep shaft, where I could watch the tall New Zealanders cautiously working at the rock face. Now and then we listened in, and heard the Germans working in their counter-saps.

Naturally our Durham miners enjoyed this heavy work immensely . . . I found it hard going enough during the eight hours when, without a break, we hoisted the sandbags of chalk on to our shoulders and staggered under them to the dump, twenty yards down the trench. But when five o'clock in the morning came, and we filed into the communication trench, sleepily finding our way back to the point where we could get out into the open, we all felt happy.

Ammonal proved the most satisfactory, as not only was it powerful but a naked flame, or even firing a bullet into it, could not set it off. It was carried either in petrol cans, the mouths sealed with pitch, or in waterproofed rubberized bags and stacked up against the face of the mine chamber from floor to roof. When the chamber was full, gun-cotton primers and detonators were inserted into the charge and the leads were run back to the shaft and surface. This was followed by tamping. The force of an explosion follows the line of least resistance, which in this case would be back along the gallery, so it had to be blocked to force the explosion upwards. Tamping was done with sandbags stacked tightly from floor to roof in the gallery and was usually a long, arduous process involving lowering the bags down the shaft and dragging them (or using a trolley) to the mine chamber. It was preferable to construct a series of these blockages with gaps in between to ensure their maximum effectiveness. However, as a rule of thumb, the tamping to be broken through should be one and a half times the distance of solid ground above. Thus if it was 20 feet to the surface, 30 feet of tamping was needed – the assembly and placing of which could be a full day's work.

Firing was done electrically, usually from reserve trenches after the infantry had evacuated the front line. The resultant destruction and size of the crater depended on the amount of explosive, the depth of the mine and the type of soil over it – details of the effectiveness of the mines at Messines are described below (page 307).

Mining on both sides was at its height in June 1916, when the British blew 79 on their front, the Germans opposing them with 73. During that year the British blew a total of 466 mines and the Germans 385, but by the end of 1917 the numbers had dropped dramatically, with the former blow-

ing 48, the latter 39. Map 59 shows the comparative simplicity, compared to the complexity in later battles, of the British mining of Hill 60 in April 1915.

The Lochnagar Crater

This British mine was packed with two charges of 24,000 lb and 30,000 lb of ammonal and located about 500 yards south-east of the village of La Boiselle – see Map 42. It was scheduled to be blown, along with 16 other mines, at 7:28 a.m. on 1 July and destroy much of the defensive strongpoint called Schwaben Höhe, which was to be assaulted by the 101st Brigade, 34th Division (Tyneside Irish). Just north of the village another large mine, known as the Y Sap mine, was set under the German defences to be attacked by the 103rd Brigade. A young RFC officer watching the Lochnagar explosion from his aircraft later recalled:

The whole earth heaved and flashed, a tremendous and magnificent column rose up in the sky. There was an ear-splitting roar drowning all the guns, flinging the machine sideways in the repercussing [*sic*] air. The earth column rose higher and higher to almost 4,000 feet. There it hung, or seemed to hang, for a moment in the air, like the silhouette of some great Cyprus tree, then fell away in a widening cone of dust and debris.

This rain of debris injured some of the attackers waiting in no-man's-land. The crater measured 300 feet across and 90 feet deep.

The Lochnagar Crater is now privately owned and is visited by some 75,000 people annually. There are a number of memorials nearby and an annual remembrance service is held at the site every year to commemorate that fateful first day of the Somme offensive.

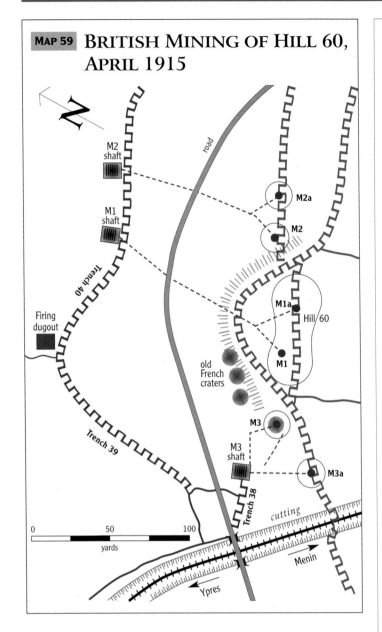

A mine crater at Beaumont-Hamel.

KEY

∿∿∿ main British trench line

⌐ British communication trench

------- British tunnels/galleries

∿∿∿ main German trench line

⌐ German communication trench

------- German counter-mine tunnel

⊙ mine location and crater

Notes for Map 59

• The earliest mining enterprise of any magnitude, in conjunction with infantry operations, was carried out against the commanding enemy positions on Hill 60, east of Ypres, in April 1915. Hill 60 was merely a large artificial mound created from the excavated earth from the nearby railway cutting. It got its name from the 60-metre contour line that encircled the summit on certain maps and it became well known as the scene of some of the fiercest fighting on the Western Front. Its importance lay in the fact that it commanded Ypres and overlooked a large area to the west.

• The French had lost the hill in December 1914 to the German 39th Division and in order to regain it had started mining and had blown several mines. In early 1915 the British 28th Division assumed control of the area. In April the 171st Tunnelling Company, under Capt E. V. C. Wellesley, RE, took over to complete the mining of the hill. Ventilation was difficult; the service blower proved too noisy, so was exchanged for a blacksmith's bellows fitted to a rubber hosepipe. Lighting was by candles until the mines were charged, when torches were used. Details of the shafts were as follows.

• **M1 and M2** Work started on 8 March and was complete by 10 April, giving an average daily progress of 9 feet, spoil being removed on trolleys. The shafts were 12 feet deep (very shallow in comparison with later mining) and 4 feet 6 inches in section. The forward galleries started at a height of 4 feet 6 inches with a width of 4 feet, but with branch lines reduced to 2 feet at the roof, 3 feet at floor level and only 3 feet 3 inches high. This was far too small and caused considerable difficulty when laying the mines. M1 and M1a were calculated to be about 20 feet below the enemy trenches, and M2 and M2a about 15 feet below. The charges in chambers M1 and M1a were 2,700 lb of gunpowder and in M2 and M2a 2,000 lb of gunpowder. Charging was done with 100-lb bags of powder, which proved very heavy and difficult to handle. Tamping consisted of three walls of sandbags each 10 feet thick with 10 feet of space between them, making 50 feet in total.

• **M3** This was an old French shaft only 3 feet by 2 feet 6 inches in section and in very poor condition, with several changes of direction and level, and full of corpses. The charges were laid directly in the galleries (no explosives chamber or tamping) and consisted of 500 lb of gun-cotton in both M3 and M3a, which were thought to be only 12 feet below the enemy position. Germans were heard working near M3 shaft on 2 April and again on the 16th, close to the junction of M3 and M3a – the reason for the lack of an explosives chamber and tamping.

• **Blowing** The mines were blown on 17 April at 7:00 p.m. (German prisoners stated they intended to blow Trench 38 two days later) and had considerable effect on the morale of the enemy, with the British infantry attacking with few losses. The craters formed by M1 and M1a joined to form a huge (for that period of the war) crater 180 feet long, 90 feet wide and 30 feet deep. The M3 crater was about 30 feet across.

• Although all troops were warned not to enter the mines until they were free of gas, two engineers who entered M3 shaft 36 hours after the explosion were asphyxiated, probably due to the large amount of gun-cotton used and the charge not being tamped.

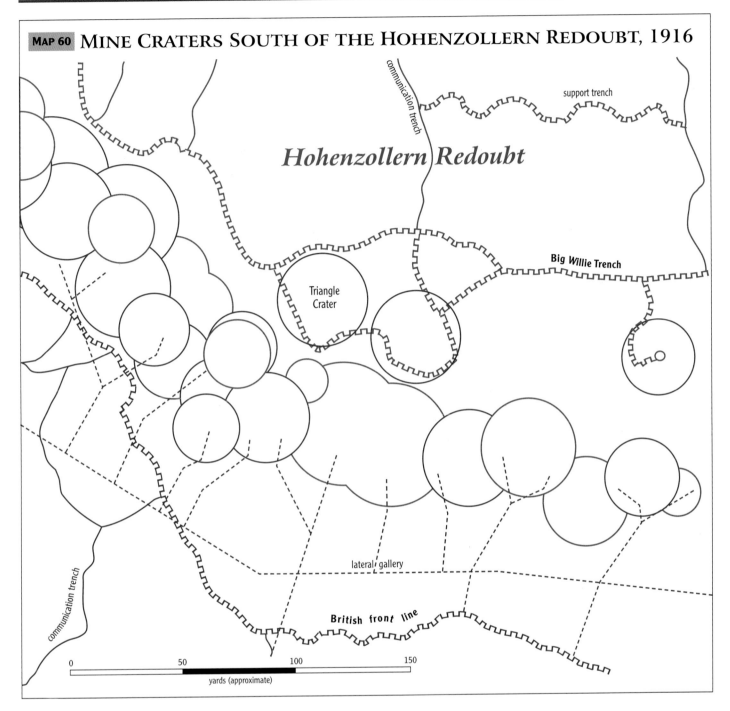

MAP 60 MINE CRATERS SOUTH OF THE HOHENZOLLERN REDOUBT, 1916

communication trench

support trench

Hohenzollern Redoubt

Big Willie Trench

Triangle
Crater

lateral gallery

communication trench

British front line

0   50   100   150

yards (approximate)

Notes for Map 60

This shows the intense level of mining in an area approx. 150 x 300 yards during a ten-month period in 1916. The mines were generally shallow (16–23 feet) owing to the water level, and the shafts were all wider towards the enemy. On the Fourth Army front during the week prior to its attack on 1 July, 51 mines were blown – 28 by the British and 23 by the Germans.

Hazards of the Underground War

Gas

One of the main dangers of tunnelling was the colourless, odourless carbon monoxide (CO) that was given off by explosions. It displaced oxygen in the blood, resulting in a slow but terrifying death as first giddiness, shortness of breath and finally loss of the use of limbs overcame the victim. Men working in a tunnel could initially be totally unaware of low concentrations of gas. A man working strenuously at the face, or hauling spoil, could start to be affected by a tiny concentration of 0.1 per cent after about forty minutes, while a level of 0.3 per cent could render him unconscious in ten minutes. With higher levels he would collapse within moments. Even if removed from the mine in a reasonable time, oxygen starvation could cause permanent damage to the nervous system. Gun-cotton explosions gave off the most CO, followed by gunpowder, with ammonal emitting the least. Underground explosions by *camouflets* (see page 303) were by far the most dangerous, as the surface was not broken and so all the gasses were trapped in the tunnel system. The experience of Captain Cecil Cropper, commanding 250 Tunnelling Company, is quoted in *The*

Tunnellers' War 1914–1918 and gives a clear picture of the deadly effect of CO gas. Cropper and his sergeant had gone down to assess the situation in a gallery after exploding 150 lb of gun-cotton to attack Germans working in a tunnel close by:

> The sergeant came with me and I told another man to stay at the bottom of the shaft and keep in touch with us. We went in slowly and cautiously and got 200 feet in when I decided we had gone far enough as it was gassy. I had no sooner started back when my head started to throb and I felt myself being overcome by gas. I said to the sergeant 'Come on man. We'll have to go for it. I'm nearly done.' He said 'So am I sir.' I crawled along that 200 feet feeling my sense giving way every second and expecting to lose all power in my limbs any moment. I yelled for help but received no reply and by this time the sergeant had collapsed altogether, and as I crawled on to the light I could see in the shaft only 50 or 60 feet away. I knew that unless I could reach the bottom of the shaft I would not make anybody hear my cries.
>
> Gasping for breath and fighting for my life I reached the shaft and yelled for the fool who should have been at his post but had left us in the lurch. I told him to come down and help me to get the sergeant out. He came down and about 50 feet in I found the sergeant. We dragged him out and got him to the surface and with artificial respiration brought him round, while I revived myself. All I can say is that it would have been a most peaceful death . . .

The requirement was early warning. This was supplied by taking caged canaries or mice down the mine, as in an atmosphere containing a percentage of CO that would begin to affect a man in half an hour, a canary or mouse would be affected in about two minutes. There was some disagreement over which gave the better warning. An affected mouse became restless, breathless, staggered and rolled over, but if trained was not so easily frightened as a canary. At least one officer always carried a mouse in his pocket when underground, holding it in his hand when checking a gallery. Tests with canaries revealed that in an atmosphere of 0.25 per cent CO the bird would show three phases of the effect of poisoning. First, it rubbed its beak against the cage or perch, shook its head and was often slightly sick. Second, it breathed with beak wide open and its legs were more widely spread to give balance. Finally, just before collapsing, the bird swayed backwards and forwards on its perch trying to keep balance, before making a wild

flight and falling to the bottom of the cage – evacuation should have been well under way by then. It was recommended that the perch should not be too small in diameter or the claws might become fixed round it and the bird would not fall. For the same reason its claws had to be kept trimmed.

An amusing incident involving a canary is given in the 1922 publication *Work of the Royal Engineers in the European War, 1914–1918: Military Mining*:

> An officer, issuing from a shaft on a front where the utmost secrecy was essential in the mining work, had the misfortune to let his canary escape. The bird flew to a bush in 'No Man's Land,' and heralded its freedom in cheerful song. The local sniper, who was at once summoned, only succeeded after several shots in making it move to another tree, nearer the German lines. The problem was finally solved by the arrival of a trench mortar officer, who grasped the situation at once, and at the first attempt bodily removed bird and tree.

Trapped below ground

Stories of miners getting trapped down a mine and dying of lack of air, flooding or being buried under a collapsed roof are not unusual in civilian mines, but when an enemy seeks to destroy tunnels or normal safety procedures are curtailed by the needs of war such events become a daily hazard. There is no better example of the horror of being trapped 100 feet below the ground in pitch blackness, facing a lingering, gasping death, than the experience of twelve men of Captain Cecil Cropper's 250 Tunnelling Company in June 1916.

The Petit Bois mine gallery under the German lines at Messines (see page 307) was exceptionally long at 1,070 feet. It had been started in late 1915 and progress of 100–150 feet a week was achieved through blue clay. However, intense pressure on the sides and roof from the expanding clay as it was exposed to air splintered the timber, and it was only with substantial reinforcement that work was able to continue, although the rate of progress slowed considerably. On 10 June the Germans blew two large mines, the northernmost directly above the British main gallery. Some 250 feet of the gallery was smashed, trapping the twelve men working at or near the face. Rescue parties were rushed to the site and began to work frantically to reach their entombed comrades. These men, stripped to the waist and bathed in sweat, had worked in relays day and night for six and a half days to bypass the wrecked part of the gallery when they finally broke through. None of the entrapped men was expected to be alive. Eleven bodies were found and it was assumed

that the twelfth was buried under the rubble. The rescuers withdrew to allow the air to clear, but when they returned they saw the incredible sight of the twelfth man, Sapper William Bedson, crawling slowly from the debris. His first words were 'For God's sake give me a drink! It's been a damned long shift!'

Bedson later related how the trapped men had assembled at the broken end of the gallery and started to take turns in a desperate but forlorn effort to dig their way out. Their exertions quickly used up energy and air, which soon became foul. Within three days all but one were dead. Bedson, who was an experienced coal miner, lay motionless at the face end, where the air was slightly less foul, and kept himself going by swilling out his mouth from his water bottle. At night he slept on a bed of sandbags. After being stretchered to the shaft on a trolley he was rested for two hours before being hauled out, only narrowly escaping death from shellfire as he was being carried along a communication trench.

Bedson lived a charmed life, as he had already been wounded in 1914 and again in Gallipoli. After a full recovery he volunteered to return to the tunnels, but the authorities considered it would be tempting fate too much so he was posted to a base depot. His eleven comrades are buried in a row in the Kemmel Chateau Cemetery.

Enemy action

Tunnellers worked in filthy, cramped and claustrophobic conditions in the knowledge that at any time flooding, roof collapse and entrapment could result in a horrible death – conditions that entitled them to a double rum ration. However, it was anticipation of the sudden explosion of an enemy mine nearby that provoked the most constant, nagging fear. Early knowledge of the enemy working close by was of paramount importance, while at the same time it was vital to try to ensure that they were unaware of your presence. Security and the ability to strike the German miners first depended on silence and the listening system – the noise of working was the great giveaway. This fear of enemy mines was felt equally by the infantryman in his trench or dugout on the surface who could be panicked by suspicious sounds. There were frequent instances of alarms being raised over what were subsequently revealed to be innocuous noises, such as digging trenches, wiring or chopping wood.

The critical importance of having trained listeners attached to every tunnelling company was soon appreciated and eventually a specialist mine-listening school was established for each army. After some experimentation, the most effective equipment was the geophone, small enough to be carried in a coat pocket, as it measured the tiniest vibrations and with it the user could 'hear the earthworms crawl and the ants walk'. The operator had two wooden sensors, connected to a doctor's stethoscope, which he moved around the walls, roof and floor of the tunnel until a sound registered equally in both ears. From this a compass bearing was taken on the noise. The distance sound travelled depended on the type of soil or rock through which the tunnel passed – much further through hard chalk than clay, and further through clay than sandy soil. With a geophone through chalk, picking could be heard 250–300 feet away; through clay 50–70 feet; and through sand only 30–40 feet. Talking was audible at 30 feet, 4–6 feet and 3–5 feet respectively. For examples of noises heard by a listening post over a period of time, see the box below. Listening reports with bearings were sent immediately to the senior trench officer and plotted on his map, then a plan of the enemy's workings compiled.

For the men underground, hearing a suspicious noise or the German language being used perhaps only 30 feet away was a traumatic experience. Listeners were known to panic, pleading for early relief and saying they couldn't stand the strain; in some cases, their nerve went completely. However, a good, experienced listener would record and interpret the sounds with considerable accuracy. The noise of a windlass making frequent lifts indicated a shaft was still being sunk, whereas if the pauses between the noises were long then it was likely the gallery was being excavated. After perhaps weeks of listening and charting a gallery's progress, it was silence that was dreaded – the mine was charged, but when would it blow?

Before this stage was reached, on the principle that offensive mining was the best defence, counter-mining was the frequent tactic. The method used to attack an enemy gallery was called *camouflet* (making an explosion underground without rupturing the surface) fighting, the aim being, if possible, to place a mine beneath the enemy. One method was to stack the charge at the face of the gallery or in a listening post and tamp it in the usual way. Alternatively, if a small explosion was required, then a torpedo-shaped mine could be placed by boring a hole with an earth auger towards the enemy gallery. Wiring leads were run back to the exploder, the nearby galleries blocked, all miners withdrawn and the infantry above ground warned. At least one torpedo was kept primed and ready for immediate use at the rear of the workings. The diagram on page 306 shows how *camouflet* fighting could be used offensively.

By the end of 1916 the scale of mine warfare had expanded to such an extent that there were insufficient trained listeners to man all the posts, so central listening stations were established. They worked electronically, like a telephone exchange, and could distinguish the signals from up to thirty-six remote sensors.

With the spread of the complex maze of underground galleries from both sides under no-man's-land, there were frequent occasions when miners broke through into an enemy gallery. This could result in the most vicious and frightening face-to-face combat, often in the dark – hand-to-hand fighting at its most brutal. The weapons carried by miners were revolvers, automatic pistols, sawn-off .303 rifles (the Canadians favoured these), knives, bayonets, knuckle-dusters, sharpened spades and clubs. The following three descriptions, quoted in *Beneath Flanders Fields* by Barton, Doyle and Vandewalle, illustrate these sudden encounters.

First, Captain Basil Sawers, 17 Tunnelling Company:

> Underground fights always followed the same pattern. The tunnels were boarded and bullets didn't ricochet off the wood. So you got two men facing each other and firing. When one man emptied his gun, he dropped down and the man behind him stepped over him and took over. You carried little automatics which were meant to shoot where your finger pointed. If the Germans broke into us we had to fight them back with guns and then blow. Eventually one side or the

Listening to German Tunnellers

At the end of May 1916 a British listening post in a shallow gallery was able to record details of the German tunnellers' activities at their shaft head right up to the blowing of a British mine. The following, taken from the 1922 publication *Work of the Royal Engineers in the European War 1914–1918: Military Mining*, is an extract of what was overheard:

Date/time	Listening results	Remarks
May 31st 2 p.m.	Listening with Geophone. Loud laughter and talking – then windlass working, and picking. Interpreter sent for.	German shift comes on enemy suspects nothing.
7 p.m.	We fix 2-in pipe against lagging board and 4 ft. of tamping put in.	
8.5 p.m.	Four or five men sit down opposite pipe. Loud laughter and talking for 30 mins. Stopped by N.C.O. and work begins.	Shaft is about 36 ft. deep – a total of 50 ft.–60 ft. below ground level.
11 p.m.	Our interpreter arrives. Pick work and winch – 18 turns up and down.	
1st June 12.5 p.m.	Conversation in German – 'Who is there? Is it the relief?' In English – 'Who is there?'	
12.50 a.m. to 1.5 a.m.	Work with pick. 15 mins of winch.	
1.15 a.m.	Winch at work.	
1.45 a.m.	ditto	
2.10 a.m.	ditto	
2.20 a.m.	Very loud knock.	Timber falling down shaft.
2.50 a.m.	Loud sounds as if pipe was being touched	Not understood.
3 a.m.	Voices and winch starts.	
3.25 a.m. to 4 a.m.	Conversation in German. 'That will soon be deep enough, will it not?' 'Yes – I do not know. I will ask the Serjeant-Major.' [Further conversations reported and then]	
9 p.m.	German officer comes down shaft.	Enemy is laying and tamping charges.
10 p.m.	German conversation – 'Quite right, but it is too heavy.' 'Very well you can have some more people.'	
11.15 p.m.	Officer comes down and says that men must work more quickly and finish the job. The Germans are unusually quiet tonight.	

Offensive Mining similar to that at the Hohenzollern Redoubt, early 1916 (not to scale)

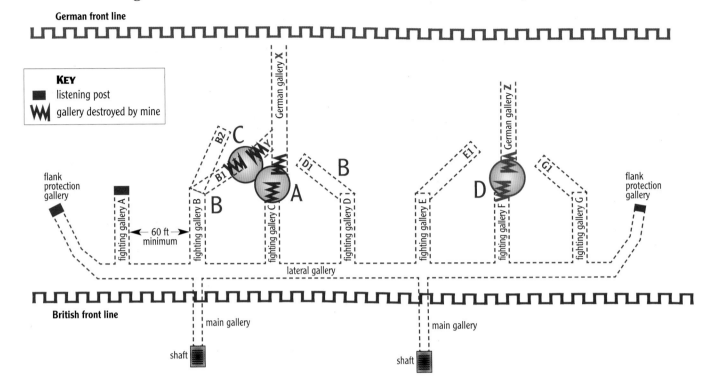

Notes

- The shafts are located well back behind the front trench in a dugout; the main galleries are driven from these and connected by a lateral gallery to give ventilation and safety. From the lateral galleries, the fighting galleries are driven forward.
- The lateral gallery is as far forward as possible to avoid unnecessary length to the fighting galleries, but sufficiently far back to secure it from mine explosions from enemy or own fighting galleries.
- The best method of defence in mining operations was to take the offensive. This was recognized by both sides.
- This policy is illustrated here by the British continuing to mine offensively despite losing two galleries.

A Denotes the British gallery **C** blown on approach of hostile Germans working in gallery **X**.

B Once the gallery is clear of gas, work starts on British fighting galleries **B** and **D**, driving them forward to positions **B1** and **D1**.

C On recovering their gallery as far as possible, the Germans drive gallery **Y**, which is blown again from **B1**. Gallery **B** is advanced again to **B2**.

D Similarly, on the enemy blowing a mine in their gallery **Z**, which destroys gallery **F**, galleries **E** and **G** are driven forward to **E1** and **G1** respectively.

Thus advantage is taken of blows on either side to force the enemy back.

---

other had to blow – there was no question of capturing [an enemy gallery].

If we broke into them, the whole thing was organized. We had our charges ready. We did it once, but never again. When you are all on the same level, you can't get a proper seal to keep the air from going through. Result is that gas might blow back on you.

Lieutenant John Westacott, 2 Canadian Tunnelling Company:

Sometimes a fight would take place in a tunnel – 4 feet x 3 feet – and in the dark you didn't know who you were fighting. The only thing was to put your hand over quick to feel if the man had any epaulettes; the Germans used to have epaulettes on the shoulder and we could tell that way. That knuckle knife was very good. One of our officers invented that. It was a specially made knife with a blade about five inches long which was

fitted to a brass frame over our hand and strapped to our wrist, so when our fist was closed the knife was at a right angle to our arm. It was silent in action – very handy, especially for raiding galleries.

Lieutenant Westacott again:

We waited until the Germans had gone a few yards past the fork so as to get enough room to get up behind them, then we crept in our stockinged feet silently up behind the enemy in single file. Ever so quietly we gained on them and in a few seconds I was only about four yards behind the last man, the officer, and then all of a sudden they saw the torches of my other two men coming towards them. Thinking they were their own men from the face they shouted in German, and they all stopped. Then, as no reply came they jabbered a bit amongst themselves for a second or two, then the NCO in front fired a shot down the tunnel. Back

came a shot from my boys right on the second. So now, being only a few yards behind the enemy I put on my torch and so did my men behind me. The man in front of me, who was the officer, turned round half facing me, he had his revolver pointed at me in a second; but he sort of hesitated, no doubt struck dumb by the grotesque sight of a hooded body coming at him. It must have been an awful sight for them to see us in a Proto set [breathing equipment; see opposite] in that dim semi-darkness. I shot him before he could recover from his shock. At the same time keeping my body in a down to the floor level to allow my sergeant in a crouching position to shoot over me, and the others behind to shoot over us . . .

The German party never had a chance, their NCO was shot in the leg and my sergeant kicked his revolver out of his hand, but he rolled over, grabbed his gun again and was starting shooting, so the sergeant shot him again. The fighting did not last more than two or three minutes, then one of the Germans shouted 'Kamerad' . . . The casualties were Germans: one officer, one NCO, two men dead; three captured alive, one very badly wounded; Canadians: three men wounded, one badly.

Rescue Operations

By the autumn of 1915 the extensive mining, the increased numbers of personnel involved, along with the frequency of mine and *camouflet* blows, meant that casualties from gas poisoning had assumed worrying proportions. In six weeks one company had sixteen killed, forty-eight sent to hospital and eighty-six minor cases treated in the unit. These represented a very serious loss, mainly of skilled miners who were hard to replace. In September 1915 Lieutenant Colonel D. Dale Logan, RAMC, was attached to the staff of the engineer-in-chief to organize a system of rescue work and protection against gas in mining. Extensive investigations were carried out into the type of gas emitted by a blow and its effect on exposed personnel. It was conclusively confirmed that carbon monoxide was the odourless killer. The way in which CO could contaminate the galleries is shown in the diagram overleaf.

By the summer of 1915 mine rescue schools had been set up both to train company rescue men and to test best practices and equipment. After considerable investigation and trials, two types of equipment proved the most satisfactory. The most commonly used was the Proto breathing apparatus, which consisted of two cylinders containing 280 litres of oxygen under pressure that were slung on the wearer's back. A reducing valve could adjust the flow of oxygen from 1.5 to 3 litres a minute along a tube to a breathing-bag worn on the chest. This equipment was bulky and heavy, but the oxygen lasted up to two hours. The alternative was the Salvus equipment, which operated on the same principle as the Proto but was lighter and less cumbersome, although its oxygen lasted only an hour. Rescue teams wearing this equipment would also carry Novita oxygen reviving apparatus, a mine stretcher on which a man could be secured, dragged along a gallery and hoisted up a shaft, as well as a canary or mouse. If dealing with a fire, an asbestos hood and apron were worn and, with smoke causing loss of visibility and sense of direction, the rescuers were often linked together by a white rope.

Men volunteering for mine rescue had to undergo stiff selection tests both before and during training. Coolness of nerve, the ability to confront sudden dangers, such as fire, a falling roof, failure of equipment or another member of the team being injured were

essential. Of equal importance was meticulous attention to detail, such as the correct adjustment of equipment or in the procedures on entry to and examination of a mine. All men were subjected to a rigorous medical and those with colds, bronchitis, low blood pressure or any heart problems were rejected.

By early 1916 the tunnelling company rescue organization had been properly established. Overall responsibility rested with the company commander but with direct control vested in the company Proto officer, who was assisted by a specially trained NCO instructor. There was also a special medical service for tunnelling companies, staffed by medical officers who had previous experience with civilian mining operations and thus knowledge of miners' ailments and of gas poisoning in mines. Mine rescue stations were established, usually in a dugout within a maximum of 200 yards from an entry shaft. At these stations were the rescue personnel and all the equipment was kept and maintained here. Where convenient, one station served a group of mines. In September 1917, on the First Army front of about 20 miles there were eight tunnelling companies and 46 rescue stations, or almost six for every company.

In frightening and dangerous circumstances, compliance with standing orders and a rapid response by the rescue teams saved many lives. In one example, eight men were underground at the time of an enemy blow. Immediately they made their way out after extinguishing lights. One reported to the NCO in charge that the man working with him at the face was partly buried in debris, and in attempting to rescue him he felt himself being overcome by gas and thought it best to come back for help. The NCO ordered all men to the surface – although the exertion of making his way out rendered the man who had been gassed unconscious.

On hearing the explosion the Proto officer had assembled the rescue team at the head of the shaft within two minutes of the men emerging. They descended and found the trapped man, whom they freed and dragged to the foot of the incline, where they placed him on a trolley and sent him to the surface. Unfortunately, despite artificial respiration and the administration of oxygen, he died.

Despite this example of failure, it was considered vital that attempts to resuscitate victims of gas poisoning were kept up for long periods. An Australian mine rescue team rushed to a shaft that had been destroyed by a German raiding party using a large mobile charge that trapped thirty-six infantrymen in the tunnel. They succeeded in rescuing and resuscitating eleven men, all of whom were unconscious. Two appeared completely lifeless, but dogged perseverance for ten hours – an incredible time – eventually revived them.

Proto mine-rescue apparatus.

Effect of Camouflet Gas on Ventilation in Galleries (not to scale)

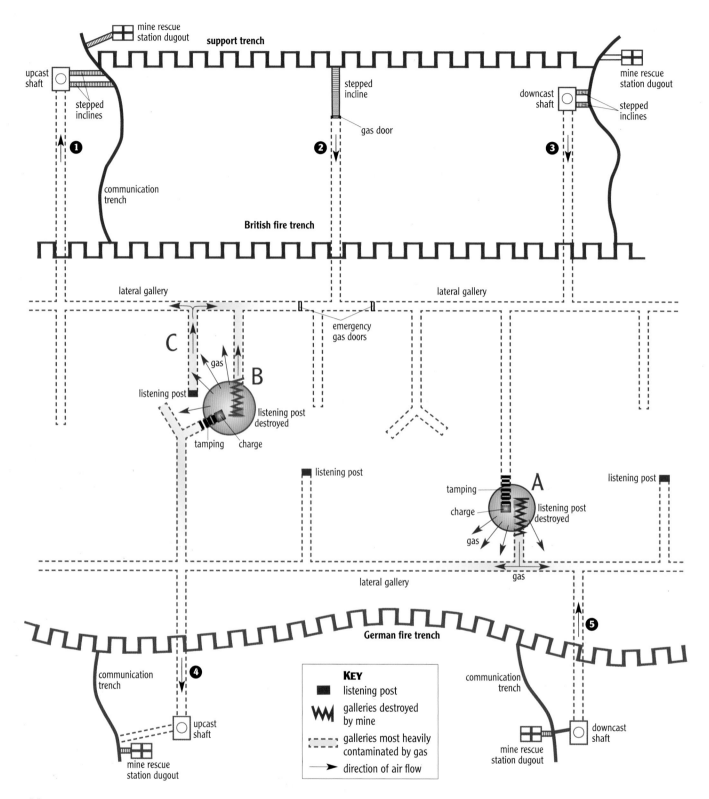

Notes

- This diagram shows a more detailed layout of a possible system of British and German listening posts and the uses of *camouflets* by both sides.
- The British *camouflet* at **A** shows the likely esape of carbon monoxide gas into the listening-post gallery and the gas seeping through the soil into the German lateral gallery.
- The German *camouflet* at **B** is likely to force gas ito two British listening-post galleries and possibly into the left branch of the German 'Y' gallery.

- The arrows ❶, ❷, ❸, ❹ and ❺ indicate the normal vertilation flow of air through the galleries.
- Note the British have installed three gas doors to block galleries.
- Note that the British gallery at **C** has been driven too close to **B**, so the German *camouflets* has forced gas through it.
- On hearing the explosions, both British and German mine rescue teams would be deployed, possibly from all four stations.

Subways

Tunnelling companies were not only responsible for mining operations but also for the construction of important dugouts and subways. The former were often elaborate, multipurpose affairs to house brigade or artillery headquarters as well as communication centres, stores and dressing stations. They all included offices, kitchens, messes, accommodation for officers and other ranks, and signal centres. Some were specifically designed to accommodate a battalion of 600 men, other smaller ones perhaps a battalion headquarters or machine-gun post. They were invariably dug below 20 feet, with the larger ones lit by electric light powered by generators. A typical layout of a brigade headquarters is shown in the diagram below. A considerable degree of comfort could be achieved, given the time and effort, with the deep German bunkers taking pride of place in this respect.

Subways, or large shelters to protect troops forming up to attack, were initially seen as a means of getting men forward to the front line from reserve trenches without exposing them to shellfire. Later developments saw them used tactically, with sealed exits to conceal units until zero hour, when the exits would be blown and the troops would pour forth to make their attack.

In the Canadian assault on Vimy Ridge in April 1917 (see Map 28, page 103) the construction of infantry subways played a crucial part in the attack plan. The task of constructing the twelve subways was given to the British 170, 173, 251, 253, 255 and the Australian 3 Tunnelling Companies. Although impeded initially by wet weather, rapid progress was made afterwards at an average rate of 12–15 feet a day. The subways were 6 feet high and 3½ feet wide – enough space for a man in full equipment to walk along them – with 'lay-bys' provided at intervals to allow men to pass. The tunnels incorporated chambers for headquarters, trench-mortar and machine-gun emplacements, ammunition and ration stores, kitchens and dressing stations, as well as providing ample accommodation for infantry units. Tramlines for a light railway were built in some subways, and all were lit by electric light (provided by the famous Australian Electrical and Mechanical Mining and Boring Company); and if connected to the mining system, gas doors were provided. It became one vast maze requiring signboards to indicate locations and hundreds of small boreholes to the surface for ventilation. The twelve subways totalled almost 11,000 yards of tunnelling and varied in length from the Grange subway, a mile long, to the small Gobron of 290 yards.

Underground caves and passages have been in use in France for hundreds of years, providing refuge for the populace in times of war. Some were so extensive that cattle and fodder were kept in them for long periods, with water supplied from wells dug in the floor. Tunnellers were tasked with developing the numerous caves on the south-eastern outskirts of Arras as part of the British Arras offensive, in conjunction with the Canadians' attack on Vimy Ridge, in early April 1917. In all some twenty-five caves were linked up and transformed into underground barracks, complete with electric light, a ventilating plant, running water, headquarters, dressing stations, stores and offices. Tunnels were driven back from the caves and incorporated part of the Arras sewer system, while tramway tracks facilitated the forward movement of ammunition and supplies. In all some 7 miles of tunnels and subways were constructed in four months by the New Zealand Tunnelling Company, assisted by two sections from 184 Company. On completion they provided safe, dry and warm accommodation for 11,400 troops (see Map 61).

Messines, 7 June 1917

The moment of zero hour on that morning at the Messines Ridge when nearly 900,000 lb of explosive erupted has been described at the start of this section. Field Marshal Haig, his staff – including Brigadier General R. N. Harvey, the inspector of mines – watched from a dugout at Kemmel. Harvey later described what he saw:

> A violent earth tremor, then a gorgeous sheet of flame from Spanbroekmolen, and at the same moment every gun opened fire. At short intervals of seconds the mines continued to explode; period which elapsed between the first and last mine, about 30 seconds [the official time was 19 seconds – those at Trenches 122 and 127 were 7 seconds early] . . . The majority of the mines showed up well with a fine flame. Others merely showed a red glow; this may have been due to their being blotted out by the smoke of the bombardment. The earth shake was remarkable, and was felt as far as Cassel.

Prime Minister Lloyd George is supposed to have felt the tremor in 10 Downing Street, 130 miles away.

The mining attack on the Wytschaete–Messines Ridge was the tunnellers' most spectacular achievement of the war and the largest military mining operation in history. Norton Griffiths originated the idea in May 1915 and a start was made against Hill 60 (see Map 59). The gallery under this hill, known as the Berlin Tunnel, experienced serious problems with flooding, requiring weeks of pumping to make it usable again. Various deep galleries were begun in 1916 and there were interruptions when the Germans blew several mines, including the one at Petit Bois that caused considerable

Basic Layout of Standard Brigade HQ Bunker

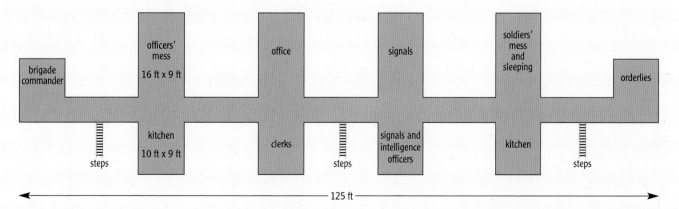

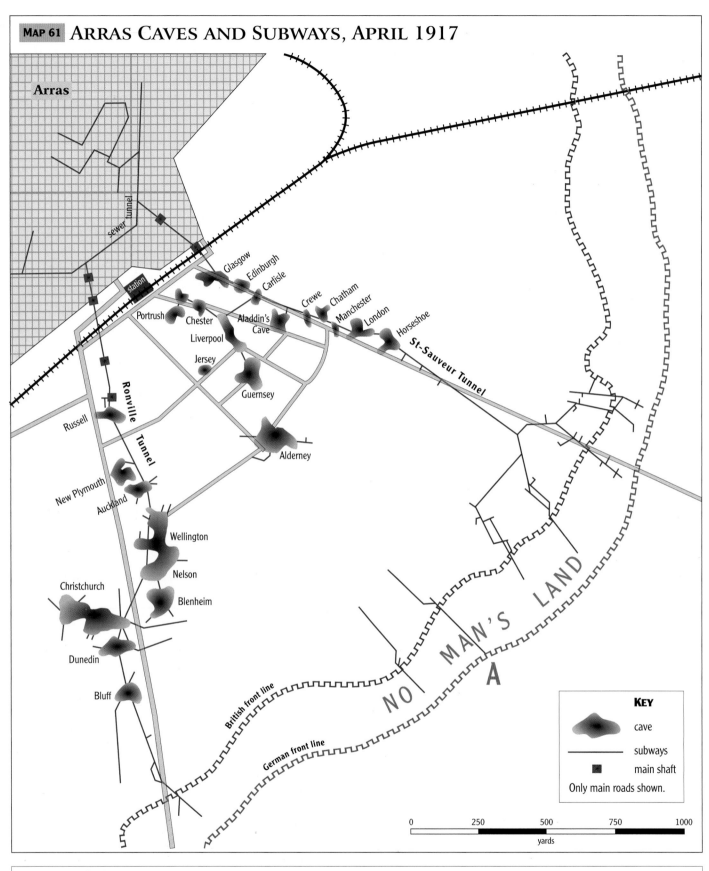

MAP 61 ARRAS CAVES AND SUBWAYS, APRIL 1917

Arras

sewer tunnel

station

Glasgow
Edinburgh
Carlisle
Crewe
Chatham
Manchester
London
Horseshoe

Portrush
Chester
Aladdin's
Cave
Liverpool
Jersey
Guernsey

St-Sauveur Tunnel

Russell

Ronville Tunnel

New Plymouth
Auckland

Alderney

Wellington

Nelson

Christchurch
Blenheim

Dunedin

Bluff

British front line

German front line

NO MAN'S LAND

A

KEY

cave

subways

main shaft

Only main roads shown.

| 0 | 250 | 500 | 750 | 1000 |

yards

Notes for Map 61

The two main subways were the St-Sauveur and Ronville Tunnels. The former linked nine of the smaller caves with accommodation for 2,000 men, while the latter linked the nine mostly large caves accommodating over 9,400, which were:

Russell	50	Blenheim	750
New Plymouth	500	Christchurch	4,075
Auckland	300	Dunedin	590
Wellington	1,500	Bluff	460
Nelson	1,200		

Note how the attackers could debouch from the subways in no-man's-land very close to the German trenches and in one case actually into them (**A**).

MAP 62 — THE MESSINES MINES, 7 JUNE 1917

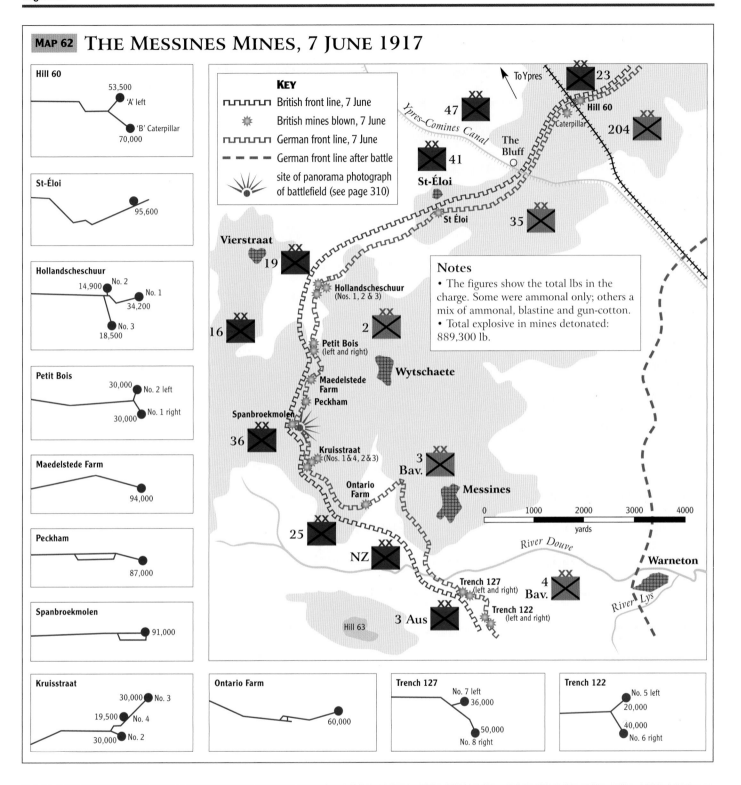

Hill 60
53,500 'A' left
70,000 'B' Caterpillar

St-Éloi
95,600

Hollandscheschuur
14,900 No. 2
34,200 No. 1
18,500 No. 3

Petit Bois
30,000 No. 2 left
30,000 No. 1 right

Maedelstede Farm
94,000

Peckham
87,000

Spanbroekmolen
91,000

Kruisstraat
30,000 No. 3
19,500 No. 4
30,000 No. 2

Ontario Farm
60,000

Trench 127
No. 7 left 36,000
50,000 No. 8 right

Trench 122
No. 5 left 20,000
40,000 No. 6 right

KEY
British front line, 7 June
British mines blown, 7 June
German front line, 7 June
German front line after battle
site of panorama photograph of battlefield (see page 310)

Notes
- The figures show the total lbs in the charge. Some were ammonal only; others a mix of ammonal, blastine and gun-cotton.
- Total explosive in mines detonated: 889,300 lb.

To Ypres
Ypres–Comines Canal
The Bluff
23
47
Hill 60
Caterpillar
204
41
St-Éloi
St Éloi
35
Vierstraat
19
Hollandscheschuur (Nos. 1, 2 & 3)
16
2
Petit Bois (left and right)
Wytschaete
Maedelstede Farm
Peckham
Spanbroekmolen
36
Kruisstraat (Nos. 1 & 4, 2 & 3)
3 Bav.
Ontario Farm
Messines
25
NZ
River Douve
Warneton
Trench 127 (left and right)
4 Bav.
Trench 122 (left and right)
River Lys
Hill 63
3 Aus

0 1000 2000 3000 4000
yards

Respirator Problems

Wearing, working or fighting in respirators was not pleasant and reduced a soldier's effectiveness very quickly – it is much the same today. Below is a quote from the despatch of a German journalist.

A salvo of gas shells whistles over [they made a distinctive noise and were thus easily recognizable], bursting 100 metres away with a weak explosion. Gas! In a trice the masks are on and nosebags filled with moist hay are drawn over the horses' mouths and nostrils. We wait until a few more salvoes arrive and then continue our route through the poisonous cloud. The eye-pieces become misty and breathing becomes difficult – we cannot see our way. And then gas! The mask makes freedom of movement impossible with its horrible pressure on the face and the eye-pieces besmirched with mud and gore. Rifles full of water. The ground on which one seeks a foothold, a sliding morass. Impossible to eat! And day and night the same!

As this makes clear, forcing troops to don respirators even if the threat of gas was false severely handicapped their physical ability – it made shooting a particularly difficult challenge.

Wytschaete

The British assault on the central sector of Messines Ridge, 7 June 1917. The ridge between the fortified villages of Wytschaete and Messines was some 6 miles in length and up to 250 feet high, enabling the German defenders to overlook the British lines. It was here that 19 mines were blown within 30 seconds at 3:10 a.m. and, in the wake of this and the massive artillery bombardment, nine British and dominion divisions attacked. By mid-afternoon the ridge was taken. German losses exceeded 25,000 and Allied losses 17,000. This photograph was taken from the southern edge of the Spanbroekmolen crater, or Pool of Peace – see Map 62 and photograph, page 259.

16th Irish Division

36th Ulster Division

damage and entombed twelve men (see page 302). Not only was the Messines operation on a scale never before attempted, but it was also the most protracted – not so much because of the time taken to drive the numerous galleries but because of the inordinate amount of time between completing fifteen of the mines and firing them. The Trench 127 mine was charged by 20 April 1916, almost fourteen months before it was blown, and fourteen others were blown during that year. The second largest of them all, however – the Spanbroekmolen with 91,000 lb of ammonal – only just made it by 6 June 1917.

The series of horrendous explosions, hurling earth, rocks and bodies high into the air, had a devastating effect on the German survivors. The number of German losses is impossible to calculate, although some 700 are thought to have died in the Hill 60 and another 400 in the St-Éloi

explosions, while some 7,000 demoralized prisoners were taken. General Ludendorff recorded in his memoirs:

> We should have succeeded in retaining the position but for the exceptionally powerful mines used by the British, which paved the way for their attack . . . The result of these successful mining operations was that the enemy broke through on June 7th.
>
> The heights of Wytschaete and Messines had been the site of active mine warfare in the early days of the war. For a long time past, however, both sides had ceased to use such tactics; all had been quiet, and no sound of underground work on the part of the enemy could be heard at our listening posts. The mines must therefore have been in position long before. The effect of the explosions on morale was simply staggering . . .

Tunnellers mid-1917 to November 1918

After Messines the work of tunnelling companies became more general. Preparations for the Fifth Army's offensive in July 1917 (Ypres) involved a large amount of dugout and subway construction during which the companies suffered severely from shellfire. One company worked with the Tank Corps, building tank crossings over canals, streams and ditches, and another had sections attached to the four corps of the Fifth Army, working with the Army Tramway Company laying and maintaining tramways to various battery positions.

The year 1918 saw the advent of more mobile warfare, first with the German attacks in March, followed by the Allied offensive and advance that ended the war. During the former the tunnelling companies were heavily committed to demolition of bridges, supply

The Struggle for Vauquois

In 1914 the tiny hamlet of Vauquois, with its small church and village school, had a population of 168 souls and sat atop the Butte de Vauquois some 900 feet above sea level. It was a picturesque rural French village some 14 miles west of Verdun and 3 miles east of the Argonne Forest (see Map 32). By 1918 it had ceased to exist. It was the scene of some of the most intense mining operations of the war, resulting in its total destruction (it is the only place where you can find surviving evidence of extreme mine warfare). Today the hill's summit is a tangle of craters and tunnel entrances (the French named their tunnels after stations on the Paris Métro), watched over by the Memorial to the Combatants and Dead of Vauquois – a French soldier holding a rifle in one hand and a grenade in the other, looking east towards Verdun. A new village is now situated below the summit, while under the hill much of the underground tangle of tunnels, barracks, command posts and storage depots has been restored.

Because the hill offered such a splendid vantage point, the struggle for its possession was bitter and bloody. The first to arrive were the Germans who took the hill in September 1914 and fortified it. From October to March 1915 the French 10th Division attempted to retake it with a series of assaults, during one of which they used a flamethrower with unfortunate results, as a strong wind blew the flame back on to their own infantry; this was the first and only time

the French used a flamethrower. Eventually the French secured the south side of the hill, while the Germans clung to the northern slopes. This was to be the situation for the next three years, with each side striving to dig deeper and exploding ever larger mines as they tunnelled towards each other. In May 1916 the Germans blew the largest mine used at Vauquois – a 3,750-lb detonation that killed 108 Frenchmen. The mining was combined with infantry bayonet attacks, but no real progress was made by either side.

The loamy sandstone was not too difficult to dig into and by the end of hostilities the French and German tunnels had a combined length of over 10 miles. By this time the Germans had exploded 199 mines, the French 320 and the village had disappeared. The Germans planned to blow away the entire hill with three supermines, the shafts of which went to a depth of over 300 feet; however, only two shafts were completed and neither was ever used. The German pioneers finally withdrew back to Varennes in mid-April 1918, leaving some 8,000 French and Germans buried somewhere on or under the hill.

When the US 35th Division arrived in September 1918 at the start of their Meuse–Argonne offensive, the village had gone and in its place was a lunar landscape of overlapping craters, shattered trenches, twisted wire and the labyrinth of tunnels.

dumps, pumping stations, wells, caves and road-cratering. Eighty-eight demolitions were blown and eighty-seven handed over ready for demolition to other units. Several tunnelling companies were tasked to work on rear-zone defences, supervision of labour, drainage, dugouts, water-supply systems and rear communications such as bridges, roads and causeways. For the last three months of the war the role of the tunnelling companies changed dramatically to bridge construction and removal or clearance of enemy mines, demolition charges or booby traps. Throughout the area of operations of the BEF, these companies constructed 149 heavy and 38 light bridges, removed 6,714 land mines, 536 booby traps, 2,718 gas shells and 1,431 British demolitions. The total weight of enemy explosives removed was a staggering 2,641,660 lb.

Immediately after the Armistice the tunnelling companies were rapidly disbanded to release men needed for essential home industries. Haig penned the following message of appreciation – the last of a number of such notes he wrote extolling their efforts:

A large number of men are now being withdrawn from Tunnelling Companies for urgent work at home.

Before they leave the country I wish to convey to the Controllers of Mines and to all ranks of the Tunnelling Companies, both Imperial and Overseas, my very keen appreciation of the fine work that has been done by the Tunnelling Companies throughout the last four years.

At their own special work, Mine Warfare, they have demonstrated their complete superiority over the Germans, and whether in the patient defensive mining, the magnificent success at Messines, or in the preparation for the offensive on the Somme, Arras and Ypres, they have shown the highest qualities both as Military Engineers and fighting troops.

Their work in the very dangerous task of removing enemy traps and delay-action charges, on subways, dugouts, bridging, roads and the variety of other services on which they have been engaged, has been on a level with their work on the mines.

They have earned the thanks of the whole Army for their contributions to the defeat of the enemy. Their fighting spirit and technical efficiency has enhanced the reputation of the whole Corps of Royal Engineers, and of the Engineers of the Overseas Forces.

I should like to include in the appreciation the work done by the Army Mine Schools and by the Australian Electrical and Mechanical Mining and Boring Company.

In June 2010 a memorial to the tunnellers, paid for from voluntary donations, was unveiled near Givenchy, close to the site where Sapper Hackett won his Victoria Cross (see box, page 296).

The Special Brigade (gas, smoke and flamethrowers)

The first to use gas on the Western Front were the French, who fired tear gas (Xylyl bromide) grenades in August 1914. The quantities delivered were small, as were the effects on the Germans, who in most instances did not even notice the gas. The Germans followed by using howitzer shells containing tear gas in their bombardment at Bolimov, west of Warsaw, on the Eastern Front – it was a failure, as the liquid gas failed to vaporize in the freezing temperature. Then in October the Germans fired shells containing an irritant gas against the British at Neuve Chapelle, but with little noticeable effect.

No gas units existed in the British Army in 1914; it had never been contemplated as a weapon of war as it was prohibited under the Hague Treaty of 1899. However, things quickly changed after the Germans used chemical warfare by unleashing chlorine gas (tear gas did not contravene the Hague Treaty) against French troops at Ypres on 22 April 1915. Several more gas attacks occurred and the Allies' initial outrage was quickly followed by makeshift defensive measures, the most primitive being cotton wadding soaked

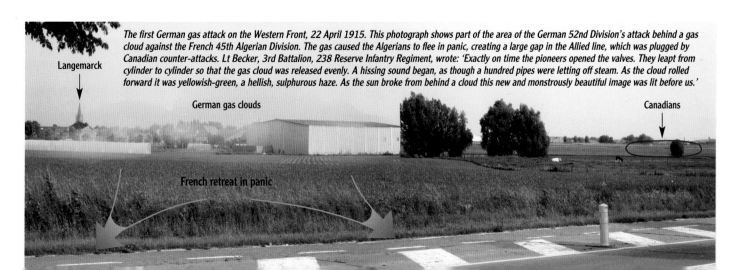

The first German gas attack on the Western Front, 22 April 1915. This photograph shows part of the area of the German 52nd Division's attack behind a gas cloud against the French 45th Algerian Division. The gas caused the Algerians to flee in panic, creating a large gap in the Allied line, which was plugged by Canadian counter-attacks. Lt Becker, 3rd Battalion, 238 Reserve Infantry Regiment, wrote: 'Exactly on time the pioneers opened the valves. They leapt from cylinder to cylinder so that the gas cloud was released evenly. A hissing sound began, as though a hundred pipes were letting off steam. As the cloud rolled forward it was yellowish-green, a hellish, sulphurous haze. As the sun broke from behind a cloud this new and monstrously beautiful image was lit before us.'

Following the Germans' first use of gas and the confused retreat of the French, the 10th Canadians (2nd Canadian Brigade) and the kilted 16th (Canadian Scottish, 3rd Canadian Brigade) were ordered to retake this wood. The 1,500 men advanced about 500 yards before being caught by heavy machine-gun and rifle fire from a trench south of the wood. Despite many casualties, the Canadians stormed forwards at the run, capturing the trench with bayonets and rifle butts. The wood was taken and four captured British guns retaken. However, strong German positions to its east and west compelled the Canadians to withdraw to the trench south of the wood.

Oblong Farm

Area of Kitchener's Wood

Juliet Farm

in bicarbonate of soda or urine tied over the mouth and nose. Local women were employed to make up rudimentary pads with string ties, and officers were sent to Paris to buy more muslin and gauze. The first basic respirators, issued initially in batches of sixteen to infantry machine-gunners, were grey flannel bags with talc eyepieces. These were followed by a more extensive distribution of the P (Phenate) gas helmet with glass eyepieces in November 1915. However, it did not give adequate protection against the phosgene gas then being used and was replaced by the PH (Phenate-Hexamine) helmet in January 1916, which was made of thicker material impregnated with various chemicals, including caustic soda and sodium phenate. A further improved box respirator that gave reasonable protection against the different gases in use was found too bulky and heavy for issue to the infantry. However, a smaller, lighter version was quickly designed and a million were ordered. These began to be issued in August 1916, although even this did not protect the body from the effects of mustard gas, introduced by the Germans in 1917.

In May 1915 Lord Kitchener authorized a British response, and experiments and trials in the use of discharging compressed chlorine gas clouds from cylinders (the method used by the Germans) were instituted. Four RE special companies, each consisting of ten sections under an officer and under the overall supervision of Major C. H. Foulkes (later brigadier general and director of gas services) were formed during July–August 1915. Personnel, including science graduates, chemical specialists and volunteers, were recruited and the four companies had a combined establishment of fifty-seven officers and 1,347 other ranks.

The first time these special companies and their cylinders were used was at the opening of the Battle of Loos on 25 September 1915. Because of a shortage of cylinders it was nec-

essary to interpose periods of smoke during the discharge to simulate more gas. Smoke was to be discharged from 11,000 smoke 'candles' and fired by the 4-inch Stokes mortar, as no gas bombs for this weapon were yet available. Loos was also the first time smoke had been used on this scale and, as it proved to be highly effective in covering the movement of the attackers, hardly any British operation took place subsequently without it (a mixture of smoke, gas and high-explosive shells became a common combination). Not until the final moment were the last of the 5,100 heavy cylinders manhandled into position in bays or 'batteries' of twelve. At zero hour, 5:50 a.m., a redoubled artillery bombardment accompanied the release of the gas and smoke. Officers or NCOs in charge of a battery of projectors and smoke candles received the following secret instructions.

0	Start the gas and run 6 cylinders one after the other at full blast until all are exhausted.
0-12 – 0-20	Start the smoke. The smoke is to run concurrently with the gas if the gas is not exhausted by 0-12.
0-20	Start the gas again and run 6 cylinders one after the other at full blast until all are exhausted.
0-32 – 0-40	Start the smoke again. The smoke is to run concurrently with the gas if the gas is not exhausted by 0-32.
	Turn off all gas punctually. Thicken up smoke with triple candles. Prepare for assault.
0-40	ASSAULT

The resultant dust, smoke and gas formed an impenetrable cloud that – except in the north where the wind was unfavourable (although gas was still released, mildly affecting over 2,000 British infantry and engineers; see page 49) – rolled steadily towards

and over the German line. Despite the gas catching the Germans by surprise, their immediate reaction was to bombard the British front line, destroying a number of emplacements and burying some of the crews. Nevertheless, overall the gas and smoke were effective. An extract from the German Fourth Army Headquarters, dated 27 September, confirms this – although much of the invisibility referred to so far behind the lines must have been due to smoke rather than to gas.

No preparation for a gas attack had been observed. The gas cloud was so strong that at 6 kilometres behind the front it was only possible to see at ten paces distance. At 1,500 metres from the enemy trenches the artillery was in great danger from gas. Breech blocks became unusable and it was impossible to give orders. By the ever-recurring gas clouds the respirators gradually became less effective.

The increasing use of gas by both sides and the experience of Loos led to the expansion of the special companies and their forming the Special Brigade, RE, in 1916 with an establishment of 208 officers and 5,306 men. It consisted of a headquarters, five battalions and four special sections, as below:

• Four Special Battalions, each of four companies, each equipped with sixteen gas cylinders as well as smoke candles. Each company had an establishment of seven officers and 218 other ranks.

• A Stokes mortar battalion of four companies, each with eighteen officers and 315 other ranks, had twelve 4-inch Stokes mortars firing gas, Thermit (from mid-1917) and smoke bombs. The mortar shell was a steel sphere containing liquefied gas and could be used to drench enemy trenches and dugouts with gas that could linger for hours or even days. Thermit bombs contained not gas but a mixture of iron oxide and powdered aluminium that, when ignited, produced molten metal that was splattered over the area when the bomb exploded.

• Z Company, with eighteen officers and 300 other ranks, had four special sections equipped with man-pack flame-projectors. Efforts to develop a longer-range (100-yard) flame-projector, although effective, and used with some success on the opening day of the Somme offensive, were later abandoned as installation in the trenches was so laborious and they were so vulnerable to enemy shellfire.

Anti-gas measures – besides the obvious one of developing effective respirators mentioned above – were taken very seriously throughout the BEF, and by 1917 a colonel had been appointed assistant director of anti-gas services at GHQ. A chemical intelligence service was set up, with trained officers at army and corps headquarters whose duty was to examine captured prisoners and documents to obtain information on any new developments in gas warfare projected by the Germans, and to ascertain the effects of British gas weapons. All ranks

Basic German Gas-shell Markings

The Germans found it necessary to mark their gas shells with distinctive coloured crosses for ease of storage and recognition by the artillery troops that handled them. The basic code was:

• **White cross** Contained gas affecting the eyes, such as tear gas, and was sometimes called a T-shell after Hans Tappen who invented them.

• **Green cross** This was a pure gas shell (not combined with HE or shrapnel) containing a suffocating gas that affected the lungs, such as chlorine or phosgene.

• **Blue cross** Contained nasal irritants such as diphenylchloroarsine – a fine dust that penetrated respirators causing pain in the sinuses and forcing the wearer to remove his mask. This was not particularly successful, as sometimes the particles were not fine enough, although the shell had a detonation and fragmentation effect as well.

• **Yellow cross** Gas affecting the skin – mustard gas.

A typical German counter-battery or long-range shoot would contain 20 per cent HE shells, 70 per cent blue cross and 10 per cent green cross. The relationship of these markings to the contents of the shell soon became known to the Allies and this proved of great value in quickly identifying the type of gas being used in an attack.

were given detailed instructions on how to deal with gas, and anti-gas schools were established at which instructors from brigades and battalions were trained. The gas warning system in the trenches involved gas sentries and alarms such as rattles, bells, horns or the banging of an empty shell case. Gas curtains and doors became an integral part of bunkers, tunnels and cellars. Inspections were frequent and rigorous to ensure that all precautions were understood and respirators checked.

When mustard gas, which burned the skin and contaminated everything it touched, was introduced, methods of decontaminating persons, clothing, weapons and ground subjected to it were implemented. More vulnerable than the troops were the horses, and although attempts were made to devise masks for them, they proved far from satisfactory, as well as being highly unpopular with the horses.

Having gas cylinders installed in a trench system awaiting use was seldom welcomed by the infantry occupants due to the ever-present possibility of them being damaged by enemy shelling. Private Frank Richards had this to say on the matter:

I had left the Battalion [2nd Royal Welch Fusiliers] in the trenches at Givenchy with two more days to do before they were relieved; on the last day the enemy had shelled hell out of our front line and some of the gas cylinders, which were still there, had been smashed. The Company had many casualties from gas. We thoroughly hated the sight of these cylinders and knew the danger we were in when the front line was being shelled. Some time later they were all removed, and our artillery sent over gas shells instead.

It was not just the close proximity of the gas cylinders that was unpopular with the infantry, but also the huge labour required to get them there. Previous experience had demonstrated the enormous effort needed to get twelve cylinders per bay positioned over a 4,500-yard frontage by one corps. During each of the first two nights' work, 106 lorries carried the cylinders from the railheads to divisional dumps, but on the third night only twenty were needed. At the railhead 120 men worked transferring cylinders to the lorries, while the final carry to the trenches required 3,560 men on the first and second nights and 900 on the third. Not until the end of 1917 had a system been devised that enabled gas to be released direct from railway trucks brought forward on tramways, giving the infantry some, but by no means complete, respite.

As with cylinders, the Germans were the

first to start firing artillery gas shells. These, containing (initially) lachrymatory (tear) gas, were increasingly used during 1915, prompting Sir John French to request that 10 per cent of all British shells for 4.5-inch, 60-pounder and 12-inch guns contain gas. Although agreed in principle, only 160,000 had been delivered by the end of 1916. For the Somme battles the British made ninety-eight separate gas attacks, releasing over 1,100 tons of phosgene-chlorine mixture (called white star) from cylinders; the small amount of gas shell used was fired by the French, who had employed artillery shells containing phosgene at Verdun. Although artillery was able to place the gas more accurately at greater depth than cylinders and was not wind-dependent, its disadvantage was the small amount of gas contained in the projectile.

While commanding Z Company in the Special Brigade, Captain William Howard Livens devised the Livens Projector – a large steel tube that could fire a gas bomb containing 30 lb of phosgene gas over a relatively short range (about a mile), but sufficiently far to be able to saturate German forward trenches with gas, while at the same time being located up to 600 yards behind the British forward trenches, thus not drawing enemy fire on to the long-suffering infantry. The tubes were dug in with muzzles flush to the ground, in batteries of twenty or twenty-five (usually under a corporal) at an angle of 45 degrees, with the range adjusted by the size of the propellant charge. Several thousand of these could be electrically fired simultaneously, with the resultant cloud released in the target area being dense and, hopefully, unexpected. The drums were sometimes filled with Thermit or inflammable oils – over 1,500 of the latter were used to set alight the woods on Messines Ridge in 1917. Other fillings included high explosive, white phosphorus or 'stinks' – foul-smelling materials to simulate gas when the latter could not be employed safely.

Although the Livens projector was not particularly accurate, and was thus deemed an area weapon, targeted mostly on villages, woods or regions containing many dugouts and strongpoints, the final two years of the war saw the drums fired in large numbers at the start of major battles, as the following examples show:

Arras, April 1917 – 2,340
Cambrai, November 1917 – 4,200, plus 3,100 Stokes mortar bombs
St-Quentin, 19 March 1918 – 2,960
Lens, 21 March 1918 – 3,730, plus 1,400 Stokes mortar bombs

A captain supervises the loading of gas projectiles into Livens projectors sunk in the ground and angled at 45 degrees towards the enemy.

The German response to the Livens projector was to fill their 18cm *Minenwerfer* bombs – known to the British as 'rum jars' – with gas. They fired out to a range of about 1,400 yards but their time fuzes emitted a stream of sparks in flight and so they were easy to follow at night.

One of the persistent myths of the Western Front was that the use of gas caused many thousands of fatalities and crippled tens of thousands more for life. Mustard gas is often highlighted as being particularly lethal, or to have condemned its victims to 'prolonged misery and an abbreviated life', but medical records show that of 4,575 severe cases sent to England for treatment, only 0.7 per cent died and 0.4 per cent were classified as permanently unfit, while under 2 per cent had their medical category reduced from A to a lower grade. Generally, poison gas proved surprisingly non-lethal – in 1915 the British suffered some 13,000 gas casualties, of whom only 307 died, or one in forty-two, whereas for every soldier hit by a bullet or shell splinter one in three were fatalities. In 1916 only 1,123 died from gas poisoning out of 100,000 total deaths, and further statistics reveal that overall some 93 per cent of gas casualties returned to full duty, many within a few weeks. Estimated total gas casualties overall were:

	Fatal	Non-fatal
British Empire (inc. Canada)	8,000	188,700
France	8,000	190,000
USA	1,450	72,800
Germany	9,000	200,00

However, death by gas poisoning was a particularly horrible one. The three main types of gas used were:

Chlorine

A fairly inefficient gas compared with those used later. It was easily smelled and visible to the eye, and tended to cling in the bottom of shell holes, trenches or dugouts, making it often possible to avoid the heavy concentrations. Even in the first German gas attack at Ypres a soldier who stuffed a handkerchief in his mouth and kept his head above his trench could avoid the worst effects. Thirty parts of gas to a million caused coughing, while a thousand parts brought death by drowning, as the gas destroyed the alveoli of the lungs and small bronchial tubes, preventing the man from absorbing oxygen. Some 60 per cent of the Canadians who faced the chlorine gas at Ypres were sent home and half remained disabled at the end of the war.

Phosgene

A derivative of chlorine, but far more powerful and invisible. It smelled faintly of mouldy hay, but even if inhaled in fatal amounts it was not immediately irritating. However, such a dose led to 'shallow breathing and retching, pulse up to 120, an ashen face and the discharge of four pints (2 litres) of yellow liquid from the lungs each hour for the 48 of the drowning spasms.'

Mustard gas

Designed to harass and disable rather than kill, this caused the most British gas casualties on the Western Front (90 per cent after its introduction at the Third Battle of Ypres in 1917), although only 2 per cent died from it – phosgene was the biggest gas killer. It was composed of ethylene in a solution of sodium chloride that looked to the soldier like sherry and smelled of onions or garlic. It evaporated slowly in trenches or woods, or in any area not exposed to sunlight, so it was a potential danger long after the shelling had ceased. It

caused awful suffering to its victims and for this reason was particularly dreaded. Even a tiny amount on the skin caused massive blisters, while higher concentrations could burn flesh to the bone, leaving survivors scared for life. A British nurse stated:

> Gas cases are terrible. They cannot breathe lying down or sitting up. They just struggle for breath, but nothing can be done. Their lungs are gone – literally burnt out. Some have their eyes and faces entirely eaten away by gas and their bodies covered with first-degree burns. We must try to relieve them by pouring oil on them. They cannot be bandaged or touched. We cover them with a tent of propped up sheets. Gas burns must be agonizing because usually the other cases do not complain even with the worst wounds but gas cases are invariably beyond endurance and they cannot help crying out.

But perhaps the most dreaded effect was blindness, caused mainly by both chlorine and mustard gas, although by no means all cases were permanent.

The most notable victim of a gas attack was Adolf Hitler, who was hospitalized and temporarily blinded. It has been suggested that his suffering, along with fears of retaliation, was the reason he refused to permit the use of poison gas on the battlefield – but not of course in the concentration camps – during World War II.

Other Special Units/Companies

Listed below, excluding some seventy-seven different types of signal and 300 transportation units, are some of the RE specialist companies in existence on the Western Front by November 1918. The list is not exhaustive, as it omits the numerous railway units (see page 322), but demonstrates the complexity and variety of work for which the corps had responsibility in addition to normal field engineering. Unless otherwise indicated, they were classified as companies.

75	AA Searchlight Sections	11	Pontoon Park
5	Army Mines Schools	1	Postal Service unit
16	Artisan Works	1	Printing
7	Electrical & Mechanical	5	RE Workshops
5	Field Survey Battalions	4	Special Brigade (Gas) Battalions
11	Forestry		
10	Foreway (formed in March 1918 to distribute engineer supplies forward of railheads)	1	Special (Gas) Brigade
		1	Special Works Park (camouflage)
		25	Tunnelling
1	Land Drainage	5	Water-boring Sections
1	Meteorological Section	5	Works

Signalling

Throughout history reliable communications have been an essential ingredient of command on the battlefield. Prior to and after World War I, commanders, including generals, had exercised control largely by voice. Although various methods of visual signalling had been in use since the ancient Greeks flashed signals from burnished shields, and later armies used flags or smoke, it was the voice of the general – who could, up to the end of the nineteenth century, usually see what was happening – that was the main means of control. The commander issued his instructions either directly to his subordinates, through liaison officers or via mounted aides-de-camp sometimes carrying written messages, sometimes verbal ones. After World War I commanders have had the ubiquitous radio set and then the magic of satellite communications, which in 1982 enabled generals in London to tell the commander in the Falklands personally what he was to do; and later every infantry soldier in Afghanistan has been issued with a personal set for close-range individual communication.

During World War I, although by 1918 big improvements had been made, lack of quick, reliable communications was often the key factor in decisions being made too late or not at all; between a gap in enemy defences being exploited or not; and in the inability to change a plan quickly during the long years of trench warfare. The problem was that once an attack was launched – particularly between 1915 and 1917 – the sheer destructive power of artillery frequently severed the link between what was happening at the front and higher-formation headquarters; thus decision-making information either failed to arrive or was out of date when it did. The deadly intensity of shellfire, machine-gun and rifle fire took a heavy toll of runners or of men repairing the endless breaks in cables, while the weather, smoke and exposure to this fire frequently rendered visual signalling impractical.

For the British, responsibility for signalling rested with the Royal Engineer Signal Service (RESS). The BEF went to France in August 1914 equipped for a short, mobile war, depending for communications on telegraph, liaison officers, despatch riders on motorcycles, visual signalling and orderlies mounted on horse or bicycle. Initially, considerable reliance was also placed on the French civil-communication network. Heavy, cumbersome and frequently unreliable wireless sets were confined to linking GHQ to the three corps (from 31 August) and the cavalry division.

Royal Engineer signal companies provided communications forward from General French's headquarters to the infantry battalions and artillery regiments, and within the battalion or battery communication was, theoretically at least, the responsibility of the unit. At GHQ the director of army signals, a brigadier general, exercised technical control, but there was nothing resembling a signals chain of command, as each unit was self-contained.

As shown in the diagram on page 312, from 31 August 1914 the BEF was served by L Signal Company, one GHQ signal company, three army corps signal companies, six divisional signal companies, a signal squadron with the cavalry division and a signal troop attached to each cavalry brigade, and an enhanced one to the independent cavalry brigade. These units were responsible for intercommunication, not only from the base on the French coast to battalion or artillery brigade headquarters, but also in some cases right up to front-line command posts.

Throughout 1915 communications on the Western Front forward of divisional headquarters were largely dependent on the field telephone. It was the primary, but not the only, instrument of control from brigade commanders to the captains commanding companies or batteries. With the passing months, and with upwards of a million miles of cable linking the thousands of command posts along and to the rear of the 450-mile front, the scale of the task of the signal services of all nations became obvious. However, it was during 1915 that voice telephone usage in the front line received its death blow with the discovery of how vulnerable it was to enemy overhearing (see page 320). This was also the year in which the carrier-pigeon service was proved to be a success.

Many experiments to tackle the insecurity of the telephone were made during 1916, including the introduction of the Fullerphone (see page 320). It also saw a revival of the use of visual signals and the beginning of the forward deployment of wireless stations. There were also message-carrying dogs and aircraft-contact patrols with klaxons and message bags. Wireless was proving successful in maintaining contact between divisional and brigade headquarters.

By 1917 trench warfare had achieved its maximum intensity and had been the catalyst for further development of signalling under these conditions. This included the use of message-carrying rockets, further employment of the wireless in the forward

areas, the success of the power buzzer and amplifier, the adoption of the daylight signalling lamp and the extensive use of the Fullerphone as the standard method of forward telegraphy. It was also the year in which listening in to German signal traffic became fully established. And with American formations starting to arrive in England and France, RESS instructors were attached to impart current signal practice. This was followed by American officers and NCOs being attached to divisional and brigade signal units in the field to gain crucial experience.

The 1918 retreats and subsequent major advances by the Allies saw a change from trench to more mobile warfare. The British retreat in March cost the signal service considerable loss of equipment captured (forty pigeon lofts were seized, for example) or destroyed, but the Hundred Days offensive saw a more sophisticated signal service, capable of leapfrogging forward to set up new networks.

The RESS also saw rapid expansion in terms of personnel, largely in the number of men in the units rather than in the number of units themselves. The allocation of one signal company to each division, corps and army remained constant throughout the war, but the number of officers and men in them increased severalfold. For example, in 1914 a divisional signal company establishment was 5 officers and 157 other ranks, rising in 1918 to 15 officers and 400 other ranks. Even more spectacular was the increase in the GHQ and L (line of communication) signal companies, whose combined establishment in 1914 was 10 officers and 344 other ranks, but in 1918 was 40 and 1,376.

A wireless operator at work inside a dugout.

BEF Signals – Outline Organization, 31 August 1914

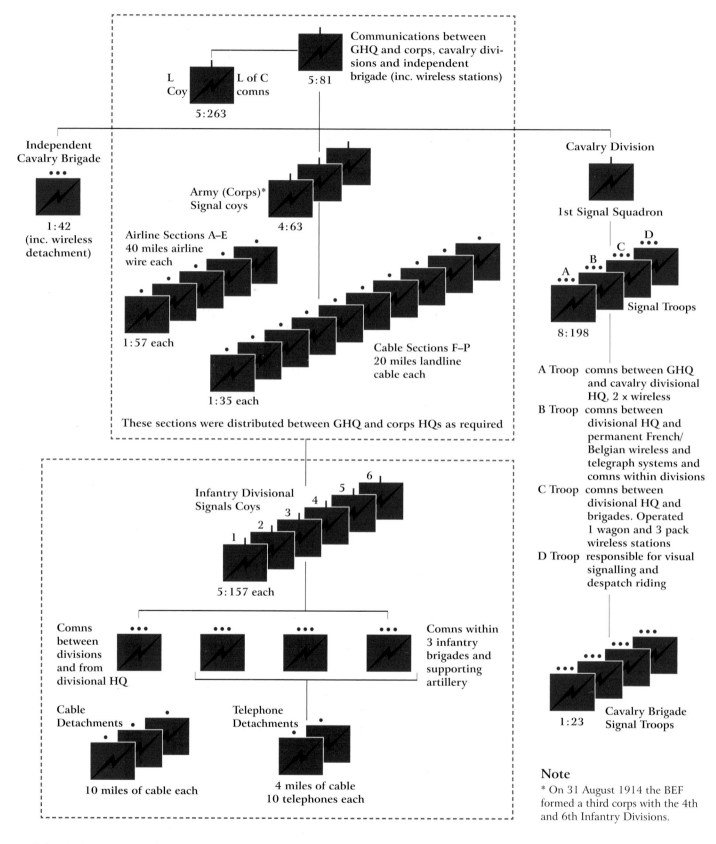

Communications between GHQ and corps, cavalry divisions and independent brigade (inc. wireless stations)

5:81

L Coy   L of C comns

5:263

Independent Cavalry Brigade

1:42 (inc. wireless detachment)

Army (Corps)* Signal coys

4:63

Airline Sections A–E 40 miles airline wire each

1:57 each

1:35 each

Cable Sections F–P 20 miles landline cable each

These sections were distributed between GHQ and corps HQs as required

Cavalry Division

1st Signal Squadron

A B C D

Signal Troops

8:198

A Troop comns between GHQ and cavalry divisional HQ, 2 x wireless

B Troop comns between divisional HQ and permanent French/Belgian wireless and telegraph systems and comns within divisions

C Troop comns between divisional HQ and brigades. Operated 1 wagon and 3 pack wireless stations

D Troop responsible for visual signalling and despatch riding

Infantry Divisional Signals Coys

1 2 3 4 5 6

5:157 each

Comns between divisions and from divisional HQ

Comns within 3 infantry brigades and supporting artillery

Cable Detachments

10 miles of cable each

Telephone Detachments

4 miles of cable 10 telephones each

Cavalry Brigade Signal Troops

1:23

Note
* On 31 August 1914 the BEF formed a third corps with the 4th and 6th Infantry Divisions.

Before looking at some of the methods of communication in more detail, a summary of the Liaison and Intercommunication Appendix to the 30th Division Operation Order No. 19 gives a picture of the variety and complexity of a communication plan for the division's attack on 1 July 1916. Attacking on its right was the French 39th Division and on the left the British 18th Division (see Map 40).

• **Liaison** At divisional headquarters were officers from the French mission, XIII Corps Heavy Artillery and 21st, 89th and 90th Infantry Brigades. The 30th Division had an officer from the French divisional headquarters, and the 89th Brigade (attacking on the right) was represented at the headquarters of the French 77th Brigade (attacking on the French left), and also at the 21st Brigade (attacking on its left) HQ. The 21st Brigade was represented at the headquarters of the 89th and 55th Brigade (attacking on the division's left). The 30th Divisional Artillery was connected to the French Divisional Artillery.

• **Alternative methods of communication** Three main and four advanced lamp stations were established, most of them continually manned. All units possessed twenty-four light Morse discs and a number of torches. Runners were to be employed in pairs. Pigeons were issued to all brigades. Two advanced wireless stations were set up for the 30th Division and another for the 18th Division.

• **Communications with aircraft and kite balloons** Each brigade had 1,500 ground flares; 220 were issued to each battalion to be carried by officers, NCOs and selected men. They were to be used only on the orders of a company or platoon commander, and only from the front line. When used they meant, 'We are here and so far as we know we are the leading infantry or within 50 yards of the leading infantry.' As with flags, flares were only to be used when brigades reached certain specified lines or objectives, or if checked before reaching that line. Mirrors were to be used to attract the attention of aircraft. The kite balloon was spotting for the artillery and would accept infantry messages only at night. A series of simple codes was arranged – for example, a series of Ns meant short of ammunition; Os meant barrage wanted; Xs meant held up by machine-gun fire. Every infantryman wore a yellow patch on his pack and a tin disc, shiny side outwards. Companies and platoons carried special flags that meant nothing unless waved to indicate the leading infantry.

An infantry battalion was largely responsible for its own internal communications and a battalion operation order was extremely detailed in this respect. The 11th Suffolk (Cambridgeshire) Battalion's order for its attack on the same date is a good example, with a separate appendix devoted to communications. In summary, the main battalion operation order under the heading Communications/Signallers stated:

• A brigade advanced signal exchange was to be established near the front line and all signallers and runners had to know its location.

• Company commanders had to organize a system of runners between platoon, company and battalion headquarters, and six runners were to be sent to brigade

headquarters. Runners all had a strip of yellow braid on both arms.

• The position of the front line of the attackers was to be indicated by lighting ground flares in a row, three or four paces apart at fifteen-second intervals, but only on the order of an officer.

• All commanders were to report to their superior once every half hour. The code word 'RAT' meant 'I have taken my objective and am consolidating', while 'RATTRAP' meant 'I have consolidated'.

• All German wires (telephone cables) not required for own use were to be cut by signallers.

The Suffolks' signallers were to maintain communications by wire (cable), which was being run out by signallers following up the advancing companies; by runners; and by visual means. Duties were as follows:

• There were two wiring parties. The one on the left consisted of Sergeant Southgate and seven named privates (of whom two were operators and two linesmen). This party carried field glasses, compass, four coils of wire, four telephones and yellow ribbon. The right-hand party, under Lance Corporal Hunt, had six privates and was similarly equipped but with only three telephones.

• There was a 'ladder' party under Corporal Lambert, with two soldiers equipped with a coil of wire, pliers and insulating tape. They were tasked with connecting the cable run out by the two forward parties using three links or joins (rungs of the ladder) at specific features (a road and German trench lines) during the attack.

• Two linesmen were to patrol each line to repair breaks.

• Two operators remained at battalion headquarters and a Lance Corporal Jones and one soldier maintained communications between the headquarters and aircraft, while another was left at the brigade visual station.

• The battalion intended to establish its own visual station once the objective was secured. It consisted of Lance Corporal Ilett and six privates, two of whom were runners, and was equipped with telescope, discs, flags, shutter and lamps.

• A number of signallers were kept with the transport as replacements for casualties.

These two examples illustrate how by mid-1916 the communication plan for a divisional offensive involved virtually the whole gamut of signalling methods available, from a signals exchange to the humble runner. In this case liaison officers, visual signalling, wireless, telephones, pigeons, aircraft and kite balloons were involved in order to provide the necessary links, back-up and alternative

means of getting information to and from the divisional headquarters, infantry and artillery command posts and the advancing infantry.

Below is a look at various ways of delivering messages.

Written messages

• **Runners** This was supposedly the method of last resort, but it had been used since history's earliest battles – as the only means available, as a back-up to duplicate another system, or when other methods had failed. It was slow and could be expensive in men, requiring the best and bravest in the battalion – which was the level at which it was most used. Casualties were high, as although communication trenches were used wherever possible, the runner had frequently to expose himself, particularly to shellfire. A through-run to his destination was preferred, but on occasions when the distance to be covered exceeded 500 yards or so a relay system was employed. Some battles in 1917 saw such a system between brigade and battalion headquarters, with runner posts marked by large coloured flags by day and coloured lamps at night. Runners normally wore red bands around the left forearm and carried their messages in the top left-hand breast pocket – so dead messengers could be recognized and the body quickly checked for undelivered messages.

Perhaps the most infamous runner was Adolf Hitler, who from December 1915 was a lance corporal in the 16th Bavarian Reserve Regiment. According to one source, a Lieutenant Horn stated that Hitler was never promoted sergeant, as it would have meant the regiment losing 'one of its best despatch carriers'. Hitler was wounded in the leg on the Somme in 1916 and gassed in 1918, and as early as December 1914 was awarded the Iron Cross 2nd Class. Three months before the Armistice he received the Iron Cross 1st Class for his bravery – on the recommendation of his regiment's Jewish adjutant, something he was later keen to conceal. At the end of the war he was guarding Russian prisoners at a camp in Bavaria.

• **Despatch riders** Another common means of delivery, particularly in the rear areas, although as with so many aspects of mobilization there was initially an acute shortage. Despatch riders were mounted on motorcycles, but orderlies delivering messages on bicycles or horseback were common. Early in the war despatch riders proved of particular value during the retreat from Le Cateau and advance to the Aisne, when almost total reliance was placed on them for operational communication between division and brigade. Packets and letters for the administrative services, along with private

A carrier pigeon is released with a message from a forward trench. The lieutenant on the right still holds his message pad and pen in his hand.

correspondence were dealt with by the Post Section of the Royal Engineers, whose activities were outside the sphere of the signal service. However, it was soon found necessary to form the Despatch Rider Letter Service (DRLS), organized by the director of signals. By October 1914 it had started running on a regular timetable between bases, depots and GHQ, but not until August 1915 was this service relieved of carrying letters not concerned with operations.

By 1917, in the rear of the buried-cable area, a semi-permanent telegraph and telephone system operated, but despatches of a less urgent nature were still handled by the DRLS, with two or three deliveries daily to all important signal offices in each formation area.

Mounted orderlies (on horses or bicycles), when available, were supplied by troops from the corps cavalry unit or a section from the corps cyclist battalion. They performed similar functions to the despatch riders.

• **Animals (pigeons and dogs)** Carrier pigeons with coded messages clipped to their legs were in service on the Western Front with the BEF in a small way from September 1914 – but only because the French provided fifteen birds; the French have a memorial to their pigeons in the Citadel at Lille. Like all other aspects of the armies, expansion was not long in coming. For the Somme offensive in July 1916 the British had 12,000 pigeons, but by 1918 some 20,000 were available, with 400 expert handlers and some 90,000 men trained to use them. In one corps attack in the Second Army offensive in June 1917, no fewer than 532 pigeons were issued to attacking units on a single day, and ninety-two operational messages were received using

them. General supervision was exercised by the officer commanding the Carrier Pigeon Service at GHQ, who advised the deputy directors of signals at army and assistant directors of signals at corps headquarters. Eventually pigeons were routinely allotted to brigade forward signal offices, artillery forward observation and liaison officers, as well as two to company headquarters of attacking battalions and to each attacking tank. Pigeon lofts were where the birds homed, while forward pigeon stations were points to which they were taken and from where they were normally released with messages. In 1917 the service consisted of stationary, motorized or horse-drawn lofts located at divisional headquarters. Stationary lofts would have 60 birds, later increased to 120; horse-drawn had 75 birds each; and the six motorized had 50 birds each. Officers involved in an attack were issued with pre-written message forms to use.

If properly trained (it took six weeks, and another two if the loft moved), pigeons were usually a successful way of delivering messages, with a bird taking on average twenty-five minutes to fly from the front to its loft. Demand for the birds often outstripped supply as their value was demonstrated again and again. Casualties were relatively high – 10 per cent were lost at Messines, with fifty birds killed by a shell hitting a distributing station. However, only in the British Second Army were they ever trained to fly at night.

Use of dogs to carry messages was favoured more by the French and Germans than by the British, and it was not until the Messines battle in 1917 that the first attempt to use 'liaison dogs', as the British then called them, was made by an artillery commander. His success led to the establishment of a War Dog Training School at Shoeburyness in Essex.

One problem with their employment was the tendency of the handlers in the field to make pets out of them and not properly understand their capabilities and limitations. This resulted in November 1917 in the centralization of the messenger-dog service under the overall control of the officer commanding the Carrier Pigeon Service, with all dogs being withdrawn to a central kennels at Étaples, France, for retraining. Interestingly, part of the training involved creating nearby explosions and smoke when feeding them so that they associated the noise with the high point of their day. Dogs had the advantage of speed over pigeons, averaging a mile in seven minutes; they could also be used at night and were quicker to train. Nevertheless, they were somewhat – understandably – unreliable under heavy shelling (something that didn't seem to bother pigeons) and their eyes were badly affected by gas. Each dog was in the exclusive care of one man and always on a lead or chained when not taking messages. Water was always available, but they were not fed until all message-taking for the day was over. When a dog arrived with a message it was immediately rewarded with a piece of meat. It was not until the spring of 1918 that a full dog-messenger service was operating on the British front, although from then on its usefulness was limited by the onset of more mobile warfare.

• **Rockets** Message-carrying rockets were intended for use instead of a runner – that is, between brigade and battalion command posts, artillery brigades and by forward observation officers to batteries. They were constructed in two parts: the head carried the propellant and a whistle, while the tail carried a smoke and flare composition with a receptacle for the message. Three range 'collars' could be fitted over the top of the whistle and came with the rocket. Fired

An Unpopular Pigeon

Field Marshal Montgomery, who was wounded on the Western Front, recalled the following story:

During the Somme battle an infantry brigade which had better remain nameless was to be the leading brigade in a divisional attack. It was important that the Brigade Commander should receive early information of the progress of his forward troops, and intense interest was aroused when it was disclosed that a pigeon would be used to carry the news.

When the day of the attack arrived the pigeon was given to a soldier to carry. He was to go with the leading sub-units and was told that at a certain

moment an officer would write a message to be fastened to the pigeon's leg; he would then release the pigeon which would fly back to its loft at Brigade H.Q.

Time slipped by, but no pigeon arrived – the Brigadier walked feverishly about outside his dug-out. The soldiers anxiously searched the skies – there was no sign of any pigeon. At last the cry went up: 'The pigeon!' And sure enough it alighted safely in the loft.

Soldiers rushed to get the news and the Brigade Commander roared out: 'Give me the message!'

It was handed to him and this is what he read: 'I am absolutely fed up with carrying this bloody bird around France.'

without a collar, the range was from 2,000–2,300 yards; with a small collar 1,600; with a medium 1,200; and with a large only 800 yards. They were set up for firing in a trough at an angle of 45 degrees and the whistling noise, smoke and flares in flight gave a clear indication of where they landed, while their continuing to emit smoke and flame for about two minutes after landing facilitated their being found quickly – although care had to be taken with recovery, as they were extremely hot.

• **Message bags** These were used successfully by aircraft, which dropped bags containing information obtained by reconnaissance flights at specially designated 'aeroplane dropping stations' near divisional or corps headquarters. These stations were often manned by signallers on loan from a pioneer battalion.

Visual messages

• **Visual signal stations** These were usually used as an alternative to other means of communications, or as a back-up, and were supplied with various equipments, including flags, lamps (initially the noisy Begbie, which was later replaced by the silent, electrical Lucas lamps), heliographs, telescopes, ground panels, discs and shutters for signalling in semaphore or Morse, and the firing of flares or rockets. None except the last was popular in forward areas, particularly during the static trench-warfare period, due to the necessary exposure of the operators unless concealed from the front. Battalion signallers were, however, issued with the means of visual signalling and an example of their use and associated problems during the Somme offensive is given by Private Frank Richards in his book *Old Soldiers Never Die*:

Eight of us and the Brigade Signalling Corporal were detailed off to form a transmitting station between High Wood and Brigade Headquarters which was situated on the fringe of Mametz Wood [a distance of about 3,200 yards]. No telephones would be carried and our station would receive messages by flag from the signallers with the attacking force; which we would transmit to Brigade by heliograph or flag. The position that we had to take up was by a large mill about 600 yards this side of High Wood [see Map 55]. The mill was built on some rising ground which made it a very prominent landmark. We had a good view of everything from here, but we also found that when we were exchanging messages with the wood, the enemy would have an equally good view of us, especially when we were flag-waving…

[We] fixed our heliograph and telescope up, and by 8 a.m. we were in communication with Brigade. Shortly after this the enemy began shelling us and by 10 a.m. they had put up one of the worst barrages that I was ever under . . . When receiving a message the smoke of the bursting shells and the earth and dust that was being thrown up constantly obscured our vision, and we could only receive a word now and then.

The five men I didn't know were sheltering in a large shell hole by the side of the mill; they were absolutely useless and terror-stricken . . . The enemy now turned a machine gun on the mill, our flag-waving had attracted their attention.

Eventually they received orders to cease visual signalling and become runners between the brigade headquarters and High Wood.

For its attack on 1 July 1916, XIII Corps ordered every platoon and company headquarters in the three attacking divisions (9th, 18th and 30th) to carry a coloured flag (different for each division). They meant nothing unless waved, and on no account were they to be stuck in the ground. When waved it indicated that that sub-unit considered itself to be the leading infantry.

• **Flares, panels, grenades and rockets** Ground flares (usually red, green or white) were mostly used to signal the position of the leading infantry to aircraft (as were panels), which could then communicate this information by message bag to artillery or infantry command posts – it was always crucially important for the gunners and brigade and divisional commanders to know exactly where the leading troops were in any advance, in order to judge progress. They were not used at night. Flares were lit only on the orders of an officer and only then at specific times or places.

The other type of flare, not used for signalling, was the illuminating flare – the flare burst at its maximum height and floated down on a small parachute, lighting up targets below. Infantry battalions were equipped with Very pistols (invented by an American naval officer, Samuel Very), which could fire coloured signal or illuminating cartridges up to a height of 1,000 feet – the latter remained alight for forty seconds. There were also occasions when they proved effective anti-personnel weapons. John Nettleton, in the Artists Rifles, described one such incident that occurred at night when figures were seen approaching his position.

The subaltern fired his Very pistol at the figures, instead of in the air [it was an illuminating cartridge], and the Very light hit one of them in the eye or on the

forehead, and stuck there, fizzing. By its light I saw an enormous Boche, ten foot high and weighing about two hundred and fifty pounds, or so it seemed coming at me…

The German was finished off by a second shot from a .45 revolver.

A more sophisticated version of the Very pistol was the star shell or rocket, which would explode at a predetermined height. Towards the end of the war the British 18-pounder gun was firing the Mark V shell containing ten stars.

The No. 32 grenade, which gave off coloured smoke, was frequently used for signalling pre-arranged messages by the colours being thrown successively in certain combinations – for example, throwing a green then a red and finally a green, which would be termed 'green over red over green'. Fourth Army's orders for the British offensive in early August 1918 stated that in III Corps green over green over green was the SOS signal; but in the Canadian Corps a No. 32 grenade red over red over red was not only the SOS but could also mean 'We are held up and cannot advance without help', in which case a smoke rocket (No. 27 grenade) would also be fired from a rifle in the direction of the problem.

Large rockets were also used by day or night to fire pre-arranged signals with a specific meaning, such as calling for the artillery immediately to fire a certain barrage. Another example was as a signal for an attack. On 2 June 1916 the signal for the 2nd Canadian Division's attack on Mount Sorrel was the simultaneous firing of six green rockets. However, several rockets proved defective and fourteen had to be fired before six ignited and fired successively rather than simultaneously. The result was confusion, with battalions starting their attacks at different times.

Audio messages

• The shouted order, the whistle blast that signalled a platoon to advance, or on occasion a bugle call were used to indicate a specific action.

• Contact patrol aircraft (see Section Eleven, page 430) were equipped with klaxon horns to communicate with infantry via a simple pre-arranged code – a succession of Morse code As might mean 'put up flares'.

Telegraph and telephone

• **Telegraph** Using Morse code, telegraph services were employed worldwide, with messages sent across oceans and countries via underwater copper cables or landlines carried on poles. Telegraph was highly successful for civilian use, but much less so on the battlefield. In the operational zone on the Western Front it was very vulnerable to shellfire, lacked the flexibility to cope with unpredictable movement of formations, and was vulnerable to tapping. Largely for these reasons, telegraph was a major means of communication only in rear areas and between large formation headquarters beyond the reach of enemy guns.

• **Telephones** They were the most common method of intercommunication, both in the forward and rear areas of the Western Front, used for direct speech or, much more commonly, with a buzzer phone for transmitting and receiving Morse-coded messages. However, telephones had to be connected to exchanges by cable, or wire as it was called at the time – the British required 13,000 miles of it for the Battle of Cambrai alone. Another indication of the size of the problem was that during a 24-hour period in July 1916 an infantry division had to process 7,000 operational messages. Cables could be carried over land on improvised poles or tree stumps; laid on the surface of, or buried (called 'buries') beneath the ground; or fixed to the side of trenches; or any combination of these. All methods – but the first two in particular – were vulnerable to breaks, caused mostly, but not always, by shellfire. It was found that only cable buried 6–8 feet deep was secure from heavy shells, but to bury so much over long distances was a monumental task that invariably required the reluctant services of 'resting' infantry battalions. During the prolonged preparations for the Somme offensive, some 43,000 miles of overhead wire was erected in rear areas and 7,000 miles buried in forward areas, as well as considerable

quantities laid over ground – quite staggering statistics. A feature of this effort was the emphasis on lateral links, or 'laddering', and multiple duplication that had been found critical to lessening the likelihood of almost instant loss of communications, certainly in the operational zone, once an enemy counter-barrage started during an attack.

Cable had usually to be laid on the surface, at least initially during an attack, by signallers following the assault and reeling it out behind them. In the majority of attacks with a limited objective, however, the German barrage came down so heavily that the lines could not be relied on and, with the front-line British trenches as well as those just captured under continuous shellfire, attempts to repair lines or lay new ones were usually discontinued as causing a useless waste of life. Ground lines, even if they survived the shelling, often fell victim to the constant stream of walking wounded, limbered wagons, stretcher-bearers and reinforcements. In these situations reliance was placed on a combination of runners, despatch riders, visual signalling and orderlies.

• **Security** Without adequate precautions, telephone conversations or buzzer messages could easily be tapped into, particularly in the forward areas. This danger was appreciated as early as mid-1915 from intelligence reports that showed information had leaked to the enemy. The French had established forward listening posts and confirmed they had heard scraps of German conversations. Steps were taken to tighten security by forbidding the naming of units, times of reliefs, movement of units, location of guns or results of enemy artillery fire when using telephones. Technical steps were taken

to improve the earthing of the lines, including using twisted cable. However, it was not until 2 July 1916 that the real seriousness of lax telephone security was revealed. On that date British troops managed briefly to occupy the fringe of the village of Ovillers-la-Boiselle (this village was not finally secured until mid-July) and discovered, pasted up in a dugout, a copy of an order that had been overheard clearly warning of the attack on the previous day. Investigation revealed it was an order repeated over the telephone by the brigade major, despite his protests, at the insistence of the brigade commander. The result on 1 July had been that the 2nd Berkshires and 2nd Lincolnshires lost forty-eight officers and 797 men between them – the former ended up being commanded by a second lieutenant.

The most effective way of minimizing security breaches was a combination of rigorous discipline and the use of the Fullerphone in forward areas. The Fullerphone was a portable DC-line Morse telegraph, devised in 1915 by a Captain A. C. Fuller of the British RESS. Its transmissions were practically immune from overhearing and had much clearer signals than those of the buzzer telegraph. By the end of 1916 the Fullerphone was well established and by 1918 most divisions had it for all forward communications circuits, including those forward of battalion headquarters. However, it was successful and secure only on buzzer circuits, so instructions were issued that the speaking set be removed from the instrument and carried by an officer for use only in dire emergencies.

Wireless messages

Wireless, or W/T (wireless telegraphy), had the great advantage over telephones or telegraph in that it needed no wire or cable in order to communicate. This was a massive advantage. However, in 1914 it suffered from numerous drawbacks from a military point of view. It was heavy, cumbersome, fragile and thus awkward to move around a battlefield. It required a ready supply of electricity, as the accumulators needed frequent recharging, and it was also highly vulnerable to tapping into by an enemy. This latter meant codes and ciphers were required, with the delays these involved, as well as the need for skilled operators. Add to this unreliability and a large degree of scepticism by many in the military, and it becomes clear why the BEF went to war with only a handful of sets that linked its headquarters forward only to the cavalry. These were three wagon and one lorry-borne sets at GHQ, three wagon sets at the cavalry divisional headquarters, and a pack

Men of the Royal Engineers laying and testing a communications cable on a stretch of the Western Front.

set with each cavalry brigade. There was no wireless with the infantry divisions.

All this changed rapidly as the war progressed. Wireless became increasingly used in the command chain at divisional, corps and army level, although the presence of large aerials was a great giveaway until the inconspicuous loop aerial became widely available. As usage became more common, the wireless sections of the corps and divisional signals companies were tasked with communicating to other corps, within the division and to flanking divisions. From early 1915, as both the intelligence (largely listening in to the enemy) and the tactical side of wireless use continued to develop, differentiation set in and the two branches grew apart, with each developing its own specialists and qualified personnel, although both continued to be controlled from GHQ. The same year saw wireless carried in balloons and some aircraft, although with the latter carrying a 70-lb set it meant there was no observer, so the pilot had to observe, fly, deal with any enemy and handle the necessary codes and ciphers – a daunting undertaking.

Continuous experimentation was aimed at getting the use of wireless forward as far as battalion headquarters, particularly during the static years of trench warfare. The first significant step was the introduction of the BF – officially known as the British Field set, but by all users as the 'bloody fool' set, as it was specifically designed to be simple, to be used by hastily trained operators and to be as near as possible 'fool-proof'. This set, combined with the Wilson transmitter and the Mark III short-wave receiver, was destined to become the standard apparatus for forward wireless communication between corps, division and brigade headquarters from 1916 onwards.

By 1917 wireless sets were used as an alternative to buried cable between divisional and battalion headquarters and trench sets were commonly used for artillery observa-tion. They were to play a key role at Cambrai and the 1918 battles.

To explain the complexity of the vast signal circuits and communication centres that by 1918 linked formation headquarters, administrative bases, divisional and brigade forward stations, report centres, and artillery and battalion command posts, as well as artillery observation posts, balloons and aircraft, is beyond the scope of this book. However, to illustrate the enormous expansion within just one army consisting of two corps of three divisions each (about the size of the BEF in early August 1914), the signal units at the Armistice comprised: 1 army signal company, 3 airline sections, 2 cable sections, 8 area signal detachments, 1 signal construction company, 1 light railway signal company, 9 army field artillery brigade signal subsections, 17 heavy artillery group signal subsections, 2 corps signal companies, 4 airline sections, 4 cable sections and 6 divisional signal companies – together totalling 168 officers and 4,380 other ranks.

Overall there were 321 individual Royal Engineer units serving on the Western Front on 1 August 1918. To mention but a few, these ranged from 155 field companies to 52 divisional signal companies, 32 heavy artillery group sections and 16 tunnelling companies down to 2 forestry companies and a printing company.

German Signalling

The Germans, and indeed all belligerents, used the same basic methods of signalling and, as with other arms, developed more sophisticated and complex systems. The Germans' final signals reorganization took place in mid-1917 and saw the Signal Service (*Nachrichtenwesen*) include all means of communication, from wireless telegraphy to messenger dogs, with a director of signals answerable to the chief of the General Staff of the field army. There were signals com-manders at all formation headquarters and the staffs of the army wireless and telephone commanders were amalgamated.

Each infantry and artillery unit had its own signalling detachment – a regimental detachment was split into telephone and visual (lamp) sections and also supplied personnel for pigeons, dogs and message-carrying rockets. The strength of this detachment was up to 150, including one officer. Telegraph units were deployed only on the lines of communication and never forward of army headquarters. At army HQ there were also two telephone detachments, each of between five and seven motor airline sections each of four lorries, an officer and forty-two other ranks, along with an army telephone park that supplied equipment. A telephone detachment was also attached to each division, with responsibility in static warfare for linking the divisional headquarters to brigades and regiments. The sections in each detachment carried about 25 miles of cable.

German listening sets were allotted to all formations, from army to division. At army level a listening detachment consisted of some fifteen officers and up to 300 other ranks. Two power-buzzer stations with sending and receiving equipment with a range of about 2,000 yards were deployed with each regiment. Wireless stations were allotted down to divisional level. These consisted of a divisional headquarters station and an infantry and artillery station, the former having thirteen sets (two large, five medium and six small), the latter twelve sets (two large, six medium and four small). The range of a divisional set was up to 60 miles, while a small trench set could manage only from 600–1,100 yards.

Extensive use was made of lamp-signalling, message-carrying rockets, dogs and pigeons. As with the British, mobile pigeon lofts were normally located near divisional headquarters with forward stations at command and observation posts.

Construction and Labour

Construction and repair on a gigantic scale was necessary in forward and rear zones and throughout the lines of communication area by both the Allies and the Germans. Initially, the former had intended to rely mainly on hiring indigenous French and Belgian workers, and large numbers were employed, but although some were used throughout the war their numbers fell dramatically as they were withdrawn to work for their own armies.

The work of construction, repair and maintenance was technically the responsibility of engineers or skilled artisans, at least to organize or supervise the work. In the forward areas it included constructing trenches, command posts, bunkers, strongpoints, gun positions, subways, tunnels, bridges, roads, timber tracks, light railways and billets, along with their inevitable expansion and repair. In the communications zone it involved building depots, stores, more billets, port facilities, training schools, camps, water-supply facilities, bridges, road and rail links and extensions. Add in forestry work to supply tens of thousands of tons of timber and quarrying stone for hundreds of miles of roads, and it becomes obvious that such a workload required enormous numbers of semi-skilled and unskilled workers – way beyond the capacity of military engineers alone.

Although not strictly an engineer task as such, labour was also needed for the offloading and loading of supplies, ammunition, materials and stores at ports, railheads, distribution points and depots. As the war progressed, the demands for labour became so strident throughout the theatre that it resulted in a wide miscellany of

New Zealand pioneers lay a new road at Messines, June 1917, just after the taking of the village and ridge.

labour units from various organizations developing on an ad hoc basis. In February 1917 the British War Office authorized most of such units being merged into a Labour Corps (see opposite).

Until late 1916 the British inspector general of communications (IGC), a lieutenant general (see diagram, page 166) had command of all units on the line of communication (LOC) except those involved in its actual defence. He was responsible for 'the disposition of all reinforcements, supplies and stores on the LOC, and for sending them up to within reach of field units'. After that date the IGC post was abolished and replaced by a director general of transportation, a major general (see Section Eight, pages 341–2). Operating under the IGC was the Works Directorate, tasked with constructing stores depots, camps and port facilities, along with the employment of indigenous labour.

The sources of labour used are summarized below:

Cavalry

During the summer of 1916 the Cavalry Corps, with considerable reluctance, found itself involved in constructing defences in the rear of the combat zone. In November they formed a number of small (250 men) pioneer battalions, mostly for work building or repairing roads and railways.

For the November 1917 British offensive a cavalry track battalion was temporarily created from 500 Indian cavalrymen, with British officers, to follow up the attack by filling in shell holes in roads and tracks.

Infantry

Front-line infantry battalions, with much grousing and grumbling, were used continuously throughout the war during their so-called rest periods out of the line on digging communication and signal-cable trenches, gun pits, repairing roads, providing burial parties, carrying supplies (food, ammunition, water, duckboards, barbed wire and engineer stores) – work often undertaken under shellfire, soaked by rain, plastered in mud and bitterly cold. It was work that never ended by day or night and was carried out by men already exhausted through lack of sleep. It was in an attempt to reduce their usage that many of the other construction/labour units were formed.

From early 1915 pioneer battalions were established and one was attached to each New Army division, and by June 1916 to the regular divisions, to support the Royal Engineers for tasks in the forward zone. Although many complained that, 'We did not join to dig for others', they remained fighting troops and often worked under shellfire or were involved in combat during German offensives. They worked under the CRE at divisional headquarters, improving communication trenches, laying light railway track, road repair and even helping French farmers with the harvest.

In July 1915 ten entrenching battalions were formed from drafts of reinforcements from infantry depots. They were not entirely satisfactory, as their numbers fluctuated wildly, and they were abandoned by the end of 1917. However, twenty-five were re-formed in February 1918, but were soon broken up as replacements for losses in the German offensive in March.

Salvage and convalescent companies formed from men temporarily unfit or under age were created in 1915 to undertake salvage work, burials and guarding headquarters.

In the spring of 1916 men below medical category A were formed into infantry labour battalions. Thirty-one such battalions served in France, mainly on road maintenance.

In 1917 men from the Training Reserve below category A were grouped into 500-strong infantry labour companies for work mostly on road and rail maintenance and unloading wagons. By the summer of that year, 128 such companies were on the Western Front.

Royal Engineers

In late 1914, 20 Fortress Company and 29 Works Company (replaced by 42 Fortress Company) RE were in support of the BEF, and in March 1915 six Territorial Force fortress companies joined them. They were composed of skilled soldiers and they were not employed as unskilled labour. Later in

1915 they were reclassified as army troops companies, RE.

Also in 1914, two regular railway companies and three Royal Monmouth and Royal Anglesey companies were deployed under the chief railway construction engineer. By 1918 there were thirty-two New Army railway companies and several Canadian railway construction battalions on the Western Front.

In August 1915, RE labour battalions began to be recruited direct from UK labour exchanges. Many were men in their forties and fifties and they were paid 3 shillings (15p) a day, with ex-foremen appointed as senior NCOs. Eventually eleven battalions served in France.

The huge amount of road building and repair, which was, like trench digging or repair, a daily task everywhere throughout the war, required vast quantities of stone. By August 1916 two quarrying companies, RE, were formed, to be followed in 1917 by another ten, with thirteen more the next year – a year in which 2.8 million tons of stone were supplied.

The widespread flooding of trenches, particularly in the flat Flanders area, saw the formation of two land-drainage companies in September 1915.

During 1916 the need for timber became as acute as that for stone. Timber was used in the trenches for revetting, duckboards, dugouts, tunnelling, making fascines and for hundreds of miles of timber tracks and railway lines. Three RE labour battalions and a Canadian forestry battalion were working in French forests, with the number of companies later rising to fifty-six.

At the end of 1916, the RE formed reinforcement companies composed of tradesmen drafted from RE depots to work under the army chief engineer. While waiting to replace casualties these men were mostly employed in constructing and repairing camps. Like their infantry counterparts, they were disbanded by the end of 1917.

Army Service Corps (ASC)

In August 1914 Nos 1 and 2 Companies, ASC, composed of labourers with former foremen as NCOs, were working in the depots at the ports supplying the BEF. By the end of the year another four companies had arrived and by 1916 thirty-four such ASC labour companies had been deployed in France.

In early 1915 two railway labour companies, ASC, with men recruited from UK railways, were working at the main railheads supplying the front.

Also in 1915, Nos 35 and 36 Naval Labour Companies were raised from dockers and stevedores to unload ships – they were later transferred to the Royal Marines.

Prisoners of war

With the huge increase in prisoner numbers during the Somme battles, it was decided to create prisoner-of-war companies for labouring duties behind the combat zone. They were composed of around 425 prisoners each, with two British officers and some sixty other ranks for administration and guards, and by September forty-seven such companies were working.

Non-Combatant Corps (NCC)

Eight NCC companies were formed of unarmed pacifists equipped with various tools for field engineering tasks.

Colonial units

In 1916 the first South African Cape Coloured Labour Battalion arrived on the Western Front – a force that eventually grew to more than 20,000 men. They were technically civilians but were employed under military law and they were contracted to work in France for a year.

The British West Indies Regiment sent seven battalions to France as labour units, along with the Bermuda Militia Artillery contingent.

The Chinese Labour Corps (CLC) was formed in early 1917, growing to over 95,000 by the Armistice (see box below).

An Indian Labour Corps, some 21,000 strong, was also formed for work in France and the Middle East, with companies composed of different races and religions.

1917 also saw the arrival of 15,000 members of the Egyptian Labour Corps on a six-month contract. They were followed by volunteers in contingents from Malta, Mauritius, the Seychelles and Fiji. This last group was only 100 strong, but they proved such good dockworkers that they were granted the official title of Fijian Labour Corps in 1918.

A major effort was made to rationalize the military 'non-technical' labour organizations in January 1917 with the formation of the Labour Corps under a director of labour, a brigadier general, at GHQ. The corps absorbed the infantry and RE labour battalions (except units permanently attached to transportation services), twenty-eight ASC labour companies and divisional salvage companies. These units also served as combat infantry as required during the crisis in March and April 1918, winning a large number of gallantry awards. Towards the end of that year they received their own cap badge – a pick, shovel and rifle bound together by a laurel wreath – and were the forerunners of the Royal Pioneer Corps, which adopted the same badge and is now part of the Royal Logistics Corps. The Labour Corps grew to 390,000 by the end of the war, with around 175,000 working in the United Kingdom and the remainder in other theatres.

The Chinese Labour Corps

The first to recruit Chinese/Vietnamese labour were the French. The first shipload arrived at Marseilles in July 1916 and were employed on road-building in northern France. The British followed suite in 1917 and employed almost 100,000 by the end of the war. They were volunteers who came mainly from Shantung or some other northern provinces and served under military discipline. They were assembled at the tiny British possession of Wei-hai-wei on the Chinese coast.

Their contracts stipulated working ten hours a day, seven days a week, although allowance was made for special Chinese festivals. They were given a number and referred to officially as 'coolies'. Each was given ten Mexican silver dollars on recruitment – many left most of them with their parents; thereafter their wages ranged from 1 franc a day for a labourer to 2.50 francs for a skilled worker, 2.60 francs for an assistant interpreter (equivalent of a sergeant) and 5 francs for an interpreter/clerk. The great majority came straight from the paddy fields of rural China and were described by one British officer as a 'very simple, very strong, very entertaining people'. To avoid fraud, all had their fingerprints registered in Scotland Yard. Chinese-speaking British personnel were recruited as officers and NCOs.

Generally the Chinese worked hard and behaved well if treated with respect and an occasional show of kindness. There were, however, some unpleasant incidents. They were particularly resentful of any bullying by British NCOs – a number who tried it on ended up being badly injured by a blow to the back of the neck with a shovel on a dark night. In an extreme case, a sergeant had his throat slit. On occasion they warned the NCO by giving him a 'Black Hand Gang' note – in which case the man was rapidly removed from his post. One of their oddities was wearing all their clothes all the time, and according to one witness never taking them off from one year's end to the next! Add to this their passion for wearing hats –

Members of the Chinese Labour Corps.

many bought several bowler hats, which they wore as a status symbol one on top of the other – and they must have presented a somewhat comical appearance.

On Christmas Day 1917 there was a mutiny by Chinese labourers which was witnessed by a Sapper David Doe, RE. His diary record of the event is quoted in Malcolm Brown's *The Imperial War Museum Book of the Western Front*:

25 December. Went to HQ for Xmas dinner and tea. After dinner we went over to the football ground to see a match at 3 p.m., but the Chinese coolies encamped just opposite put a stop to it. They murdered their NCOs and fled the camp armed with sticks, iron and the tops of picks. They came across our ground and then the artillery camp turned out and commenced firing rifles at them. Several shots missed me by not much! The police sent us all back to camp to get *our* rifles and we all had to turn out to shoot the Chinese to help stop the mutiny. About eight were shot on our footer ground. Some had got very far away and we had to help round them up. In all we captured 93 prisoners. *Some* Xmas believe me!

Apart from the above shootings, ten Chinese were executed by the British between 1918 and 1920 (Chinese labour was retained after the war for the huge clearing-up operations).

The Chinese, who were kept strictly segregated from Europeans, provided an essential component of the overall labour force on the Western Front during the final two years of the war and for some time afterwards. The graves of most of the 1,612 Chinese who died are scattered among twenty military cemeteries across France. The Chinese War Cemetery at Noyelles-sur-Mer contains the graves of 838 and commemorates forty-one who have no known grave. In 2010 a monument to the Chinese Labour Corps was unveiled at Poperinghe.

Supplies arriving at the railhead at Écurie in 1915.

Section Eight

Supply and Transport

The more I see of war, the more I realize how it all depends on administration and transportation . . . It takes little skill or imagination to see where you would like your army to be and when; it takes much knowledge and hard work to know where you can place your forces and whether you can maintain them there. A real knowledge of supply and movement factors must be the basis of every leader's plan . . .

Field Marshal Earl Wavell

The above quote by the distinguished World War II commander encapsulates the critical importance of logistics, the continuous supply and movement of men and materials without which any army is quickly crippled. Logistical support for an army can be very roughly regarded as meaning the three 'Ms': men, munitions and movement. Logistics was the primary responsibility of the administrative and service staff at a headquarters and service or administrative units on the lines of communication. Despite being derided by many, these staff and units ultimately proved highly successful in overcoming the monstrous problems they faced (the BEF trebled in size during 1915 and doubled again the following year), although there were, of course, times when soldiers went hungry, were cold, wet and miserable, went short of ammunition or lacked some equipment. This is inevitable for some units at some time during a war – it still happens today.

It was with the realization in late 1914 and through 1915 that this was to be a war of a scale and type never previously seen or contemplated that brought home to politicians and commanders the immense shortfall in virtually every aspect of logistics. It was within days of the war on the Western Front starting that the vagaries of battle, of advance and withdrawal, exposed the problems of maintaining supplies for both sides. The danger of losing a line of communication, and therefore the potential collapse of the means to fight, is well illustrated by the German First Army's threat to the exposed BEF's line of communication in August 1914 when it was compelled to retreat from Mons (Map 63). This threat forced the evacuation of Le Havre in great haste and confusion to establish a new base at St-Nazaire–Nantes. Major General A. Forbes, who served as a senior ordnance staff officer throughout the war, later described this evacuation:

The position then, when the order to evacuate Havre was received in the afternoon of the 29th August, was as follows: Scattered about the gigantic Hanger au Coton and other sheds or wharves were some 20,000 tons of clothing, ammunition and stores of unknown quantities, with more arriving daily. The articles were in miscellaneous heaps often buried under piles of forage; wagons had been dismantled for shipment, the bodies had not yet been erected on their wheels, machine guns had not been assembled with their mounts or cartridge belts, guns with their mechanisms, cases of horse-shoes with those of nails . . . horses were stabled among the stores and French and Belgian soldiers encamped there [inside the enormous shed] . . .

A telephone message from the Port Naval Officer that all unloading was to cease instantly and everything to be bundled back on board ship with the utmost despatch, some small-arm ammunition being put as deck cargo on each vessel. This was followed by an order from the Base Commandant detailing the priority of loading; firstly ammunition according to its nature – small arm, then 18-pounder and so on; then guns, next engineering equipments, and lastly general stores, clothing, vehicles, etc., according as time might admit. Everything not on board by the 3rd September was to be abandoned. One result of this it will be noticed that the most vital fighting equipment went to the bottom of the hold . . .

The stores loaded in this haphazard way, were in hopeless confusion. There were cases of service dress caps, parts of guns and machine guns, bales of horse rugs and blankets, ammunition, tentage, signalling gear, etc. – much in broken packages – mingled with forage, medical, veterinary, and other goods . . . to sort out this chaos was a lengthy and tedious operation, accompanied by a considerable amount of looting.

Sandbags

According to the history of the Royal Army Ordnance Corps, no category of commodities, except for ammunition, approached sandbags in bulk (although statistics seem to show fodder was also greater). Demands for sandbags increased in leaps and bounds and, to supplement supplies from home, large contracts were placed in France. It was thought at the time that when a firm of sack-makers in Flixecourt undertook to provide 30,000 a day a major breakthrough had occurred. Later the consumption rate for the BEF was calculated at a million a day and, on one occasion in 1916, 10 million were sent to the front in four days. They fast became such desirable items that soldiers even requested sandbags along with other items in letters home. This was because they were not just required to construct trenches and bunkers, but to wrap around puttees to keep out the mud, to lie on or use as extra blankets in winter, as cleaning rags and as carrier bags for ration or ammunition parties.

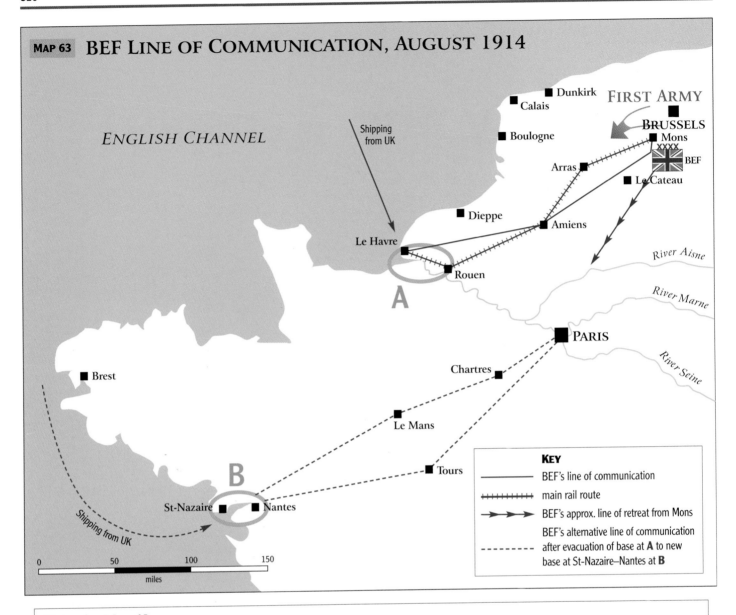

MAP 63 BEF LINE OF COMMUNICATION, AUGUST 1914

ENGLISH CHANNEL

Dunkirk
Calais
FIRST ARMY
Boulogne
BRUSSELS
Mons
XXXX
Arras
BEF
Le Cateau
Dieppe
Amiens
River Aisne
Le Havre
Rouen
River Marne
A
PARIS
River Seine
Brest
Chartres
Le Mans
Tours
B
St-Nazaire
Nantes
Shipping from UK
Shipping from UK

0   50   100   150
miles

KEY

——————— BEF's line of communication

++++++++++ main rail route

→→→→→ BEF's approx. line of retreat from Mons

- - - - - - - BEF's alternative line of communication after evacuation of base at **A** to new base at St-Nazaire–Nantes at **B**

Notes for Map 63
• The BEF's retreat from Mons exposed its line of communication to Kluck's advancing First Army, so French had no alternative but to order an immediate change of base from Le Havre to Nantes.

• The new line of communication with the IGC's headquarters at Le Mans added considerable distance to both the shipping and land routes to the front. Fortunately, the Germans were defeated on the Marne

and driven back to the Aisne, and the BEF was able to regain Le Havre and other bases on the French coast as the front stabilized and then became static at the end of the year.

There was similar confusion and loss of equipment during the German offensives of March 1918. But the great shell shortage of 1915, when artillery batteries had to be rationed and many shells were found to be defective, as has already been discussed (see pages 238–40), was one of the most public and potentially damaging supply problems for the British. Nevertheless, despite these setbacks, the British soldier at the front was seldom, if ever, without the basic means to keep fighting for prolonged periods.

It is normally easier to keep a static army maintained than one advancing, with ever-lengthening supply lines and distance from secure bases. For the Germans it was the

rapid advance that exposed serious weaknesses in their logistical arrangements. The most obvious example was the right-wing army of the Germans' offensive through Belgium and northern France in August 1914. Had the Germans won on the Marne their further advance would have been extremely problematic without a prolonged halt to allow supplies to catch up. Even Moltke's modified invasion plan – with a weaker right wing and shorter distances (300 instead of 400 miles) to march, due to Kluck's army turning south at Brussels rather than his grenadiers' sleeves brushing the coast – did not have sufficient logistical back-up to maintain delivery to many lead-

ing formations. Numerous units had to supplement their rations by living off the countryside, plundering or capturing enemy stocks. Fortunately for the Germans, the Belgian retreat had been rapid and they had failed to destroy many supply dumps. Also, the French countryside was rich and it was the harvest season. At Liège and Amiens large stocks were seized, and after the battle at Le Cateau British dumps were looted. However, no army the size of the German one – especially an army heavily dependent on so much technical armament and equipment – could march and fight over hundreds of miles indefinitely without a properly functioning supply and replacement system.

While most men's stomachs were reasonably full, the same could not be said for the horses upon which the movement of men and equipment at the front depended. Kluck's First Army alone had around 85,000 horses requiring about 2 million lb of fodder every day, and although it was harvest time, feeding on green corn weakened many animals. Proper arrangements for feeding horses had been neglected and the veterinary service was largely non-existent, with the result that during the advance through northern France many horses were suffering from exhaustion and dying. This had a hugely adverse effect on cavalry operations, with large numbers of animals unable to carry their riders. Heavy artillery units were similarly affected and unable to keep up with the advance.

By the time the Germans reached the Marne, the physical and mental effects of exhausting marches, a growing shortage of supplies and the dire situation with horsepower were of acute concern to the German High Command – and this despite Kluck having further cut the distance marched by turning east of Paris rather than crossing the Seine between that city and Rouen as originally planned.

By winter 1914/1915 warfare was becoming extremely complex in terms of the quantity and varied types of supplies, weapons, munitions and equipment, as well as men required to keep armies functioning in the field. At the outbreak of the war the ration strength of the BEF was about 120,000 men and 53,000 animals, while at the Armistice some 3 million persons and 500,000 animals had to be fed daily. With battle consuming men and materials at a rate never dreamed of, increased production and importation was only half the solution; the other half, and often the most difficult, was the ability to move requirements to the right troops at the right place at the right time. It was at ports and base depots and along an army's lines of communication that supplies of all kinds were offloaded, stored, broken into formation or unit loads and moved forward again. Use was made of existing rail, roads and waterways, along with their expansion and adaptation for distribution to troops, not just at the front but also to the ever-expanding numbers of rear-area units. This dependence on lines of communication has dominated military campaigning in varying degrees since wars began. A key objective of generals has frequently been to sever an enemy's lines of communication, as to do so for any length of time could starve him of the means, and weaken his ability and will, to fight.

The remainder of this section examines logistics under the separate headings of Supply and Transportation, although each was entirely dependent on the other to keep the soldier fighting. Space prevents a close look at each belligerent's logistical arrangements, so discussion concentrates on the British system, with much briefer reference to those of the French, Americans and Germans.

Supply

Lines of communication consisted of sea lanes, inland waterways, railways and roads. These were the conveyor belts that delivered supplies and personnel to the field armies from the home base and elsewhere, and along which the seriously wounded, soldiers going on leave, damaged equipment and empty vehicles returned. There was always a need to offload, break bulk and reload supplies at various stages of the journey – at ports, main base depots (regarded perhaps as the wholesalers of the supply system), advanced depots (the retailers or distributors), regulating stations, railheads and refilling points before delivery to the units (see diagram, pages 346–7). It was at these locations that supplies of all types were stockpiled, broken down into specific packages to meet the detailed demands of formations and units, and reserves built up and maintained.

The BEF's strategic supply base was the United Kingdom – the source of the overwhelming majority of its needs. Thousands of different items were required and had to be manufactured, requisitioned or imported and stocked, kept in depots around the country for movement to ports for the cross-Channel journey to France – almost 25.5 million tons of supplies ranging from food, ammunition, timber and tanks to canteen goods (see box, page 467) were shipped to France during the war. The general term 'supply' covers anything needed by the army,

German Supply and Transportation Organization

The German system of supplying their armies was extremely complex and the detail is beyond the scope of this book. However, the principles of lines of communication using railways, railheads, bases and depots and both motor and horse transport were the same as with the Allies. The supply of armies in the field was carried out mainly through a branch known as the Intendance (*Intendantur*), which was ultimately controlled by the army administration department of the War Ministry. Responsibility for the overall supply of the army rested with the quartermaster general, whose immediate subordinate was the intendant general. Each army in the field had an intendant, as did each corps and division, whose task was to coordinate the supply of his formation whether it came from local sources or through line of communication units such as supply columns, parks, bakeries, etc. These military officials roughly corresponded to British supply and administrative staff. At the headquarters of regiments there was a transport officer and with the battalions a supply officer (equivalent to the British quartermaster).

All personnel of the medical and supply units, except for professional/technical personnel, belonged to the train that provided the men, horses and vehicles of transport, of supply units and of regiments (nearest British equivalent was the Army Service Corps). Ammunition, transport, supply and bakery columns, as well as bridging trains, were formed into divisional and corps trains allotted to specific formations. In 1916, because it had proved vital to be able to move divisions from one sector of the front to another with increasing frequency and this transfer of administrative and supply units was complex, a reorganization was undertaken of supply arrangements. The use of MT was increased, with several such units being attached to each army, and army MT columns were allotted to corps temporarily as required; the only divisional MT column moved with its division to a new area. The front was divided into sectors and all horsed ammunition, transport and supply columns became sector units grouped permanently under sector staff with one staff to each divisional sector and corps headquarters. On this basis, a divisional sector would usually be allocated two artillery-ammunition columns, a supply column, a supply park, a field bakery column and a divisional bridging train. Corps headquarters were similarly constituted and additionally controlled a field hospital, veterinary and field butchery.

MAP 64 ENGLAND – MAIN WESTERN FRONT SUPPLY BASE, 1914–1918

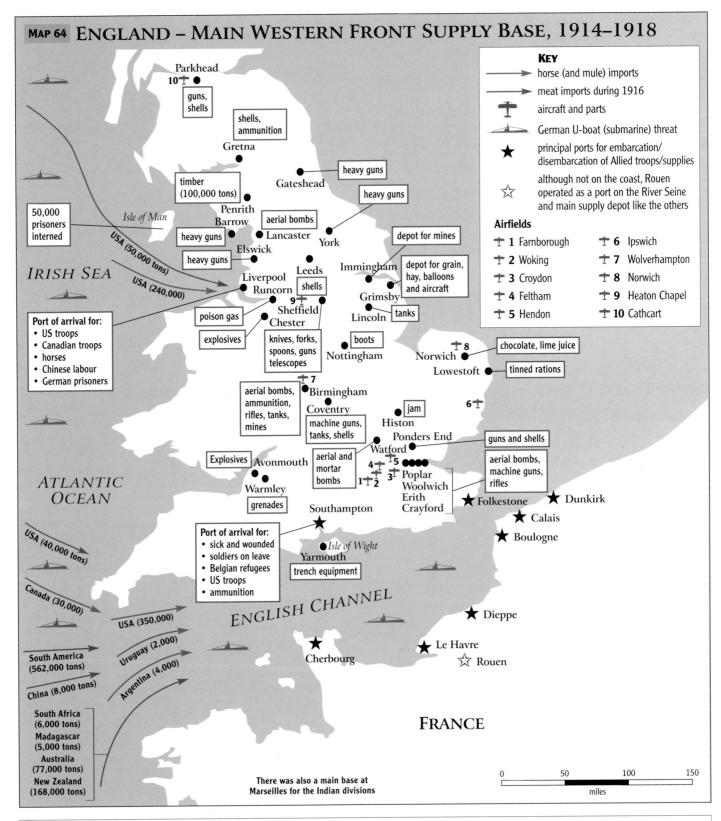

KEY

→ horse (and mule) imports
→ meat imports during 1916
✈ aircraft and parts
⊷ German U-boat (submarine) threat
★ principal ports for embarcation/disembarcation of Allied troops/supplies
☆ although not on the coast, Rouen operated as a port on the River Seine and main supply depot like the others

Airfields
✝ 1 Farnborough   ✝ 6 Ipswich
✝ 2 Woking   ✝ 7 Wolverhampton
✝ 3 Croydon   ✝ 8 Norwich
✝ 4 Feltham   ✝ 9 Heaton Chapel
✝ 5 Hendon   ✝ 10 Cathcart

Parkhead — 10 — guns, shells

shells, ammunition — Gretna

timber (100,000 tons) — Penrith Barrow — heavy guns — Elswick — heavy guns

heavy guns — Gateshead
heavy guns — York
aerial bombs — Lancaster

depot for mines

Leeds — shells
Immingham — depot for grain, hay, balloons and aircraft

50,000 prisoners interned

Isle of Man

USA (50,000 tons)
USA (240,000)

IRISH SEA

Liverpool — Runcorn — 9
Sheffield
Chester
poison gas
explosives

knives, forks, spoons, guns telescopes

Grimsby
Lincoln — tanks
boots
Nottingham

Norwich — 8 — chocolate, lime juice
Lowestoft — tinned rations

Port of arrival for:
• US troops
• Canadian troops
• horses
• Chinese labour
• German prisoners

ATLANTIC OCEAN

aerial bombs, ammunition, rifles, tanks, mines — 7 — Birmingham
Coventry
machine guns, tanks, shells
Histon — jam
6

Ponders End
Watford — guns and shells

Explosives — Avonmouth
aerial and mortar bombs
4 — 5
1 — 2 — 3 — Poplar Woolwich Erith Crayford
aerial bombs, machine guns, rifles

Warmley
grenades

Southampton

Folkestone — ★ — Dunkirk ★
★ Calais
★ Boulogne

USA (40,000 tons)

Canada (30,000)

USA (350,000)

Port of arrival for:
• sick and wounded
• soldiers on leave
• Belgian refugees
• US troops
• ammunition

Isle of Wight
Yarmouth — trench equipment

ENGLISH CHANNEL

Uruguay (2,000)

South America (562,000 tons)

China (8,000 tons)

Argentina (4,000)

★ Dieppe

★ Le Havre
☆ Rouen

Cherbourg ★

FRANCE

South Africa (6,000 tons)
Madagascar (5,000 tons)
Australia (77,000 tons)
New Zealand (168,000 tons)

There was also a main base at Marseilles for the Indian divisions

0   50   100   150
miles

Notes for Map 64

• This map shows some, but not all, of the sites of production and storage depots for supplies of all kinds primarily destined for the Western Front. Many items were imported, but the map shows only meat and horses – the meat tonnage only for 1916.

• Britain depended for survival on her merchant fleet and the ability of the Royal Navy to protect it, but it was not until June 1917 that a convoy system of merchant vessels with warship escorts began to be employed – and another six months elapsed before it became fully effective. Between

1914 and 1918 the German U-boats sank almost 8 million tons of British shipping, the majority of it in the English Channel, Irish Sea and the Atlantic Ocean south of Ireland.

• Initially the three French ports at which the BEF disembarked and supplies were offloaded, and which were developed into main bases, were Le Havre, Rouen and Boulogne, known as Nos. 1, 2 and 3 Bases respectively. As the war progressed, supplies crossing the Channel were offloaded at all six French ports shown. From these ports/bases the BEF was fed with men and materials along road, rail and waterway lines of communication.

but most items came under the five headings of munitions (weapons, ammunition, explosives and military equipment), food (rations for men and fodder for animals), clothing, fuel (coal, coke, anthracite, wood for fuel, oil and petrol) and motor vehicles (including motorcycles, lorries, locomotives and wagons, tanks and aircraft). It took many months for Britain's industries to expand or convert to war production and the country was never self-sufficient, meaning considerable reliance was placed on imports (particularly for meat and horses) from around the world (see Map 64). Also, within the United Kingdom, government appeals to the public for voluntary donations of extra items of clothing or small luxuries for troops at the front met with a huge, at times overwhelming, response – some 230 million cigarettes, 45 million medical dressings, 12 million bandages, 16 million books, 4 million pairs of socks and 2 million mufflers were among items supplied in this way. Further supplementation of supplies came with large-scale local purchase, especially of food and fodder, in France. Although the bulk of supplies from the United Kingdom went to the Western Front, she also had at times to maintain British forces in Mesopotamia, the Dardanelles and Salonica, primarily from a main base in Egypt. Over the period of the war Britain also supplemented the supplies of her allies in Europe (France, Belgium, Italy, the USA, Russia and Romania). As just a few examples of many items, she supplied France with around 14,000 machine guns, almost 5 million grenades, 416,000 tons of explosives and 101 tanks; Belgium with 50 million bullets, 878 lorries and ambulances and 34 aircraft; Italy with 50,000 rifles, 950,000 tons of iron and steel and 213 trench mortars; the USA with 164 heavy guns, 11 million bullets, 452 aircraft and 18 tanks; and Russia with 500 medium guns, 27,000 machine guns, 650 aircraft engines and 6 airships.

Before looking at the mechanics of how troops' material needs were stored, issued and moved to the soldiers that needed them, some background information on their basic requirements will be helpful. In Britain the government contracted out the production of the army's requirements and they will be examined under the headings of food (including forage), water, munitions, clothing, fuel, remounts and then a look at salvage.

Food

The prime comfort for the soldier of any army, particularly if in a trench or dugout in the front line, was food. Food included the ability to brew a mess tin of tea. This could be done at any odd moment and would take about fifteen minutes using a 2-inch candle in a bully-beef tin, or about eight minutes with a cigarette tin filled with whale oil and a piece of flannelette as a wick. However, by 1916 most men had small individual 'Tommy cookers' with solid fuel tablets (still used today), or they had a primus stove, so that a brew was usually constantly available when not under fire.

The theoretical ration scale per man was laid down in regulations and for British troops on the Western Front it entitled him each day to:

Meat (fresh or frozen) – 1¼ lb; or preserved (tinned) – 1lb; the former was reduced to 1 lb and the latter to 12 oz in October 1915.

Bread – 1¼ lb, cut to 1 lb in January 1917; or biscuit or flour – 12 oz.

Bacon – 4 oz.

Cheese – 3 oz, reduced to 2 oz from January 1917.

Vegetables – 8 oz fresh or 2 oz dried.

Jam – 4 oz (usually Tickler's plum and apple).

Sugar – 3 oz.

Salt – ½ oz.

Tea – just over ½ oz.

In addition, a tin of condensed milk and small amounts of mustard and pepper were supposed to be shared among up to twenty men. Pickles were issued at 1 oz a week per man; oatmeal was given three times a week; while butter was issued as an extra until 1 July 1917. Added to this was the eagerly awaited daily tot of powerful rum, usually carefully doled out into the soldier's mess tin or enamel mug by the platoon sergeant. The small reductions for front-line soldiers in 1917 were introduced at the same time as somewhat more substantial ones in the rations of line of communication troops.

In full, the ration contained 4,193 calories a day, but the soldier in the front-line trench frequently failed to get his full entitlement due to enemy action or other delays and disruptions in the supply chain. The German ration initially contained slightly more bread and vegetables but less meat and had a calorific value of 4,083, while the Americans received 4,714 calories, with more generous portions of meat and vegetables. The ration was adequate provided it reached the soldier. German troops were issued with mineral water, but if medical officers considered it necessary they were allowed a small daily amount of rum, brandy, arrack, wine or beer.

Australian soldiers resting around a cookhouse that has been set up in the field.

Tommies bargaining with locals over geese for their Christmas dinner in the market at Bailleul, December 1916.

For the British the most common dish prepared in the field from rations was the all-in stew (familiar to the present writer and soldiers the world over). Preference was usually given to tins of Fray Bentos, regarded as the best brand of bully beef, which could be put in the stew-pot with dried vegetables, made into a hash, or eaten cold with bread or biscuit. A common variation was the Maconochie tin of meat and vegetables (referred to as M and V), which could also make the basis of a reasonable stew. A Private Harold Horne of the Northumberland Fusiliers interviewed in 1978 recalled:

Sometimes we got Manconochie [*sic*] rations. This was a sort of Irish stew in tins which could be quickly heated over a charcoal brazier. When it was possible to have a cookhouse within easy reach of the trenches, fresh meat, bacon, vegetables, flour, etc., would be sent up and the cooks could produce reasonably good meals. Food and tea was sent along in 'dixies' [large iron containers the lid of which could be used as a frying pan].

There were times, when out of the line or during quiet periods, when the troops ate reasonably well, but when the enemy was active things were different. As Harry Patch, the 'last fighting Tommy', who died aged 111 and 38 days on 25 July 2009 (see box, page 190), said, 'Our rations – you were lucky if you got some bully beef and a biscuit. You couldn't get your teeth into it. Sometimes if they shelled the supply lines you didn't get anything for days on end.'

If practical, officers invariably supplemented their rations with local purchase of items such as fish, tinned fruit, eggs or different meats, as their higher pay enabled them better to afford the exorbitant prices often charged by storekeepers behind the lines. It was not uncommon for a company officers' mess of perhaps five or six to place a weekly order with a London store for a food parcel. One major writing to his family considered, rightly it seems, that he and his fellow officers ate well:

I give you a day's menu at random: Breakfast – bacon and tomatoes, bread, jam and cocoa. Lunch – shepherd's pie, potted meat, potatoes, bread and jam. Tea – bread and jam. Supper – ox-tail soup, roast beef, whisky and soda, leeks, rice pudding and coffee. We have provided stores of groceries and Harrods have been ordered to send us out a weekly parcel. However, if you like to send us an occasional luxury it would be very welcome.

Most soldiers depended on parcels from home for extra luxuries to relieve the monotony, with items such as fruit cake, ham, sardines, sweets, chocolate and, most popular of all, Woodbine cigarettes. As in the recent wars in Iraq and Afghanistan, friends and relatives were generous with their gifts and many sent additional amounts for distribution to their soldier's comrades – and it was not uncommon for a recipient not to know the sender.

If General Sixt von Armin, commander of the German Fourth Army during the third Battle of Ypres, is to be believed, the German troops' ration was deteriorating, certainly in quantity, during the latter part of the war when there was severe rationing in Germany due to the British naval blockade. As early as January 1915 German food restrictions began at home with the introduction of bread cards, and in October two meatless and fatless days a week were introduced. In a report Armin stated:

All troops were unanimous in their request for increased supplies of bread, rusks, sausage, tinned sausages, tinned fat, bacon, tinned and smoked meat, and tobacco, in addition. There is also urgent need for solidified alcohol for the preparation of hot meals [this latter item, now called 'hexamine', is still issued for individual cooking in today's British Army].

In various quarters, the necessity for a plentiful supply of liquid refreshments of all kinds, such as coffee, tea, cocoa, mineral waters etc., is emphasized still more. On the other hand, the supply of salt herrings, which increase the thirst, was to be found, as a general rule, very undesirable.

The French Army ration consisted of 26 oz bread or 24 oz biscuits, 18 oz fresh or tinned meat, 3½ oz vegetables, 1¾ oz salt pork or 1 oz salt, 1 oz lard, small amounts of coffee and sugar and 0.25 litre wine. Generally, in the earlier part of the war supplies of food to the front were erratic and meals commonly arrived cold or not at all, causing considerable grumbling.

Food was fresh (frozen) or tinned and for front-line troops of all armies was either cooked behind the lines in the battalion cookers (one per company), wheeled horse-drawn wagons fitted with dixies – large, open iron pots that were heated by a fire below. It was then carried forward at night by fatigue parties, meaning it usually arrived cold or at best lukewarm. A better way was to take the food forward in hay boxes – large, double-skinned, straw-lined metal boxes designed to keep food hot on the same principle as a Thermos flask. Central cooking, being the most popular, was used as often as possible, with the cooks' wagon behind the lines and the company cooks (usually two) preparing the all-in stew, which was sent up to the trenches after dark along with the dry rations. These would be carried in dirty sandbags with tea and sugar shaken into separate corners and tied in place. When available, tins of jam, cheese, bully beef, bacon, butter, biscuits, bread and mail were placed on top. With the carrying party stumbling, tripping over wire and perhaps dodging shells in the dark, loads were not infrequently dropped in the mud and those items not in tins were less than appetizing on arrival – but woe betide the man who spilt the rum!

Charcoal braziers were another common method of cooking, but when the charcoal ran out wood from duckboards or trench revetments was often used, to the serious detriment of the condition of the trenches. Sometimes a group of men would acquire a small primus stove on which – again, if they could obtain the fuel – a meal could be prepared. With minor differences, this was how the soldiers of any army fed in the forward area.

An emergency ration, called an 'iron ration', was carried by every man in all armies for use if cut off from regular food supplies for a long period. It was supposed to be eaten only on the orders of an officer. For the British it consisted of 1 lb preserved meat (bully beef), 3 oz cheese, 12 oz biscuits, ⅝ oz tea, 2 oz sugar, ½ oz salt and two meat-extract (Oxo) cubes. From October 1915 there was no cheese, salt or meat extract.

The journey forward from source to the British soldier on the Western Front was a long one, with most of the meat, for example, originating thousands of miles away. To facilitate its collection, handling and storage, bulk meat supply was frozen and at the outset of the war meat ships were permanently allotted to each of the overseas base ports for use as store ships. Subsequently, in many places cold-storage facilities were built. Initially stocks were purchased or requisitioned from within the country, but it soon became obvious that large-scale importation was essential. The British Board of Trade arranged contracts with South America (Argentina, Paraguay, Uruguay, Brazil and Venezuela), Australia, New Zealand, the USA, China, South Africa and Madagascar (see Map 64) for meat supplies – a total of 866,000 tons was imported in 1916 alone.

From the first, bread for the BEF was baked in field bakeries at each base port in France – the bakers' work being facilitated by the introduction of steam ovens in 1915. Capacity was further enhanced when various forms of automatic machinery were introduced in the base bakeries and women workers were employed, thus relieving the Army Service Corps (ASC) men for other duties. These automatic bakeries were supplied by the appropriately named firm of Messrs Baker and Sons, of Willesden, each being able to produce a daily average of 50,000 lb. As noted above, fresh bread often arrived in the trenches dirty or wet or both, and then had to be cut up and divided among a group of four or five soldiers. However, this number fluctuated almost daily because of deaths, or men suddenly absent due to wounds or sickness, so that a loaf could be split only two or three ways as the missing men's rations were delivered until the system registered their absence. Bread was a staple and popular item, much preferred to the alternatives of hardtack biscuits (often referred to as dog biscuits) or oatmeal or rice, and whenever possible it was purchased locally. The biscuits have been almost, but not quite, universally condemned as virtually inedible due to their concrete-like consistency. A soldier in the Royal Artillery had this to say about them:

> The biscuits were so hard that you had to put them on a firm surface and smash them with a stone or something. I've held one in my hand and hit the sharp corner of a brick wall and only hurt my hand. Sometimes we soaked the smashed fragments in water for several days. Then we would heat and drain, pour condensed milk over the stuff and get it down.

Another way of rendering the biscuits edible was to boil a mess tin full of water and then add the biscuits. When they had dissolved into a sort of porridge a tin of plum and apple jam was stirred in and the result eaten with a spoon. It was also not uncommon for biscuits to be burnt as fuel rather than eaten.

Despite frequent, if relatively brief, shortages in the trenches there was a huge wastage of food behind the front line. Richard Holmes illustrates this by describing tented artillery headquarters' floors and

French Rations

Initially the French planned to continue the usual peacetime system whereby soldiers got at least one hot meal every evening, cooked on a company basis in a mobile kitchen and prepared by cooks who did duty on a roster like any other fatigue. In garrison or on manoeuvres this worked fine – at the end of the day the meal would be prepared and served hot to the men as they queued up with their mess tins. However, during the first few weeks of the war the Germans captured a considerable amount of stores, many mobile kitchens proved defective, were lost or damaged and rations became scarce. With the development of trench warfare this system of company cooking became unworkable for troops in the front line.

In the trenches, particularly if fighting was in progress, French soldiers, as in most armies, were forced to exist on a tepid or cold meal at around 4:00 a.m. that was cooked well behind the lines and brought to the trenches by carrying parties or by mule, usually along with the ammunition and other supplies. Invariably it was a vegetable soup (*la soupe*) or some sort of stew that was not easily distinguishable from the soup. Bringing forward the heavy containers of food on carrying frames, often in open tins, was not a popular task as it often meant negotiating ground pitted with shell holes in the dark and with the likelihood of being hit by pre-planned enemy harassing fire.

The soldiers were supposedly entitled to 0.5 litre of wine daily (increased in 1915 from 0.25) and most regarded this and cigarettes as the most important part of the ration when, or if, it arrived. The wine, which was held in a 2-litre canteen (as were water and coffee), was cheap and rough (*pinard*) and not infrequently arrived in the form of a solidified jelly that had to be melted – this was of a particularly poor quality. In severe winter weather or prior to a major attack the troops might be issued with a powerful spirit (*gniole*) – the equivalent of the British rum ration.

The standard ration for troops in the rear or out of the line resting consisted of a fourteen-day menu with meat, vegetables, fruit, bread and other baked foods, although there was no set calorific entitlement. Messing facilities could be established near supply railheads, bases, medical facilities and rest camps or training camps to provide reasonable meals for those troops lucky enough to get them. As with all soldiers in rear areas, there was the opportunity to supplement rations with locally purchased items or meals at cafés. The field ration whose problematic delivery has been described above usually consisted of salted meat, fish, various pâtés made of meat scraps, lard, cheese, vegetables, rice, potatoes and beans – many of which went into the stew.

Like other armies, the French had a reserve or iron ration usually consisting of two tins of boiled or corned beef, tinned sardines, twelve hardtack biscuits, two packets of dried soup and two coffee tablets. The standard meat ration packed in tapered or straight tins was the Madagascar (a French colony) brand '*Boeuf Bouilli*', which the French soldiers assumed contained monkey meat; since then the French Armed Forces have called all tinned meat '*singe*' (monkey) meat. The British reversed the words *boeuf bouilli* and called tinned meat 'bully beef'.

One of the many complaints by the French Army mutineers of 1917 (see box, page 128) was the poor quality and quantity of the food and its improvement was one of the reforms brought in by Marshal Pétain that helped halt the discontent. British and later American units serving in French formations were initially unhappy with French rations but later, while still describing them as queer, got used to them.

paths being paved with unopened bully-beef tins – no doubt because better alternatives were more readily available to purchase in the rear areas.

Bacon was popular and was usually of good quality. Cheese was an important part of the ration, the supply of which was arranged by the Board of Trade through contracts for the entire supply from Australia, New Zealand and Canada. It gave the army what it wanted, leaving the balance for the civil populace.

The critical importance of horses and mules for the functioning of all armies is discussed below under 'Remounts' (page 339); here it is sufficient to note that in November 1918 there were 305,664 horses and 76,602 mules in France, giving a total of 382,266 draft, riding and pack animals with the BEF. The tonnage of oats and hay shipped to France from August 1914 to November 1918 amounted to 5,438,602 tons – a total that exceeds even the tonnage of ammunition shipped by 185,264 tons and dramatically illustrates the supply problem for this item alone. For Germany the inability to import fodder (it sometimes had sawdust mixed in to ease the feelings of hunger – also resorted to by other nations) was ultimately to lead to the death of thousands of horses through semi-starvation combined with overwork, causing serious movement and hence tactical and supply problems.

Hungry and thirsty animals were the norm on the Western Front for much of the time, as the required daily ration – for heavy draught horses 19 lb oats and 15 lb hay, and 12 lb each for other horses, along with some bran at least once a week – could seldom be sustained in the forward area; it was not uncommon for ravenous horses to chew at wagon wheels. During the retreat from Mons, horses suffered severely, as Gunner J. W. Palmer explained:

> The position over the rations for both men and horses was rather precarious. These were the days when we went without rations of any kind or water. The horses were more or less starved of water. On the retreat we went to various streams with our buckets, but no sooner had we got the water half way back to them, than we moved again.
>
> We had strong feelings towards our horses. We went into the fields and beat the corn and oats out of the ears and brought them back, but that didn't save them. As the days went on, the horse's belly got more up into the middle of its back, and the cry was frequently down the line, 'Saddler – a plate and a punch!' This meant the saddler had to come along and punch some more holes in the horse's leather girth to keep the saddle on.

Initially, oats for the BEF were procured under arrangements made by the government's director of contracts, supplemented by shipments from Canada. However, with monthly requirements growing to about 85,000 tons, additional shipments were arranged from the USA and Central and Southern America. As only the oats from Canada were bagged, the rest being loose in bulk, floating pneumatic suction plants were erected in early 1917 at the base ports.

Like oats, hay was initially obtained under contract locally, supplemented by shipments from Canada. However, hay had necessarily to be shipped in compressed form (bales) and the only pressing establishment under War Office control was at Woolwich, which was able to press only limited quantities. Fortunately, for the first six months most of the BEF's requirements could be met by local purchase. By the end of 1914 an organizing committee was appointed by the Army Council to facilitate the purchase of forage (fodder) by the military authorities direct from the farmer. At about the same time, a forage department was established along with advisory committees in each English county, and the purchase and pressing of hay was started throughout the country, supervised by officers from the Forage Department. This resulted in large quantities becoming available. A vital part of the labour required to harvest the hay was provided by the Women's Forage Corps (see box below), which was formed in 1915 and attached to the Army Service Corps. In November 1915 a forage committee replaced the organizing committee for the supply of forage and other farm produce to troops at home and overseas. Six forage department companies (ASC) for England, and one each for Scotland and Ireland, were formed. By 1916 shipping difficulties from overseas (the German U-boat threat) direct to France meant that shipments from Britain had to be substantially increased – the entire crop for that year, some 14 million tons, was taken over by the War Department; of it, over a million tons was required by the army, the remainder being released for use by farmers and the public.

The Women's Forage Corps (WFC)

This little-known unit of the ASC eventually numbered 6,000 women who worked throughout the UK gathering forage for army horses. It was controlled from the War Office under the overall direction of a superintendent of women, Mrs Athole Stewart. The country was divided into areas under an area administrator and area inspector of women. Each area was then subdivided into districts under an assistant superintendent of women, along with a district purchasing officer.

The women worked in several capacities. In the field they were involved in the whole process of harvesting. Gangs of six worked on baling, feeding the machine by forking hay from the stacks, tying the bales with wire and

Members of the Women's Forage Corps feed a hay-baler on a British farm.

checking the weight of each bale as it left the machine. Horse-transport drivers in charge of teams of horses and wagons took the bales to the nearest railway station, where forwarding supervisors checked the bales' weight and supervised loading. There were also officials dealing with correspondence and quartermistresses who drove machine supervisors around on their inspections of the hay-baling machines and issued rations.

It was invaluable and extremely strenuous work that involved considerable hardship. The women wore a khaki-and-green uniform with an ASC cap badge and 'FC' shoulder titles. The corps was disbanded at the end of the war.

Water

The demand for water for men and animals was immense – both could survive and work without food much longer than they could without water. Water was required for drinking, cooking, washing, laundry and baths. For men it invariably needed purification. In rear areas much use was made of the civil water-supply system, which was improved and developed by army engineers. Responsibility for supply to the BEF rested with the Royal Engineers. The installation of water-supply facilities, including sinking bore holes (wells), was carried out by field companies supplemented by labour units in the divisional areas, and by army troop companies in the corps areas. The objective was to establish water-supply points all along the front, and that water be provided as far forward as possible by means of pumps and piping – these supplies were supplemented by motorized water tankers. A water-supply committee was set up at GHQ in 1915 and a water-supply officer was attached to the chief engineer at each army and corps headquarters as an adviser, and to take responsibility for the issue of all water-supply stores.

Space prevents discussion of this subject in detail, but a brief look at water-supply arrangements for the Somme offensive gives a clear indication of what was involved.

The first requirement was to assemble the large quantity of extra water-supply plant and equipment from England – including powerful steam fire-engine pumping sets from the London County Council. More boring plant was acquired and two water-supply barges equipped with purification plant and pumps for forcing filtered water through pipes were sent to the Somme area. A pump-repair shop was established at Varennes, near Acheux, and arrangements made for the extension during the advance of the system of 4-inch and 6-inch piping, which was laid on the ground or in 2½-foot trenches, and for the provision of water points. A typical water point consisted of 2,000-gallon canvas tanks on the ground (later made of galvanized iron and raised on a scaffolding platform), provided with a hose for filling vehicles and taps for water bottles. Each attacking corps was given eighty additional horse-drawn water carts and the provision of a water tank column (ASC) consisting of 192 3-ton and 111 one-ton lorries, carrying 550- and 135-gallon tanks and equipment for the purification of water on the surface or in shallow wells. These vehicles were available to take water up to 10 miles from water points to fill unit water carts. At the height of the battle, water was provided for 300,000 men and 150,000 animals. In the event, 1.25 million

A water cart, stuck in the mud up to its axle, with one wheel and one horse gone over the edge of the brushwood track, at St-Éloi, during the Battle of Pilckem Ridge, August 1917.

gallons were pumped daily and 10,000 gallons carried forward by road.

The preparations for water supply for the British attack on Messines Ridge in June 1917 illustrate the ingenuity of the engineers in utilizing surface water in an area unsuitable for boring wells. On the left the task was comparatively simple, as Zillebeke and Dickelbusch Lakes provided unlimited quantities; in the centre water was trapped by dams to form reservoirs on the slopes of hills; and on the right it was pumped from sterilizing barges on the River Lys.

Appendix F to 30th Division's Operation Order of 1 July 1916, issued on 21 June, said:

(v)   Every man starts with a full water-bottle. Great importance is attached to supervision by regimental officers and NCOs of the use of water-bottles.

(vi)   It is hoped there will be Water Points ready at: Talus Boise
              Willow Trees near
                Machine Gun Wood
              Copse Valley

There are [water] tanks in Chateau Redoubt, Maricourt, and two 400-gallon tanks on trucks on Metre Gauge railway at Carnoy.

Tanks are also being placed in assembly trenches.

(vii) Carriage of water from Water Points by petrol tins and on mules.

8 mules per Battn. carrying 12 gallons each (6 petrol tins).

400 petrol tins per Bde. For hand carriage in addition to the 48 carried on mules.

(viii) If supply fails owing to damage to pipes by shell fire, supply will be by water carts as far as Maricourt and 'U' Works, thence forward by hand.

The divisional RE field company would establish three main water points that would be supplied by pipes, along with a series of water tanks from which unit water carts, mules and personnel could fill up. The intention was to get as many water points and tanks established as close as possible to the front, with a number of tanks actually in the assembly trenches. Battalions were given eight mules, each carrying six petrol cans of water (soldiers always moaned that drinking water tasted of petrol), and perhaps another hundred cans to be carried by hand. All these cans would be taken forward to create a reserve stock of water in the trenches.

Munitions

The term 'munitions' embraces ammunition, guns, weapons and military equipment but is most commonly associated with ammunition and it is the supply of this that concerns the bulk of the following discussion. Several aspects of the BEF's problems with artillery ammunition supply, faulty fuzes and the 'munitions crisis' of 1915 have already been touched on above in Section Five, pages 238–40. As with virtually every other aspect of logistics, British industry was hopelessly unprepared for the volume of demand and lacked the skilled workers necessary for mass production of sophisticated, technical weaponry and ammunition.

Ammunition included not only shells for several different calibres of guns, howitzers and mortars, but also each piece of ordnance eventually needed stocks of HE, shrapnel, smoke or gas projectiles along with their appropriate fuzes. With small-arms ammunition (SAA), the requirement was for rifles and machine guns, tracer rounds, armour-piercing bullets, bullets for sniper rifles and several types of pistol or revolver ammunition. Add to these HE and

Comparative BEF Artillery Ammunition Expenditure in Major Offensives/Battles

This table illustrates the magnitude of the task of supplying shells for the guns and howitzers. The most rounds fired in one period of twenty-four hours by the BEF (the attack on the Hindenburg Line from noon 28 September to noon 29 September 1918) was almost a million, of which 18-pounders firing 553,765, 4.5-inch howitzers 164,267, and 8-inch howitzers 15,340 accounted for 733,372.

A British soldier stands amongst a dump of empty shell cases near Domart, April 1918.

Comparative Usage

Offensives	Period	Approx. expenditure	
		Rounds	Tons
Somme	26 June–9 July 1916	3,526,000	75,000
Arras	9 April–6 May 1917	4,261,500	109,800
Messines	3–10 June 1917	3,280,000	85,500
3rd Ypres	30 July–7 Oct. 1917	2,011,000 (weekly average)	53,400 (weekly average)
Autumn offensive	18 Aug.–27 Oct. 1918	2,203,400 (weekly average)	53,100 (weekly average)

smoke grenades, Very pistol cartridges, rockets, flares and aerial bombs and the size of the problem is clear. Not only were armies rapidly expanding in manpower, but the weapons they used (quick-firing artillery and machine guns) multiplied the quantities of ammunition a hundredfold. Over 5.25 million tons of ammunition were shipped to the BEF in France during the war, but it was not until 1916 that it was possible for British generals to be reasonably confident of having reserves of artillery shells, in particular, on the lines of communication to sustain a major battle.

It was the First Battle of Ypres that brought home the realization of the sheer volume and variety of ammunition needed in modern war. Although the new Ministry of Munitions was formed in early 1915 under Lloyd George, it took a year for industry to expand and begin to catch up with demand. New factories had to be built, machinery made and skilled workers trained. Alongside each factory an ordnance

depot was formed and the ammunition taken on charge by the army immediately it was ready. However, this storage proved inadequate to cope with the increasing quantities and it was necessary to build additional storage facilities at Bramley and Altrincham, each to hold 240,000 tons (the former was later increased by 125,000 tons). The shell shed at one depot had an area of over 9 acres. The depot at Bramley eventually covered an area 1½ miles long and over ½ mile wide. There was another large depot at Didcot and numerous smaller depots were opened elsewhere.

During 1915 it became increasingly evident to all belligerents that massive artillery support by hundreds of guns well stocked with shells was the prerequisite of success for both offensive and defensive operations. For the BEF the shell shortage resulted in 18-pounder shells being rationed on a *per diem* basis as early as 25 October 1914. In the last two weeks of December howitzer shells were restricted, first to 250 rounds

and then to 200 rounds per division – fewer than three shells a day per howitzer. This minimal allocation was extreme, but the continuing overall shell shortage severely handicapped all planning throughout 1915 – the BEF had massive injections of manpower that year but not enough guns and shells to support them effectively for anything other than battles on narrow fronts of short duration. Even as late as February 1916, if an army commander wanted to mount an operation and use more shells than the daily allowance he had to get the authority of GHQ – a thoroughly unsatisfactory state of affairs.

Part of the problem was the emphasis placed in England on manufacturing more and more guns, particularly the heavier type, but with insufficient spare parts and ancillary equipment, so it was not uncommon, for example, for batteries to arrive in France without the tools to set their fuzes. As with most things, the Germans were initially better prepared than the Allies and it

A British ammunition dump for the Battle of Albert, July 1916. The photograph shows empty 18-pounder cases.

Supply of Ammunition for 30th Division, 1 July 1916 (not to scale)

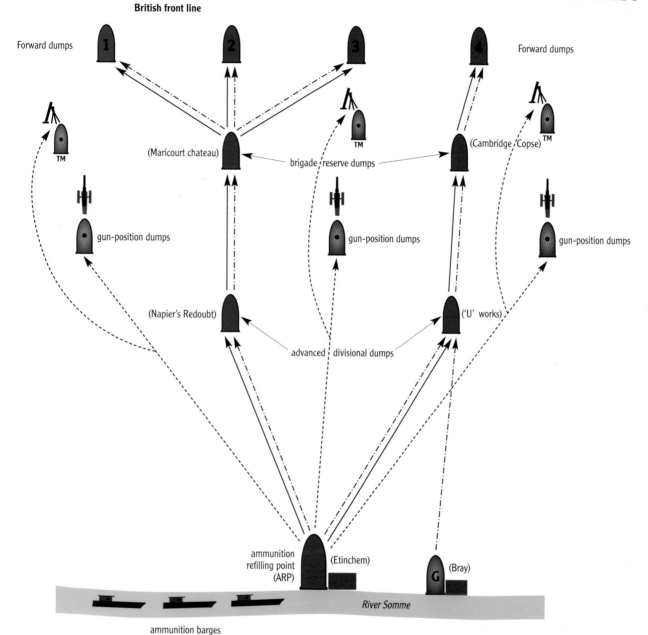

British front line

Forward dumps

1   2   3   4   Forward dumps

TM

(Maricourt chateau)   brigade reserve dumps   TM   (Cambridge Copse) TM

gun-position dumps   gun-position dumps   gun-position dumps

(Napier's Redoubt)   advanced divisional dumps   ('U' works)

ammunition refilling point (ARP)   (Etinchem)   G   (Bray)

River Somme

ammunition barges

Notes

- The divisional ARP at Etinchem received all types of ammunition by barges coming up the Somme. These were then distributed to the advanced divisional dumps, except for artillery and trench-mortar ammunition, which went straight to dumps by the battery positions.
- Small-arms ammunition and grenades went forward from the advanced divisional dumps via the brigade reserve dumps and thence to forward dumps close behind the forward trenches.
- Grenades had their detonators inserted at Etinchem and Bray.
- Nos 1, 2 and 3 are the forward dumps for the 89th Brigade and No. 4 for the 21st and 90th Brigades.

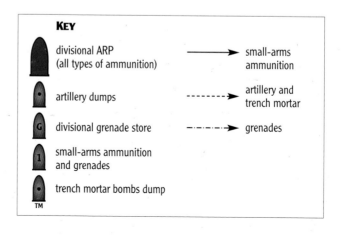

KEY

- divisional ARP (all types of ammunition)
- artillery dumps
- G   divisional grenade store
- 1   small-arms ammunition and grenades
- trench mortar bombs dump   TM

→ small-arms ammunition

---→ artillery and trench mortar

—·—·→ grenades

was not until after the Marne that ammunition conservation orders were issued. However, it was not just quantity that was the problem, but type. In August 1915 the BEF had just under 1.2 million artillery rounds in France, of which 72 per cent were 18-pounder shells, but of these only 4.4 per cent were HE – the great majority, shrapnel, being ineffective in destroying trenches and bunkers.

It was not only artillery ammunition that was lacking but also SAA and grenades, of which phenomenal amounts were needed with the arrival of the new (Kitchener) divisions and the increasing use of heavy and

Dismantling Shells

It was the RAOC that became responsible for dealing with the vast amount of unexpended ammunition held by the BEF at the end of the war. The *Cologne Post* published an article on the subject, part of which is quoted below:

Three hundred and fifty thousand tons of shell! When the War ended such was the amazing quantity of ammunition we had on our hands in France. In a single heap were 60,000 rounds of 6-in shells, representing 2,300 tons of steel, about 20 tons of copper and more than 240 tons of high explosives.

What was to be done with so vast an accumulation of 'superfluous' material? Was it to be fired aimlessly into the air or be cast into the sea, there to provide a nine-days wonder for the fishes! No. The lot was bought for £2,000,000, and ever since the work of converting it into material useful to our manufacturers has gone on steadily . . .

To obtain [this] result – in connection with which as many as 10,000 men and women have been engaged at one time – special methods are necessary. An unusual feature of the work is that cranes and other mechanical lifters are not employed. Every shell, after being raised by hand, is transported by gravity . . .

In the case of the high explosive shell, the distinctive operation is removing the bursting charge. This is generally done by 'washing out.' The shell is inclined at an angle of 40 degrees, with its nose opposite a jet from which hot water and steam are fed into the interior. The steam causes the explosive to break up, and flow into suitable receptacles. In from three to thirty minutes, according to the size of the shell, the interior is clear; but, as it is important that it should be quite free from explosive, it is inspected three times before it is passed.

light machine guns and grenades (the British started the war with no grenades; the Germans with around 170,000 hand and rifle grenades) for close-quarter trench fighting and raiding. Manufacturing output for Vickers machine guns in 1915 was 2,405 and for Lewis guns 3,650; in 1918 it was 39,473 and 62,303 respectively. As an example of the SAA problem, in May 1915 there were only 100 rounds per rifle in reserve on the lines of communication when the requirement was for 200. Just to maintain 100 rounds required a supply of 20 million a week, and in September GHQ urgently requested another 43 million, followed soon afterwards by another 54 million to build reserves to the required 200 per rifle. The rate at which machine guns came to consume ammunition is well illustrated by the British Second Army's three corps' (IX, X and II ANZAC) assault at Messines on 7 June 1917. Of over 700 machine guns, 454 were allocated for the machine-gun barrage on that day. The estimated requirement for machine guns was some 15 million rounds, or 5 million per corps – 1 million for harassing fire and 2 million each for barrages and SOS calls. For the two days at the start of the attack this meant 15,000–20,000 rounds per gun per day. With artillery ammunition, the bombardment for the three corps from 26 May to 6 June required over 3.5 million shells at an estimated cost of £17.5 million. Feeding the Second Army for this operation were twenty-six railheads, plus seven more for ammunition, with narrow-gauge lines in some areas taking materials to within less than a mile of the front-line trenches.

In the months immediately preceding the Somme, offensive stocks of ammunition and other supplies were pouring into France in such quantities that there was no space at the main bases at the ports (at times ships were queuing at the docks to offload) to store them, and frantic negotiations with the French were needed to secure additional suitable sites. With the huge losses on the Somme (it lasted for almost five months), the situation of the BEF in 1915 – when, in general terms, the manpower was available but not the ammunition – was reversed, with ammunition being available but the most worrying shortage being manpower. However, although enough ammunition was supplied to sustain the initial offensive on the Somme, such a long and costly battle requiring so much logistical support had not been anticipated. The need to stockpile huge reserves of supplies of all kinds and then to sustain the continuous fighting exposed weaknesses in the transportation system on the lines of communication (see pages 346–7). The system of supplying the 30th Division with its ammunition for its

attack on 1 July 1916 is shown in the diagram on page 335.

By 1918 the British logistics organization was superior to those of her allies and the Germans. Huge stocks of supplies of all descriptions were held at bases and dumps on the lines of communication and at the Channel ports. The scale of the increase is demonstrated by a comparison between the number of shells of all calibres held in France in early July 1916 with that held in February 1918. On the former occasion just under 6.5 million rounds were available and on the latter almost 16.5 million. When the German offensive in March drove back the Fifth Army with the objective of taking ports such as Calais and severing supply lines there was a realization among the British High Command that if this happened only a fraction of the stores and equipment could be saved. However, the Germans' impetus waned and they were halted, but not before the retiring British had lost and abandoned a vast quantity of weapons, ammunition and other supplies. Nevertheless, the fact that the thousands of troops that needed refitting were armed and kitted out again efficiently and quickly is proof of the amount of supplies held in France at that time.

Some final statistics on munitions demonstrate the enormity of supplying just the artillery effort of the BEF on the Western Front. There were fifteen different calibres of guns and howitzers in action, ranging from the 13-pounder to the giant 14-inch gun. The approximate expenditure during the war totalled 170,385,295 rounds, of which the 18-pounder fired over 99 million, the 4.5-inch howitzer over 25 million and the 6-inch howitzer over 22 million; the 14-inch gun fired a mere 235. In one day (28/29 September 1918) the British fired almost a million rounds in their attack on the Hindenburg Line. During the war the French fired approximately 200 million shells; the Germans (on all fronts) 275 million; Austria–Hungary 70 million; and Russia 50 million.

Clothing (including web equipment)

The present writer has been unable to find the figures for British clothing and personal equipment supplies issued for the Western Front alone, but the statistics for all theatres and home forces, bearing in mind that the Western Front received at least 80 per cent, illustrate graphically the size of the manufacture and distribution task. The figures below, showing a selection of items, are taken from *A History of the Army Ordnance Services*, Vol. 3: *The Great War* by Major General A. Forbes, published in 1929.

Personal equipment (sets)

Infantry	6,785,000
Other arms	3,093,000
Water bottles	10,037,000
Mess tins	16,110,000
Waterproof sheets or capes	13,516,000
Blankets	35,690,000
Boots (pairs)	39,822,333
Shirts	45,485,205
Socks (pairs)	107,872,068
Jackets	26,798,933
Trousers	26,900,656
Greatcoats	9,263,192
Caps	23,811,507
Leather jerkins and fur undercoats	4,860,407
Rubber trench boots	2,608,930

An important item, not strictly part of a soldier's equipment but upon which his ability to keep his rifle functioning depended, were the rolls of flannelette with which he cleaned his weapon. No less than 50 million yards was issued during the war.

August 1914 and the months that followed saw enormous deficiencies in virtually every item of personal clothing and equipment needed to kit out the hundreds of thousands of men being recruited. The war reserves of clothing served for little more than the fitting out and upkeep of the BEF for a few weeks. During peacetime the manufacture of clothing had been confined to only a few firms. The large expansion needed could be obtained only gradually and, before clothing could be made, the cloth had to be manufactured. Trivial as it may seem, the clothing trade was initially wholly unable to meet the demand for buttons. By mid-December 1914 delivery of boots was almost 700,000 pairs in arrears. The normal peacetime requirement was around 245,000 pairs, made by firms in Northamptonshire. As indicated above, some 40 million pairs were supplied (exclusive of the orders placed for allied governments) during the war and these were obtained by enlisting the aid of a civilian expert who was tasked with coordinating the resources of the whole country. The result was that boots were made in Northampton, Kettering, Rushden and numerous smaller towns and villages in Northamptonshire, and also in Leicester, Leeds, Bristol, Scotland and Ireland.

Temporary expedients were initially required to clothe the men during the first rush of recruits. A supply of 500,000 suits of blue serge uniforms was acquired (most from Post Office stocks), this material being the only colour available in sufficient quan-

tities. Greatcoats of blue and grey were obtained and several hundred thousand civilian-pattern greatcoats were purchased. In addition, in the early stages resort was made to buying 1.3 million jackets and 900,000 greatcoats from Canada and the United States. Another desperate measure was to pay 10 shillings to every recruit who reported with a greatcoat, boots and a suit of clothes to wear until a uniform was available. Commanding officers were authorized to make local purchases of boots, mess utensils and other items deemed essential for their units. It was a time of frantic improvisation. The supply of these and other items improved dramatically as factories expanded and mass production with large numbers of women workers took hold. By early 1919 the British government had spent £295 million on cloth, serge, flannel and other material on clothing sixty-nine divisions with the various expeditionary forces, and another £29 million on clothing for allies. Britain supplied Australian, New Zealand, Portuguese and American forces with clothing and much equipment. The Indian divisions, as noted above (see page 114), arrived at Marseilles in summer uniforms. Finally, the introduction of labour units from China, South Africa and elsewhere increased yet further the quantities required.

For the handling of clothing and boots, additional accommodation was obtained by the construction of buildings in Battersea Park and by hiring large premises in London (such as at Olympia, Aldgate and White City), Manchester, Southampton, York, Leeds and elsewhere. There were sub-depots at Sheffield, Glasgow and Edinburgh, with clothing stores at Bradford, Shipley, Huddersfield and Manchester. By mid-1918 the total floor space for clothing depots in the United Kingdom exceeded 2 million square feet.

Winter clothing posed a particular problem in 1914 when the cold weather arrived early. Special arrangements had to be put in hand as the need had not been anticipated. All these additional requirements involved the handling of huge quantities of goods of varied descriptions; for example, 3 million goat and other skins, plus several million square feet of sheepskin leather, had to be obtained for the manufacture of fur and leather undercoats, and large numbers of long, fur-lined coats were obtained from the United States and Canada.

The standard pattern of infantry equipment was the 1908 webbing (belt, pouches, haversack and large pack). Prior to mobilization only two firms had the machinery capable of making the webbing to meet annual requirements. With the hugely increased

Indian Army Equipment

The arrival of Indian divisions at Marseilles in early 1915 generated considerable problems regarding clothing, feeding and equipping the troops. The British officer (Captain A. Forbes, later a major general and author of *A History of the Army Ordnance Services*, Vol. 3: *The Great War*) sent to Marseilles to make administrative arrangements for their arrival was horrified by what he found. On asking a British supply officer who had arrived in advance how their uniforms would be replenished, his response was that he assumed the regiments would write to India and have them made up in the bazaar! India had made no provision for uniform resupply.

From guns to boots, the reserves sent from India were paltry and it was obvious that the BEF would have to maintain all Indian troops, native or British, while they served on the Western Front. Among the difficulties was that the rifle issued to Indian troops was not the same as that used by BEF units and it fired different ammunition. Rifles, bayonets, machine guns and ammunition had to be sent to re-equip the whole force, and they had to be trained in their use. This was by no means all. The Indian groundsheet was not waterproof and telephone apparatus was not compatible with British equipment. The cavalry regiments provided their own swords, so they varied from regiment to regiment and none would fit the British cavalry scabbard. The Indian government furnished officers with neither tents nor saddler, so there was a huge variety of shapes and sizes of privately purchased tents that required replacement. On top of all this came problems with food, cooking, eating and drinking utensils – to supply the wrong type could deeply offend religious customs or caste.

demand, several others began to learn the process, but no firm except these two possessed or could obtain the machinery to make certain parts of the equipment. Consequently the number of complete sets obtainable continued to be limited and a modified form of equipment had to be devised, made partly of leather and partly of webbing. Large orders for this equipment, along with water bottles, mess tins, picks, shovels and artificers' tools were placed in the United Kingdom, Canada and the United States. The BEF went to war in soft service-dress peaked caps (SD caps) and, although there were various experiments, it was not until 1916 that satisfactory steel helmets ('tin hats' or 'battle bowlers') were universally available on the front line. The average number of sets of personal web

Steel Helmets

The BEF started the war with soft caps and it was not until 1 July 1916 that a million helmets, enough to equip all front-line troops, had been issued. The French had a helmet made in four parts issued early the previous year and this resulted in GHQ requesting some samples. Trials in the UK, however, considered that the 500 helmets tested gave insufficient protection. After further experiments samples of a heavier helmet were sent to France in September 1915. Some 3,500 were issued, although further trials were made with a helmet of the same design but made of hardened manganese steel and weighing 2 lb, which was able to resist shrapnel travelling at up to 750 feet a second. Full-scale manufacture was agreed in November and by March 1916 140,000 had reached France.

It was found that wearing this helmet reduced the number of head wounds by 75 per cent. It would not stop a direct hit by a bullet, but was often effective against shrapnel. The 'tin hat' or 'battle bowler', as it became to be known, had the distinctive wide brim that was on occasion sharpened and used as a cutting weapon in hand-to-hand fighting. GHQ requested the urgent delivery of sufficient to equip all troops in France. This helmet was issued to all dominion troops and about 1.5 million were given to the Americans as they arrived in France. The total output by the end of the war was well over 7 million – and the same helmet continued to be issued during World War II.

equipment issued annually was 11,000 in 1914, a number that by 1919 exceeded 10 million (all theatres, including the UK).

Obtaining sufficient personal equipment to keep up an ever-increasing flow of supplies to France was only half the problem. The other half was equipping the hundreds of thousands of horses and mules with the necessary saddlery and harnesses. There were two basic difficulties: first, the shortage of leather, more particularly the leather required to withstand the hard usage of active service; second, the limited number of firms capable of making the military pattern of saddlery and harness. It was necessary yet again to turn to the United States, Canada and India for saddlery. At one time these equipments were being made in twenty-four different cities scattered throughout America. Even when production had increased and substantial supplies were arriving from overseas at the end of February 1915, congestion at the ports and on the railways in the United Kingdom delayed distribution and shipment to France. Not until December 1915, when the number of sets of harness in use had increased from 40,000 to 518,000, had supply more or less caught up with demand.

Once in France, clothing and other items of equipment were stored and moved forward by the transport system described below.

Fuel (petrol, coal and timber)

Fuel of various types was required for motor transport (MT), ships, barges, aircraft, tanks, locomotives and engines for equipment such as pumps and generators. The outstanding feature of MT was its phenomenal growth, as shown in the table below.

In the case of aircraft, total production during the war of 54,957 represents the average from several sources, and the present author was unable to find a figure for those in use in France at the Armistice. Nevertheless, the numbers show the massive amount of fuel (petrol and aviation fuel) needed to keep vehicles moving or aircraft flying.

Initially supplies of petrol were obtained by contracts with petroleum companies in the United Kingdom and requirements were at the modest level of 250,000 gallons a month, but demands rose steadily and rapidly to culminate in the astronomical amount of 10.5 million gallons a month. By the end of the war over 758,000 tons of petrol had been shipped to France. Supplies destined for France obtained from the Asiatic Petroleum Company amounted eventually to 2 million gallons of petrol and 600,000 of aviation fuel a month, with the balance coming from the United States.

To begin with, petrol for lorries was supplied in 50-gallon steel drums and for cars and light vehicles in 2- or 4-gallon tins packed in wooden cases. Until the middle of 1916 petrol tins used by the BEF were filled in England, at Portishead, near Bristol, from where it was shipped to overseas bases. At this time, with the requirement then standing at 2 million gallons a month, it became evident that if it continued to be transported in tins and wooden crates the enormous bulk would exceed the capacity of the petrol-discharging berths at French ports. Arrangements were therefore made to establish filling installations in France and for a tanker steamer service direct from the United States – this resulted in approximately 11,000 tons of empty petrol tins being sent to France for filling by the end of the war. Tank storage was acquired at Calais and Rouen and filling machines transferred from Portishead. Both these facilities were expanded to meet demand, and by late 1916 shipment of filled cans from England had ceased except for occasional replenishment of reserves.

The filling of aviation spirit that required special supervision continued to be carried out at Portishead until the spring of 1918, when consumption rose to such an extent that it had to be done at Calais and Rouen under the supervision of inspection staff from the Air Ministry.

The methods of getting fuel distributed in France are shown on pages 346–7.

Coal and timber were both used as fuel in huge quantities by all armies, particularly for powering the engines of the thousands of locomotives deployed by the French and for the use of the BEF. The British Army Service Corps shipments from all ports to the BEF from 14 August 1914 to 1 May 1920 amounted to over 2 million tons of coal and timber (for use as fuel). The demands for timber were especially high, as not only was it used as a fuel but also for trench supports, bunker and tunnel roofs, hutting, railway sleepers and many hundreds of miles of duckboards and plank road. Production in the United Kingdom could not meet the demands for home use (3 million tons in 1918 for collieries alone) and for the army, although by the end of the war almost 25,000 people were employed in the Timber Supplies Department in the United Kingdom – these included forty companies of the Canadian Forestry Corps (7,160 men), 2,288 Portuguese, 3,695 prisoners of war and 1,683 women cutters and measurers.

Increase in Motor Transport, 1914–1918

Type	Available 1914	In use in France November 1918
Lorries/tractors	1,141	31,770
Cars/vans	213	7,694
Motor ambulances	–	3,532
Motor cycles	131	14,464
Buses	–	370
Tanks (not MT)	–	1,976 (total output 2,818)

To meet demands, timber was imported from Canada, Russia and Sweden. However, a substantial proportion of the BEF's needs came from French forests.

By mid-1916 the difficulties in agreeing the allocation of local timber resources, the urgent demands for increasing amounts and the shortage of freight to move stocks led to the extension of the authority of the inter-Allied commission charged with overseeing supply – the *Commission Internationale d'Achat de Bois* (Timber Purchasing Commission). The commanders-in-chief of British, French and Belgian armies had to submit their timber requirements to the commission several months in advance and keep it informed of work in British and French forests. Any foreseen shortfalls were to be made up by imports. This led to the BEF holding monthly conferences to establish needs. At the first, held on 1 September 1916, it was realized that for the coming winter, out of a total timber requirement of some 100,000 tons, 72,000 could not be met by existing contracts, and the bulkiness of timber and high cost of importation allied to freight shortages presented the British planners with a serious problem. More urgent meetings with the French took place. The result was that by the end of October 1916 agreement had been reached to establish a Franco-British War Timber Commission in London, and the French agreed to hand over sufficient local woodland to occupy up to forty-six Canadian Forestry Corps companies at no cost to the British, but with a sharing agreement on the timber produced. Buying would still be done through the Commission Internationale d'Achat de Bois, to which additional British members were appointed.

By 1915 the German occupation of French territory had cut the supplies of pig iron by 64 per cent, steel manufacturing by 24 per cent and coal by 40 per cent, including the large coal-mining area around Lens, resulting in a serious, but not crippling, setback for French industry. In the UK, although massive tonnages had to be made available to the BEF, the bulk of home production was needed for British industry, rail transportation and domestic use, with the latter being rationed. The worst shortage came in 1918, with UK reserves cut to seven days' supply, partially alleviated with experiments combining anthracite (40 per cent) with bituminous coal, which was successful in closed stoves. Also, a factory was converted to produce peat briquettes that could be used as a substitute for charcoal as fuel in the trenches. Despite the difficulties, coal shipments to France totalled almost 4 million tons by the end of the war.

Remounts

Without horses, and to a lesser extent mules, no army on the Western Front could function – the supply of these animals was absolutely critical for movement of cavalry, guns, wagons for supplies and munitions, and ambulances. There were four categories of horse – riding, light and heavy draught and pack – but with mules only draught or pack. In general terms, the riding horses carried the cavalry, horse artillery, most other artillery officers, senior officers, staff officers and orderlies. Light draught horses (in teams of two, four or six) pulled the artillery limbers, wagons and ambulances. Heavy draught pulled heavy artillery, although by 1918 most had been replaced by tractors, motor vehicles or locomotives for the super-heavy guns. Mules pulled lighter carts, while both horses and mules were used to carry packs of ammunition, supplies or stores, particularly in the forward area. For the British, the best breeds for the military were the Suffolk, Clydesdale and Welsh carthorses and the American Percheron.

As with men, the British had devised a system of reserves for horses before the war. Responsibility for the Remount Service had rested with the Army Service Corps (ASC) since 1891. In 1914 there was a director of transport and remounts at the War Office who answered to the quartermaster general, and an assistant director of remounts (at that time Colonel C. H. Bridge). In each home command there was a deputy assistant director of remounts with the responsibility for collecting information on the horse population in his area – he had the authority to

enter farms and stables to classify animals (horses from six to ten years old and from 15.2 to 16 hands were needed). This was part of the pre-war horse registration scheme or Army Horse Reserve (not operative in Ireland). It was a voluntary scheme in which owners registered their animals with the remount service and, in return for an annual payment of £4 for an artillery horse and 10 shillings for others, agreed to their horses being requisitioned by the army if necessary.

At the outbreak of war the establishment for horses in the army was raised from the existing 25,000 to 165,000 (an estimated three months' supply), a further 25,000 of which had been registered in the Horse Reserve. Purchasing officers were despatched around the country and within twelve days some 115,000 additional horses had been acquired through compulsory purchase and the overall target of 165,000 had been achieved. The prices paid by the government for a cavalry troop horse was £40 and for an officer's charger £60.

However, with the wastage of animals in the first months of the war running at almost 20 per cent, followed by the recruitment of the New Armies in 1915, it was immediately evident that the purchase of very large numbers of horses and mules from overseas was critical. Pre-war planning had included arrangements for the immediate despatch of a Remount Commission to the United States and Canada to buy animals for the army and this was increased with additional purchasing officers. Mules were also to be acquired in the United States and Spain. The Indian government was asked to undertake the buying of horses on Britain's

A shell-carrying pack mule advancing through the mud at the Battle of Pilckem Ridge, August 1917.

behalf, as well as their own, in Australia. Remount purchasing officers also went to New Zealand, Portugal and China.

The major overseas source of horses and mules was the United States, which along with Canada provided two thirds of the animals used by the British Army. The British purchasing officers, all of whom had to have considerable equine experience, travelled throughout the West and Midwest buying thousands of animals, usually at large fairs. After purchase the animal was branded with a broad arrow indicating British War Office property and taken to the nearest railhead. During the long, slow journey to the east coast ports of embarkation, the animals were taken off the trains at regular intervals for watering and feeding at specially constructed depots. There they were also checked for sickness or injury. On arrival at the port they were loaded on to transports and secured in stalls for what was a thoroughly unpleasant voyage both for the animals and for those looking after them below decks. In addition to sickness causing losses, an estimated 6,500 animals were drowned or killed by shellfire when their transport was attacked during the voyage. Once in the UK it was the job of the Remount Service and Veterinary Corps to get the animals fit again before the much shorter voyage to France.

The ASC operated four remount depots in the UK before the war (Woolwich, Dublin (two), and Lusk in Ireland), but by late 1915 there were forty-two. A remount squadron of 200 all ranks commanded by a major ran each depot, with a Veterinary Corps officer attached. They were able to train up to 500 horses at a time. A base remount depot with 2,600 animals and two advanced remount depots each with 300 animals were sent across the Channel with the BEF in 1914. This soon proved woefully inadequate and further base remount depots were established at all base depot ports and one of the advanced depots was discontinued. The number of animals received in remount depots in the UK from overseas, the great majority going to the Western Front, was as follows:

	Horses	Mules
1914	38,867	109
1915	55,113	10,695
1916	52,258	21,520
1917	93,847	36,613
1918	76,404	26,567
Totals	316,489	95,504

The figures for 1917 show a dramatic jump in the requirement for remounts. This is in line with the heavy losses in manpower that year in the gruelling struggles in the Arras offensive, at Messines, Passchendaele and Cambrai – the animals suffered as much as the men.

The Americans, who did not launch major offensives until 1918, were desperately short of animals towards the end of the war. General Pershing was forced to ask the French for 25,000 horses – his request was refused – as shipping space from America was so limited, and towards the end of their Meuse–Argonne offensive the Americans faced a shortage of 100,000 animals that virtually immobilized their artillery. Pershing's senior supply officer complained, 'The animal situation will soon become desperate'. Nevertheless, the Americans fought on successfully without replacements.

Before the war the Germans had developed state-sponsored stud farms to breed horses and mules for the military and thus they began the conflict better prepared than their adversaries in this respect – as they did in many others. This policy of building a considerable reserve of animals meant that in 1914 the ratio of horses to men in the army was approximately one to three. These breeding programmes enabled the Germans to mobilize 715,000 horses and the Austrians around 600,000. Nevertheless, these would not prove sufficient to take them through the massive expansion of the war and slaughter on all fronts. Eventually, despite extensive use of animals seized in Belgium and France, the Germans ran out of horses with the consequent immobility of many guns and supply columns – by 1918 it had become a definite contributing factor to their defeat.

Salvage

An obvious way of easing production difficulties and shortages was salvage. Although initially the BEF had no salvage organization, it was soon appreciated that steps needed to be taken to prevent excessive wastage. In 1915 divisional salvage companies were formed with a duty to search the area behind the trenches and abandoned billets for derelict and damaged items of all descriptions, and to form a dump where material could be sorted for reissue or taken to corps or base dumps for repair in France or shipment back to the UK. For materials from the trenches, reliance was placed on good discipline and administration within units. They were responsible for salvaging materials and dumping at convenient points from which the salvage company could collect them or from where they could be taken back by returning empty ration or ammunition vehicles. In 1917 the formation of employment companies with a dedicated salvage section of an officer and fifty other ranks, and the attachment of an officer and forty-four other ranks to each corps headquarters, was a substantial advance in coordinating the, by then, huge salvage activities. However, it was not until November 1917 that an Army Salvage Board in the War Office under the chairmanship of the QMG was established to coordinate the overall war effort. A controller of salvage (Brigadier General Evan Gibb, formerly ASC) was appointed at GHQ, with salvage staff officers at subordinate headquarters down to divisional level.

The ASC dealt with all salvage under the headings of supplies and transport. The former included the collection of empty containers such as sacks, boxes, crates, empty bottles, jars and drums – anything that could be re-used, repaired and refilled. This included the collection and repair of damaged and abandoned motor vehicles and associated accessories – all of which involved the setting up of maintenance depots and workshops in France. The responsibility for the salvage, repair and reissue of other weapons and equipment rested with the AOC, who operated returned stores depots at Graville (Le Havre) and Valdelièvre (Calais). These were huge clearing houses where items easily repaired went to be mended; things that needed skilled repairs went to a workshop; and those to be sent back to the UK went to the transit branch for shipment. The balance beyond repair was sold off or sent home as scrap metal – anything left was burned. Colonel W. N. Nicholson in his book *Behind the Lines* describes a visit to the depot at Le Havre in July 1917:

All the salvage from the battlefields of two armies came down to this depot. In one place rose a mountain of ammunition boxes and shell cases, which German prisoners were busy loading on board ship. Further up the river many thousands of empty ammunition boxes lay in long lines. Ship succeeded ship as fast as she could be loaded; as soon as filled another empty one moored alongside. The disposal of all other sorts of salvage, from cast iron fragments to equipment, interested me particularly. Here in some twenty long sheds, 1200 French women under two British Ordnance officers were employed cleaning leather equipment, water bottles, rifles, bayonets; everything except clothing, which went to Rouen. The salvage came down from the battle area indescribably dirty, old and broken, and practically everything was made use of; empty cartridge cases found a purchaser in the French Government. Unfired S.A.A. had first to be cleaned and then sent home for reboxing.

A dump of war-torn cars on the Western Front awaiting repair.

Equipment was brushed [scrubbed], polished and made up into new; so that for the previous six months no unused equipment had been required from home . . . Everything found a niche. Leather that could be made up in the workshops was sold by weight to the French. At the time of my visit about sixty truckloads a day came from the two armies this base served.

The repair of boots amazed a Russian war correspondent, who wrote in *The Times* on 15 June 1916 of what he had seen:

It is most marvellous to see the things that are done here. Take, for instance, boots. Our boots when they are worn out are thrown away by the soldiers. We saw heaps of these cast offs near the Russian trenches in Galicia and Poland, and indeed what use could be that leather torn in pieces and hard as wood? Here, however, things are different. We saw sheds full of old boots, piles of rubbish, and I could not understand what they were going to do with it all; but here we saw, stage by stage, this rubbish turned again into splendid boots, soft and strong.

There were laundries and disinfectors close behind the front where the clothing of men attending the bath houses could be washed and exchanged. Greatcoats not needed in the summer were repaired and stored for reissue. Major General Forbes, in his *History of the Army Ordnance Services*, describes the ingenuity shown in making use of the most unlikely materials:

Laces were cut from the uppers of old boots and the residue of leather used as fuel, solder was recovered from old tins, lead from the linings of tea chests, nosebags and cooks' clothing were made from old tentage, worn out ground sheets and waterproof capes reappeared as ration bags and cap covers, old oil drums became braziers, kerosene tins fire buckets, arm or leg baths for hospitals were made from petrol tins and the spokes of old wheels turned into legs for tables and chairs. The blood of slaughtered bullocks was even commandeered from the A.S.C. butchery and used in place of linseed oil for making paint.

The Paris firm of Joly Fils was given a contract in the spring of 1915 to wash, disinfect and repair greatcoats, blankets and horse blankets and a nearby building was found to store these items for reissue in the autumn. Joly Fils was quickly swamped by the work and other firms in or near the city were soon involved. Debenham & Freebody of London took on the specialist cleaning of fur- or sheepskin-lined coats and leather jerkins. Cartridge cases by the thousands of tons were shipped back to the UK after being checked for serviceable live rounds by Frenchwomen.

The salvage of technical items was undertaken at AOC base and mobile workshops under the overall control of the chief ordnance officer. King George V and Queen Mary visited the former at Le Havre and Calais. It was here that items were actually manufactured or altered in the light of operational experience, examples being gun sights, reconstructing the filtration system on water carts that had failed the test of front-line service, or devising new axles for mobile kitchens. A major achievement was the manufacture of 8,000 anti-aircraft sights before any arrived from the UK, and of 108 95mm mortars and their bombs from locally obtained steel piping and gun-cotton – the bombs were eventually produced at a rate of 1,400 a day. Hosts of items were made in their thousands, from intricate trigger mechanisms through pistons to tentpoles and wheelbarrows. Concurrent with manufacture went the salvage and repair of gun parts, rifles, machine guns and mortars, and virtually every type of military equipment. The boot-making and repair factory at Calais became the largest such organization in the world. Its workforce of 180 in the autumn of 1915, turning out 350 pairs a week, had grown by 1918 to 800 staff (including German prisoners) producing 30,000 pairs a week.

By the end of the war this vast salvage and repair organization had saved tens of millions of pounds and crucially speeded up the supply of many critical items to the front-line soldier.

Logistics

In France the huge logistical organization involved in fighting the war came under the overall direction of GHQ. Details of the staff at GHQ are shown in the diagram on pages 166–7, but in summary the General Staff (G) Branch were responsible for planning, operations and intelligence; the adjutant general (AG) for personnel, medical, casualties and discipline; and the quarter-master general (QMG) dealt with supplying the army. However, because of the complexity and size of logistics and the large area occupied by the lines of communication, the post of inspector general of communications (IGC) was created at lieutenant general level. He was not part of GHQ staff and his headquarters was not located with GHQ – largely due to the size of both.

The IGC's task was the control and co-ordination of all transportation on the lines of communication, for moving every item of supplies and all troops from the ports and bases to the point where they were received by the fighting units – often forward of the railheads. He also commanded all line of communication units other than purely defensive ones. For this task he had his own staff and also those of the relevant directorates located at his headquarters (railways, works, ordnance services, remounts, veterinary and postal). Difficulties arose, as although these directors got their instructions from the IGC they were technically under the command of the QMG at GHQ. The potential for duplication, conflict and confusion was serious if the most senior officers responsible for supplying the army with the troops and means to fight (AG, QMG and IGC) were squabbling over who was responsible for what. Fortunately for the BEF, the officers concerned saw the problem and were sufficiently professional to make the system work – not infrequently in a somewhat ad hoc manner. However, the near breakdown of transportation during the Somme offensive (see page 347) brought about a simplification of the system with the appointment in late 1916 of a director general of transport (DGT, a major general) in late 1916 who was located at GHQ. He relieved the IGC of responsibility for ports, docks, shipping and railways, leaving the IGC with little to do, and he was replaced by an officer solely responsible for commanding the defensive units on the lines of communication.

It was the Army Ordnance Corps (AOC), using labour from several sources, that had primary responsibility for storing, issuing, maintenance, repair and accounting for practically all war material apart from rations, forage, petrol and hospital equipment. The first three were the responsibility of the ASC, while medical and surgical stores were supplied from base depots of the Royal Army Medical Corps (RAMC).

The AOC was granted the prefix 'Royal' for service during the war and its motto was *Sua tela tonanti*, usually translated as 'To the Warrior his Arms'. The AOC in the field was organized into companies, not battalions, and took instructions from an ordnance officer at the appropriate headquarters. With the need to form corps and armies between GHQ and divisional by the end of 1914, the usual ordnance representation at the various headquarters developed as follows:

GHQ – under the QMG a director of ordnance services (DOS), a major general

Army HQ – a deputy director of ordnance services (DDOS), a brigadier general

Corps HQ – an assistant director of ordnance services (ADOS), a colonel

Divisional HQ – a deputy assistant director of ordnance services (DADOS), a lieutenant colonel

Brigade HQ – an ordnance staff officer, often a captain

Regimental/battalion HQ – a quartermaster, normally a lieutenant or captain who had risen through the ranks and been given a quartermasters' commission, and who was deemed a non-combatant officer except in dire emergencies

This seemingly straightforward system had its complications. Initially all fighting units were part of a division, but as the number of units serving directly under a corps or army commander (such as heavy artillery and a plethora of administrative units) rapidly increased, so corps or army ordnance officers were appointed to cater for them. Corps troops, for example, could number up to seventy units, with technical equipment of all kinds and conditions needing repair and replacement, illustrating how an ordnance officer, corps troops (OOCT) became a key appointment. Often an army had two, even four (First Army) ordnance officers, army troops.

The American Services of Supply (SOS)

Responsibility for the supply and transportation services of the AEF rested initially with what was somewhat vaguely termed the 'line of communication' formed in July 1917. This system proved unworkable and in February 1918 a board was set up to devise a complete overhaul. For a brief period the new organization was called 'Service of the Rear', a title that invited obvious ridicule and was quickly abolished for that reason by General Pershing, who substituted 'Service of Supply'. The American supply lines started in the US and entered France mostly through, from north to south, the ports of Brest, St-Nazaire, La Pallice, Bordeaux and Marseilles, with the SOS headquarters in Tours (where the telephone-exchange operators were ultimately 250 French-speaking American ladies known as the 'Hell Girls'). Troops and supplies arriving from England used the ports at Calais, Le Havre and Rouen. The rail lines running north to the main areas of US operations were chosen to avoid the congestion around Paris, where many of the French factories and supply depots were located.

Until the end of July 1918 the commander of the SOS, responsible directly to General Pershing, was Major General Francis J. Kernan. Major General James G. Harbord (formerly commander of the 2nd Infantry Division at Belleau Wood) replaced him, but the chief of staff of the SOS, Colonel Johnson Hagood, remained. It was Hagood, who had been placed in charge of the advanced section of the supply service in the autumn of 1917, who was shocked by the chaos he discovered when trying to get supplies to the right division at the front. Examples he gave were of the French supplying the 42nd Division with 900 horses but no fodder, and after this had been secured the horses never arriving; or of the 26th Division receiving crates full of baby clothes addressed to a Boston department store; and of trainloads of wagon bodies arriving with no wheels. In his book *Over There: The American Experience in World War I*, Frank Freidel recounts how, in desperation, Colonel Hagood wrote to General Harbord (then chief of staff to Pershing) on 15 November 1917:

> If the United States does not actually fail, its efficiency is certainly going to be tremendously decreased by the sheer incompetence of its line of communication, beginning in the U.S. and ending at the French front. This incompetence not only applies to the machine as a whole but, we may as well admit, applies to the individual officers and employees, none of whom had had experience in solving such a problem as this. In this, of course, I include myself.

> I am informed that a ship lay at one of our base ports in France for forty-two days waiting to be unloaded . . . One of the brigade commanders told me that his men had gone as long as twelve days without potatoes, eight days without any vegetable component at all, and that it was a common experience to have no bread. French and Canadian officers seeing the men in this pitiable position have come to their rescue and helped them out. At one time ninety per cent of all the transportation of one American division had been borrowed from a French captain, who had secured it by a personal appeal to his own division commander.

Supreme efforts were made to improve the system and, as noted above, in July 1918 General Harbord was put in command to galvanize and reorganize the still-struggling and recently named Service of Supply. This he did by embarking on a tour of inspection in a special train with the commander-in-chief. Part of the problem was that there was poor morale amongst SOS personnel, with many of the officers having failed in the front line and been reassigned to supply duties to become what are now sometimes vulgarly called in soldiers' slang 'REMFs' (rear echelon motherfuckers). Many were incapable of handling troops or were totally untrained in the duties they were expected to perform. There were also difficulties when the white officers and NCOs treated thousands of black soldiers as second class, although this improved when black soldiers began to get promoted.

Despite the many shortcomings, by late 1918 the SOS had succeeded and the enormous shortfalls, due in part to a shortage of shipping from the US, had been alleviated by massive local purchase – some 10 million tons of material were acquired in Europe for the use of the American Army from June 1917 to December 1918, while in the same period about 7,675,000 tons were shipped from the US and England. During their comparatively short period on the Western Front, SOS units milled 200 million feet of timber, cut 4 million railway ties, baked 800,000 lb of bread a day and repaired 30,000 vehicles. At the Armistice over 2 million Americans were serving in France and 650,000 of them belonged to the SOS.

MAP 65 MAIN BEF SUPPLY BASES AND LINES OF COMMUNICATION, 1916

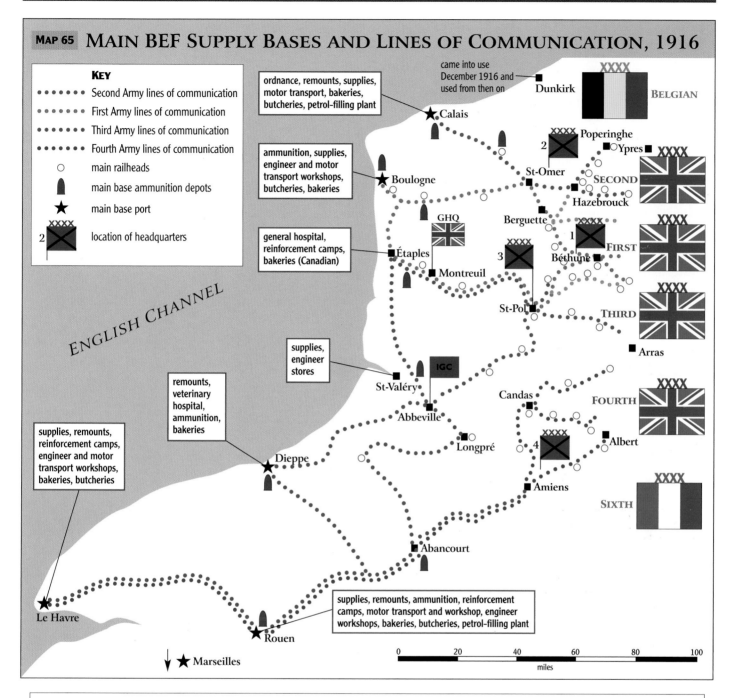

KEY

- • • • • • Second Army lines of communication
- • • • • • First Army lines of communication
- • • • • • Third Army lines of communication
- • • • • • Fourth Army lines of communication
- ○ main railheads
- main base ammunition depots
- ★ main base port
- location of headquarters

ordnance, remounts, supplies, motor transport, bakeries, butcheries, petrol-filling plant

ammunition, supplies, engineer and motor transport workshops, butcheries, bakeries

general hospital, reinforcement camps, bakeries (Canadian)

supplies, engineer stores

remounts, veterinary hospital, ammunition, bakeries

supplies, remounts, reinforcement camps, engineer and motor transport workshops, bakeries, butcheries

supplies, remounts, ammunition, reinforcement camps, motor transport and workshop, engineer workshops, bakeries, butcheries, petrol-filling plant

came into use December 1916 and used from then on

ENGLISH CHANNEL

BELGIAN
Dunkirk
Calais
Poperinghe
Ypres
St-Omer
SECOND
Boulogne
Hazebrouck
GHQ
Berguette
FIRST
Étaples
Béthune
Montreuil
St-Pol
THIRD
Arras
St-Valéry
IGC
Candas
FOURTH
Abbeville
Longpré
Albert
Dieppe
Amiens
SIXTH
Abancourt
Le Havre
Rouen
Marseilles

0   20   40   60   80   100
miles

Notes for Map 65

• In 1915 there had been two lines of communication, northern and southern, the former based on Boulogne and Calais, the latter on Le Havre, Rouen and Dieppe. On arrival at these ports, the system was for supplies to be sent by rail to regulating stations (the northern line initially did not need one, as the ports were comparatively near the front where trains from the bases were directed to appropriate railheads). With four armies in the field, separate regulating stations and lines of communication were allotted to each army. The system was not rigid and considerable cross-traffic occurred. The map shows the basic system of

bases and lines of communications (railways) that developed during 1916 under the command of the Inspector General of Communications (IGC) Lt Gen. Sir F. T. Clayton, and the Director of Works Maj. Gen. A. M. Stuart, RE, at Abbeville some 40 miles south of GHQ at Montreuil.
• Preparations for the Somme offensive, as for any major offensive, necessitated the stocking of advanced depots for all supplies, ammunition, water and engineer stores in depth behind the front, with smaller dumps near the front trenches. This map can show only the main railheads and the base ammunition depots.

In 1914 the DOS was located at GHQ, initially at Le Cateau, and the IGC from whom he took his orders was at Amiens. His deputy represented him at GHQ. As discussed above, this cumbersome arrangement meant that policy and command decisions (decided at GHQ) were divorced from the main means of execution (the IGC). The result was duplication, particularly among the staff. Even when the DOS moved to Montreuil in early 1917, bringing him into a closer relationship with the heads of other staff branches, he was

not fully absorbed into GHQ and every department of the DOS's office had its counterpart in that of the QMG at GHQ.

As with every branch of the army, the AOC saw rapid and extensive expansion during the war. From thirty officers and 1,360 other ranks in France in 1914 there were 800 officers and 15,000 other ranks at the Armistice. Once the front had stabilized by the end of 1914, there was a vast increase in demand for AOC services. Apart from ammunition and replacement of damaged or lost weapons and equipment, there developed a continuous need for weapons and stores needed for the new trench warfare: machine guns, hand grenades, barbed wire, sandbags and periscopes. During the first six months of 1916 a million steel helmets were issued. The list given in the British *Official History of the War*, Vol. I, demonstrates the variety of articles and huge quantities issued by the AOC from its base depot in Calais alone during the first ten months of 1916: 11,000 compasses; 7,000 watches; 40,000 miles of electric cable; 40,000 electric torches; 3.5 million yards of flannelette (for cleaning personal weapons); 1.25 million yards of rot-proof canvas; 26,000 tents; 1.5 million waterproof sheets; 12,800 bicycles; 5 million anti-gas helmets; 4 million pairs of horse and mule shoes; 447,000 Lewis-gun magazines; and 2.25 million bars of soap. By October 1918 the AOC was controlling eight large depots holding almost 340,000 tons of ammunition feeding over 120 ammunition railheads. By this time some 25.5 million tons of materials had been landed in France for distribution.

Again, taking the Somme offensive as an example, the supply flowed forward to the front along four lines of communication grouped in pairs – the 'northern' and 'southern' lines. A deputy director of communications, aided by an assistant and deputy assistant, controlled the operation of each pair. The base supply depots for the northern line were Boulogne and Calais and for the southern Dieppe, Rouen and Le Havre. From these base depots the daily supplies went forward through advanced supply depots, regulating stations, railheads and refilling points to unit quartermasters who distributed to the troops (see the diagram on pages 346–7). On the northern line no advanced supply depot was needed until January 1917 owing to the proximity of the bases to the front.

What did all this mean in terms of essential supplies for a British infantry division preparing to attack? The orders for the 47th Division, IV Corps, attacking at Loos on 25 September 1915, gives an example:

- Carried on the man – 200–220 rounds of ammunition, haversack, current day's ration and iron ration, two or three sandbags, two gas helmets and a proportion of wire-cutters, billhooks and hedging gloves.

- Small-arms ammunition (SAA) – dumps in support lines of 100 rounds per man, plus fifty rounds per man in the brigade reserve in the trenches, another fifty rounds (part of the brigade reserve) at Maroc in the support lines and 128 boxes in the divisional reserve.

- Maxim guns – 16,500 rounds per gun: 3,500 with the gun, 8,000 in battalion reserve in the trenches, 5,000 in brigade reserve at Maroc; plus 128 boxes in divisional reserve.

- Grenades – grenadiers with between twelve and twenty each, 1,750 in the trenches, 6,400 in brigade or divisional dumps.

- Rations – no problems were foreseen and one day for every man (13,500) in dump at Maroc was considered sufficient.

- Water – petrol tins and canvas carriers with small cisterns stored full in the trenches, and 20,000 gallons at Maroc.

- RE stores – small depots in the trenches, three brigade depots in Maroc and a mobile depot with bridging material on nine wagons (lorries). The contents of the depots were sandbags, corrugated-iron sheets, billhooks, axes, pickets, barbed wire, mauls, shovels, picks, crowbars, wire-cutters and tracing tape.

The second critical half of logistics was moving all these men and materials from the recruiting depot or factory gate to the units that needed them.

Transportation

The organization for transporting men, vehicles and materials from camps or factories at home to the front in France in ever-expanding numbers was highly complex, involving many thousands of civilians, staff, sailors, soldiers and labour from a variety of units, as well as French staff and personnel. The diagram on pages 346–7 shows the journey and means of transportation, in simplified form with no attempt to show how the means often overlapped, were used simultaneously or were sometimes omitted from the chain. However, it does represent the basic journey used for most supplies, certainly in the middle and later years of the war. The notes on transportation that follow refer to the stages shown on the diagram.

Within the UK

The movement of men and materials from camps and factories or dumps to embarkation or loading ports within the UK was by rail and, to a much lesser extent, by road. Supplies were mostly handed over to the military at the factory gate and they became responsible for loading and movement. At the War Office overall responsibility rested, for almost all the war, with the QMG (Lieutenant General Sir John Cowans). However, in September 1916 a deputy to the QMG, known as the director general of military railways (DGMR), was appointed with responsibility for provision of personnel and materials for railways, canals, docks and roads (excluding MT vehicles). Sir Eric Geddes accepted this post as well as that of director general of transport (DGT) in France; however, this soon proved unworkable and a deputy DGMR was appointed to act for him in London. There was also a director of movements (DM) at the War Office tasked with controlling ports and movements in the UK, including home railways and movements by sea, who was initially responsible to the QMG rather than the DGMR. This was changed in January 1917 so that the DM was responsible to the DGMR and the latter ceased to be a deputy to the QMG. Within four months the final change took place, whereby the DGMR became a full member of the Army Council. This series of changes (described only briefly) at the War Office is included to illustrate how complex and how long it took to reach satisfactory overall command and control arrangements for transportation at the highest level.

By Sea

From British ports – mostly, but not exclusively, along the south coast – everybody and everything had to cross the Channel. Under *Field Service Regulations, Part I: Operations, 1909,* this was the responsibility of the Royal Navy, who provided the various ships, barges (useful only in calm weather) and ferries. In view of the extensive canal system in Belgium and France, a barge service for the BEF was organized with a depot, initially at Dover. By January 1916 this depot was congested so Richborough was developed as an alternative and by 1918 it was a seaport able to handle 30,000 tons of cargo a week. There was also a coastal barge service running from Le Havre northwards to Dieppe, Fécamp, Le Tréport, St-Valéry, Boulogne, Calais and Dunkirk, and back – all short hops of a maximum of 30 miles.

Many barges were specially built to ensure they were strong enough for the Channel crossing and were of the maximum dimensions to operate on the inland waterways (see page 350). Initially the cross-Channel barges could carry 180 tons, but by the end of the war 1,000-ton barges were in use that could go up the Seine, though not the northern waterways; instead they discharged cargoes at quays not normally used by seagoing vessels. In two years (1917 and 1918), although often adversely affected by the weather, sixty tugs and 160 barges delivered 10,000 bargeloads to France – 1.4 million tons. In 1918 a train ferry service to carry loaded railway wagons from UK railways to those in France was established from Southampton to Cherbourg and Dieppe, and from Ramsgate to Calais and Dunkirk, with a 3,600-ton ferry being able to transfer 300 wagons a month (see Map 68).

This short stretch of water was continuously crowded month after month by scores of vessels delivering men, horses, mules and supplies, then returning with leave personnel, wounded, German prisoners and salvage. The statistics are revealing. From August 1914 to April 1919, 10,785,126 personnel were embarked for France from British ports. These included British drafts, complete units, personnel returning from leave, as well as Royal Navy, American troops, other Allied men and nurses. The number of animals transported exceeded 804,000. These figures show just how vital a link in the transportation chain the Channel was, and how tempting a target for German submarines and enemy minelaying, particularly when Germany resorted to unrestricted submarine warfare in 1917.

The naval transport department of the Admiralty was responsible for the berthing of vessels at overseas ports, the discharge of cargoes on to the quays (including the labour working in the ships' holds) and arranging with the French port authorities for the use of cranes and other landing equipment. The Royal Navy representative in France was the principal naval transport officer (PNTO), with naval transport officers (NTOs) at each main port who worked closely with the military landing officers (MLOs) and French port authorities.

Railways in France

Base depots were established at the Channel ports and other places on the lines of communication (see Map 65). Here goods arrived in bulk by ship to be broken down into wagonloads and sent forward by train. General base depots were the centres for collecting and despatching reinforcements. No. 1 General Base Depot (for Royal Garrison Artillery), No. 2 General Base Depot (for

The steamship Stockport moored in a French port as supplies are unloaded by hand.

Royal Horse Artillery and Royal Field Artillery) and No. 3 General Base Depot (for Canadian forces) were established at Le Havre. Also there were the base depots of the ASC, AOC and Army Veterinary Corps (AVC). No. 4 General Base Depot (for RE) and No. 5 General Base Depot (for Cavalry and RAMC) were at Rouen, while the Indian General Base Depot was at Marseilles. Most infantry divisions had base depots, including those for Australian and New Zealand divisions at Étaples; in October 1916 these last two and the Canadians moved to Le Havre.

Railways carried 95 per cent of the traffic from these depots along trunk routes on the lines of communications. As the diagram on pages 346–7 shows, standard double- or single-gauge railways brought the great bulk of men and all types of supply from the ports to advanced supply depots (it was sometimes possible to omit these and take supplies straight to regulating stations), then on to regulating stations and finally to railheads. At regulating stations commodities were unloaded and reorganized into mixed quantities for each division before being sent on to the railheads.

It is no exaggeration to say that without the extensive use of railways no army on the Western Front could have functioned effectively for more than a few days. Most railheads catered for several types of commodities, such as ammunition, supplies (rations, fodder and fuel) or engineer stores, and were the places from which motorized divisional supply columns (see page 350) collected the packs (loads) of their division's needs. Map 66 shows railheads in use in April 1916 during the British build-up for the offensive on the Somme. At this time forty-four railheads were operating, stocking fifty-two supply, thirteen ammunition, eight engineer stores and two GHQ dumps. The logistical planning for the Third and Fourth

Armies, totalling forty-two divisions, envisaged a daily requirement of 9,500 tons of ammunition, 6,000 troop reinforcements, 1,440 remounts and two trainloads of engineer stores and spare parts. It was calculated that all this would require seventy-one trains daily, and at times another fifty-seven permanent and temporary ambulance trains. The importance of having railheads as close as possible to the refilling point, or even located along with it, is obvious but was rarely possible, particularly for heavy ammunition.

It was the French authorities that provided railway locomotives, wagons and personnel in support of the BEF at the start of the war under previously agreed arrangements. The French also undertook railway maintenance and construction with their ample number of railway troop units. The main double- and single-rail tracks of the standard-gauge served the principal cities and towns, with narrower-metre gauge lines serving more remote country districts (Belgian railways were the same). In addition, light steam tramways, often following roads and using road bridges, were in use. Except for a period of a few months in 1918, metre-gauge lines were of minor importance and initially were referred to as 'light railways' until light railways proper came to be built in forward areas (see page 352).

French box-trucks or wagons, frequently the cause of much grumbling amongst troops travelling in them, were identical whether carrying people or horses. Their capacity was supposedly forty men or eight horses – numbers that were often scrawled on the sides of the wagons. To pack a train with troops with kit hung from hooks in the roof often took up to four or five hours. The occupants usually had no idea where they were going, how long it would take, or if they would get food (it was not uncommon for iron rations to be eaten against orders). Often the train would crawl along at such a slow pace that men could get out and walk alongside with no danger of being left behind. Sometimes the driver would be asked for hot water for tea, while at halts or when the train was moving particularly slowly opportunity would be taken to defecate by the track – followed by a short run as the man caught up with his wagon.

The system of having fixed numbers of men or animals in a wagon certainly simplified load-planning for railway staff, as thirty wagons would carry either 240 horses or 1,200 men, or 160 horses and 400 men or 80 horses and 800 men, and so on. For most of the war the French used three types of trains, the first for ordinary fighting units, the second for units with numerous vehicles, and the third for tactical moves of units without regimental transport. However, in early 1917 these three were combined into trains consisting of one passenger coach, thirty covered wagons (men and horses), seventeen flatbed trucks (vehicles) and two brake vans. It was found that, with units usually under full strength, almost every unit (British or French) could be moved by rail in this omnibus-type train, so although units varied in composition, no alteration to the train was allowed.

As the war effort expanded, so demands for rail transportation increased along with the need for more and more rolling stock,

locomotives and ambulance trains. This requirement led inevitably to the British heavily supplementing the French system, including undertaking the construction of new lines, light railways, sidings, railheads and their maintenance, along with the provision of workshops. These duties mostly devolved on to the Royal Engineers, supported by a large labour force (29,000 men worked on railways alone at the end of the war). From the 'No. 1 Railway Company' (8th Railway Company, RE) that embarked in August 1914, the RE railway units on the Western Front had multiplied many times by November 1918 to include:

26 railway construction companies
41 broad-gauge operating companies
1 signal and interlocking company
6 broad-gauge workshop companies
5 broad-gauge miscellaneous trades companies
6 wagon-erecting companies
13 railway traffic sections
3 electrical sections
1 steam-boiler repair company

From November 1914 the expansion of BEF transportation systems was divided into two phases: the first lasted until September 1916, by which time the Battle of the Somme had exposed an inadequate system. The crisis caused the Prime Minister to send

Sir Eric Geddes, a professional civilian railway expert (deputy general manager of the North Eastern Railway, which employed 50,000 men), to investigate into and report on the entire British transportation organization behind the Western Front. The second started with the arrival of the same man, now Major General Sir Eric Geddes, as DGT at GHQ and lasted until the end of the war.

As planned, the first two years of the war saw the French authorities meeting the British rail transport requirements (in practice, the *Chemins de Fer du Nord* or Northern Railway Company) – but with mounting difficulties. By the middle of 1916 wastage had seriously depleted the company's resources. Traffic essential to the life of the country had also to be maintained with an inadequate rail network, depleted personnel and shortages of locomotives, rolling stock and equipment. With the ever-increasing tonnages of supplies, munitions and stores arriving at the ports for the BEF, not only from the UK but from other parts of the world too, the needs of the armies began to overwhelm facilities for their reception and onwards transportation. The BEF was obliged to take on more and more responsibility for the working, maintenance and expansion of rail facilities for its own armies. As early as February 1916 the French had asked for 2,500 railway wagons and in

Troops detraining at Poperinghe, September 1917.

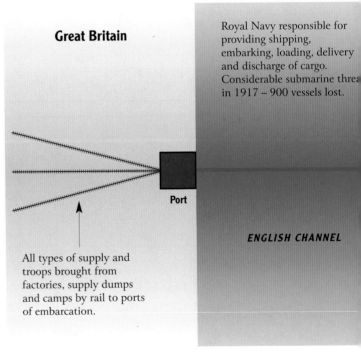

Simplified Layout of Supply Chain in Use b

Great Britain

Royal Navy responsible for providing shipping, embarking, loading, delivery and discharge of cargo. Considerable submarine threa in 1917 – 900 vessels lost.

Port

ENGLISH CHANNEL

All types of supply and troops brought from factories, supply dumps and camps by rail to ports of embarcation.

Notes
• This was the basic system of supply as required by regulations; however, it was adapted to meet particular circumstances.
• No attempt has been made to show supplies transported by inland waterway or those obtained by local purchase.

May suggested the British supply all wagons needed by the BEF. By November the French wanted locomotives as well as wagons, maintenance workshops and assistance in railway construction. This was the background to the BEF's transportation difficulties of 1916.

By August 1916, in the middle of the Somme battle, another munitions crisis appeared to be developing. The problem lay on the lines of communication, where huge bottlenecks had developed, with congestion on both roads and railways where the volume of traffic had more than doubled during the year; much of it had to be funnelled into a small portion of the BEF's front. The average of loaded railway wagons moved daily in January was 2,484; by December it was 5,202. Geddes summarized the problem thus:

> The organization was bad; responsibility was divided, and no-one realized the need for Transportation until they broke the machine which was never designed to stand the strain. They blamed the Ports; they blamed shipping . . . the bottleneck was between the rail head and coast. They had no statistics, they were short of material; short of foresight; short of programmes; short of labour and imagination; and they never pushed the rail heads far forward enough.

When Geddes arrived as DRT he brought with him several senior civilian railway managers, all, like himself, given temporary military ranks – an issue that rankled with some but had the backing of Lloyd George and Haig. The improvements put in place by Geddes were gradual, but in time proved decisive. To give just two examples of the scale of developments: first, by November 1918 about 54,000 wagons had been imported to France, 30,000 of them released from British home stock, 23,000 specially built and 1,000 privately owned; second, hundreds of miles of light railways and tramways had been laid (see page 352).

Finally, the extent of the increase in the BEF's use of rail transportation is revealed in the following figures of weekly averages:

BEF Use of Railways

	March 1917	October 1918
Imports (tons)	184,336	189,446
Locomotives in use (standard gauge)	401	1,376
Wagons in use	10,546	48,186

Note Although imports barely increased, there had been a threefold increase in locomotives and a fourfold one in wagons (figures include both British and French). This, along with the construction of additional lines, the expansion of light railways and inland waterways, planned and overseen efficiently, produced the best transportation network on the Western Front.

A supply train steams towards a railhead, with supply lorries moving alongside.

EF, Middle and Later Years

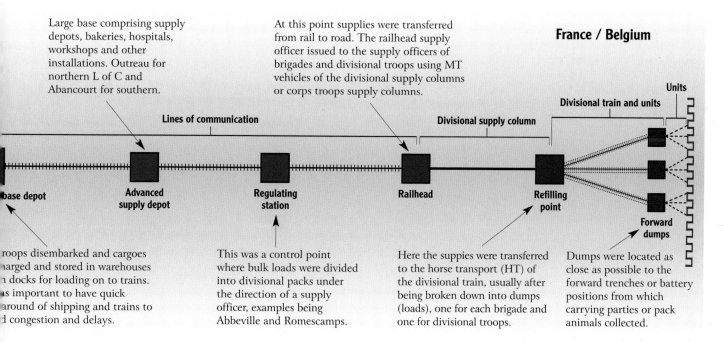

France / Belgium

Large base comprising supply depots, bakeries, hospitals, workshops and other installations. Outreau for northern L of C and Abancourt for southern.

At this point supplies were transferred from rail to road. The railhead supply officer issued to the supply officers of brigades and divisional troops using MT vehicles of the divisional supply columns or corps troops supply columns.

Lines of communication

Divisional supply column

Divisional train and units

Units

base depot

Advanced supply depot

Regulating station

Railhead

Refilling point

Forward dumps

roops disembarked and cargoes
harged and stored in warehouses
n docks for loading on to trains.
s important to have quick
around of shipping and trains to
d congestion and delays.

This was a control point where bulk loads were divided into divisional packs under the direction of a supply officer, examples being Abbeville and Romescamps.

Here the suppies were transferred to the horse transport (HT) of the divisional train, usually after being broken down into dumps (loads), one for each brigade and one for divisional troops.

Dumps were located as close as possible to the forward trenches or battery positions from which carrying parties or pack animals collected.

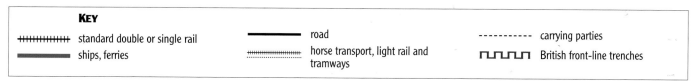

KEY

┼┼┼┼┼┼┼┼ standard double or single rail	──── road
═══ ships, ferries	┈┈┈┈ horse transport, light rail and tramways
---------- carrying parties	⊓⊔⊓⊔ British front-line trenches

Buses on the Western Front

The naval division sent to Antwerp in October 1914 did not have sufficient motor transport for an infantry division, so the Admiralty provided it with a number of omnibuses, each capable of carrying twenty-five men, from the London General Omnibus Company with volunteer drivers to supplement its needs. Later that month the BEF took over these buses from the Admiralty and during the Race to the Sea, when the BEF had to move north from the Aisne, the French lent sufficient buses to transport up to 10,000 troops. At the same time GHQ requested another 300 buses from England with the idea of enabling infantry units to accompany cavalry. These buses were

initially used without modifications but were later painted khaki, had their windows removed and were fitted with 2-inch-thick planks to provide limited protection. Some eventually had anti-aircraft guns attached to them and others carried pigeon lofts.

Eventually an omnibus park was formed at a headquarters company and five army sections of twenty-five buses, as well as six omnibus companies. Excluding the army sections, the park consisted of 324 buses, each carrying twenty-five men and 271 seated lorries each carrying twenty men – a total capacity of 13,520 men. This unit was able to move the infantry and dismounted engineers of an entire division.

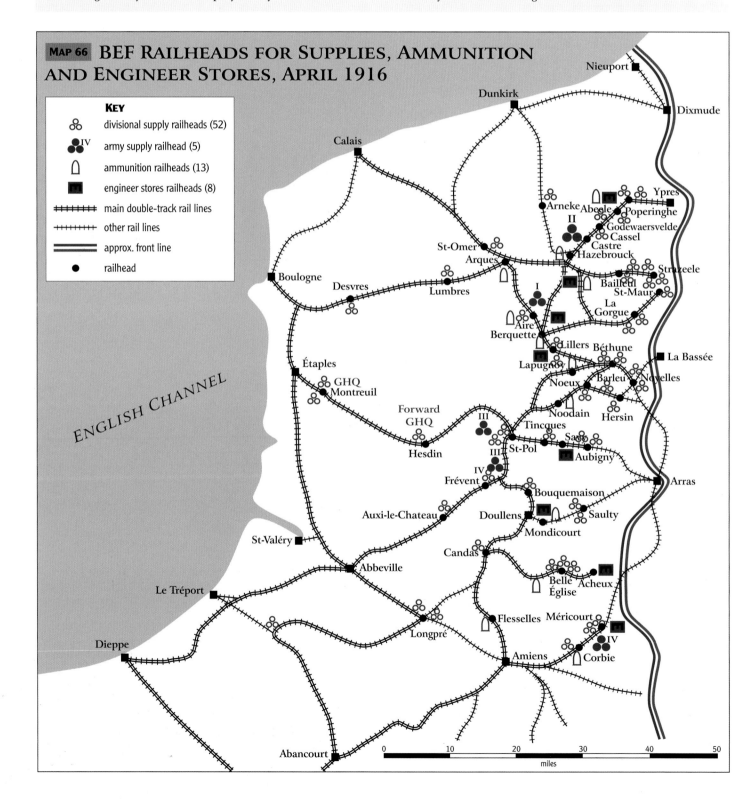

MAP 66 BEF RAILHEADS FOR SUPPLIES, AMMUNITION AND ENGINEER STORES, APRIL 1916

KEY
- ⚙ divisional supply railheads (52)
- ⚙IV army supply railhead (5)
- ⌂ ammunition railheads (13)
- ▣ engineer stores railheads (8)
- ┼┼┼┼ main double-track rail lines
- ┼┼┼┼ other rail lines
- ═══ approx. front line
- ● railhead

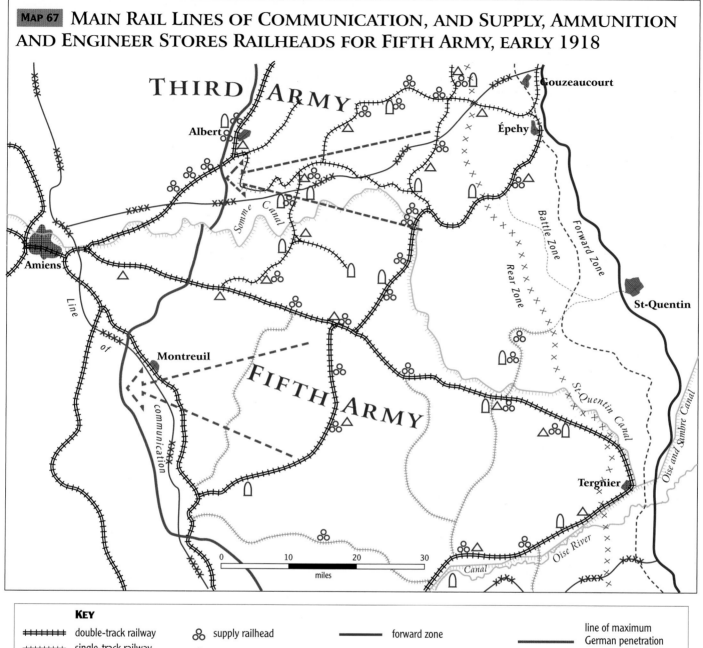

MAP 67   MAIN RAIL LINES OF COMMUNICATION, AND SUPPLY, AMMUNITION AND ENGINEER STORES RAILHEADS FOR FIFTH ARMY, EARLY 1918

THIRD ARMY

Gouzeaucourt

Albert

Épehy

Somme Canal

Battle Zone

Forward Zone

Rear Zone

Amiens

St-Quentin

Line of

Montreuil

St-Quentin Canal

FIFTH ARMY

Oise and Sambre Canal

communication

Tergnier

Oise River

Canal

0   10   20   30

miles

KEY

┼┼┼┼┼┼┼ double-track railway

┼┼┼┼┼┼ single-track railway

┼┼┼┼┼┼ metre-gauge railway

- - - - - railtrack not used

⚘ supply railhead

⌂ ammunition railhead

△ engineer stores railhead

——— forward zone

- - - - battle zone

× × × × rear zone

——— line of maximum German penetration

⟩⟩⟩ German advance during March 1918 offensive

Notes for Map 67

• This simplified map shows just the railheads for supplies, ammunition and engineer stores operating in the rear zone of the Fifth Army (and part of the Third Army) prior to the German offensive in March 1918. There were 20 supply, 12 ammunition and 13 engineer stores railheads serving this one army. It was from the railheads that supply and ammunition columns took the requirements to the formations in the army (see pages 346–7).

• What has not been shown for reasons of clarity and space is that many railheads were multi-purpose and were used for troop movements and supplying remounts, stone, tanks or for collecting salvage. Note how the German offensive drove the Fifth Army almost to the gates of Amiens and overran almost the entire rear area, with the consequent loss or destruction of huge quantities of every type of supply.

A working party of British troops moving forward on a light railway near Ypres, February 1917. Note the materials were loaded first and then the troops found what space they could.

Inland Waterways

The flat area of Belgium and northern France already had well-developed inland waterways before the war, with Belgian canals and rivers carrying some 50 per cent of that country's commerce. Map 68 shows the three networks used by the BEF – mostly after 1916. North-east of a line from Arras to Calais was the most extensive network, linking the ports of Calais and Dunkirk to the Belgian and northern half of the British sectors of the front. The second line was the canalized River Somme from St-Valéry past Abbeville and Amiens to Péronne. This system was connected to the northern network via the Canal du Nord and the St-Quentin Canal, although for much of the war these links were in enemy territory. Another problem with this central system was that a railway swing bridge spanned the Somme at Abbeville and rail traffic from Abbeville northwards was both heavy and continuous, so could not be interrupted often. The bridge was opened only two or three times, so the river traffic beyond Abbeville was local craft only. The third system was the River Seine, which was navigable from Le Havre through Rouen to Paris.

To start with the use of inland waterways was not considered seriously as it appeared to have several disadvantages as compared with the railway network. Routes were fixed and repairs to waterways damaged during operations would take far longer to mend than railway tracks. Traffic was largely restricted to daylight and might be suspended during fog, frost or gales. Similarly, flooding might raise the water level and prevent barges going under bridges. And finally, movement was slow. A loaded barge would not cover more than about 10 miles a day if horse-drawn, or 25 if hauled by tugs. However, it became apparent that barges could be useful in carrying large, bulky cargoes such as hay, oats and stone for road repairs; or timber, sleepers and, in some circumstances, ammunition, when there was no great urgency for delivery. There were advantages in storing some reserve stocks on barges, which then became floating reserve parks or depots that could be moved near the front or withdrawn if necessary. Barges were also to prove invaluable for transporting seriously sick or wounded soldiers who could not withstand the jolting of lengthy road or rail journeys. Eventually specialist barges were operating mobile water-treatment plants using filtration and chemicals, and some were used for carrying floating bridges.

Although the commander-in-chief wrote home in December 1914 suggesting more use of barges (he had in fact hired a number), it was not until 1915–16 that the service devel-oped on an organized footing. The Inland Water Transport (IWT) service, initially under the director of railway transport, was established in early 1915 under Colonel G. E. Holland (ex-commander Royal Indian Marine) with the title of deputy director of inland water transport (DDIWT). In October 1915 the IWT ceased to be a branch of the railway directorate and Holland became answerable directly to the QMG.

The service was divided into two branches, one for the working and control of water transport, the other for maintenance and reconstruction of waterways. By September 1916 the IWT was operating on just over 200 miles of waterway, using 528 craft (38 tugs, 336 self-propelled and towed barges, 36 water barges, 28 bridge barges, 24 hospital barges, 18 salvage barges, 10 barrack barges and 38 others). The self-propelled and towed barges had a dead-weight carrying capacity of 76,000 tons. The average weekly weight carried in the last two months of 1916 was approximately 22,000 tons of cargo and no personnel. In 1917 this average had grown to approximately 46,000 tons and 3,700 personnel.

Roads

Roads (including many hundreds of miles of timber corduroy roads), supplemented by light railways and tramways (see page 352), provided the means by which motor transport (MT) and horse transport (HT) conveyed the great bulk of supplies (in their general sense) forward from the railheads to the troops. The link in the chain from railhead to refilling point was provided by MT and was the responsibility of the ASC.

The ASC (RASC in 1918) had a total of 6,431 all ranks in 1914, rising to 325,881 by the Armistice, some 144,000 being in France along with many thousands of labourers working under its directions. In total, in all theatres and the UK, at the end of the war the RASC was operating 56,659 lorries, 23,133 cars and vans, 7,045 ambulances, 5,400 tractors, 1,285 steam wagons (steam-powered heavy-haulage road vehicles) and 34,865 motorcycles in 715 horse-transport, 654 motor-transport and 346 supply units. In 1965 the RASC was merged with the RE transportation branch (railways, inland waterways, port operations) to become the Royal Corps of Transport (RCT). In 1993 the RCT and RAOC were amalgamated to form today's Royal Logistic Corps (RLC).

On the Western Front the ASC was normally organized into companies, each fulfilling a particular role as follows:

- HT companies – including companies in divisional trains

- MT companies – including companies in the divisional supply columns, ammunition parks, omnibus companies (see page 348), companies attached to heavy artillery, motor-ambulance convoys, bridging and pontoon units and workshops

- supply companies – including bakeries, butcheries, auxiliary (petrol) companies and remount depots

- labour companies

The task of getting supplies from the railhead to the refilling point using MT belonged to the ASC supply columns. There were army troops (67 all ranks and 8 lorries); corps troops (81 all ranks and 13 lorries) and divisional supply columns (342 all ranks and 65 lorries) – each division normally had a supply column, divisional train and an ammunition park). Ammunition, particularly artillery ammunition, required specialist, separate transportation units – ammunition parks and sub-parks.

The build-up to a major offensive such as the Somme entailed weeks of preparation in bringing forward and stocking large tonnages of supplies and ammunition of all kinds. By 1 July 1916 additional ASC units had been formed. For non-divisional artillery an additional company was provided and attached to each army and heavy-artillery headquarters – responsible for the ammunition supply of tractor-driven siege batteries. Also formed were mobile repair companies, workshops, and omnibus and water-tank companies (both GHQ units). During that July supplies, ammunition and stores were taken forward from railheads by the supply and ammunition parks in three ways:

- supplies and light ammunition: by MT and thence to destination by HT

- light- and medium-artillery ammunition and engineer stores: by MT to a dump and thence to a battery or engineer depot by light railway/tramway

- heavy-artillery ammunition or engineer stores to siege battery or engineer depot by MT all the way

In all, during the build-up the Fourth Army employed some 1,200–1,300 lorries daily on ammunition supply alone.

This massive volume of daily traffic in all weathers required hard surfaces on which to park (called 'stabling'). These were far from easy to find and consequently many stabling places were several miles from the routes over which the lorries were required to work. The *British Official History of the War: Transportation on the Western Front* gives several examples, one of which was III Corps' ammunition park in July 1916. The

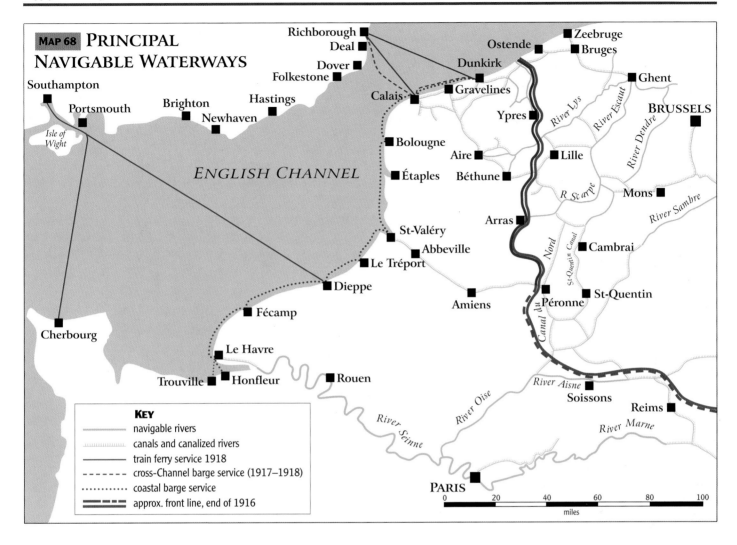

MAP 68 PRINCIPAL
NAVIGABLE WATERWAYS

ENGLISH CHANNEL

KEY

————————	navigable rivers
··············	canals and canalized rivers
————————	train ferry service 1918
– – – – –	cross-Channel barge service (1917–1918)
··············	coastal barge service
══════	approx. front line, end of 1916

park was stabled at Franvillers while part of its work was to carry ammunition from Edge Hill to a dump 2 miles distant from that railhead. The lorries ran empty from Franvillers to Edge Hill (7 miles), carried the ammunition for 2 miles, then returned to Franvillers empty – a total of 18 miles, only 2 of which was carrying a load. The worst example was a divisional supply column in the Third Army that ran 40 miles a day and carried a load for only 4 or 5 of them, then deposited it 2 miles further away from the unit it supplied than the railhead from which it had picked it up!

These long runs meant massive petrol consumption, great wear and tear on vehicles, drivers and roads, along with bottlenecks and congestion leading to tailbacks and delays. On 1 September 1916, during intensive Somme fighting, the Fourth Army was operating 4,671 lorries, 1,145 cars and ambulances and 1,636 motorcycles, and the amount of supplies taken from railheads in a day was almost 2,000 tons, of which over 1,200 tons was ammunition of all types. A traffic census taken at Fricourt Cemetery on 22 July 1916 showed some 7,300 motor and horsed vehicles passing every twenty-four

hours, or about five per minute. Petrol consumption, assuming an average daily journey of 15 miles at 5 miles a gallon and allowing for vehicles off the road for repair, was estimated at 12,000 gallons for the Fourth Army alone.

Traffic planning was extraordinarily complex and detailed, and was based on road circuits drawn up by each corps to suit their needs, taking into account the location of their railheads and dumps. 'Normal' and 'operation' circuit maps were compiled for each army. Normally, red roads were usable in both directions by all traffic; blue roads in both directions by cars and motorcycles, and by other traffic only in the direction of the blue arrows; uncoloured roads were not to be used by lorries, buses or steam tractors; horses were not to be exercised on coloured roads. On operation circuit maps motor ambulance routes were shown by red and blue dotted lines. Wherever possible, tracks away from metalled roads were earmarked for animals and horse transport.

Control posts were essential to keep traffic moving. The twenty-five military police in a division, of whom only about half were available for traffic duties, were reinforced

during operations by one or two officers and up to ninety other ranks. It was found necessary to take men from other divisional units to form permanent traffic-control companies under the overall charge of the assistant provost marshal.

Road repair was a constant daily duty for thousands of soldiers and labourers, due not only to damage caused by the traffic and bad weather but also by enemy shelling. As the size of the BEF grew, so the British took over from the French more and more responsibility for maintenance in the 'tactical' zone behind the front. By December 1915 the British had undertaken to provide the 3,370 tons of metal required daily for road repairs in their area. In addition to repairing or improving existing roads, new ones had to be constructed. Railheads had to be accessible to hundreds of lorries operating continuously for prolonged periods, which entailed the building of hard-standing station yards and approach roads. Station yards had to be some 450 yards long and 40 feet wide, necessitating 5,000–6,000 tons of stone delivered by about twenty trainloads. This often meant the railhead could not be used until these facilities were completed.

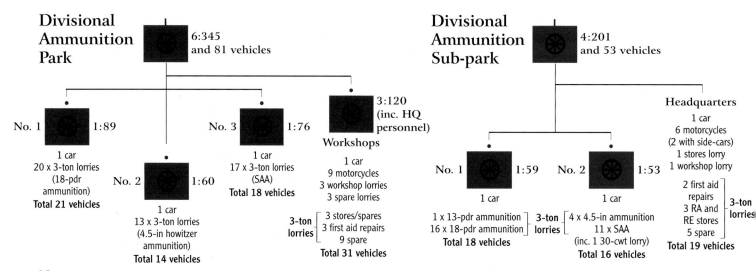

Divisional Ammunition Park — 6:345 and 81 vehicles

No. 1 — 1:89
1 car
20 x 3-ton lorries
(18-pdr ammunition)
Total 21 vehicles

No. 2 — 1:60
1 car
13 x 3-ton lorries
(4.5-in howitzer ammunition)
Total 14 vehicles

No. 3 — 1:76
1 car
17 x 3-ton lorries
(SAA)
Total 18 vehicles

Workshops — 3:120 (inc. HQ personnel)
1 car
9 motorcycles
3 workshop lorries
3 spare lorries

3-ton lorries [3 stores/spares
3 first aid repairs
9 spare]
Total 31 vehicles

Divisional Ammunition Sub-park — 4:201 and 53 vehicles

No. 1 — 1:59
1 car
1 x 13-pdr ammunition
16 x 18-pdr ammunition] 3-ton lorries
Total 18 vehicles

No. 2 — 1:53
1 car
4 x 4.5-in ammunition
11 x SAA
(inc. 1 30-cwt lorry)
Total 16 vehicles

Headquarters
1 car
6 motorcycles
(2 with side-cars)
1 stores lorry
1 workshop lorry
2 first aid repairs
3 RA and RE stores] 3-ton lorries
5 spare
Total 19 vehicles

Note

In preparation for the Somme offensive divisional supply columns were placed under the command of corps rather than the IGC. Divisional communication parks (also L of C units) were broken up and reserve units called 'GHQ ammunition parks' formed instead, with a GHQ corps ammunition park allotted to each corps and a sub-park to each division. The corps administered these units and were responsible for ammunition.

Horse Transport, Light Railways and Tramways

The next leg of the journey for supplies was from the refilling point to dumps close to the unit or, in the case of heavy artillery, direct to the guns. Initially this was the responsibility solely of the divisional train and ammunition column with horse-transport companies of the ASC, but during 1916 increasing use was made of light railways (60cm gauge), initially using the French lines but soon constructed by the British using the same gauge. The final development saw the use of tramways to supplement and extend light railway lines to within a short distance of the unit, or in some cases direct to artillery batteries, with duckboard tracks leading to most infantry units. By late 1917 an extensive network of light railways and tramways with lateral links was established. These were invaluable for the transport of wounded, who would otherwise have to be carried by relays of stretcher-bearers.

The task of the divisional train was to carry the baggage of the units in the division and bring up supplies of food, fodder and other commodities to locations where they could be manhandled or taken by pack animals to the trenches. Separate units – ammunition columns – brought ammunition forward. The train was commanded by a lieutenant colonel and had an establishment, less detached personnel, of 428 all ranks. It was divided into four companies, three of which each carried the baggage and supplies of an infantry brigade and one field ambulance, and the fourth of which did the same

for artillery, divisional troops and headquarters. However, the complete establishment, including personnel with the transport of the divisional ammunition columns that were detached in the field, totalled 657 all ranks. Vehicles included four motor cars for requisitioning purposes, bicycles, carts and wagons drawn by two draught horses (including one Maltese cart drawn by one horse for the medical officer). Most vehicles were GS (general service) four-wheeled wagons capable of carrying 1½ tons.

The development of light railway tracks came about due to the need to take the immense pressure off the roads, as the growing dependence on motor transport was causing so much congestion, delay and endless road maintenance. To alleviate this problem, it was intended wherever possible to locate the railhead beside the refilling point or at a dump within reach of the horse transport of the divisional train, thus cutting out the use of MT entirely. The first light railway (as distinct from trench tramways) worked by the British was a 60cm laid by the French in an area subsequently taken over by the British in February 1916. The Germans were also well ahead of the British, in that their mobilization equipment included large stocks of light-railway material. For convenience, this 60cm gauge was adopted when the BEF began construction of their own tracks along their entire front later that year.

It was the slow struggle to advance of the Somme battle – when supplying the army by means of MT over roads which had given out under the traffic and which in captured areas were non-existent – that brought matters to a head. Orders were placed for over 600 miles of track, 120 tractors and locomo-

tives and over 1,600 wagons, with construction under the director of railways and the work being carried out by railway construction troops. In August the QMG instructed that light railways were to be used along the whole front for carrying munitions and materials in order of priority – heavy-artillery ammunition, light-artillery ammunition, engineer stores and supplies. Experience on the Somme showed that for an advance on a 12-mile front loads totalling some 20,000 tons had to be delivered daily – a practical impossibility using just MT, and the few isolated lines and the wooden corduroy roads were completely inadequate.

It was in 1917 that light railways were to play a crucial part in British offensives. At Arras in April a considerable tonnage was conveyed from standard-gauge railheads to light-railway railheads and from there taken forward by road transport, but it was at Messines in June that light railways played a truly major part. Ammunition was delivered direct to heavy batteries and much of the light-gun ammunition was taken to artillery-group stations within 3,000 yards of the front line. At the start of the Ypres offensive at the end of August up to 7,000 tons of ammunition a day was carried by light railways. During August it was calculated that in just one month (July) light railways had moved some 60,000 tons of supplies a week – the work of around 1,350 lorries. At Cambrai in November, advancing troops were followed closely by light-railway construction units that had a track into Marcoing village the day after its capture. Most of these lines were vulnerable to heavy German shelling, so continuous maintenance, often under fire, was essential. In late 1917 the decision was taken to build a lateral line some 6,000 yards in the rear of the front to connect all the various corps systems, and this was completed by March 1918. One unanticipated problem of the expansion of light-railway tracks was the damage caused by their being used by troops and pack animals as pathways over shell-torn areas – the French even resorted to protecting stretches of track with barbed-wire fences.

During 1917 1,000 miles of light-railway track were laid, and by September they were carrying 20,000 tons and 30,000 men every day. These light railways were organized, managed and worked as a complete railway system under its own directorate and by experienced railway personnel. The directorate employed up to twenty-three operating companies, five train crew companies, two trades companies and three workshops.

Alongside the development of light railways came the construction and use of tramways, so that eventually the two systems merged into a complex spider's web of lines that covered the area from the reserve trenches to the railheads and refilling points and effectively supplemented the use of motor and horse transport. Both the French and Germans had seen the advantages of tramways, but with the British only a few units, notably the Canadians, made efforts to install them, using light rails and hand-pushed trolleys. However, in March 1915 the supply of ammunition and stores for the British attack on Neuve Chapelle was facilitated by the laying of tramlines to within a few hundred yards of the front line. These tramlines had wooden rails and sleepers and the trucks, taken from the Béthune tramways, had iron wheels. Construction was carried out at night, with the noise minimized by the use of wood. It was the 8th Division that first utilized these wooden tramways, the idea originating with Lieutenant Colonel H. M. de F. Montgomery the divisional AA and QMG, who had seen similar tramways in use on French farms.

In September 1915, in a circular instruction from the QMG, trench tramways were to be extended backwards from the front to the most forward point that could be reached by horse transport to alleviate the amount of supplies that had to be carried by hand to the trenches. The expansion of tramways continued apace during 1916 and into 1917. The artillery light railways delivered heavy and medium ammunition from railheads to dumps near the batteries, from where it was removed in push-trolleys over light, unballasted tramways to immediately behind the guns. These tramways were in addition to the trench tramways provided under corps arrangements and worked by divisions leading forward from refilling points.

By late 1917 there were nine army tramways companies and one army troops company working on tramways; they were named 'foreways' companies. In early March 1918 it was stipulated that light railways would lay, maintain and operate lines up to artillery-group stations in the medium-artillery zone, and that the foreways engineer service would operate forward from the group stations. The intention was that the latter's duties would include distribution of ammunition to medium-battery locations; distribute trench mortar, SAA, engineer and ordnance stores and rations; evacuate wounded; remove salvage and transport personnel if it did not detract from other responsibilities. However, this scheme was never completely operative due to lack of sufficient personnel and the German offensive of March 1918. Later attempts finally to rationalize the system were frustrated by the abandonment of static trench warfare, for which tramways were primarily intended, with the Allied advance in the summer that culminated in the German surrender.

Despite all the above use of ships, barges, railways, motor and horse transport and tramways, carrying supplies over the last few hundred yards to the infantryman's trench had invariably to be done by men and pack animals. Exhausted carrying parties staggering through the mud along slippery duckboard tracks in the dark, falling into shell holes, stumbling over bodies and strands of wire and constantly exposed to enemy harassing fire were among the more horrific memories of any infantryman who survived the war. Nevertheless, as Ernest Parker describes in his book *Into Battle 1914–1918*, being involved with mule transportation had its moments. After the Battle of Loos he was transferred from the Durham Light Infantry to transport duties:

> At the transport camp we lived a peaceful life by day and enjoyed abundant rations prepared by our own cook. Grooming mules was often exciting. One of us at least never quite mastered the art of picking up their hind legs. When evening came we paraded with our mules, balancing two large panniers on each side of the pack saddles. With these ponderously swaying from side to side we journeyed in crocodile formation to the dump at the Dickebusch communication trench. Once we had unloaded the stores, pleasure began and seated astride the iron bars of the pack saddles, we cantered off merrily into safety. Thoughtfully our leader would halt us half-way so that pipes could be loaded and the mules rested. One occasion the jolting of the beast's awkward trot flung my pipe onto the roadway. I managed to dismount a hundred yards further on, but the miserable beast refused to return. Listening with cocked ears to the rest of the troop clattering off down the cobbled road, he suddenly jerked me off my feet and in a mad gallop raced towards his brothers.

German soldiers transport provisions through Doullens with locally requisitioned horse-drawn vehicles, September 1914.

Nurses and RAMC orderlies care for British, French and German wounded soldiers at No. 29 Casualty Clearing Station, Gézaincourt, in April 1917 during the Battle of the Lys.

Section Nine

Medical, Chaplains, Veterinary

*Many of the wounded Germans seemed half demented; some laughing inanely,
others crying; and I noticed more than one of our own men who had lost their
wits and were shedding tears like children. It is painful to see full-grown men
lose their nerve to that degree, but it seems that the shock of wounds, or seeing
wounds inflicted, has that effect on some people.*

D. W. J. Cuddeford, *And All for What? Some Wartime Experiences*

Medical

Virtually any casual mention of the Western Front or World War I instantly conjures up in the public's mind the horrendous, seemingly senseless, slaughter and maiming of hundreds of thousands of young men. The casualty statistics, although often varying substantially depending on the source consulted, always frighteningly expose the scale of the losses and the suffering, both physical and mental, they represent. The Western Front saw fighting at least somewhere along its 450-mile length every hour of every day for over four years, with an average daily death toll of around 5,000. The total casualty count of killed, wounded, 'shell-shocked' (see box, page 361), missing and prisoners on all fronts almost certainly exceeded 15 million. On the first day of the Somme over 57,000 British soldiers fell, nearly 20,000 of them dead. To any overall casualty figure must be added the men who died of disease, or who were evacuated sick and therefore absent from the front for varying periods of time. However, the large number of soldiers that succumbed to the deadly influenza pandemic that struck Europe from 1918 to 1920 (over 50 million people died worldwide in one of the worst natural disasters in history) is not included in the casualty figures. With all belligerents, the size of their losses mounted dramatically year by year, spiking during major battles but never for a single hour ceasing. The following table for the BEF demonstrates the increasing toll of dead, wounded, missing and prisoners.

British Casualties 1914–1918

Year	Monthly average casualties	Total
1914 (August–December)	19,131	95,654
1915	24,757	297,083
1916	53,529	642,353
1917	68,150	817,795
1918 (January–November)	77,533	852,866
Total		**2,705,751**

However, this section is concerned only with the wounded and the sick – the responsibility of the medical services of each nation whose priority was always treatment in and speedy evacuation from the forward zone. As with other sections, there is insufficient space to include more than brief reference to armies other than the British, but the medical services of other nations operated in much the same way.

Injuries and Illnesses

Before explaining the organization of the British Royal Army Medical Corps (RAMC) to see how it grew in size and complexity, it is worth examining the prevalent types of wound or sickness that occurred and the treatment.

Wounds

Military surgeons worked by one rule of thumb: patch up and move on (see 'Casualty Evacuation', page 362). At front-line aid posts or dressing stations time was not spent on the hopelessly injured – they were normally given painkillers and left on their stretchers to die. This system of prioritizing the wounded is known as 'triage', and remains a basic element of dealing with mass casualties today. A soldier badly wounded in no-man's-land on the Western Front might have to lie in a shell hole, cold, wet and shocked, for many hours before being found, or alternatively try to crawl back to his own lines before he received attention from medical staff – by which time many such men were beyond saving. One who survived such an ordeal was New Zealander Second Lieutenant Frank McKenzie, who was hit in the leg during an attack in late September 1916:

Thoroughly scared and crippled I crawled on two hands and one knee about half a mile to our original front line. However the barrage still pursued me and I crawled gradually another half mile until we came to our 18-pounder line. The officer in charge tried to get me into an empty ammunition limber, but the pain in that crampt [*sic*] space was too severe, and I decided to crawl back to the first field dressing station along the limber track. The attack took place

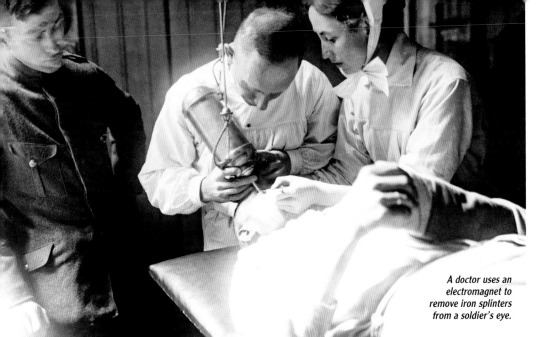

A doctor uses an electromagnet to remove iron splinters from a soldier's eye.

at noon, and it was dark when I got to the artillery line. I crawled all night with rests in the mud, and arrived at the field dressing station at day-light.

Shell, mortar or grenade fragments, shrapnel or bullets caused most wounds. To these must be added the less numerous gas casualties; crushing injuries and being buried alive (both caused by collapsing bunkers or tunnels); aerial bombing; exposure; or stab wounds (these were a fairly rare occurrence). Battlefield wounds were classified as either penetration or laceration injuries – frequently they were a combination of the two. It was not uncommon for the contents of the soldier's pockets to cause secondary injuries, as the blast from the bomb or shell could drive penknives, coins or pencils into his body. Occasionally outside objects such as pebbles, bits of masonry or even the bones of a nearby victim caused wounds. Invariably, whatever the cause of the injury, grease, dirt and bits of clothing were driven into wounds and it became axiomatic for the medical services to regard every wound as infected.

When a bullet fired from comparatively close range (up to 500 yards, and most bullet wounds on the Western Front came into this category) hits a man, it makes a small penetrating entry wound. If not deflected it is likely to exit the body or limb through a larger wound, having followed a straight line. However, pointed bullets are easily deflected by bone or tough muscles, making them tumble and causing considerable tearing of tissue before they exit. Also, these turning bullets frequently damage organs, arteries or break bones. An American surgeon writing in 1939 on bullet wounds on the Western Front stated:

A surgeon must explore the internal track of all penetrating bullets, no matter how tiny the entering wounds may seem.

If he meets an abdominal wound, for instance, he must first cut off all jagged infected surface tissue. Without damaging important nerves, veins, arteries, he must then pull out the intestines 'foot by foot', looking for bullet perforations, and stitching them up. If he neglects the exploration, his patient is almost certain to die of hemorrhage or peritonitis.

Ricocheted bullets were a common cause of serious wounds as they struck the body with an enlarged irregular surface and a tearing, bruising action, carrying with them material from clothes or even particles of soil.

Artillery and mortars caused substantially more deaths and wounds than any other weapon. Shells came in two main types – shrapnel or high explosive. With the former the explosion flung what were essentially round bullets forwards and downwards. Compared to the rifle or machine-gun bullet they were of small weight and low velocity and could be compared with the old smoothbore bullets. In general they inflicted comparatively slight injuries such as contusions or incomplete perforations – that is, the projectile remained in the body in what was called a 'cul-de-sac' wound. However, it was the bursting high-explosive shell, the mortar bomb and the grenade that usually caused the greatest and most traumatic damage. Their ghastly lacerating wounds could rip huge chunks out of the victim's body and when this happened to a limb the only way to save the man's life was a tourniquet and speedy amputation. To be struck in the body or head by a jagged shell splinter was invariably fatal.

Whatever the cause of the wound, it was commonly followed, even if trivial, by 'wound shock' or lowered vitality, which, if untreated, could lead to death. Wound shock resulted from pain, loss of blood, loss of body heat and fluids, and toxaemia. Its

best treatment was found to be small doses of morphine for pain relief, keeping the soldier warm with blankets and hotwater bottles and plenty of hot, sweet tea to drink. By 1918 a casualty clearing station would have a resuscitation tent where severely shocked and apparently dying cases were warmed in heated beds before an operation.

The wound most soldiers welcomed was the so-called 'Blighty' wound. The word was slang for 'Britain' or 'home' and was derived from the Hindustani word for 'foreigner'. Such a wound was serious enough to get the man evacuated to his home country but not so bad as to leave him permanently disabled. Many soldiers wrote home about the prospect of a Blighty. An officer in 1917 reported, 'I saw a fellow get a lovely wound in the head with a bit of shrapnel. He was so pleased he made me laugh.'

The *British Official History of the War: Medical Services, General History*, Volume III, gives an analysis of the nature of wounds admitted to BEF casualty clearing stations in twenty-four hours (21 September 1917) during the Third Battle of Ypres. Of the 10,789 wounded, the causes were 3,867 HE shell; 2,933 bullet; 2,142 shrapnel; 1,544 uncertain causes; 209 gassed; 77 grenade; and 17 bayonet. Discounting the undetermined cases, artillery caused almost two thirds of the wounds. The total number of British Army individuals wounded in action on the Western Front, including those wounded on more than one occasion (over 5,000 men were wounded three times or more) and accidental injuries, was 2,272,998.

A Brave Rescue

After the Battle of Loos in September 1915, Captain Ernest Parker, 10th Durham Light Infantry, recounted how a battalion runner stopped briefly to tell of his 'personal' visit to the German front line on the day following the fruitless British advance:

In no-man's-land were scores of our own men whose pitiful appeals tore the hearts of their helpless comrades. At last overcome by pity Comberland sprang over the parapet and, waving his handkerchief, approached the German wire, where a tortured man was spreadeagled on the tenacious barbs. Below in the enemy trench an officer's head appeared, and with perfect sang-froid Comberland sprang smartly to attention and saluted, afterwards carrying his wounded comrade back.

Parker, who was awarded the MC, described this extraordinary incident in his book *Into Battle, 1914–1918*.

Treatment

During an attack a wounded soldier was expected either to treat himself or, if that was impossible, to await the arrival of stretcher-bearers or, if capable of walking, to make his own way back. His comrades in the attack were under strict orders not to stop to assist any man who fell. From an enemy's perspective it is often better to wound than kill, as the wounded soldier requires other fit soldiers to remove and treat him.

Soldiers were provided with a field dressing, with larger shell dressings available within the platoon (even if the shell dressing was applied quickly an abdominal wound was usually fatal). This individual dressing was a cotton bandage to which was attached a cotton-wool pad treated with an antiseptic. There was a safety pin for fastening the bandage. Provided the soldier was capable of applying it himself, or it was done by a comrade, it was largely successful in stemming non-arterial blood flow and kept out the worst of the dirt. Unfortunately, whatever the projectile, foreign material was almost always driven or carried into the wound and it was this deeply embedded matter that could cause serious problems in the form of tetanus (lockjaw). The tetanus spore was prevalent in the soil of France and Belgium, but the large-scale inoculation of wounded troops with an anti-tetanus serum dramatically reduced the incidence of infection. In 1914 the infection rate among the BEF was around 8 per 1,000, reduced to 1.47 per 1,000 by 1918. There were only 2,529 British cases by the end of the war.

Much more common – and dreaded by wounded men – was the onset of gas gangrene. The dry version was caused by the loss of blood supply to some or all of a limb, and wet gangrene resulted from the presence in the wound of the clostridium bacteria common in the manured farming soil of France. The onset of gangrene could be rapid, starting at the site of the wound and characterized by the swelling of the limb, air under the skin, blisters containing a red-brown fluid, fever, sweating and pain, along with an unpleasant smell. If the swelling was pressed there was a crackly sensation which came from the gas underneath. The only possible treatment, if caught early enough, was called 'debridement' – the complete removal of damaged or infected tissue. This meant the wound was enlarged and left open, drained and treated with antiseptics. Later in the war maggots were often placed on an infected area as they attacked only dead or damaged tissue and simultaneously sterilized it. As gangrene spread rapidly, and as it was often

many hours or even days before a wounded soldier reached a surgeon, frequently the only solution was amputation if his life was to be saved. It was not only wounded soldiers that contracted gangrene but also those suffering from severe trench foot (see page 358) or even frostbite, both of which could cut off blood supply.

The treatment of men exposed to gas poisoning was primarily palliative, with survival dependent on the recuperative power of the individual. The great majority eventually recovered, although those seriously gassed were affected for the rest of their lives. The introduction of mustard gas later in the war meant victims had huge burn blisters on exposed skin and had to have their clothes carefully removed and decontaminated. The problem with treatment was that a small amount of mustard gas on clothing or skin was not necessarily noticed immediately, as it took time to develop into painful burns. If its presence was known quickly after contamination, then clothing could be removed and the skin rubbed with a paste of bleaching powder and water to neutralize the toxic chemicals.

A serious handicap to treatment of all types of wound was the huge influx of casualties experienced during a major battle, which frequently threatened to swamp the surgical capacity available. Surgical teams were rushed in from areas not involved in the battle to assist and were often grouped in threes with duty periods rotated on a shift system. Nevertheless, the situation at the start of the British Amiens offensive in August 1918, described by Captain John Hayward, RAMC, in *Everyman at War*, reflects a common situation in a casualty clearing station:

The stretchers filled the numberless rooms, and then flowed out into the corridors which became blocked except for a narrow passage. Every unit, except those engaged with the nine operating surgeons, was occupied in sorting, dressing and doing what was possible for the masses of wounded, but the numbers were too great and many had to lie for hours without help, or die unattended.

A quick surgeon might get through from fifteen to twenty cases in a spell of twelve hours. I certainly could not do more than ten or twelve.

Medical procedures/drugs

A number of life-saving procedures were employed that contributed significantly to the success rate of operations and the relief of suffering.

• **X-rays** By 1914 many hospitals in many countries already had X-ray machines, but they were all far removed from the battlefields. X-ray machines had been available during the Boer War and motorized units with trailers of X-ray equipment were deployed with the BEF in May 1915 on the basis of one to each army. An X-ray unit was eventually sent to each casualty clearing station. The French were fortunate to have the services of the first woman professor at the Sorbonne, Marie Curie, who had received Nobel Prizes for physics and chemistry. She devoted herself to a project to launch a radiological service for the French Army, obtaining vehicles for conversion to X-ray units and working with electrical manufacturers to produce portable electric generators. She became director of the army's radiological service, which by 1918

The aftermath of a gas attack: men of the 55th West Lancashire Division suffer the effects of the deadly new weapon.

had twenty mobile units and which in the final two years of the war took over a million X-rays and saved thousands of lives.

• **Blood transfusions** These were not practised by the majority of surgeons in Britain prior to the outbreak of war, although experiments in methods and techniques had started before the turn of the century. It was only during the final two years, when the RAMC was reinforced by American medical expertise, that the practice spread throughout the army. As well as replacing blood loss, it was found to reduce considerably the amount of shock suffered by the casualty.

• **Painkillers** The most common drug used throughout the army was morphine, which was an effective way of reducing both suffering and shock. The problem was it came to be used to such an extent that many wounded soldiers became addicted to it – morphine created the first great wave of drug addiction in America and Britain after the war. Regimental medical officers had supplies of this drug, although early in the war it was also issued to British infantry company commanders in a tube of ¼ grain tablets – one to relieve pain, two to render semi-insensibility and three to render unconsciousness until death.

• **Anaesthetics** The general anaesthetics used were ether, chloroform, ethyl chloride and a nitrous oxide/oxygen mixture, all normally applied by drop masks. Although ether was the most commonly used because it was safe, it was also slow to take effect, did not relax the muscles and was not well tolerated by severely shocked casualties. Chloroform was more potent and took effect quickly, but was less safe than ether and extremely hazardous to use on wounded men in severe shock, so it was avoided if possible. Ethyl chloride and nitrous oxide were used for short surgeries (operations of under an hour), especially those involving joint manipulation. An American surgeon commented that it was sometimes hard to tell how men would react to anaesthesia, stating that some, even though quiet and sickly, took large quantities of anaesthetic and became 'excitable and troublesome', while other 'rough looking and vigorous' soldiers needed very little. Local anaesthesia with novocaine was used for minor surgery, with stovaine for operations on the pelvis or legs.

• **Inoculations** All British soldiers were routinely inoculated against typhoid (enteric fever). However, at the front the inoculation in greatest demand was the anti-tetanus serum for the wounded. It eventually became routinely held as far forward as the regimental aid post, as preventative action against this potentially deadly infection was necessary as quickly as possible after injury. The use of this serum reduced fatalities from tetanus from 63 per cent in 1914 to 38 per cent in 1918, by which time the number of cases had also been substantially reduced.

• **Mobile laboratories** From 1915 the BEF, in addition to the mobile X-ray units already discussed, was supplied with one hygiene and two mobile bacteriological laboratories for each army. In May 1916 a motorized dental laboratory was offered through the British Red Cross by the Civil Service Motor Ambulance Fund and sent to the Third Army. Eventually each army was supplied with a mobile dental laboratory through the generosity of donors.

Hygiene and Sickness

Personal hygiene for soldiers living in the front-line squalor of a filthy, waterlogged trench required huge efforts of self-discipline and continuous enforcement of hygiene discipline within units and by the medical authorities. To exhaustion, poor diet and often contaminated water were added the rain, the mud and, as early as the winter of 1914/15, freezing weather. As trench warfare developed, the rotting corpses of men and horses, refuse and unprotected open latrines gave rise to flies in their billions and rats in their millions, to which were added the ever-present body lice. These were the health hazards faced by every soldier in every army on the Western Front, in addition to the danger from the enemy.

Disease and illness produced both deaths and sickness that required evacuation – although, perhaps surprisingly in view of the living conditions, not on the scale of that caused by enemy action. This was certainly the case in the BEF, with medical advances such as inoculations and with strict hygiene discipline at regimental level. Special sanitary squads were responsible for latrine management (digging, covering and filling in), provision of potable water, bathing and delousing arrangements. At higher level, RAMC sanitary units, water purification and staff officers with sanitary responsibilities at all headquarters from division upwards, together with the establishment of the RAMC School of Health Instruction (it trained over 3,000 men), ensured that sickness levels were kept as low as possible. This was in contrast to previous wars where losses to sickness often far outstripped those from military action. The table on the right shows the numbers of seriously sick BEF soldiers evacuated from the Western Front.

Comparing this total with that of wounded in action (1,838,935; see page 152), the ratio of evacuated sick to wounded was 1:1.84. During the period 1 July–10 November 1917 the BEF had 42,704 men evacuated to bases through sickness and 104,847 wounded, giving a ratio of 1:2.45. Many soldiers who reported sick to their unit medical officer were given a tablet and had their sick note marked 'M and D' (Medicine and Duties), while some who developed a fever or diarrhoea, for example, struggled on regardless.

In addition to complaints such as flu and diarrhoea, three illnesses are especially linked to Western Front trench warfare – although all were known before the war – along with one timeless disease associated with periods away from the line: trench foot, trench fever and trench mouth, plus venereal disease. Each one was the cause of debility and a drain on unit strengths in terms of morale and loss of manpower.

Trench foot

This condition was brought about by continuous exposure to wet and cold, leading to a lack of circulation in the feet. If untreated it quickly became cripplingly painful and could ultimately lead to gangrene and amputation. In late 1914 and into 1915, during a grim winter, the hastily dug trenches in the fields of Flanders soon flooded, forcing soldiers to stand immobile for many hours with their feet in freezing water. Their leather ammunition boots gave no protection and it was impossible to dry feet or change socks. Feet became swollen, turning first red then black, and were agony to walk on. Andrew Macdonald, in *On My Way to the Somme*, quotes a New Zealand soldier telling of his experience:

> The night was horribly cold and our feet were wet, yet we were left to stand in that mud until morning. In the morning we moved round to another trench but it was even worse for it had both water and mud. We stayed there all that day and the next afternoon I could stand it no longer as I could hardly walk. I went round to the doctor and he said I had trench feet, so he said I had better go back to the transport for a couple of

Rates of Sickness Evacuation

Year	Officers	Other Ranks	Total
1914	892	25,013	25,905
1915	5,558	121,006	126,564
1916	12,818	219,539	232,357
1917	15,311	321,628	336,939
1918	12,654	265,735	278,389
Totals	47,233	952,921	1,000,154

days. I managed to struggle back and found our Q.M.S. [quartermaster sergeant]. He gave me a dry pair of socks and I felt a new man. My feet swelled up so much that I could not get my boots on again and in the morning I couldn't walk. A couple of chaps carried me down to the Dr and I went away to hospital in Rouen.

During that first winter over 20,000 cases were reported in the BEF – something that stimulated coordinated preventative action. Additional socks were issued to the infantry and frequent foot inspections became mandatory. Whale oil was issued and soldiers made to rub it into each other's feet to stimulate circulation, while the grease would hopefully prevent feet becoming waterlogged. The Germans were generally dug in on higher ground and so had less acute drainage problems, and from early on their trenches were considered as more permanent features than those of the Allies, whose main objective was to attack and drive the Germans back. However, the BEF soon resorted to supplying gum boots or waders to the worst areas, and it became commonplace to install duckboards raised up on inverted A-frames in trenches, and to pump out excessive water. The orders for the 7th Bedfordshire Regiment to relieve another battalion in the line on 14 January 1917 included the following:

9. GUM BOOTS The two Companies holding the front line (A & D) will draw a pair of Gum Boots per NCO and man at Crucifix Corner, any Gum Boots remaining after A & D have been supplied will be drawn by 'B' and 'C' Companies. These boots will be carried over the shoulder into the trenches.

10. FEET CARE OF OC Companies will ensure that every man changes his socks once every 24 hours and that feet are to be well rubbed with whale oil at least once a day.

All these efforts saw a steady decline in the incidence of trench foot. The total recorded cases among British troops in the war was about 74,000, although it is likely that many cases were unrecorded – it was a chargeable offence to neglect the feet.

Trench fever

Body lice (as distinct from head lice or nits) caused this sickness, which became a universal plague for troops in the front line as it was impossible to eradicate the lice completely from the folds and seams of clothes without recourse to heat sterilization of clothing, fumigation, hot baths and frequent changes of uniform – facilities established only in rear areas. The fever was transmitted by the soldier scratching his itching skin and forcing infected faeces from the louse into the lesion caused by the bite; the louse, utterly dependent on human blood for sustenance, caught the fever by biting an infected soldier and moving on. After infection there was a latent period of between eight and thirty days. The fever struck with high temperature, severe headaches, uncontrollable giddiness and pains in the leg muscles and particularly the shins. Shivering attacks were common and sometimes a pink rash appeared for a few hours. The fever lasted around five days (it was sometimes called 'five-day fever') but then invariably recurred after another five or six days. These recurrences could be repeated up to twelve times.

Treatment was only symptomatic and little could be done apart from rest and nursing care in hospital. There were virtually no deaths from the fever, but it took the majority of sufferers away from duty for up to three months – something that made it considered well worth the suffering by many soldiers, as it was almost as good as a Blighty wound.

Some 800,000 cases of trench fever were reported during the war in the British Army, with comparable numbers in other armies.

Trench mouth

The medical term for this complaint was acute necrotizing ulcerative gingivitis – the eroding of the gums, bleeding and ulceration, along with the sloughing off of gum membrane with accompanying foul breath. The resultant pain made biting, swallowing and even talking difficult. In severe cases the glands in the throat and neck would swell. The cause was a combination of very poor oral hygiene, heavy smoking, poor diet and stress. The treatment consisted of rest, good mouth hygiene and a balanced diet, together with a reduction in smoking. It is said trench mouth was the cause of so many toothless former soldiers in the decade after the war.

Venereal diseases (VD)

A revealing statistic taken from the *British Official History: Medical Services* states that on 31 December 1914 of the 13,731 sick and wounded in medical charge of the BEF in France, 1,230 were cases of VD. This equates to 9 per cent and is a startling indication of the seriousness of the problem from the start of the war. Venereal diseases proved to be a constant drain on all forces on the Western Front to the extent that eventually special VD hospitals had to be opened at several bases (Le Havre, Étaples, Rouen, Calais, St-Omer and Boulogne), which had to be expanded to accommodate the large number of cases that accumulated in France – these men were not evacuated to England. When the Portuguese contingent disembarked in 1917 numerous cases already existed among them, necessitating sending the officers to the hospital at Le Havre and the other ranks to Étaples. Similarly, the 9th Battalion of the British West India Regiment, which was mainly recruited from Jamaica, had signed up men who already had the disease.

In the latter part of the war fifty men were required as stretcher-bearers at casualty clearing stations for the arduous work of loading and unloading wounded into motor ambulance cars and ambulance trains. In 1917 these men were replaced with convalescent VD cases and a small camp was pitched for them at each station.

The French Army did not have the problem, as in France they accepted *maisons tolérées* (houses of tolerance) which were regularly inspected by medical officers and entrance to which was controlled by military police. The British military authorities tended to view VD as a self-inflicted disability and a General Order stated that NCOs infected could be punished by reduction in rank and officers forced to resign their commissions (which would mean serving on as a private). However, although a number of officers contracted VD, the present author was not able to find any statistics. Overall, just over 153,500 British cases were treated on the Western Front – a substantial number of 'casualties'.

The Royal Army Medical Corps

The RAMC was formed in June 1898 and after mobilization it had an effective strength of some 18,700 all ranks, but no dental surgeons. The number increased steadily throughout the war, reaching a peak in April 1918 with 145,401 (12,432 officers and 132,969 other ranks), of which 769 were dental surgeons.

The few dentists available from the end of 1914 were quickly overloaded, as neglect of teeth and gums was commonplace in the trenches, along with wounds to the jaw. While the Australians had one dentist for every 1,000 men, the British had one for every 10,000 and they were deployed back at base hospitals. One claimed to have an average of forty patients every morning, but could do little except extractions. Things slowly improved over the coming years as the number of dentists and dental technicians increased, so that over a six-month period in 1918 they filled over 40,000 teeth, extracted nearly 80,000 and made or repaired 25,000 sets of dentures in the BEF.

Shortage of Medical Officers

The rapidly expanding army of 1915 and 1916 experienced an acute shortage of medical officers. There were several problems in getting civilian doctors to join up. First was the maximum age limit of thirty-five, then the difficulty experienced by many general practitioners in finding a suitable locum to take their place, and those who did enlisted on contracts of one year or the duration of the war, whichever was the sooner. A number of doctors whose contracts ran out in August 1915, for example, returned home. There was also considerable discrepancy with pay. A special reserve RAMC lieutenant was paid 14 shillings a day while a civilian volunteer received 24 shillings, though many of the latter were recently qualified and lacked experience.

For medical officers working under intense pressure in a CCS during a major battle, lack of relief could seriously compromise their ability. A report on the matter to Kitchener in late 1915 stated:

apart from the fact that cases coming to the Clearing Hospitals have to wait unnecessarily long before their wounds are dressed, I have frequently seen Medical Officers who have been working for such prolonged periods, without sleep or proper food, that they are not in a fit condition to attend serious cases.

The age limit was extended, with doctors aged between forty and forty-five serving at home to release the younger ones for overseas service, but problems persisted. During the Somme offensive around 400 medical officers became casualties, while no fewer than 142 refused to renew their yearly contracts; it was not until late 1917 that this rule changed so that when a yearly contract expired the doctor was automatically called up for the duration of the war. However, an appeal to the USA for volunteer doctors resulted in a heartening response – an immediate offer of 1,000 doctors and 500 nurses. By 1918 several units had American medical officers, some of whom received the Military Cross for gallantry.

By the end of hostilities the RAMC had lost 470 officers and 3,669 other ranks killed in action or died of wounds. It has been estimated that the British medical services, in all theatres, were responsible for some 1.6 million wounded returning to duty. According to the *British Official History: Medical Services*, 64 per cent of all wounded in all theatres returned to full duties, 18 per cent returned to line of communication or sedentary work, 8 per cent were discharged as invalids and 7 per cent died of their wounds. These remarkable figures were achieved through RAMC personnel of all ranks working alongside military nursing services, various civil nursing services and volunteers (see pages 373–5), along with drivers from the ASC and tradesmen from the RE. RAMC personnel were non-combatants and were not issued arms – today when on parade they do not fix bayonets and officers never draw their swords. The corps has no colours or battle honours, although personnel were present on every battlefield of the war, not just the Western Front. On the Western Front RAMC personnel won seven Victoria Crosses for exceptional gallantry when attending wounded under fire. Captain Noel Chavasse won a bar to his VC (see box opposite) and Captain Arthur Martin-Leake a bar to his first, awarded for gallantry in the Second Boer War.

The size and complexity of the medical facilities on the Western Front are shown in the table on the right. Not all these units

were present at the same time; there was a steady build-up to cater for the rapid growth in the size of the armies and the flood of casualties resulting from every major offensive – including large numbers of gas and shell-shock casualties that had not been anticipated. Similarly, a few units were withdrawn for service in other theatres – the Indian medical units departed when their divisions were sent to Palestine, and several British units went to Italy later in the war. Nevertheless, the overwhelming majority of medical units sent to the

Western Front remained there, and all the units listed spent many months or years there. Details of most of these units' functions are explained under 'Casualty Evacuation', see page 362.

Not all these units were provided by the RAMC. Voluntary organizations contributed substantially, with the British Red Cross Society (BRCS) providing thirteen of the voluntary hospitals and the St John Ambulance and Australian Voluntary Aid one each. The Maharaja of Gwalior donated a motor ambulance; an ambulance train was the gift of Lord and Lady Michelham; two more were given by the UK Flour Millers' Association and another by the Princess Christian's Fund; a mobile X-ray unit was presented by Cheltenham College; and when the Americans arrived in late 1917 they took over the running and staffing of eight general hospitals.

As with all other branches of the BEF, the medical service that went to France in 1914 was totally inadequate for the years of static trench warfare that quickly followed. By 1916 the system of command, control and administration of the BEF's medical services was as shown in the diagram on pages 362–3. At GHQ were the director general of medical services, his deputy and subordinate staff responsible for medical arrangements and units serving the forward area. All headquarters at army, corps and divisional level had the appropriate grade of medical staff and administrative personnel. At the headquarters of the line of communication was a director of medical services with a deputy and staff responsible for medical arrangements and RAMC units serving the lines of communication and base areas.

Medical Facilities on the Western Front

Unit	British	Australian	Canadian	N. Zealand	S. African	Indian	Total
Field ambulances	54	15	14	4	1	17	105
Casualty clearing stations (CCS)	57	4	4			3	68
Sanitary sections	70	5	5	1		4	85
Motor ambulance convoys (MAC)	31						31
Ambulance trains	45						45
Ambulance flotillas	5						5
Stationary hospitals	28		10	1		2	41
General hospitals	39	3	6		1	6	55
Voluntary hospitals	14	1					15
Convalescent depots	16					2	18
Advanced depot medical stores	17		1				18
Base depot medical stores	5						5
Mobile laboratories	26						26
Mobile X-ray laboratories	5						5
Mobile dental units	5						5
Totals	**417**	**28**	**40**	**6**	**2**	**34**	**527**

Captain N. G. Chavasse, VC and Bar, MC, RAMC

Captain Noel Chavasse was the medical officer of the 10th (Liverpool Scottish) Battalion, the King's (Liverpool) Regiment during the first three years of the war. He was the only man to win the Victoria Cross twice during World War I. Only two other men have achieved this incredible distinction: Captain Arthur Martin-Leake, RAMC, was awarded his first VC during the Second Boer War and his second in Belgium in November 1915; the third was Second Lieutenant Charles Upham, 20th Battalion, 2nd NZEF (Canterbury Regiment), who won his first in Crete in 1941 and second in North Africa in 1942.

Captain Chavasse gained an MC for gallantry during the fighting around Hooge in June 1915, although he did not receive it until almost a year later. On 8 August 1916, at Guillemot, France, Captain Chavasse attended the injured under heavy fire, frequently in view of the enemy, and during the night searched for wounded, at times within 25 yards of enemy lines. The next day he took a stretcher-bearer and under heavy shellfire carried a badly wounded man 500 yards to safety, being wounded in the back by two shell splinters on his return journey. That night, with twenty volunteers, he rescued three more wounded from a shell-hole, buried the bodies of two officers and collected many identity discs. During this period he saved the lives of at least twenty men. This incredible bravery gained him his first VC.

A year later, between 31 July and 2 August 1917 in the Wieltje sector of the Ypres salient, Captain Chavasse earned his second VC. Although severely wounded early in the action while carrying a wounded officer to the dressing station, he refused to leave his post. He continued his duties and repeatedly went out under heavy fire to search for and attend the wounded. During this time, although exhausted and faint

from his wound, he also helped carry in badly wounded men. At about 3:00 a.m. on 2 August a shell hit the aid post, killing or seriously wounding everyone inside. Chavasse received several more wounds, including a gaping one in his stomach, which bled profusely. Nevertheless, he managed to crawl up the steps out of the dugout and along a muddy track to another dugout. He was sent to No. 32 CCS at Brandhoek where he was operated on. He regained consciousness and spoke to a Colonel Davidson, who stated, 'He seems very weak but spoke cheerfully.' Regrettably, Captain Chavasse died on 4 August, never knowing he was to be awarded a second VC, and was buried at the Brandhoek Military Cemetery the following day. The entire Liverpool Scottish Battalion and all the medical officers at the hospital attended the funeral. Even today the base of his remarkably moving headstone, with its two carved images of the VC and inscription 'Greater love hath no man than this', is always covered by small wooden remembrance crosses and poppies (left).

In 2007 the present writer visited the grave in the company of two of Captain Canvasses' nephews, Christopher and Patrick Chavasse. On 17 August 2008 a bronze memorial to Captain Chavasse was unveiled in the grounds of Liverpool University, in Abercromby Square, opposite the house where he lived from the age of fifteen. It depicts Captain Chavasse, together with a stretcher-bearer, helping to carry a wounded man from the battlefield. The names of fifteen other VC holders with strong Liverpool connections are engraved on the base. The drumhead service was attended by over 1,000 people, including fifty members of the Chavasse family, along with the Lord Mayor of Liverpool, dignitaries, and the bandsmen and pipes and drums of the Liverpool Scottish.

Shell Shock

In 1917 a Captain Charles Myers, RAMC, was the first to use the expression 'shell shock' to describe psychiatric casualties who would today be termed post-traumatic stress disorder cases. The armies of World War I went to war in ignorance of the fact that the prolonged stresses or a sudden horrific event in battle could cause mental illness every bit as debilitating as physical injury, although it might not manifest itself for months or even years afterwards. It was initially thought that close proximity to shell explosions might, sometimes in the absence of physical wounds, be the cause of 'nerves', as some called it. At first it was believed that the man's nerves had been damaged by exposure to heavy bombardment. Victims were often hysterical and could neither eat nor sleep. Symptoms included extreme anxiety, paralysis, dizziness, nightmares, limping and muscle contractions, heart palpitations, loss of speech and even blindness or deafness – all of which rendered the soldier unfit for duty.

This battle fatigue – the constant exposure to fear, stress and witnessing horrific deaths and wounds – soon became a serious cause of casualties, with four out of five victims never returning to front-line duty. During the war the British Army dealt with some 80,000 so-called shell-shock cases (including the poets Wilfred Owen and Siegfried Sassoon), with around 20,000 men discharged in 1918 still suffering from it. One soldier, Private Arthur Hubbard, who was evacuated to England, is an example of how witnessing a 'terrible sight' could trigger lasting psychological trauma. When in hospital he wrote to his mother (punctuation and grammar amended slightly) of his experience on 7 July during the Somme battle:

We had strict orders not to take prisoners, no matter if wounded. My first job, when I had finished cutting some of their wire away, was to empty my magazine on three Germans that came out of one of their deep dugouts, bleeding badly, [in order] to put them out of their misery. They cried for mercy, but I had my orders, they had no feeling whatever for us poor chaps . . . it makes my head jump to think about it.

Hubbard had reached the fourth line of German trenches but was forced to retreat under shellfire (which at one stage buried him) and under heavy machine-gun fire – it all proved too much for him and he collapsed.

There was not much sympathy for shell-shocked soldiers among medical staff or commanders, many of whom considered these men to be showing signs of emotional weakness or cowardice. Some were charged with offences such as desertion, cowardice or insubordination, while treatment was often harsh and included solitary confinement, disciplinary punishments and electric shocks. Although mild cases recovered quite quickly with suitable rest and good food away from the battle area, most serious cases ended up in hospitals in England. There was also controversy over whether shell-shock cases should be regarded as 'sick' or 'wounded' – if the latter, the man would qualify for a wound stripe on his uniform. In 1916 GHQ instructed that all cases be first sent to special centres in each army area for careful diagnosis. A report would then be sent to the man's commanding officer, who would report back to the centre on whether he had been subjected to exceptional stress. Only then would the man be classified as sick or wounded.

General Plan for Medical Administration of BEF after Formation of Four Armies, 1916

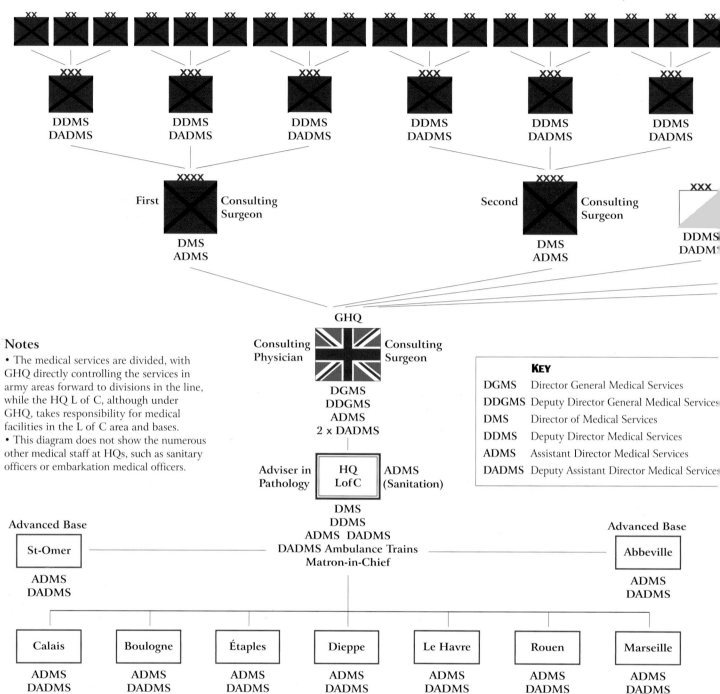

Notes
• The medical services are divided, with GHQ directly controlling the services in army areas forward to divisions in the line, while the HQ L of C, although under GHQ, takes responsibility for medical facilities in the L of C area and bases.
• This diagram does not show the numerous other medical staff at HQs, such as sanitary officers or embarkation medical officers.

KEY

DGMS	Director General Medical Services
DDGMS	Deputy Director General Medical Services
DMS	Director of Medical Services
DDMS	Deputy Director Medical Services
ADMS	Assistant Director Medical Services
DADMS	Deputy Assistant Director Medical Services

Casualty Evacuation

A wounded man's chances of survival depended on the speed with which his wound was assessed and treated. Modern warfare produces vast numbers of casualties requiring professional treatment at the same time, something impossible in the front line under fire. The only way to achieve a satisfactory measure of success was to have an efficient chain of evacuation where wounded were graded according to seriousness (triage), given appropriate treatment and moved quickly back, but no further than necessary, to where surgeons could operate and where they could rest and convalesce. This process divided the wounded into three categories: those with relatively minor injuries who could afford to wait for further treatment; those with serious but potentially treatable wounds who required rapid attention to optimize their chances of recovery; and those whose injuries were untreatable or with a poor chance of useful recovery who were simply kept as comfortable as possible until they died.

For the seriously wounded this system would often mean a casualty ultimately being sent by hospital ship to a UK hospital for long-term treatment, followed by either full recovery and return to front-line duty; being medically downgraded for limited duties; or being discharged. The primary task of the medical services was to get as many men as possible fit for duty as quickly as possible. Virtually the same systems applied to the sick, although they tended to be separated from the wounded and invariably recovered in theatre.

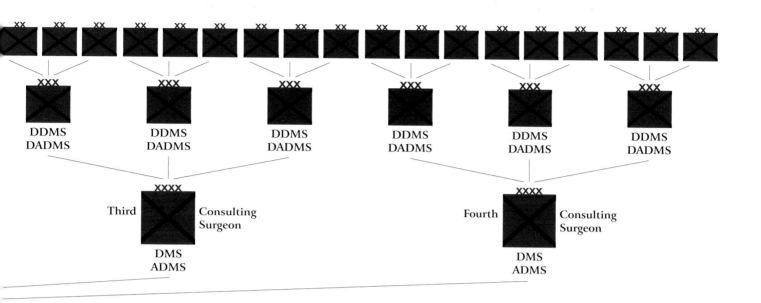

DDMS DADMS — DDMS DADMS — DDMS DADMS — DDMS DADMS — DDMS DADMS — DDMS DADMS

Third — Consulting Surgeon — DMS ADMS — Fourth — Consulting Surgeon — DMS ADMS

Field Ambulance Personnel Tasks

On 12 January 1916 the war diary of No. 56 Field Ambulance records the duty roster for the day. Out of the 155 men (excluding officers) assigned duties, only 32 were employed on the eight wards: a sergeant wardmaster and corporal assistant wardmaster for each of the two blocks in a ward. The others were on the fatigues and duties as follows:

5 on pack-store duties	1 in ablution room
6 on rifle and kit cleaning	1 fumigator
3 on hospital fatigues	1 in cleaning yard
3 on bath-house duty	2 bootmakers
6 at RAMC cookhouse	1 horsed-ambulance driver
3 on men's dining hall	1 tailor
5 on patients' cookhouse	1 barber
4 on canteen	2 at ASC refilling point
3 on patients' dining hall	3 water-cart orderlies
3 billet cleaning	5 loaders
4 in dispensary	1 sick-officer's cook
6 in wash-house	1 sick-officer's orderly
7 on sanitary squad	5 in permanent police squad
4 at bathing establishment	2 in sergeant's mess
9 in drying room	8 in officers' mess
4 in quartermaster's stores	11 not detailed
2 whitewashers	

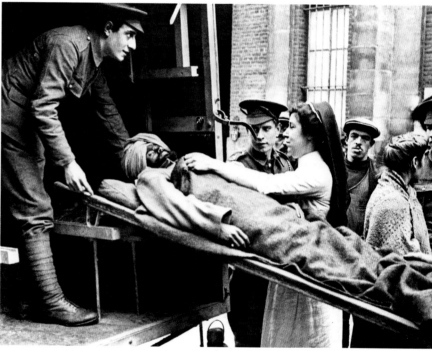

A wounded Indian soldier is lifted aboard a motor ambulance on the Western Front, October 1914.

Within a British infantry or cavalry division there were three RAMC field ambulances (FA; medical units, not vehicles); in normal circumstances each was responsible for the casualties of one brigade. Its theoretical capacity was 150, but in a major battle it was invariably overwhelmed and had to be reinforced. The field ambulance unit had a heavy responsibility and could be required to open and operate a number of posts on the evacuation chain. These could be some or all of the following, which are listed in probable order from the front to the rear, although some could be co-located:

- bearer relay posts up to 600 yards behind the regimental aid posts (RAP)
- divisional collecting posts
- advanced reserve bearer posts
- advanced dressing stations (ADS)
- rear reserve bearer posts
- walking-wounded collecting stations (WWCS)
- sick-collecting posts (SCP)
- main dressing station (MDS)
- local sick rooms and rest stations in back areas (separate ones for officers)

However, the critical function of the field ambulances was normally to establish one ADS per brigade and one MDS per division. The diagram on page 364 shows the basic establishment of a field ambulance at the end of 1914 after the addition of seven motor ambulances (later increased to ten). From early 1915 a workshop to service these vehicles was added to each division, along with a sanitary section consisting of a subaltern, two sergeants, two corporals and twenty-one privates. This RAMC section was responsible for maintaining water supplies, cooking facilities and living and sleeping accommodation in a reasonably hygienic condition – something of an uphill task in front-line trenches. These sections were placed under corps or army control from April 1917. In addition, each infantry battalion, artillery brigade or cavalry regiment had its own sanitary squad of an NCO and eight privates.

Although there was considerable flexibility in how the bearer and tent divisions were used for reinforcing other field ambulances, it was normal practice in battle for the tent division (all three subdivisions) to form an MDS and to employ the stretcher-bearers of the bearer division (all three bearer subdivisions) in bringing the wounded to it from the RAPs through

an ADS established at a point to which the ambulance transport could come up.

The three field ambulances in a division were divisional troops and did not belong to brigades – they were controlled by the assistant director of medical services (ADMS) at divisional headquarters. Medical arrangements for the three field ambulances of the 3rd Division for the first Battle of the Scarpe on 9 April 1917 illustrate this, and show the kind of pre-planning and flexibility needed when an advance was expected in order to keep the evacuation chain functioning. In this case all the bearers of one field ambulance were sent to reinforce the RAPs, while

the tent division formed an ADS in the conveniently located Cave Girls' School. The second ambulance was packed ready to advance, with all necessary equipment broken down into sandbags for hand carriage. The third was held further back, packed with its wagons ready to advance.

The various stages and posts through which a casualty might expect to be evacuated are explained below. The diagram on the facing page shows the basic chain of evacuation within a division, along with the type of transportation that, in ideal circumstances, moved the wounded man from being hit to removal to the UK on a hospital

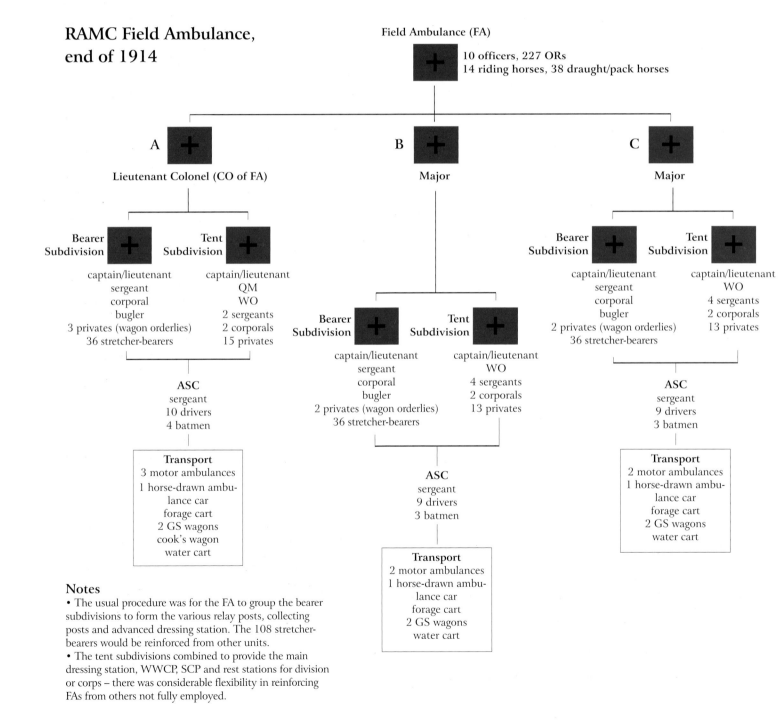

RAMC Field Ambulance, end of 1914

Field Ambulance (FA)

10 officers, 227 ORs
14 riding horses, 38 draught/pack horses

A — Lieutenant Colonel (CO of FA)

Bearer Subdivision
captain/lieutenant
sergeant
corporal
bugler
3 privates (wagon orderlies)
36 stretcher-bearers

Tent Subdivision
captain/lieutenant
QM
WO
2 sergeants
2 corporals
15 privates

ASC
sergeant
10 drivers
4 batmen

Transport
3 motor ambulances
1 horse-drawn ambulance car
forage cart
2 GS wagons
cook's wagon
water cart

B — Major

Bearer Subdivision
captain/lieutenant
sergeant
corporal
bugler
2 privates (wagon orderlies)
36 stretcher-bearers

Tent Subdivision
captain/lieutenant
WO
4 sergeants
2 corporals
13 privates

ASC
sergeant
9 drivers
3 batmen

Transport
2 motor ambulances
1 horse-drawn ambulance car
forage cart
2 GS wagons
water cart

C — Major

Bearer Subdivision
captain/lieutenant
sergeant
corporal
bugler
2 privates (wagon orderlies)
36 stretcher-bearers

Tent Subdivision
captain/lieutenant
WO
4 sergeants
2 corporals
13 privates

ASC
sergeant
9 drivers
3 batmen

Transport
2 motor ambulances
1 horse-drawn ambulance car
forage cart
2 GS wagons
water cart

Notes
• The usual procedure was for the FA to group the bearer subdivisions to form the various relay posts, collecting posts and advanced dressing station. The 108 stretcher-bearers would be reinforced from other units.
• The tent subdivisions combined to provide the main dressing station, WWCP, SCP and rest stations for division or corps – there was considerable flexibility in reinforcing FAs from others not fully employed.

Chain of Evacuation for a Corps of Three Divisions from Front Line to Main Base

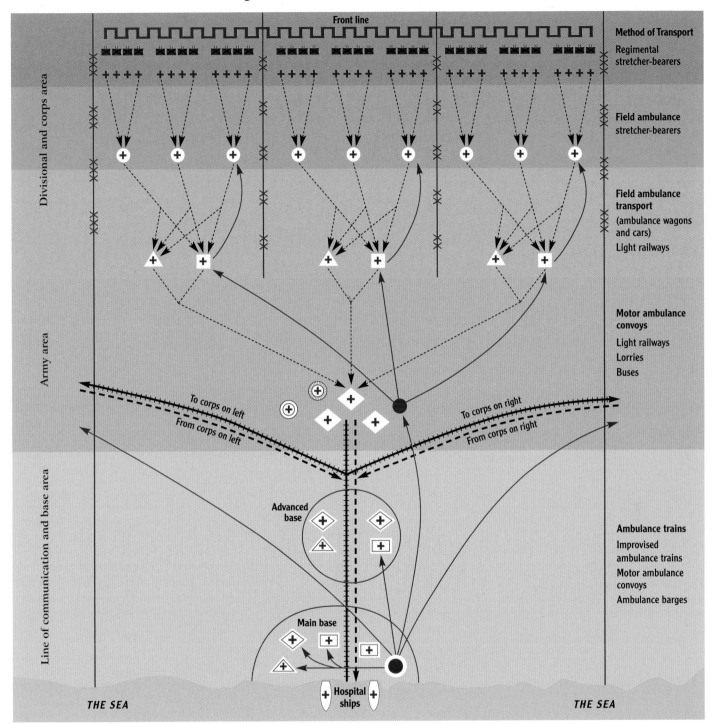

Notes
• This diagram does not attempt to show every post that was at times necessary for the effective evacuation and treatment of casualties – for example, the separate facilities made for the sick, or all the bearer posts often needed in getting wounded to the CCS. Similarly, divisional collecting posts are not shown.
• It does, however, show the basic evacuation chain for a corps and the likely transport used for the evacuation. Note that regimental and field ambulance stretcher-bearers took wounded from the battlefield back to the CCS. On some occasions it was possible to get transport to an RAP.
• Although not to scale, it does indicate the likelihood of congestion during a major offensive of both casualties and transport.
• For large-scale operations, the number of field ambulances serving attacking formations would be reinforced by formations not involved.

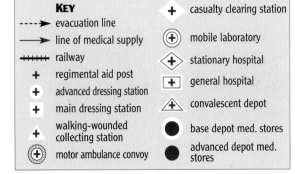

KEY
- - - → evacuation line
——→ line of medical supply
++++++ railway
+ regimental aid post
+ advanced dressing station
+ main dressing station
+ walking-wounded collecting station
⊕ motor ambulance convoy

✚ casualty clearing station
⊕ mobile laboratory
◆ stationary hospital
⊞ general hospital
△ convalescent depot
● base depot med. stores
● advanced depot med. stores

A Stretcher-bearer at Loos

Patrick Macgill was a stretcher-bearer in the London Irish Rifles at Loos in 1915. He later described two incidents not untypical of his duties.

Up near the German wire I found the company postman sitting in a shell-hole, a bullet in his leg below the knee and an unlighted cigarette in his mouth. 'You're the man I want!' he shouted on seeing me. And I fumbled in my haversack for bandages.

'No dressings for me yet,' he said with a smile. 'There are others needing help more than I. What I want is a match.' As I handed him my match-box a big, high-explosive shell flew over our heads and dropped fifty yards away in a little hollow where seven or eight figures lay prostrate, faces to the ground. The shell burst and the wounded and the dead rose slowly into the air to a height of six or seven yards and dropped slowly again, looking for all the world like puppets worked by wires.

Macgill went on to describe coming across a dying man:

'Is there any hope for me?' [he asked]. 'Of course there is matey,' I lied. 'You have two of these morphia tablets and lie quiet. We'll take you in after a while, and you'll be back in England in two or three days time.'

I placed the morphia under his tongue and he closed his eyes as if going to sleep. Then, with an effort, he tried to get up and gripped the wire support with such vigour that it came clean out of the ground. His legs shot from under him, and, muttering something about rations being fit for pigs and not men, he fell back and died.

other buildings or cellars were often used, while during a retreat or an advance sunken roads or embankments provided some shelter from enemy fire. Two medical orderlies assisted the MO, with sixteen stretcher-bearers found from within the battalion. This was an exceptionally dangerous, demanding and traumatic job. The poet Robert W. Service (see also page 455) worked as an ambulance driver for the Canadian Red Cross on the Western Front and later wrote 'The Stretcher-Bearer', the first verse of which is:

My stretcher is one scarlet stain,
And as I tries to scrape it clean,
I tell you wot – I'm sick with pain
For all I've 'eard, for all I've seen;
Around me is the 'ellish night,
And as the war's red rim I trace,
I wonder if in 'Eaven's height
Our God don't turn away 'Is Face.

In battle it was the custom to distribute these battalion stretcher-bearers to the companies. However, by July 1916 it became necessary to double the number of bearers as a reserve directly under the MO – bandsmen, pioneers and any such others that were available were used. The duty of these bearers was to bring the wounded to the RAP, which was usually located near battalion headquarters. Here were kept stretchers, blankets, means of heating food and water, splints, shell dressings, field dressings, painkillers (morphine) and various ointments, all in addition to the MO's medical equipment. Before a major battle it was common for field ambulances to provide extra manpower and equipment. Using the Scarpe battle as an example, each RAP within the division received one officer, one NCO and eighteen extra men from field ambulances seventy-two hours before the attack. They also supplied each RAP with fifty tins of water, candles, sixty stretchers, eighty blankets, twenty waterproof sheets, as well as extra dressings, splints and rations.

The MO's primary task was to patch up casualties to make them fit enough for the move back along the first stage of the evacuation chain by hand carriage, wheeled stretchers, trolley lines or, whenever possible (usually only at night), by horsed or motor ambulance wagons. Special communication trenches were used wherever possible for the removal of wounded. The MO gave basic first aid to stop blood flow, splinted broken bones, applied dressings and injected casualties with anti-tetanus serum or morphine. Additionally, the first treatment for shock occurred here in the form of keeping men warm in blankets and giving hot drinks and food, or indeed a swig or two of rum. From the RAP walking wounded were sent back to the ADS either directly or, more usually, via a walking-wounded collecting station, the

remainder being taken directly by bearers (possibly through a bearer relay post) or transport – both methods provided from the field ambulance. If the MO was himself a casualty, then a doctor from the field ambulance replaced him.

Bearer relay posts

The number of bearer relay posts depended on circumstances, but one would always be formed if the expected carry exceeded 1,000 yards. Over difficult and dangerous ground a carry of 500 or 600 yards even with four men per stretcher was often the limit, meaning that relay posts would be set up at 500, 600 or 1,000 yards back from the RAP to a divisional collecting post or the ADS. Normally between sixteen and twenty-four men under a sergeant would be at each post, but when casualties were heavy these men had to be reinforced from field ambulances or units not directly involved in the operation. It was unusual for the number of stretcher cases to exceed 40 per cent of the wounded, but they could either be lying or sitting wounded. The bearers at each post used shell holes, dugouts, trenches or other shelters, with the routes between posts marked by flags and at night by transparency lamps. In a letter home in 1915 Lance Corporal Harold Chapin, RAMC, emphasized the sheer physical effort involved: 'It took six of us to carry one man. You have no idea of the physical fatigue entailed in carrying a twelve stone man a thousand yards across muddy fields'; it sometimes needed eight men.

It was not uncommon for stretcher-bearers to bring in German wounded and they usually received the same treatment at a CCS, or at other rear-area medical facilities, as British wounded. However, human nature being what it is, stretcher-bearers would invariably give priority to their own comrades when it came to carrying wounded back from where they had fallen. Second Lieutenant D. W. J. Cuddeford, 12th Highland Light Infantry, described an incident of this during the battle of Flers-Courcelette in September 1916:

I remember seeing a German officer who with his men had apparently made a good hand-to-hand fight of it against the KOSB [King's Own Scottish Borderers]. At the time I came up it was all over, and there were eight or nine Germans lying in the trench all bayoneted. The officer himself, though badly wounded in more than one place, judging from the mess he was in, was sitting up in the midst of his men and in quite good English was shouting for assistance, at one moment imploring our boys, and at the next offering money to any of our stretcher

ship. Wounded were initially grouped into three categories – lying, sitting and walking cases. The first two required transportation of some sort for their entire journey (sitting took up less room in vehicles and were often moved on wheeled trolleys) and while a man slightly wounded in the arm or shoulder might walk initially, most needed transport at some stage. The object of separating the walking wounded from the rest was to avoid congestion and delays in assessing the seriously wounded.

Regimental aid posts

When a battalion occupied the front line an RAP was established by its medical officer (MO) in a shelter or dugout capable of accommodating twenty to thirty men at a time. In the early stages of the war cottages,

bearers who would take him back to a dressing station. One couldn't help feeling sorry for even a German in his plight, but I'm afraid nobody took the slightest notice of him, except to tell him he could 'bloody well wait' until our own wounded had been attended to.

Divisional collecting posts

These would be required in a major offensive where the distances to some ADSs were excessive and as the advance progressed their number was likely to increase. They were established at points where the wounded could be transferred from hand carriage on stretchers to some form of wheeled transport, such as ambulance wagons, trucks or light railway cars. They were composed of an NCO and twenty-four men, with one or more medical officers from the bearer division of a field ambulance to check the casualties and supervise loading (none shown on the diagram on page 365).

Reserve bearer posts

The number of bearers in a field ambulance was 108, giving a total within a division of 324. With a minimum of four men needed to carry a stretcher any distance, this was sufficient when the number of wounded expected was fairly light, but inadequate for a major battle. In that case the RAMC bearers had to be reinforced by a reserve of men from other units of the division or corps. It was the practice for divisional and corps commanders to place 200 men (in some instances up to 600 were needed), under their own officers, at the disposal of the divisional ADMS. It was found best to send half to form an advanced reserve bearer post near the divisional collecting post and to use them for reinforcing the relay posts further forward – although it was important to have trained RAMC bearers forming the first relay from RAPs.

Advanced dressing stations

This post became probably the most important of the tactical posts formed by a field ambulance. One such post was formed for each division, or one for each brigade in the line, depending on road approaches for ambulance transport and suitable protected sites for personnel. It was often located in large dugouts or in the cellars of buildings and in the vicinity of light railways. Accommodation for 100 casualties was considered the minimum requirement. It was staffed by the tent division of one or more field ambulances and was stocked with reserves of blankets, stretchers, pyjamas and hotwater bottles, oxygen cylinders, splints and oil stoves. In the latter stages of the war blood transfusion equipment was included.

With the large number of wounded on the Western Front it was realized that an ADS could be swamped if all casualties were brought to it. Consequently, walking wounded were directed to walking-wounded collecting stations; however, many walking wounded arrived at the ADS and it was found necessary to divide the dressing station into two sections, one for stretcher cases and the other for walking wounded. This was all the more necessary as the former were carried back in motor ambulance cars and the latter in motor lorries, so two separate posts and road approaches were needed to avoid congestion. The system evolved whereby the transport was parked some distance away and only one or two ambulance cars were sent at a time, an empty one being despatched whenever a loaded car passed the park on its way back.

Walking-wounded collecting stations

The war correspondent Philip Gibbs watched men arriving at a walking-wounded collecting station during the Battle of Arras in April 1917:

I saw these walking wounded coming back; tired brave men, who bore their pain with stoic endurance, so that there was hardly a groan to be heard between them . . . They formed up in a long queue outside the dressing-station, where doctors waited for them, and where there was a hot drink to be had.

The Most Decorated NCO of the War

William Harold Coltman, VC, DCM and Bar, MM and Bar, won all his decorations for gallantry without firing a shot. He served as a regimental stretcher-bearer in 1/6th Battalion, North Staffordshire Regiment. As a lance corporal in October 1918 his actions gained him the coveted Victoria Cross to complete his outstanding array of decorations. His official citation states:

For most conspicuous bravery, initiative and devotion to duty. During the operations at Mannequin Hill, north-east of Sequehart, on the 3rd and 4th Oct. 1918, L.-Corp Coltman, a stretcher bearer, hearing that wounded had been left behind during a retirement, went forward alone in the face of fierce enfilade fire, found the casualties, dressed them and on three successive occasions, carried comrades on his back to safety, thus saving their lives. This very gallant NCO tended the wounded unceasingly for 48 hours.

His first DCM was awarded for actions during a period of several days in July 1917 – his citation reads:

Conspicuous gallantry and devotion to duty, in evacuating wounded from the front line at great personal risk under shell fire. His gallant conduct undoubtedly saved many lives, and he continued throughout the night to search for wounded under shell fire and machine gun fire, and brought several in. His absolute indifference to danger had a most inspiring effect upon the rest of his men.

The citation to his Bar to the DCM states:

On the 28th September, 1918, near the St. Quentin canal, near Bellenglise, he dressed and carried many wounded men under heavy artillery fire. During the following day he still remained at his work without rest or sleep, attending the wounded, taking no heed of either shell or machine gun fire, and never resting until he was positive that our sector was clear of wounded. He set the highest example of fearlessness and devotion to duty to those around him.

Coltman was awarded his first MM for rescuing a wounded officer from no-man's-land in February 1917. His second award was for outstanding conduct behind the lines in June 1917. He was also awarded the *Croix de Guerre* by the French Army and had, previous to any of his later awards, been Mentioned in Despatches for his excellent work.

This exceptional man survived the war and returned to Staffordshire, where he worked as a groundsman in the Parks Department in Burton-on-Trent. During World War II he commanded the Burton-on-Trent Army Cadet Force in the rank of captain. He died in 1974, aged eighty-two, and is buried with his wife in St Mark's Church in Winshill. His medals are on display in the Staffordshire Regimental Museum, Whittington Barracks, Lichfield. There is a memorial to him in the barracks and a road is named after him in Tunstall.

They were covered in mud, and were too weary and spent to talk. That long line of silent wounded men will always remain in my memory.

Outside in the sunlight, waiting their turn to enter the dressing station, some of the men lay down on the bank in queer distorted attitudes very like death, and slept there. Others came hobbling with each arm round the neck of the stretcher bearers, or led forward blind, gropingly. It was the whimper of these blind boys and the agony on their faces which was the most tragic in all this tragedy, those and the men smashed about the face and head so that only their eyes stared through white masks.

It was common practice in major operations with divisions operating on comparatively narrow fronts for walking-wounded collecting stations to be organized at corps level to receive wounded from all divisions, although the diagram on page 365 shows divisional stations for these casualties to clarify the various stages of evacuation. Walking wounded were brought to these stations from advanced dressing stations or divisional collecting posts usually by light railways or motor lorries, but if this was impossible then on foot. A corps WWCS would normally be set up by the bearer division of one of the field ambulances of the reserve division in the corps. It would contain ample accommodation for the reception, a buffet for refreshments (often run by the YMCA) and separate accommodation for those wounded waiting to be sent further back. Here their wounds were checked and dressings adjusted, their particulars recorded and, if not already received, anti-tetanus injections given. Troops were able to rest, get hot meals, drinks and some sleep. Wounded went from these stations either to a CCS or, for the lightly wounded, to a divisional or corps rest station from which they would return to their units when recovered. Evacuation from this station was normally by buses and lorries under corps control, each of which could carry up to twenty-five lightly wounded.

Sick-collecting posts

During a major battle the number of sick was comparatively small. They were usually collected at a reception and evacuation point separate from, but close to, the WWCS and evacuated by the same means. Sick-collecting posts are not shown on the diagram.

Main dressing stations

The establishment of the MDS was the primary function of the tent division of a field ambulance. If only one was formed for a corps, then four or more tent subdivisions from elsewhere reinforced it. It was formed to deal with the reception of stretcher cases brought from the ADS by motor ambulance cars – horse-drawn ambulance cars were still used if journeys off roads or tracks were essential – and so required more facilities than for walking wounded. Emergency operations were performed and wounded suffering from severe shock or gas poisoning had to be treated and retained until able to be evacuated further. Up to 100 seriously wounded and thirty gassed would be accommodated in buildings, huts or marquees prepared as wards. In addition, reception, evacuation and dressing rooms were needed, along with an operating room, mortuary, cemetery and reserve stocks of stretchers, blankets, hotwater bottles and splints.

Local sick and rest rooms

These were set up in the rear areas of divisions and corps and were of great value in expediting the return to duty of sick and slightly wounded personnel. The urgent need for them was evident after the Battle of Neuve Chapelle in 1915 when large numbers of trivial cases had been evacuated unnecessarily to base hospitals and to England. It became the practice to form large convalescent depots on the lines of communication able to accommodate up to 1,000 cases and providing dining, recreational and ablution facilities.

Motor ambulance convoys

The formation of these convoys took place after the Battle of the Aisne in September 1914 to replace the empty supply lorries that up to that time were the only means of taking wounded from the MDS to a CCS or railhead. In the later stages of the war one motor ambulance convoy was allocated to each corps in an army and one as army reserve. Further reserve convoys were held at GHQ and at the advanced base – for the Somme offensive there was a reserve convoy at Abbeville, the advanced base, as well as at GHQ. An MAC consisted of three sections: 'A' (headquarters section) with twenty ambulance cars and 'B' and 'C' each with fifteen cars and a workshop unit. Each section could be split into smaller groups of five if necessary. The number of these ambulance convoys grew from fourteen in 1915 to thirty-one by 1918, twenty-five of which were employed at the front.

Casualty clearing stations

The CCS was the first large, well-equipped medical facility that a wounded soldier would visit. Its three functions were:

1. To receive and treat until fit for further evacuation all seriously wounded and sick.
2. To expedite the immediate evacuation to base hospitals of those fit to travel.
3. To retain for early return to duty wounded or sick likely to recover in a few days.

It was usually in a tented camp, although in static trench warfare it might be in huts. They were often grouped in clusters of two or three in a small area, close to a rail link and several miles behind the front. A typical CCS could hold from 500 to 1,000 casualties, with the operating marquee usually containing six operating tables. The quantity of stores and equipment held was correspondingly large, which had a limiting effect on the mobility of the unit – it needed between 100 and 200 lorries to move location. At the end of September 1916 a CCS had to be so organized that each prepared a schedule of equipment enabling a light section to advance or retire with sufficient equipment and tentage, using a maximum of nine 3-ton lorries, to ensure it could treat up to 200 wounded without delay in a new position.

Essex Farm Advanced Dressing Station today.

A wounded German prisoner is assisted and given a drink by his British captors at the Battle of the Somme, 1916.

Serious operations, such as amputations, were carried out at the CCS and it had an establishment that included eight officers (one of them a quartermaster), three chaplains and seven nursing sisters. When preparing for a major offensive a CCS was reinforced with surgical teams from units not actively engaged, so that the CCS had at least two surgical teams. In 1917 as many as six such teams would be available, two formed by the CCS itself, the others brought in from other units. When Lance Corporal Harold Chapin first worked in a CCS the experience was almost too much for him:

> I had a nasty spell last Monday, stood by at a long (hour and a half) operation on the skull and brain trephining [sic] it is called. I nearly fainted twice but pulled myself together and went back as soon as I had got a breath of fresh air and a drink of water outside the room. The blood did not affect me at all. The infernal snoring and groaning of the poor devil under the anaesthetic seemed to hypnotise me. Moreover the room was very hot and I was holding a bowl of Methylated spirit – the smell from which is no help to a faint-feeling man. It was touch and go with the man. A piece of shell and some fragments had penetrated the skull. After the operation hope was expressed that he would only be paralysed. The next morning he was reading 'Punch'! I felt better than I've felt for years when I saw him holding the paper in both hands.

Regrettably, Chapin was shot through the head and killed while going to attend wounded at the Battle of Loos.

A Captain John A. Hayward, RAMC, a newly arrived assistant surgeon, graphically recorded his early experience in a CCS on the Western Front:

> It was extraordinary that in this charnel house of pain and misery there was silence, and no outward expression of moans or groans or complaints . . .
>
> Even the badly wounded asked for a smoke. Here were lying uncomplaining men with shattered heads or ghastly disfigurement of their faces, others with shell and bullet wounds of the chest, spitting blood and gasping for breath; and worst of all, those quiet, afraid-to-be-touched cases, with the innocent tiny little mark where the bullet had entered the abdomen, but already with the thready [sic] pulse, drawn corners of the mouth, anxious look, and rigid muscles that betoken hopeless disaster within . . .
>
> 'Resuss' was a dreadful place. Here were sent the shocked and collapsed and dying cases, not able to stand as yet an operation, but which might be possible under the warming-up under candles in heated beds or transfusion of blood. I have seen men already like corpses, blanched and collapsed, pulseless and with just perceptible breathing, within two hours of transfusion sitting up in bed smoking, and exchanging jokes before they went to the operating table.

An example of what could be achieved in just one day under pressure occurred on 11 April 1917 when Captain Donaldson, RAMC, of No. 19 CCS, successfully performed seventeen operations, all gunshot wounds – fifteen leg, one shoulder and one buttock injury.

The number of CCSs on the Western Front corresponded to the number of divisions, but the actual number allotted to an army at any one time was not necessarily the same as the number of its divisions. For example, at Loos the First Army had eighteen divisions but only twelve CCSs; at Vimy in 1917 the First Army had eleven divisions but fourteen CCSs. Experience showed that ten CCSs with the capacity to hold 1,000 were sufficient to cope with the bigger battles. By the end of the Somme offensive in November 1916 over 295,000 wounded had been evacuated to CCSs. By the end of the war sixty-five casualty clearing stations had served most of their time on the Western Front.

The diagram on page 370, taken from the *British Official History of the War: Medical Services*, shows the layout of a tented CCS with 500 beds in 1918.

Ambulance trains

Initially ambulance trains were mobilized in the proportion of one for each division in the field, but as with everything else this was found woefully insufficient. In February 1915 a demand was made on the War Office for twenty-four trains, followed in September with a request for another twelve. By 1 July 1916 there were thirty trains in France and by the end of the war forty-one had been sent to the Western Front, although a number spent some time operating in Italy. They were used to transport lying and sitting wounded from CCSs to the advanced base hospitals and to the main base hospitals at or near the ports; ambulance trains also ran in England from the ports to military hospitals. The capacity of the trains varied, with some carrying more lying than sitting wounded and others the reverse. For example, No. 1 Ambulance Train had a capacity for 308 lying but only 17 sitting cases, whereas No. 24 was equipped for 162 and 320 respectively. The carrying capacity was insufficient to relieve CCSs during a major offensive. Consequently, use was made of empty supply trains to take sick or wounded able to sit up.

A typical ambulance train would have fifteen carriages, composed of a brake and boiler at each end; six with bedded wards in bunks; one for sitting cases (the proportion of these last would vary); one operating theatre, pharmacy and store; one fitted as combined cookhouse and dining room; and two as accommodation for medical staff. Doctors, nurses from Queen Alexandra's Imperial Military Nursing Service (QAIMNS) and RAMC orderlies staffed them. Emergency operations were performed on many of these trains, despite the cramped conditions, movement of the train and poor lighting.

Ambulance flotillas

The use of barges for conveying sick and wounded was initiated by a Mr Douglas Hall, who organized a British water ambulance fund for equipping barges on the Seine early in the war. He formed a flotilla of six barges at Rouen, one for personnel, one for stores and four with thirty beds for hospital use. After Neuve Chapelle in March 1915 GHQ ordered the construction, or rather the conversion, of barges for ambulance use on canals. By the Armistice five flotillas were operational on the Western Front. Each barge was fitted with thirty beds and had a dispensary, kitchen and toilets. The staff consisted of one medical officer, two QAIMNS nurses and nine RAMC orderlies, with three REs from the Inland Water Transport for navigation; a sergeant was the sailing skipper. These barges, towed by tugs, were intended to carry the more seriously wounded who could not stand the jolting of a train journey – these included head, abdominal and chest injuries. They were taken on the northern canal system to hospitals at St-Omer or Calais, and on the Somme to Amiens or Abbeville.

The conversion of these mostly coal or cargo barges involved cutting access hatches through the roof and constructing hand-operated lifts to enable stretcher cases to be lowered into the hold. Electric lights (turned off at night) were installed, along with stoves for heating in winter and fans for the summer. All barges were painted white inside and grey on the outside, with large red crosses on each side, and normally they avoided moving at night due to the difficulty in passing under very low bridges.

Medical-store depots

Base depots for medical stores were formed at Boulogne, Rouen, Étaples, Abbeville and Le Havre; this last moved to Calais in late 1915. These depots received their stocks from the UK or by local purchase and supplied medical and surgical stores, dentistry and special equipment and vaccines to hospitals at the base and on the lines of communication. They also supplied advanced depots of medical stores in army areas. There were normally three advanced depots for each army, usually located in convenient buildings from which they supplied the CCS and field ambulances. Until July 1916 a medical officer commanded each depot, but thereafter command was given to a medical quartermaster.

Mobile laboratories

There were four types:

• **Hygiene and bacteriology** None existed on mobilization of the BEF, but both types were being constructed and during 1915 they were deployed on the basis of one hygiene and two bacteriology for each army.

• **X-ray** These were mounted on a lorry chassis and allocated one to each army, with the intention of deploying to a CCS as required. However, in practice this meant the laboratory remaining with the first CCS and eventually an X-ray outfit was sent to each.

• **Dental** Initially the only dentists with the army were those with the CCSs and all men needing artificial teeth or mechanical work connected to dentistry had to be evacuated to a base hospital. In May 1916 a motor dental laboratory was offered to the BEF through the British Red Cross Society (BRCS) by the Civil Service Motor Ambulance Fund and was sent to the Third Army. Its success prompted donations of further laboratories for each of the five armies in France. Dentistry for dominion and American troops was always on a more advanced scale than for the British. The Canadians had a dental surgeon with each field ambulance, infantry and artillery brigade and divisional headquarters. The Americans deployed a dentist and dental equipment with every infantry battalion.

Sanitary sections

Initially sanitary sections were deployed only at bases and no provision was made for sanitary work with the field army. This was rectified in early 1915 when sanitary sections were attached to divisions and formed part of the divisional troops. A section had an officer and twenty-five other ranks, plus a

motor lorry with the necessary equipment such as shovels, wheelbarrows, disinfectants, sprays and notice boards. Their tasks included incinerating rubbish, filling latrines, disposal of horse manure and sanitation of towns and billets in the divisional area.

Ambulance transport at the bases

The taking of wounded to the base hospitals from the ambulance trains and from the hospitals to the hospital ships for embarkation was the responsibility of ambulance cars, operated and organized by the Joint Committee of the BRCS and Order of St John. Many of these fleets were staffed by members of the women's Voluntary Aid Detachment (VAD), who provided the drivers and undertook the care and management of the cars. This organization had its headquarters in Boulogne. By 1918 these fleets of ambulance cars had grown to 491, divided between Boulogne (129), Rouen (90), Étaples (81), Le Havre (67), Le Tréport (38), St-Omer (31), Calais (30) and Trouville (25).

Hospitals

It was in hospitals and convalescent depots on the lines of communication (or in the UK) that the seriously wounded and sick were treated, rested and, if fully fit, returned to duty. The main types were the general and stationary hospitals, but as the war devel-

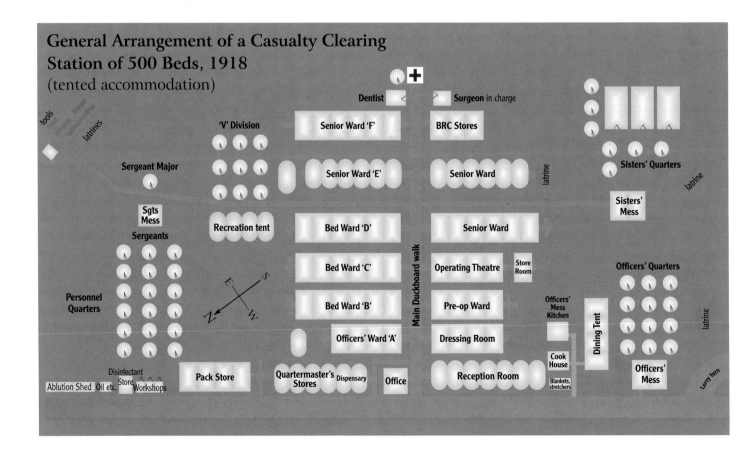

General Arrangement of a Casualty Clearing Station of 500 Beds, 1918 (tented accommodation)

Disposal of Sick and Wounded Received into Hospitals and Convalescent Depots

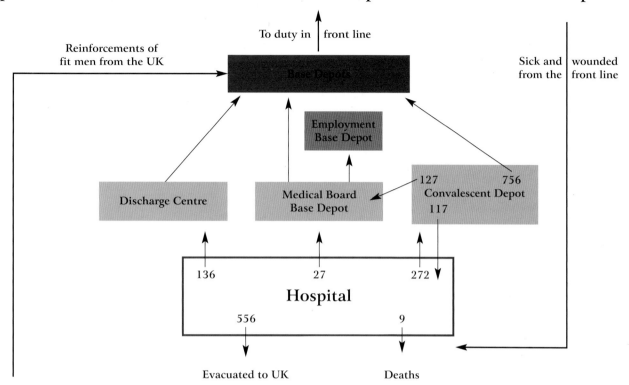

Notes

- The numbers indicate the proportion per 1,000 admissions into hospitals and convalescent depots on the lines of communication in 1917.

- Just one half of admissions into hospital were evacuated to the UK. About one quarter were discharged to convalescent depots; the remainder were discharged direct to duty or to employment at the base.

- Three quarters of cases admitted to convalescent depots were discharged fit for duty at the front.

oped different types were needed to cater for men in detention and for native labour. Isolation hospitals, voluntary Red Cross hospitals and hospitals for various types of disease, such as VD, were also required. The dominion and Indian forces mobilized their own general and stationary hospitals.

- **General hospitals** Initially intended to provide 520 beds, they were deployed on the basis of two for each division. However, this was soon found to be too small and uneconomical in terms of resources, so new types were organized in France in 1915 to take 1,040 beds. It was later found that hospital centres were the best way of caring for the mass casualties that were inevitable during major offensives. These saw the grouping of general hospitals, such as the one at Trouville in 1917, where there were three such hospitals each able to provide 2,500 beds.

- **Stationary hospitals** These were originally intended to provide relatively small hospitals (200 beds) for posts on the lines of communication or for reception of infection cases in army areas, acting as intermediaries between the forward medical units and the base. But, due to the comparative shortness of the distance between front and base, little

use was found for stationary hospitals as such, so they expanded and became fully equipped, making them virtually identical to general hospitals except in number of beds.

- **Hospitals for labour contingents** Seven hospitals (one went to Italy) for sick native labour contingents (Chinese and South African) were established. Each was staffed by RAMC personnel with native assistants. The largest was No. 3, the Chinese general hospital at Noyelles, which had 1,500 beds and a staff of fifteen officers, sixty-four British other ranks and 161 Chinese, including an interpreter.

- **Voluntary hospitals** Except for the St John Ambulance Brigade hospital, all voluntary hospitals were numbered from 1 to 10 as hospitals of the BRCS. They were generally small, with a maximum of 350 beds; three (Nos 1, 2 and 8) were reserved for officers. Organizations or individuals providing some of these hospitals included the Friends Ambulance Unit (took over No. 3); Sir Henry Norman (No. 4); Lady Hatfield's Anglo-American (No. 5); the Liverpool Merchants' Hospital (No. 6); the Baltic and Corn Exchange Hospital (No. 8); Millicent Duchess of Sutherland's (No. 9); and Lady Murray's (No. 10).

Convalescent depots

Only one convalescent depot, organized to accommodate 1,000, went to France with the BEF in 1914. The intention was for most sick and lightly injured to be retained in division, corps or army areas rather than on the lines of communication where convalescent depots would be located. By 1915 these arrangements had proved inadequate. There was congestion in the forward hospitals, and too many casualties were being evacuated to England, causing considerable unnecessary loss of manpower for prolonged periods. These factors led to the establishment of convalescent depots on the lines of communication at Boulogne, Wimereux, Rouen, Le Havre, Étaples, Dannes-Camiers and Le Tréport, and for Indians at Boulogne and Marseilles. In 1917 a new type of depot was established, able to accommodate up to 5,000 with facilities and staff for physical and military training programmes to get men fit for duty. In all, fourteen convalescent depots for other ranks and one each for Australians and Indians were operating in 1918. These were able to accommodate over 60,000 convalescents at the time of the Allied advance to victory. There were separate, much smaller, convalescent homes for officers and nursing sisters.

The diagram on page 371 shows the outcome in 1917 of the inflow of sick and wounded from the army areas to the base hospitals. It depicts the proportionate outflow from the base hospitals to the UK, to convalescent depots, to duty direct, to employment at the base, or by death during 1917 for every 1,000 cases admitted.

Second Army medical arrangements, Messines

The Second Army's casualty evacuation planning for the Battle of Messines is a good example of how arrangements for dealing with anticipated heavy losses had progressed since the early days of the war.

The Second Army had IX, X, and II ANZAC Corps, each with three divisions in the line and spread about equally along a 17,000-yard frontage in the battle area. Each corps had a fourth division in reserve. In all, the army had some 300,000 all ranks, of whom just over half were the infantry who were to make the assault and conduct follow-up operations. Map 69 shows the location of the main medical units in the army area tasked with evacuating the wounded to the CCSs and thence to the hospitals on the lines of communication. The ADMS at division were responsible for clearing wounded from the firing line to the corps main dressing stations and corps collecting posts; the DDMS at corps from these posts to the CCSs; while the DMS of the army coordinated evacuation to the lines of communication. The comprehensive plan included:

Regimental aid posts

These were mostly situated in communication trenches and were increased in number to thirty (from only twelve battalions in line initially) and strengthened. Arrangements were made for each division to assemble 80–100 additional stretcher-bearers at forward brigade headquarters, with supplies of stretchers kept at RAPs for them. Most RAPs were connected to advanced dressing stations by trench tramways and in the event most wounded were brought back by this means.

Walking-wounded collecting stations

Their locations were selected so that walking wounded could be directed away from the ADSs to avoid congestion, which meant most could be reached by cross-country tracks from the front marked by red cross flags and lanterns. From these stations walking wounded were transferred by horse transport, lorries, buses or returning supply and ammunition trains.

Advanced dressing stations

The majority of these were situated near a narrow-gauge field railway that had been constructed along the whole front. These eighteen stations were located as close as possible to the RAPs. The three in Ploegsteert and Ploegsteert Wood were less than a mile behind the RAPs, with the furthest away being the dressing station at Dickebusch in X Corps' area. The station 2 miles west of Ypres was X Corps' divisional collecting post for walking wounded. Divisional trench tramway officers were located at or near each ADS and were responsible for the trolleys – fitted to carry stretchers and drawn by mules – that were supplied to the RAPs as fast as the number of casualties required.

Main dressing stations

II ANZAC Corps had two at Pont d'Achelles and Westhof Farm; IX Corps three at Dranoutre, Locre and Westoutre; X Corps three, one on the La Clytte–Zevecoten road and the other two at Brandhoek some 4 miles west of Ypres. All of them possessed seven sets of equipment for treating gas casualties. Wounded were conveyed to the MDS by divisional motor and horse ambulances. In the event, large numbers of lightly wounded that arrived at the MDSs were transferred directly to divisional rest stations (not on Map 69).

Motor ambulance convoys

One MAC was allotted to each corps (two at Bailleul and one at Poperinghe) for the evacuation of seriously wounded from the MDSs to the CCSs. Also, a fleet of thirty lorries was put at the disposal of each corps DDMS. The MAC worked on the continuous chain principle, whereby a car was sent to each main dressing station every six minutes during the main phase of the attack. This system was able to evacuate 2,200 cases to CCSs from 7 to 10 June.

Casualty clearing stations

There were eleven in all, three at Bailleul and one just south-east of the town; four at Remy Siding; and two at Mendinghem (off map) and the Australian CCS at Trois Arbres. No. 11 CCS south-east of Bailleul and No. 3 (Canadian) at Remy Siding were intended to receive walking wounded only. There was also a reserve CCS in the back area at Mont des Cats and one at Hazebrouck (off map) to which sick and wounded could be transferred if necessary. Each CCS was expanded to take up to 1,000 wounded and reinforced with additional personnel and operating tables and 100 fully equipped hospital beds two days before the attack. The additional personnel

included three surgical teams, three medical officers, from six to twelve nurses and twenty RAMC other ranks. A labour company was allocated to each CCS for loading and unloading ambulance trains. Except for those taking lightly wounded, each CCS received patients in rotation, 150 at a time, enabling operations to be carried out with minimum delay. During the first three days of the battle some 2,400 operations were performed.

Ambulance trains

During the first three days of the battle thirty-five ambulance or temporary ambulance trains were used, with sixteen being garaged in the army area before the battle. These trains conveyed the wounded from the CCS to base hospitals.

The British wounded at Messines

Although there was congestion initially in II ANZAC Corps' medical units, as this corps suffered more than the other two, overall the number of wounded was lower than expected and the evacuation system worked smoothly. The first three days of the fighting saw over 17,000 wounded admitted to the medical units of the three corps, the details of which are set out below.

Many wounds were severe, caused mainly by explosive shells and shrapnel, with only 5 per cent attributable to rifle or machine-gun bullets. A substantial number of men were also gassed, mostly in II ANZAC Corps. From records kept in divisions of the proportion of stretcher cases to walking wounded collected by field ambulances, the average of these figures shows the percentage of walking cases to be 64.2 and of lying cases 35.8, or about two walking cases to one stretcher case.

By way of comparison, in the Fourth Army during the first three days of the Somme offensive 34,909 wounded were received by fifteen CCSs – almost exactly double the number of wounded at Messines. These fifteen CCSs had 174 MOs, 137 nursing sisters and about 1,900 other ranks. By the end of the first week in July they had treated around 42,000 cases – an average of 400 cases per CCS every day and about 35 for each MO. By the end of July the Fourth Army CCSs had admitted, treated and evacuated almost 100,000 wounded.

Second Army Wounded at Messines, 1917

Date	II ANZAC	IX Corps	X Corps	Total
7 June	4,414	2,368	1,963	8,745
8 June	3,103	898	2,097	6,098
9 June	1,350	339	1,027	2,716
Totals	**8,867**	**3,605**	**5,087**	**17,559**

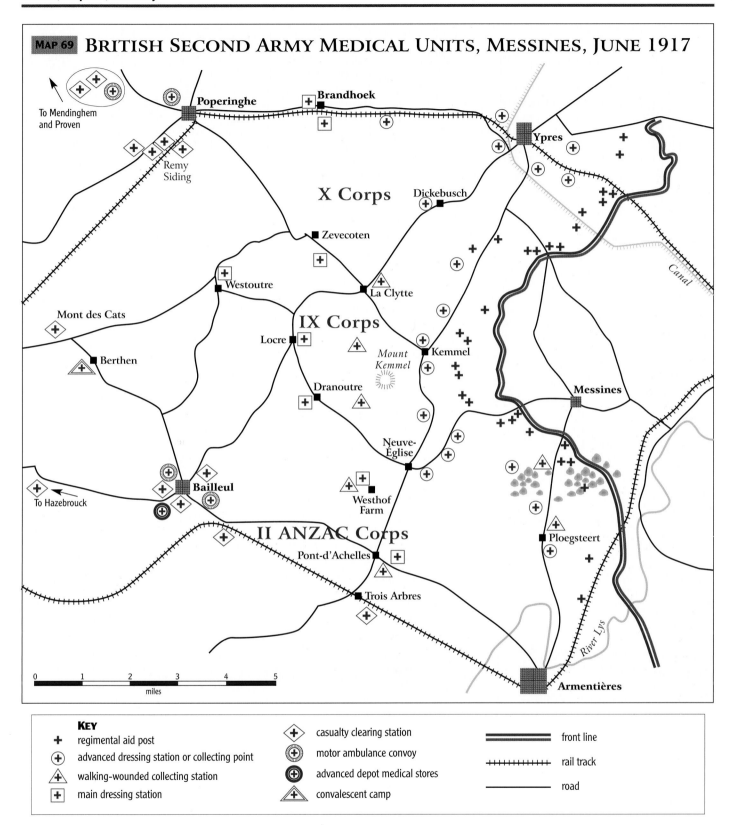

MAP 69 BRITISH SECOND ARMY MEDICAL UNITS, MESSINES, JUNE 1917

KEY

- ✚ regimental aid post
- ⊕ advanced dressing station or collecting point
- △ walking-wounded collecting station
- ▣ main dressing station
- ◈ casualty clearing station
- ⊛ motor ambulance convoy
- ⊚ advanced depot medical stores
- △ convalescent camp
- ▆▆▆ front line
- ┿┿┿ rail track
- ─── road

British Women in Medical Services

Women in the medical services eventually played a hugely beneficial role in the treatment and recovery of hundreds of thousands of patients. However, it proved extraordinarily difficult to get them fully accepted in the male-run medical establishment. There was continuous opposition to their employment, and tension surrounding their position and responsibilities. Even when eventually recognized as vital to the welfare and care of the wounded and sick, in theatre as well as at home, women nurses were always subordinate to male physicians, and British nurses were not allowed to look after Indian troops.

At the start of the war many women doctors volunteered their services, only to be turned down by the RAMC and War Office. However, by 1916 the increasing shortage of medical staff and the huge increase in the number of casualties overcame official resistance and reluctantly women doctors were allowed to join the regular military establishment, but effectively as associate members with no military rank and thus junior to all male doctors in uniform; they were also expected to travel third class by train. Most were employed at hospitals in the UK or at bases overseas, although some were attached to the RAMC in the field – even then they were never, despite considerable pressure, commissioned. Meanwhile other women, although not qualified doctors, had found different ways to serve the military medical organization. The main organizations were:

• **Queen Alexandra's Imperial Military Nursing Service (QAIMNS)** This was the 'regular' military nursing service formed in 1902 to replace the Army Nursing Service that had provided nurses for military hospitals since 1861. Very high professional and social standards (only 'ladies' were considered for membership) were required for entry into the QAIMNS, so at the outbreak of war there were only 297 members – matrons, sisters and staff nurses. It was decided that with the inevitable and dramatic wartime expansion further recruitment should be temporary, so the many thousands of nurses who joined were given short-term contracts. By the Armistice there were over 7,700 trained nurses in the QAIMNS, with many married and from the lower social orders; over half were serving overseas. On the Western Front they served in field hospitals, ambulance trains, hospital ships and barges and eventually as far forward as casualty clearing stations. Their service was magnificent and saved countless lives, as well as providing care to the sick and convalescents and great comfort to men in terrible pain or dying.

• **Territorial Force Nursing Service (TFNS)** This organization was established in 1908 and was intended to provide nurses for the twenty-three Territorial Force UK hospitals in the event of war. The intended establishment for each hospital was one principal matron, two matrons, thirty sisters and eighty-eight staff nurses. They were civilian nursing personnel with considerable experience (some were working in St Thomas' Hospital, London, and the Edinburgh Royal Infirmary) but intended for home service. In 1913 TFNS personnel were given the option of volunteering to serve overseas and some accompanied the BEF to France in 1914. As the war progressed, so many more went overseas and a number proved capable of nurse management at a high level in large hospitals, casualty clearing stations and field ambulances. During the war over 8,000 women served in the TFNS, almost 2,300 of them overseas.

• **First Aid Nursing Yeomanry (FANY)** This body was established in 1907 with the task of 'tend[ing] British soldiers in the field'. The women had to be between seventeen and thirty-five years of age and at least 5 feet 3 inches tall. They undertook a training programme that included first aid, home nursing, horsemanship, veterinary work, signalling and camp cooking. When they offered their services to the British Army they were turned away on the grounds that there was no practical use for them, even for driving ambulances. The British Red Cross Society declined to recognize FANY. However, the head of FANY, Grace Ashley-Smith (later Mrs McDougall), chanced to meet the Belgian Minister for the Colonies, who suggested FANY might help his country, so in late October 1914 the first FANY ambulance convoy, consisting of a motor ambulance, six 'Fannies', three nurses, two orderlies and Ashley-Smith's brother crossed to Belgium and set up a small hospital in a school. This tiny unit was slowly reinforced with more personnel, ambulances and a mobile kitchen and bath unit. Another request to be recognized and utilized by the British Army in mid-1915 was again rejected, despite the fact that their convoy, although supporting the Belgians, was now located in the British base at Calais. Nevertheless, the shortage of ambulances meant that before long the RAMC were using the FANY convoy, although the organization's priority remained with the Belgians.

The Director of Medical Services at Calais, Surgeon General H. R. Whitehead, quickly realized the value of FANY and, initially in defiance of the British authorities, agreed to the establishment of a FANY ambulance convoy at Calais to work entirely for the British and to take over ambulances previously operated by the BRCS. The army supplied rations and the BRCS funded the maintenance of the vehicles, but FANY personnel continued to find their own uniforms and travel expenses. The success of the Calais convoy led to the setting up of several others to support the French Army. The War Office made another effort to disband FANY convoys in France and Belgium, but the BRCS delegation sent to do so was rebuffed by the Belgians, and thereafter the Belgian and French authorities took direct control of the convoys. The exception came in January 1918 when a British FANY convoy was established at St-Omer.

Although the number of FANY personnel never exceeded about 450, decorations for bravery were awarded to 52 of them: 19 Military Medals, 27 *Croix de Guerre*, a *Légion d'honneur* and 5 Belgian *Croix Civique*.

• **Voluntary Aid Detachment (VAD)** In 1909 the War Office established an organization whose members (men and women) could provide voluntary aid to sick and wounded soldiers – its units became known as Voluntary Aid Detachments. These detachments were managed by the BRCS and St John Ambulance, with each having an establishment of twenty-three. By the time war was declared the organization had grown to over 55,000, of whom almost two thirds were women. Personnel were trained in basic nursing by the BRCS (first aid, changing dressings, bedmaking, giving a blanket bath and ward cleanliness). However, others were expected to tackle any sort of work connected with the running of hospitals, including driving, cooking, laundry, storekeeping, clerical duties and operating canteens. Despite all this, it was not until 1915 that they received any pay and then only a miserable £20 a year.

Although intended only for employment in hospitals in the UK, where they cared for wounded soldiers in a variety of wards and convalescent hospitals, the first detachment

A Voluntary Aid Detachment (VAD) worker starts the engine of a motor ambulance at Étaples, 1917.

Mademoiselle Emilienne Moreau

The following is a short extract from Colonel Rawnsley's (ADMS, 15th Division) report on the medical services after the Battle of Loos.

I wish to place on record the courageous and devoted services rendered to the British Army by Mdlle. Emilienne Moreau, the particulars of which were furnished me by Captain F. A. Bearn, RAMC, the officer in medical charge of the 9th Black Watch. This girl who is only 17½ years old, was living with another woman in a shop at Loos in the Church Square. These premises were taken as a regimental aid post by Captain Bearn and these two women spent the whole day and night (25th–26th September) in helping to carry in the wounded and carry out the dead, also preparing food and coffee for all, refusing payment. This work was done continuously for twenty-four hours. When the British troops were making ineffective efforts to dislodge two German snipers from the next house, who were firing on the stretcher bearers, this young girl seized a revolver from an officer and went into the back of the house and fired two shots at the snipers. She came back saying, '*C'est fini*', and handed the revolver back to the officer.

Because of her bravery, Emilienne Moreau became a national heroine in France, known as 'the Lady of Loos'. She was awarded the *Croix de Guerre* and the *Croix du Combattant* by the French, and from the British she received the Military Medal, the Royal Red Cross (1st Class) and the Venerable Order of St John – one of the very few women to have been awarded this last. In World War II she played an important part in the French Resistance. She died in 1971, aged seventy-two.

went to France as early as October 1914. Led by the first commandant of the BRCS VADs, Mrs Katherine Furse, the No. 1 British Red Cross VAD Unit Rest Station was established at Boulogne, where it catered for wounded in transit. By November 1918 VAD personnel had grown massively to 90,000 women and some 40,000 men, serving in the UK and every theatre. Of these, some 23,000 were nurses and 18,000 nursing orderlies.

• **Scottish Women's Hospitals (SWH)** British officialdom's initial determination to reject the services of women volunteers did not deter Dr Elsie Inglis, who in 1914 founded the Scottish Women's Hospitals, an organization linked to the women's suf-frage movement in Scotland. Her offer of help to the military authorities was reportedly rebuffed with the words, 'My good lady, go home and sit still.' The French and Serbian Armies, however, welcomed her offers of assistance and the SWH (staffed entirely by women) set up field hospitals, dressing stations and other medical units in France and Serbia from 1914 onwards. Later they moved into Russia, Romania and Salonika, providing doctors, nurses, orderlies, cooks and drivers.

Eileen Crofton, in her book *The Women of Royaumont*, describes the grim scenes experienced in a hospital run by the SWH. During the Somme offensive Royaumont was a French auxiliary base hospital attached to the French Army some 20 miles north of Paris and only 25 miles from the front.

> At that time it had about 400 beds. Over 24 hours 2nd–3rd July 1916, 121 casualties were sent in, and they kept coming; over 200 altogether in the first week. Their wounds were terrible, many of the men were wounded dangerously in two, three, four or five places . . .
>
> That first night, the surgeons operated through until 7.00am, exploring and debriding (cutting away infected flesh) wounds and amputating shattered limbs. The urgent need was to prevent the spread of gas gangrene, which was already developing or established in 90% of the cases. The gas could be seen on the x-rays, the bacteria could be seen microscopically on the wound smears, the putrefaction could all too easily be smelt. The stench was very bad.

The French developed a gas gangrene anti-serum that was trialled at Royaumont from 1915, although by 1918 it was still not generally available.

German Medical Units

The German Army medical organization in the field resembled that of the British – indeed those of all armies on the Western Front – as the general principles of evacuation, triage and treatment, then speedy return to duty, were much the same. At the German GHQ was a director general (lieutenant general) of medical services, who controlled the medical services in the theatre of operations and on the lines of communication; at army HQ was a director of medical services (major general); at corps a deputy director (colonel) and a civilian consulting surgeon; at division an assistant director (lieutenant colonel); at regimental level a senior medical officer (major); and with each battalion two medical officers, four medical NCOs (one with each company) and sixteen non-combatant stretcher-bearers wearing Red Cross brassards.

In the trenches each company set up an aid post in a dugout, while further back a larger regimental aid post was established in the support trenches or in well-constructed dugouts or cellars capable of accommodating up to thirty wounded. These aid posts were well stocked, with supplies for five days, extra dressings and medical stores, as well as being well lit and connected by telephone to the rear. Three of the battalion medical officers and a detachment of stretcher-bearers would staff these regimental posts. Similar aid posts were built for artillery regiments.

The next unit to the rear was the bearer company, or field ambulance, commanded by a major. There were 208 stretcher-bearers divided into two sections under non-medical officers. The bearer company was tasked with establishing a wagon rendezvous about 4,000 yards behind the regimental aid post, a main dressing station and a collecting station for walking wounded. The next stage in evacuation was to a field hospital – in effect a CCS – of which there were two for each division and two for corps troops. Usually they were opened in villages in back areas, staffed with six medical officers and appropriate medical staff with about 200 beds. They were normally organized to deal with special cases, with advanced operating centres often located near to main dressing stations.

The Germans also made use of ambulance convoys and ambulance trains, and established base hospitals and depots for medical stores. As with all armies, expansion during the four years of trench warfare was dramatic. By 1918 on all fronts there were 314 medical companies (field ambulances), 592 field hospitals (CCS), 72 base or line of communication hospitals, 62 ambulance trains and another 100 for lightly injured or sick, as well as 85 auxiliary hospital trains and 23 medical stores depots. It has been estimated that overall the German medical services treated over 4.2 million wounds (many men received more than one or were wounded several times) during the war.

The future Field Marshal Erwin Rommel was an infantry company commander fighting the French in the Argonne Forest in September 1914. On 24 September he was wounded and he later described the incident, which took place during an attack (he had run out of ammunition so was relying on his bayonet), and his evacuation in his book *Infanterie Greift An* (*Infantry Attacks*):

> As I rushed forward, the enemy fired. Struck, I went head over heels and wound up a few paces in front of the enemy. A bullet, entering sideways, had shattered

my upper left leg; and blood spurted from a wound as large as my fist. At any moment I expected a bullet or bayonet thrust. I tried to close the wound with my right hand and, at the same time, to roll behind an oak. For many minutes I lay there between the two fronts. Finally my men broke through the bushes and the enemy retreated.

Lance Corporal Rauch and Private Rutschmann took care of me. A coat belt served as a tourniquet and they bandaged my wound. Then they carried me back to the hut in a shelter [tent] half . . .

It was a tough time leaving these brave men. As the sun set two men carried me back to Montblainville in a shelter half attached to two poles. I felt but little pain, yet I fainted from loss of blood.

When I regained consciousness in a Montblainville barn, Schnitzer, the battalion surgeon, was working over me . . . my wound was dressed again, and I was loaded into an ambulance beside three wounded, groaning comrades. We left for the field hospital, the horses trotting over the shell-torn road; and the jolting which resulted caused me great pain. When we

arrived around midnight one of the men beside me was already dead.

The field hospital was overcrowded. Blanketed men lay in rows along the highway. Two doctors worked feverishly. They re-examined me and gave me a place on some straw in a room.

At daylight an ambulance took me to the base hospital at Stenay, where a few days later I was decorated with the Iron Cross, Second Class. In the middle of October after having had an operation, I was taken home in a private car that had been placed at the Army's disposal.

Chaplains

At the outbreak of war the Army Chaplain's Department, administered on the Church of England side by the Chaplain General, Bishop John Taylor Smith, was small, with only 117 commissioned chaplains (89 Church of England, 11 Presbyterians and 17 Roman Catholics). There were also a number of temporary acting chaplains, including Wesleyan, Baptist and Congregationalist. On mobilization 63 chaplains went to France with the BEF, on the basis of one Church of England for each brigade (infantry and cavalry), one Presbyterian for each division (provided it contained a Scottish unit) and four (two Church of England, one Roman Catholic and one Presbyterian) at each of the two main bases and advanced base. In 1915, as the size of the army continued to grow, the number of chaplains with each division was increased from 12 to 14 (later to 17) and chaplains were appointed to each stationary and general hospital. The chaplains with the divisions were attached, one each, to infantry battalions and artillery brigades. This meant that most English battalions had a Church of England chaplain, southern Irish regiments a Roman Catholic and Scottish a Presbyterian. For free church Christians and Jews, chaplains of these denominations were attached to division or corps to act in a roving capacity. By the end of the war 878 Church of England chaplains and 820 of other denominations had served on the Western Front and of these 176 gave their lives.

The role of the chaplains – normally referred to as 'padres' or, somewhat irreligiously, as 'sky pilots' – was that of the spiritual welfare of the troops. This duty included holding services in the field, particularly on the eve of a battle and for burials; giving comfort to the wounded and dying (for Roman Catholics this invariably involved giving the Last Rites), including attending military executions; and often writing letters to the next of kin of soldiers killed in action. They were

also involved in material welfare matters ranging from the running of canteens through organizing entertainment behind the lines to the distribution of sweets and cigarettes 'for the boys'– at least one chaplain was nicknamed 'Woodbine Willy'. Regimental padres in the front line would normally be found at the RAP or at a dressing station.

Their overall effectiveness in improving morale was patchy, ranging from the outstandingly good to the decidedly ineffective. The degree of effectiveness depended mostly on the personal example they set – whether they were commonly or rarely seen in the front-line trenches was the primary factor on which most soldiers judged them. Colonel W. N. Nicholson wrote in *Behind the Lines*:

> In my experience when the padres were good, they were very very good; but when they were bad they were awful. Selfish and inefficient. Perhaps it was because the Church of England is out of touch with the manhood of England; but undoubtedly the Roman Catholics and Nonconformists had a much closer relationship with the rank and file and made the most of the opportunity war brings . . .

As to the importance of religion on morale generally for the men of the BEF on the Western Front, John Baynes in his book *Morale: a Study of Men and Courage* reveals some interesting results from extensive interviews and correspondence on the subject. This was carried out with the officers and men who served with the 2nd Scottish Rifles (Cameronians) in 1915 up to, and including, the Battle of Neuve Chapelle in March. Baynes concluded that the influence of religion on morale had three possible effects:

> It could be an important influence, giving immense strength and inspiration; it could be of no importance at all; or it could be something rather vague and intermittent. I

offer the following table to show the percentages included in each of these three categories.

	To officers (%)	To soldiers (%)
An important influence	50	10
No importance	15	50
Vague and intermittent	35	40

Officers were more likely to be more influenced by religion than the men because, with a regular battalion at that stage of the war, the officers were almost entirely upper middle class, the product of public schools and Sandhurst, where Christianity and churchgoing had been one of the constants underlying their upbringing and training. This was far less the case with the soldiers, many of whom came from poor urban areas where religion played little if any part in their life outside the army. Many men got little comfort from religion, as Private J. Bowles, Queen's Westminster Rifles, explained in 1916:

> Before we left England our Chaplain preached several sermons on the effect of danger and suffering on men out there. He said that being constantly in danger of losing one's life made men think of the serious side of life and fly to religion as the only source of comfort. My own experience is quite the contrary. In the bombing raid I was on recently the language was so bad that even the men themselves commented upon it. Men go to their deaths with curses on their lips and religion is never mentioned or thought of. Why is it? I can only put it down to the fact that life out here is one of continual hardship and suffering, that in war there is no place for a God of Love, no time for the softer emotions, and no inclination to worry about a future when the present is a hell that the devil himself would be proud to reign over.

With the greater social levelling of the New Armies, however, the contrasting influence of religion on individuals was less obvious, with more of the officers and other ranks coming into the 'vague and intermittent' category. Nevertheless, it was a minority of soldiers of any rank that would not offer up prayers while under shellfire or during the moments before going 'over the top'.

Regarding the effectiveness of chaplains in improving morale, Baynes agrees with Nicholson 'that the padres of the Protestant Churches proved to be rather inadequate, but that the Roman Catholic padres were of an averagely high level.' One of the Cameronian officers, Lieutenant J. P. Kennedy, recalled the battalion's Christmas communion service in a barn in 1914, but apart from that had no recollection of seeing a padre at all during his time in France, and certainly not at the front – however, Kennedy's experience was limited as he was killed at Neuve Chapelle.

The padres' influence for the good depended not only on the soldiers seeing his sharing the dangers but also on his ability to relate on a personal level to individuals, and to be seen to be doing his best to improve their material well-being through acts of kindness, and physically assisting with the wounded or helping to dig a grave, for example. It was no use 'walking about a trench filled with flies feeding off a disintegrating tin of marmalade shouting the odds about believing in Jesus! It would go down even less well than the marmalade.' Much more effective for gaining soldiers' respect, apart from his presence in the line, would be small acts of assistance such as helping to carry ammunition, rations or a stretcher. The padre of the 9th Loyal North Lancashire was favourably regarded for helping to bring forward a machine gun, while the Roman Catholic chaplain Willie Doyle with the 8th Royal Dublin Fusiliers was always to be seen in the firing line (he received the MC) and was almost as likely to be bringing up ammunition as the Host; he was killed in August 1917.

If the run-of-the-mill Church of England chaplain was somewhat mediocre in his effectiveness, a number were regarded with a huge amount of respect and affection. Three chaplains won the Victoria Cross (two on the Western Front and one in Mesopotamia) and many more were awarded the Military Cross for gallantry under fire.

The first to gain the Victoria Cross was Captain The Reverend Edward Noel Mellish, who in 1900, aged twenty, had fought as a trooper in Baden-Powell's police against the Boers in South Africa. After a spell in England he returned to South Africa to work in the diamond mines at Jagersfontein. Later he studied at King's College, London, before being ordained in 1912. In March 1916, while padre of the 4th Battalion the Royal Fusiliers, he became involved in the action at St-Éloi craters after the blowing of six mines under the German lines. During 27–29 March Mellish went back and forth under continuous heavy shell and machine-gun fire between the original trenches and those captured by the Fusiliers in order to tend and rescue the wounded. He brought in ten badly injured men on the first day from ground swept by machine-gun fire. The next day he returned and repeated his actions, this time bringing in twelve men. On the third night he took charge of a party of volunteers and went back to rescue the remaining wounded. A story tells that one of the men he brought back was a Cockney soldier known for his dismissiveness of religion who, when recovering in hospital, asked of the padre, 'What religion is 'e?' When told he replied, 'Well I'm the same as 'im now, and the bloke as sez a word agin our church will 'ave 'is bloody 'ead bashed in.' Mellish received the Victoria Cross, to add to his Military Cross, from the King at Buckingham Palace in June 1920. During World War II he served as an air raid warden. He died in July 1962, aged eighty-two.

Probably the best-known chaplain to gain the Victoria Cross was Captain The Reverend Theodore Bayley Hardy who, with a DSO and MC as well, was the second most decorated non-combatant of the war (after Captain Noel Chavasse, RAMC, with the VC and Bar and MC; see box, page 361). With poor health and at over fifty years old, the Reverend Hardy had difficulty in persuading the authorities to accept him as an army chaplain. However, his persistence was rewarded in mid-1916 when he was given a posting to the base at Étaples. Determined to serve at the front, he continued to pester people until in December 1916 he was finally sent as padre to the 8th Battalion, the Lincolnshire Regiment. In less than a year he was awarded the Distinguished Service Order, Military Cross and Victoria Cross. For the DSO the citation in the *London Gazette* reads:

> For conspicuous bravery and devotion to duty in volunteering to go with a rescue party for some men who had been left stuck in the mud the previous night between the enemy's outpost line and our own. All the men except one were brought in. He then organized a party for the rescue of this man, and remained with it all night, though under rifle-fire at close range, which killed one of the party. With his left arm in splints, owing to a broken wrist, and under the worst weather conditions, he crawled out with patrols to within seventy yards of the enemy and remained with wounded under fire.

For the MC:

> For conspicuous gallantry and devotion to duty in tending the wounded. The ground on which he worked was constantly shelled and the casualties were heavy. He continually assisted in finding and carrying wounded and in guiding stretcher bearers to the aid post.

And for the VC for three separate actions, the citation reads in part:

> For conspicuous bravery and devotion to duty on many occasions. Although over fifty years old, he has, by his fearlessness, devotion to the men of his battalion, and quiet, unobtrusive manner, won the respect and admiration of the whole division . . . His valour and devotion are exemplified in the following incidents:
>
> He followed the patrol, and about four hundred yards beyond our front line of posts found an officer of the patrol dangerously wounded. He remained with the officer until he was able to get

New Zealand soldiers taking Communion before going into battle, 1916.

assistance to bring him in . . . an enemy shell exploded in the middle of one of our posts . . . [Hardy] made his way to the spot despite shell and mortar fire and set to work to extricate the buried men. He succeeded in getting out one man who had been completely buried. He then set to work to extricate a second man who was found to be dead. During the whole time that he was digging out the men this chaplain was in great danger . . .

[Hardy] asked the men to help get in a wounded man. Accompanied by a sergeant, he made his way to the spot where the man lay, within ten yards of a pill-box . . . occupied by the enemy. The wounded man was too weak to stand, but between them the chaplain and the sergeant eventually succeeded in getting him to our lines.

Hardy's incredible courage so impressed the King that he appointed him Honorary Chaplain to His Majesty, hoping this would persuade him to take a more secure post, but Hardy refused all offers to leave 'his boys'. Sadly, during the German offensive in March 1918, he was hit by a burst of machine-gun fire and died of his wounds in hospital at Rouen on 18 October 1918, aged fifty-five. An extract from the letter of condolence from his commanding officer to his family reads:

What his loss has meant to us is more than I can express, but his name will always be recalled with reverence and to those of us who knew him intimately a great blank has appeared, though thank God we shall meet him again under happier surroundings.

Veterinary

On the Western Front the overwhelming majority of animals with the BEF needing care were the horses and mules. The others – dogs and pigeons for message-carrying; cats, mostly kept as pets by the troops and used to catch rats; and canaries and mice used by tunnellers to detect gas – rarely required the services of veterinary personnel. The supply of horses and mules has been discussed above in Section Eight under 'Remounts' (page 339) but the scale and complexity of the task confronting the Army Veterinary Corps (AVC) needs further explanation.

Horses were classified into three types according to the work required of them. Riding horses were, as their name suggests, used solely for riding by officers, staff, or in the cavalry and horse artillery, and for some personnel in artillery regiments, supply or medical units. Light draught horses were the most numerous as they were the animals used to work in teams of pairs to draw the field-artillery guns or ammunition, ambulance and supply wagons. They performed the bulk of the really arduous tasks in the field in the most exposed and exacting circumstances – consequently they suffered more casualties and sickness than the others. The heavy draught horses required to haul big guns and howitzers were English Shire horses. They initially suffered badly from pneumonia, required larger amounts of fodder and water than the smaller horses or mules and could not well withstand forced marches. During the first year of the war it appeared doubtful whether the use of these animals should continue. Fortunately, by the end of 1915 their excessive mortality had been considerably reduced and the static nature of trench warfare, combined with the ability of these animals to do twice the work of a similar number of mules, meant that the enormous hauling capacity of the Shire horse remained an important factor in tackling the transportation of heavy loads. Finally, there was a relatively small number of packhorses for carrying ammunition, food and water over difficult ground to front-line positions.

For approximately every four horses with the BEF there was one mule, used for hauling light loads and carts or employed as a pack animal. Mules proved more resistant than horses to the adverse conditions of the frequently atrocious winter weather, deep mud and the consequent poor animal management often unavoidable at the front. Also, they could remain reasonably fit on 25 per cent less fodder than horses. Their mortality rate was about half that of horses.

At the end of the war there were 382,266 horses and mules in service in France, divided by type as shown below.

The number of these animals in France peaked in April 1917 when a total of 436,000 were in service (there were over a million working animals, including numerous camels, in all theatres).

The total mortality from all causes (see opposite) on the Western Front from August 1914 to November 1918 was 269,000 out of an overall total in all theatres of over 500,000 mortalities. The weekly average wastage in France was 2 per cent of the total – meaning that 200 replacement animals were required weekly for every 10,000 in the field. This 'wastage' included all those sick or injured animals evacuated to veterinary hospitals for treatment of temporary disabilities. These animals required replacements, but when cured were discharged to remount depots for conditioning and re-issue to units. The average sick rate was around 11 per cent of total strength, with a mortality rate varying from almost 21 per cent a year in 1914 down to nearly 10 per cent in 1916. Due to the severe conditions in the first half of 1917 (there were snow blizzards in April) it rose again, but had dropped to normal by midsummer. Between the start of the war and the Armistice, 859,178 horses and mules were admitted to BEF veterinary hospitals and convalescent depots, of which 534,744 were discharged cured – just over 63 per cent, a figure that is a tribute to the high standards of veterinary work achieved by the corps. Overall total admissions to veterinary hospitals on all fronts, including the home front, were 2,562,549, of which 78 per cent, or approximately 2 million, were returned to duty.

The chief causes of animal deaths were battle casualties (including gas), other injuries or surgical conditions leading to the destruction of the animal; debility and exhaustion; respiratory diseases; glanders and mange.

- **Battle casualties** These were either bullet or shell wounds. Lieutenant E. H. Wylie, AVC, described an incident in 1915:

a German shrapnel shell burst on percussion among the trees, killing four horses outright (all thoracic wounds) and wounding ten others, two of these so severely that I shot them immediately. Of the others one had a bullet wound on the near side of the neck . . . It entered here and passed through to the other side as far as the skin and then became deflected downwards over the shoulder and along the thorax leaving its course

Horses and Mules on the Western Front, November 1918

	Riding	Light draught	Heavy draught	Draught	Pack	Total
Horses	93,830	141,770	64,980		5,084	305,664
Mules				74,369	2,233	76,602

clearly demonstrated like the weal produced by the cut of a whip.

By palpation I traced this with my hand as far as the fourteenth or fifteenth rib where I could distinctly feel the bullet rolling about subcutaneously. From this situation I removed it with a scalpel quite readily.

Wounds inflicted by bullets that did not hit a vital organ or break a bone but passed cleanly through the body or limb usually healed quite quickly and did not affect the utility of the animal. As with human casualties, wounds inflicted by shell fragments or bullets striking bones or vital organs were often fatal or untreatable – something that resulted in the destruction of the animal. Some shell wounds could be enormous and immediate destruction was the only humane course. Wounds containing a number of shell splinters could cause problems leading to death from septicaemia or gas gangrene. However, despite these difficulties veterinary surgeons successfully carried out thousands of operations on all parts of an animal's anatomy, including the head, neck, thorax and abdomen.

Considerable efforts were made to devise satisfactory protection from gas by means of horse respirators, which were issued on the basis of a third of the animal's strength. They were not particularly successful as, while giving some protection against chlorine gas, they were useless against the mustard gas that largely replaced it, and in practice the overall number of animal gas casualties was relatively few and declined rapidly in the latter part of the war.

During the first two years on the Western Front battle losses of animals were not great. It was the large offensives that began in 1916 that saw casualty lists rise alarmingly. For the Somme offensive from July to November 1916 the number of animal casualties was 10,004, of which 3,941 were killed or destroyed and 6,063 wounded by shells, bombs or bullets; of these, gas losses amounted to 385, of which only 33 were killed or destroyed. During a six-month period in 1917, which included Messines, of the 34,054 animal casualties 10,590 died of battle wounds but only 68 from gas. The final Hundred Days Allied offensive that ended the war saw the BEF incur 46,023 animal casualties of which 23,251 died from battle wounds but a mere 26 from gas.

• **Debility and exhaustion** Casualties from this cause were the result of shortages of food or water or both, overwork, exposure to cold and wet weather, and poor animal management (see below). In the circumstances of the battlefields on the Western

Front none of these factors could ever be eliminated; the best that could be achieved was to alleviate some of them some of the time. The Arras offensive of April 1917 saw huge losses among draught horses in particular. The 167th Brigade, RA, recorded that 'many horses died of sheer fatigue'. A gunner described the advance:

We moved forward but the conditions were terrible. The ammunition that had been prepared by our leaders for this great spring offensive had to be brought up with the supplies, over roads that were sometimes up to one's knees in slimy yellow-brown mud. The horses were up to their bellies in mud. We had to put them on picket line between the wagon wheels at night and they'd be sunk in over their fetlocks the next day. We had to shoot quite a number.

Mules suffered as well as horses. Lieutenant R. G. Dixon, RGA, later wrote:

Heaving about in the filthy mud of the road was an unfortunate mule with both of his forelegs shot away. The poor brute, suffering God knows what untold agonies and terrors, was trying desperately to get to its feet which weren't there. Writhing and heaving, tossing its head about in its wild attempts, not knowing that it no longer had any front legs.

I had my revolver with me, but couldn't get near the animal, which lashed out at us with its hind legs and tossed its head unceasingly. The Jerry shells were arriving pretty fast – we made some desperate attempts to get the mule so that I could put a bullet behind its ear into the brain, but to no avail.

By lingering there trying to put the creature out of its pain I was risking not only my life but also my companions. The shelling got more intense – perhaps one would hit the poor thing and put it out of its misery.

April 1917 saw some of the bitterest weather conditions experienced in France for many years, resulting in the forage ration being reduced for the 195,000 animals engaged in the arduous Arras offensive. These combined factors saw animal losses due to debility reach unprecedented levels. In February 5,317 animals were admitted to veterinary hospitals for this reason, 9,427 in March and a staggering 20,319 in April.

• **Care and management** The prevention of animal wastage from debility and exhaustion called for unremitting effort by the

AVC. A major problem to overcome was that, unlike the old Regular Army, the New Army personnel of all ranks had virtually no experience or training in animal care and management – essential preventative medicine. Training courses were instituted at veterinary hospitals for ten officers and fifty NCOs at a time, and although they only lasted ten days at least they imparted the basic elements of animal management, such as grooming, exercise, watering and feeding routines, clothing, clipping, picket lines, saddles and harness, signs of disease, sore backs and shoeing. All this helped, but it was understandably hard always to get men to attend closely to animals – for example, in matters of watering and feeding in the pouring rain, with a biting wind and horse lines deep in mud. There was also a substantial, unavoidable, wastage of forage in these circumstances as the hay became soiled and was rejected, with every bit of fodder that fell from the nosebag being lost in the mud.

• **Respiratory disease** The disease known at the time as 'contagious pneumonia' was the cause of mortality in remounts, especially heavy draught horses, during the first twelve months of the war. Intensive research revealed that this disease was not contagious under ordinary conditions, and that most deaths occurred as a result of moving, entraining or shipping animals while they were in a state of unsuspected high temperature. Losses were subsequently much reduced by the simple expedient of keeping animals under observation for two weeks and moving them only once their temperatures were normal. With this preventative measure implemented at the heavy draught remount depot at Swaythling near Southampton, the deaths from pneumonia during the first six months of 1916 fell to 163 out of 3,504 admitted from the previous year's 1,287 and 7,999 respectively. This precaution of ensuring horses had normal temperature before shipment saved thousands of animals during the voyages from America.

• **Glanders** Fortunately this unpleasant disease to which horses and mules are particularly susceptible did not take hold on the Western Front, although the Germans deliberately attempted to spread it among Russian animals on the Eastern Front. It is an infectious disease often caused by ingesting contaminated food or water. It causes lesions of the lungs, coughing, fever and the development of infectious nasal discharge and can result in the animal's death in a matter of days. On mobilization and thereafter all animals, whether purchased by the British Remount Commission in the USA or in Canada, were as far as possible tested using mallein injections before shipment. The only serious outbreak occurred in 1915 in the mule remount depot at Taunton when the disease was introduced by an infected shipload from California.

• **Mange** This skin disease is the result of mites infesting domestic animals. The mites become embedded in the skin and hair follicles, causing the animal to kick and bite the infected area, often leading to secondary infection. Outbreaks of mange were practically confined to the first three years of the war. Although comparatively easy to control with dips, the rapid expansion in animal numbers in France outpaced the provision of facilities for dipping and good horse management. Consequently mange spread steadily from autumn 1915 to spring 1917, when 16,624 animals were under treatment – almost 4 per cent of total strength. However, increased dipping arrangements and an improvement in preventative measures resulted in the incidence falling to 0.4 per cent by the war's end.

The incidence of mange invariably grew during winter months owing to the animals' long coats and fewer facilities for grooming.

The Army Veterinary Corps (AVC)

At the end of the war the Quartermaster General wrote:

The Corps by its initiative and scientific methods has placed military veterinary organisation on a higher plane. The high standard which it has maintained at home and throughout all theatres has resulted in a reduction of animal wastage, an increased mobility of mounted units and a mitigation of animal suffering un-approached in any previous military operation.

During World War I the Army Veterinary Corps (which was granted the prefix 'Royal' on 27 November 1918) was under the overall control of a director of veterinary services (major general) based at GHQ, with a deputy director at the headquarters of the IGC. Initially AVC personnel were armed only with swords, something that caused some concern, as the diary of No. 11 Mobile Veterinary Section (MVS) for September 1914 makes clear:

The section is armed with swords only, and a firearm is necessary in view of the close proximity of the enemy. A revolver would appear to be the most useful weapon; it would serve as a defence and as a means of

destroying horses incapable or useless for further service, which individuals of the section are sent out to collect.

On about the same date, No. 9 MVS had to borrow three rifles in order to capture five Germans discovered eating in a nearby farm. In November 1914 approval was given to issue arms to MVS personnel on the basis of revolvers to sergeants and rifles to everyone else.

The AVC was the equivalent for animals of the RAMC for personnel, tasked with keeping animals fit and evacuating sick and injured animals as quickly as possible. In general terms this involved preventing contagious or infectious diseases, prompt treatment of minor ailments, advising units on animal management and, in many cases, surgery on wounded animals. As with the RAMC for soldiers, the objective of the AVC was also to provide convalescent facilities for animals recovering and to release them for further duty through remount depots. From a strength of 122 officers and 797 other ranks in 1914 responsible for 53,000 animals, the corps at its highest in France (in 1918) was 651 and 15,000 respectively, with an animal strength of over 475,000. In addition, dominion forces provided 114 officers and 1,446 other ranks.

The AVC in France and Belgium was ultimately organized as follows:

• **Staff officers** at formation headquarters down to divisional level. At GHQ a director of veterinary services with an assistant and deputy assistant; a deputy director at each army headquarters and for the northern and southern lines of communication; a deputy director for the cavalry corps; an assistant director at each divisional headquarters and cavalry division; and a deputy assistant director at each infantry division.

• **Veterinary officers** with field formations and lines of communication. These executive officers were allocated to cavalry regiments, artillery brigades, divisional ammunition columns and divisional trains, horse transport depots and remount depots. There were also executive veterinary officers at Marseilles, Le Havre, Rouen, Abbeville, Amiens and Calais. In addition, an AVC sergeant was attached to each infantry brigade, artillery battery and numerous other units.

• **Mobile veterinary sections** consisting of an officer and twenty-four soldiers, including a staff sergeant, shoeing smith, cook, clerk and dresser (reduced to an officer and eighteen soldiers when some personnel were transferred to veterinary evacuation stations after they were instituted). An MVS was allotted to each cavalry brigade and infantry division. Their duty was to collect all sick or

wounded animals within the formation and to clear them from the fighting area as quickly as possible – these duties roughly equate to those of an RAMC CCS.

The MVSs were linked to divisional headquarters by telephone. Duties included the admission of sick animals – except in urgent cases, animals were not admitted unless accompanied by a certificate from a veterinary officer and one day's forage. A system of triage was implemented to decide which animals must be dressed and evacuated and which retained. During periods of stationary warfare bi-weekly evacuation by rail of thirty-two animals, accompanied by a conducting NCO, was normal (it varied with circumstances). During the Somme operations arrangements were made to run special sick-horse trains on certain days. Barge and road transport were also used as available. In 1917 there were 85 MVSs in France (68 British regular and Territorial force, 6 Indian, 5 Australian, 5 Canadian, and 1 New Zealand).

• **Veterinary evacuation stations**, initially entitled 'corps mobile veterinary detachments', first came into being in 1916 when it was found that the MVSs could not keep pace with the number of casualties to be evacuated. Their duties were similar to those of the divisional MVS, but their primary function was to relieve it of entraining and conducting obligations. Their establishment was an officer (from corps HQ), a sergeant, corporal and six privates from the RAVC, and twenty to thirty soldiers from the line of communication for conducting duties. By the end of the war there were sixteen British and two dominion VESs on the Western Front.

• **Veterinary hospitals**. Initially, in 1914, six veterinary hospitals each with a capacity for 250 animals went to France, with two each established at Le Havre, Rouen and Amiens. This number was soon found inadequate and in November of that year approval was given for their expansion to accommodate 1,000 animals each. Serious problems were encountered in finding adequate stabling and hard standings, the provision of which was a task for engineers rather than for AVC personnel. By 1916 and the start of major offensives, this provision was again seriously insufficient and by 1917 there were twenty-one British, two dominion and two Indian hospitals each accommodating up to 2,000 animals on the Western Front.

As far as possible these hospitals on the lines of communication or at bases were organized to work in groups, each comprising a reception hospital, a mange hospital and two general hospitals. A hospital accommodating 2,000 animals was commanded and administered by a lieutenant colonel, a major, four other technical officers (captains or subalterns) and a quartermaster, with two warrant officers and 631 other ranks. The hospital usually operated with eight subdivisions each able to accommodate 250 animals under the command of a captain or subaltern.

• **Reception hospitals** received animals directly evacuated from the front and had admission, retention, transfer and disposal sections. Each animal was 'triaged' in the admission section. This meant observation for forty-eight hours before going to one of the other sections. In the retention section animals were classified as needing surgical, medical or convalescent treatment. The treatment section contained all animals ready for transfer to other hospitals by road or train. In the disposal section were animals considered too old or so disabled as to make them unfit for further military service. Provided their maladies allowed, serious cases were sold to local butchers or contractors for human consumption. Other cases were sold by auction to local farmers.

• **Mange hospitals** Treatment involved clipping, although by 1918 clipping of only the legs and bellies had become standard practice, as many clipped animals had been lost to exposure during winter weather. Animals were dipped three or four times a week, groomed and exercised. When all signs of itchiness had gone and a fresh coat was growing they were allowed to convalesce before discharge.

• **General hospitals** were subdivided for reception, lameness, surgical foot cases, other surgical cases, pneumonia and catarrh, debility, isolation for any contagious disease except mange, and discharge.

• **Convalescent horse depots** Two were established on the Western Front, each capable of accommodating 1,200 animals and with an establishment of three officers and 128 other ranks. The commanding officers of the veterinary hospitals were responsible for ensuring that only animals free from any disease or affliction requiring veterinary treatment were transferred – these depots were entirely for the purpose of providing rest for debilitated and worn-out horses. When fit they were discharged to remount depots.

• **Base depots** Two were established in France for the receipt and issue of veterinary stores to hospitals and other units.

• **Veterinary bacteriological laboratories** The first one in the field was set up at Rouen in 1917 and others followed in all theatres. They all proved useful in investigating the causes of pneumonia, skin parasites and the treatment, management, feeding and well-being of military animals generally.

• **Schools of farriery** The first was set up at Aldershot in June 1915, to be followed by one at Woolwich and another at Romsey. A fourth was established at Abbeville, consisting of an officer and fifty-three other ranks, including twenty-five farrier sergeants. It was initially under canvas but moved to specially constructed premises in January 1917. It was able to train up to 234 British and 26 Indian personnel at a time. At the time of its closure in August 1918, 2,353 British and 181 Indian personnel had been trained.

• **Royal Society for the Prevention of Cruelty to Animals (RSPCA)** When war was declared the RSPCA came forward to offer its resources in personnel and funds to the War Office. Many of its inspectors and other staff joined the AVC and the Army Council gave its approval to the formation, as an auxiliary of the AVC, of the RSPCA Fund for Sick and Wounded Horses, to be used primarily for the provision of stabling for veterinary hospitals in France. It supplied a host of gifts to the BEF, including stabling for 12,500 animals, buildings for 4 veterinary hospitals, 80 horse and 28 motor ambulances, 107 horse tents, 4,000 manure skips, 18 corn- and 3 bone-crushers and a host of other equipment. In addition, the RSPCA financed a fully equipped research laboratory at the Army Veterinary School at Aldershot.

Men and Horses

It is perhaps appropriate to end this section with a brief look at the strong affection that so often developed between a soldier and his horse. As J. M. Brereton wrote in *The Horse in War*, 'the soldier came to regard his horse as an extension of his being.' In the 2012 television documentary *The Real War Horse*, the 105-year-old Bill Cotgrove, who fought in the Royal Field Artillery, spoke of his devotion to his wartime companion:

> I was the one who named my horse Alfie. I remember washing him down when he got muddy. I used to make sure he wouldn't get loose to roll around in the mud . . . I took care of him properly. I looked after a mare too. I always made sure they were fed and watered and had their hay before I packed down for the night.

Another old soldier, Alfred Henn, formerly in the Royal Horse Artillery, kept a photograph of his horse until he died in 2000, aged 103. As his horse had lost an eye he was named Nelson. Henn recalled:

> One night, the horses stopped mid-track. They wouldn't walk a straight line, they

Wounded horses – some of them with bandages – are taken aboard a barge in France for transport to a veterinary hospital.

kept swerving about, and I thought, 'What has happened?' We couldn't see anything in the dark, but we'd just walked into an area where a shell had dropped. There was smoke coming up and the wall was covered in pieces of flesh. It was a terrible sight, I tell you, and the poor horses were more frightened than we were.

Finally, Max Arthur's *Forgotten Voices* quotes a recording made by the Imperial War Museum of Gunner H. Doggett recalling an incident in 1917:

> Our ammunition wagon had only been there a second or two when a shell killed the horse under the driver. We went over to him and tried to unharness the horse and cut the traces away. He [the driver] just kneeled and watched this horse.
>
> A brigadier then came along, a brass hat, and tapped this boy on the shoulder and said, 'Never mind sonny!' The driver looked at him for a second and all of a sudden he said, 'Bloody Germans!' Then he pointed his finger [at the horse] and he stood like a stone as though he was transfixed. The brass hat said to his captain, 'All right, take the boy down the line and see that he has two or three days' rest.' Then he turned to our captain and said, 'If everyone was like that who loved animals we would be all right.'

A tank prepares to descend a ridge at the Tank Driving School, Wailly, where more than 400 tanks were gathered for training in preparation for the Battle of Cambrai, 1917.

Tanks

I consider the tanks a most magnificent weapon, and I cannot understand why we have none of them to speak of. If only we had a large number you would never have advanced as you have done.

German company commander captured in 1918

In October 1918, just prior to Germany's capitulation, the German High Command issued a long explanation to political leaders giving the reasons for impending defeat. An extract reads:

Two factors have had a decisive influence on our decision [that the war was unwinnable], namely, tanks and our reserves.

The enemy has made use of tanks in unexpectedly large numbers. In cases where they have suddenly emerged from smoke clouds our men were completely unnerved . . . Solely owing to the success of the tanks we have suffered enormous losses in prisoners . . .

Field Marshal Haig, in a despatch concerning the final push for victory, wrote:

Since the opening of our offensive on 8th August tanks have been employed on every battlefield, and the importance of the part played by them in breaking up the resistance of the German infantry can scarcely be estimated . . . in 1918 fifty-nine British divisions defeated ninety-nine German divisions, an achievement which would have been impossible without the aid of tanks. Truly the 10,000 fighting men of the Tank Corps were easily worth an extra dozen divisions to the British Army.

Both the German High Command and Haig were referring to the last stages of the war, involving the final breaching of the German front and the subsequent hundred days of Allied advance across ground that had not been pulverized by months of shellfire and bombing. To get to this situation had involved a steep learning curve, including a period when some had condemned tanks as virtually useless and the whole tank-production process in Britain had almost been cancelled. This curve was relatively short as well as steep. It occurred between 15 September 1916, when tanks made a generally disappointing first appearance on the Somme battlefield, and 20 November 1917 when they achieved a spectacular, if temporary, success at Cambrai. It involved a change of attitude by senior commanders, mechanical improvements to the tank itself, and considerably improved tactical handling and cooperation with other arms.

Tanks Built 1916–1918

British

Mark I: 75 male, 75 female

Mark II: 25 male, 25 female

Mark III: 25 male, 25 female

Mark IV: 1,166 – 950 fighting tanks, 205 supply and 11 experimental; the fighting tanks were roughly in the proportion 2 female to 1 male

Mark V: 200 male, 200 female

Mark V*: 579

Medium A (Whippet): 200

Total: 2,595

French

Schneider: 400

St-Chamond: 377

Renault FT17: 3,177

Total: 3,954

German

A7V: 20 – of approximately 100 tanks used by the Germans, the bulk were captured British Mark IVs

Early Tanks and Tactics

The tank was the product of the impasse on the Western Front. Neither vast numbers of infantry, massed artillery fire, gas, nor any combination of these had enabled either side to break through their opponent's deep defensive zones. In particular, the tank was the long-sought answer to the 'dreadful trinity' of trench, wire and machine gun. It became the tool to bring back some sort of mobility, especially cross-country mobility, to the stagnant battlefields of France and Belgium. The Tank Corps Memorial at Poelcapelle, near Ypres, encapsulates their achievement: 'From mud, through blood to the green fields beyond' – words reflected in the colours of the corps flag (green over red over brown).

Before the endless trench barrier existed, wheeled motor vehicles had been fitted with machine guns and sent by the Belgians, French and British to harry the German cavalry screening their great wheel towards Paris. These cars soon became 'armoured cars' when they took to carrying steel plates to improve protection. Their raiding and ambushing inflicted considerable loss to the Germans at little cost to themselves. However, they were road-bound and once the front solidified their usefulness was negated.

In October 1914 Lieutenant Colonel Ernest Dunlop Swinton, who was acting as an official military correspondent with the BEF, suggested that an armoured car mounted on the American Holt Company caterpillar track system and armed with a gun and machine gun would be capable of breaching wire entanglements, spanning trenches and crushing machine guns. The idea of the tank was born, but it was not to appear on a battlefield for some twenty-three months. This was a period of frustration, delays and experimentation, and a strong degree of scepticism by officials at the War Office, who thought the war would be over in another year and thus time and money would be better spent on other, more pressing matters.

Nevertheless, it was Swinton, with the backing of Winston Churchill, then First Lord of the Admiralty, who saw the potential for 'landships' and pressed for their development. A Landship Committee was set up in February 1915 and, directed by Swinton, experimental construction began with some Holt tractors. By September 1915 the first product, nicknamed 'Little Willie', had appeared. This was not entirely satisfactory, so work was started on 'Big Willie', a wooden model of which was inspected at Wembley in late September that year and accepted. Production was given to Messrs Foster of Lincoln, with the first tank being demonstrated to an audience that included Lloyd George and Lord Kitchener on 2 February 1916. It generated considerable excitement and, although Kitchener described it as a 'pretty mechanical toy', forty were ordered by GHQ France, a number soon increased by the War Office to a hundred.

Great secrecy was necessary to prevent the enemy being forewarned of this new weapon. Names for the mechanical monster included 'caterpillar machine gun destroyer', 'landship' and 'land cruiser', and for a while 'water-carrier', to conceal its real purpose. It was quickly realized that the initials of the latter would be ridiculed, so 'tank' was finally agreed. In March 1916 the Heavy Section Machine Gun Corps was established under the command of Lieutenant Colonel Swinton and training began at Elveden, near Thetford, with enthusiastic volunteers from other regiments. In mid-August the first detachment of thirteen left for France and by early the next month fifty had been assembled at Abbeville under command of Colonel H. J. Elles, DSO. The tank was about to undergo its first ordeal by fire.

The Mark I Tank

This was the first tank ever to go into action and, although numerous improvements were eventually made, up to and including the Mark V, the standard shape and design for the hulls remained much the same throughout the war. From the side it was a parallelogram with rounded corners. In the Mark I the two caterpillar or crawler tracks, each of ninety steel plates with lips for gripping the ground, running around rollers, passed completely round the body of the machine. The weight of the tank was carried upon the tracks by means of these rollers, which ran right across the underside. The tracks and rollers needed continual lubrication – the latter by grease guns. This tank had a hydraulic stabilizer or 'tail' at the rear. It consisted of a pair of heavy wheels designed to facilitate steering the tank by pulling on steel ropes – in fact, they were more trouble than they were worth and they made little difference to the steering when shot away. Captain D. G. Browne, MC, who commanded a tank in France, described such an event in his book *The Tank in Action*:

> a projectile burst under the stern and blew the tail away without doing any other damage: amid the general uproar no one was aware of what had happened; and the tank moved forward and was in action for some time before the loss of this absurd appendage was discovered.

In order to turn – or swing – the tank, the tail had to be raised off the ground, an operation that could take anything from five to thirty minutes, and the verdict of most, including Captain Browne, was that they were an 'abomination'. These tails were scrapped by the end of 1916.

The space inside the steel hull between the tracks was extremely cramped, as it had to contain the large engine, other machinery and ammunition, as well as the crew of eight. The Mark I was 26 feet long (32 feet 6 inches with tail), 13 feet 9 inches wide and 8 feet 5 inches high. It had a maximum speed over level ground of about 3.7 m.p.h. – brisk walking speed; however, conditions were seldom ideal and an average speed of 2 m.p.h. was the norm. The armour at the front was 12mm thick, on the sides 10mm and on the roof 6mm, giving it an overall weight of 28 tons for a male and 27 for a female (see details of armament below). It was powered by a 105-h.p. Daimler petrol engine, giving it a theoretical radius of action of 12 miles, or about 6 hours of continuous movement, although tanks often exceeded both by substantial amounts. The engine's greatest asset was its comparative simplicity, although it took up an immense amount of space, leaving only a very narrow gangway on either side between the engine and the sponson (see below). In the first tanks the whole of the petrol supply was carried inside, and in a vulnerable position, with a tank on either side of the front cab, which meant a direct hit by a shell would almost certainly condemn the commander and driver to a horrific death. As the petrol was fed to the carburettor by gravity, if a tank became ditched nose first in a deep crater petrol supply was cut off and the crew had to resort to the dangerous business of feeding the carburettor by hand.

This tank was able to cross trenches up to 11 feet 6 inches wide and surmount a vertical obstacle 5 feet high. It could crawl up a slope of 1 in 1.2 on firm, dry ground; on wet ground 1 in 2.5; and on very wet ground 1 in 4. It could negotiate a sheer drop of 12 to 15 feet, depending on the skill of the driver – provided it was not waterlogged and full of mud. Shell craters presented no problem. It could knock down trees with diameters of 20 inches, although if the roots came up underneath the tank it could be 'bellied' – its tracks could not grip the ground. The tank could not cross marshy ground or streams with swampy banks. It could, however, negotiate water up to 18 inches deep if the bottom was firm. It was reluctant to travel on hard cobbled roads, as they tended to break the track plates, and narrow sunken roads were avoided if possible. In the early model there was no silencer, so the noise and sparks from the exhaust pipe were a great giveaway even at comparatively long distances. Crews attempted to devise makeshift silencers out of oil drums, or used wet sacks to damp out the sparks.

The armoured body protected the crew from rifle and machine-gun bullets and shrapnel bursts, but bullet splash – the flaking off of tiny slivers of hot metal from the inside of the tank when the bullet struck, or bullets entering between the chinks of the armour plate fittings – caused the crew to wear protective metal 'splash' masks with a chainmail apron protecting face and neck. The mild steel-plate armour of these early tanks was vulnerable to armour-piercing bullets – something that the Germans were quick to discover and they supplied their units accordingly.

Another problem with the Mark I male was the two heavy sponsons (a form of projecting gun casemate borrowed from the navy), which were bolted on to the side of the tank and had to be removed for entraining (as today, no tank was expected to move long distances under its own power), then refitted after detraining. This was a laborious and lengthy process involving unbolting the sponsons and hoisting them with a girder and tackle on to a rail trolley.

Visibility was extremely limited when the commander's and driver's hatches were closed, as they were forced to use several double glass prisms set into the armour, making target indication and fire control problematic (and they splintered badly if hit). In smoke or darkness the tank was virtually blind, which often meant an officer had to walk in front at enormous risk to act as a guide – Captain Clement Robertson won a posthumous Victoria Cross for doing just that (see box overleaf). The means of entering and exiting were also unsatisfactory. The doors in the sponsons, particularly in the female tank, were only about 2 feet high, necessitating crawling in head first or exiting feet first, which meant a quick escape was frequently impossible.

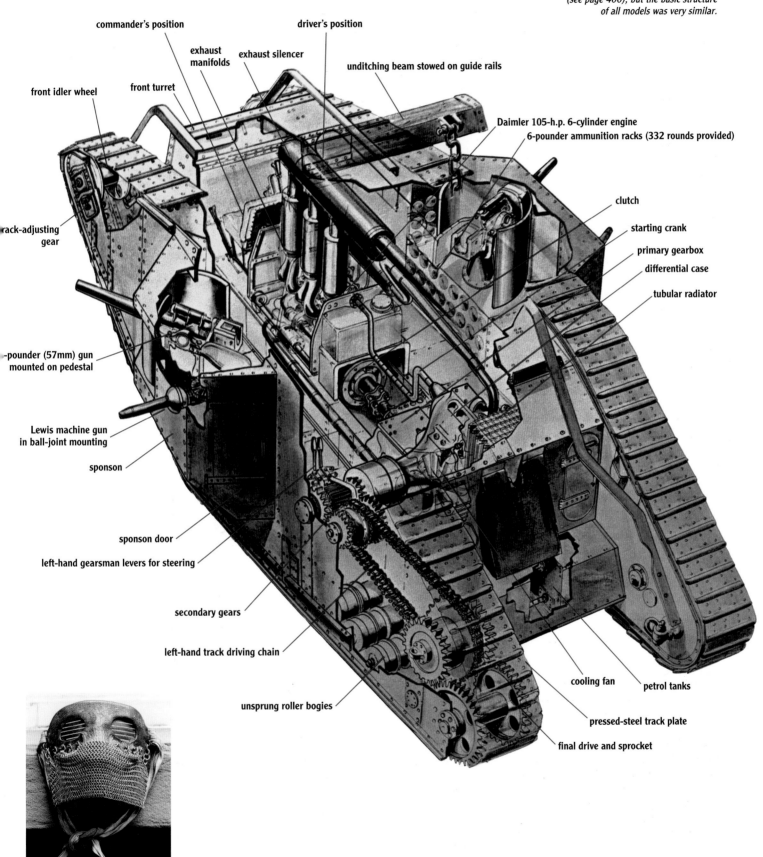

This illustration shows the layout of a World War I tank. The particular features are those of a male Mark IV (see page 400), but the basic structure of all models was very similar.

commander's position

driver's position

exhaust manifolds

exhaust silencer

unditching beam stowed on guide rails

front idler wheel

front turret

Daimler 105-h.p. 6-cylinder engine

6-pounder ammunition racks (332 rounds provided)

track-adjusting gear

clutch

starting crank

primary gearbox

differential case

tubular radiator

-pounder (57mm) gun mounted on pedestal

Lewis machine gun in ball-joint mounting

sponson

sponson door

left-hand gearsman levers for steering

secondary gears

left-hand track driving chain

unsprung roller bogies

cooling fan

petrol tanks

pressed-steel track plate

final drive and sprocket

A splinter-proof face mask designed to be worn by the crews of British Mark IV tanks.

Captain Clement Robertson, VC

In preparation for an attack on Reutel, Ypres, on 4 October 1917 (see Map 71), Captain Robertson, assisted by a Private Allen, his batman (servant) who had volunteered to assist, spent three days and nights planning, reconnoitring and taping the route forward for his section of four tanks. The problem was the dreadful state of the ground, as damage to nearby streams had caused serious flooding and rendered much of the ground boggy and unsuitable for tanks.

On 1 October Allen was badly shaken by an exploding shell but continued to assist his officer. Not until 9.30 p.m. on 3 October was the route finally taped, by which time both men were exhausted through lack of sleep. Nevertheless, Captain Robertson, determined that all his tanks would get into action, elected to lead them forward on foot, as despite the tape there was every chance of them losing their way in the dark.

To attack Reutel involved crossing the Reutelbeek stream by a bridge, which was under direct enemy fire but, unlike the surrounding countryside, had remained unscathed by the previous intense bombardments. Robertson, accompanied by Allen, walked forward ahead of the tanks and guided them to their starting point by 3:00 a.m. on 4 October. After only two hours' rest he set off again to walk his tanks into battle. Soon they came under heavy fire from guns, machine guns and rifles, but they continued to walk forward undeterred. On arrival at the bridge Captain Robertson calmly walked across under a hail of fire and signalled his tanks forward as though he were a traffic policeman. Once across, the tanks were close to their objective and Robertson could now have sought shelter in a tank. He did no such thing, but continued to walk ahead, to the amazement of his crew. Just as he reached a position where the objective was unmistakable he was hit in the head by a bullet and fell forward, dead before he hit the ground. Allen, on seeing his captain fall, went to his side and removed all maps and papers from his officer's pockets before he sought shelter in a tank.

Captain Robertson's sacrifice had enabled the tanks and supporting infantry to get forward and was the primary reason for the success of this attack. He was awarded a posthumous Victoria Cross and Allen the Distinguished Conduct Medal (DCM), but regrettably he too was not to survive the war.

A major problem that affected all tanks was the lack of any ability to communicate effectively with other tanks (apart from walking over to speak) or with higher command other than by flag or pigeon (wireless sets were installed in a few later models but only for communication with higher headquarters or aircraft). Once launched into battle each tank operated very much as an individual machine and on the initiative of its commander. Each was given a detailed briefing as to routes, timings, enemy positions, obstacles and objectives (and later rehearsals with the infantry) before zero hour. However, although commanders carried out such a reconnaissance whenever possible, once a tank rolled forward it was very much on its own, with little prospect of further instructions or guidance from a higher commander.

The armament carried decided whether the tank was a Mark I male or Mark I female. The former was armed with two Hotchkiss 6-pounder, quick-firing, shortened naval guns on recoil mountings behind a revolving shield, and four Hotchkiss machine guns (one spare); the latter with five Vickers, one spare and one Hotchkiss (for the commander). The 6-pounder could be loaded and fired by one man if necessary. It fired a percussion shell or case-shot out to 2,600 yards, although actual firing was normally at much closer range. A normal load of ammunition for the male was 200 6-pounder and 10,000 machine-gun rounds, and for the female 24,000 machine-gun rounds, although both these numbers were sometimes exceeded. The 6-pounders and machine guns (except the commander's) were contained in the sponsons on either side of the tank. In the male the sponsons projected further out than those on the female, as they had to contain the 6-pounders and these needed to be able to fire to the front as well as to the side (they had an arc of 120 degrees). The machine guns in the male were positioned one on each side in the sponson and one operated by the commander at the front; the female had two in each sponson and one at the front. A manhole in the roof had small loopholes through which revolvers could be fired – revolvers being the personal weapons of the crew.

A crew consisted of an officer and eight other ranks – four primarily involved in driving, steering and gear changes, and four in firing the guns. All wore overalls, had anti-splash masks and were armed with revolvers. The officer, as commander, sat at the front on a slightly raised seat on the left of the driver. He gave orders as necessary for the direction of the tank, manipulated the handbreaks for small adjustments of steering in either direction, and fired the forward machine gun, which was mounted between the commander and driver. The latter, in the right-hand seat, drove the machine and controlled the gear changes. Both of them had rectangular windows that could be closed by a steel flap from the inside.

To drive a tank well required not only a skilful driver but considerable teamwork from three other crew members. The machine had forward speeds ranging from ¾ m.p.h. in bottom gear to 4 m.p.h. in top gear, and reverse. However, the driver himself could change only from first to second. To go faster he required the assistance of the two gearsmen sitting on either side at the rear of the tank. Because of the noise, he had to bang on the engine cover with his right hand to get their attention, then, with the gearsmen alerted, he raised one or two fingers to indicate the speed he wanted. The gearsmen operated the gearlevers accordingly while the driver operated the clutch. All this required good coordination and was often the cause of much grinding of gears and cursing by those involved. In his book *The Tank in Action* Captain D. G. Browne, MC, states, 'Two men were required to work these gears; and no member of any tank crew who took a Mark I or Mark IV into action is ever likely to forget the sweat and tears and blasphemy expended over this atrocious system.'

To make a full turn, called 'swinging', the tank was stopped and the driver locked the differential and raised a closed fist to signal, say, to the right-hand gearsman to put his gears in neutral and thus disconnect the right-hand track. The commander then applied the right-hand break and, with that track immobilized, the tank swung round to the right. It was a clumsy and often frustrating process, and one to be avoided in the heat of battle if possible. It could be performed on the move, but this was even more fraught with difficulties and required an exceptionally experienced driver.

The 6-pounder gunner in the sponson knelt on the floor to peer through a telescopic sight searching for a target. When fired, the noise was shattering, and with both guns and machine guns firing the din was indescribable. The empty shell cases were thrown outside through a small opening in the floor. The gunner's No. 2 reloaded, and either he or the gearsman also fired the machine gun when suitable targets appeared.

With poor ventilation, the crew of all tanks suffered to some extent from the heat, which could reach 50°C, and from noise and carbon-monoxide fumes, quite apart from any injuries inflicted by the splash of bullets on the sides. With time, many crew members became somewhat 'acclimatized' to the conditions, but despite the rotary fan situated in the rear, virtually all suffered at some time from severe headaches, giddiness, vomiting, mental confusion or even unconsciousness. Exhaustion, after hours operating in the confined space and poisoned air, affected all crews in action – it was not unknown for a man to have convulsions and collapse after many hours in these conditions. Pigeons, taken into action in baskets which, for lack of space, were invariably placed on top of the engine, sometimes became decidedly groggy.

Early Organization and Tactics

In August 1916 GHQ issued notes on tank organization and equipment, which are incorporated in the diagram below.

The first tanks to leave England were half of C Company on 13 August 1916, then the remainder on the 22nd, followed by D and finally A and B. E and F remained at Thetford and formed the nucleus of the tank battalions that were created when expansion was authorized later that year. Although nominally under the Machine Gun Corps, in practice these four companies were self-contained and unattached when they assembled in great secrecy at Yvrench, near Abbeville, for intensive train-

ing. Extra training was an urgent priority, as many drivers had spent no more than an hour or two in a tank before arriving in France. One tank commander later wrote:

> I and my crew did not have a tank of our own the whole time we were in England . . . ours went wrong the day it arrived. We had no reconnaissance or map reading . . . no practices or lessons on the compass . . . we had no signalling . . . and no practice in considering orders. We had no knowledge of where to look for information that would be necessary for us as tank commanders, nor did we know what information we should be likely to require.

Because of the overriding need to prevent their presence being known to the Germans, no attempt was made to discuss or practice

Mark I Tank Organization, August 1916

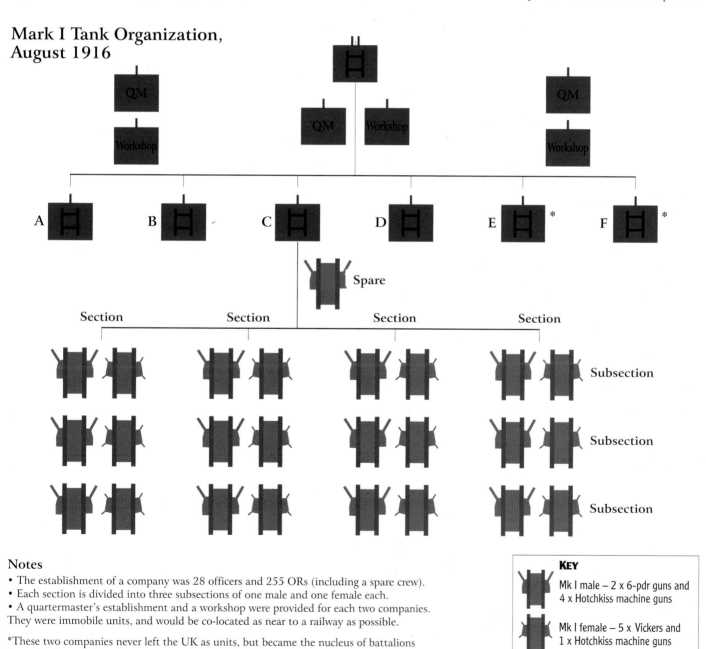

Notes
• The establishment of a company was 28 officers and 255 ORs (including a spare crew).
• Each section is divided into three subsections of one male and one female each.
• A quartermaster's establishment and a workshop were provided for each two companies. They were immobile units, and would be co-located as near to a railway as possible.

*These two companies never left the UK as units, but became the nucleus of battalions formed at home when the expansion of the corps was authorized later that year.

KEY

Mk I male – 2 x 6-pdr guns and 4 x Hotchkiss machine guns

Mk I female – 5 x Vickers and 1 x Hotchkiss machine guns

methods of cooperation or tactics with the infantry units they were to support. Captain Browne, who commanded a tank from May 1917 onwards, was particularly scathing of this lack of liaison in the field:

> a fuller comprehension by other arms, a more liberal interchange of views, and especially some tuition of the infantry who were to cooperate in action, might have saved much disappointment and many lives. Nothing of the kind was attempted; and the companies had to think out and master other people's problems in addition to their own in the field . . . Not only was experience of this new warfare yet to [be gained], but many of the officers and a large proportion of the men actually were in France for the first time and knew nothing of normal battle conditions.

The only guidance on tactical principles available to GHQ was Lieutenant Colonel Swinton's *Notes on the Employment of Tanks*, written and approved in February 1916, the main points of which were:

• The key to success would be achieving surprise, so the tanks should not be used in 'driblets' and secrecy was essential.

• Initial assembly positions should be about 2 miles behind the British line with routes forward carefully reconnoitred. The next move should be at night to bring the tanks forward to their start point in rear of the front trenches, with the attack starting just before dawn.

• Tanks should advance about 100 yards apart either in what was in effect an extended line or initially in groups before spreading out to work laterally in breaching wire and locating and destroying machine guns.

• Tanks should precede the infantry and draw rifle and machine-gun fire. The following infantry should reach the enemy front trench as the tanks were climbing the parapet to enfilade the line. Once the infantry were secure, the tanks should continue, preferably following communication trenches to the next objective, with fresh infantry following close behind.

• The whole infantry tank attack should move quickly to keep ahead of the German barrage. As tanks would be particularly vulnerable to artillery fire, counter-battery fire would be of paramount importance. Every possible means was to be used to neutralize or destroy enemy guns, including gas shells and bombing by aircraft.

• Using these methods it was thought feasible for the attackers to break through the German defensive zone within a day, but that tanks were an auxiliary to the infantry and should be under overall infantry command during an operation.

Tanks at Flers-Courcelette

The battle of the Somme had begun on 1 July, but progress had been painfully slow, expensive in manpower and by mid-September the ground had been pulverized by artillery fire from both sides, which created countless thousands of craters and much loose soil. On the plus side, the weather during the two weeks prior to 15 September had been mostly fine, so the 'going' for tanks was not as treacherous as it might have been. The main British attack supported by the tanks would be made by the three corps of the Fourth Army under General Rawlinson, and the Canadian Corps of General Gough's Reserve Army on the left, with the French Second Corps of their Sixth Army advancing on the British right. The British intention was to break through the German line with the Fourth Army, seizing Morval, Les Boeufs, Gueudecourt and Flers, while the Reserve Army took Martinpuich and Courcelette. The hoped-for resultant gap would be exploited by the Cavalry Corps. Haig, who was a strong supporter of the new weapon, had GHQ call for vigorous and bold action in a message that included:

> On the front of the attack, besides a superiority of at least four to one in infantry, we have a more numerous artillery, practical superiority in the air and a large mass of cavalry immediately available to exploit to the full a successful assault by the other arms.
>
> In addition we have a new weapon of war that may well produce great moral and material effects.

The forty-eight available tanks were allocated as follows:

Fourth Army
XIV Corps (on the right):
C Company, less one section – 16
    56th Division – 3
    6th Division – 3
    Guards Division – 10
(one to assist 14th Division on its left)
XV Corps (in the centre):
D Company, less one section – 17
    14th Division – 3
    41st Division – 10
    New Zealand Division – 4
III Corps (on the left):
one section D Company – 8
    47th Division – 4
    50th Division – 2
    15th Division – 2
Reserve Army: one section C Company – 7
    2nd Canadian Division – 6
    (the seventh in reserve)

Eight of the nine attacking infantry divisions had at least one subsection of tanks

each, while two (Guards and 41st) had five each. Because of the shortage of numbers, a frontage of over 13,000 yards and the need for all attacking divisions to have tank support in this first tank assault, the machines were allocated in 'penny packets', but with more of a concentration in the centre for the attack on Flers. The following extracts from instructions relating to the tanks of the 41st Division (given mainly for the benefit of the infantry) are taken from Operation Order No. 42, dated 13 September, followed by orders specific to the tanks that had been issued by that division the previous day.

TANKS

Ten tanks Heavy Section M.G. Corps will operate in the attack and will be in position in rear of our front line trenches by 4 a.m. 15th instant.

Those tanks will act in accordance with the special orders issued to them and will usually precede the Infantry. Their role is to destroy hostile machine guns and Strong Points and clear the way for the Infantry.

The Infantry must follow behind the tanks and should any strong point succeed in holding up the Infantry they will call a tank to assist them. The signal will be the signal for 'Enemy in sight' with the rifle.

An escort of 1 N.C.O. and 10 men will be detailed to remain with each tank, and should the tanks get in rear of the Infantry or for any reason be obliged to withdraw across ground over which the Infantry has passed, the escort will remove any wounded which happen to be in the path of the tank.

The escort will also protect the tank from close assault by the hostile Infantry, or from attack by explosive charges.

The above escorts will not join the tanks until after they reach the first objective (green line). Should the tanks become out of action . . . the Infantry are on no account to wait for them . . .

The following signals will be used from tanks to Infantry and Aircraft:

Flag Signals
Red Flag = Out of action
Green Flag = Am on objective
Other flags are inter-tank signals

Lamp Signals
Series of T's = Out of action
Series of H's = Am on objective

These were the first rudimentary instructions, received by the infantry only hours before the attack, on how to work with tanks. Extracts of orders given to the tanks are as follows:

MOVEMENT TO POSITIONS OF DEPLOYMENT

1. . . .

2. Ten tanks have been allotted to the 41st Division, and will be distributed for tactical purposes, as follows:

Group C   1 Tank.
Groups D, E & F   3 Tanks each.

3. 123rd Inf. Bde. will provide a party of guides for conducting the Tanks to their positions of assembly and deployment, and for reconnoitring and marking out routes to same . . .

4. On the night of 13th/14th Sept. the Tanks will move into position of assembly in the GREEN DUMP VALLEY . . . Arrangements for placing of tanks into position and camouflaging them against aerial observation will be made by C.R.E. 41st Division.

5. An advanced dump of petrol, ammunition etc., for the use of tanks will also be established in the GREEN DUMP VALLEY . . .

6. In the early morning, 14th inst., guides and tank Officers will reconnoitre the routes to be taken to the positions of deployment . . . Guides will study the ground between these points . . . the route detailed will be marked by notice boards and tape. Compass bearings will be taken . . .

IN OFFENSIVE

1. Ten Tanks have been allotted to 41st Division. These will be divided into Groups as follows:

Group C – 1 tank [male]
Group D – 3 Tanks [2 female, 1 male]
Group E – 3 Tanks [2 female, 1 male]
Group F – 3 Tanks [1 female, 2 male]

2. ...

3. ...

4. Gaps 100 yards wide will be left in the Creeping Barrage for the passage of Tanks. Stationary barrages will lift off their objectives before the Tanks arrive.

5. The objectives, routes and responsibility for dealing with Strong Points encountered by each group of tanks will be as follows: . . .

There followed detailed instructions on how the tanks would fight their way forward through to the fourth objective just north of Gueudecourt. These orders were extraordinarily precise regarding timings, routes and action on objectives, presumably because it was realized that communication between individual tanks and their section commanders would be virtually impossible once battle was joined.

The hoped-for breakthrough did not take place. Once again the cavalry trooped back to their lines unused and the tanks' performance had been mostly, but not entirely, disappointing. Of the forty-eight allotted, only thirty-one made it to their start points. The tanks had therefore lost almost a third of their strength due to mechanical breakdowns or ditching before any of them saw action. Of the thirty-one that arrived at their start points, fifteen returned safely, although a number were damaged. The statistics of the day show that of the forty-eight allocated, eight failed for mechanical reasons, fourteen were ditched or 'bellied' and eleven were destroyed by shellfire, some of them catching fire. Losses by shellfire amounted to exactly a third of overall losses. Of those that clashed with the enemy, nine had pushed ahead of the infantry as planned and caused considerable damage, and the remaining nine, although they never caught up the infantry, did good work crushing wire, destroying machine-gun posts and clearing German pockets that were still holding out. Casualties to tank personnel were comparatively insignificant. Overall, the tanks working with the Reserve Army and the III and XIV Corps failed to achieve much, while those with XV Corps secured better results as they were instrumental in the taking of Flers – a solitary tank driving up the main street being the highlight. At the same time a tank was driving up both the eastern and western sides of the village.

Overall, the first appearance of the new wonder-weapon did not produce impressive statistics, but it was by no means a failure (brief details of individual tank actions are described in the notes to Map 70). Haig, however, was happy with their performance and saw not just their weaknesses, but also their potential. He sent his deputy chief of staff to London to press for another 1,000 – a mission that was to produce only a fraction of this number.

After-action critique

The tank action at Flers inevitably exposed the weaknesses and strengths of this novel machine. The main ones are summarized under the headings of structural/mechanical, personnel and tactical/administrative.

Structural/mechanical

• The concept of the machine was basically sound and the structure of the Mark I tank, although needing technical alterations and improvements, remained the basis of tank design for the rest of the war. The Mark II and III tanks incorporated some of the necessary improvements, but very few were produced as they were quickly superseded by the Mark IV and then the Mark V (see pages 400 and 408). These were the versions that saw, respectively, the successes at Cambrai in late 1917 and in the more mobile battles from August 1918.

It was confirmed that the enemy of the tank was a direct hit from a high-explosive shell. Captain Frank Mitchell, MC, described such an event in the attack on Bullecourt in April 1917 (a bad day for tanks) when a Mark II tank (little different from a Mark I) was hit:

> a shell hit the petrol tank, which in these tanks (Mark II) were situated forward, near the driver and the officer. The tank immediately burst into flames. The officer and driver, caught like rats in a trap, were burnt alive. Only a sergeant and two men succeeded in escaping from that raging inferno.

• The mild steel plates of the armour were only just bulletproof and certainly did not stop armour-piercing bullets.

• The number of mechanical breakdowns was excessive. That 34 per cent of the tanks allotted to the attack never reached their start points (not all due to mechanical problems), and that another nine broke down when they advanced, dramatically weakened the attack before it had properly started. Most of these breakdowns were due to design faults and to the unexpected wear and tear on track rollers and sprockets outstripping the supply of spare parts.

• Tanks had ditched far too easily. Once its tracks were unable to grip the ground, for whatever reason, a tank had no means of righting itself and was out of the battle – unless able to give supporting fire from a possibly vulnerable, stationary position (for details of ditching and unditching, see box, page 392).

• The 'tail' was vulnerable and unnecessary.

• The lack of communications with other tanks and with higher headquarters other than by flag or pigeon was a serious, and never entirely solved, drawback once an attack was under way.

Personnel

• Apart from enemy action, crews were always subjected to extremely debilitating conditions inside a tank. For hours they endured deafening noise, petrol fumes, heat, and inhaled carbon monoxide, with the consequences of blinding headaches and nausea as a minimum. The nervous strain also took its toll. According to a letter to *The Times* dated 16 September 1976 by the late Sir Basil Henriques, who commanded a tank in September 1916, these conditions could have dire consequences for some crew members as described on page 392.

Notes for Map 70

The map shows that 48 tanks (41 with the Fourth Army and 7 with the Reserve Army; numbers in parenthesis on map) were earmarked to make the first tank attack in the history of warfare. Of these, 31 went into action (numbers not in parenthesis). It also depicts the approx. route of each tank and whether it was disabled in some way or returned. Individual performances were as follows.

Fourth Army

XIV Corps

56th Division Three tanks allotted. Right-hand tank attacked Loop Trench but was disabled by a shell, although its machine guns kept German bombers away for five hours. Eventually destroyed by fire and abandoned by the crew. Of the two tanks on the left, one split a track coming forward and did not advance; the other advanced 20 minutes before the infantry to the northern end of Bouleux Wood, cruising around before becoming ditched in front of an enemy trench. Attacked by bombers and abandoned after all crew hit.

6th Division Three tanks allotted to attack the Quadrilateral. Only one reached the start point (one broke its tail, the other had engine trouble); it advanced ahead of the infantry along the railway track at about 5:50 a.m. but possibly fired on waiting British troops by mistake. It continued west of the target before returning low on fuel. Crew wounded by 'splash' and armour-piercing bullets.

Guards Division Ten tanks allotted. Of the right subsection (first objective Straight Trench), one broke its tail and could not start; the other two headed east to Straight Trench, making good use of the 6-pdrs and machine guns. Both returned having knocked out several machine guns. In the centre subsection, none reached the start point (one detained in Trones Wood with mechanical problems, but sent to assist the Guards in a later attack; the other two became stuck in shell craters). Of the left subsection, one (tasked with assisting XV Corps) was halted by track problems in Ginchy, another was stuck in Trones Wood with mechanical difficulties. The final two started late. One was ditched and the other returned low on fuel. Both claimed to have knocked out several machine-gun posts and aided the capture of prisoners.

XV Corps

14th Division Four tanks allotted. One (Capt. H. W. Mortimore) began its advance at 5:15 a.m. (so becoming the first tank in history to enter battle), 15 minutes ahead of the infantry. It advanced just north of Ale Alley, giving great assistance to the infantry before being disabled, probably by a British shell hitting its steering gear. Of the left-hand subsection of three, one was ditched in Delville Wood on its way to the start point. Another, advancing a little ahead of the infantry at 6:20 a.m., was damaged beyond repair by shellfire at Tea Support Trench. D5 (2nd Lt A. Blowers) broke its tail wheel in a shell hole but was rescued by another tank and arrived late at the start point with restricted steering. Despite this, the tank advanced almost 3,000 yards up Gas Alley and along Watling Street, well ahead of most of the infantry. Turning back, he was knocked out by a shell, probably from a German battery in Bull's Road, but his action had allowed the infantry to advance to a considerable depth.

41st Division 10 tanks allotted for the important and difficult task of taking Flers. It was planned to divide them into four groups and attack up both eastern and western sides as well as through the village. The groups were to assemble at the northern end of Longueval and the north-western corner of Delville Wood. In the event, only five got into action. The other five were either ditched before reaching their start point or within a few yards of starting. D6 (2nd Lt R. C. Legge), a male tank, was able to penetrate as far north as Bull's Road, where it engaged a German gun battery before being hit by shells and catching fire. Legge and three men were killed, one was captured and three escaped. D15 (Lt J. L. Bagshaw), a female, reached the Tea Support Trench then was disabled by shellfire that wounded Bagshaw and the driver. As the crew scrambled out, one was killed and the rest wounded by firing from Switch Trench. D17 (Lt S. H. Hastie), a male, achieved lasting fame by driving up the main street of Flers, reportedly followed closely by cheering British infantry – a rather exaggerated account from an aircraft released to the press. In fact, the infantry were few and some way behind. Hastie himself reported that when in the middle of the village he 'could see no signs of the British Army coming up behind me so I slewed the tank round and made my way back to Flers Trench'. Here the engine of his damaged tank packed up. D16 (Lt A. E. Arnold) and D18 (2nd Lt L. C. Bond), both female, succeeded in penetrating up the west side of Flers, giving valuable support to infantry, and returned relatively unscathed. At the end of the day Flers was in British hands.

New Zealand Division All four tanks allotted reached their start point just north of Longueval. D8 (Lt H. G. F. Bown), a male, reached his third objective, Flers Support; although the tank was damaged it continued to fight and eventually was able to withdraw. Another tank (D11) was able to reach the northern end of Flers, where it remained overnight to assist the New Zealanders in defending the village; it would advance again the next day. One tank was set on fire by shells having got only as far as the Switch Line, while the fourth progressed up Fish Alley before also being set on fire by shelling. The crew remained to fight on with the infantry.

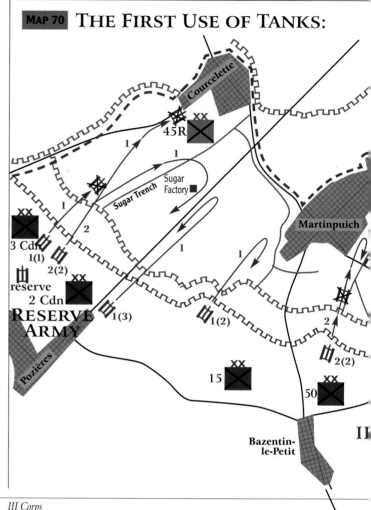

MAP 70 THE FIRST USE OF TANKS:

III Corps

47th Division Four tanks allotted with the unenviable task of helping the infantry take High Wood – a really tough nut to crack, with an infamous reputation for the hellishness of the struggle for its possession. It had been reduced to a matchwood tangle of stumps and branches, pitted with thousands of shell craters in which were numerous German positions, including the inevitable machine-gun posts. It was a nightmare for tanks, with the likelihood of being 'bellied' or ditched as well as the crew being flung around like rag dolls inside. Tank commanders advised strongly against their use but were overruled. However, the tank attack was not a complete failure. One was ditched crossing the British trench, another at the edge of the wood. One was forced out on the eastern edge and mistakenly fired on the 6th (City of London) Rifles before becoming ditched in a British trench and requiring 14 hours of labour to recover. The fourth got through the German lines in the wood – at one stage Germans clambered on the roof, firing through loopholes. It managed to clear the wood before halting with engine trouble, but was set on fire by shelling. The crew scrambled out, taking shelter in a German trench where about 75 enemy surrendered. Lt W. H. Sampson, its commander, received the MC.

50th Division Two tanks allotted, both arriving at their start point. Having crossed the German first line, one was disabled by shells; the crew abandoned it but fought on with the infantry. The second caused much loss to the enemy and advanced up the east side of Martinpuich before turning back short of petrol. It returned safely.

15th Division Two tanks allotted. One was disabled with a broken track before reaching the start point; the other played a limited role, although it did destroy two machine-gun posts before lack of fuel forced a return.

Reserve Army

2nd Canadian Division Six tanks allotted (another held in reserve), split into three groups. Two did not make it to their start point. One ditched in a shell hole with damaged steering; the other came forward but developed track problems and was hit by a shell. One gave effective support to the infantry assault on the sugar factory before retiring, damaged but safe. Another barely moved forward at about 10 yards a minute before being 'bellied' – its tracks turned, but there was no movement. The fifth was also prominent in the capture of the sugar factory, having advanced up the road from Pozières; it later returned with a captured German colonel. The sixth reached the outskirts of Courcelette, having been dug out once en route only to be ditched again, with the crew spending the rest of the day unsuccessfully trying to free it.

ATTLE OF FLERS-COURCELETTE (SOMME), 15 SEPTEMBER 1916

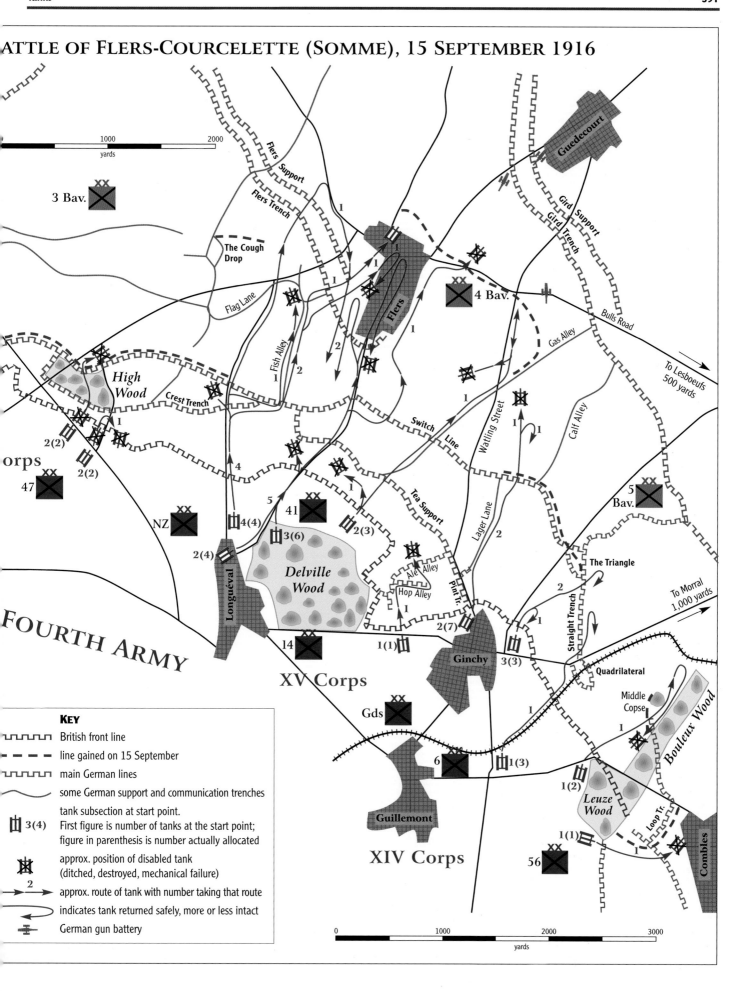

3 Bav.

Guedecourt

Flers Support

Flers Trench

The Cough Drop

Gird Support

Gird Trench

Flag Lane

Flers

4 Bav.

Bulls Road

To Lesboeufs 500 yards

Gas Alley

Fish Alley

High Wood

Crest Trench

Switch Line

Watling Street

Calf Alley

2(2)

2(2)

Lager Lane

5 Bav.

orps

47

NZ

4(4)

2(4)

41

5

3(6)

2(3)

Delville Wood

Ale Alley

Hop Alley

Tea Support

Pint Tr.

The Triangle

Straight Trench

To Morral 1,000 yards

Longuéval

14

2(7)

1(1)

Ginchy

3(3)

Quadrilateral

Middle Copse

Bouleux Wood

FOURTH ARMY

XV Corps

Gds

6

1(3)

1(2)

Leuze Wood

Loop Tr.

Combles

Guillemont

XIV Corps

56

1(1)

KEY

- ⊓⊔⊓⊔ British front line
- – – – line gained on 15 September
- ⊓⊔⊓⊔ main German lines
- ∿∿∿ some German support and communication trenches
- 🁢 3(4)   tank subsection at start point.
  First figure is number of tanks at the start point; figure in parenthesis is number actually allocated
- ✠ approx. position of disabled tank (ditched, destroyed, mechanical failure)
- →² approx. route of tank with number taking that route
- ↪ indicates tank returned safely, more or less intact
- ⊢✠⊣ German gun battery

Ditching

Ditching occurs when a tank gets itself into a position with its tail down in a wide and very deep trench, so that, although the tracks grip the surface, the engine power is insufficient to pull it out. Alternatively, the belly, with a dead weight of nearly 30 tons on top of it, is resting on comparatively hard ground, while the tracks, on softer ground, churn round without gripping at all.

A British tank stuck in a trench near Ribécourt, Battle of Cambrai, November 1917 – a problem solved by the use of fascines.

The need was for something that would give the tracks a more secure grip or leverage. After the experiences on the Somme, two separate devices were adopted. First, for use on soft ground, iron shoes or 'spuds' were clamped at intervals along the tracks. Second, each tank carried a pair of what were known as 'torpedo-booms' – cigar-shaped bars of wood and iron about 6 feet long to be clamped to each track by chains when it became ditched. As the tracks revolved, these booms would be pulled round underneath the tank until they jammed in the ground, when, the tracks being stopped, the tank would be able to climb out over them in the normal way. This was the theory. In practice, although these booms were useful on numerous occasions, they were often found to be too weak and too small. In soft ground

they could be dragged round and up to the surface again, or in hard ground the chains sometimes broke under the strain.

The above relates to the Mark I tank, but for the Mark IV a much improved version of the boom was devised. Instead of the two booms each tank was fitted with a single squared boom about 12 feet long and strengthened with steel; its only drawback was its weight of 9 cwt, making it extremely difficult to manhandle. A pair of longitudinal rails kept it clear of obstructions on the roof and it was secured at right angles across these. When required for unditching, it was attached to the track plates on either side by chains or clamps. Two men sheltering behind the tank could effect this attachment. Then the heavy boom was carried forward as the tracks revolved and was carried under the tank. Its length and stiff resistance transversely to the direction of the tracks' movement enabled the machine to climb out of almost any position. Only if the heavy Mark IV was very badly ditched did the weight of the boom and the spuds sometimes mean the engine was not powerful enough for this device to succeed.

The nervous strain in this first battle of tanks for officers and crew alike was ghastly. Of my company, one officer went mad and shot his engine to make it go faster; another shot himself because he thought he had failed to do as well as he ought; two others had what I suppose could be called a nervous breakdown.

• Crews had not had sufficient training in either driving or the use of the weapons. Limited visibility, coupled with the constant lurching of the tank, made target acquisition problematic and hitting a target at anything other than close range extraordinarily difficult unless stationary. Similar problems confronted tank commanders in navigating along a particular route, avoiding major obstacles or ground that could ditch the tank, and locating an objective. Once in action they could see so little, and maps were almost useless in a devastated landscape, so each officer had to memorize beforehand the look of almost every tree-stump, crater or pile of rubble. A night attack was an impossibility.

• Tanks drew away much of the fire from the infantry and had as great an encouraging effect on our own troops as they had a demoralizing one on the enemy (see German reaction to tanks, page 412).

Tactical/administrative

• On 15 September tanks had been used in driblets with from two to five subsections attached to each infantry division. This was the consequence of the new weapon being seen in an infantry support role under infantry command, and only forty-eight being available to spread around the eleven attacking divisions. This, coupled with the numbers that never participated at all, substantially diluted the tank's physical impact and its effect on morale. There has been much criticism of the High Command for frittering away the tank asset in penny packets when attacks en masse were the most likely way to achieve a breakthrough. The difficulty, often ignored by critics, was that the thousand tanks wanted by Haig never materialized – indeed, by March 1917 only sixty usable tanks were available for the Battle of Arras.

• The overriding need for careful and thorough reconnaissance by tank commanders, not only of the route forward from assembly area to start point but also from start point onwards. Sufficient time had to be allowed in planning for this and for the marking of the routes with tape and lamps in planning – even then it was usually necessary for an officer to guide the machine forward on foot to the start point.

• The administrative back-up for tanks in terms of fuel, ammunition, recovery and repair was extensive and essential. It was realized that tanks needed their own supply system and workshops.

Tanks at Arras

Sixty Mark I and II tanks were involved in the First Battle of the Scarpe, which began after a four-day artillery bombardment on 9 April as part of the Arras offensive. Of these sixty, eight were allotted to the First Army, forty to the Third and twelve to the Fifth, so they were divided over a 25-mile front. On the night before the attack the bitter wind picked up to gale force and it poured with rain that turned to snow, making the ground waterlogged. It was under these evil conditions in the pitch black that the tanks had to move to their start points.

As time was short and movement inordinately slow, the eight tanks with the First Army tried to take a shortcut to the line along a track made of brushwood and sleepers. It gave way under their weight and six tanks slithered into a morass. For the remainder of the night the crews, desperate to get forward to support the waiting infantry, floundered about in the swamp, drenched and freezing, trying to get their tanks moving. They were unsuccessful, and although with daylight they were eventually extracted, they were not in time to take part in the attack, though they were used later.

The forty tanks with the Third Army, although spread over a wide front, were able to provide effective assistance to the infantry. They crushed wire entanglements, destroyed machine-gun posts and provided fire support, enabling the infantry to capture the ½-mile-long stronghold known as The Harp and another strongpoint named Telegraph Hill.

The twelve tanks allotted to the Fifth Army were due to attack with the 4th Australian Division at Bullecourt (see Map 30, page 111) on 10 April, but the day before it was suddenly decided the tanks should attack at dawn without any preliminary warning bombardment in order to achieve surprise – the bombardment would arrive after the tanks had passed through the enemy wire. The tanks would be concentrated on a narrow, one-division front in what was to be the first attempt to introduce this tactic in tank warfare. However, the move to the assembly area, made in one long column (by then eleven machines) led by an officer walking cautiously in front of each tank, was subjected to a violent blizzard of driving snow that reduced visibility virtually to zero and the pace to a tentative crawl. At dawn the tanks were still a long way from their assembly position and the attack had to be postponed. The language of the Australian infantry who had been lying out most of the night in the freezing weather only to be recalled because the tanks had not appeared can well be imagined.

A pigeon is released from the port-hole in the side of a tank near Albert, August 1918.

Tank Battle History Sheets

These sheets, or report forms, were first instituted for the Battle of Arras in April 1917. They were issued to crew commanders before each engagement and were to be filled in after its completion. They were forwarded to Tank Corps headquarters, where they provided valuable information on how the crew and machine had functioned in battle. The following example from the Battle of Arras is taken from Colonel Fuller's book *Tanks in the Great War*:

BATTLE HISTORY OF CREW NO. D6 TANK NO. 505. DATE 9/4/17
COMMANDED BY LIEUTENANT A ———

Unit to which attached	14th Division
Hour the tank started for action	6.20 a.m., April 9, 1917.
Hour of zero	5.30 a.m. (14th Division attacking at 7.30 a.m.)
Extent and nature of hostile shell fire	Increasing as tank worked along Hindenburg Line.
Ammunition expended	3,500 rounds S.A.A.
Casualties	Nil.
Position of tank after action	Caught in large tank trap and struck by shell fire.
Condition of tank after action	Damaged by shell fire.

Orders received. – to attack Telegraph Hill with infantry of 14th Division at 7'30 a.m. on April 9, 1917, then proceed along Hindenburg Line to Neuville Vitasse. To wait at Rallying-point N.E. of Neuville Vitasse until infantry advanced again towards Wancourt. To proceed with infantry to Wancourt and assist them whenever necessary.

Report of action. – Tank left starting point at Beaurains at 6'30 a.m. on April 9, 191, crossed our front line at 7.27 a.m, attacking Telegraph Hill at 7.30 a.m.; then worked towards Neuville Vitasse along the Hindenburg Line. At a point about 1,000 yards N.E. of Neuville Vitasse, the tank was caught in a trap consisting of a large gun-pit carefully covered with turf. I and Sergeant B ——- immediately got out and went to guide other tanks clear of the trap in spite of M.G. and shell fire.

(Signed) A ———, Lieut.
O.C. Tank D.6.

The next day, 11 April, the tactics of the attack were reversed and the infantry led under cover of the usual artillery barrage. The tank attack was a failure. All eleven tanks either suffered mechanical failure or were disabled or destroyed – being silhouetted against the snow made them particularly easy targets for enemy gunners. In one tank a shell came through the front, decapitated the driver and exploded in the engine. The officer was blinded and stunned and a corporal wounded. As the crew crawled out through the narrow sponson doors the tank was hit again. One machine bore to the right and moved outside the zone of attack and, although putting up a splendid fight, was ultimately put out of action at Bakery Trench by streams of armour-piercing bullets. Another reached the edge of Bullecourt village but was halted by gear problems. It continued to fire, but when the Germans brought up a field gun and with no infantry support the crew abandoned their tank. Reports that one or two tanks reached Riencourt and Hendecourt (off Map 30 to the north) have been discounted. Although the Australian infantry secured part of the German second line, sustained enemy counter-attacks and shortages of ammunition forced a withdrawal on 12 April with very heavy casualties – the 4th Australian Brigade was almost destroyed. The Australians were vocal in voicing their opinion that the tanks had let them down. For many months the Australians distrusted tanks and not until Amiens sixteen months later was confidence restored.

However, the tanks had done all they could and their crews had displayed exemplary courage, with the result that the Bullecourt attack gained this company two MCs, one DCM and three MMs. The army commander, General Gough, sent the following message to the tank company involved in this attack:

> The Army Commander is very pleased with the gallantry and skill displayed by your company in the attack today, and the fact that the objectives were subsequently lost does not detract from the success of the tanks.

Within two months the Mark I and II tanks had been almost entirely replaced by the Mark IV (the Mark III was experimental and never saw action, being used as a training tank).

Later Tanks and Tactics

Tank Corps Reorganization

From the autumn of 1916 to November 1918 the Tank Corps, as it was officially named on 28 June 1917, was in a continuous state of change, expansion and reorganization. Having started with six companies – two of which did not leave England – under a lieutenant colonel, it ended up in mid-1918 under a major general with five tank brigades (fourteen tank and one armoured car battalions) in France. This force had workshops, schools and supply depots in both countries; had sent detachments to Ireland and Egypt; and in the final months it not only led the infantry of three British armies in almost every attack but also dictated in important respects how those attacks were to be delivered. These tank battalions of the final victorious advance in 1918 were equipped primarily with Mark V, Mark V* and Mark A Medium (Whippet) tanks, as well as supply and gun-carrying tanks (see pages 408–10). Tank Corps headquarters was established at the small village of Bermicourt 28 miles north-west of Arras and remained there for the rest of the war, although expansion meant the main gunnery and driving schools had eventually to relocate.

The maximum number of usable fighting tanks ever available in France was 435, so full-scale massed armoured attacks were never feasible. It was a case, so common in World War I, of supply not meeting demand. Only fifty each of the Mark II and III tanks were ever produced, as while being manufactured their design was superseded by the Mark IV and 1,000 of these had been requested. There were only sixteen tanks in full working order in France in December 1916 and, as stated above, only sixty could be assembled at the end of March the next year for the Battle of Arras. The reasons for this overall shortage were partially explained in the notes on a War Cabinet discussion held on 22 March 1917 (War Cabinet No. 102; CAB 23/2), quoted by John Terraine in *The Smoke and the Fire*:

> The Minister of Munitions [Dr Christopher Addison] reported considerable delays had occurred in the completion of the original estimate for the output of Tanks. A serious miscalculation had been made in the original estimate. Tanks had been first used in September 1916. The final design, however, had not been approved until the 23rd November, and the drawings had not been ready until the 7th January 1917 . . .
>
> The Minister of Munitions further stated . . . that everything was being done to speed up the supply . . .
>
> The Master-General of Ordnance informed the War Cabinet that only about 60 Tanks were in France, although Dr Addison stated the total deliveries amounted to 250. This discrepancy was explained by Lieutenant Colonel [A. G.] Stern [chairman of the Tank Supply Committee] as partly due to losses on the Somme, partly to the difficulty in supplying sufficient spare parts, and partly to heavy wastage, particularly among those retained in this country for instructional and experimental purposes . . .

The War Cabinet observed with concern that the number of tanks available in the immediate future for offensive operations of the Western Front is less than the number available last September. They took note of Lieutenant Colonel Stern's anticipations that when deliveries commenced they would take place in considerable quantities . . . The Minister of Munitions, however, wished it to be clearly understood that if the rate of wastage and the requirements for spares in respect of the 1,000 Mark IV Tanks on order should prove on the same scale as for those already supplied, it would be quite impossible to keep anything like that number available for service.

And so it proved. Planned production for the first nine months of 1917 was 1,460, of which 1,000 were to be the new Mark IVs, and from August the much-improved Mark Vs would become available. However, no Mark IVs were available in France until after the Battle of Arras in April 1917, and only 378 fighting tanks were assembled for the Cambrai attack in November. No Mark Vs appeared at the front until March 1918. In October 1917 Churchill, by then Minister of Munitions, wrote, 'I consider a year has been lost in Tank development, and the most strenuous efforts will now be made to repair this melancholy state of affairs.'

However, it was not just production problems that kept tank numbers down – the Germans played a substantial role. At Cambrai 179 tanks (47 per cent) were destroyed by enemy fire or immobilized, with many more damaged. At Amiens on 8 August 1918, 360 Mark V and V* and ninety-six Mark A Whippets took part on the only other occasion when tanks make a big contribution to victory, although the price was again high. On 9 August only 145 were still in action; on 10 August eighty-five; on 11 August thirty-eight and the next day a mere six were able to fight and all crews were utterly spent. While the tanks achieved some spectacular successes, the attrition rate kept fighting numbers well below those needed to keep unit strengths up to establishment until the Armistice.

By April 1917 the approved establishment in France was three brigades (1st, 2nd and 3rd Tank Brigades), each under a colonel, each of three battalions – a battalion, commanded by a lieutenant colonel, consisting of three numbered companies with four sections of four fighting tanks and one spare or supply section. This gave a total

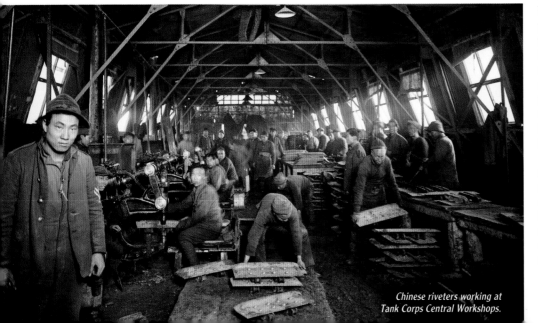

Chinese riveters working at Tank Corps Central Workshops.

C Battalion Tank Corps at Third Ypres, 2 August 1917

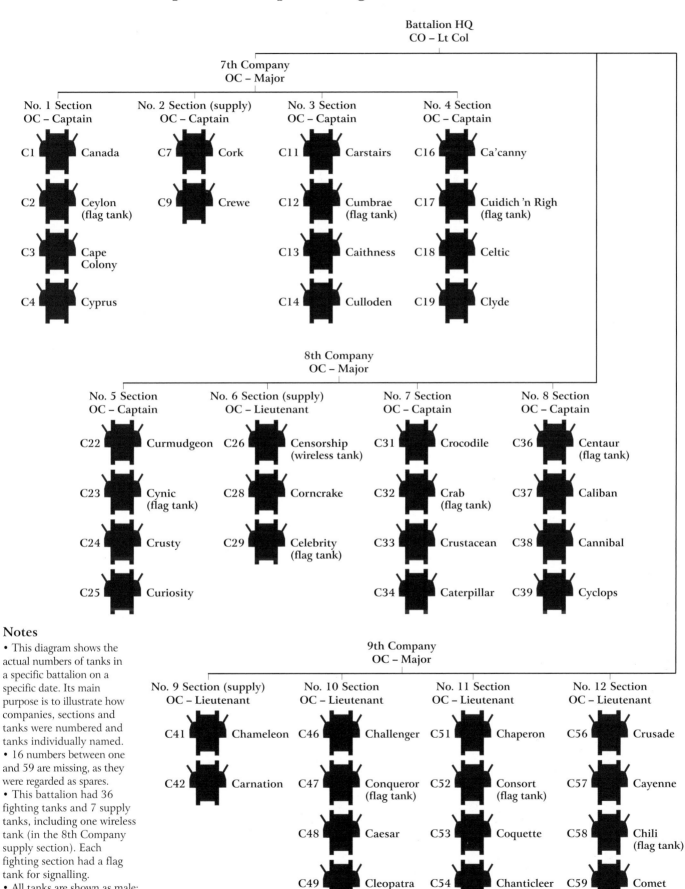

Battalion HQ
CO – Lt Col

7th Company
OC – Major

No. 1 Section
OC – Captain

C1 Canada
C2 Ceylon (flag tank)
C3 Cape Colony
C4 Cyprus

No. 2 Section (supply)
OC – Captain

C7 Cork
C9 Crewe

No. 3 Section
OC – Captain

C11 Carstairs
C12 Cumbrae (flag tank)
C13 Caithness
C14 Culloden

No. 4 Section
OC – Captain

C16 Ca'canny
C17 Cuidich 'n Righ (flag tank)
C18 Celtic
C19 Clyde

8th Company
OC – Major

No. 5 Section
OC – Captain

C22 Curmudgeon
C23 Cynic (flag tank)
C24 Crusty
C25 Curiosity

No. 6 Section (supply)
OC – Lieutenant

C26 Censorship (wireless tank)
C28 Corncrake
C29 Celebrity (flag tank)

No. 7 Section
OC – Captain

C31 Crocodile
C32 Crab (flag tank)
C33 Crustacean
C34 Caterpillar

No. 8 Section
OC – Captain

C36 Centaur (flag tank)
C37 Caliban
C38 Cannibal
C39 Cyclops

9th Company
OC – Major

No. 9 Section (supply)
OC – Lieutenant

C41 Chameleon
C42 Carnation

No. 10 Section
OC – Lieutenant

C46 Challenger
C47 Conqueror (flag tank)
C48 Caesar
C49 Cleopatra

No. 11 Section
OC – Lieutenant

C51 Chaperon
C52 Consort (flag tank)
C53 Coquette
C54 Chanticleer

No. 12 Section
OC – Lieutenant

C56 Crusade
C57 Cayenne
C58 Chili (flag tank)
C59 Comet

Notes

• This diagram shows the actual numbers of tanks in a specific battalion on a specific date. Its main purpose is to illustrate how companies, sections and tanks were numbered and tanks individually named.

• 16 numbers between one and 59 are missing, as they were regarded as spares.

• This battalion had 36 fighting tanks and 7 supply tanks, including one wireless tank (in the 8th Company supply section). Each fighting section had a flag tank for signalling.

• All tanks are shown as male; about half would be female, but it is uncertain which.

establishment of forty-eight fighting tanks to a battalion and 144 in a brigade. Command of the tank formations with the BEF was given to Brigadier General Elles. The facts that the rank for a brigade commander, for what was in effect a tank division, was a grade lower than the infantry or cavalry equivalent and that colonels commanded brigades caused some rancour. However, with the official forming of the Tank Corps in late June the post was upgraded to major general.

Initially every battalion had its own workshop company, commanded like the other companies by a major, until these were amalgamated to form brigade (and later divisional) workshops responsible for all repairs that could be affected in the field. Each battalion also had a reconnaissance officer (a captain) with three assistants. By this time (August) there had been further slight changes and a typical tank company would now comprise three fighting sections of four tanks each, and a fourth section of one wireless and two supply tanks (twelve fighting tanks, one wireless and two supply). Tanks had since the start been given War Department (WD) identification numbers, but in the field they were also given what might be called battalion numbers and names. In many cases, but not universally, these numbers were painted on the roof and sides. For example, A Battalion's tanks had names beginning in A, B Battalion's B and so on. C Battalion, going into action at the Third Battle of Ypres on 21 August 1917, was numbered and named as on the diagram on page 395, although as was the norm with practically every unit, it did not exactly fit the establishment mould.

Expansion included a tank signals branch using both wireless and pigeons, and a few cable-laying machines. Wireless was tried in tanks specially fitted for the purpose and used as command machines, but was not strikingly successful. However, despite the conditions inside a tank, according to Captain Browne pigeons remained the best means of communicating with a headquarters during an action, until the final advance in 1918 when the lofts could not keep up. Writing in 1920, he recalled:

Two birds, when available, were carried in each tank; and their behaviour in the most trying circumstances imaginable was truly exemplary. I shall never forget the placid, and almost *blasé* air in which a couple in my own tank continued to sip their water, and take apparently an intelligent interest in the proceedings, while in a sweating atmosphere of petrol fumes, high explosive, and decomposing humanity, we were crashing over fallen tree-trunks along the Poelcapelle road.

By August 1918 the Tank Corps organization was as follows:

• **In England** A training centre at Wool, Dorset, where recruits were trained for four months and either drafted to a new battalion forming at Wool or despatched to the Tank Corps Depot at Mers in France. There they remained for about six weeks before joining a battalion at the front. The Tank Testing Section was at Newbury under the control of the Mechanical Warfare Supply Department. All machines were sent there from the manufacturers, and thence shipped by ferry from Richborough to Le Havre. From there they went to the Central Stores at Erin to be finally prepared for handing over to the battalions.

• **In France** A Tank Corps headquarters taking orders direct from GHQ. It was organized on the same lines as an infantry division headquarters with a major general and the G, A and Q branches of the staff. G Branch was responsible for establishing various training schools including a Six-pounder School; a Hotchkiss, .303 Machinegun and Revolver School; a Mechanical Maintenance and Driving School; an Anti-Gas School; and a Wireless Signalling School. By this time there were five tank brigades with the BEF. Besides the brigades there was a headquarters carrier unit controlling five tank supply companies (twenty-four supply tanks each) and two gun-carrier companies (sixteen carriers each). The technical organization consisted of a central workshop; a central stores; five advanced workshops; and two tank field companies for salvage work. In addition, 711 Company, ASC, and 8 Squadron, RAF, were attached.

There had been another change before the attack at Cambrai in late November 1917 and that involved tank companies changing from three sections of four fighting tanks to four sections of three – the organization shown in the diagram on page 399.

Tank Tactics

Tank tactics, like those of other arms, evolved over a period of many months. Tanks were the new weapon and their first actions were very much trial and error against a tenacious enemy that soon bolstered every means available for anti-tank defence. Nevertheless, by late 1917 it was possible to set out some tactical guidance based on experience to give a combined infantry and tank assault the best chance of success. These were incorporated in an official confidential publication known as *Weekly Tank Notes*, which covered a host of tank matters apart from tactics. It had the

following to say on the underlying principle involved:

An attack carried out by Tanks and infantry should be considered as one combined operation . . . Offensively this means that each of these two arms must be employed against the weapon it can most easily destroy . . .

The weapon chiefly dreaded by the infantry is the machine gun [in the attack perhaps] and by the tank the field gun, therefore, the tactical basis of co-operation between tanks and infantry should be – that Tanks must protect infantry from machine gun fire, and infantry must protect Tanks from field gun fire.

Several simple actions for a section of four tanks attacking a single trench system are as shown in the diagram opposite.

In order to prevent the surviving enemy appearing after tanks had passed by, it was vital that infantry should follow up closely behind with clearing (bombing) parties to deal with trenches and dugouts. Tanks would crush the wire, making narrow paths for the infantry, then some would turn laterally along the line of the trench and use both guns and machine guns to destroy or neutralize opposition. There should be virtually no time between the tanks arriving at the enemy trench and the infantry winning the 'race for the parapet' – in theory there should be no race. Behind the clearing parties would come the stop parties with the task of securing the trench system and dugouts and setting up blocks in trenches (fire and communication) to prevent enemy infiltrating back. Behind them would be further supports or reserves.

These tactics, in use by November 1917, are illustrated in the diagram overleaf, along with a method used to overcome a fire and support trench system with trenches too wide for tanks to cross without the use of fascines. Fascines were huge bundles of branches tightly bound with chains (put together by Chinese labour); they were carried on top of the tank and could be dropped in a trench to fill it sufficiently for the tank to cross. After the first objective had been secured, reorganization took place during which the surviving tanks would rally before pushing on to secure the next line, with fresh infantry moving through the captured enemy position.

The diagram on page 399 shows a tank company and two infantry battalions formed up prior to an attack without a creeping artillery barrage.

Artillery barrages and concentrations continued to be of critical importance in most advances. The primary aim of the heavier guns or howitzers was counter-battery fire to

Possible Actions of Sections and Subsections Attacking a Single Trench

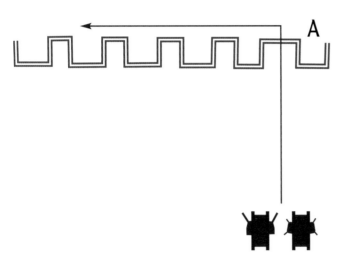

The subsection of two tanks (a male and a female) advances to cross the trench at roughly the same place and together, before turning, in this case to the left, to shoot up the trench and drive the enemy away.

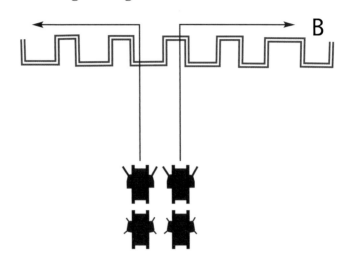

A section of four advances, with the subsections turning in opposite directions on crossing the trench at different locations but close together.

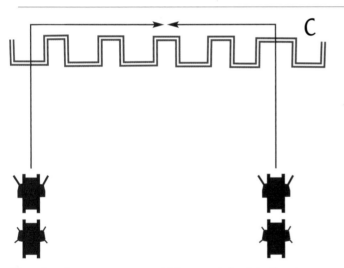

The subsections cross at more widely separated points, then turn inwards to squeeze out a strongpoint in the centre.

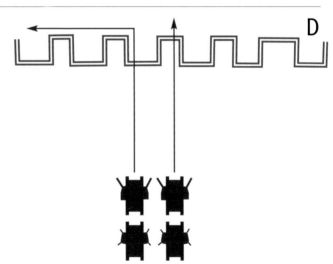

Here the left-hand subsection turns left, while the right-hand one presses straight on to threaten retreating enemy.

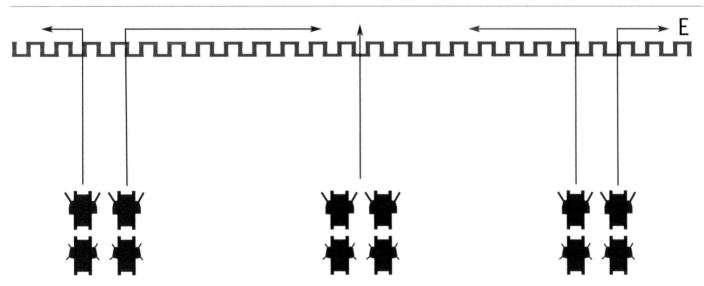

Here the sections – in practical terms likely to be a company – attack a longer trench line. Each section strikes the trench at fairly widely separated points. The centre section forges ahead while the flanking sections move both inwards and outwards.

Infantry/Tank Tactics for Attacking a Trench System, November 1917

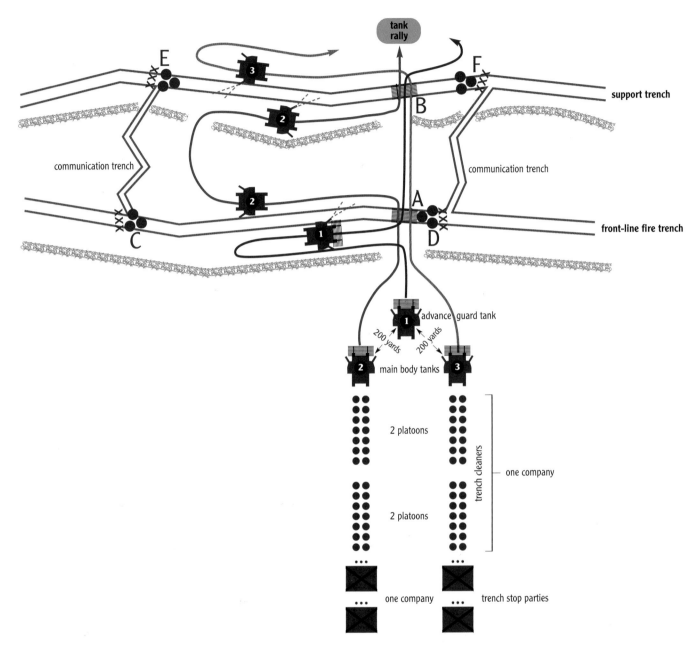

Notes

• This diagram shows one of several tactics used by November 1917 for a section of three tanks with two infantry companies to capture a specific section of German trench and the support trench. The tanks all have fascines to enable them to cross trenches up to 15 feet wide. Each trench is protected by a wire obstacle.
• The advance guard tank (No. 1) crushes the wire and swings left before crossing the trench. It proceeds along the parapet, shooting up any enemy with gun and machine guns before returning to cross the trench at **A** and **B** and moving to the rallying point.
• The left-hand main body tank (No. 2) advances next and drops its fascine at **A**, crossing the trench before turning left and moving along the rear of the fire trench. It then turns right and forces a gap through the second wire obstacle, moving along the support trench to cross it at **B** to come to the rallying point.

• The right-hand main body tank (No. 3) crosses the trench over the fascine at **A**, crushes a gap in the wire in front of the support trench and drops its fascine in the support trench at **B**, then crosses over and turns left to rake it before returning to make for the tank rallying point.
• The infantry cleaners (four platoons) clear the trenches from right to left (two platoons per trench). They are followed by the four stop-party platoons, who secure the trenches (two platoons per trench) and man stops (barricades) at **C**, **D**, **E** and **F**. They would also widen the gaps in the wire through which reserves could pass to attack the next objective.
• The above assumes all went well and no tanks were disabled. If that happened, then the remaining tanks would act on their own initiative, but at all times supporting the infantry to secure the trenches by their fire. A disabled tank was often able to act as a strongpoint and still provide considerable protection to the infantry.

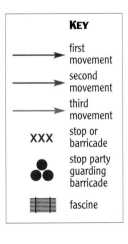

KEY

→	first movement
→	second movement
→	third movement
XXX	stop or barricade
⬤⬤⬤	stop party guarding barricade
▦	fascine

Tanks and Infantry Battalions Formed Up Prior to an Attack, November 1917

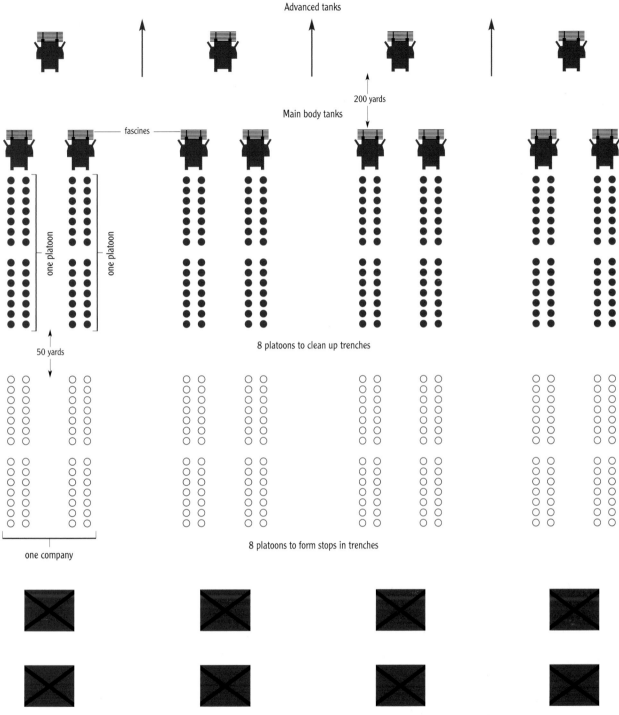

Advanced tanks

200 yards

Main body tanks

fascines

one platoon

one platoon

50 yards

8 platoons to clean up trenches

8 platoons to form stops in trenches

one company

one battalion in support

Notes

• Here a tank company with four sections of three tanks is leading an attack by an infantry battalion with eight platoons tasked with cleaning up the trenches, and eight providing the stops. Another battalion is advancing in support. This attack is not preceded by an artillery creeping barrage.

• Each tank section and following company would generally be given a specific tactical point to capture. If possible, the section area should be free of communication trenches. The tank advance is divided into two waves or lines – the advanced and the main body tanks.

• The advanced tanks threaten the enemy and keep down his fire, while the main body tanks, followed by the infantry, advance and cross the enemy wire and trenches. Once this duty is finished, the advanced tanks become a reserve to the main body. The task of the main body tanks is to assist the infantry, to protect them while capturing the objective and subsequently to remain in close touch with them while the position is secured.

• The general objective of this tank/infantry attack is to penetrate at several points, place the infantry through these points and then protect them as they clear the trenches and depots.

hit German guns able to take on the tanks – this would often be in addition to the usual timed or creeping barrage by field artillery moving ahead of the tanks and infantry. In this case the British shells would fall about 100 yards ahead of the tank section, which would be advancing in line abreast with the infantry in file close behind. High Command would have to make the decision as to whether a creeping or standing barrage was likely to be more advantageous than a surprise attack without close artillery support. Once the Hindenburg Line had been breached in the summer of 1918 and the Allied advance moved into more open country, tank and infantry formations were more open, with the combined infantry/tank firing line having infantry Lewis-gun sections up level with the tanks followed by the rifle sections.

However, as with all battles, these neat tactical formations rarely survived shots being fired, unforeseen delays and subsequent losses. Formations became broken up, with tank sections of three or four often reduced to two or only one machine, although sometimes such individual tanks made spectacular advances. Nevertheless, in the months leading to the end of the war, infantry–tank cooperation, along with that of artillery and air-craft, had developed into an all-arms battle – something that was the core of battlefield tactics in any major engagement during World War II and remains so to this day. It is illustrated in Section Thirteen.

The Mark IV Tank

The Mark II had only a brief appearance on the battlefield at Arras, while as a training tank the Mark III had none. They were replaced by the Mark IV, which became the fighting tank of the BEF during most of 1917. Male and female were almost the same as the Mark I in terms of length, weight, speed, engine and requiring a crew of an officer and seven men. However, the new tank incorporated a number of improvements:

• Though its armour plates were the same thickness as the Mark I, they were made of hardened steel that kept out the German armour-piercing 'K' bullet – although it did not stop the 'splash' inside.

• It incorporated signalling between the driver and the gearsmen by electric lights, and it carried a compass.

• A new large, single petrol tank replaced the two located near the driver and officer. It contained 70 gallons of fuel and was located outside at the rear and so reduced the risk of fire turning the cab into a fiery deathtrap. The extra fuel enabled it to increase its radius of action from 12 to 15 miles.

• It was also possible for the crew to make a faster escape from female tanks, as a double door underneath each sponson replaced the one only 2 feet high. The male sponsons were lighter and could be unbolted and, with a shortened 6-pounder gun, could now be pushed inside the tank. This facilitated moving the tank by rail, as it did away with the tedious, time-consuming business of having completely to remove the sponsons at the start and replace them at the end of every journey.

• Detachable 'spuds' were provided for the tracks to improve their grip on soft, wet ground.

• The track rollers and links were now made of cast iron, enabling them to withstand more wear.

• A more efficient silencer was installed, with the long exhaust carried to the rear of the machine. This meant less noise, and the sparks and flames that were previously emitted on the roof, creating a great giveaway, were no longer so visible.

• After Messines these tanks were fitted with an efficient unditching system (see box, page 392) to give individual tanks a reasonable chance of unditching themselves rather than waiting to be rescued.

The only change that was not beneficial was with the machine guns. Against the advice of tank officers and a military committee, which decided a Lewis gun would be ineffective in a tank, the War Office decided to replace the Hotchkiss with the Lewis gun. Thus a male Mark IV had two 6-pounders and four Lewis guns, and a female had six Lewis guns. It was not until the arrival of the Mark V in 1918 that this error was rectified and the Hotchkiss reappeared.

A British Mark IV tank is guided across a trench, 1917.

Tanks at Messines

The attack on the Messines–Wytschaete Ridge in early June 1917 was the first phase of a much grander plan to drive the Germans off the entire coastline as far as the Dutch border; the second phase of this would be the attack on Passchendaele Ridge (Third Battle of Ypres), scheduled for July. The Messines attack was a limited one aimed at taking the ridge that dominated the Ypres salient. It was carefully planned over many months and included the exploding of twenty mines (nineteen were detonated) under the German front line (see Map 62, page 309). A ten-day bombardment by 2,266 guns and howitzers preceded the 7 June assault by the three infantry corps of the Second Army under General Herbert Plumer. The assault would be covered by massive creeping and standing barrages and counter-battery concentrations (see Maps 49–52, pages 258–61), as well as machine-gun barrages for which it was estimated some 5 million rounds would be needed. All this meant that tanks would play a comparatively minor role, as the combination of the mine explosions coming on top of the prolonged artillery pounding destroyed and demoralized most Germans, enabling the infantry to advance rapidly and take the ridge as planned.

However, this was the debut of the Mark IV tank and the 2nd Tank Brigade, consisting of A and B Battalions with seventy-two fighting tanks, was allotted to the Second Army. Each battalion had two spare tanks and six of the old Mark IIs employed as supply tanks (it was also the first time supply tanks were used). The seventy-two were divided between the three corps as follows:

X Corps – 12 for the attack on the ridge

IX Corps – 28: 16 for the ridge and 12 for the second objective, the Oosttaverne Line

II ANZAC Corps – 32: 20 for the ridge and 12 for the Oosttaverne Line

The tank operations were to be entirely subsidiary to the infantry attack. For the previous three weeks the weather had been fine, and had this not been so the tanks would never have been able to advance over the pulverized ground; a short, sharp thunderstorm on the night before the attack did not appreciably affect the ground. At zero hour on 7 June forty tanks (eight having for various reasons not made the start) were launched in the attack on the Blue Line or first objective, which was the German second line just beyond the crest of the ridge. Of these, twenty-five reached it and covered the consolidation. Twenty-four tanks took part in the attack on the Oosttaverne Line, of which sixteen reached it.

The effectiveness of the mines and creeping barrage resulted in Messines being taken by 7:00 a.m. and Wytschaete by midday, with tanks being required to give only minimal support – in some cases they were unable to keep up with the infantry, so fast was the advance. Tank highlights included a tank with II ANZAC Corps crossing the enemy trenches at a very rapid rate and arriving at the objective in an hour and forty minutes, having covered 3,000 yards and having destroyed an enemy machine gun on the way. Another one, appropriately named the 'Wytschaete Express', led the Ulster Division into that village and was instrumental in helping persuade a large number of Germans to surrender. A third came into action effectively near Fanny's Farm, where infantry were held up for a time. As darkness approached, and with the Oosttaverne Line secured, two of the tanks that had taken part in that attack became ditched near a place called Joye Farm. They were both well placed to deal with any counter-attack in that area, so the crew were told to stop unditching efforts and remain inside their tanks. Some time after 4:30 a.m. the next day it appeared that a counter-attack was developing, so two 6-pounders were brought to bear while the Lewis-gunners took their guns into nearby shell holes to fight from there. From 6:00 a.m. the enemy made repeated attacks, shooting at the tanks with armour-piercing bullets that failed to penetrate, and in all cases they were beaten off with heavy loss (with more Lewis-gun ammunition being supplied by the infantry). At 11:30 a.m. they were finally dispersed by artillery fire.

Tank personnel losses were nineteen killed and ninety-nine wounded or missing. Of the machines, eleven were disabled by direct hits from German 77mm field guns and forty-eight were ditched, two being hit after disablement. The main lesson learned was the unacceptable level of disablements, frequently due to inadequacies of the current unditching equipment – its replacement was given priority (see box, page 392). Apart from that, the Mark IV had handled better than its predecessors and the improvements listed above were universally welcomed by the crews.

Mark IV Tanks at Passchendaele

As Colonel (later Major General) J. F. C. Fuller, a staff officer at the headquarters of the Heavy Branch, MGC, wrote, 'From the tank point of view the Third Battle of Ypres is a complete study of how to move thirty tons of metal through a morass of mud and water.'

The First Battle of Ypres in late 1914 held the German attempt to break through in Flanders but left them occupying the Messines Ridge to the south of the town and the higher ground to the east. The Ypres salient had been created. The second battle of that name in April 1915 saw the Germans push back the Allied force even further so that the front lines were much closer to the town. The Allied offensive, officially known as the Third Battle of Ypres but more commonly called Passchendaele, was launched to secure the higher ground as a step towards an eventual advance on Bruges. For the British it started as a two-stage operation – the first to secure the Messines Ridge (see pages 257–9 and 307–10); the second, with Messines secure, to overrun the enemy defences on the Pilckem Ridge and Gheluvelt plateau east of the town and then take the Passchendaele Ridge to the north-east (see Map 71).

The land occupied by the British was flat, with Ypres and the canal being a mere 70 feet above sea level. Even the Germans on the plateau to the east were mostly on the 170-foot contour line, with the highest point being not much over 400 feet. The ridges were, in effect, quite gentle rises (the shading on the map is somewhat deceptive in this respect), although possession of even this small elevation gave them every advantage in terms of observation and the ability to seek protection on reverse slopes. In Haig's after-battle despatch he wrote, 'On no previous occasion had the whole ground from which we had to attack been so completely exposed to the enemy's observation.'

In peacetime this land possessed a good drainage system, a vast spider's web of dykes and ditches largely destroyed in the fighting of 1915–16, despite constant repair efforts by land-drainage companies sent out for the purpose. The soil was patchy, sometimes clay, sometimes sand or a mixture, but with the water table mostly close to the surface so that trenches and dugouts invariably contained water and needed the constant use of pumps and lining with duckboards. Ypres, which a century earlier had been a sea port, sat in part of what was aptly called the 'Low Countries'. Tanks could be expected to operate successfully over this terrain, even when pitted with shell craters, provided the ground was still reasonably firm. Unfortunately this was not to be, as the tremendous and prolonged pounding by the guns of both sides throughout most of June and July, coming on top of the usual, if much less intense, shelling of the previous two years, totally destroyed the drainage system.

General Gough's Fifth Army undertook the main offensive that started on 31 July 1917. Preparations for the attack included the use of 3,000 artillery pieces on the Fifth Army's front. It was the largest bombardment ever carried out by the British Army and marked the zenith of these prolonged

MAP 71 THIRD YPRES: INITIAL ASSAULT, 31 JULY 1917

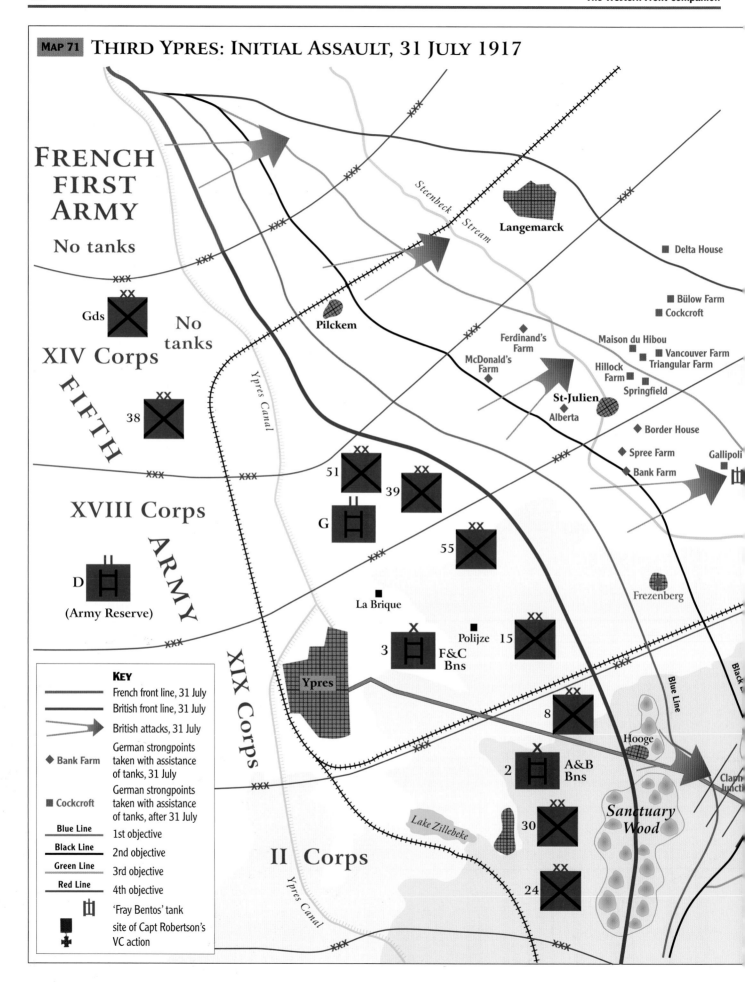

FRENCH FIRST ARMY

No tanks

Gds

XIV Corps

No tanks

FIFTH

38

ARMY

XVIII Corps

D

(Army Reserve)

51

G

39

55

3 F&C Bns

15

8

2 A&B Bns

30

24

XIX Corps

Ypres

II Corps

La Brique

Polijze

Hooge

Sanctuary Wood

Lake Zillebeke

Frezenberg

Langemarck

Steenbeck Stream

Pilckem

Ferdinand's Farm

McDonald's Farm

Delta House

Bülow Farm

Cockcroft

Maison du Hibou

Vancouver Farm

Triangular Farm

Hillock Farm

Springfield

St-Julien

Alberta

Border House

Spree Farm

Bank Farm

Gallipoli

Ypres Canal

Blue Line

Black Line

Clapham Junction

Ypres Canal

KEY

French front line, 31 July

British front line, 31 July

British attacks, 31 July

◆ Bank Farm   German strongpoints taken with assistance of tanks, 31 July

■ Cockcroft   German strongpoints taken with assistance of tanks, after 31 July

Blue Line   1st objective

Black Line   2nd objective

Green Line   3rd objective

Red Line   4th objective

'Fray Bentos' tank

site of Capt Robertson's VC action

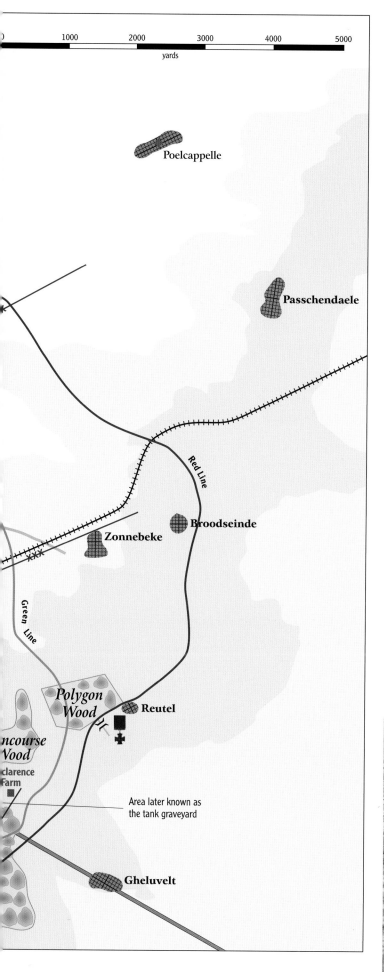

1000 2000 3000 4000 5000
yards

Poelcappelle

Passchendaele

Red Line

Broodseinde

Zonnebeke

xxx

Green Line

Polygon Wood

Reutel

ncourse Wood

clarence Farm

Area later known as the tank graveyard

Gheluvelt

Notes for Map 71

• This map shows the initial deployment of the British Fifth Army under Gen. Gough at the opening of the Third Battle of Ypres (Passchendaele) – a battle that lasted until November and became infamous for the appalling conditions in which men and machines struggled to function. Only the initial assault divisions are shown.

• Most tanks drowned in the mud but some managed to advance with huge difficulty and at a snail's pace. The map highlights a number of German strongpoints at which tanks played an important part in their destruction or capture on that first day, and some of the others that were taken subsequently before all remaining tanks were withdrawn from the battlefield.

• At the start, the entire tank force in France – three brigades of Mark IV fighting tanks – was committed to the attack. No. 1 Tank Brigade, consisting of D and G Battalions, was under command of XVIII Corps, but D Battalion was initially held back as Army Reserve. No. 2 Tank Brigade, of A and B Battalions, was attached to II Corps and No. 3 Tank Brigade, of F and C Battalions, to XIX Corps. XIV Corps and the French on the left had no tanks allocated, as the front line was too close to the Ypres Canal and the German front line to allow the construction of bridges or causeways for the tanks to cross. The number of tanks allotted to each corps was 72 to each of II and XIX Corps, 36 to XVIII Corps with 36 in reserve.

• The final objectives were as follows:

II Corps – attacking on the right to capture the Broodseinde–Gheluvelt Ridge and protect the right flank of the Fifth Army.

XIX Corps – attacking north-east of Ypres to secure a section of the enemy's third line (Red Line) known as the Gheluvelt–Langemarck Line.

XVIII Corps – main objective was the Green Line; seize crossings over the Steenbeek, establish a line beyond the river and advance on the Gheluvelt–Langemarck Line.

A wrecked tank left behind on the battlefield at Ypres.

This rare photograph, taken during combat in Flanders, shows a tank bursting into flames after being hit by shellfire. In the background another tank crashes through barbed wire, accompanied by infantrymen. Note the ground is strewn with helmets and weapons, while a fallen soldier lies almost under the tank.

artillery bombardments by the BEF on the Western Front – eight days of counter-battery work (a primary task of the British heavy guns, but one that was far from successful) being followed by sixteen days' intense bombardment. During this period some 1,500 German guns and howitzers were responding. All this shelling made the vital preparatory work of the RE doubly difficult. Their tasks included building gun platforms, constructing tracks, repairing roads, bridging streams and building causeways over the Ypres Canal so that the tanks could move forward to their final start points. This work was completed by the 184th Tunnelling Company, RE, attached to the Heavy Branch, MGC, under spasmodic shelling.

The overall plan is explained in Map 71 and the accompanying notes. The following paragraphs use the experiences of two companies of G Battalion (1st Tank Brigade) during their move from their assembly area to the start point of their advance on 31 July and the subsequent failure of the attack (see Map 72). This is followed by the highly successful tank attack on 19 August on the Maison du Hibou, Triangle Farm, Vancouver, Hillock Farm and The Cockcroft strongpoints (see Map 73). The facts and quotations are taken from Captain (then a lieutenant) Browne's book *The Tank in Action*, published in 1920. Browne, who won the Military Cross, commanded tank G46 'Gina' in No. 10 Section of 21 Company, G Battalion of No. 1 Tank Brigade on 31 July and C47 on 19 August.

G Battalion was attached to XVIII Corps, commanded by Lieutenant General Sir Ivor Maxse, with D Battalion earmarked as army reserve, for the attack on the German lines on the Pilckem Ridge and to secure crossings over the Steenbeek stream and then, hopefully, on to the Passchendaele Ridge – the ultimate objective being a complete breakthrough. The Germans, worried that they

would be subjected to a massive explosion of mines as at Messines, had reorganized their defences so that front lines were thinly manned by a few sentries and observation posts, behind which were well-defended lines strengthened by dozens of concrete-reinforced strongpoints usually dug into the rubble of destroyed farm buildings. Maps 71 and 72 show some, but certainly not all, of these strongpoints that featured in the fighting.

Oosthoek Wood, the assembly area for the Fifth Army's three tank brigades, covered several hundred acres about 4 miles west of Ypres (Map 72). It was bisected by a wide, timbered military road and a rail link enabled tanks to be offloaded after dark on the edge of, or near to, the wood. G Battalion arrived by rail at the wood a company at a time over three nights, to be met by the reconnaissance officers and advance parties and guided into the wood. Parking dozens of tanks in a wood in the middle of the night was fraught with frustrations, as Captain Browne explained:

Parking tanks (especially Mark IVs) among timber at night is always a noisy and trying operation, resembling in sound and destructiveness the gambols of a herd of inebriated elephants. The tank-driver, unaided, can see nothing whatever, and has to be guided by the flashings of an electric torch, with which refinements of signalling are difficult and generally misunderstood. The trees, which appear to be harmless and nicely spaced in daytime, become endued with a malignant spirit and (apparently) have changed their positions since last seen. It was as black as a coal-pocket in Oosthoek Wood that night; and for an hour or so it rang with curses and exhortations and the crash and rending of ill-treated timber . . .

Spasmodic German shelling of the wood resulted in personnel being taken by lorries back to a tented camp at Lovie Chateau out

of artillery range, leaving the tanks under guard in the wood. Every day the tank crews marched down from Lovie Chateau to do their work in the wood, returning in the late afternoon. As soon as G Battalion had settled down in the wood, reconnaissance of the area and routes forward by tank commanders, NCOs and drivers began.

The major obstacle between the tanks and the British front-line trenches was the Ypres Canal, which was targeted regularly, day and night, by German guns. North of Ypres it had been bridged by several earthen causeways with the one known as Marengo being earmarked for the tanks to use. The obvious danger was that a tank disabled on the causeway would block the route for all those behind. The plan was to move forward by stages over several nights along the track called Rum Road, first to a tree-lined enclosure known as Halfway House. From there they would continue forward over Marengo causeway to Frascati Farm – another place with plenty of trees and bushes – where the tanks could be under camouflage nets and the trees to await the time to move to their start points just in rear of the British front line at Forward Cottage. The intention was to spend X day (the day but one before the battle) at Halfway House and during the night X/Y move forward again to Frascati Farm. From there to Forward Cottage was about a mile, and as it was too dangerous to walk over this ground in daylight it would be marked by white tape by reconnaissance officers on the final evening.

For the attack G Battalion had been split, with 19 and 21 Companies supporting the infantry of XVIII Corps and 20 Company being held as corps reserve. Prior to the move forward every tank commander and driver had walked the route forward two or three times. Captain Browne explained how the officers would make their reconnaissance of the enemy lines, and the ground beyond their own front line, from a specially constructed observation post called Wilson's Post. They would come forward by vehicle to Reigersberg Chateau, then walk via Bridge No. 4, La Brique, and then along a very shallow disused trench to Wilson's Post.

Wilson's Post . . . was a small two-storied tower embedded literally to its eyelids in the earth, its cranium concealed in willows and other shrubs. It was approached from La Brique by an unfinished trench about the depth of a roadside gutter. In the bottom storey, illuminated by a candle, an orderly sat over a telephone; in the upper chamber – about five feet square and reached by a ladder – a telescope peered through two shallow slits on the ground level and swept from an angle the whole front from which my battalion was to attack. Sitting on a little bench with one's feet dangling over the trap-door, one could see the brown slope of the Pilckem Ridge, seamed with light-coloured lines which marked the enemy's trenches, the foliage of Kitchener's Wood appearing over the crest, and, away to the left, the debris of the estaminet called Boche Castle and a few clumps of skeleton trees which, on that obliterated countryside, served us for landmarks.

On another occasion when observing with another officer from another location, Captain Browne described the state of the ground over which tanks fought in the Ypres salient.

[We] peered out through our binoculars upon a barren and dun-coloured landscape, void of any sign of human life, its dreary skyline broken only by a few jagged stumps of trees. From this desolation clouds of dust shot up where our shells were falling. It was much the same as any other battlefield, to all appearance. But even then the duckboards under foot in the trenches were squelching upon water; and a few hours rain [as fell on 31 July] dissolved the fallacious crust into a bottomless and evil-smelling paste of liquid mud. And rain was the least offender. It was our own bombardment [and that of the Germans] which finished the work of ruin, pulverized the ground, destroyed what drainage there was left, and brought the water welling up within the shell-holes as fast as they were formed.

The attack was originally scheduled for 25 July but was postponed for three days, with the final postponement to 31 July being made at the last moment. Last-minute preparations of G46, a brand-new tank, included washing and scrubbing as it came from the workshops in a filthy condition, cleaning the Lewis guns and filling the 276 drums with ammunition. Track plates, spuds, camouflage nets, petrol, oil, water and grease had to be obtained from advanced stores dumps. Officers studied aerial photographs and maps and, in addition to frequent reconnaissance of the route and enemy positions, attended briefings that included studying a large model made of sand and brick of the area to be attacked. Crews took two days' rations, iron rations, supplemented by a few additional luxuries such as oranges, chocolates and biscuits, and each tank had one water bottle full of rum and another of whisky – Captain Browne took two bottles of whisky.

The assault by XVIII Corps was to be made on a two-division frontage – the 39th Division on the right and the 51st Division on the left. The two companies of G Battalion were allocated as follows – 19 Company plus No. 10 Section of 21 Company (Browne's section), sixteen tanks in all, was to attack in a single wave with the 39th Division. The remaining two sections of 21 Company, eight tanks, would operate with the 51st Division. Captain Browne's section received orders to split up after crossing the German front line. The left-hand pair (G45 and G46) were to advance on the northern end of Kitchener's Wood (see Map 72), giving special attention to Boche Castle strongpoint; then to move round the wood with the infantry and mop up any resistance before pausing for the barrage to lift prior to further advance. The right-hand pair (G47 and G48) would move on the southern end of Kitchener's Wood and when the barrage lifted support the infantry attacking the Alberta strongpoint.

During the night of 24/25 July the tanks of 21 Company (less No. 10 Section) moved from Oosthoek Wood to Halfway House, but the postponement of the attack meant that 19 Company and Captain Browne's section did not begin their move until after dark on the 28th, when the long line of sixteen tanks crawling along the military road was watched with considerable curiosity from infantry bivouacked near the edge of the road. After two minor mishaps the tanks joined the rest of 21 Company at Halfway House. When work on camouflage was completed, the crews, less a guard, went back by lorry to Lovie Chateau in the early hours of the 29th for a final brief rest.

That evening the crews returned for the move to Frascati Farm. Rain had fallen, it was cloudy and very dark as, with 21 Company leading, they set off. G46 developed clutch problems and the resultant delay caused some anxious consulting of watches. The reconnaissance officer of 19

Company told Browne that 'things were very serious' – if the tanks were caught in the open in daylight east of the canal the whole operation could be jeopardized. The march continued, with officers walking ahead of their tanks and their drivers peering desperately through their flaps to keep the faint white patch on the officer's back in sight. The column crossed the Marengo causeway without incident and from there on the route had been taped, although a lot of loose wire, debris and shell holes continually caused officers to stumble or fall. To fall in front of a tank only a few feet behind you in these circumstances was highly dangerous. Browne described one tank commander's terrifying experience:

[He] had a very narrow escape from death or injury that night through becoming entangled in a mass of wire. His tank cleared him by inches while he was still struggling to get free, and then the track caught the wire and pulled him helplessly after. He was carried onto the roof when the driver somehow discovered what had happened and pulled up.

During the final part of the march the Germans began to bombard the area with gas shells – fortunately not mustard gas – interspersed with a few rounds of high explosive. This shelling lasted about half an hour but caused no obvious problems, and the tanks arrived at Frascati Farm just before first light and camouflaged up in the bushes under the trees. The journey had taken seven hours.

That evening of the 30th, Major Fernie, 19 Company commander, arrived to give final instructions and to establish his headquarters in Hill Top Farm, while Lieutenant Colonel E. B. Hankey, commanding G Battalion, moved into divisional headquarters in Oosthoek Wood. For the crews it was the time for final preparation for battle, which involved filling up with petrol from a dump in the trees and leaving behind all

Three British tanks stuck in the mud east of Zillebeke, 1917.

MAP 72   G BATTALION, TANK CORPS (19 AND 21 COMPANIES) – MOVEMENTS AND

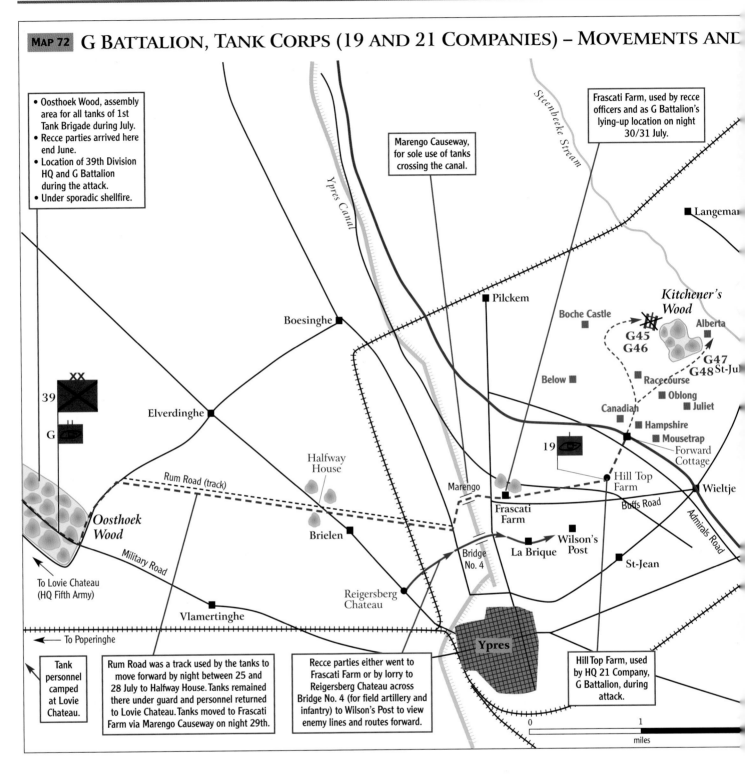

- Oosthoek Wood, assembly area for all tanks of 1st Tank Brigade during July.
- Recce parties arrived here end June.
- Location of 39th Division HQ and G Battalion during the attack.
- Under sporadic shellfire.

Marengo Causeway, for sole use of tanks crossing the canal.

Frascati Farm, used by recce officers and as G Battalion's lying-up location on night 30/31 July.

Steenbeeke Stream

Langema

Ypres Canal

Pilckem

Boesinghe

Boche Castle

Kitchener's Wood

Alberta

G45
G46

G47
G48 St-Ju

Below

Racecourse

Oblong

Juliet

Canadian

Hampshire

XX

39

G

Elverdinghe

19

Mousetrap

Forward Cottage

Wieltje

Halfway House

Marengo

Hill Top Farm

Rum Road (track)

Frascati Farm

Oosthoek Wood

Brielen

Buffs Road

Admirals Road

La Brique

Wilson's Post

Military Road

To Lovie Chateau (HQ Fifth Army)

Bridge No. 4

St-Jean

Reigersberg Chateau

Vlamertinghe

To Poperinghe

Tank personnel camped at Lovie Chateau.

Rum Road was a track used by the tanks to move forward by night between 25 and 28 July to Halfway House. Tanks remained there under guard and personnel returned to Lovie Chateau. Tanks moved to Frascati Farm via Marengo Causeway on night 29th.

Recce parties either went to Frascati Farm or by lorry to Reigersberg Chateau across Bridge No. 4 (for field artillery and infantry) to Wilson's Post to view enemy lines and routes forward.

Ypres

Hill Top Farm, used by HQ 21 Company, G Battalion, during attack.

0   1

miles

---

spare kit such as camouflage nets and tarpaulins. Fixing the spuds to the tracks occupied a considerable time – a tank carried forty-four of these in a box and at least thirty were required on the tracks to be properly effective. It was a tedious and irksome task, with stiff nuts and bolts and too few spanners; so much so that G46 managed to fix only half the necessary number in time, dumping the rest in a ditch.

At 10.45 p.m. the final move forward began. One tank of 19 Company was halted by mechanical problems while the rest inched their way towards the front line, again with officers walking ahead. Well ahead of time the column halted for half an hour near Hill Top Farm and watched the dozens of Very lights, rockets and flares that burst and hung in the sky all round the salient. When they moved forward again this illumination assisted the drivers and commanders, who had now climbed into their tanks, to follow the machine in front and the tape on the ground. With plenty of time the

tanks inched cautiously forward to halt fifteen minutes before zero hour (set for 3:50 a.m.) some 300 yards from Forward Cottage, where they would cross the front line.

Precisely at 3:50 a.m. some 3,000 guns opened fire:

shells of every calibre burst virtually together in two great semi-circles on or over the enemy's first and second lines – ten miles or so of sudden flame and horror. A few hundred yards in front of

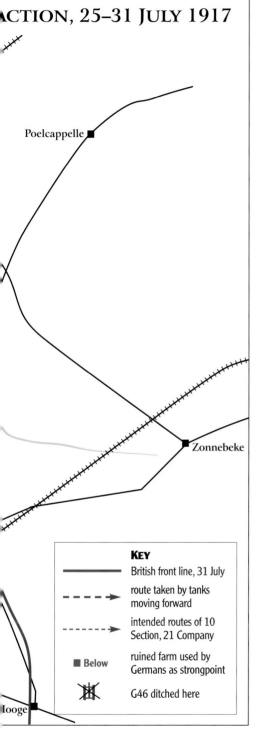

CTION, 25–31 JULY 1917

Poelcappelle

Zonnebeke

KEY

——	British front line, 31 July
- ->	route taken by tanks moving forward
- - ->	intended routes of 10 Section, 21 Company
■ Below	ruined farm used by Germans as strongpoint
✕	G46 ditched here

looge

our leading tank the very earth seemed to erupt. It spouted fire and fragments like a volcano. The mist which hung over the trenches was rent to tatters in a blaze of orange light, while hundreds of shrapnel bursts sparkled above . . . Far behind where the 9.2 barrage fell along the crown of the ridge, great tongues of flame leapt and wavered in volumes of scarlet smoke. And out of this instantaneous inferno arose streams of green and crimson rockets the S.O.S. calls of the enemy.

The tanks of the two G Battalion companies advanced behind the infantry. As G46 slowly moved forward across the obliterated German first line heading north, the atrocious state of the ground and almost total lack of recognizable features rendered normal navigation impossible – everywhere was just a brown waste of mud and waterlogged craters littered with debris. Browne commented that 'my compass was chasing its tail and generally behaving as if it was drunk; and after we had swung a dozen times to avoid the more dangerous craters . . . we might have been heading in any direction.'

Nevertheless, after sighting a recognizable lone tree G46 crawled on in the direction of Boche Castle, still well behind the attacking infantry. A German shell fragment cut the lashing of the unditching boom on the roof and it fell off, and as it proved too heavy for the crew to lift it was abandoned. Browne passed near G45, which had ditched in a huge crater near Boche Castle, and proceeded towards Kitchener's Wood, trying to avoid the remains of a road that he had been told was mined.

On all hands [sides] lay these brimming pools . . . I tried at once to get back to the road . . . but in that amphibious world the engine was not powerful enough to induce the tank to reverse or swing. She would only plough her way slowly forward through the mud. The end was inevitable . . . immediately in front were two or three large shell-holes, full to the brim. It being impossible to avoid, the G46, like a reluctant suicide, crawled straight into the first . . . The water rushed in through the tracks and sponson doors, covered the floor boards and flooded the sump: the fly-wheel thrashed through it for a second or two, sending showers about the interior; and then the tank, not having been constructed for submarine warfare, gave up the struggle.

It was then around 10:00 a.m. and in four hours G46 had advanced about 2 miles, was still behind the infantry and had fired only a few short bursts from two Lewis guns that had been quickly stopped by Browne, who thought they might hit British troops. The experience and fate of G46 (and G45) was typical of so many tanks, committed against the advice of senior tank officers to ground hopelessly unsuited to their employment. Browne and his crew plastered mud over the number on the roof, camouflaged the tank as best they could and remained with it until the following night before making their way back to Frascati Farm. Of the four tanks of 10 Section, three were ditched on the 31st but one, commanded by Lieutenant Alden (the officer who was nearly killed when

entangled with wire), reached its objective and assisted the infantry and another tank in taking Alberta strongpoint. He returned safely and was later awarded the MC.

The result of the day's fighting from the tank perspective was generally regarded as a failure – and that tanks were unsuitable for swamp warfare!

• **II Corps** Of the forty-eight tanks detailed to assist this corps only nineteen came into action and those that did suffered crippling losses. Their problems were not only the state of the ground, which compelled them to advance down the Menin Road, but that this route led straight through a narrow defile in the woods and the infantry had been unable to take the strongpoint just north of Clapham Junction that commanded the road. The tanks were picked off easily and the area became known as 'the tank graveyard', with seventeen hulks out of action.

• **XIX Corps** Several successes were achieved, with two tanks playing a crucial role in the capture of Frezenberg village redoubt, one tank supporting the capture of Bank Farm and two others Spree Farm. They were also instrumental in beating off several enemy counter-attacks, and one tank reached as far forward as Border House.

• **XVIII Corps** Here success was limited to assisting in the capture of McDonald's and Ferdinand's Farms. The Alberta strongpoint threatened to hold up the advance until two tanks arrived as described above, crushed the wire and by their fire drove the garrison under cover until dealt with by the infantry.

Despite these successes the two southern tank brigades had sent in 107 tanks, including ten supply, two wireless and one cable-laying machines, but by the end of the day thirty-three had been disabled by shellfire, a similar number had ditched and twenty-two were disabled by mechanical problems – around 88 lost out of 107 was a grim result. It was bad enough to make a number of senior commanders, including General Gough, seriously question the value of the Tank Corps. Gough's damning report on the operation could be paraphrased as: tanks cannot operate on bad ground; ground on a battlefield will always be bad, therefore tanks are no use on a battlefield. There was deep pessimism within the Tank Corps and rumours of abolition abounded. However, the High Command eventually decided to give it a further lease of life – a decision that was fortunate indeed and undoubtedly influenced by a brilliant little action on 19 August when a force of nine tanks, of which seven saw action, from G Battalion were instrumental in taking five strongpoints of exceptional strength with little loss to themselves or the supporting infantry.

The Cockcroft operation

The details of this small but important operation are given in Map 73 and its notes. The weather had been foul for August since the beginning of the month, with almost daily downpours of rain. Combined with the shelling, the result was to render the ground one vast quagmire of liquid mud pitted with a myriad water-filled shell craters. The plan was to capture five German concrete strongpoints that were blocking progress by XVIII Corps up the road to Poelcappelle, the strongest being The Cockcroft. Garrisons varying from 30 to 100 or more men with multiple machine guns defended each. Because of the virtual impossibility of tanks leaving the roads, the plan was a simple one: a column of nine tanks would advance up the Poelcappelle road with each tank having been given a specific strongpoint to attack. Infantry would follow to storm each position. There would be no conventional covering barrage; instead the area on the far side of the objectives would be blanketed in smoke.

One point after another was taken, with the tanks intimidating the garrisons until they fled, or driving them under cover, enabling the infantry to storm the posts virtually unscathed. It was almost certainly this action that saved the Tank Corps from disbandment. Losses among tank personnel were just thirteen and the infantry, which would normally have expected anything from 500 to 600, had only fifteen.

From this date to 9 October tanks took part in eleven further actions, the majority being on XVIII Corps' front on the Poelcappelle road. On 22 August tank F1 (a male), called 'Frey Bentos' after the ration tinned meat and commanded by a Lieutenant

The Influence of Tanks on British Troop Morale

The following is an extract from *Weekly Tank Notes*, No. 4, dated 31 August 1918, on the positive influence tanks' presence had on British morale.

Casualties – the most striking achievement of the Tanks in these operations [between 21 and 25 August] has been the low figure of our infantry casualties, which have in very few cases exceeded the number of prisoners captured. This result has been effected not only by the offensive power of the Tank in destroying enemy machine gunners, but also on its morale effect causing the enemy to surrender when otherwise he would continue to fight. The fact that all the enemy's offensive weapons concentrate against the Tank tends to diminish the casualties amongst the infantry.

Morale – The tank has in these operations become a most powerful factor in the morale of our own troops. Our infantry appear to realize that, when working with Tanks in front of them, their casualties in the attack will only be in hundreds, whereas formerly without Tanks their casualties would be in thousands . . .

Barrage – Artillery Officers state that a barrage can be arranged now very much more quickly than formerly, owing to the fact that with the use of Tanks occasional gaps are not of such great importance, and the gunners have therefore only to make sure of the range.

Hill, but with his section commander Captain Richardson on board as a passenger, put up an exceptional fight. It became ditched close to an enemy strongpoint called Gallipoli (see Map 71) and for seventy-two hours the crew fought on, although under continuous bombing and shelling and beating off storming parties until almost out of ammunition. Then, with every man wounded, they abandoned their tank and crawled back to their own lines. The two officers received the MC, the sergeant and a gunner the DCM and the remainder the MM.

On 22 August tanks were involved in fighting south of Fortuin (18 tanks), in front of St-Julien (16 tanks) and on the Menin Road (16 tanks); on 27 August north of St-Julien (12 tanks); on 20 September on the Menin Road Ridge (52 tanks); on 28 September at Polygon Wood (15 tanks); and

on 4 October at Broodseinde (12 tanks) – of that action the corps commander commented, 'the tanks in Poelcappelle were a decisive factor in our success on the left flank'. Thereafter the much depleted and utterly exhausted tank brigades were withdrawn from the fighting – Passchendaele itself was left to the infantry and the guns.

Within a matter of weeks, at Cambrai on 20 November, the Mark IV proved itself to the many doubters. Here they were attacking over suitable ground with the advantage of surprise, as the operation was not signalled to the enemy with a preliminary bombardment. This action is described as part of the all-arms battle in Section Thirteen.

The Mark V, Mark V*, Medium A (Whippet) and Other Tanks

Mark V

This tank was a considerable improvement on the Mark IV, with a better all-round speed and ease of manoeuvre. Although the dimensions and weight were similar to its predecessor and the hull still looked much the same as the Mark I, it was driven by a 150-h.p. Ricardo 6-cylinder engine. It could reverse at all speeds of the four-speed gearbox and all the means of movement were under the direct control of the driver. This was due to the use of epicyclic gears, which allowed one man to drive and steer the tank, thus releasing three others to man the guns and allowing the commander to concentrate solely on directing activities. To steer the tank at any speed the driver had merely to raise the gear lever on the side on which he wanted to turn, which had the

A tank bogged down and with a track lost near St-Julien during the Third Battle of Ypres.

MAP 73 TANK SUCCESS AGAINST THE COCKCROFT AND OTHER STRONGPOINTS, 19 AUGUST 1917

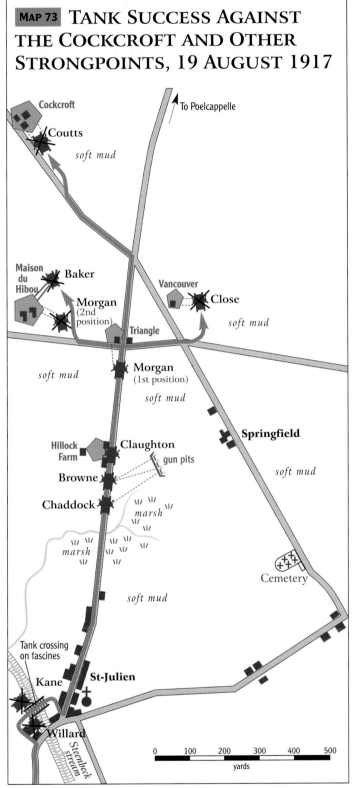

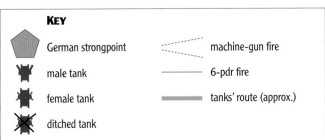

KEY

⬠ German strongpoint

🯅 male tank

🯅 female tank

✖ ditched tank

- - - - machine-gun fire

——— 6-pdr fire

━━━ tanks' route (approx.)

Notes for Map 73

• In mid-August 1917 a cluster of five German strongpoints was holding up the progress of XVIII Corps' advance up the St-Julien–Poelcappelle road. It was decided to use nine tanks from G Battalion, Tank Corps, to lead against these strongpoints with infantry supporting, and to attack without the usual artillery preparation – this time it would be a smoke barrage only, with the tanks advancing in single file up the Poelcappelle road as the ground on either side was totally unfit for tanks. The attack was planned to start at dawn on 19 August.

• The Germans were defending concrete pillboxes with walls at least 3 feet thick and so impervious to small-arms fire. The largest and strongest, with a garrison of around 100 men, was the Cockcroft. Of the others, Maison du Hibou was the second strongest with 60–80 men; the remainder (Vancouver, the Triangle and Hillock Farm) had smaller garrisons. There were also a number of well-defended gun pits about 150 yards opposite and east of Hillock Farm.

• The planned objectives were as follows (the tank commanders were all subalterns from 19, 20 and 21 Companies). Whether the tank was male or female is shown in parenthesis:

Coutts (F) and **Willard** (M) – the Cockcroft
Baker (M) and **Kane** (F) – Maison du Hibou
Morgan (F) and **Close** (F) – the Triangle and Vancouver
Claughton (F) – Hillock Farm
Browne (F) – the gun pits
Chaddock (F) – reserve, but to push through and assist Coutts and Willard at the Cockcroft if possible

• The potential weaknesses were that there were only two male tanks with 6-pdrs and that one of them, Willard's, was not running well.

The outcome was as follows:
Cockcroft Willard's tank ditched by the crossing over the Steenbeek, so Coutts faced a solitary attack on the strongest position with only Lewis guns. However, he left the road as he approached and struggled to within 50 yards before he bogged down, but his presence and the spraying of the apertures in the walls with machine-gun fire caused a panic departure of the garrison. However, the supporting infantry from the 33rd Brigade refused to acknowledge his success signal and would not advance until first his sergeant and then Coutts himself had gone back and personally told the commanding officer.
Maison du Hibou Only Baker's tank was available, as Kane's had also ditched at the crossing over the stream. Baker had the only remaining 6-pdr and, finding the walls of this two-storey strongpoint too strong, plunged into the mud and crawled to the rear before becoming ditched. Fortunately, one 6-pdr could be brought to bear on the rear door, and after pumping 30–40 rounds into it the garrison came rushing out, mostly to be shot down or surrender to the infantry who were in close support.
Triangle and Vancouver The Triangle put up a far stronger resistance and the German armour-piercing bullets caused problems with Morgan's tank, although with his help the infantry were able to get inside and bayonet or shoot the occupants. Meanwhile, Morgan attempted to go to Baker's assistance but ditched when he slid off the road, although he was able to bring Lewis-gun fire on to escaping Germans and eventually to unditch himself. Close managed to convince the occupants of Vancouver to abandon their position, although he too ditched off the road within 50 yards of the strongpoint.
Hillock Farm Claughton drew up alongside the position and opened fire, which was sufficient for the Germans to flee.
Gun pits Browne engaged them from the road for about 15 minutes, then German artillery began firing on their own position and supporting infantry were able to take the gun pits after it ceased.

• All five strongpoints were taken and losses were exceptionally light. Four tanks had ditched, of which one (Morgan) returned; two men were killed; and one officer and 10 men were wounded. Infantry losses were very slight (15) but the Germans lost many killed, wounded and captured, as well as at least 50 machine guns.

effect of interrupting the drive to that track so that, being driven by the other track, the tank would turn to the 'idle' side. When a sharp turn was needed, application of the foot brake would check the 'idle' side. The cooling of the engine was improved and it was completely enclosed in sheet-iron casing from which the foul air was exhausted through the roof. The petrol tank's capacity was increased to 75 gallons, giving it a radius of 25 miles, and was divided into three compartments so that if one was hit by shellfire the tank could, hopefully, continue to function. The larger engine gave it a maximum speed of 5 m.p.h.

There was better all-round observation with the installation of an observation cab in the roof instead of the previous manhole. Armament was improved by the reintroduction of the Hotchkiss machine gun and the addition of one to fire through the rear wall. The better all-round vision made it possible for the unditching beam to be fitted to the tracks from inside the tank (see box, page 392). It was, however, noisier than the Mark IV, and more extensive arrangements had to be made to disguise the noise by artillery or machine-gun fire or low-flying aircraft.

The Mark V first went into action at the Battle of Hamel on 4 July 1918. Five companies of sixty tanks were employed, attacking in two waves: the first of forty-eight, the second, or reserve, of twelve. The artillery provided a creeping barrage and smokescreens, behind which came the Australian infantry followed by the tanks – this arrangement was at the behest of the Australians, who had not yet lost their mistrust of tanks gained at Bullecourt. The intention of this arrangement was for the tanks to come forward when the infantry were held up. Unlike so many previous occasions, all the tanks were on their start points on time – an indication of the improved reliability of the new machines. The greater manoeuvrability of the Mark V enabled the tanks to drive over enemy machine-gun posts before the gunners could escape – this happened a number of times and was a particular feature of this attack. The assault achieved surprise, and the cooperation between the tanks and infantry was excellent, with all objectives secured. Bullecourt was forgiven, if not forgotten, and from then on the Australians were much in favour of the armoured arm.

Mark V*

As with all tanks, there were male and female versions. This tank was 6 feet longer than the Mark V, with the weight of the male being about 33 tons. It had the same armament and crew of eight as the Mark V but could carry twenty or twenty-five additional troops and had the ability to cross a 14-foot trench as compared with 10 or 11 feet. It was powered by the same engine and had the same mechanical arrangements, although it incorporated an adapted transmission system to cater for the additional length. In effect, it was a stretched version of the Mark V and the first ever purpose-designed armoured personnel carrier – although it was disappointing when used as such, as the infantry suffered from carbon-monoxide poisoning and so were unable to function properly when they dismounted. It could, however, be used to bring up supplies or bring back wounded personnel.

Medium A (Whippet)

This was the British light tank (sometimes called the 'cavalry tank' because of its mobility) and was primarily a personnel, animal or soft-vehicle destroyer. It weighed just 16 tons, was capable of a maximum speed of 8 m.p.h. on good, flat surfaces and had a radius of 35 miles. Armour over the vital parts was 12mm thick. It was 23 feet long, 8 feet 7 inches high and 8 feet wide. It was able to cross a 7-foot-wide trench and carried a crew of an officer and two men. Armament consisted of four machine guns (Hotchkiss) with 5,400 rounds of SAA. The tracks were almost as long as those on the larger tanks but did not go over the entire machine, only round the chassis. It had two 45-h.p. four-cylinder Tylor engines, which were positioned at the front under the armoured bonnet, giving it a climbing ability of 1 in 2. The fighting cab was perched at the back and it was from there that the three Hotchkiss machine guns were fired. The Whippet called for a particularly skilful driver, otherwise stalling one of the engines was a common occurrence. Steering was affected by varying the speed of either engine, which was controlled by a steering wheel connected to two carburetor throttles, the movement of the wheel producing acceleration of one engine and simultaneous deceleration of the other.

Whippets first saw action on 26 March 1918 during the German offensive. Twelve were instructed to advance on the village of Colincamps, and as they rattled down the main street they encountered a large body of Germans approaching from the opposite direction. The Germans mistook these weird-looking machines for their own tanks and began to cheer enthusiastically until the Whippets opened fire and charged, causing the enemy to flee in panic. This was one of the very few tank successes during that German offensive. Some 370 British tanks were involved in the British retreat – almost half broke down and were abandoned without firing a shot.

In extreme circumstances a Whippet could remain in action with only one crew member. This happened on 23 August 1918 when a tank officer and sergeant were wounded; the remaining soldier placed the wounded in a shell hole and drove on into the fight, locking the steering and opening fire with two machine guns. He continued to alternate driving and firing for some four hours before bringing his tank safely back. His action that day was all the more extraordinary when it is recalled that, because the Whippets were small, the heat inside built up, despite the fans, to an almost unbearable intensity – often machine guns were too hot to hold and ammunition swelled enough to jam the guns.

Specialist tanks

Used for the first time at Messines in April 1917, specialist supply tanks included some gun-carrying tanks originally designed to carry into action a 60-pounder gun or 6-inch howitzer with ammunition. They required a four-man crew and were powered by a six-cylinder 105-h.p. Daimler engine. Situated between the inner walls of the hull at the front was a 'skid', or platform, that could be drawn out and its front lowered to the ground to provide a ramp up which the gun was hauled.

Many of these were converted into supply tanks. In June 1917 each tank battalion had six supply tanks, two in each company, and special sledges were built to be towed behind them, carrying a wide variety of stores and ammunition. Supply tanks (twelve old Mark Is) were used for the first time at Messines, with each carrying sufficient petrol, oil, grease, water and ammunition to replenish five fighting tanks. For the Cambrai offensive 110 sledges were constructed for supplies to be towed behind tanks. Special infantry carrier companies were formed in 1918 of old Mark IV tanks, but these were, much to the crews' annoyance, used to carry supplies for infantry and fighting tanks.

Tank Notes, September 1918, give examples of the capacity of supply and gun-carrier tanks, and their value in saving manpower in just one operation:

• sixteen supply tanks (usually Mark IVs converted) transported 120,000 lb, including grenades, mortar and small-arms ammunition; pickets, barbed wire, picks and shovels and other stores. For such a load at 56 lb per man, 2,143 men would be needed.

• six gun-carrier tanks transported 925 rounds of 6-inch howitzer, 4.5-inch howitzer and 18-pounder ammunition, 113 boxes of small-arms ammunition, barbed wire and other stores in total weighing 97,752 lb – a load requiring 1,745 men to move. Some were also used purely as supply tanks.

Wireless tanks were experimented with for command purposes from a tank battalion to brigade or divisional headquarters or with aircraft, with, at Cambrai and Third Ypres for example, one per battalion. However, they were far from satisfactory and the tank had to stop and erect an aerial in order to transmit. The first wireless tank was the old female Mark I, suitably adapted with the armament removed and the sponsons partly plated over, and with the wireless and operator in the sponson. It is likely that by Cambrai in late 1917 some Mark IVs had been adapted.

There were also bridge-building tanks, and tanks of any sort were frequently used for improvised salvage work, sometimes for cable-laying, and with grapnels for dragging away wire obstacles.

Mark V, V* and Whippets at Amiens

Map 26 (page 77) gives a general outline of the opening day of the battle on 8 August 1918 (the 'Black Day' of the German Army), although the representation of the tanks and cavalry is only generally indicative of their operations. The twelve tank battalions were allotted as follows:

Canadian Corps – 1st, 4th, 5th and 14th Battalions

Australian Corps – 2nd, 8th, 13th and 15th Battalions

III Corps – 10th Battalion

General Reserve – 9th Battalion

Cavalry Corps – 3rd and 6th Battalions

The 17th Armoured Car Battalion operated independently.

The 602 tanks were made up of 288 Mark V, 72 Mark V*, 96 Whippets, 124 supply and 22 gun-carriers. The total of fighting tanks was 456, of which some 415 went into action at zero hour. On 8 August all objectives were gained except on III Corps' front. The complete surprise (there was no long preparatory bombardment) was made doubly effective by the fog. In all, some eighty-two brigades of field artillery, twenty-six brigades of heavy artillery and thirteen batteries of heavy guns and howitzers opened fire at zero hour, with the heavies concentrating on enemy gun batteries. The crossing of the Luce river – a difficult operation – was successfully accomplished and a large number of machine guns were engaged and overcome, and within two hours some 16,000 prisoners were taken. Both Whippet battalions had a good deal of fighting with German cavalry divisions around Le Quesnel and Harbonnières. By that evening the maximum penetration had been over 7 miles in the centre, and the tanks had rallied with about 147 out of action due to ditching, mechanical problems and enemy fire. All crews were utterly exhausted by the great distances covered in the heat, and composite companies had to be formed for the next day.

The Whippets had often been forced to mark time, as the cavalry with whom they were working were held up by solitary machine guns, and a number of tanks dropped out of action from various causes. When they were acting on their own, however, they could achieve remarkable results, as shown by the adventures of the Whippet called 'Musical Box', which was commanded by Lieutenant C. B. Arnold of B Company, 6th Battalion, Tank Corps. He was able to run amok behind German lines for nine hours despite the heat and fumes inside the machine, destroying a gun battery, an enemy hutted camp, numerous vehicles, horses and men. In his report, written in 1919 after his release from captivity, Arnold describes the highlights of his day:

The gun battery I ran diagonally across the front of the battery, at a distance of about 600 yards. Both my guns [machine guns] were able to fire on the battery, in spite of which they got off about eight rounds at me without damage . . . I turned full right and engaged the battery from the rear. On observing my appearance . . . the gunners, some thirty in number, abandoned their guns and tried to get away . . . Gunner Ribbans and I accounted for the whole lot.

The camp I entered the valley (between Bayonvillers and Harbonnières) . . . [and] many enemy were visible packing kits and others retiring. On our opening fire on the nearest, many others appeared from the huts, making for the end of the valley . . . We accounted for many of them.

Conditions inside I would here beg to suggest that no petrol be carried on the outside of the machine, as under orders we were carrying nine tins of petrol on the roof . . . The perforated tins allowed the petrol to run all over the cab. These fumes, combined with the intense bullet splash and the great heat after being in action (by this time) nine to ten hours, made it necessary . . . to breathe through the mouthpiece of a box respirator, without actually wearing the mask.

It was here that Lieutenant C. B. Arnold, commander of the tank 'Musical Box', stopped to confer with Australian infantry during his advance.

At this bridge over the railway just south of Harbonnières 'Musical Box' ambushed a German lorry, shooting the driver and watching the vehicle fall into the ditch.

German gun battery
in this area

This photograph is taken from the bridge over the A29 motorway north of the village of Marcelcave. 'Musical Box' engaged a German gun battery in the area indicated, forcing the gunners to abandon their weapons.

Vehicles, horses and soldiers Over the top of another bridge I could see the cover of a top of a lorry coming in my direction. I moved up out of sight and waited until he topped the bridge, when I shot the driver. The lorry ran into the right-hand ditch . . . I could see a long line of men retiring on both sides of the railway, and fired at these at ranges of 400 yards to 500 yards, inflicting heavy casualties. I passed through these and also accounted for one horse and driver of a two-horse canvas-covered wagon . . . [we] came in view of a large horse and wagon line . . . Gunner Ribbans fired continuously into motor and horse transport moving on three roads . . . I fired many bursts at 600 yards to 800 yards at transport blocking roads on my left, causing great confusion . . . There were about twelve men in the middle aisle of these lines. I fired a long burst at these. Some went down . . .

'Musical Box' is hit Two heavy concussions closely followed one another and the cab burst into flames. Carney [the driver] and Ribbans got to the door and collapsed. I was almost overcome, but managed to get the door open and fell out onto the ground, and was able to drag out the other two men . . . The fresh air revived us and we all got up and made a short rush to get away from the burning petrol. We were all on fire. In this rush Carney was shot in the stomach and killed. We rolled over and over to try to extinguish the flames. I saw numbers of the enemy approaching from all round. The first arrival came for me with a rifle and bayonet. I got hold of this and the point of the bayonet entered my right forearm. The second

man struck at my head with the butt end of his rifle, hit my shoulder and neck and knocked me down. When I came to, there were dozens all round me, and anyone who could reach me did so, and I was well kicked; they were furious.

German Anti-tank Tactics

When the British tanks first appeared on the battlefield on 15 September 1916 the Germans were surprised, shocked and frightened. With none of their own, the High Command was compelled to concentrate on anti-tank defence. In 1916 this meant constructing obstacles, and it was not until after Arras the following spring that German anti-tank activity increased substantially and included the single-shot, 13mm, anti-tank rifle firing large, armour-piercing bullets of .530 calibre. It was 5½-feet long and weighed about 36 lb, and had the kick of a mule – making some soldiers reluctant to use it. German instructions on its use included advice that multiple hits were needed to kill or injure the crew, and that hitting the tank at an angle smaller than 60 degrees would result in a ricochet. However, the British Mark IV that went into action at Messines was far less vulnerable to armour-piercing bullets than the Mark I.

Bundles of grenades were also used to damage tracks – although the tank was merely converted into a stationary pillbox. Mines, iron stockades and concrete walls were all also brought into use, but it was soon realized that the best tank-killer was artillery firing armour-piercing shells – a captured German document stated that 'the first duty of field artillery is to keep off

enemy tanks. All other duties must give way to this.' The successful counter-attack at Cambrai in November 1917, when a number of derelict British tanks were captured, somewhat reassured the Germans that the tank could be defeated. By September 1918 a captured German document gave the following advice on anti-tank barriers:

> See that the cement blocks are firmly seated; otherwise the tank will push them over. The tank is not stopped by blocks which are less than 6½ feet high. It is advisable to dig, in front of the block, a ditch 3 feet deep, forming an acute angle at the base of the block.
>
> If barriers are constructed by means of agricultural machines, they must be entangled with a quantity of wire; make use of the pointed metal portions (harrows &) which will catch in the track. These barriers will only fulfill their purpose if they are drawn up in narrow streets to a depth of 30–60 feet. Stretched wires are no use, the tank breaks them down.
>
> A cart placed across a road cannot stop a tank unless it is large and filled with stones. Small ordinary carts are useless.

Use was also made of tank traps, often laid out in chequerboard fashion. These were deep, wide pits, sometimes filled with water, which were covered with branches and wood over which was spread earth and mud.

The greatest anti-tank activity, however, was developed after French attacks in July 1918 employing large numbers of tanks. In an official note to his armies, General Ludendorff wrote, 'It is to the Tanks that the French owe their success on the first days.' From that time on, as the Germans never possessed substantial numbers of their own tanks, that anti-tank defence became of paramount importance. The value of water as a tank obstacle came to the fore at the beginning of August that year, when the lines of the Ancre and Avre rivers were taken up as major anti-tank obstacles. The general tone of High Command instructions to divisions was that sacrifices of guns and labour must be made to develop anti-tank defences. Behind all this was the belief that if the enemy tanks could be stopped, the attack would fail. In an official communiqué dated 22 August 1918 an NCO was mentioned by name for having knocked out tanks. The naming of individual officers in such a way was very rare, and the special mention of an NCO almost unprecedented. It was done to emphasize the need for gunners to remain with their guns and to fire at advancing tanks at short ranges.

Orders from the LI Corps contained the following instructions:

A captured German tank named 'Elfriede'.

Each Division will detail from the Reserve Field Artillery one Anti-Tank Battery, which will be 'Standing To'. The limbers will contain armour piercing shell. Guns belonging to the Artillery in the Line fire over open sights at tanks [indirect artillery fire was largely ineffective against moving tanks] that have broken through. Heavy Batteries must be given a definite strip of country in which they will fire on Tanks. All machine guns, including those kept in reserve, must be provided with armour-piercing ammunition. Every heavy machine gun has as its first duty to fight any Tank appearing within its radius.

Anti-Tank Rifles should normally be placed in the main line of resistance.

Anti-Tank Mines complete the Anti-Tank defence. They will most particularly be dug in front of the line and also laid in large numbers in front of the strong points and support points.

Special Note. As soon as the Tank attack is launched, all Anti-Tank weapons have this one aim, to fight until the last Tank has been put out of action. As soon as the Tanks are destroyed the whole attack has failed. This must be brought to the common knowledge of the troops.

Wooden tank models were supplied to many divisions for instruction of troops in the areas most vulnerable to attack by artillery, trench mortars and machine guns. Special anti-tank groups or companies were formed in the forward areas, each consisting of a field gun, machine guns, anti-tank rifles and trench mortars. Virtually every infantry battalion in the line had dedicated tank-killing squads and an anti-tank mine-laying section consisting of an NCO and five soldiers. A captured document reveals clearly the seriousness with which the High Command regarded the British and French tank threat:

On the approach of Tanks all means of communication are to be freed for the passing of news. Codeword 'Panzerwagen'. On receipt of special light signals one will be chosen to mean, 'look out tanks.' In the case of tank attack the advance zone will be evacuated as far back as the main line of resistance to a breadth corresponding to the tank attack, in order to enable the artillery to fire freely into the evacuated advance zone.

Counter attacks against hostile infantry, advancing under cover of fire from the Tank, does not hold out any chances of success and demands unnecessary sacrifice; they must therefore only be launched after the Tank has been put out of action.

German Tanks

The Germans put their emphasis on anti-tank defences and tactics rather than the construction of large numbers of their own tanks. This was primarily because by 1917 manufacturing capacity in Germany was suffering acutely from shortages of raw materials and skilled workers as well as problems with transport. Production therefore had to concentrate on really essential items to keep the war effort functioning, such as aircraft, submarines, munitions, artillery, motor vehicles and railway material. Tank production had a lesser priority and progressed slowly during 1917. After several failures during testing at the Motor Transport Testing Company at the Berlin Lankwitz Barracks, the model A7V tank (*Panzerkraftwagen*) was passed for service.

The chief characteristics and problems related to this machine were:

- 24 feet long, 10 feet 6 inches wide and a maximum height of 11 feet. It weighed 40 tons and had a maximum speed of 8 m.p.h. on a good surface, 3 m.p.h. across reasonable country. It had 20mm of armour plate on the sides and 30mm at the front; however, the roof was not armoured. The steel was not hardened, which reduced its effectiveness. It was powered by two centrally mounted four-cylinder petrol engines delivering 100 h.p. each, and carried 110 gallons of fuel. A decided advantage over the British tank was that it was provided with sprung bogeys and this use of springs for so heavy a tank was the one progressive feature in the German contribution to tank design.

- The armament consisted of a 57mm gun mounted at the front and six 7.92mm machine guns, with the female version having just eight machine guns. Around 40–60 ammunition belts each containing 250 rounds were carried, as well as 180 shells for the gun – these were split 90:54:36 between canister, anti-tank and high explosive. It normally had a crew of sixteen – an officer, eleven NCOs and four privates – twice the size of a British crew.

- Inability to cross large trenches or heavily shelled and muddy ground due to its shape (large overhang at the front) and lack of much ground clearance were serious disadvantages, which, coupled with its weight, restricted its cross-country mobility.

- The crew was vulnerable to internal 'splash' of even ordinary SAA, as there were many crevices and joints in the armour plate. The driver had a blind spot out to about 12 yards from the front of the tank – a major problem when manoeuvring over difficult ground, or at night or in fog or smoke.

New Zealand soldiers examine captured anti-tank artillery.

The Germans captured and salvaged between twenty-five and thirty British Mark IV tanks which they used against the Allies – they preferred them to their own A7V. A High Command document dated 7 July 1918 gives the German tank organization in the field as three sections of five A7V tanks each and five sections of five British tanks (Mark IVs – two male and three female). It was proposed to increase these forty tanks to seventy-five.

The A7V was first used on 21 March 1918. Five tanks under the command of a Captain Grieff were deployed north of the St-Quentin Canal. Three broke down with mechanical problems before getting into action, but the remaining pair assisted in halting a British attack in the area.

Summary of German tank actions in 1918

24 April The most successful German tank operation. Of fourteen tanks brought forward, twelve got into action. The tactically important village of Villers-Bretonneux was captured. One British male tank hit a German tank and the others withdrew. Two British female tanks were hit by German tanks. A counter-attack restored the situation and two derelict German tanks were left on the battlefield. This was the first tank versus tank action ever fought – see opposite.

24 May (French front) Tanks were again used on the first day of the Aisne offensive. None succeeded in passing a large trench – the Dardanelles Trench – in the second line.

1 June (French front) Fifteen tanks operated with little success in the Reims sector and eight tanks were abandoned in the French lines.

The memorial to the first tank versus tank clash of the war, near the village of Cachy.

31 August Three tanks approached British lines east of Bapaume. On being engaged by artillery, they withdrew. Two A7Vs became ditched in the enemy's line and were captured in a subsequent British advance.

8 October About fifteen captured British tanks were used in the Cambrai sector and were at first mistaken for friendly machines and not engaged. However, when it was clear they were hostile, three were disabled by British tanks and several others by a captured German gun used against them.

11 October A few tanks were used at St-Aubert, four of them being hit by British artillery fire.

The First Tank versus Tank Clash

By 24 April the German spring offensive seemed to have got a second wind and had advanced to within 7 miles of Amiens, threatening to take the higher ground overlooking the town. There was a danger that it would cut the Amiens–Paris railway line. The front where the tank clash took place was about 8 miles east of Amiens, between Villers-Bretonneux (in German hands) and the small village of Cachy, less than 2 miles to the south-west. Allied troops in the woods behind the line here were a mixture of the French Foreign Legion, Moroccans and Australians. The British tanks of A Company, 1st Tank Battalion, were located in the Bois de l'Abbé immediately west of Villers-Bretonneux. On the night of 23rd April the Germans shelled the woods with mustard gas. With a German assault imminent the order was received to proceed to the Cachy switch line (trench) and hold it at all costs.

Among the tanks was a male Mark IV commanded by Captain Frank Mitchell, the British officer destined to participate in the first ever tank versus tank action. What follows are extracts from his book, *Tank Warfare*:

> We put on our masks once more and plunged, like divers, into the gas-laden wood. As we struggled to crank up, one of the three men collapsed. We put him against a tree, gave him some tablets of ammonia to sniff, and then, as he did not seem to be coming round we left him, for time was pressing. Out of a crew

Tanks in the One Hundred Days Campaign

Tank Notes Weekly, No. 4, gives an informative picture of tank operations during August 1918.

> Practically the whole Tank Corps has been either in action or trekking to new scenes of operations, continuously since 8th August.
>
> The great heat, the long distances travelled, and amount of fighting has been a very severe trial for the Tank crews, while the strain on Commanders and Staffs has been enormous, with the constant necessity of making hasty arrangements with infantry formations.
>
> The Tank Corps is now deficient of about 250 Officers and 2,000 other ranks (representing about 30 per cent of the fighting strength) . . . though several Tanks have been hit, it should be noted that a direct hit on a tank does not necessarily mean that all the crew are killed or wounded. A large percentage of the direct hits on Tanks inflicted many fewer casualties on the crews than might have been expected. On 23rd August, 8 Tanks in one sector received direct hits, but only one man was slightly wounded. The Tanks themselves are generally put out of action for only a short period. This is, of course, particularly the case during a successful advance, when it is possible to get up to the Tanks and repair them in peace.

In just over three months between the British offensive that started on 8 August 1918 and the Armistice on 11 November, the British Tank Corps had fought in twenty-six battles and major engagements and had almost been brought to a standstill. Since 8 August some 2,000 individual tank engagements had taken place and practically the whole of this number had been put out of action in some way – over 1,000 tanks had been repaired and made fit for service again. Casualties to personnel were comparatively light. According to the *Order of Battle of Divisions* compiled by Major A. F. Becke, 1,848 tanks were engaged and 565 were knocked out between 8 August and 24 October 1918. Tank crew casualties were 472 killed, 2,347 were wounded and 367 missing. The number of tanks in action on 8 August was 430 – the greatest number of tanks ever in action on one day during the war.

An example of the severity of the tank operations during this period is illustrated by the 5th Tank Brigade, which was not formed until March 1918 but nevertheless fought in fifteen battles or engagements. Of the initial 576 tanks, no fewer than 310 reached their objectives and only twenty-six failed to reach their start line – a huge improvement on their debut eighteen months before. The only tank brigade still in action on 4 November was the 2nd Tank Brigade. It fought in the final battles of the war on the Sambre.

of seven [plus Mitchell] there remained only four men, with red-rimmed bulging eyes, while my driver, the second reserve driver, had had only a fortnight's driving experience. Fortunately one gearsman was loaned to me from another tank.

The three tanks [in his section] . . . crawled out of the wood and set off over the open ground towards Cachy . . .

I informed the crew [that enemy tanks were expected] . . . Opening a loophole, I looked out. There some three hundred yards away, a round squat looking monster was advancing; behind it came waves of infantry, and farther away to the left and right crawled two more of these armed tortoises.

So we had met our rivals at last! For the first time in history tank was encountering tank! . . .

[My] right gunner peering through his narrow slit, made a sighting shot. The shell burst some distance beyond the leading tank. No reply came. A second shot boomed out, landing just to the right, but again there was no reply. More shots followed.

Suddenly a hurricane of hail pattered against our steel wall, filling the interior with myriads of sparks and flying splinters! Something rattled against the steel helmet of the driver sitting next to me, and my face was stung with minute fragments of steel. The crew flung themselves flat on the floor. The driver ducked his head and drove straight on.

Above the roar of our engine sounded the staccato rat-tat-tat-tat of machine guns, and another furious jet of bullets sprayed our steel side, the splinters clanging against the engine cover. The Jerry tank had treated us to a broadside of armour-piercing bullets!

Taking advantage of a dip in the ground, we got beyond range, and then turning we manoeuvred to get the left gunner on to the moving target. Owing to our gas casualties the gunner was working single-handed, and his right eye being swollen with gas, he aimed with the left. Moreover, as the ground was heavily scarred with shell holes, we kept going up and down like a ship in a heavy sea, which made accurate shooting difficult. His first shot fell some fifteen yards in front, the next went beyond, and then I saw the shells bursting all round the tank. He fired shot after shot in rapid succession every time it came into view.

Nearing the village of Cachy, I noticed to my astonishment that the two females [in his section] were slowly limping away to the rear. Almost immediately on their

arrival they had both been hit by shells which tore great holes in their sides, leaving them defenceless against machine gun bullets . . .

Then came our first casualty. Another raking broadside from the German tank and the rear Lewis gunner was wounded in both legs by an armour-piercing bullet which tore through our steel plate. We had no time to put on more than a temporary dressing, and he lay on the floor bleeding and groaning, while the 6-pounder boomed over his head and empty shell cases clattered all round him . . .

The left gunner, registering carefully, began to hit the ground right in front of the Jerry tank. I took a risk and stopped the tank for a moment. The pause was justified; a well-aimed shot hit the enemy's conning tower, bringing him to a standstill. Another roar and yet another white puff in front of the tank denoted a second hit. Peering with swollen eyes through his narrow slit, the gunner shouted words of triumph that were drowned by the roar of the engine. Then once more he aimed with great deliberation and hit for the third time. Through a loophole I saw the tank heel over to one side; then a door opened, and out ran the crew. We had knocked the monster out.

Quickly I signed to the machine gunner, and he poured volley after volley into the retreating figures.

French Tanks

If the British father of the tank was Lieutenant Colonel (later Major General) E. D. Swinton, then Colonel (later General) Jean-Baptiste Estienne was the father of the French version. On 12 December 1915 Estienne set out his theory of armoured, mechanized warfare to the French GHQ. This was followed by a visit to the Schneider engineers in Paris before returning to his artillery command at Verdun. At the end of February 1916 the Department for Artillery and Munitions placed an order with Schneider for 400 armoured vehicles. However, there were to be conflicting lines of development, as in April Estienne learned that a similar number of armoured vehicles of a heavier type were being manufactured by the St-Chamond works.

During the summer Estienne visited England and saw the British Mark I demonstrated; it was a visit that convinced him of the necessity of having large numbers of light tanks. On his return he put his views to the Renault firm and urged the ministry to adopt a light machine. Initially his idea was rejected, although design drawings for the vehicle were prepared. Promoted to major general on 30 September, Estienne was able to convince Marshal Joffre to authorize the construction of a large number of light armoured vehicles. Meanwhile, during the summer the Ministry of Munitions had approved the establishment of four battalions each of Schneider and St-Chamond tanks. However, it was not until May 1917

A French Renault FT17 tank, armed with a machine gun and revolving turret, heads for the front.

that the ministry was finally convinced and ordered 1,150 light tanks to be built by Renault. A summary of the specifications of each follows:

• **Schneider tank M16** Almost 20 feet long, weighing 13½ tons with armour plate at the front and sides 11.6mm thick and capable of 4.5 m.p.h. on a good surface. It was powered by a 60-h.p. engine, had a crew of six and was armed with a shortened 75mm gun and two Hotchkiss machine guns. This was impressive armament with the gun being the most powerful used by an operational tank until 1941. However, the tracks went only round the chassis, not the whole body of the tank like the British, and this meant there was a long hangover of the hull at the front, giving the tank severe problems in crossing even comparatively narrow trenches and limited its climbing ability. It had a range of 27 miles and came into service in December 1916. A heavier model, weighing up to 23 tons, with thicker armour, a maximum speed of 6 m.p.h. and a crew of nine, armed with a long 75mm gun and four machine guns, was produced for 1917. It was, like the 1916 version, too long in the body compared with the tracks and in the field proved prone to breakdowns.

• **St-Chamond tanks** This was the French heavy tank, weighing 24 tons and being more heavily armed than the Schneider, with a 75mm gun and four machine guns. Armour plate was 11.4mm thick at the front and 8.5 at the sides (the later model had thicker armour). It was powered by a 9-h.p. engine, giving it a maximum speed on the flat of 6 m.p.h. with a range of about 34 miles. It had a crew of nine. It suffered from the short tracks round the chassis and the consequent serious disadvantages of the Schneider.

• **Renault FT17** This was a true light cavalry machine – an armoured skirmisher. It was tiny compared to the heavies, weighing only 6.4 tons and had 16mm of armour at the front with 8mm on the sides. Overall length was just over 16 feet. It had a crew of just two – a driver who sat on the floor and a gunner who fired either a 37mm gun or Hotchkiss machine gun from a 360-degree revolving turret – a huge advantage. It was powered by a 35-h.p. engine and could travel at a maximum speed of 5 m.p.h. with a range of 20 miles. It was highly manoeuvrable and could spin round like a top.

On 16 April 1917 French tanks went into action for the first time. This was the opening day of the French Fifth Army's attack on the Chemin des Dames ridge and involved eight companies (128) of Schneiders. Of these, three companies failed to get into action and suffered heavily from German artillery on higher ground. The others managed to get ahead of the infantry and in places to reach the enemy third line, but only after having problems crossing trenches and at a heavy cost. Twenty-eight tanks broke down, fifty-two were knocked out by shells, more were damaged, some abandoned, and only a few came back unscathed – it was not a promising start.

On 15 July 1918 the Germans launched their last major offensive of the war between Château-Thierry and Reims. At 4:35 a.m. on 18 July, in a slight fog, the French launched their counter-attack with seven heavy and nine light tank battalions (337 tanks, of which the 110 light tanks were in reserve) available to their Tenth Army. These were allocated as follows:

I Corps	3rd Heavy Tank Battalion (27 Schneider tanks) to 153rd Division
XX Corps	12th Heavy Tank Battalion (30 St-Chamond tanks) to 2nd US Division
	11th Heavy Tank Battalion (30 St-Chamond tanks) to 1st US Division
	4th Heavy Tank Battalion (48 Schneider tanks) to Moroccan Division
	1st Heavy Tank Battalion (48 Schneider tanks) to 1st US Division
XXX Corps	10th Heavy Tank Battalion (24 St-Chamond tanks) to 38th Division
Army Reserve	1st Light Tank Battalion (45 Renault tanks)
	2nd Light Tank Battalion (40 Renault tanks)
	3rd Light Tank Battalion (45 Renault tanks)

Not all these tanks were available for the Tenth Army's actual attack on 18 July. However, it achieved complete surprise and resistance was not sustained. The heavy tanks and infantry were able to advance to a considerable depth. At 7:00 p.m. the 1st Light Battalion came into action and succeeded in leading the infantry forward about 2 miles. Of the 337 tanks allocated to the Tenth Army's front, only 225 were engaged on 18 July. Of these, 102 were casualties, sixty-two of them being hit by artillery shells. Tank personnel losses amounted to 25 per cent. The next day composite tank units with 105 machines were assembled to continue the attack, although by then the German resistance had stiffened and the tank battalions suffered heavily, with the 3rd Heavy Battalion losing all but two. Nevertheless, overall the attack was a success, although by the end of the day fifty of the 105 had been knocked out by shellfire and 22 per cent of personnel had become casualties.

On 20 July thirty-two tanks took part in local counter-attacks in which seventeen were hit and 52 per cent of the crews became casualties. On 21 July further assaults were made without artillery preparation by 100 tanks, during which another thirty-six were hit and 27 per cent of personnel lost. The next day tanks were withdrawn and regrouped for a final attack on the 23rd against enemy positions that were strongly supported by a powerful artillery force. It was another bad day for the tanks in terms of losses, with forty-eight out of eighty-two being knocked out.

A French tank and a dead German soldier are left behind by US troops as they run for cover under enemy fire during the Meuse–Argonne offensive, 1918.

Meanwhile, on the Sixth Army's front, eight companies of light tanks and three of heavies had been in action successfully, and when the fighting in what was to be called the Battle of Soissons ended it was considered that the tanks, particularly the light Renaults, had been the weapon that had brought overall success. The last action fought by French tanks occurred on 25 October when Renaults operating in open country made an advance of 8½ miles on a front of 3 miles.

According to Colonel (later Major General) J. F. C. Fuller in his book *Tanks in the Great War*, 3,988 individual French tank actions took place during 1918 – 3,140 by Renault, 473 by Schneiders and 375 by St-Chamonds.

American Tanks

The United States entered the war in April 1917 and by September had plans to create a Tank Corps of five heavy battalions and twenty light, a target that was increased in May 1918 to fifteen heavy and thirty light battalions, making up fifteen tank brigades of one heavy and two light battalions each. The heavy battalions were to have a new Mark VIII model powered by Liberty aero-engines built at Neuvy-Pailloux, 200 miles south of Paris, and the light version would be the French Renault, but manufactured in America. This programme proved far too ambitious; it was found impossible to produce these numbers and in the event no tank of American manufacture was used in the war. This compelled American armoured units to rely, as they did for so much equipment and most weapons, on their Allies – in this case mainly the French Renault light tank, but also some heavies. In the last months of the war the Americans also fielded a battalion of British Mark V and Mark V* in the Somme sector.

The American Tank Corps first saw action at St-Mihiel in September 1918 in operations conducted by the US First Army. Here I Corps operated with two battalions of the 304th Tank Brigade, equipped with 144 French Renaults with American crews and commanded by Lieutenant Colonel George S. Patton. It was supported by two units of Schneider and St-Chamond heavy tanks crewed by the French. In all, the First Army deployed 419 tanks, including three battalions of Renaults, with two more companies of heavy tanks, all with French crews, supporting IV Corps. Although the Americans succeeded in their objective of eliminating the St-Mihiel salient, it was something of a debacle for the tanks, as so many failed due to mechanical breakdowns or became ditched in the mud.

However, by 26 September the Tank Corps had been made up to strength for the Meuse–Argonne offensive. Because tanks had frequently run out of fuel at St-Mihiel, Patton ordered the crews to strap two 52-gallon fuel drums on the back of the machines – despite the obvious danger of fire if they were hit; he instructed that the drums should be tied on with ropes so that, hopefully, they would burn through and the drums fall off before endangering the crew. The other main concern was the frequency of mechanical breakdowns and shortages of spare parts. A private soldier suggested that one tank in each company should be loaded up with spares and towing equipment to act as a mobile workshop – an idea that Patton immediately implemented. Despite this, the Meuse–Argonne offensive, which lasted to the end of the war, saw huge losses to the Tank Corps, with an attrition rate of 123 per cent due primarily to mechanical failures and ditching. By the end of the war there were only fifty operational tanks available to the corps.

Lieutenant George S. Patton with a French-built Renault light tank, July 1918.

A rare photograph of an aerial dogfight over the Western Front.

Section Eleven

Aviation

*Let us remember also those who belong to the most recent military arm,
the keen-eyed and swift-winged knights of the air, who have given to the
world a new type of daring and resourceful heroism . . .*

King George V's address to Parliament and
Representatives of the Dominions, November 1918

The Royal Flying Corps (RFC) was the air arm of the British Army during most of the war. During the early part of the fighting on the Western Front its responsibilities centred on reconnaissance flights, which came to include spotting for artillery and aerial photography. These duties led RFC pilots into aerial clashes with German aircraft and later into strafing enemy infantry, trenches and gun emplacements, as well as bombing military airfields and strategic transportation and industrial facilities.

At the outbreak of war the Royal Naval Air Service (RNAS) was under Admiralty control and tasked with fleet reconnaissance, patrolling the coasts for enemy ships and submarines and attacking enemy coastal territory. Eventually, like the RFC, it conducted strategic bombing raids. However, the RNAS did a considerable amount of work with the army and ultimately maintained a number of squadrons on the Western Front. Initially it established only a small unit of twelve planes on the Belgian coast, but by the time it was amalgamated with the RFC to form the Royal Air Force (RAF) on 1 April 1918 it had 55,000 personnel, almost 3,000 aircraft (including seaplanes), 103 airships and 126 coastal stations. The RAF was then under the control of the newly formed Air Ministry and had some 114,000 personnel and 4,000 combat aircraft in 150 squadrons. The Royal Navy regained its own air service in 1937 when the Fleet Air Arm of the RAF was returned to Admiralty control. Throughout the war the RFC relied on army logistical support except for the supply of aircraft and aeronautical stores.

This section is mostly concerned with the RFC, with reference to the French and German equivalents when appropriate.

RFC Organization

The War Office branch responsible for the RFC was the Directorate General of Military Aeronautics. It was independent of the other four main branches, with a director general (at first a brigadier general, eventually a lieutenant general) who dealt directly to the Secretary of State. Its formation was not complete on the outbreak of war, and only by stripping other units of personnel and aircraft was the BEF able to field an HQ RFC (including a wireless unit), four squadrons (Nos 2, 3, 4 and 5) with a total of sixty-three aircraft and an aircraft park, all under the command of a brigadier general. As with most types of military equipment, the French and Germans started with numerical advantages, the French having over 100 and the Germans over 300 military aircraft and thirty Zeppelin airships.

Covert Operations

One of the more usual operations of the RFC was to deliver spies behind enemy lines. The first attempt, on 13 September 1915, was a failure, as the aircraft crashed, injuring the spy and the pilot, Captain T. W. Mulcahy-Morgan. Both were captured, although two years later Mulcahy-Morgan escaped and managed to get back to England. Later missions proved more successful.

In addition to delivering spies the RFC was responsible for supplying these agents with carrier pigeons, which were used to send reports back to army headquarters. In 1916 a special flight was formed as part of the Headquarters Wing to handle these and other unusual assignments.

With the arrival in France of No. 6 Squadron in October 1914, one squadron was placed under the control of the HQ RFC (Brigadier General Sir David Henderson) and the other four were grouped into two wings commanded by lieutenant colonels, the 1st Wing being attached to the First Army and the 2nd Wing to the Second Army. As the BEF and RFC expanded so did the number of wings, and by November 1915 there were eight. By 1916 further expansion had led to the establishment of RFC (now under Major General Sir Hugh 'Boom' Trenchard) brigades, with one attached to each army. Each brigade was commanded by a brigadier general and contained a 'corps wing' of one squadron per corps for artillery reconnaissance and photographic work on the immediate front, and an 'army wing' of several squadrons for bombing, fighting and long-range reconnaissance. The brigades also had a balloon squadron (by 1917 three or four) and an aircraft park. On the formation of the RAF in April 1918, brigades incorporated an air ammunition column, lorry park and salvage unit. In October 1917 the RFC was tasked with strategic bombing that entailed hitting targets in Germany. For these duties HQ VIII Brigade, based in France, controlled three wings each with three bomber squadrons – by June 1918 this had become an independent strategic air force under its own major general.

The squadron was the basic operational unit of the RFC, commanded by a major (the RFC retained army ranks), while the French usually had flights (*escadrilles*) of ten aircraft commanded by captains. The Germans also had flights (*Fliegerstaffeln*) of six, twelve or eighteen aircraft (the size depending on the role), which were commanded by a major. The RFC squadron was divided into three flights, each under a captain and each with four aircraft, with an establishment of nineteen officers and 138 other ranks. This was increased in 1916 when a flight's strength was augmented to six machines (eighteen in the squadron) and again in March 1917 when corps flights had eight (twenty-four in the squadron). This higher establishment applied to all fighter squadrons in 1918, although due to shortages of both pilots and aircraft only a few squadrons were that strong at the end of the war. By this time a squadron also included an intelligence section, an adjutant, technical officer, assistant equipment officer and recording officer, in addition to flying personnel. Details of the aircraft and roles are explained in the remainder of this section, but in summary at the end of hostilities the RAF had the following squadrons on the Western Front:

1 communications squadron
20 corps reconnaissance squadrons
7 fighter reconnaissance squadrons
19 day bomber squadrons
6 night bomber squadrons
38 single-seater fighter squadrons

The order of battle of the RFC for the Battle of Arras in April 1917, in the diagram on pages 424–5, shows how the corps had developed over the previous two and a half years.

By the end of the war the French, under General Maurice Duval, head of the *Service Aeronautique*, had massively expanded their air arm to a force of almost 3,000 up-to-date aircraft and several hundred obsolescent. These were organized into twelve *groupes de combat* (fighters), each of sixty-six squadrons, seven *groupes de bombardement* (bombers) of nineteen squadrons and five *groupes de bombardement de nuit* (night bombers) of fourteen squadrons. These were deployed in brigade and divisional structures (the *Division Aerienne*).

German aviation organization in the field by 1918 had an aviation and a balloon commander at each army headquarters and an aviation group commander at corps headquarters. Each army had an aircraft park that received machines from Germany, a store for issuing spares and carrying out minor repairs, and maintained a pool of pilots, observers and machine-gunners who were posted to units to replace casualties. The 'flight' was the standard aviation unit. These flights were designated in accordance with the tasks they performed. Reconnaissance, protective and fighting flights normally had six machines, whereas bombing flights had from ten to twelve and pursuit flights from fourteen to eighteen aircraft. For their attack on Verdun, the Germans were the first to employ the majority of their air force to create a massive air umbrella to dominate the skies: 170 aircraft, fourteen balloons and four Zeppelins – a concentration that for early 1916 was an impressive effort.

Aircraft

Types of Aircraft

From late 1914 until the Armistice, each belligerent developed a confusing number of different types of aircraft to cater for the widely different tasks given to them. With most types of machine, later models had various modifications to improve their performance. The United Kingdom had produced over forty different models by 1918, including twenty-two types of fighter, eleven bombers and ground-attack machines and eleven reconnaissance or contact patrol aircraft. The French built more than twenty different models and the Germans at least as many. It was common for one type of machine to be used in two or more roles, particularly in the first eighteen months of the war, but specialization of a particular type of aircraft or designated squadrons for a specific role – such as aerial reconnaissance and photography, contact patrols or bombing – was virtually universal by 1918.

Aircraft could be of the monoplane type (one pair of wings), or biplanes (two sets of wings) or triplanes (three sets), although the great majority were biplanes made of wood and canvas. This type of seemingly flimsy construction had the advantage that, unless a vital part of the engine, or the controls or the pilot were hit, bullets would pass through, leaving a small hole and no serious damage – countless planes returned safely, peppered with scores, if not hundreds, of holes. One of the most striking examples was Captain G. A. K. Lawrence, who returned from a flight on

30 September 1915 and counted 300 holes. However, the lightness of these machines meant that they were vulnerable to strong winds and often had to be tied down while parked. Failure to do so could mean aircraft being severely damaged. Lyn Macdonald, in her book *1914*, quotes from No. 2 Squadron diary for 12 September:

> Before anything could be done to make the machines more secure, the wind shifted, and about half the number of machines were over on their backs. One Henry Farman [aircraft type] went up about thirty feet in the air and crashed on top of another Henry Farman in a hopeless tangle. The BEs [aircraft type] of No. 2 Squadron were blowing across the aerodrome, and when daylight arrived and the storm abated, the aerodrome presented a pitiful sight.

British pilots had to be wary of the prevailing strong westerly winds; if a pilot became too distracted by the action and events going on around him, he could find himself drifting far behind enemy lines and perhaps short on fuel, facing a strong headwind as he tried to return to his own lines and therefore very vulnerable to attack from behind.

An aircraft was either a single-seater or a two-seater, the latter having an observer as well as the pilot. They sat in tandem, some with the pilot in front and some the observer. The single-seater was lighter than the two-seater and therefore faster and able to climb more quickly. They were called

'scouts' but later were used as fighters and for ground attack. Early examples were biplanes, small and lightly armed by later standards. Their disadvantage was that the pilot had to do everything – fly, manoeuvre, navigate, aim, fire and reload his machine gun. An extreme example of what could happen is described in Major Charles C. Turner's book *The Struggle in the Air, 1914–1918*. In May 1915 a British pilot in pursuit of a German, trying to fly and fire his machine gun at the same time, lost control of the steering gear and the plane turned upside down. The belt round his waist was loose and the jerk of his turn almost threw him out of the machine, but he saved himself by clutching hold of the rear centre strut while the belt slipped down round his legs. While he hung there, head downwards, the plane fell from about 8,000 feet to around 2,500 feet, spinning round like a falling leaf. At last he succeeded in freeing his legs and reaching the control lever with his feet. He then managed to right the machine, which turned slowly over and he was able to slide back into his seat.

The two-seater was primarily for reconnaissance, including aerial photography and spotting for artillery. Having a fixed, forward-firing gun for the pilot and another with the observer, who had a better field of fire, often made up for its slowness (see page 430). For this reason it was mainly a defensive aircraft, but it was also employed on bombing raids, preferably escorted by fighters.

British Aircraft in World War I

The total number of aircraft of all forty-six types delivered to RFC and RAF (excluding RNAS, but including the Independent Air Force) service and training units during hostilities were: 1914 – 144; 1915 – 507; 1916 – 2,320; 1917 – 4,965; 1918 – 8,145; total 16,081. The ten most important were:

Type	1914	1915	1916	1917	1918	Total
AW			17	213	547	777
Bristol Fighter				308	626	934
De Hav. 4			1	340	323	664
De Hav. 9					933	933
FE.2b	1	18	315	269	396	999
Morane	3	92	223	96		414
Nieuport Scout			194	256	8	458
RE.8			18	1,114	1,025	2,157
Sopwith Camel				471	1,669	2,140
SE.5 and 5a			1	335	1,663	1,999

• The FE.2b (Farman Experimental) two-seater tractor biplane was the aircraft that ended the 'Fokker Scourge' over the Somme (see page 433). It was a pusher fighter/bomber with the observer sitting far forward in the nacelle, directly in front of the pilot. This configuration made it vulnerable to attacks from the rear and it was frequently shot down. During the summer of 1916 the Germans captured a new FE.2b when the pilot inadvertently landed on an enemy airfield. The introduction of more advanced machines made this aircraft ineffective as a fighter and by 1917 it was primarily used for night bombing raids and photographic work.

Key characteristics included a maximum speed of 91 m.p.h.; ceiling 11,000 feet; endurance 2½ hours; armament two Lewis guns for the observer and one for the pilot and six bombs (20 lb or 25 lb).

An observer in an FE.2d demonstrates how he has to stand up to fire his Lewis gun.

• The Sopwith Camel (called 'Camel' because of the humped fairing over the twin machine guns) was a highly manoeuvrable, single-seater, tractor biplane that secured more aerial victories than any other Allied aircraft on the Western Front, being credited with almost 2,300 kills. However, it was a difficult aircraft to learn on, mainly due to the small wingspan, making it somewhat unstable, which in turn could cause it to flip over into a spin at low speeds. It was therefore a tricky machine in which to take off or land – it was the cause of a high number of fatal accidents. Nevertheless, once the techniques of flying (applying hard right rudder on take-off, for example) were mastered it was a highly effective fighter – the Canadian ace Captain Alexander Shook accounted for fifty-four enemy with this machine.

Key characteristics included maximum speed 118 m.p.h.; ceiling 19,000 feet; endurance 2½ hours; armament two Vickers machine guns or one Vickers and one Lewis machine gun, or two Lewis guns.

• The SE.5 (Scout Experimental) was a single-seater scout biplane, initially disliked by pilots, but the 5 model was quickly replaced by the improved 5a type. When it entered service in 1917 it proved superior to its German opponents. The SE.5a was often preferred by pilots to the Sopwith Camel, as it was easier to fly (particularly for novice pilots), its engine was surprisingly quiet and it performed well at high altitudes. It was also slightly faster than the Camel, thus making it easier for the pilot to break off action at will. Mick Mannock was one of the aces who handled this fighter with deadly effect, although it was the South African pilot Captain Anthony Proctor, with fifty-four kills, who downed more Germans with this machine than any other pilot.

Key specifications included maximum speed 120 m.p.h.; ceiling 19,500 feet; endurance 2½ hours; armament one Vickers gun (port side of fuselage) and one Lewis gun atop the upper wing.

• The Bristol Fighter was a heavily armed two-seater tractor biplane that became one of the more successful fighters of the war, although it had a bad start when it was introduced in April 1917. It was initially flown by inexperienced pilots and observers, who were advised that the aircraft might be structurally weak and so should avoid violent manoeuvres in combat. This combination caused a flight of six Bristols to lose four in a clash over Douai with the Red Baron's Jasta 11 squadron – a result that almost resulted in the machine being withdrawn from service. However, it was ultimately regarded as one of the decisive aircraft of the war. A Canadian pilot, Captain Andrew McKeever, achieved the highest score of thirty-one in this aircraft.

Key characteristics included maximum speed 123 m.p.h.; ceiling 21,500 feet; endurance 3 hours; armament one Vickers gun (synchronized forward firing), two or three Lewis guns (in rear cockpit mounted on a ring) and up to 240 lb of bombs.

Engines varied slightly in power, but more particularly in their positioning on the aircraft. An engine at the rear behind both pilot and observer was said to push the machine forward; these aircraft were called 'pushers'. Those with the engine in front, pulling the aircraft forward, were termed 'tractors' and if they were two-seaters the pilot sat in the front cockpit. Although by 1917 the British had produced a powerful pusher, the FE.2d, the tractor type dominated the skies due to its greater speed and climbing ability once the solution to firing through the propeller had been found – see page 427.

All aircraft had open cockpits, exposing the occupants to all weathers – something that made for extreme discomfort in winter. This could range from struggling to see through rain-splashed goggles to loss of feeling in frozen fingers and feet that sometimes led to frostbite, particularly when, by 1917, combats often took place at an altitude of 15,000 feet or more rather than 2,000–3,000 as in 1914. The following extract from a letter written by an RFC observer in a reconnaissance appeared in the *Morning Post* in the winter of 1914/1915 (exact date unknown):

When we left the ground it was freezing hard, and en route we encountered two snow-storms. The cold was absolutely excruciating, my eyes got frozen up; the water in my eyes turned to ice. I had to keep on brushing it out of my eyes. A great sheet of ice formed over the mouth outlet of my mask, so that I had to smash it to breathe . . . We arrived back, and the pilot being nearly dead with cold crashed the machine on landing. Fortunately neither of us was damaged.

Airco DH.2 The first RFC single-seat fighter. A 'pusher' aircraft with one Lewis light machine gun mounted on the nose. When flown by experienced pilots it proved an excellent combat aircraft and was instrumental in winning back control of the skies in the summer of 1916. However, by December the German Albatros D.III had proved superior.

Vickers FB.5 A British twin-seater 'pusher', designed initially for a scouting role. It was the first scout aircraft to be armed and had a Lewis gun fired by the gunner/observer seated in front of the pilot.

Sopwith 1½ Strutter British fighter and bomber. The first British aircraft to have synchronized a Vickers machine gun firing through the propeller. In the twin-seater version the gunner/observer was seated at the rear firing a Lewis gun. It carried up to 224 lb of bombs.

Sopwith Camel British single-seater fighter armed with twin Vickers machine guns. Highly manoeuvrable and accounted for more aerial victories than any other Allied aircraft during the war. Often used in low-level ground-attack role with small bombs for trench strafing.

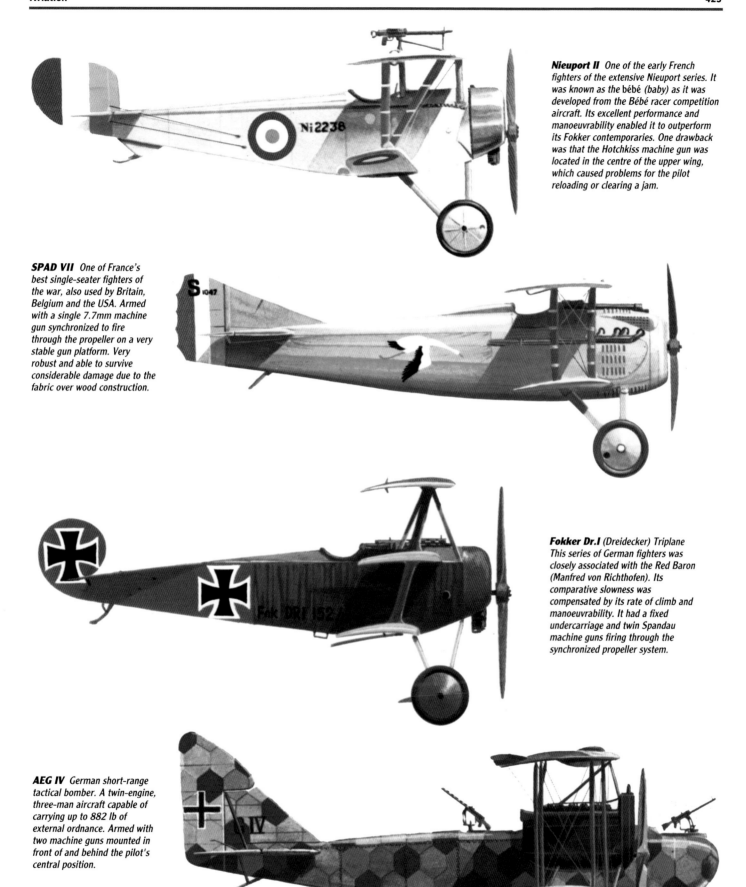

Nieuport II One of the early French fighters of the extensive Nieuport series. It was known as the *bébé* (baby) as it was developed from the *Bébé* racer competition aircraft. Its excellent performance and manoeuvrability enabled it to outperform its Fokker contemporaries. One drawback was that the Hotchkiss machine gun was located in the centre of the upper wing, which caused problems for the pilot reloading or clearing a jam.

SPAD VII One of France's best single-seater fighters of the war, also used by Britain, Belgium and the USA. Armed with a single 7.7mm machine gun synchronized to fire through the propeller on a very stable gun platform. Very robust and able to survive considerable damage due to the fabric over wood construction.

Fokker Dr.I (Dreidecker) Triplane This series of German fighters was closely associated with the Red Baron (Manfred von Richthofen). Its comparative slowness was compensated by its rate of climb and manoeuvrability. It had a fixed undercarriage and twin Spandau machine guns firing through the synchronized propeller system.

AEG IV German short-range tactical bomber. A twin-engine, three-man aircraft capable of carrying up to 882 lb of external ordnance. Armed with two machine guns mounted in front of and behind the pilot's central position.

RFC Order of Battle for
Battle of Arras, 9 April 1917

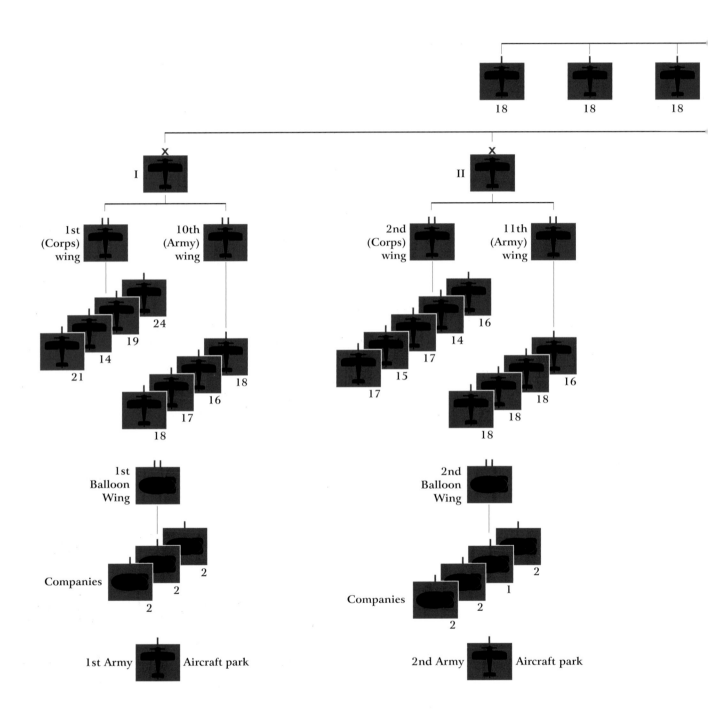

Notes
- Each RFC brigade operated with the corresponding numbered army.
- The number of aircraft in each squadron is shown.

- The total strength of the RFC was then 50 squadrons, 903 aircraft and 35 kite balloon sections (one balloon per section).
- No attempt has been made to indicate the types of aircraft, as there was considerable mixing of multiple types.

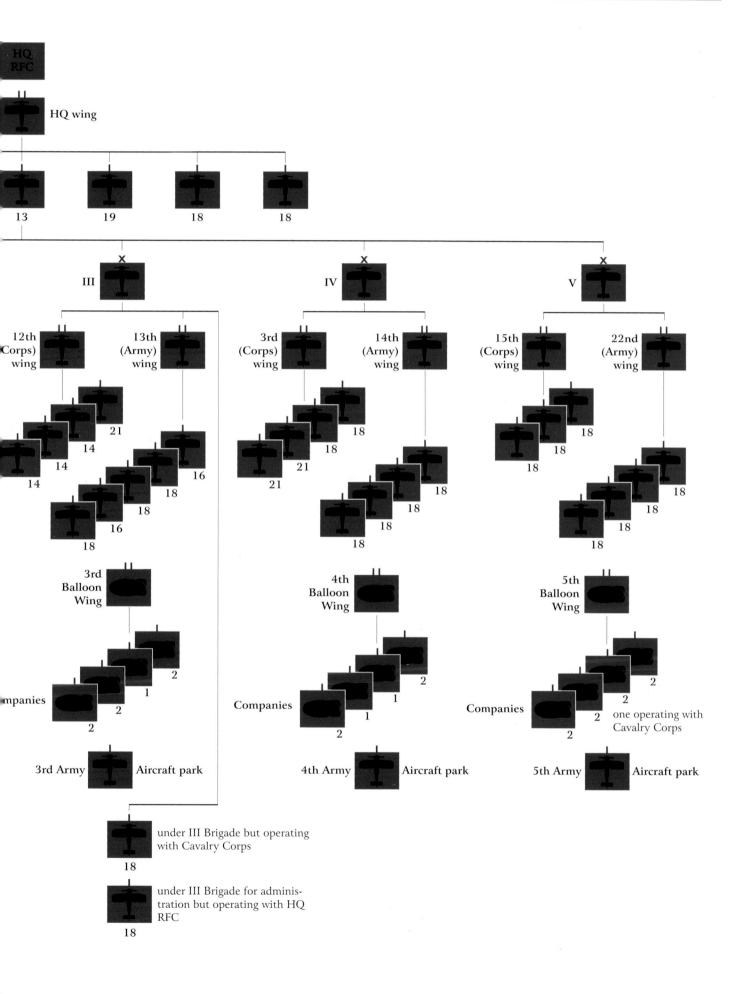

HQ
RFC

HQ wing

13

19

18

18

III

IV

V

12th
(Corps)
wing

13th
(Army)
wing

3rd
(Corps)
wing

14th
(Army)
wing

15th
(Corps)
wing

22nd
(Army)
wing

21

14

14

14

16

18

18

16

18

18

21

18

18

18

18

18

18

18

18

18

18

18

18

18

3rd
Balloon
Wing

4th
Balloon
Wing

5th
Balloon
Wing

2

1

Companies

2

2

2

1

Companies

2

2

2

Companies

2

2

one operating with
Cavalry Corps

3rd Army   Aircraft park

4th Army   Aircraft park

5th Army   Aircraft park

under III Brigade but operating
with Cavalry Corps

18

under III Brigade for administration but operating with HQ
RFC

18

A Zeppelin – probably L.50 – coming out of its hangar.

Dirigibles, airships and Zeppelins

The other type of 'aircraft' was the 'dirigible' – a name that came from the French word *dirigeable* meaning anything 'steerable' but in practice has been largely replaced by the more common name of 'airship'. These were designed for reconnaissance or night bombing raids but proved one of the big disappointments of the war – certainly for the Germans, who were the primary users on the Western Front – when aircraft were able to reach their height and shoot them down with incendiary bullets. In 1914 there were two basic types – the rigid and the non-rigid (often called 'Blimps'). The rigid type had a solid framework supporting an external fabric and containing a number of bags of hydrogen; the engines and control car were suspended from the framework. The non-rigid had no framework and the pressure of the gas inside maintained the outer envelope. The engine and control car were either attached directly to the envelope or suspended directly from it. Rigid or non-rigid, their purpose was reconnaissance and bombing, especially the latter.

The Germans had experimented with airships for many years before the war and by 1914 had a considerable fleet of Zeppelins (named after their designer, General Ferdinand Graf von Zeppelin). They were rigid airships filled with the highly inflammable hydrogen, which was held in from sixteen to twenty compartments in the long cylindrical hull. The outside of the hull was a sheath of aluminium built as a trellis girdle, the whole covered with fabric. The first airships were 520–560 feet long with a gross lifting capacity of 28–38 tons. The best could reach a maximum speed (discounting help from the wind) of 55–60 m.p.h., although the most economical speed was around 40 m.p.h. They could climb to a height of about 9,000 feet by discharging ballast (water), but their usual navigating height was 4,000–6,000 feet. They were crewed by between ten and twenty-eight men in the forward and rear gondolas (cars) and armed with four or six machine guns and bombs – the early types could carry only one ton of the latter and had a distance radius of about 450 miles.

The birth of strategic bombing came in World War I when German Zeppelins started bombing Britain from bases in Belgium (see page 436). By late 1916 the Germans had developed 'super' Zeppelins, the largest being an outstanding feat of engineering 775 feet long, with a gas capacity of almost 2.5 million cubic feet. She was powered by seven 250-h.p. engines, giving this lumbering monster a maximum speed of 77 m.p.h.. Her maximum altitude was 18,000 feet. She was able to carry a load of 19 tons and was armed with four large-bore machine guns and six maxims as well as 4 tons of bombs.

The first German airship to be destroyed in the air by an Allied flier was the LZ.37. It occurred at around 3:00 a.m. on 7 June 1915 when Flight Sub-Lieutenant R. A. J. Warneford, RNAS, flying a Morane (French-designed) monoplane, sighted a Zeppelin returning from a raid on England. He chased it for some considerable time as the airship dumped ballast and rose rapidly while continually firing at Warneford with her machine guns. Warneford struggled to gain altitude and pursued his prey into the early hours of the morning before succeeding in getting close to and above his target. His only armament was a carbine and six 20-lb bombs attached to an undercarriage rack. He began to drop his bombs singly by pulling a toggle on the right-hand side of the fuselage, but only after the last bomb did the airship disintegrate in a massive ball of fire. Incredibly, out of a crew of ten there was one survivor. This was Alfred Mühler, the helmsman, who stayed in the forward gondola as the flaming wreck spiralled down. It smashed through the roof of a building and deposited Mühler on to a bed! Mühler survived the war, opened a *Bierkeller* and enjoyed countless free beers while relating his story.

Warneford was so close that the blast overturned his aircraft and stopped the engine. He righted his machine and was able to glide down to make an emergency landing in German-occupied territory. Incredibly, within thirty-five minutes he managed to restart the engine, take off and then return to base. On hearing of his achievement King George V sent him the following message:

> Most heartily congratulate you upon your splendid achievement, in which you, single-handed destroyed an enemy Zeppelin. I have much pleasure in conferring upon you the Victoria Cross for this gallant act.   George R I

Warneford also received the French *Légion d'honneur*, but regrettably died in an air crash within days of receiving it.

As with so many things, the British were slow to build and develop airships. It was not until 1912 that the government agreed that some were required, with the result that in 1914 only a small fleet of non-rigid airships was available. Until submarine war developed, these were of little value for offensive operations, their sole use being for reconnaissance. This type consisted of an aeroplane fuselage and engine attached to a streamline-shaped gas container with about 60,000 cubic feet capacity. Although very small, it had the advantage of speed over the much larger Zeppelins. The British Army had abandoned airship development in favour of aircraft by the start of hostilities, but the Royal Navy recognized the potential value of these small, non-rigid airships to counter the mine and submarine threat in coastal waters. Operated by the RNAS, a number of classes of this type, armed with bombs and machine guns, were developed for scouting, mine-clearance and submarine-attack duties.

The French preferred the non-rigid type and operated them throughout the war.

Aircraft Armament

At the outbreak of the war there was considerable scepticism as to the value of aircraft over the battlefield and the first aircraft to take to the skies above Belgium were unarmed and deployed merely on scouting duties. They were expected to avoid combat during these reconnaissance flights, and there were stories of rival aircraft exchanging nothing more than waves as they flew past each other. However, this behaviour soon gave way to more hostile action, including the use of revolvers, rifles, grenades and occasionally machine guns – the latter usually manhandled with some difficulty by the observer in a two-seater. Nevertheless, the first victim of aerial combat occurred as early as 5 October 1914 when a German Aviatik scout was shot down near Reims by a forward-mounted Hotchkiss machine gun operated by Corporal Louis Quenault, the observer, in a two-seater French Voisin piloted by Sergeant Joseph Frantz – note that neither was a commissioned officer, unlike the RFC where at least one if not both occupants of an aircraft were officers.

These usually futile attempts to cause serious damage quickly developed into a far more deadly game of catch-up as each side in turn produced new and superior aircraft in terms of speed, manoeuvrability and armament. It became a struggle with two elements that lasted until the end of the war: first, to produce the best fighter; and second, to develop the best bomber, which in turn required better fighters to protect it, and so on. Perhaps the most important aspect from the pilot's point of view was the effectiveness of his machine's armament compared with that of his enemy, in particular the ability to fire his machine guns successfully for aerial combat – the British Vickers Maxim and Lewis, the French Hotchkiss or the German Maxim or Spandau. From early 1915 onwards this became an aerial arms race.

A critical moment came with the realization that the most effective way of shooting down an opponent was by flying towards him and firing a forward-pointing machine gun aligned to the aircraft's axis. The problem was that, while observers could handle a machine gun in a two-seater – especially when ring-mounted, which enabled them to swivel guns easily – in pusher aircraft the observer's field of fire was restricted by the struts and rigging required to secure the tail unit. Pilots needed to be able to fire forwards without destroying the propeller blades – above all what they wanted was to be able to aim their guns by pointing the machine at the target and then pulling a trigger or pushing a button. One solution was to position the gun or guns on the top plane (wing) of biplanes to fire over the propeller

arc, although this made it awkward for the pilot to reload or to clear a jammed gun. A solution, called the Foster mounting, was eventually found for Lewis guns. It enabled the gun to slide back for drum-changing and also allowed the gun to be fired at a slight upward angle, which was a great advantage if attacking an aircraft in its blind spot under the tail. Another solution with pusher aircraft such as the British Vickers FB.2 was to have the gun mounted on the front of the fuselage with the breach mechanism right in front of the pilot's face.

Before the war only a few – none of them in the United Kingdom – had given thought to the possibility of actually firing through the spinning propeller; some experiments to this end had been made in Germany and France. In the former Franz Schneider, a Swiss engineer, had patented such a device a year before the outbreak of war, but his work was either ignored or forgotten by the government in 1914. The French aircraft designer Raymond Saulnier patented a similar device, but this was found unworkable with the Hotchkiss machine gun due to 'hang fire' – the firing cycle causing the bullet to leave the gun too late to synchronize the gunfire consistently with the spinning propeller.

The French answer to this problem was to introduce a 'deflector' system whereby the propeller blades had steel wedges fixed on them at the point where a proportion of the bullets would strike, deflecting them without damage. The French pilot Roland Garros trialled this system in a Morane-Saulnier L in March 1915 and managed to down several enemy aircraft within a month, causing consternation among German aviators. However, the system was far from foolproof as bullets could be deflected in all directions, hitting other parts of the propeller or even coming back at the aircraft. Also, this repeated striking of the propeller put a strain on the crankshaft that could possibly cause engine failure. On 19 April Garros was forced down behind enemy lines (whether due to engine failure or enemy action seems uncertain) and was captured along with his machine, despite his attempts to burn it. His aircraft was immediately handed over to the Dutch aircraft designer Anthony Fokker and his engineers to investigate, and if necessary adopt, the French method of firing through the propeller with a view to using it for the new, air-cooled German Parabellum MG14 machine gun.

However, Fokker quickly rejected this method as unsuitable and instead revisited the idea of a synchronizing gear. He designed a system whereby the spinning propeller operated the gun so that the bullet was fired only when the slower moving propeller blades were out of the way. The effectiveness of this was to change aerial warfare on the Western

Front completely. This was quickly illustrated in the summer of 1915 when the future German aces Oswald Boelcke and Max Immelmann began downing aircraft with this deadly new technique flying the Fokker E.I single-seater monoplane (*Eindecker*). It was the start of the so-called 'Fokker Scourge', which became even deadlier later in the year when the Germans introduced their improved E.III model. The rate of British losses was driven up and some pilots and observers began to consider themselves 'Fokker fodder'.

German superiority was reversed, however, with the Allied introduction of the British D-type fighter and French Nieuport scout, and by the time of the Somme the Allies had air superiority. But by the end of the year the pendulum had swung again in the German's favour, culminating in 1917 with 'Bloody April' (see page 433), before new Allied machines like the Sopwith Camel (see page 422) and SE.5 again recaptured the advantage. However, from mid-1916 these air-supremacy swings were not so much due to armament alone as to the combination of armament with speed, climb, manoeuvrability and the resultant aerial combat tactics discussed below.

The ammunition used by the British was .303 for the Lewis gun, with a larger magazine containing ninety-six rounds, and for the Vickers, which was belt-fed – a belt contained 250 rounds. Tracer (bullets that burn in flight enabling the firer to see how to adjust his aim) and incendiary bullets were developed for attacks on balloons and airships.

A French-built Morane-Saulnier monoplane with bullet deflectors on the propeller blades.

The RFC's need for tracer was accepted early on, but experiments were initially unsatisfactory. The length of the trace was insufficient and there was too high a percentage of 'blinds' or 'prematures'. Not until July 1916 was satisfactory tracer ammunition supplied to the RFC. The first .303 incendiary ammunition for attacking airships was called the 'Buckingham Bullet' as it was designed by J. F. Buckingham at his Coventry works. It was issued to the RNAS in December 1915 and the RFC the following spring. The original pointed-nose bullet was later superseded by one with a flattened nose that made a larger hole in the fabric of the airship or balloon and allowed more gas to escape.

The only other type of incendiary bullet used on the Western Front was the 'Brock Bullet', which resulted from experiments instigated by Commander Frank Brock, in charge of the Intelligence Section of the Air Department at the Admiralty. It was designed to explode between the first and second fabrics of the airship and had an effective range of 800 yards. It was first issued in late 1916 but was superseded by an improved version for the RFC in early 1917, although the RNAS continued to use it until the end of the war.

For bombing airships, the early armament for an aircraft was not only bombs, but also *Le Prieur* rockets or Ranken darts. The bombs were the 20-lb Hales high-explosive and the 16-lb incendiary; two of each were normally carried. Experience showed that the chances of seeing an airship from above at night were small and of hitting it even smaller. The Lewis gun was used, but all that was expected was that after several drums of ammunition had been fired into the airship it might be so punctured that it would be forced down through lack of gas.

With rockets, three were attached to the interplane struts on each wing. They were fired by means of an electric bell-push on the pilot's seat and if they hit the balloon they were guaranteed to send it down in flames provided the pilot was sufficiently resolute to restrain from firing until within 150 yards of his target, as the range of the rockets was short. Also, the extra load made the machine sluggish when fighting and approaching the balloon, usually at an altitude of about 3,000 feet, exposed the aircraft to heavy gunfire from the ground.

The Ranken dart, named after its inventor Lieutenant Commander Francis Ranken, was a slender, drogue-stabilized, 1-lb bomb with a sharp steel nose and four pivoting vanes at the rear. When the dart hit the airship's skin the head would punch through while the vanes caught on the envelope and fired the detonator. These darts were dropped from a 24-round box at the rear of the aircraft.

There was another, somewhat outlandish, weapon called the 'fiery grapnel', consisting of four grappling hooks packed with an incendiary composition and attached to a length of cable. The attacking aircraft was supposed to troll above the Zeppelin until the hooks snagged on its covering, which was then ripped and set alight; unsurprisingly, it was not a success.

All the initial types of ammunition could be used only if the aircraft was flying above the target. With the aircraft of 1914 and 1915 this was invariably difficult, as they had so little chance of getting above airships that could rise to 18,000 feet in a matter of minutes, whereas the aircraft would take some two hours to reach 14,000 feet. In these circumstances the aircraft had to rely on surprise and catching its prey when flying low.

However, by the summer of 1916 efficient explosive and incendiary bullets meant that the Zeppelin's days were numbered.

Observation Balloons

Captive round balloons filled with hot air had been used for observation of the battlefield during the Napoleonic, American Civil, Boer and Russo-Japanese Wars. By the start of the twentieth century hydrogen was replacing hot air and most modern armies had balloon sections on their establishment. In 1911 Britain had an Air Balloon Battalion of the Royal Engineers but this was taken over by the RNAS and subsequently, when the overwhelming importance of observation from balloons on the Western Front became self-evident, the RFC took over all land sections and started its own training centres in England. However, in 1914 the BEF went to war without any balloons and it was not until early May 1915 that the first British balloon section arrived on the Aubers Ridge part of the front.

The Germans went to war with eight balloon companies equipped with the *Drachen* (dragon) sausage-shaped balloon with a single stabilizer (balloonet) under, and curved over, the tail. The French initially deployed spherical balloons that proved highly unsuitable, as they tended to rotate, making observation or photography extremely difficult. A considerable improvement was the French Caquot balloon, designed by Lieutenant Albert Caquot – an elongated, streamlined balloon with three round, rear-mounted stabilizing fins that could operate in winds in excess of 60 m.p.h., whereas other types were not sent up in winds of over 35 m.p.h. The original Caquot was over 9 feet long, 32 feet in diameter and had more than 23,00 cubic feet of hydrogen gas in chambers inside the

A kite balloon goes down in flames.

canopy. The basket could carry a crew of two – the captain and observer – and in clear weather at 4,000 feet (maximum operating height) could spot large objects up to 40 miles away through binoculars. This type of kite balloon (a general term for virtually all balloons on the Western Front) was soon copied by the Germans, the British and then the Americans, and by the end of the war had replaced the Drachen type in all armies.

Balloons were tethered by a cable attached to the underneath by a number of branch ropes. On the ground the cable was wound round a winch powered by a petrol engine fixed to the back of a lorry. To get two men airborne required a ground crew of around forty-five. These men had to be highly trained in handling the balloon on the ground as well as launching it and hauling it down – at times this had to be done quickly, a task facilitated by the crew having access to a nose valve that could release gas and to a 'ripper panel' that, if removed, could speed up the process considerably in an emergency. The ground crew also had the normal military duties of administration and guard, as well as attending the plant for making hydrogen and being able to move the balloon periodically in accordance with the operational situation.

The function of the balloon crew was to observe their given section of the front, and in particular to undertake artillery spotting. The balloons were normally sited about 3 miles behind the front to make them less vulnerable to enemy ground fire. If launched singly they would be positioned 12–15 miles apart, although sometimes a group would be sited together. Major Charles Turner, RFC and RAF, has described in his book *The Struggle in the Air, 1914–1918* what it was like to ascend in a balloon:

The observer having entered the basket, the crew of men handling the guy ropes and cables get ready to let up, and the order is given to the winch hands. The balloon . . . has so much lift that it unwinds the cable on the drum. Directly the balloon gets clear of the ground, if there is any wind it begins to swing to and fro, and this motion is too much for bad sailors. Up aloft there is no sensation of giddiness, and the only discomfort comes from the rolling of the basket [made of woven bamboo or willow] and the curious twitches and jerks caused by some winds. Sailors say this is worse than the worst ship. One's fancies also may roam unpleasantly at times to questions of security of the gear . . . Many an aeroplane pilot has told the author that he feels much more nervous in a kite-balloon than in a flying machine. Landing in a high wind may be exciting, and the crew who have to secure the guy ropes are sometimes bowled over. One has been in a basket swinging through nearly 180 degrees . . .

Part of the training of the observation balloon officer was a course of free ballooning, in order that he might learn how to make use of ballast and valve in the event of the balloon breaking adrift.

As noted above, the primary task of the observer was artillery spotting, for which certain equipment was essential. In the basket would be two telephone handsets to communicate with ground crew or artillery battery via a telephone cable that was sometimes fixed to the main winch cable. Also required were binoculars, compass, barometer, air-speed indicator, pressure gauge, notebook, maps and map board, code book and a long-range camera – until aerial photography was mostly taken over by aircraft; and, most importantly for crew morale, two parachutes. The spotting was in two parts: first, to spot the muzzle flashes of enemy guns; and second, to observe the trajectory of the large friendly shells (spotting for field artillery was not a task) and reporting their accuracy. To do this they reported the fall of shot by indicating if it was 'over', 'under', 'left', 'right' or 'on target'.

Because of their importance as spotters for enemy and friendly artillery, balloons were always considered important targets and were often subjected to concentrated attack by the opposing side. To encourage pilots to attack enemy balloons both sides counted downing a balloon as an air-to-air kill with the same value as shooting down an aircraft. Some pilots seemed to specialize as 'balloon-busters', such as Major Willy Coppens, DSO, MC, *Croix de Guerre*, a Belgian pilot who became the top scorer of the war with thirty-seven kills. On 18 June 1918 he was hit in the shin by a dum-dum bullet that smashed the bone, tore away the muscles and severed an artery. With a collapsed leg and in excruciating pain Coppens managed to pull his machine out of a spin and crash land. He was rushed to a field hospital and then to a hospital at La Panne, where his leg was amputated. It was because of their vulnerability and importance that the defence of balloons became critical, involving batteries of anti-aircraft guns and heavy machine guns; later in the war fighter aircraft were tasked to patrol the area for their protection.

With balloons being such obvious and important targets, the life expectancy of crews was often very short. Towards the end of the war, when balloon-busting by pilot aces became quite commonplace, the crews hanging precariously in their baskets were called 'balloonatics', as their life expectancy on an active front could be as low as two weeks.

Unlike air crews, these men had parachutes and were expected to leap from the basket and float down to safety if their balloon caught fire. Allied air crew were not given parachutes, as the High Command considered it would encourage them to abandon their aircraft needlessly! However, this lack of parachutes was not always common knowledge to their infantry comrades on the ground. In September 1916 Lieutenant Colonel J. L. Jack, commanding the 2nd Battalion, West Yorkshire Regiment, wrote in his diary that the two crew on a downed British aircraft 'jumped out too late for their parachutes to open properly, and dropped like stones before our eyes . . .' In fact they had almost certainly jumped to avoid being burned alive.

By the spring of 1916 kite-ballooning had become recognized as one of the most hazardous of duties and crews wore their parachutes at all times, ready for a speedy exit from a blazing wreck. On 21 October 1916 Lieutenant T. W. Nops was in a balloon with his observer when they were attacked by an aircraft. Nops opened fire with a rifle and in his excitement failed to notice that the balloon had caught fire on the top until the flames spread and the basket began to fall. Nops helped his observer to jump with his parachute and he landed safely. Nops, however, had not left enough time to save himself; he crashed to the ground in the basket and was killed.

The German balloon service was controlled by the general commanding the air forces and the supply of personnel and equipment was the responsibility of the Inspectorate of Balloon Troops in Berlin through six depots throughout Germany. The headquarters of each army had its commander of balloon troops, and a balloon detachment of staff employed in connection with photography, signals and maps was located at each corps headquarters. Each detachment controlled two or three balloon sections, with a section comprising two balloons. Normally one section on a corps front observed for the infantry divisions and was in direct communication with them; the remainder was employed on artillery observation.

A British kite balloon on the Western Front, April 1916.

RFC Recruitment and Training

Many pilots were initially seconded from their original regiments and some RFC ground crew also volunteered for flying duties – everyone who qualified received additional flying pay. All that was required of volunteers was that they pass the usual army medical, except that the eye test was more rigorous. There was no formal training for observers until 1917, and many went on their first mission with only the briefest of instructions from the pilot. In a two-seater the pilot was in command (this had not been so at the outset of the war) and, as aircraft of this period did not have dual controls, if the pilot was killed or incapacitated the observer would usually be doomed as well. The great fear of air crew was of being burned to death and a number took a revolver with them to avoid such a fate.

Schools of Instruction (called Schools of Military Aeronautics in October 1916) were established at Reading and Oxford and after theoretical work the pilots went to training squadrons either in the UK or overseas. In March 1916 official standards required for pilots were:

• fifteen hours' solo flying (increased in December to twenty and up to twenty-eight according to the type of aircraft) before he was passed for overseas duty

• cross-country flight of at least 60 miles and during the flight to have landed at two landing places under supervision

• climb to 6,000 feet and remain at that height for fifteen minutes, after which land with the engine stopped, the aircraft first touching the ground within a circle of 50 yards' diameter

• two night landings assisted by flares

However, before he could wear his wings a pilot was also required to pass tests in gunnery, artillery observation, bomb-dropping and photography.

The rapid expansion of the RFC, the urgent need for more and more pilots, led to standards of both recruits and training slipping, which resulted in an unacceptable number of fatalities during 1915–16. Lieutenant Colonel Robert Smith-Barry, the former commander of 60 Squadron, formulated a more comprehensive and practical training scheme at the Advanced School of Flying at Gosport. A programme of theory and flying training in dual-control aircraft with an experienced instructor soon weeded out the unsuitable. Smith-Barry was an Irishman and a great 'character', as well as being able to perform the most amazing aerial antics. His batman was a French boy called Doby, a refugee from Lille, whom he dressed in RFC uniform and called Air Mechanic Doby; in France Doby

excelled at scrounging luxuries for the mess from his compatriots. After a year and some changes of command nobody knew Doby's history, so he was regarded as a genuine member of the RFC!

A Smith-Barry innovation was to encourage his students to perform potentially dangerous manoeuvres in a controlled environment so that they learned to rectify errors of judgement safely. Of these manoeuvres, the aircraft going into an uncontrolled spin was the most dreaded. Captain Ronald Sykes, DFC, recorded the sensation – his description is held in the Imperial War Museum voice archives:

> It was the most sickening sensation. You were thrown violently to one side of the cockpit with a fierce blast of wind on one cheek. You had to switch off the engine and straighten everything – the control stick and the rudder. You usually didn't come out of the spin quickly. You just had to put everything central and wait. Eventually you entered a nose dive and you pulled the stick back slightly and you were all right.

Another student's first attempt was nearly a disaster:

> He told me what to do and how to get out of a spin, but when I saw the world turning round on an axis directly below me, I absolutely froze on the controls and I couldn't do anything at all. The instructor was swearing and cursing and he overcame the pressure I was putting on the controls and he got us out of the spin about 500 feet above the ground.

As the war progressed the RFC increasingly drew on men from the British Empire (by the end of 1918 a third of aircrews were Canadians). Although training became safer, by the Armistice some 8,000 RFC personnel had been killed while training or in flying accidents – an appalling statistic.

As a broad generalization, and bearing in mind that many aircraft performed dual or secondary roles, the tasks of the RFC and the air forces of other belligerents can be divided into three: reconnaissance (including artillery spotting and aerial photography), aerial combat and ground attack (bombing and supporting ground forces).

Reconnaissance

The need to know what is happening on the other side of the hill had been a priority for generals since wars began and in World War I, with both sides dug in along a front of hun-

dreds of miles, the traditional eyes of an army, the cavalry, were impotent. The answer lay in the air, and reconnaissance – or the prevention of it by the enemy – became the primary task of aircraft on the Western Front.

There were two basic types of aerial reconnaissance: tactical and strategic. The former provided information for corps, divisional or lower commanders through ascertaining the strength and dispositions of the enemy in a limited area of the front by locating his trenches, gun batteries, headquarters, reserves, forward supply dumps and railheads. The latter involved much deeper penetration behind enemy lines to seek out his lines of communication bottlenecks, supply dumps, reserve positions and large-scale movement of troops or transport – information needed by higher command for planning a major offensive.

The RFC launched its first aerial reconnaissance on 19 August 1914 when two two-seater aircraft went up without observers, got lost in poor weather and only one completed its task. Of much more value was the strategic surveillance flight on 22 August by Captain L. E. O. Charlton (observer) and Lieutenant V. H. N. Wadham when they reported the German First Army attempting to outflank the BEF, allowing Sir John French to realign his force and save his army around Mons. French's despatch on 7 September included the following tribute:

> I wish to bring to your Lordships' notice the admirable work done by the Royal Flying Corps under Sir David Henderson. Their skill, energy and perseverance has been beyond all praise. They have furnished me with complete and accurate information, which has been of incalculable value in the conduct of operations. Fired at constantly by friend and foe [recognition was a problem at this time], and not hesitating to fly in every kind of weather, they have remained undaunted throughout.

Similarly, on 3 September French aerial observation spotted the German First, Second and Fifth Armies moving towards Paris, information that enabled General Joseph Gallieni, the defender of the city, to react quickly enough to check the advance.

The most effective aircraft was the two-seater, with the pilot able to concentrate on flying and the observer either spotting for artillery, marking his map, taking aerial photographs or defending against enemy aircraft to the rear with his machine gun. As the war progressed, the skills of and demands on the observer became as intense as those of the pilot. A good observer needed an extensive military knowledge to decide what objects to look for and where to look for them, and the ability to read a map quickly in order to navigate and mark positions on it. In fine weather the difficulties were formidable, but in the driving rain or snow, with temperatures below zero and being buffeted around by the wind, they became immense. Communications between observer and pilot were always difficult in open cockpits. Simple signals, such as movement of the head or hands to left or right, and touches on back or shoulders were used, as were speaking tubes. Sometimes boards with coloured discs to which the pilot could point were fixed to the rear edge of the top plane each with a specific meaning such as 'It's an enemy' or 'It's friendly'.

Particularly for artillery-spotting, it was air-to-ground communications that were critical – the observer had to be able to signal to the battery with which he was working. By the end of 1914 the headquarters wireless unit had the role of supplying wireless-equipped aircraft to the RFC squadrons working with the army. Later flights were allotted to each wing in an RFC brigade and eventually each squadron had a wireless-equipped flight. This was a one-way wireless telegraphy and it was not until towards the end of the war that limited wireless telephony was introduced.

The use of wireless aircraft prior to the Somme had been restricted to one every 2,000 yards of front, which was the maximum that could be employed without signals clashing. However, by the spring of 1917 technical advances and better organization enabled the number of wireless observers to be increased to one every 1,000 yards, doubling the number of aircraft able to support the artillery on any section of the front. The reorganization that took place from late September 1916 saw a wireless station attached to each heavy- or siege-artillery battery, counter-battery group and corps headquarters, with five stations for each divisional artillery group. All RFC wireless stations would accompany the artillery units when they moved. Additionally, a central wireless station was established in each corps area, near the headquarters of the corps heavy artillery, to monitor the wireless progress of all shoots. If communication between a battery and an observer broke down it would act as a relay station by the use of a telephone to the battery commander so that the shoot could continue.

When observing for artillery the observer needed to know about gunnery, including such matters as the time taken for a shell to travel a given distance – it enabled him to attribute a given burst to a particular battery. If, for example, the range from the guns to the target was 5 miles, the observer would expect to see the burst near the target after about thirty seconds. The ability to send wireless signals enabled an effective 'drill' or procedure to be established for artillery-spotting, taking advantage of the discovery early in the Somme offensive that artillery wireless stations on the ground picked up signals best when the aircraft was flying towards the battery. As a result, the method of ranging guns was as follows. The aircraft initially flew towards the target and then turned towards the battery and signalled it to fire. On seeing the flash the observer started his stopwatch and the aircraft turned to fly towards the target in time to see the burst and note any corrections needed. Again the aircraft turned back towards the battery and the corrections were passed to it. This cycle of events could continue until the shoot was on target.

Aerial reconnaissance was not just for artillery-spotting or ranging but involved a far more complex combination of tasks, particularly in the build-up to a major offensive. For example, for the opening of the BEF offensive in April 1917 the work required of aircraft included observation of fire on batteries involved in counter-battery tasks, observation of fire on trenches and wire obstacles, and trench reconnaissance and contact patrols (making contact with and reporting the location of the foremost friendly or enemy infantry). All this required the most careful planning and management, with specific flights being given specific tasks.

To be of maximum value to ground headquarters both strategic and tactical reconnaissance involved the extensive use of aerial photography. Photographs could be taken from both static balloons and moving aircraft.

The advantage of the stationary platform of the former tended to be nullified by the distance from the area under observation, and by the fact that pictures were taken at an oblique angle that made judging distance accurately problematic. The aircraft could cover greater distances and penetrate to targets of strategic as well as tactical importance, taking vertical as well as oblique pictures. The problem was that initially there was no suitable camera and efforts were very amateurish, with the pilot trying to take photographs of the right target while also flying low and having to risk heavy ground fire. Although a two-seater with an observer improved things, rain, sleet and freezing temperatures (the observer had to wear gloves, which made handling difficult), coupled with primitive cameras, made the whole task often more miss than hit.

In early 1915 the British produced their first camera designed for aerial photography, called the A-type camera. It weighed about 10 lb and was contained in a wooden case that could be gripped by the observer, who leaned over the side to take his picture. An improvement was the strapping of the camera to the outside of the aircraft. It was this camera that was used to take the first aerial photograph trench map of the German front line, to a depth of about 1,500 yards, in preparation for the Battle of Neuve Chapelle in March 1915 – something that convinced doubters of the immense value of aerial photography and stimulated further improvements and expansion. This early model was followed by the B- and C-types; with the latter eighteen pictures could be taken in succession by either the pilot or the observer pulling a cord and turning a handle forward and then back to reload. This camera was used extensively for the Somme battles.

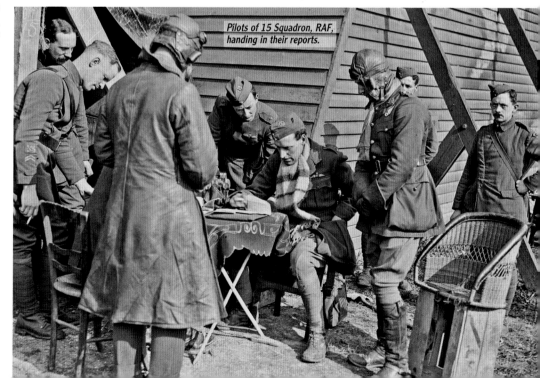

Pilots of 15 Squadron, RAF, handing in their reports.

The best height for taking photographs was around 6,000 feet; the disadvantage was that this was within the range of 'archie' (anti-aircraft) fire and the pilot had to keep a steady, straight course and maintain the same altitude, thus making himself a far easier target to hit. Nevertheless, photographs from this height showed details such as barbed wire; even footprints in grass, invisible to the eye, sometimes came out in an enlargement. Cable trenches when left open appeared straight and narrow, while air lines were shown as tiny white dots – the displaced earth where the poles had been inserted. If the enemy expected an attack, new lines of wire would appear, with trenches and dugouts behind and new battery positions made. If they intended to mount an attack there would be increased artillery activity, more communication trenches constructed and saps pushed forward. Behind the lines the rapid construction of more light railways invariably meant a build-up of supplies. These tens of thousands of photographs enabled cartographic units to produce up-to-date trench maps with a scale of 1:10,000 or even 1:5,000, as well as photographic maps that quickly became the essential tools for the planning and conduct of every operation from small patrols to major offensives.

All these countless thousands of artillery observation and photographic flights were the routine duties of the RFC (and other nations' air forces) throughout the war. As an example of the extent of these operations, from 14 to 21 August 1916 the RFC assisted the guns to range on 730 German batteries, resulting in 128 gun pits being totally destroyed and causing 321 explosions among the batteries. That week they flew over 1,200 hours; took 5,000 photographs of enemy positions; dropped over 2,000 bombs and fired more than 30,000 bullets at German ground forces. By 1918 RFC activity was even more intense. On 16 February it carried out 33 reconnaissance flights, of which 8 were long-distance photographic flights; 83 enemy batteries were destroyed and 6 neutralized; 9 gun pits were destroyed and 33 damaged; 29 explosions and 26 fires were caused; and 2,547 photographs were taken – a record for one day. In 1918 the French claimed to have printed 100,000 photographs each night and during four days of the Meuse–Argonne offensive to have made 56,000 aerial prints to hand over to the Americans.

Any flight over enemy lines, especially if the task required flying below the ceiling of anti-aircraft batteries, required the pilot to display exceptionally cool nerves and great courage. Below is an extract from a soldier's admiring letter to *The Times*, published in September 1915 and quoted in Charles C. Turner's *The Struggle in the Air*:

The airmen are a new race of human beings. Five of the super-avian birds yesterday evening utterly distracted the Hun batteries along our front. The air spaces above were spotted with shrapnel puffs, regularly, in the proportion of currants to a well-made 'plum-duff' (I can think of no better illustration), and back and forth passed the hawks with the most perfect and practical indifference. You hear the muffled 'plop' up aloft about eight seconds after you have seen the sparking flash of the bursting shell . . .

When the batteries are really busy you see flash upon flash away up there, four and five together, and soon the flashes merge into a wild confusion of irregular 'plops.' The hawks, if low down, and in great danger, dodge the shells by continually shifting their angle of flight, darting about here and there, and it must need a cool head, and hands and feet, which work automatically up there.

We have seen flights where it seemed impossible for the hawk to miss a shell, and then, when the hawk had reached safety, we have seen him deliberately turn back and return to the same danger zone. It looks like bravado, but it is not. That hawk had not finished the task he had set himself to finish, so he went back. One hawk did this five times while we watched from the front trench, and when he finally decided to go home to roost, and regained safety, it was great relief to cheer him, and I hope he heard that bottled-up explosion of relief we gave him.

In the evenings, after sundown, by twilight, and against the sunset pinks and yellows, the hawks, from all points of the Hun front, come home to roost. Gliding in with engines stopped, they swoop in long gradual slants . . .

If a German hawk ever passes over us, he is hunted and harried, unhappy thing, which very soon 'scoots' for home and lagerland. You never see them at their ease and serene.

Just one example by an RFC pilot will serve to illustrate the thousands of acts of gallantry displayed by air crews of all nations on the Western Front. On 31 July 1915 Captain John Liddell was severely wounded while flying on a reconnaissance mission over the Ostend–Bruges–Ghent area. His right thigh was smashed, which caused momentary unconsciousness, but making a great effort he regained partial control after his machine had dropped 3,000 feet. Despite the intense pain and loss of blood, and still under continuous fire, he proceeded on his course and brought the aircraft down safely half an hour after being wounded.

The official report stated:

The difficulties overcome by this officer in saving his machine and the life of his observer cannot be readily expressed, but as the control wheel and throttle were smashed, and also one of the under carriage struts, it would seem incredible that he could have accomplished what he did.

Captain Liddell was awarded the Victoria Cross.

Aerial Combat

The fighting in the skies above the Western Front saw a fluctuating struggle for air supremacy. As the war progressed a critical factor in the planning and success of battles was control of the air space over both enemy and friendly territory to a depth of several miles. With both sides seeking this control, numerous air-to-air combats became a daily occurrence. The tasks of single-seater and two-seater fighters grew rapidly to include attacking enemy machines on reconnaissance or artillery observation, escorting and defending friendly reconnaissance two-seaters and attacking enemy balloons. Quickly added to these roles were strafing ground targets; defending air space from enemy bombers; and conducting contact patrols that involved reporting progress of infantry on the ground.

By the end of 1916 fighting in the air had become a highly specialized business with techniques and tactics continuing to evolve along with improved aircraft performance and armament until 1918. Before looking at the tactical techniques used, a brief summary of how the fortunes of the air war favoured one side and then the other up until the final months of the war will provide a helpful background.

1914–1915

It was during this period that the realization came that aerial combat was going to play a crucial part in the land battle and that fighter aircraft, or scouts as they were usually called, needed machine guns able to fire to the front and rear. The forward-firing gun of the pusher aircraft provided some offensive capability and the mounting of a gun firing to the rear from a two-seater gave some defensive capability. With the single-seater tractor aircraft the ability to fire forwards was essential. As noted above, the French developed the deflector system that allowed bullets that struck the propeller to be deflected, but it was the Germans who went one better and made the real breakthrough with synchronized machine guns. British attempts to use the Lewis gun in this way were unsuccessful.

The Elation of the Kill

Major (later Group Captain) Alan Scott, who commanded 60 Squadron, RFC, during the German March offensive of 1918 described the elation of seeing an enemy go down in flames:

> We simply had it all over the Boche for speed and, as we had the height, they could not possibly get away. I picked my man out as he was coming towards me, and dived straight at him, opening fire with both guns at close range. He suffered the same fate as his companion [shot down in flames].
>
> A burning machine is a glorious but terrible sight to see – a tiny red stream of flames trickles from the petrol tank, and then long tongues of blazing petrol lick the sides of the fuselage and, finally, a sheet of white fire envelops the whole machine, and it glides steeply towards the ground in a zigzag course, leaving a long trail of black smoke behind it, until it eventually breaks up. There is no doubt that your first Hun in flames gives you a wonderful feeling of satisfaction. I can well image what the big game-hunter must think when he sees the dead lion in front of him. Somehow you do not realize you are sending a man to an awful doom, but rather your thoughts are all turned on the hateful machine which you are destroying, so fascinating to look at and yet so deadly in its attack.

The Maxim guns (Vickers) used by both the Allies and Germany (as the Parabellum MG 14 and Spandau LMG) had a firing cycle that was far easier to synchronize. By late 1915 German aces (pilots with over ten kills) such as Max Immelmann and Oswald Boelcke flying the Fokker E.I Eindecker gave the Germans a period of air superiority that lasted until the following spring. Although the Allies suffered losses, the 'Fokker Scourge' was partially contained by obsolescent Allied pushers until the synchronized gear could be matched by the RFC (the FE. 2b and DH.2) in March 1916. The French flying the single-seater Nieuport II (see page 419) tractor biplane, with its gun firing outside the arc of the propeller, also proved capable of bringing down the Fokker.

1916–1917

For the Somme offensive the RFC, although still mostly equipped with the old BE.2c, began to receive new aircraft such as the Sopwith 1½ Strutter (see page 422). These, combined with an offensive attitude to all flights, enabled the RFC to win back air superiority in the weeks prior to the offensive. The RFC took on the role of 'trench strafing' (in modern terms 'close air support'), which included bombing munition and supply dumps – roles that quickly became commonplace. The Allied successes in the air over the Somme battlefields prompted the German High Command to galvanize production of the Albatros D.I and reorganize their air formations, which eventually produced the strategic bombing squadrons that caused such consternation in England during 1917 and 1918.

By late 1916 the Germans were operating specialist close-support squadrons, which gave the British infantry considerable trouble at Cambrai, along with fighter squadrons equipped with the new Albatros fighter. These 'hunting squadrons' (*Jagdstaffeln* – shortened to *Jasta*) were not attached to a ground formation but moved around as needed and were mobilized in response to enemy sightings. These Jasta missions were aggressive aerial warfare.

By the end of the year the pendulum had swung back to favour the Germans and for the first half of 1917 they again achieved domination of the skies. April that year became known as 'Bloody April' when the RFC suffered significantly higher losses than their opponents. Despite a considerable numerical advantage, the RFC lost a third of its fighter force in a month, with the flying life expectancy of pilots being, at one point, a mere eighteen hours. Although new and better Allied fighters – such as the Sopwith Pup, Sopwith triplane and SPAD S.VII – were coming into service, at this stage their numbers were small and the Germans had deployed their Albatros D.III, described by some as the best fighting scout on the Western Front despite its structural problems. Nevertheless, by the end of 1917, as the British introduced their improved fighters in increasing numbers along with the Bristol F.2b, and with the Germans' disappointment over their latest Albatros and Fokker Dr.I (more structural problems), the RFC had regained control.

1918

This year saw increasing shortages of supplies – such as metal and rubber – for the Germans, who resorted to cannibalizing captured Allied aircraft for spares and materials, even to the extent of draining lubricants from damaged engines. Their morale suffered when Manfred von Richthofen (the Red Baron), their number-one ace, was killed in April (see pages 444–5) and when the Americans began entering the war in rapidly increasing numbers; by mid-1918 all-American squadrons operated in the skies above the trenches.

The first awards of the Victoria Cross to two aircrew of the newly constituted Royal Air Force were announced on 1 May 1918. The citation for Second Lieutenant Alan McLeod describes a dogfight against heavy odds that involved outstanding airmanship as well as exceptional courage:

> Second-Lieutenant A. A. McLeod, whilst flying with his observer (Lieutenant A. W. Hammond, MC) attacking hostile formations by bombs and machine-gun fire, was assailed at a height of 5,000 feet by eight enemy triplanes which dived at him from all directions. By skilled manoeuvring he enabled his observer to fire bursts at each machine in turn, shooting three of them down out of control. By this time Lieutenant McLeod had received five wounds, and whilst continuing the engagement a

Australian Vickers gunners of No. 4 Section, 22 Machine Gun Company, firing at an enemy aircraft, May 1917.

A Bristol fighter takes off from Vert Galand Aerodrome.

bullet penetrated his petrol tank and set the machine on fire. He then climbed out on to the left bottom plane, controlling his machine from the side of the fuselage, and by side-slipping steeply kept the flames to one side, thus enabling the observer to continue firing until the ground was reached.

The observer had been wounded six times when the machine crashed in 'No Man's Land,' and Second-Lieutenant McLeod, notwithstanding his own wounds, dragged him away from the burning wreckage at great personal risk from heavy machine-gun fire from the enemy's lines. This gallant pilot was again wounded by a bomb while engaged in this act of rescue, but he persevered until he had placed Lieutenant Hammond in comparative safety, before falling himself from exhaustion and loss of blood. The observer, Lieutenant Hammond, was awarded a bar to his MC.

McLeod survived and returned to his native Canada to recover from his wounds, but died of Spanish flu in November 1918.

Combat tactics

Major Edward 'Mick' Mannock, VC, DSO, MC, when explaining air-to-air combat to his pilots, summarized successful tactics with the words, 'Gentlemen, always above; seldom on the same level; never underneath.' To start an attack above an enemy aircraft was usually the key to achieving surprise – a factor in any form of combat that frequently rewards the weaker side with success. If height was the main factor it could be re-inforced by skilful use of clouds for concealment and by approaching with the sun behind the attacker – the phrase 'Beware the Hun in the sun' was a common British maxim. The principles of air-to-air combat were drummed into German pilots by their ace Oswald Boelcke, whose eight *Dicta* were:

Secure an advantage before attacking Advantages could include altitude, speed, surprise, performance or numerical superiority – the more you had the better.

Speed: usually the pilot in the fastest machine had control over the combat – he had the choice of continuing the fight or breaking off in the knowledge that the slower machine could not catch him. The pilot in the slower aircraft was forced on to the defensive. The faster machine could perform more elaborate manoeuvres and was able to climb to gain a height advantage faster – climbing cut air speed by a half, while diving increased it by about 50 per cent.

Altitude: being above an opponent gave a pilot control over when and where to make his attack. He could dive on his enemy, which gave him a considerable speed advantage.

Surprise: attacking out of the sun or cloud or from a greater height were the best ways of getting in the first shot. Most air victories were won at the first pass. In practice this usually meant attacking single-seater scouts from above and two-seaters from below their tails – the observer's blind spot.

Performance: knowledge of the strengths and weaknesses of your own and the enemy's machine was vital. Who was faster, who could turn quicker or where were the blind spots could make all the difference to the tactics used or the decision to attack or retreat and how best to do it.

Always continue an attack you have begun New, inexperienced pilots tended to start a fight and then if not immediately successful break off and run. To turn tail was to surrender all or most of your original advantages and invariably presented your tail to the enemy's guns. It was better to continue the fight and wait for your opponent to make a mistake or flee. Continuous

practice of quick turns was required, as this manoeuvre was crucial and used more frequently in a dogfight than any other. Never fly straight in a dogfight unless firing.

Open fire at close range and when the enemy is clearly in your sights Opening fire at much over 100 yards was usually useless and merely wasted ammunition, as well as giving your enemy warning of your presence and position and time to react. To hit a fast-moving, fleeting target from a bouncing platform was hard enough without the range being excessive. The amount of ammunition carried was limited to several hundred rounds – perhaps only a minute of continuous firing – so it had to be conserved. Reloading was always difficult and sometimes dangerous, so making the first burst effective by ensuring the range was short and the target squarely in the sights was the best way of securing an early victory.

Always keep your opponent in sight and never be deceived by his ruses Unless a conscious effort was made, keeping your eye on your enemy was often easier said than done in the excitement of combat and amid the distractions of flying and manoeuvring. If a pilot 'lost' his enemy he was likely to have lost his advantage. A common ruse was for a pilot to feign being hit and deliberately go into a spin, hoping his attacker would think him finished and break off the attack before he had to pull out of the spin at the last moment. Pilots should always follow their enemy down to ensure their opponent crashed; if he didn't they should continue the fight.

In attacking, always do so from behind Firing across the path of a fast-moving aircraft requires a 'leading' shot aimed ahead of the target. For most pilots, even after practice, this was often a waste of ammunition, particularly if combined with excessive range. Again, this was initially a common mistake among new pilots. Head-on or tail-on attacks required virtually no deflection and the target would remain in the cone of fire for much longer. The latter method was by far the most effective and the most feared – having an enemy on your tail and firing at close range usually had fatal consequences. In two-seaters it was the task of the observer to defend the rear, which is why an attack was best made from the blind spot just under and behind the tail.

Fly to meet a diving attacker The instinctive reaction of a novice pilot on discovering an attacker diving down on him was to turn away or flee. This reaction was usually disastrous, as it continued to present your tail to the enemy. Instead the aim should be to turn towards the attacker and put him on the defensive. Although climbing was slow, there was a chance the attacker would over-shoot and have to pull out of his dive, per-haps giving the initial defender time to circle round and counter-attack with his own dive.

When over the enemy lines, always remember your line of retreat A pilot operating over enemy lines who decided to flee in the face of a numerically superior enemy or because his machine was dam-aged had to remember the shortest route back over friendly territory. This was not always easy if he had previously been involved in violent manoeuvres and changes of direction, which could quickly lead to disorientation. Other relevant factors were the need to watch fuel and the strength and direction of the wind – Allied pilots making for home often faced a westerly headwind.

When possible, attack in groups of four or six aircraft, and avoid two machines attacking the same enemy During the early months of the war aerial combat was com-monly a one-on-one affair, but as the struggle progressed the number of aircraft in the skies over the Western Front grew enormously. Reconnaissance aircraft, even if several were flying together, had to be escorted by fighters above them. Attacking in a group became the most effective method, with the leader able to concentrate on his target knowing that his rear was guarded. Later air battles could involve scores of machines turning and twist-ing in a bewildering tangle. When one side was numerically weaker it was important not to double up in attacking a single enemy, as it was likely that each would get in the other's way and leave an unmarked enemy able to attack the tail of one of your side.

Although not specifically mentioned in the *Dicta*, pilots needed to sight their guns and constantly practise gunnery at fleeting tar-gets. The golden rule of opening fire only at close range could occasionally be ignored if the pilot was a crack shot. Captain George E. McElroy, RFC, was such a man. It was largely his excellent shooting that gained him forty-eight victories, making him one of the top British aces of the war. Not only was his long-range shooting accurate, but his vic-tim was inclined to think that his attacker was a novice in opening fire at such ranges and was often fooled into taking what turned out to be fatal risks. Connected with shooting was the need to practise judging distances in the air – no easy matter when travelling at speed at varying heights. Good shooting and judging distance had to be combined with being able to distinguish friend from foe quickly and, having identi-fied the machine as hostile, then to know its performance and blind spots.

In November 1916 the RFC's *Notes on Aeroplane Fighting in Single-Seated Scouts* had the following to say on opening fire:

> Do not let the enemy adjust his fire. If the enemy attempts to fire, do not fire yourself, and do not make for him in a straight line, for a cool gunner firing at a machine making straight for him has the greatest chance of hitting it and bringing it down.
>
> Make for your opponent in a zigzag course which obliges him to change the aim of his gun from side to side. Keep also a little above him, and as you approach get ready to start firing; then when about 100 yards off, and when the conditions are favourable, e.g. when the enemy gun is still pointed to port, and you yourself have turned and are already slightly on the starboard side, charge straight at him, firing a rapid burst. The shots should be fired at about 50 yards from the target.
>
> Under these conditions 15 to 50 rounds can be fired, after which you must swerve to avoid a collision.

The same notes also recommended the fol-lowing action if caught unawares:

> If surprised in an unfavourable position it is by no means easy to shake off the adversary. If time permits it should be the invariable rule to turn and attack before he comes to close quarters. If, however, he succeeds in doing so the best chance lies in a side-slip, or a fall out of control. A turn will expose the broad side of the machine to his fire, while to dive straight away is to court disaster.

For a description of an air-to-air combat it is hard to beat that of the German ace Manfred von Richthofen's account of how he brought down Major Lanoe George Hawker, DSO, one of the early British aces, on 23 November 1916:

> The Englishman tried to catch me up in the rear while I tried to get him behind. So we circled round and round like madmen after one another at an altitude of about 10,000 feet. First we circled 20 times to the left, and then 30 times to the right. Each tried to get behind and above the other.
>
> Soon I discovered that I was not meeting a beginner. He had not the slightest intention to break off the fight. He was travelling in a box [a De Havilland 2 pusher] that turned beautifully. However, my packing case was better at climbing than his. But I succeeded at last in getting above and beyond my English waltzing partner.
>
> When we had got down to about 6,000 feet without having achieved anything in particular, my opponent ought to have discovered that it was time for him to take his leave. The wind was favourable to me, for it drove us more and more towards the German position. At last we were above Bapaume, about half a mile behind the German front. The gallant fellow was full of pluck, and when we had got down to about 3,000 feet he merrily waved to me as if he would say, Well, how do you do?
>
> The circles which we made round one another were so narrow that their diameter was probably no more than 250 or 300 feet. I had time to take a good look at my opponent. I looked down into his carriage and could see every movement of his head. If he had not had his cap on I would have noticed what kind of face he was making.
>
> My Englishman was a good sportsman, but by and by the thing became a little too hot for him. He had to decide whether he would land on German ground or whether he would fly back to the English lines. Of course he tried the latter, and after endeavouring in vain to escape me by loopings and such tricks. At that time his first bullets were flying around me, for so far neither of us had been able to do any shooting.
>
> When he had come down to about 300 feet he tried to escape by flying in a zigzag course, which made it difficult for an observer on the ground to shoot. That was my favourable moment. I followed him at an altitude of from 250 to 150 feet, firing all the time. The Englishman could not help falling. But the jamming of my gun nearly robbed me of my success.
>
> My opponent fell shot through the head behind our line. His machine gun was dug out of the ground and it ornaments the entrance of my dwelling.

Richthofen is said to have fired over 900 rounds in this duel.

Ground Attack: Bombing

Before the outbreak of war the French, Germans, Russians and Austro–Hungarians were developing aircraft for bombing. As noted above, by 1914 the Germans had built a powerful bombing force around Zeppelin airships and used them extensively early in the war. The obvious potential for aerial bom-bardment was not lost on the UK, although they did not build machines especially for this role until after hostilities had started.

A Pilot's Diary, November 1915

As a young pilot, Lieutenant Colonel Louis Strange, DSO, MC, RFC, flew the two-seater Avro aircraft on early bombing missions and later recorded a typical week's flying over the Ypres area of the front.

November 1. – 7 a.m., repaired engine and flew to Bailleul, twenty-five minutes. 10 a.m. chased a German machine for forty minutes and fired fifty rounds from a Maxim, but he went down over his own lines, apparently undamaged. 11.30 a.m., started flight of thirty minutes' duration, dropped 25 bombs on bivouac around Q— and Lille and eighteen on a kite balloon, which went down although we did not actually hit it. 2 p.m., reconnaissance round Ypres, Roulers, Courtrai, Menin and back to Bailleul. Dropped eleven bombs on bivouacs; this makes a record of thirty-six in one day. Also I made a record of my longest time in the air for a day five hours and fifteen minutes. Lieut. Vaughan [his observer] wounded.

November 2. – 8 a.m., reconnaissance as passenger in Lieut. Creed's machine, observing for one hour and ten minutes round Quesnoy, Messines, etc. 12 noon, up again observing over battle in progress between Ypres and Armentières. The line is now an extraordinary sight, as the trenches are very close to one another and the ground all round them is pitted with shell holes.

November 3. – 9 a.m., chased German machine for twenty minutes. 11.40 a.m., reconnaissance round Béthune and Lille, drove a German machine down at L—, dropped twenty-two bombs on ammunition columns at Renardes in course of a one hour forty-five minutes' flight.

November 4. – Dull, misty day. Due attention paid to machine.

November 5. – 10 a.m., reconnaissance with Lieut. Wilson round Messines for one hour thirty-five minutes' flight. 2 p.m., flew for one hour fifty-five minutes after German machine and drove it down at Lille, where I dropped nine bombs on the aerodrome. Fired fifty rounds from a Maxim at a balloon, dropped five bombs at Doulemont and got a very close burst from anti-aircraft guns.

November 6. – Thick mist all day. No flying.

November 7. – . . . The district comprising Courtrai, Roubaix, Quesnoy, and Menin, seems very full of troops, especially cavalry. The latter's camps show up more clearly on account of the rings the horses make when they are exercised. I find it pays to do a sharp left or right-hand banked turn when under shell fire, as you gain a few clear minutes before the gunners get onto you again . . . The Germans seem to get more and more anti-aircraft guns; the more you get used to being shelled, the more they shell you. I think I must have seen a good two or three thousand shells burst at our machine in the air today, and reckon that at least fifty of them were fired at me.

With the BEF, early bombing of an opportunistic nature by individuals was undertaken from aircraft in front-line squadrons. These initial attempts merely involved the pilot (or observer) leaning over the side and dropping the bomb (grenade) by hand. Tentative successes included stampeding German cavalry horses and Captain Louis Strange destroying two trucks with home-made petrol bombs. In March 1915 Captain Strange took part in the RFC's first planned bombing raid of the war. He was flying a modified BE.2c carrying four 20-lb bombs on wing racks that were released by pulling a cable in the cockpit. Flying at low level, he succeeded in causing seventy-five casualties on a troop train in Courtrai station. See also box above.

On 25 April Second Lieutenant William Rhodes-Moorhouse became the first airman to win the Victoria Cross, albeit posthumously. Like Strange he was attacking Courtrai rail junction, but with a 100-lb bomb. He swept in very low and released the bomb, but was immediately caught in a heavy barrage of small-arms fire from rifles and a machine gun in the belfry of Courtrai church. He was hit in the thigh and his machine was badly damaged. During his return flight to Allied lines he was hit again twice, but managed to bring his aircraft back despite the agonizing pain and loss of blood. He then insisted on making his report before being taken to a casualty clearing station where he died the next day. Rhodes-Moorhouse is buried at his family home,

Parham House, Dorset. Interred alongside him are the ashes of his son, Flying Officer William Rhodes-Moorhouse, killed in action during the Battle of Britain.

The first genuine bomber used in combat was the French Voisin aircraft, a pusher biplane with a steel airframe that bombed the Zeppelin hangars at Metz–Trascaty on 14 August 1914. Successive designs had increasingly powerful engines, and its carrying capacity rose from 132 lb to 660 lb by the end of the war. The French High Command organized these machines into bombing squadrons that later contained over 600 aircraft. However, the French were extremely reluctant to bomb behind German lines, as they did not wish to drop bombs on German-occupied France.

All countries used bombers in a tactical role as they could reach areas beyond artillery range. When an offensive was being planned, behind-the-lines activity, including the build-up of traffic and munitions dumps, presented an ideal target. Strategic bombing targeted factories and mines supporting the war effort as well as rail junctions and communication centres and later cities. An example of what might be called 'revenge' bombing occurred after the April 1915 dropping of chlorine gas on Allied trenches. The French response was to despatch bombers to destroy what they believed to be the gas factory at Ludwigshafen.

Long-range bombing of civilians in towns and cities by airships and aircraft,

although not directly a part of the Western Front battles, requires a brief mention as it had considerable effect on morale, and as far as the UK was concerned eventually compelled the use for home defence of air assets that might have been deployed at the front. German Zeppelin raids on civilians began on 19 January 1915 when two Zeppelins dropped twenty-four 110-lb high-explosive and incendiary bombs on Great Yarmouth, King's Lynn and Sheringham, killing four and injuring sixteen people. These raids continued with a further nineteen in 1915, twenty-three in 1916 (including the accidental bombing of London) and eleven during 1917 and 1918. By the time the last raid was made on 5 August 1918, in which the commander of the German Naval Airship Department was killed, fifty-four raids had been made on the UK, resulting in 557 deaths and 1,358 injured. These attacks, along with those by aircraft which began in 1917 (see below), resulted in at least one recruiting poster that capitalized on the raids on London. It consisted of a nighttime skyline of London showing a Zeppelin over St Paul's Cathedral lit up by a searchlight with the following words underneath:

IT IS FAR BETTER TO FACE THE BULLETS THAN TO BE KILLED AT HOME BY A BOMB – JOIN THE ARMY AT ONCE AND HELP STOP AN AIR RAID – GOD SAVE THE KING.

During 1917 the Zeppelin attacks were supplemented by the large German Gotha G bombers, the first heavier-than-air bombers to be used for strategic bombing. This three-seater aircraft had two 260-h.p. Mercedes engines, three machine guns and a wing span of over 77 feet. It could carry 1,000 lb of bombs, which could be dropped through an oblique shaft through the bottom of the machine that also allowed the rear gunner to fire his machine gun at any enemy below. Twenty-one of these bombers raided Folkestone on 23 May 1917, killing ninety-five people. Daily raids on London followed during August and the population became highly critical as the RFC seemed unable to halt them. The British were forced to deploy some twelve squadrons and around 10,000 men on home defence, but despite the Germans resorting to night attacks, by the end of the war the raids had ceased. Nevertheless, there were in all twenty-seven Gotha attacks on the UK, with 835 reported deaths and 1,990 injured.

The British retaliated, and in October 1917 No. 41 Wing, consisting of two squadrons, was established as a strategic bombing formation for attacks on Germany. The first raid was on 17 October on Saarbrücken, and a week later one squadron returned to the same city while the other bombed railway marshalling yards nearby – both by night. The wing was expanded with the addition of two more squadrons flying the DH.4 and this strategic bomber force became the Independent Air Force.

Bombers operated by day or night. With the former, in addition to attacking ground targets, another, often more important, aim was to induce the enemy to divert his fighting strength from the main area of operations. By day bombers had to drop their load from great heights to avoid the increasingly effective German anti-aircraft fire, and therefore attacks against such small targets as ammunition dumps or railway junctions could seldom be done with sufficient accuracy to make them of direct military value. With night bombing, while their effect on morale might be less powerful, it was not necessary to have such high-performance aircraft (about three times the weight per horsepower was carried by night bombers) and these machines could fly lower as they were not so vulnerable to ground fire. Additionally, targets were more plentiful at night as important troop and supply movements were usually made during darkness, and attacks on enemy airfields would often catch aircraft in their sheds.

A bombing raid required an escort of fighters to keep the enemy at a distance, and for local protection of the bombers should any enemy succeed in getting to close quarters. The bomber aircraft had to keep in close formation even under heavy anti-aircraft fire, as any tendency to straggle or open out rendered the escorts' task impossible. When near their objective, the bombers flew in line-ahead formation to drop their bombs, but a rallying point was always selected beforehand where they would reassemble and resume their formation. The escort normally consisted of two-seater fighters disposed around the bombers for close protection, especially on the flanks and rear, with single-seater machines flying well above the formation. While the bombs were being dropped, the escort circled round above the bombers ready to dive on any enemy machines that appeared.

It is interesting to look at two examples of bombing missions. The first is a British tactical one, taken from Major Charles Turner's *The Struggle in the Air*:

> During the tremendous battles of 1918, at times there were more than 300 of our machines up together on a front of perhaps 15 miles; and a great many of these would be engaged in bombing from low altitudes the enemy's communications and troops – an amazing spectacle . . .
>
> On August 16th and 17th, raids were made on Habourdi and Lomme aerodromes, near Lille . . . In the first place [Habourdi] our machines attacked from a height of no more than 200 feet, and two enemy machines were fought in the air and crashed. Machine-guns and anti-aircraft guns were attacked from above with our machine-guns as soon as they tried to open fire, and were silenced. Hundreds of bombs were dropped. Three large hangars, containing numbers of aeroplanes, were burned out, and several others were badly hit. Two machines outside the sheds on the ground were destroyed. Fires were caused in the officers' and men's quarters, and a building supposed to be the officers' mess was blown up. A number of out buildings and an ammunition shed were set on fire. During the return journey a train was shot at until it stopped; a Staff motor-car was shot at in the road, and it turned over in the ditch . . .
>
> In the raid on Lomme aerodrome more than 100 bombs were dropped from less than 100 feet. This was too low, and the concussion damaged some of our machines. Four sheds were set on fire, and it is believed others were damaged. A number of outbuildings were wrecked, and the personnel running for shelter in all directions suffered many casualties.

The second example is a German nighttime strategic raid against Dunkirk, taken from the *British Official History of the War: The War in the Air*, Volume V, by H. A. Jones:

> The first attack began about 8 p.m. on the 24th September [1917] on the Naval Air Service depot at St. Pol. Aided by a parachute flare, which burned for several minutes, the German pilots got many hits. The pump-house, which supplied the water for the fire mains, was put out of action, and no hose could be used when the engine repair-shed was set on fire by an incendiary bomb. About a thousand men were organized to save material from the adjacent buildings, but in spite of their work great damage was caused. The engine repair-shop, saw-mill, machine-shop, spare engine-shop, engine packing-shed and the drawing and records offices were destroyed. In the engine packing-shed one hundred and forty engines were lost. The raids on the depot were repeated each night for a week and ended with a severe attack on the 1st of October. Between 9.30 p.m. on this evening and 2 a.m. on the 2nd, about one hundred bombs were dropped. It is now known that the attack on this night was made by twenty-two Gothas and by two smaller type bombers . . . the weight of the bombs dropped was approximately ten tons. A direct hit on the aircraft erecting shop started a fire, which consumed twenty-three aeroplanes.

Messines

The RFC played a crucial role in the success by the Second Army on 7 June 1917 at Messines Ridge. Its objective was to win air superiority over the battle area up to a depth of 10,000 yards behind the German front line to enable the corps to give maximum assistance to the British guns while at the same time blinding the enemy intelligence-gathering efforts. It was the first time the RFC was specifically tasked with providing almost real-time information on enemy activity to the British batteries. Concurrent with this primary role was the requirement to provide daily photographic coverage of the entire enemy trench line – an example being No. 53 Squadron, which photographed all the trench line in X Corps' area every day during the week preceding the attack. Every evening the counter-battery staff used these pictures to produce the programme of targets for the next day. To do this the squadron kept three aircraft in the air on artillery work throughout daylight hours from 1 to 7 June, with two providing support for heavy-artillery batteries and the other checking damage to German trenches and wire.

The main British bombardment started on 31 May and, apart from a thunderstorm on the evening of 6 June, the RFC had favourable weather for all their activities. Two flights from each of the three corps were used for counter-battery fire, with the third (called the bombardment flight) working with the guns engaged on the destruction of trenches, wire and strongpoints (see Map 74). These last aircraft switched to contact patrols to give ground support and to report progress on the opening day of the infantry attack. Photography to show the results of British gunfire was a duty of all flights, with responsibility of the corps' squadrons extending to a depth of 5,000 yards behind the enemy front – beyond that it was the duty of army squadrons. In the week prior to the attack Second Army aircraft observed for destructive fire on 231 German batteries, observed 225 trench bombardments and sent 716 'zone calls' for opportunity targets. If during a flight an aircraft spotted a worthwhile target not previously registered, a request via wireless giving map references could be passed to a battery, which, if not engaged on a priority task, could switch to this opportunity target. For a number of reasons not all zone calls could be answered: on 4 June when the artillery was heavily involved in the massive preparatory bombardment, only sixteen out of seventy-five zone calls could be observed, whereas on 7 June, when the bombardment was largely over, 398 calls were made and 165 were responded to and observed.

The Second Army Report Centre at Locre was the central receiving station for information and as such had nearby dropping places for aircraft to deposit messages and was connected with RFC aircraft lines, field survey companies and balloon units, as well as anti-aircraft and wireless stations. It also had direct communication by telephonic and telegraphic means via buried cable with the three corps report centres, corps heavy artillery and divisional headquarters – all underlining the growing sophistication of communications technology.

During the run-up to the attack the Germans, although seriously outnumbered in the air, made determined efforts, particularly on the British northern flank, to register their own guns with observation from the air. On the Second Army front enemy activity was most marked on 4 and 5 June, when seventy-four British batteries were engaged through German aircraft causing damage to twenty-seven guns, and the destruction of three battery ammunition dumps. These enemy air activities were revealed through the expansion of wireless intercept stations, known by the British as 'Compass Stations', which had been adopted in October 1916. They enabled the rapid location of enemy aircraft working over the lines by taking bearings on any aircraft using wireless, and when they had by intersection determined

its position, passed the information to RFC forward ground stations. These stations then displayed code-strip signals on the ground, indicating to friendly aircraft the areas in which enemy aircraft had been reported. They were unable to send this information direct to aircraft as the powerful wireless sets needed for this interfered with all other wireless traffic in the front-line area. However, the system generally gave good results and by May 1917 each army had two aeroplane compass stations and one aeroplane intercepting station. Throughout the week ending 7 June compass stations intercepted signals revealing sixty-two German aircraft directing fire from batteries opposite the Second Army's front. On forty-seven occasions RFC fighter squadrons were allocated to deal with these aircraft. The Germans had a similar organization for intercepting aircraft wireless calls that on occasion warned gun batteries that they were shortly to be targeted, giving the detachments time to seek shelter.

During the preparatory phase leading to the battle there were daily dogfights over the front lines as the RFC fought for mastery of the skies and the Germans fought to prevent it. Not all of these swirling and confused actions resulted in British success. In the morning of 5 June a flight of eight Sopwith two-seaters on a photographic mission near Menin was attacked by superior numbers of Germans, including five Albatros scouts. The ensuing melee resulted in the RFC losing two aircraft destroyed, another forced to land behind German lines and two others were so badly shot up that, although they landed behind British lines, they had to be written off.

This action saw only one Albatros go down in flames. During the afternoon the Germans were less successful, losing Lieutenant Karl Schäfer, an ace with thirty victories to his credit. Seven FE.2ds from No. 20 Squadron became entangled with some fifteen Albatros scouts above the Menin–Ypres road. Lieutenant Schäfer, flying a red aircraft, shot and mortally wounded Lieutenant W. W. Sawden, who dived for home closely pursued by the German. Another FE.2d, piloted by Lieutenant Harold Satchell with his observer Second Lieutenant Thomas Lewis, went to Sawden's assistance and after an exciting and aerobatic display a burst of fire at close range caused the Albatros to break up in the air.

The Messines battle also saw the extensive use by the RFC of contact patrols flying along the front reporting the progress of the infantry by dropping messages at designated dropping places at corps and army headquarters, and the use of fighters in the ground-attack role. These aircraft sought out opportunity targets, such as machine-gun posts, gun emplacements, trenches and

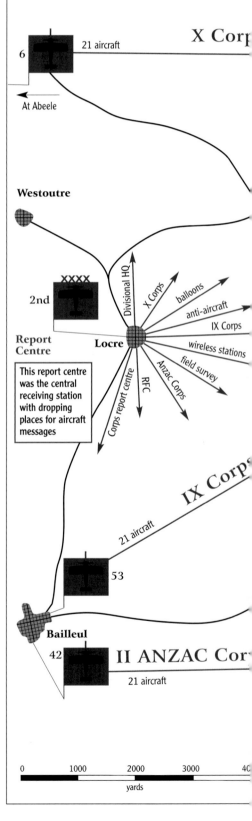

MAP 74 **MESSINES – DISPOSITION OF RFC SQUADRONS, 7 JUNE 1917**

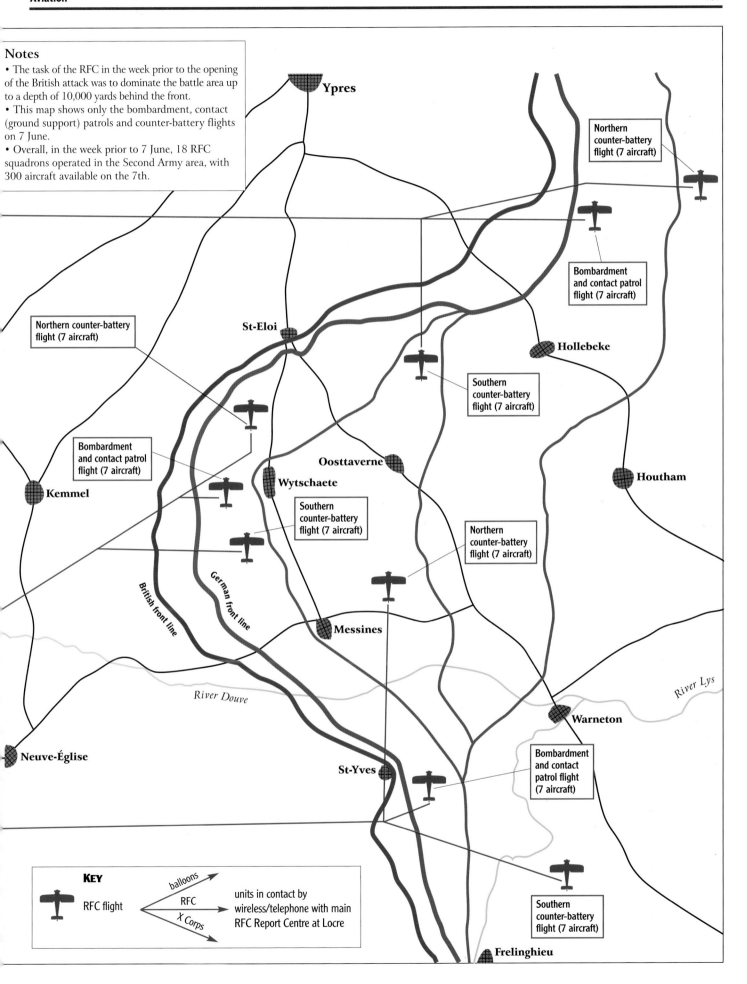

Notes

- The task of the RFC in the week prior to the opening of the British attack was to dominate the battle area up to a depth of 10,000 yards behind the front.
- This map shows only the bombardment, contact (ground support) patrols and counter-battery flights on 7 June.
- Overall, in the week prior to 7 June, 18 RFC squadrons operated in the Second Army area, with 300 aircraft available on the 7th.

Ypres

Northern counter-battery flight (7 aircraft)

Bombardment and contact patrol flight (7 aircraft)

Northern counter-battery flight (7 aircraft)

St-Eloi

Hollebeke

Southern counter-battery flight (7 aircraft)

Bombardment and contact patrol flight (7 aircraft)

Oosttaverne

Houtham

Kemmel

Wytschaete

Southern counter-battery flight (7 aircraft)

Northern counter-battery flight (7 aircraft)

British front line

German front line

Messines

River Douve

River Lys

Neuve-Église

Warneton

St-Yves

Bombardment and contact patrol flight (7 aircraft)

KEY

RFC flight

balloons

RFC

X Corps

units in contact by wireless/telephone with main RFC Report Centre at Locre

Southern counter-battery flight (7 aircraft)

Frelinghieu

troops in the open, then dived low and sprayed them with machine-gun fire. Before first light on 7 June General von Armin's Fourth Army was attacked by several British squadrons who bombed and machine-gunned artillery, infantry and transport for several hours. Others strafed troop trains at a height of 50 feet, and skimmed over the heads of infantry units, sending them rushing in wild confusion for the nearby woods. Although these very low attacks exposed the aircraft to heavy ground fire, 'infantry strafing' was far from unpopular with pilots – many found it both exhilarating and rewarding. One pilot saw a car with five occupants going along the Menin road and dropped so low for his attack that his machine almost grazed the vehicle as he flew directly over it, guns blazing. The car swerved wildly into a bank and overturned. Shortly afterwards he fired on four gun teams dispersing the drivers and then, further up the same road, flew over and scattered a column of infantry marching to the front. If a pilot ran out of ammunition it was not unknown for him to fire Very lights at a worthwhile target.

Other types of mission of a more strategic nature were also daily occurrences before the battle. One of these was strategic air reconnaissance of German rail communications as far east as Bruges and Ghent, paying particular note to the lines converging on Menin and Courtrai. Single-seater DH.4 aircraft, flying at between 16,000 and 21,000 feet, usually made these distance strategic reconnaissance flights. The second type of mission involved day bombing to divert enemy air activity away from the impending battle area. Examples of these raids included the attack on 3 June on a large ammunition dump at Vijfwegen, which was hit by four 112-lb bombs. The next day the same squadron attacked the airfield at St-Denjs-Westrem, where thirty-nine lightweight (25-lb) bombs damaged a shed. These flights often, but not always, met hostile aircraft prepared to attack the formation. One occasion when they did was on 6 June, when ten German single-seater fighters attacked six DH.4s from No. 55 Squadron on their way to bomb the railway yards at Ingelmunster. The action saw each side lose an aircraft, but the British bombers continued on their mission, dropped their bombs and fought their way home. There were also tactical night bombing raids that dropped their bombs from a few hundred feet and thus scored many more hits than their high-flying comrades, their targets often being trains and railway stations just behind the front.

Aces

The number of official 'kills' needed for a pilot to be deemed an 'ace' was just five (the Germans required ten). Scores of pilots far exceeded this number, but the precise figure of 'official credits' was always, and remains, controversial, as the circumstances of these aerial battles was often confused and invariably stressful. These factors, coupled with the natural inclination of pilots to enhance their claims and with two pilots often claiming the same victim, have meant the exact figures are often uncertain. For example, the leading French ace Captain René Fonck is credited with 75 kills although he claimed 126; and the top British ace Major Edward 'Mick' Mannock, VC, according to recent research, should score 61 not 73.

Taking the best figures available, the top ten British aces downed some 472 enemy aircraft; the Germans 506; the French 382; and the Americans 170. Space prevents this book detailing the numbers of kills of even the highest-scoring aces (20 or above) of all belligerents, but the list of the top ten given below includes five nationalities. Their country's highest decoration for gallantry is shown where awarded.

Captain Manfred von Richthofen, Germany: 80, *Pour le Mérite*
Captain René Fonck, France: 75, *Légion d'honneur*
Lieutenant Colonel William A. Bishop, Canada: 75, *Victoria Cross*
Lieutenant Ernst Udet, Germany: 62, *Pour le Mérite*
Major Edward 'Mick' Mannock, United Kingdom: 61, *Victoria Cross*
Lieutenant Colonel Raymond Collishaw, Canada: 60, *DSO and Bar*
Major James T. B. McCudden, United Kingdom: 57, *Victoria Cross*
Captain Anthony Beauchamp-Proctor, South Africa: 54, *Victoria Cross*
Major Donald R. MacLaren, Canada: 54, *DSO*
Captain Georges Guynemer, France: 54, *Légion d'honneur*

Other countries' aces included Captain Robert A. Little (Australia), 47; Second Lieutenant Willy Coppens (Belgium), 37; and Captain Edward V. Rickenbacker (United States), 26, Congressional Medal of Honor. Some exploits of the top aces of Britain, France and Germany are described below.

Major Mick Mannock

With sixty-one, or possibly more, credited victories, Major Edward 'Mick' Mannock, VC, DSO and 2 Bars, MC and Bar, was the highest-scoring British ace of the war and also the most decorated for gallantry and leadership. He was born in Ballincollig, Co. Cork, Ireland (hence his nickname 'Mick'), on 24 May 1887. He was the son of a corporal in the Royal Scots Greys who was a hard-drinking, brutal father who deserted his family when Mick was twelve (he reappeared twenty years later). At the age of ten Mick developed an eye infection that supposedly left him blind in the left eye. However, that his vision was permanently impaired is discounted by later reports from comrades that he had exceptional eyesight and was an outstanding marksman, albeit at close range. Whatever the truth, with his background few would have foreseen him as a future major with such an outstanding record as a combat pilot. The family moved to Canterbury, where as a youngster he took any sort of job and at twenty he joined the Labour Party, having developed a great sense of anger at the prevailing social injustices. Notwithstanding this, according to his friend Jim Eyles Mannock remained deeply patriotic and a strong believer in the British Empire.

60 Squadron, RAF, Celebrates

In August 1917 when the news that Canadian Captain (later Air Marshal) William Bishop, DSO and Bar, MC, DFC, had been awarded the Victoria Cross was received it called for celebrations, described by a fellow pilot:

There was tremendous excitement in the squadron yesterday, as our 'stunt merchant' has been awarded the VC . . . We celebrated it last night by one of the finest 'busts' I have ever had. There were speeches and lots of good 'bubbly', consequently everyone was in the best of spirits.

After dinner we had a torch light procession to the various squadrons stationed on the aerodrome. This was led by our Very lights experts. Luckily for us the night was very dull and cloudy, or else I expect old man Boche would have had a hand in it too. We charged into one mess and proceeded to throw everyone and everything we came across out of the window. We then went over to the other squadron. The wretched lads were all in bed, but we soon had them out, and bombarded their mess with Very lights, the great stunt being to shoot one in through one window and out the other. I can't imagine why the blessed place didn't go up in flames. After annoying these people for a bit, we retired to our own mess, where we danced and sang till the early hours of the morning. I have still got a piece of plaid cloth about six inches square, which was the only thing left of a perfectly good pair of 'trouse' that belonged to one of our Scotch compatriots.

Major Mick Mannock (far left, with pipe) with fellow pilots of No. 74 Squadron.

The outbreak of war found him employed as a telephone linesman in Turkey on a cable-laying project for his employer, a firm based in Wellingborough, Northamptonshire. Along with other Britons he was thrown into a Turkish jail as an internee and his health deteriorated alarmingly under the harsh conditions. Within eight months he was so near death that the Turkish authorities agreed his repatriation through the British Red Cross on 1 April 1915.

After a period of recuperation Mannock joined the RAMC, but quickly found its non-combatant role was not for him and transferred to the RE, in which he secured a commission exactly a year after his repatriation from Turkey. This brought action no nearer and in August 1916 he again requested a move, this time to the RFC. A number of sources describe how in order to pass the stringent eye test required for pilots he sneaked into the medical hut when it was unoccupied and memorized the eye-test chart. This seems highly improbable if one accepts that he did not have permanent damage to one eye. In February 1917 he joined the Joyce Green Reserve Squadron for flying training, after which he was sent to France to join No. 40 Squadron, equipped with the French-built Nieuport 17 scouts.

On his first night in the mess he inadvertently sat down in the empty chair that a newly fallen flyer had occupied until that day. It was not a good start, and for some time his background, his age (at twenty-nine he was well above the average age of his brother flyers) and reserved nature made it difficult for him to fit in. He was not a natural flyer and did not become a first-class shot at moving targets without constant gunnery practice. However, coupled with his acquired shooting skill was his determination to keep his nerve and always to force himself to get as close as possible to an enemy before opening fire. Later, after one kill he described how 'I was only ten yards away from him – on top so I couldn't miss. A beautifully coloured insect he was – red, blue, green and yellow. I let him have 60 rounds, so there wasn't much left of him.' In 1918, as an instructor he would tell his flyers, 'Sight your own guns. The armourer doesn't have to do the fighting.' A fellow pilot was later to comment on one of Mannock's unique successes: 'Four in one day! What is the secret? Undoubtedly the gift of accurate shooting combined with the determination to get to close quarters before firing. It's an amazing gift, for no pilot in France goes nearer to a Hun before firing . . .'

However, Mannock was a nervous, cautious flyer to begin with – so much so that some of his fellow pilots thought his holding back in the air indicated cowardice. He later admitted that aerial combat terrified him, particularly the horror of being burned alive – a dreadful death that he saw and inflicted often enough as the months passed. This abiding fear resulted in his keeping a revolver in a pocket on the inside of his cockpit, claiming, 'They'll never burn me.' Despite this he had little pity for those Germans he sent to a fiery death; in fact, he seemed to relish the idea, on one occasion exclaiming, 'I sent one to hell in flames today . . . I wish Kaiser Bill could have seen him sizzle.' This cold callousness towards his victims contrasted starkly with his weeping at the death of comrades such as Captain Albert Ball, VC, and later of his friend and top ace Captain James McCudden, VC. The strains these men had to overcome were huge. During the Battle of Arras in 1917, the life expectancy of a new pilot fell to eleven days. On one occasion while on home leave Mannock completely broke down in front of his friend Jim Eyles, who subsequently described what happened:

> We were sitting in the front talking quietly when his eyes fell to the floor, and he started to tremble violently. This grew into a convulsive straining. He cried uncontrollably, muttering something that I could not make out. His face, when he lifted it, was a terrible sight. Saliva and tears were running down; he couldn't stop it. His collar and shirt-front were soaked through. He smiled weakly at me when he saw me watching and tried to make light of it; he would not talk about it at all.

Despite the fear, the emotion and a somewhat inauspicious and late start, Mannock eventually proved himself a superlative fighter pilot, although it was not until 7 May 1917 that he got his first kill – not an aircraft but an observation balloon. Of the six aircraft in this attack the flight commander was shot down and all other aircraft damaged, Mannock being the only one to make a safe landing. Two days later he came close to being downed himself when he chased a German towards Courcelles. Attacked by three enemy, his gun jammed and his engine failed at the critical moment when he started evasive action. Luckily he was at 16,000 feet and was able to escape by nose-diving and spinning towards Allied lines. His first victory over a single-seater came in early June, and from then on his successes mounted along with his morale and confidence. At the same time his ruthless streak became ever more evident; on several occasions he deliberately machine-gunned helpless crew on the ground; when questioned about this he replied, 'The swines are better dead – no prisoners.'

In January 1918 the strain of combat flying and the inner terror of being roasted alive were taking their toll and Mannock was sent on leave, followed by a period with a training squadron. It was as an instructor that he made a lasting impression for instilling aggression and the techniques of aerial combat (the Mannock Rules) that had proved so successful in France. After a further spell in France he went on another well-deserved leave with fifty-nine kills to his credit and on his return took command of No. 85 Squadron with the rank of major. By this time Mannock was firmly convinced he would not survive the war. On 22 July, after he had downed another victim, a fellow flyer remarked that there would be a red carpet waiting for him after the war, to which he replied, 'There won't be any "after the war" for me.'

The end came four days later, after his shooting down of a German two-seater that crashed behind the enemy lines. Lieutenant D. C. Inglis, a newly arrived pilot whom Mannock had offered to help get his first kill, described what happened:

> Falling in behind Mick again we made a couple of circles around the burning wreck and then made for home. I saw

Mick start to kick his rudder, then I saw a flame come out of his machine: it grew bigger and bigger. Mick was no longer kicking his rudder. His nose dropped slightly and he went into a slow right-hand turn, and hit the ground in a burst of flame. I circled at about twenty feet but could not see him, and as things were getting hot, made for home and managed to reach our outposts with a punctured tank. Poor Mick . . . the bloody bastards had shot my Major down in flames.

Whether Mannock used his revolver remains uncertain. He was brought down behind German lines by ground fire hitting the engine, and according to one unconfirmed account his body was reportedly found without gunshot wounds (although this remains unproven) some 250 yards from the wreckage – perhaps he was thrown clear or jumped. His body has never been recovered by the Commonwealth War Graves Commission and he has no known grave. His name is commemorated on the RFC Memorial to the Missing at the Faubourg d'Amiens CWGC cemetery in Arras. There is also a plaque in his honour in Canterbury Cathedral.

After the war intensive lobbying by many of his former comrades resulted in Mannock's being awarded the Victoria Cross posthumously. It was presented to his father at Buckingham Palace in July 1919. His father was also given his other medals, despite Mick having stipulated in his will that his father should get nothing from his estate. Shortly afterwards this magnificent set was sold for £5 – fortunately the medals were later recovered and are now displayed at the RAF Museum, Hendon.

French ace René Fonck.

Captain René Fonck

Ending the war as the top Allied ace, with seventy-five officially recognized kills to his credit (seventy-two solo and three shared), Captain René Fonck, *Légion d'honneur*, *Médaille militaire*, *Croix de Guerre*, Military Cross, Military Medal, Belgian *Croix de Guerre*, was never wounded and boasted, 'I put my bullets into the target as if by hand.' The fact that he was a braggart who lost no opportunity for self-promotion – he claimed many more kills than his official tally – did not endear him to his comrades. Nevertheless, Fonck was an outstandingly skilful flyer, and an excellent shot who conserved his ammunition until close to his target. His accuracy was such that a short burst of a few rounds was often sufficient to bring his victim down. He developed an intimate knowledge of enemy aircraft, their engines and their capabilities – knowledge that became a vital part of his success in stalking and outmanoeuvring his opponents. Fonck carefully planned his own missions, exercised regularly, pressed his own uniforms and didn't drink – he was very much a loner, another thing that did not make his fellow flyers warm to him. Another French ace, Lieutenant Claude Haegelen, said of Fonck:

> He is not a truthful man. He is a tiresome braggart, and even a bore, but in the air, a slashing rapier, a steel blade tempered with unblemished courage and priceless skill . . . But afterwards he can't forget how he rescued you, nor let you forget it. He can almost make you wish he hadn't helped you in the first place.

René Paul Fonck was born in 1894 in Saulcy-sur-Meurthe, a village in the mountains of the Vosges region of north-east France. He was conscripted in August 1914 and, despite an early interest in aviation, opted for the combat engineers, where he spent much of his time digging trenches or repairing roads and bridges. The boredom of these duties eventually convinced him to apply for a transfer and he was trained as a flyer at St-Cyr and then at Le Crotoy, qualifying as a pilot in May 1915. His initial front-line posting was to Escadrille (squadron) Caudron 47, in which he flew the cumbersome-looking two-seater bomber/reconnaissance biplanes. Although twice mentioned in despatches for his work, it was not until July 1916 that he claimed his first kill. That August he captured an enemy aircraft without firing a shot. He attacked the German, and by extraordinarily skilful manoeuvres kept out of his adversary's fire, while gradually forcing him lower and lower until the German had no option but to land behind French lines – presenting the Allies with an undamaged enemy machine for inspection. This action saw Fonck awarded

the *Médaille militaire*. By May 1917 he had attained the status of an ace.

On 11 September 1917 the top French ace at that time, Captain Georges Guynemer, went missing and never returned, an event that was a huge shock to French aviators, including Fonck. The Germans claimed that their ace Lieutenant Kurt Wissemann had shot him down. On 30 September Fonck was convinced he had exacted revenge. In his autobiography, *Mes Combats*, published in Paris in 1920, he described the encounter as follows:

> Ten minutes after I took off, I spotted a plane in the distance. I recognized it immediately as a two-seater photo-reconnaissance job. Absorbed in their work, its two occupants had not seen my approach. As usual, I climbed very high in order to dive on the enemy. This tactic, instinctive to birds of prey, always seemed to me to be the best strategy. I surprised them in an attitude of complete security, the pilot still at his controls, and the observer in the act of taking photos, bending over the cockpit waist-high.
>
> I swooped down but waited until I was a few metres away before opening fire. With my eyes fixed on the sight, I quickly saw all the details growing rapidly in size. Aiming directly for the middle of the plane, my bullets raked the area which housed the motor and the aircraft's crew.
>
> It wasn't long before I saw the results. Undoubtedly killed by the first burst, the pilot must have slumped in his seat, jamming the controls in his agony, for the plane immediately began to spin. While rapidly banking to avoid collision I saw the body of the observer, still alive, falling from the upside-down plane. For a split second he had tried to remain in his seat. He passed only a few metres from my left wing, his arms frantically clutching at the emptiness. I shall never forget that sight.
>
> But the incendiary bullets had done their job, and the plane, like a gigantic torch, went down at full speed, crashing to the earth where the body of the observer had preceded it.

The aircraft fell behind French lines and the pilot's papers showed him to be a Lieutenant Wissemann. Was he the man who had killed Guynemer? Fonck immediately assumed he was and told a journalist, 'By killing the murderer of my friend [he was not Guynemer's friend] I am the tool of retribution.' However, his victim was in all probability a different Kurt Wissemann, as the killer of Guynemer had been downed on 28 September flying a single-seater.

By 1918 Fonck was flying the highly successful SPAD XIII, the first fighter to mount twin Vickers machine guns. On 9 May he downed six Germans, a spectacular achievement, especially when one considers this was accomplished within three hours. It resulted from an early-morning bet with two American pilots as to whether they could bring down an enemy before Fonck. One American took off and shot down a machine before Fonck had taken off – he was delayed by misty weather. Fonck persuaded the winner to change the wager to who would shoot down the most that day. Not until 3:00 p.m. was it clear enough for him to get airborne. At around 4:00 p.m. he attacked and killed three enemy two-seater reconnaissance planes; two hours later he repeated it.

Fonck survived the war, claiming his aircraft were only ever hit by one bullet. In September 1926 he attempted to be the first to fly the Atlantic but crashed on take-off when the landing gear collapsed – the prize went to Charles Lindberg the following year. Back in the military he rose to be a colonel and inspector of French Fighter Forces from 1937 to 1939. During the inter-war years he was in contact with his former enemies Hermann Göring and Ernst Udet, which aroused suspicions of his being sympathetic to the Nazis; however, this proved not to be the case and by the time of the occupation of France in World War II his loyalty to the Vichy regime was questioned to the extent that he spent a period in the Drancy internment camp. Furthermore, after the war a police inquiry into his supposed Nazi collaboration found no evidence to support the allegation; in fact, it revealed he had been a member of the French Resistance and he was awarded the Certificate of Resistance in 1948. He died in Paris, aged fifty-nine, and is buried in his home village, Saulcy-sur-Meurthe.

Manfred von Richthofen

The most outstanding ace of World War I, an ace among aces, was Rittmeister Manfred Albrecht, Freiherr von Richthofen, *Pour le Mérite*, Iron Cross First and Second Class, with eighty confirmed kills and the likelihood of well over a hundred if unconfirmed ones are included. Until he reached sixty, each time he shot down a plane he ordered a silver cup from a Berlin jeweller inscribed with the date and type of aircraft he had downed. He became widely known as the 'Red Baron', a title that combined his Prussian title of nobility *Freiherr* (literally 'free lord' or baron) with his having his aircraft painted red or partially red.

Originally a cavalryman, Richthofen transferred to the Imperial German Air Service (*Luftstreitkräfte*) in 1915, where he eventually distinguished himself as a fighter pilot, resulting in his becoming, in April 1917, commander of Jasta 11. This was followed in June by appointment as leader of a larger unit, *Jagdgeschwader* 1 (fighter group or wing), consisting of four squadrons, although he was still only a captain. It was this unit, which operated independently and so could be moved rapidly from one part of the front to another, that became known as Richthofen's 'Flying Circus'. By the latter part of 1917 he was a national hero in Germany and well known and feared by Allied airmen. It was a severe blow to the morale of all Germans, military and civilian, when he was finally shot down and killed near Amiens on 21 April 1918. He has been the subject of numerous books and films, and discussion has raged up to the present day on various aspects of his career and character, and especially on the exact circumstances of his death.

Manfred von Richthofen was born near Breslau, Lower Silesia (now part of Poland), into an aristocratic Prussian family on 2 May 1892. Until the age of eleven, when he went to a military school, he was educated at home. After completing cadet training in 1911 he joined a Uhlan (lancer) cavalry regiment and after the outbreak of war served on both the Eastern and Western Fronts, in Russia, Belgium and France. However, lack of action prompted his transfer to the German Army Air Service, and from June to August 1915 he served as an observer on reconnaissance missions over the Eastern Front. Back in the west he claimed his first victim while still an observer when he shot down a French biplane from his rear cockpit – but as it fell behind Allied lines Richthofen did not get the credit. Determined to qualify as a pilot, he attended flying training but initially did not appear to have the aptitude, wrecking his aircraft on landing after his first solo flight. Despite this setback he qualified on Christmas Day 1915.

It was not until after another brief spell on the Eastern Front that Richthofen was granted his first official kill when, on 17 September 1916, he downed a British two-seater pusher (an FE.2b). After initially attacking by diving on his enemy's tail and being met by a hail of bullets from the British observer, who stood up in his cockpit to fire, Richthofen broke off and, using cloud cover, reappeared below and behind his victim – in the blind spot. He riddled the British machine from very close range (the two aircraft almost collided), mortally wounding the pilot (Second Lieutenant L. B. F. Morris) and the observer (Lieutenant T. Rees). Richthofen's report read:

> I singled out the last machine [in the formation] and fired several times at close range (10 metres). Suddenly the enemy propeller stood still. The machine went down gliding and I followed until I had

Manfred von Richthofen.

Manfred von Richthofen's 'Flying Circus' – Albatros D.IIIs of Jagdstaffel 11, La Brayelle, near Douai, 1917.

killed the observer who had not stopped firing until the last moment. My opponent went downwards in sharp curves . . .

Most of Richthofen's victories occurred when flying aircraft of the Albatros model and it was while flying an Albatros D.II on 23 November 1916 that he had won probably the hardest dogfight of his career against the British ace Major Lanoe Hawker, VC, DSO – see page 435.

In January 1917 Richthofen was awarded the *Pour le Mérite* and his score steadily mounted. He took command first of the fighter squadron Jasta 11, followed in June by the fighter wing or Flying Circus – so called because the aircraft of its squadrons were painted in a variety of flamboyant colours, although Richthofen's machine had first appeared in its red paint that January. However, he did not always escape unscathed. On 2 December 1916 bullets punctured his petrol tank, forcing him to shut off his engine and make an emergency landing; and on 6 July 1917 a bullet grazed his skull, causing temporary blindness from which he recovered only blurred vision after falling some 6,000 feet. He struggled desperately to remain conscious and was just able to land before 'I tumbled out of the machine and could not rise again.' His wound required surgery to remove bone splinters, followed by a month in hospital. He was able to return to active duty in August, although with his head still partially bandaged. By the end of the year his score had reached sixty-three.

Richthofen was not a spectacular pilot in terms of aerobatics, but rather a notable tactician and squadron leader who chose his fellow pilots with care, quickly weeding out those who failed to meet his standards. He was an excellent marksman, but one who avoided unnecessary risks, always seeking to

MAP 75 THE SHOOTING DOWN OF THE RED BARON, 21 APRIL 1918

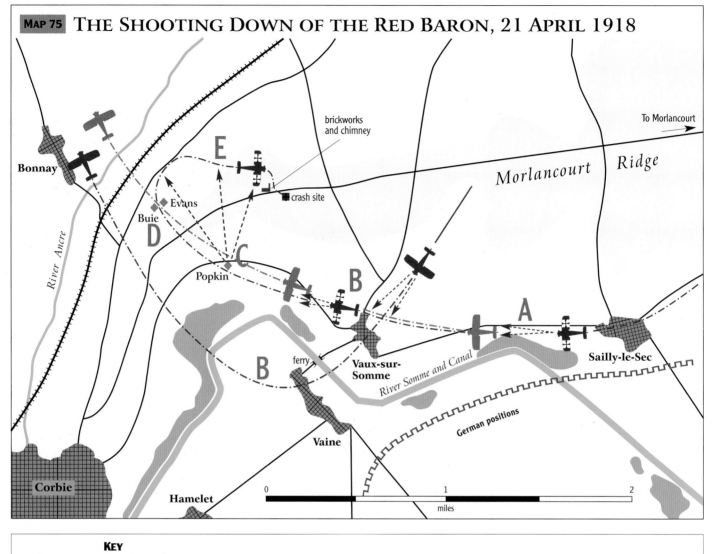

KEY

Red Baron and approx. route	Lt May and approx. route	Capt. Brown and approx. route

machine-gun fire

Notes for Map 75

• As noted in the text, there are a number of claimants to killing the Red Baron and it is impossible to be 100 per cent certain who succeeded despite the considerable research done, particularly in Australia. This account, which appears to the present writer to give the most likely story, is based on an article that appeared in the *Journal of the Australian War Memorial* in April 1988.

A – Richthofen gets on the tail of Lt Wilfrid May at low level and opens fire, but with no effect.

B – Richthofen closes the gap and continues firing on May. Capt. Arthur Brown dives down steeply to attack Richthofen, opens fire but misses and has to pull up sharply to avoid hitting the ground.

C – Sgt Cedric Popkin, with a Vickers anti-aircraft machine gun, allows

May to over-fly his position and then opens up on the approaching German, but without visible result. To avoid Brown's attack, Richthofen begins to turn hard right.

D – Gunners William Evans and Robert Buie fire on Richthofen with a Lewis gun but probably miss, as the angle of fire is not consistent with the wound caused. May continues his flight to safety.

E – Richthofen makes his tight turn over Morlancourt Ridge, still at a very low level. Popkin opens fire for a second time with a series of long bursts from slightly below and at the right-hand side of the German. A single bullet hits Richthofen, entering near the right armpit and mortally wounding him. He survives for about 30–40 seconds – enough time to make an emergency landing in a field near the modern brickworks.

---

attack by diving on his target out of the sun if at all possible. He also had a ruthless killer streak, writing 'I never get into an aircraft for fun. I aim first for the head of the pilot, or rather the head of the observer if there is one.' He endeavoured to get close before firing, and after killing or disabling the crew sought to break up their machine in the air

by aiming at the wing spars and struts – that way there could be no doubting his claim.

The great German offensive in March 1918 saw Richthofen score his final seventeen kills during the six weeks 12 March–20 April, taking his officially credited score to eighty. On Sunday, 21 April, the legendary Red Baron made his last flight. He took off

that morning flying his red Fokker Dr.I triplane (see page 423), along with five other pilots, all wearing parachute harnesses – the Germans were the only nation to adopt the use of parachutes for airmen during the final months of the war on the Western Front. The weather was cloudy, with mist along the River Somme. At around 10:30 a.m. a

The brickworks near the village of Vaux-sur-Somme at which Manfred von Richthofen was shot down by an Australian machine gun on 21 April 1918. His squadron was taken over by Herman Göring, later to become Hitler's deputy and head of the Luftwaffe in World War II.

swirling dogfight developed between British and German patrols. A novice Canadian pilot, Lieutenant Wilfrid May from No. 209 Squadron, RAF, flying a Sopwith Camel, became separated from his squadron and, with a jammed machine gun, was heading home when Richthofen spotted this isolated machine and dived in pursuit. The Red Baron was in turn seen by another Canadian, Captain Arthur Brown, who dived steeply at high speed to intervene, fired a burst (later claiming to have seen Richthofen flinch as though hit), but then had to climb steeply to avoid crashing. Richthofen turned to avoid this attack and resumed chasing and overhauling May, both aircraft now only a few hundred feet above the Somme and well into British territory (something totally out of character for Richthofen, who spoke strongly against such risk-taking), with the German now exposed to ground fire. It was almost certainly during this extremely low-level chase (at the end both aircraft were only 50 feet or so above the ground) that a .303 bullet hit Richthofen. However, in his last few moments of life he made an emergency landing in a field, close to a brickworks just north-west of the village of Vaux-sur-Somme in an area occupied by Australian troops. The Australians who reached the aircraft claimed Richthofen was still just alive and a Sergeant Ted Smout reported that his last word was a mumbled '*Kaputt.*' His aircraft was more or less intact on landing, but was quickly taken apart by souvenir hunters.

It is now generally accepted that Richthofen was killed by ground fire when a single bullet, entering at the right armpit from slightly behind and exiting close to the left nipple, damaged his heart and lungs. Clearly such a wound could not have been caused by the shots from Captain Brown, as the angle (he was firing from above) was

wrong (see Map 75), and he could not have survived the injury he received for more than thirty to forty seconds, whereas he continued the pursuit of May. Some sources consider the shot may have come from Gunner Robert Buie or Gunner W. J. 'Snowy' Evans, both of 53 Battery, 14th Field Artillery Brigade, Royal Australian Artillery, but again they seem to have fired at an angle that does not appear to fit the wound. Most sources now favour Richthofen having been hit by a bullet fired by Sergeant Cedric Popkin of the Australian 24th Machine Gun Company with his Vickers anti-aircraft gun. He fired at Richthofen twice, the second time from the right as he turned, and only a few moments before he came down.

The truth is that we will never be absolutely sure who finally nailed the Red Baron, as it could have been a lucky shot by a rifleman, a number of whom fired at him.

Richthofen's body was treated with great respect and he was given a full military funeral the next day. The burial took place at

the village of Bertangles, near Amiens. Six airmen with the rank of captain served as pallbearers and a guard of honour fired a salute. Nearby squadrons presented wreaths, one of which read, 'To Our Gallant and Worthy Foe'. In the early 1920s the French moved his body to a military cemetery at Fricourt. In 1925 his youngest brother recovered the body with the intention of burying it in the family grave at Schweidnitz (now in Poland), but the authorities persuaded him to allow its final resting place to be the Invalidenfriedhof cemetery in Berlin, where many German military heroes lay. The Nazis erected a massive tombstone over this grave, inscribed with the single word 'Richthofen'. However, this cemetery was on the Soviet-zone boundary during the Cold War and the tombstone was damaged by bullets fired at East Germans attempting to flee to the West, so his body was moved yet again to a family plot at the Südfriedhof, Wiesbaden, where he lies alongside his brother Bolko, his sister Elisabeth and her husband.

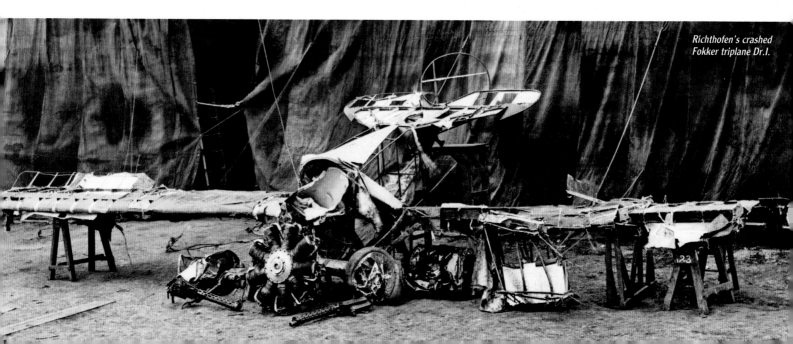

Richthofen's crashed Fokker triplane Dr.I.

Men of the 1st Battalion, Lancashire Fusiliers, in a trench fixing bayonets prior to the attack on Beaumont-Hamel during the Battle of Albert, Somme, 1 July 1916.

Section Twelve

Trench Warfare

When all is said and done, the war was mainly a matter of holes and ditches.
Siegfried Sassoon, *Memoirs of an Infantry Officer*, 1930

The boast of every good battalion was that it had never lost a trench.
Robert Graves, *Goodbye to All That*, 1929

*A slit trench, after all, is the nearest thing to a grave we'll be in
while we're alive. It* is *a grave.*
R. M. Wingfield, *The Only Way Out*, 1955

Trench warfare involving a series of opposing fighting lines that consisted mainly of trenches, dugouts and strongpoints is for ever associated with the Western Front in World War I. It has become a byword for attrition warfare, for stalemate, for seemingly futile attempts to break through opposing trench lines that merely gained a few hundred yards at the cost of appalling slaughter. However, trenches were not new in 1914. Roman legions constructed field works to protect their marching camps every night, and the digging of saps had been a part of siege operations for hundreds of years. The Duke of Wellington constructed many miles of such lines at Torres Vedras in the Peninsular War, and trenches and breastworks were a common feature during the American Civil War. More recently Boers defended a trench line at the Battle of Magersfontein in 1899 that defeated the Highland Brigade, and many military observers, especially the Germans, studied the elaborate trench systems of the 1904 Russo-Japanese War battlefields. And prior to the outbreak of war British training manuals, such as the 1909 *Field Service Regulations* and *Infantry Training 1914*, contained instructions on trench construction and siting.

On the Western Front trench systems that eventually stretched for hundreds of miles were soon forced on armies by the military revolution in firepower, which was not matched by mobility and protection for troops until the advent of the tank in large numbers. The trench offered protection from the fire of rifles and machine guns and – provided it wasn't subjected to a direct hit – from the shells and bombs of guns and mortars.

Trench warfare, akin to siege warfare, was employed on the Western Front from September 1914 up to the final weeks of the war. By October 1914 the entire front in France and Belgium had solidified, and as the months and years passed so the trench systems became deeper and vastly more elaborate, so that they formed defensive zones rather than lines – the emphasis being on defence in depth. As the German trenches were on French and Belgian soil, the Allies were compelled to take the offensive with the objective of breaking through in order to defeat the invaders. The advantages seemingly lay with the defenders, and the tactics of the attacker became a series of trial-and-error efforts to break through either by a single, powerful thrust that invariably failed, or more gradually by 'bite-and-hold' operations. However, lessons were learned; the problems of trench warfare were recognized and, after the disastrous results of 1 July 1916 on the Somme, technical and tactical innovations saw major all-arms offensives with artillery, infantry, tanks and aircraft cooperating fully. These ultimately led to the breaching of the Hindenburg Line and the mobile warfare of the Allies' general advance to victory from August to November in 1918.

The so-called 'lying trenches' (shallow scrapes that gave minimal protection to a lying man) and the small, unconnected rifle pits of August and September 1914 had by Christmas become trenches. They were joined up wherever possible, but were still rudimentary, often lacking traverses and frequently packed with troops, leading to heavy losses from artillery fire. These hastily dug trenches were gradually replaced and improved over the many months that followed so that they became huge areas of interlocking defensive works, built to resist artillery bombardments and infantry attacks. Each side constructed similar systems, although the Germans, mostly on the defensive and thus tending to remain in the same locations for long periods, were able to build more elaborate, much deeper works, reinforced by concrete with overhead cover impervious to direct hits from 60-lb heavy shells or even to continuous pounding – such dugouts or shelters were regarded as

The Misery of a Waterlogged Trench

John Baynes, in his superb book *Morale*, quotes from the diary of Captain Malcolm Kennedy on the subject of this particular misery during the winter of 1914/15:

As time wore on the weather conditions grew steadily worse. Trenches became waterlogged . . .

Thanks to the issue of gumboots which was made after a time, it was possible to wade about in most of the trenches without getting soaked through. In some parts, however, even this form of protection was of no avail, as the boots only came to the knees [thigh-length boots were issued later] whereas the water came over them . . .

This constant immersion in icy cold water played havoc with the feet, and made them swell to such an extent it was agony to keep on one's boots. To take them off, however, to gain relief would have been fatal, as it would have been impossible to pull them on again . . .

Paddling about by day, sometimes with water above the knees; standing at night, hour after hour on sentry duty, while the drenched boots, puttees and breeches became stiff like cardboard with ice from the freezing cold air. Rain, snow, sleet, wind, mud and general discomfort added their bit to the misery of trench life.

A German soldier in a waterlogged trench near Ypres, 1915.

'bombproof'. Where terrain and time permitted, the Germans' defensive stance allowed them to employ considerable engineering efforts in improving their defences. The ground between the opposing lines of trenches was 'no-man's-land' and could vary in width from only a few yards, such as at Guillemont (50 yards) and Zonnebeke (8 yards), to, typically, between 100 and 400 yards (at Cambrai over 500 yards), much of which was quickly covered in a jungle of barbed-wire entanglements, shell craters, decomposing bodies and the detritus of war. In some areas, however, no-man's-land could be over 1,000 yards wide.

On parts of the front – notably in the low-lying areas of Flanders, where the high water table prevented digging – a recognizable trench was impossible to construct, so protection in the form of sandbag breastworks was built up – 10 feet of earth was needed to give adequate protection, or a combination of sandbags and earth. Flooding of trenches became commonplace and the misery this caused is discussed below (page 464); here it is sufficient to note the words of George Coppard, a machine-gunner at Festubert in winter 1915: 'the front-line area was flooded and the communication trenches had vanished under water. There was no front-line

trench. Instead, earthworks, consisting of sandbags piled on top of the original parapet had to be made.' The same problem arose when the ground was frozen hard. In the southern Vosges area the French and Germans frequently resorted to building *sangars* (breastworks of rocks and stones). Lieutenant Erwin Rommel, the future field marshal of World War II, was a German company commander in the Argonne in early 1915 and described this situation in his book *Infantry Attacks*:

> The position consisted of a continuous trench reinforced by numerous breastworks . . . In general the position was poorly developed, and surface water had kept the trench depth to three feet or less in some places. The dugouts, built to accommodate eight to ten men, were of necessity equally shallow, and their roofs stuck out above the ground level making them excellent targets.

Trench warfare included major attacks involving many divisions, or the more mundane small-scale operations between these offensives and in quiet, or comparatively inactive, sectors of the front. A major attack is discussed in some detail in Section Thirteen, while this section is concerned with the technicalities of trench warfare, life in and out of the line and the tactics of minor operations such as sniping, patrols and raids.

The Trenches

Siting, Layout and Types of Trench

Siting of front-line trenches depended on the defensive line decided upon by the High Command, but the detailed tactical siting was, within limits, largely the responsibility of unit commanders with advice from the engineers. The factors considered would include observation, the facility for forming up for an attack, drainage, concealment, field of fire and the ability to give and receive mutual support from flanking units, particularly with machine guns and trench mortars.

The importance of occupying higher ground if at all possible was often the critical factor – for much of the time the Germans in many areas overlooked the British. On higher ground, even if only a comparatively slight rise, the choice was whether to entrench the forward or reverse slope. The forward slope usually gave better observation and field of fire but was impossible to conceal and thus exposed to direct enemy fire. A reverse-slope position had the advantage of concealment

from direct observation and, if combined with a forward artillery observation post with telephone communications on the crest, was often the best option. The important factor was to prevent the enemy gaining the observation advantage. If this was impossible, the only satisfactory solution was to mount an attack to secure the dominating ground. The Allied attacks on Lone Tree Ridge at Loos in 1915 (British), and in 1917 at Messines Ridge (New Zealand and British), Vimy Ridge (Canadian), Chemin des Dames (French) and Passchendaele Ridge (Canadians finally took the town) are but a few of innumerable examples of attacks large and small on entrenched and fortified areas of high ground that dominated Allied positions.

By 1916 the general layout of a British trench system would comprise a front line of the main fire trench and about 20–30 yards behind it a 'supervision' trench. These two were linked together with short communication trenches at frequent intervals. The fire and supervision trenches, and any shelters, headquarter dugouts, latrines or saps (small trenches or tunnels running forward from the

fire trench), or machine-gun posts connected to them, were deemed to be included in a front line. From the supervision trench longer communication trenches would lead back to the support line, which was similarly constructed, with perhaps the incorporation of small strongpoints but no supervision trench. The support line would usually be about 100 yards behind the front line. Further back, perhaps from 400 to 600 yards, was the reserve line. This whole trench system usually incorporated a series of works, variously known as 'keeps', 'strongpoints' or 'redoubts', constructed for all-round defence. It was where the infantry fought and died – see the diagrams opposite and on page 450.

The French system often varied from this, as they used the power of their quick-firing 75mm guns to compensate for lack of a reserve line. Their system included a front-line trench system segmented with fully garrisoned and fortified trenches alternating with sectors garrisoned only by sentries. Two belts of wire with a 5-yard gap between usually protected this line. The French support trench was fully manned with numerous dugouts.

Front-line fire trenches

The best fire trenches consisted of the actual trench with a sloping parapet on the enemy side that increased the height of the trench by about 9 inches, and a slightly higher parados in the rear. The trench (including the parapet) would be deep enough to allow men to move along it without stooping, and sufficiently wide to allow movement of fully equipped men and those carrying stretchers. The bottom would have a drainage channel, covered with duckboards, leading to a sump from which water could be pumped as necessary. The walls were revetted to hold crumbling soil in place with timber supported by stakes or angle iron pickets, frames of woven willow or special revetment frames of wood lined with strong wire mesh. The parapet was normally constructed with sandbags and soil and was bulletproof, and allowed every soldier to fire his rifle to the front. It was irregular in shape in order better to conceal men firing or observing over it. Similarly the parados behind was irregular and higher than the parapet to prevent heads showing against a skyline. It was often made from earth thrown up during the digging of the trench, its main purpose being to give protection against the back blast of shells landing behind the trench.

With the trench being so deep it was vital to have a firestep on the enemy side. This ledge was about 4 feet 6 inches below the crest of the parapet and could be cut out of the side of the trench when it was being dug or built up with sandbags later. The best had a duckboard cover. The firestep had many other uses apart from enabling the soldiers to fire their weapons. Professor Richard Holmes in *Tommy* quotes the view of Private David Jones, who served in the 15th Royal Welch Fusiliers on the Somme:

The firestep was the front-fighter's couch, bed-board, food-board, card-table, workman's bench, universal shelf, only raised surface on which to set a thing down, above water level. He stood upon it by night to watch the enemy. He sat upon it by day to watch him in a periscope. The nature, height and repair of firesteps was of great importance to the front-line soldier, especially before adequate dugouts became customary in all trenches.

The trenches of all combatants had firesteps. Although captured trenches were often put to use by their captors, with the firestep being on the wrong side it was impossible for the trench to be used to fire from; it had to be 'reversed' and a firestep cut out of the oother side or built up with sandbags filled with earth – the reason why shovels and empty sandbags were carried in an assault, certainly by follow-up troops if not by the attackers.

Traverses were a vital part of any length of fire trench. They were buttresses of earth jutting out, normally from the front of the trench, dividing the trench line into a series

Parapets Built of Bodies

Private Frank Richards, DCM, MM, who served in the 2nd Royal Welch Fusiliers, described this horror in his book *Old Soldiers Never Die.*

Some part of the parapet had been built up with dead men, and here and there arms and legs were protruding. In one bay only the heads of two men could be seen; their white teeth were showing so that they seemed to be grinning horribly down at us. Some of our chaps who had survived the attack on 20th July [1916] told me that when they were digging themselves in, the ground being hardened by the sun and difficult to dig away quickly, if a man was killed near them he was used as head cover and earth was thrown over him.

British Arrangement of a Defensive Line, 1916 (not to scale)

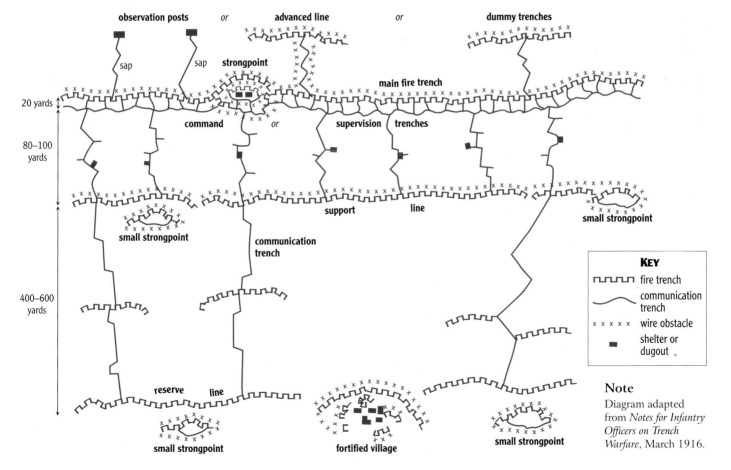

Note

Diagram adapted from *Notes for Infantry Officers on Trench Warfare,* March 1916.

British Front Line with Supervision and Communication Trenches, 1916 (not to scale)

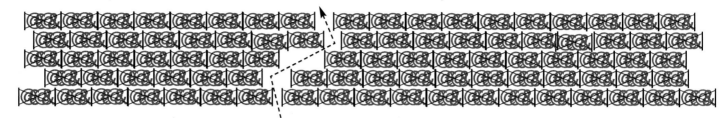

Path for patrols to exit and return – gap could
be blocked by movable knife rest barriers.

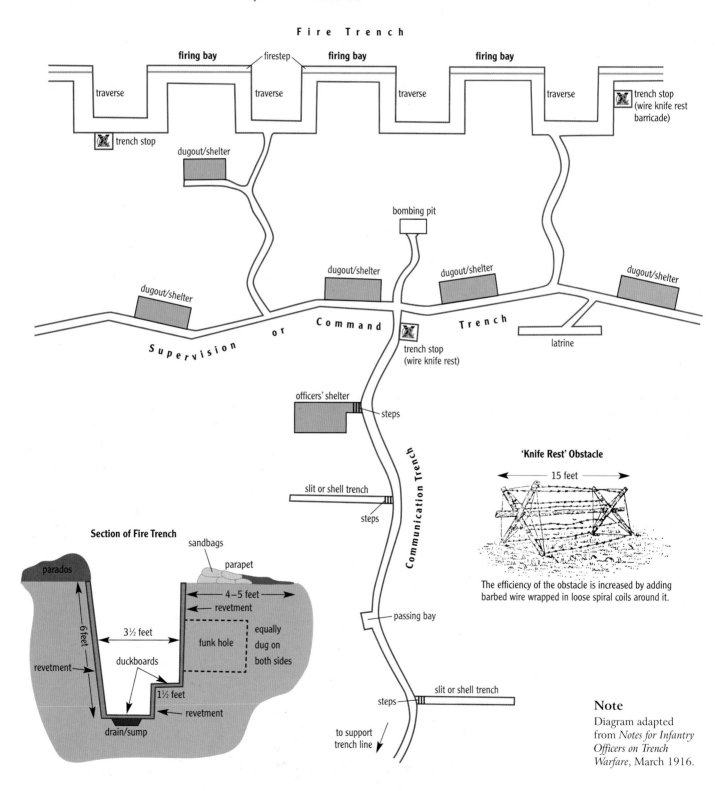

Fire Trench

firing bay   firestep   **firing bay**   **firing bay**

traverse   traverse   traverse   traverse   ☒ trench stop
                                                                                                                       (wire knife rest
                                                                                                                       barricade)

☒ trench stop

dugout/shelter

bombing pit

dugout/shelter   dugout/shelter   dugout/shelter

dugout/shelter

S u p e r v i s i o n   o r   C o m m a n d   T r e n c h

☒ trench stop   latrine
(wire knife rest)

officers' shelter

steps

slit or shell trench

steps

'Knife Rest' Obstacle

◄─── 15 feet ───►

The efficiency of the obstacle is increased by adding
barbed wire wrapped in loose spiral coils around it.

Communication Trench

passing bay

Section of Fire Trench

sandbags

parapet

parados

4–5 feet
revetment

6 feet   3½ feet

equally
dug on
funk hole   both sides

revetment   duckboards

1½ feet

revetment

drain/sump

steps   slit or shell trench

to support
trench line

Note

Diagram adapted
from *Notes for Infantry
Officers on Trench
Warfare*, March 1916.

Men of the Border Regiment resting in a front-line trench, Thiepval Wood, August 1916.

of firing bays. They were spaced from 20 to 30 feet apart and were designed to limit the number of casualties caused if a shell hit the trench. Bomb stops of timber 'knife rests' (see diagram opposite) wrapped with barbed wire were kept ready in a recess to drop into a trench to block it or seal off a section that had been occupied by the enemy. The disadvantage was that the traverses aided bombing attacks along the length of a trench, as bombs could be thrown from under cover of a traverse into the next bay. To guard against this it was recommended that some stretches of trench should be straight without traverses, with the end traverse loopholed for defenders to fire along the trench at any enemy who had occupied it.

To the rear of almost every other firing bay was a communication trench to allow for easy and swift movement to and from the supervision trench. It was common practice for small shelters called 'funk holes' to be dug either into the front or rear walls of the trench. These could be large enough to permit one man to lie in to rest or shelter during a bombardment. They were far from comfortable, but were common during the early part of the war. They bore no comparison to properly constructed shelters or dugouts but remained in use throughout the war in many areas, although they weakened the trench and a collapse would bury an occupant. In order to enable soldiers to climb out of a trench when fully laden for an attack, short wooden ladders were provided.

Running forward at right angles to the front trench were saps – narrow, shallow trenches (sometimes tunnels) – at the end of which was a small bay capable of holding two or three men. These were normally listening posts about 30 yards from the trench and just behind the wire obstacle. Often, slightly larger saps were used as exits and entrances for friendly patrols going out at night across no-man's-land, or for the covering party for a patrol. The men in the listening post were tasked with reporting enemy movement, patrols, wiring parties or sniper positions – they were in effect advanced sentry posts.

If a portion of a front-line trench system were lost a 'switch' trench would be dug to connect the second system to the still held section of the first. On Map 43 (page 212) the Mouquet Switch connects the strongpoint of Mouquet Farm on the third line with the Schwaben Redoubt on the second, so that if Thiepval and the German trench line to the south were captured, and those to the north remained in German hands, there would still be an unbroken line connecting Mouquet Farm and the Schwaben Redoubt with the fortified village of St-Pierre Divion. The Mouquet Switch was also used as a communication trench.

The initial construction of a fire trench required an immense amount of digging, a task in the front line that normally fell on the infantry occupants. In theory, digging a front-line system at night took 450 men about six hours to complete 275 yards. Trench maintenance required a constant daily grind and the supply of duckboards, timber or iron pickets, prefabricated dugout frames and several hundredweight of nails. The more elaborate rearward defences required the same, plus engineer expertise, stores and equipment, although infantry working parties reluctantly provided much of the labour. This meant that an infantryman's spade (or pick) was used a hundred times more frequently than his rifle. The BEF apparently started out with around 2,500 spades but ended up with some 10.6 million.

The general line of front-line trenches was seldom straight for any great length and often followed a feature such as the edge of a wood, a track, a stream or the contour of a hill or ridge. This could create salients jutting out towards the enemy. Some were large ones of considerable strategic significance, such as the infamous Ypres salient; others were much smaller tactical bulges in the line that gave the defenders the opportunity to bring flanking machine-gun and rifle fire on to attackers, but which could also be fired into from the

flanks as well as the front. The actual trenches could be constructed in a series of approximately rectangular firing bays alternating with traverses, as described above, or in a zigzag or winding, twisting pattern – sometimes a combination of all. If a front trench was on a reverse slope it was sometimes necessary to dig the firing bays forward in the shape of a T or inverted L with the crosspiece on the crest line. Whatever the manner of their construction, emplacements for machine guns able to sweep the front with interlocking fire were incorporated into them.

Supervision trenches

The supervision or command trench, dug some 20–30 yards behind the fire trench, formed the second part of the front line. This was a continuous, usually slightly zigzagged, trench affording easy lateral communication close behind the firing bays and connected to them at frequent intervals. The best position for these communication trenches to join the fire trench was behind a traverse, and ideally for every alternate traverse there should be one such mini-communication trench. The supervision trench would accommodate platoon and possibly company headquarters in shelters (as distinct from deep dugouts) for troops resting or during an enemy bombardment. Outside the company headquarters shelter would be a stand set up with signal rockets ready to fire. These would be the signal that their position was under attack and that the artillery should fire on its SOS target – usually in no-man's-land beyond the defenders' wire. Additional shelters were likely to be found off the communication trenches running forward to the fire trench. From the supervision trench were dug stores for reserves of ammunition and latrines.

Private Berry, 5th Bedfords, wrote of the problems of living in the front line on the Somme even if not actually under fire,

New Zealand troops in a front-line trench near Fleurbaix, near Armentières, June 1916. Note the periscope rifle resting on the parapet.

An old British communication trench in Ploegsteert Wood.

though there may be some exaggeration here regarding the implied length of time spent continuously in the front line:

> Once we were in the line, we set to work to make ourselves comfortable, making little 'dug-outs' for cover against splinters from shells, and then having something to eat. It was a painful affair making a cup of tea in the front line, as it had to be done without making any smoke and we tried all sorts of dodges. One way was to stick a bayonet into the side of the trench, to hang the Dixie on, under which we lighted a smashed up candle, which was wrapped in a piece of sandbag. This was a favourite way. Another idea was to sit in a dug-out with a blanket over the entrance, to make a small fire out of pieces of wood cut up like matches; we would sit with the tears running down our faces for about half an hour, for we dared not let the smoke out . . .
>
> Winter was coming upon us at a great pace now. Rain was falling almost daily and it was impossible to describe all the minor discomforts we went through. We were soaked to the skin week after week; covered in mud from head to foot . . . We often had to go for over a week without a wash or shave; it was a job to keep our rifles clean, but we had to spend our whole time doing this. I have heard many jokes about the Somme mud, but it was no joke in those days . . . Our rations were often uneatable, being either covered in mud or wet through. At the same time, we were in a very unpleasant state; our clothes also our bodies being infested with live insects, which were known to the tommies as Chats . . . Can you wonder at the Government supplying the men with rum?

Latrines were of course essential throughout the trench system and it was a matter of unit pride to keep them in good order and prevent men from relieving themselves in the trenches. In the front line they would usually be located off the supervision trench and would consist of a short sap leading to a T-shaped trench with a bucket or 'deep drop' hole with a pole across the top. There was a sanitary NCO in each company who often acquired the nickname of 'NCO i/c shit-wallers [*sic*].' Trench latrine buckets were regularly emptied at night into shell holes and covered with earth and chloride of lime. The deep latrines had a light sprinkling of soil thrown into them.

The support line

Support trenches accommodated troops who provided the first support to the garrison of the front line, and were available immediately for reinforcement or local counter-attack. They also provided cover to which the bulk of the front-line troops could be temporarily withdrawn during an enemy bombardment. The support line was always constructed as a second line of resistance if the first line was lost. As such, it was dug with fire bays and traverses, but normally without a supervision trench. In order not to be caught in a bombardment of the front it was located some 80–100 yards to its rear and connected to it by communication trenches (see right). It was in the support line that the deeper dugouts giving good protection against artillery fire and offering more comfort were located – in the forward line deep dugouts were said to detract from the ability of the troops in them to man the firing line rapidly. There would be more machine-gun posts, bays for trench mortars and often at least one strongpoint in this line.

Leading off the communication trenches that ran back from the supervision trench were a number of bombing and 'slit' or shell trenches. The former were trenches dug within easy bomb-throwing distance of the front line to enable defenders to drive out any enemy that had occupied that section of the front line by lobbing bombs into it. The slit trenches were intended to give additional shelter for men when under bombardment. They were dug at right angles to the communication trench and were long enough to hold from ten to twelve men. They were very narrow (only 1–2 feet wide), about 7 feet deep and strutted across the top to help prevent collapse. They provided good protection against most shelling, except for a direct hit. Similar provision was often made further back along the communication trenches for reserves brought up to support a counter-attack. For a major attack, special assembly trenches were often dug to form a jump-off line for the assault units to await zero hour and thus avoid overcrowding in front-line trenches.

The reserve line

Behind the support line, located 400–600 yards to its rear and connected to it by communication trenches, lay the reserve line. It could consist of a line of trenches, but more often of dugouts or strongpoints sometimes formed by the use of natural cover such as woods, buildings, embankments and gullies or small villages. It was here that a battalion headquarters was usually found, along with the RAP and the reserve company available for local counter-attacks.

Communication trenches

These were the links that stitched together the three defensive lines described above and any associated dugouts or strongpoints. As such, they formed a crucial part of the trench system as they permitted movement under cover from one line to another. All movement above ground during the day in the forward area risked an almost instant and often deadly response from enemy snipers or guns. These trenches were the arteries along which flowed reinforcements, reliefs, counter-attack units, all supplies of food and ammunition, along with runners, stretcher-bearers and walking wounded. Some communication trenches wound their way over extensive distances – one called Convent Lane was about 3 miles long – and the 1,500-yard Turk Lane trench dug by New Zealand pioneers near Montauban during the Somme offensive earned them the name 'Diggers', a term later adopted by the division and then by all ANZAC soldiers.

Because of all this traffic, communication trenches had to be around 3 feet wide and follow a gently winding course – sharp angles would usually prohibit the carrying of wounded on a stretcher. At intervals down a long trench, slit or shell trenches would be dug, as well as passing places – the trench

Assembly Trenches

For any major attack where a considerable number of troops were to advance in depth, it was usually necessary for assembly trenches to be dug to accommodate these supports and reserves, who would often advance in successive waves. The control of these extra troops moving up to the front-line jump-off positions along communication trenches was a tricky one, especially if done at night. The possibility of delay and chaos was ever present.

 In August 1917 an instruction for the training of divisions for offensive action was issued and its paragraphs on the organization of trenches to the rear of the front-line trench illustrate the complexity of the detailed preparations needed:

The system of assembly trenches must conform as far as possible to the existing trench system in order to obtain concealment . . . The ideal system to aim for is as follows:

On each brigade front of attack, within 800 yards of the front line, one 'IN' and one 'OUT' trench. On each battalion front of attack within 800 yards of the front line, one 'IN' and one 'OUT' trench. On each company front of attack, one 'IN' and one 'OUT' trench for the depth of the company zone of assembly. Trenches allotted as 'OUT' trenches, unless specially dug for the purpose, must have the corners of the traverses or zig-zags rounded off to allow the passage of stretchers. If desired special trenches can be allotted for wounded only. A map showing 'IN' and 'OUT' traffic in communication trenches must be prepared and issued down to company commanders, trenches available for stretchers being specially marked. This map need not be accurately drawn to scale; a diagrammatic sketch with distances marked on it is sufficient.

All traffic in communication trenches must be regulated, and regimental police told off for this duty . . .

Trenches must be clearly labelled with clearly marked signboards. 'IN' and 'OUT' trenches in addition to this their names must be marked with special boards: black letters on a white ground for 'IN' trenches, white letters on a black ground for 'OUT' trenches. All lettering to be 6 inches high and each board to have a directing arrow.

For leading waves, which move in line and must therefore leave the trenches simultaneously, ladders or steps are necessary. Stakes 3 to 4 feet long, driven into the parapet to act as handles when climbing ladders, are useful . . .

Provision must be made for bridges over the front-line trenches for the rear waves.

equivalent of a lay-by. Except in chalk, communication trenches that were required to remain serviceable for extended periods (which was the vast majority) required both revetting and a proper drainage system – all of which demanded considerable labour to dig and a great many materials to construct, as well as a constant effort to maintain from the effects of shelling and poor weather.

Special efforts were required to defend against enemy bombers working their way down a communication trench to attack the lines behind. One way of doing this was to ensure the last 40 yards of the trench entering a support line were straight, with a machine-gun post or fire trench able to fire down it. These communication trenches were frequently valuable if prepared for use as fire trenches in repelling a flank attack that had penetrated the front line. This was best done by having T-shaped firing bays dug off the communication trench and wire obstacles on either side.

Enemy shelling, water, mud and congestion combined to make a journey along these trenches something of a nightmare. When troops were moving up to the front line to take part in a major attack, congestion could delay progress forward or to the rear for hours. Careful timing and route-planning by the staff was essential but not always apparent – in some cases a one-way system was enforced, with certain communication trenches reserved for wounded. Lieutenant (later Brigadier) F. P. Roe's experience on 1 July 1916 is typical:

Every single yard of the communication trench up to the front line was impassable and the confusion was indescribable. Reinforcement troops and working parties with materials and ammunition were trying to make their way forward against a stream of troops coming out of their line, including stretcher-bearers with casualties, walking wounded and exhausted troops coming out after a spell in the front line. To make matters worse, many of these sections of communication trench had been destroyed by heavy artillery fire from the German lines, and this was unceasingly active.

Trench names

The vast fishing net of Allied and German trenches that eventually spread over hundreds of miles of the Western Front became a hugely complex maze. Without naming the trenches (and frequently numbering them as well) like the streets in a city, finding a particular location would have been a frustrating and often impossible task, particularly at night when much movement took place. It was the task of the engineers to erect signboards on trenches and produce many thousands of trench maps (see Maps 76 and 77) with many trenches named. For security reasons, Allied maps of German trenches did not show or name most of their own. German trenches were usually given English or French names depending on who held that sector of the front and when the British took over trenches previously occupied by the French just south of the Somme they sometimes kept the same names used by the French for the German trenches (see Map 76).

However, even with the trench maps, guides were inevitably needed to bring fresh troops forward to mount an attack or relieve another unit in the line. With the

A communication trench is dug through Delville Wood.

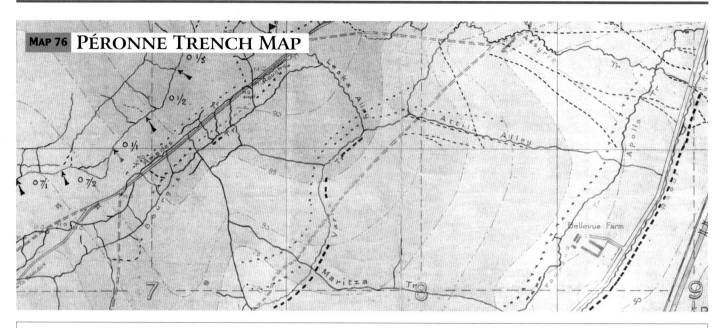

MAP 76 PÉRONNE TRENCH MAP

Note for Map 76

This map of the German trench system south of the Somme and just south-west of Péronne in 1917 shows part of an area taken over by the British from the French. The trench names are still those used by the French, such as Amedes Trench and Attila Alley. It also clearly shows how the German defensive zone was divided into three lines, with a front line (Amedes Trench) with its supervision/control trench immediately behind (Bourgas Trench), the two being connected by numerous short communication trenches. About 500 yards to the rear is the support line (Varna Trench) and then over 1,000 yards further back the reserve line, which in this case consisted of two trench lines (Fourche and Apollo Trenches and then the Raul Trench). The main communication trenches connecting these lines are shown and named (Leska Alley, Attila Alley and Maritza Trench). Likely German machine-gun, trench mortar and listening posts are also marked.

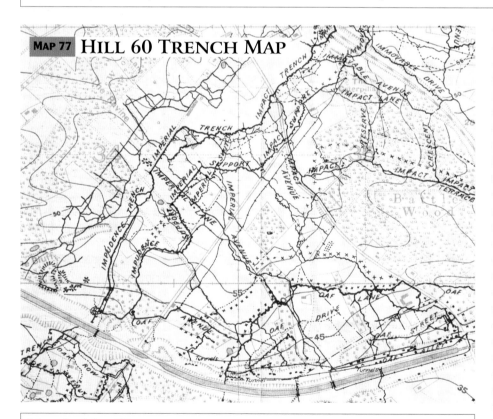

MAP 77 HILL 60 TRENCH MAP

Note for Map 77

This map is an example of the extensive network of German trenches that existed around Hill 60 in April 1917. The names given by the British clearly distinguish between fire and communication trenches, and the map shows how all trenches in a specific sector of the front were often given names beginning with the same letter, in this case an 'I'. The front line has Impudence, Imperial and Impact Trenches connected by short communication trenches to Impudence, Imperial and Impact Supports. Leading back from the support line are communication trenches named Imperial Lane and Imperial and Impact Avenues. For security reasons, only the British front and supervision trenches are shown.

Moving Up the Line, 1915

Ian Hay, in his book *The First Hundred Thousand*, gives us a revealing description of his first journey up to the front line:

Presently we find ourselves entering upon a wide but sticky path cut in the clay. At the entrance stands a neat notice board, which announces, somewhat unexpectedly: OLD KENT ROAD.

. . . we soon find ourselves tramping along below the ground-level, with a stout parapet of clay on either side of us. Overhead there is nothing – nothing but the blue sky, with the larks singing, quite regardless of the war.

'Communication trench,' explains the guide . . .

Every hundred yards or so comes a great promontory of sandbags, necessitating four right-angle turns . . . Now we are crossing a stream . . . spanned by a structure of planks – labelled, it is hardly necessary to say – LONDON BRIDGE. The side street, so to speak, by which the stream runs away is called JOCK'S JOY. Why we ask?

'It's the place where the Highlanders wash their knees,' is the explanation.

Presently we arrive at PICCADILLY CIRCUS, a muddy excavation in the earth from which several passages branch . . . We take the turning marked SHAFTESBURY AVENUE, and after passing through TRAFALGAR SQUARE – six feet by eight – find ourselves in the actual firing trench.

A German barbed-wire entanglement at Beaucourt-sur-Ancre, Battle of the Ancre, November 1916.

movement of large numbers of men, supplies and stores for a major offensive, and to deal with the expected heavy losses, traffic along the trenches was controlled by military police, and the staff drew up timetables indicating how long it would take to get from point A to point B. Some communication trenches would be designated forward movement and others for rearward evacuation of wounded.

The actual naming of trenches developed in a somewhat haphazard manner, although there was a discernible effort to call a fire trench such and such 'Trench' and a communication trench 'Lane', Alley', 'Road', 'Street' or 'Avenue'. Some reflected the region of origin of the first troops to occupy them, with street names from London, Glasgow or Edinburgh, for example, while others might indicate a particular danger or event in that part of the line, such as Bone and Carrion Trenches and Cemetery Alley or Suicide Road. Alcoholic drinks were popular, with Beer, Bitter, Rum, Hop and Pilsen Trenches. Others indicated the state of a trench at some time in its existence, as with Slither, Slimy and Slum Trenches.

It was not only trenches that were named. Many junctions, farms, woods and ammunition or supply dumps were given names, examples being Piccadilly Circus, Bloody Farm, Tremble Copse and Dead Man's Dump.

The French sometimes named trenches after individuals, such as *Tranche* (trench) *Capitaine du Page* or *Boyau* (communication trench) *Garibaldi*. Around Hill 60 some of the names given to German trenches clearly indicated their purpose, as in Impact Trench, Impact Support and Impact Reserve, with communication trenches linking these lines called Impact Lane, Impact Avenue and Impact Terrace (see Map 77).

The Living and the Dead

With death a daily occurrence and bodies everywhere, it is hardly surprising that where fighting was heavy and prolonged the corpses piled up. The living often ate and slept surrounded by bodies. Sergeant Léger, who fought in the bitter struggle to defend the Bois des Caures near Verdun (see page 130), later wrote:

My main concern was to avoid having a corpse close by me. I made the mistake of digging the hole to rest my head a little too deep. I uncovered two feet with shoes on, it was the body of a Frenchman (the Hun only wore boots). I dug a little further along to try and find a better spot. There was nothing doing. There were human remains everywhere.

Barbed Wire

Robert W. Service was a Canadian stretcher-bearer and ambulance driver on the Western Front whose poems were published under the title of *Rhymes of a Red Cross Man* (see also page 366). In one of them, entitled 'On the Wire', the final verse tells how the torment of a wounded man left entangled in the wire finally drives him to end his agony himself:

> Hark the resentful guns!
> Oh, how thankful am I
> To think my beloved ones
> Will never know how I die!
> I've suffered more than my share;
> I'm shattered beyond repair;
> I've fought like a man the fight,
> And now I demand the right
> (God! how his fingers cling!)
> To do without shame this thing.
> Good! there's a bullet still;
> Now I'm ready to fire;
> Blame me, God, if You will,
> Here on the wire . . . the wire . . .

Corporal George Coppard, who enlisted on 27 August 1914 while still only sixteen, spent most of the next four and a half years as an infantryman and machine-gunner on the Western Front. His description of the dead and wounded on the German wire in the La Boisselle sector following the attack on 1 July 1916 gives a grim picture of the reality of that awful day:

Hundreds of dead, many belonging to the 37th Brigade [Coppard may have been confused here, as the 37th Infantry Brigade, 12th Division, was not involved on 1 July], were strung out like wreckage washed up to a high-water mark. Quite as many had died on the enemy wire as on the ground, like fish caught in a net. They hung there in grotesque postures. Some looked as though they were

praying: they had died on their knees and the wire had prevented their fall.

From the way the bodies were evenly spread out, whether on the wire or lying in front of it, it was clear there were no gaps in the wire at the time of the attack . . . The Germans must have been reinforcing their wire for months. It was so dense that daylight could barely be seen through it. Through the glasses it looked almost solid.

A Captain Leeham never forgot the appalling stench of dead bodies piled up in a trench that he experienced on 1 July 1916:

The trench was a horrible sight. The dead were stretched out on one side, one on top of each other six feet high. I thought at the time I should never get the peculiar disgusting small of the vapour of warm human blood heated by the sun out of my nostrils. I would rather have smelt gas a hundred times. I can never describe that faint sickening, horrible smell which several times nearly knocked me up altogether.

There is no doubt that intact barbed wire (razor wire was also introduced) erected in front of an enemy position, laid in two or three irregular belts each 10–15 feet deep, was the direct cause of countless attackers dying and assaults failing. Most major offensives were based on the success or otherwise of artillery blowing gaps in the wire well before the actual attack, and maintaining that fire periodically during the night to deter repairs. The attacking side sent out nightly patrols to check on the effectiveness of this shelling, the location and size of the gaps and to cut more wire with wire-cutters. By day aircraft photographed the wire, again to locate gaps but also to identify new belts and to confirm the layout. As noted above, it was not until tanks were employed in numbers to crush or drag away the wire with grapnels that a reliable solution was found, at least where tanks were available. Colonel (later Major General) J. F. C. Fuller compared the effectiveness of tanks and artillery in cutting wire when he wrote, 'You *know* you can cross a belt of wire over which a tank has passed, you *hope* you can pass through a belt of wire on which the artillery has played for a couple of days.'

One method of breaching a wire obstacle was to use a bangalore torpedo – a long pipe filled with explosive that was pushed under the wire and detonated to create a narrow gap. Another, for use without cutting low wire entanglements, was to throw coils of rabbit wire over the obstacle to create a bridge.

Like trenches, the use of barbed wire on the battlefield was not new in 1914: it had been employed in the American Civil War and extensively in the Boer and Russo-Japanese Wars. It was used on the Western Front by all nationalities in ever-increasing amounts, with the original belts in front of fire trenches 10 yards deep rapidly increasing to 30 yards or more. It was sited, along with trip wires to set off flares, rattle tin cans or discharge warning guns, so that an enemy bomber on the far side could not simply lie down and lob bombs into the trench.

Every night wiring parties went out to erect new wire obstacles and to strengthen or repair existing ones. It was one of the most unpopular types of working party, particularly early in the war when the wire was strung between wooden posts that required hammering into the ground – the noise, even with muffled hammers, inevitably resulted in enemy flares going up and bursts of machine-gun fire. This problem was partially solved by the introduction of steel pickets that could be screwed into the ground.

The near edge of the entanglement was supposed to be at least 20 yards from the trench and generally between 3 and 5 feet high. The obstacle was often positioned to canalize attackers into the killing zones of machine guns and thus often ran in long slants across the front. To be sure of success against sudden surprise attacks, the wire defences needed to consist of several thick belts and to be erected in irregular patterns. In December 1917 this lesson had been re-learned, as recorded by General Byng in his report to GHQ after Cambrai:

> Wire must be put down in such masses that it forms a series of impenetrable hedges along which field and machine guns can sweep. Wire must be irregular and placed in thick bundles which are impervious to wire-cutters. All lines must be wired to a depth hitherto considered quite unnecessary. Providing the enemy does not adopt a form of tank, this should ensure safety from a surprise attack.

Wire was also placed in disused trenches, ditches, in woods and scrub and in shell craters – anywhere it might cause problems to advancing troops. Friendly wire obstacles always had narrow passages through them to allow patrols or attacking troops to exit their own wire. These passages were not straight but angled to confuse any enemy who found them in the dark – they could also be temporarily blocked with wire knife rests.

Sergeant Arthur Mothersole, MM, took part in a trench raid near Beaumont-Hamel in July 1916 and later described the frustrating and dangerous experience of encountering uncut enemy wire:

> Mr. A. [his officer] is with the rush. We are at the wire. And then —
>
> I believe every heart stopped for a moment. No lights now; Fritz was too busy. But our legs and hands were scratched and bleeding. We knew there was no gap.
>
> I could hear many of the boys cursing and swearing for their wire-cutting tools. Somebody was bashing the strands with a rifle. A. and I walked along to find a weak place. The enemy was silent – too silent. Something lobbed over and burst. 'Egg-shell bomb!' muttered somebody. Three star shells were in the air, and they showed up a score of the party struggling through the wire. Then the point-blank rifle-fire, the flashes striking hot to our very faces. 'Nothing for it, sir; men don't stand an earthly. They'll get hung up on this damned wire.'
>
> A. agreed, and the long-short, long-short blasts of the whistle sounded a retirement.

Other Defensive Structures

Dugouts

It was not until 1915 that dugouts to protect troops from shellfire became commonplace, for the most part, but not entirely, replacing the funk holes of the earlier months of the war, many of which were expanded into more substantial shelters. Dugouts were built to house virtually all types and levels of headquarters forward of divisional headquarters, such as medical aid posts, forward supply dumps or signal centres, and to provide shelter for troops not required on the firing line, including machine-gun and trench-mortar crews. Their objective was to protect the occupants from both shrapnel and high-explosive shells – the latter requiring much thicker overhead protection than the former.

Dugouts could be constructed either by the digging of a large, deep pit, which was roofed using timber or concrete and then covered with earth, or by mining – that is, excavated via a sloping tunnel, which was later provided with steps that formed the entrance. Either way they could start as basic rudimentary shelters but be developed over time into large, and in many cases reasonably comfortable, accommodation.

British General Staff *Notes for Infantry Officers on Trench Warfare*, issued in March 1916, recommended the following for roof construction over deep dugouts:

> a) Every deep dugout must have two or more separate exits to facilitate rapid egress and in case one gets blocked [many lives were lost when a collapsing roof buried its occupants].
> b) Roof timbers must always be made three or four times stronger than is necessary to support merely the load due to the thickness of the roof for which they are designed. This is necessary to allow, not only for the shock of the burst of a shell, but for the possibility that a fresh garrison may take it into their heads to put another 2 or 3 feet of earth on top of the existing roof.
> c) …
> d) …
> e) A 'burster' layer, of 6 inches to 1 foot of brick or stone, should always be provided near the top surface of the roof. Over this 'burster' layer should be a layer of not less than 6 inches of earth to decrease danger from the scattering of the stone or brick by the burst of the shell. As the object of 'burster' is to explode the shell near the surface, it will be to a large extent defeated if the layer of earth above it is made more than 12 inches thick.

The large dugouts invariably led off the support or reserve trenches. Ernest Shephard, who as a regular soldier joined the 1st Battalion, the Dorset Regiment in July 1909, was by 1916 a company sergeant major and in his diary described his company headquarters on the Somme:

> [It was] the best I have ever been in, about 80 feet long, 10 feet wide, 100 feet below ground [doubtful accuracy], two entrances down steps. We have all the Company Staff together. Dugout is parted in three. One part for the telephone and operators, Officers' servants and trench mortar battery attached. Centre part for the Officers, and third part for the stretcher-bearers, Company and platoon orderlies, sanitary men and myself.

Machine-gun posts

The firing of the Lewis light and the Vickers heavy machine guns differed in that the former was usually fired over the parapet without any fixed emplacement, while the latter heavy weapon was invariably fired from a specially constructed post. However, the Lewis gun was often fired from a specific 'firing place', such as a loophole or depression in the parapet, and when not in action it was kept under cover during a bombardment.

The heavy Vickers guns were positioned in all three defensive lines to bring crossfire to bear in front of the trenches that they protected. The key element in the construction of their emplacements was concealment, as both sides were constantly searching for machine-gun posts so they could be registered

and targeted as a matter of priority in any bombardment. This meant an emplacement must look like any other part of the parapet and should not project above it; it needed to be over 6 feet thick if made only of earth.

The ideal arrangement was that each gun should be in a bombproof shelter with overhead cover and in advance of, and to a flank of, the part of the line it was to cover. The gun would be set up on a platform or ledge behind the parapet and either fire on fixed lines or be able to traverse. Guns providing barrage fire would be fixed to fire at an appropriate angle to give overhead fire. Alternative firing positions were constructed where possible, and each firing post had an adjoining dugout for the crew, often with elephant shelters (semi-circular sheets of corrugated iron) used as a framework for the roof,

A Lewis-gunner on the banks of the Lys Canal during the 1918 German spring offensive. The gunner fires through the bank via a wooden box-type loop, while the sergeant stands ready with a fresh magazine.

along with ammunition recesses cut into the emplacement walls. The diagram below shows an ideal layout of an early 1918 machine-gun emplacement for a Vickers, in this case set up to fire a barrage.

Redoubts/strongpoints/ pillboxes

There is really little distinction between a strongpoint and a redoubt, although generally the former was a smaller affair with a smaller garrison. Both were common features of defensive systems and could be sited in any or all trench lines – or, equally often, particularly during the latter two years of the war – in the deep defensive zones such as the German Hindenburg Line. For the sake of clarity, these positions will be referred to as redoubts no matter what their size.

Redoubts were usually sited in, around or on features whose loss would weaken the general defensive line. They were developed for all-round defence, the garrison of which was expected to hold out long after flanking trenches were lost to facilitate counterattacks. An example of this was the extensive, triangular Schwaben Redoubt, which was garrisoned by an entire German regiment (see Map 43, page 212). It was briefly captured by the 36th Ulster Division on 1 July 1916 but lost the same day to heavy counter-attacks and not finally taken until 14 October. This redoubt was positioned on the summit of a low ridge and was the centre point of the German second line between the rubble of Thiepval on the ridge overlooking the Ancre valley to the immediate south and the Somme river in the north, which was guarded by another redoubt built around the tiny village of St-Pierre Divion. By 1 July the ruins of Thiepval could well be termed a fortress, with deep dugouts in converted cellars and numerous concrete machine-gun posts. It resisted all attempts to take it for almost three months, finally falling to the 18th Division on 27 September – an event that facilitated the final attacks on the Schwaben Redoubt.

Machine-gun Emplacement for Barrage Work (not to scale)

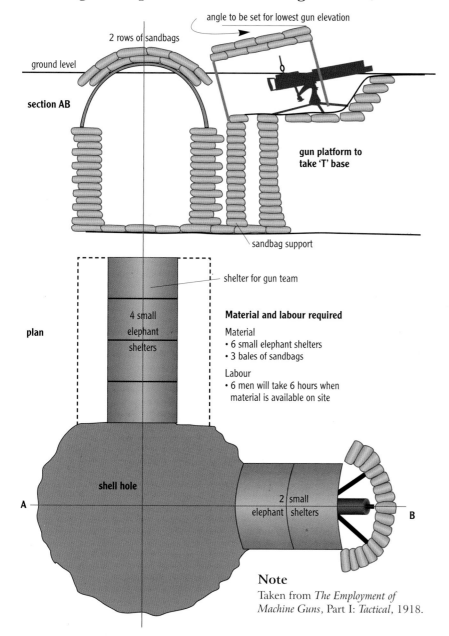

angle to be set for lowest gun elevation

2 rows of sandbags

ground level

section AB

gun platform to take 'T' base

sandbag support

shelter for gun team

plan

4 small elephant shelters

Material and labour required

Material
- 6 small elephant shelters
- 3 bales of sandbags

Labour
- 6 men will take 6 hours when material is available on site

shell hole

A

2 small elephant shelters

B

Note

Taken from *The Employment of Machine Guns, Part I: Tactical*, 1918.

Strongpoint/Redoubt for about 50 Men

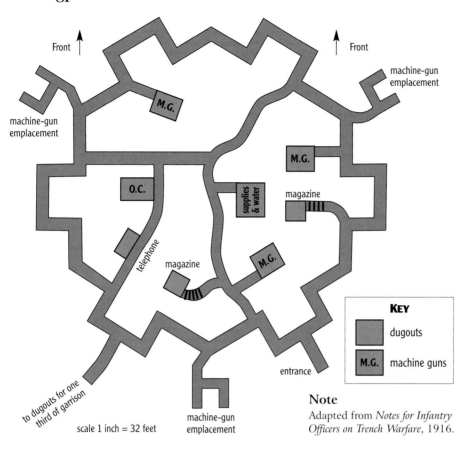

Front ↑   ↑ Front

machine-gun
emplacement

machine-gun
emplacement

M.G.

O.C.

supplies
& water

magazine

telephone

magazine

M.G.

M.G.

to dugouts for one
third of garrison

scale 1 inch = 32 feet

machine-gun
emplacement

entrance

KEY

| | dugouts |
| M.G. | machine guns |

Note

Adapted from *Notes for Infantry Officers on Trench Warfare*, 1916.

many survived heavy artillery bombardments to inflict severe losses on advancing infantry. Map 73 (page 409) shows the attack by British tanks on a series of strongpoints based on pillboxes defending the St-Julian–Poelcappelle road in August 1917. The tanks' guns and machine guns were useless against the 3-feet-thick walls, so they had to resort to attacking from the rear at the entrances. The British built very few machine-gun pillboxes themselves, perhaps feeling that such solid defences would make the troops less offensively minded.

Life In and Out of the Line

Oh, the rain, the mud, and the cold,
The cold, the mud, and the rain;
With weather at zero it's hard for a hero
From language that's rude to refrain.
With porridgy muck to the knees,
With sky that's a-pouring a flood,
Sure the worst of our foes
Are the pains and the woes
Of the RAIN,
THE COLD,
AND THE MUD.

Robert W. Service,
'A Song of Winter Weather'

Map 43 shows about 4,000 yards of the Somme front on 1 July and clearly illustrates the use of redoubts by the Germans in all three lines of trenches, with the front line having the Leipzig salient and Thiepval; the second line the Wundtwerk, Thiepval again, the Schwaben Redoubt and St-Pierre Divion; and the third line Mouquet Farm, Goat and Stuff Redoubts – all linchpins of an extremely strong defensive zone.

Another example of the Germans converting a village into a redoubt was Gommecourt (see Map 45, page 220). Here the entire village is surrounded by fire trenches with a network (not all on the map) of communication trenches running through the village. The south-western area, called the Kern Redoubt and incorporating the eastern edge of Gommecourt Park, was a particularly strong area. Most woods in the battle area were soon reduced to matchwood, but they were still invariably converted into strongpoints that required many costly attacks to capture – examples such as Delville Wood, High Wood, Mametz Wood and Trones Wood abound. Map 34 (pages 130–1) shows how the French under Lieutenant Colonel Driant had based the defence of the Bois des Caures on a series of strongpoints linked by communication trenches which, although not officially called a redoubt, was precisely that.

The British also constructed numerous redoubts. An excellent example is the defence of Manchester Hill in March 1918 by the battalion headquarters and D Company of the 16th Battalion, the Manchester Regiment, under Lieutenant Colonel Wilfrith Elstob, VC, DSO, MC. Map 78 shows the layout of this redoubt, which incorporates a quarry and consists of a series of section firing and machine-gun posts sited for all-round defence, with thick belts of wire not only all round but also running across the centre of the position. The Manchesters were about to face part of the Germans' great offensive of 21 March and were ordered to hold their hill to the last man. They did as commanded, in the end fighting hand to hand before being overrun. Elstob, wounded three times, was one of the last to be killed after emptying his revolver and firing a rifle as the Germans closed in.

Pillboxes, or blockhouses, were miniature forts developed by the Germans to give added strength to their defensive lines. The British used the term 'pillbox' because the reinforced concrete construction was the same shape as the boxes in which chemists supplied tablets during the war. German machine-gunners were often housed in pillboxes and the thick concrete walls and roof made them impervious to most shells –

Life in the front line meant time spent in the front, support or reserve trenches or dugouts. It is a commonly held belief that the infantry spent the majority of their time in the front-line trenches with little relief from the horrors of war and the weather. This is far from the truth. The BEF took great pains to ensure that men and units rotated regularly between front-line positions and billets in the rear. In his book *Mud, Blood and Poppycock: Britain and the Great War* Gordon Corrigan compiled the statistics of five regular battalions, showing how much time they spent in the trenches (front, support and reserve), the longest continuous period in trenches (days) and the longest period in the front firing line during the month of January in 1915, 1916, 1917 and 1918. In summary, his results were:

Average Time in Trenches

	Number of days in trenches	Longest continuous period in trenches	Longest continuous period in firing line
January 1915	10	5.4	2
January 1916	6	4.2	3
January 1917	2	2	0.8
January 1918	6	5.2	2.4

MAP 78 THE MANCHESTER HILL STRONGPOINT, 21 MARCH 1918

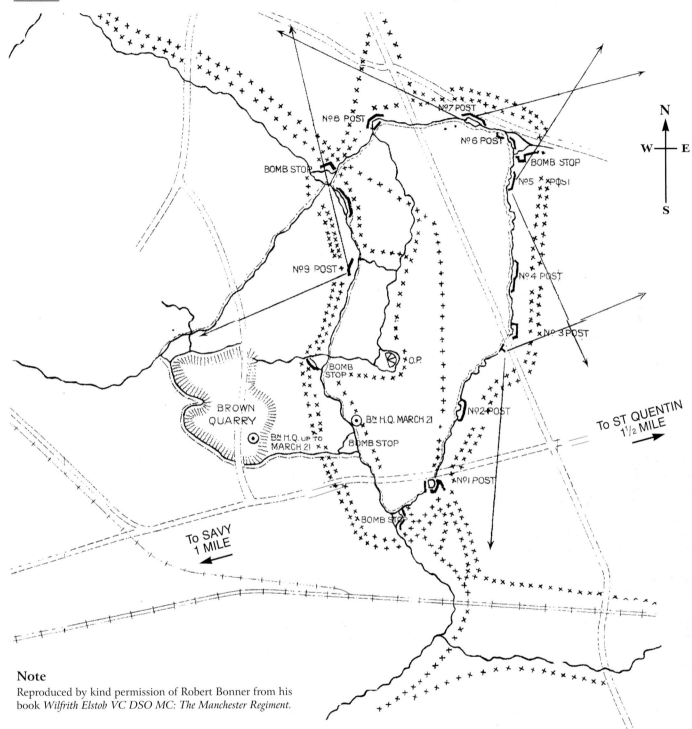

N
W ┼ **E**
S

NO 8 POST

NO 7 POST

NO 6 POST

BOMB STOP

BOMB STOP

NO 5 X POST

NO 9 POST

NO 4 POST

NO 3 POST

O.P.

BOMB STOP

BROWN QUARRY

BN H.Q. MARCH 21

NO 2 POST

BN H.Q. UP TO MARCH 21

BOMB STOP

To ST QUENTIN 1½ MILE

NO 1 POST

BOMB STOP

To SAVY 1 MILE

Note

Reproduced by kind permission of Robert Bonner from his book *Wilfrith Elstob VC DSO MC: The Manchester Regiment.*

In January 1915 the maximum number of days spent in the trenches by these five battalions was thirteen by the 1st South Wales Borderers, but in January 1917 they were not in the trenches at all. Overall a British battalion on the Western Front could expect to serve an average of about ten days in the front line in one month. However, because Indian battalions had about 250 fewer men than the British they,

of necessity, spent longer in the trenches – one Gurkha battalion spent three weeks in the line.

The system was flexible, and the time spent in the line or out varied according to the tactical situation. A division with three brigades might have two in the line and one out. When in the line a battalion was given responsibility for a sector that included the front, support and reserve lines. A common

deployment of its four companies was two in the front line and one each in the support and reserve trenches. Great care was taken that a company that was forced to spend more time in the front trenches during the battalion's time in the line spent less time when next at the front – the same applied to battalions within a brigade.

A battalion normally moved up to the line partly by train and partly by marching.

Law and Order in the BEF

It has been suggested that the purpose of having discipline in any army is twofold: first, to ensure staunchness in battle; second, to keep order in the army. In World War I the British Army, dominion and colonial troops, along with Chinese and native labourers from South Africa, were subject to military law. Military law and discipline was enforced through the Army Act, which was reviewed by parliament annually, and the detailed application of the law and procedures was set in the Manual of Military Law – this system still operates today.

Discipline can be either entirely imposed through strict enforcement of military law, or it can be largely individual self-discipline. The latter is normally the best and is associated with high morale in a unit, but imposed discipline is usually needed in some degree to underpin self-discipline and obtain conformity in times of great danger and stress. It has always been the case that infringements of military law are punished more severely on active service than when committed at home. This was true during 1914–18, when service overseas counted as active service, as indeed it was, while being stationed in Britain was not. The ultimate example was the death penalty – of the 346 death penalties carried out, none was for a soldier serving at home.

For serious offences that could not be dealt with within a unit the usual procedure was for the case to be heard by a court martial. Three types were in use. The District Court Martial (DCM) had to have a minimum of three members, with a major or above as president. It had limited powers, as it could not try an officer, but for soldiers it could impose imprisonment with hard labour, reduce an NCO to the ranks and discharge a man from the army.

For more serious offences a General Court Martial (GCM) would be convened. It could try officers and sentence a man to death, impose penal servitude for life and any lesser punishment. This court had a minimum of five members, the president being a full colonel.

The third type was the Field General Court Martial (FGCM), which had three members (in very exceptional circumstances it could be two), with the president being a major. This court was used in the forward areas where either it was usually impossible to convene a GCM as sufficient court members were not available, or it was impractical for operational reasons to withdraw witnesses or court members for a prolonged period. It had the same powers as a GCM and it was FGCM that tried almost 95 per cent of the court-martial cases heard overseas during the war – 154,399 out of 163,147.

Overall, both at home and overseas, 304,262 cases were tried by a court martial during the period 4 August 1914 to 31 March 1920; of these, 5,952 involved officers.

The most significant offences that usually went for trial by court martial were (with the most prevalent first): absence without leave, drunkenness, insubordination and desertion. The death sentence could be awarded for murder, cowardice in the face of the enemy, mutiny, desertion, wilful disobedience, striking a superior officer, sleeping on post or quitting it, and casting away arms in the face of the enemy. If a man was sentenced to death – and by no means all those found guilty of the above offences were – there was the possibility of appeal, and the findings of the court and all associated documentation were forwarded to higher authority for confirmation. This was the procedure for all court-martial convictions and the higher authority had the power to quash the conviction or reduce the sentence. For death-sentence cases the papers were submitted to GHQ for examination by the judge advocate general (the senior military lawyer) before being passed to the commander-in-chief for final confirmation or otherwise. Sir Douglas Haig, contrary to general belief, confirmed the sentence only with considerable reluctance and after much thought, as is evidenced by the following figures.

Between 4 August 1914 and 31 March 1920, 3,080 death sentences were passed (on British, dominion, colonial troops and labourers) but only 346 (11 per cent) were carried out. The offences for which the sentence was carried out were:

Desertion	266	Disobedience	5
Murder	37	Mutiny	3
Cowardice	18	Sleeping on post	2
Quitting post	7	Casting away arms	2
Striking/violence	6		

Three officers were sentenced to death and executed, two for desertion and one for murder, during the war. Of the soldiers executed, ninety-one were already under a suspended sentence and of these forty had been previously sentenced to death, in thirty-eight cases for desertion, one for quitting his post and one for disobedience.

Victor Silvester, the famous dance-orchestra leader who died in 1978, took part as a boy soldier (he enlisted at fifteen after absconding from school and giving a false age) in five executions. After being wounded in 1917 he was discharged, but resumed a military career, spending some time at the Royal Military Academy, Sandhurst. In an interview just before he died he described the first execution:

> The victim was brought out from a shed and led struggling to a chair to which he was then bound and a white handkerchief placed over his heart as our target area. He was said to have fled in the face of the enemy.

Captain Ernest Parker, 10th Durham Light Infantry (then a private), described his journey with a draft of reinforcements up the line to the Ypres salient in 1915:

> Our cattle truck, like its neighbours, was marked plainly *Hommes 40: Chevaux 8,* but by a wonderful feat of compression squeezed fifty of us into it, and it was with difficulty that we converted our packs into seats.
>
> Before leaving the station the engine screamed in a blood-curdling manner and began jerkily to tug the train forwards, jolting the trucks together with such violence that we were all piled into a heap on the floor. The engine, after this display of energy, now came to a standstill while the gamins [children] dolefully intoned

> 'Boolee bif – Biskwi' until we were irritated into audible protest. At this sign of recognition the plaintive wailing grew more persistent and to relive our ears we aimed a fusillade of iron rations, reserved for emergencies, through the open door . . . The snail's crawl of the engine had at least one advantage, for it allowed us to stretch our cramped limbs by walking alongside the cattle trucks . . .
>
> At the halting places a few lucky people obtained hot water from the engine driver, while the rest of us looked on in envy as it was turned into strong Dixie tea.

After leaving the train the Durhams bivouacked in the fields of a farm near Vlamertinghe, where they were drenched in a downpour, before marching up to the front:

> Towards midnight we turned out to go up to the line . . . After some miles of heavy marching . . . we saw between the twin rows of staggered poplars a mass of battered towers and steeples thrusting skywards in black jagged outlines against a background of fire and smoke. Before us stood the city of Ypres, grimly menacing our passage . . . Passing through the town, we came to the mounds of rubble on the flanks of the Cloth Hall . . . and as we noticed its remaining masses of heavy masonry, the wags were in great form – until, travelling rearwards from the guide, came the news that brought an awed silence. Underneath us lay deeply buried a complete company of the Cornwalls [Duke of Cornwall's Light Infantry]

The tears were rolling down his cheeks as he tried to free himself from the ropes. I aimed blindly and when the gunsmoke had cleared away we were further horrified to see that, although wounded, the man was still alive. Still blindfolded, he was attempting to make a run for it still strapped to the chair. An officer in charge stepped forward to put the finishing touch with a revolver held to the poor man's temple.

He had only once cried out and that was when he shouted the one word 'mother'. He could not have been much older than me. We were told later that he had been suffering from shell-shock, a condition not recognised by the army at the time. Later I took part in four more such executions.

The great majority of minor offences were dealt with within the soldier's own unit, by either his company or equivalent commander or his commanding officer. The former could award a soldier seven days confined to barracks or camp, extra guards or piquets and forfeiture of pay for absence of less than a week – he could only admonish or reprimand a junior NCO. Cases he could not deal with went before the commanding officer, who had a wide range of powers including twenty-eight days' detention, fines for drunkenness, deductions of pay for loss or damage to equipment, up to twenty-eight Field Punishments No.1 (FP No. 1 – see below), and removal of acting or lance rank from an NCO. For offences that carried a higher maximum penalty the case would be passed to higher authority, normally brigade, or for a court martial. Apart from the award of extra duties, cases against officers went automatically to brigade or to a court martial.

Field Punishment No. 1 could involve a soldier being kept in irons or handcuffs and secured to a fixed object for not more than two hours a day, but not for more than three out of four consecutive days. He could be required to perform manual labour in the same way as a man undergoing a sentence of imprisonment with hard labour. The use of this punishment varied in frequency and length, depending on the unit's commanding officer's views and the seriousness of the offence. Field Punishment No. 1 was an alternative to detention or imprisonment (when awarded by a court martial), as such a punishment would remove the soldier from the risk and stress of the front line – something that some men might regard as welcome, and would certainly antagonize their better-behaved comrades.

Hundreds of thousands of men applied for exemption from military service for a number of reasons apart from medical. Perhaps the most common was that their civilian job was essential for the country's war effort. They were all considered by local tribunals, which – largely because of the huge numbers – frequently rejected applications. The ones that caused most difficulties were the conscientious objectors. Charles Messenger, in his book *Call-to-Arms*, gives the figure of around 16,500 during the period 1916–18. Of these he states that some 6,000 had their objection upheld and were totally exempt and almost 5,000 more were granted exemption from combat service, with the remainder being rejected.

Lieutenant Colonel Reginald Brook, commandant of the Military Detention Barracks at Wandsworth, had his own way of inducing a change of mind in those who refused to put on a uniform, which he explained in a letter to the *Daily Express* on 4 July 1916:

Conscientious objectors usefully employed in the construction of a military road, August 1917.

I had them placed in special rooms, nude, but with their full army kit on the floor for them to put on as soon as they were so minded. There were no blankets or substitutes for clothing left in the rooms, which were quite bare. Several of the men held out for several hours but they gradually accepted the inevitable. Forty of the conscientious objectors who passed through my hands are now quite willing soldiers.

recently entombed by a hurricane bombardment.

Through the gaping streets we followed the guide until at the Menin Gate we wheeled right and halted under the shelter of the ramparts. Here Regimental Sergeant Major Noble turned out to welcome the new draft, and by means of a few staccato shouts divided us into four groups; each of which was allotted to a company.

Parker later described his first experience in the firing line:

At last our turn came for duty in the firing line, and there we found our duties allotted in a cycle of three hours, the first hour on sentry, the second sitting alert beside the standing sentry, while the third was set aside for rest or miscellaneous duties. In my case the third hour was seldom spent in rest. I was taken away to draw rations from the support line, and often I went out into the listening post, reached by a sap running out towards the German lines. I believe it is a fact that the section lance corporal responsible for the distribution of duties was already out of his mind. During this wretched tour of duty he ate up most of the section's rations, and for five days I was nearly starved and felt giddy for lack of sleep. This NCO was reported missing when we left the front line and months afterwards he was arrested in the disguise of a Belgian peasant while engaged in the pleasant pastime of bombing the peasant's pigs.

Parker's experience of duty rosters (although not necessarily with three-hour duties) was universal in all units, not just the infantry. In a front-line trench the men were on duty rosters divided into hours, often two hours on and two or four off, according to the number of posts to be manned and the number of men available. Two on and two off was not popular, as it gave men little time for rest – two hours in a dugout filled with other bodies and continual coming and going was hardly conducive to sleep. By day in the support line soldiers could work only under cover, so most work had to be done at night. As gunners were tied to the servicing of their guns, which had to be able to fire for twenty-four hours every day, the duties of gun detachments were usually on a twenty-four hour on and twenty-four hour off basis.

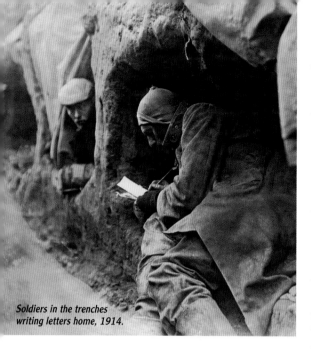

Soldiers in the trenches
writing letters home, 1914.

Standing orders

Units at the front invariably had comprehensive 'standing orders' covering every detail of routine. A Major North, the brigade major of the 124th Infantry Brigade, issued standing orders for 1915–16 for the units in the brigade – the important instructions are summarized below. They give a clear picture of the detail required in a properly organized defensive sector of the front-line trenches.

Reliefs

The day prior to the unit taking over the position in the line, an officer from every company and platoon would visit the trenches to be taken over to gain as much information of the position and enemy activity as possible – this was often preceded by a visit by the company commander and his sergeant major. On the day of the relief an officer from each company would go forward and take over all items of trench stores being left behind by the outgoing unit. These included such items as SAA, picks, shovels, pumps, Very-light cartridges, grenades, braziers, Vermorel sprays (anti-gas tool), gas gongs, barbed-wire rolls, pickets and steel loophole plates.

Machine-gunners, bombers, snipers and signallers of the outgoing unit would remain for twenty-four hours in order to brief their reliefs fully. The relieving companies, platoons and machine-gun and bombing posts would be led forward after dark by guides. On arrival in the trenches the platoon being relieved climbed on to the firestep and the reliefs filed in behind. On the word 'Pass' being sent along, the changeover would take place.

The company commander of the relieving company would then ensure sentries were posted and orders for all the posts correctly handed over before establishing communications with flanking companies or units. Within twenty-four hours he would report the condition of the trenches and the ammunition situation to battalion headquarters.

Sentries

As a general rule, although this could vary according to circumstances, there should be one sentry by day for every three firing bays, exclusive of machine-gun and bombing posts. By night or in fog or smoke there would be a sentry in every bay. These sentries were posted and relieved by an NCO under supervision from the platoon commander.

Sentry duty was obviously critical, even during quiet periods. Standing alone in the dark, desperately cold, especially in the dreadful winter of 1916/17, was a never-to-be-forgotten experience. Occasionally the stillness would be broken by the rat-tat of a machine-gun burst, or the distant rumble of transport bringing up both sides' supplies and ammunition. The Ypres salient was special in that flares and rockets invariably lit up the sky, while machine-gun fire and shellfire were at times almost continuous. If the sentry system was well organized the man coming off duty would have hot tea (perhaps laced with rum) to drink when he stood down.

In early March 1918, when a major German offensive was expected, Sir Douglas Haig issued an Order of the Day concerning sentries. It emphasized the seriousness of the general situation, stressing that there had been recent cases where sentries found asleep had been court-martialled and sentenced to death (he had in some cases commuted the death sentence), and that no further clemency could be expected – in other words, sleeping sentries must die. A few nights later Lieutenant R. J. Martin, 2/10th Londons, was inspecting sentry posts and later recorded this incident:

> [I was] visiting the posts for which I was responsible [when] I saw a sentry, head resting on the parapet, fast asleep. I took his rifle away and awakened him. I sat on the parapet and talked to him, emphasising that I would break my trust if I were to overlook the offence. I reminded him of the punishment that awaited him and asked, 'Do you have anyone at home?' He replied, 'I have a mother. This will kill her too.' I thought of our two mothers, each in those midnight hours, praying for the safety of her son on the battlefield. I said to him, 'If you give me your solemn word not to mention this incident to any living creature, I will do the same, let us forget it.' He broke down in tears and I went on my way. True, I was part of the military machine, but in fact only a bank clerk in uniform.

Apart from detecting enemy activity or impending attacks, the sentries were also responsible for warning of gas attacks. All men had to carry their smoke helmets (respirators) on their person or within reach at all times. At the first hint of gas the sentries would sound the alarm gongs, triangles or bells that were hung up at intervals throughout the trenches. Where gas attacks were known to be likely it was sometimes necessary to post wind sentries whose task was to spot wind changes that were likely to herald an attack. They were often equipped with wind vanes mounted on the parapet as direction indicators during a gas attack. Company Sergeant Major Ernest Shephard, while in the front line at Ypres in May 1915, noted:

> We now have 'wind sentries' who carefully watch wind to see when it turns favourable to enemy using gas. A very keen lookout has to be kept because we are so close that once wind [is] favourable to [the] enemy they could put gas into our trenches within about 3 seconds, so we have to spot it at once or go under.

Some wag put up the following ditty at a Royal West Kent sentry post in 1915 – it effectively stated what was required in the event of a gas attack:

> *If a whiff of gas you smell,*
> *Bang your gong like bloody hell,*
> *On with your googly, up with your gun –*
> *Ready to meet the bloody Hun.*

Listening posts

A universal feature on all sectors of the front, pushed out into no-man's-land, these were in effect advanced sentry posts. They were expected to give early warning of attacks, raids or patrols. Sergeant Major Shephard, this time on the Somme front in autumn 1915 in a quiet sector, explained:

A German s
stands guar
trench, wearing
armour and armed
his gas-mask conta

The enemy trenches vary in distance [from us] from 80, 100, 150 to 250 yards. Where they are 150 yards upwards we have 'listening posts', and advanced posts pushed forwards, so that our line resembles a large crab, claws and legs to the front feeling the way.

Officers and NCOs of the watch

It was the responsibility of all company commanders in the front line to ensure the officers took turns to be on 'watch' (duty) throughout every twenty-four hours. Platoon commanders would detail an NCO of the watch. The officer and NCOs on duty would have to visit all sentries, bombing posts and machine guns in the area once every hour by day and night – this was a particularly arduous task for the officer, who would get no sleep for twenty-four hours. At night the officer would carry a Very pistol. It was noted that the time to put up flares was when the Germans were not sending any up.

Standing to arms

All troops would stand to one hour before daylight and one hour before dark. They would man the firestep and the bombing and machine-gun posts. Officers would check that all the posts were manned and that each man had two smoke helmets and 120 rounds of rifle ammunition. Weapons, ammunition and equipment would be inspected and it would be ascertained that every soldier was able to fire at the bottom of his own wire. In the morning troops would not be stood down until the enemy front line was visible, and at night only when it was completely dark. At both these times sentries would take over.

Gas attacks

All personnel were to carry two smoke helmets at all times which were to be inspected at morning and evening stand-to. Sentries would bang the alarm gong and everyone would put on a smoke helmet and man their posts. Nobody was to remain in a dugout. Officers in command of trenches opposite enemy positions from which the gas was coming would send the SOS call to the artillery and order rapid fire on enemy trenches. If the gas cloud was thick enough to hide the enemy's front parapets, machine guns and rifles were to fire short bursts on fixed lines.

In a letter to a friend Private Alfred Mayes of the 1st Bedfordshires described the effects of getting gassed but still having to carry on fighting:

A peculiarity of this gas is that one rarely loses consciousness. I will endeavour to describe the sensation. When the wind is right, the Germans fire a shell over us and you see a green cloud of smoke rolling along the ground towards you. When it envelops you, all the air disappears and you start gasping for breath and as you gasp this stuff fills your lungs until you haven't the strength to gasp at all, or move hand or foot. All the time one's brain is clear and you know what is going on all around you, but you cannot breathe and all your strength seems gone. If the gas does not blow away it is all up with you. When it does some are too far gone and gradually sink. Personally, I could not walk ten yards without being 'done up'. I have seen fellows six feet high being fed with milk and having air pumped into them to keep them alive, I have seen them die two days later with their faces as black as a nigger's.

Fixing of bayonets

Bayonets were to be fixed during the hours of darkness, during a snowstorm or thick mist, or when the proximity of the enemy made it advisable.

Counter-attacks

As soon as possible after taking over a sector of the line the commanding officer had to send to brigade headquarters his plan for counter-attacking the enemy should they capture any part of the battalion's line.

Mines

In the event of the Germans firing a mine in or near the line, the side of the crater nearest the British line was to be immediately occupied by the nearest troops.

Firing by day and night

Indiscriminate firing by day or night was forbidden. By day men would fire only when a target offered itself. Enemy appearing briefly at specific locations would be pointed out to the battalion sniper officer. By night, if the enemy was thought to be working on his trenches or wire, the company commander would authorize the firing of five rounds rapid at certain times – provided no friendly patrols were out in the area. A certain number of fixed rifles would be positioned in each trench laid on (aimed at) specific targets and to be fired by sentries in accordance with their orders.

Company meetings

These were to be held each evening with the company officers and NCOs, although not all together. They were what the modern army terms 'O-groups' (orders groups), at which the company commander gives out his orders for the night, including administrative instructions and work to be done in the following twenty-four hours.

Discipline

This section consisted mostly of what soldiers were not permitted to do, such as cooking, washing and shaving or sleeping in a front-line trench. They were also forbidden to leave a trench without an officer's permission or to remove their equipment while in a front-line trench. They were required to keep all ammunition clean and to carry arms at all times when moving about.

Returns

No battalion or other unit in the line could escape paperwork. The following reports were required daily by 124th Brigade HQ:

At 5.15 a.m. – Situation and wind – by orderly
At 11.00 a.m. – Strength and casualty return – by ditto – Artillery intelligence report – by ditto
At 4.00 p.m. – Situation and wind – by telephone
At 5.30 p.m. – Intelligence report – by orderly or telephone
At 9.00 p.m. – Return of material required for trench construction to be sent up the following evening – by telephone

There were a further twenty-two headings to these standing orders, including tactical matters such as sniping, patrols, artillery support and prisoners, as well as administrative ones concerning rum issue, rations, water and care of the feet.

Daily routine

The routine of the 1/4th Loyal North Lancashire Regiment in the Ypres salient in late 1916 was slightly different from the one outlined above. At 'stand-to' an hour before dawn everybody manned their fighting positions on the firestep in full equipment. They waited as it slowly got fully light, alert to a possible attack. When it was light and no hostile movement was detected, the company commander's order of 'stand-down' was passed along the trenches.

All sentry posts remained manned. Each post had an NCO and from four to six men. The post's standing orders were usually pinned to a board with a duty roster showing each man's work for twenty-four hours. Each post – which included Lewis guns, and bombing as well as rifle posts – also had a sheet for recording intelligence observations concerning enemy activity. The intelligence officer collected these records daily when he visited sniper posts.

Shortly after stand-down the ration party, led by an officer from the reserve company, arrived with the breakfast meal carried in knapsack food containers or dixies and the

Two soldiers cooking in a trench at Orvillers, July 1916.

words 'Breakfast up' were passed around. Before this, however, one man from each sentry post was waiting at the distribution point carrying a mess tin for every man in his post. On the occasion described, the Lancashire lads were getting bacon, tea and dry rations for the day. Sentries were relieved for their meal as soon as one man had finished. The officers ate from tin plates either in the company headquarters bunker or in their own personal shelter – often with rations supplemented by local purchase.

Typical Fatigue Parties

Normal practice was for supplies in the forward area to be delivered to a convenient crossroads by regimental transport to the waiting battalion quartermaster. From there a fatigue party would carry them to the front line in sandbags along communication trenches or, if there was a tramway, by pushing loaded trucks across the open – a duty that often exposed the men to machine guns traversing the area.

Another duty that had to be done continuously was the digging of telephone cables. This often devolved on to the infantry of a reserve brigade, who were marched, often several miles, to some road corner beside open fields across which telephone cables leading to a forward headquarters or other critical location were to be laid. For example, in May–June 1916 a whole system of underground telephone lines was being established throughout the forward area of the ANZAC Corps. The cable had to be laid 5 feet deep, unless water prevented it, and each man in the working party was given a specific task, usually to dig 3 yards of trench. When all was finished an engineer officer would lay the cable, the trench was refilled and turf replaced. In this way 200 men would lay 600 yards of cable every night, with the work completed by around 2:30 a.m. The 1st Australian Division had dug 26,400 yards of cable trench by the end of June 1916.

After breakfast came weapon cleaning and an inspection by platoon commanders. The company commander issued instruction for the work for the day through the sergeant major, and sent his 'trench state' (report on the condition of the trenches and ammunition held) by runner to battalion headquarters before setting out on his tour of inspection with the sergeant major. 'Dinner's up' was the signal for a break and the issue of the midday meal in the same way as breakfast, although this was usually stew or roast meat and potatoes.

At 1:30 p.m. casualty returns and any special indent for stores, equipment or ammunition had to be sent to battalion headquarters, and two hours later a report on the wind strength and direction. During this period the soldiers had washed and shaved the best they could and had their feet inspected by the company duty officer of the day – whale oil was usually rubbed into the feet at this time to help prevent trench foot (see page 358). Work continued until tea, which was followed by stand-to again for about an hour as it began to get dark. Although not mentioned by the Loyal North Lancashire Regiment, it was common practice, especially on active fronts, for the hot meal of the day to be brought up by ration parties during darkness after stand-down.

Private F. A. Berry of the 5th Bedfordshires was not too fond of being part of ration parties, especially when they involved wearing a gas mask:

Rations used to be brought up to within a mile and a half of the front line by our transport, then a party of men would be sent from the front line to fetch them. This meant going in battle order, with rifles and perhaps on top of that a man would have to carry two petrol tins of water, so you can imagine what it would be like with a gas mask on as well.

Night routine meant that the men working all day hopefully got some intermittent and disrupted rest. During darkness wiring parties would wriggle over the parapet with coils of wire and posts to repair or improve the wire obstacle, and any patrols, wearing boilersuits and cap comforters (soft woollen hats), would depart on their mission (see page 470). On their return the company commander had to debrief the officer and send off a written report. With the patrols' return operations closed down until the duty officer (they did four-hour shifts), having sent in another situation and wind report, ordered stand-to.

If the reader thinks this a rather gentle routine he would be right for six days out of seven in the front and support trenches. Enemy shelling, snipers or gas alarms could

Digging a Man from the Mud

In his book *Behind the Lines*, Colonel W. N. Nicholson described the incredible efforts needed to release a man from the grip of deep mud. The incident occurred in a trench on the Somme:

The trenches in front got worse, and rose from knee to waist deep in glutinous mud and water. One man was stuck for sixty-five hours. When his battalion left the trenches he was 'handed over' to the relief, who continued the attempt of freeing him, keeping him alive with food and drink and cigarettes.

It was exceedingly difficult to scoop the mud from a man thus caught, often it could only be done by two men at a time, each using his hands, and as fast as they scooped mud out, more flowed in. We purchased ropes to haul the men out, and found that when at last freed the mud had stripped them of every stitch of clothing, they came out naked. So a reserve of boots had to be provided to prevent men walking back barefoot.

upset things, and the weather could ensure disruption and misery. In the rain everything got soaked and it was impossible to dry anything out; often the drainage could not cope, trenches and dugouts became flooded, trench walls or dugouts could collapse during prolonged rain, trapping – and not infrequently crushing – the occupants. All of which meant men often sloshed about ankle deep, or deeper, in water or mud, which, if prolonged, led to trench foot. The literally deadly morass of the Third Ypres (Passchendaele) battlefield in 1917 consumed men, animals, guns and vehicles at a staggering rate. The effects of the weather on the morale and health of the men of both sides has already been touched on in Sections Four and Nine, but this short extract from Sergeant Major Shephard's diary gives us the reality of even a quiet periods:

Friday 19th [November 1915]

Fairly mild night, bitterly cold from 2 a.m. onwards. One case of frostbite in D Coy. I took trench patrol duty [tour of trenches] from 7 a.m. to 9 a.m. The trenches are in an appalling state. The rain, followed by the frost, has caused the trenches to crack up. The men's dug-outs are two-thirds unfit for use (either falling in, or full of water). Consequently the men have to be in the open trench continually, sleeping (when possible) on the fire platforms [steps]. The trench floors are very muddy, at one place it is up to the ankles. The worst point is that the trenches are so deep that it is impossible to throw the thick clay mud over, and to get up to haul with buckets in daylight would be, well, asking for the Huns to put daylight into one, so we can only do a little at night. Parts of [one trench] are 3 feet deep in mud, and we are hard at work damming the parados and revetting.

Quiet sectors and truces

The impression of many people today is that the fighting on the Western Front was virtually continuous, and that troops in the front line seldom had a break from the terror and physical demands of battle – a concept that is far from accurate. Time spent out of the line well to the rear will be discussed below, but in the front line large-scale battles where units suffered horrendous losses were not taking place all the time. There were many parts of the front where fighting on a large scale seldom, if ever, occurred – new divisions were routinely sent to quiet sectors to be broken in gently to trench warfare. In many areas, to a greater or lesser degree, a live-and-let-live situation existed at least for some of the time. This did not mean no casualties occurred, but rather that there was a steady drip, drip of losses rather than mass casualties.

Unofficial, localized truces occurred throughout the war, particularly when the trenches were only a matter of a few yards apart. This was quite common when troops were manning forward saps well out into no-man's-land and within bomb-throwing distance of each other – a mutual understanding to refrain from any aggressive action was reached. Short truces were also occasionally arranged for the collection of wounded. When the 5th Seaforth Highlanders moved into a quiet sector in July 1915 the opposing trenches were very close and the Germans greeted their new opponents by shouting, 'We Saxons, you Anglo-Saxons, don't shoot.' A few days later they announced they were being replaced by Prussians and the British should 'Give them hell!'

Groups of individuals from German and British (and to a lesser extent French) trenches ventured out into no-man's-land for impromptu meetings on many parts of the front during the war. Often this was for the burying of dead. In one incident British and Germans were buried alongside each other near Lille. Gifts of food were sometimes exchanged, with the British giving chocolate and receiving sausages or sauerkraut in return. During quiet periods it was occasionally possible to cook food in the front line without the smoke or smell arousing a hostile response.

The unofficial truce of Christmas 1914 is well known. A letter published in *The Times* from a British medical officer described the British losing a football match 2–3 to a Saxon regiment. Corporal John Ferguson of the 5th Seaforth Highlanders recalled:

> What a sight; little groups of Germans and British extending along the length of our front. Out of the darkness we could hear the laughter and see lighted matches. Where they couldn't talk the language, they made themselves understood by signs, and everybody seemed to be getting along nicely. Here we were laughing and chatting to men whom only a few hours before we were trying to kill.

At midnight in some sectors the firing of pre-arranged flares signalled both sides to return to their trenches. Private Jones of the Queen's Westminster Regiment commented, 'Altogether we had a great day with our enemies, and parted with much hand-shaking and mutual goodwill.' Bruce Bairnsfather in his book *Bullets & Billets* described his Christmas experience as follows:

> I wouldn't have missed that unique and weird Christmas Day for anything . . . I spotted a German officer . . . I intimated to him that I had taken a fancy to his buttons . . . I brought out my wire clippers and, with a few deft snips, removed a couple of his buttons and put them in my pocket. I then gave him two of mine in exchange . . . The last I saw was one of my machine gunners, who was a bit of an amateur hairdresser in civil life, cutting the unnaturally long hair of a docile Boche, who was patiently kneeling on the ground whilst the automatic clippers crept up the back of his neck.

At the following Christmases truces were far less common and artillery bombardments on Christmas Day were sometimes ordered to deter them. However, in 1915 a German soldier, Richard Schirrmann, serving in the Vosges mountains, recalled that when the church bells in the villages behind the line rang out, French and German troops visited each other and exchanged wine and cigarettes for black bread, biscuits and ham.

New Year's Eve in 1914 is well remembered in Brigadier General J. L. Jack's diary for a unique incident involving a company's rum issue. The company sergeant major of A Company, 1st Cameronians, had replaced the storeman who had become a casualty with a Private McN., as General Jack calls him. His job involved taking charge of various stores, food and water, including the rum jar. This proved too much of a temptation for McN., who, after taking several swigs, climbed out of his trench and started staggering around in no-man's-land still clutching his jar. General Jack recorded:

Nothing abnormal was noticed till dawn next day, when posts of 'A' Company were petrified to see a very drunken soldier, minus his equipment, lurching along in No Man's Land to the cheers and laughter of Germans who sportingly did not fire. The entreaties and orders of friends passed unheeded, the delinquent merely pausing occasionally to take a mouthful of rum . . . Pursuing his unsteady way, McN. came opposite the trenches of an adjacent battalion, where he received a peremptory warning to come in, or he would be arrested. This last being too much for our storeman's dignity, he turned towards his threatener [*sic*], took another swig and coolly remarked 'Come oot and fetch us' – an offer which was, needless to say, declined.

Any form of truce or fraternization was officially forbidden and several General Orders were issued on the subject, with many unit standing orders reinforcing them. To be found guilty of such activities resulted in punishment, even when on occasions they were arranged to collect wounded. An officer in the Scots Guards was court-martialled for allowing this to happen in his company. However, Haig annulled his reprimand – possibly because he was related to the prime minister, Herbert Asquith.

On active fronts where patrols and raids were regularly and aggressively carried out, fraternization was rare. However, on quiet sectors after weeks of comparative inactivity the live-and-let-live routine would extend not just to infantry activities but also to those of

Christmas 1915: German soldiers in a trench with a Christmas tree, parcels and 'angel's hair' made of cotton wool.

the artillery and trench mortars. These included one side or another establishing an obvious routine of firing (or not firing) at certain times of the day or night; or they might fire the same number of shells at the same target at the same time each day. The object of this was to establish a routine that was recognized by the enemy and reciprocated. Ration parties, mealtimes and certain locations such as crossroads or trench junctions were singled out for these arrangements. Tony Ashworth, in his book *Trench Warfare 1914–1918*, quotes a German soldier whose unit was facing the French describing this tacit, mutual, routine firing by artillery after many weeks on a quiet sector by the same units:

and so the routine continued with unbroken monotony . . . The way the war was carried out in the Champagne was really ludicrous . . . At 7.22 a.m. half a dozen coal boxes [shells that exploded with a dense cloud of black smoke] of the six-inch variety landed in a bunch on our front line; at 7.25 six of

The French Army in the Trenches

Relations between officers and men in the French Army were significantly different from those in either the British or German Armies. The officers of all the armies tended to keep their distance from their soldiers except when in battle, but the British officer's code of putting his men's welfare first was seldom the practice in the French Army, where NCOs and men were expected to look after themselves to a much greater extent.

French soldiers were required to move everywhere on foot and to carry bedding, clothing, food and drink (including the wine ration), equipment and ammunition. The weight of the backpack containing all these was around 88 lb, while the British one was nearer 66 lb.

French soldiers were notoriously poor at maintaining good standards of hygiene. Taking over French trench lines was not popular with the British, as invariably they were in a neglected state requiring hours of work to clean up. Low standards of personal hygiene were the cause of considerable suffering by French troops through cold, wet and lice. It was not until General Pétain's shake-up of French conditions of service after the mutinies in 1917 that better provision was made for amenities and leave.

The French had several penal battalions in each division where even quite minor defaulters were ruthlessly exposed to the most dangerous tasks around the battlefield, such as being in the leading wave of an attack or being in a party chosen to carry out a hazardous raid.

ours returned the compliment. Promptly at noon each side sent over a heavy mortar shell. By way of an evening blessing there was a mutual exchange of coal boxes, beginning precisely at 7.22 . . . when the exchange of compliments was due, we retired . . . to our famous concrete shelters . . . On the other side of No-Man's-Land things were presumably just the same. It was all very comfortable.

Rotation

The individual soldier's time in a front-line trench was usually brief as, certainly within the BEF, the staff established an effective system of rotating divisions. It was an extremely complex system to organize and maintain so that units had, over time, a fair share of front-line duties and rest. The fact that units only rarely spent longer than a week in the line even during major offensives gave a considerable boost to morale and is a positive reflection of the efficiency of the much-maligned staff. A fairly typical infantryman's year could be divided approximately as follows:

Front line 15%
Support line 10%
Reserve line 30%
Rest area in billets 20%
Hospital/sick, travelling, leave or training courses 25%

The way the British system normally operated was that a sector of the front would be allocated to an army corps, usually containing three divisions. The sector would be divided into two with two adjacent divisions occupying the front and the third in reserve. This allocation of duty would continue down through the divisions, with two of the three infantry brigades on a divisional front, the third in reserve. Within a brigade of four battalions (German regiments) two would occupy the front with two in reserve, and so on down to companies and platoons.

Rotation in the French Army was a far more haphazard affair until Verdun, when a system of regular relief from the line was arranged for divisions. However, there was still a problem at unit and sub-unit level, where long periods in the front line and the general lack of an effective welfare system were contributory factors to the 1917 mutinies (see box, page 128). It was much improved from then on due to the reforms instituted by Pétain.

Away from the line

Life out of the line in billets at least offered a break from the filth, sleeplessness and risk of imminent death or injury, but not necessarily from hard work, drill, route marches, kit inspections, training and formal discipline, all of which caused much grumbling.

That said, the vast majority of soldiers welcomed their time away from the line with considerable relief.

The first requirement of most infantrymen coming out of the line was a hot bath (shower) and complete change of clothes. If these simple requirements were met efficiently – and mostly they were – then spirits rose dramatically. However, not everyone was happy with these basic services. Andrew Macdonald in his book *On My Way to the Somme* quotes a New Zealand soldier who was disappointed with the bathing arrangements on leaving the Somme battlefield:

we were marched to a place called Albert . . . for a supposed hot bath . . . To our disgust when we got there, we stripped off our dirty clothes, and made our way into the buildings to find the showers consisted of a few drops of lukewarm water, not even running, but dripping and you had to fight your way to get your hands to get a few drops let alone underneath it. I managed to get a lather over my body with soap and then could not get enough water on to wash it off . . . They gave us clean shirts and underpants and socks, but we had to put on our lice infested tunics . . .

Invariably units had to march some miles out of the line to their rest area, where billets were arranged in advance to accommodate them. Finding billets was a job given to one of the battalion's officers, who went on his search, often with an interpreter, in advance of his unit. Under billeting regulations civilians were obliged to house troops and officers but could not be forced to provide accommodation for officers' messes. This was where a good interpreter who had a way with the ladies was seemingly useful. Such a man was Second Lieutenant John Nettleton's interpreter, whom Nettleton recalled saying to a reluctant Frenchwoman: 'Surely in a big house like this you can find a room for three officers? I will send you only *des officiers très gentils; pas des Canadiens ou Australiens.*'

Life in billets behind the lines included better and more varied food, with the possibility of buying eggs, milk, fruit and vegetables from the farms – all run by women, as the menfolk were in the French Army. However, the military authorities invariably found work such as road-mending or sometimes even working as farm labourers. These activities were interspersed with route marches, inspections and the always popular concert parties or sporting competitions, which included football, swimming, cricket and tugs-of-war. Training also featured high in any programme of activities. For example, the 1st Battalion, the Bedfordshire Regiment arranged five days of rifle-firing competitions – called in their

Expeditionary Force Canteens

On mobilization no field-force canteen, such as had been deployed in the Boer War, was organized. When it was suggested in August 1914 Lord Kitchener refused, saying, 'This war is not going to be a picnic.' The need was soon obvious, however, and when the army was on the River Aisne cars were sent to Paris to obtain small quantities of matches and cigarettes. When the BEF moved to Flanders Paris was too distant and the local supplies of luxuries were not to British taste – French cigarettes were unpopular and the Belgian beer was so weak the soldiers resorted to adding rum.

Early in 1915 the Canteen and Mess Co-operative Society was authorized to establish a branch in France, and the Expeditionary Force Canteens, managed by the society, came into being. Depots were set up at Le Havre, St-Omer, Poperinghe, Armentières and Bailleul, and in the six months from January to June 1915 the takings amounted to well over 3 million francs; profits made were used for the benefit of the soldiers. The organization greatly expanded the range of

Inside an Expeditionary Force canteen, Abbeville, June 1916.

goods available to the men and ventured into the operation of officers' clubs.

Nearer the front the organization established divisional canteens in order to protect the troops from the exorbitant prices charged by the local cafés and shops. In addition to the usual cigarettes and toilet requirements, goods such as wines, spirits, cigars, boots, underwear, footballs and a host of other items were available, so these canteens became universal providers. In the half year to December 1918 takings had risen to well over 223 million francs. Many brigades or even battalions also acquired their own dry canteens.

During this period there were 295 canteens operating in France, and the staff of officers and other ranks of the organization exceeded 5,000. In 1917 the organization in France was augmented by 700 members of Queen Mary's Army Auxiliary Corps, better known as WAACs (Women's Army Auxiliary Corps).

---

war diary a 'Miniature Bisley' – from 23 to 27 July 1917; the winning teams of various events got 3 francs a man as a prize.

Less popular was the commanding officer's inspection that took place for one company each day during the same period, from 8:30 a.m. to 11:15 a.m. The main activities the commanding officer checked were bomb-throwing, the firing of rifle grenades, techniques of attacking a trench, an assault course and musketry (rapid firing and snapshooting). NCOs were tested on fire control and map-reading. A typical day of recreational activities for this battalion in a rest area at Écurie Wood Camp was Monday, 23 July:

2:00 p.m. to 4:30 p.m. A Company v. B Company – football
C Company v. D Company – cricket
Those not playing sport – 'Roberts Competition' (musketry)
5:30 p.m. to 6:30 p.m. C Company v. B Company – boxing
The regimental band to play every afternoon except Fridays from 2:30 p.m. to 4:30 p.m.

Out of the line the troops needed some time to relax off duty and this invariably meant the availability of estaminets for cheap wine, cafés, canteens and girls. The first two were available in all French and

Belgian towns and in most villages behind the front line. Canteens, however, were gradually established by the Canteen and Mess Co-Operative Society (see box above), the forerunner of the Navy Army Air Force Institute (NAAFI).

Various religious bodies set up their own canteens and other recreational facilities. By the end of 1914 the first in the field was the Young Men's Christian Association (YMCA), which established centres in base camps and later on the lines of communication, in rest camps and at army training schools. Buffets were set up at important railway junctions for the use of troops in transit. By the end of 1916 the YMCA was

Football matches provided respite away from the front line. Here the 1st Battalion, Wiltshire Regiment, play at Bouzincourt, 1916.

An Australian Comforts Fund canteen provides a cup of tea for a soldier during the Battle of the Somme.

operating a chain of canteens close to the front line where troops could buy hot drinks, cake, biscuits, cigarettes and basic toilet requirements – the Church Army canteen at Poperinghe was typical of these near-front canteens. YMCA staffs were mostly men and women volunteers either over service age or of a low medical category, and they numbered around 1,500. An example of the scale of the facilities provided was the canteen at the Étaples railway siding, which distributed some 200,000 cups of tea monthly to troops passing through.

Other religious bodies providing canteens and recreational facilities in France and Belgium included the Church Army, the Salvation Army, the Church of Scotland (the present writer recalls the 'Church of Jocks' mobile canteen arriving on the firing ranges in Germany long after World War II as the highlight of the day), the Women's Catholic League and the Catholic Club.

Minor Operations

The type of small-scale operations, as distinct from a major attack, that dominated the lives of front-line infantry of all nationalities and caused a considerable and continuous number of losses in both killed and wounded, were three in number, namely sniping, patrolling and raiding. This section looks at each in turn and then at the tactics of a battalion attack.

Sniping

Prior to World War I a sniper was known as a sharpshooter – a proven expert shot with a rifle. The word 'sniper' comes from the game bird known as the snipe, a very small bird that is difficult to see as it blends well into the landscape. Saying that a marksman could hit a snipe at 200 yards with a rifle was the last word in praise, so men whose accurate shooting was exceptional became known as snipers.

Sniping was a deadly game played by both sides every day along active sectors of the line and it took a constant and deadly toll – to be hit by a sniper's bullet was

A sniper team from the 4th Royal Berkshires at their station in a ruined roof.

invariably fatal, although in quiet sectors ritualized firing could be part of a tacit live-and-let-live. Normally the slightest exposure during daylight was taking a huge risk (snipers seldom worked at night). A soldier hit by a sniper's bullet usually received a head wound through being careless – being spotted peering over the parapet or through a firing loophole for too long. A rare survivor of such a wound was a sergeant in the 2nd Oxfordshire and Buckinghamshire Light Infantry in the Ypres salient: while observing, he was sniped by a bullet that hit a sandbag, ricocheted into three pieces, one of which hit him on the nose while the other two split his helmet. It was not unknown for either side to play 'games' with sniper fire by waving a shovel from side to side above the parapet to signal a miss.

Special sniper schools were established; the BEF had five, one for each army, by 1917. However, at the start of the war, while a German battalion might have up to eighteen trained snipers, there were none in a British battalion. This was later rectified and a battalion would have between thirty-two and forty trained snipers working under the intelligence officer, as their task was not only to shoot enemy but also to submit a daily report. This would include the number of casualties inflicted, the number and location of sniper posts, any alterations to the enemy trenches or wire and any enemy movements. With thirty-two snipers (sixteen pairs) it would be normal to expect eight teams to be in sniper posts (hides) for two hours during daylight before being relieved – they would usually be excused all duties at night.

Captain Herbert W. McBride served in the 21st Battalion, Canadian Expeditionary Corps, first as a private, then as an NCO and finally as an officer. He was considered by his commanding officer to be 'one of the best machine gunners in the Allied Army. Also one of the best shots with a rifle'. In 1935 the American Small Arms Technical Publishing Company published his *A Rifleman Went to War*, in which he described how snipers best operated in his experience. Some of his salient recommendations are summarized below – most of them were used during the course of the war as 'best practice' by the BEF.

The Pistol in War

One of the most experienced infantry weapons experts of the war was Captain H. W. McBride, the American who joined the Canadian Army and went to the Western Front in 1915 and later served in the United States Army. He was a convinced advocate of the pistol for close-quarter combat.

If a man really knows how to handle his pistol, he can whip – yes, kill – five men within the last ten yards of any assault. He may be killed, often is, by a shot from the side or by someone behind his immediate adversaries, but he can, with the utmost confidence, undertake to handle at least three enemy bayonet men . . .

The case for the pistol may be summed up in 'I don't want this thing often, but when I do I want it damn bad' . . . The Germans had launched a sudden and intensive drive against the Princess Pats [Princess Patricia's Light Infantry] at Hooge and a large forest nearby called Sanctuary Wood. In this latter forest were two [Canadian] guns, placed to cover an exposed approach, with orders to stay there and fight to a finish. And they did – they worked those two guns until the last man was killed *by German bayonets*. This was one of the exceedingly rare instances of where the bayonet was actually used in the war. Those gunners had no arms at all excepting the two eighteen-pounders, yet every one of them was bayoneted at the guns, after having shot down many times their number of the enemy. BUT – had those gunners all been equipped with pistols, there is no doubt in the world that most of them would have been able to make their getaway.

Field Glass versus Telescope

Major H. Hesketh-Pritchard, 40th Pathans and commandant of the First Army Scouting, Observation and Sniping School, often had to demonstrate to his disbelieving students the superiority of the telescope over field glasses. He wrote:

One point that was noticeable was the good focusing power of the German snipers of certain regiments, who shot very well before dawn and towards dark. In the crack Jaeger regiments . . . in which were a large percentage of Forest Guards, this was very noticeable. But for long distance work, and the higher art of observation, the Germans had nothing to touch our Lovat Scouts. This is natural enough when one comes to consider the dark forests in which the German Forest Guards live, and in which they keep alert for the slightest movement of deer or boar. Mostly game is seen within fifty or seventy yards, or even closer, in these sombre shades, and then it is only the twitching of an ear or the movement of an antler . . . Compare the open Scottish hills. It is the telescope against the field glass, and the telescope won every time. In fact, in all the time I was in the trenches, I never saw a German telescope, whereas I saw hundreds and hundreds of pairs of field glasses . . .

Now the best field glass cannot compare with the telescope . . . I had great difficulty in convincing some of our officers, who were used to field glasses, of this fact, but there was by the place at which I was quartered in early days the carved figure of a knight in armour standing on the top of a chateau. This knight had very large spurs, and I would ask student officers to try and count the rowels with their field glasses. They never could do so. I would then hand them one of my beautiful Ross glasses [telescope], and there always came the inevitable question, 'Where can I get a glass like this?'

• Snipers should operate in pairs. Of the two it was not essential that both be expert marksmen. It was often found effective for the best shot to do the shooting while his comrade used a telescope to locate the target and indicate its location quickly and accurately to the firer, with the observer taking over for only brief periods.

• It was often better to locate sniper posts behind the front line, possibly in the support trenches and if possible on rising ground, and to construct several different sniping positions. Such a location would give a far wider and deeper field of view and fire than one in a front-line trench, and the additional range would not affect the accuracy of a good marksman. For obvious reasons of concealment, snipers should not use easily identifiable features such as buildings.

• Once the post was completed the next task was to mark out a range card or diagram with the exact range to all identifiable landmarks in the sniper's arc of responsibility. These could be a bush, a tree stump, a gap in the wire, a different coloured sandbag in the enemy parapet – anything that could be quickly used by the observer as a known reference point from which to describe the position of the target. Provided the sniper did not fire near a location where he thought a target might appear, it was possible to fire some 'ranging shots' to verify distances, particularly if there was random firing by others along the front. These should be made at objects such as a water-filled shell crater or piece of debris rather than an obvious can or bucket left lying on or near the enemy parapet.

• The crucial importance of concealment was always as important, if not more so, than accuracy of shooting, as the slightest movement, dust from firing a shot or the flash of sunlight on a lens could bring a quick response from the enemy. The Germans had the advantage in the early morning on a fine sunny day, as the sun would be shining into the eyes of the British snipers and could easily be reflected off the lens of telescopic sights or binoculars; the reverse was true on a clear evening.

Early German Snipers

By 1916 Major H. Hesketh-Pritchard (see box above) had put British sniper training on a professional basis and British snipers had become a match for their German opposite numbers. However, this had not always been the case. As Major Hesketh-Pritchard explained in his book *Sniping in France*, in 1914 and well into 1915 things were very different.

That the Germans were ready for a sniping campaign is clear enough, for by the end of 1914 there were already 20,000 telescopic sights in the German Army, and their snipers had been trained to use them. To make an accurate estimate of how many victims the Hun snipers claimed at this period is naturally impossible, but the blow which they struck for their side was a heavy one . . .

At this time [1914 to early 1915] the skill of the German sniper had become a byword, and in the early days of trench warfare brave German riflemen used to lie out between the lines, sending their bullets through the head of any officer or man who dared to look over our parapet . . . From the ruined house or the field of decaying roots, sometimes resting their rifles on the bodies of the dead they sent forth a plague of head wounds into the British lines . . . the hardiest soldier turned sick when he saw the effect of the pointed

A German sniper position on the Butte de Vauquois.

German bullet, which was apt to keyhole so that the little hole in the forehead where it entered often became a huge tear, the size of a man's fist, on the other side of the stricken man's head.

At that time in the German Army there was a system of roving snipers; that is, a sniper was given a certain stretch of trench to patrol, usually about half a mile, and it was the duty of sentries along his beat to find and point out targets for him . . .

One point cropped up over and over again [during a German prisoner's interrogation], and that was the ease with which German snipers quite frankly owned that they were able to distinguish between our officers and men in an attack, because, as one naively said, 'the legs of the officers are thinner than the legs of the men' . . . It's no use wearing a Tommy's tunic and a webbing belt, if the tell-tale riding breeches are not replaced by more common-place garments . . .

There was one protection [against sniper fire] which was always sound . . . and that was to teach our men to hang as many rags as possible upon our wire, and whatever else they could in the region of our parapet. These fluttering rags continually caught the Germans' eyes [distracting them, or fooling them into thinking they were firing at men] . . . It is possible that, if the truth were recognized, those simple little rags saved many a life during the course of the war.

• The sniper must be trained for quick snap-shooting. The ability to get off an accurate shot within a few seconds made all the difference in achieving a kill or not, as the average time a target was visible was usually less than ten seconds. During this brief period the sniper had to locate the target from the observer's directions, align on it and fire.

• At ranges over 700 yards it was difficult with the weapons then available to secure a hit, although McBride considered that, if all conditions were favourable and there was time to sight properly, a hit out to 1,000 yards was feasible.

• The role of the sniper pair was not just to shoot enemy but also to gather and record information on any changes to, or movement in, the enemy lines and pass it back to headquarters. McBride recalled his frustration when information was not acted on:

> I have lain, day after day, watching through the big telescope the construction of concrete emplacements, the digging of new trenches and the movements of men far behind the enemy front line. The worst of it was that when we reported a lot of these things, they were not heeded or believed by our superiors.

One of the most famous Canadian snipers was Lance Corporal Henry Louis Norwest, MM and Bar, who served three years on the Western Front with the Canadian 50th Battalion. He was descended from French–Cree (Native American) ancestors and had been a ranch hand and rodeo rider before enlisting in January 1915 under the name of Henry Louie. He was discharged within three months for misbehaving; nevertheless, within eight months he was back in uniform under a new name. A former comrade said:

> Henry Norwest carried out his terrible duty superbly because he believed his special skill gave him no choice but to fulfil his indispensable mission. Our 50th [Battalion] sniper went about his work with passionate dedication and showed complete detachment from everything while he was in the line . . . Yet when we had the rare opportunity to see our comrade at close quarters, we found him pleasant and kindly, quite naturally one of us, and always an inspiration.

Norwest was awarded his first MM for showing 'great bravery, skill and initiative in sniping the enemy after the capture of the Pimple [Vimy Ridge; see Map 28, page 103]. By his activity he saved a great many lives'. The following year he was awarded the Bar. Norwest did well again during the Amiens offensive in August 1918, where he succeeded in destroying several machine-gun posts with his

incredibly accurate shooting. However, on 18 August, while trying to locate another post, he was killed instantly by a German sniper. His personal score was then 115 kills.

Patrolling and Raiding

Patrols and raids are grouped together in this section as the latter were often, and still are in the modern army, a larger version of the former (usually called a 'fighting patrol'). On the Western Front both sides used them to try to dominate no-man's-land and seek information about the enemy. Haig was a strong proponent of vigorous and sustained patrolling, and during the months preceding the Somme offensive GHQ took over control of the overall raiding policy at the front. Battalions were required to institute regular raids as part of this policy of active trench warfare, the aim being to wear down the opposition and confuse him as to the intentions of the BEF, whose patrols and raids outnumbered those mounted by the Germans. The *British Official History* points out that, from 19 December 1915 to 30 May 1916, of the sixty-three British raids forty-seven were successful, compared to only twenty out of thirty-three German raids. The tempo increased as the start of the Somme offensive neared. In the nights preceding 1 July the BEF mounted 310 patrols, with the First Army conducting fourteen raids to the Germans' one, the Second Army seventeen (the I ANZAC Corps seven) to two, and the Third Army twelve to one.

Patrol tasks included ambushing enemy patrols, protecting wiring parties, observing enemy activities, checking on gaps in enemy wire, wire-cutting, locating the position of enemy listening or machine-gun posts. Raids could consist of up to 200 or more men tasked with gaining information by assaulting trenches and bunkers and capturing prisoners for identification and interrogation purposes. Other tasks might include locating and destroying mine shafts or machine-gun posts.

Although active patrolling and raiding was the official policy, it was by no means always a popular one with those carrying it out, as it could, and often did, stir up considerable unwelcome retaliation and at times resulted in substantial loss, both of which could cause resentment. In quiet sectors where a live-and-let-live attitude had developed, patrolling could be perfunctory, with little attempt made to fulfil its task, or with false reports given. Sometimes a patrol might deliberately refrain from firing on an enemy patrol. Tony Ashworth quotes a subaltern called Herbert Read in the 10th Green Howards, who recalled:

We suddenly confronted, round some mound or excavation, a German patrol . . . we were perhaps twenty yards from each other, fully visible. I waved a weary hand, as if to say: what is the use of killing each other? The German officer seemed to understand, and both parties turned and made their way back to their own trenches. Reprehensible conduct no doubt.

Patrolling and raiding prior to a major battle was invariably aggressive. On 4 March 1918 Brigadier General H. C. Jackson, commanding the 175th Brigade, who was shortly after-

A Patrol Report

Lieutenant C. E. Pumphrey, 10th Durham Light Infantry, submitted the following patrol report of a reconnaissance of the STRAND communication trench at 4:55 a.m. on 4 August 1915. It was obviously a meticulously conducted patrol and illustrates the sort of detail required when planning a raid or attack.

About 40 yards on our side of the junction of FLEET STREET and THE STRAND, the Germans have built a barricade, two sandbags thick, with a large sandbag loophole. There was no sentry at this barricade. At all points above our barricade our shells have damaged the trench, and for the last 30 yards before the junction the parapet is mostly gone.

There is a very strong barricade at the junction.

The defences are:
1. The lower barricade already named. Presumably this is manned at night, though I could see no evidence of this.
2. The trench is filled in, 4 yards in length, thus cutting off a traverse which might shelter an attacking party.
3. There is a small loophole on the left side on this barricade. I saw the sentry behind this loophole.
4. Three yards to the right is a large steel plate – possibly 3 ft. by 2 ft. It is so placed that a gun behind it will command the maximum length of trench. Presumably it shelters a machine gun.
5. I did not see any wire – but there may have been some. There is a general mix-up of sandbags etc. which would slightly delay a rush.
6. An intensive bombardment of the junction of THE STRAND and FLEET STREET would be a great help to an attack. From the appearance of the parapet, I suspect a second machine gun at the left corner, covering the open field to the left of the communication trench.

Lieutenant Pumphrey attached a neat diagram to illustrate his report.

wards to lead his men forward blowing a hunting horn, instructed the commanding officers of the 2/10th and 12/10th Londons:

> it must now be realised that identification is absolutely essential for Higher Command. Identifications all along the line at the same time are vital to enable Intelligence to locate units, and find out how the line is held, and how many Divisions there are in reserve. We must therefore . . . take risks that would not be justified at any other time . . . There is much to be said for the big raid – the valuable results being out of all proportion to the increased risks.

On 11 March Lieutenant General Richard Butler, commanding III Corps, issued instructions on the importance of information on the German wire obstacles:

> On most parts of the Corps front, German wire is sufficiently good to necessitate it being cut preparatory to attack. Patrols, by ascertaining constantly whether or no the German wire is intact, can find out whether the enemy are making preparations for surprise attacks . . .
>
> As far as possible, therefore, it should be the aim of every Company Commander in the front line to have German wire examined every night to ascertain whether cut or not. It may be possible in this way to locate a prospective [German] raid and ambush it.
>
> Originals of all patrol reports are carefully scrutinised by my staff, and raid routes entered on a map; reports and map are inspected by me personally every day.

7th Canadian infantry raid, 1915

One of the best examples of a successful raid, illustrating the complexity, detailed planning and preparation required, was carried out by parties of the Canadian 7th Battalion with the 5th Battalion (2nd Canadian Brigade) on the night of 16/17 November 1915 – see Map 79. The following account is based on commanding officer Lieutenant Colonel K. W. Oldham's Operation Order, dated 15 November 1915.

The 2nd Canadian Infantry Brigade was tasked with mounting two raids on the enemy front line some 1,000 yards south of Messines on the night of 15/16 November 1915. However, due to the River Douve still being in flood but subsiding fast, these raids were postponed for twenty-four hours. The 7th Battalion was to attack the German strongpoint immediately south of La Petite Douve Farm and the 5th Battalion the

MAP 79 7TH BATTALION, 2ND CANADIAN BRIGADE RAID, PETITE DOUVE FARM, 17 NOVEMBER 1915

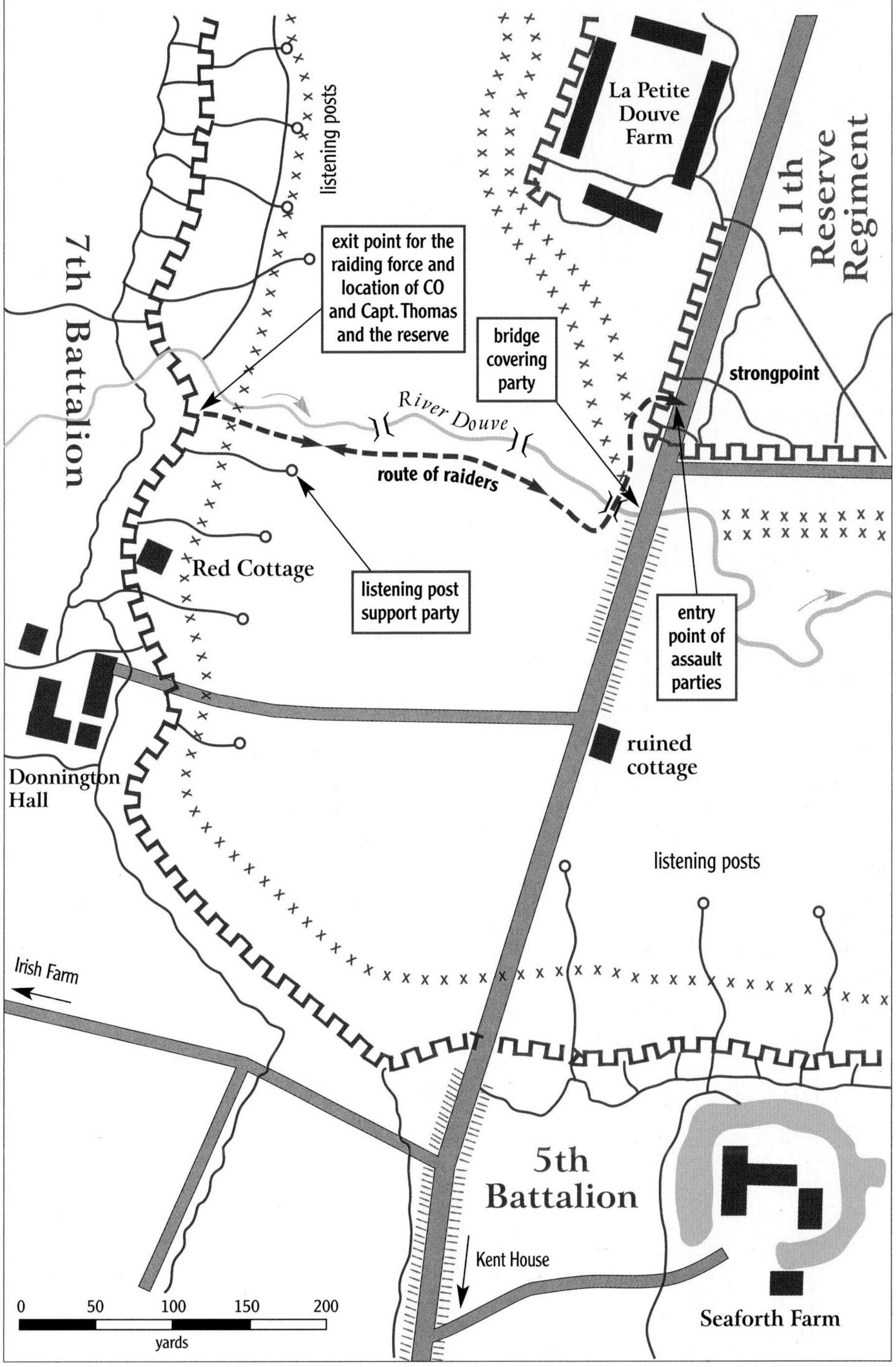

German trenches immediately south of the River Douve, north-east of Seaforth Farm (off map). The latter raid was unsuccessful, as the leading men fell into a previously undetected flooded area that concealed a wire obstacle. Although they were extracted, the enemy were alerted and opened fire, and despite desperate searching no gaps could be found, so the raiders were forced to retire. The following paragraphs all refer to the highly successful 7th Battalion raid.

The objectives of this raid were primarily to capture prisoners for identification and interrogation, but also to cause losses by inducing the enemy to bring up reserves and thus offer good targets for the artillery, while at the same time damaging his morale. The strongpoint south of La Petite Douve Farm was selected as the target because a covered line of approach existed along the right bank of the River Douve (as the floods rapidly decreased it would be only 10 feet wide and

3 or 4 feet deep). This route was to some extent protected, as the ground adjacent to the river was in a slight depression and bordered in places by bushes – the modern photographs of La Petite Douve Farm and the route of the raiders along the stream (see opposite) show that the ground has not changed much apart from the Douve being smaller. This point of attack was in range of the Canadians' trench mortars and rifle grenades and the area had been heavily bombarded by artillery several times before without an attack following: it was thought that this, and the fact that the enemy position was protected by the Douve and a double wire obstacle, might lead the Germans at this point into a false sense of security.

Preparation

Infantry preparation began ten days before the raid for the five officers and seventy-nine NCOs and men who had volunteered. These volunteers were largely from the company in the support trenches and were quartered in a comfortable billet close behind the line; they were excused other duties apart from training for the raid. A facsimile of the German trenches was laid out on a field and over this the attacking party worked by day and night. Bombing attacks, blocking of trenches and the withdrawal were all practised. Bridging ladders (for the river crossing) were constructed, tested and trained with, as were 'tra-

versor' mats for throwing over wire. It was said that the men entered into this constant practice as though they were training for a football match.

Supporting fire played a critical role in the preparation and during the raid itself. On the 15th and 16th, A Battery, Royal Canadian Heavy Artillery, were to cut the wire in front of the battalion's attack. At the same time the 118th Howitzer Battery was to bombard the enemy front line and communication trenches and breach the parapet of the trenches.

At 5:00 p.m. on the 15th, the 14th Trench Mortar Battery registered on La Petite Douve Farm; the next day it bombarded the farm between 4:00 p.m. and 6:00 p.m., targeting the machine-gun position, and between stand-down and midnight it continued to fire at these targets occasionally – it was important to hit the farm hard, as the garrison was in a position to bring flanking fire on to the attackers, and the mortars were to continue firing on the farm while the assault party was in the enemy trenches. Machine guns fired in cooperation with the trench-mortar battery, especially to cover the preparation of the raiding parties by firing on the flanks and targets in the enemy rear. Finally, snipers and fixed-rifle batteries (several rifles permanently fixed to fire on specific targets) were to increase their fire and endeavour to prevent the enemy using his

communication trenches. From stand-down, firing at a slow rate was to be employed to cover the noises made during the final preparations for the advance.

No man would wear a greatcoat or gumboots and no water bottles or haversacks would be taken. All ranks in the assault party were to wear black veiling masks, and means of identification such as pay books, identity discs, badges, letters, anything liable to give away information, were removed by all ranks. Electric pocket torches were attached to the rifles of bayonet men.

During the afternoon of the 16th a final daylight reconnaissance by two men was to be made along the bank of the Douve to discover if the wire had been effectively cut and the trench parapets broken down. After dark the reconnaissance officer would take out a patrol to ascertain the width of the Douve at the point to be crossed, the damage done to the wire and the most practical route through it, and to report any other obstacles that might delay progress.

Organization

• **Command** This rested with Captain L. J. Thomas, although he remained in the forward Canadian trench during the raid with telephone communications to the assault party to control the situation as it developed and to deal with the unexpected once the attack started.

Method Used by Bombing Party to Clear Sections of Trench (not to scale)

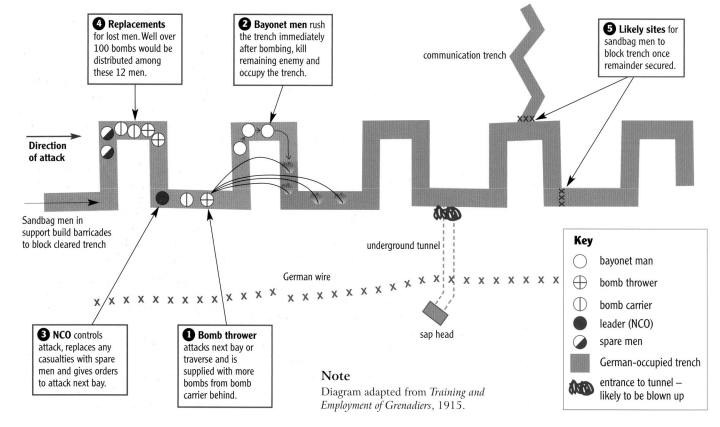

❹ Replacements for lost men. Well over 100 bombs would be distributed among these 12 men.

❷ Bayonet men rush the trench immediately after bombing, kill remaining enemy and occupy the trench.

communication trench

❺ Likely sites for sandbag men to block trench once remainder secured.

Direction of attack

Sandbag men in support build barricades to block cleared trench

underground tunnel

German wire

sap head

❸ NCO controls attack, replaces any casualties with spare men and gives orders to attack next bay.

❶ Bomb thrower attacks next bay or traverse and is supplied with more bombs from bomb carrier behind.

Note

Diagram adapted from *Training and Employment of Grenadiers*, 1915.

Key

○ bayonet man
⊕ bomb thrower
◍ bomb carrier
● leader (NCO)
◐ spare men
▬ German-occupied trench
🌀 entrance to tunnel – likely to be blown up

e stream followed by e successful left acking party to proach the German sition, seen from the ge of their defensive sition, looking west.

Route of Canadian raiding party

Petite Douve Farm and the trench system to its south were heavily defended by the Germans, forming a salient that jutted out towards the Canadian line.

German strongpoint

Point at which Canadians enter German position

German trenches

- **Scouts/bridging/wire-cutting party** One officer (Lieutenant W. Holmes), four NCOs and six men were tasked with scouting the position first, then positioning the bridges and carrying out any necessary wire-cutting – the wire-cutters were armed with revolvers.
- **Assault party** This consisted of two bombing and blocking parities (left and right) and the trench rifle party, all under the overall command of Lieutenant R. H. Wrightson. The left bombing and blocking party was composed of an officer (name unknown), 2 bayonet men, 2 throwers (of bombs), 2 carriers (of bombs), a spare bomber, 4 wire men each with 20 bombs in sandbags and 2 shovel men also with 20 bombs each but with revolvers not rifles – total 1 officer and 13 men. The right bombing and blocking party consisted of an officer (name unknown) with the same personnel, except there were 3 bayonet men instead of 2 but only 2 wire men with bombs – total 1 officer and 12 men. The other element of the assault party was the trench rifle party. This was composed of Lieutenant Wrightson, 5 riflemen, a telephonist with an instrument, a linesman and 2 stretcher-bearers – total 1 officer and 9 men. It was the assault group that actually attacked the enemy trenches and bombed their way along them, blocked off counter-attacks and captured the prisoners – for the general tactics employed for trench clearing, see the diagram opposite.
- **Bridge-covering parties** These consisted of a right and left party each of three riflemen positioned on the left bank of the Douve to keep down enemy fire from La Petite Douve Farm, take charge of prisoners brought back by the scouts and send them to the listening-post support party. They were to hold their position until the entire assault party had withdrawn.
- **Listening-post support party** An NCO and ten men, plus a telephonist with instrument and a linesman – in total thirteen men. Their task was to place a bridge over the

Douve, position themselves on the left bank and be prepared to reinforce the assault party if required, take charge of the prisoners and escort them back to Canadian lines, then assist with the removal of any wounded.

- **Trench reserve party** This party, which remained in the front-line trench with Captain Thomas, consisted of two NCOs and twenty men.
- **Withdrawal** The assault party would be withdrawn from the enemy trenches not later than twenty minutes after the assault had been delivered, or before at the discretion of Lieutenant Wrightson. There were two signals for withdrawal: one was two long blasts followed by three short ones repeated several times; the other was a succession of red Very lights fired from the point of entry – both would be used, but one was sufficient for the withdrawal to start. If no signal was made by the expiry of twenty minutes, the officers in charge of the bombing and trench parties were at once to withdraw independently. When withdrawal was complete the artillery fire would immediately revert from firing on the German rear trenches to those in the front line.
- **Administration** Communications would be by telephone between Captain Thomas (along with the commanding officer, who was located with Thomas during the operation) back to battalion headquarters and forward to the officer commanding the assault party and the listening-post support party. An aid post was to be established at Irish Farm and a dressing station at Kent House. A reserve of bombs was dumped at the front-line trench and listening post to be sent forward in sacks of twenty as required. During the preparatory bombardment all men from the front-line trenches except sentries, signallers and machine-gunners would be withdrawn. They would return for stand-to but again withdraw during the assault – this was to avoid the expected enemy counter-bombardment.

The raid

On 16 November the preparatory fire plan was implemented, starting at 9:00 a.m., and during the early part of the night slow rifle fire to the flanks was commenced to conceal the noise of the scouts cutting wire and bridging. At 4:00 p.m. the scouts went out to examine the artillery's wire-cutting efforts, only to discover that the trees along the Douve had interfered with the bursting of many shells so that the wire was largely uncut. They reported that this wire could not be crossed with 'traversor' mats and should be cut by hand.

Early in the night the bridging parties of four men to each placed the bridges in position, working when the moon was clouded over. As each bridge weighed 60 lb this was a slow and difficult task, but all three bridges were in position by 2:00 a.m.

Meanwhile, four men started their cutting task at about 9:15 p.m., working steadily when the moon was obscured, lying motionless when it was not, until 11:45 p.m. Their task was extremely perilous and difficult, made worse by the bitterly cold night with a hoar frost on the ground, as they were working within 30 yards of the enemy position. Wearing leather gloves and lying on their stomachs, one man carefully cut the strands while another held the ends and slowly moved them aside. When finished they had made two diagonal lanes through the wire.

The other parties, led by scouts, left the Canadian front line at the following times:

Left bombing and blocking party	1:45 a.m.
Right bombing and blocking party	2:00 a.m.
Bridge-covering parties	2:05 a.m.
Trench rifle party	2:08 a.m.
Listening-post support party	2:15 a.m.

They moved along the right bank of the Douve, crossing to the left bank over the bridge nearest the German lines and went quickly through the lanes cut in the wire.

An Enemy Raid Repulsed

Lieutenant Colonel F. N. Butler, commanding the 1st Battalion, Bedfordshire Regiment, submitted the following report to 15th Brigade Headquarters on 17 February 1917.

About 4.45 a.m. the enemy managed to enter our lines between islands 30 and 28, both garrisoned by Lewis guns. The distance between these two islands is about 150 yards. The night was very dark and the ground in NO MAN'S LAND is very broken and affords good concealment.

The garrison at 30a were first alarmed by the enemy bombing our wire to the right. They put up lights and saw a party of about 30–40 Germans in file getting through our wire between 30a and 30b. (The 30b is not garrisoned.) They opened fire with their gun and most of the enemy retired. However, an officer and about six determined men rushed forward and got through the wire. They bombed toward 30a island. The officer was killed close to this island and the remainder of this party proceeded between 32 Strong Point and COVER TRENCH and entered our breastwork at

about Post 33 from behind. Meanwhile the whole Company had stood to and Lieut. G de C. MILLIAS organised a bombing party and kept them out of the Strong Point. Sergeant GROOM was killed here. At the same time 2nd Lieut. A. A. CREASEY mounted a Lewis gun at the junction of SHETLAND ROAD and COVER TRENCH and so pinned the enemy in the straight piece of breastwork between 32 and 34. Two Germans were killed by this fire and the remainder wounded. The wounded managed to scramble over the parapet and get away . . .

CASUALTIES
ENEMY. 1 Officer, 3 Other Ranks (confirmed)
OUR OWN. 1 Sergeant killed.

Of the enemy casualties one Officer and two Other Ranks were left in our hands, and several were known to have been wounded.

The conduct of 2nd Lieut. A.A. CREASY and Lieut. G de C. MILLAIS deserve mention. It was entirely due to their alertness, personal courage and initiative that a big enemy raid was foiled.

At 2:32 a.m. the assault parties, led by their officers, jumped into the enemy trench almost on to a German sentry, who was taking shelter from a shower of rain that had just started. He was instantly shot by the officer of the right party, while the officer of the left shot three more and then bombed down the trench for three bays until joined by his party. Thereafter they pulled or bombed the enemy out of his dugouts or drove them into communication trenches. After shooting the first man the officer of the right party seized the next German, took his rifle and with it clubbed a third, after which his party joined him and they began bombing down the trench. This party captured eight of the twelve prisoners taken.

Within two minutes of jumping into the trench telephone communications had been established and the message 'In and all going well' was passed to the commanding officer. The blocking parties carried out their tasks in the front and communication trenches while the trench rifle party covered them to check

any local counter-attacks. The assault had secured about 40 yards of trench. Meanwhile, the prisoners had been passed back over the parapet to the scouts. The whole operation went exceptionally well and the whistle signal for withdrawal was given just nineteen minutes after entering the enemy trench. The assault party withdrew, taking with them twelve prisoners and leaving behind at least thirty Germans dead or wounded. They returned by the same route, taking up all bridges but one (recovered the next night) and also the spare bombs. Canadian casualties amounted to one man killed accidentally by another man firing as he stumbled and one slightly wounded.

The German resistance was negligible: they were caught by surprise and no officers were seen, so leadership was poor and no initiative shown. It was forty minutes after the retirement before any counter-attack was organized and this was halted by artillery fire. The Germans had failed to counter the raid due to lack of active patrolling, lack of

early warning from listening posts, sentries too few and not alert, absence of officers and lack of leadership by NCOs.

German raids

The Germans patrolled and conducted raids for the same reasons and using almost identical techniques to other nations. They paid particular attention to ambushing Allied wiring parties that had come out at night to repair gaps created by artillery or trench-mortar fire. Like their opponents, they relied mostly on bombs and side arms, bayonets and knives or clubs for the close-quarter fighting that these raids invariably involved. Like the British, their patrols were usually composed of volunteers led by an officer. Raids penetrating behind enemy lines were not supposed to spend more than fifteen minutes completing their task and the whole operation, including withdrawal, was supported by artillery, mortars and machine guns. Engineers sometimes accompanied raids to blow up dugouts or mine shafts.

Trench-warfare Tactics

The tactical training of the old British Army involved infantry platoons advancing in open order in short rushes covered by the fire of others, with guns often firing over open sights on the flanks. Having built up a strong firing line and won the firefight, the attackers would assault the enemy position with fixed bayonets. The British soldier was taught to choose suitable cover, estimate ranges and then shoot fast and straight, although the ultimate object was always to close with the enemy.

These tactics were still considered sound in the early months of the war on the

Western Front. The German attempts to advance in dense formations against the British rapid rifle fire resulted in disastrous repulse, although for the British the Battles of Mons and Le Cateau were largely defensive ones that did not give commanders experience of the effectiveness of employing official offensive tactics. However, once the fighting had stagnated, with both sides dug in, the British were initially seriously disadvantaged by the small number of machine guns in infantry battalions as well as the lack of coordination in their fire, as opposed to the Germans who were better

equipped in this respect. It was a similar case with artillery.

The problem was compounded by the Allies having to take the strategic and therefore tactical offensive, as there was no alternative if the German invaders were to be driven from occupied territory. Until mid-1918 the fighting on the Western Front became a bloody struggle to overcome the inherent technological advantages given to the defenders in strong positions over attackers desperately trying to cross no-man's-land without being destroyed in the process. This was eventually achieved,

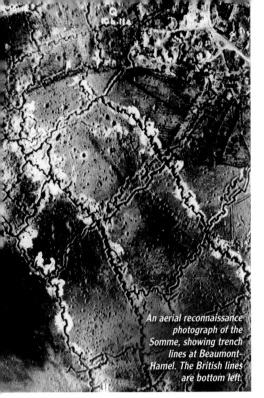

An aerial reconnaissance photograph of the Somme, showing trench lines at Beaumont-Hamel. The British lines are bottom left.

although the learning curve was steep and long, with countless thousands of lives lost as a result of having to endeavour to breach the ever-thickening defensive zones. By early 1915 it had developed into what might be described as the longest and most costly siege operation of all time.

During 1915 not only had the front solidified but also British pre-war regulars were being replaced by large numbers of the new Kitchener armies and territorials, and the overall standard of musketry and training was being rapidly diluted. In that year the BEF began to distribute tactical manuals (many copied from the French) as they sought to establish a tactical doctrine to be taught at the various tactical and weapon training schools that were being set up. The comparatively small battles of 1915, such as Neuve Chapelle, Festubert, Aubers Ridge and Loos, were largely experimental in terms of finding a successful tactical formula that combined infantry, artillery, gas, trench mortars, and Vickers and Lewis guns in a coordinated assault that could overcome the problems of a well-dug-in defender protected by wire and supported by machine guns and artillery.

At Loos (see Map 14, page 48) the 15th Scottish Division's successful advance of at least 2 miles into the enemy defences was described as a scene resembling 'nothing so much as a cross-country race . . . Men ran as if for a prize.' A breakthrough had almost been achieved, but the opportunity was missed due to heavy losses, counter-attacks and British reserves being too far in the rear to intervene quickly. Nevertheless, the battle seemed to vindicate the tactics of infantry attacking in successive linear waves, advancing by rushes or by walking steadily forward under covering artillery fire, and after heavy bombardments by the guns to cut wire and destroy or demoralize the enemy. These tactics involved the waves leapfrogging through those ahead to continue the momentum of the attack as necessary. At Loos the leading brigade of the 9th Scottish Division attacked and took the Hohenzollern Redoubt, advancing with two brigades in line, each with two battalions in front and each battalion in three waves. These two battalions were followed by two more, also in three waves, ready to leapfrog through. The third brigade followed in reserve. This doctrine of successive waves in the assault had been well established by the end of 1915 and was to remain so, with slight variations, for much of the war – at least until the advent of large-scale tank attacks and the more mobile warfare of the final hundred days. It was the basis of the attack on the Somme on 1 July 1916.

As with virtually all battles on the Western Front, attackers had to overcome the first obstacle – the wire in front of the enemy position. By July 1916 the Germans had enjoyed about eighteen months of comparative peace in the Somme sector and they had taken full advantage of this to construct strong defences. The *British Official History* described the German position astride the Somme as follows:

> Altogether, from its natural position and the skill with which the defences had been developed in 18 months' work, the sector was of extraordinary strength, requiring all the art of the gunner and of the engineer to dislocate and destroy its strongpoints and obstacles before there could be any hope of a successful infantry assault.

In the week-long preparatory bombardment some 500,000 shells rained down on the German positions.

Before looking at the tactics employed by the British infantry to overcome these defences, it is revealing to look again briefly at what the Germans had prepared for them – in particular, as an example, the defences opposite the 34th Division on 1 July (see Map 42, page 208). This division faced an enemy front-line trench some 2,000 yards long, but with a significant salient backed by the heavily defended La Boiselle village, which was by then just piles of rubble but with deep enemy bunkers and machine-gun posts still occupied. In the centre was the Schawben Höhe, a complex strongpoint of trenches and bunkers, and on the right the Sausage Redoubt. The distance of this front line from the British trenches varied from less than 100 yards opposite the La Boiselle salient to 750 yards on the right in Mash Valley.

From 800 to 1,000 yards to the rear was what the Germans called the first intermediate line (the line of the first objective of the 34th Division attack), running north-west from Bailiff Wood. This line was as strong and heavily wired as the front line. Communication trenches led back to the Germans' second intermediate line fronting the fortified village of Contalmaison and then running north-west to Pozières (the 34th Division's second objective). Between these three lines were numerous machine-gun posts and small strongpoints such as Peak and Bailiff Woods. Further back was another line, in places over 2,000 yards to the rear, although this was incomplete at the start of the Somme battle (the 34th Division's third objective was to seize a line about 500–1,000 yards short of this final German position). The 34th Division thus faced a series of strong lines bolstered by several major redoubts and strongpoints, as well as numerous smaller ones, most reinforced with concrete.

By July 1916 the Germans had vastly strengthened their wire defences. The original entanglements of 5–10 yards wide had now grown to two massive belts each about 30 yards broad and 15 yards apart. These masses of wire were interlaced with iron stakes and

German troops just visible behind wire defences in a front-line trench.

trestles 3–5 feet high, making an impenetrable barrier except for the small gaps left for their own patrols. The so-called front line, from being a single trench, had become in some places three lines of trenches about 100–150 yards apart. The first was for sentry groups, the second for the front trench garrison and the third for local support troops. Concrete recesses had been dug deep into the parapet from which sentries could observe either directly, or more often with a periscope. The dugouts had been tunnelled to a depth of 20–30 feet and at intervals of about 50 yards, each capable of sheltering some twenty-five men during a bombardment.

The 34th Division's assault was to be made in successive waves by the full weight of the twelve infantry battalions. It was to attack in four 'columns', each column being three battalions deep on a frontage of 400 yards. Between the third and fourth columns opposite La Boiselle there was to be a gap. This key part of the salient was not to be attacked directly, the two left columns passing on either side. The division formed up to

advance from the trenches on Tara Hill in the formation shown in the diagrams below.

There is not space here to describe in detail the preliminary bombardment or the artillery and other support provided to the attacking infantry of the 34th Division on 1 July. It is sufficient to note that creeping barrages had yet to be refined, and the gunner's basic plan was to fire a series of eight timed lifts. The following paragraphs will be limited to explaining the intended tactics of these attacking battalions as being typical of those current at that time (see Map 42).

The divisional plan involved the taking of three objectives, with the leading two brigades securing the first and second (the third German trench line on Map 42). These brigades were to consolidate on this line while the third reserve brigade, which had been following up, leapfrogged through to take Contalmaison and secure a line running north from the east of the village. The first objective was to be taken by 8:18 a.m. (forty-eight minutes after zero) and the second by 8:58 a.m. The 103rd Brigade was to take the

third objective, including Contalmaison, by 10:10 a.m. The division was to advance and fight its way through over 3,000 yards of well-developed enemy defences in a matter of two hours and forty-eight minutes. The tactical formation for the advance is shown in the diagrams below, with the divisional infantry advance described in the *British Official History* as:

> the whole of the infantry of the division, except the head of the second column, rose as one man, the front line going 'over the top' and the rear lines moving down the slopes of Tara-Usna ridge, even the reserve 103rd Brigade leaving their trenches . . .

The leapfrogging tactics used by divisional command to push through to the final objective was also used within brigades. In the 101st Brigade, for example, the two leading battalions, the 15th Royal Scots and 10th Lincolns, were to secure as their objective the Scots Redoubt and the German trench line running north from it (second German line on Map 42), and the 16th

34th Division Attacking Formations, 1 July 1916 (not to scale)

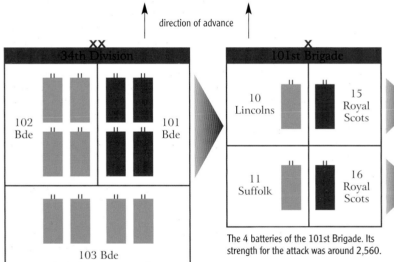

The division formed in 4 columns each of 3 battalions. It would have sent some 8,700 men into the attack.

The 4 batteries of the 101st Brigade. Its strength for the attack was around 2,560.

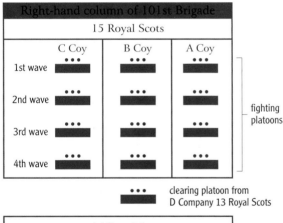

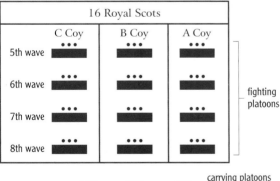

Each of these battalions put around 650 all ranks into the attack with an average strength in the platoons of 49 men. Each of the attacking battalions occupied about 400 yards of frontage, giving about a yard between each with 120 men in a company – slightly more in practice, as not every member of a platoon would be in one long line. According to the 11th Suffolks' Operation Order, waves would be about 150 yards behind each other.

The Battle of Albert: the 103rd (Tyneside Irish) Brigade, 34th Division, advancing from the Tara-Usna Line to attack La Boisselle on the morning of 1 July 1916.

Royal Scots and 11th Suffolks would leapfrog through to take the Bailiff Wood line (the divisional first objective).

The Suffolks' battalion operation order dated 26 June 1916 covers twelve closely typed pages of A4 paper, including seven appendices detailing matters such as communications, bombing, use and deployment of Lewis guns, ammunition supply, the carrying platoons and the action of the attacking waves if held up. The basic idea was that if a leading wave were held up, then those following should push forward to reinforce and support it. The Suffolks' orders state:

> Should an assaulting battalion fail to win its allotted objective, waves of C and D battalions [in this case 16th Royal Scots and 11th Suffolks], and finally if necessary, waves of the Divisional Reserve [103rd Brigade] must be pushed forward without hesitation, so as to break down the enemy's resistance.

The success of this method of attack was, other things being equal, dependent on the infantry keeping up with the timed lifts of the supporting barrage. Changing the artillery timings at the last moment was invariably difficult due to unreliable communication between the leading infantry and the guns, and the time needed to make changes. To lose the barrage was fatal, and to lessen the chances of this happening at the outset the leading two waves of the 15th Royal Scots and 10th Lincolns were ordered to creep forward into no-man's-land under cover of the barrage, ready to advance at zero hour.

The attacking riflemen went over the top carrying two extra bandoliers of ammunition, two Mills bombs, four sandbags, a pick or shovel, gas helmets but no large packs. Battalion bombers, moving with the carrying company, were to carry a bucket with twenty-four bombs each. The Suffolks had one company bombing party deployed on the right flank of the third wave and another company's on the left flank. The carrying companies were laden down with extra ammunition and stores that would be vital during the consolidation phase – they were not expected to join in the fighting for the objective. The Suffolks' orders for this company were:

3 Platoons will carry stores as follows:
10 men each 24 bombs in sandbags.
10 men each one coil of wire and one pick.
4 men each one coil of wire and one maul.
6 men each three large angle irons and 2 sandbags.
3 men 2,000 rounds of S.A.A. in sandbags divided between them.
4 men each 80 sandbags.
1 Platoon will carry Stokes [mortar] ammunition as follows:

30 men will carry Stokes ammunition (1 carrier to 2 men).
Attached to the Carrying Company will be the following:
Bn. Bombers
Bn. Police
Reserve Lewis Gunners carrying Lewis Gun S.A.A.

As the reader will be aware, the British assault on 1 July was, with one or two comparatively minor exceptions, a major disaster. The *British Official History* describes the 34th Division's failure succinctly:

> In a matter of ten minutes some 80 per cent of the men in the leading battalions were casualties; for directly the artillery barrage lifted off the German front line, an ever-increasing number of machine guns – mostly in the rear of the front line, well-sited and hidden, and untouched by the bombardment – came into action, sweeping No Man's Land, which was 200–800 yards wide, and the front slopes of the Tara-Usna ridge. There was no surprise: the Germans were ready. Warned by [an] order that had been overheard, and well drilled at manning the parapet, they came up out of their deep dug-outs as if by magic directly the barrage moved, and established a rough firing line before the British had got across No Man's Land.

The crucial lesson learned by the British during the long months of the slugging match that was the Somme after the first day was that if the infantry lost the barrage it lost the attack. Nothing could replace the need for the most meticulous preparation between these two arms, with every effort made to achieve tactical surprise. There was a rethink of both infantry assault tactics and supporting artillery techniques – notably the refinement and adoption of the creeping barrage as the best way of enabling the infantry to win the race for the parapet.

However, it was not just the British that had suffered heavily and needed to learn lessons. The Germans regarded the severity of the Somme battles as having cost the army losses from which it never fully recovered, particularly in experienced officers, NCOs and men. A number of their regimental histories have chapters entitled 'The Hell on the Somme' and attribute their losses to the rigid tactical orders issued by Falkenhayn that 'not a foot's breadth of ground must be voluntarily abandoned. Only over our bodies may the enemy advance.' The history of the 16th Bavarian Regiment recorded that the tragedy of the Somme battle 'was that the best soldiers, the stoutest-hearted men were lost; their numbers were replaceable, their

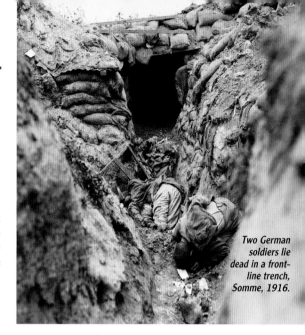

Two German soldiers lie dead in a front-line trench, Somme, 1916.

spiritual worth never could be'. Captain von Hentig, a staff officer of the Guard Reserve Division, wrote, 'The Somme was the muddy grave of the German field army, and of the faith in the infallibility of the German leading [High Command].' Thus both sides used the closing weeks of 1916 and the opening months of 1917 to recoup, reorganize and rethink. The result was a new tactical concept for both the attacking British and the defending Germans.

For 1917 the basic change for British tactics within units was that, although leapfrogging waves through was still legitimate tactics, a new technique saw the leading wave going as deep as the unit's final objective. Another unit or formation could then move through to another series of objectives. Leapfrogging thus tended to be between units rather than within them. The first wave would go for the last objective. With the first line moving close to a creeping barrage, and the barrage moving at the speed of the infantry (not easy to achieve), there would be no fighting until the barrage had lifted from the relevant part of the German line, because the defenders could not emerge while being shelled – thus ensuring the attackers got to the parapet first. It meant that the defenders could not emerge from their dugouts until the attackers, following perhaps only 40 yards behind the barrage, had overrun their position.

By 1917–18 this worked most of the time, the shining example being the initial British attack at Arras – see below. However, the further into an enemy position an attack went, the greater the risk of timings getting out of kilter and of the infantry losing the barrage and with it the battle – hence the importance now attached to pausing on phase lines, or having a barrage 'stand' on a line while the next attacking unit caught up. The actual fighting on the objective was to be done by the 'moppers-up'. These needed to be 'front-loaded' so that captured ground would be

A Battalion Formed Up to Attack Four Successive Objectives, *c.*1917

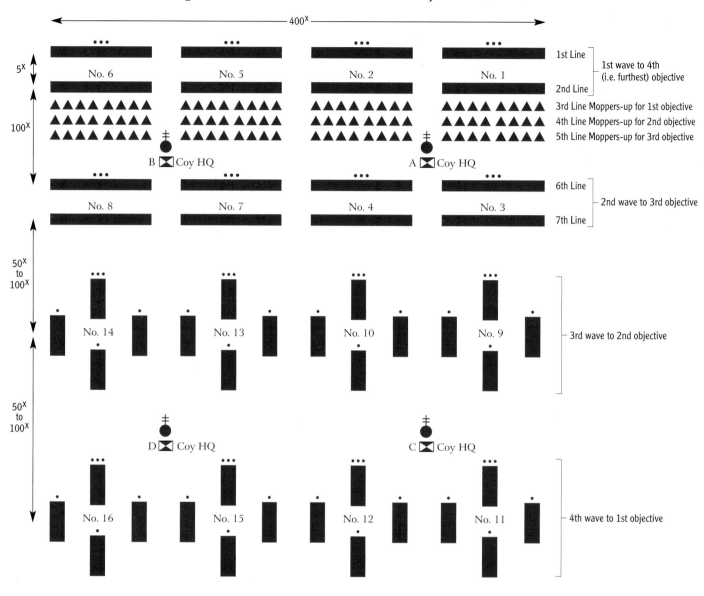

	1st Line	1st wave to 4th (i.e. furthest) objective
No. 6 / No. 5 / No. 2 / No. 1	2nd Line	

3rd Line Moppers-up for 1st objective
4th Line Moppers-up for 2nd objective
5th Line Moppers-up for 3rd objective

B Coy HQ   A Coy HQ

No. 8 / No. 7 / No. 4 / No. 3 — 6th Line / 7th Line — 2nd wave to 3rd objective

No. 14 / No. 13 / No. 10 / No. 9 — 3rd wave to 2nd objective

D Coy HQ   C Coy HQ

No. 16 / No. 15 / No. 12 / No. 11 — 4th wave to 1st objective

Measurements: 400ˣ (top width), 5ˣ, 100ˣ, 50ˣ to 100ˣ

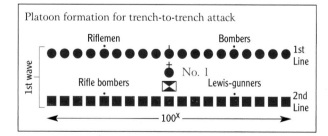

Platoon formation for trench-to-trench attack

Riflemen — Bombers — 1st Line
No. 1
Rifle bombers — Lewis-gunners — 2nd Line
1st wave
100ˣ

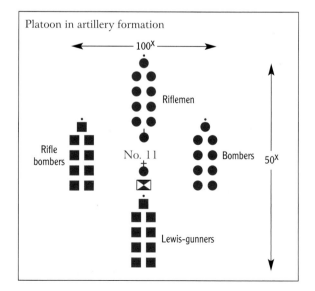

Platoon in artillery formation

100ˣ

Riflemen

Rifle bombers   No. 11   Bombers

Lewis-gunners

50ˣ

Notes
• This battalion moves in four waves, each direct to its objective close behind a creeping barrage, and is distributed in depth on attaining them.
• C and D Companies start the advance in 'artillery formation' but deploy into lines for the final assault.
• This battalion has platoons of 4 officers and 40 men, but if seriously understrength the moppers-up would be found from another battalion.

Key

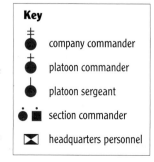

‡ company commander

• platoon commander

| platoon sergeant

•■ section commander

⊠ headquarters personnel

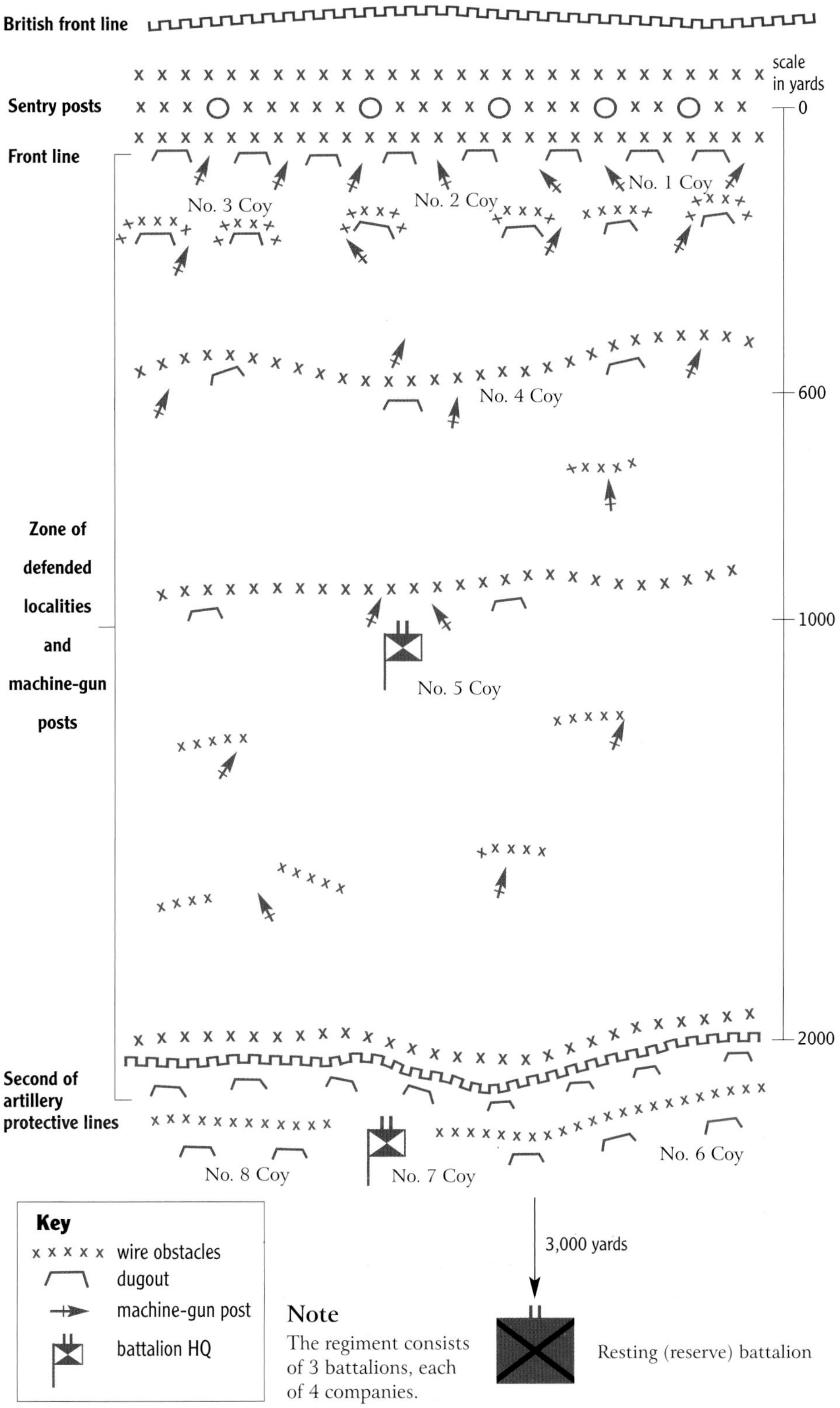

saturated with troops immediately after the first assault wave had passed over on its way to its objective – any lull would be fatal (see diagram opposite). Thus the assault waves and moppers-up had fundamentally different tasks. The former cleared fire trenches and dugouts; the latter manned captured trenches and dealt with any local counter-attacks.

The British set-piece attack at Arras on 9 April 1917 tested the BEF's new tactics for both artillery and infantry against the new German defensive doctrine set out in their *Conduct of the Defensive Battle*, issued to all divisions in early December 1916. It stated that the lines of trenches should be replaced by a zone of fortified localities – machine-gun posts and 'island' infantry positions each prepared for all-round defence (when the British later adopted these positions they called them 'birdcages'). These strong-points, occupied by the regiments of the front-line divisions, were to be spread over an area 1,200–2,000 yards deep, reaching back to the second, or artillery, protective line. Near this second line were to be the *Eingriff* divisions – immediate counter-attack divisions ready to throw back the enemy if they breached the frontal zone.

In setting out this new doctrine, General Ludendorff intended the garrisons of this forward zone to have freedom of movement. Writing in the forward to the new textbook he said, 'The infantryman will no longer have to say to himself, "Here I stay and here I die": he will have the right to give ground to a certain extent within the defence zone if hard pressed.' However, such teaching aroused powerful opposition from men like General Falkenhayn, who considered that on the modern battlefield such instructions to the young, half-trained troops that were replacing the dreadful losses of the Somme battles would lead to a fatal slackening of discipline. Within a month the opposition was sufficiently strong to compel Ludendorff to withdraw the flexibility given to the front-zone infantry. In January 1917 the German infantry training manual stated:

The final occupation of the front zone will depend on the success of the counter-attacks, but until they arrive every man of its garrison and the crew of every machine-gun must hold his post and stand his ground even though surrounded.

The right to give ground had been abolished – 'Here I stay and here I die' was to remain the motto of the frontal-zone defenders. Isolated garrisons were expected to hold out for hours as attacking waves swept past and beyond them, until the attackers were eventually forced back by the counter-attack divisions. These *Eingriff* divisions were to be

positioned close up behind the front zone whenever a large offensive seemed imminent. Such was the scheme of the German forward zone for the Battle of Arras in April 1917 – see the diagram above.

A key element of this new German defensive doctrine was the role given to the forward

battalion commanders. When a regiment went into a ground-holding role alongside the other two regiments in the division, its three battalions assumed differing tasks. The forwardmost battalion commander was termed the *Kampftruppenkommandeur* (commander of forward troops) or KTK; commanding the

Defence Layout of German Regiment, April 1917

Key
x x x x x wire obstacles
⌐\ dugout
→ machine-gun post
battalion HQ

Note
The regiment consists of 3 battalions, each of 4 companies.

Resting (reserve) battalion

second supporting battalion in the next zone some 600–800 yards to the rear was the *Bereitschaftstruppenkommandeur* (commander of supporting troops) or BTK. The third or reserve battalion occupied the rear line under the command of the *Reservetruppenkommandeur* (reserve troop commander) or RTK.

It was the KTK officer who held the critical appointment (and he was sometimes only a captain). With a gunnery officer and communications, he was located in a concrete dugout between the main defensive line and the gun lines and had total control over all units that came forward into his sector during the battle. The supporting troops close behind were at his disposal; he decided when to use them, and when they came forward he commanded them. Similarly, although the regimental commander decided the moment to use the reserve battalion when it went forward, it came under the KTK's command – any written orders sent back by the KTK to an officer his senior would be obeyed, as in the German Army it was invariably the appointment rather than the rank that decided seniority. Once additional units came within his jurisdiction the KTK became responsible for all their casualty and resupply arrangements – putting huge responsibility on an officer who could be commanding numbers way above normal for his rank.

The new tactics of both the German and British armies were tested at the Battle of Arras, which started on Easter Monday, 9 April 1917 and is more accurately called the first Battle of the Scarpe. It was a small part of what was the most formidable and, as it turned out, the most successful British offensive hitherto launched. Fourteen divisions of the First and Third Armies were lined up for the attack. In the Third Army area of 20 square miles (a 10-mile frontage 2 miles deep) some 200,000 troops were amassed, with another 150,000 in the rear. Over 1,700 artillery pieces provided the preparatory

bombardment that started on 5 April and continued up to Z-day, 9 April. The number of pieces engaged during the actual attack by the Third Army and the Canadian Corps rose to over 2,000. The main task of the 18-pounders, along with trench mortars, was to breach the massive belts of wire within their range, and for the former to provide creeping barrages during the attack. The 4.5-inch howitzers were to assist the 18-pounders and the 6-inch howitzers in bombarding the second and third German positions, while the heavier pieces attacked such targets as billets, light railways, railheads, supply depots and headquarters.

Overall the attack on the 9th was an outstanding success, with the most successful and longest advance being made by the 9th and 4th Divisions of XVII Corps (see Map 80). By evening the Third Army had taken over 5,000 prisoners and 36 guns – numbers that rose to over 7,000 and 112 respectively by 12 April. The three days 9–11 April cost the Third and First Armies a combined total of approximately 13,000 casualties, or only about a quarter of the 57,000 lost by the same number of attacking divisions on just the first day of the Somme.

The three major lessons learned by the British on the opening day at Arras were, first, the effectiveness of a carefully planned creeping barrage in enabling the infantry to arrive on an enemy parapet before the defenders; second, the importance of counter-battery fire (some 80 per cent of German heavy artillery was neutralized); and third (but not for the first time), the unreliability of preparatory bombardments in breaching the wire effectively in enough areas. A soldier in the 4th South African Infantry later wrote of the opening barrage:

> These 18-pounder shells were not more than three feet above our heads [not surprising as they were landing only

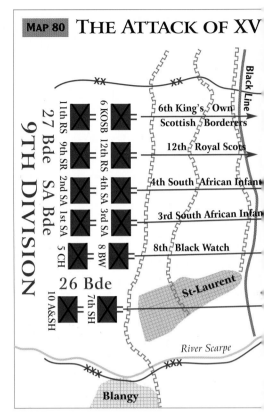

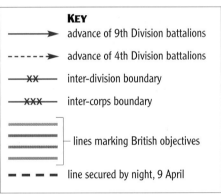

KEY

advance of 9th Division battalions

advance of 4th Division battalions

inter-division boundary

inter-corps boundary

lines marking British objectives

line secured by night, 9 April

40–50 yards in front of him], and yet I never saw a person duck on that account, such was our confidence in the artillery . . . The [creeping] barrage was like a big brother to us, metaphorically taking us by the hand.

With regard to the German wire, Brigadier General F. S. Dawson, commanding the South African Brigade, wrote of the attack on the Brown Line:

> The position was an exceedingly strong one and when the infantry arrived at the wire, they found it uncut by our artillery and so thick that they could not cut it. They had to stop and look about for the passages which the Germans used and eventually found two, one for each regiment. If the position had been held [the Germans had fled or surrendered] those two regiments [1st and 2nd South African Infantry] would have been wiped out.

A rare photo of the moment of attack: an officer of the 9th Battalion, the Cameronians (Scottish Rifles), leads the way out of a sap at Arras, 11 April 1917.

ORPS, 9TH (SCOTTISH) AND 4TH DIVISIONS, ARRAS, 9 APRIL 1917

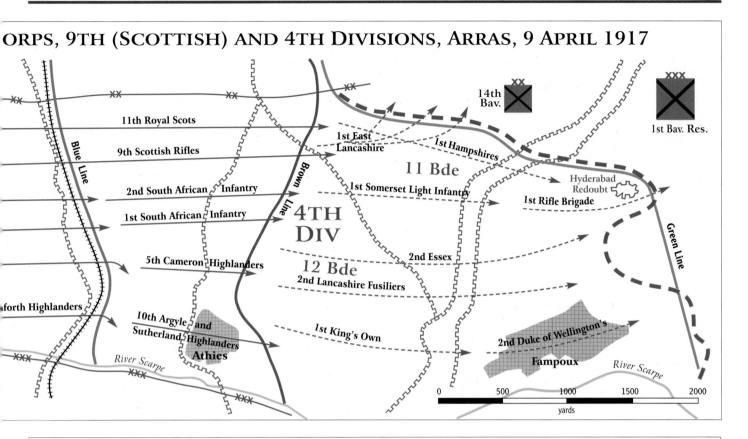

Notes for Map 80

• This map shows the attack of, first, the 9th (Scottish) Division and then that of the 4th Division on the deep German defensive zone just north of the River Scarpe on 9 April 1917 – part of the British Arras offensive. It clearly illustrates the new tactical concept of the use of creeping and protective barrages and the use by the infantry of the attack formations and tactics depicted in the diagram on page 478.

• The German defences were based on the concept shown in the diagram on page 479, with battalions of the 14th Bavarian Division deployed in the defences. To avoid confusion, no German communication trenches are shown; nor are the scattered machine-gun and defended localities between the trench lines.

• The 9th Division had three objectives – the Black, Blue and Brown Lines – although four trench lines must be taken or crossed before the Brown Line was reached. The division was to consolidate on the Brown Line, while the 4th Division passed through and took the Green Line.

• Because the front was almost 2,000 yards wide, the 9th Division attacked with three brigades in front, each brigade having two battalions leading and two in support, with either two or three companies up. The South African Brigade, for example, advanced on a two-battalion frontage, each with a two-company frontage, each company with two platoons leading; and each battalion, company and platoon had its equivalent in support – deployed as in the diagram on page 478.

• Advancing behind creeping barrages of high-explosive shells, with one in four being smoke, the leading battalions advanced to take the Blue Line on the railway embankment, where they reorganized under the protection of standing barrages. With some minor modifications the next phase saw the supporting battalions leapfrog through and advance under cover of a creeping barrage to secure the Brown Line. By 8:00 p.m., the 9th Division had taken all its objectives and captured 51 officers and 2,046 other ranks with comparatively small losses.

• To take the Green Line the 4th Division passed through the 9th and advanced with two brigades leading, the 11th on the left and 12th on the right – both following within 50 yards of a creeping barrage and using similar formations and tactics to the 9th Division. In the 11th Brigade, the 1st East Lancashires swung left to guard the flank while the 1st Hampshires pushed on to the Green Line. The 1st Somerset Light Infantry took the final German trench line, while the 1st Rifle Brigade advanced through them and took the Hyderabad Redoubt. In the 12th Brigade, the 2nd Essex and 2nd Lancashire Fusiliers pushed through almost to the Green Line. On their right the 1st King's Own consolidated on the enemy trench line as the 2nd Duke of Wellington's advanced to take Fampoux.

• This attack was a complete success, with advances of up to 6,000 yards (the Hyderabad Redoubt) being the deepest of the war so far, and confirmed the effectiveness of the close cooperation between the infantry, using their new tactics of attacking, and the supporting artillery, with the 18-pounder batteries firing carefully timed creeping barrages.

The Battle of Arras lasted until mid-May and included the three Battles of the Scarpe, the capture of Vimy Ridge, the two battles of Bullecourt and the Battle of Arleux. The initial British objective was to divert German divisions from the French Nivelle offensive in the Aisne sector, take the German occupied high ground that dominated the plain of Douai and, it was hoped, achieve the long-sought break-through. By the standards of the Western

Front, the gains of the first two days were nothing short of spectacular. A considerable amount of ground was won for relatively few casualties and a number of strategically important features were taken, notably Vimy Ridge (see page 102). However, by the end of the battle these gains had been offset by more than 150,000 casualties, no break-through had been achieved and the French offensive at the Aisne had failed – the original stalemate returned.

For the Germans the battle on 9 April on British XVII Corps' sector had in many cases caught them unawares and, as noted, many prisoners were taken. In some places they had surrendered half-dressed as they were clambering out of deep dugouts, and in others without boots, which they had lost in the thick mud as they tried to escape. The failure on this first day was due, according to Crown Prince Rupprecht, to the bulk of the German reserve counter-

A German machine-gun position in Caterpillar Wood, Messines.

attack divisions not being brought up close enough to the front prior to the attack as intended. Having these divisions available for immediate counter-attack was a fundamental requirement for the success of the German defensive strategy – but, on 9,10 and 11 April they arrived piecemeal. The Sixth Army's five counter-attack divisions, instead of being readily available behind the second line, were in their billets between twelve and twenty-four hours from the battlefield. The result was that the entire front zone on a 10-mile front, including Vimy Ridge, was lost. The Crown Prince commented as follows:

The defence can be divided into two distinct categories: that in which efforts were made to carry out orders under the new scheme, and that in which local commanders tore up the scheme. In the former, the 'island' positions with few exceptions surrendered or were abandoned by their garrisons. In the latter, where battalion commanders extended on a line which caught up the troops streaming back and gave them a rallying position, which was reinforced by any available garrisons of strongpoints in rear, the British advance was in several cases held up for considerable effect and with damaging effect.

Where the British attack succeeded, two battalions of each German regiment were accounted for, the foremost destroyed and the second either destroyed or driven back fighting, generally with heavy loss. The third battalions were in billets three to six miles from the battlefield, and arrived individually, to form the nucleus that evening and next morning. The leading troops of the reserve divisions [there were six, two of which were 25 miles away] in a few cases made an appearance that night, but in no case were they in action before the following day.

The new German system depended on early action by the reserve or counter-attack divisions. These, as the British knew, were too far away to intervene. Consequently the defence collapsed almost everywhere, except where the Hindenburg Line made defence an easy matter under any system.

The British also had not made good use of their reserves at the start, and this was probably the main reason why XVII Corps did not quite achieve a breakthrough on 9 April. Had the advance to the Green Line been made by the highly successful 9th Division, with the 4th Division being used to push through beyond, assisted by cavalry (unfortunately positioned south of the Scarpe), the attack might have been even more spectacularly successful. As it was, the overall results of all the Arras battles were disappointing.

The next great testing of the British attacking and German defensive methods came during the Flanders campaign from 31 July to 9 November 1917 during which the BEF struggled to take the muddy southern slopes of the Passchendaele Ridge in the Third Battle of Ypres. The treacherously waterlogged condition of the ground east of Ypres created almost insuperable problems for the Germans in constructing defensive positions and it was common for strong breastworks to replace trenches. Fortified localities were often either shell-hole nests or concrete shellproof shelters (pillboxes) scattered throughout the front zone to hold machine guns and infantry garrisons in the same way as deep dugouts had done at Arras. The troops manning these positions were in effect 'sheep for the slaughter', to be sacrificed. They would be regarded as having done their duty so long as they compelled the attackers to use up their supports, cause delay and generally disorganize the attack and await the arrival of the counter-attack divisions.

It was considered that the reverse slope of the Passchendaele Ridge would provide the ideal place for these formations to assemble. The Germans had anticipated the British launching a major offensive in this sector as early as June, and by the time it was launched on 31 July there were approximately two counter-attack divisions immediately behind the ridge for every three holding the front zone, and behind these counter-attack divisions were more reserve formations. The real battle divisions were the counter-attack divisions, whose task it was to fight the battle behind the front zone, and eventually recapture it.

The British attacks towards Pilckem Ridge on 31 July (see Map 22, page 66), which formed the opening of Third Ypres, had been preceded by a two-week bombardment requiring an enormous expenditure of ammunition pounding the German frontal zone, thinly manned by troops more or less written off as expendable. In addition, this prolonged bombardment warned the Germans of the location of the offensive and gave them time to position their counter-attack divisions accordingly. Another consequence that affected both sides, but much more so the British, was that this continuous deluge of shells churned the ground into an appalling morass that was to exhaust the advancing infantry in crossing it.

In a similar vein to Arras, the attackers broke into and through the frontal zone and by around midday were moving on beyond with their objective the ridge, believing the battle virtually over. At this moment the German counter-attack divisions advanced over the ridge and bore down on them. This was the stage when the British timetable for the attack was almost finished and the allotted artillery ammunition expended. For the Germans, however, the real fight was just beginning, and they had the advantage of catching the British in unfavourable locations with a mass of churned-up ground behind them. At 2:00 p.m. the rain started. Within two hours it was sheeting down, creating a vast quagmire that trapped both sides and forced the battle to come to a halt. By this time the British, although holding some areas they had taken, had in others been pushed back 1,000–2,000 yards. The overall British advance on the Pilckem–St-Julien–Zonnebeke front was up to 2,000 yards but at a cost of over 30,000 casualties.

As a result of their July experience, the Germans decided to reduce the front-zone garrison along their whole front from the North Sea to the River Lys. In the Ypres sector this meant only six regiments deployed in the frontal zone, covering some 4½ miles of front, but it enabled another counter-attack

The Approach to Passchendaele

The correspondent Philip Gibbs described trying to approach Passchendaele Ridge:

I had no heavy kit like the fighting men, but fell on the greasy duckboards as they fell, and rolled into the slime as they rolled. The rain beat a tattoo on one's steel helmet. Every shell-hole was brimful of brown or greenish water; moisture rose from the earth in a fog. Our guns were firing everywhere through the mist and thrust sharp little swords of flame through the darkness, and all the battlefields bellowed with the noise of these guns. I walked . . . past enormous howitzers which at twenty paces distance shook one's bones with the concussion of their blast . . .

division to be added to the sector. The Germans also copied the British in reorganizing their artillery into two categories, one of which was to be employed only during a major battle and otherwise kept hidden from view. With these exceptions the German defence to meet the second British offensive on 16 August remained unchanged.

The attack at Langemarck on 16 August saw a substantial modification of overall British tactics by the Fifth Army. Owing to the state of the ground and the consequent difficulty in bringing forward supporting artillery, objectives of approximately 2,000 yards deep, instead of 3 or 4 miles as in July, were selected. With these limited objectives timings were speeded up, with units expected to have taken objectives by 8:00 a.m. In the event this thoroughly disrupted the German plans. The counter-attack divisions, waiting behind the ridge for their enemy to come on, were eventually launched into the attack with some 2 miles of mud to cross before they met the British. What they found was that the frontal-zone garrison had been lost and the British had had time to consolidate their new positions well before the counter-attack divisions appeared. Few of these attacking German battalions reached the British line. The Fifth Army had employed 'bite-and-hold' tactics with considerable success.

The Germans' response to their frontal divisions being gradually eaten up and the ground permanently lost, made extremely quickly, was to hold the frontal zone more strongly, as at Arras. Front-line divisions were to place all three regiments in the front zone, with each having a battle battalion, support battalion and reserve battalion, which were all to be involved in the fighting in the frontal zone. Additionally, these units were not just to sit in their pillboxes come

what may, but were to adopt a flexible defence as decided by the forward commander. The KTK had regained his control. To this the British replied with yet more bite-and-hold operations, with less deep bites and quicker holding and using only twenty-four-hour preparatory bombardments. By using these tactics the British had inched their way forward at enormous cost in appalling conditions, and by early October had strengthened their grip on the southern part of the ridge astride the Menin Road and were approaching the northern, Passchendaele, end.

From the German perspective, the problem was that British offensives with limited objectives gave them virtual immunity from counter-attacks and enabled these divisions to be broken up by massed artillery fire before they began the fight to retake captured ground. The answer appeared to be to strengthen yet further the frontal zone by moving the support and reserve battalions up nearer the front battalion, and sending forward a battalion from the counter-attack division to occupy the position formerly occupied by the reserve battalion. Every available machine gun was sent up to the front part of the front zone, many forming machine-gun batteries of four to eight guns at 250-yard intervals along the front. The aim was to check the attackers using immediate local counter-attacks and then launch properly prepared counter-strokes within twenty-four or thirty-six hours.

This method of defence was applied to meet the attack by I and II ANZAC Corps at Broodseinde on 4 October 1917. However, the day was a disaster for the Germans. The German 4th Guards Division, which had

been brought forward to retake the Grote Molen spur lost on 26 September, was caught lying out in the open waiting to advance and decimated by the surprise opening barrage of the British attack. Elsewhere the well-planned and executed creeping barrages destroyed or demoralized the closely packed German front-line infantry units. The grave concerns of many German divisional commanders at packing the frontal zone with defenders were vindicated, but at a high cost. At last the British found themselves within striking distance of Passchendaele itself.

Another change was urgently needed in German defensive tactics, and this was forthcoming within a matter of days. The new proposals advocated by General Ludendorff were based more than ever on the artillery barrage, but equally on freedom of movement in the battle zone. The defence was to be conducted on some recognizable feature that became the main line of resistance some 500–800 yards from the enemy's front. This strip of no-man's-land was termed the advanced zone, and in this strip, 200–300 yards in front of the line of resistance, were the outposts, comprising a piquet line with a line of sentries beyond. Both these lines contained light machine guns and the groups manning these positions consisted of an NCO and six or eight men with one or two light machine guns. Two such groups would be positioned in front of each company sector of the main line. This light covering force was to drive away enemy patrols, give early warning of enemy activity, but withdraw immediately if a major attack was launched to avoid the defensive artillery barrage – it was found necessary to fire this barrage on the advanced zone, timed to allow the troops

A German position destroyed near Honnebeke during the Battle of Menin Road Ridge, Passchendaele, September 1917.

Notes for Map 81

- In this case a German regiment with three battalions (each of 12 companies) was deployed, with a forward battalion forming a main line of resistance on part of the Passchendaele Ridge astride the Passchendaele–Keiberg road. A line of outposts some 200 yards in front of the main line consisted of an outer line of sentry posts supported by a piquet line of light machine guns and infantry groups (two per company). This zone was the barrage zone into which the defensive barrage would fire when the outposts signalled a major attack. It would be fired on a set time to allow these troops to withdraw to the main line.
- The forward battalion garrisoned the main line and the outposts with its companies in line and the men sheltering in deep dugouts until attacked.
- A second battalion was in position to the rear in support, with two of its companies (5 and 6) at the disposal of the forward battalion commander, who was the KTK in command of all troops sent forward into the fight. The divisional heavy machine guns were sited to cover the second line, behind which would be some field artillery batteries.
- The third battalion of the regiment was held back in reserve, in this case in and around Moorslede. It would be sent forward in a local counter-attack role if requested by the KTK (with the approval of the regimental commander) and then would become subject to the KTK's orders in the battle area.

KEY

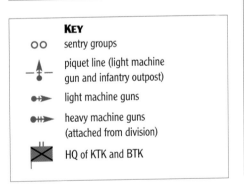

oo	sentry groups
	piquet line (light machine gun and infantry outpost)
	light machine guns
	heavy machine guns (attached from division)
	HQ of KTK and BTK

MAP 81 LEHR (3RD GUARDS DIVISION) DEFENSIVE ORGANIZATION, 26 OCTOBER 1917

to withdraw, in order to engage a quick enemy attack.

The remainder of the front-line battalions of each regiment garrisoned the main line of resistance. It was not necessarily occupied, but the men lay in dugouts or shell holes ready to do so. Two companies of the support battalion were at the disposal of the front battalion commander (KTK) for immediate local counter-attacks. The framework of the defence was built around machine guns, with the light guns of the front and support battalions (twelve each) covering main lines of resistance and with the infantry filling the gaps. The heavy machine guns attached to each division were grouped in nests of between two and four guns to cover the second line. The reserve battalion was behind the second line and behind that were the counter-attack divisions (see Map 81).

Higher commanders had been compelled to put their faith firmly back in the hands of the regimental officers, as the *Reichsarchiv* monograph (quoted in the *Army Quarterly Magazine*, March 1936) states:

All the threads of battle passed through the KTKs . . . They were responsible for their 500 yards of battle frontage. All reinforcements arriving in their zone came at once under their command. The artillery directed their fire according to their instructions. On their reports the higher commanders issued their orders, regimental and other commanders might add their opinions to the report as it passed back through their hands but the divisional commander relied on his KTK's judgement of the situation.

This new system of defence was in place by the time the British launched their final attacks on 12 October (First Battle of Passchendaele) and 26 October (Second Battle of Passchendaele). The first, by the II ANZAC Corps, was a chaotic disaster due to the horrendously muddy conditions that prevented the forward movement of supporting guns and resupply of ammunition. The unfortunate Australians lost 3,000 men in a few hours. The second, by the Canadian Corps, finally took Passchendaele, but not until 10 November and only at a cost of over 12,000 casualties. In three and a half months the BEF had suffered some 260,000 casualties while fighting in some of the most shocking physical conditions of the entire war – the name 'Passchendaele' is used to this day to encapsulate the horrors of the Western Front.

The next major offensive was a series of powerful thrusts launched by the Germans against both the British and French sectors of the front, beginning on 21 March 1918. In Operation Michael I, II and III, three German armies were able to crush the British Fifth Army and advance almost 40 miles before being halted on the River Avre (see Map 24, page 72). The two underlying tactical reasons for this initial German success that caused considerable consternation, not to say some panic, among the Allies were the inappropriate defensive tactics of the British and the new offensive tactics of the Germans.

The British had captured a German tactical pamphlet on which they modelled their new defensive system. The problem was that they adopted the techniques set out in the German General Staff instructions issued on 15 August 1917 – techniques the Germans were to abandon as useless. The radical changes made by the Germans in the following months were not understood sufficiently, and without trials the complicated and discredited zone of fortified localities was adopted. The British Fifth Army was deployed to meet the great offensive on Amiens with tactics similar to those with which the German Sixth Army had faced the British Arras–Vimy offensive a year before. The Fifth Army made matters more problematic as its front-line battalions were in some cases required to hold double the frontage held by the Germans at Arras.

By the end of the first day the *British Official History* has this to say: 'of the battalions [of Fifth Army] in the Forward Zone many had entirely ceased to exist as units, while in the majority of the others few officers and men remained' – almost an identical repeat of the German story at Arras on 9 April 1917. The important difference was that Ludendorff never intended his 'birdcages' to halt a determined attack on their own. In all major battles in which the system

had been used it had acted only as a slight check and at a heavy cost. The counter-attack divisions were meant to play the crucial role in the system, but the Fifth Army attempted to hold its long line with birdcages only. There were no counter-attack divisions in the rear, and no warning was given to brigade or battalion commanders that there might be an ordered retreat. Units were expected to hold out when surrounded, and it is to the credit of many units that they did so until overwhelmed or forced into precipitate retreat.

The second factor was the Germans' use of new offensive tactics, which saw strongpoints bypassed by squads of specially trained stormtroopers who advanced along lines of least resistance, and which contained machine guns, flamethrowers and trench mortars. These stormtrooper squads were supported by special field artillery units and were closely followed by assault units comprising infantry, machine guns, trench mortars, engineers, sections of field artillery and ammunition carriers. Their task was to exploit the successes of the stormtrooper squads, destroy strongpoints and repel any local, small-scale counter-attacks. The essence of these tactics, which would have the support of 'hurricane' artillery bombardments, was speed – no obstacle was to hold them up for long.

However, these tactics could succeed only if weak spots could be found in a defensive system, and the Fifth Army was spread wide in semi-isolated strongpoints many of which were blinded by mist, just as sleet had blinded the Germans when the British attacked at Arras–Vimy. There was therefore an element of luck in both these attacks and, despite the flawed British defensive layout and the new German offensive tactics, 21 March was not the out-

standing triumph Ludendorff had anticipated – the Germans suffered some 40,000 casualties of which over 10,000 were dead.

Once the Allies took the offensive all along the Western Front in August 1918 and breached the Hindenburg Line, the British were able to employ mobile all-arms battle tactics of infiltration and open warfare, with the infantry encouraged to revert to the pre-war principles of fire and movement with more flexible formations against a crumbling enemy.

Since early 1916 British infantry companies had advanced in waves (extended lines), with individuals eventually spaced 5 yards apart and following a 'creeper' (creeping barrage). Follow-up units in reserve usually moved forward in 'artillery formation' (file or single file) until they were actually assaulting. In 1918, although waves or lines continued to be employed, there was a growing tendency for the use at platoon level of section groups, sometimes in diamond, square or blob formation. These formations were not specified officially until the issue of an Inspectorate of Training pamphlet in October 1918 which gave junior commanders the option of using them according to the circumstances. Nevertheless, platoon fire and movement had become commonplace in the more open warfare of the Hundred Days campaign. When dealing with a machine-gun post or pillbox a platoon would engage it with a section and Lewis gun while simultaneously moving round to assault from the flank or rear with the remainder of the platoon. Alternatively, a section could be used to engage an enemy position in a firefight while the remainder exploited a gap. The platoon then continued its advance, leaving the enemy position to be dealt with by follow-up units.

A wiring party carrying gear to set up a new barbed-wire line. Note the corkscrew metal posts, which could be screwed into the ground more quietly than hammering in straight posts.

At Cambrai tanks came into their own in breaking down the German wire defences.

Cambrai

The moral effect of the support given by tanks to the attacking infantry is very great. He says his men felt the utmost confidence in the tanks and were prepared to follow them anywhere. The effect of the advancing line of tanks on the enemy infantry was extraordinary. They made no attempt whatever to hold their trenches, and either bolted in mad panic or, abandoning their arms, rushed forward with hands uplifted to surrender.

A battalion commander reporting what he was told by one of his infantry subalterns who took part in the attack at Cambrai; quote in Colonel (later Major General) J. F. C. Fuller's *Tanks in the Great War*, 1920

The Battle of Cambrai, from 20 November to 7 December 1917, was the final British offensive of that year. At the end little had been achieved strategically by either side; the initial highly successful attack by the British Third Army was ultimately driven back by powerful German counter-attacks, and at the end casualties were around 45,000 each, with 11,000 Germans and 9,000 British taken prisoner. In terms of territory, the Germans recovered most of their early losses and gained a little elsewhere, albeit with a net loss of ground.

However, the opening day of the battle has been chosen for the final section of this book as the British attacks that day show that even the formidable trench, wire and strongpoint defences of the Hindenburg Line could be overcome by a surprise artillery–infantry assault, using newly available methods and equipment combined with a mass tank attack. It is a clear example of just how successful an all-arms operation could be if meticulously planned, rehearsed and executed – as such it was a significant milestone in the operational progress of the BEF. The first day was so successful in breaking deeply and quickly through the enemy defences that a British victory was, somewhat prematurely as it turned out, celebrated by the ringing of church bells throughout England.

This section will look in particular at the extensive planning and preparation leading to Z-day, 20 November. To simplify this complex battle plan the section is subdivided into: the outline plan, the German defences, and then the planning and preparation of the infantry, artillery, tanks, cavalry, air, medical, supply and engineering aspects of the initial offensive. These summaries will be followed by a more detailed look at the attack on the St-Quentin Canal crossings by the 29th Division and a brief resume of the day's achievements. The section will end with an outline of how and why the Germans were able to turn the tables during the following two and a half weeks.

Outline Plan

The planning for a British attack by General Sir Julian Byng's Third Army in the Cambrai sector of the front had been ongoing while the BEF was still embroiled in the Third Battle of Ypres – there was no possibility of launching it while this battle continued. The seemingly endless struggle through the mud for the Passchendaele Ridge ended just ten days before the attack at Cambrai on 20 November – an attack that had been discussed with the French as early as April as the British part of an Allied offensive near St-Quentin proposed by General Nivelle. The keys to overall success would be surprise, and therefore total secrecy in all preparations; and the employment of new techniques and technologies that demanded full cooperation between infantry, artillery, tanks and aircraft. Cavalry also had a role to play, but only if the Hindenburg Line were breached. In all, nineteen infantry and five cavalry divisions were at General Byng's disposal.

Special Order of the Day to the Tank Corps

Brigadier H. J. Elles, who, ignoring orders to the contrary, led his Tank Corps into action on 20 November, issued the following Special Order No. 6 on the evening prior to the assault:

1. Tomorrow the Tank Corps will have the chance for which it has been waiting for many months – to operate on good going in the van of the battle.
2. All that hard work and ingenuity can achieve has been done in the way of preparation.
3. It remains for unit commanders and for tank crews to complete the work by judgement and pluck in the battle itself.
4. In the light of past experience I leave the good name of the Corps with great confidence in their hands.
5. I propose leading the attack of the centre division.

HUGH ELLES
B.G. *Commanding Tank Corps.*

Elles arrived in H Battalion lines just five minutes before the tanks moved off and as they were warming up their engines. He was smoking a pipe and had the extra large Tank Corps flag rolled up round a stick under his arm. He walked up to 'Hilda', commanded by Lieutenant Leach, tapped it with his stick, declaring it to be the centre of the line and that he would join its crew for the attack. He unfurled the flag, fixed it to the tank and climbed on board.

'Hilda' was later ditched in a trench near Ribécourt and Major G. Huntbach recalled seeing Elles walking back 'still pulling at his pipe, and with his fondest theories vindicated, exultant. He gave us a cheery wave with the now shot-riddled victorious banner. Behind him, at a respectful interval, came several crowds of German prisoners.'

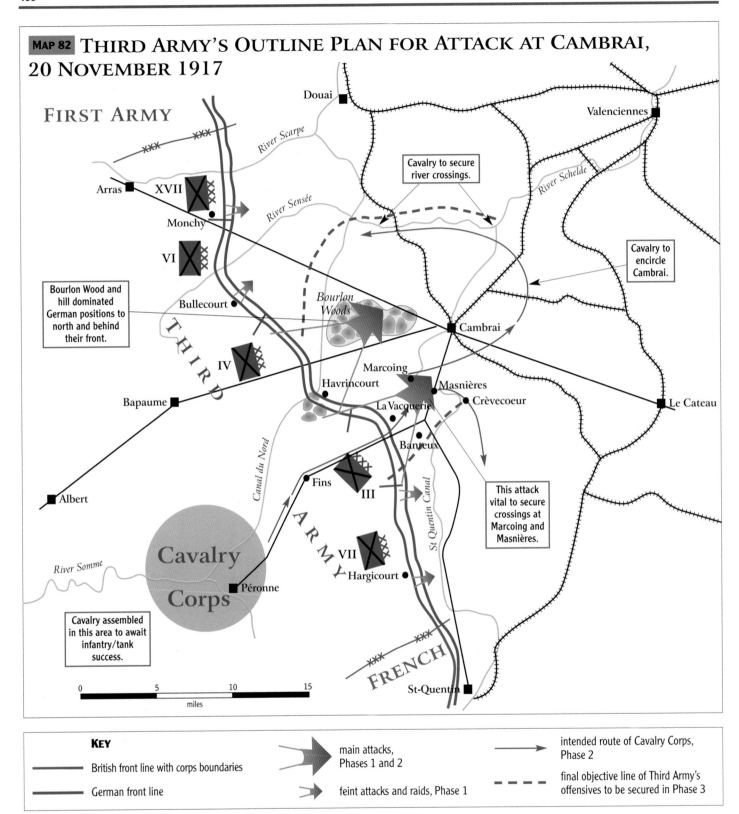

MAP 82 THIRD ARMY'S OUTLINE PLAN FOR ATTACK AT CAMBRAI, 20 NOVEMBER 1917

FIRST ARMY

Douai

Valenciennes

River Scarpe

Cavalry to secure river crossings.

River Schelde

Arras

XVII

River Sensée

Monchy

Cavalry to encircle Cambrai.

VI

Bourlon Wood and hill dominated German positions to north and behind their front.

Bullecourt

Bourlon Woods

THIRD

Cambrai

IV

Marcoing

Masnières

Bapaume

Havrincourt

Crèvecoeur

Le Cateau

La Vacquerie

Canal du Nord

Banteux

This attack vital to secure crossings at Marcoing and Masnières.

Albert

Fins

III

St Quentin Canal

Cavalry

ARMY

VII

Corps

Hargicourt

River Somme

Péronne

Cavalry assembled in this area to await infantry/tank success.

FRENCH

St-Quentin

| 0 | 5 | 10 | 15 |

miles

KEY

—— British front line with corps boundaries

—— German front line

➤ main attacks, Phases 1 and 2

➤ feint attacks and raids, Phase 1

→ intended route of Cavalry Corps, Phase 2

- - - final objective line of Third Army's offensives to be secured in Phase 3

For the main attack and immediate follow-up the Third Army intended to use:
• III Corps (Lieutenant General Sir William Pulteney) – 6th Division, 12th (Eastern) Division, 20th (Light) Division and 29th Division

• IV Corps (Lieutenant General Sir Charles Woollcombe) – 36th (Ulster) Division, 62nd

(West Riding) Division, 51st (Highland) Division and 56th (London) Division

• 1st, 2nd and 3rd Tank Brigades – a total of 376 fighting tanks in nine battalions

• Cavalry Corps (immediate follow-up and exploitation role; Lieutenant General Sir Charles Kavanagh) – 1st, 2nd, 3rd, 4th and 5th Cavalry Divisions

The following had supporting roles:
• VI Corps – 3rd, 16th and 34th Divisions

• VII Corps – 24th and 55th Divisions

• XVII Corps – 4th, 15th and 61st Divisions

• V Corps (in reserve) – Guards, 40th and 59th Divisions

The plan was codenamed 'Operation GY' and the Third Army's orders were issued at 7:00 a.m. on 13 November. An abbreviated summary is given below:

• The object is to break the enemy's defensive system by a *coup de main*; with the assistance of tanks to pass the Cavalry Corps through the break thus made: to seize Cambrai, Bourlon Wood and the passages over the Sensée River and cut off the troops holding the German front line between Havrincourt and that river.

• Surprise and rapidity of action are of the utmost importance.

• The operation will be in three phases:

1. The infantry attack, to include the capture of the crossings over the St-Quentin Canal at Masnières and Marcoing, and of the Masnières–Beaurevoir Line east of those places.
2. The advance of the cavalry to isolate Cambrai, and to seize the crossings over the Sensée river, and of IV Corps to capture Bourlon Wood. (Although not of quite the same importance as the securing of the crossings at Marcoing and Masnières to get the cavalry over the St-Quentin Canal, the seizure of Bourlon Wood and ridge was regarded by Haig and Byng as a key objective for Day One).
3. The clearing of Cambrai and of the quadrilateral St-Quentin Canal–Sensée River–Canal du Nord, and the overthrow of the German divisions thus cut off.

• The operation will start on Z-day at zero hour – to be notified separately (the former was 20 November and the latter 6:20 a.m.).

• To distract enemy attention, VII, VI and XVII Corps will undertake subsidiary operations.

• The preliminary task of breaking through the enemy line is allotted to III and IV Corps.

• As soon as a passage through the Masnières–Beaurevoir Line has been opened by III Corps, the Cavalry Corps will pass through to isolate Cambrai and seize the Sensée river crossings. At the same time IV Corps will capture Bourlon Wood on Z-day.

There were further instructions for the widening of the breach, the guarding of the flanks of the operation, and the role of VII, VI and XVII Corps in advancing as the main attack progressed. Reference was also made to separate instructions issued to the artillery, cavalry and RFC. Haig had instructed that if the operation were not successful within forty-eight hours he would call a halt.

The German Defences

The Cambrai sector was under General Georg von der Marwitz commanding the Second Army, with the defences of the Hindenburg Line that faced Byng belonging to General Theodor Freiherr von Watter's Caudry Group. This sector had been dubbed the Flanders sanatorium by the Germans as it was mostly used for rest and recuperation by formations depleted and exhausted in the bitter struggle east of Ypres. Watter's command on 20 November consisted of:

• In the north, responsible for a sector some 6,000 yards wide, was the 20th Landwehr Division (Infantry Regiments 77, 79 and 92) under Lieutenant General Freiherr von Hanstein. It was numerically weak, with a high proportion of elderly and young conscripts, and had only been in the line for eight days.

• In the centre was the 54th Division (Infantry Regiment 84 and Infantry Reserve Regiments 27 and 90) commanded by Watter. It was an experienced division but had recently been transferred to recuperate from a hammering in the north. It was responsible for some 10,000 yards of trench line that included the villages of Havrincourt on the right and La Vacquerie on the left. It was one of the few divisions that had received specialist training in dealing with tanks, which involved moving their 77mm guns out of their gun pits and taking on tanks with direct fire. This was the division that would face the brunt of the main British attack.

• In the south was the 9th Reserve Division (Infantry Regiment 395 and Infantry Reserve Regiments 6 and 19) under Lieutenant General Hildermann. This was another second-rate formation, responsible for a wide 8,000-yard frontage (mostly off the map to the south).

• Fortuitously, arriving on 19 November was the majority of the107th Division (Reserve Infantry Regiments 52, 227 and 232) commanded by Major General Havenstein. This division had been released from the Russian front and was no doubt hoping for an easy time. They were abruptly disappointed the next day as they were rushed to defend the third, incomplete defensive line from Anneux to Rumilly (the Masnières–Beaurevoir Line to the British, but known as Siegfried II, or SII, to the Germans) south-west of Cambrai as the British attack overran the forward positions. This line was some 8,000 yards long and units arrived in dribs and drabs, straight from their overnight billets in or around Cambrai or directly they detrained.

• Artillery firepower comprised three howitzer and six gun batteries (thirty-four pieces in all); a medium battery of 5.9-inch howitzers and one (captured) French, Belgian and Russian battery – all short-range (5,500-yard) pieces. There was also a heavy mortar battery, and the 107th Division brought an additional five field artillery batteries, although they had been ordered to leave their ammunition behind in Russia. In total, a meagre seventy or eighty pieces which, coupled with a shortage of ammunition – the field batteries had 1,000–1,500 rounds with the guns and a reserve stock of 4,600 – was hopelessly inadequate in a major battle. The batteries were mostly positioned in the rearward battle zone; those shown on Map 83 are representative of these and do not purport to show exact locations.

If the Germans were weak in infantry and artillery, they were confident that the deep Hindenburg defences would compensate.

Unusually for the Western Front, the British positions, for the most part, overlooked those of the Germans, although east of Havrincourt the German front-line trenches were concealed from direct observation by being sited on the reverse slope of slightly rising ground. However, this sector had been virtually undisturbed thus far, so the numerous small villages remained intact and the woods had not been reduced to matchwood. The area that saw the bulk of the fighting in the forthcoming battle was between the Canal du Nord in the west and the St-Quentin Canal, linking St-Quentin and Cambrai with the River Sensée, in the north. The Canal du Nord had been constructed in 1914 and was dry, but still provided a formidable obstacle of which the Germans made full use. The countryside was rolling farmland that had not been ravaged by shellfire.

The German defensive system varied from 6,000 to 8,000 yards deep and included an outpost, battle and rearward battle zones, behind which was the partially constructed Masnières–Beaurevoir Line. The outpost zone, its forward edge well wired, consisted of disconnected lengths of trench 6 feet deep and 5½ feet wide at the top. In this area, and also in the battle and rearward battle zones, self-contained centres of resistance were sited chequerwise (these included farmhouses and other isolated buildings). This zone included the fortified village of La Vacquerie, the north-eastern arm of Havrincourt Wood, a stretch of the Canal du Nord west of Havrincourt and the 'Spoil Heap' – a feature 400 yards long and 60 feet high. Most dugouts and machine-gun posts were reinforced with concrete, providing excellent protection for their occupants.

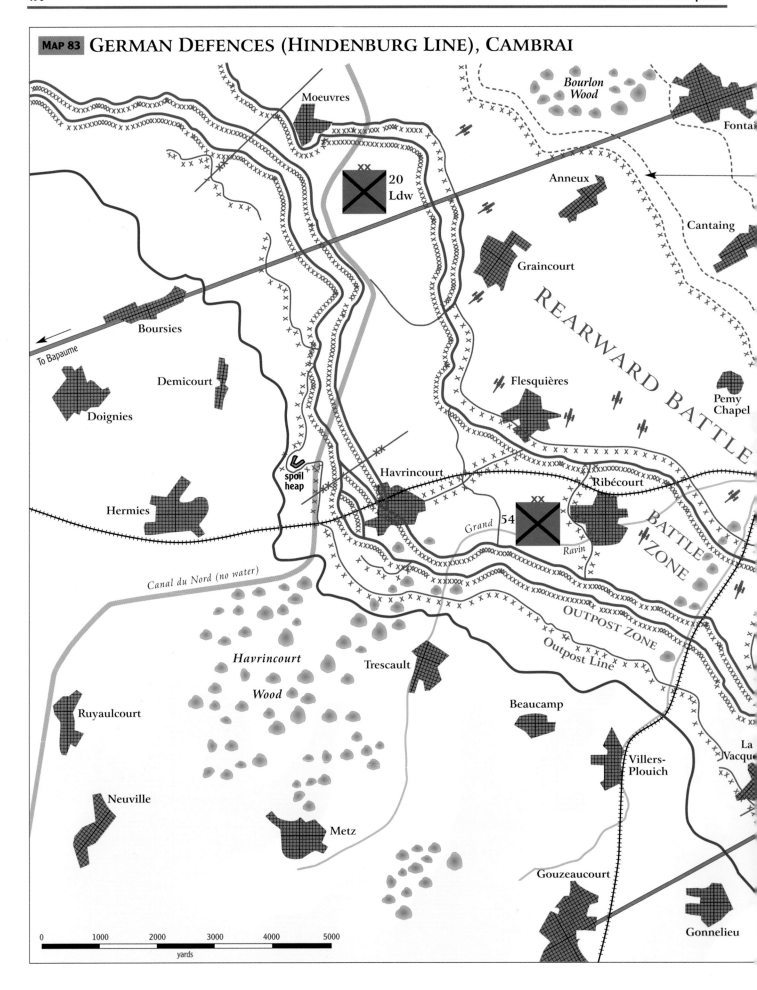

MAP 83 GERMAN DEFENCES (HINDENBURG LINE), CAMBRAI

Bourlon Wood

Moeuvres

Fontai

20 Ldw

Anneux

Cantaing

Graincourt

REARWARD BATTLE

Boursies

To Bapaume

Demicourt

Flesquières

Pemy Chapel

Doignies

spoil heap

Havrincourt

Ribécourt

Hermies

Grand 54

Ravin

BATTLE ZONE

Canal du Nord (no water)

OUTPOST ZONE

Outpost Line

Havrincourt

Trescault

Wood

Beaucamp

Ruyaulcourt

La Vacque

Neuville

Villers-Plouich

Metz

Gouzeaucourt

Gonnelieu

0   1000   2000   3000   4000   5000

yards

An aerial photograph of part of the battlefield at Cambrai, from the British front to Bourlon Wood. It shows the intact condition of the countryside prior to the British advance.

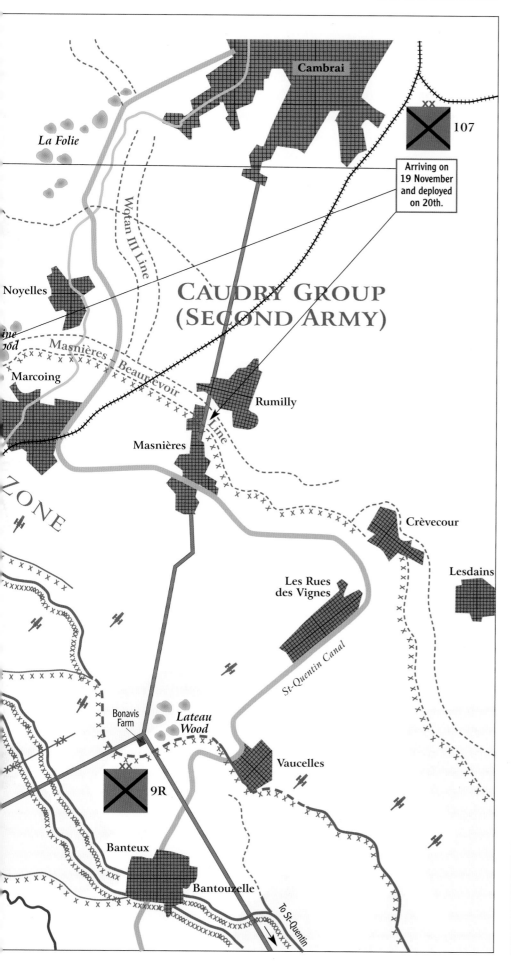

CAMBRAI

La Folie

Wotan III Line

Noyelles

Masnières — Beaurevoir

CAUDRY GROUP (SECOND ARMY)

107

Arriving on 19 November and deployed on 20th.

Marcoing

Rumilly

Masnières

Crèvecour

Lesdains

Les Rues des Vignes

St-Quentin Canal

ZONE

Bonavis Farm

Lateau Wood

Vaucelles

9R

Banteux

Bantouzelle

To St-Quentin

The front-line trench system that formed the front edge of the battle zone was a serious obstacle. The average fire trench was over 10 feet wide at the top (some over 12) and very deep to make them tank-proof. They ran along the reverse slopes of low spurs where possible and incorporated the eastern arm of Havrincourt Wood and the village itself. However, it was the wire that presented the most obviously daunting obstacle. Four belts of wire with large triangular projections were spaced at regular intervals from the foremost belt. Each belt was 10–12 yards wide and 3–4 feet high, very dense and forming a zone 100 yards deep. Such a barrier would require a bombardment of two or three weeks and the expenditure of a million shells to have any chance of making usable gaps for an infantry assault. The support (or supervision) trench was of similar construction. A British officer described the German wire in front of their defences at Cambrai as:

> winding away over the ridges in three [often four] broad belts, clean cut and separated by narrower avenues of grass; miles upon miles of it. With great patches red with rust after any rain, and looking in the distance where it climbed some final crest to the horizon like zigzag strips of plough or trimmed and level vegetation.

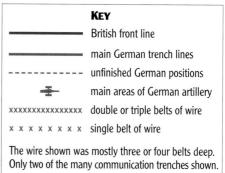

KEY	
———	British front line
———	main German trench lines
– – – –	unfinished German positions
✈	main areas of German artillery
xxxxxxxxxxxxxx	double or triple belts of wire
x x x x x x x	single belt of wire

The wire shown was mostly three or four belts deep. Only two of the many communication trenches shown.

Trees cut down by the Germans and laid across a road near Havrincourt to hinder the British advance.

Masnières, Marcoing, Noyelles and Cantaing were organized for defence.

On 16 November General von der Marwitz reported to higher command that 'hostile attacks on the Army front are not to be expected in the near future'. However, on the night of the 18th/19th prisoners were taken in raids on the British 55th, 20th and 36th Divisions, and while no information was gleaned from the first two it became clear from the captives from the 36th Division that an attack in the Havrincourt area was to be expected soon. This tended to confirm German suspicions aroused by the low-level flying over their lines on the 19th by British reconnaissance aircraft. On the same day a fragment of telephone conversation, 'Tuesday Flanders . . .' was intercepted. No date for a British attack was known but it was anticipated that any major assault would be heralded by the usual prolonged artillery bombardment which would reveal the location and likely timing. Nevertheless, at midnight on 19 November General Watter issued a warning that the anticipated attack on the Havrincourt sector would probably include tanks.

The support system, forming the rear of the battle zone, also consisted of a front and support trench, each with four or even five belts of wire and with numerous dugouts in the support trench. The main communication trenches that crossed the battle zone were wired on both sides. In this zone was the fortified village of Ribécourt, through which ran the Grand Ravin (a large drainage ditch) and Lateau Wood. Many of the German battery positions were close behind this Hindenburg support system in the rearward battle zone.

Finally, this support line was backed by a further line of incomplete defences – Siegfried II or the Masnières–Beaurevoir Line, 3½ miles south of Cambrai. A single belt of wire fronted it, and although the trenches were not especially deep they were well provided with dugouts. The villages of

Planning and Preparation

Infantry

The infantry attack plan is shown on Map 84, with success depending on surprise and shock. The extremely tight secrecy of the planning and assembly of the troops, tanks, guns and supplies beforehand, and the complete lack of any preparatory barrage, were crucial in obtaining surprise. The shock would come in the unexpectedness of the assault coupled with the lack of any preliminary bombardment and the mass use of tanks.

Secrecy was critical to every formation, arm, unit or soldier from GHQ through the staff down to the rifleman, tank crew or transport driver. The precautions taken were elaborate. Even senior operations staff officers at GHQ were kept in the dark until the last possible moment. False rumours of an attack in the Amiens area and elsewhere were circulated, along with a story that an infantry/tank training school was being established at Albert. Leaving two wireless tanks in the area to send fictitious messages masked the withdrawal of tanks from around Lens. Tank officers visiting the front were disguised – Colonel Fuller, the Tank Corps' chief staff officer, claimed to have worn blue-tinted glasses, while General Byng supposedly visited units dressed as a Canadian private. Officers and soldiers working in rear areas who might make obvious deductions about all the preparations and movement were told the secret in the strictest confidence. All talk of what was, or might be, happening in clubs, cafés or messes was strictly forbidden.

Apart from curbing loose talk, the other key element of secrecy was concealment – of the assembly, which started two weeks before Z-day, of troops, guns, tanks, equipment and supplies, all of which required the extensive use of camouflage. Details are given below of the engineer involvement in this; it is sufficient here just to mention the need for considerable extra shelter and accommodation for the troops, particularly with winter approaching. Front-line trenches had to be widened to accommodate the extra troops assembling for the attack or for reserves waiting to advance. Maximum use would be made of woods, such as the large Havrincourt Wood, for concealing tanks and the construction of shelters for troops.

Much of the preparation and movement had to be done at night, although the week up to 19 November was mostly dull and overcast, with poor visibility limiting enemy observation. In order to help conceal all this activity, areas were divided into three zones.

The 'daylight zone' ran about 2 miles behind and parallel with the front, on the enemy side of which no parties of more than two men were allowed, and then they had to be at least 100 yards apart – although in some hidden localities working parties of ten men were allowed. In the 'central zone' restrictions were not so severe, as it could only be observed from enemy balloons on a fine day. In the 'rear zone' only German aircraft could spot activities, so restrictions could be considerably more relaxed.

For the officers and men in the infantry battalions involved in the attack, priority was devoted to training with the tanks. Tanks were going to lead the assault, certainly as far as the Brown Line. For the infantrymen and most tank crews this made it vital to have at least some working knowledge of how the other arm operated in terms of tactics for dealing with enemy wire, trenches and bunkers. They also needed to know what mutual assistance could be expected in battle, and how they were to communicate with each other.

Training and rehearsals started in early November, with each division training with the tank brigade with which it was to operate. The 51st and 62nd Divisions trained with the 1st Tank Brigade at Wailly (4 miles south-west of Arras), as did the 29th Division with part of the 2nd Tank Brigade; and the 6th Division trained at Beaufort (11 miles east of Arras) with the remainder of the 2nd Tank Brigade. The 12th and 20th Divisions worked together with the 3rd Tank Brigade in the area between Bray and Fricourt on the Somme. Use was made of full-scale models of the relevant parts of the Hindenburg Line, with a trace of each sector taped out on the ground. Particular attention was given to the infantry assembling behind tanks, advancing to attack behind tanks, passing through wire crushed by tanks and clearing a section of trench under the protection of tanks. However, due to time constraints, each infantry battalion could be allowed only two days for infantry/tank training, which meant it was often rudimentary.

The infantry companies and platoons had to practise different tactical procedures from those used when attacking behind a creeping barrage and without tanks leading the way. These are set out in diagrammatic form in the diagrams on pages 398 and 399, which illustrate the tactics used by three of III Corps' divisions. However, Major General George 'Uncle' Harper, commanding the 51st (Highland) Division (nicknamed by some until November 1916 'Harper's Duds' from its divisional sign 'HD') insisted on a different technique for his infantry. He made the leading wave of tanks split into two, the wire-cutters advancing first followed by a second wave of fighting tanks, with the infantry following at least 100 yards behind rather than 25, in two extended ranks not files, as Harper believed that tanks attracted fire. However, this caused some difficulties when the infantry had to pass through the narrow gaps made in the wire by tanks, but

as infantry divisional commanders had the final word on tactics used within their command this was the way the 51st (Highland) Division trained.

Advancing infantry could not afford to be in doubt about where the tanks had crushed a path through the wire, so the troops following immediately behind carried flags to mark the paths for those further back to locate easily. Similarly, with tanks using fascines to cross wide trenches, the tank crew would throw out a red-and-yellow flag which the first infantryman passing had to stick in the ground some 20 yards on either side of the crossing – to plant it opposite would invite it being crushed by any follow-up tanks.

The infantry also had to learn various inter-tank–infantry signals. These were made with coloured discs using the following code:

Green	Wire cut or crushed
Red	Wire uncut
Red Green or Green Red	Have reached my objective
Helmet held above head on a rifle	'Tank wanted' by infantry

The assembly of the attacking infantry required careful planning and coordination in order to get the divisions in the line without attracting attention. They arrived in the general area by road and rail. On 15, 16 and 17 November the 6th, 12th, 29th and 51st Divisions reached Péronne by rail and moved into II and IV Corps areas on the following nights. The 62nd Division, which had been training in the Wailly area, marched on the night of 13th/14th and

concentrated west of Havrincourt Wood three nights later.

In III Corps sector the 20th Division had held the whole of the front line, and on the night of the 17th/18th the left part of its line was taken over by the 6th Division. It was forbidden for any unit to send out patrols, apart from standing patrols on its own wire. On the same night in IV Corps area, which until then had been held by the 36th Division, the 62nd Division sent three battalions forward to take over its battle-front, although the outpost line was still held by the 36th. During the night of 18th/19th the 12th Division relieved the right of the 20th and thus III Corps had its three attacking divisions in position just a day before Z-day. As the right portion of IV Corps front had good covered approaches (Havrincourt Wood), the 51st Division was able to take over its trenches in daylight on the morning of 19 November.

The infantry divisional attack plans involved advancing behind the tanks at Z-hour (6:20 a.m.) on 20 November under cover of a series of timed lifting barrages, with a series of objectives (phases) denoted by the Blue, Brown and Red Lines on Map 84. As each objective was secured, another wave of tanks and infantry would leapfrog through to the next one. Details of which brigades would form the leading or support waves was left to divisional commanders, resulting in all having two brigades up and one in support except for the 20th Division, which had all three attacking brigades in line to take the Brown Line as the 29th Division was following with its own tank support to take the key crossings over the St-Quentin Canal.

Men of the 4th Battalion, Gordon Highlanders (51st Division), crossing a trench at Ribécourt, 20 November 1917.

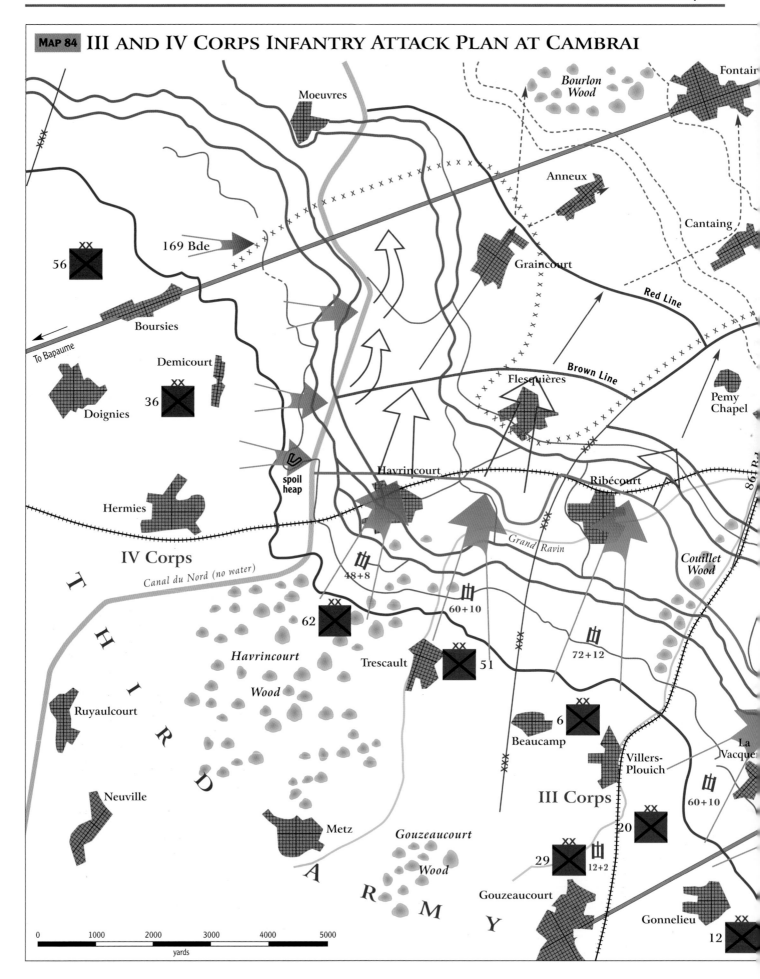

MAP 84 III AND IV CORPS INFANTRY ATTACK PLAN AT CAMBRAI

Moeuvres

Bourlon Wood

Fontair

Anneux

Cantaing

169 Bde

Red Line

56

Boursies

To Bapaume

Graincourt

Demicourt

Brown Line

Flesquières

Pemy Chapel

36

Doignies

spoil heap

Havrincourt

Ribécourt

Rd 98

Hermies

Grand Ravin

Couillet Wood

IV Corps

Canal du Nord (no water)

48+8

62

60+10

Havrincourt

72+12

Wood

Trescault

51

Ruyaulcourt

6

Beaucamp

La Vacque

Villers-Plouich

60+10

Neuville

III Corps

Metz

Gouzeaucourt

Wood

20

29

12+2

Gouzeaucourt

Gonnelieu

12

THIRD ARMY

0   1000   2000   3000   4000   5000

yards

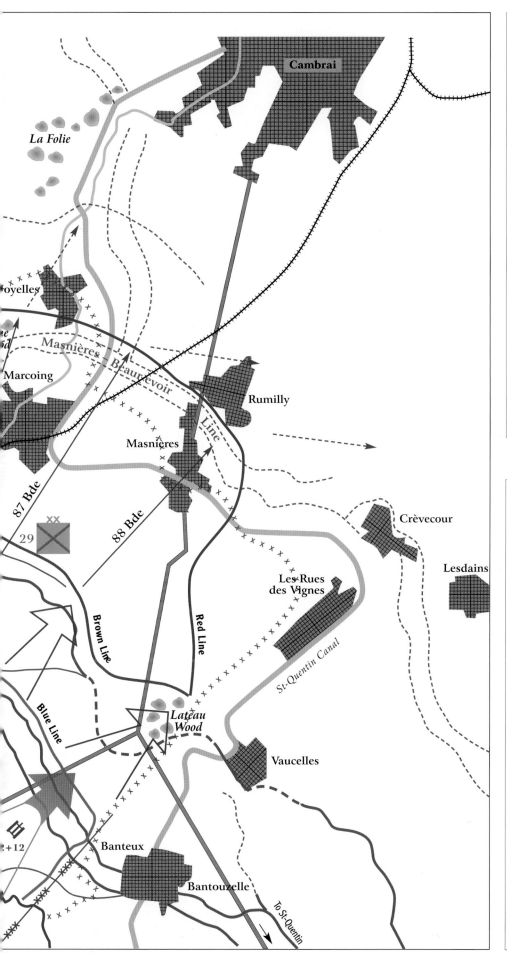

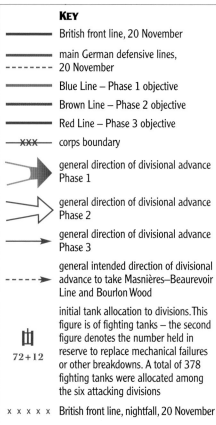

British front line, 20 November

main German defensive lines, 20 November

Blue Line – Phase 1 objective

Brown Line – Phase 2 objective

Red Line – Phase 3 objective

corps boundary

general direction of divisional advance Phase 1

general direction of divisional advance Phase 2

general direction of divisional advance Phase 3

general intended direction of divisional advance to take Masnières–Beaurevoir Line and Bourlon Wood

72+12 initial tank allocation to divisions. This figure is of fighting tanks – the second figure denotes the number held in reserve to replace mechanical failures or other breakdowns. A total of 378 fighting tanks were allocated among the six attacking divisions

x x x x x British front line, nightfall, 20 November

Notes for Map 84

• This shows the general plan of attack for 20 November for III and IV Corps. III Corps would make the brunt of the attack on the right, with the key task of securing the crossings over the St-Quentin Canal at and between Marcoing and Masnières that would allow the cavalry to exploit and advance east and north of Cambrai.

• Six divisions were involved in the taking of the Blue and Brown Lines. On the left a brigade from the 56th Division would advance to secure the flank of the 36th Division but would not make a major attack. The advance to the Red Line would be made by a fresh division, the 29th Division, whose task it was to take the all-important St-Quentin Canal bridges. On the left the advance to this line would be the three original attacking divisions (the 6th Division from III Corps and 51st and 62nd Divisions from IV Corps). Further exploitation was intended to take Bourlon Wood, the Masnières–Beaurevoir Line and the villages of Anneux, Containg and Fontaine. Operations to secure the right flank of the attack would be made by the 12th and 20th Divisions.

• The number of fighting tanks allocated to each division, including replacement reserves, is shown. The infantry attack in phases would be based on formations and units leapfrogging forward to take their designated objectives.

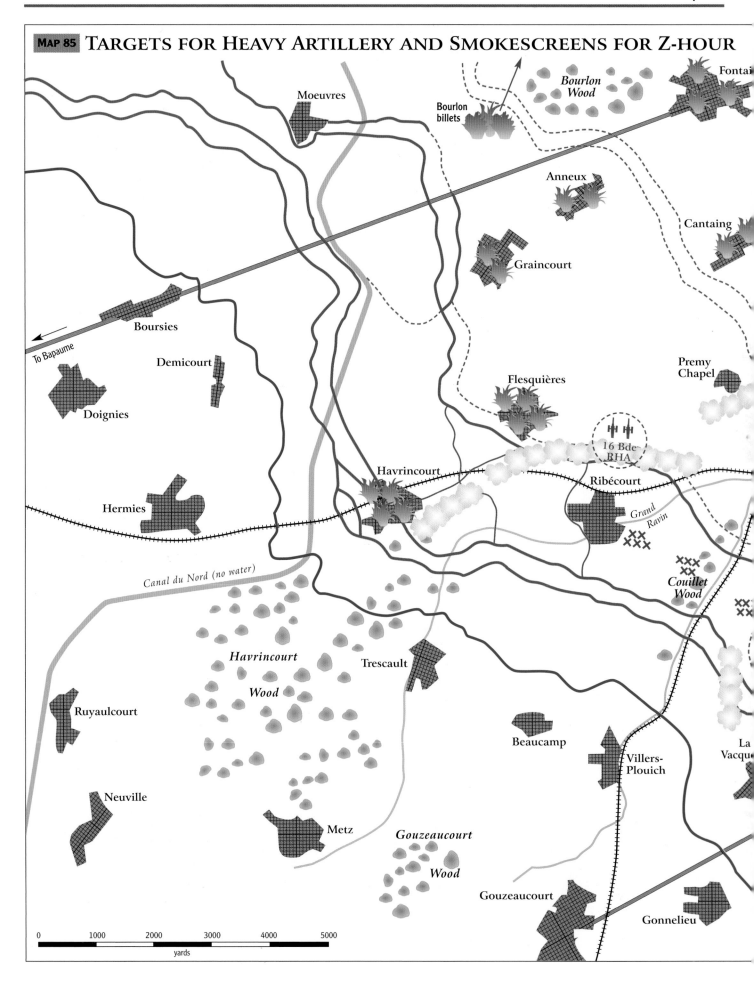

MAP 85 **TARGETS FOR HEAVY ARTILLERY AND SMOKESCREENS FOR Z-HOUR**

Bourlon Wood

Fonta

Bourlon billets

Moeuvres

Anneux

Cantaing

Graincourt

Boursies

To Bapaume

Premy Chapel

Demicourt

Flesquières

16 Bde RHA

Doignies

Havrincourt

Ribécourt

Grand Ravin

Hermies

Couillet Wood

Canal du Nord (no water)

Havrincourt

Trescault

Wood

Ruyaulcourt

Beaucamp

La Vacqu

Villers-Plouich

Neuville

Metz

Gouzeaucourt

Wood

Gouzeaucourt

Gonnelieu

0   1000   2000   3000   4000   5000

yards

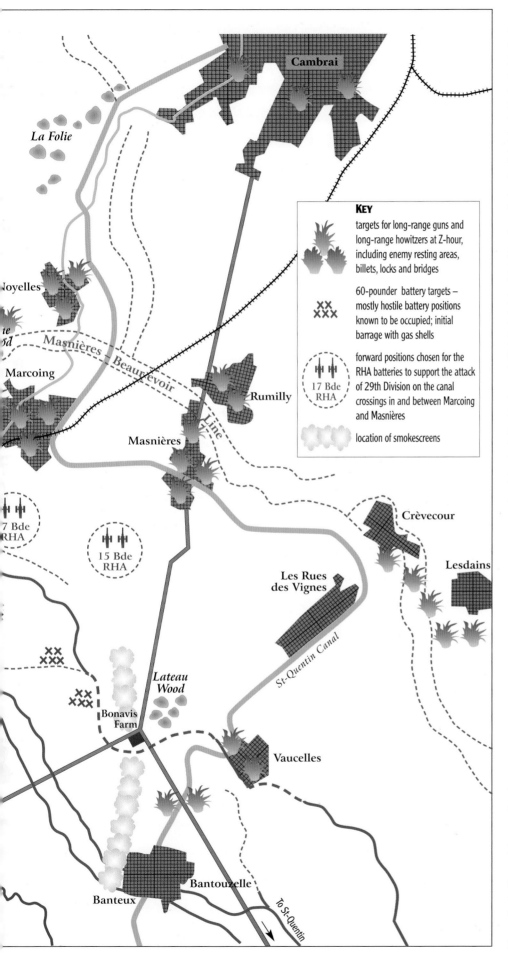

KEY

targets for long-range guns and long-range howitzers at Z-hour, including enemy resting areas, billets, locks and bridges

60-pounder battery targets – mostly hostile battery positions known to be occupied; initial barrage with gas shells

17 Bde RHA — forward positions chosen for the RHA batteries to support the attack of 29th Division on the canal crossings in and between Marcoing and Masnières

location of smokescreens

Artillery

On 4 August 1917 Brigadier General Hugh Elles, commander of the Tank Corps, and his chief of staff Lieutenant Colonel J. F. C. Fuller submitted a plan for a raid or reconnaissance in force in the Cambrai sector of the front. It was to be led by tanks and made without any preliminary artillery bombardment. Shortly after this Brigadier General Henry Hugh Tudor, Commander, Royal Artillery (CRA) of 9th Division, put forward a similar plan for an attack with the artillery firing at Z-hour without any previous registration of targets (thus firing entirely off the map), with tanks being used to cut the enemy wire. This novel use of artillery was aimed at achieving complete surprise. General Byng, commanding the Third Army, approved this idea and proposed enlarging its scope. The Tudor plan was agreed by GHQ on 13 October and became the basis for the Cambrai attack on 20 November, with the artillery element heavily reinforced from army resources and formations not involved with the main assault.

The planning of the artillery contribution to the Cambrai battle, along with the movement and positioning of over 1,000 guns and howitzers, forward ammunition dumping and target selection, was one of the most complex aspects of the operation, as the following paragraphs will illustrate. The artillery made available to III and IV Corps is shown in the table below.

Artillery at Cambrai

	III Corps	IV Corps	Total
13-pdr (RHA batteries)	36	18	54
18-pdr	264	234	498
4.5-inch howitzer	66	66	132
60-pdr	54	42	96
6-inch gun	8	4	12
6-inch howitzer	72	68	140
8-inch howitzer	14	16	30
9.2-inch gun	1	1	2
9.2-inch howitzer	16	12	28
12-inch howitzer	4	4	8
15-inch howitzer	2	1	3
Totals	**537**	**466**	**1003**

Three artillery instructions were issued by the Third Army on 29 October and 10 and 14 November and are summarized below:

29 October

• **Camouflage** At the start of planning the erection of camouflage to hide work and tracks was to start immediately, before any other work.

• **Battery boards** Battery positions had to be selected and sites surveyed and marked so that the preparation of battery boards could be put in hand without delay. This included selecting positions to which it was intended to move batteries during operations. The surveying of these battery positions was the task of the field survey companies of the Royal Engineers and involved the technical 'surveying in' of the guns and targets on to the same map grid. The barrels of all guns when laid on the same bearing had to be exactly parallel.

• **Calibration and grouping** As much calibration as possible had to be carried out without increasing the volume of fire that should take place in the line. Additional calibration was to be done at the artillery ranges at Quinconce (III Corps) and Fricourt (IV Corps). Guns and howitzers were to be inspected by munitions officers and grouped in batteries according to barrel wear and subsequent loss of muzzle velocity.

• **Artillery fire** The need for fire to cover deep into the enemy defences meant that battery positions had to be as far forward as possible – but no firing would take place from them before Z-hour.

• **Communications** The selection of observation posts (OPs) for the reinforcing batteries was a priority. OPs beyond the German trenches had to be chosen from the map, as artillery observers would need to advance with the attacking formations. Details of the reinforcing and improvement of telephonic communications were issued separately.

• **Trench mortars** No specific allocation was deemed necessary, but all available mortars were to be targeted on enemy positions on the immediate flanks of the attack.

• **Outline artillery plan** Siege and heavy artillery would neutralize rather than attempt to destroy enemy batteries, OPs, assembly areas, main movement routes, telephonic communication lines, rest billets and command posts. Attention was to be paid to villages and approaches on the flanks that might be used as assembly areas for a counter-attack. Smoke, to be fired at Z-hour, was required to screen off high ground, OPs and the Hindenburg Line. The barrage covering the attack of the tanks and infantry would be provided by 13-pounders, 18-pounders firing shrapnel, HE and smoke. Any 4.5-inch howitzers not firing smoke-screens and any 6-inch howitzers that could be spared from the counter-battery programme would fire HE instantaneous-fuze ammunition. Some field and heavy batteries were detailed to switch firing on to any counter-attacks or large bodies of troops spotted by aircraft or balloons.

10 November

• This concerned the allocation of artillery to the Cavalry Corps and the reversion of Royal Horse Artillery (RHA) batteries to cavalry control, with the addition of field howitzer batteries after the second objective was taken. It also dealt with the allotment of artillery liaison officers to infantry formations.

• It specified the rates of fire for 18-pounders and 4.5-inch howitzers for continuous and protective barrages as one round per gun per two minutes; for 6-inch howitzers as one round per howitzer per three minutes; and for 8-inch and 9.2-inch howitzers as one round per howitzer per five minutes. For the super-heavy howitzers and medium and heavy guns the rate was to be according to circumstances. For the lifting barrage fire to support the infantry and tank attacks, the rate for the 18-pounders was to be 2–4 rpm (the latter rate not to be continued for over ten minutes), the 4.5-inch howitzers one round per howitzer per minute, and for the 6-inch howitzer also one round per howitzer per minute.

• It included general arrangements for the forward movement of batteries (which would involve the drawing up of complex movement tables not just for guns but for all other arms as well). Gaps in the wire for the forward movement of guns where they could not follow the tanks were to be cut by the gunners, and about 700 fascines were provided for the batteries to fill in trenches as necessary to get guns across. General instructions for artillery intelligence and cooperation with the RFC (see page 505) were included.

• The allocation of ammunition held per piece was as shown in the table below:

Artillery Ammunition

	At guns	Corps reserve dumps	Army reserve dumps
18-pounder	100	100	100
4.5-inch howitzer	100	50	100
60-pounder	100	50	100
6-inch howitzer	100	50	100
6-inch gun	100	50	100
8-inch howitzer	75	25	100
9.2-inch howitzer	75	25	100
12-inch howitzer	50	–	50

• For air defence, twenty-eight anti-aircraft guns were deployed in a chequerboard manner, the forward edge covering an area 3,500 yards ahead of the British front line.

14 November

• All guns, howitzers and trench mortars were to open fire on their targets at Z-hour (6:20 a.m.). Detailed target allocations were confirmed for long-range guns and howitzers in III and IV Corps (see Map 85). The 60-pounder batteries were to open fire with gas shells on all enemy battery positions known to be occupied and then switch to enemy reserve or resting areas near Crèvecoeur, Masnières, Marcoing, Cantaing and Noyelles, while the 6-inch guns continued to bombard the German batteries. All 13- and 18-pounder guns, along with those 4.5-inch howitzers not employed in the smoke barrage, would be employed in the frontal lifting barrage preceding the tanks and infantry. Howitzers were to use the largest proportion of the new instantaneous 106 Fuze and concentrate fire on machine-gun posts, OPs and communication trenches. Map 86 is the barrage map for IV Corps' attack starting at Z-hour on 20 November, showing how it lifted from trench line to trench line on a specific, but by no means a uniform, timetable.

A 6-inch howitzer concealed under snow-coloured camouflage netting on the Cambrai front, 1917.

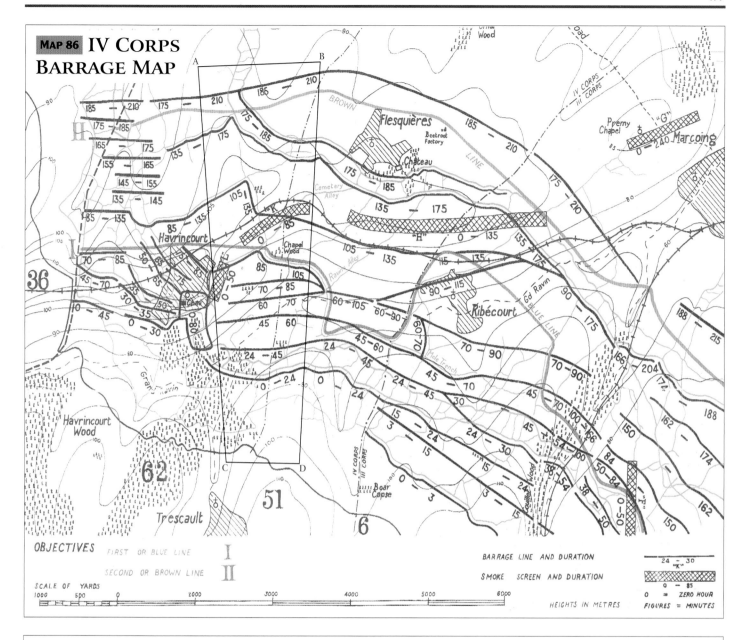

MAP 86 IV CORPS BARRAGE MAP

OBJECTIVES

FIRST OR BLUE LINE   I

SECOND OR BROWN LINE   II

SCALE OF YARDS

BARRAGE LINE AND DURATION

SMOKE SCREEN AND DURATION

24 — 30 "K"

0 — 85

0 = ZERO HOUR

FIGURES = MINUTES

HEIGHTS IN METRES

Notes for Map 86

• This shows the barrage map required for the attack of IV Corps that started at Z-hour on 20 November. That such an intricate fire plan for the guns was practical without any previous registration is a remarkable example of how the technical aspects of gunnery had progressed by late 1917. This was a lifting barrage rather than a creeping one, and the shells 'stood' on the lines indicated for the period of time in minutes shown on each line, which varied in accordance with the estimated time it would take for the attackers to reach that particular trench from the previous one. Wherever possible the barrage conformed to the actual line of a trench. Beyond the attackers' main objectives, the Blue and Brown Lines, the barrage became a 'protective' barrage, in that it 'stood' for a comparatively long period while the attacking troops reorganized and supports and reserves moved forward to take over the advance, as well as protecting against any local counter-attack.

• The barrage within the rectangle ABCD provides a typical cross-section of how it worked. The starting point for the attacks was their front line CD. At Z-hour the advance started, as did the barrage, which stood on the first main trench line for 24 minutes – the time given for the attackers to cross the 900–1,000 yards of no-man's-land. This allowed for an advance of 100 yards every 4 minutes – a task that would probably include dealing with several enemy positions in their outpost line. The infantry and tank commanders were well

aware of the timings of the barrage, and if they arrived close to their objective early then they had to wait for the barrage to lift before making their final assault. Conversely, however, if they were late the barrage would not wait.

• Progressing from south to north up the rectangle, the first lift stood for 21 minutes (24–45), the time allowed for the attackers to take the front-line trench and its supervision trench just 150 yards behind. There followed four more lifts to the first main objective, the Blue Line. This allowed a period of one hour to advance 1,100 yards and it was likely to involve some serious fighting. The next lift occurred 105 minutes after Z-hour and became a protective barrage beyond the Blue Line for 30 minutes (note the smokescreen 'K' in this area lasted from 0–85 minutes). Two more lifts took the barrage to the Brown Line (135–175 and 175–185), with a final protective barrage beyond this lasting from 185–210 minutes.

• The attack on Havrincourt illustrates the flexibility of the barrage plan. The initial barrage lasted from 0–30 minutes, with a box barrage around the chateau strongpoint continuing for 80 minutes while the attack by the infantry continued through the village. The infantry were given five lifts for this attack, taking them through the complex system of trenches and ruined buildings, with the village being taken and the Blue Line reached by 85 minutes after Z-hour.

Clandestine preparations: a fatigue party carrying duckboards over a support-line trench at night, Cambrai.

Tanks

Every available tank on the Western Front was assembled for the attack at Cambrai on 20 November. The total of 476 working tanks comprised 378 fighting tanks (Mark IVs), 54 supply tanks or gun-carriers used for supply, 32 wire-clearing grapnel tanks, 2 bridging tanks, 9 wireless tanks and 1 telephone-cable-carrying tank. It was to be the first mass use of tanks by the BEF in the war, with all three brigades (nine battalions) involved. The two crucial tasks that tanks had to undertake were:

• To crush the enemy wire for the infantry and cavalry. This was a role usually undertaken by the artillery and requiring many days of preparatory bombardment that produced variable results. At Cambrai there would be no such bombardment, so the infantry advancing behind the fighting tanks relied entirely on the tanks to crush paths for them to file through. For the cavalry, whose horses needed much larger and more complete gaps than the infantry, this duty was assigned to the thirty-two specialist wire-clearing tanks (they had large letters 'WC' painted in white on the back) fitted with grapnels (see opposite).

• To give close machine-gun and gun support to the infantry in suppressing enemy resistance during the fight for the trenches and dugouts. They were also required to deal with machine-gun posts and pockets of resistance that were holding up the advance.

The Tank Corps, like the other arms and services, had an immense amount of work to do in preparation, all of which had to be carried out with the utmost secrecy. This can be summarized as concentrating the three brigades at Wailly (4 miles south-west of Arras) and their dispersal to detraining areas behind the Cambrai front; training and rehearsals with the infantry; the construction of various devices for dealing with wire, bridging the wide trenches of the Hindenburg Line, and bringing up supplies to keep the tanks moving and fighting; and the establishment of forward ammunition and petrol dumps.

The withdrawal of a tank brigade from the Ypres salient and another from Lens was announced as being done for winter training purposes and this seemed to convince the British tank crews as well as the Germans. Two wireless tanks were left at the front to send bogus messages that could easily be intercepted to persuade enemy listeners that the brigades had not moved. The forward Tank Corps headquarters at Albert was disguised as the corps training centre, and officers visiting the front removed any visible distinctive badges and wore helmets and trenchcoats. It was only two or three days before Z-day that section and tank commanders got to know the plan.

It was a great triumph for the staff and railway units that the thirty-six trains required to bring forward the nine battalions almost simultaneously to their respective concentration areas was achieved without any major hitch. It was found necessary to borrow extra, but smaller, trucks from the French in order to entrain upwards of 450 machines at Beaumetz (near Wailly). Twenty-seven trainloads were concentrated at Plateau, near Albert, by 14 November, with the remaining nine arriving the following night. The period of training and rehearsals with the infantry has been described above, but the tanks themselves needed to practise the new tactical drills for trench-crossing and fighting through the enemy positions (see the diagram on page

• Smoke ammunition to be fired was calculated on the assumption of favourable wind – south-west 10–15 m.p.h. The smokescreens were intended to blind observation from the flanks and the Havrincourt–Flesquières Ridge in particular (Map 86). The lifting barrage in front of the advancing tanks and troops was confirmed as a third shrapnel, a third HE and a third smoke. At midnight before Z-hour army HQ would decide if the wind was favourable or not and would send a signal saying 'Fire full ration', 'Fire half ration' or 'Fire no smoke'.

• A heavy artillery group (one 60-pounder and one 6-inch battery) was allotted to each attacking division, and a 60-pounder battery was allotted to the CRA of 29th Division for exploitation beyond the Hindenburg Line to support the attack on the Masnières–Marcoing line. Forward locations for the field artillery supporting this operation were selected and are shown on Map 85. Covering the hoped-for cavalry break-out presented a problem as the RHA batteries could do little other than follow until tasks became clear. The 1st Cavalry Division, whose task would involve decisive and energetic action, allocated only one section of H Battery, RHA to its leading brigade – hardly adequate.

Movement of the batteries into their final positions – some as close as 2,000 yards from the front trenches – began on the night of 7 November. The flow of guns of all calibres intermingled with the ammunition columns, marching infantry, and ambulance cars and cavalry units moving into position through the darkness in accordance with the marching schedules. The last batteries arrived in their locations on the night of 17 November.

Trains loaded with Mark IV tanks with fascines at Plateau Station, awaiting despatch to the forward area prior to the opening of the Battle of Cambrai.

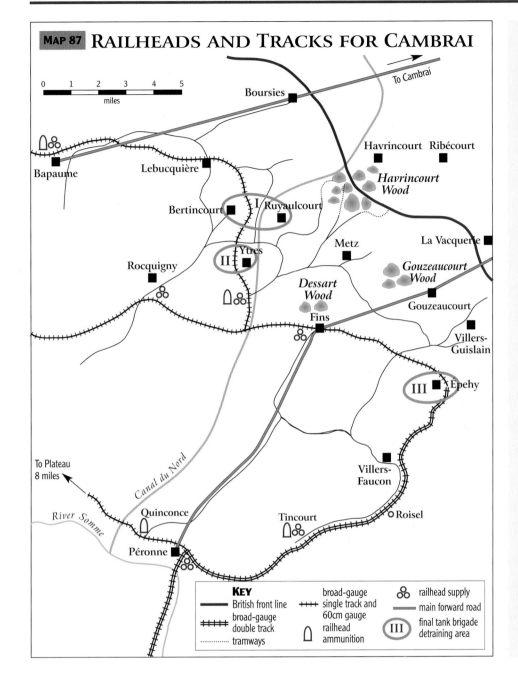

MAP 87 RAILHEADS AND TRACKS FOR CAMBRAI

KEY
— British front line
broad-gauge double track
.... tramways
+++++ single track and 60cm gauge
railhead ammunition
broad-gauge
railhead supply
main forward road
final tank brigade detraining area

Wire-pulling Tanks

An official report on wire-pulling operations was issued after the Battle of Cambrai. In commenting on these specialist tanks, which led the attack in their sectors, the report stated that some failed to reach the wire in time:

> The work therefore fell upon the remainder, so that in at least one case the tank functioned seven distinct times, the grapnel being cut out after each pull with the wire cutter, lifted on to the petrol tank and released again when the next belt was encountered . . . in no case did the grapnel break or fail to grip the wire.
>
> The wire before our own line was of the usual type, not a serious obstacle, very straggled and unsatisfactory to pull. In some cases several attempts were needed before the ground was cleared.
>
> The strongest belts of wire were constructed of wooden and iron stakes and all were interconnected. This pulled very satisfactorily in every case . . .
>
> After pulling the wire away the ground is absolutely clear of every scrape of wire or obstruction such as posts etc.

The above appears something of an exaggeration, as the Marquess of Anglesey's *A History of the British Cavalry* quotes from the history of the 4th Dragoon Guards as follows:

> the difficulties of negotiating the abandoned trenches was horribly time consuming. Further, in spite of the claims made by the wire-pulling tanks, it appears that the broken coils were hazardous to horses legs. Indeed it was frequently necessary to dismount and use wire-cutters.

398). The tank brigades' final detraining areas were at the following railheads, all of which had to be built or repaired: 1st Brigade at Bertincourt-Ruyaulcourt, 2nd Brigade at Ytres and 3rd Brigade near Épehy, which at 5 miles from the front was the furthest away from the start line (Map 87). From these areas all the tanks had moved into assembly points 2–4 miles from the front by 18 November.

Perhaps the key new technique that the fighting tank crews had to master was the use of fascines, as the real obstacle in the Hindenburg Line was not just the width of the trenches but their depth. When a tank was halfway across, but not yet balanced on the parados, the tail left the parapet and dropped to the bottom of the trench, shifting its centre of gravity and leaving the machine at an angle near the vertical. The tracks could

not grip sufficiently to lift the dead weight and the tank became ditched and its guns virtually useless. The object of the 4 feet 6 inch diameter fascines was not to fill the trench and make a bridge, but rather to prevent the tail of the tank from dropping so far as to make recovery impossible. The fascines weighed 1¾ tons and were frustratingly difficult to handle and move – twenty Chinamen were employed to push them along the ground, and each required mechanical hoisting to lift them on and off rail trucks and on to tanks. Once fixed to a tank they increased its height considerably, something that resulted in numerous overhead telephone cables being knocked down on 19 November. The fascines were dropped into a trench over the nose by the use of a release mechanism inside the tank. At Cambrai the deepest and

widest trenches proved no obstacle to a fascine-carrying machine – in fact, in some cases a wide firestep in a trench served the same purpose as a fascine in stopping the tail dropping to the floor.

At the same time that the fascines were being made, 127 tanks were repaired and thirty-two were being fitted with enormous four-pronged grapnels for wire-clearing for the passage of cavalry. Their use was entirely new and involved a special drill. They worked in threes; the centre one went straight ahead through the wire to cut a narrow gap, then the flank tanks dropped their grapnels and gathered up the ends before turning left and right and dragging the wire to either side to widen the gap. This technique usually ensured that every stand and picket was uprooted and a clean gap was created in a few minutes. Their orders were to cut gaps of 60 yards in each belt of wire across the planned routes of the cavalry. Once their tasks were completed the crews could cut the cable and release the massive tangle of wire – some were then instructed to rejoin the action as a fighting tank.

For re-supply, 110 heavy timber, load-carrying sledges were built to bring forward ammunition and petrol to sustain the attack. The main forward supply dumps for the tanks – in total containing 165,000 gallons of petrol, 55,000 lb of grease, 5 million rounds of SAA and 500,000 rounds of 6-pounder shell – were established at Havrincourt Wood, Dessart Wood and Villers-Guislain, all made possible by the extensive system of light railway tracks behind the front. From these dumps fuel and ammunition were taken forward by supply and gun-carrying tanks towing the sledges.

The three tank brigades moved forward by night and were concealed in their assembly areas as follows: 1st Brigade with D, E and G Battalions hidden in the western end of Havrincourt Wood; 2nd Brigade with B and H Battalions in Dessart Wood; and 3rd Brigade with A, C, F and I Battalions concealed under brick-coloured camouflage nets in and around Gouzeaucourt and Villers-Guislain. Each battalion had earmarked a few fighting tanks to be held in reserve to replace mechanical breakdowns. The numbers attached to each infantry division and their planned infantry objectives are shown on Map 84.

The tanks had to be ready to move forward before 6:00 a.m. on 20 November and actually to move off ten minutes later, followed by the infantry. At Z-hour, 6:20 a.m., the barrage of HE, shrapnel and smoke would fall on the enemy outpost line before moving forward in lifts of about 250 yards on a timed programme. This massive tank assault would be led, contrary to his orders, by their commander, Brigadier General Hugh Elles, in his tank ('Hilda'), flying a huge Tank Corps flag. For his Special Order for the day, see box, page 487.

Tank D51 ('Deborah') at Cambrai

Second Lieutenant Frank Heap commanded tank D51, which was knocked out by a field gun just as it left the comparative shelter of Flesquières. For his action that day Heap was awarded the Military Cross, the citation for which reads:

Tank D51 'Deborah'.

> In Cambrai operations near Flesquières on 20 November 1917, he fought his tank with great gallantry and skill, leading the infantry on to five objectives. He proceeded through the village and engaged a battery of enemy field guns from which his tank received five direct hits, killing four of his crew [recent research states that it is possible five crew died in the battle]. Although then behind the German lines he collected the remainder of his crew and conducted them in good order back to our own lines in spite of heavy machine gun and sniper fire.

D51 was discovered the following day by Scottish infantry and the dead crew were buried beside their tank. After the war their bodies were re-interred in the Flesquières Hill British Military Cemetery.

The tank was abandoned and lay buried for eighty years before historian Philippe Gorczynski discovered her under a field, with wire still entangled in her tracks, in 1998. It was something of a puzzle as to why D51 was buried some 900 yards from where she was finally knocked out. Gorczynski seems to have established beyond much doubt that the British, using other tanks, dragged 'Deborah' to her resting place in the field and buried her to form part of a shelter.

On 20 November 2009 relatives of the crew of D51, including Second Lieutenant Heap's great-grandson Mr John Heap, made a pilgrimage to Flesquières to honour the bravery and sacrifice of the crew. They were able to trace the path taken by D51 that morning and attend a church service. The remains of 'Deborah' now reside in a barn only a few yards from where she was knocked out.

Cavalry

Even with well over 400 tanks, the only arm capable of exploiting gaps created by others was the cavalry. Only they could move rapidly and far enough in the open country behind the enemy defences to disrupt his rear areas and communications. At Cambrai the entire Cavalry Corps of five divisions (1st, 2nd, 3rd 4th and 5th) was earmarked for this role, along with flank protection for any major penetration of the Hindenburg Line. However, it could be launched only if the infantry had secured the bridges over the St-Quentin Canal at Marcoing and Masnières. To exploit success, the cavalry would need to act aggressively and be ready to cross the canal the moment those bridges were taken.

Lieutenant General Sir Charles Kavanagh commanded the Cavalry Corps (well over 27,000 horsemen), but for this operation his 1st Division was placed under command of IV Corps and the Lucknow Brigade from the 4th Cavalry Division was attached to III Corps. Another, unique, unit was formed from the same division for a special task. This was the so-called Cavalry Track Battalion, created some three weeks prior to the attack and comprising twenty British officers and over 500 recently arrived dismounted Indian cavalrymen. It was commanded by Lieutenant Colonel R. C. Bell of the Central India Horse, and its task was to follow the infantry and create gaps in the wire (along with wire-clearing tanks), fill in or bridge trenches and shell holes and create the broad tracks necessary for the passage of the cavalry divisions. In this task they would work in conjunction with the infantry pioneer battalions. This battalion's method of operation is explained below (page 508). The crucial importance of Bell's task was made clear to him by General Kavanagh when he told him, 'If you don't do your job, I can't do mine.'

Below is a summary of orders issued by the Third Army to the Cavalry Corps on 13 November. All tasks, somewhat optimistically, were to be undertaken on Z-day (Map 88).

• To surround and isolate Cambrai, blocking all exits and destroying means of communication – this task to be given priority if it proved

Dismounted Lancers wait by the side of the road while artillery go forward near Trescaut, 20 November 1917.

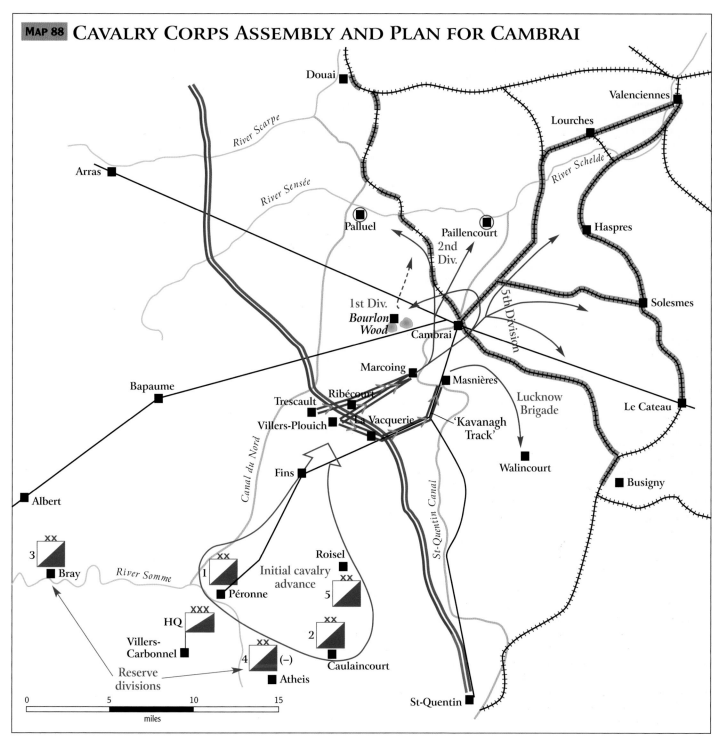

MAP 88 CAVALRY CORPS ASSEMBLY AND PLAN FOR CAMBRAI

Douai

Valenciennes

River Scarpe

Lourches

Arras

River Sensée

River Schelde

Palluel

Paillencourt
2nd
Div.

Haspres

1st Div.

Bourlon Wood

Cambrai

5th Division

Solesmes

Bapaume

Marcoing

Masnières

Trescault   Ribécourt

Villers-Plouich   La Vacquerie

Lucknow Brigade

Le Cateau

'Kavanagh Track'

Fins

Canal du Nord

St-Quentin Canal

Walincourt

Albert

Busigny

3 ××
Bray

River Somme

Roisel

1 ××
Péronne

Initial cavalry advance

5 ××

HQ ×××

Villers-Carbonnel

2 ××

4 ×× (−)

Caulaincourt

Atheis

Reserve divisions

St-Quentin

0   5   10   15
miles

A Problem with a Fascine

A tank commander during the Battle of Cambrai gave an account of using a fascine to cross a wide trench:

The Hindenburg Trench was a truly formidable obstacle, and we naturally had a few exciting moments. First, poised over the deep and wide excavation; then releasing the fascine – would it drop alright? – we saw it lumber beautifully into the bottom. But could we get over? One can imagine our doubts, as we had witnessed a few ghastly failures at Wailly [during training]. Anyhow, down we dropped and up, up, up – and no one thought of the balance point – until we crashed upon the other side, splitting open my section commander's head, and petrol cans, oil cans and ammunition boxes scattered all over the place. However we had done the first part of our job successfully . . .

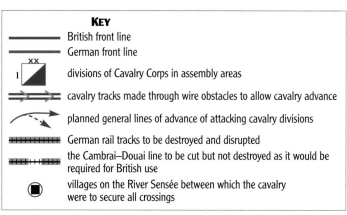

KEY

British front line

German front line

1 ×× divisions of Cavalry Corps in assembly areas

cavalry tracks made through wire obstacles to allow cavalry advance

planned general lines of advance of attacking cavalry divisions

German rail tracks to be destroyed and disrupted

the Cambrai–Douai line to be cut but not destroyed as it would be required for British use

villages on the River Sensée between which the cavalry were to secure all crossings

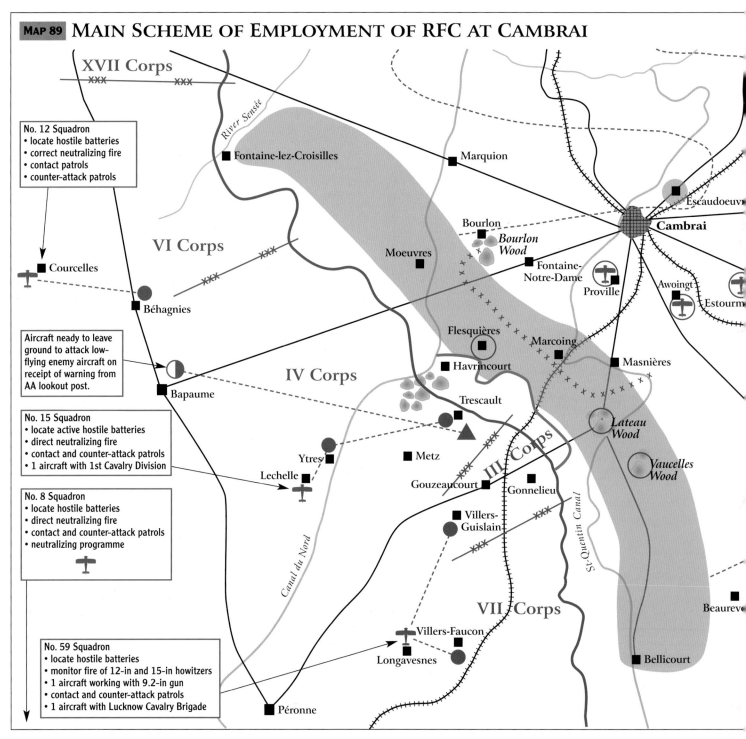

MAP 89 **MAIN SCHEME OF EMPLOYMENT OF RFC AT CAMBRAI**

XVII Corps

River Sensée

No. 12 Squadron
• locate hostile batteries
• correct neutralizing fire
• contact patrols
• counter-attack patrols

■ Fontaine-lez-Croisilles

■ Marquion

■ Escaudoeuv

Cambrai

VI Corps

● Bourlon

■ Moeuvres

Bourlon Wood

■ Courcelles

Fontaine-Notre-Dame

Awoingt

■ Béhagnies

Proville

Estourm

Aircraft neady to leave ground to attack low-flying enemy aircraft on receipt of warning from AA lookout post.

■ Flesquières

Marcoing

IV Corps

■ Masnières

■ Bapaume

■ Havrincourt

No. 15 Squadron
• locate active hostile batteries
• direct neutralizing fire
• contact and counter-attack patrols
• 1 aircraft with 1st Cavalry Division

Trescault

Lateau Wood

▲

● Ytres

■ Metz

Vaucelles Wood

Lechelle

III Corps

No. 8 Squadron
• locate hostile batteries
• direct neutralizing fire
• contact and counter-attack patrols
• neutralizing programme

Gouzeaucourt

● Gonnelieu

■ Villers-Guislain

St-Quentin Canal

Canal du Nord

VII Corps

■ Beaurev

No. 59 Squadron
• locate hostile batteries
• monitor fire of 12-in and 15-in howitzers
• 1 aircraft working with 9.2-in gun
• contact and counter-attack patrols
• 1 aircraft with Lucknow Cavalry Brigade

Villers-Faucon

Longavesnes

■ Bellicourt

■ Péronne

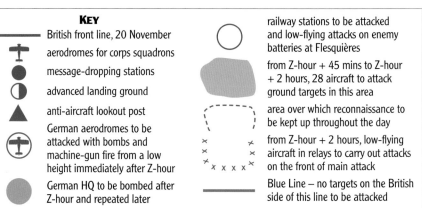

Notes for Map 89
• This map does not claim to show all targets or the timings of RFC operations on 20 November, but rather to indicate the main bombing ones, the areas over which reconnaissance, contact and low-flying attacks were to be made.
• It also shows the airfields from which RFC corps squadrons operated, the arrangements for message-dropping and location of the anti-aircraft lookout post.
• The duties of Nos 8, 12, 15 and 59 Squadrons are indicated in general terms, which include contact and counter-attack patrols, locating hostile batteries and monitoring neutralizing fire, and the bombardment of the enemy's super-heavy gun and howitzers.

KEY
— British front line, 20 November
✈ aerodromes for corps squadrons
● message-dropping stations
◐ advanced landing ground
▲ anti-aircraft lookout post
⊕ German aerodromes to be attacked with bombs and machine-gun fire from a low height immediately after Z-hour
● German HQ to be bombed after Z-hour and repeated later

○ railway stations to be attacked and low-flying attacks on enemy batteries at Flesquières

from Z-hour + 45 mins to Z-hour + 2 hours, 28 aircraft to attack ground targets in this area

area over which reconnaissance to be kept up throughout the day

from Z-hour + 2 hours, low-flying aircraft in relays to carry out attacks on the front of main attack

Blue Line – no targets on the British side of this line to be attacked

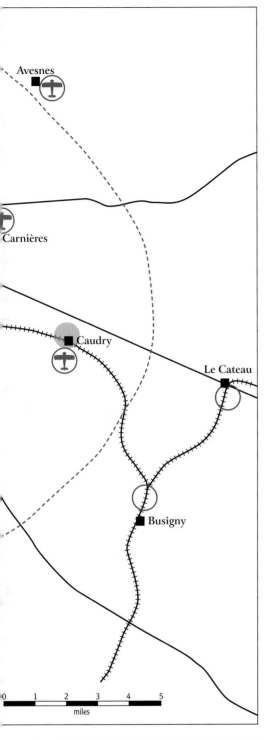

An Airman's View at Cambrai

Squadron Leader A. S. G. Lee, described flying over the battlefield:

We flew very close to the ground . . . having to rise to pass over tanks moving through the thick haze of smoke. One retains vivid pictures of little groups of infantry behind each tank, trudging forward, of flames leaping from disabled tanks . . . of ludicrous expressions of amazement on the upturned faces of German troops as we passed a few feet above their trenches.

impossible to achieve the others. The railway lines from Cambrai to Douai, Busigny, Le Cateau, Solesmes, Lourches and Solesmes–Haspres–Valenciennes were to be disrupted.

- To secure the crossings of the Sensée between Paillencourt and Palluel (inclusive).

- To secure the flank of the forces engaged in clearing the quadrilateral St-Quentin Canal–River Sensée–Canal du Nord (see Map 82).

To fulfil these tasks, the Third Army's instructions emphasized that the leading cavalry divisions must pass through as soon as the crossings at Masnières and Marcoing, or between them, were secured on Z-day: this could be any time after Z-hour plus four and a half hours (10:50 a.m. onwards). The Cavalry Corps was to move its leading divisions to forward concentration areas behind the front, but the decision to move from these advanced positions would rest with the corps commander (Kavanagh). This meant close contact with the attacking infantry.

Three routes or passages were to be opened up through the enemy defences under the arrangements of III and IV Corps to allow the forward and timely movement of the Cavalry Corps. Of these three tracks, two converged on the crossings of the St-Quentin Canal at Marcoing and one on the crossings at Masnières (Map 88). They were:

- Villers-Plouich–Marcoing.

- Trescault–Ribécourt–Marcoing (the first mounted formation to use this track was to be the 1st Cavalry Division). The pioneers of the 6th Division were told that clearing this track had priority over all other tasks, and they would have wire-clearing tanks to assist.

- Villers-Plouich–La Vacquerie–Masnières. For this track – the 'Kavanagh Track' – twelve wire-clearing tanks were under command of the Cavalry Corps, twenty under infantry command for use on the other two tracks.

To summarize: the cavalry plan envisaged the 1st, 2nd and 5th Divisions as the formations to make the initial advance and attacks, with the 3rd Division and the 4th Division (less the Lucknow Brigade) moving up in reserve. The 1st Division would cross the canal at Marcoing and sweep round east and north of Cambrai to isolate it before assisting in attacking and securing Bourlon and its wood; it would then rejoin the corps. The 2nd Division would also cross at Marcoing and then attack to the west of Cambrai and secure the crossings over the Sensée, while the 5th would cross at Masnières, advancing north and east of Cambrai to disrupt and destroy German communications – particularly the rail lines from Cambrai. On the right flank the Lucknow Brigade (4th Division) would conduct a raid towards Walincourt after crossing at Masnières or nearby.

Air

III Brigade, RFC, reinforced for the battle, comprised six corps squadrons, seven fighter squadrons, a fighter-reconnaissance squadron, and part of a day-bombing squadron (two DH.4 flights of No. 49 Squadron). These totalled 289 aircraft (125 for corps work, 134 single-seater fighters, 18 Bristol fighters and 12 DH.4s). This gave the British a huge numerical advantage over the Germans, who could muster only around 78 aircraft, only 12 of which were fighters. The British also had six sections of kite balloons available to work with the corps of the Third Army – they were specifically tasked with reporting the movement of enemy troops to the artillery.

Concealment of air activity prior to Z-day was as important for the RFC as for other arms and their flying time was restricted to flights over the British sector. Fortunately, German observation by balloon or aircraft was severely hampered by overcast and misty weather in the days before 20 November, except on the 19th, by which time it was too late for the enemy to make any major changes in their defensive arrangements. On 9 November Third Army issued general instructions to the RFC for their roles in the offensive, which are summarized below (see also Map 89).

- **General** The essence of the operation was secrecy. No attempt was to be made to screen the preparations before Z-day by having more aircraft on the front affected than had been the case for the previous four months. No machine was to cross the front line before Z-hour. The following instructions applied to Z-day.

- **Medium-distance reconnaissance** This was to be carried out of roads and railways around Cambrai, the area east and south-east of the front of operations; special attention was to be paid to approaches from the north.

- **Bombing** The following targets were to be attacked: enemy aerodromes opposite Third Army front, south of the River Scarpe (off map to the north); headquarters at Caudry and Escaudoeuvres (by corps squadrons from VII and XVII Corps); railway junctions in order of importance – Douai (off map), Somain (off map), Busigny, Le Cateau and Valenciennes (off map).

- **Ground targets** As many squadrons as possible were to attack ground targets, specifically selected groups of batteries, troops and transport beyond the range of the British barrage.

- **Fighting patrols** These patrols were to be maintained throughout the day, paying particular attention to the vicinity of enemy aerodromes.

• **Hostile balloons** Those opposite the front to be attacked at intervals throughout the day.

• **General aircraft activity** Air activity was to be displayed over the whole front of the main and subsidiary operations up to Z-hour plus two hours (in order to deceive the Germans about the area of the main attack); thereafter efforts must be concentrated on the front of the main operation.

There would be no time for the deliberate observation of the fire of British artillery, but it was vital that the positions of active German batteries was reported, and to save time air observation was to be confined to correction of fire for neutralization rather than destruction. To supplement the artillery fire, four fighter squadrons were detailed to attack ground targets such as active batteries, troops and machine-gun positions. There were to be low-flying attacks by four Sopwith Camels on each of

six aerodromes. To facilitate the work of the fighting squadrons a forward aerodrome was established at Bapaume and stocked with fuel, ammunition, bombs and spares. The attacks on troops and transport were to start forty-five minutes after Z-hour (7:05 a.m.) and for an hour and a quarter were to be made along an extended front from Fontaine-lez-Croisilles to Bellicourt, after which they would concentrate on the front of the main attack.

Medical

Medical preparations for the battle revolved around reinforcing with personnel, particularly surgical teams, the medical facilities available to III and IV Corps that were to bear the brunt of the fighting. As with all preparation, it had to be done in great secrecy. Initially Byng, the army com-

mander, insisted that only his surgeon general, Major General Sir James Murray Irwin, be informed of his plans, but he was persuaded that it would be impossible to obtain the necessary extra support at the casualty clearing stations without at least the deputy director of medical services at GHQ knowing what was going on. It was this critical need to reinforce the casualty clearing stations with both personnel and equipment that was so difficult to achieve without alerting personnel to the fact that a major offensive was imminent. In the event the movement of medical units to Italy that was taking place at the same time was successfully used as a cover.

Thirteen casualty clearing stations were established (see Map 90) to support the offensive, with 18 extra surgical teams (73 medical officers, 64 nursing sisters and 447 other ranks). The doctors came from other armies and the nurses from base and line of communication hospitals. Wounded from the Tank Corps were to be evacuated according to the arrangements of the division in whose area the tanks were operating, and from the Cavalry Corps to the nearest casualty clearing station.

Each corps was allocated one motor ambulance convoy supplemented by fifty motor ambulance cars sent from the First Army. Seventy buses or charabancs were allocated – thirty to III Corps, thirty to IV Corps and ten in reserve – for evacuating sitting casualties. Reserve stocks of stretchers and blankets were positioned at dumps at Ytres (750 stretchers), Tincourt (500 stretchers) and Grevillers (1,000 stretchers and 3,000 blankets). Not until 18 November were four lorryloads of medical stores and 30,000 bandages allowed forward. All medical arrangements were in place by the 19th.

In III Corps' area the main dressing station on the road south of Fins was hutted, well equipped with electric light, operating theatre, gas treatment centre and could accommodate 500; it also had a walking wounded station alongside it. The advanced dressing station at Gouzeaucourt was in cellars and well protected, but the one at Villers-Guislain was cramped. Maximum use was to be made of the narrow-gauge (600mm) Decauville network of tracks (see Map 90) for evacuation. Decauville was a manufacturing company founded by Paul Decauville that made sections of light track fastened to steel sleepers; by the end of the war it had been used by both the British and the French to construct many thousands of miles of track on the Western Front. The corps had at its disposal four covered ambulance wagons on the Decauville railway fitted with equipment and heated by oil stoves. This railway system connected two of the

Cambrai – Evacuation Scheme for Sick and Wounded

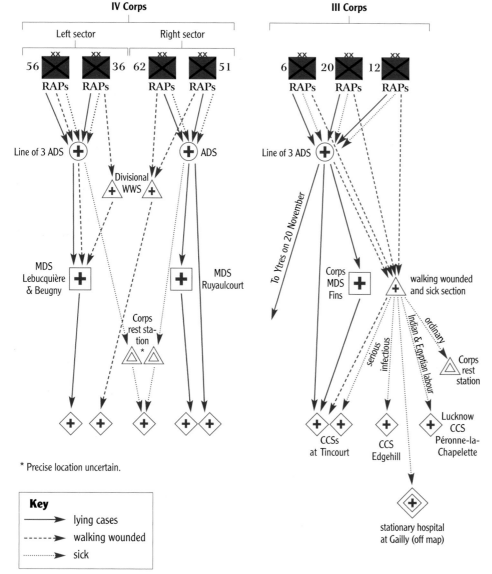

* Precise location uncertain.

Key
→ lying cases
- - -→ walking wounded
········→ sick

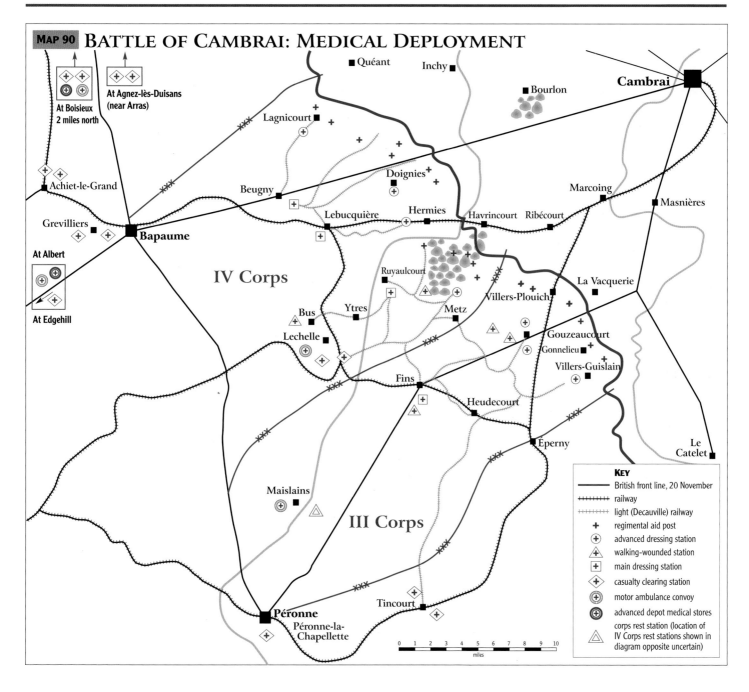

MAP 90 BATTLE OF CAMBRAI: MEDICAL DEPLOYMENT

KEY
— British front line, 20 November
+++++++ railway
+++++++ light (Decauville) railway
+ regimental aid post
⊕ advanced dressing station
△ walking-wounded station
⊞ main dressing station
◈ casualty clearing station
⊚ motor ambulance convoy
◉ advanced depot medical stores
△ corps rest station (location of IV Corps rest stations shown in diagram opposite uncertain)

three advanced dressing stations with the main dressing station, the walking wounded station and all the casualty clearing stations. Decauville trains and motor ambulance cars were available for stretcher cases, and for walking wounded there were buses.

In IV Corps the divisions on the northern sector were not considered likely to become engaged in major fighting, so the normal arrangements for casualty evacuation and treatment were considered sufficient. On the southern sector it was likely that losses would be heavier, so maximum use was to be made of the Decauville rail network run by the two light railway companies with headquarters at Ytres and Bapaume.

For the Cavalry Corps, plans envisaged the brigades being accompanied by pack-mounted sections of the cavalry field ambulances, which were located at Fins with the corps forward headquarters. These sections carried stretchers, medical equipment, water and blankets and were intended to form brigade collecting posts in touch with regimental medical officers and aid posts. They were to keep the wounded in groups near a road until the situation allowed them to be cleared to an advanced dressing station. Light sections would follow these pack sections with dismounted stretcher-bearers in the ambulance wagons, followed by the heavy sections and motor ambulance cars. The pack-mounted section would supplement the regimental aid posts and collect wounded alongside roads, preferably in houses or barns.

Engineers

Much, although not all, engineer planning revolved around the completeness of the arrangements for opening and controlling communications. Roads and tracks leading to the British front line had to be prepared as completely as concealment permitted prior to Z-hour. All infantry, artillery and tank routes had to be cleared and signed with noticeboards, and boards were also required for routes on the other side of the German defences. Detailed instructions had to be issued about the numbers of personnel – mostly pioneer working parties from divisional pioneer battalions under Royal Engineer supervision – for specific tasks on specific roads or tracks. The guiding principle was that roads had first to be cleared for the passage of guns and limbered wagons and only after this had been completed would further work be done for general traffic.

The other vital task, mentioned above, fell to the field survey companies of the Royal Engineers. They were responsible for the surveying of numerous battery positions for the new artillery units coming into the army area. Without these surveys, which were pegged out and located accurately on a grid, the guns would not be able to prepare battery boards, and predicted firing – on the accuracy of which depended the success of the opening of counter-battery fire and the lifting barrage at Z-hour – would be impossible.

Very considerable effort went into the planning and preparation for the advance through and beyond the German defensive positions. For any exploitation of success it was essential for routes forward for artillery, cavalry and supplies of fuel and ammunition to be designated and cleared as rapidly as possible. Planning went so far as to have infantry divisions position men with drag ropes at trench crossings and other difficult spots to help guns and vehicles forward. For the purpose of clearing

passages behind the enemy lines parties of engineers and pioneers were to follow immediately behind the rear battalions of assaulting brigades, as it was deemed critical to have routes cleared quickly up to the Brown Line. Cavalry routes were the designated cavalry tracks shown on Map 88; specific formations or units were made responsible for clearing these with the aid of wiring-clearing tanks (see page 501). An example was the 6th Division pioneers, who were responsible for making the road between Ribécourt and Marcoing passable to the cavalry with the assistance of wire-clearing tanks.

The 'Kavanagh Track' was the responsibility of the Cavalry Track Battalion, and plans were drawn up from aerial photographs, which showed that the track would be over 5 miles long and would cross at least twenty-six trench lines. A replica of this trench system was constructed, with each trench numbered and squads of men detailed off to each trench. As this work would have to be carried out with material found nearby, 'collecting parties' were told off and instructed to work out what material was needed for their trench crossing. A 'track leader', an officer, would accompany the infantry attack along with twenty-six

men carrying noticeboards with the numbers of the trenches from one (British front-line trench) to twenty-six (the Hindenburg Line). As the officer identified the trenches he would place the noticeboard in position so that the appropriate squad (equipped with shovels, picks, sandbags and rammer) would recognize its particular trench and could set to work

In the 29th Division, tasked with securing the crossings over the St-Quentin Canal at Marcoing and Masnières, the pioneer battalion working under the orders of the divisional commander, RE, was to be employed in the construction of a tramway system from Gouzeaucourt to Marcoing to connect up with the German system near La Vacquerie.

Another equally important task, and very much a part of route-clearance, was the securing and making usable of river and canal crossings. Two field companies RE, the 497th (Kent) and 455th (West Riding), were tasked with the preservation or restoration of all river and canal crossings from Marcoing to Masnières inclusive. Three pontoon detachments, augmented by six pontoon wagons, were kept in reserve on the Fins–Gouzeaucourt road in case this bridging was needed.

29th Division Attack on the St-Quentin Canal Bridges

Securing the bridges across the St-Quentin Canal was vital to the success of the whole concept of breaching the Masnières–Beaurevoir Line and allowing the cavalry to exploit around Cambrai and beyond.

The 29th Division, nicknamed the 'Incomparable 29th', was the last regular division to be formed and the only one to fight in Gallipoli. It was certainly considered an elite division with an impressive fighting record: after Gallipoli, where the 1st Lancashire Fusiliers won six Victoria Crosses, came the Somme (the division lost 5,240 men on 1 July); the Arras offensive in April 1917; Third Ypres in November – all prior to

Cambrai. By the war's end the division had won twenty-seven Victoria Crosses. It was commanded on 20 November 1917 by Major General Sir Beauvoir de Lisle and was composed as shown in the table below.

At 1:30 p.m. on 18 November Lieutenant Colonel F. H. Moore, divisional chief of staff, issued written orders for the attack, which are summarized as follows (see Map 91):

- After the securing of the Brown Line by the 12th, 20th and 6th Divisions, the 29th Division would advance and pass through the leading division to secure the crossings over the St-Quentin Canal at, and between, Masnières and Marcoing, and capture the

section of the Masnières–Beaurevoir Line north of the canal to allow the cavalry to pass through and exploit the gap.

- 88th Brigade, with one section of 497 Field Company, RE and a bearer division of 88 Field Ambulance, was to take the crossings over the canal at Masnières with the assistance of four tanks. It was then to seize and consolidate the defence of the Masnières–Beaurevoir Line from east of the sugar factory to the Masnières–Cambrai road. 59th Brigade, 20th Division, would protect the right flank.

- 87th Brigade, with a section of 455 Field Company, RE and a bearer division of 87 Field Ambulance, was to take the crossings east of Marcoing with the assistance of four tanks. It was then to seize and consolidate the Masnières–Beaurevoir Line from the Masnières–Cambrai road (exclusive) to the canal just south of Flot Farm.

- 86th Brigade, with one section of 510 Company, RE and the bearer division of 89 Field Ambulance, was to capture and consolidate the Masnières–Beaurevoir Line from the canal near Flot Farm and north of Nine Wood to the Premy Chapel hill. 18th Brigade, 6th Division, would protect the left flank.

86th Brigade	87th Brigade	88th Brigade
(Brig. Gen. G. R. H. Cheape)	(Brig. Gen. C. H. T. Lucas)	(Brig. Gen. H. Nelson)
2nd Royal Fusiliers (2RF)	2nd South Wales Borderers (2SWB)	4th Worcestershire (4 Worc)
1st Lancashire Fusiliers (1LF)	1st King's Own Scottish Borderers (1KOSB)	1st Essex (1 Essex)
16th Middlesex (16 Mdx)	1st Royal Inniskilling Fusiliers (1 Innsk F)	2nd Hampshire (2 Hants)
1st Royal Guernsey Light Infantry (1 RGLI)	1st Border (1Bord)	Newfoundland Regiment (Nfd R)

- 2nd Monmouthshire (2 Mon) as divisional pioneers
- A section of 455, 497 and 510 Field Companies, RE
- Twelve tanks from A Battalion (four for each brigade)
- In support: 15th, 16th and 17th Brigades, RHA

- A 60-pounder battery and a horse-drawn 6-inch howitzer battery
- Bearer divisions of 87, 88 and 89 Field Ambulances
- A contact aircraft to fly over corps area at specified intervals

The objective of the 87th Brigade. The taking of Flot Farm would mean breaking the Masnières–Beaurevoir Line south-east of Noyelles.

Flot Farm was in front of these trees

Sugar factory

• Three cavalry divisions were to pass through the 29th Division once the crossings and the Masnières–Beaurevoir Line were secured – the 5th followed by the 2nd Cavalry Division at Masnières and Marcoing, while the 1st would advance on Noyelles and Cantaing to the north.

• As soon as sufficient cavalry had passed through to screen the infantry, the 88th Brigade was to push forward to a spur about 1,200 yards north of Crèvecourt, leaving two battalions in the Beaurevoir Line. The 87th Brigade would advance one battalion to the eastern and northern fringes of Rumilly, with another on a knoll a mile further north, keeping two in the Beaurevoir Line. The 86th Brigade was to become the divisional reserve after being relieved by the 6th Division.

• A brigade of Royal Horse Artillery field guns would move to the locations shown on Map 91 to support the crossings over the canal and advance beyond as required.

• The 29th Division heavy artillery group and the super-heavy guns and howitzers would fire concentrations until 10:15 a.m. on Marcoing, 10:30 a.m. on Masnières, 11:30 a.m. on Rumilly and until 11:40 a.m. on Lesdain (off map, immediately south-east of Crèvecourt).

By 10:15 a.m. that morning the Brown Line had been secured and Major General de Lisle gave the order by bugle call for his division to advance. At that stage it was regarded as more of a pursuit than an attack, as little serious opposition was expected. Previously, in the early hours of that morning, the division had marched 7 miles from just north of Péronne to its waiting area to the south of La Vacquerie.

The 88th Brigade, which was led by four tanks and the 1st Essex, soon ran into serious opposition from a German field battery and two machine guns in a strongpoint on Welsh Ridge. Three of the tanks and guns exchanged fire, with the result that one enemy gun was knocked out, but at the cost of three tanks. Although the fourth developed engine trouble, the infantry were able to take the position and capture seventy prisoners. This delay resulted in the 4th Worcesters overtaking the Essex, and they were able to get two companies over the canal at the bridge opposite the Masnières sugar factory, although heavy fire prevented further progress. At around 12:40 p.m. a tank (named 'Flying Fox') supporting the 59th Brigade (the reserve of 20th Division) tried to cross the damaged main bridge but it collapsed under the weight – the crew were lucky to escape under heavy fire from close range.

At about 2:30 p.m. the Canadian Cavalry Brigade (5th Cavalry Division) arrived just south-west of Les Rues Vertes and the Fort

Garry Horse were ordered forward. By this time the 2nd Hampshires had located a lock crossing a few hundred yards south-east of the sugar factory bridge by which the Worcesters had crossed, and although subject to rifle and machine-gun fire began to get men across in single file. During this process their commanding officer, Lieutenant Colonel C. S. Linton, was shot dead by a sniper. It was decided to try to get the Fort Garry across at the same place, although considerable work had to done by the machine-gun squadron, aided by civilians, to make the lock negotiable by horses.

At around 3:30 p.m. the rain that was to continue all night started as B Squadron crossed over. Lieutenant Harcus Strachan, the squadron second in command, reported that:

> The squadron, taking horses in single file at a distance, crossed the bridge, which was under fire and very precarious. Several men fell into the canal, and a number were drowned, but by the blessing of Providence, we reached the other side and away we went at a gallop at 3:45 p.m.
>
> While cutting through some wire obstacle several men and Captain Duncan Campbell were killed and command devolved on to Strachan. On reaching the higher ground east of Masnières the squadron charged an enemy gun battery of four guns with drawn swords, cutting down most of the gunners as, all except for one detachment that continued to fire, fled. Advancing further the squadron overtook a number of German infantry retiring in disorder towards Rumilly and the squadron rode right over them as they discarded arms and equipment right and left. They offered no opposition, but they protected themselves as well as they could by lying down or hiding behind piles of rubbish, etc., where we could not reach them with the sword. Batches of from fifty to a hundred put their hands up, but the squadron could not stop to collect them . . .

Having reached a sunken road east of Rumilly a halt was called to rest the exhausted horses. It was then discovered that only forty-three men and mounts remained, and of these all but seven horses were wounded and all the pack animals lost. Darkness was approaching and patrols failed to discover any of the regiment following up their advance. Telephone lines were cut, but in cutting a power line one man was electrocuted. It was then reported that a strong force of Germans was advancing along the road towards them. A brisk firefight drove them away, but a much larger force appeared to be trying to cut them off.

Strachan decided he must withdraw, as it was dark, there was no sign of support and a number of horses had died of wounds and exhaustion. The journey back took all night, involving a halt for an hour for a little rest and sleep in a large crater. Despite becoming separated into two groups, the remnants of the squadron finally returned, bringing a number of prisoners with them – Strachan's group remained by the broken bridge with the tank stuck in the centre. Strachan, who already had the Military Cross, was awarded the Victoria Cross for his exploits.

By 10:00 p.m. the 88th Brigade had the 2nd Hampshires, two companies of the Worcesters and one of the Essex over north of the canal.

B Squadron, Fort Garry Horse crossed the bridge at this lock, then charged uphill into the German line, cutting down many Germans and overrunning an artillery position. Lieutenant H. Strachan won the VC for his skill and gallantry in withdrawing the remnants of the squadron back over the canal.

The objectives of the 29th Division on the opening of the Battle of Cambrai. This view from the divisional start line, some 2,500 yards behind the British front line (near the Brown Line), shows the approximate axis of advance of the 86th (left) and 88th (centre) Brigades. The 86th Brigade advanced beyond Bois Couillet, led by tanks, with the object of securing crossing places over the St-Quentin Canal at Marcoing and Masnières. The 20th Division had cleared up to the Brown Line earlier that morning, leaving the 29th Division the formidable task of breaking the last line of German defences – the Masnières–Beaurevoir Line.

Bourlon Wood

Marcoing

Bois Couillet

87th Brigade

MAP 91 **29TH DIVISION ATTACKS THE BRIDGES AT MARCOING AND MASNIÈRES**

KEY

- Masnières–Beaurevoir Line
- Brown Line
- 4 tanks lead each brigade
- intended line of advance of battalions
- 86 area where brigades were to consolidate
- 15 RHA field artillery brigades' location to support the advance
- approx. route of Lt Strachan's squadron of Fort Garry Horse
- x x x x British front line at nightfall

To Cantaing

To Cambrai

Sugar Factory

Flot Farm

Noyelles

86

Nine Wood

Lock

Rumilly

German attack

Premy Chapel

1GNSY
2 RF

16Mddx

Marcoing

Lock

Station

87

German artillery battery

Brown Line

16 RHA

1LF

copse

Lock

Masnières

88

Ribécourt

1 KOSB

1 Bord

2 SWB

Les Rues Vertes

Sugar Factory

Mount Plaisir Farm

Lock

Crèvecœur

Innsk

Lock

Courillet Wood

17 RHA

Nfland

1 Essex

2 Hants

4 Worc

Lock

15 RHA

Les Rues des Vignes

Lock

86

Brown Line

87

88

St-Quentin Canal

Lateau Wood

29TH DIVISION

Villers-Plouich

Bonavis Farm

Vaucelles

La Vacquerie

XX

At Gouzeaucourt
1 mile

0   1000   2000   3000   4000
yards

Masnières

88th Brigade

The 87th Brigade attack made better progress on the left than the right. The KOSB had little problem in entering Marcoing and pushed a company over the canal by the main railway bridge and secured the town. Following behind came the 1st Border, who also attempted to cross by the railway bridge but were checked by a troublesome German machine gun that had been overlooked by the KOSB. As the leading platoon advanced from the bridge, this lone gunner opened fire from the station platform. Sergeant C. E. Spackman immediately rushed forward, shot two of the crew with his rifle and bayoneted a third, capturing the gun. This action won him a Victoria Cross.

By 12:30 p.m. three companies of the 1st Border were across, although further progress was prevented by very heavy flanking fire from the Rumilly spur on the right. Meanwhile two tanks had crossed the canal and were able to reach the area of Flot Farm, which they drove round, silencing several machine guns. At about 2:00 p.m. the 7th Dragoon Guards (Secunderabad Cavalry Brigade, 5th Cavalry Division) arrived in Marcoing and were able to cross and reinforce the Borders but could advance no further.

The 2nd South Wales Borderers had managed to cross the canal by the lock east of Marcoing Copse under considerable rifle fire, and were later followed by the Inniskillings. Despite a further advance during which the Inniskillings successfully fought through several defended ammunition pits with bullet and bayonet, they were unable, even in cooperation with the 1st Border, to break into the Masnières–Beaurevoir Line trenches before darkness halted further attempts.

By mid-afternoon the 5th Dragoon Guards (1st Cavalry Division) had arrived; their orders required them to advance east of the canal in a turning movement around Noyelles and Cantaing. Although one squadron crossed the canal and moved forward towards Flot Farm, it was checked by fire and wire and withdrew west of Marcoing where the regiment waited, saddled up all night.

On the left of the divisional attack, the 86th Brigade's assault on Nine Wood was led by four tanks and the 16th Middlesex. They were fired on from within the trees, but fire from the tanks quickly suppressed the opposition and the wood was occupied. On the left the Guernsey Battalion, which had played a part in securing Nine Wood, established itself facing north and west and linked up with troops of the 6th Division near Premy Chapel. To the right rear of the Middlesex, the 2nd Royal Fusiliers assisted the KOSB in clearing part of Marcoing and helped take 100 prisoners and several machine guns. By 3:00 p.m. it had advanced and taken up positions between Nine Wood and the canal.

At around 3:45 p.m. a squadron of the 7th Dragoon Guards advanced on Noyelles and, despite some fire, galloped at the village, took it and captured fifteen Germans at no loss to themselves. The Royal Fusiliers sent a company forward to occupy the village, but found it impossible to reach the canal as the river bridges (not shown on map) were all broken. The rear battalion of the brigade, the 1st Lancashire Fusiliers, had little to do in 'mopping up' Marcoing, so advanced to take up a position south-west of Nine Wood to strengthen the left flank.

Sometime after 3:00 p.m. the 4th Dragoon Guards (1st Cavalry Division) advanced, with one squadron heading for some woods north of Noyelles and another for Cantaing village. The latter was halted by wire and heavy machine-gun fire, although two troops galloped as far as La Folie Chateau beyond the woods, cutting down a number of Germans on the way and taking several prisoners at the chateau. Germans advancing in large numbers through the woods forced a retreat, during which the squadron commander was killed.

Two companies of the 1st Border Regiment crossed this railway bridge and the lock at Marcoing on 20 November 1917.

old railway station platform

the station building was located in these trees

German machine gun

Sergeant Spackman's charge

On crossing the railway bridge the leading platoon of the Border Regiment was confronted by a large German machine-gun post on the station platform. Sergeant Spackman went forward, shot two of the crew, bayoneted a third and captured the gun. He was awarded the VC, survived the war and died in 1969.

A British tank, 'Flying Fox', crashed into the bridge over the St-Quentin Canal at Masnières, destroying the vital river crossing.

Nightfall, 20 November

The line reached by the 29th Division by nightfall is shown on Map 91. The break-in attacks by III and IV Corps had gone well. Secrecy combined with predicted artillery fire and massed tank assault had resulted in spectacular (in Western Front terms) gains of between 3 and 4 miles (see Map 84). Two strong trench systems covered by an outpost zone had been carried in not much more than four hours, with heavy losses inflicted on the Germans. Some 7,500 prisoners had been taken and 120 guns destroyed or captured at a cost of around 4,000 British casualties.

Nevertheless, as in so many previous battles, a break-out had not been achieved. III Corps had closed up to the St-Quentin Canal and crossed it at Marcoing, but the 'Flying Fox' tank crashing through the main bridge at Masnières undoubtedly slowed progress and by nightfall only a small toe-hold north of the canal had been achieved in this area.

In IV Corps' sector Flesquières remained in German hands, as the attack by the 51st Division had stalled, largely due to the infantry becoming separated from the tanks. By the time fighting ceased, and with the troops destined to spend a debilitating, sleepless night in the pouring rain, the Masnières–Beaurevoir Line was largely unbroken and Bourlon and its wood – important objectives of the first day – were still firmly in enemy hands. So although church bells rang out in England, real victory still eluded the Third Army. The offensive, successful in its first phase due to the new tactics combined with meticulous preparation and secrecy, made possible by brilliant staff work, had achieved a surprise attack that in many places the enemy had found irresistible. But instead of the offensive gathering momentum, the exhausted force had come to a standstill.

Today the Royal Tank Corps celebrates 20 November every year as Cambrai Day. It is one of their most famous battle honours, as it was the first time tanks had been used in really large numbers and on ground favourable to their movement. They achieved remarkable results, and the Tank Corps had proved they could master two of the deadly enemies of their infantry comrades, namely barbed wire and machine guns, although they remained very vulnerable to the main killer of the Western Front – artillery. However, by nightfall on the 20th the tank brigades had no reserves for the next day, crews were utterly exhausted and losses had been high. Of the 378 fighting tanks involved, 179 (47 per cent) were out of action – sixty-five by direct hits from artillery fire, seventy-one through serious mechanical faults, and forty-three through ditching or other causes.

Captain D. G. Browne, MC, writing in 1920 of his personal experiences, described the state of the tank battalions at the end of the first day. He starts by quoting from the *Weekly Tank Corps Notes*:

> By 4 p.m. on the 20th November one of the most astonishing battles in all history had been won, and as far as the Tank Corps was concerned, tactically finished, for no reserves existing, it was not possible to do more than rally the now very weary and exhausted crews, select the fittest, and patch up composite companies to continue the attack on the morrow.

Browne continued:

> I have pointed out before the actual physical exhaustion, due to extreme heat, cramped quarters, jolting, and other causes, entailed in any prolonged operation in a tank. Of the machines which rallied on the evening of November 20th nearly all had been running for at least sixteen hours. Some had covered distances undreamt of in

any previous tank action. All were out of petrol, water and ammunition, and many had mechanical troubles that needed attention . . . For the brigade and battalion staffs there was the task of calculating losses and effectives, and of arranging the formation of composite companies for the continuation of the battle next day. There was not an additional man or tank to be had: all had been in action . . .

Unteroffizier Theodor Kruger at Flesquières

The attack of the 51st (Highland) Division on Flesquières was eventually driven back, and a number of tanks approaching up Cemetery Alley trench were knocked out by a German artillery battery. The German guns belonged to a battery of the 108th Field Artillery Regiment, 54th Division, whose gunners had received special training in anti-tank gunnery – specifically, by firing over open sights at close range. The tanks in question belonged to the 4th (D) Battalion and had been knocked out before penetrating the enemy wire. The wrecks of these tanks were scattered about the Flesquières ridge.

A report that the German battery had been destroyed except for one gun, which was manned by a single German officer, who had eventually been killed by his own gun, gave rise to the story that he had been responsible for knocking out ten or more tanks. This report, or rumour, was even mentioned in Haig's despatch on the battle. The British press seized upon the story, and then the Germans sought to identify this man praised so highly by the enemy, eventually naming Unteroffizier Theodor Krüger as their hero. Years later Hitler had a monument to him and the German Artillery erected in Cologne – it was destroyed in World War II.

However, it is virtually certain that one gun and one man could not have inflicted all these losses. What is perhaps more likely was that Krüger's gun knocked out a number of tanks, but that the exact number will never be known with certainty. The war diary of the 4th (D) Battalion, Tank Corps, recorded nine tanks knocked out or disabled on 20 November: D6, D11, D28, D32, D41, D45, D47, D49 and D51 (see box, page 502). All suffered direct hits and two, D6 and D11, were also burned out. All except D47 were female tanks. Clearly the German guns in the Flesquières area had some easy targets that morning and a number of the kills undoubtedly were attributable to Unteroffizier Krüger – but probably not all.

The Endgame

It is not for this book to go into the subsequent arguments of soldiers and historians about why the cavalry was seemingly so cautious in its advance on 20 November, but there is probably much truth in the suggestion that had they been commanded by a real 'thruster' instead of the somewhat pedestrian Kavanagh the cavalry would have suffered unjustifiable losses for little gain.

The next fourteen days saw the usual Western Front battle develop, with the British trying to advance against rapidly stiffening resistance as the Germans rushed reserves to the threatened sector. On 30 November the Germans launched a major counter-attack with two thrusts, both aimed at retaking the British salient created in their defences during the battle. The main thrust came first from the east, on both sides of Lateau Wood towards Villers-Guislain and Gouzeaucourt, and the other from the north through Bourlon. This latter attack made virtually no progress, but the southern one took Gonnelieu and Villers-Guislain, and for a while held Gouzeaucourt. At one stage a German attack towards Les Rues Vertes and Marcoing threatened to cut off the 29th Division. It was not a good day for that division, as it nearly lost its commander, who had to make a hasty departure – although not as rumoured in his pyjamas – from his headquarters on the outskirts of Gouzeaucourt.

At Les Rues Vertes a section of 497 (Kent) Field Company, RE were caught asleep in the brewery on the southern edge of the canal and captured while the troops of the German 30th Division pressed on towards the canal bridge. The 86th Brigade rear headquarters was located near the southern end of the broken bridge – with the disabled tank still stuck in the middle. Captain Robert Gee was a staff officer at the headquarters and, with a handful of signallers and orderlies armed with rifles and a Lewis gun, hastily barricaded the street with

The crossroads in Masnières, site of the former village of Les Rues Vertes, where on 30 November Captain Robert Gee led a group of signallers and orderlies against the counter-attacking Germans. His gallantry saved the village and culminated in Gee, revolver in hand, charging a machine gun, capturing it and turning it against the Germans. Although wounded in the knee, the next day he escaped capture by swimming the canal. He was awarded a well-deserved VC.

German advance
Gee's advance
barricade

furniture from a nearby house. From there they opened up a heavy fire on the startled Germans, forcing them back. Running short of ammunition, Gee went to collect more from the brigade dump in another house. There he was surprised by two Germans and in the ensuing struggle Gee managed to kill one by clubbing him with an iron-tipped stick, while the second was dealt with by two of his men who arrived just in time. With the arrival of reinforcements from the Guernsey Light Infantry Gee was able to strengthen his barricade and then push forward with a bombing party to drive the enemy further back. The Germans withdrew, but left behind a machine gun at the southern edge of the village to hold the British until reinforcements could be summoned. Captain Gee brought up a Stokes mortar to give fire support and, with one orderly, worked round to a flank to attack the machine gun. The mortar's first bomb was hopelessly inaccurate, so Gee, armed with a revolver in each hand and accompanied by the orderly, rushed the position. The orderly was killed, but Gee was able to account for the machine-gun crew Wild West-style with

his revolvers. Shortly afterwards he was wounded in the knee. In the words of his brigade commander, 'by his heroic conduct, his energy, his fine leadership and utter neglect of himself, Captain Gee certainly saved the 86th Brigade'. Captain Gee was awarded the Victoria Cross. After the war he moved to Perth, Australia, where he died in 1960, aged eighty-four.

The fighting south of Cambrai had fizzled out by 4 December, with both sides exhausted and with the results about evenly balanced as regards territory gained or lost and casualties inflicted. Nevertheless, despite its being a comparatively small-scale encounter, the first day marked a critical moment in the overall context of how the fighting on the Western Front was conducted. Credit for the startling British success on 20 November has been claimed by both the tanks and the artillery, but in truth it was the tactical combination of all arms, careful planning, preparation and excellent staff work that together secured that key to success in an all-arms battle that has remained the same since man first fought man – surprise.

The inhabitants of the captured village of Noyelles take refuge in Marcoing, 22 November 1917.

The coffin of the Unknown Warrior is carried from HMS Verdun on arrival in Dover on 10 November 1920.

Epilogue

'We Will Remember Them'

O Valiant Hearts, who to your glory came,
Through dust of conflict and through battle flame;
Tranquil you lie, your knightly virtue proved,
Your memory hallowed in the land you loved.

Sir John Stanhope Arkwright,
The Supreme Sacrifice, 1919

The Armistice

Very early on the morning of 11 November 1918 Major Hugh Shadbolt, RA was watching his men dragging heavy howitzers into a clearing in a wood near the Forest of Mormal (close to the French–Belgian border) when a despatch rider rode up and handed him a message form. 'Hostilities will cease at 11 a.m. today. A.A.A. [Acknowledge] No firing will take place after this hour.' Mark Severn, in his story 'The Advance, 1918', recorded Major Shadbolt's immediate reaction.

He sat down on a tree stump. In any case the order did not affect them as the enemy was out of range, and they could move no further.

This then was the end. Visions of the early days, their hopes and ambitions, swam before his eyes. He saw again his prehistoric howitzer in the orchard at Festubert, and Allington's long legs move towards him through the trees. He was back with the Australians in their dugout below Pozières. He saw the long slope of the hill at Heninel [5 miles from Arras], covered with guns, ammunition dumps, tents and dugouts. Ypres, the Salient, Trois Tours, St. Julien – the names made unforgettable pictures in his mind. Happy days at Beugny and Beaussart, they were gone, and the bad ones with them. Hugh was gone, and Tyler and little Rawson; Sergeant Powell, that brave old man; Elliot and James and Johnson – the names of his dead gunners strung themselves before him. This was the very end. What good had it all been? To serve what purpose had they all died? For the moment he could find no answer.

His brain was too numb with memories.
'Mr. Straker.'
'Sir.'
'You can fall the men out for breakfast. The war is over.'
'Very good, sir.'

By the end of October 1918 Germany was on the point of collapse, both militarily on the Western Front and at home. On the night of 29 October a naval mutiny broke out in the port of Wilhelmshaven and the revolt spread across the country within a matter of days, leading to the proclamation of a republic on 9 November, along with the abdication of Kaiser Wilhelm II. The new German government was headed by Friedrich Ebert.

The Armistice was the result of a desperate and hurried process. The German chief of staff, Paul von Hindenburg, had already requested a meeting with Ferdinand Foch by telegram on 7 November as he was under huge pressure – revolution in Berlin and elsewhere across Germany seemed imminent, as millions of people were desperately war weary and thousands were on the verge of starvation

The German delegation, headed by the politician Matthias Erzberger, crossed the front line in five cars and was escorted on a ten-hour journey across devastated northern France. They were taken to a railway siding in the Forest of Compiègne, where the negotiations were to take place aboard Foch's private train. The Allied delegation was composed of Marshal Foch (although he appeared only briefly on three occasions during the three days of negotiations), General Maxime Weygand (Foch's chief of staff), Admiral Sir Rosslyn Wemyss (First

Sea Lord and British representative), Rear Admiral George Hope, RN, and Captain John Marriott, RN. Representing Germany were Matthias Erzberger, Count Alfred von Oberndorff (from the Foreign Ministry), Major General Detlof von Winterfeldt (army) and Captain Ernst Vanselow (navy).

The Germans tried unsuccessfully to argue for conditions less stringent than what amounted to demilitarization and

The Allied representatives at the signing of the Armistice on board a train in the Bois de Compiègne. Left to right (first row): Admiral Hope, General Weygand, Admiral Wemyss, Marshal Foch, Captain Marriott.

total surrender, as well as the continued crippling naval blockade of Germany (which would not end until an official peace was signed). They could, of course, do little except protest at the harshness of the Allied terms. On 10 November the German delegation was shown newspapers from Paris reporting that the Kaiser had abdicated and, despite desperate attempts, they were unable to receive instructions from Berlin. However, they were ordered to sign the Armistice by Hindenburg. The signing took place between 5:12 a.m. and 5:20 a.m., Paris time, on 11 November, to come into effect at 11:00 a.m.

Just a small part of the conditions was that the German armies were to hand over in good condition 5,000 guns (2,500 heavy and 2,500 light); 25,000 machine guns; 3,000 *Minenwerfer* and 1,700 aeroplanes (fighters, bombers and night-bombing machines).

Foch issued a General Order to the armies at 10:50 a.m.: 'Hostilities will cease on the whole front as from November 11 at 11 o'clock French time. The Allied troops will not, until further orders, go beyond the line reached on that date and at that hour.' The actual peace between the Allies and Germany (this was only officially an armistice, not a peace treaty) would not be settled until 1919 by the Paris Peace Conference and the Treaty of Versailles.

In London the news brought vast crowds on to the streets. Trafalgar Square and the Mall were one huge sea of people. They surged down to the gates of Buckingham Palace where they sang the National Anthem, 'Land of Hope and Glory' and 'Tipperary' over and over again until the King and Queen came on to the balcony.

The war that had lasted 1,564 days was over – but the suffering and grief continued for generations to come.

The Cost

The total losses suffered by all the belligerents in World War I can never be calculated precisely, as records were incomplete and the methods of recording differed from nation to nation. Although the numbers quoted in the paragraphs that follow cannot be regarded as absolutely definitive, they do give an approximate idea of the scale of military casualties.

The Thiepval Memorial, bearing the names of more than 72,000 men who fell on the Somme and have no known grave.

On the Western Front the total British Army deaths from all causes (including those from Canada, Australia, India and other places) amounted to 648,376, of which 32,098 were Royal Navy and RFC/RAF losses.

In 2009 the Commonwealth War Graves Commission issued the following figures for World War I for British Army soldiers who have no known grave:

No known grave but listed on a memorial to the missing	526,816
Buried but not identifiable by name	187,861
Therefore not buried at all	338,955

According to figures produced in the 1920s and given in the *British Official History: Medical Services*, total British Army wounded were as follows:

Wounded in action and other causes	2,272,998
(RN and RFC/RAF 16,862)	
Proportion returned to duty	64%
Proportion returned to duty but not front line	18%
Proportion discharged as invalids	8%
Proportion died of wounds	7%
Unknown	3%

The above figures include those wounded twice or more. The number of British personnel wounded twice was 34,651 and three or more times 5,097.

In all theatres of the war, the Central Powers sustained over 14 million casualties, of which almost 4 million were deaths (from all causes).

Horrendous as these figures are, they bear no comparison with the overall losses in World War II, where the Soviet Union alone had well over 13 million military deaths.

It is difficult even to estimate how many of the overall losses occurred on the Western Front. Taking into account the bitter struggle on the Eastern Front, the heavy losses in the Italian campaign, the Balkans and against Turkey, the casualties in France and Belgium cannot much exceed half. Nevertheless, the Western Front saw the most intense, protracted and bloody battles involving the main Allied powers. John Terraine, in his book *The Smoke and the Fire*, compared the daily British losses in five major battles in the period 1916–18 (see below).

It is worth noting from these figures that the two battles that represent in many British eyes the true horror of the Western Front in terms of losses – namely the Somme and Third Ypres (Passchendaele) – cannot be compared in terms of their daily casualty rate with Arras, nor with the German offensive of March 1918 where for forty-one days the average daily loss was 5,848.

British Losses in Five Major Battles, 1916–1918

Battle	Duration	Days	Casualties	Daily rate
Somme	1 July–18 November	142	415,000	2,950
1917 Arras	9 April–17 May	39	159,000	4,070
3rd Ypres	31 July–12 November	105	244,000	2,121
1918 Picardy, Lys (German offensive)	21 March–30 April	41	239,793	5,848
Final offensive	8 August–11 November	96	350,000	3,645

In Memoriam

When war shall cease this lonely unknown spot
Of many a pilgrimage will be the end,
And flowers will shine in this now barren plot
And fame upon it through the years descend:
But many a heart upon each simple cross
Will hang the grief, the memory of its loss.

from 'A Soldier's Cemetery' by Sergeant John William Street, York and Lancaster Regiment, killed in action on the Somme, near Serre, on 1 July 1916

Britain and the Commonwealth

British and Commonwealth memorials and war cemeteries were erected and maintained by the Commonwealth War Graves Commission (CWGC), established by Royal Charter as the Imperial War Graves Commission on 21 May 1917. A uniform headstone was designed, 2 feet 6 inches high and 1 foot 3 inches wide, bearing the regimental badge, name (where known), rank, number, date of birth and death, religious emblem (Christian, Latin Cross, Star of David or other) and any personal inscription, which the family could choose. The headstones were laid out mostly in straight lines to represent a battalion on parade. In almost every cemetery stands the towering 'Cross of Sacrifice' surmounted by a bronze crusader's sword – this is now plastic, as many bronze swords were stolen. In the larger cemeteries is an imposing 'Stone of Remembrance' with the words Rudyard Kipling chose from Ecclesiasticus: 'Their Name Liveth for Evermore'. He also chose the inscription that appears on the headstone of every unidentified burial: 'A Soldier [or Sailor or Airman] of the Great War, Known unto God'. Twenty-three of these cemeteries in Belgium and eighty-nine in France hold the graves of Victoria Cross winners.

There are several hundred cemeteries and memorials scattered all over what was the Western Front, with many of the memorials built to honour a national contingent, a division, a brigade or a regiment, even an individual artillery battery, of the fallen of a particular battle. Those men whose bodies were never recovered have their names inscribed on the pillars or walls of special memorials. The names of British and Commonwealth missing in the Ypres salient are recorded on the Menin Gate at Ypres – perhaps the best-known memorial in the world. It was constructed astride the road up which countless thousands of troops marched to the front and takes the form of a triumphal arch. On its pillars are the names of 54,896 men from the United Kingdom, Australia, Canada, India (and what is now Pakistan) and South Africa who died before 16 August 1917 and whose bodies were never found. The Menin Gate does not hold the names of the New Zealand or Newfoundland missing as they opted for separate memorials on the battlefields over which they fought.

Every evening at 8:00 p.m. under the pillars of the Gate the Last Post is sounded by buglers of the Belgian Fire Service. This moving ceremony has taken place uninterrupted since 1928 (except during the Nazi occupation) and always draws a large crowd, many of whom lay wreaths and spend time searching for their relatives or regimental name on the pillars.

However, it was discovered on completion of the Gate that there was insufficient room for all the names, so the cut-off date noted above had to be imposed. Those who died after this date (most of them during Third Ypres) are commemorated at the Tyne Cot Memorial and cemetery near Zonnebeke. This is the largest British and Commonwealth cemetery in the world, with almost 12,000 graves and close to 35,000 names of the missing inscribed on the wall panels. An impressive and unusual feature of Tyne Cot is that inside the visitor centre the names and ages of all those commemorated are read out continuously from a recording at the rate of about seven every minute.

The missing from the Somme battlefields are commemorated on the Thiepval Memorial, which, standing 150 feet high, dominates the surrounding countryside and is the largest British battle memorial in the world. On the stone piers are engraved the names of over 72,000 soldiers who have no known grave. A large inscription on an internal wall reads:

> Here are recorded the names of officers
> and men of the British Armies who fell on
> the Somme battlefields between July 1915
> and March 1918 but to whom the fortune
> of war denied the known and honoured
> burial given to their comrades in death.

The Thiepval Memorial also serves as an Anglo-French battle memorial to commemorate the joint nature of the Somme offensive. In recognition of this, a small cemetery containing the bodies of 300 Commonwealth and 300 French graves lies at the foot of the memorial. On the French headstones is the single word '*Inconnu*' (unknown). On top of the archway is the inscription: '*Aux armées française et britannique, l'Empire britannique reconnaissant*' ('To the French and British Armies, from the grateful British Empire').

France

The Ministry for War Veterans and Victims is responsible for administering and maintaining France's war cemeteries, of which there are 108 in the country. French graves are marked with stone crosses with metal plates bearing the inscription '*Mort pour la France*' ('Died for France') and the name, rank, regiment and date of death of the soldier. A mass grave, or ossuary, is a feature of some French cemeteries, and in all chapels relatives have put up many commemorative plaques.

The Douaumont Ossuary at Verdun is the largest French cemetery and ossuary in the country. It is located on the battlefield where the French and Germans were locked in combat for 300 days in 1916. The ossuary is a memorial containing the remains of both French and German soldiers who died on the battlefield. Inside the vaults are the skeletal remains of some 130,000 unidentified bodies from both nations. The bones and skulls can be glimpsed through windows set at intervals low in the outside walls. The tower is 150 feet high and contains a bronze bell weighing over 2 tons, which is rung at official ceremonies. From the tower a magnificent panoramic view of the battlefield and the 15,000 crosses marking the graves of additional fallen soldiers is obtained. On top of the tower a rotating red and white 'Lantern of the Dead' shines out over the battlefield at night. The cloister is almost 150 yards long and contains forty-two alcoves, each with information on the area of the battlefield from which the bodies in that tomb were recovered. The first floor is a war museum with weapons and relics of the surrounding villages destroyed in the battle.

United States

In 1923 the American Battle Monuments Commission was set up to erect and maintain memorials and graves for American war dead in the United States and overseas, although this was later restricted to overseas sites only. There are seven American cemeteries, each with its chapel, in Belgium and France commemorating 29,265 burials, 1,655 burials where the identity of the fallen is unknown, and 4,452 missing men. These are: Belgium – Flanders Fields at Waregem; France – Aisne–Marne at Bellau, Meuse–Argonne at Romagne, Oise–Aisne at Fère-en-Tardenois, St-Mihiel at Thiaucourt, and the Somme at Suresnes. Those not buried or commemorated at these places were repatriated.

Every man whose body was identified had his name, rank, organization, state and date of death (but not of birth) inscribed on the headstone. These headstones were either white marble crosses or Stars of David for Jews – there was nothing that recognized any other faith, and occasionally there is a Star of David marking the grave of an unknown soldier. As crosses are used, there is no room for any personal messages as there is on British headstones. All unknown dead were buried with headstones bearing the words: 'Here rests in honored glory an American soldier known but to God'. On Memorial Day each grave is decorated with the Stars and Stripes and the national flag of the host country. Missing soldiers have their names and details inscribed in one of the chapels.

The largest and most impressive American cemetery in Europe is the Meuse–Argonne one at Romagne-sous-Montfaucon. It contains 14,240 graves,

forming an immense field of white crosses on the slope of a hill with the chapel on the summit. Almost every unit of the AEF is represented here, virtually all having fallen during America's biggest battle in World War I. The cemetery measures 600 yards between the two main entrances, and the surrounding wall is 1½ miles long. Inside the chapel the stained-glass windows depict the insignia of American divisions and other formations that served in Europe. On the panel of the west loggia is a coloured map showing the ground captured by each division during the offensive.

Germany

The German War Graves Commission, based in Kassel, performs the function of maintaining the cemeteries of German war dead from World War I onwards. After

World War I there was a need to concentrate the burials from many scattered, neglected and makeshift cemeteries into fewer larger ones, and over time this was achieved. Now the main cemeteries in Belgium are at Vladslo (25,644 burials), Langemarck (over 44,000), Menen (47,864) and Hooglede (8,247). In France they are located at Fricourt (Somme), Vermandovillers (Somme Department) and Neuville-St-Vaast (Arras).

All feature mass graves. At Langemarck a mass grave containing over 29,900 bodies is located near the entrance, and more than 10,000 soldiers, including two British killed in 1918, are buried in graves containing up to eight men whose names and ranks are inscribed on the flat, black marble markers on the ground over the grave. These German cemeteries have a gloomy and sombre appearance, with no flowers of any sort.

The Unknown Warrior

The British Unknown Warrior lies in a tomb beneath a slab of black Belgian marble edged with a mass of red poppies in Westminster Abbey. The inscription, in brass lettering made from melted-down cartridge cases from the front, is shown in the photograph below:

Only since the Falklands War in 1982 has Britain brought its fallen servicemen or women who died on active service home for burial, and even then relatives have had the option of leaving them in their original resting place – an option taken up by many. In all previous wars the accepted, and only practical, course was for burial to take place in the country where they died. The numbers were too great, the means of speedy transportation did not exist, and the cost was huge – all of which combined to ensure that Britain's military cemeteries are scattered in virtually every corner of the world where the British Army has served.

In 1916 Padre David Railton, MC, had just finished a burial service near Armentières and was returning to his billet when he came across a solitary grave marked by a wooden cross on which was written, 'An Unknown Soldier of the Black Watch'. This had a profound effect on him and he wrote to Sir Douglas Haig suggesting that a body should be returned to England for burial to represent all those killed on the Western Front. He received no reply, but after the war Railton continued to promote the idea of such a shrine in Westminster Abbey. He was backed by the Dean of the Abbey and the prime minister, Lloyd George; with their help and a powerful and favourable press campaign the idea gained massive public support. It was known that the French proposed the burial of an Unknown Warrior at the Arc de Triomphe and this, together with the growing public demand, convinced King George V to give his approval. The burial was to coincide with the King's unveiling of the permanent Cenotaph in Whitehall on 11 November 1920.

The arrangements were put in the hands of Lord Curzon of Kedleston, who prepared, in committee, the service and location. But it was only on 7 November that instructions were sent to the British GOC in France, Brigadier General L. J. Wyatt, to make immediate arrangements to select the body. Four motor ambulances, each with an officer and two soldiers, were despatched to the battlefields of Arras, Aisne, Somme and Ypres to exhume the body of an unidentifiable British soldier and bring his remains to a Nissen hut, hastily converted into a temporary chapel, at St-Pol, near Arras. Great care had to be taken that the remains would be British and that there was no means of identifying his name, arm of service or regiment. The parties were careful to choose graves in areas where only the British had fought, and that the grave contained pieces of British equipment, such as boots, belt or buckle, or bits of uniform, but nothing else.

The remains were put in sacks, laid on stretchers and covered with the Union Flag, then placed in front of the altar in the chapel under guard. At midnight on 7 November Brigadier General Wyatt and Lieutenant Colonel E. A. S. Gell of the Directorate of Graves Registration and Enquiries arrived at the chapel. Neither officer knew from which battlefield the bodies had come. Wyatt walked forward and touched one stretcher, thus deciding which one was to be Britain's Unknown Warrior. The other bodies were removed for reburial and the one selected was placed in a coffin and a short service held. The coffin, under a Union Flag, was driven under escort to a chateau near the harbour at Boulogne where it remained under French

Marshal Foch salutes the body of the Unknown Warrior on its arrival at the quay in Boulogne.

guard overnight. Also taken to Boulogne were six barrels of Ypres soil for use in the burial.

The send-off from Boulogne was entirely arranged by the French, except for the bearer party. Two undertakers from Britain had arrived with the special coffin made from Hampton Court oak, and with a crusader sword presented by the King fixed to the lid by a shield. On it were inscribed the words:

A British Warrior who fell in the Great War
1914–1918
For King and Country

The coffin under its flag was borne by eight British soldiers (a sergeant major RASC, a sergeant RE, a gunner RGA, a trooper Australian Light Horse, a private Canadian infantry, a private 21st London Regiment, a private RAMC and a private MGC) and placed on a French gun carriage drawn by six black horses. The escort leading the cortège was a detachment of the 6th Lille Chasseurs. French soldiers carrying enormous wreaths of white lilies from the French government followed the casket; French cavalry trumpeters and a French Army band led the procession. The gun carriage was followed by detachments from every branch of the French Army, local dignitaries, French veterans and schoolchildren.

Marshal Foch, the French commander-in-chief, and Lieutenant General Sir George Macdonogh, the King's representative, joined the long column. The route was lined by more French troops and many thousands of French citizens. At 9:45 a.m. the bells of every church in Boulogne rang out, the trumpeters sounded *Aux Champs* and then the band struck up with Chopin's funeral march as the procession began its slow, sombre journey to the harbour. As the gun carriage passed by, the officers of the detachments lining the route saluted with their swords and the troops presented arms.

At the quayside was the British destroyer HMS *Verdun*, whose motto was 'They shall not pass' (the motto of the French defenders of Verdun). Marshal Foch made a speech of thanks and farewell on behalf of France and the French Army, in which he said, 'I express the profound feelings of France for the invincible heroism of the British Army.' Macdonogh replied in French and accepted the body on behalf of the King and country.

As the coffin was carried up the gangway it was met by the captain and his officers, the entire ship's company drawn up along the rails and the Royal Marine detachment with fixed bayonets. When the bearer party had almost reached the deck it was greeted by the sharp shrill and screech of the bosun's pipe sounding the traditional naval salute as the marines presented arms and the officers saluted. The coffin was placed on the quarterdeck, still covered with the Union Flag and made invisible as the lily wreaths were placed over it. As *Verdun* drew slowly away, Foch remained a solitary figure standing on the edge of the quay at the salute as the band played the British National Anthem and a gun battery began firing the final farewell, a nineteen-gun salute.

In mid-Channel *Verdun* was met by six destroyers to escort the Unknown Warrior to Dover – selected as it was the port through which scores of hospital ships had docked when bringing wounded and sick from the front. The destroyers formed up three ahead and three astern of *Verdun*. The sea was calm, but it was an overcast and dull November day. As the ships approached Dover the escorting destroyers stopped engines and *Verdun* proceeded on its own as the guns in Dover Castle began to fire their nineteen-gun salute. Every vantage point, including the cliffs, was packed with people. Dover was at a standstill. *Verdun* docked at Admiralty Pier to be met by the mayor and corporation, a guard-of-honour from the Royal Irish Fusiliers (RIF) with their colours and band. A new bearer party of six warrant officers carried the coffin ashore as it was once more saluted by the bosun's pipe and the ship's company. The RIF band struck up 'Land of Hope and Glory', its colours were lowered and the guard presented arms.

Led by General Macdonogh, the procession marched to Dover station, from where the coffin was to be taken to London in a carriage attached to the rear of the Dover–London boat train. The carriage had been painted white so that it could be recognized as the train passed through the Kent countryside on a dark November evening. It stopped briefly at every station along the route so that it could be seen by the hundreds of people who had turned out, many of them dressed in black. At Faversham and Gillingham contingents of ex-servicemen and

British Honours Conferred for Gallantry and Leadership in the Field

The decorations for gallantry in action awarded to British forces during the period 14 August 1914 to 31 May 1920 were the Victoria Cross (VC) awarded to all ranks; the Distinguished Service Order (DSO) awarded to officers; the Military Cross (MC) awarded to officers and warrant officers; and the Distinguished Conduct Medal (DCM) and Military Medal (MM) awarded to other ranks. The list below gives the number of each awarded for service in the field or in connection with air raids or coastal bombardments.

Award	Number of recipients in World War I
VC	579
Bar to VC	2
DSO	9,002
1st Bar to DSO	709
2nd Bar to DSO	71
3rd Bar to DSO	7
MC	37,104
1st Bar to MC	2,983
2nd Bar to MC	168
3rd bar to MC	4
DCM	24,620
1st Bar to DCM	472
2nd Bar to DCM	9
MM	115,589
1st Bar to MM	5,796
2nd Bar to MM	180
3rd Bar to MM	1

The coffin of the Unknown Warrior in Westminster Abbey with the Actors' Pall.

Boy Scouts, and at Chatham naval ratings, were paraded on the platform. As the train moved slowly through the outskirts of London the gardens of the houses lining the track were full of people standing in the drizzle in order to catch a glimpse of the carriage bringing their Warrior home.

At Victoria the carriage was shunted on to Platform 8 – the platform from where countless thousands of men had set off for war, and where leave and hospital trains had brought men home. The carriage with the coffin remained at Victoria overnight under a guard provided by the Grenadier Guards.

At 8:30 a.m. on 11 November eight bearers from the Coldstream Guards entered the carriage, draped the coffin with the Union Flag used by Padre Railton as an altar cloth on several battlefields and fixed a helmet, side arm (bayonet) and belt on top. The cortège formed up with four mounted policemen ahead, followed by massed bands of the Foot Guards, then the gun carriage, drawn by six black horses with twelve pall-bearers (six each side: four admirals of the fleet, four field marshals, three generals and an air marshal). A seemingly endless column of detachments provided by the RN, Army and RAF followed the carriage, marching six abreast, with more contingents of soldiers and hundreds of ex-servicemen and veterans. As they started the 2-mile march to the Abbey, Néry Battery, RHA (whose actions at that village are described in Section Five, page 244) began firing a nineteen-gun salute from Hyde Park.

The route (Buckingham Palace Road–Grosvenor Gardens–Hyde Park Corner–Constitution Hill–The Mall–Admiralty Arch–Trafalgar Square–Whitehall–the Cenotaph) was lined with troops. The entire route was also packed with silent crowds six or eight deep on either side, while thousands more watched from windows, roofs and any possible vantage point (there were reported to be 50,000 in Trafalgar Square). In the distance they heard the steady thump of the bass drum and pipers playing a lament. People had come from every part of the country to witness the homecoming of the Unknown Warrior. Inevitably it crossed the minds of family members who had a son, brother or husband reported missing that the unidentified soldier passing before them could just conceivably be their relative. As the gun carriage passed the troops reversed arms, men removed their hats and bowed while many in the crowds, including men, wept openly.

The carriage halted at the new, permanent Cenotaph, which was concealed under two massive Union Flags. It was met by the King, who placed a wreath of red roses on the coffin and saluted. Bands played 'O God, Our Help In Ages Past', which was sung by the Abbey choir, although the crowds remained silent. The Archbishop of Canterbury said the Lord's Prayer, which was followed by a long silence as all awaited Big Ben to strike the first note of eleven o'clock. On the first stroke the King pressed a button and the flags fell away to reveal the Cenotaph as we know it today. This signalled the start of a two-minute silence. It was virtually a complete national silence. In every town, village and workplace people paused to reflect. Traffic stopped, trains stopped, shops ceased business and the Stock Exchange and banks ceased to trade. Courts stopped as judges and prisoners stood, as did prisoners in their cells, while British warships and liners at sea stopped their engines. At the end of the silence eight Guards buglers sounded the Last Post. This was followed by the laying of wreaths by the King and dignitaries, after which the procession moved down Whitehall to the Abbey, with the King walking behind the gun carriage. This was the signal for the crowds to be allowed forward to lay their personal wreaths; within a short time the whole of the base of the Cenotaph was a mountain of wreaths and flowers. Within five days it was estimated that over 100,000 wreaths and bunches of flowers had been laid.

At the Abbey the bearer party of Coldstream Guards NCOs carried the coffin down the nave, lined with 100 men decorated for gallantry in the war, seventy-four of them holders of the Victoria Cross, all commanded by Colonel Bernard Freyberg, VC. The coffin was placed on bars over the open grave. The congregation consisted of the King, ministers, service chiefs and other dignitaries, but most of the seats had been reserved for over 1,000 war widows. The first rows were given to 100 widows who had lost their husbands and all their sons. Then came mothers who had lost their only or all sons, and finally those women who had lost their husbands. They were given seats in accordance with the dreadful price they had paid. Seats were also reserved for 100 nurses wounded or blinded at the front, and a twelve-year-old boy who had written to say, 'The man in the coffin might be my daddy.'

The Dean of Westminster conducted the burial service with the King standing at the head of the grave and the pall-bearers on each side. At the finish of the service the bearers removed the helmet, bayonet and belt, and as the coffin was lowered the King stepped forward to sprinkle soil taken from the battlefields into the grave. More prayers followed and then the hymn 'Abide With Me'; then came a roll of drums that built up to a crescendo before gradually fading away. As the drummers finished, buglers sounded the Last Post, followed by the Long Reveille that signalled the end of the service.

After the Abbey was empty the doors were closed while the grave was covered with a funeral pall given by the Actors' Church Union and the Union Flag, and four sentries, one each from the RN, RM, Army and RAF, were posted at each corner with arms reversed; these sentries were changed every twenty minutes. When this was completed the doors were reopened and the crowd, which stretched four deep back to the Cenotaph, was allowed in to file past on either side. This was the start of what became known as 'The Great Pilgrimage', which by 27 November had seen about 1.5 million people come to the Abbey.

All the next of kin of British war dead received what became known as the 'Dead Man's Penny' – a large bronze medal with Britannia holding a laurel wreath of victory standing with a lion and the words 'He Died for Freedom and Honour' round the edge.

Britain and France were by no means the only nations to create tombs for unknown

The 'Dead Man's Penny'.

warriors or soldiers. In 1921 tombs were unveiled in the United States (Tomb of the Unknowns, Arlington National Cemetery, Virginia); Portugal (Monastery of Batalha, near Leiria, which holds two unknown soldiers of World War I, one from Flanders and one from the African theatre); and Italy (Piazza Venezia, Rome). Most other former Allied nations that fought on the Western Front have subsequently unveiled tombs containing the remains of an unknown soldier, including Australia (Australian War Memorial, Canberra); Belgium (at the foot of the Colonne du Congrès, Brussels); Canada (only as recently as 28 May 2000, in the Hall of Honor, Parliament Buildings, Ottawa); Greece (Syntagma Square, Athens); India (India Gate, New Delhi); and New Zealand (National War Memorial, Wellington). Russia has a tomb of the Unknown Soldier placed in Alexander Garden in Moscow.

Former Central Powers have also all created tombs: Austria (Heldenplatz, Vienna); Bulgaria (Eternal Flame, Sofia); Germany (Unter den Linden, Berlin); Hungary (Heroes' Square, Budapest); and Turkey (Canakkale Martyrs' Memorial, Gallipoli).

The Last Combat Deaths on 11 November 1918

Perhaps among the bitterest tragedies of the war struck those close relatives of the men who were killed on the final day. On the Western Front several hundred men died and several thousand were wounded in the hours between the signing of the Armistice at shortly after 5:00 a.m. and the ceasefire coming into effect at 11:00 a.m. The precise numbers will never be known, but the United States accepts that some 3,000 of its troops became casualties during that time. The great majority of these would never have occurred if it were not for several generals ordering attacks knowing that the Armistice was to take place later that morning. After the war a Congressional Commission was established to investigate this, but its findings were never published.

It has been established as far as is possible that at least four Allied soldiers (one British, one Canadian, one Frenchmen and one American) died just a few minutes before the ceasefire. They are as follows:

British

Private George Ellison was a pre-war regular soldier, a former coal miner from Leeds, recalled to the colours in 1914 at the age of thirty-six, serving with the 5th Royal Irish Lancers. On 11 November 1918 he was back near Mons where his war had started four years earlier. He had been incredibly lucky so far, in that he had escaped injury. That final morning he was on the outskirts of Mons scouting a wood reportedly occupied by Germans when a single shot rang out, killing Ellison instantly about an hour before the ceasefire He is buried in the St-Symphorien Military Cemetery at Mons – as is Private John Parr, the first British soldier killed in the war, who died on 21 August 1914 at Obourg.

Canadian

Private George Price was born in 1892 and conscripted into the Canadian Army in October 1917 to serve in the 28th Battalion of the Canadian Expeditionary Force. On 11 November 1918 he was part of an advance to take the town of Ville-sur-Haine, near Mons. Price and his patrol came under machine-gun fire and advanced to attack the position. On entering the house from which they thought the fire had been coming, they found the Germans had fled through the back door. The patrol entered a second house, which was also free of the enemy, but as Price stepped back into the street he was shot through the heart by a sniper. He was killed just two minutes before 11:00 a.m.

Like Ellison, Price is buried in the St-Symphorien Military Cemetery. On the fiftieth anniversary of his death in 1968 surviving members of his former company journeyed to Ville-sur-Haine to place a plaque in his memory on the wall of a house near where he fell. The house has since been demolished but the plaque is now on a stone monument on the same site. In 1991 the town of Ville-sur-Haine erected a footbridge over the nearby canal and named it the George Price Footbridge.

Augustin Trébuchon

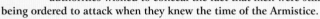

George Ellison

George Price

Henry Gunther

French

Private Augustin Trébuchon was born in 1878 and was a shepherd before the war. He volunteered for the army in August 1914, joining the 415th Infantry Regiment as a messenger. He served in the Second Battle of the Marne, Verdun, Artois and on the Somme before arriving in the Ardennes at the end of the war. During his time at the front he had been wounded twice by shellfire, and by late 1918 had been promoted to *Soldat de Première Classe*.

Early on the morning of 11 November Trébuchon's unit had crossed the River Meuse near Vrigne-sur-Meuse and at around 10:30 a.m., when the fog cleared, the French found themselves exposed and under fire from Germans on higher ground. Trébuchon, who knew the ceasefire was to occur at 11:00 a.m., was killed while he carried a message that read *'Rassemblement à 11h 30 pour le ravitaillement'* ('Assemble for food at 11:30 a.m.').

Trébuchon is buried in the cemetery at Vrigne-sur-Meuse along with seventeen of his comrades. A street in the town has been named after him. Strangely, the date of his death on his memorial at Malzieu-Forain records 10 November 1918. It is said to have been changed, for him and for others killed on the 11th, as the French authorities wished to conceal the fact that men were still being ordered to attack when they knew the time of the Armistice.

American

Private Henry Gunther was born in 1895 in Baltimore into a family of German descent – something that provoked anti-German feelings against him when America joined the conflict. He worked in a bank before being conscripted into the US Army in April 1917. Within five months he was made a supply sergeant in the 313th Infantry but was soon demoted to private when the censors intercepted a letter he had written to a friend urging him not to enlist.

Sometime before midday on 11 November 1918 the 313th was ordered to advance towards Metz, despite word spreading that the Armistice would come into effect at 11:00 a.m. Gunther's platoon, commanded by a Sergeant Ernest Powell, took cover when several warning shots were fired on them by a German machine-gun position near the village of Chaumont-devant-Damvillers. Gunther seemingly flew into a rage, leapt up and, despite Powell's shout to get down, charged the enemy position. The Germans waved him back and refrained from firing until he was within a few yards of their position. He was then shot dead. Most accounts give the time as 10:59 a.m.; if so, Gunther was almost certainly the last man to be killed on the Western Front, if not in the war.

Gunther was posthumously awarded the Distinguished Service Cross and in 1923 his remains were returned to Baltimore and buried in the Holy Redeemer Cemetery. A French memorial placed near the spot where he fell was dedicated in 2008, and on Veterans' Day in 2010, the ninety-second anniversary of his death, a memorial plaque was unveiled at the site of his grave.

Bibliography

Official Manuals, Pamphlets and Journals

Cavalry Journal, XIII, October 1923, Lt Col Paterson, Fort Garry Horse

Field Artillery Training, 1912

Field Artillery Journal, Vol. IV, No. 3, July–September 1914

Notes on Artillery, June 1916 (compiled by the General Staff)

Notes on Gunnery Issued by General Staff 1918, May 1918

Royal Engineers Journal, December 1919; extracts from the report of Lt Col J. P. Macksey, DSO, RE, CRA, 31st Division

Royal Engineers Journal, March 1932; 'Demolitions at Mons'

Royal United Services Institute Journal, Vol. LXIV, No. 454, 1919; 'The Fight at Néry, September 1st 1914' by Major A. F. Becke

Field Service Pocket Book, 1914, General Staff, War Office, HMSO, 1914

Notes for Infantry Officers on Trench Warfare, General Staff, HMSO, March 1916

Consolidation of Trenches, Localities and Craters after Assault and Capture, with a Note on Rapid Wiring, 1916, General Staff, HMSO, 1916; reissued by Naval & Military Press, Uckfield, 2004

Notes on Trench Warfare for Infantry Officers, December 1916, General Staff, HMSO, 1917

The Tactical Employment of Lewis Guns, January 1918, General Staff, HMSO, 1918; reissued by Naval & Military Press, Uckfield, 2008

The Employment of Machine Guns, Part 1: Tactical, General Staff, January 1918

Fighting in the Air, April 1918, General Staff, HMSO, 1918; reissued by Naval & Military Press, Uckfield, 2008

Weekly Tank Notes, 10 August–2nd November 1918, Vol. I (Nos 1–13), General Staff, 1919

Field Service Regulations, Vol. II: *Operations, 1924*, War Office, HMSO, 1924

63rd (RN) Division Trench Standing Orders (2nd edition) 1917; reissued Naval & Military Press, Uckfield

SS 119 – *Preliminary Notes on the Tactical Lessons of Recent Operations*, GHQ, July 1916

SS 120 – *Provisional Instructions for Cooperation between Aeroplanes and Artillery during an Advance*, GHQ, September 1916

SS 123 – *Notes on the Use of Carrier Pigeons*, GHQ, August 1916

SS 135 – *Instructions for the Training of Divisions for Offensive Action*, General Staff, December 1916; reissued as *The Training and Employment of Divisions*, January 1918; *The Division in Attack*, November 1918

SS 143 – *Instructions for the Training of Platoons for Offensive Action*, General Staff, 1917 and 1918

SS 144 – *The Normal Formation for the Attack*, General Staff, February 1917

SS 164 – *Notes on the Use of Tanks*, General Staff, May 1917

SS 174 – *Notes on Communications during Recent Operations on the Front of Second Army*, GHQ, July 1917

SS 175 – *Notes on the Use of Smoke*, GHQ, 1917

SS 184 – *Gas Warfare, Monthly Summary of Information*, No. 1, General Staff, July 1917

SS 191 – *Intercommunication in the Field*, General Staff, November 1917

SS 592 – *Catechism for Artillery Officers*, General Staff, March 1918

Books

Publication was in London unless otherwise stated.

American Armies and Battlefields in Europe, American Battle Monuments Commission, Washington, DC, 1938

Anglesey, Marquess of, *A History of the British Cavalry*, Vol. 7: *The Curragh Incident and the Western Front 1914*; and Vol. 8: *The Western Front 1915–1918*, Leo Cooper, Barnsley, 1997

Arthur, Captain Sir George, *The Story of the Household Cavalry*, Vol. III, Heinemann, 1926

Ashworth, Tony, *Trench Warfare 1914–1918: The Live and Let Live System*, Pan Books, 2000

Baker, David, *Manfred von Richthofen: The Man and the Aircraft He Flew*, Outline Press, 1995

Banks, Arthur, *A Military Atlas of the First World War*, Heinemann Educational Books Ltd, 1975

Barton, Peter, Doyle, Peter, and Vandewalle, Johan, *Beneath Flanders Fields: The Tunnellers' War 1914–18*, Spellmount, Stroud, 2004

Baynes, John, *Morale: A Study of Men and Courage*, Cassell, 1967

Becke, Major A. F., *History of the Great War: Order of Battle of Divisions*, Part 1: *The Regular British Divisions*, Naval & Military Press, Uckfield, 2007

Becke, Major A. F., *History of the Great War, Order of Battle of Divisions*, Part 4: *The Army Council, GHQs, Armies and Corps, including Tank Corps*, Naval & Military Press, Uckfield, 2007

Berton, Pierre, *Vimy*, Pen and Sword Books, Barnsley, 2003

Bethell, Colonel H. A., *Modern Artillery in the Field*, Macmillan & Co., 1911

Blenkinsop, Major General L. J. (ed.), *History of the Great War Based on Official Documents: Veterinary Services*, HMSO, 1925

Bond, Brian, et al., *'Look to Your Front': Studies in the First World War*, Spellmount, Staplehurst, 1999

Bonner, Robert, *Wilfrith Elstob VC DSO MC: The Manchester Regiment*, Fleur de Lys Publishing, Knutsford, 1998

Brereton, J. M., *A History of the 4th/7th Royal Dragoon Guards and their Predecessors 1865–1980*, The Regiment, Catterick, 1982

Brereton, J. M., *The Horse in War*, David & Charles, Newton Abbot, 1976

Brown, Ian Malcolm, *British Logistics on the Western Front, 1914–1919*, Praeger, Westport, Connecticut, 1998

Brown, Malcolm, *The Imperial War Museum Book of the Western Front*, Pan Books, 1993

Brown, Malcolm, *Tommy Goes to War*, Tempus Publishing, Stroud, 2001

Browne, Captain D. G., *The Tank in Action*, William Blackwood & Sons, Edinburgh, 1920

Bull, Dr Stephen (compiler), *An Officer's Manual of the Western Front 1914–1918*, Conway, 2008

Bull, Dr Stephen, *Trench: A History of Trench Warfare on the Western Front*, Osprey, 2010

Butler, Simon, *The War Horses*, Halsgrove, Wellington, Somerset, 2011

Cave, Nigel, *Battleground Europe: Ypres – Sanctuary Wood and Hooge*, Leo Cooper, Barnsley, 1993

Cave, Nigel, *Battleground Europe: Arras – Vimy Ridge*, Leo Cooper, Barnsley, 1996

Cave, Nigel, *Battleground Europe: Ypres – Passchendaele*, Leo Cooper, Barnsley, 1997

Cawston, Lieutenant Colonel, E. P., *Personal Reminiscences of Incidents in the Kaiser War 1914–1918*, Vols 1 and 2, Canterbury Quartos, St Leonards-on-Sea, 1968

Charrington, Major H. V. S., *The 12th Royal Lancers in France*, Gale & Polden, Aldershot, 1921

Clarke, Dale, *British Artillery 1914–1919 – Field Army Artillery*, Osprey, 2004

Clarke, Dale, *British Artillery 1914–1919 – Heavy Artillery*, Osprey, 2005

Clayton, Anthony, *Paths of Glory: The French Army, 1914–18*, Cassell, 2003

Coppard, George, *With a Machine Gun to Cambrai*, Cassell, 1999

Corrigan, Gordon, *Mud, Blood and Poppycock: Britain and the Great War*, Cassell, 2003

Creveld, Martin Van, *Supplying War: Logistics from Wallenstein to Patton*, Cambridge University Press, 1977

Crofton, Eileen, *The Women of Royaumont: a Scottish Women's Hospital on the Western Front*, Tuckwell Press, East Linton, 1997

Cron, Hermann, *Imperial German Army 1914–18*, Helion & Company, Solihull, 2006

Cuddeford, D. W. J., *And All for What? Some Wartime Experiences*, Heath Cranton, 1933

Darling, Major General J. C., *The 20th Hussars in the Great War*, privately published, Lyndhurst, 1923

Digby, Peter K. A., *Pyramids and Poppies: The 1st SA Infantry Brigade in Libya, France and Flanders, 1915–1919*, Ashanti Publishing, Rivonia, South Africa, 1993

Donovan, Tom (compiler), *The Red Hazy Hell*, Spellmount, Staplehurst, 1999

Dunn, Captain J. C., *The War the Infantry Knew 1914–1919*, Jane's Publishing Co., 1987

Edmonds, Brigadier General J. E. (ed./compiler), *History of the Great War Based on Official Documents: Military Operations in France and Belgium, 1914*, Vols I and II; *1915*, Vol. I; *1916*, Vols I and II; *1917*, Vols I, II and III; *1918*, Vol. IV, Macmillan and Co. and HMSO, 1922–1948

Ellis, John, and Cox, Michael, *The World War I Databook*, Aurum Press, 2001

Farndale, General Sir Martin, *History of the Royal Regiment of Artillery: Western Front 1914–1918*, Royal Artillery Institute, 1986

Finnegan, Colonel Terrence J., USAF Reserve, *Shooting the Front: Allied Aerial Reconnaissance and Photographic Interpretation of the Western Front*, NDIC Press, Washington, DC, 2006

Forbes, Major General A., *A History of the Army Ordnance Services*, Vol. 3: *The Great War*, Medici Society, 1929

Foulkes, Major General C. H., *Gas!: The Story of the Special Brigade*, William Blackwood & Sons, 1934

Fuller, Colonel J. F. C., *Tanks in the Great War, 1914–1918*, John Murray, 1920

Fuller, Steven, *1st Bedfordshires*, Fighting High, Hitchin, 2011

Gavaghan, Michael, *The Story of the Unknown Warrior*, M & L Publications, Preston, 1995

German Army Handbook of 1918, Frontline Books, Barnsley, 2008

Gibbs, Philip, *From Bapaume to Passchendaele, 1917*, William Heinemann, 1918

Gilbert, Martin, *The Routledge Atlas of the First World War*, Routledge, 1994

Grieve, Captain W. Grant, and Newman, Bernard, *Tunnellers: The Story of the Tunnelling Companies, Royal Engineers, during the World War*, Herbert Jenkins, 1936

Griffith, Paddy, *Forward into Battle*, Crowood Press, Swindon, 1990

Griffith, Paddy, *Battle Tactics of the Western Front*, Yale University Press, New Haven and London, 1996

Griffith, Paddy (ed.), *British Fighting Methods in the Great War*, Frank Cass, 1996

Hammerton, Sir John (ed.), *The Great War – I Was There!*, Vols I, II and III, Amalgamated Press, 1938

Hammond, Bryn, *Cambrai 1917*, Weidenfeld & Nicolson, 2008

Hanson, Neil, *The Unknown Soldier: The Story of the Missing in the Great War*, Doubleday, 2005

Harding, David (ed.), *The Complete Encyclopedia of Weapons*, Macmillan London, 1980

Harper, Lieutenant General Sir G. M., *Notes on Infantry Tactics and Training*, Sifton, Praed & Co., 1919

Hay, Ian, *The First Hundred Thousand: Being the Unofficial Chronicle of a Unit of "K(1)"*, Grosset & Dunlap, 1916

Henniker, Colonel A. M. (compiler), *History of the Great War Based on Official Documents: Transportation on the Western Front, 1914–1918*, HMSO, 1937

Hesketh-Pritchard, Major H., *Sniping in France*, Hutchinson & Co., 1931

Hickey, Captain D. E., *Rolling into Action: Memoirs of a Tank Corps Section Commander*, Naval & Military Press, Uckfield, 2007

Hogg, I. V., and Thurston, L. F., *British Artillery Weapons and Ammunition, 1914–1918*, Ian Allan, 1972

Holmes, Richard, *Firing Line*, Jonathan Cape, 1985

Holmes, Richard, *The Western Front*, BBC Worldwide Ltd, 1999

Holmes, Richard, *Tommy: The British Soldier on the Western Front 1914–1918*, HarperCollins, 2004

Horne, Alistair, *The Price of Glory: Verdun*, Penguin Books, Middlesex, 1964

Institute of Royal Engineers, *The Work of the Royal Engineers in the European War, 1914–1919 – Military Mining*, Institute of Royal Engineers, Chatham, 1922

Jack, Brigadier General J. L., *General Jack's Diary 1914–1918*, Eyre & Spottiswoode, 1964

Jones, H. A., *The War in the Air*, Vols III and IV, Oxford University Press, 1934

Keech, Graham, *Battleground Europe: Arras – Bullecourt*, Leo Cooper, Barnsley, 1999

Keegan, John, *The Face of Battle*, Jonathan Cape, 1976

Levine, Joshua, *Fighter Heroes of World War I*, Collins, 2009

Lengel, Edward G., *To Conquer Hell: The Battle of Meuse–Argonne 1918*, Aurum Press, 2008

Lloyd, R. A., *A Trooper in the 'Tins': The Autobiography of a Lifeguardsman*, Hurst & Blackett, 1938

Lucy, John F., *There's a Devil in the Drum*, Faber & Faber, 1938

Lumley, L. R., *The Eleventh Hussars (Prince Albert's Own) 1908–1934*, Royal United Services Institute, 1936

Lunt, James, *Charge to Glory!*, Heinemann, 1960

McCarthy, Chris, *The Somme: The Day-by-Day Account*, Arms & Armour Press, 1995

Macdonald, Andrew, *On My Way to the Somme*, HarperCollins (New Zealand), Auckland, 2005

Macdonald, Lyn, *1914*, Michael Joseph, 1987

Macdonald, Lyn, *Somme*, Michael Joseph, 1983

Macksey, Kenneth, and Batchelor, John H., *Tanks: A History of the Armoured Fighting Vehicle*, Purnell Book Services Ltd, 1970

Macpherson, Major General Sir W. G., *History of the Great War Based on Official Documents: Medical Services, General History*, Vols II and III, *HMSO*, 1923 and 1924

McBride, H. W., *A Rifleman Went to War*, Lancer Militaria, Mt Ida, Arkansas, 1987

Masefield, John, *The Old Front Line*, Heinemann, 1917

Messenger, Charles, *Call-to-Arms: The British Army 1914–18*, Cassell, 2005

Middlebrook, Martin, *The First Day on the Somme*, Allen Lane/Penguin, 1971

Mitchell, F., *Tank Warfare: The Story of the Tanks in the Great War*, Spa Books/Tom Donovan Publishing, Stevenage, 1987

Moran, Lord Charles, *The Anatomy of Courage*, Constable & Robinson, 1945

Mosier, John, *The Myth of the Great War*, Profile Books, 2001

Neillands, Robin, *The Great War Generals on the Western Front, 1914–1918*, Robinson Publishing, 1998

Nettleton, John, *The Anger of the Guns*, William Kimber, 1979

Neumann, Major Georg Paul (compiler), *Official History of the German Air Force in the Great War*, trans. J. E. Gurdon, Naval & Military Press, Uckfield, n.d.

Nicholson, Colonel G. W. L., *Canadian Expeditionary Force 1914–1918: Official History of the Canadian Army in the First World War*, Queen's Printer and Comptroller of Stationery, Ottawa, 1962

Nicholson, Colonel W. N., *Behind the Lines*, Jonathan Cape, 1939

North, John (ed.), *Men Fighting: Battle Stories*, Faber & Faber, 1958

Oldham, Peter, *Battleground Europe: Ypres – Messines Ridge*, Leo Cooper, Barnsley, 1998

Parker, Ernest, *Into Battle, 1914–1918*, Longman, 1964

Passingham, Ian, *Pillars of Fire: The Battle of Messines Ridge, 1917*, Sutton Publishing, Stroud, 1998

Passingham, Ian, *All the Kaiser's Men*, Sutton Publishing, Stroud, 2003

Pidgeon, Trevor, *The Tanks at Flers*, Vols I and II, Fairmile Books, Cobham, 1995

Pidgeon, Trevor, *Battleground Europe: Somme – Flers and Gueudecourt*, Leo Cooper, Barnsley, 2002

Priestley, Major R. E., *The Signal Service in the European War of 1914 to 1918*, W. & J. Mackay, Chatham, 1921

Pritchard, Major General H. L.(ed.), *History of the Corps of Royal Engineers*, Vol. V, The Institute of Royal Engineers, Chatham, 1952

Pollard, Captain A. O., *Fire-Eater: The Memoirs of a V.C.*, Naval & Military Press, Uckfield, 2005

Purdom, C. B., *Everyman at War: Sixty Personal Narratives of the War*, J. M. Dent, 1930

Richards, Frank, *Old Soldiers Never Die*, Naval & Military Press, Uckfield, 2001

Rommel, Erwin, *Infantry Tactics*, Greenhill Books, 2006

Scott, Group Captain A. J. L., *Sixty Squadron, R.A.F.*, Naval & Military Press, Uckfield, 2003

Service, Robert W., *Rhymes of a Red Cross Man*, Fisher Unwin, 1916

Severn, Mark, extract from 'The Advance, 1918'; from *Fifty Amazing Stories of the Great War*, Odhams Press, 1936

Sheffield, Gary (ed.), *War on the Western Front*, Osprey, 2007

Shephard, Ernest, *A Sergeant Major's War*, Crowood Press, Ramsbury, Marlborough, 1987

Sheppard, Major E. W., *The Ninth Queen's Royal Lancers, 1715–1936*, Gale & Polden, Aldershot, 1939

Simpson, Andy (ed.), *Hot Blood and Cold Steel*, Tom Donovan Publishing, 1993

Simpson, Andy, *The Evolution of Victory: British Battles of the Western Front, 1914–1918*, Tom Donovan Publishing, 1995

Stedman, Michael, *Battleground Europe: Somme – La Boisselle*, Leo Cooper, Barnsley, 1997

Sylvanus Lewis, W., 'In a Kite Balloon'; from *Everyman at War*, 1930

Takle, Patrick, *Battleground Europe: The Affair at Néry*, Pen & Sword, Barnsley, 2006

Terraine, John, *The Western Front 1914–1918*, Hutchinson & Co., 1964

Terraine, John, *The Smoke and the Fire: Myths and Anti-myths of War, 1861–1945*, Sidgwick & Jackson, 1980

Terraine, John, *White Heat: The New Warfare 1914–18*, Leo Cooper, Barnsley, 1982

Thomas, Cecil, *They Also Served: The Experiences of a Private Soldier as Prisoner of War in German Camp and Coal Mine, 1916–1918*, Hurst & Blackett, [1918?]

Toland, John, *No Man's Land: The Story of 1918*, Book Club Associates/Eyre Methuen, 1980

Turner, Major Charles C., *The Struggle in the Air, 1914–1918*, Edward Arnold, 1919

Wade, Aubrey, *Gunner on the Western Front*, Batsford, 1959

War Office, *Statistics of the Military Effort of the British Empire during the Great War, 1914–1920*, HMSO, 1922

Warner, Philip, *Passchendaele*, Sidgwick & Jackson, 1987

Watson, Major W. H., *A Company of Tanks*, William Blackwood, Edinburgh and London, 1920

Winter, Denis, *Death's Men: Soldiers of the Great War*, Penguin, 1978

Winter, Denis, *Haig's Command: a Reassessment*, Penguin, 1992

Young, Michael, *Army Service Corps 1902–1918*, Leo Cooper, Barnsley, 2001

Index